Eric Arnould
Linda Price
George Zinkhan

second edition

9 780072 537147

CONSUMERS

McGraw-Hill Irwin

Boston Burr Ridge, IL Dubuque, IA Madison, WI New York San Francisco St. Louis
Bangkok Bogotá Caracas Kuala Lumpur Lisbon London Madrid Mexico City
Milan Montreal New Delhi Santiago Seoul Singapore Sydney Taipei Toronto

Series in Marketing McGRAW-HILL/IRWIN

Arens
Contemporary Advertising
Ninth Edition

Arnould, Price, & Zinkhan
Consumers
Second Edition

Bearden, Ingram, & LaForge
Marketing: Principles & Perspectives
Fourth Edition

Belch & Belch
Advertising & Promotion: An Integrated Marketing Communications Approach
Sixth Edition

Bingham & Gomes
Business Marketing Management
Second Edition

Boyd, Walker, Mullins, & Larreche
Marketing Management: A Strategic Decision-Making Approach
Fourth Edition

Cateora & Graham
International Marketing
Eleventh Edition

Cole & Mishler
Consumer and Business Credit Management
Eleventh Edition

Cravens, Lamb, & Crittenden
Strategic Marketing Management Cases
Seventh Edition

Cravens & Piercy
Strategic Marketing
Seventh Edition

Crawford & Di Benedetto
New Products Management
Seventh Edition

Dolan
Marketing Management: Text and Cases
First Edition

Duncan
IMC: Using Advertising and Promotion to Build Brands
First Edition

Dwyer & Tanner
Business Marketing
Second Edition

Eisenmann
Internet Business Models: Text and Cases
First Edition

Etzel, Walker, & Stanton
Marketing
Twelfth Edition

Forrest
Internet Marketing Intelligence
First Edition

Futrell
ABC's of Relationship Selling
Eighth Edition

Futrell
Fundamentals of Selling
Seventh Edition

Hair, Brush, & Ortinau
Marketing Research
Second Edition

Hawkins, Best, & Coney
Consumer Behavior
Ninth Edition

Johansson
Global Marketing
Third Edition

Johnston & Marshall
Churchill/Ford/Walker's Sales Force Management
Seventh Edition

Kerin, Berkowitz, Hartley, & Rudelius
Marketing
Seventh Edition

Kerin, Hartley, & Rudelius
Marketing: The Core
First Edition

Lehmann & Winer
Analysis for Marketing Planning
Fifth Edition

Lehmann & Winer
Product Management
Third Edition

Levy & Weitz
Retailing Management
Fifth Edition

Mason & Perreault
The Marketing Game!
Third Edition

McDonald
Direct Marketing: An Integrated Approach
First Edition

Mohammed, Fisher, Jaworski, & Cahill
Internet Marketing: Building Advantage in a Networked Economy
Second Edition

Monroe
Pricing
Third Edition

Pelton, Strutton, & Lumpkin
Marketing Channels: A Relationship Management Approach
Second Edition

Peppers & Rogers
Managing Customer Relationships to Build Competitive Advantage
First Edition

Perreault & McCarthy
Basic Marketing: A Global Managerial Approach
Fourteenth Edition

Perreault & McCarthy
Essentials of Marketing: A Global Managerial Approach
Ninth Edition

Peter & Donnelly
A Preface to Marketing Management
Ninth Edition

Peter & Donnelly
Marketing Management: Knowledge and Skills
Seventh Edition

Peter & Olson
Consumer Behavior
Sixth Edition

Purvis & Burton
Which Ad Pulled Best?
Ninth Edition

Rayport & Jaworski
Introduction to e-Commerce
Second Edition

Rayport & Jaworski
e-Commerce
First Edition

Rayport & Jaworski
Cases in e-Commerce
First Edition

Richardson
Internet Marketing
First Edition

Roberts
Internet Marketing: Integrating Online and Offline Strategies
First Edition

Spiro, Stanton, & Rich
Management of a Sales Force
Eleventh Edition

Stock & Lambert
Strategic Logistics Management
Fourth Edition

Ulrich & Eppinger
Product Design and Development
Second Edition

Walker, Boyd, Mullins, & Larreche
Marketing Strategy: A Decision-Focused Approach
Fourth Edition

Weitz, Castleberry, & Tanner
Selling: Building Partnerships
Fifth Edition

Zeithaml & Bitner
Services Marketing
Third Edition

McGraw-Hill Irwin

CONSUMERS
Published by McGraw-Hill/Irwin, a business unit of The McGraw-Hill Companies, Inc., 1221 Avenue of the Americas, New York, NY, 10020.

This book is printed on acid-free paper.

domestic 1 2 3 4 5 6 7 8 9 0 VNH/VNH 0 9 8 7 6 5 4 3
international 1 2 3 4 5 6 7 8 9 0 VNH/VNH 0 9 8 7 6 5 4 3

ISBN 0-07-253714-0

Publisher: *John E. Biernat*
Associate sponsoring editor: *Barrett Koger*
Developmental editor I: *Anna M. Chan*
Marketing manager: *Kim Kanakes*
Media producer: *Craig Atkins*
Senior project manager: *Kimberly D. Hooker*
Senior production supervisor: *Michael R. McCormick*
Lead designer: *Pam Verros*
Photo research coordinator: *Judy Kausal*
Photo researcher: *Mike Hruby*
Supplement producer: *Betty Hadala*
Senior digital content specialist: *Brian Nacik*
Cover design: *Pam Verros*
Interior design: *Pam Verros*
Typeface: *10/12 Times New Roman*
Compositor: *TechBooks*
Printer: *Von Hoffmann Press, Inc.*

Library of Congress Cataloging-in-Publication Data

Arnould, Eric J.
Consumers / Eric Arnould, Linda Price, George Zinkhan.—2nd ed.
p. cm.—(McGraw-Hill/Irwin series in marketing)
Includes bibliographical references and index.
ISBN 0-07-253714-0 (alk. paper)—ISBN 0-07-121426-7 (international : alk. paper)
1. Consumer behavior. 2. Consumer behavior—United States. I. Price, Linda. II. Zinkhan, George M. (George Martin) III. Title. IV. Series.
HF5415.32 .A76 2004
658.8'342—dc21 2002041065

INTERNATIONAL EDITION ISBN 0-07-121426-7

www.mhhe.com

DEDICATION

For my mother and daughter, who believe the world is wonderful and mysterious and share great hope for humankind. Like bookends, their optimism frames the content of this book.

Linda L. Price

Written in hopes of living up to the spirit of two great educators, my late uncle Robert S. Brumbaugh, professor of philosophy (and so much more) at Yale University, and the late Robert Netting of the University of Arizona, an inspiration to a generation of cultural anthropologists.

Eric J. Arnould

To my family and friends.

George M. Zinkhan

PREFACE

This book is an invitation to the diverse, intriguing, dynamic, global world of consumers. The world of consumers seems both smaller and larger than it did last year or even yesterday. Human societies have always mixed and changed, but people, ideas, and goods move farther and faster today than in previous decades. Cell phones, the Internet, mobile commerce, and global satellite communications bring us together quickly, frequently, and almost effortlessly. In the last decade, Internet communications have more than doubled every year. The global marketplace is a fact of life. The world seems smaller.

At the same time, the magnitude of our differences, our vibrant and unique traditions, values, desires, and ways of living are more salient than ever. Cultures are resourceful, resilient, and unpredictable. We meet Buddhist monks breakfasting at Denny's in L.A.; order an orthodox Hindu menu at the McDonald's in Mumbai, India; purchase Yasser Arafat–brand potato chips in Cairo; and celebrate Chinese values and traditions with *Sesame Street* in Shanghai. In our own neighborhood, we find people, beliefs, and consumption behaviors that seem strange, unfamiliar, and confusing. Retail strips are adorned with signage not only in foreign languages but in alphabets from every corner of the globe. The world seems larger, more diverse, and perhaps more intimidating. Local marketers can no longer assume that their local customers will share their particular views on the world. This book can help students bring order into this dynamic world of consumption.

Our intent with this revised edition of *Consumers* is to assist readers in making sense of consumers as culture-bearers, social beings, families, and individuals. We are interested in behavior but also in what consumers think, feel, and say. We are interested in what consumers purchase but also in their consumption dreams and plans, their unfolding consumption experiences, and their consumption satisfaction and memories. We are interested in the meanings consumers attach to consumption and possessions. We are interested in how people dispose of things they no longer want and precious things they can no longer keep. We offer theories and tools borrowed from all the social sciences, including areas as diverse as neuroscience, cognitive psychology, and evolutionary anthropology, to enable readers to thrive in a global marketplace.

Thriving in the global marketplace means looking closely at the cultures from which consumer desires emerge, the rituals and patterns associated with products, services, and experiences. Such an approach is especially important when cultures are in turmoil and technologies are disrupting established economic and social patterns of behavior. We believe that the best marketing courses teach students to be sensitive to cultural dynamics.

To research and write this book we brought together the multidisciplinary skills and viewpoints of three consumer researchers. All three of us have traveled extensively and engaged in multicountry consumer research. We are committed deeply and resolutely to understanding and teaching consumer behavior. Each of us is blessed (or cursed) with an eclectic vision of consumers. However, we are grounded in different traditions. Eric Arnould brings to the project a cross-cultural approach to consumer behavior derived from anthropological training and many years of overseas work. Linda Price contributes perspectives from social psychology and more generally the intersections between cognition, society, and culture. George Zinkhan adds his many years of experience with issues in mediated communications, advertising, and marketing to his enduring interests in the literary arts. As authors, we are passionate and active teachers and researchers. The book offers a cutting-edge treatment of research and practice related to consumers with a wealth of contemporary, real-world examples and marketing applications.

OBJECTIVES

The second edition of *Consumers* is intended to serve as a textbook for undergraduate and graduate courses in consumer behavior. The book could also be used as a supplementary text in courses desiring to offer a global perspective on marketing. The tone of the text is conversational, and we offer copious examples and applications of consumer theory and research in various regions of the world.
The objectives of this book are

- To highlight the importance and necessity of a global approach to understanding consumers. To offer a book that emphasizes and illustrates the relationships between individuals and the communities and cultures in which they live.
- To provide a comprehensive understanding of consumers adopting a culturally relative orientation. To illustrate how culture affects internal, individual variables such as perception, emotions, memory, and decision making as well as self-concept, lifestyle, values, and family organization.
- To illustrate the impact of the Internet and other technological advances on consumers' lives and actions. To illustrate the ways in which mediated communications such as television, the Internet, and e-mail influence consumers and consumer culture.
- To use simple language and examples to integrate complex contemporary discussions about consumers from a diverse number of disciplines.
- To provide a clear and wide-ranging treatment of the entire cycle of consumption from preconsumption thoughts, feelings, and actions, to consumption and postconsumption thoughts, feelings, and actions.
- To offer explicit treatment of topics often neglected or given cursory investigation in consumer behavior texts, including chapters dedicated to global market segments, consumer satisfaction, and consumer disposition behaviors.
- To highlight the connections between understanding consumers and good marketing practice.
- To create a book that conveys our own enthusiasm and wonderment about consumers and their cultures.

Based on feedback and reviews of the first edition of *Consumers*, additional objectives for the second edition are

- To provide a more user-friendly organization to the book.
- To highlight ethical and policy dilemmas experienced by consumers and marketers in the marketplace.
- To bring every chapter up to date with current research and global examples.

SUPPLEMENTS

We understand that new approaches can be foreboding; change is risky. So this package offers instructors comprehensive supplements and a full array of multimedia materials to use in the classroom. We blend the new and exciting features of global consumer behavior with the important features of other consumer behavior texts. Our approach incorporates the latest developments in instructional technology to facilitate efficient organization and delivery of concepts and information. We hope that the book will feel familiar but with a new and exciting flavor.

- An Instructor's Manual, written by Cathy Hartman of Utah State University and Pamela Kiecker of Virginia Commonwealth University in conjunction with the text's authors, goes beyond providing solutions to end-of-chapter questions and problems. It incorporates additional, new material and examples for professors to use with students. Sample course syllabi also are included.
- Our PowerPoint Presentation, also created by Pamela Kiecker in conjunction with the text's authors, is available on the book's website and on the Instructor's CD-ROM. It provides over 350 slides of text material and additional resources for use in class lectures and discussion.
- The Test Bank, written by Ronald Weir of East Tennessee State University, includes over 1,300 multiple-choice, fill-in-the-blank, and essay questions. Many of the test questions have been class-tested by the text's authors over several semesters.
- The accompanying Video Package includes a professionally produced collection of stories shared by consumer behavior teachers and researchers from around the world. These stories bring to life a variety of concepts from the textbook. Other video segments in the package include segments relating consumer behavior to marketing strategy, illustrating consumption in different parts of the world, and providing examples of consumption within subcultures and communities.
- Our book-specific website at www.mhhe.com/Arnould04 offers complete classroom support for both students and professors. For students, the site provides student quizzing, an e-learning session, interactive activities, links to companies used as examples in the book, and Internet exercises. For professors, we provide downloadable supplements, a link to PageOut, and updated *Business Week* articles. Pamela Kiecker of Virginia Commonwealth University will provide updates to the website during the school semester.
- Our Instructor's Presentation CD-ROM provides professors with the Instructor's Manual, computerized test bank, video clips, links to company sites, and our PowerPoint slides.

ORGANIZATION

The revised edition of *Consumers* is organized into five parts as shown in the exhibit on the next page. The first part of the book is composed of four chapters. Chapter 1 introduces our perspective on the nature and scope of consumer behavior. We explore the significance of consumption in daily life, introduce two concepts that broadly structure the content of our book, and suggest several reasons why studying consumers is important. The two organizing concepts are the domain of consumption and the wheel of consumption, both of which we describe. Chapter 2 overviews the changing world of consumption and illustrates consumption in different regions of the world with numerous examples. This chapter contrasts consumption patterns in less-developed countries with those of the post-industrial world and the transitional economies of Eastern Europe. In this chapter we also outline several important trends that shape global consumer behavior. In Chapter 3, we outline the meaning and nature of

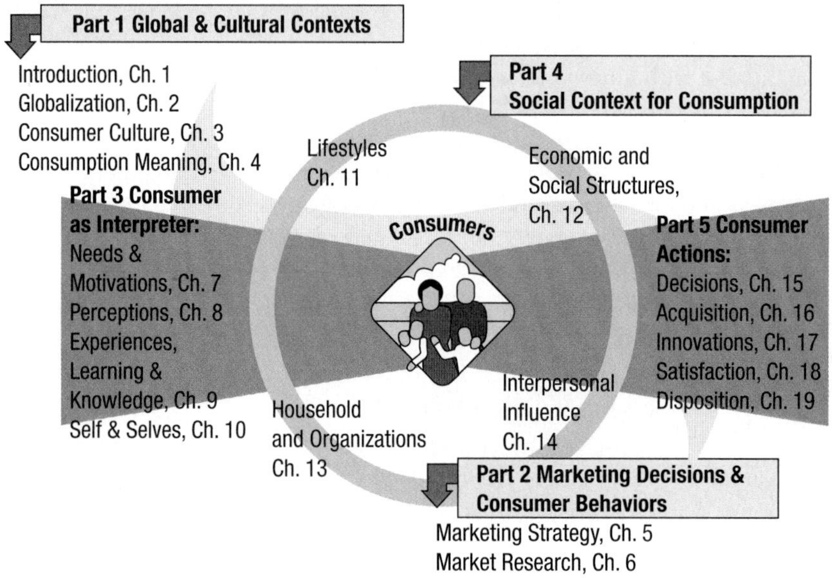

consumer culture and how it influences consumer behavior. This important chapter provides many basic ideas that are referred to throughout the text. Chapter 4 focuses on what consumption means to consumers. We hope you find this chapter to be one of the richest in the book. Multinational firms are interested in predicting whether or not consumers will purchase, but they are also interested in what their products or services mean to consumers. We introduce many new ideas in this chapter and describe cutting-edge theories about consumer meaning. We employ numerous commonsense examples that help the reader understand the importance and nature of consumer meanings.

Part 2 of *Consumers* zeros in on the relationship between marketing and consumer behavior. In the exhibit these strategic and managerial issues are shown in constant dynamic interaction with the issues discussed in Part 1 of the book. Indeed, the global distribution of consumer behavior, the shape and dynamics of consumer culture, and the meanings of things to consumers strongly affect marketing strategy, policy, and research, and in turn are affected by these managerial practices. If managerial issues are not central to your interests, they can be skipped without a loss of continuity or coherence with the rest of the book. Chapter 5 provides the crucial link between understanding consumer behavior and marketing strategy, and is organized around the ideas of the marketing imagination, and market segmentation, targeting, and product positioning tactics. Throughout the book we give additional examples and illustrations of the connection between understanding consumers and effective marketing strategy. Chapter 6 describes and illustrates a wide range of market research strategies and includes extensive discussion of the impact of new technologies (e.g., the Internet) and globalization on the effective and ethical conduct of market research. As compared to other textbooks, we provide more discussion of anthropological and sociological techniques and describe details of Internet-based and multicountry market research.

Part 3 of *Consumers* begins to unpack the nature of consumer behavior at the individual level, the traditional focus of consumer behavior studies in marketing. It approaches individual consumers as sense makers and meaning makers, as beings who take in information from their environment and use it to make sense of their environment and themselves. Chapter 7 draws on our newest understandings of how humans develop in their cultural environments to cast new light on the important topic of motivation. Although we cover the usual array of motivational techniques and research, we also emphasize the goal-oriented nature of consumer behavior and cross-cultural differences. Chapter 8 provides a basic and provocative overview of consumer perception. Again, our intent is to show how something as individual as perception is shaped by culture and environment. Appropriately, this chapter is rich with sensory examples. Chapter 9 follows on the heels of Chapter 8 by emphasizing how context and culture influence what consumers experience, learn, and remember. In contrast with other textbooks, we emphasize an understanding of consumer learning and how that relates to knowledge rather than focusing predominantly on knowledge per se. We also consider how new technologies might affect what, when, and how consumers learn. Chapter 10 provides an overview of how consumers' self-concepts and personalities relate both to the environments in which they live and their consumption behavior. We introduce a discussion of a number of personality traits that have drawn recent attention from researchers, and suggest how ideas of the self differ in different world areas.

Part 4 addresses the social contexts in which consumption decisions are made and consumption and disposition typically occur. The issues discussed in this part of the book are depicted in the exhibit, and frame the sense making that we discuss in Part 3 of the book, and the actions consumers take, discussed in Part 5. Chapter 11 follows up on Chapter 10 with a far-ranging discussion of consumer lifestyles, the self-conscious choice to live and consume in certain ways. It discusses lifestyles in other parts of the world such as Japan and France; it discusses how consumer lifestyle is connected to constellations of products and services and cultural beliefs and values. Chapter 12 provides a thorough overview of how economic and social structures affect consumer behavior. This chapter is the longest chapter in the book, but other books frequently include multiple chapters on this topic. Rather than deal with these topics in a piecemeal fashion, we have integrated our discussion across the related topics of social class, ethnicity, gender, and age. While some texts cover the material in this chapter in two or more chapters, we feel a single chapter coverage allows semester-length classes to deal with the full range of topics covered in the text. Chapter 13 investigates the processes by which individuals and informal groups influence others' acquisition behaviors. We discuss the behavior of market mavens, celebrity endorsers, and reference groups, for example. In Chapter 14 we explore the role of households and formal buying groups in the acquisition and consumption process. We show how the structure of these groups affects acquisition. We summarize how internal resource pooling affects acquisition and consumption.

Part 5 focuses on consumer purchase, acquisition, and evaluation, the traditional heart of consumer research. These actions are seen as a consequence of the thoughts and feelings consumers develop and that we discuss in Part 3 of the book. At the same time, the actions we discuss in Part 5 affect consumers' sense- and meaning-making activities discussed earlier. Part 5 provides an in-depth treatment of several of the most important topics in consumer theory and research. This part is formulated around the consequences and outcomes of consumer acquisition. In five action-packed chapters we cover traditional topics plus some new material. Some of these topics are given only cursory treatment, or no discussion, in other consumer behavior texts. For example, drawing on the latest research in psychology and consumer research, Chapter 15 summarizes theories about consumer decision making and attitude models. Again, we stress the power of situation and context for altering and framing how consumers decide what to believe, buy, or do. Although we cover conventional ideas about consumer decision making, we emphasize how consumers creatively construct choices to respond to particular situations. While some texts cover the material in this chapter in two or more chapters, we feel single-chapter coverage allows semester-length classes to deal with the full range of topics covered in the text. Chapter 16 describes the many ways that consumers acquire products, services, and ideas. In contrast with conventional treatments, we emphasize gift giving and secondary markets (e.g., yard and boot sales) as important ways that consumers acquire things. In this chapter we also include many leading-edge ideas about how and why people shop and how we can understand and predict purchase behavior. Chapter 17 overviews how, why, and when consumers purchase new services and products and then discusses how and whether they integrate these innovations into their everyday lives. Chapter 18 describes what we know about consumer satisfaction. Although consumer satisfaction is considered a key to business success, this is still the only consumer behavior book with an entire chapter dedicated to the topic. In one chapter we compress the most recent research on how to deliver value and satisfaction to consumers. Chapter 19 concludes the book with a discussion of consumer recycling, reuse, and disposition behaviors. That is, we address what becomes of things when consumers' needs for them dissolve. In Chapter 2, we identify ecological concerns as a global trend; the final chapter addresses the micro and macro consequences of consumption. Sympathetic to the calls for sustainable consumption, we argue that both marketers and consumers need to pay more attention to what happens after purchase and consumption, and provide examples of how marketers can profit from understanding postacquisition attitudes and behaviors.

CHAPTER STRUCTURE

On the basis of extensive teaching and writing experience, we have included a number of features in each chapter that should help students learn about consumers. First and foremost, each chapter is global in theory and scope and up to date with reference to both contextual factors such as new technologies and topical theory and research. In addition, we offer a unique blend of old and new.

- Introductory Vignette. Each chapter opens with a consumer story that overviews many essential aspects of the chapter. Many of the vignettes are new to this edition of the book. The vignettes often draw from the authors' own experiences and are typically global in character. We refer back to these vignettes throughout the chapter to make subsequent theories more tangible for the reader.
- Learning Objectives. Each chapter begins by outlining a few essential learning objectives that readers can use to gauge their comprehension of the text.
- Consumer Chronicles. Each chapter includes several boxed and detailed consumer examples that help to illustrate a particular theory or idea with the real thoughts, feelings, and experiences of consumers around the world.
- Good Practice. Each chapter uses set-aside examples of marketing/management good practice related to consumers. Sometimes the Good Practice refers to what companies can, should, and are doing. Sometimes it provides a hands-on

opportunity for readers to apply a good practice of their own. These sections are target opportunities for in-class discussion and exercises.

- Industry Insights. Each chapter includes examples from industry that help to highlight the application of consumer theory and research to the practice of marketing and management. As in the case of Consumer Chronicles, these set-aside illustrations help to texture readers' understandings; many are new to this edition.
- Ethical Dilemmas. Each chapter includes examples of ethical and policy problems that face consumers and marketers everyday. New to this edition, these set-asides provide opportunities for classroom discussion of real-world problems.
- You Make the Call. In addition to a set of end-of-chapter questions and exercises, each chapter concludes with a short case that can help students grasp the big picture and elaborate on their own understandings of the chapter material. Many of the cases are new to this edition. The cases are fun vehicles for class discussion, chapter review, and mini projects. They may even generate some future research.
- Abundant Use of Full-Color Material. This book draws on a wide array of visual materials. We include author-developed charts, graphs, and exhibits but also cartoons, photos of billboards, packaging, advertisements, and consumers. More than simply eye-catching and aesthetic, this material is intended to convey the richness and complexity of global consumer behaviors. Numerous examples illustrate the Internet and emerging technologies, but other examples illustrate the many places that high technology has not yet penetrated.

ACKNOWLEDGMENTS

Since this project is now in its 15th year, a lot of people share the credit for coaxing us along. Mary Fisher and Bill Schopf of Austen Press, a short-lived experimental arm of Irwin Press, initially talked Linda and Eric into doing the book as part of a close-working team. Both have since gone on to pursue other dreams. Managerial staff at Irwin and later Irwin/McGraw-Hill have patiently nudged us forward, including Barrett Koger, Kim Kanakes, and Anna Chan. In fact, the whole team associated with McGraw-Hill/Irwin worked patiently with us to bring the second edition of this book and pedagogical package to fruition. Linda and Eric put up with and encouraged each other as part of their ongoing personal/professional experiment. Colette Price put up with Linda and Eric. Linda and Eric are grateful to co-author George Zinkhan, who has brought his energy and insight to the entire second edition of the book. Austen Arnould (University of Nebraska), Michelle Morrison (University of Georgia), and George Zinkhan IV (Rice University) provided useful insights on drafts of the first edition. Feedback from several generations of undergraduates at the Universities of Georgia and Nebraska who collected new materials, wrote out cases, and responded to exams and assignments have helped to highlight needed improvements.

A number of reviewers, some of whom appropriately offered highly spirited commentary in response to first edition manuscript and finished product, and others who gracefully offered more gentle comments, played a role in the development of the second edition. In particular, we wish to thank

M. Wayne Alexander, *Minnesota State University*
Barry J. Babin, *University of Southern Mississippi*

James R. Bettman, *Duke University*
Mark Blake, *York College of Pennsylvania*
Marjorie I. Bonavia, *University of Maryland, College Park*
Jerome Christia, *Coastal Carolina University*
Ruth Clottey, *Barry University*
Robin A. Coulter, *University of Connecticut*
John E. Crawford, *Lipscomb University*
Robert Farris, *Mt. San Antonio College*
Terrance G. Gabel, *Truman State University*
Mary Margaret Galligan, *Shepherd College*
David Gerth, *Nashville State Technical Institute*
Douglas Hauskrecht, *University of Akron*
Mark E. Hill, *Lynchburg College*
Gary L. Hunter, *Illinois State University*
Alican Kavas, *Winston-Salem University*
William C. LaFief, *Frostberg State University*
Marilyn Lavin, *University of Wisconsin–Whitewater*
Matt Meuter, *California State University, Chico*
James M. Munch, *University of Texas at Arlington*
Jeff B. Murray, *University of Arkansas*
Mark Neckes, *Johnson & Wales University*
Barney Olson, *Central College*
Barbara Ross-Wooldridge, *University of Tampa*
Dennis Sandler, *Pace University*
Victoria Seitz, *California State University, San Bernadino*
Michael J. Shapiro, *Dowling College*
Richard D. Shaw, *Rockhurst University*
L. J. Shrum, *Rutgers University*
Leigh Southward, *Tennessee Tech University*
Eric R. Spangenberg, *Washington State University*
Paul Wellen, *Roosevelt University*

ERIC ARNOULD, *University of Nebraska–Lincoln*

Dr. Eric Arnould is Professor of Marketing at the University of Nebraska–Lincoln despite the fact that he holds a Ph.D. degree in cultural anthropology from the University of Arizona (1982). He also has taught at Odense University, Denmark; the University of South Florida; California State University, Long Beach; and the University of Colorado at Denver. From 1975 to 1990, he worked on economic development in more than a dozen West African nations. Since 1990, he has been a full-time academic. Occasionally, he undertakes a consulting assignment. His research investigates consumer ritual (Thanksgiving, New Year's, football bowl games, Halloween, inheritance), service relationships (friendship and betrayal), West African marketing channels, and the uses of qualitative data. His work has appeared in the three major U.S. marketing journals (*Journal of Consumer Research, Journal of Marketing*, and *Journal of Marketing Research*) as well as many other social science periodicals and books. Dr. Arnould is a frequent presenter at national and international conferences. He speaks French and Hausa and enjoys running, do-it-yourself work on his old house, and being a parent.

LINDA PRICE, *University of Nebraska–Lincoln*

Dr. Linda L. Price is E. J. Faulkner Professor of Agribusiness and Marketing at the University of Nebraska–Lincoln. She received her Ph.D. degree in marketing from the University of Texas–Austin in 1983. She also has been on the faculty at the University of South Florida; the University of Colorado, Boulder; the University of California, Irvine; Odense University, Denmark; and the University of Pittsburgh. Dr. Price has published over 50 research papers in areas of marketing and consumer behavior. Many of these papers appear in leading journals such as *Journal of Consumer Research, Journal of Marketing, Journal of Public Policy and Marketing*, and *Organization Science*. Linda is a frequent speaker at national and international conferences, universities, and community forums. She has consulted for several large multinationals but also for small enterprises, national and regional agencies, and not-for-profit organizations. Dr. Price's research focuses on consumers as emotional, imaginative, and creative agents and on the relational dimensions of consumers' behaviors. Her major areas of teaching include consumer behavior, market research, and marketing theory.

GEORGE ZINKHAN, *University of Georgia*

Dr. George Zinkhan is the Coca-Cola Company Chair of Marketing at the University of Georgia, Terry College of Business. He received his Ph.D. degree in marketing from the University of Michigan in 1981. Besides the University of Michigan, he also has taught at the University of Houston, University of Pittsburgh, and the Madrid School of Business. Dr. Zinkhan has published more than 100 research papers in the areas of marketing, advertising, and electronic commerce. These papers appear in leading journals such as *Journal of Marketing, Journal of Marketing Research, Journal of Consumer Research, Strategic Management Journal, Journal of Applied Psychology, Decision Sciences*, and *Journal of Advertising*. Among his recent co-authored books are *Electronic Commerce: The Strategic Perspective* (Harcourt, Inc., 2000) and *Advertising Research: The Internet, Consumer Behavior, and Strategy* (American Marketing Association, 2000). As indicated by the themes of these books, Dr. Zinkhan's research interests focus on consumer behavior, communication, electronic commerce, and knowledge development.

brief CONTENTS

CONTENTS

Part THREE

Consumers as Interpreters

Chapter SEVEN

Consumer Motives, Goals, and Involvement

Chapter EIGHT

Perception: Worlds of Sensations

Chapter NINE

Experience, Learning, and Knowledge

Part FIVE

Consumer Action

Chapter FIFTEEN

Consumer Attitudes and Decisions

Chapter SIXTEEN

Acquiring Things

Chapter SEVENTEEN

Consumer Innovation

Chapter EIGHTEEN

Consumer Satisfaction

CONSUMERS

chapter 1

LEARNING OBJECTIVES

After completing this chapter, you should be able to:

- Describe examples of the importance of consumer behavior in people's daily lives.
- Describe what consumer behavior is.
- Give examples of the domain of consumer behavior.
- Know generally why the circle of consumption is significant for marketing strategy.
- Identify some of the elements of social context that influence consumers.
- Know various approaches to the study of consumers.
- Understand some reasons why knowledge of consumer behavior is of value to you.

INTRODUCTION:
The World of Consumers

EVENING ROUTINES FOR TWO CONSUMERS

Denver, Colorado Peggy checks her e-mail one last time and tucks a report into the front of her briefcase, hoping she can find time to read it before tomorrow's 9:00 A.M. sales briefing. As usual, Peggy is running late. Her *Timex* watch reads 5:20 P.M. as she walks to the parking garage. With traffic, she'll be lucky to retrieve Sam and Sarah from daycare by the 6 P.M. deadline, and that's without stopping for milk. She'll have to drag the children with her into the local *Albertson's,* or forgo milk for cereal in the morning. A tough choice! She retrieves her new *Toyota Sienna* minivan from the four-story parking garage and heads for the daycare center, en-route home. The *Toyota Sienna* advertising campaign promises she'll "feel safe just looking at it," and she does. She doesn't feel this car fits her, but her children and their friends fit in it, and that's what's important for now. Dave teases her that soon she'll be the typical soccer mom.

Peggy listens to *All Things Considered* on National Public Radio as she fights evening traffic and braces herself for the most stressful two hours of her day. The children will be tired, hungry, and demanding her attention. Sam and Sarah like their daycare, but Peggy still feels guilty about the long hours they spend away from parents and home. Two more days until the weekend, then they'll do something special as a family. She mentally reviews the contents of the refrigerator and pantry. What can she cook quickly, that will still be a healthy balanced meal—not a frozen entrée or take-out? Pasta, salad, and chicken are her usual standby. She wishes she had time and energy to produce interesting meals. She has lots of 20-minute recipes she's gleaned from magazines such as *Redbook* and *Woman's Day,* but even they require a little advance ingredient planning.

As she pulls up to the daycare door, she pulls out her cell phone and calls Dave. He can stop for milk and eat with the family if he gets home by 7:30 P.M.

The children are hardly in the door before begging Peggy to turn on the TV. She relents. They love to watch *Dragon Tales* on PBS, and it is educational TV, but the truth is Peggy needs a break—it's almost 6:30 and the children should be bathed and in bed by 8:30 P.M. She puts a pot of water on the stove to boil. She's opting for instant linguine pasta tonight. She always buys the same brand of instant pasta and keeps a selection of different kinds in the freezer—it has a red label, but she can't remember the name. She pulls a jar of marinara sauce out of the pantry just as the phone rings—another telemarketing call. She should just let the answering machine pick up, but can't seem to break the habit of reaching for the phone. Peggy always buys the same kind of chicken too—air-chilled, boneless, skinless, chicken breasts, but doesn't remember the brand. She'll throw on some spices and marinate it with some white wine and olive oil while the oven preheats. She pulls out her wooden salad bowl. After 20 years of nearly daily use, she still loves this bowl—a wedding gift from a friend—the marriage didn't last, but the bowl did. Now, for the instant salad! *Earthbound,* organic herb salad, prewashed in a bag. She'll toss in some sliced cucumbers, shredded organic carrots, and sliced mushrooms to make it a little more interesting. Oh, and she'll heat some frozen peas in the microwave for the children.

Dinner is ready, the table is set, and the candles are lit. Peggy can spend a few minutes cuddling on the couch with the kids. Dave arrives with milk and a fresh baguette—a perfect addition—and surprises the family with the gift of a new DVD of *Harry Potter and the Sorcerer's Stone*. *Albertson's* now puts a rack of fresh baguettes by the checkout aisles each evening for last-minute shoppers like Dave. Having dinner together as a family is important to Peggy. It's the best chance they have to review their day together and plan tomorrow. They finish their meal with *Ben and Jerry's Chocolate Chip Cookie Dough* ice cream. The back label says they oppose recombinant bovine growth hormone, which seems like a good thing, but a single serving still has 130 calories from fat and that seems very bad. Peggy silently promises to run in the morning and serve fresh fruit for dessert tomorrow night.

Zinder, Niger At 5 P.M. Balla gives the cowhides soaking in a tanning bath of water and vegetal tanning agents a final stir, rinses his hands in the liquid, rises from his heels, tucks his pack of *Mai Zobe* cigarettes into his ragged pocket, and strides stiffly from the tannery. He walks down a narrow unpaved lane towards his home, stopping along the way to purchase a small plastic bag of roasted peanuts in the shell to give to his young son waiting for him at home.

Once home, he greets his second wife curtly at the door asking if she's bought water from the public pump. He directs her to place some in the sheltered outdoor bathing area, playing quietly with his son, and cracking peanuts for him, as he waits. After a few minutes, Balla heads for the bathing area, and using a bar of *Palmolive* soap and a fiber loofa washes off the grime of the workplace. He uses a tin teakettle to pour rinse water over his head. Then, wrapped in a striped Chinese bath towel, he heads into one of the three doorways of his dark three-room house, where he dresses in a long blue gown and drawstring pants tailored from polished cotton damask cloth made in the Netherlands, and claps a locally knitted skullcap on his head. He doses his clothing with a liberal shot of *Binta-el-Sudan* brand perfume, a big seller locally, and leaves the house en route for the neighborhood mosque for regular evening prayer.

Aisatou, Balla's senior wife, is in charge of cooking duties this evening. Realizing she is out of *Maggi* bouillon cubes (a Nestlé's brand), she sends her 10-year-old daughter Mariama out to the tiny kiosk at the corner with a 25-franc coin to purchase a single cube for use in the evening sauce. Maggi has been a popular seller in Niger for decades; Aisatou's friends all use them although *Amora* cubes (a Unilever brand) have recently entered the market. Mariama often helps out Aisatou in this way, making fill-in purchases from the local kiosk or ambulatory peddlers as the need arises. Meanwhile Aisatou tends her outdoor stove, basically an iron ring to hold the coals, with ventilation holes and supports for her aluminum pot locally manufactured from old oil drums.

A small congregation of neighborhood men celebrates the evening prayer. Balla returns from the mosque in the dark. As he passes, his friend Moussa, who is sitting in the porch that provides a doorway to the interior of his home, greets Balla. Woven plastic mats manufactured in Nigeria protect his clothes from the dusty floor. Balla removes his backless shoes and joins Moussa. After some minutes of chatting, Moussa's teenage daughter emerges silently from the interior of the house, kneels, and pushes towards her father an enameled metal tray on which are three matching covered enamel dishes, and retreats. Moussa and Balla ignore her. A few minutes later, the same young woman places a lit, Chinese-made, *Rooster* brand kerosene hurricane lamp on the porch.

Mysteriously, about 10 minutes later, Mariama arrives, carrying a similar set of enameled dishes on her head, and Balla's son trailing behind her. Moussa then turns to his tray, opens the smallest dish, and pours the contents, a tomato and squash–based sauce, over the contents of the largest dish, cooked spaghetti. He hands a spoon to Balla, and repeating the words, "Bismilla," they dig in. After eating some, Balla offers his neighbor Aisatou's dish, boiled millet cake with dried okra sauce seasoned with Maggi and peanut oil, which they share, eating with their right hands. Balla is especially pleased with this traditional dish as it is one of his favorites, and Aisatou prepares it with care. The dish also sends a subtle message about their family values and Aisatou's role as a careful and caring wife to Moussa, a message of which Balla approves. Balla also feeds a few bites of the meal to his son, who plays nearby as they dine. After finishing their meal, they access the final dish on the tray that contains cool tap water for them to drink. As they sip, a small boy, a student from the *madrasa* (Koranic school), passes begging for charity. Moussa and Balla spoon some of their leftovers into the student's begging bowl.

OVERVIEW

As the opening vignettes suggest, the subject of this book is people's acquisition, use, and disposal of products, services, ideas, and experiences—their behavior as consumers. The vignettes help to illustrate that people around the world are consumers to varying degrees, and that consuming is an ever-present aspect of daily life, sometimes affecting us in surprising ways. The first chapter of this book introduces you to the study of consumers. First, we describe the broad range of consumer activities in daily life. Even as a consumer, you may not have given much thought to the significance of these activities in our lives. Next, we outline what we mean by consumer behavior. One key idea to retain from this discussion is how diverse consumers are, and how varied are their consumption activities. The next section of the chapter outlines different ways to study consumers. These approaches are based in basic social science disciplines such as anthropology, economics, sociology, and psychology. While we integrate these approaches in the book, specialists in each subject area pursue their interests in consumers vigorously. The final topic we address is the question of why you should study consumers. We suggest a number of reasons: managerial, personal, and policy-oriented.

CONSUMER ACTIVITIES IN DAILY LIFE

If you stop and think for a moment, you'll realize that during a large part of your day you are involved in consumer activities. If you are anything like the two consumers we describe in the introductory vignettes in this chapter, the early evening hours of your day include lots of consumer activities. Take a few moments right now and think about your early evening hours. For many, this is a time of transition from the workday, where the focus is on productive activity, to a time at home with family and friends with a focus on consumption activity. What are your evening consumption routines and habits? Is this a time when you make certain kinds of purchases, and make them in certain places with some regularity? Are the products or brands you use different than the ones you use during the workday? Are some of these brands that you regularly use, that you feel loyal to? Do some of them have special meanings for you, or remind you of certain people and events in your life? Are you consuming alone or with others?

The two consumers in the opening vignettes (Peggy and Balla) live in different parts of the world, and obviously engage in some different consumption activities. To explain the consumer activities of Peggy and Balla, we need to understand how their cultures and geographic location inform their behaviors. In the first part of this book, especially Chapters 2 and 3, we will talk about important cultural differences in virtually every aspect of consumer activity.

Balla's wife Aisatou encourages him to wash off the odors of the tannery every day with sweet smelling Palmolive soap every evening before evening prayer. The frequency of this ***grooming ritual,*** a topic we discuss in Chapter 3, varies in different cultures.[1] Grooming rituals are important because they prepare us to enter public, private, and other significant social environments, and allow us to communicate specific messages about ourselves. Consider the managerial implications of grooming in a different context. Many Hungarians believe it is unhealthy to wash their hair more often than once or twice a week.[2] Proctor & Gamble would like to grow the shampoo market in Hungary, where P&G is the market leader, by encouraging Hungarians to engage in the hair-washing ritual more frequently. In the second part of the book, we discuss marketing strategies and how marketers try to identify target markets and position their products to deliver benefits to them.

Peggy and Balla's consumer behaviors also reflect a number of processes that reflect their interpretations of information about the world and their place in it, such as their ***self-concepts*** (Chapter 10); their ***motivations*** (Chapter 7); and past ***experiences, learning, and knowledge*** (Chapter 9). Thus, piety is an aspect of the self-concept that motivates Balla to purchase a fine gown and perfume to wear at the mosque, and to dispose of leftovers as alms to a begging Koranic student. Peggy feels torn between her work role and desire to be a good mother. She struggles to prepare a "balanced but fast" meal for her family and relies on trusted brands of pasta and chicken to help. Her experience and knowledge lead her to trust them. For similar reasons, Aisatou trusts the quality of Maggi bouillon cubes, while her knowledge of eating behaviors leads her to send her husband's meal to him to consume at Moussa's house.

Evening **rituals** also reflect variations in the social context in which Peggy and Balla live their lives, including their ***lifestyles*** (Chapter 11), ***household structures,*** and stage in the ***family life cycle.*** Peggy and Dave juggle a career and family and Peggy is a member of a two-career family like a growing number of consumers in Europe and North America; Balla too is a family man, as are most people in his country.[3] Household influences on consumption are described in Chapter 13. The growth in dual-career households in affluent consumer societies leads to demand for products such as the Toyota Sienna that facilitate suburban lifestyles and healthy convenience products such as instant pasta and instant salad. The presence of a preteen daughter leads Aisatou to entrust her with much of the family shopping. Peggy and Balla's consumption routines would change if they were single. For example, Peggy might frequent fast-food shops and dine with female singles like herself. Balla would probably live in his father's

The minivan is a great example of a product with a strong life-style appeal, here positioned to stimulate beliefs and feelings about safety.

household; he would tend to eat with a peer group. It's also important to observe that behaviors such as cooking and eating are strongly influenced by ***gender, social class, ethnicity,* and *age.*** The impact of social and economic structures on consumer behavior is the topic of Chapter 12.

The study of consumer behavior includes a focus on relationships between what people think, feel, and do. These matters are the focus of the final part of the book. For example, the vignette describes Peggy's ***beliefs and feelings*** about her minivan. Peggy thinks that her brand of minivan facilitates her lifestyle, and also feels good using it because of its safety features. Thus, Peggy has a positive **attitude** toward her minivan (Chapter 15), although it's not a perfect expression of her sense of self (Chapter 10). Her beliefs and feelings are compatible, and these beliefs and feelings are also consistent with her **purchase behavior.** Many of the chapters in this book will help untangle how choices are made. For example, Chapter 8 describes how perceptions influence attention and processing of advertisements and product packaging and Chapter 15 describes some different choice rules or **heuristics** that consumers employ in making purchase decisions. In consideration of these issues, we could describe Peggy as ***brand loyal*** in her pasta purchases.[4] **Brand loyalty** *is more than just repeat purchase behavior. It also includes a preference for a particular brand and a positive emotional response to the brand.* Very often other people influence our attitudes and behaviors (Chapter 14) such as the case of Aisatou's brand loyalty to Maggi bouillon cubes.

www.maggiworld.com

www.amora.com

Peggy and Balla use and reuse products in new ways to solve particular consumption problems. Peggy does mental inventories of her cupboards and refrigerator in deciding how to create an interesting meal from the ingredients on hand. Balla uses a plastic kettle as a tool for washing. They engage in **use innovativeness.**[5] That is, *they are con-*

stantly on the lookout for novel ways to solve familiar problems or address familiar needs. Many consumers and organizations are concerned with creating innovative solutions to consumption problems. The **diffusion** and **adoption** of innovative products in consumer and industrial contexts is an important field within consumer behavior. **Diffusion** *refers to the spread of a new product through a population.* Balla's wearing of Dutch cloth while eating off of Nigerian enamelware to the light of a Chinese kerosene lamp, and Aisatou's use of an "improved stove" are good examples of the effects of diffusion and are related to the fact that Niger was a European colony and borders Nigeria. Innovation and resistance to innovation are the subject of Chapter 17. Notice too that Balla's shower is a kettle ***recycled*** for this purpose. In Chapter 19 we focus on consumers and organizations' recycling, reusing, and disposal behaviors.[6]

WHAT IS CONSUMER BEHAVIOR?

Peggy and Balla probably share other consumption activities with you, including producing and sharing a routine meal, making purposeful choices, engaging in habitual purchase and consumption behavior, using branded consumer products, consuming products imported from different countries, using and enjoying gifts (Dave's DVD purchase), and so forth. Consumer researchers may study each of these activities. So what is consumer behavior; is it everything? No, we define **consumer behavior** as *individuals or groups acquiring, using, and disposing of products, services, ideas, or experiences.* But what does this definition really mean? In this section of the chapter we try to answer this question in three ways. In the first part, we simply take apart this definition, and explain each of its parts. In the second part, we introduce the idea of the circle of consumption and its relationship to marketing strategy.

The Domain of Consumer Behavior

Exhibit 1.1 provides a graphic illustration of the **domain of consumer behavior.** Consumers may consist of individuals or groups. Parts 3 and 5 of the book focus on individual consumers. Consuming groups include families, clubs and organizations, purchasing units within corporations, and governments. Organizations range from consumer cooperatives to nonprofit advocacy groups like Amnesty International. Government organizations that purchase and consume may vary in size from small rural communities to nation-states. Part 4 of the book focuses on groups.

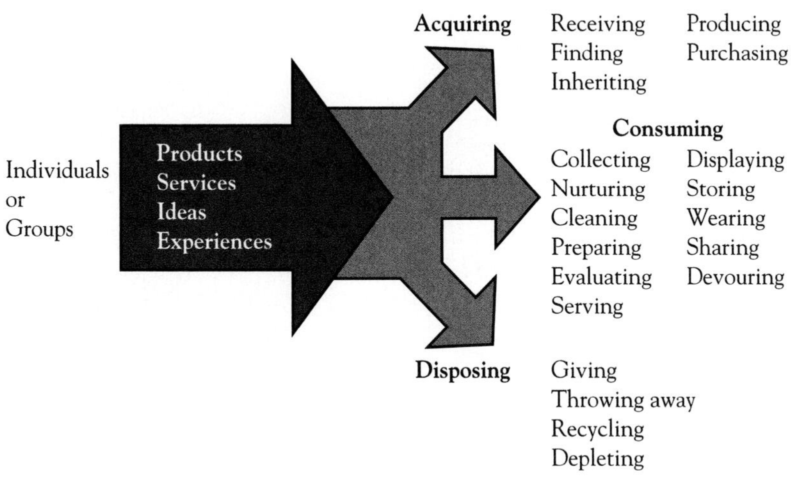

EXHIBIT 1.1

The Domain of Consumer Behavior

Acquiring includes a range of activities such as receiving, finding, inheriting, producing, and, of course, purchasing. The first two chapters in Part 5 focus on these issues. Consuming encompasses many different behaviors too, such as collecting, nurturing, cleaning, preparing, displaying, storing, wearing, sharing, evaluating, devouring, and serving. We discuss some of these activities in Chapter 4, concerned with consumption meanings, while Chapter 18 deals extensively with consumers' evaluations of goods and services. Finally, disposition spans a range of behaviors that includes giving, throwing away, recycling, and depleting, which we discuss in Chapter 19. As pointed out in the next section of the chapter, each of these activities provides marketers with multiple opportunities to develop distinctive market offerings and product positionings.

As indicated in Exhibit 1.1, each activity can involve products, services, ideas, and experiences. For example, many private homes include *products* such as furnishings and appliances that have been received as gifts, recycled, purchased, and inherited. Some travelers such as back-packers and mountain climbers collect *experiences,* talking about places they have traveled and mountains they have climbed. For instance, a recent ad for the nation of Turkey promotes the natural mystery tourists experience in this ancient land. Prior to a long-distance move, many consumers visit their doctors, dentists, hairdressers, and restaurants to acquire services that will tide them over until new service relationships are established in a new community. We might almost say these consumers are trying to store *services.* Some corporations have disposed of the old functional specializations (e.g., research and development, engineering, marketing, customer service, materials handling) and have adopted new organizational forms such as parallel engineering, quality circles, and the marketing orientation (see Chapter 5). Others purchase research data that profiles potential or actual customers. These corporations are disposing of and acquiring *ideas and information!*[7]

Because the subject is so far ranging, topics that consumer behavior researchers study are limited only by their imagination. For example, a consumer behavior researcher employed by a commercial firm may study how individuals differentiate among and

Promoting Consumption Experiences: Turkish Tourism

choose brands of pasta sauce. Consumer behavior researchers also study how individuals and families acquire a pet or a preference for particular species of pet; plan, take, and remember a family vacation; celebrate the Chinese Midsummer Festival; use their refrigerator as a family altar to display photos and accomplishments; and dispose of old telephone books. Consumer behavior researchers are also likely to study how firms choose and evaluate suppliers, or even how a city chooses a landfill engineering company. Further, they are likely to study how these decisions are related to other psychological, demographic, sociological, cultural, and economic factors. For example, a number of researchers have sought to relate changes in households' acquisition of consumer durables such as microwave ovens or microcomputers to changes in gender and work roles.[8] Thus, as we discuss below, many academic disciplines provide insights for understanding consumer behavior.

The Circle of Consumption and Marketing Strategy

Exhibit 1.2 illustrates the **circle of consumption.** The circle of consumption provides an approach to the study of consumption and developing marketing strategy that focuses on consumption activities. The circle of consumption is based on the fact that *the production and acquisition of goods and services, their consumption, and the disposal of used goods are part of a cycle of managerial and socioeconomic activities.* We refer to this description of the consumption process at various points in the text to illustrate marketing opportunities. Understanding each phase and the relationships between them is useful for marketers and others interested in understanding consumers.

The processes of production, acquisition, consumption, and disposal are universal. In every society, consumption is organized into behavioral systems involving varying groupings of goods and persons. As suggested by Exhibit 1.2, the order in which the processes of production, acquisition, consumption, and disposal occur and the participants in the processes vary both within and between societies. Some are commercial processes and some are not. In marketing, we ordinarily think of the circle of consumption as moving from production by a manufacturer to distribution through an array

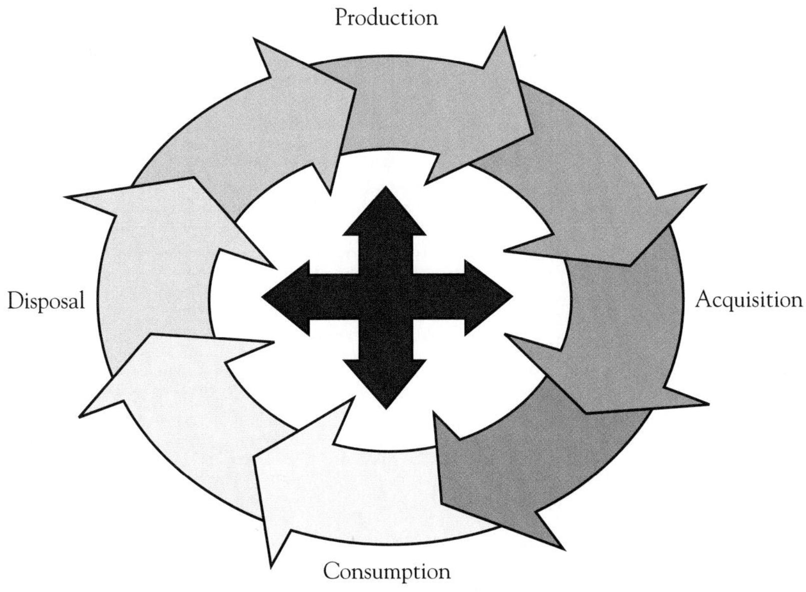

EXHIBIT 1.2

Circle of Consumption

of marketing intermediaries (distributors, wholesalers, and retailers), to acquisition by an industrial buyer or end consumer, who then consumes the product in further production activities or in final consumption. Both types of consumers then dispose of the waste generated by their consumption activities in some way. Indeed, we focus primarily on this type of consumption cycle in this book. However, the number of steps in the circle of consumption, as well as the order of the steps, varies.

Much of the attention of marketers has focused on **acquisition** as the critical phase in the circle of consumption. In the past, marketers focused mostly on one kind of acquisition—purchase decisions. They have studied how consumers and organizational buyers gather information, evaluate it, and decide which products, services, and ideas to buy. This psychological approach to purchase behavior imagines that consumers engage in search and evaluation of product and brand alternatives and judge their purchase decisions in terms of how well the purchases solve their consumption problems. You can probably think of many of your own purchase decisions that fit this model. For example, perhaps you decided that you needed easier access to the Web to better manage your schoolwork and your job, so you decided to purchase a personal digital assistant (PDA). You learned about brands in *PC Magazine,* evaluated them at an online website sponsored by a consumer testing organization, and then made your choice at a local retailer.

Exhibit 1.2 also invites you to think about products—physical products, services, ideas, and celebrities, for example—as having **biographies.**[9] Think of your collection of possessions. How were your possessions acquired? Consumption is not a simple outcome of a single purchase, but may involve a host of activities. For example, a consumer

An appeal based on the idea of the biography of possessions is illustrated in this ad for American Girl dolls.

An appeal based on the idea of the biography of possessions in this ad for Patek Philippe.

may purchase a koala bear doll on a holiday taken in Australia. She may then display the doll in her home. Perhaps following a move or a lifestyle change, the consumer may give the koala doll away to a young niece. It's conceivable that someday the doll could become what people call "a collectible." At this point, the niece may decide that she would prefer to sell the doll on the eBay website rather than keep it. The biography of things can contribute value to objects beyond the value of consumer goods that are merely offered for sale. As suggested by the text of their ads, The American Girl Collection shown on p. 12 and Patek Philippe ads shown above both use the idea that things may have a biography to promote different categories of consumer goods—a line of collectible dolls and high-end watches, respectively.

The idea that products have a biography may apply to industrial goods as well. Consider steel printing machinery, the kind used to print this book or your newspaper. It may be purchased new, then resold as used equipment to a lower-tech producer, even donated to a charity, and, finally, end up lovingly restored and preserved in a museum of arts and industries such as the Smithsonian Institution in Washington, DC, or the Musée d'Arts et Industries in Paris, France. Sixty-six percent of steel of the kind used in printing equipment in the United States is in fact recycled at some point. The figure for the United Kingdom is about 40 percent.[10]

You have probably already realized that for both consumer and industrial products, each of the transfers and the associated behaviors presents businesses with entrepreneurial opportunities to manage the movement, use, and disposition of the goods. In the last few years, managerial focus has evolved from its preoccupation with acquisition to include the full circle of consumption. Understanding acquisition, which is very important to marketers, requires an understanding of the other steps because consumer beliefs, values, and attitudes are affected by these links. By understanding the links between these phases, managers can implement strategies to influence the timing and sequence of these phases, which, in turn, can affect demand for their product. For example, **disposition** *refers to those processes by which consumers divest themselves of consumer goods*. By looking at disposition, the circle of consumption highlights the importance of "thinking green" and the value to organizations of developing sustainable marketing practices (e.g., practices that are environmentally friendly and do not unnecessarily deplete the planet's resources).[11] A quick search of the Internet will also introduce you to dozens of companies that offer for-profit solutions to consumers' waste production processes. The following examples are presented to help you understand the managerial implications of the circle of consumption.

FROM DISPOSAL TO ACQUISITION In the Netherlands, thousands of bales of used, unwanted clothing are collected from individual households through a public works program for the unemployed and shipped to less developed countries where they are refurbished and resold. Private dealers in the United States have been buying beat-up old British sports cars such as MGs, Triumphs, and Austin Healeys and shipping them to Europe for restoration and resale at premium prices. In the United States, parts dealers scavenge consumer durables such as washers, refrigerators, and air conditioners. Very few of these machines end up in landfills. On the consumer side, young married couples often put new households together from extra and leftover housewares retrieved from their parents' garages and basements.[12]

www.aertinc.com

http://207.122.589.com/68850

www.safetykleen.com

http://www.webcon.net.au/quilts/links.html

FROM DISPOSAL TO PRODUCTION An Arkansas firm called Advanced Environmental Recycling Technologies recycles waste materials including ground up plastic and wood chips to make termite- and weather-resistant window frames and trim (see the brochure photo below). Many companies (for example, Tee-Gee) now recycle old newspaper and cardboard to make pencil bodies. Safety Kleen Corporation rinses the used industrial solvents it collects so that the solvent can be reused; the solid waste products are incinerated and used in making concrete. In Senegal, craftsmen mold empty tuna fish and beer cans into attaché cases for resale. On the consumer side, consumers have long produced new products from old ones such as women who make use of fabric scraps to create beautiful quilts. The Australian website given in the margin provides links to quilting groups and commercial raw material dealers.

A.E.R.T. uses recycled waste materials to develop an innovative product.

FROM DISPOSAL TO CONSUMPTION In a world-wide advertising campaign, Patek Philippe watches, mentioned above, suggests that consumers think of giving their watches as heirloom gifts; one consumer's disposition is another's consumption. In the United States, Second Harvest coordinates nationwide donations in food, cash, and kind from corporate partners and restaurants that provide assistance to the hungry and homeless. Donors receive tax benefits. For a fee, old pencils and pencil-making technology can be revisited at your leisure in the Cumberland Pencil Museum, in Cumbria, United Kingdom. On the consumer side, one of the authors owns a photograph showing a paper 7-Eleven Slurpee cup holding flowers placed on a grave on the Mexican Day of the Dead in Arizona. Cast-off rubber tires are used as planters and children swings in the United States and as hoops in children's games in the **less affluent world (LAW).**

@ www.secondharvest.org

@ http://museum@pencils.co.uk

FROM PRODUCTION TO CONSUMPTION Many firms make component parts such as ball bearings that are consumed in the course of further industrial production, such as the manufacture of conveyor systems. Farmers in the less affluent world produce and consume an important fraction of their own food, shelter, and clothing. On the consumer side, Señora Gonçalves, a middle-class Portuguese consumer, produces her family's evening meal from "scratch," by baking a casserole in her gas oven. Rick, a mild mannered professor from Edmonton, Canada, makes several trips to his local Home Depot and builds a deck for his family to enjoy on summer evenings.

FROM ACQUISITION TO CONSUMPTION This process affects items received for immediate consumption. Power plants purchase coal, oil, and gas for immediate consumption. On the consumer side, take-out (or "take away," as they say in the United Kingdom) meals are an example of this process. Hunter-gatherer groups in Greenland harvest natural products for immediate consumption, as do amateur game hunters and mushroom gatherers in North America. The Noyes Museum in Oceanville, New Jersey, recently ran an exhibit entitled ReCreation/Recreation that featured 50 artists from around the United States, delighting in the artistic possibilities found in trash. A recent issue of *Utne Reader* magazine suggested that collecting found objects as a means of creative expression has become a bonafide trend. The Online 'zine *Found* is devoted to the pastime.[13]

@ www.foundmagazine.com

FROM ACQUISITION TO DISPOSAL Many firms thrive in this niche. The U.S. $6 billion gift industry involves the purchase of goods for immediate disposal through gift giving. Japanese tourists take the purchase of *omiyage,* souvenirs of foreign travel, as gifts to friends at home to a high art.[14] In Mexico girls celebrating their 15th birthday, called "Quinceaños," may receive Hallmark greeting cards. In Singapore, a teacher might receive Hallmark's Forever Friends–branded gift products to enjoy on Teacher's Day, September 1st. Some people frequent garage sales and flea markets to provision their own subsequent selling activities. Some impulse shoppers purchase expensive clothing for the thrill of the purchase and later return the goods unused to the retail store or even hide them away in drawers and closets unused.[15]

HOW DO YOU STUDY CONSUMERS?

To be successful, marketers and policy makers need to understand the role of consumption activities in the daily lives of consumers such as Peggy, Balla, and you. And increasingly they need to have a broadened understanding of consumption as we have described it above. For example, Wolfgang Schmitt, chairman and CEO of Rubbermaid, Inc., stresses this very thing: the need to understand consumer trends in their broadest sense, including not just demographics or lifestyle, but also fashion, color, technology, government, and law. He also stresses the necessity for firms to gain real insight into consumers' lives. Rubbermaid doesn't just use marketing communication tools to sell product; of equal importance to the firm is sharing experiences about how to use those products—how consumers might organize their kitchen or solve space problems in their child's room. This approach to understanding consumers' "life worlds" and positioning products as central to their lives is one of several newer approaches to marketing adopted by consumer products companies as diverse as Dockers, Levi's, and Pepsico Co.'s Mountain Dew brand. You can find out more about Rubbermaid's provision of consumer solutions at their website.[16]

www.rubbermaid.com

Learning about consumers is the key to successful marketing. We outline different ways to learn about consumers in Chapter 6. Consider a simple decision such as the purchase and use of salad ingredients. Peggy, who we met above, is loyal to her Earthbound prewashed, organic salad mixes and is willing to pay a substantial price premium, but other consumers may experiment with different salad mixes, or choose the cheapest brand, or buy one they saw advertised on television. Companies such as Dole who produce a variety of salad mixes and distribute them internationally are interested in research to establish how consumers around the world evaluate different brands and make such decisions.

Peggy is part of a **market segment** of consumers that desires products that are "healthy" and "natural." Companies in different parts of the world have found it profitable to ***target*** this segment with marketing appeals. For example, Wild Oats market targets this segment in North America, while a multitude of retailers target this segment in the United Kingdom and Europe.[17] Throughout this book and especially in Chapters 5 and 6 and Part 4, we will discuss how marketers identify, select, and target market segments.

www.wildoats.com

http://www.organicsmart.co.uk

Of course, it is also important for marketers to learn about customer needs and wants in business-to-business settings. Some examples of business needs include low cost, high quality, prompt delivery time, inventory management, and profit maximization. If business-to-business marketers have a good understanding of their customers, then they have a better chance to build a relationship that will last a long time and be mutually beneficial for both buyer and seller.

Making sense of consumer behavior is important in a number of professions, and professionals make sense of consumer behavior on the basis of an array of approaches and to serve many different goals. Think about the principles that you learned in your coursework in anthropology, sociology, economics, history, or psychology, for example. They can be useful in explaining consumer behavior.[18] In fact, consumer researchers examine consumer behaviors from five orientations that are based in several social sciences:

1. Anthropology. Its influence on marketing is relatively recent. This perspective has tended to focus on consumers' behaviors and practices to help organize our understanding of phenomena such as consumption rituals, myths, and symbols, and contributes a concern with the meaning and significance of consumption to consumers. Anthropology is the source of the meaning transfer framework used to explain some aspects of acquisition discussed in Part 1 of the book. It has contributed the ethnographic method to market research discussed in Chapter 6.
2. Economics. Macroeconomics provides indicators of consumption behaviors very useful to understanding global differences in consumption. We discuss consumption indicators in Chapter 2. Classical microeconomic theory is the

source of the utility-maximizing framework used to explain some aspects of information processing and product choice making and to model purchase behaviors discussed in Part 5 of the book. Economics has helped us understand how consumers respond to prices and pricing tactics.[19]

3. History and geography. The influence of these disciplines on marketing is relatively minor. Their focus is on the origins and development of consumer culture, including marketing communications and advertising, and the impact on urban and suburban landscapes of marketing institutions and practices, especially retail spaces. Geographical models of market system structure and retail placement are influential, however. McDonald's Corporation chooses retail sites primarily on the basis of geography and population density, and shopping mall owners plot the effect of the "retail gravity" exerted by the mall on surrounding populations, for example.
4. Psychology. Perhaps the most influential social science in marketing is psychology. From psychology derive the ideas of personality, the self, and the individual, ideas essential to the study of "the consumer." More specifically, the decision-making, experiential, hedonic, and behavioral influence perspectives on consumer learning, attitude formation, decision making, and choice discussed in Parts 3 and 5 of this book derive from psychological theories. So too does work on ***darkside consumption behaviors*** such as addictions and compulsive consumptions such as gambling.[20]
5. Sociology. Sociology has contributed insights into the social forces that influence consumption such as religion and social structural concepts such as social class, ethnicity, gender, and lifestyles that help organize our understanding of social context effects on individual and group consumption behaviors. In addition, sociologists pay a lot of attention to the blending of marketing and popular culture including fashion, popular music, and literature. Sociologists have also pioneered study of the moral and symbolic significance of consumption activities and have been in the forefront of those critical of the downsides of consumer society such as excessive materialism and waste.[21]

This book tries to integrate these approaches and goals. But it's a good idea to have a sense of these approaches and goals at the outset. One way to get a sense of the diversity of approaches to consumers is taking an example and thinking about how different people might view it given their different backgrounds, perspectives, and goals. Consider the two pictures of consumers, one a family from Mali in West Africa, a part of the less affluent world, and the other of a family in Russia, a country with a **transitional economy,** one moving between a state-dominated economy and a market-dominated one. What different questions might marketers with a background in these five different disciplines pose in response to the photos on pages 18 and 19.

Let's take as an example the bicycles that are one of the few common elements between the two photos. An anthropologist might be interested in the meanings of the bicycles to the two consumer families. She might ask if bicycles are associated with freedom of movement in Mali and with health and exercise in Russia. She might also wonder about the nature and significance of bicycle excursions for members of the two households. She might also wonder whether these values could explain the consumption of other products in the two cultures. Or she might wonder whether the families were members of a particular ethnic or tribal group and if this factor could influence the meaning and use of bicycles. Such information could be useful for product positioning, of course.

Household consumer goods in Mali, a country in the less affluent world include a bicycle.

A macroeconomist might ask what the bicycles represent as relative shares of the households' discretionary income and how large the average household's discretionary income is in the two countries. He might be interested in generating an estimate of total national demand for bicycles and other discretionary goods in the two countries from this information. Such estimates might be of interest to firms considering market entry with other discretionary consumer goods. A microeconomist might be interested in the question of what trade-offs each household made to purchase the bicycle and how they arrived at the decision that a bicycle would best suit their needs relative to other alternatives. He might wonder if bicycles are considered a luxury, and wonder about the reasons for such a luxury purchase in Mali, where the inventory of consumer goods is otherwise so modest. An economic orientation might also lead to inquiry into the frequency of bicycle and bicycle part purchase and replacement, given the environmental differences between frigid Russia and arid Mali.

A marketer with a background in geography might be interested in the nature of the retail landscape for bicycles. She might wonder if bicycle specialty shops exist in these countries, or if bicycles are sold in other retail environments. She might also be curious about the country of origin of these bicycles. Are they locally made or imported, and if imported how? A historian might wonder when Russians and Malians first began to bicycle and how this practice spread to Russia and Mali, and from where.

A contemporary consumer researcher with a background in psychology might be very interested in the decision process that led to the bicycle purchase in each country. He might wonder whether and how this purchase was a planned behavior and if so, what sort of planning was involved. How was information gathered and assessed? Who was the decision maker? The psychologically oriented researcher might also wonder what consumer goals drove this purchase. Were these goals functional, emotional, or perhaps status-oriented?

A sociological perspective might well inspire a researcher to inquire about the obvious differences in family size represented in the two photos and wonder about the structure of these families. He might wonder who is the decision maker for bicycles in

Household consumer goods in Russia, a country with a transitional economy, include bicycles.

the two households and if this might vary depending upon the financial importance of the decision to the household. He might also be struck by the larger number of bicycles per family member in the Russian context and inquire about the social class of the two families. He might wonder whether these are both "middle class" families and, if so, how large the Russian and Malian middle classes are. He might also inquire about who rides bicycles and whether this varies by age and gender in the two cultures. Finally, he might wonder how bicycle ownership affects or is affected by social status in the two countries.

The different types of questions researchers with different disciplinary orientations ask lead them to different views of the nature of consumers and consumer behavior.

WHY STUDY CONSUMER BEHAVIOR?

Studying consumer behavior is exciting and fun, but it can be important to you for a number of reasons. First, if you plan to go into business, understanding consumer behavior is critical, as our examples from movements around the circle of consumption above suggest. In market economies, businesses stay in business not by producing products, building accounting systems, generating dividends for their owners, or managing employees. To restate the definition of marketing in functional terms, we can say that businesses stay in business by *attracting and retaining customers.* They attract and retain customers by engaging in exchanges of resources (including information, money, goods, services, status, and emotions) with consumers, exchanges that both businesses and their customers perceive to be beneficial.[22] When companies ask Who are our customers? How do we reach them? What should we sell them? What will motivate them to buy? What makes them satisfied? they are asking questions that require a sophisticated understanding of consumers.

Let's take one more everyday example. A knowledge of the principles of perception and learning discussed in Part 3 in this book can help you design a restaurant menu to encourage people to notice and choose some items more than others. The placement on a page, vividness of presentation, and use of various kinds of perceptual surprises such as the large size of some of the items shown in the Hard Rock Cafe® menu can influence diner's choices. For example, items featured in the photos may be highly profitable for the restaurant, and merely by picturing them on the menu customers may be more likely to purchase them. See Exhibit 1.3 for an example of such a menu.

Marketers can benefit both from understanding what problems consumers have and from how consumers themselves solve these problems. In this spirit, Microsoft Corp. uses a slogan "Where do you want to go today?" claiming, "We do a lot of our best work trying to keep up with your imagination." Many companies have learned that successful marketing often means keeping up with their customers' imaginations. Similarly, Apple Computer's and Nokia's newest computing products cater to emerging needs for portability, systems integration, and management of a broad range of digital contents including sound, image, and text.

http://www.apple.com/imac

http://www.nokiausa.com/communicator

As the world grows smaller and the global reach of businesses expands, the job of attracting and retaining customers grows ever more challenging. As in many other aspects of human behavior there are important universal elements, but equally important local differences governing consumer behaviors. For example, companies may have a hint that their customers are dissatisfied (e.g., sales may be declining), but they may

EXHIBIT 1.3

Hard Rock Cafe Menu. Its design incorporates many principles of consumer behavior.

not know the exact nature or content of this dissatisfaction. For instance, if Ford Motor Company notices that sales of Ford Lasers in Thailand in the most recent quarter are much lower than expected, they know that there is a problem in the marketplace. However, they don't know the specific cause of the problem. Do changing consumer tastes, preferences for new competitive products, economic conditions, engineering mistakes, or something else cause it? To see how Ford promotes its vehicles in Thailand, take a look at Ford's marketing communication campaign.

@ http://www.ford.co.th/advertisement/fordtoday.htm

Even if you don't plan to go into business, there's a good chance that understanding consumer behavior will be an important tool in your job. Many not-for-profit organizations (governments, arts organizations, and charities) define their mission in terms of satisfaction of human needs and wants of some sort. Knowledge of consumer behavior helps nonprofit organizations understand donors' motivations, produce effective communication programs, and change behaviors (e.g., public service announcements that encourage the use of seat belts or discourage smoking). As private individuals, we "market" ourselves to firms and other members of society (e.g., to attract a sponsor for our skateboarding obsession, to solidify personal relationships, or to get a job). If you think this seems extreme, just have a look at "marketing communications" to be found in the personals pages of any daily or weekly newspaper.[23] Thus, to imagine ourselves in another person's shoes—to think about other people's needs and motivations—is not only good practice; it's a marketing skill.

A third reason to take an interest in consumer behavior is its importance to many important debates in **public policy.** Government regulators, lobbyists for industry groups, and nonprofit organizations and activist organizations seek to influence myriad government and corporate policies and consumer activities.

Public policy defends consumer rights from perceived threats through the application of remedies that are formalized in laws and regulations. Consumers' rights are often taken to include four rights enunciated by President John F. Kennedy in the early 1960s in the **Consumer Bill of Rights:** the rights to safety, to be informed, to choose, and to be heard. In recent years, consumers' right to privacy has been added to the list of the concerns of policy makers and advocates. The Canadian government has recently adopted some relatively strong laws protecting consumers' privacy rights. You may have encountered discussions of the laws and regulations designed to defend these rights in classes in introductory marketing, business law, international business, or consumer science.

@ http://www.privcom.gc.ca/legislation/index_e.asp

Threats to consumer rights abound. For example, harmful product ingredients, faulty manufacturing processes, or even marketing campaigns that target "vulnerable" consumers may negatively affect consumer safety. An example is tobacco marketing and merchandising directed at consumers in the less affluent world who cannot afford health care and are ignorant of tobacco's health effects (see photo on page 59 in Chapter 2). Note that this example also concerns a threat to the right to be informed. A website devoted to the conflict is sponsored by the United Nations World Health Organization.

@ http://www5.who.int/tobacco/index.cfm

Threats to the right to choose are extremely varied. For example, monopolies that control and limit products offered to consumers constrain choice. State and federal governments recently sued Microsoft Corporation because its Windows software was felt to constrain choice of Internet browsers. Suits are pending in Europe as well. Product counterfeiting, a rampant problem in Eastern Europe and Asia, constrains consumers' access to authentic products. It has led to conflict among World Trade Organization members, and to the labeling of consumers who download songs and movies as thieves and criminals. Psychological problems such as compulsive consumption behaviors also inhibit choice. These include eating disorders such as anorexia or obesity (recently recognized as a global health problem); compulsive shopping and gambling; and addictions to alcohol, tobacco, and drugs.

Remedies to threats to consumer rights take the form of industry rules, government regulations, and laws, including international treaties and conventions. Most governments in the developed world have consumer protection agencies that formulate and monitor regulations designed to protect consumers. Usually their policy remedies do one of three things: They inform consumers; they mandate certain consumption choices; and, sometimes, the regulations also constrain or limit consumer choices.[24] Labeling food products to identify whether they contain genetically modified ingredients or have been produced in accordance with organic standards is an example of a remedy that informs consumers. Restricting the amount and content of marketing communications to children who may lack the cognitive resources necessary to separate commercial content from noncommercial content in targeted TV programs is an example that constrains advertisers' choices in the interests of protecting a vulnerable group. For example, the European Parliament has banned companies from sending promotional products to children in the European Union.[25]

A final reason why studying consumers is important comes from a personal perspective. We live in a marketing age where almost anything can be offered to someone as a possible object of consumption. For example, in the aftermath of the terrorist attacks in New York City on September 11, 2001, the U.S. market was flooded with flag-themed merchandise. Meanwhile all sorts of Osama Bin Laden merchandise quickly appeared in markets globally. Products ranged from cologne to toilet paper featuring images of

Thai anticounterfeit officials use a steamroller to crush hundreds of thousands of counterfeit products ranging from fake Rolex watches to Disney Winnie the Pooh dolls worth a total of 28 million baht ($620,000) at a police headquarters in Bangkok on May 11, 2001. Despite regular police raids, fake watches and pirated brand-name clothes are openly on sale throughout Thailand.

this notorious figure. You can easily imagine that these products would appeal to very different consumer groups! Further, thousands of organizations and organizational groups work hard to persuade people to consume in ways beneficial to their goals. People need tools to help them understand the persuasive tactics that bombard them and to devise strategies for sorting out what products are meaningful to them and what are not. After completing this course, you will be better informed and prepared to exercise more effective control over your own consumer behavior. You will know more about the strategies and tactics marketers use to influence your behavior in the marketplace. You might also relate your ideas (e.g., through a website that solicits consumer comments, a letter-writing campaign, or even a protest) to companies so that they can improve their offerings and, in the long run, enhance overall life quality. Consumer activism affects company practices. Nike has recently moved to become more transparent in response to attacks on its Asian labor policies. You will also begin to understand more of the *why* behind some of your own consumption activities. Understanding the *why* can be useful. In this book, we invite you to think about how marketing activities relate to your own patterns of consumer behavior and consumption. Some consumer behavior specialists have even helped juvenile offenders reevaluate their criminal behavior and motives by discussing the ways in which marketing had influenced them.[26]

http://cbae.nmsu.edu/~dboje/nike.html

SUMMARY

Welcome to the world of consumer behavior! We define consumer behavior as individuals or groups acquiring, using, and disposing of products, services, ideas, or experiences. This definition includes the search for information and actual product purchase. The study of consumer behavior includes an understanding of consumers' thoughts, feelings, and actions and an understanding of relevant marketing strategies. Topics that consumer behavior researchers study are limited only by their imaginations. Anthropologists, psychologists, sociologists, economists, geographers, and historians each has a valuable perspective to contribute.

Consumer behavior includes or is related to a wide variety of human activity. Consumers in different parts of the world lead very different lives. However, they share many patterns of consumption, including brand and service loyalties, using and enjoying gifts, rituals, making choices, and purchasing products to name a few.

Consumer behavior is exciting and fun, but it is also important to you for a number of reasons. Organizations stay in business by attracting and retaining customers. However, even if you don't plan to go into business, knowledge of consumer behavior is useful in any job where the mission includes satisfaction of human needs and wants. Understanding consumers is also important to groups and organizations seeking to influence public policies that affect consumers' rights. Finally, understanding consumer behavior will make you a better-informed consumer.

Consumer culture reflects a general shift in the basic emphasis of economic systems from exchange or production to consumption. The nature and dynamics of consumer behavior vary widely from place to place depending upon historical, macroeconomic, and cultural factors. The production and acquisition of goods and services, their consumption, and the disposal of used goods are part of a cycle of social and economic activities that we call the circle of consumption. The processes of production, acquisition, consumption, and disposal are universal, but the order in which the processes occur and the participants in the processes vary widely both within and across social

SUMMARY

systems. Much marketing attention has focused on one aspect of acquisition—purchase decisions. However, purchase decisions are just one part of the wheel of consumption. In recent years, managerial interest has evolved to include the full circle of consumption. Links that are important for marketers to understand and manage include disposal to acquisition, disposal to production, disposal to consumption, production to consumption, acquisition to consumption, and acquisition to disposal.

KEY TERMS

acquisition 12
adoption 9
attitude 8
biography 12
brand loyalty 8
circle of consumption 11
consumer behavior 9
Consumer Bill of Rights 21
diffusion 9
disposition 14
domain of consumer behavior 9
heuristics 8
LAW (less affluent world) 15
market segment 16
public policy 21
purchase behavior 8
ritual 7
transitional economies 17
use innovativeness 8

REVIEW QUESTIONS

1. Think of one of your important possessions. Write out its biography or life history from production to the present, paying special attention to its movement in and out of the marketplace.
2. Describe two purchase decisions that you have made primarily for the experience you expected to have. Can you describe these consumption experiences?
3. Describe an object you found and kept for personal consumption. How did you find it? What factors made you decide to keep it?
4. List several examples of products you have acquired both through various kinds of markets—retail outlets, flea markets, garage sales, wholesale warehouses—and through other acquisition processes mentioned in the text. Can you identify patterns of acquisition associated with particular product categories? Explain.
5. How do you and your family or roommates use your refrigerator? Pick three of the social sciences discussed in the text and describe how each of them might explore consumers' uses of their refrigerators.
6. List various ways in which you have disposed of particular products recently. Identify patterns of disposition associated with particular product categories.
7. Pick an important social problem in your community. In what ways (if any) does this problem relate to the Consumer Bill of Rights or other aspects of consumer behavior?
8. How do you handle "the last little bit" of hair gel, ketchup, toothpaste, or hand soap? Describe the techniques you use (or don't!) to use that last bit.

"YOU MAKE THE CALL"

MANAGING CONBINI

Hidetoshi Nakatz is a Japanese soccer star who has been playing for Rome in a European football league. He is asked by the press to name the one thing that he most misses about Japan. His answer . . .? "Conbini!"

Conbini are Japanese neighborhood convenience stores. They are very popular with customers, and their popularity has been increasing in recent years. The 50,000 convenience stores have a special place in the Japanese economy where frequent shopping is a necessity, since consumers often don't have much space to store things in their homes. Conbini are open 24/7, and they are much smaller (average size only 100 meters) than the typical convenience store in the United States. An average conbini receives 700 to 900 customers per day, and the average customer visits once every other day. Major corporations that operate chains of conbini in Japan include Seven-Eleven (8,000 stores), Lawson's (7,100 stores), Family Mart, Circle K (UNY Corp), and Daiei Inc. In Japan, the "Seven" is spelled out in the corporate name, in contrast to the name that is widely used in the United States (7-Eleven).

Conbini are always looking for new products and services to add to the store selection. In the late spring, for example, all of the summer products start appearing on the shelves of conbini around town. Many of these new items are simply variations on a theme, taking a twist to accommodate whatever lifestyle fad is current. In 2001, it was blueberries and cranberries—drinks, chocolates, yogurt, ice cream, and pastries. You must try the new things while you can—most of them will be one-hit retail wonders, just like the sadly missed Jet, a gin-flavored tonic soda from the summer of 1996. In 2002, new sports drinks included WELL, which is full of vitamins and good stuff but not so

A convenience store at dusk in Yokohama, Kanagawa Prefecture. Photo by Sakai Nobuhiko.

full of flavor. According to one venturesome customer, it tastes like watered-down grapefruit without the bite. Another drink, Concept-san (Mr. Concept), gets right in your face with its experimental nature. It's a notch up on flavor, a fantasia of grapefruit and sweet peach nectar that's not as awful as it sounds.

However, there is a problem with new products because shelf space is so limited in the small stores. One recent solution is to add virtual products to the shelves through the introduction of an in-store Internet service (called Loppi). In each store, Loppi appears as a terminal that connects to a portion of the Internet, thus forming a compact e-commerce system. Using Loppi, customers can order concert tickets, train/plane reservations, books (Yahoo!, Seven-Eleven, and a leading Japanese book distributor are part owners of the book-ordering system), hot meals, a horoscope forecast, and other offerings. Each of these services is delivered to the customer in a different way. For instance, customers pick up small appliances or books at the same conbini where they ordered them, a few days later. The hot meals, where the children of older, home-bound parents are the target market, are delivered to customers' homes. The concert tickets or the plane tickets can be printed out on the spot. At present, what do you think is the most popular service offered over Loppi? It turns out to be the horoscope forecasts. "The Loppi terminals have been a hit," gushes Naoyuki Kiriyama, manager of Lawson's New Business Development. "On some days, we have sold more than 100,000 sporting event and concert tickets online, and when popular computer game software goes on sale, we've received up to 3,000 orders a minute."

What are the major challenges for a fledgling e-commerce firm? Among others, marketing expenses are high for start-up firms; and it is difficult and expensive to attract attention in an increasingly crowded market. Conbini are good partners for new e-commerce ventures, because in-store promotional expenses are low. In January 2000, Seven-Eleven Japan Co. teamed up with NEC, Nomura Research, Sony Corp., and others to form a "Japanese-style e-commerce" venture, called 7dream.com.

Loppi provides a way to overcome existing barriers to e-commerce in Japan, where the technology and infrastructure are not as developed as they are in the United States and where regulatory hurdles can sometimes be a problem. Loppi is online shopping with a twist, since most purchases are still in cash at the register. Shoppers sign on the terminal, select a product, and receive a paper receipt. They take this to the cash register to pay for the item in either cash or with a special Lawson card. According to Lawson, this face-to-face contact with customers is critical and seems to be overcoming some of the resistance to electronic commerce. In addition, when consumers order products online, they not only pay for but receive merchandise at conbini rather than at the home or work. This is actually more convenient for many consumers who aren't home during the day and don't want to accept deliveries at the workplace (as a rule, Japanese parcel delivery firms won't leave packages unattended on residential doorsteps). Delivering parcels to the final destination in Japan is akin to the "last mile" problem in telecommunications. Stringing that copper to each house is very expensive—and so is delivering each parcel to each individual residence. Consolidating packages at central locations significantly reduces costs. In addition, as indicated by Hidetoshi Nakatz, customers flock to conbini. For all of these reasons, conbini make attractive e-commerce partners for start-up firms.

QUESTIONS

1. What is it that makes an American invention (i.e., the convenience store) so popular in Japan?

CASES

2. How has the original concept of the convenience store evolved to fit the local culture and circumstances?
3. What do Japanese buyers like about conbini?
4. What other kinds of new products or services could be introduced in the conbini?
5. How should these new offerings be distributed (e.g., in store, delivered to the home, delivered over the local Internet)?
6. How might conbini's innovations in e-commerce be adapted to e-tailing in the United States? (Hint: Search online information about Circuit City.)

This case is adapted from Kumiko Aoki, "Cultural Differences in E-Commerce: A Comparison between the U.S. and Japan," First Monday *5 (November 2000), http://firstmonday.org/issues/issue5_11/aoki/index.html; Tim Clark, "What's the Difference between E-tailing and Mail Order?"* Japan Internet Report, *no. 40 (July/August 1999) (TKAI, Inc., and Digitized Information, Inc.), http://www.jir.net/jir7_99.html; Kevin Osborne, "The Future of E-Commerce: Conbini,"* Computing Japan *5 (October 10, 1998); Stephanie Strom, "E-Commerce the Japanese Way,"* New York Times, *March 17, 2000, pp. A1, A4; http://users.telerama.com/~kristen/blog/2002_archive.html.*

ENDNOTES

1. For a discussion of grooming rituals, see Dennis Rook, "The Ritual Dimension of Consumer Behavior," *Journal of Consumer Research* 12 (December 1985), pp. 251–64.
2. This is based around an interview with the Proctor & Gamble marketing manager for shampoo in Hungary. As a note of comparison, the average French person bathes or showers 4.4 times a week, compared with 3.7 times in Britain and 3.8 times in Italy, according to the *Tampa Tribune,* October 23, 1998, p. 20A.
3. Genaro C. Armas, "In the 'Burbs, Singles Outnumber Families," *Lincoln Journal Star,* February 26, 2002, p. 3A.
4. Jacob Jacoby and Robert W. Chestnut, *Brand Loyalty: Measurement and Management* (New York: John Wiley & Sons, 1978).
5. For a discussion of use innovativeness, see Elizabeth C. Hirschman, "Innovativeness, Novelty Seeking and Consumer Creativity," *Journal of Consumer Research* 7 (December 1980), pp. 283–95; Nancy M. Ridgway and Linda L. Price, "Development of a Scale to Measure Use Innovativeness," in *Advances in Consumer Research,* ed. Alice Tybout and Richard Bagozzi (Provo, UT: Association for Consumer Research, 1983); and Nancy M. Ridgway and Linda L. Price, "Creativity Under Pressure: The Importance of Consumption Situations on Consumer Product Use," *Proceedings of the American Marketing Association Summer Educator's Meetings* (1991), pp. 361–68.
6. Marta E. Savigliano, "Tango in Japan and the World Economy of Passion," in *Remade in Japan,* ed. Joseph J. Tobin (New Haven, CT: Yale University, 1993), pp. 235–52.
7. For a discussion of attempts to store services, see Robin A. Higie, Linda L. Price, and Julie Fitzmaurice, "Leaving It All Behind: Service Loyalties in Transition," in *Advances in Consumer Research,* ed. Leigh McAlister and Michael L. Rothschild, vol. 20 Provo, UT: Association for Consumer Research, 1993, pp. 656–61.
8. R. S. Oropresa, "Female Labor Force Participation and Time-Saving Household Technology: A Case Study of the Microwave from 1978 to 1989," *Journal of Consumer Research* 4 (March 1993), pp. 567–79.
9. Igor Kopytoff, "The Cultural Biography of Things: Commoditization as Process," in *The Social Life of Things,* ed. Arjun Appadurai (Cambridge: Cambridge University Press, 1986), pp. 64–94.
10. See http://www.steel.org/environment/ and www.issb.co.uk for more information.
11. Don Fuller, *Sustainable Marketing: Managerial-Ecological Issues* (Newbury, CA: Sage, 1999).
12. Some of the examples in this section can be found in William Rathje and Cullen Murphy, *Rubbish! The Archaeology of Garbage* (New York: HarperCollins Publishers, 1992).

13. Jon Spayde, " 'Found Art' and Finding Yourself," *Utne Reader,* July–August 2002, pp. 76–80; http://www.greenworks.tv/rough_terrain/noyesmuseum.
14. Terrence H. Witkowski and Yoshito Yamamoto, "*Omiyage* Gift Purchasing by Japanese Travelers in the U.S.," in *Advances in Consumer Research,* ed. Rebecca H. Holman and Michael R. Solomon (Provo, UT: Association for Consumer Research, 1991), pp. 123–28.
15. Thomas C. O'Guinn and Ronald J. Faber, "Compulsive Buying: A Phenomenological Exploration," *Journal of Consumer Research* 16 (September 1989), pp. 153–54.
16. Doug Holt, "Why Do Brands Cause Trouble? A Dialectical Theory of Consumer Culture and Branding," *Journal of Consumer Research* 29 (June 2002), pp. 70–90; and "Grand Masters of Marketing," *Marketing Management,* Summer 1998, pp. 22–28.
17. See the website www.itaiep.doc.gov/eebic/countryr/hungary/research/cos97.htm for a profile of the cosmetics industry in Hungary.
18. Daniel Miller, *Acknowledging Consumption* (London and New York: Routledge, 1995).
19. Ben Fine, "From Political Economy to Consumption," in *Acknowledging Consumption,* ed. Daniel Miller (London and New York: Routledge, 1995), pp. 127–63.
20. Peter Lunt, "Psychological Approaches to Consumption," in *Acknowledging Consumption,* ed. Daniel Miller (London and New York: Routledge, 1995), pp. 238–63.
21. Colin Campbell, "The Sociology of Consumption," in *Acknowledging Consumption,* ed. Daniel Miller (London and New York: Routledge, 1995), pp. 96–126.
22. Richard Bagozzi "Marketing as Exchange," *Journal of Marketing* 39 (October 1975), pp. 32–39; George Homans, *Social Behavior: Its Elementary Forms* (New York: Harcourt Brace and World, 1961); and John O'Shaughnessy, *Why People Buy* (New York: Oxford University Press, 1987).
23. Elizabeth C. Hirschman, "People as Products: Analysis of a Complex Marketing Exchange," *Journal of Marketing* 51 (January 1987), pp. 98–116.
24. Jagdish N. Sheth, Banwari Mittal, and Bruce I. Newman, *Consumer Behavior: Consumer Behavior and Beyond* (Ft. Worth, TX: Dryden, 1999), pp. 125–32.
25. http://wwwdb.europarl.eu.int/oeil/oeil_viewdnl.ProcedureView?lang=2&procid=5595.
26. John F. Burns, "When Seeing Osama Is Not Enough," *New York Times,* Week in Review, January 6, 2002, p. 2; and Julie Ozanne and Ron Paul Hill, "Juvenile Delinquents' Use of Consumption as Cultural Resistance: Implications for Juvenile Reform Programs and Public Policy," *Journal of Public Policy and Marketing* 17, no. 2 (1998), pp. 185–96.

LEARNING OBJECTIVES

After completing this chapter, you should be able to:

- Discuss how economic indicators and global markets shape consumption.
- Outline some basic global trends influencing consumption.
- Define the major world consumption areas, including North America and western Europe; Japan and the newly industrialized countries; transitional markets in eastern and central Europe; and developing and Third World countries.
- Explain something about consumption patterns and preferences in major world areas.
- Describe some patterns in cultural values in major world areas.
- Identify trends and likely changes in consumer behavior for several different parts of the world.

OF CONSUMPTION

MEET GARY

Meet Gary. Gary's snail mail is delivered to a spacious, high-rise condominium located on Bay Shore Drive in Tampa, Florida, but it might be a stretch to say he lives there. Gary is in his mid-30s and is currently in Hong Kong working on a six-week project for a Scandinavian-based telecommunications company. Gary has worked for this company for almost three years. He's part of an international team. Although the work team will communicate using English, Gary is the only native speaker on the team. Gary loves the challenges of his job and enjoys sampling the unique sights, sounds, and tastes of Hong Kong, but he's looking forward to a break in the constant rhythm of international project management. The month of August will offer a chance for him to just kick back and spend time with friends. He's planning a bike tour in the south of France with his good friend, Bernard. This will give him a chance to use up some frequent flyer mileage he's accumulated with *United* Airlines—not to mention a chance to revisit that charming French B&B he remembers from a couple years back. He can almost taste the distinctive cheese and hard French rolls they served the first morning of his last visit. Bernard will drive up from Italy with his fiancée to meet him. Gary met Bernard some years ago when they both worked with a fledgling software developer that has since gone bankrupt. Over the years, they've kept in touch through e-mail, but it will be nice to reconnect in person. Gary will use the last few days of August to follow up on a job lead that would land him in Frankfurt, Germany, for a couple years. In fact, he's already booked a room at a Loew's Hotel in Frankfurt. He knows Loew's will offer just the right mix of local character and amenities for the global business traveler. Although he likes to sample local fare on vacations, when he's working he prefers predictability. The Frankfurt firm offers a good professional opportunity, and, coincidentally, a college buddy is currently living nearby. Reconnecting with Chris was a fluke—they were both on a recent e-mail from a mutual friend.

Gary is an important target for marketing communications, but marketers have to work hard to catch him. They certainly can't catch him with direct mailings to his home address. But there are other ways, and he's worth some effort. Not only does Gary spend a lot of his own money, but he also makes spending decisions for his multinational company. He books international airline travel, stays in business hotels around the world, and relies on technology to connect him to colleagues, clients, family, and friends. He enjoys expensive adventure travel and what he calls "the good life" and he labels himself "cosmopolitan." Marketers would like to understand him better, but how? What's important to Gary when he's booking an airline reservation or deciding where to stay in Hong Kong, what restaurants to visit in Frankfurt, and where to vacation next summer? Gary's parents, who live in a small town in rural Pennsylvania, don't understand him at all. They are beginning to lose hope that his is just a life stage, and doubt that Gary, their only son, will ever settle down and return home. Gary shrugs when asked about home. He loves his parents, but he certainly doesn't think of rural Pennsylvania as home.

OVERVIEW

The purpose of this chapter is to describe consumer behavior within a global context. The above vignette illustrates a consumption world that is molded by two important forces: globalization and localization. **Globalization** is a process in which consumers, firms, and governments are increasingly interconnected across national borders by a variety of actors (such as multinational firms and regulatory agencies) and agencies (such as multinational advertising and public relations firms). Increasingly rapid movements of money, information, media, goods, services, and people across national borders fuel globalization. Globalization creates social links and networks that cut across national boundaries such as global market segments that consume global brands. For example, *Cosmopolitan* magazine is now published in 50 countries including new editions in Latvia and Kazakhstan and claims a readership of 8.2 million worldwide. Cosmo appeals to a would-be cosmopolitan segment of young adult women who can sample adult pleasures in its pages without becoming enmeshed in adult worries. Cosmo's sex-and-glamour message is global, but local editors tailor images and stories to address local concerns. The Internet plays an important role in globalization, enabling business-to-business, business-to-consumer, consumer-to-consumer, and even government-to-consumer transactions across national and temporal borders go to ourbrisbane.com to see an example.[1] Globalization is a social process where geography's effect on social and cultural relations and actions is diminished.[2] For example, consumption ideas and trends move easily across geographic space and national borders. Consumer Chronicles 2.1 shows that the current generation of young people may represent a global consumer generation.

www.ourbrisbane.com.au

At the same time, however, localization is also an important force. We gave several examples in Chapter 1 of ways in which consumer behavior, marketing strategy, and consumer research are customized to particular cultures and settings. **Localization** is about *preserving a sense of identity, home, and community.*[3] There is a revival of local culture. Consumers are expressing a return to their roots and adapting global consumer goods and meanings to fit their local cultures. Globalization produces a revaluing of local cultures in terms of consumption values. A commercial illustration of this revaluing of local cultures is the promotion of the ancient Maya civilization of Belize, Guatemala, and Mexico as an exotic tourist destination. Renewed identification with the ancient Occitanian language and culture by citizens of southwestern France and northwestern Spain provides a noncommercial illustration. Globalization also promotes "third cultures." An example of this is backpacking tourism targeted to middle-class youth and supported by a global network of hostels, Internet cafes, and literature such as the *Lonely Plant* guidebook series.[4]

The development of taste and demand for such items as Vietnamese restaurants, Jamaican reggae music, Chinese films, and Afghan jewelry in the United States and Europe illustrate a dialogue between unique local identities and global flows of people, money, technology, media, and ideologies. The Swiss firm Nestlé offers a

The Consumer Generation

CONSUMER CHRONICLES 2.1

The young global consumer has arrived. That's what emerges from a survey by UNESCO and the UN Environment Program of 5,322 young adults between 18 and 25 conducted in 30 cities in 24 countries, both rich and poor. Sixty percent of the sampled admitted they bought too many things, but nearly half said they would be happier if they had more. For 78 percent of those asked, quality is what counts most when they buy things, then the price (71 percent) and then fashion (48 percent). Buying something environmentally friendly or "humanly correct" is important to 40 percent. Brand names have become very important to this group, as has tracking the latest styles in fashion and music. According to a UNESCO spokesperson, what most distinguishes subgroups in the survey is that some have the money to fulfill their desires, while others do not.

Source: The Consumer Generation by Agnes Barden. The Teacher/M&G Media, *Johannesburg, January 2002* http://www.teacher.co.2a/200201/consumer.html.

AP-Potato chip bags featuring a picture of Palestinian leader Yasser Arafat are on sale at a grocery store in Cairo on Tuesday May 28, 2002. This product reflects the globalization of consumer culture.

EXHIBIT 2.1

Global and Local Blends

Source: Nestlé S.A.; from map insert in *National Geographic*, August 1999.

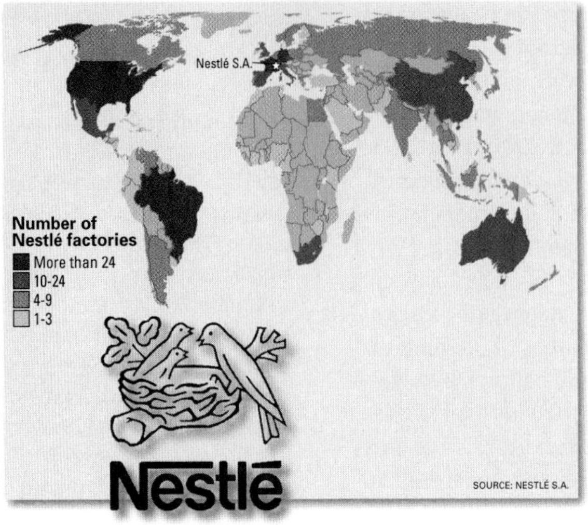

prominent example of the dialogue. Exhibit 2.1 illustrates the global production and consumption of this brand. Notice that while Nestlé is a global company, it also helps spread localization by, for example, making Asian noodles in Latin America. Similarly, Coca-Cola may taste pretty much the same in California and in Veracruz, Mexico, but the meanings and uses may vary dramatically between locales. In Brisbane, Australia, Coca-Cola is sometimes advertised as "the first long black," a reference to a double expresso in local slang. The photo on page 35 illustrates the use of a Coca-Cola bottle to give a young Olmec boy jaguar spots for a ritual dance in Veracruz. To understand and predict consumer behavior in Peoria, Illinois, or Harare, Zimbabwe, requires knowing something about global trends and flows and also local tastes and preferences. We will discuss both in this chapter.

This chapter begins with an overview of the global economy and describes some important global trends. In the previous chapter we described globalization and the Internet and other technologies as being significant forces. This chapter outlines some other important global trends. The second portion of the chapter outlines some basic information about consumption patterns and preferences in different parts of the world. In Chapter 6 we describe how secondary data can be used to learn some basics about different cultures. Here, we draw on secondary data along with other information to describe consumers in different parts of the world. We briefly describe consumption patterns and preferences in North America and western Europe, Japan and other countries in the Pacific Rim, the transitional economies of central and eastern Europe, and developing countries and the less affluent world. As you read through this information, it is important to remember that these are oversimplified sketches of consumption around the world, but they are intended to give you a feel for the variety of consumer wants, behaviors, and abilities.

THE GLOBAL ECONOMY

Understanding consumers requires a basic understanding of the distribution of economic power and potential around the world. The nature of the economic system within a country affects nearly every facet of consumer behavior. As economies grow, markets become diverse, larger, and more demanding. With improved economies, the range of tastes, preferences, and variations of products sought by consumers increases.

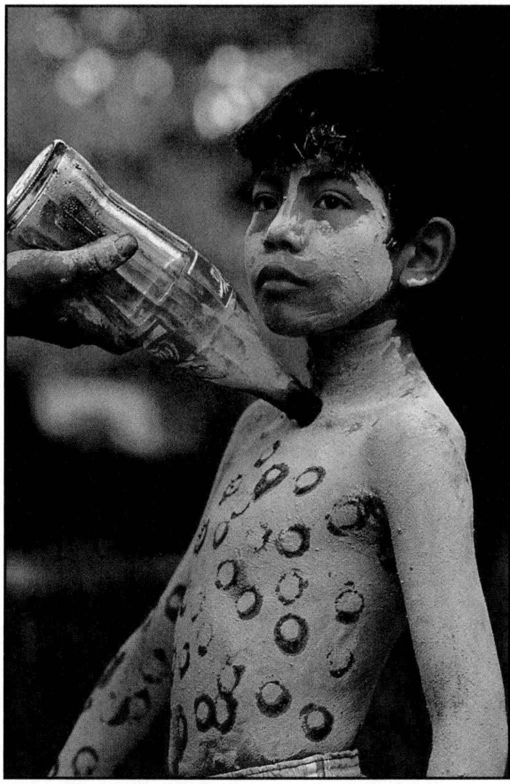

The globalization of markets spreads products widely. Locally, consumers use them for their own purposes. An empty Coca-Cola bottle is re-appropriated to apply paint to this young Olmec boy.

Economic Indicators

GROSS DOMESTIC PRODUCT AND GROSS NATIONAL PRODUCT **Gross domestic product (GDP)** and **gross national product (GNP)** are two measures of a country's economic activity. GDP is *a measure of the market value of all goods and services produced within the boundaries of a nation.* GNP includes *the market value of goods and services produced by all that nation's business operations, including those in foreign countries.* In the U.S., consumer spending accounts for about two-thirds of the GDP. Business investments and government spending are also included. Evidence of sustained growth in GDP provides evidence of potential consumer demand. For example, Vietnam's sustained growth in GDP of over 4 percent per year is unleashing new consumer and business demand. Similarly, because of rapid growth in the GDP, Australia, India, China, and even Russia are receiving increased attention from marketers.[5]

Another useful indicator is the **average GNP per capita,** which can be represented as *the dollar value of a country's final output of goods and services in a year, divided by its population.*[6] The average GNP per capita in selected nations is shown in Exhibit 2.2. These figures indicate the purchasing power for each resident, that is, the amount of money an average person has to spend on consumer goods and services. While the United States ranks first in GNP, average purchasing power is greatest in the European Community. Average GNP per capita provides important information about consumer demand, but it can be misleading. It depends further on how GNP is distributed, how and what infrastructures support GNP, and what kind of growth in GNP is expected. Consider first an example of the impact of GNP distribution. According to Exhibit 2.2,

Country	GNP in $ per Capita	Country	GNP in $ per Capita
Argentina	$ 9,530	Hungary	$ 6,730
Armenia	2,160	Mexico	7,660
Australia	19,870	Nigeria	870
Austria	21,650	Russian Federation	4,190
Canada	21,380	South Africa	15,290
China	3,330	Sweden	18,770
Denmark	22,120	Turkey	6,060
El Salvador	2,790	United Arab Emirates	17,000
France	21,510	United Kingdom	19,960
Germany	21,110	United States	28,020
Guatemala	3,820	Vietnam	1,570

Source: The World Bank, *World Development Indicators* (Washington, DC: International Bank for Reconstruction and Development, 1998), pp. 12–15.

EXHIBIT 2.2

Average per Capita Income for Selected Countries

China has only about $3,300 per capita GNP. Yet, Levi is able to sell $75 pairs of jeans to the youth culture of China because extended families there, as in other places, are showering money on their children.[7] India has a massive middle class, but looking at average income alone in that country is misleading because there are wide differences in education, social mobility, exposure to media, and so on.

Two additional examples help illustrate the effects of GNP distribution on consumer culture. In Abidjan, Ivory Coast, hundreds of laundry workers toil at their own individual rocks cleaning thousands of garments each day. Almost no garments are lost, despite the apparent chaos. Clothes arrive at hotels and homes the next day, cleaned and pressed, for a small fee. In Abidjan, those who could afford to buy washing machines have little incentive to purchase them, since they can also easily afford to have someone else do their laundry. When eastern Europeans first began visiting Western Europe in large numbers after the fall of communism, they were dazzled by the huge department stores and the seemingly never-ending array of lovely things to buy. At the same time the poor and the homeless they saw on the streets shocked them. Under communism, everybody was equal in poverty.[8]

Infrastructure represents *capital goods that support the activities of many industries.* This would include paved road, seaports, energy supplies, and so on. If infrastructure does not develop with an expanding population and economy, then countries begin to lose economic ground. For example, shallow harbors and inadequate port equipment make it more expensive to ship computer equipment from Miami to San Antonio, Chile (less than 4,000 miles), than from Miami to Yokohama, Japan (about 9,000 miles). Only about 20 percent of the Chinese who live in the more affluent cities are accessible because of a poor distribution system for products in the interior of the country. However, recent rapid development of a national rail and highway system is changing this.

Growth in GDP and GNP is also an important factor. In 1960, east Asia accounted for just 4 percent of world economic output. The newly industrialized countries of east Asia accounted for 25 percent by 1998. While GNP in Europe and the United States

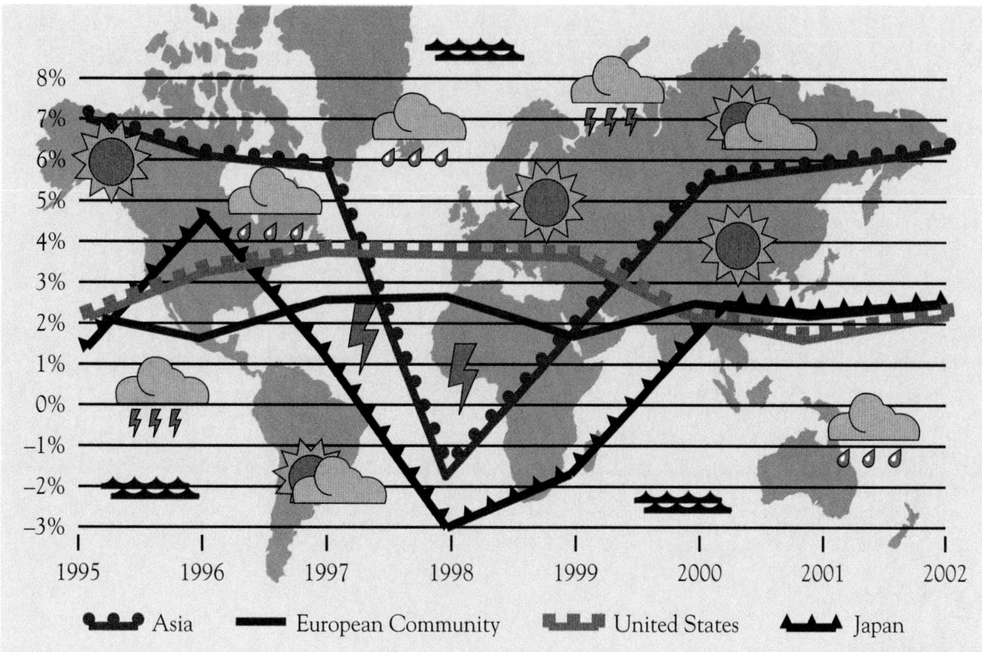

EXHIBIT 2.3

World GDP Growth, 1995–2002

Source: The World in 2000 (London: The Economist Publications, 1999), p. 13.

has grown at about 3 percent or less per year over the past 25 years, many east Asian economies are growing at more than twice that rate, a trend that is expected to resume after a recent economic downturn.[9] Transitional economies in central Europe such as Hungary, Poland, and the Czech Republic offer additional examples. Although average per capita GNP is still quite low, many sectors of these economies are growing rapidly and there is a lot of entrepreneurial activity. Exhibit 2.3 illustrates world growth in GDP for Asia, the European Community, the United States, and Japan. Note the enormous growth in GDP in Asia.

Another limitation of average GNP per capita is that it does not take into account government welfare programs that provide services to consumers. These are quite extensive in many European countries, for example. Such programs free up individual income for discretionary consumption expenditures. Nor do these figures take into account the extent to which consumers acquire goods and services through informal markets, as in the Russian Federation's barter economy (see Chapter 16), or through nonmarket means, such as gifts within or between extended family households, as in Nigeria. Researchers must take into account these factors and many others when determining consumer demand for any particular good or service.

INCOME DISTRIBUTION The distribution of income within countries is also important in determining demand. Income distribution gives us a better idea of the size and purchasing power of potential market segments than does per capita income. Consider the cases of the United States, the United Kingdom, and India. Most consumers in India make less than $5,000 per year, but only 18 percent in Britain and 8 percent in the United States make less than $5,000. However, 83 percent of British consumers make less than $15,000 per year, compared to only 33 percent of U.S. consumers. Fully 55

Country	Gini Index	Country	Gini Index
Argentina	—	Hungary	27.9
Armenia	—	Mexico	50.3
Australia	33.7	Nigeria	45.0
Austria	23.1	Russian Federation	31.0
Canada	31.5	South Africa	58.4
China	41.5	Sweden	25.0
Denmark	24.7	Turkey	—
El Salvador	32.0	United Arab Emirates	—
France	32.7	United Kingdom	32.6
Germany	28.1	United States	40.1
Guatemala	59.6	Vietnam	35.7

*A dash indicates no data.

Source: The World Bank, *World Development Indicators* (Washington, DC: International Bank for Reconstruction and Development, 1998), pp. 68–71.

EXHIBIT 2.4

Gini Index for Selected Countries*

percent of American consumers make over $20,000 per year, as compared to only 9 percent of British consumers and an insignificant number of Indian consumers. Thus there is a larger, wealthier consumer segment in the United States than in the UK, and a larger, wealthier segment in the UK than in India.

One way of comparing the distribution of income within countries is called the **Gini index.** Its measures the extent to which the distribution of income deviates from a perfectly equal distribution. A Gini index of zero represents perfect equality, whereas an index of 100 implies perfect inequality. Thus the higher the index, the more unequal is income distributed. Exhibit 2.4 provides Gini indexes for selected countries. The Gini index provides marketers guidance on the distribution of appropriate price points for consumer goods, for example.[10]

Variations in the Gini index imply different aspirations and possibilities for consumers in different nations. Exhibit 2.2 shows that the per capita income of Sweden is about $18,770 (in world purchasing equivalent terms), and we also know from the table that this income is fairly evenly distributed over the population of Sweden as a whole. The per capita income of El Salvador, by contrast, is only $2,790, but that income is more highly skewed with a smaller percentage of the population controlling a larger proportion of the national wealth. Sweden represents a large middle-class market, whereas El Salvador has a large low-end market and a small elite market.

ENGEL'S COEFFICIENT Another useful measure of purchasing power is Engel's coefficient. This coefficient measures the percentage of an average household's income spent on food. For example, in the United States about 18 percent of expenditures go for food and beverages; comparable figures of just over 20 percent are reported in Japan and France. In China, India, and Turkey, three developing nations, the percentage is over 50 percent. As economies develop, Engel's coefficient goes down, indicating an increase in disposable income to spend on other things than food. For example, between

1992 and 1995, Engel's coefficient in South Korea declined from 30.4 to 28.5. In Japan, it declined from 24.8 percent in 1987 to 22.2 percent in 1996.[11]

Global Markets

The globalization of markets, trends toward economic cooperation such as development of the **North American Free Trade Agreement (NAFTA)** and expansion of the **European Community (EC),** and increased global competition make it important to view the global economy in the context of regions of the world. There have been economic links between almost all parts of the world since the sixteenth century. However, it is only in the latter half of the twentieth century that the world has truly become a global marketplace. The global movement of people, capital, information, materials, and products has gathered speed. Gary, who you met in the vignette, is in some ways a product of these processes. The world of the twenty-first century is divided not into countries but into market areas. These market areas often share common characteristics that influence consumer behavior such as similar levels of income, culture, official languages, and rules concerning the conduct of business.

The three **Triad regions**—Europe, the Americas, and the Asian Pacific Rim—constitute a new economic order for trade and development. Global companies that are located in the Triad regions have *significant market power.*[12] At the economic center of each Triad region is an economic industrial power. In Europe it is the European Community; in North America it is the United States; and in Asia it is Japan. Each of these regions has strong single-country markets or multicountry markets that are bound together by economic cooperative agreements. We have already mentioned the EC and NAFTA partnerships. The introduction of a unified currency, the euro, and the expansion of the European Community to include 21 countries have increased its importance as a market area. Two important multinational trading groups encompass the Asian Pacific Rim. **ASEAN** is the *Association of Southeast Asian Nations.* The group has a combined population of 480 million and a combined GDP of $560 billion. As of 1997, ASEAN countries included Brunei, Indonesia, Malaysia, the Philippines, Singapore, Thailand, Vietnam, Myanmar (Burma), and Laos. This is the primary cooperative agreement for that Asian Pacific Rim. **APEC** was formed in 1989 and is the *Asia-Pacific Economic Cooperation.* The APEC provides a formal structure for the major governments of the region, including the United States and Canada, to discuss mutual interests for trade and economic collaboration.

In addition to these Triad powers, there are emerging trading powers in the southern hemisphere such as the **Newly Industrialized Countries (NICs)** of Asia (Singapore, South Korea, Thailand, Indonesia, Taiwan), South Africa, Brazil, Nigeria, and Saudi Arabia. These developing countries now also contain important consumer markets. These countries have rapidly industrialized in targeted industries and have per capita incomes that exceed other developing countries. NICs are impressive exporters of many products such as steel, machine tools, electronics, and clothing. They have instituted significant free-market reforms and are attracting trade and foreign direct investment. Brazil offers a great example of the growing importance of NICs in world trade by becoming a successful niche marketer of small commuter jets, for instance.

Goods, services, and information are produced and consumed in every nation. The flow of goods, services, and information is global, but the distribution of production and consumption varies significantly. The developed countries consume more than twice the value of imported goods and services than do the developing countries ($33.6 versus $14.7 trillion).[13] The economies of some countries are dependent on the production and export of one or a few commodities such as oil, copper, or agricultural goods. Many Middle Eastern, African, and Central American countries are dependent in this way. The so-called banana republics get their name from this kind of product dependence. Thus, the economy of the island nation of Grenada is largely dependent on exports of the spices nutmeg and mace in addition to tourism. This concentration of production is often coupled with an uneven distribution of wealth and purchasing power. Those people who manage production and export are often elite consumers whose tastes and preferences resemble those of consumers in North America and Europe. The bulk of their fellow consumers, however, have a relatively small share of the nation's total purchasing power. Their consumption behavior may be molded by more local tastes and preferences and constrained by limited purchasing power.

GLOBAL TRENDS

Four trends influence consumption patterns around the world. Of course, these trends are more evident and accelerating more quickly in certain parts of the world. They represent areas of opportunity for consumer marketers.

The Service Economy

It is often said that countries in the Triad regions are moving toward a **service economy.** In fact, of the 1,000 largest corporations in the world today, almost 200 of them are service firms. North America, followed by Japan and the European Community, dominates the world market for the services that are consumed in the other nations of the world. They are likely to dominate the information boom as well. Nonetheless, developing countries' exports of services grew at an average annual rate of 12 percent in the 1990s, twice those of the Triad nations.

What does the shift to a service economy mean? It means that the share of the nation's productive output is shifting from the manufacture of tangible products to the management of the movement of services and information. Gary is a good example of a service economy worker. Services include a wide range of activities, including accounting, management, and engineering services provided by firms such as KPMG, Deloitte and Touche, and Bechtel; insurance on an oil supertanker; logistics functions provided by firms such as Mitsui Lines or Consolidated Freight; global information networks being designed by Time Warner or Vodaphone; and fax and photocopying services provided by manufacturers such as Xerox and neighborhood copy centers such as Kinkos or Kwik Kopy. The shift to a service economy is also reflected in consumer behavior. Services typically account for between one-third and one-half of household consumption.[14] E-services such as Orbitz (travel), eBay (auctions), and specialized medical diagnostic services illustrate how the Internet is promoting the growth of the service economy.

Green Marketing

Increasingly, global concern for the environment extends beyond issues such as industrial pollution, hazardous waste disposal, and deforestation to include issues that focus directly on consumer and industrial products. Historically, business has not given great thought to where its raw materials come from nor to where its products go after they have been purchased. Now all that is changing with the advent of **green marketing.** By one estimate, only 20 percent of Triad nation companies can be described as proactive in their commitment to improve environmental performance.[15] Nevertheless, some firms have adopted what is called triple-bottom-line accounting in which corporate profits, the community, and the environment are given consideration.

Industry is faced with the fact that raw materials are finite. For example, world reserves of a number of important minerals will last for less than a century at current rates of industrial consumption. Many companies have adopted the concept of eco-efficiency, including 3M, Procter & Gamble, and SC Johnson Wax. A program established at SC Johnson Wax has cut the company's manufacturing waste by half, reduced virgin packaging waste by 25 percent, and reduced the use of volatile organic compounds by 16 percent; at the same time, production has increased by more than 50 percent. One plant extracts methane from a nearby landfill for energy production; another continuously reuses 95 percent of its wastewater. The company has realized a more than $20 million annual cost savings.[16]

The recycling industry is another response to the recognition that resources are finite. Nearly 90 percent of the raw materials that go into an average automobile are recyclable, and firms are scrambling to do more. BMW is striving for the fully recyclable vehicle. Recently, one of the big three American automobile manufacturers found a way to recycle soft bumpers into taillight plastic.[17] In California, over 80 percent of all aluminum cans are recycled.

In some cases, environmental activists have moved aggressively against corporations with a poor green profile. For example, Mitsubishi has been targeted for its efforts to build salt plants in a Mexican bay where gray whales breed. Three major forest products producers—MacMillan Bloedel, Interfor, and Western Forest Products, all in British Columbia—were criticized for their clear-cutting of old-growth forests. They recently sought timber certification, indicating that they harvest in an environmentally sound way. Certification can provide competitive differentiation in the marketplace.[18]

Growing Gap between Rich and Poor

Another trend of significant concern is the growing gap between rich and poor nations of the world and between the rich and poor within nations of the world. The rapid economic growth in east Asia during the past two decades has been accompanied by worsening inequality. In the United States, the income of the wealthiest one-fifth of the population has increased by 21 percent since 1980, while real wages of the bottom 60 percent of the population have stagnated. In Europe, immigration of poor foreign workers has fueled an anti-immigrant backlash in many countries. The poorest tenth in Britain are 13 percent worse off than they were in 1979 and the richest tenth are now 65 percent better off.[19] Although an increase in marketing activity has the general effect of delivering goods and services to consumers more effectively, market economies are not necessarily effective in providing for an equitable division of consumption possibilities. Thus, one response of marketers to the widening gap between rich and poor has been the development of two-tier marketing. That is, brands and retail formats are developed to cater to the top and the bottom of the market. Meanwhile, mid-priced brands and stores may suffer.

A discussion of the growing gap between rich and poor must draw attention to the African continent.[20] Although in the mid-1990s there were signs of improvement, with

Varied Voices on the Web

INDUSTRY INSIGHTS 2.1

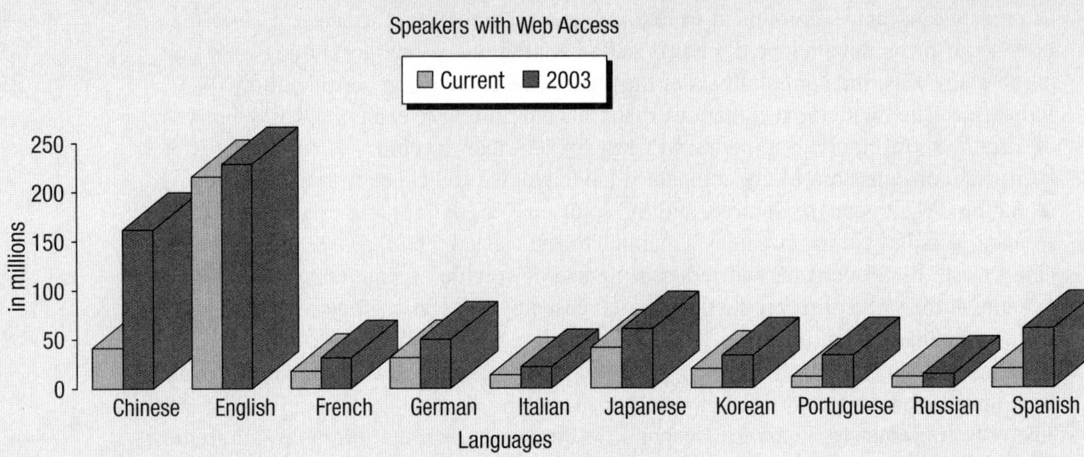

In today's global economy, the Internet is the ideal medium for businesses to increase worldwide awareness of their companies and products or services. And experts agree that marketing strategies, especially those that are Web-based, should take place in the language of the target market. But many companies have yet to realize the importance of multilingual sites and haven't yet made theirs available in languages other than their own. While English is the dominant language on the Web today, the number of non-English speakers on the Web will skyrocket in the next two years. As Internet penetration rates rise in other areas of the world, it will become increasingly important for marketers not only to get their message out, but also to make sure it is understood.

Source: Paula Lyon Andruss, "Speak the Language and Be Heard," Marketing News, *June 4, 2001, p. 3.*

some African countries showing growth rates of more than 6 percent, in 2002 the picture is very gloomy. African countries are at the bottom in World Bank compilations of GDP and GNP, and the gap between them and the rest of the world is widening. At least 45 percent of Africans live in poverty, and only 15 percent of Africans live in environments minimally adequate to sustain growth and development. The growth rate in sub-Saharan Africa as a whole was only 2 percent in 1999. The continent is plagued with floods; famine; diseases, especially HIV and AIDS; and wars. Moreover, the next generation of Africans will be more numerous, poorer, less educated, and more desperate.

Earthscaping

The final and perhaps most dramatic trend concerns **earthscaping,** *the accelerated movement of people, ideas, goods, capital, information, services, and popular culture around the world.* Investment in or buy-out of regional or national brands or retail chains is an example of global earthscaping caused by the movement of capital. For

Global telecommunications have brought the world closer even to consumers and small business owners in remote parts of Africa through call centers like the one pictured here.

example, the Dutch firm Ahold has bought up many grocery chains in the eastern United States such as Giant Foods and Stop & Shop. Similarly, Wal-Mart bought up the British retail chain Asda.[21] The global spread of the Internet is an example of technological earthscaping. Industry Insights 2.1 suggests one strategic implication. Cell phone technology has had a similar effect in many less affluent countries as isolated villages have been linked to the outside world.[22] This accelerated movement has led to the uprooting of many consumption habits from their local context and their commercialization on a global scale. Consider the exchange of hamburgers for sushi and rock music for karaoke between Japan and the West; or the appearance of Islamic consumption habits of dress and cuisine in northern Europe and North America to balance Western habits in Islamic North Africa and the Middle East.

Global earthscaping also results in the **creolization** of global consumer institutions, *a blending of local and global meanings.* Fast-food restaurant franchises provide an example, one that has mutated into a myriad of forms in particular local markets. Also illustrative are theme parks, of which Disney World is merely one example. Over local protests, Romania has recently announced plans to create a Dracula theme park in Transylvania. Another example is the Christmas consumption holiday now celebrated around the world, including in non-Christian countries such as Turkey and Japan. Creolization is discussed in more detail in Chapter 3.

Globalization is also producing an **anti-globalization** movement among some segments of consumers. Anti-globalization leads to demonstrations and boycotts of foreign customs and high-profile multinational firms. Hindu nationalists smashed card shops in northern India on Valentine's Day 2001 in protest against greeting cards they considered immoral, for example. Adidas and Nike have been repeatedly attacked by human rights and labor groups for alleged sweatshop tactics employed by their suppliers in Southeast Asia. Protests have prompted expensive reforms that have not appeased all critics. McDonald's has been particularly hard-hit. During the mad cow disease scare of the late 1990s, Europeans falsely accused McDonald's of using tainted beef. This followed protests against McDonald's that accused the firm of undermining French culinary traditions and farming practices. In response, McDonald's France staged a months' long public relations campaign in 2001 that invited French consumers to visit McDonald's suppliers and corporate headquarters to learn about the firm's operations. A rumor in India that McDonald's french fries were flavored with beef extract led Hindu nationalists to trash some outlets, as consumption of any animal product is a violation of Hindu dietary laws. Vegetarians in the United States filed a lawsuit against the use of beef flavoring in McDonald's french fries as well. Multinational firms can expect these trends to accelerate in the twenty-first century and will need to adopt proactive policies to address the concerns of anti-globalization activists.[23]

CONSUMPTION IN NORTH AMERICA AND WESTERN EUROPE

The discussion of consumer behavior and consumption norms in North America and western Europe should also make reference to Australia, New Zealand, and other nations with substantial populations of European origin such as Chile or South Africa. However, we generally limit the following discussion to countries with average annual per capita incomes ranging from $5,000, as in Spain, to over $18,000, as in Sweden.

Consumption Patterns and Preferences

Four main topics highlight the consumption patterns in this group of nations: consumer skills, recreational shopping, experiential consumption, and luxury fever. Countries in North America and Europe reflect a distinct consumption ideology.

CONSUMER SKILLS Choice making, even for complex products such as pharmaceuticals, is a highly developed skill among consumers in North America and western

The Toorang Mall in Brisbane, Australia, promotes positive experiences by combining exciting architecture, shops, and eateries.

Europe. Gary's preference for a Loew's Hotel reflects these skills. As a result, many consumers are extremely price and value conscious. Highly developed choice-making skills fuel the growth of retail discount chains and do-it-yourself outlets. Consumers are accustomed to making fine distinctions between similar brands, and they are adept at detecting new uses for products offered by major manufacturers. Many consumers in these nations develop sophisticated relationships with favored brands that endure and change over their life span.[24]

RECREATIONAL SHOPPING The role of shopping and purchasing has taken on dramatic new meaning in these countries. Ever since the invention of the department store in nineteenth-century France, there has been a growing trend toward recreational shopping. The modern, self-enclosed shopping mall in all its variant forms has become a site to which consumers make frequent pilgrimages to satisfy a wide variety of needs, including those for aesthetic enjoyment, problem solving, and personal display. Consumers in Japan spent almost $8,000 per person in retail stores in 1990. Americans spent just over $8,000. By contrast, residents of Argentina spent only $662; residents of Malaysia spent $790; and residents of Iran spent $804 per person.

These trends achieve expression in malls such as the West Edmonton Mall (Canada), theme parks such as Universal Studios, and themed retailers such as ESPN Zone where consumers may participate in both real and virtual sporting challenges. These retail environments combine, in a seamless whole, both shopping and entertainment. In addition, we see the phenomenal persistence of a wide variety of occasional marketplaces such as arts and crafts shows, festivals, flea markets, swap meets, farmers' markets, street vending, and garage sales where people buy, sell, socialize, and are entertained.[25]

Gambling: A Dark Side of Consumer Behavior?

ETHICAL DILEMMA 2.1

Organized gambling has been a boon for the economies of a few Native American tribes who are free to organize gaming on their reservations. However, many tribes are concerned that the presence of gambling threatens their cultural values. States like the taxes generated by gambling. But some are concerned about the effect of gaming money on state legislators, with millions of dollars going into pro-gaming lobbying efforts. Finally, compulsive gambling is recognized as a disease, and one that is increasing. Do you think some forms of gambling should be more closely regulated or even prohibited?

EXPERIENTIAL CONSUMPTION A distinctive feature of North American and European economies is the importance of leisure and tourist consumption. After a brief downturn following the events of September 11, 2001, adventure and ecotourism operators reported an upturn in bookings, returning the industry to the growth it had been experiencing throughout the 1990s.[26] Organized gambling is commonplace in Europe and North America as well. It has quietly become one of U.S. consumers' favorite forms of entertainment, generating more revenue than movies, spectator sports, theme parks, cruise ships, and recorded music combined. Now, 37 states sponsor lotteries and 27 offer casino gambling. U.S. consumers wagered $550 billion in 1996. However, as suggested in Ethical Dilemma 2.1, gambling has a dark side.

The increasing importance of experiential consumption can be seen in many areas of life. Cities as diverse as Brisbane, Australia; Stockholm, Sweden; and San Antonio, Texas, have been remodeled to provide intense touristic experiences along their central waterways. Recreational shopping has been mentioned above. And experiential benefits rather than attributes and features are now the focus of advertising for many

By the year 2000, global brands had become part of the consumption landscape in Miskolc, Hungary.

products and services. One popular business book describes a new marketing paradigm that focuses on providing consumers with high value and highly profitable experiences as the **experience economy.**[27]

The Japanese and elite consumers in other cultures have swelled the ranks of world tourism in recent years, but North America and Europe have traditionally had large tourist markets. The motives that inspire tourist consumption are diverse, ranging from nostalgic visits to historic towns and villages, to escapist entertainment at Mardi Gras, to romance at a Club Med or on a cruise, to extraordinary adventures through African safaris, Himalayan trekking, or Outward Bound trips. The RV ad shown on page 47, clearly targeted for parents of preschoolers, suggests recapturing the experiences of childhood through a family trip in a recreational vehicle.

LUXURY FEVER Some experts argue that luxury is experiencing an incredible boom.[28] In 1999, luxury spending in the United States was growing four times as rapidly as spending overall. The trend toward luxury auto purchases is accelerating, and the purchase of sport utility vehicles with sticker prices over $30,000 grew by 260 percent between January 1995 and October 1997. Luxury travel grew 130 percent between 1990 and 1995. There are long waiting lists for everything from premium wine to luxury jets. Suites costing from $750 to $1,800 a night at the Four Seasons Resort in Palm Beach are booked months ahead. The Four Seasons Hotel is one of many luxury service establishments benefiting from the luxury boom.

Family size has gone down, but house square footage has gone up. The average U.S. house at the end of the 1990s was nearly twice as large as its counterpart from the 1950s. U.S. consumers eat fewer meals at home, but they do so on more elaborate cooking equipment. One California executive admits that she cooks maybe seven times per year, but she has a $7,000 stove. Between 1995 and 1996, overall merchandise sales increased by only 5 percent, but U.S. spending on luxury goods—defined as goods in a category exceeding a given price threshold (such as $200 for a pair of shoes)—increased by 21 percent.

The United States is not the only economy exhibiting luxury fever. For example, Japan, with fewer than half as many people as the United States, consumes over half the U.S. volume of luxury goods. Countries in Europe and Asia and even Russia and other transitional economies appear to have big and growing appetites for luxury goods. Luxury spending is a trend not just among the rich; it's found among middle and lower-income earners as well. There is considerable evidence that in the United States and other countries consumers are spending beyond their means.

Important national differences between consumers persist in the Triad nations. The vignette that opens Chapter 3 highlights the danger of presuming that all highly developed consumer societies are the same. Britons and Americans are often jokingly but tellingly described as two peoples separated by a common language. Similarly, marketers who treat Canadians like ice-bound Americans, for example, will run into trouble. For example, Canada has two distinct dominant cultures, one French Canadian and one English Canadian. The former are very sensitive to language issues and insist on French language advertising and packaging. Canadian consumers are relatively less biased in favor of innovative marketing programs than are U.S. consumers. Perhaps because of less retail competition, Canadians are somewhat less apt to be deal-prone bargain hunters as well. Thus, consumer loyalty programs such as frequent purchaser or frequent flyer programs are less well accepted. Slower rates of intake into such programs, lower overall rates of participation, and an appreciation of soft rewards such as discounts over hard rewards may be expected. Finally, privacy laws are stricter in Canada than in the United States, reflecting Canadian consumers' attitudes about protecting their personal information.[29]

Trends and Changes in Consumer Behavior

What trends will dominate as the twenty-first century unfolds?[30] Some experts predict that a move out of the industrial age and into the information age will alter culture and lifestyles in important ways. Some call it the era of fragmentation, or the culture of subcultures, where people can take a menu approach for their lifestyle, picking and

This ad for recreational vehicles reflects one of the important consumption trends in the Triad countries: strong growth in experiential consumption. The ad suggests that RVing is a means to strengthen family ties and get in touch with what matters in life.

choosing from day to day according to mood and current fashion. Because of advances in technology, marketers can cater to smaller and smaller niche segments, customizing products and services to individual tastes. In some ways, the information age connects people with each other; in other ways, it leads to isolation. In the developed countries, consumers can interact with the world via interactive TVs and computers. Tens of millions of people around the world are connected to electronic bulletin boards, and this number is growing at 10 percent monthly. Cyberspace lifestyles have the potential to make centralized offices obsolete. More and more people are beginning to work at home. This trend may make home and neighborhood much more important in developed countries than they have been for the last several decades. Incidentally, this trend also makes provision of information, entertainment, and home shopping via the Internet and television growth industries.

CONSUMPTION IN JAPAN AND THE NEWLY INDUSTRIALIZED COUNTRIES OF THE PACIFIC RIM

The newly industrialized countries of the Pacific Rim usually refer to South Korea, Taiwan, Singapore, and Hong Kong. These four countries are also referred to as the Asian tigers. However, driven by aggressive investment from Japan and China among

This ad for Four Seasons hotels reflects one of the important consumption trends in Triad countries—luxury fever.

others, Malaysia, Thailand, Indonesia, and the Philippines (the "tiger cubs" or "little tigers") too are candidates for joining this group. China also is rapidly growing economically.

In the late 1980s Vietnam also adopted free markets. It is now flooded with Japanese comic books and karaoke, Hong Kong television dramas, French fashion, Chinese cultural goods, Hollywood movies, and Western-style billboards. Fifteen to 20 million Vietnamese are poised to enter the middle class with disposable incomes of $1,000 or more. Still marketers must build basic brand awareness and knowledge. The economic crisis that closed out the twentieth century (i.e., the Asian flu) interrupted the growth trend in the NICs but has not reversed it.[31] For example, South Korea's GDP increased at a 5.7 percent rate in the first quarter of 2002. Liberal credit policies are fueling a consumer spending boom. Pop culture and the Internet are thriving. Koreans are mad for fantasy role-playing games, for example.

Japan is one of the Triad nations, not a newly industrialized country. Economically it shares more with North America and western Europe than with countries of the Pacific Rim. For example, it is becoming a service economy in which younger people are increasingly embracing consumption rather than production and savings.[32] As one of the wealthiest nations in the world, Japan represents a huge market, changing quickly to a culture of consumption.[33] Moreover, the direction of Japan's economic progress since World War II foreshadowed the changes we now see expanding in other countries of the Pacific Rim. Japan's direct investment and development aid to Southeast Asia have been instrumental in fueling the growth in this region. Japan shares many values with other countries of the Pacific Rim, where Confucianism forms the foundation for ethics and morality in business as well as in social and personal lives.

For international businesses attempting to penetrate the Pacific Rim it is tempting to lump the countries in the region together, as we have done. Nevertheless, culture and values and related opportunities differ across these nations. For example, cosmological belief systems vary greatly across the Pacific Rim, influencing both culture and consumption patterns. Although Buddhism and Confucianism are broad influences across the Pacific Rim, Indonesia has the largest Muslim population of any country in the world. These ideological differences have implications for market segmentation and product positioning strategies (see Chapter 6). Similarly, the geography, population, and resource base of the countries differ greatly. For example, Vietnam is a country of 76 million citizens. Malaysia, by contrast, has a population of just 19 million. In addition, some of these countries have relatively homogeneous populations with no significant minority groups such as those found in Japan and Korea. Others such as Indonesia and the Philippines experience significant conflict between religious, ethnic, and language groups within the nation. Such differences complicate segmentation, positioning, and marketing communications.

The annual per capita income in the NIC countries ranges from about $8,500 to about $24,000, lower in the "tiger cubs" and higher in Japan (more than $36,000). Most consumers in the NICs are rapidly becoming more educated and their household incomes are growing. More women are entering the workforce, especially in Japan, increasing the number of dual-income families. Many working-age Asian children live at home until marriage, so their disposable incomes have increased. With the acceleration of economic affluence, consumer interests are moving beyond basic necessities to include consumer appliances, electronic products, cars, and cosmetics. Exhibit 2.5 shows how some European firms are moving aggressively to cater to rising consumer demand in the MCS.

EXHIBIT 2.5

European Firms' Retail Operations in the NICs

	Carrefour (France)	Auchan (France)	Casino (France)	Metro (Germany)	Tesco (U.K.)	Ahold (Netherlands)	Makro (Netherlands)	Delhaize (Belgium)
Japan	1			Considering	Considering			
South Korea	20				7			
China	27	1		7	Considering	Withdrawing	4	
Taiwan	24	Considering	10		1		8	
Hong Kong	Withdrawing							
Singapore	1					Withdrawing		30
Malaysia	6				Considering	39	7	
Indonesia	7						10	20
Thailand	11	1	24		24	41	19	20
Philippines	Considering			Considering				

European firms are attracted to open new businesses in the NICs because of rising personal consumption and because the modern retail sector is relatively underdeveloped with few major players. The absence of regulations has made it easier for foreign firms to enter most of these countries, with the exception of Japan where large retailers are regulated to protect small firms. The world's largest retailer, Wal-Mart, has announced intentions to operate stores in Japan, China, and Southeast Asia, but is running behind European competitors.

Source: Shigehisa Shibayama, "European Retail Chains Link with Asia," *The Nikkei Weekly*, March 12, 2001, p. 18.

Consumption Patterns and Preferences

As in North America and Europe, the general attitude in the Pacific Rim toward consumption is extremely diverse. Much of the development of markets in the NICs has resulted from the twin themes of modernization and rationalization. These nations have striven to replicate standards of living modeled on European and North American patterns. However, these two themes have also been, in part, responsible for the predominance of savings relative to consumer spending among consumers in the NICs.

In recent years, there has been a rapid adoption and localization of Western consumption styles. Thus, Tokyo features a number of tea salons modeled on French pastry shops. In a number of the NICs, the focus of consumer spending has, until quite recently, been on consumer durables. In China, for example, the six "big things" are VCRs, televisions, washing machines, cameras, refrigerators, and electric fans. Most consumers in NICs depend on reputable brands and track records. In addition, consumers want information about products and brands rather than fancy packaging, displays, or promotional gimmicks. In markets such as Japan and Hong Kong, a wide variety of image-based, luxury consumer goods also enjoy healthy growth, and the most up-to-date marketing methods are appropriate.

Consumers in the NIC countries are open to foreign goods, but as in Europe and North America, they are selective in what they choose. For example, the European image is represented by traditional brands such as Mercedes Benz and Wedgewood china; the U.S. image is represented by brands and products such as Coca-Cola, jeans, cigarettes, and chain restaurants.[34] In China, Western imports have a very positive image among wealthier segments. Chinese consumers may even reject Western products manufactured in China if the packaging used does not resemble that used in international markets. Chinese consumers are also selective in how they consume Western products. For example, teens love hip-hop music but prefer romantic and self-expressive varieties to gangsta rap.[35]

Trends and Changes in Consumer Behavior

Dramatic changes are underway in the NICs of the Pacific Rim. Many of these nations are made up of youthful consumers; and the populations of these countries are growing rapidly. In almost all, we see a shift away from a savings orientation that characterized the years after the end of World War II toward a consumption orientation. Nonetheless, financial services that provide savings opportunities, such as life insurance plans offered by the American International Group (AIG), remain popular.[36] One effect of this change is a boom in the auto market in China. Car sales are expected to grow 15 percent annually over the next few years to five million cars a year by 2010. In many of these countries, aggressive adoption of foreign goods, images, and products—everything from Coca-Cola to Levi's, and from KFC and McDonald's to Disneyland—by consumers is accompanied by aggressive marketing attempts to redefine these goods in ways that make them compatible with national cultural heritage and identity. In many countries, from Taiwan to Thailand, U.S.-style suburban shopping malls are mushrooming.[37]

Many leaders of Asian countries are concerned that the influx of Western culture will undermine traditional values. As a result, while Thailand, the Philippines, and Indonesia are moving to deregulate broadcasting, China, Malaysia, Singapore, and Vietnam continue to ban private ownership of satellite dishes. India is trying to impose restrictions on Western films and commercials deemed indecent.[38] Japan has launched an initiative to promote cultural exchanges among Asian nations. Another kind of problem associated with the development of consumer culture in the NICs is described in Ethical Dilemma 2.2.

Product Counterfeiting Is a Big Headache in the NICs

ETHICAL DILEMMA 2.2

The marketing of product counterfeits is a big problem in the NICs. Unscrupulous manufacturers knock off everything from designer watches and suitcases to motorbikes. Sometimes the headquarters of these unscrupulous firms is located in one country while manufacturing and marketing take place in others. Not only does product fakery infringe on the intellectual assets of firms such as Rolex, Vuitton, Honda, and Yamaha, but it also undercuts their market share and profitability, degrades their products' brand image, and delivers inferior value to customers. For example, Chinese-made motorbikes have now captured over 50 percent of the Vietnamese market, many of them marketed under fraudulent Yamaha, Suzuki, and Honda nameplates. Consumers have flocked to the knock-off models because they sell for one-third the prices of the real thing. In response, Japanese manufacturers and the Chinese government are taking legal action and revising their legal codes to crack down on counterfeiters. Part of what makes the problem difficult to resolve in Vietnam is that some of the offending local firms are state-owned or owned by powerful government officials. The Vietnamese government doesn't want to abandon its stance of protection for state-owned firms. In Japan, the problem is complicated by the fact that scrupulous shell firms in Japan license manufacturing rights to possibly unsuspecting firms in China. Establishing legal jurisdiction is half the battle here.

Sources: Mituso Toga, "Japan Firms Set to Take on Fakes," Nikkei Weekly, *February 26, 2001, p. 24; and Ryuichi Ushiyama, "Chinese Motorbikes Overrun Vietnam,"* Nikkei Weekly, *February 26, 2001, p. 24.*

CONSUMPTION IN TRANSITIONAL ECONOMIES: EASTERN EUROPE

The term **transitional economies** refers primarily to the *countries formerly dominated by centralized command economies.* These include Albania, Bulgaria, the Czech Republic, Estonia, Hungary, Latvia, Lithuania, the Slovak Republic, Poland, Romania, the former Yugoslavia and East Germany, Russia, and the 10 republics of the Commonwealth of Independent States. Some include Turkey in this group of countries. This sector represents a population of 430 million and about 15 percent of global GDP. However, there are parallels between these transitional economies and nations in other parts of the world that are shedding state-controlled economies and adopting free markets such as China.

The most advanced in the creation of market-led economies include Hungary, Poland, Turkey, and the Czech and Slovak Republics. Others such as Russia, Bulgaria, Romania, and Albania are well behind. The per capita income in these countries remains relatively low, ranging from lows of $700 in Albania, $1,124 in Romania, $1,390 in Bosnia, and $1,951 in Russia, to $2,503 in Poland and $4,072 in Hungary. Marketing executives in Hungary, Poland, and Bulgaria agree that consumers are becoming more demanding, which means that companies must refine their market segmentation and develop customized products. As competition increases, retailers are becoming more powerful and product life cycles are becoming shorter.

Consumption Patterns and Preferences

After the fall of communism in 1989, protected and subsidized economies began to liberalize. Industries were privatized, there was a dramatic influx of foreign goods and foreign investment, and national economies experienced a long period of inflation. At the same time, state-managed distribution systems declined in importance. In these

Key Factors for Market Success in Transitional Economies

INDUSTRY INSIGHTS 2.2

Percentage Ranking 1 or 2	Total Sample (n = 2,309)
Competitive pricing	37.9%
Product quality	32.3
Company/brand reputation	15.2
Speed of reaction to customer requirements	14.6
Product performance	13.7
Close links with key customers	13.6
Product range offered	10.7
Prior market research	10.3
Product design	9.1
Finance and credit offered	9.0

Source: Graham J. Hooley, "Raising the Iron Curtain: Marketing in a Period of Transition," European Journal of Marketing *27 (November–December 1993), pp. 6–20.*

transitional economies, consumers' standards of living eroded under the impact of price inflation and the loss of guaranteed employment.[39]

Consumers have responded through a variety of strategies. For example, they get second jobs, spend more time producing their own food for consumption, and sell private products and produce directly to other consumers. Estimates from 1989 suggest that three-fourths of Hungarian households participate in secondary forms of employment.[40] Many consumers have also reduced consumption or learned to do more comparative shopping. But consumers have also changed their consumption patterns in unexpected ways. **Engel's law** states that *as real income goes down, so does the share devoted to luxury products.* However, in 1990 as real income decreased in Czechoslovakia, Hungary, and Poland, the demand for perceived luxury products increased. This may be explained by the nonavailability of luxury goods in the past or by the luxury boom gripping the United States, Japan, and other countries. This trend continues.

Industry Insights 2.2 lists what some marketing executives view as the key factors for success in reaching consumers in transitional economies in eastern Europe. Competitive pricing is most important in those countries where market transition is most advanced, such as Hungary. Product quality issues figure importantly in successful marketing as

In the years following the collapse of communism in 1989, street markets like Budapest's "China market" supplied consumers with new, foreign products.

well. As competition between local and foreign products increases, product quality issues become more important.

Trends and Changes in Consumer Behavior

At this stage, multinational consumer products companies such as Unilever, Nestlé, Procter & Gamble, and Colgate-Palmolive and numerous European firms such as the German publishing giant Bertelsmann have experienced dramatic sales growth in eastern Europe.[41] However, real household incomes in much of this region are stagnating, and penny-pinching is the norm. Moreover, shoppers in these transitional countries no longer view imported brands as necessarily superior. For example, perceptions of "made in Poland" are increasingly positive, and many shoppers in central and eastern Europe are looking for homegrown quality products. Some local firms have transformed themselves into successful marketing companies. Media are revolutionized; scores of consumer-oriented magazines are now available, as is commercial satellite television. Producers in almost all fast-moving consumer goods categories are offering smaller unit sizes to accommodate local budgets and little-and-often purchasing habits. For example, Unilever markets its upmarket OMO and Coral brands in single-use packets to lower the price barrier for trial purchases.

One clear trend is that the priorities of western Europe, which include the emergence of green segments and a voluntary simplicity movement, are not likely to characterize this part of the world in the short run. Consumers in transitional economies have been denied things for such a long time that there is a large demand for consumer products. As one eastern European woman remarked when she purchased a fur coat, "I do not think that you can apply First World ecological philosophy to Third World women." Simpler, more resource-conscious packaging may be a trend in western Europe; but in transitional economies, consumers first want to taste the privileges of a better standard of living before they work to save the planet.

The growth of Internet use is dramatic in eastern Europe. The Polish Public Opinion Research Center estimates that 2.5 million Poles (6 percent of the population) have access to the Internet, with approximately half of those considered active users. The popularity of the Internet in Croatia is fast approaching that of Western levels. The latest Croatian broadcaster to put its programs online is HRT, Croatian Radio and TV.

@ www.hrt.hr.

Old downtown shopping districts across Europe have been spruced up to promote positive experiences in charming settings.

Hungarian Consumers in Transition

CONSUMER CHRONICLES 2.2

Judit, a 40-year-old school teacher, is typical of Hungarian consumers of her generation. In the new era of market liberalization, she feels she "must change" her appearance, attitude, health, reading habits, politics, and so on to keep her job, and support her children—"I hope my children will live better and easier, I hope." She has quit smoking and taken up swimming; she's purchased a personal computer and is enthusiastic about e-mail. She believes the socialist political system "had to change," but her post-socialist life is more difficult. She observes that more cars in the street "pollute the air." There are "nicer shops and wider assortments, but the people don't have much money." Describing the public transportation that she relies on, "It got worse in the past two or three years, much worse," and "You couldn't see homeless people, for example, ten or twelve years ago." Now "it's a luxury to buy books." She bemoans the lack of funding for education and educators, and is trying to "get more money . . . to buy different things for the children or for me." Judit's approach to consumerism is fraught with contradictions. Judit's children and friends pressure her to try new products and change her socialist attitudes, but she is uncomfortable with shopping and brands. After a lengthy and enthusiastic promotion of California Fitness cosmetics, she concludes, "But forget about California Fitness. It isn't that important. . . . I use their things more often than the [other cosmetics manufacturers]."

Source: Robin Higie Coulter, Linda L. Price, and Lawrence F. Feick, "Origins of Product Involvement and Brand Commitment: Women and Cosmetics in Post-Socialist Central Europe," working paper (Storrs, CT: University of Connecticut, 2002).

These trends have provided growth markets for industrial computer suppliers like Unisys and personal computer makers like Compaq.[42]

The advertising industry has grown dramatically in transitional economies in the past decade. In Kazakhstan, a former Soviet Republic, Kazakh-language television is leading a charge for Kazakh-language advertising, for example.[43] Nonetheless, consumers remain skeptical of heavy-impact, high-frequency advertising, as it reminds them of communist propaganda techniques. While western Europeans expect to be informed about brand differences, eastern Europeans expect advertising to provide information about products per se and expect variety in product range.

It is difficult to predict the future of consumer behavior in the transitional economies, and some will fare better than others. For example, the shallowness of Russia's democratic culture, primitive economic regulation, and hostility toward individual initiative constitute significant obstacles to the implementation of a market economy.[44] Furthermore, consumers in many of these economies have described a negative evolution in their experience of Western consumerism. It starts with an immense greed, a kind of fever, a wish to buy everything. Then, consumers discover powerlessness and relative poverty. Because of their poverty, many of these consumers view displays of Western consumer goods to be more like exhibits in a museum than the fruits of participation in a marketing economy.[45]

In a number of transitional economies, a consumer lifestyle reflecting local culture and history has begun to take hold despite some persistent market distortions. As in the Triad countries, consumer products firms seek to segment markets into groups with which they associate their products. Examples include young adult women targeted by *Cosmopolitan* magazine in Romania or the youth market targeted by Alima AG, a Gerber subsidiary in Poland that manufacturers fruit drinks. Consumer Chronicles 2.2 documents

http://www.cosmopolitan.ro/index.htm

B2-4B Spells Profits

INDUSTRY INSIGHTS 2.3

Whether its called B2-4B (business to 4 billion) or selling to the bottom of the pyramid, companies such as HP, Unilever, and Citibank are latching on to the idea that they can turn a profit while having a positive effect on the sustainable livelihoods of people not normally considered potential consumers. For example, last year Palo Alto–based Hewlett-Packard Co. launched an initiative called world e-Inclusion, which, working with a range of local partners, aims to sell, lease, or donate a billion dollars' worth of satellite-powered computer products and services to underserved markets in Africa, Asia, Eastern Europe, Latin America, and the Middle East. Hindustan Lever (HL), a subsidiary of Unilever, introduced single-use sachets of high-end detergents and personal care products that sell for pennies. HL distributed the sachets through a network of pushcarts and kiosks. The sachets have contributed to disproportionate growth for Hindustan Lever in many product categories thanks to high margins on the small packages. Unilever has now transferred this successful marketing principle from India to Brazil. At the end of 2001, Grameen-Phone, the Bangladesh cell phone company that provides cell phone services to over 12,000 villages through individual entrepreneurs, turned $27 million in pretax profits after just five years. In the HL and Grameen Phone cases, product demonstrations and positive word-of-mouth proved persuasive to aspiring consumers in the less affluent world.

Source: Dana James, "B2-4B Spells Profits," Marketing News, *November 5, 2001, pp. 1, 11–12; Susan E. Reed, "Helping the Poor, Phone by Phone,"* New York Times, *May 26, 2002, Section 2, p. 2. Copyright © 2000 by the New York Times Co. Reprinted with permission.*

the story of Judit, a Hungarian woman interviewed in 1998 about her experiences as a consumer. It is clear that Judit, like many consumers in transitional economies, has mixed feelings about the new consumer identity marketers are urging on Eastern Europeans.[46]

CONSUMPTION IN DEVELOPING AND LESS AFFLUENT COUNTRIES

We use the terms *developing world* and *less affluent world (LAW) countries* primarily to refer to nations in the Southern Hemisphere in Asia, Africa, and Latin America. We somewhat arbitrarily define the developing countries as those in which the annual per capita income is more than $1,500 and less than $5,000. These countries are primarily in Latin America and Asia. The LAW countries include those in which the annual per capita income is less than $1,500. These countries are primarily in Africa and Latin America.[47] LAWs are increasingly attractive because growth in the GDP tends to be higher than in the Triad countries, between 3.5 percent and 3.8 percent compared to 1.0 percent to 1.5 percent growth in Triad nations in 2002, for instance. Industry Insights 2.3 suggests how some firms are moving to serve the four billion less affluent consumers. Some of these markets are attractive because of their large populations, 535 million in Africa alone. In many of these nations, access to basic necessities, adequate food, clean water, appropriate clothing, and sanitary housing are unavailable to a large part of the population, creating opportunities for sales of basic infrastructure to local companies and governments. However, the distribution of consumer incomes tends to be highly skewed, creating *small segments of very wealthy and large segments of very poor consumers,* or **dual income distribution.** For example, in Peru, 1 percent of the population accounts for nearly half of the national income. Marketers who cater to the middle class are likely to do less well in these countries than do those who cater to the wealthy and the poor. Still, the middle class is growing rapidly, even in developing countries such as India, where it numbers approximately 250 million people.[48] Consumer Chronicles 2.3 describes McDonald's successful strategy in India.

Consumption Patterns and Preferences

Marketers seeking to do business in the less affluent world must be prepared to deal with less stable economic environments than in developed countries, the NICs, and even some countries with transitional economies. Sales tend to follow a boom-and-bust cycle. The payoff for investing in developing countries can be great, but so can the risks. For example, Whirlpool has invested hundreds of millions of dollars to modernize and cut costs in Brazil and solidify its position as the market leader in refrigerators, room air conditioners, washers, and other white goods. Many white goods, like microwaves, in the maturing or declining phase of the product life cycle in North America or Europe are in the growth phase in Brazil and other developing countries. Thus, only 15 percent of Brazilian households own a microwave oven, compared to 91 percent in the United States. Sales at Brasmotor, Whirlpool's local subsidiary, soared 28 percent from 1994 to 1995 and 15 percent more in 1996. Forty years of operations in Brazil have earned strong brand loyalty. Whirlpool's refrigerators have 60 percent of the market.[49]

Marketers must be prepared to meet the needs and respond to the particularities associated with traditional consumption sets, complexes of goods preferred in these countries. For example, many West African women like to decorate their sleeping huts or houses with collections of matched enameled bowls, basins, and platters. In relatively wealthy homes, these may be

McDonald's in India

CONSUMER CHRONICLES 2.3

The first McDonald's opened in India in 1997, with two outlets at Bombay and New Delhi. Since then, the company has added four in New Delhi and two more in Bombay and plans to open several outlets across India. The selling point for the Indian success is that McDonald's represents all things American. Despite the crowd that gathers around these outlets paying steep prices for a taste of the American icon, this represents the growing trend toward fast foods. This trend has seen entrants such as Kentucky Fried Chicken and Domino's, which not only offer the product, but present the service so far unexplored in India.

The average price for a burger at McDonald's in India is 31 rupees, which is an equivalent of 80 cents in the United States. McDonald's doesn't serve up an all-beef patty, however. In order to appeal to the Hindus in India (who do not eat beef), McDonald's has centered marketing attention on the Maharaja Mac (comprised of two lamb patties, special sauce, lettuce, cheese, pickles, onions, and a sesame seed bun). In addition, McDonald's has introduced a vegetable burger and nuggets with chili and masala sauces to cater to the Indian palate.

Source: Adapted from L. S. Kadaba, "McDonald's Has No Beef in India," Houston Chronicle, *Dining Guide, April 10, 1997.*

Snack products like this yogurt drink, sold in plastic sachets for a few cents, appeal to consumers in the less affluent world.

PepsiCo in Mexico

INDUSTRY INSIGHTS 2.4

Late last year, PepsiCo, Inc., CEO Roger Enrico entered a *changarro* in Mexico City that is smaller than his bedroom at home. Inside the crowded store, he congratulated the bemused shop owner on becoming the 8,000th retailer in Mexico to adopt the company's "Power of One" strategy, the large colorful displays that unite snacks and soft drinks that has led to average sales increase of 36 percent for PepsiCo products. Enrico's trip also underscored the snack-food supremacy of Frito-Lay Co. in Mexico, where its Sabritas brand boasts an 81 percent share of the salty-snack market. That's why PepsiCo is exporting its business model for Mexico to other emerging nations, from India to China, where it now has three snack-food plants. Much is at stake because the company's greatest growth prospects for its all-important snack-food business are outside the United States. In this arena, it's not merely a game of capturing market share but of increasing consumption of snacks by keeping prices as low as 1.5 pesos or 16 cents. This is a key part of the success formula in Mexico. "Our focus is being the lowest-cost producer because our success is based on making our product more affordable to consumers," says Roger Rebolledo, who leads Frito-Lay's operations in Latin America and Asia Pacific.

Source: Reprinted with permission from Johan A. Byne, "Today, Mexico, Tomorrow . . . ," Business Week, *April 10, 2000, p. 184, copyright ©2000 by* The McGraw-Hill Companies, Inc.

stacked from floor to ceiling. Such goods symbolize women's mastery of the domestic domain. Another dramatic example of the influence of local values on consumption processes comes from Indonesia. The consumption of clove-flavored cigarettes is a big business in Indonesia, so important that the central bank once intervened to maintain prices of cloves to benefit small producers.[50]

It may be useful to separate market strategies for different types of consumption behaviors involving subsistence necessities, social investments, and luxury expenditures. Many Third World people produce a larger share of their subsistence necessities for direct consumption than do those in the First World. As a result, there is a historical pattern of limited reliance on the marketplace for acquisition of basic goods and services. Associated with this is the tendency of many consumers to find sources of personal identity in productive roles. Nevertheless, marketing opportunities abound. For example, in the Ivory Coast, Nestlé introduced Bonfoutou, a product made entirely from local yams, at a cost of $4.6 million. Bonfoutou is very close to the original pounded yam dish, the traditional foutou. Its appeal is to urban working families.

In addition, limited means and a history of price inflation make many consumers in the developing world acutely price conscious. As a result, in Brazil, Argentina, Mexico, and China, the hypermarket concept—broad selections of inexpensively priced consumer necessities housed under one roof—has proven highly successful. Large, mixed retailers accounted for 12 percent of retail sales in Brazil in 1990 and 11 percent in Mexico, the latest year for which figures are available. The numbers have surely increased since then.[51] Industry Insights 2.4 shows a growing trend in Mexican retailing and describes how the successful strategy developed by PepsiCo in that country is being exported to other developing nations (e.g., India, China). In the LAW very small inexpensive packages do well. Wealthy consumers in developing countries often aspire to Euro-American consumption patterns. Using a global marketing strategy, targeting upper-income consumers, L'Oréal was able to introduce its Plénitude skin care line into the Ivory Coast. Never-

The World Health Organization is fighting the spread of cigarette consumption in the less affluent world, but this small businessman seems delighted with his bright, mobile Rothman's kiosk.

theless, L'Oréal emphasized products suited to the expectations of African women, such as a nongreasy skin care moisturizer suited to the climate.[52]

Among the more numerous poorer consumer segments, consumption choices are often faithful to patterns that are perceived to be traditional. These patterns do represent marketing opportunities. To illustrate, L'Oréal developed a line of inexpensive shampoos, soaps, and shower gels tailored to African tastes that emphasize skin softness, something to which West African women are sensitive. In a number of Middle East nations, the *chadour,* or veil, has increasingly become required dress for women. In Algeria, beautiful lace veils become one of the few permissible outlets for fashion expression among middle-class women. Indian women continue to wear the traditional *sari.* The sari symbolizes cultural continuity and "correct" female attitudes. Minor modifications in blouse and *pullu* (the loose end that hangs over the shoulder or is pulled over the head) are considered daring fashion statements.[53]

Another distinctive type of consumption behavior in many developing or Third World nations is the tendency to devote considerable amounts of disposable income to social investments designed to contribute to social status and prestige. The Hindu social order and in turn the cosmic order, or dharma, is even predicated on an interdependence between and circulation of gifts and commodities among the various social castes in India. Diverse examples of social consumption expenditures include the Saints' day fiestas of Central America and the charitable donation of mosques and public buildings in Islamic communities in Africa. Throughout the less affluent world, expenditures on dowry and bride wealth are an important form of social investment that involves constellations of consumer goods. The nature and value of goods and services purchased and consumed as social investments are the object of group evaluation, decision making, and, of course, gossip.[54]

Finally, consumers in developing countries make important purchases of luxury goods of foreign origin, especially consumer electronics and motorbikes, that may symbolize a cosmopolitan orientation to them. For example, battery-operated televisions and gas-fueled refrigerators are common in rural areas of Central America where many like to watch the evening soap operas.[55] Coca-Cola's phenomenal distribution and advertising system has made it a common feature of the consumption landscape in many developing and LAW countries. Many can occasionally afford this luxury. Provincial Argentineans exhibit considerable loyalty to Western brands and may travel long distances to Bolivia's duty-free markets to obtain designer goods more inexpensively than in Argentinean shops. Leisure consumption patterns continue to be influenced by the colonial experience in Third World nations. French-speaking Africans consume a high proportion of French luxuries, and English-speaking Africans consume more English luxury goods. English-speaking

The Parable of the Red Shoes

CONSUMER CHRONICLES 2.4

Some years ago, I found myself waiting in the Algiers airport for an Air Algérie flight from Algiers, Algeria, to Paris, France. I waited for many hours; there was no posted flight schedule, and the only information given was occasional announcements in Arabic on an absolutely unintelligible public address system. When I asked some employees for information I was brusquely advised to return to my seat. Hence, I had ample time to observe my fellow travelers.

One group in particular drew my attention. This was a large family of Algerians waiting for the same flight as I. The group included two men. They wore tan jellaba, or ankle-length, long-sleeved, open-necked, embroidery-trimmed gowns. Pointed yellow leather, backless slippers protruded from under one gown; dark Western business shoes from under the other. There were also four women. The women were covered from head to toe. Their faces were veiled. Their gowns too were in neutral colors. Their veils were distinctive in that they were made of exquisite white lace. I was intrigued by the presence of a pair of bright red, stiletto-heeled shoes under the hem of the gown of one of these otherwise shapeless forms.

Finally, our flight was called and I proceeded to my seat on the plane. I was just settling back for a long-postponed nap when out of the corner of my eye, I caught a flash of the red stiletto heels moving briskly up the aisle. I looked up and instead of a shapeless form, I now saw a beautiful young Algerian woman, hair freshly coifed, and wearing a short, stylish Parisian dress. She had a lovely smile. She had lost no time in switching outfits as consumption contexts changed.

Caribbean islanders enjoy the British game of cricket and its attendant consumption rituals, whereas French-speaking Caribbean islanders prefer soccer.[56] Quite often, consumers in these nations adopt different patterns of purchase and consumption, depending on the context. This is consistent with patterns of creolization that we discuss further in Chapter 3. Consumer Chronicles 2.4 provides an example of consumer creolization from the personal experience of one of the authors of this book.

Trends and Changes in Consumer Behavior

The developing countries are in the throes of a dramatic mutation. Changes in macroeconomic and demographic factors (e.g., economic liberalization, the growth of a monetary economy) have transformed customary modes of acquisition. Populations are growing rapidly, and there is a visible gap between basic needs and ability to meet them. For example, in Mongolia, half of the population is younger than 21. After a decade of liberalization, the United States has become the strongest influence on Mongolian consumer culture. Expansion of commercial radio and satellite TV results in new desires for novel consumption goods. In many LAW nations, marketers must proceed with care in promoting exotic consumer goods in order to avoid becoming the target of antiforeign sentiments. Some consumers in Latin America and Asia see the recent miraculous explosions of Euro-American consumer goods as evidence of **cultural imperialism,** *the imposition of foreign values and practices through the power* *of advertising hype.* Thus, Kentucky Fried Chicken has been picketed in India because of concerns about health and violations of Hindu vegetarian values.

One interesting Third World trend is the creative recycling and reconsumption of goods produced in the First World (see Chapter 17). Often, these are instances of the movement of goods on the wheel of consumption from disposal to consumption. For example, kerosene lamps made of cast-off Pepsi cans are common in rural Malaysia. Recycled Western clothing provides some young African men with the means to make a rebellious fashion statement, not unlike their teenage counterparts in the Triad nations. In many countries in the Southern Hemisphere, 20-foot steel shipping containers are recycled into retail shops, warehouses, and even housing.[57]

In many parts of the less affluent world, civil servants and other new elites act as a relay for the diffusion of Western styles of consumption. In Brazil, soap opera stars are so influential that product placement in the soap operas, or *novelas,* is an important market communications strategy for products such as Kellogg's Corn Flakes, Johnson's Wax, Tang, or computer games. In San Salvador, El Salvador, the evening hangouts of choice for many more affluent people are full-service gas stations run by Esso, Shell, and Texaco. Open air, security guards, lots of foreign imports, and an opportunity "to copy the gringos" provide the draw. Social comparison possibilities and the motive to integrate with perceived elite consumer patterns fuel the fad.[58]

Elite consumers in the less affluent world often adopt "modern," or Euro-American, consumption orientations. But they do not simply mimic idealized Euro-American styles of consumption. Because **nationalism,** *the idea of the nation-state as the sovereign authority,* often developed at the same time as former colonies achieved their independence, consumption preferences often take on blended or creolized styles. Such consumption patterns combine elements of local, traditional consumer behavior with cosmopolitan or imported consumer behaviors. Consumers may wear both foreign designer sunglasses and traditional dress; they may preserve traditional tastes in food but drive Peugeot and Mercedes Benz automobiles. In Argentina, the traditional idea of shopping—*hacer compras*—conveys an image of tedious, functional buying. The English word *shopping,* however, conjures up images of the American good life. Thus, the creolized name of one shopping center in provincial Argentina is *Paseo Shopping.* The name combines the image of North American lifestyle shopping with the traditional idea of the *paseo,* a leisure stroll or tour of the sights.[59] Creolization is an outcome of the acculturation of people to different cultural settings, discussed more fully in Chapter 3. Good Practice 2.1 shows how a local movie industry that is very responsive to market conditions in the LAW has prospered.

GOOD PRACTICE 2.1

Nigerian Video Marketing Is Responsive to Local Conditions

Nigeria's domestic film industry, known here as "home video," is one of the great African success stories of the last 10 years. The movies are shot on video, with production budgets ranging from $10,000 to $60,000, and marketed to the home audience, rental shops, and streetside video clubs charging pennies a head for admission. The movies deal with the real issues of African life: crime and corruption, family conflict, religion, and witchcraft. Last year Nigeria's Film and Video Censors board certified 640 new movies for distribution. Marketers like Emmanuel Isikaku are the reigning powers of the home video industry. But it has taken a while for them to get the knack of running it. Legend has it that consumer electronics dealers began to make cheap movies only because Nigerian consumers wouldn't buy blank videotapes. "It's true it started as a way to sell videocassettes," says Emmanual Eriobu of Infinity Merchants, producers of thrillers like *Children of Terror.* In March, the industry declared a recess to get control over production and distribution and rationalize personnel policies and pay scales. Nigerian home video has conquered West Africa, and its entrepreneurs hope to carve out a niche internationally.

Source: Matt Steinglass, "When There's Too Much of a Not-Very-Good Thing," New York Times, *May 26, 2002, Section 2, p. 16. Copyright © 2002 by the New York Times Co. Reprinted with permission.*

SUMMARY

This chapter outlines the basic contours of the global market economy and identifies opportunities and constraints created by the global economy. Average GNP per capita is a useful indicator of aggregate purchasing power, but it has many limitations as a tool in estimating consumption (e.g., does not take government welfare programs into account). Important trends in global consumption include the move toward a service economy, global concern for the environment, a growing gap between rich and poor, and a number of earthscaping processes.

A global perspective of consumer behavior is important because both marketers and consumers face a global marketplace. In North America and western Europe, consumers thrive in an information-rich environment. Consumption patterns and preference are defined by the enormous consumption possibilities that exist in these countries, and consumers are accustomed to making fine distinctions between similar brands. Experts predict important trends and changes in consumer behavior as we move into the twenty-first century. Perhaps most important is the fragmentation into smaller subcultures and customized consumer segments.

Consumption patterns in Japan and the newly industrialized countries of the Pacific Rim differ somewhat from those in the Western world. Japan is such a dominant influence in the Pacific Rim that the success of this region is closely tied to Japan. Cultural values and economic problems and opportunities differ greatly across these nations, but it is still possible to characterize some of the commonalities in this region of the world. Access to market information is expanding dramatically with the introduction of new telecommunications satellites and the Internet. Consumption patterns and preferences are extremely diverse. In a number of the NICs, the focus of consumer spending has, until quite recently, been on consumer durables. In other markets, especially Japan and China, a wide variety of luxury goods and services enjoy healthy growth.

One of the most dramatic changes in the late twentieth century was the shift of the centralized command economies in former communist states to market economies. Each of these countries has its own special economic problems and differs in its evolution to a market-driven economy. The transformation has been dramatic, but the future remains unpredictable. Consumers are definitely learning to discriminate quality and now have access to the same explosion of media options as North America and western Europe.

Many less affluent nations have ancient and well-developed market institutions but lack modern marketing infrastructures. The recent spread of global satellite communications has had a dramatic effect on access to marketing communications. Third World consumers are remarkably loyal to local values. In these countries, the future is likely to be mapped by the continued clash between foreign goods and values and local traditions and beliefs. An especially interesting aspect of consumption in these countries is creolization—adapting foreign products and services to local needs and tastes.

You will learn more about global consumption throughout this book. The purpose of this chapter is to set the tone for thinking about marketers and consumers interacting in a very fast-paced, global world.

KEY TERMS

KEY TERMS

Engel's law 53
European Community (EC) 39
experience economy 46
Gini index 38
globalization 32
global structure of common difference 43
green marketing 40
gross domestic product (GDP) 35
gross national product (GNP) 35
infrastructure 36
localization 33
nationalism 61
Newly Industrialized Countries (NICs) 39
North American Free Trade Agreement (NAFTA) 39
service economy 40
transitional economies 52
Triad regions 39

REVIEW QUESTIONS

1. Discuss likely advantages and disadvantages of introducing strong U.S. brands in developing country markets.
2. Collect three or four examples of green marketing. What messages are being communicated by the manufacturer? What claims support those messages?
3. Outline five or six ways in which the information age is likely to change aspects of consumer behavior.
4. Outline some consumption behaviors characteristic of a trend toward green consumerism.
5. There seems to be a growing preference among many women in Budapest, Hungary, for Avon cosmetics. Avon is a U.S. company that offers a full line of moderately priced women's cosmetics products. An unusual feature of the company is that the product line is distributed through Avon representatives who are most often women who sell the product to friends, relatives, and acquaintances as a part-time job. Considering the information you have about consumer behavior in eastern and central Europe, analyze Avon's success.
6. What recommendations would you offer to a U.S. company planning on introducing computer games in China?
7. What recommendations could you offer to a U.S. company planning to introduce its brand of toothpaste in central and eastern Europe? (Assume that the toothpaste is commonly available in U.S. markets.)
8. What recommendations could you offer to a U.S. company planning to introduce its brand of toothpaste in the Third World? (Assume that the toothpaste is commonly available in U.S. markets.)
9. What ethical issues are raised by Philip Morris subsidiary Rothman's provision of colorful cigarette kiosks to African entrepreneurs?

CASES

YOU MAKE THE CALL

CHEAPER DRUGS ATTRACT BUSLOADS OF ELDERLY CITIZENS OVER THE BORDER

Nogales, Mexico: It may not look like much but it's a lifeline for many Americans. Fifty miles south of Tucson, Arizona, Nogales is Pancho Villa country. He can hardly have imagined that one day the cross-border raids would not have to do with cattle rustling or revolution, but with the price of Klonapin and Glucophage, and that the ill people of Mexico's wealthy northern neighbor would be seeking help south of the border.

We are on a drug run. There are more than 20 people involved and there are potentially tens of thousands of dollars at stake. The border into the United States has to be crossed, but we have been assured that we have nothing to fear from the customs officers. All we have to do is get on the bus and sit tight.

This drug run from the Mexican border town of Nogales to Phoenix in Arizona is completely legal. The drugs being purchased are prescription drugs and there are even a couple of licensed American pharmacists on board to answer questions and give advice. This is the Prescription Express, a mobile symptom of a health crisis in the United States where more than 40 million people have no medical insurance and the soaring cost of drugs means that some of them now have to make a choice between taking their medication and eating. The drug companies charge whatever they think the local market will take, which in the United States leads to skyrocketing prices. The cost of drugs is going up by 15–20 percent a year. Most of the drugs in Mexico cost less than half the price in the United States, some as little as a tenth.

The Prescription Express takes people who need medicinal drugs across the border into Mexico, where the same drugs can cost a fraction of the price in the United States. This is only the second fortnightly run from Phoenix, but the enterprise's founder, Ron Swager, hopes that it will soon be running much more frequently. Interest in the idea is already intense from both would-be passengers and politicians. Those on board the bus have paid $25 for annual membership and a further $40 for the trip from Phoenix or $20 from Tucson. By the end of the day, some will have saved themselves as much as $800 in prescription charges.

Swager, a marketing man who was born in Connecticut but has made his home in Tucson, thought of the idea after hearing a pharmacist at a heart patients' support group he attends talking about how the cost of drugs was now so high that people were crossing into Canada to buy them. "A light bulb went on in my head," said Swager over breakfast in Tucson before the bus set off on the second leg of its journey. "I thought—why isn't anyone doing that here?" As a marketing man, he decided that he needed "product differentiation." Hence the traveling pharmacist, who reassures passengers and gives free advice. South of the border, he found a Mexican pharmacist, Francisco Cervantes, who had a store away from the town center where the bus could park. "The coach provides safety and comfort," he said. "People can pay with a dollar check—they're not exposed to Mexico except for a 10-foot walk."

In Nogales, up a winding street opposite a taco stand, Cervantes and four colleagues are waiting to serve the customers. He owns three other pharmacies in town and said 85 percent of his business is now from Americans crossing the border to save money. The 60-mile trip through the Sonoran desert, past ranches and trailer parks, takes little more than an hour, during which the pharmacists, Marty Wicker and Saul Rutin, stand in the bus aisle answering questions and cracking jokes. Those on board are mainly women, the oldest 91 but most in their 60s. Some younger people on board have come with their parents' prescriptions. The novels of Danielle Steele seem to be the favored travel reading.

"It's a political issue," said Merry—"as in Christmas"—Mohr, one of the passengers. "It's disgraceful that we have to be bussed to another country. I'm a 67-year-old widow of 20 years and my resources are limited. Our government should be looking at protecting our own citizens and letting Israel and the Palestinians take care of their own business. The government should be examining the enormous profits that the drug companies are making. It would be a good issue for the loyal opposition [the Democratic party] to get involved in." Marsha Mizelle, a physiotherapist, was buying drugs for her mother and mother-in-law. "This trip saves about $320. One day every three months is worth it to me."

For some, the bus trip is about more than saving dollars. Susan Harris, who moved to Tucson from Colorado, said, "Of course, it's to save money, but part of it is the adventure. Maybe being alone, it is a nice way to get here. We thought it would be a bunch of grey-haired old bats, which it hasn't been. You have to be a little bit brave to sign up cold. I've probably saved $200—it's kind of fun for a day's adventure."

Once everyone has bought their drugs, the journey back across the border begins. Customs officers check the drugs bought against the prescriptions carried by the passengers. Swager said he does not allow any controlled substances in and that he screens out young people who might be looking for drugs for reasons other than medicinal. "This is going to become very commonplace," predicts Mr. Rutin of the express. He said the Prescription Express had already brought rewards that were not financial. "I've never had so many 'God bless yous' from people in my life," he said. "It's fulfilling."

Source: Duncan Campbell, "This Is Nogales, Mexico. It May Not Look Like Much But It's a Lifeline for Many Americans: Cheaper Drugs Attract Busloads of Elderly Citizens over the Border," The Guardian *(United Kingdom), May 2, 2002, http://search.ft.com/.*

QUESTIONS

1. What globalization trends can you identify in this case?
2. If you wanted to compete with Ron Swager, what features and benefits might you add to a competing service?
3. If you were Francisco Cervantes, how might you take fuller advantage of the business opportunity represented by U.S. consumers seeking relief from high drug prices?
4. How widespread is the cross-border search for cheap pharmaceuticals? (Hint: search the Web and look for Canadian and other Mexican examples.)

1. David Carr, "Romance in Cosmo's World Is Translated in Many Ways," *New York Times International,* May 26, 2002, Section A, pp. 1, 8; and Jude Munro, "Building OurBrisbane.com," Paper presented at the 2nd International Services Marketing Conference, July 5, 2002, Australian Marketing Institute, University of Queensland, Brisbane, Australia.
2. Malcolm Waters, *Globalization* (London and New York: Routledge, 1955), p. 3.
3. See Daniel Miller, *Worlds Apart: Modernity through the Prism of the Local* (London and New York: Routledge, 1995); and Thomas L. Friedman, *The Lexus and the Olive Tree: Understanding Globalization* (New York: Farrar, Straus, Giroux, 1999). A good discussion of globalization and localization as related to marketing strategy is included in Güliz Ger, "Localizing in the Global Village: Local Firms Competing in Global Markets," *California Management Review* 41 (Summer 1999), pp. 64–83.
4. Ulrich Beck, *What Is Globalization?* trans. Patrick Camiller (Cambridge, UK: Polity Press, 2000); and Cathy Pryor, "Sign of the Times," *Weekend Australian Magazine,* July 6–7, 2002, p. 10.
5. Dana James, "Mixed Messages," *Marketing News,* July 22, 2002, pp. 1, 7–8.
6. The World Bank Group, May 4, 2000, www.worldbank.org/depweb/english/modules/economic/gnp/map1.htm.

7. Philip R. Cateora and John Graham, *International Marketing,* 10th ed. (New York: Irwin/McGraw-Hill, 1999). See, also, Sheila Tefft, "Xu's Have Western Taste," *Advertising Age,* April 18, 1994, pp. 1–10.
8. Slavenka Drakuli, *How We Survived Communism and Even Laughed* (New York: Harper Perennial, 1993).
9. Anthony Pecotich and Clifford J. Shultz II, *Marketing and Consumer Behavior in East and South-East Asia* (New York: McGraw-Hill, 1998).
10. The World Bank, *World Development Indicators* (Washington, DC: International Bank for Reconstruction and Development, 1998), pp. 68–71.
11. "Major Economic Statistics," *Kotra Trade and Investment* 16 (March–April 1998); and *Report on the Family Income and Expenditure Survey* (Tokyo: Statistics Bureau, Management and Coordination Agency, October 1997).
12. Kenichi Ohmae, *Triad Power* (New York: Free Press, 1985).
13. United Nations, *International Trade Statistics Yearbook,* vol. II (New York: Department for Economic and Social Information and Policy Analysis Statistics Division, United Nations, 1996), p. S2.
14. The World Bank, *World Development Indicators,* pp. 27, 170.
15. World Resources Institute, *World Resources, 1998–99* (New York: Oxford University Press, 1998), p. 166.
16. Ibid., p. 167.
17. This story was broadcast on "Marketplace," *American Public Radio,* April 15, 1993.
18. Marguerite Holloway, "Will It Be Timber for Green Logs?" *Business Week,* October 19, 1998, pp. 81, 84.
19. *The Guardian,* November 25, 1996, p. 12.
20. "Africa, the Heart of the Matter," *The Economist,* May 13, 2000, pp. 22–24.
21. William Echikson, Amy Borrus, and Wendy Zellner, "Now for Its Next Course," *Business Week,* January 24, 2002, pp. 62, 64; and Kerry Capell, Heidi Dawley, Wendy Zellner, and Karen Nickel Anhalt, "Wal-Mart's Not So Secret British Weapon," *Business Week,* January 24, 2000, p. 132.
22. "Cell Phones Transform Bangladesh," *Lincoln Journal Star,* February 23, 2000, p. 7A.
23. Michael Arndt, "A Misguided Beef with McDonald's," *Business Week,* May 21, 2001, p. 14; Journées Rencontres McDonald's campaign found at www.mcdonalds.fr; "Right Wing Youths Attack Valentine Card Shops," Reuters (2001), http://dailynews.yahoo.com/h/nm/20010212/od/valentine_dc_2_html.
24. Patricia Braus, "Selling Drugs," *American Demographics,* January 1998, pp. 26–29; Susan Fournier, "Consumers and Their Brands," *Journal of Consumer Behavior,* 1997, pp. 31–39; Albert Muniz and Thomas O'Guinn, "Brand Community," *Journal of Consumer Research* 27 (March 2001); and Barbara Olsen, "Brand Loyalty and Consumption Patterns: The Lineage Factor," in *Contemporary Marketing and Consumer Behavior,* ed. John F. Sherry Jr. (Beverly Hills: Sage Publications, 1995), pp. 245–81.
25. Robert V. Kozinets, John F. Sherry, Benet DeBerry-Spence, Adam Duhachek, Krittinee Nuttavuthisit, and Diana Storm, "Themed Flagship Brand Stores In The New Millennium: Theory, Practice, Prospects," *Journal of Retailing* 78 (Spring, 2002), pp. 17–29; and George M. Zinkhan, Suzana de M. Fontenelle, and Anne L. Balazs, "The Structure of São Paulo Street Markets: Evolving Patterns of Retail Institutions," *Journal of Consumer Affairs* 33, no. 1 (1999), pp. 3–26.
26. Susan Stellin, "They're Strapping on the Backpacks," *New York Times,* March 3, 2002, Travel, p. 8.
27. Joseph Pine II and James H. Gilmore, *The Experience Economy* (Boston: Harvard Business School Press, 1999).
28. Robert H. Frank, *Luxury Fever* (New York: Free Press, 1999).
29. Paula Lyon Andruss, "Understanding Canada," *Marketing News,* March 12, 2001, pp. 1, 11, 15;
30. For a summary, see Irene Lacher, "The Era of Fragments," *Los Angeles Times,* January 2, 1994, pp. E3–E4.

31. Brian Brenner and Moon Ihlwan, "CODI Korea," *Business Week,* June 10, 2002, pp. 54–58; Dana James, "Back to Vietnam," *Marketing News,* May 13, 2002, pp. 1, 13–14.
32. For information on Japan's move to a service economy, see D. Kilburn, "In Japan, Voice of Authority, or Flattery, a Call Away," *Advertising Age,* February 1, 1988, p. 46. For a discussion of Japan's move to a culture of consumption, see Laurel Anderson and Marsha Wadkins, "Japan—A Culture of Consumption?" in *Advances in Consumer Research,* vol. 18, ed. Rebecca H. Holman and Michael R. Solomon (Provo, UT: Association for Consumer Research, 1991), pp. 129–34.
33. C. Smith, A. Rowley, D. Givson, L. doRosario, C. Perry, and S. Anwanohara, "Japan 1990," *Far Eastern Economic Review* 148 (June 21, 1990), pp. 37–66.
34. "Asia's New Consumers: Pamper Them," *The Economist,* February 16, 1992, pp. 56–57; and Tom Eglinton, "Asia Lifestyles Special Report," *Far Eastern Economic Review,* July 30, 1992, pp. 37–52; August 27, 1992, pp. 29–40; September 10, 1992, pp. 37–51.
35. Martin Fackler, "Young Chinese Nip to American Pop Culture," *Lincoln Journal Star,* February 15, 2002, p. 7A.
36. Salah S. Hassan and Roger D. Blackwell, *Global Marketing: Perspectives and Cases* (Fort Worth: Dryden Press, 1994), pp. 359–80; and Dexter Roberts and Alysha Webb, "Motor Nation," *Business Week,* June 17, 2002, pp. 44–45.
37. Mary Yoko Brannen, "'Bwana Michey': Constructing Cultural Consumption at Tokyo Disneyland," in *Re-Made in Japan,* ed. Joseph J. Tobin (New Haven, CT: Yale University Press, 1992), pp. 216–34; and Alison Jahncke, "Thailand's Super Shoppers Get U.S.-Style Superstores," *Christian Science Monitor,* July 16, 1997, p. 8.
38. Sheila Tefft, "Contest over Asia: Satellite Broadcasts Create Stir among Asian Regimes," *Christian Science Monitor,* December 8, 1993, pp. 12–13.
39. Graham J. Hooley, "Raising the Iron Curtain: Marketing in a Period of Transition," *European Journal of Marketing* 27, November/December 1993, pp. 6–20.
40. Istvan R. Gabor, "Second Economy in State Socialism: Past Experience and Future Prospects," *European Economic Review* 33 (1989), pp. 597–604.
41. David McQuaid, "Poland: After the Gold Rush," *Business Eastern Europe,* October 24, 1994, p. 7.
42. Bureau of Economic and Business Affairs, *Country Commercial Guides* (Washington, DC: U.S. Department of State, 1997), www.state.gov/www/issues/economic/html.
43. BBC Monitoring Service, "TV Experts Call for Half of Adverts to Be in Kazakh Language," March 18, 2002, http://scarch.ft.com.
44. Andrew Kopkind, "From Russia with Love and Squalor," *Utne Reader,* May–June 1993, pp. 80–89.
45. See Drakuli, *How We Survived Communism,* p. 121.
46. Elizabeth Dunn, "Slick Salesmen and Simple People," *Uncertain Transition: Ethnographies of Change in the Postsocialist World,* ed. Michael Burawoy and Katherine Verdery (Lanham, MD: Rowman & Littlefield, 1999), pp. 125–50.
47. Peter Menzel and Charles C. Mann, *Material World* (San Francisco: Sierra Club Books, 1994), p. 248.
48. G. Koretz, "Why Asian Countries Blossomed while Latin America Wilted," *Business Week,* August 28, 1989, p. 16; Robert C. Schmults, "The African Market: A Lion Awakes," *Insight,* August 9, 1993, pp. 18–21; and Amy Kaslow, "World Bank Says to Poor Nations: Be More Efficient," *Christian Science Monitor,* June 22, 1994, p. 8.
49. Ian Katz, "Whirlpool: In the Wringer," *Business Week,* December 14, 1998, pp. 83–84.
50. Eric J. Arnould, "Toward a Broadened Theory of Preference Formation and the Diffusion of Innovations: Cases from Zinder Province, Niger Republic," *Journal of Consumer Research* 16 (September 1989), pp. 239–67.
51. *International Marketing Data and Statistics* (London: Euromonitor, 1997), p. 356.
52. Nathalie Boschat, "Catering to Africa's Consumers," *World Press Review,* June 1993, p. 40.
53. Naseem Khan, "Asian Women's Dress from Burqah to Bloggs—Changing Clothes for Changing Times," in *Chic Thrills: A Fashion Reader,* ed. Juliet Ash and Elizabeth Wilson (Berkeley: University of California Press, 1992), pp. 61–74.

54. Eric J. Arnould, "Toward a Broadened Theory of Preference Formation and the Diffusion of Innovations: Cases from Zinder Province, Niger Republic," *Journal of Consumer Research* 16 (September 1989), pp. 239–67.
55. Carlos Denton, "Marketing Myths of Central America," *Marketing News,* January 21, 2001, p. 12.
56. Constance Classen, "Sugar Cane, Coca-Cola and Hypermarkets: Consumption and Surrealism in the Argentine Northwest," in *Cross-Cultural Consumer Behavior,* ed. David Howes (London and New York: Routledge, 1996), pp. 39–54.
57. Anna Husarka, "The First Casualty," *The New Yorker,* April 19, 1993, pp. 57–65.
58. "Salvadorans Find Fun, Fuel at Gas Stations," *Long Beach Press-Telegram,* January 3, 1993, p. A3; and Philip Cateora, *International Marketing* (Homewood, IL: Irwin, 1993), p. 526.
59. Clayton Jones, "From Carpet Bombing to Capitalism in Laos," *Christian Science Monitor,* November 19, 1993, pp. 10–11.

LEARNING OBJECTIVES

After completing this chapter, you should be able to:

- Understand the meaning and nature of culture.
- Discuss the ideas of cultural blueprints, categories, and principles.
- Explain why the fact that culture is learned is significant to marketers.
- Describe the importance of cultural values to consumer behavior and some ways of measuring cultural values.
- Give some examples of cultural myths and symbols and marketing's role in reproducing them.
- Explain and identify some examples of consumer rituals.
- Recognize some guidelines for cultural awareness.

THE MEANING AND NATURE OF CULTURE

THE BABY JOGGER

While living in Denmark, we purchased a California-style jogging stroller (shown on page 72) so that we could be together with our three-year-old daughter while we ran in the city of Odense's lovely river park. We wondered how likely the Danes we encountered were to adopt jogging strollers. To us it seemed to be a product in harmony with our understanding of Danish culture, although we rarely saw one in Denmark. We wondered what people were saying about the jogger as we ran past them in the park. And we wondered why it attracted attention. So the question became, Would Danish culture favor the spread of the baby jogger among consumers, or not?

Consider some findings. The Danes we encountered on the island of Fyn love to do things outside. They treasure their rustic summer beach houses. They like to bicycle, run, ride, and swim. Fyn and the city of Odense are crisscrossed with paved bicycle paths. In the winter, we often saw elderly people walking in the park using walking aids. Year-round, babies nap in snug cribs that are kept in unheated porches in Danish day care centers. In addition, Rollerblades™ became quite popular while we were in Denmark. Doing things in family groups, such as eating breakfast, exercising, drinking in pubs, or summering at a beach house, is important in Fyn. Strange as it may sound to North Americans, Danes tend to express individualism primarily through membership in particular groups, for example, as members of the freshman class, jogging or football clubs, and so on. That is, U.S.-style individualism is not well regarded in Denmark. And it doesn't pay to stand out from the crowd too much. Finally, Danes on Fyn currently favor big fancy baby buggies with springs and chrome wheels. They say this is for comfort and durability, but we detected a certain amount of subtle showing off in a family's choice of baby carriage. Families like to stroll with baby carriages through the downtown shopping streets on Saturday mornings, as they take advantage of the morning shopping hours, and through the parks in the afternoons. Rows of babies in big buggies often sleep contentedly in front of stores while their parents shop inside. So what is your prediction? Would baby joggers become popular items among Danish consumers?

As it turned out, our jogging stroller scandalized many Danes. A Danish friend confided to us that people we gaily passed commented that our daughter was probably handicapped and that we were probably not very good parents for confining her to such an uncomfortable stroller. Indeed, they felt it was individualistic on our part to do so. Apparently, walking with your child in a snug, cozy buggy in the middle of winter is a good thing, but running with your child in a light, airy jogging stroller is not. Things do not look good for the baby jogger in Denmark.

Contrasting consumer reactions to the baby jogger in the United States and Denmark emphasize the subtle impact of culture on consumers' preferences.

OVERVIEW

The chapter will provide you with an introduction to the nature of culture. We pay particular attention to consumer culture. As the opening vignette illustrates, when we visit another culture, we are often surprised by the experience. Things we take for granted—that babies might enjoy an outing in a jogging stroller, for example—do not necessarily hold true in a different cultural context. Our discoveries help to show us the limits of our own cultural assumptions—that, for example, some Danes believe that a jogging stroller is a bad thing for babies. In the case of the jogging stroller, a difference in cultural values results in a difference in preferred consumption patterns. In this chapter, in order to help you understand and manage the interaction of culture and consumer behavior, we discuss the meaning of culture and its expression in cultural values, myths, symbols, and rituals. We also introduce you to some ideas about the evolving relationship between marketing and culture.

THE MEANING AND NATURE OF CULTURE

Social sciences such as sociology, anthropology, and psychology offer varying definitions of culture. Marketers also hold varying conceptions of culture. A traditional marketing view is shown on the left in Exhibit 3.1. In this perspective, culture is viewed as a relatively unchanging precursor of individual behavior. In this model, culture consists primarily of values and norms. **Values** are *enduring beliefs about desirable outcomes that transcend specific situations and shape one's behavior.* If asked, people can usually state important values: honesty, dependability, and so forth, for example. Cultures vary in the strength of members' beliefs in a limited number of universal values. **Norms** are *informal, usually unspoken rules that govern behavior.* Waiting one's turn in an orderly line for a cashier is an example of a normative behavior in a retail

EXHIBIT 3.1

Two Views of Culture and Consumer Behavior

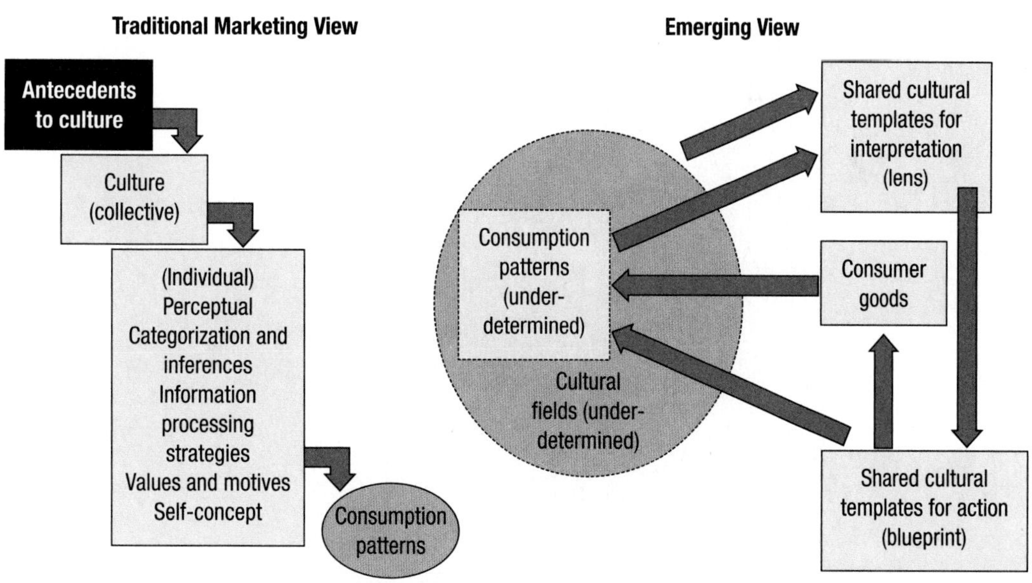

Sources: Daniel John McCort and Naresh K. Malhotra, "Culture and Consumer Behavior: Toward an Understanding of Cross-Cultural Consumer Behavior in International Marketing," *Journal of International Consumer Marketing* 6, no. 2 (1993), pp. 91–127; Douglas B. Holt, "Consumers' Cultural Differences as Local Systems of Tastes: A Critique of the Personality/Values Approach and an Alternative Framework," *Asia Pacific Advances in Consumer Research* 1 (1994), pp. 178–84; and Mary Douglas and Baron Isherwood, *The World of Goods* (New York: W. W. Norton, 1979).

context. People may not be able to articulate norms, and cultures vary widely on the norms that people obey.

The diagram on the left provides a linear view of culture. Causality flows from top to bottom. Values and norms help to determine perceptual and cognitive principles that, in turn, influence people's attitudes to marketing offerings and consumption practice. In this perspective, the key questions for marketers are to what extent should they adapt market offerings to other cultural contexts, and how should they do it.[1]

Our view of culture and consumer behavior differs from the traditional view and is shown on the right in Exhibit 3.1. Following some anthropologists (scientists who study human cultures), we define a society's **culture** as *dynamic blueprints for action and interpretations that enable a person to operate in a manner acceptable to other members of the culture*. The blueprints or frameworks vary between cultures, although they always incorporate frameworks both for action and for interpretation. Members of a culture use knowledge of these models as a lens to perceive their world, as a set of rules for making sense of it, and as a repertoire of taken-for-granted ways to act on it. Habits and customs such as greetings are examples of cultural blueprints. So too are rules for fan behavior at sports events, as shown in the photo of Japanese soccer fans below, and many other ritual behaviors (discussed later in the chapter) we engage in. Blueprints include nonverbal communication skills such as how to claim a place in a line at a check-out counter. Thus, culture consists of shared blueprints. Both individuals and firms that wish to operate successfully in a culture require these kinds of knowledge. The frameworks vary between cultures, but they always incorporate a variety of elements that we will discuss later in the chapter. Consumer Chronicles 3.1 illustrates what can happen when companies fail to adapt to local blueprints for action.

The rules for fan behavior at sports events exemplify cultural blueprints.

Costs of Not Adapting to Cultural Blueprints for Action

CONSUMER CHRONICLES 3.1

When Carrefour SA opened its megastore in a Tokyo suburb in December 2000, customers swarmed in. But 10 months later, there is barely a line for most of the day at cash registers of most Carrefour stores there. The company never adequately adjusted its business to the buying patterns of Japanese consumers and it has not capitalized on the curiosity of local consumers about products that hold the allure of hailing from France, analysts say. Since their opening, each store has been posting losses of about $830,000 a month. And overall sales have been about 20 percent lower than anticipated. "It's different from France, where people got to a megastore once a week and do bulk buying," said Mr. Saotome of Mitsubishi Research Institute. Refrigerators and storage space in Japanese homes are limited, so housewives often carry out the task of shopping. They make it their routine to visit a familiar nearby supermarket where other friends congregate almost daily rather than to drive to a hypermarket on the weekend with the family to stock up. Further, Japanese department stores have traditionally invested heavily in consumer education, initiating consumers into the mysteries of new and exotic products, something discounter Carrefour failed to do.

Sources: Miki Tanikawa, "French Supermarket Struggles to Fit In," International Herald Tribune *online, October 5, 2001, www.iht.com/articles/34613.html; and Millie Creighton, " 'Something More: Japanese Department Stores' Marketing of 'a Meaningful Human Life,' "* Asian Department Stores, *ed. Kerrie L. MacPherson, (Honolulu: University of Hawai'i Press, 1998), pp. 206–32.*

Blueprints for action and interpretation are constructed by culture from two components. First is through **cultural categories,** which *define and organize time, space, nature, the sacred, and society*. For example, occupation, class, ethnicity, gender, and age (discussed in Chapter 12) are examples of cultural categories. Others include parents and children (social categories), cleanliness and filth (natural and sacred categories), and work and leisure (temporal categories), for example. These categories help organize a system of social distinctions that arranges the world of consumption. Apparently, our use of a jogging stroller did not fit with Danish cultural categories of baby strollers or family leisure time. Before the development of consumer culture, cultural categories such as these were more rigid than they are today. As an example of quickly changing cultural categories, consider that many of today's information technology occupations such as "content provider" did not exist in the recent past. Other occupations such as printer or bookbinder either no longer exist or are radically altered from what they once were because of technological change. Especially in the Triad countries, cultural categories are subject to frequent change. The globalization of markets has increased the pace of change in the nature and meaning of cultural categories. Consumer Chronicles 3.2 shows what can happen when social categories (native and foreigner) and categories of the natural and sacred (cleanliness and dirt) come into conflict.

One kind of complex cultural category is referred to as a cultural field in Exhibit 3.1. Several examples of cultural fields could include family leisure time, shopping trips, or birthday parties, as suggested by the photo of a British birthday shown on page 76. Consumer goods and consumption patterns help to define cultural fields of interest to marketers and consumers alike. Thus, many people like to buy club or team merchandise

Consequences of Cultural Category Confusion

CONSUMER CHRONICLES 3.2

The Japanese are far too polite to say it out loud. But every foreigner knows, deep in his heart, that he fails to measure up to Japan's dauntingly high standards of personal hygiene. In short, *gaijin* (foreigners) smell bad. So imagine the disappointment of one poor white man on being denied entry to a public bathhouse on Hokkaido, the most northerly of Japan's main islands. Foreigners, said the proprietor flatly, were not welcome.

There then followed a period of confusion as Debito Arudo (né David Aldwinckle) in fact claimed to be Japanese and had a passport to prove it. After some discussion, the bathhouse owner still refused Mr. Arudo entry, on the grounds the Japanese customers would think he was foreign. Mr. Arudo lost his patience and decided on the un-Japanese step of filing suit.

As soon as Mr. Arudo's intentions become clear, the bathhouse owner modestly adjusted tack. Foreigners would, after all, be allowed to bathe, but only if they met four conditions: they must have lived in Japan continuously for more than one year; they must sufficiently understand bathing customs; they must understand Japanese; and they must not cause any inconvenience to other customers—that is, they must not stink. Since *gaijin* do, as every Japanese knows, smell bad, Mr. Arudo continues his search for justice, and a bath, in the courts.

Source: "Bathroom Blues," The Economist, *February 10, 2001, p. 44.*

to wear to a sports event, eat special kinds of stadium foods, and engage in various kinds of spectating activities within the field of a sports event. Our purchase of a baby jogger fit the field of family leisure time as we understood it, but the Danes use different goods and consumption practices in this context, such as large strollers.

A birthday party exemplifies a complex cultural category or field.

Cultural principles for action at sporting events inform us of how to participate in the "wave."

In addition to cultural categories, blueprints for action and interpretation are shaped by another component, **cultural principles.** Cultural principles *allow things to be grouped into cultural categories, ranked, and interrelated.* They include *values and ideals, norms, and beliefs,* for example. Cultural principles enable us to classify products into categories such as "minivans" or "salty snacks," and identify products and brands as belonging to these categories. Cultural principles also lead to the identification of some brands as exemplars of a category. Thus, Jeeps or Land Rovers may exemplify the category of SUV; Wal-Mart may exemplify the category of discount department store. Some cultural principles allow us to identify and act in accordance with norms such as the rules for fan behavior at a sports event, for example. We use such principles to know how to participate in "the wave" (see photo, above) or to hurl insults at referees, but not bottles. Other cultural principles take the form of the rules for recreation that our baby jogger violated in Denmark, for example. Cultural principles are sometimes expressed in sayings and folk wisdom such as "hard work pays," "there is virtue in loyalty to the state," "you get what you pay for," "seeing is believing," "possession is nine-tenths of the law," or "the nail that sticks up gets hammered down."

Some cultural principles operate at very basic levels. For example, in a sequence of advertising images, Western viewers will tend to see those at the right as coming later in time than those at the left. The same would not necessarily be true for members of Arabic cultures for whom text may wrap around the page, or of Chinese cultures where text may flow in columns down the page. In summary, cultural principles structure understanding and action. Exhibit 3.2 summarizes distinctions between cultural categories, principles, and blueprints.

EXHIBIT 3.2

Cultural Principles, Categories, and Blueprints

Principles	Categories	Blueprints
Values and ideals Norms Beliefs Folk wisdom	Concepts that organize nature, time, space, and society	Combination rules Interpretive lens Active knowledge —Customs —Habits —Rituals —Customary skills —Nonverbal communications

In the emerging view, values, norms, habits, customs, and other cultural elements differ in kind, not merely in strength, between different cultures. To complicate matters, culture cannot be reduced to a list of norms, values, consumer goods, consumption patterns, or other cultural elements, although all of these are important in a culture. Our list of facts about the Danes did not enable us to correctly predict the acceptability of baby joggers, for example. This is what leads us to state that consumption patterns and even cultural fields are **indeterminant,** or not fully predictable. Culture is indeterminant because the actions of firms and consumers, including their marketing and consumption behaviors, produce changes usually small, but sometimes large in culture itself. For example, Australian Rules Football (see photo below) is a recent innovation with its own characteristic consumption patterns and merchandise. At the same time it is a cultural field whose norms, values, and rituals would be pretty familiar to the European soccer fan or the North American football fanatic. Diffusion of the microwave oven, on the other hand, is widely thought to have transformed North American cooking and eating habits, social roles in the household, and even the cultural category "meal time." Some believe that the Internet will revolutionize Chinese society and culture, in dramatic and unpredictable ways, by flooding it with a democracy of new ideas and values. Remember, as the model on the right side of Exhibit 3.1 indicates, culture is a set of dynamic models for action and understanding.[2]

The unique configuration of cultural categories and principles that produces Australian rules football illustrates the indeterminate nature of consumer culture.

The issue of language comes up in a number of the examples we use in this chapter. Language has a significant influence on our blueprints for action and interpretation. The view of the world that people have depends very much on the character and structure of the language they speak. Users of different languages (a set of cultural principles and categories) are led toward different types of observations and different evaluations of similar observations (interpretations). Language is not only an instrument for describing events, it also shapes events. Observers using different languages will present different facts in the "same" situations, or they will arrange similar facts in different ways.

For example, Dutch and Scandinavian languages have words for "togetherness" that express much more than "being together" and that do not exist in the Anglo-American world. The words are *gezellig* (Dutch), *hyggelig* (Danish), *mysigt* (Swedish), and *kodikas* (Finnish). The Danes use it even in combinations like *hyggetime* (together time) and *hyggemad* (together food). These terms imply sharing one's feelings and philosophies in a very personal way while being together in a small group. Members of other cultures will not understand the concept. Asked about *gezellig,* an Englishman living in the Netherlands might say, "It's so intrusive." As a template for action, the concept means Dutch people prefer a small dinner party to a larger group, for example. A small group is not even considered a "dinner party" by the British, who tend to apologize if there are not more than two couples for dinner. These shared cultural principles of togetherness help to account for the greater collective orientation of the Dutch and the Scandinavians when compared to the more individualistic Anglo-Americans, for example (see the discussion of cultural values).

For the Dutch and Scandinavians, the togetherness concept can be effective in advertising for the type of product used during get-togethers, such as coffee, candies, pastries, and drinks. During the past century, Sara Lee/Douwe Egberts has used it successfully for advertising the company's brand of coffee in Holland and has earned a substantial market share through its use.

Language is much more important than many international marketers realize. It is common knowledge among those who are bi- or trilingual that advertising copy carrying cultural values is difficult to translate. People who speak a single language do not understand this. If translations are needed, particularly for research purposes, the best system is translating and back-translating the questions (translating the foreign language version back into the original language version) to be sure that at least the questions have the same meaning. Yet, the values included in the words cannot be translated easily, and sometimes, equivalent words and meanings are not found.[3]

The diagram on the right side of Exhibit 3.1 suggests that one of the ways that cultural categories are established is through material objects. Objects, especially consumer goods, contribute to the construction of the culturally constituted world because they are a visible record of blueprints for action and interpretation. Products provide tangible markers and symbols of meaning. Consumer goods give cultural meanings concrete forms. People's ways of acquiring, using, and disposing of goods and services enable them to act out cultural blueprints. The baby stroller vignette illustrates how consumer goods, like material objects in general, make blueprints for action and interpretation tangible. In other words, Danish baby carriages symbolize certain cultural values and impose certain cultural ways of behaving (norms). At the same time, they exclude other ways of believing and behaving. Thus, a big baby buggy imposes a certain pace on how one walks, keeps a baby cozy, and encourages sleep. Consumer goods also provide symbols of membership in, and boundaries around, consumption communities. Goods provide others with symbols of these identities as well. To oversimplify a bit, we could say that big, fancy baby buggies symbolize coziness and status to Danes, whereas lightweight baby joggers symbolize health and fitness to Californians. And in the Danish mind, Californian jogging strollers may symbolize poor parenting as well.

As the vignette suggests, cultural categories and cultural principles are expressed simultaneously in consumer goods. You cannot have one without the other. When consumer goods show a distinction between two cultural categories, they express the cultural principles that distinguish the categories. For example, in the United States horses are not food. This categorization expresses the principle that animals may be divided into at least two groups: domestic animals and livestock. It would violate the cultural principles that define the categories to eat horses or other domestic animals such as dogs, cats, canaries, and gerbils. Hence, most North Americans do not. Dogs are not classified as domestic animals in some parts of the Philippines, nor are cats among the Gourmantché people of Burkina Faso, Africa. Hence, the flesh of these animals is appropriate for consumption. Many examples of differences in categories and principles could be provided.

Clothing, like other publicly consumed products, is valuable in separating cultural categories of time, space, gender, ethnicity, and class. Clothes represent cultural principles—we agree on some of their meanings. For example, formal attire and cocktail dress imply time and action categories as well as categories of appropriate settings; evening wear is not worn to work, for instance, and may involve an atmosphere that encourages chitchat and alcohol consumption, for example. In many developing countries, the category of Western dress contrasts with traditional dress. The former represents categories such as cosmopolitan, elite, educated, and foreign; traditional dress represents categories such as local and authentic.

Clothing represents many other cultural categories and principles. Trousers and dresses represent not only gender differences but also cultural principles that distinguish the

Women's professional dress enables them to express the blueprints for action and interpretation associated with the business world.

The Western Business Suit

CONSUMER CHRONICLES 3.3

Fashion trends are fast changing and often difficult to predict. Nonetheless, the Western business suit communicates that the wearer is a serious person who is ready to conduct business. The appropriate style for men remains fairly constant over time. In contrast, there is not a consistent "uniform" for women. When male executives were asked to rate the ability of ensembles to create an "executive look" for women, they came up with the following ranking, from most favorable impression to least favorable impression:

- Skirted suit
- Dress or skirt with blazer
- Dress with matching jacket
- Man-tailored pants suit
- Simple dress
- Skirt and blouse
- Slacks and blouse
- Skirt and sweater
- Slacks and sweater

Women who rely on mass-media images for ideas about work clothing perceive a wider range of acceptable outfits. Women who rely on work associates' and superiors' ideas about appropriate clothing for work have a narrower range of acceptable outfits. As mentioned at the outset, fashion trends evolve over time. As more and more firms introduce the idea of casual Friday (or everyday casual, as in Silicon Valley), standards of acceptable business attire continue to change. Nonetheless, manner of dress remains as an important tool for impression management in all cultures.

Source: Sex Roles 15 (1986), pp. 197–205, "Women's Adoption of a Business Uniform: A Content Analysis of Magazine Advertisements," Carol S. Saunders and Bette A. Stead. Copyright ©1986. Reprinted with kind permission of Kluwer Academic Publishers.

behavior of these categories of persons. When Western women began wearing business suits, as shown in the photo on page 80, it was a way for them to express the blueprints for action and interpretation associated with the business world—seriousness, authority, efficiency, and the like—and asserted their position in a category from which they had been excluded before. Consumer Chronicles 3.3 adds some details to how the symbolic system of business dress codes is developing.[4]

Acting in conformity with cultural blueprints, members of a community or market segment constantly reinforce the distinctions between cultural categories through their purchase choices and consumption decisions. Members of consumer cultures are constantly engaged in making the cultural categories and principles by which they live. Through our consumer behavior, we define and redefine the meanings of self, community, and products and services themselves. When we encounter devoted members of a Harley-Davidson owner's group, a Winnebago-Itasca traveler's group, a fan club (e.g., a Trekkie or Deadhead), a new religious sect, or a political party, we can often see these behaviors pretty clearly.

Consumers' expressions of likes and dislikes (cultural principles) distinguish both goods and consumers from one another. In this way, consumers are also divided into cultural categories. Thus, in the Central American nation of Belize, a distaste for eating traditional country dishes (cultural principle) like cowfoot soup categorizes someone as a member of the urban middle class. In the same way, a dislike for eating imported foods such as pizza or tuna fish sandwiches (cultural principle), coupled with a preference for cowfoot soup, categorizes someone as a Belizean neotraditionalist. As these examples suggest, consumer likes and dislikes and the market segments they define have important implications for marketers.[5]

Our vignette provides an example of cultural blueprints in action with regard to rules for choosing and using baby strollers in Denmark. In our view of culture, a key question for marketers becomes how to align their products with cultural blueprints, categories, and principles. To successfully communicate how to use products, who should use them, and what benefits their use provides, marketing communications should build on cultural blueprints. A challenging question for marketers concerns whether and how the introduction of new products and services may contribute to the development of blueprints, categories, and principles.

As the discussion of cowfoot soup illustrates, while we talk of culture as widely shared blueprints for action and understanding, culture is really a systematic collection of values, norms, behaviors, and so on that also reflects *substantial variability.* Thus, we did see one or two Danish couples using baby joggers, but not many. The diversity that may exist in a particular culture is fostered by many factors, including ethnic and class differences (Chapter 12), individuals' lifestyles (Chapter 11), family and household traditions (Chapter 13), and personal experience.[6] For example, some research suggests that the values of managers working in global business environments may reflect professional values that contrast somewhat with the values most characteristic of their national cultures.[7] You may also recall from Chapter 2 that as a result of the globalization of marketing practices, consumers in many developing countries and those in transitional economies confront clashes between Euro-American and traditional cultural beliefs and behaviors. Cultural variability often leads to the development of differences in consumer lifestyles within and across national borders, a topic we discuss in Chapter 8.

Having given you a basic introduction to culture, we now turn to a more specific discussion of several aspects of culture and their relationship to marketing and consumer behavior. These topics include cultural values, myths and symbols, and rituals.

CULTURAL VALUES

Consumer researchers interested in culture have devoted most of their attention to understanding cultural values. And cultural values are a good example of what we have called a template or cultural blueprint for action. Values include **instrumental values,** *shared beliefs about how people should behave,* and **terminal values,** or *desirable life goals.* Examples of instrumental values include competence, compassion, sociality, and integrity. Ambition is an instrumental value that might help one attain a comfortable life, which is a terminal value.[8] An example of an instrumental value widely held in Western consumer cultures is a belief that people have choices and that free choice is good. Terminal values include social harmony, personal gratification, self-actualization, security, love and affection, and personal contentedness. The desire for security is used to promote many products ranging from insurance to breath mints and deodorant; many products and services are positioned to appeal to other terminal values.[9]

Cultural values are shared broadly across a society. They are learned, reinforced, and modified within subcultures, ethnic groups, social classes, and families. Values are organized into systems that differ in their importance to consumers. They transcend particular situations. Some believe that behaviors develop from attitudes, which in turn derive from more general or abstract cultural values. This is referred to as the **value-attitude-behavior hierarchy.** According to this model, within any given consumption choice situation, *abstract values affect midrange attitudes that lead to specific* *consumer behaviors.* Therefore, some researchers believe that values could influence and explain a variety of individual and collective consumer behaviors. For example, the abstract values of security and self-confidence may be linked to attitudes about preventing cavities and providing clean, white teeth, respectively. Consumers with these attitudes may seek these benefits in the toothpaste they buy.[10]

Consistent with the traditional view of culture shown on the left side of the diagram in Exhibit 3.1, attempts have been made to identify and measure a universal set of values. This would allow researchers to compare consumers in one country with those in another. Results of these comparisons, in turn, would enable marketers to adjust the marketing mix to suit the value preferences of different markets.

Among the frequently used value measures are the List of Values and Hofstede's worker values. Researchers have found considerable cross-cultural differences in levels of these general sets of values. In addition, researchers have sought to correlate these values with consumer behaviors such as how they rank product features, or attributes, and the way they respond to advertising claims.[11]

Researchers at the University of Michigan Survey Research Center developed the **List of Values (LOV)** measure.[12] The LOV includes eight values: sense of belonging, fun and enjoyment, warm relationships with others, self-fulfillment, being well respected, a sense of accomplishment, security, and self-respect. Differences in the strength of these values between regions of the United States and between the United States, Norway, and Germany have been detected.[13] In the United States, the LOV has been related to a number of important measures of mental health, well-being, and adaptation to society.

The LOV has been related to some U.S. consumer behaviors, including shopping, spending, nutrition attitudes, natural food choice, fashion items, and gift giving. For example, people who value warm relationships with others give gifts for "no occasion." In an international study, Israeli thrill and adventure seekers scored higher on three values—warm relations with others, fun and enjoyment, and self-respect—than thrill-avoiders. However, a study that attempted to test the degree to which consumers from two different cultures, the United States and Germany, would identity LOV values in TV advertisements ran into trouble when the value-based terms were translated into German. German subjects viewed the terms differently than did the Americans and consequently interpreted the meanings of advertisements differently. Some terms were difficult to translate from English to German, and some that could be translated did not really share the same set of meanings in the two cultural settings. Not surprisingly, therefore, measures linking the LOV and particular patterns of consumer preferences are often weak or inconsistent across cultures and contexts. This problem of translation limits the usefulness of the List of Values and lends support to the view that cultural blueprints differ in kind between cultures.[14]

Another general value dimension of considerable interest to marketers involves individualism versus collectivism. This dimension derives from **Hofstede's worker values.** His study of people from 40 countries revealed that the United States and the English-speaking countries have high levels of individualism (competition is high, independence and separateness are valued, and people believe individual status and position are earned and changeable). By contrast, Latin American and east Asian countries such as Japan and China have lower levels of this social value. We have already mentioned that Danes are more collectivist in their value orientation than are U.S. citizens.[15]

One intriguing study conducted with a student sample in Hong Kong may help explain the effect of interdependent value orientation on the processing of advertising messages.[16] (You will learn more details about processing strategies in Chapters 9 and 15.) In one experiment, researchers found that only consensus information (others' evaluations of a product) influenced Hong Kong consumers' evaluations. Interestingly, only product characteristics guide evaluations in similar experiments conducted in the United States. The pattern of findings could be interpreted in two ways. First, consumers with different cultural backgrounds may differ in their preference for advertising processing strategies. For example, heuristic-based processing (simplifying rules to make judgments) using consensus cues may be more preferred in interdependent cultures like that of Hong Kong. Or systematic (extensive use of product cues) and heuristic processing may occur across different cultural contexts, but the information that is perceived as most important may vary across cultures.

The results from a second experiment that manipulated the accessibility of cues provided support for the second hypothesis. This pattern of results suggests fundamental similarities in the ways in which both Hong Kong and North American consumers process advertising content. However, cross-cultural differences found in importance of cues—specifically elaborate consensus information—may lead to the differences in attitudes. Information of this type is useful to marketers in helping them tailor advertising messages to different cultural contexts.

Confusing and inconclusive results are unfortunately typical of studies that have sought to link consumer behaviors and Hofstede's abstract cultural values. Part of the problem is that values do not translate well. The blueprints for action and interpretation that would express values such as individualism or collectivism vary between cultures. In addition, specific behaviors linked to these values also differ between cultures. These limitations complicate the use of schemes of abstract values by international marketers.[17]

Researchers have identified less universal values than those found in the LOV and Hofstede's research. Culture-specific sets of core values help define a particular culture's blueprints for action and interpretation. Understanding core cultural values may be useful even if cross-cultural comparisons of values are not always useful. The reason is that consumers' purchases are indirectly connected to fulfilling core values. Core values are like goals that can motivate action (see Chapter 10). For example, results of a recent study of advertising effects using Japanese and American samples confirmed that when advertising cues are processed at a low level, cultural-value-based differences in consumer preferences exist. Therefore, understanding these values may be useful for product positioning purposes, including marketing communications.[18] Exhibit 3.3 compares a constellation of U.S. values with one of Japanese values. A chrysanthemum and rose, significant symbols in Japan and the United States, respectively, represent them. Like the petals of the flowers, within a culture core values are connected with each other and together they make up a whole constellation of values that differ one from the other. For example, materialism is a significant value in the United States. For many citizens, the quantity and quality of their material possessions convey achievement and success. Achievement and success are obtained in turn through applying the instrumental values of individual competitive effort. A terminal value for many U.S. citizens is that all people should have equal opportunities for achievement; they believe that through effort, entrepreneurship, and courage (instrumental values), anyone can succeed. Not surprisingly, then, one common motive for purchasing in the United States is rewarding oneself for personal achievement. Similarly, *wa* (harmony) is a Japanese terminal value that strongly affects advertising, product design, and packaging, as suggested by the photograph of the boxed lunch on page 99. Face-saving is a related terminal value in many Asian NICs, including Japan. The values of harmony

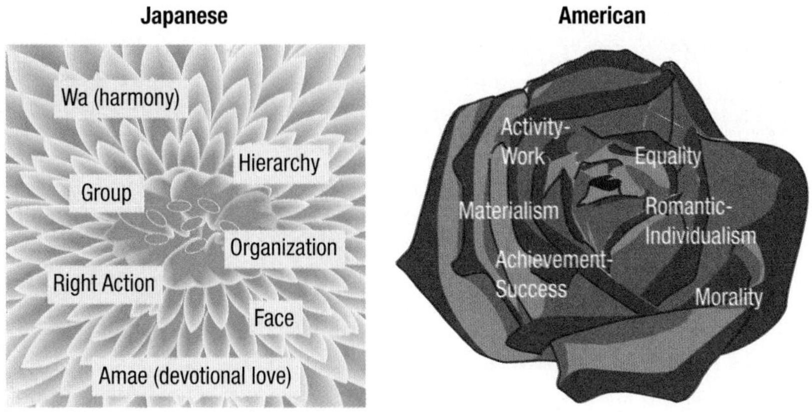

EXHIBIT 3.3

Japanese and American Cultural Values

and face-saving lead Japanese and Koreans to give gifts that are chosen from established brand names, on set occasions, and that reflect widely recognized status differences in their societies. In this way, misunderstandings in giving that might provoke a mutual loss of face are avoided; harmony is maintained.[19]

Researchers have identified other terminal value clusters in other countries. For example, a study in Bangladesh found five important values: gratification, love and tranquility, harmony, hedonism, and spiritual orientation. In contemporary mainland China, diligence, face-saving, frugality, tolerance, pride in Chinese history, tradition, modernity, technological sophistication, and, above all, a warm and loving family are important values. Because of their persuasive force, the latter four are frequently used in Chinese television ads to position products.[20]

Another value concept that interests marketers is **consumer ethnocentrism.** Ethnocentrism may be thought of as an instrumental value that helps provide a template for action. It is *a belief that one's own system of tastes and preferences is better than that of another cultural group.* This value influences consumers to purchase goods produced in their home country, regardless of actual product quality. Thus, consumers' views of foreign countries influence their perception of the quality of products designed or produced in those countries. In a recent study, highly ethnocentric U.S. consumers rated both the status and quality of a car designed, engineered, and manufactured in America more highly than one produced in Japan. They also expressed positive attitudes toward buying U.S.-made cars. By contrast, low-ethnocentric consumers appeared to favor foreign cars.[21] Marketers may wish to diminish the foreign associations with their products when marketing to ethnocentric consumer segments.

Good Practice 3.1 provides a scale to measure consumer ethnocentrism. Each of the 17 items is scored on a 7-point scale, with 1 meaning strongly disagree and 7, strongly agree. Highly ethnocentric consumers have high average scores. To measure ethnocentrism in other countries, researchers can substitute different country references for the U.S. references in the scale items, as some have done for France, Japan, Germany, and Russia.[22]

Consistent with our dynamic perspective on culture outlined in Exhibit 3.1, we do not want to leave you with the impression that cultural values, however important they may be, are unchanging. In fact, cultural values are subject to influence by marketing practices. For example, by manipulating the level of ease of recall of value-based associations embedded in marketing communications, some research provides evidence that cultural preferences may be relatively pliable. For example, when value-based

The CETSCALE: How Ethnocentric Are You?

GOOD PRACTICE 3.1

1. Americans should only buy American-made products.
2. Only those products that are unavailable in the United States should be imported.
3. Buy American products. Keep Americans working.
4. American products first, last, and foremost.
5. Purchasing foreign-made products is un-American.
6. It is not right to buy foreign products.
7. A real American always buys American-made products.
8. We should purchase products manufactured in America instead of letting other countries get rich off of us.
9. It is always best to purchase American-made products.
10. There should be very little trading or purchasing of goods from other countries, unless out of necessity.
11. Americans should not buy foreign products because this hurts American business and causes unemployment.
12. Curbs should be put on all imports.
13. It may cost me more, but I prefer to buy American products.
14. Foreigners should not be allowed to put their products on our markets.
15. Foreign products should be taxed heavily to reduce their entry into the United States.
16. We should buy from foreign countries only those products that we cannot obtain within our own country.
17. American consumers who purchase products made in other countries are responsible for putting their fellow Americans out of work.

Source: Terry A. Shimp and S. Sharma, "Consumer Ethnocentrism: Construction and Validation of the CETSCALE," Journal of Marketing Research *24 (August 1987), pp. 280–89.*

associations were subtle and not easy to recall, an experiment demonstrated that Japanese preferred peacefulness associations (e.g., peaceful, mild, shy) with a brand. By contrast, U.S. participants preferred a ruggedness appeal. However, when the value-based associations were made more vivid and easier to recall, a different pattern of results occurred. Culture-based differences were eliminated.

From a manager's perspective, these findings suggest that global brands based on culturally distinct associations (e.g., BasuKurin bath salt in Japan, Marlboro cigarettes in the United States) still may use global advertising campaigns. But such campaigns should aim to increase the accessibility of the associations (e.g., ruggedness in Japan) rather than shift the meaning of the brand (imbuing Marlboro with less rugged but more exciting associations in Japan). Or a campaign could aim to increase the value of the associations (attempting to make ruggedness more important in Japan). The implication is that such campaigns may eventually alter the structure of cultural values across cultures.[23]

Finally, a value of interest to marketers is **materialism.** Materialism is a terminal value defined as *the importance a consumer attaches to worldly possessions* or as *a consumption-based orientation to happiness seeking.* Further, materialism is a combination of other value orientations, including nongenerosity, possessiveness, envy, and preservation (a tendency to hang on to things).

Materialism has generally been seen as a Western trait that achieved an elevated place with the development of industrial and postindustrial life. Most researchers see the spread of materialism and consumer culture as going hand in hand. Some cross-cultural research has found higher levels of materialism in Western cultures and in urban samples in non-Western cultures where consumers are more exposed to marketing. High levels of materialism comparable to those in the United States and New Zealand, for example, can be found in places experiencing an explosion of new consumer goods and culture such as Romania, the Ukraine, and Turkey. But this research has also found that materialism is not identical across cultures. Consumers in countries that have experienced dramatic increases in the supply of consumer goods, for example, formerly communist countries such as Romania or the Ukraine, focus more on tangible evidence of consumer wealth such as consumer electronics and cars. The materialism of western Europeans who enjoy greater social stability relates more on the consumption of experiences, art, and aesthetics.[24]

Value-based approaches to culture have been criticized. Faced with problems such as those encountered in the study of German and American interpretations of the values in ads (see page 83), some argue that values differ qualitatively between cultures. Hence, they cannot meaningfully be compared across cultures where different languages are spoken. Others maintain that even if you can get consumers to provide rankings of values, those values are not necessarily the values that matter in a particular culture. Critics also argue that values such as in the LOV or Hofstede's work are too abstract to provide much help in understanding particular consumption patterns. Can they really help managers account for the Danish distaste for California-style jogging strollers discussed in the vignette, the peculiar popularity of the Argentine tango in Japan, or other preferences we discuss below? Finally, critics argue that the procedures used to develop scientifically valid, cross-cultural measures of values remove the cultural aspects from the instruments, rendering them practically useless.[25]

More work is needed to understand how cultural values relate to consumer behavior and how they vary cross-culturally. Better understanding of the relationships between culture, value preferences, consumers' evaluation of product or service offerings, and purchase and consumption behavior would be useful for more effective cross-national marketing. Without understanding basic values, it is unlikely that marketers can influence specific behaviors within a culture. Of course, marketers need to understand how an individual's values stem not only from shared cultural values but also from regional, social (ethnic and religious), and family values and personal life experiences. And as our introductory vignette makes clear, marketers need to understand how values interact to produce consumption preferences. In future chapters we will discuss these influences and how they vary with consumption lifestyles.

CULTURAL MYTHS AND SYMBOLS

In addition to values, societies also possess sets of myths and symbols. Myths and symbols are an example of what we have called a template or cultural blueprint for interpretation because they help us understand what we observe in social life. **Myths** are *stories containing symbolic elements that express shared emotions and cultural values.* In traditional cultures, people conveyed cultural knowledge to their children through myths, legends, and fairy tales. The Chinese moon cake tradition, discussed later (see "Cultural Rituals") is based on the myth of Chang E, a beautiful woman who lives on the moon with her pet rabbit. Today, many popular culture media such as television programs, advertisements, movies, comics, cartoons, and novels build on mythic themes and convey cultural knowledge to consumers. Knowledge of myths and fairy tales and how they work is useful to marketers.[26]

Myths serve several important functions in culture. First, they emphasize *how things are interconnected.* The recent U.S. movie *You've Got Mail* is built on a myth that emphasizes interconnections. Much as in Shakespeare's 500-year-old comedic plays *A Midsummer's Night's Dream* and *As You Like It,* people in the movie who are "meant to be together" overcome enormous odds and numerous comic obstacles to come together. The success of the widely syndicated television show *The X-Files* may be due in part to its combination of the myth of the heroic quest for truth, "the truth" as the show has it, with mythic themes from Christianity such as the "miraculous" pregnancy of one of the show's principal characters, and other religious traditions.[27]

Second, myths *maintain social order by authorizing a social code.* Richard Wagner's operas, such as *The Ring Cycle,* draw on ancient Norse myths and reinforce ideas of heroism and national destiny for many Germans. French comic books about the mythical Asterix the Gaulois who lives in Roman times use hilarious caricatures to reinforce French social values and poke fun at the behavior of other Europeans. The European Cinderella myth teaches us how a miserable but deserving person can be blessed with wealth and happiness. This rags-to-riches story resonates with the U.S. immigrant experience. Therefore, variants of the Cinderella myth reappear in many media products, including recent films such as *Pretty Woman* and *Working Girl.* The Cinderella rags-to-riches story also has special meaning for the Japanese, who see this story as relating to the post–World War II Japanese experience. Indeed, Tokyo Disneyland chose to feature Cinderella's castle instead of Sleeping Beauty's castle as at the original Disneyland. In the Middle East, several fanciful Egyptian soap operas of recent years have provided a mythical vehicle to work out conflicting models of behavior related to women's roles in society and the place of Islam in a modern nation.[28]

Consumer Chronicles 3.4 illustrates a modern form of mythmaking, an urban legend that authorizes a social code. **Urban legends** are *stories passed by word of mouth that purport to be nearly firsthand accounts of real events but are fictitious. They contain a moral lesson.* We know the story about the cookie recipe is a myth: A world-class retailer would not behave this way, and internal contradictions like the price of the salads (too low) detract from the truth claim. Reality is not the point however. This is a moral story about the rules of market exchange and how customers may reasonably resist retailers' violations of these taken-for-granted rules. In short, it is a story about the rules of fair play. Other common examples of urban myths with implications for marketers include product tampering and adulteration scares. When poorly handled, such as the 1999 Belgian Coke scare, urban myths like these can lead to panic and costly product recalls. Myths are powerful![29]

Third, myths provide *psychological models for individual behavior and identity.* Many myths teach models of heroic or right action. Disney films such as *The Lion King, Mulan,* and *Tarzan* are examples of films whose heroes act out models where individualism and personal integrity are promoted. The actor Harrison Ford has starred in a string of Hollywood movies that promote the value of male heroism and the protection of the nuclear family. The late Toshiro Mifune starred in scores of Japanese movies that dealt with cultural themes of duty and honor. Similarly, the late film actor Marcello Mastroianni became an icon of sophisticated European male values of the 1950s and 1960s.

Urban Retail Legend

CONSUMER CHRONICLES 3.4

This is a true story, this is not a joke . . .

My daughter and I had just finished a salad at Neiman-Marcus Cafe in Dallas and decided to have a small dessert. Because both of us are such cookie lovers, we decided to try the Neiman-Marcus cookie. It was sooo excellent that I asked if they would give me the recipe and the waitress said with a small frown, "I'm afraid not but, you can buy the recipe." Well, I asked how much, and she responded, "Only two-fifty, it's a great deal!" I agreed, just add it to my tab I told her.
Thirty days later, I received my Visa statement from Neiman-Marcus and it was $285. I looked again and I remembered I had only spent $9.95 for two salads and about $20 for a scarf. As I glanced at the bottom of the statement, it said, "Cookie Recipe—$250." That's outrageous! I called Neiman's accounting department and told them the waitress said it was "two-fifty," which clearly does not mean two hundred and fifty dollars by any possible interpretation of the phrase. Neiman-Marcus refused to budge. They would not refund my money, because according to them, "What the waitress told you is not our problem. You have already seen the recipe. We absolutely will not refund your money at this point." I explained to her the criminal statutes that govern fraud in Texas. I threatened to refer them to the Better Business Bureau and the state attorney general for engaging in fraud. I was basically told, "Do what you want, it doesn't matter, and we're not refunding your money."
I waited, thinking of how I could get even or even trying to get any of my money back. I just said, "Okay, you folks got my $250, and now I'm going to have $250 worth of fun." I told her that I was going to see to it that every cookie lover in the United States with an e-mail account has a $250 cookie recipe from Neiman-Marcus . . . for free. She replied, "I wish you wouldn't do this." I said, "Well, you should have thought of that before you ripped me off," and slammed down the phone on her. So here it is!!!
Please, please, please pass it on to everyone you can possibly think of. I paid $250 for this. I don't want Neiman-Marcus to ever get another penny off of this recipe.

Neiman-Marcus Cookies

Recipe may be halved

2 cups butter

4 cups flour

2 tsp. soda

2 cups sugar

5 cups blended oatmeal (measure oatmeal and blend in a blender to a fine powder)

24 oz. chocolate chips

2 cups brown sugar

1 tsp. salt

1 8 oz. Hershey Bar (grated)

4 eggs

2 tsp. baking powder

2 tsp. vanilla

3 cups chopped nuts (your choice, but we liked pecans best)

Cream the butter and both sugars. Add eggs and vanilla; mix together with flour, oatmeal, salt, baking powder, and soda. Add chocolate chips, Hershey Bar, and nuts. Roll into balls and place two inches apart on a cookie sheet. Bake for 10 minutes at 375 degrees. Makes 112 cookies.

Have fun! This is not a joke; this is a true story.
Ride free, citizens!
Please pass this to every one you know!

What constitutes heroic or right action varies between cultures. The Japanese movie *Masseur Ichi and a Chest of Gold* illustrates a Japanese version of heroic behavior that differs from U.S. myths. In this movie, the hero, a blind samurai, is motivated to save face and protect the honor of a superior. These motivations lead him to help struggling farmers, who have been disloyal to their superiors, retrieve a chest of gold from some

New Spells from Timeless Fairy Tales

INDUSTRY INSIGHTS 3.1

An eerie parallel universe teeming with monks, gnomes, elves, witches, wizards, and knights lives anew in movies and television, in a flurry of recent advertising campaigns, and on fashion runways and retail displays as artists, film directors, photographers, and designers plunder the imagery of fairy tales to weave a spell on an ever-susceptible public. A vein of escapism runs through television hits such as *Buffy the Vampire Slayer, Witchblade,* and *Charmed*. And it can be seen in Louis Vuitton's print advertising that depicts Snow White followed by seven monkish dwarfs carrying her LV luggage (see www.vuitton.com).

"There is a deep disquiet among people today that stems from the artificiality of modern life," said Joseph Pearce, a writer in residence at Ave Maria College in Ypsilanti, Michigan. "Some people dream of a society free from machinery and technology."

The obsession with fairies and magic may well have evolved from Harry Potter, J.K. Rowlings' magical wand–wielding child in her series of best-selling books and, now, on film. To say nothing of *The Lord of the Rings,* J. R. R. Tolkien's wildly popular saga of the diminutive denizens of Middle Earth, and the movie it inspired that received 13 Oscar nominations.

"Fairy tales and myths represent a poignant idealism," said Rick Owens, a Los Angles fashion designer whose romantically hooded, medieval-style gowns owe a common debt to Romantic German opera composer Richard Wagner and the swirling style of Art Nouveau painting and architecture. "All these myths are about youthful utopian dreams," Mr. Owens said.

Tolkien and the literature of fantasy offer escape from contemporary life, Theodore Sherman, editor of *Mythlore,* a scholarly quarterly devoted to the study of fantasy, said. On a deeper level they also offer a model for coping, "for confronting life's non-too-pleasant realities," he said. They also address a recurring fantasy of fusing with nature, the better to harness mystical power. "We want to recover our sense of the wind, the waves, and the oceans," Dr. Sherman said. "There is a feeling that if we understand these things, we might be able to . . . rediscover our sense of wonder."

Fairy tales are particularly stirring to a public increasingly focused on magic, real or metaphorical, as weapon of last resort such as Harry Potter's wand, Frodo's ring, or the demon-defeating gauntlet of *Witchblade* that come to the rescue when real-life solutions fail.

Source: Ruth La Ferla, "Designers Weave New Spell Out of Timeless Fairy Tales," New York Times, *Sunday Styles, February 24, 2002, pp.1, 2.*

thieves. In this case, the unassuming hero's inner strength of character allows him to overcome great odds.

Understanding myths is useful for creating successful media and fashion products. Industry Insights 3.1 suggests that a desire for simple and powerful connections is making fairy tales a source of value to consumers. Further, myths can play a role in building the image of a company and products. McDonald's ran a series of advertising campaigns that replayed U.S. myths. In one, an elderly couple enjoys a romantic meeting at McDonald's. In another, a man demonstrates his commitment to fatherhood by taking his son to breakfast at McDonald's. In a third, an elderly man (with a Protestant work ethic) gets a job after retirement at McDonald's. In a fourth, a young boy stops in at McDonald's for his (now deserved) breakfast after finishing his paper route. Each of these stories features primary U.S. values such as work and activity, the value of individual effort, and equality.

Industry Insights 3.2 provides an example of global mythmaking. It suggests that *Star Wars* not only drew on Western mythology for its plot elements and heroes but that the film has actually contributed a kind of secular mythology to world consumer culture.

Global Mythmaking in Popular Culture

INDUSTRY INSIGHTS 3.2

To make *Star Wars,* [George] Lucas began by studying the mythology of other cultures, noting recurring plot twists and cruxes and moments-of-no-return that reappeared in the stories humans told themselves. He took elements from myths found in *The Golden Bough,* Sufi legends, *Beowulf,* and the Bible and tried to combine them into one epic story. He ransacked Joseph Campbell's books on mythology, among other sources. It was a kind of get-'em-by-the-archetypes-and-their-hearts-and-minds-will-follow approach to screenwriting. One could go through *Star Wars* and almost pick out the chapter headings from Campbell's *The Hero with a Thousand Faces:* the hero's call to adventure, the refusal of the call, the arrival of supernatural aid, the crossing of the first threshold, the belly of the whale, and the series of ordeals culminating in a showdown with the angry father, when at last, as Campbell writes, "the hero . . . beholds the face of the father, understands—and the two are atoned"—which is precisely what happens at the end of *Jedi.*

I asked Jack Sorensen [the president of LucasArts] if he could explain the appeal of *Star Wars* as culture, and he said, "I'm as perplexed by this as anyone, and I'm right in the midst of it. I travel all the time for this job, and I meet people abroad, in Italy or in France, who are totally obsessed with *Star Wars.* I met this Frenchman recently who told me he watches it every week. I don't really think this is caused by some evil master plan of merchandisers and marketers. The demand is already out there, and we're just meeting it—it would exist without us. . . . I feel like *Star Wars* is the mythology of a nonsectarian world. It describes how people want to live. People all view politics as corrupt, much more so in Europe than here, and yet people are not cynical underneath—they want to believe in something pure, noble. That's *Star Wars."*

The marketing is the culture and the culture the marketing. The space that the marketing of *Star Wars* takes up in the culture . . . is validation for the fans of the movies—a kind of return on their investment—just as, in a smaller way, the marketing of the WASP lifestyle by Ralph Lauren is a validation of . . . preppy culture. *Star Wars* is both something to buy (marketing) and something to be (culture), through the buying: becoming a *Star Wars* fan.

Source: John Seabrook, Nob®ow: The Culture of Marketing—the Marketing of Culture *(New York: Alfred A. Knopf, 2000), pp. 143, 145.*

The box office success of *Attack of the Clones* testifies to the success of global mythmaking. Today, marketing and merchandising have become deeply involved in building culture.[30]

Important behaviors in any society can be better understood by reference to shared **cultural symbols,** *objects that represent beliefs and values.* Culture is well reflected in **core symbols,** symbols that are *emotionally powerful and that contain multiple meanings.* In the United States, core symbols include George Washington and the Wild West. In Japan, core symbols include the rising sun image worn by the soccer fans shown in the picture on page 74. The Danish flag, Danbø, is a core symbol, commemorating a miraculous, long-ago victory over the Poles.

People use core symbols in different ways. The U.S. flag is a public symbol, typically used to mark official places and events. Danes use their flag as an intimate, domestic symbol. A Danish traveler returning from abroad might expect to be met at the airport by his friends waving small Danish flags. And no birthday is complete without Danish flags as part of the celebration.

Marketers can use cultural symbols to help position products and services. Because of positive symbolic associations, French wine and cheese are often stamped with the French flag, for example. The Taj Mahal, a famous Indian building, is a popular name for Indian restaurants all over the world. An animated George Washington (who resembles the image on the paper dollar) has been used in a U.S. government television ad campaign to reassure consumers that the "golden dollar" coin is OK with him. Mayflower uses an image of the pilgrims' ship to symbolize the positive benefits of moving with this company. The examples are endless.

Not only can products and services be positioned using key cultural symbols, but consumer goods can also become cultural symbols. For example, the blue and white BMW logo and the Mercedes circle emblem have become global high-status symbols of distinctive German engineering. Harley-Davidson motorcycles too enjoy a special symbolic status globally.

Consumer goods may become national symbols. French symbols include the old DS (pronounced déese, the French word for goddess) luxury-model Citroën, the favorite car of the war hero and president General de Gaulle, as well as the famous 2CV Citroën. 2CV fan clubs have formed everywhere in France. McDonald's Golden Arches redesigned with a traditional Serbian cap, a *sajkaca,* jauntily perched over one of the arches has become a symbol of national pride in Serbia (former Yugoslavia). This symbol reinforces the identification of McDonald's as a Serbian company. In Egypt, religious commodities provide symbolic protection to believers, such as a copy of the Qur'an (Koran) encased in a velvet box, covered in shrink-wrap, and set in the back window of a taxi. Singha Beer provides a good example of a brand to which many Thai beer drinkers are highly loyal. It has strong associations with Thai national identity due to a long promotional campaign on the slogan "our beer, our nation." "Authentic" Thai restaurants abroad often serve Singha Beer.

www.members.tripod.co.uk/~BARRS_IRN_BRU/main.htm

Consumer goods may also become regional symbols. One example is a soft drink called Irn Bru, made in Glasgow, Scotland, for the past half century. Glaswegians "know" it to have remarkable curative qualities for illnesses induced by hard drinking. It has a special, well-guarded formula. It sells incredibly well locally and is the preferred soft drink of many young people. Irn Bru has been the subject of songs, stories, jokes, films, and more. It became famous because of its ads that poked fun at those of Pepsi and Coke, positioning it as an alternative to these U.S. brands. There is even a Church of Irn Bru website.[31]

Some categories of consumer goods are apt to convey important symbolic meanings, and certain types of symbolic meanings are apt to be conveyed by consumer goods. Food is a flexible symbol of identity, capable of symbolizing fine distinctions. What an individual eats may tell others that the person is young or old; male or female; high status or low status; or sick or well. For example, an old joke from the 1970s stated, "real men don't eat quiche." At the same time, food may also reference wider cultural identities, for example, implying that the person is a Jew, Muslim, or Hindu, or French, British, or Brazilian. On some occasions the food a person chooses to eat might tell something about his or her self-image and how that person wishes to be perceived by others. These meanings are evoked in different social contexts and at different times through particular food items. One study found people chose more ethnic foods when dining with members of the same ethnic group than when dining with consumers of mixed ethnicity. For example, a person of Italian heritage living in New York City may be more likely to eat Italian with other Italians than when dining with non-Italians.[32] On Robert Burns night (commemorating the Scottish poet), a citizen of the United Kingdom might eat haggis (stuffed sheep stomach) and mashed neeps (potatoes) to symbolize a regional Scottish, rather than British, identity. Recently, boycotting Coca-Cola and consuming Iranian-made Zamzam-Cola, named after a sacred spring in Mecca, has become a symbol of support for Palestinians in Israel.[33]

Some places become symbols of quality, with value linked to products from particular areas. The BMW and Mercedes Benz symbols have already been mentioned. The districts of Champagne and Cognac in France have been successful at protecting their specific regional product names. This enables producers of champagne and cognac to charge higher prices because of the attached symbolic value of these regions. In Beijing, McDonald's is an attraction because it offers a fulfilling experience symbolic of U.S.–fast-food culture. From the tourist industry we know souvenirs often symbolize place. Japanese tourists desire *omiyage* (souvenir) gifts that capture *meibutsu,* or the essence of place. Other goods become symbols of domestic places, such as home-cooked meals.[34]

Consumers use goods in many transitional or developing societies to symbolize modernity or their ability to participate in global consumer society. Consumers' **conspicuous consumption** of status symbols is a frequent by-product of economic development. Conspicuous consumption is the *acquisition and visible display of luxury goods and services to demonstrate one's ability to afford them.*[35] In Thailand and other parts of Asia, in part through the promotion activities of part-Thai player Tiger Woods, playing golf has become an aspirational symbol of modernity and internationalism. In China, in successive waves of conspicuous consumption, the *san dajian,* "three big items," that convey the most status on their owner have changed. During the 1960s and 1970s, they were wristwatches, bicycles, and sewing machines. In the 1980s, these gave way to color TVs, refrigerators, and washing machines. In the 1990s, the three big items were telephones, air conditioners, and VCRs. Of course, conspicuous consumption of symbols of wealth and power is not limited to consumers in developing economies; it is also common among newly rich consumers in developed economies.[36] We will have more to say about how symbols (shared blueprints for interpretation) work in Chapter 12 and about the symbolic meanings of goods in Chapter 14.

CULTURAL RITUALS

In Chapter 1, using the example of grooming, we introduced the concept of rituals and briefly described their importance in consumer behavior. **Cultural rituals** are a good example of activities that combine blueprints for action and understanding. They consist of *behaviors that occur in a relatively fixed sequence and that tend to be repeated periodically.* Knowledge of rituals simplifies behavioral choices such as how to behave at a wedding, for example. In addition, a ritual makes symbolic statements about the social order, often by dramatizing cultural myths and often linking the present with the past. U.S. Thanksgiving Day and the Mexican Day of the Dead, for example, dramatize cultural myths and link the present with the past.

Rituals organize people's feelings and facilitate and simplify group communications. That is, rituals organize life experience and give it meaning. They are particularly useful in handling situations involving risk, whether the risk is social, emotional, or physical. One outcome of holidays such as U.S. Thanksgiving or the Chinese Moon Festival, for example, is family togetherness. Family unity is often threatened by members' migrations and life-cycle changes. Shared family consumption rituals reinforce or repair the social fabric.

Cultural rituals propose principles and blueprints for consumer behavior that provide marketers with many opportunities for product positioning. Thanksgiving and the Moon Festival reinforce cultural values for people in the United States and China, respectively. Both are widely celebrated. Both celebrate consumption values of abundance and fullness; in both, fat—butter in the United States, lard in China—are consumed in unusual amounts. Christmas is another widely celebrated consumption ritual. It celebrates a principle of family generosity in the United States and Britain, serving as a blueprint for group generosity among the Inuit peoples of Greenland, courtship among Japanese couples, and family generosity to the community in Trinidad.[37]

In Chapter 1 we presented a vignette that focused on ritual behavior that is the product of individual motives and emotions—evening grooming rituals that move participants from the public space of work and activity to the private domestic space of leisure. At the other extreme, rituals can be stimulated by a culture's cosmological belief system, by cultural values, or as a source of group learning. One possible typology of ritual experience is provided in Exhibit 3.4.[38]

In rituals, consumers manipulate objects and symbols. In taking ritual action, people in consumer societies naturally have recourse to consumer goods, the ready-to-hand material of consumer culture. Rituals, like goods, help to establish and stabilize culture categories and principles. Rituals activate the relevant social meanings of consumer goods. Without ritual, categories and principles remain latent and consumer goods rest inert. Marketers may use marketing communications to initiate ritual use of goods, but consumers develop their own household and community rituals as well. The objects and symbols that people manipulate allow them to give form to ritual experience and to associate a shared emotion with these experiences. Subsequently, this shared emotion can develop motivational force (see Chapter 7) that may shape purchase and consumption decisions and behaviors.[39]

Four important types of *consumer rituals* are those relating to possession, grooming, divestment, and exchange (we discuss these at further length in Chapter 4). People

EXHIBIT 3.4

Kinds of Rituals

Primary Behavior Source	Kinds of Rituals	Examples
Cosmology	Religious	Baptism, meditation, mass, Feast of the Sacrifice, Passover, Christmas
	Magical	Healing, channeling, gambling
	Aesthetic	Performing arts
Cultural values	Rites of passage	Graduation, marriage, school entrance exams
	Calendrical	Festivals, holidays (Christmas, New Year, World Cup, Super Bowl, May Day, U.S. Thanksgiving)
Group learning	Civic	Parades, elections, trials
	Small group	Fraternity initiation, business negotiations, office parties, gift giving, integration rituals
	Family	Mealtime, bedtime, birthday and holiday celebrations, moving, gift giving, disposition
Individual aims and emotions	Personal	Grooming rituals, possession rituals, household rituals
Biology	Ethological	Greeting, mating

Source: Dennis Rook, "The Ritual Dimension of Consumer Behavior," *Journal of Consumer Research* 12 (December 1985), pp. 251–64.

undertake **possession rituals** when products move from the marketplace to the home or workplace where they are consumed. Possession rituals also occur when people move into a new home or take possession of preowned goods, which may involve cleansing, customization, or making offerings such as the Jewish custom of tacking a *mezuzah* to the door frame. Removing tags and packaging, customizing, placing, arranging, monogramming, relabeling, framing, storytelling about special possessions, and so on are some of the ritualized activities people engage in to symbolize ownership.

Grooming rituals tend to be private behaviors that aid in the transition from private to public self and back again (see Chapter 10). Clean/dirty, public/private, work/leisure are three of the symbolic transformations that are often involved in grooming rituals. Numerous beauty products (shampoos, cosmetics, perfumes) and personal services (salons, spas, health clubs, fat farms, resorts, etc.) are marketed on their contribution to making grooming rituals successful. Grooming rituals may also be related to possession rituals, as when people clean, polish, restore, or renovate things they own. Hence the marketing success of Pledge furniture polish, for example.

Divestment rituals occur when consumers relinquish possession of objects. These rituals are discussed in Chapter 19, where we explore the topic of disposition.

Exchange rituals, like holiday gift giving, are widespread ritual type that we discuss in Chapter 16. An important class of exchange rituals involves **rites of passage.** In rites of passage, such as college graduation, participants mark events that symbolize changes in their social status. Rites of passage symbolize the permanence of a change in social status and the behaviors associated with that change. We classify them with exchange rituals because participants often exchange gifts. Debutante balls provide an example of a Western high-society rite of passage that is experiencing renewed popularity. It formalizes coming of age for young women and their entrance into the matrimonial market. Through the ball, the women are "given" to high society.[40]

Many rituals involve the consumption or exchange of goods that have symbolic value: baby clothes, food and drink, jewelry, stationery, diplomas, candles, household furnishings, or ceremonial clothing, such as gowns worn by brides or first communion celebrants. Moon cakes, exchanged as gifts in huge numbers during the Chinese Midsummer Festival, are a good example. Häagen Dazs has come out with an ice cream version to capitalize on the tradition. Ritual goods are indispensable to the meaning of the ritual experience and are used to communicate symbolic messages.[41]

For marketers, providing ritual goods has many pluses. For example, vendors at some Shinto temples in Japan that specialize in childbirth blessings do a thriving business in protective charms and support garments. Stationery and party supply stores provide all sorts of goods for calendrical rituals such as birthdays, Carnival, or Halloween. Other retailers provide symbolic goods that allow fans to express their affiliation with sports teams and contests. Sometimes, a consumer product becomes almost identical with a ritual or even triggers the ritual. For example, Mother's Day was created in order to sell more flowers. And it works. For florists, Mother's Day is the biggest revenue-producing day of the year.[42]

Rituals have life cycles; they decline and gain in popularity, and new cultural rituals emerge as others fade. One by-product of the globalization of marketing is the emergence of global consumption rituals. Christmas and the World Cup soccer championship provide examples of the few ritualized celebrations that are widely celebrated around the world. The Christmas exchange ritual is even celebrated in countries without a Christian tradition, such as Japan and Turkey, and among Greenland's Inuit peoples. And, of course, both Christmas and the World Cup induce a flood of consumer spending.

GUIDELINES FOR CULTURAL AWARENESS

For marketing managers, our model of culture presented on the right in Exhibit 3.1 offers many advantages over the traditional marketing model. To help you become more culturally aware, we present some additional guidelines here. It is important to note that although culture is shared, people hardly ever notice their own culture. This is because culture is an all-encompassing phenomenon like gravity. People don't notice gravity. Nor do they notice a host of behavioral norms of significance in consumer behavior until they are confronted with the different norms or beliefs of members of another culture. For example, consider the cultural blueprints for action concerning verbal communication as reflected in television commercials. In the UK, the United States, and Germany, one of the preferred formats is the "personalized lecture" style in which a celebrity endorses a product. The focus is on the celebrity's persona and its rub-off on the product (see Chapter 14). This format is consistent with a cultural emphasis on personal identity and individualism. By contrast, much of the advertising in Japan is entertainment oriented, with nonverbal rather than verbal communications emphasized. If celebrities are involved, they rarely address the audience explicitly. They play a more symbolic role, associating with the product rather than directly endorsing it. Such a style is compatible with a collectivist culture, where maintaining face is important.[43]

Failure to appreciate such differences because of the all-encompassing quality of culture causes global marketing blunders. For example, U.S. airlines with routes between Japan and Hawaii initially experienced erratic success. Some days the flights were full; others, the planes flew nearly empty. Eventually the airlines figured out the problem. Japanese consider certain days especially lucky for weddings. Honeymoons naturally follow these lucky days, and Hawaii is a favored destination. To even out loads, airlines began offering discounts when honeymooners were not flying.[44]

Different norms governing the use of time, interpersonal interaction, personal space, and body language, among other things, are also primary reasons consumers from one culture often misunderstand service experiences in other cultures. In Africa, most people don't treat time as a resource to be saved or wasted. The idea of buying time—the theme of a North American commercial campaign for a major telecommunications company a few years ago—would not have popular appeal in most of Africa. Western tourists may encounter this important difference in templates for action and interpretation the first time they wait half a day in line for service at an African bank or post office! Similarly, the European expectation that meals will take a long time to serve and to eat drives time-conscious Britons and Americans to distraction and makes them believe (incorrectly) that European waiters are inattentive. Europeans generally dislike American waiters' professional smiles and phony intimacy ("Hi, my name is George and I'll be your waiter today"). Similarly, Asian waiters' unwillingness to smile makes Americans think they are unfriendly. All these examples reflect differences in taken-for-granted cultural templates for action or norms about service interaction. These differences become significant for marketers when firms operate internationally or when they serve customers of different cultural backgrounds. Adaptation of marketing mix elements is then required.

Even though people don't notice their own culture very often, and generally don't remember learning about it, culture is learned. *Learning a culture by growing up in it as a native* is called **enculturation.** Like enculturation in general, consumer enculturation begins early. Marketing communications and marketing mixes can provide sources of enculturation. Thus, many North American three- to four-year-olds recognize and express a preference for McDonald's french fries. Danish children of that age enjoy liver paté as a snack. The Disney kids' movies mentioned in the section on cultural myths enculturate U.S. values of individual initiative.

A major source of multinational marketing blunders is a lack of appreciation for the learned nature of culture and the tenacity of learned preferences. Many food products have required taste modifications to appeal to local consumers. For example, Nestlé makes dozens of versions of its popular instant coffee to suit national tastes. Failure to adapt is costly. The French hypermarket chain Carrefour recently suffered losses in Southeast Asia because it failed to tailor product assortments to local tastes.[45]

Marketing is playing an increasingly active role in the enculturation process. For example, marketers in the UK have used cultural meanings associated with women's changing roles and increased economic activity in attempts to position products in the so-called women's market. Marketers target women by symbolically associating products with lifestyles and images that reflect, reinforce, and propagate these cultural meanings. For example, PPP Health Care's 1997 "Women's Plan" and The Prudential's recent "Wanna Be" campaign are built on the cultural assumption that women of the 1990s are independent. This value of independence draws on liberal feminist thinking in British and North American culture that promotes women's freedom from male domination. This independence is symbolized in the insurance companies' promotional literature as the outcome of the contemporary trend toward high divorce rates and single-parent households. The insurance companies then position their financial products on the risks (lack of male financial support) and benefits (freedom of choice) associated with women's financial independence. As a result, marketing practices are involved in creating behaviors (purchasing financial services products) that reinforce and propagate cultural values and norms associated with one kind of woman's consumer identity.[46]

www.ppphealthcare.co.uk

Learning a new or foreign culture through direct or indirect experience of others is known as **acculturation.** Through changes in consumption, immigrants learn new cultural templates for action and interpretation. One study found that some U.S. retailers play a role in acculturation among Mexican immigrants and earn the loyalty of these new customers in the process. Sometimes immigrants overshoot some aspect of the new consumption behavior, which then becomes an exaggerated version of that of natives. One study found Mexican Americans overspending on choice meats compared to the native U.S. population. Complete acculturation is impossible, and natives often detect cultural differences in the consumer behaviors of acculturating immigrants. When foreign corporations or media promote foreign templates for action and interpretation, they are encouraging acculturation. For example, MTV, which has affiliates in Brazil, India, China, Europe, and North America, has helped to create a global youth culture.[47]

As you can tell from many of the examples, culture supplies boundaries on our behavior, often with implications for consumer behavior. For example, culture conditions basic biological functions and body image, tells us who and how to marry, sets norms for family relationships, and guides how we believe power and resources should be distributed. Some are concerned that fashion advertising plays too strong a role in establishing blueprints for acceptable body images. Fads in body manipulation test some body image boundaries; see the *Body Play* magazine website to learn a lot about such fads. The Japanese are frank about bodily functions; Japanese commercials provide graphic and humorous ads for products like hemorrhoid remedies. In Ghana, funerals are an important event for elaborate display and consumption of consumer goods; funerals in many other cultural contexts are not.[48]

www.bodyplay.com

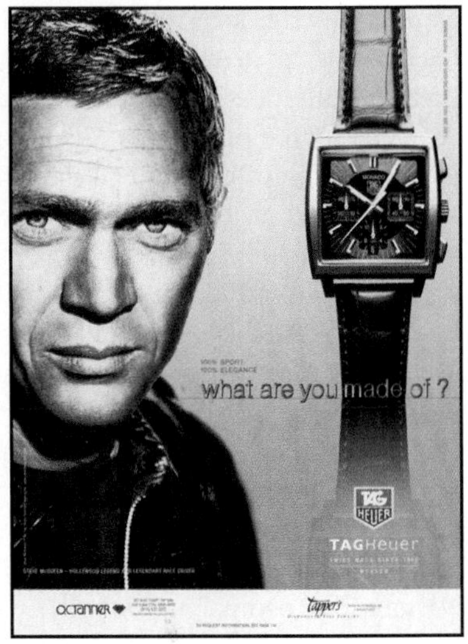

Individualistic heroes: Steve Jobs, James Bond, and the late Steve McQueen.

Cultural boundaries are formalized through social institutions that impose punishments and provide rewards to encourage us to conform to expected cultural behaviors. In Scandinavia, for example, government taxation and income subsidies level and equalize citizens' consumption possibilities. In the United States, retailers, schools, and the police often limit youth culture fashions and behaviors with negative sanctions. Some commonly seen signs in the United States read "No shirt, no shoes, no service," or "No skateboarding or in-line skating in mall." In such ways, consumption and consumer goods figure in the policing of cultural borders.

Another point is that culture is patterned. Cultural blueprints for action and interpretation are patterned in at least three slightly different ways. First, *they are repeated and reinforced throughout the society,* contributing to a pattern of culture. This is done, in part, through stories, myths, and symbols, including those used in commercial media.

Oriental carpets.

Danish design furniture.

Japanese boxed lunch.

Thus, the American value of rugged individualism is repeated in the mythical lives of action heroes such as James Bond, industry tycoons such as Steve Jobs, and even cartoon characters such as the Energizer Bunny! As shown in the photo on page 98, individualistic heroes such as the late Steve McQueen help firms position products to appeal to would-be adventurers.

Second, blueprints for action and interpretation are *reaffirmed and renewed through ritual consumption experiences.* The typical Dutch or Swedish *kafferep,* a get-together over coffee, is a widespread ritual that reinforces values of equality, ironic humor, and community.

Third, culture blueprints *tell people what things connect with what other things.* Children learn early what consumption objects go with different occupational roles in their culture; the stethoscope goes with the nurse and doctor, the hardhat goes with the construction worker, and the microphone goes with the pop star, for instance. They learn what boys consume and what girls consume, who wears what kinds of uniforms, and what kinds of people drive particular types of cars or live in particular types of houses.

1950s American appliances.

People also learn the aesthetics typical of their culture, what consumer goods it is tasteful to pair together. Preferred colors, smells, tastes, and sounds differ between cultures. The patterning of sensory elements gives Bakhtiari carpets (Iran) their distinctive look, differentiates Chinese from Italian opera, and provides Danish furniture, Japanese lunch boxes, and American appliances of the 1950s their distinctive flair. In Chapter 4 we illustrate how Danes and Britons have different but strong ideas about what kinds of furnishings should go together in a tasteful living room. Consumer Chronicles 3.5 provides an illustration of the learning, patterning, and the taken-for-granted, all-encompassing qualities of consumer culture.[49]

Patterns of consumption aesthetics impose normative pressure on consumers. This is called the **Diderot effect.** The Diderot effect is *the motive "force that encourages an individual to maintain a cultural consistency in his/her complement of consumer goods."*[50] The Diderot effect is quite common. For example, a woman may buy a new outfit on sale and then reflect that she doesn't have anything to go with it. She may then search for shoes and other accessories to go with the piece of clothing. By the time she is through shopping, she has a complement of consumer goods that "go together," but perhaps she has spent more than she expected.

The Diderot effect seems to be a motivational force that has something in common with motives to maintain psychological balance and order discussed in Chapter 7. The Diderot effect may also be explained in part by reference to the image congruence hypothesis. This theory holds that consumers who imagine their presence in social situations process information about the kind of image called for by normative cultural convention in those situations. They then use that information to construct an image of themselves through their strategic use of consumer goods. In a purchase situation, we can imagine that a consumer compares the perceived self-image outcome of the purchase with expectations about the self. Similarly a couple or group making a purchase may compare the outcome with expectations about the group. The objective of this process is an evaluation of the relative "goodness" of the perceived image outcome of the purchase. In turn, this process is mostly guided by principles such as the value of self-respect or a need for self-esteem. If the self-image outcome is better than expected, the outcome is said to have a self- (or group-) enhancing effect, and cues additional purchases that further enhance self-respect or esteem. Consumer experience influences the recognition and learning of self-enhancing product symbolism. Over time and across product-related situations, product/self- (or group-) perceptions may even contribute to the formation and change of the consumer's self-concept or the extended self that consumers recognize through sets of related consumer goods, sometimes called **Diderot unities,** they own. Of course, the consumer's recognition and learning of product symbolism and his/her self-image are culturally specific.[51]

In addition to the marketing of clothing (outfits) and home furnishings (matched sets), the Diderot effect comes into play in lifestyle marketing and sports merchandising. Team regalia sold in team colors and carrying sports team logos fuels demand for a virtually endless array of merchandise. The Manchester United Football Club (UK), founded in 1878 and renowned the world over, offers an array of gear for fans such as the merchandise shown on page 103, for example.

A final contrast to draw between our model of culture presented in Exhibit 3.1 and the traditional marketing model is that we emphasize that culture is adaptive and dynamic. This point is illustrated in the discussions of evolution in the women's market and the pliability of values in advertising. A society's culture does evolve in a given environment combining people, materials and objects, resources, and ideas and beliefs. But

Culture in Your Toast

CONSUMER CHRONICLES 3.5

Assuming for the moment that bread or toast is an acceptable part of your breakfast, what do you like to put on it? In Italy and parts of France and the UK, Nutella is one popular product. Nutella is a creamy spread made from chocolate and hazelnuts. In Australia, Vegemite could be the spread of choice. Vegemite is a yeast-based product with a pungent, sour flavor. In Denmark, liver paté manufactured by a number of firms is commonly spread on a slab of fine dark bread as a morning treat. And North Americans are infamous the world over for their inexplicable taste for peanut butter. So perhaps Jif is your spread of choice. The answer to the question of what you like on your morning bread (and by the way, do you like your toast warm as in North America or cold as in the UK?) nicely illustrates a number of points about culture made in the text. Our tastes are cultural patterns that we learn through enculturation. We often take our tastes for granted unless or until we are exposed to alternatives (did any of our choices cause you to make a face?). Culture supplies boundaries on our behavior that in some respects are arbitrary. That is to say, there's nothing inherently proper about paté, Vegemite, Nutella, or peanut butter as a breakfast spread. And our tastes are embedded in broader patterns of behavior that are likewise learned through enculturation. If you'd like to learn more about the products we've mentioned, or even join a product fan club, check the Internet. You'll be surprised by what you find.

Jif Peanut Butter

Nutella

cultures are **open systems,** meaning that *they influence and are influenced by changes in their environment.* Culture changes, although it usually doesn't change quickly. For example, American culture has been described as materialistic since the early 1800s. Consumer Chronicles 3.6 suggests that American culture may become less materialistic and the cultures of developing nations more materialistic as they are exposed to more marketing communications and consumer goods.[52]

Some now claim that marketing is changing cultures dramatically. The global spread of branded consumer goods such as Nike, Benetton, or The Gap spreads powerful new symbols. Entertainment products made in Hollywood, Bollywood, and Hong Kong have diffused heroic new global images such as kung-fu and the kung-fu warrior. The globalization of retail formats such as Wal-Mart or Carrefour spreads norms about

Comparing Turks and Americans on Materialism

CONSUMER CHRONICLES 3.6

Materialism has been defined as the importance a consumer attaches to worldly possessions. Materialism has generally been seen as a Western trait that achieved an elevated place in industrial and postindustrial life. A surprising new study, however, shows that Turks are more materialistic than Europeans or Americans. One way of explaining this surprising result is by looking at cross-cultural research on the Protestant work ethic. These studies find that the Protestant work ethic is now strongest in Third World countries, regardless of dominant religion, and weakest in highly developed, postindustrial nations. Once wealth is achieved by devotion to the Protestant work ethic, the motivation to commit to that ethic dissolves. Similarly, some argue, high-level materialism also contains the seeds of its own destruction, because such consumption is ultimately unfulfilling.

Source: Güliz Ger and Russell W. Belk, "Measuring and Comparing Materialism Cross-Culturally," in Advances in Consumer Research, *vol. 17, ed. Marvin E. Goldberg, Gerald Gorn, and Richard W. Pollay (Provo, UT: Association for Consumer Research, 1990), pp. 186–92.*

product and service quality and economic value. The globalization of fast-food franchises such as McDonald's, Pizza Hut, or Jolibee changes customary ways of eating and influences dietary norms. Some argue that the globalization of consumer holidays such as Christmas; popular culture forms such as hip-hop, reggae, and world music; and institutions such as beauty pageants is changing the very nature of culture. These new global cultural forms provide consumers with common templates for action and interpretation through which to express national and local cultural diversity. Thus, in the era of globalization, cultures are no longer separate from one another and relatively unchanging. Instead, they are overlapping dynamic systems that conform to new social boundaries that are formed through the spread of consumer goods and global marketing communications that promote them. We discuss this further below.[53]

GLOBALIZATION, CONSUMER CULTURE, AND CULTURAL CREOLIZATION

The concentration, expansion, and internationalization of the consumer goods industries, the growth of affluent consumer segments in every nation, democratization, loosening of class boundaries, and a quickened flow of information through the commercial media all contribute to global market expansion. These developments have led to the development of global consumer culture.

Consumer culture refers to an organized social and economic arrangement in which markets govern the relationship between meaningful ways of life and the symbolic and material resources on which they depend.[54] Consumer culture may be characterized first by *the global marketing of virtually every good, service, image, idea, and experience.* In other words, in consumer culture everything from Beanie Babies to politicians is evaluated in terms of its market value. A second defining characteristic is *the increasing importance of materialism among new consumers.* A third element is *a parallel change in personal identity.* A number of authors argue that in advanced consumer cultures personal roles and identities assume an apparently elective quality, and are subject to frequent and significant changes. The elective quality of personal identity means that consumers may declare or claim the cultural categories or lifestyles (see Chapter 11) they inhabit. Given the fluidity of personal identity, individuals satisfy the freedom and responsibility of self-definition through the meanings of consumer goods they acquire and consume.[55]

A fourth element that spreads consumer culture is the *rapid movement of economic migrants, religious pilgrims, and guest workers between even remote villages in the*

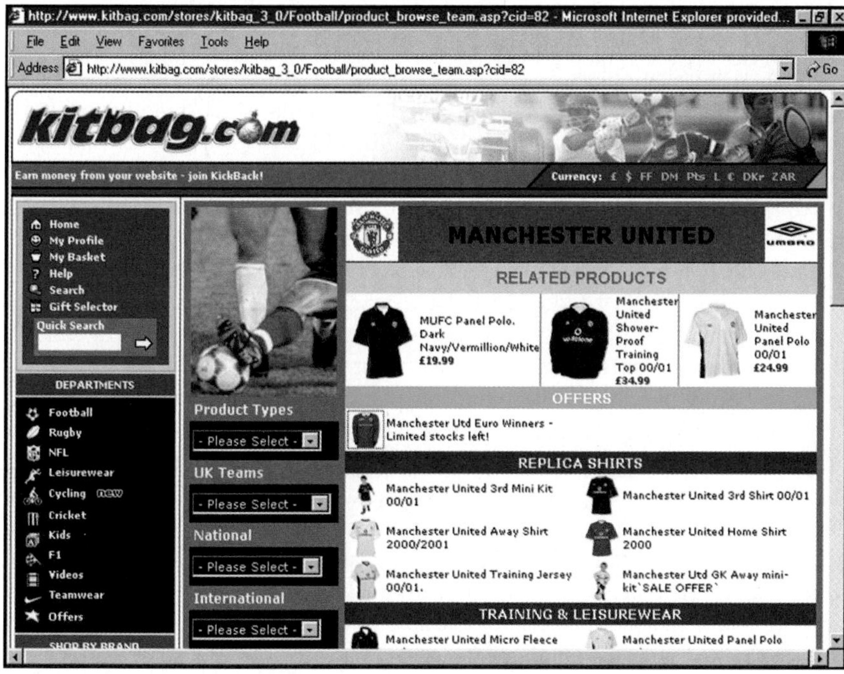

kitbag.com offers Manchester United Football Club fans the opportunity to purchase a wide range of merchandise.

developing world and cosmopolitan centers in the Triad nations. Not only do these migrants purchase airline tickets, but also they return from their travels with suitcases stuffed with novel consumer goods and often with a positive change in attitudes toward those goods.[56]

A final defining characteristic of consumer culture is the exceptional influence of the fashion industry and *the rapid pace of turnover in fashions* of every kind. In fact, an important source of consumer culture is the fashion industry, an industry that now includes movies, music, food, advertising, and interior design as well as clothing. High fashion "is challenging to our time," says Japanese designer Issey Miyake. This means that high-fashion designers borrow from around the world to create new cultural meanings and to associate new products with available meanings. In summer 2000, Victoria's Secret promoted silk sarong skirts, for example, a cloth and style borrowed from Southeast Asia. Shared taste in particular national markets then becomes an active force in a process of selection, setting limits on and guiding the development of consumer culture locally. Simultaneously, cultural values, norms, and beliefs undergo refinement and organization through attachment both to novel goods and specific social groups. We'll say more about the fashion industry in Chapter 4.[57]

One significant trend in consumer culture is the global spread of brands and consumption practices (see Chapter 17 for more discussion of diffusion and adoption). Pepsi has the goal of developing one global image that is powerful for everybody. Fast-food outlets, especially McDonald's, provide consumers everywhere one route to express some shared consumption values and preferences. Global brands such as Nivea, Nescafé, Coca-Cola, or Sony are marketed globally with few local market adjustments and have a wide appeal. However, while there are global brands, there really are not global people. The success of the Sony Walkman, for example, is based on distinct templates for action in the Eastern and Western worlds. Western consumers purchase

Walkmans to enjoy music without being disturbed by others. Consistent with Japanese values, however, the Japanese inventor of the Walkman wanted a way of listening to music without disturbing others.[58]

A second trend in global consumer culture is the creolization of consumption patterns. **Creolization** refers to *consumption patterns that combine elements of local and foreign consumption traditions.* Creolization concerns consumers in all nations. Thus, Jolibee enjoys a 59 percent market share in the Philippine fast-food market thanks to its local modifications of the global McDonald's formula. Similarly, traditional Turkish fast food called *kepab,* or shish kebab, has experienced a revival in modified retail formats as Western-style fast-food outlets have penetrated the Turkish market. These choices allow Philippine and Turkish consumers to express varying degrees of cultural conformity and cultural difference through their fast-food choices.

Similarly, the beauty pageant has become a popular consumer celebration in Belize in Central America. Some pageants judge contestants according to Euro-American ideals of beauty; others use local ideals of feminine accomplishment. Both also celebrate Caribbean values of respectability and reputation and express tensions between different ethnic groups in Belizean society that hold different value orientations. The Belizean beauty pageant is a good example of a creolized consumption event.[59]

Creolization is evident in some areas of consumer behavior in Europe and North America. Examples include the blended musical forms common in world music and creolized cuisines. A Turkish entrepreneur in Germany even offers something called McDöner Kepab—Turkish shish kebab in a McDonald's-like setting. Why do people engage in creolized consumption? One reason is that it allows consumers to experience other cultural values and beliefs without necessarily sacrificing their own.[60]

Ethical Dilemma 3.1 highlights the darkside of the creolized commodification of world musics. First, popular musical styles are often torn from their classic musical contexts that languish in obscurity. Second, the music is often adapted to Western tastes rather than the other way around. Third, financial and other rewards do not necessarily flow to deserving artists in less affluent nations in need.

Some creolized global consumption forms such as Christmas, the beauty pageant, and perhaps the Olympics become what some have called a **global structure of common difference**—*a consumer performance or ritual that enables people to play out different, yet related values through a shared collection of cultural practices.* This is easiest to understand in the context of an example. In all cultures, Christmas involves gift giving and families. But in Japan, Christmas is a gift-giving holiday that primarily concerns unmarried, dating couples. In Britain, exchanges of Christmas cards usually link only nuclear family members. Among Anupiaq Inuit of Greenland, Christmas gift giving is used to link everyone in a wider kin group that deemphasizes the nuclear family. In Trinidad, Christmas gift giving is employed to enhance the respectability of nuclear family households, vis-à-vis their neighbors. In all instances, these gift-giving patterns create opportunities for marketers, who can provide the goods and services that match this desire to give just the right gift. Creating and sustaining global structures of common difference provide global marketing opportunities.[61]

Some consumers react to globalization and creolization in an ethnocentric manner, rejecting the globalization of consumption patterns and values. This represents a third trend in global consumer culture: a nostalgic defense of so-called traditional consumption values. This can lead to boycotts of foreign consumer products. Thus, religious groups in some Middle Eastern countries adopt various versions of traditional consumption norms and reject Western products. Another example is the recent revival of interest in local and regional food products in Great Britain. Growth in attendance

Stop the World Music, I Want to Get Off

ETHICAL DILEMMA 3.1

World music is being turned into a commodity—and when you look at CD sales for the Cuban boom, for example, it's easy to see why. So far, no one seems to mind—certainly not the critic who recently wrote these dismal words: "World music doesn't require the quasi-religious commitment of jazz fans. Much of the time it is just another kind of pop music for grown-ups, a rich array of sounds for people who don't expect every piece of music to be sung in English over a predigested backing track." Yes, that's exactly how most newspapers treat it—as a party-adjunct, a feel good frippery.

This complacent cultural imperialism is widespread, and it's a global insult. For what does this term—originally coined to help shops move product—actually mean? It means all music that is neither Western classical music, nor Western jazz, nor Western pop, nor Western folk. It means, to be precise, almost all the music in the world. From our Eurocentric [ethnocentric] pinnacle, we stick a label on it, and then reduce it to an "array of sounds." Can this rot be stopped? The real antidote to the prevailing culture-blindness would be fundamental: a realization that beyond Western classical music lie a dozen other classical musics—and a myriad folk forms—many of which are of much greater antiquity, and no less refinement, than ours. Think of the infinite sophistications of Indian classical music, and of the Indonesian gamelan tradition that entranced classic composers Debussy and Britten. Drink in the exaltation of praise-singers from Azerbaijan; savor what Turkish and Persian musicians can do with their variants on the lute. And when you listen to the seductive music of Mali, bear in mind its 400-year-old roots in the Mande Empire. It may well be that around 1600 something uniquely amazing happened in European music, but that should not blind us to other discreet musical miracles—Albanian polyphony, or Vietnamese Ca Tru—in other parts of the world.

As it happens, the two above-mentioned musics are both under threat of extinction: both survive in grindingly poor societies, whose populations are currently looking to salvation by the rich West. Both these musics are unique; once lost, they will never be resuscitated. That's where the awards and the record contracts should urgently be sent. Is there any hope they will?

Source: Michael Church, "Stop the World Music; I Want to Get Off", first published in The Independent, *December 31, 2001. Reprinted by permission of* The Independent.

at local history and cultural festivals and museums in many countries, including Japan, Denmark, and the United States, may be another sign of nostalgic consumption.

Finally, there is a trend, especially in the Triad nations, toward the consumption of presumably authentic cultural products and experiences from transitional and Third World cultures. Direct mail catalogs feature an array of "authentic" products, from Soviet-era military gear and medals to foods and handicrafts produced by different native peoples. The Eziba website offers authentic craft objects from all over the world. So does the Nature & Découvertes retail chain in France. Similarly, the Polynesian culture center in Hawaii markets several versions of authentic Polynesian cultural experiences. A Galleria mall in Istanbul, Turkey, even offers a U.S. cultural experience complete with KFC, McDonald's, and a bowling alley. These examples suggest that culture itself is becoming a consumer good through global marketing.[62]

www.eziba.com

Despite the fact that customs and behaviors are moving very quickly from one culture to another, consumer behavior researchers and marketers must be careful not to fall into the trap of **self-referencing.** Self-referencing refers to *using your own experiences or intuitions to try and understand and predict the behaviors of others.* Sometimes,

The Eziba website offers cultural artifacts for sale.

such intuitions can be quite accurate. However, when the intuitions are about people in another culture, self-referencing can turn into a trap that leads to erroneous conclusions. For instance, it would be very easy to assume that Christmas gift giving in Trinidad or Greenland is very similar to customs in the United States. However, as described in a preceding paragraph, there are important differences. As customs and rituals move from one culture to another, the importing culture frequently puts its own unique stamp on the new constellation of behaviors that surround the ritual. Our erroneous assumption about the acceptability of the baby jogger in Denmark is a good example of a self-referencing error.

SUMMARY

A culture is a shared template for behavior and interpretation. Although people hardly ever notice their own culture, culture supplies important boundaries on behavior. Culture is adaptive, dynamic, and patterned. People learn culture either by growing up in it as natives or through the process of acculturation.

Although there is substantial intracultural variability, it is possible to identify core values that seem to define a culture. Many different approaches to measuring cultural values have been developed. The most famous is Hofstede's worker values; another is the List of Values. All these have been related to some consumer behaviors.

In addition to values, myths, symbols, and rituals also help to define culture. Important consumer behaviors in any society can be better understood by referencing shared myths and symbolic meanings. Consumer goods often become core symbols in a society. Consumer rituals are an important aspect of how cultures reinforce blueprints for action and interpretation. Among the different types of rituals are those that relate to possessions, grooming, divestment, and exchange. The use of ritual objects, often consumer products, accompanies these rituals.

Finally, the globalization of consumer culture seems to be producing a variety of creolized cultural forms expressed through consumer goods and behaviors.

KEY TERMS

acculturation 97
conspicuous consumption 93
consumer ethnocentrism 85
core symbols 91
creolization 104
cultural categories 75
cultural principles 77
cultural rituals 93
cultural symbols 91
culture 74
Diderot effect 100
Diderot unities 100
divestment rituals 95
enculturation 96
exchange rituals 95
global structure of common difference 104
grooming rituals 95
Hofstede's worker values 83
indeterminant 78
instrumental values 82
List of Values (LOV) 83
materialism 86
myths 87
norms 73
open systems 101
possession rituals 95
rites of passage 95
self-referencing 105
terminal values 82
urban legends 88
value-attitude-behavior hierarchy 82
values 73

REVIEW QUESTIONS

1. Outline an example of the Diderot effect in your own consumption behavior. Describe how it happened and the time frame over which it happened. For example, perhaps you collected the objects over a short period of time (one or a few days) or over several months or even years.
2. Draw on your knowledge of movies, stories, and fairy tales in your culture to describe a myth that

   a. Emphasizes how things are interconnected.
   b. Maintains social order.
   c. Provides a model for individual behavior and identity.

   A single story may serve all these purposes, but try to come up with three different examples.
3. Select a sporting event. Describe characteristics of that event that illustrate important cultural values. Be sure to discuss shared symbolic meanings, rituals, and cultural artifacts.
4. Select a time in your life when you experienced an important social status change. What made this status change important? Describe the types of rituals and ritual artifacts that symbolically marked this change. What was the role of consumption and consumer objects during this status change?
5. Select a cultural ritual that you and the community around you share (e.g., Halloween, Valentine's Day, etc.). Describe the ritual. Indicate how you think the ritual relates to important cultural values.
6. Pick an instrumental or terminal value you believe is important in your culture. Describe what type of products and what type of advertising appeals might be used to successfully represent that value.
7. Pick a symbol that is important in your culture. Describe one or two appropriate ways to use and enjoy the symbol. Describe one or two inappropriate ways to use and enjoy the symbol.

YOU MAKE THE CALL

BEER WARS IN EAST AFRICA

Is the decision by South African Breweries (SABI) to close down Castle Brewing in Kenya bad news? Three years after its entry into the Kenyan market, Castle has barely managed to scratch the surface of East African Breweries Limited's (EABL) monopoly. In Kenya the beer market has declined by 29 percent since 1996, with a similar fall in Tanzania, an EABL statement said. Before Castle entered the Kenyan market, EABL had enjoyed an uninterrupted monopoly of the market for 75 years with over 90 percent share of the local beer market. Castle's market share remained under 8 percent as EABL's Tusker maintained its ascendancy, estimated at 46 percent; Pilsner, 31.7; and fast-growing Citizen, 12. SABI's US$30 million investment is no small operation, and the damage from this development will be far-reaching. After the World Bank froze aid to Kenya five years ago, the economy has been declining and the Castle brewery in Thika was seen as a symbol of hope for Kenya's quest to attract foreign investors.

EABL is involved in the production and distribution of alcoholic beverages. Its operations include Kenya Breweries, Kibo Breweries in Tanzania, Port Bell Breweries in Uganda, and Central Glass Industries.

Tusker is the best known of its brands, and the highest selling beer in Kenya. Tusker has been brewed in Kenya since 1922. The company does not brew traditional African maize beers. Tusker is a fine pilsner. It's said to be well-balanced, full-bodied, and delicious. It has an almost Dutch character, but with a delicate sweet twist. EABL also protects their product well. The 6-pack container is made of corrugated cardboard.

As one travel author writes: "The most common beer is Tusker. Even at a game lodge a single bottle costs only sixty cents cold. The label is white and gold and black, with a trumpeting, poorly drawn bull elephant positioned between two generalized barley ears. Because they are reused for years, the bottles are thick and worn, squat and baobab-shaped brown glass with a faint band of white abrasion on all of the body's rounded edges. As you sit with one loosely balanced on your leg, picking at the label like a scab, little pulpy strings of paper will pile up where your shorts meet your thigh."

EABL promotes its brands through print, outdoor, and electronic media. Recent TV commercial themes for the Tusker brand include: Is your Tusker line up ready? Are you stocked up for this half? Take a refreshing Tusker break; A great goal deserves a great beer; and My Country, My Team, My Tusker! MILELE! These and other commercials can be viewed at http://www.eabrew.com.

@ http://www.eabrew.com

EABL is also involved in corporate social marketing campaigns. For example, Kenya had been facing a severe famine situation that resulted in starvation and death in places like Turkana. As a responsible corporate citizen, Kenya Breweries Limited, through the flagship Tusker brand, decided to help alleviate this sad situation by donating 25 cents for every Tusker bottle purchased by loyal customers during the Christmas season of 1999. The campaign generated about US$60,000, which was handed over to African Medical and Research Foundation (AMREF), who were taking care of distribution of food in the affected areas.

So far, only the Kenyan consumer appears to have reaped substantially from the price stability and product innovation encouraged by the competition between East African Breweries and Castle. When news of Castle Brewing's pullout broke, many revelers in bars toasted to the "routing of the South Africans."

Forgotten in the partying was that as many as 1,000 Kenyans had been rendered jobless as a result of the pullout. Also conveniently ignored was that the principal interest (almost 50 percent) in East African Breweries is held by a foreign firm, Guinness Plc of London.

But the revelers' sentiments were without doubt a tribute to EABL's successful marketing that has maintained its leadership in Kenya despite a vicious assault from the multinational SABI. At the end of the day, Castle Brewing had to close shop because it was unable to "push its boxes in the market." Its beers simply collapsed on the bar counters if they ever got there.

It failed to get the formula right on two critical Ps in the marketing of fast-moving consumer goods: promotion and place. And the South African firm, which is the world's fourth largest brewer and one of Africa's few transnationals with resources to match, paid the ultimate price.

Castle Brewing's forceful foray into the Kenyan market in October 1998 virtually stirred Kenya's beer monopoly, a sleeping giant, to activity. EABL responded with one of the most well-oiled marketing campaigns seen in the country. At the height of the so-called beer wars in 2000, almost US$11 million was allocated to the firm's marketing department. A vicious advertising and merchandising crusade was taken to bars, to restaurants, on television, on radio and in the print media. It included "the Win a Pub [bar]" promotion, Kenya's so far most expensive, with a US$600,000 budget. And there were the nasty asides, like the accusations and counteraccusations of defacing of each beer firm's billboards. EABL continues to be one of Kenya's largest advertisers. In 2001, the firm used US$1.5 million on its Tusker and Pilsner brands to become the biggest spender in advertising after mobile telephone company KenCell. It is significant that Castle did not even feature among the top 20 spenders, a sorry state for SABI, the sixth largest brewer in the world, and a strong multinational operator.

In addition, for the first time, the Ruaraka, Kenya–based EABL hired sales representatives and allocated them territories. This was a radical departure for a company whose products were hitherto just supplied to the points of purchase. Castle also lost the battle on place: Its beers were simply unavailable in key retail outlets, forcing those who had developed a taste for them to settle for what was available—EABL brands. This inefficiency in distribution cost the firm would-be customers. It was a case of out of sight, out of mind.

Many believe that the battle was finally won and lost in the minds of the consumer. While Castle advertising put more emphasis on the attributes of its products, EABL went for the emotional in an ambitious brand-building process. EABL's copywriters did a masterstroke, appealing to patriotism with the emotional "My Country, My Beer" line for its flagship Tusker brand. It did not help matters for Castle that Kenyan-based EABL had been denied entry into the South African market dominated by SABI through a well-publicized trade dispute. From that moment on, it became "us versus them." Even Tusker's present "My team, My Husker, Milele" line remains true to this emotional, timeless proposition.

Sources: www.allafrica.com; Washington Akumu, "Nairobi Breweries' Marketing Campaign Won the Battle," The Nation *(Kenya), May 15, 2002;* East African Standard *website, Nairobi, in English, May 15, 2002; http://www.eabrew.com/; Charles Hood, "Tusker,"* The Journal of African Travel-Writing *4 (April 1998), p. 66; http://mbendi.co.za/orgs/camm.htm; Peter Munaita, James Mwakisyala, Alfred Ngotezi, and Paul Redfern, "Winners and Losers in EABL, Castle Tie Ups,"* The East African, *May 20, 2002; http://www.nationaudio.com/News/EastAfrican/current; http://search.ft.com; and http://news.bbc.co.uk/hi/english/business/newsid_1987000/1987479.stm.*

QUESTIONS

1. What role did symbols play in the success of EABL over SABI?
2. Can you speculate about the values celebrated in Tusker's commercials?

CASES

3. What role do you feel that nationalism or ethnocentrism played in the failure of SABI's Castle Brewing in Kenya?
4. Is it possible that superior distribution alone was responsible for EABL's triumph?
5. Building on what you've learned from Chapters 2 and 3, what might SABI have done to turn failure into success?
6. From a marketing perspective, is SABI's withdrawal from the Kenyan market good or bad news?

ENDNOTES

1. Naresh Malholra, James Agarwal, and Mark Peterson, "Methodological Issues in Cross-Cultural Marketing Research," *International Marketing Review* 13, no. 5 (1996), pp. 7–43; Daniel John McCort and Naresh K. Malhotra, "Culture and Consumer Behavior: Toward an Understanding of Cross-Cultural Consumer Behavior in International Marketing," *Journal of International Consumer Marketing* 6, no. 2 (1993), pp. 91–127; and Shalom H. Schwartz and Warren Bilsky, "Towards a Universal Psychological Structure of Human Values," *Journal of Personality and Social Psychology* 53 (1987), pp. 550–662.

2. Ward H. Goodenough, "Cultural Anthropology and Linguistics," in *Report of the Seventh Annual Round Table Meeting on Linguistics and Language Study,* ed. P. Garvin (Washington, DC: Georgetown University, 1957), pp. 167–73; Edward T. Hall, *The Hidden Dimension* (New York: Anchor Books, 1982); Douglas B. Holt, "Consumers' Cultural Differences as Local Systems of Tastes: A Critique of the Personality/Values Approach and an Alternative Framework," *Asia Pacific Advances in Consumer Research* 1 (1994), pp. 178–84; Douglas B. Holt, "Post-Structuralist Lifestyle Analysis: Conceptualizing the Social Patterning of Consumption in Post-Modernity," *Journal of Consumer Research* 23 (March 1997), pp. 326–50; and David Sheff, *China Dawn* (New York: HarperCollins, 2002).

3. Marieke de Mooij, *Global Marketing and Advertising: Understanding Cultural Paradoxes* (Thousand Oaks, CA: Sage Publications, 1998), pp. 53–55.

4. Carol S. Saunders and Bette A. Stead, "Women's Adoption of a Business Uniform: A Content Analysis of Magazine Advertisements," *Sex Roles* 15, no. 3–4 (1986), pp. 197–205; and Craig J. Thompson and Diana L. Haytko, "Speaking of Fashion: Consumers' Uses of Fashion Discourses and the Appropriation of Countervailing Cultural Meanings," *Journal of Consumer Research* 24 (June 1997), pp. 15–43.

5. Dorinne Kondo, "The Aesthetics and Politics of Japanese Identity in the Fashion Industry," in *Re-Made in Japan,* ed. Joseph J. Tobin (New Haven: Yale University Press, 1993), pp. 176–203; and Richard R. Wilk, "'I Hate Pizza': Distaste and Dislike in the Consuming Lives of Belizeans," working paper, Indiana University, Department of Anthropology, Bloomington, IN, 1994.

6. James Clifford, *The Predicament of Culture: Twentieth Century Ethnography, Literature, and Art* (Cambridge: Harvard University Press, 1988).

7. Geert Hofstede, "The Quality of Life Concept," *Academy of Management Review* 9 (1984), pp. 389–98.

8. Milton Rokeach, *Understanding Human Values* (New York: Free Press, 1979). See also Wagner A. Kamakura and Jose Afonso Mazzon, "Value Segmentation: A Model for the Measurement of Values and Value Systems," *Journal of Consumer Research* 18 (September 1991), pp. 208–18.

9. Milton Rokeach, *The Nature of Human Values* (New York: Free Press, 1973).

10. Pamela Homer and Lynn A. Kahle, "A Structural Equation Test of the Value-Attitude-Behavior Hierarchy," *Journal of Personality and Social Psychology* 54, no. 4 (1988), pp. 638–46; and de Mooij, *Global Marketing and Advertising,* pp. 117–18. See also Madhav N. Segal, Uma A. Segal, and Mary Ann Palmer Niermezycki, "Value Network for Cross-National Marketing Management: A Framework for Analysis and Application," *Journal of Business Administration* 27 (May 1993), pp. 65–83.

11. Zhengyuan Wang, C. P. Rao, and Angela D'Auria, "A Comparison of the Rokeach Value Survey (RVS) in China and the United States," in *Asia-Pacific Advances in Consumer Research,* vol. 1, ed. Joseph A. Cote and Siew Meng Leong (Provo, UT: Association for Consumer Research, 1994), pp. 158–90.
12. Lynn R. Kahle, *Social Values and Social Change: Adaptation to Life in America* (New York: Praeger, 1983). See also Lynn R. Kahle, Sharon E. Beatty, and Pamela Homer, "Alternative Measurement Approaches to Consumer Values: The List of Values (LOV) and Values and Life Style (VALS)," *Journal of Consumer Research* 13 (December 1986), pp. 405–9.
13. Sharon E. Beatty, Lynn R. Kahle, Pamela Homer, and Shehkar Misra, "Alternative Measurement Approaches to Consumer Values: The List of Values and the Rokeach Value Survey," *Psychology and Marketing* 2, no. 3 (1985), pp. 181–200, Pamela M. Homer and Lynn R. Kahle, "A Structural Equation Test of the Value-Attitude-Behavior Hierarchy," *Journal of Personality and Social Psychology* 38 (1988), pp. 50–56; and Lynn R. Kahle, Ruiming Liu, and Harry Watkins, "Psychographic Variation across United States Geographic Regions," in *Advances in Consumer Research,* vol. 19, ed. John F. Sherry Jr. and Brian Sternthal (Provo, UT: Association for Consumer Research, 1992), pp. 346–52.
14. Frauke Hachtmann, "German and American Students' Perception of Social Values as Depicted in Magazine Advertisements," doctoral thesis, University of Nebraska, Lincoln, 1997; Ronald E. Goldsmith, Jon B. Freiden, and Jacqueline C. Kilsheimer, "Social Values and Female Fashion Leadership," *Psychology and Marketing* (1993), pp. 399–413; Aviv Shoham, Bella Florenthal, Frederic Kropp, and Gregory M. Rose, "The Relationship between Values and Thrill- and Adventure-Seeking in Israel," in *European Advances in Consumer Research,* vol. 3, ed. Anna Olofsson and Basil Englis (Provo, UT: Association for Consumer Research, 1997), pp. 333–38.
15. Geert Hofstede, *Cultures and Organizations: Software of the Mind* (London: McGraw-Hill, 1990).
16. Jennifer L. Aaker, "The Influence of Culture on Persuasion Processes and Attitudes: Diagnosticity or Accessibility?" *Journal of Consumer Research* 26 (March 2000), pp. 340–57.
17. A. Wolfe Kapoor and J. Blue, "Universal Value Structure and Individualism-Collectivism: A U.S. Test," *Communication Research Reports* 12, no. 1 (1995), pp. 1112–13; de Mooij, *Global Marketing and Advertising;* S. Schwartz, "Universals in the Content and Structure of Values: Theoretical Advances and Empirical Tests in Twenty Countries," *Advances in Experimental Psychology* 25 (1992), pp. 25, 1–65; Sarah Todd, Rob Lawson, and Hadyn Northover, "Value Orientation and Media Consumption Behavior," in *European Advances in Consumer Research,* vol. 3, ed. Anna Olofsson and Basil Englis (Provo, UT: Association for Consumer Research, 1997), pp. 328–32; and Harry Triandis, C. McCusker, and C. Hui, "Multimethod Probes of Individualism and Collectivism," *Journal of Personality and Social Psychology* 59, no. 5 (1990), pp. 1006–20.
18. Jennifer L. Aaker and Durairaj Maheswaran, "The Effect of Cultural Orientation on Persuasion," *Journal of Consumer Research* 24 (December 1997), pp. 315–28; Russell W. Belk and Richard W. Pollay, "Images of Ourselves: The Good Life in Twentieth Century Advertising," *Journal of Consumer Research* 11 (March 1985), pp. 887–98; and Sang-Pil Han and Sharon Shavitt, "Persuasion and Culture: Advertising Appeals in Individualistic and Collectivistic Societies," *Journal of Experimental Social Psychology* 30 (1994), pp. 326–50.
19. Geert Hofstede, *Culture's Consequences* (Beverly Hills: Sage, 1980).
20. Hong Chen and John C. Schweitzer, "Cultural Values Reflected in Chinese and U.S. Television Commercials," *Journal of Advertising Research* 36 (May–June 1996), pp. 27–46; James W. Gentry, Sunkyu Jun, Gyungtai Ko, and Heesuk Kang, "Korea," in *Marketing and Consumer Behavior in East and South-East Asia,* ed. Anthony Pecotich and Clifford Schultz II (Sydney: McGraw-Hill, 1998), pp. 371–412; de Mooij, *Global Marketing and Advertising;* and Mohammed Abdur Razzaque, "Demographics, Psychographics and Consumer Value Dimensions: A Study of Consumers in a Traditional Asian Society," in *Advances in Consumer Research,* vol. 2, ed. Flemming Hansen (Provo, UT: Association for Consumer Research, 1995), pp. 183–92.
21. Glen H. Brodowsky, "The Effects of Country of Design and Country of Assembly on Evaluative Beliefs about Automobiles and Attitudes toward Buying Them: A Comparison between Low and High Ethnocentric Consumers," *Journal of Consumer Marketing* 10, no. 3 (1998), pp. 85–113.

22. Srinivas Durvasula, J. Craig Andrews, and Richard G. Netemeyer, "A Cross-Cultural Comparison of Consumer Ethnocentrism in the United States and Russia," *Journal of International Consumer Marketing* 9, no. 4 (1997), pp. 73–93; Richard G. Netemeyer, Srinivas Durvasula, and Donald R. Lichtenstein, "A Cross-National Assessment of the Reliability and Validity of the CETSCALE," *Journal of Marketing Research* 12 (January 1991), pp. 5–21; and Terry A. Shimp and S. Sharma, "Consumer Ethnocentrism: Construction and Validation of the CETSCALE," *Journal of Marketing Research* 24 (August 1987), pp. 280–89.
23. Aaker, "The Influence of Culture on Persuasion Processes and Attitudes."
24. "Ready to Shop until They Drop," *Business Week,* June 22, 1998, pp. 104–16; Güliz Ger and Russell W. Belk, "Measuring and Comparing Materialism Cross-Culturally," in *Advances in Consumer Research,* vol. 17, ed. Marvin Goldberg, Gerald Gorn, and Richard Pollay (Provo, UT: Association for Consumer Research, 1990), pp. 186–92; and Güliz Ger and Russell W. Belk, "Cross-Cultural Differences in Materialism," *Journal of Economic Psychology* 17 (1996), pp. 55–77.
25. Holt, "Consumers' Cultural Differences as Local Systems of Tastes"; and Holt, "PostStructuralist Lifestyle Analysis."
26. Craig S. Smith, "Moon Cake Madness Hits Again," *The Globe and Mail,* October 31, 1998, p. A21.
27. Joyce Millman, "'The X-Files' Finds the Truth: Its Time Is Past," *New York Times,* May 17, 2002, Section 2, pp. 34, 41.
28. See Mary Yoko Brannen, "'Bwana Mickey': Constructing Cultural Consumption at Tokyo Disneyland," in *Re-Made in Japan,* ed. Joseph J. Tobin (New Haven: Yale University Press, 1992), pp. 216–34; and Lila Abu-Lughod, "The Objects of Soap Opera: Egyptian Television and the Cultural Politics of Modernity," in *Worlds Apart,* ed. Daniel Miller (London and New York: Routledge, 1995), pp. 190–210.
29. "Belgians Close Coke Probe," *Lincoln Journal Star,* April 23, 2000, p. 5G.
30. John Seabrook, *Nob®ow: The Culture of Marketing—the Marketing of Culture* (New York: Alfred A. Knopf, 2000), pp. 143–45.
31. Robert Block, "How Big Mac Kept from Becoming a Serb Archenemy," *The Wall Street Journal,* September 3, 1999, pp. B1, B3; Gregory Starrett, "The Political Economy of Religious Commodities in Cairo," *American Anthropologist* 97 (March 1995), pp. 41–50; and Douglas Brownlie, Philippe Jourdan, Kritsadarat Wattanasuwan, and Einar Brevik, personal communications.
32. Douglas Stayman and Rohit Deshpandé, "Situational Ethnicity and Consumer Behavior," *Journal of Consumer Research* 16 (December 1989), pp. 361–71.
33. Alison James, "Cooking the Books: Global or Local Identities in Contemporary British Food Cultures," in *Cross-Cultural Consumption,* ed. David Howes (London and New York: Routledge, 1996), pp. 77–92; and http//news.bbc.co.uk/hi/english/world/middle_east/newsid_2000000/2000574. st.
34. Søren Askegaard and Güliz Ger, "Product-Country Images: Towards a Contextualized Approach," in *European Advances in Consumer Research,* vol. 3, ed. Anna Olofsson and Basil Englis (Provo, UT: Association for Consumer Research, 1997), pp. 50–58; Güliz Ger and Per Østergaard, "Constructing Immigrant Identities in Consumption: Appearance among Turko-Danes," in *Advances in Consumer Research,* vol. 25, ed. Joseph W. Alba and J. Wesley (Provo, UT: Association for Consumer Research, 1998), pp. 1–4; Raj Mehta and Russell W. Belk, "Artifacts, Identity, and Transition: Favorite Possessions of Indians and Indian Immigrants to the United States," *Journal of Consumer Research* 17 (March 1991), pp. 398–411; and Yunxiang Yan, "McDonald's in Beijing: The Localization of Americana," in *Golden Arches East,* ed. James L. Watson (Stanford: Stanford University Press, 1997), pp. 77–109.
35. John Brooks, *Showing Off in America* (Boston: Little, Brown, 1981); and Thorstein Veblen, *The Theory of the Leisure Class* (New York: Macmillan, 1899).
36. Russell W. Belk and Janeen Arnold Costa, "The Mountain Man Myth: A Contemporary Consuming Fantasy," *Journal of Consumer Research* 25 (December 1998), pp. 218–40; Andrew Tanzer, "Tiger Woods Played Here," *Forbes,* March 10, 1997, pp. 96–97; and Yan, "McDonald's in Beijing.
37. Daniel Miller, ed., *Unwrapping Christmas* (Oxford: Clarendon Press, 1993); Victor Turner, *The Ritual Process* (Chicago: Aldine, 1969); Judith Waldrop, "Same Stuffing Next Year," *American Demographics* 13 (November 1991), p. 4; Melanie Wallendorf and Eric J.

Arnould, "'We Gather Together': The Consumption Rituals of Thanksgiving Day," *Journal of Consumer Research* 18 (June 1991), pp. 13–31; and William D. Wells and Qimei Chen, "Melodies and Counterpoints: American Thanksgiving and the Chinese Moon Festival," in *Advances in Consumer Research,* vol. 26, ed. Eric J. Arnould and Linda Scott (Provo, UT: Association for Consumer Research, 1999), pp. 555–61.

38. Dennis W. Rook, "The Ritual Dimension of Consumer Behavior," *Journal of Consumer Research* 12 (December 1985), pp. 251–64.

39. Mary Douglas, *Purity and Danger* (New York: Praeger, 1971); Mary Douglas and Baron Isherwood, *The World of Goods* (New York: W. W. Norton, 1979); Tom F. Driver, *Liberating Rites* (Boulder, CO: Westview Press, 1998); Ronald L. Grimes, ed., *Readings in Ritual Studies* (Upper Saddle River, NJ: Prentice Hall, 1996); Douglas B. Holt, "Examining the Descriptive Value of 'Ritual' in Consumer Behavior: A View from the Field," *Advances in Consumer Research,* vol. 19, ed. John F. Sherry Jr. and Brian Sternthal (Provo, UT: Association for Consumer Research, 1992), pp. 213–18; and Victor Turner, *The Ritual Process: Structure and Anti-Structure* (Baltimore, MD: Penguin Books, 1969).

40. Jennifer Edson Escales, "The Consumption of Insignificant Rituals: A Look at Debutante Balls," in *Advances in Consumer Research,* vol. 20, ed. Leigh McAlister and Michael L. Rothschild (Provo, UT: Association for Consumer Research, 1993), pp. 709–16; and Clifford J. Schultz II and Gary Bamossy, "Vicarious Fanatic Consumption: The Consumption Experience and Consummations of Soccer Fans and Hooligans," presented at the Annual Conference of the Association for Consumer Research, October 1–4, 1998, Montreal, Canada.

41. Rook, "The Ritual Dimension of Consumer Behavior," p. 253; and Mary Douglas and Baron Isherwood, *The World of Goods: Toward an Anthropology of Consumption* (New York: Basic Books, 1979).

42. Rika Houston, "Through Pain and Perseverance: Liminality, Ritual Consumption, and the Social Construction of Gender in Contemporary Japan," in *Advances in Consumer Research,* vol. 26, ed. Linda Scott and Eric J. Arnould (Provo, UT: Association for Consumer Research, 1998), pp. 542–48.

43. de Mooij, *Global Marketing and Advertising,* pp. 162–63.

44. David A. Ricks, *Blunders in International Business* (Cambridge, MA: Blackwell Business, 1993), p. 30.

45. Ricks, *Blunders in International Business,* p. 25; and Salah S. Hassan and Roger D. Blackwell, *Global Marketing: Perspectives and Cases* (Fort Worth: Dryden Press, 1994), pp. 359–80.

46. Pamela Odih, "The Women's Market: Marketing Fact or Apparition?" *Consumption, Markets, Culture* 3, no. 2 (1999), pp. 165–93.

47. Güliz Ger and Per Østergaard, "Constructing Immigrant Identities in Consumption: Appearance among the Turko-Danes," in *Advances in Consumer Research,* vol. 25, ed. Joseph W. Alba and J. Wesley Hutchinson (Provo, UT: Association for Consumer Research, 1998), pp. 48–52; Thomas C. O'Guinn, Wei-Na Le, and Ronald J. Faber, "Acculturation: The Impact of Divergent Paths on Buyer Behavior," in *Advances in Consumer Research,* vol. 13, ed. Richard Lutz (Provo, UT: Association for Consumer Research, 1986), pp. 579–83; Lisa Peñaloza, "*Atravesando Fronteras*/Border Crossings: A Critical Ethnographic Exploration of the Consumer Acculturation of Mexican Immigrants," *Journal of Consumer Research* 21 (June 1994), pp. 32–54; Harry Triandis, Vasso Vassilou, George Vassilou, Yasumas Tanka, and A. Shanmugan, *The Analysis of Subjective Culture* (New York: John Wiley, 1972); and Melanie Wallendorf and Michael D. Reilly, "Distinguishing Culture of Origin from Culture of Residence," in *Advances in Consumer Research,* vol. 10, ed. Richard Bagozzi and Alice Tybout (Provo, UT: Association for Consumer Research, 1983), pp. 699–701.

48. Sammy Bonsu and Russell W. Belk, "Death Becomes Us: Funerary Rituals and Products for Negotiating Consumer Identities in Ghana," working paper (Greensboro: University of North Carolina, 2002); and Jean Kilbourne, *Deadly Persuasion: Why Women and Girls Must Fight the Addictive Power of Advertising* (New York: Free Press, 1999).

49. Russell W. Belk, Kenneth D. Bahn, and Robert N. Mayer, "Developmental Recognition of Consumption Symbolism," *Journal of Consumer Research* 9 (June 1982), pp. 4–17.

50. An excellent discussion of the Diderot effect can be found in Grant McCracken, *Culture and Consumption* (Bloomington, IN: Indiana University Press, 1988), p. 123.
51. Russell W. Belk, "Possessions and the Extended Self," *Journal of Consumer Research* 15 (September 1988), pp. 139–68; Robert E. Burnkrant and Thomas J. Page Jr., "On the Management of Self Images in Social Situations: The Role of Public Self-Consciousness," *Advances in Consumer Research,* vol. 9, ed. Andrew Mitchell (Provo, UT: Association for Consumer Research, 1982), pp. 452–55; Newell D. Wright, C. B. Claiborne, and M. Joseph Sirgy, "The Effects of Product Symbolism on Consumer Self-Concept," *Advances in Consumer Research,* vol. 19, ed. John F. Sherry, Jr. and Brian Sternthal (Provo, UT: Association for Consumer Research, 1992), pp. 311–18; and M. Joseph Sirgy, "Self-Concept in Consumer Behavior: A Critical Review," *Journal of Consumer Research* 9 (December 1982), pp. 287–300.
52. Ger and Belk, "Measuring and Comparing Materialism Cross-Culturally." See also Albert O. Hirschmann, *Shifting Involvements: Private Interest and Public* (Princeton: Princeton University Press, 1982); and *Utne Reader,* no. 90 (November–December 1998).
53. Arjun Appadurai, "Disjuncture and Difference in the Global Cultural Economy," in *Global Culture: Nationalism, Globalization and Modernity,* ed. Mike Featherstone (London: Sage Publications, 1990), pp. 295–311; Mike Featherstone, *Undoing Culture: Globalization, Postmodernism and Identity* (London: Sage Publications, 1995); Daniel Miller, ed., *Worlds Apart* (London and New York: Routledge, 1995); *James L. Watson,* ed. *Golden Arches East: McDonald's in East Asia* (Stanford: Stanford University Press, 1997); and Richard Wilk, "Rituals of Difference and Identity: Connecting the Global and the Local," presented to the Ph.D. course "Modern Times, Modern Rituals," Department of Ethnography and Social Anthropology, University of Aarhus, Aarhus, Denmark, 1997.
54. Don Slater, *Consumer Culture and Modernity* (Cambridge: Polity Press, 1997), p. 8.
55. Dominique Bouchet, "Marketing and the Redefinition of Ethnicity," in *Marketing in a Multicultural World,* ed. Janeen Arnold Costa and Gary J. Bamossy (Thousand Oaks, CA: Sage Publications, 1995), pp. 68–104; Mary Douglas and Baron Isherwood, *The World of Goods* (New York and London: Routledge, 1996); and Kenneth J. Gergen, *The Saturated Self* (New York: Basic Books, 1991).
56. Anna Husarka, "The First Casualty," *The New Yorker,* April 19, 1993, pp. 57–65.
57. This paragraph paraphrases Herbert Blumer, "Fashion," *International Encyclopedia of the Social Sciences* (New York: Macmillan, 1968), pp. 341–45.
58. Akita Morita with Edwin M. Reingold, *Made in Japan* (New York: Dutton, 1986); and Leon E. Wynter, "Minorities Play the Hero in More TV Ads as Clients Discover Multicultural Sells," *The Wall Street Journal,* November 24, 1993, pp. B1, B7.
59. Richard Wilk, "Learning to Be Local in Belize: Global Structures of Common Difference," in *Worlds Apart,* ed. Daniel Miller (London and New York: Routledge, 1995), pp. 110–33.
60. Carol Hendrickson, "Selling Guatemala: Maya Export Products in U.S. Mail Order Catalogues," in *Cross-Cultural Consumption,* ed. David Howes (London and New York: Routledge, 1996), pp. 106–24.
61. Daniel Miller, ed., *Unwrapping Christmas* (Oxford: Clarendon Press, 1993); Colleen Ballerino Cohen, Richard Wilk, and Beverly Stoeltje, eds., *Beauty Queens on the Global Stage* (New York and London: Routledge, 1996).
62. Fuat Firat, "Consumer Culture or Culture Consumed?" in *Marketing in a Multicultural World,* ed. Janeen Arnold Costa and Gary Bamossy (Thousand Oaks, CA: Sage, 1995), pp. 105–23.

LEARNING OBJECTIVES

After completing this chapter, you should be able to:

- Explain why meaning is an important issue for marketers.
- Describe the basic process of semiosis and the semiotic triangle.
- Have a working knowledge of the meaning transfer model.
- Appreciate the role of advertising and fashion in linking meanings to products.
- Describe both ordinary and ritualized processes through which consumers transfer meaning from products to themselves.
- Explain why spokespersons are important and describe the link between spokesperson selection and marketing success.
- Recognize the kinds of meanings that consumers value.
- Know why questions of meaning are important in cross-cultural contexts.
- Recognize the significance of collecting for consumers and marketers.
- Identify a variety of behaviors through which consumers derive meaning and value from consumption.

CONSUMPTION MEANINGS[1]

DAY OF THE DEAD[2]

An interesting celebration takes place in Mexico and in many Chicano communities in North America during the first two days in November. These two days are set aside to remember the dead. November 1 is called *El dia de los santos,* or All Saints' Day, and is dedicated to the children who have died, and November 2 is called *El dia de los muertos,* All Souls' Day, and is for the mourning of adults. In the homes, families remember the children by preparing an altar, or *ofrenda,* decorated with flowers. The families that have lost a child are visited by relatives and friends who participate in the ceremony, which consists of a meal and perhaps some prayers. The meal includes a *tamal* seasoned with seeds, which symbolize happiness. The parents of the dead child place toys and foods that children like on the altar. The ceremony for the adults who have died that follows on November 2nd is similar, except that the offerings include a special kind of sweet bread decorated with skulls and crosses called *pan de muerto.* The bakeries offer *pan de muerto* in various forms, including human beings and animals.

Since this is a grassroots celebration, the presence of death is manifested in all kinds of folkloric objects, including candies made of white sugar in the form of skulls, crosses, coffins, tombs, spirits, animals, fruits, and birds; wooden or clay toys in the form of coffins lined black; wire skeletons painted white in the form of devils, dancers, musicians, bullfighters, drunkards, salesmen, and *charros* (Mexican cowboys); funeral processions; as well as tables set with skulls, candles, food, and drink. For the children there are white masks, skeletons, or toys in the form of a coffin from which a skeleton jumps out when a string is pulled and skeletons that dance when the little boards from which they hang are pressed.

The main activity on November 2 is a visit to the cemetery to bring offerings to the dead. This custom is kept alive in provincial towns and the countryside. The island of Janitzio on Lake Patzcuaro (state of Michoacán) is famous for its celebration. On the night of November 1, men, women, and children, holding candles in their hands, form a procession that winds slowly up the steep island streets to the hilltop where the cemetery is located. The church as well as the tombs is adorned with the yellow brilliance of the *cempasuchil* or *flor de muerto,* the flower of death. Yellow symbolizes death, and marigold petal crosses adorn many graves. Upon a framework of reeds people place fruits, squash, ears of corn, little figures of white sugar in the form of skulls, and little baskets of *pan de muerto.* The women sweep the graves and watch over the dead while the men turn the soil so the dead can "breath" and then partake of a little *charanda,* a native liquor. In the houses, an offering is prepared of those foods that the dead person liked best. The table for this offering is decorated with flowers, fruits, sweets, bread, and lighted candles.

OVERVIEW

In this chapter, we focus on the meanings that animate consumption behavior. Consumer motives for purchase, consumption, and possession (see Chapter 7) stem in great measure from the meaning of consumption acts and objects and the value that meaning provides. Some consumption activities seem to be primarily about the evocation of important meanings and values. The vignette on the Day of the Dead illustrates that the production, marketing, and consumption of a wide variety of toys, ornaments, food, drink, and even cleaning products help consumers to express the meanings of this old and deeply felt Mexican holiday. Tourists from other parts of Mexico may even visit the island of Janitzio to consume vicariously the values expressed in the local celebration. Understanding consumers—why they buy things, why they retain some possessions and dispose of others—requires an understanding of meaning and value.

The idea that the purchase and consumption of goods is meaningful implies that goods and services are media of interpersonal communication; they are social phenomena conveying meanings that are shared by at least some others. Products also can be personalized. Because people can form strong links with products and services they buy, they are important communicative devices. The Japanese wedding cake described in Consumer Chronicles 4.1 is illustrative. From one perspective, the cake is just an example of consumer acculturation (see Chapters 2 and 12) and clever marketing by hotels and reception halls. Nonetheless, only a few Western consumption practices are integrated into Japanese weddings. Rice is never thrown at Japanese weddings given Japanese reverence for this product, for example. For the Japanese, the sweet (*amai*) cake provides a perfect symbolic association for children, and the "entering of the sword" makes a suitably discrete sexual reference to reproduction. A symbolic analysis thus reveals that the cake signifies reproduction and children. It marks the primary purpose of marriage in Japan, thus reinforcing other traditional symbols of union, such as the *san-san-ku-do,* or exchange of *sake.*[3]

Nonmarket Sources of Meaning

There are many sources of meanings for the products and services that people consume. Marketing communications are one such source, and marketed consumer products one

The Japanese Wedding Cake

CONSUMER CHRONICLES 4.1

The scene is a modern Japanese wedding reception, a contemporary version of the traditional wedding feast that in prewar times often lasted three days. In the modern Shinto version of the Japanese wedding ceremony, during the *san-san-ku-do* ritual, *sake* (rice wine) is poured for the bride and groom by two young girls serving as shrine maidens, each of whom holds a vessel containing sake. Both vessels are decorated with *mizuhuki,* a decorated string made from paper, and a piece of origami representing a stylized butterfly, one male and the other female. Sake from both vessels is poured into the same cup, which is then shared by the bride and groom in succession.

One of the central objects in this ceremony is something entirely new. It is a wedding cake, of the kind one might expect to find at any American church wedding: three-tiered, frosted in white, topped with the inevitable miniature figures of a bride and groom in Western wedding dress. Behind it stand the real groom and his bride—perhaps also in Western dress or perhaps in traditional wedding kimono—the groom's hand steadying hers as she guides a be-ribboned sword into the cake. Cameras flash, and the guests applaud. As Japanese sensitivity to word play prohibits the use of the word "cut" at weddings, the emcee is forced to announce in stilted highly formal Chinese-style language: "The entering of the sword into the wedding cake has been performed." The bride and groom return to their seats and the celebrations continue, the cake forgotten. It is not divided and shared by all present, nor are pieces preserved—by freezing, as in the modern American custom—by the bridal couple as souvenirs of the event. More often than not, and as if to confirm our suspicion that it is all show and no substance, the Japanese version of the wedding cake, it turns out, is inedible.

Source: Walter Edwards, "Something Borrowed: Wedding Cakes as Symbols in Modern Japan," American Ethnologist 9 *(November 1982), pp. 699–711.*

source of meaningful possessions.[4] However, many of people's most meaningful possessions are not marketplace commodities at all, but things without much monetary value, such as heirlooms received from parents, photographs of family and friends, exchanges of dinners and parties, gardens, and collections. A comparative study of favorite possessions in North America and West Africa identified gifts, handmade crafts, religious writings, and collections. The father of one of your authors artfully made her a bed stand from scrap lumber. The bed stand is meaningful, but these meanings could not be purchased. Meaning derives from the creative act of conception, the labor required to make it, and feelings conveyed from parent to child in the presentation of the bed stand. Over the years, memory also adds meaning to the bed stand. Recognizing the emphasis consumers in advanced consumer culture place on personal meanings, marketing managers are keen to determine meanings consumers value. Managers strive to provide consumers with value by linking apparently authentic meanings with their market offerings. For example, Starbucks went to considerable lengths to design its original coffeehouses to recreate the coffeehouses of Milan, Italy.[5]

Marketing Success and the Loss of Meaning

In consumer culture, marketers try to offer as many goods, services, images, ideas, and experiences as possible. This expansion happens by making more different things more widely exchangeable with each other. The concentration, expansion, and globalization of the consumer goods industries, the growth of affluent consumer segments in every nation, democratization, the loosening of class boundaries, and the greatly quickened flow of information through the commercial media contribute to market expansion and the quickened movement of consumer meaning.

The success of the global market system has some unintended consequences. One is that it tends to homogenize meaning and value. If the value of every product can be reduced to money, then there is a danger that things will come to mean little more than demonstrating that consumers have the money to obtain them. This fear seems justified since consumers often seem unable to find enduring meaning in mass-marketed goods.[6] Both marketers and consumers face the problem of unsatisfactory meaning. Designers are strongly motivated to produce new and original products to satisfy restless consumers. Marketers strive to create differential meanings for what are often quite similar goods. To create and sustain differentiated positionings for products that are mostly similar, such as soap powders and packaged foods, they must promote brands heavily. Linking products to nonmarket meanings often through stories is one useful way of creating differentiation. A heroic brand story about Dyson cyclone vacuum cleaners can be found at the company website. Consumers wish to define a clear social or personal identity. Therefore, they strive to create a differentiated world of personal meanings from arrays of meaningful commercial products and through nonmarket mechanisms, such as customization, home production, and collecting. These ideas will be explained in more detail, but first we should explain *consumer meaning.*

@ www.dyson.co.uk

WHOSE MEANING AND MEANING FOR WHOM? SEMIOSIS

Consumers behave on the basis of the meanings that they ascribe to marketed products, services, and experiences. But what do we mean by **meaning?** When thinking about meaning and value, it's important to distinguish *the value in use to the consumer,* that is, the extent to which the consumer holds something dear, as distinct from a product's price, cost, and other measures of marketplace value. This value in use is what we call meaning.[7] A young child's irreplaceable but inexpensive favorite stuffed animal or blanket provides an example.

To understand consumer meaning, researchers draw on the science of meaning, called semiotics. Semiotics argues that communication depends on **semiosis,** *the process of communication by any type of sign.* A **sign** is *anything that stands for something else.* For example, a series of Greek letters such as $\phi\beta K$ is a sign that stands for the honorary fraternity Phi Beta Kappa. A simple marketing example of a sign would be a corporate logo, brand symbol, or brand name. Thus, the Intel logo found on many computer products stands for the Intel Corporation and its products. Similarly, Bibendum, the Michelin Man, stands for the Michelin tire company and its products. Some of the meanings of Bibendum are described in Industry Insights 4.1.[8]

Brand Image

The symbolic nature of brands has been recognized since the 1950s. In those years, marketers began to recognize that products have a social and psychological character as well as a physical one. Researchers recognized that the sets of feelings, ideas, and attitudes that consumers have about brands were crucial to purchase behavior. They found that brands consist of both objective or intrinsic attributes such as package size and raw materials used, and the intangible beliefs, feelings, and associations that con-

Bibendum, the Michelin Man

INDUSTRY INSIGHTS 4.1

Bibendum was born in France in 1894 when Edouard and Andre Michelin were searching for a logo and spokesperson for their tire company. Edouard noticed a pile of tires and told his brother, "It would look like a man if it had arms!" Eventually, the illustrator Marius Rossillon created a poster of a character composed of 40 narrow tire rings. Today, Bibendum is a friendly faced, 22-tire character.

In the early years, Bibendum's appearance varied considerably. Sometimes he was stout and prosperous. Other times, he was extremely thin and looked something like a mummy. He was so popular that similar characters emerged for other European manufacturers—steel man, paper man, and so forth. In the early years, Bibendum often spoke to the audience in the posters and newsletters where he appeared. His adventures were recounted in children's books. At one point, he had both a wife (Bibette) and a baby (Bebib).

Today, every Michelin tire is embossed with a tiny white Bibendum on its side wall, indicating the amount of wear on the tire. Through this practical service and others, Bibendum has lasted as long or longer than most company logos or symbolic representations. In essence, Bibendum provides a way to make modern technology concrete and understandable to consumers. Bibendum is the soul of the organization that he represents—Michelin Tires.

Source: Brad Herzog, "They're Great!" Attache *(August 1999), pp. 54–59.*

geal around them. These associations may extend to the kinds of people who use the brand and situations in which consumption is appropriate. Today, **brand image** may be defined as *a brand-specific collection of product-, brand-, and consumer-related attributes (knowledge, feelings, and attitudes towards a brand) that an individual holds in memory,* a subset of which becomes active depending on specific cues and contexts.[9] Brands, trademarks, product symbols, and packages can be tremendously effective product symbols, and ones of great value to firms. The Marlboro cowboy, RCA's dog Nipper, Harley-Davidson's wings, Disney's Mickey Mouse, and Royal Dutch Shell's shell are just a few examples of the shorthand symbols linking product and meaning for millions of consumers. Since the 1950s research has shown that as symbols, brands impact consumer's status and self-esteem. Research across cultures suggests that brands are more likely to be purchased and consumed if consumers recognize some symbolic link between the brand's image and their own actual or ideal self-image (see Chapter 10 for a discussion of the actual and ideal self). The links between brands and identity can be seen in youth gang members' adoption of branded team sports merchandise as their exclusive costume. Indeed, one British poll showed that younger people are more likely to be influenced by brand image than older people. Nonetheless, the link between brand and identity may lead to intergenerational brand loyalties. Brands can symbolize quality and predictability. This is true when consumers are unfamiliar with brands, as in some developing and transitional economies, and may partially account for McDonald's and Coke's global success. In Japan, brand names possess a mystique that connotes sophistication, internationalism, and taste. A novel called *Nantonaku kirisutaru* that consisted largely of lists of brand-name goods and discussions of them sold three-quarter million copies.[10]

At a minimum, brand names and logos improve memory and product recall. Managers can strengthen brand image by using marketing communications and loyalty programs to emphasize brand qualities consumers' value, and managers can revitalize a mature brand by creating or strengthening associations that will bring the brand to mind when new consumer goals are activated. For example, post–September 11, 2001, several U.S. brands emphasized country of origin to enable consumers to express their patriotism through product purchase. Unfortunately, there are scores of different ways to measure brand image and no agreement exists as to the best way.[11]

Semiotic Process of Interpretation

Interpretation comes about through a three-part process called semiosis. This semiotic process is how people obtain meaning from signs. Semiosis involves a sign, some object, and an interpretant, which is the meaning of the sign. This three-part system is also called the **semiotic triangle.** Exhibit 4.1 illustrates the semiotic triangle and gives an example using the advertisement shown on p. 124. The black clarinet and sheet music shown in the ad are a sign of the scotch brand. And in the advertisement, the clarinet is an interpretant that conveys certain meanings to the target market. A few of these meanings are listed in Exhibit 4.1. By grouping the object and interpretant (see Chapter 8 for a discussion of grouping), the advertiser trusts the target will associate the interpretant with the object. Importantly, each semiotic triangle exists within a particular cultural context. This context provides consumers with the cultural knowledge (categories and/or principles) they need to interpret the signs they encounter. In the advertisement Johnny Walker Black Label Scotch Whisky is the object.

To further explain the links between the three components of a semiotic triangle, consider a print ad for Prescriptives™ Comfort Cream, a skin cream, that ran a few years ago. The first component of the semiotic system is the product or service that is the object of the communication. In this advertisement, the object was the Prescriptives Comfort Cream. The object was identified in the copy of the ad and in the label of a photograph of an open jar. The object is also represented by the second element of the semiotic triangle, the sensory image called a sign. This ad showed at least two significant signs: a small glass jar and a large teddy bear. The third element is called the interpretant. It is the meaning derived from the image.

EXHIBIT 4.1

Semiotic Triangle

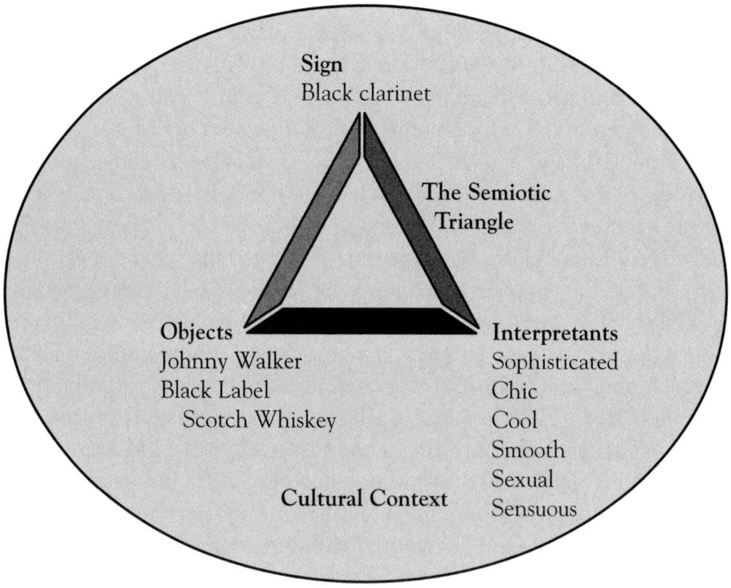

The Prescriptives ad also illustrates that signs may be of several types or bear (pun intended!) several kinds of relationships with the object (a product or service) it represents. In this case, the teddy bear is an *index* of the product. An indexical sign may share some attributes with the product or service. Thus, teddy bears are thought to be a source of security. An indexical sign has an existential or causal connection to its object. A lemon scent added to a number of household cleaning products in North America is an example of an indexical sign since the citric acid contained in citrus fruits is a cleaning agent. Ralph Lauren's polo pony logo is an indexical symbol of elite status to some consumers.

The small glass jar with the silver top is also a sign. It, however, is just a *symbol.* A symbol is related to the object through a purely conventional association or rule. Many brand names are symbols. According to their website, Virgin–the third most recognized brand name in Britain—stands for value for money, quality, innovation, fun, and a sense of competitive challenge. The association of the Virgin name with these values is purely conventional. Most corporate logos such as the Nike swoosh, McDonald's golden arches, and Mercedes Benz' star are symbols too. Marketers commonly employ size, shape, color of packaging, and other attributes to make symbolic suggestions about products. The clear Prescriptives jar might suggest value, simplicity, purity, and even costliness to Western consumers.

The final type of sign is what is called an *icon,* a sign that is similar to or resembles the product in some way. Thus, a teddy bear bears an iconic relationship to the presumed effects of Prescriptives in that it is soft, youthful, ageless, comforting, cuddly, and, like our skin, bare (bear)! A plastic lemon or lime used for packaging lemon or lime juice would be an iconic sign. Clothing trademark emblems that represent animals (Izod alligator, Munsingwear penguin, Vanderbilt swan, Brooks Brothers sheep, Ralph Lauren polo pony) are iconic emblems of animals. Commercial Japanese boxed lunches, called *bento* or *Ekiben,* often employ iconic signs as containers: one containing crab meat resembles a crab; one containing chestnuts is shaped like a nut; one containing scallops is shaped like a scallop shell.[12]

The relationships between sign, object, and interpretant are conventional. That is, meanings are relative to particular **communications communities** responding to them. Because they *share cultural knowledge* (see Chapter 12), members of a communications community agree, more or less, on these meanings. The clarinet as symbol of cool jazz requires a cultural knowledge of jazz that is not shared by everyone. Thus, product and brand meanings can vary between market segments.

We identify three different approaches to understanding the meanings of goods to consumers. First, we can examine the role of possessions in defining the self and creating a sense of identity. In other words, possessions embody personal values and meanings. In the Day of the Dead vignette, offering up flowers, candles, toys, and candies to the memory of the dead is a poignant way of expressing personal values. The self is defined in part by reference to one's ancestors, and the products consumed link mourners to ancestors. As suggested in Chapter 10, narrative is one way that people make sense of their lives. Research has shown that consumers spontaneously construct life stories that involve brands. Drama ads, discussed later, encourage their use in stories. Stories may arise in brand-use situations. Brands can then become symbols of personal life stories. In these ways, they serve a referent or **indexical meaning.**[13]

The importance of consumer goods in providing a sense of self varies between areas of the world. As consumer societies become more complex and diverse, more identity choices are available. This leads to more upheaval, ambiguity, and uncertainty. These tensions attach themselves to attributes such as age, gender, physical beauty, social

Using symbolic conventions to create brand meaning.

class, and race. As discussed in Chapter 10, people experience different and even conflicting identity choices; they use consumption to reveal different aspects of themselves. Consumers in developed economies strive to create a distinctive sense of self through consumption choices and the meaning transfer activities, which we will explain, including consuming, customizing, personalizing, grooming, and arranging goods.

Even in developing and transitional economies, in which identities of person and place remain more sharply etched in conventional roles, many consumers are involved with consumer goods and concerned with public display. Venezuelans, for example, rank first among countries in their concern for personal beauty, and Venezuelan households spend a fifth of their income on personal care and grooming products.[14]

The meanings of possessions involve not only personal but public values as well. Thus, a second school of thinking about consumer meaning emphasizes the use of goods within a culture's social communication system. In other words, consumer goods convey public messages about identity and status. For example, Chevy trucks are "like a rock," and their performance supports this belief. Hence, an individual who is hardworking and who drives a Chevy truck will more likely be perceived, and perhaps perceive him or herself, as being dependable and always there—like a rock.[15] Residents of the island of Janitzio mentioned in the vignette make a dramatic public statement about their traditional, regional Tarascan identity to other Mexicans through their unique way of celebrating the Day of the Dead. Similarly, the wedding cake and sake consumed at Japanese weddings and described in Consumer Chronicles 4.1 communicate public values.

Within particular cultural contexts and communications communities, consumers are usually able to decode the meaning of things. As we discuss in Chapter 12, consumers make inferences about social class, social status, and ethnic affiliations based on other consumers' displays of products. The implication is that the meanings of consumer goods are defined with regard to sets of recognized similarities and differences in goods. Research identifies many differences between ensembles of goods consumers within a given cultural context use to identity and differentiate groups from one another. For example, in China, color television ownership is a representation of self-worth. In one study, some consumers claimed that the purchase of the appropriate, that is, Japanese, TV was more important than having furniture when considering marriage. It also represents freedom from oppression and the wealth and promise of the new China. And the television represents an escape from everyday life in most of China and the opportunity to experience the formerly forbidden West.[16]

Across cultural contexts, people may draw mistaken inferences about the symbolic meanings of goods. For example, Danes and English consumers were shown the pair of pictures of English and Danish living rooms presented below. Not only did the two groups of consumers find the taste of the other group distasteful, Danes incorrectly guessed that the English owners of this consumption set were older than they were, and the English incorrectly guessed the Danes were both younger and poorer than they were. An example such as this reinforces the importance of tailoring promotional content to the target market's cultural context in order to convey desired meanings. An example of the social costs of mistaken inferences about the symbolic meanings of goods is shown in Ethical Dilemma 4.1.[17]

A third approach looks for the particular meanings of products and brands that give them value. Retro products and brands such as the BMW mini, Restoration Hardware, or even movie versions of old comics such as *Spiderman* can evoke past values or even just nostalgia. Restoration Hardware markets some products to convey the traditional value of thrift, for example. Referring to Consumer Chronicles 4.1, white is associated with death in traditional Japanese culture. The white of the Western-style wedding cake

Modern Danish living room

Traditional English living room

Social Costs of Misunderstanding the Meaning of Curtains

ETHICAL DILEMMA 4.1

The convention within the Bradford, UK, British community, was to drape windows inside the home with curtains. Often there were two sets of these. The nearest to the window were "net" curtains, which allowed the person inside to see out, but prevented the person outside from seeing in. Inside the net curtains was a more substantial and totally opaque pair of curtains; these were drawn at night and opened during the day. The position of the curtains gave, in the native British tradition, a very clear message to the outside world about the state of the household. If the curtains were drawn closed during the day, then either somebody was asleep when they should not be (slovenly, lazy), or had forgotten to open the curtains (slovenly, lazy), or was doing something that respectable people did not do during the day (having sex? adultery? prostitute at work?), or was working night-shifts (this at least the neighbors would understand and tolerate).

The immigrant community had no understanding of these symbolic niceties. For the Pakistani immigrants the windows in their houses in Pakistan were for the purpose of getting fresh air and the sunlight. The windows in their houses always looked into a courtyard, and were neither visible to, nor overlooked by, the general public. There was no need for putting curtains on them, particularly since this could stop the inflow of fresh air and light into the rooms. In Bradford, however, it became necessary to cover windows to keep out the gaze of strangers. It became common to see, in immigrant households, windows that were veiled, inside, by more-or-less-permanent hangings, not necessarily symmetrically hung or matching in color. To keep the world out, this was effective. As a means of communicating with the host population about the state of the household, it was disastrous.

The overall effect of semiotic miscues represented by alternative uses of curtains, gardens, fences, and home exteriors gave the British host community a very poor idea of the immigrant Pakistani community; the immigrant community seemed to be giving out consistent signals that it was lazy, dirty, and contemptuous of propriety and decency. The result was that the members of the host society left the areas where immigrants started to live. Phenomena of the kind described have tended to keep the two populations, immigrant and host, apart, even when they live (as is often the case) next door to one another. The effects of this upon housing patterns are clear: the English do not want to live in the areas dominated by the Pakistani households and tend to move into "white only" areas; reciprocally, the Pakistanis create enclaves of their own. Ethnic segregation results.

Source: Malcolm Chapman and Ahmad Jamal, "Acculturation: Cross Cultural Consumer Perceptions and the Symbolism of Domestic Space," in Advances in Consumer Research, *vol. 24, ed. Merrie Brucks and Deborah MacInnis (Provo, UT: Association for Consumer Research, 1997), pp. 138–44.*

and dress make sense because on her wedding, the Japanese bride was traditionally felt to be lost to her birth family. The goods displayed, cleaned, consumed, and decorated on the Day of the Dead are meaningful. They convey meanings about family, tradition, religion, and the purpose of life. Another example of the conventional and context-specific meaning of goods is described in Consumer Chronicles 4.2.

Of course, product meaning is changeable. One aspect of this is that it changes with time. For young people anything that is "bonzer" (Australian), "in," "hip," "phat," "fly," or "holic" (Japanese) changes as rapidly as youth-culture slang. The pace of change in meaning makes youth marketing especially difficult, as discussed in Chapter 12.

As already illustrated by the household furnishings and Ethical Dilemma 4.1 examples, meaning is also unstable across market segments. Marketers can never be certain that their images convey the meanings they wish. Consumers extract their own meanings. Idiosyncratic interpretations drawing on personal experience are common. In one study, only half the people questioned identified the most commonly given meaning for a familiar product. For example, the most frequent association with James Bond movies was "sexy girls," but only 38 percent of the subjects mentioned this meaning; the most frequent association with Breyer's ice cream was "natural," which 55 percent of subjects mentioned. Researchers have also discovered that males and females see different themes of print ads, and they even provide radically different descriptions of the advertising images themselves. This instability of meaning emphasizes the importance of carefully targeting marketing communications.

The meanings of things are sometimes contested by social groups and market segments. In 2000, the web portal Yahoo! was taken to court in France for allowing access to Nazi collectibles auctioned on eBay. French law forbids broadcast of Nazi-related materials, having determined that they are highly objectionable. However, some collectors may simply find them of historic interest. Clearly different groups contest the meanings of Nazi collectibles. The antimarketing websites mentioned in Chapter 18 also represent disagreements about the meaning of brands and firms. Firms must consider and respond when the meanings of their brand or firm are in question. An area on Procter & Gamble's website is devoted to dispelling rumors about its man-in-the-moon logo. We'll discuss the malleability of meaning further, but first we need to describe what kinds of meanings products may convey to consumers.[18]

> **CONSUMER CHRONICLES 4.2**
>
> **The Meaning of Blue Jeans**
>
> Authentic used U.S. blue jeans, especially those dating from the 50s and 60s, command thousands of dollars from some Tokyo consumers. What is it about blue jeans that (still) makes them so valuable? Certainly not the worn denim from which the jeans are made. Jeans' underlying symbolic appeal derives from their original antifashion significance. Blue jeans make visual allusions to rural democracy, simplicity, unpretentiousness, and the romance for the American West with its free-spirited, self-reliant figures such as the cowboy and the biker. For many consumers, these meanings are still associated with old blue jeans, and are still strong.
>
> *Source: Fred Davis,* Fashion, Culture, and Identity *(Chicago: University of Chicago Press, 1992), p. 71.*

www.pg.com/rumor/index.html

TYPES OF MEANINGS

Consumers' market choices are determined by a variety of values or meanings. Without prior research, marketers rarely know in advance which meanings are pertinent to a specific consumption behavior. Most consumption objects, services, and experiences have multiple meanings, both public and private. The meanings derive from a variety of sources.

Utilitarian Meanings

Traditionally, marketers viewed market choices and consumer preferences as driven by functional or utilitarian value. **Utilitarian meaning** is the *perceived usefulness of a product in terms of its ability to perform functional or physical tasks.* **Functional value** derives from *functional or physical attributes.* The attributes considered generally relate to performance, reliability, durability, number and type of product features, and price. For example, for some farmers an important functional attribute of genetically modified corn (or maize) seed is its resistance to the herbicides they also employ to control noxious weeds.

Functional meanings are important both for product category and brand-choice decisions. For instance, a consumer with no dependents will perceive little functional value

This ad for Lava hand soap conveys the functional value of the product.

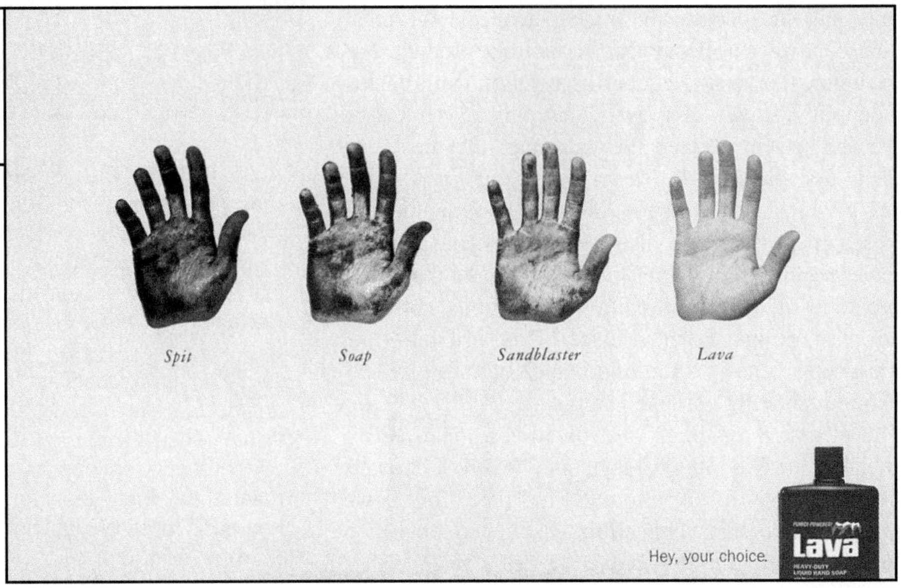

in term life insurance designed to provide financial protection to survivors. This same person might see value in a long-term annuity, which contributes to financial security at retirement. Toothpaste brands are promoted on the differential presence of such functional attributes as fluoride, baking soda, antitartar substances, and breath fresheners. In business-to-business marketing situations, purchasing agents might choose suppliers on the basis of ISO 9000 quality standards, delivery times, credit terms, price, and other functional attributes.

Utilitarian or functional themes are commonly found in advertisements such as that shown above. In a recent study of over 400 ads from the People's Republic of China, informational cues of this type predominated. Availability was emphasized in 99 percent of ads. Performance, a functional attribute, appeared in 48 percent of ads; quality appeared in 23 percent. Price was explicitly mentioned 17 percent of the time. To the majority of low-income, highly involved consumers, utilitarian information is highly valued because most Chinese are just learning to consume. Chinese governmental policy stresses the importance of conveying utilitarian meanings in ads.

Similarly, a study of Saudi Arabian television commercials found product performance and quality were the most frequently employed cues. Again, this is appropriate in a cultural context in which consumers are unfamiliar with many consumer goods. In addition, use of advertising portrayals of emotional family relationships would be inappropriate in spite of the central place family assumes in Saudi society. Many Saudis would view this as a profane use of sacred relationships. In contrast, ads in the United States and Japan contain significantly less utilitarian content meanings. By one estimate, only 39 percent of U.S. print ads contain at least two informational cues, in contrast to 77 percent of the ads in China.[19]

Utilitarian or functional meanings are also associated with the things that people own. In a recent study of North American consumers, functional meanings including financial value accounted for almost 27 percent of responses to questions about objects' meanings. In a study of West Africans, new to the world of mass-produced consumer goods, 22 percent indicated that functional utility accounted for their favorite object preferences.

In the Triad countries, utilitarian meanings are commonly ascribed to everyday shopping experiences as well. Many see shopping as a kind of work. Some consumers also view museums and art galleries primarily as a means to acquire useful skills or ideas.[20]

Sacred and Secular Meanings

Another way to approach consumer meanings is to consider the concepts of the sacred versus the secular. Consumers sometimes express certain aspects of the sacred in their consumption behaviors. Sacred properties are summarized in Exhibit 4.2. Not all sacred things share all of these properties, but to be sacred a thing must share some of them. **Sacred meaning** adheres in those *things that are designed or discovered to be supremely important.* Marketers may benefit by positioning products on sacred characteristics. Products that link consumers to one another and to nature and family or those offering emotional (always mysterious) benefits are positioned near the sacred pole of consumer meanings. For example, because mothers are widely revered, both the Mother's Day holiday and gifts purchased to mark the holiday have been a global success.

A variety of consumption phenomena can be experienced as sacred. These fall into six categories.[21] These categories and some examples are summarized in Exhibit 4.3. Marketers may benefit by linking consumption to sacred phenomena of the types discussed in Exhibit 4.3, such as the paraphernalia sold at religious shrines. In addition to products related to categories identified in Exhibit 4.3, a "sacred" positioning is useful for marketing health, green, and organic products.

Islamic commodities in Cairo, Egypt, provide a striking example of sacred commodities. Among ordinary people, the consumption of prayer beads, Islamic posters, banners, cards, and stickers bearing verses from the Koran become automatic triggers for devotional acts and are responded to as physical manifestations of God's presence. Similarly, in a study among some West Africans, nearly half of the male informants indicated

EXHIBIT 4.2

Sacred Qualities

1. Things seem to belong to a different order of reality.
2. Things elicit strong approach as well as strong avoidance reactions.
3. Objects are contaminated with sacredness.
4. Communication with the sacred is established through sacrifice.
5. Sacred things stand apart from what is ordinary.
6. Individuals feel a focused emotional attachment to sacred things.
7. The sacred is often made concrete in a tangible representation.
8. Ritual surrounds the contact of ordinary persons with the sacred.
9. Often repeated myths document the status of sacred things.
10. Sacred things cannot be understood logically but are mysterious.
11. The spirit of *communitas* (status equality) emerges between participants in sacred experiences.
12. The sacred is capable of producing ecstatic experiences.
13. Sacred things are often inalienable; they cannot be bought and sold.

Source: Russell W. Belk, Melanie Wallendorf, and John F. Sherry Jr., "The Sacred and Profane in Consumer Behavior: Theodicy on the Odyssey," *Journal of Consumer Research* 16 (June 1989), pp. 1–38.

1. **Places:** Sacred sites include cities such as Jerusalem, Lourdes, Mecca, Axum (Ethiopia), and the Forbidden City (China); might also include battlefields (Verdun, Gettysburg) and locations of massacres (My Lai, Wounded Knee); dwellings and buildings (the Parthenon, the Louvre); and certain natural settings (the [Wild] West, National Parks).
2. **Times:** Sacred times include past events such as D-Day or Christian Easter; cyclically occurring events such as Islamic prayers, the secular weekend, and harvest festivals; birth and naming days; and episodes in certain otherwise secular consumption events, such as the playing of national anthems during sporting events.
3. **Tangible things:** Included here are relics (both religious and secular), religious objects, and things identified as sacred because of their rarity and beauty, such as certain art works; things that represent the great ideas, such as the Magna Carta or the U.S. Constitution; natural objects symbolizing life, creation, and renewal; and family heirlooms.
4. **Intangible things:** Included here are magic formulas, dances, names, songs, fraternity and sorority rituals, recipes, and secrets.
5. **Persons or other beings:** Gods, prophets, and saints are religious examples. Military and athletic heroes, film, TV, and rock stars (Elvis, John Lennon, Madonna, Michael Jackson) and a variety of celebrities provide secular examples.
6. **Experiences:** At sacred times and places, experiences such as pilgrimages—both religious (Mecca) and secular (Graceland)—may be sacred. Certain ritual meals (Thanksgiving, Id-l-Fitr) are sacred. Participants and spectators regard certain extreme athletic activities (river rafting, high-altitude climbing) and spectator sports (World Cup, Tour de France, Super Bowl) as sacred.

Source: Russell W. Belk, Melanie Wallendorf, and John F. Sherry Jr., "The Sacred and the Profane in Consumer Behavior: Theodicy on the Odyssey," *Journal of Consumer Research* 16 (June 1989), pp. 1–38.

EXHIBIT 4.3

Sacred Categories and Examples

that items with Islamic or magical connotations were among their favorite possessions. Similarly, more than 50 percent of a sample of Indians residing in Mumbai, India, cited religious items, a family shrine, a family idol, or a guru's photo as favorite possessions.[22] Consumers are more likely to interpret experiences as involving the sacred than products. Some Canadian museum patrons characterize museum going as a sacred event. The reasons for this feeling are not surprising. Similar to holy places (see Exhibit 4.3), museums enforce special codes of conduct, make formal use of space, employ dramatic and specialized architecture, dispense specialized knowledge, and set people and objects apart from everyday life (i.e., the objects in museums may not be touched). Shopping malls have also been conceived as creating sacred space through use of the same architectural techniques as museums. In some cases, retail designers attempt to evoke an aura of sacredness through use of edenic signs—plants, fountains, fishponds, and large birdcages.[23] We may think of the secular properties of things as the reverse of sacred ones. As an example of a product with a **secular meaning,** Static Guard spray is promoted as a technological solution designed to reduce static electric cling of some garments. Note that static cling is a potentially embarrassing but natural phenomenon. Similarly, Oil of Olay skin moisturizer is represented as a technological intervention that can overcome the natural aging process, which many in Western consumer culture see as undesirable. Oil of Olay helps the consumer fight nature. Similarly, Nuprin is a pain reliever that works "even on the worst headache pain." As such, it is a solution to an undesirable natural event, headache. From these examples, you might conclude that products most likely to benefit from positioning near the secular pole of meaning are those that can be used by consumers to counteract unwanted natural events (e.g., personal grooming products) and to conquer or dominate relevant others (e.g., sports equipment, apparel, high-performance products and services, financial products).[24] Secular and functional meanings overlap.

Hedonic Meanings

The value of goods, services, and experiences can also be based on hedonic or aesthetic values. Products acquire **hedonic meaning** when *associated with specific feelings or when they facilitate or perpetuate feelings.* Exhibit 4.4 shows one model that suggests the hedonic meanings of consumption can be positioned in a quadrant consisting of four emotional elements. For example, the excitement of an amusement park ride is made up of pleasure and arousal components, whereas the contentment associated with drowsing at a sunny resort beach consists in pleasure and sleepiness components.

Music, art, and religious artifacts and the places they are consumed are associated with emotional value and hedonic meaning. These products may also symbolize past times and significant others. Products that affect self-image such as clothing, cosmetics, plastic surgery, health foods, tattoos, and other items on public display also provide hedonic value. Demand for popular music released on cassette tapes in developing countries, karaoke players and clubs, oldies-oriented music radio stations, and recreational and home entertainment equipment may all be explained with reference to emotions such as passion, excitement, romance, and nostalgia. Seemingly utilitarian items may also be associated with hedonic meanings. In a recent North American study, hedonic meanings accounted for at least 22 percent of responses to questions about the meaning of objects. We discuss nostalgia and remembered consumption in Chapter 9.[25]

Many consumer products arouse feelings of comfort and security through their associations with pleasant childhood experiences, remembered places, and loved ones. Consumers have fond associations with remedies such as Vicks Vaporub or foods such as Nutella used in childhood. Comfort meaning lies somewhere in the pleasure/sleepiness quadrant of Exhibit 4.4.

A potent source of hedonic meanings available to consumers is experiences. Travel, leisure, and tourist firms and recreational services are all primarily in the business of delivering hedonic meanings to consumers. These meanings often take the form of stories. Shopping too may be valued for its entertainment value and emotional worth. Street markets, themed retail spaces such as Niketown and ESPN Zone, and even Internet auction sites such as eBay are noted for their hedonic meanings. One study showed that young girls found that going to the store with other children unsupervised was charged with emotion. Hanging out in commercial malls may also provide poor, inner-city consumers with entertainment not available on public streets. In these experiences, perceived freedom, fantasy fulfillment, personal growth, experimentation with identity, and escapism may all be part of the meanings derived.[26]

Emotional meanings of consumption are not always positive. Research on addiction, **compulsive consumption,** and **terminal materialism** (or greed) illustrate this dark

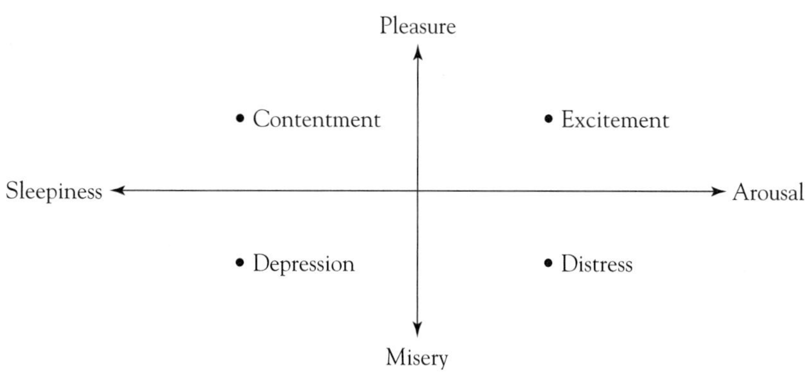

EXHIBIT 4.4

A Model of Hedonic Meaning

Source: Adapted from James A. Russell, "A Circumplex Model of Affect," *Journal of Personality and Social Psychology* 39, no. 6 (1980), pp. 1161–78.

side of consumer meanings. Compulsive consumers have extremely intense material cravings that they project onto purchase or consumption without experiencing any enduring satisfaction. Some consumers engage in compulsive consumption due to feelings of inadequacy, others due to strong impulsive drives. Addicts represent an extreme case where addictive products (e.g., drugs, alcohol) or experiences (e.g., gambling) are used to create and maintain a stable, if distorted, sense of self. People afflicted with terminal materialism, a less debilitating affliction than addiction or compulsive consumption, include those who amass great collections of art, crafts, books, and so forth. They invest goods with the power to attain some sort of personal immortality.[27]

Social Meanings

As discussed in Chapter 12, social values exert a strong influence on many product and brand decisions. There is a **reflexive relationship** between social relationships and the goods individuals consume. Reflexivity means that in consumer society, *people intentionally communicate statements about who they are, what groups they identity with, and those from which they are different primarily through consumer goods. Others tend to see what people consume as expressions of who those people are.* Thus, products can be expressive of who consumers are and to whom they are connected socially (e.g., heirlooms and family photographs).

Consumer goods can be used to express social meanings. To use a historical example, the European colonial powers often enforced Western dress codes on school children in their former colonies as part of their "civilizing" mission. Western dress symbolized acceptance of Western civilization and values. To use a contemporary marketing example, Apple Computer has become a badge of membership in the commercial arts community. Using Cannondale bikes conveyed commitment to serious mountain biking just as Burton boards and clothes express commitment to the snowboarding lifestyle. Some consumers organize around their interactions with brands and simultaneously create meaningful social relationships and negotiate brand meanings. They do this by using the brand to build the social group and sharing personal experiences with the brand, emphasizing some aspects of brand meaning while rejecting others. For example, a group of young Englishwomen formed around the consumption of Häagen-Dazs ice cream. Elaborating on a sexually suggestive ad campaign, consuming the brand became an occasion for getting together, and the ads became part of the group's shared fantasy life.[28]

Consumer goods can be used to alter social meanings. For example, Mountain Dew was an early sponsor of the extreme sports movement in the early 1990s and became linked to the emergence of that lifestyle. Goods and services may acquire social value through their association with positively or negatively valued groups (as we discuss in Chapter 16), and may in turn promote social values. So Tommy Hilfiger clothes became identified with the hip-hop lifestyle for a time and helped spread the popularity of that lifestyle. Similarly, through careful sponsorships Nike became associated with serious professional athletes and athletic performances and helped promote athleticism among some amateur athletes.[29]

The consumption of symbolically charged goods can fuel debate, as when brand names or products associated with gang membership or the Islamic veil associated with fundamentalism are banned in public schools and uniforms are imposed. In these cases people try to control what they fear through symbolic means. Controversy about the social meanings of goods extends into fields such as law enforcement and health care, where studies show that uniforms and civilian clothing influence consumers' perceptions of the quality of service delivery differently.[30]

Brand equity involves the accumulated beliefs, history, sentiment, and value consumers attach to particular brands. We could say it comprises the sum of the brand meanings just described plus consumers' confidence in and loyalty to the brand. Brand equity is enduring. For example, the German cleaning product Persil halted production during World War II. Nonetheless, thanks to residual brand equity, it was successfully reintroduced in the postwar period and resumed its leadership position rather quickly. Brand equity is a crucial asset for firms because of the proliferation of similar products, especially in Triad nations. Large amounts of brand equity differentiate their brands from generic products. Brand equity enables firms to charge price premiums that contribute to corporate profits. Managers' interest in brands is evidently not misplaced, as some authors show that consumers' evaluations of brand quality positively affect company stock valuations. Consequently, marketers aggressively pursue brand equity through integrated marketing communications strategies involving packaging, advertising, promotions, and retail placements. The acquisition of brands and trademarks and their residual brand equity often motivates corporate purchases. Again taking a German example, the Bluna soft drink brand was trademarked in 1939, but ceased production in the 1970s. Nevertheless at the end of 1994, the firm Mineralbrunnen AG spent a considerable sum to acquire this brand, although it was generating no income at the time.[31]

MOVEMENT OF MEANINGS: ORIGINS OF MEANING[32]

From where does the meaning of goods and services come? Fundamentally, meaning is a product of consumer experience. Meanings usually develop from an initial vague state to a state of refinement and stability. Once formed, meanings also may decay and disintegrate. They are formed in social interactions and respond to other consumers denials and agreements. People thrown into interaction, having similar ranges of experience and cultural knowledge, develop common meanings about consumer goods and experiences. In fact, as we have said, consumption involves both the formation and expression of collective meanings. Innovative marketers, designers, artists, and everyday consumers themselves may develop new goods and services, or new arrangements of goods and services, through which meanings can take definite form. Collective taste will be an active force guiding the development of meaning. At the same time, meanings undergo refinement and organization through attachment to products, services, and experiences and to specific social groups.[33]

The **meaning transfer model** is shown in Exhibit 4.5. This model suggests that consumer meanings move between three locations: (1) the culturally constituted world, (2) the good (product, service, or experience), and (3) groups of consumers. Meaning moves between the world and good, and good and consumer or consuming unit. As discussed in Chapter 2, this world is constituted by culture through categories and principles. Cultural categories segment time, space, nature, and the human community. Class, status, gender, age, and occupation (as discussed in Chapter 12) are examples of cultural categories that create a system of distinctions that organize the world. In addition to the cultural categories that compose the scaffolding of consumer meanings, meaning is also shaped by cultural principles. Cultural principles are the concepts, values, assumptions, and organizing ideas that allow phenomena to be distinguished, grouped into categories, ranked, and interrelated.

Acting in conformity with the cultural blueprints comprised of cultural categories and principles, members of a community or market segment constantly play out the utilitarian,

EXHIBIT 4.5

Meaning Transfer Model

Source: Grant McCracken, "Culture and Consumption: A Theoretical Account of the Structure and Movement of the Cultural Meaning of Consumer Goods," *Journal of Consumer Research* 13 (June 1986), pp. 71–84.

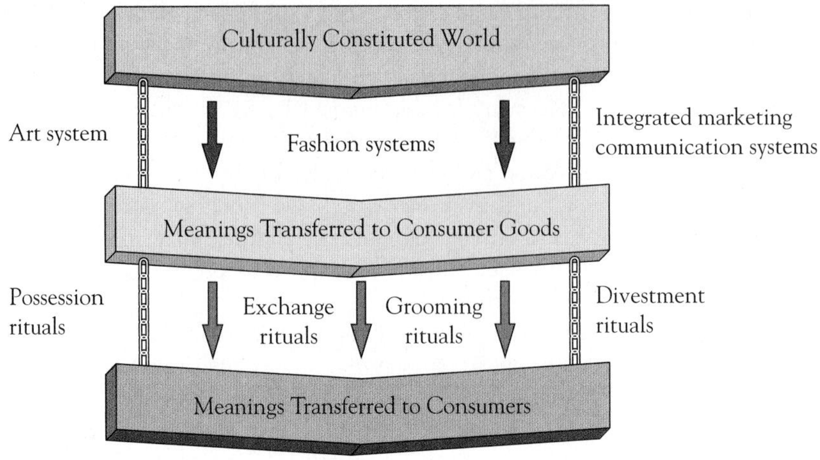

personal, sacred, secular, hedonic, and social meanings of things through their purchase and consumption decisions. In an important sense, members of consumer culture are constantly engaged in the construction of the world in which they live: defining and redefining the meanings of self, community, and products and services themselves.

The Harley-Davidson Company has mastered this meaning transfer process. Managers use product design; staged events such as the famous Sturgis, North Dakota, rally; and sponsorships to create the idea that Harley is an old-fashioned company whose heart remains in the 1950s. The company carefully cultivates ties to outlaw bikers to convince mainstream consumers that Harley upholds the outlaws' moral code that values independence, individualism, loyalty, and masculinity. This imaginative transfer of meanings from the culturally constituted world to the Harley brand allows its customers to experience Harley's version of masculinity, for example, an aura that its marketing communications imbue with authenticity. Through ownership of motorcycles and branded merchandise, care and maintenance of the bike, and participation in rallies and events that foster the exchange of experience and insider knowledge, consumers absorb the brand's meaning.[34]

Consumers' expression of likes and dislikes (cultural principles) not only distinguishes goods from one another but also distinguishes consumers from one another. In this way consumers are also divided into cultural categories. Thus, in Japan where people dress to meet social roles, students, businessmen, bureaucrats, intellectuals, office ladies, and youth-culture persons are all easily recognized through stereotypical clothing choices. In this context consumer likes and dislikes tend toward fine and subtle distinctions to which marketers are finely attuned.[35]

LINKING CULTURAL MEANINGS AND PRODUCT MEANINGS[36]

Marketers use marketing communications to connect cultural meanings to consumption objects. As shown in Exhibit 4.5, cultural production systems such as the advertising, retailing, and fashion industries actively influence the meanings that are associated with goods. For example, Japanese retailers invented the cultural category of early autumn fashions to create a new product positioning.[37]

Marketing communications work to transfer meaning by successfully bringing together a consumer good, fashion, for example, with a culturally particular representation of the world, the early autumn season, for instance. To effect the transfer, the advertiser typically begins with the advertised product or service. Then, a communication plan is created that identifies particular meanings to be associated with the brand. The advertiser also identifies where the desired meanings to be associated with the brand are resident in the world in terms of categories of time, place, emotion, and person. He or she must choose from the alternatives established by the available network of cultural categories and principles recognized by the intended audience. Advertising formats (e.g., humor, fantasy, or slice-of-life) and treatments (e.g., drama, lecture, soap opera; one- or two-sided portrayal) are selected to portray the world in a way that associates the desired meanings with the product. Verbal and visual conventions are used to provide the target of the advertising message with the chance to decode the intended link between the representation and the consumer good portrayed.

Advertising Texts and Consumption Meanings

Advertising texts are symbolic statements that link signs, interpretants, and meanings together. The message presumes or instructs consumers about meaningful relationships. Details about various message forms are shown in Exhibit 4.6. Remember, the transfer of meaning supposes consumers who understand these message forms and can interpret the meanings presented within them.

Turning now to message content, it might be useful for you to imagine that advertising serves as a kind of **culture/consumption dictionary.** Its entries are *products, services, and experiences, and their definitions are cultural meanings.* Advertising typically does not draw on the entire range of meanings available in a culture but on a narrower,

EXHIBIT 4.6

Advertising Treatments

1. **Lecture:** Informational content is emphasized. The message source implicitly is speaking directly to the reader. The ads use arguments to establish the validity of asserted claims; provide structured reasons in support of claims.
2. **Report:** Specific data are reported to support a claim or general principle that supports a claim. Comparative advertising for appliances and industrial equipment often adopts this mode to establish the claim of product superiority. Sometimes, these ads take the form of testimonials.
3. **Syllogism:** Claims and findings are advanced, and the reader is invited to deduce the implicit claim of product superiority. This category includes the simple announcement ad, which is common in retailing and in marketing bland industrial products.
4. **Drama:** Employs narrative, metaphor, and other literary devices to convey meaning. Dramatic ads tell a story. There is no explicit message source. For example, American Tourister asserts bellboys are gorillas when it comes to handling luggage. Merrill Lynch invokes the "herd apart" with its lone bulls. The pink bunny's (long-lasting) Energizer batteries enable it to escape King Kong.
5. **Allegory or fable:** In ads of this type, a claim is argued by deduction, but the terms employed are symbolic rather than factual. The parable of ring-around-the-collar resolved with soap powder is an example. The traveler's checks (American Express) lost or stolen in a foreign land is also an advertising fable.
6. **Myth/transformation:** Here, the object of the ad emphasizes the value or interpretation to be given to an event. The event is recounted figuratively rather than literally. In argumentation by myth, the story transforms the event's meanings. For example, Bombay Sapphire gin turns into (priceless) gemstones as it splashes out of the glass.
7. **Soap opera:** Uses episodic, ongoing narratives, whose ostensible subject is domestic relationships in real time. These ads feature simple, unidimensional characters, and assume traditional, middle-class values and a feminine aesthetic.

Who could resist the refreshing feel of natural herbs grown in the Swiss Alps?

widely understood set in order to communicate to as many members of a target market as possible. Meanings must not be too hard for consumers/readers to understand. For example, animal characters are widely used brand symbols because most consumers understand animals' cultural meanings. Animal logos facilitate meaning transfer. However, as the technological ability to measure media preferences and customize messages increases, the constraints on symbols and meanings used in marketing communications too may loosen.[38]

The ad for Ricola Swiss Herb Lozenges pictured above provides an example of what we've just said. This print ad uses a humorous format and a fable type of treatment to associate the desired brand meanings with the brand. The figure in the ad is a widely recognized fictional figure from horror films symbolic of death and destruction. The joke resides partly in his/her light-heartedly skipping through an alpine meadow blowing bubbles. And it depends partly on mockery of conventional celebrity endorsers. The humor is ironic. The slasher's joyous attitude resonates with the field of fresh wildflowers and gleaming snow atop the Matterhorn Mountain, shown in the background to convey the core meaning of refreshment. Ricola relies on text and image to convey the conventional meanings of health, naturalness, and freshness and pleasure associated with flowers, bubbles, the Alps, and snow-capped mountains to the target audience. The implication is that if Ricola can transform the slasher's mood, it can transfer the target's mood. The firm hopes that when consumers are looking for natural refreshment and fun, they'll think Ricola.[39]

The full details of meaning transfer in advertising are still being worked out. But we can discuss some figures of speech at the core of the culture/consumption dictionary employed in ads. Referring back to the semiotic triangle addressed earlier, we distinguished sign, interpretant, and object. Ads use figurative language to develop links between sign, object, and interpretant. For example, ads often use **similes,** *figures of speech that explicitly use a comparative term such as "like" or "as."* Citizen Nobilia ads use similes to link wristwatches (the object) with animals (the sign), such as "As beautiful as a peacock." The ads aim to transfer the evocative associated meanings (the interpretant) of peacocks (the object) to their wristwatches.

Advertising copy also makes extensive use of **metaphors,** which are *like similes but with the comparative term omitted.* Examples include "Foster's is Australian for beer," "Alitalia is Italy," and the Jaguar XJ-S "is the stuff of legends." In these cases, Australia, Italy, and legend are the meaningful signs the advertisers wish to associate with the products. Visuals are typically employed to remind or instruct readers/consumers of the meaningful associations the signs are meant to evoke. In the Ricola ad shown on the opposite page, the happy slasher is a visual metaphor for refreshment. See if you can find other examples of ads that use metaphors in this text.

Symbols are a powerful form of sign used in advertising. Unlike the other two figures of speech, symbols *omit any explicit expression of comparison between sign and object.* Sports team mascots are of this type, such as the Amsterdam Ajax soccer team that uses the image of an ancient Greek warrior or the Toronto Maple Leafs ice hockey team. Symbols are powerful mechanisms of meaning transfer because when readers/consumers expend the mental effort to interpret the meaning of the symbol, they become actively involved and in some sense accept the associations evoked by the symbol. Of course, not all associations between sign, object, and interpretant are possible. Instead, the linkages must be plausible. Exaggeration and simplification of meanings on the basis of relatively well-known cultural principles and categories help convey symbolic meaning.[40]

Visual Conventions and Consumption Meanings

Responses to marketing communication draw on a shared, learned vocabulary of visual conventions. The selection and combination of visual symbols to achieve persuasive effects is becoming increasingly important in marketing communications. In the Triad countries there is a trend toward using less language in advertising, especially print media.[41]

Visuals in marketing communications are symbolic. Their significance stems from the culturally constituted world of meaning, not from any resemblance they may have to nature. This is easy to understand in the case of the slasher pictured above, since he/she is purely fictitious. But, in marketing communications, everything from the most literal portrait to the most fanciful image is equally symbolic. The visual viewpoint, focus, graphics, and layout work together in specific ways to communicate a particular meaning. Graphic elements within the pictorial field of an advertisement suggest a concept, create a fiction, or refer to other images and texts with which marketers hope the target reader is familiar.

To interpret these images, consumers/readers must recognize advertising visuals as examples of figurative communication rather than true representations. Consumers engage in symbolic thought to interpret the visual message and decode its meaning. Consumers often encounter entirely fictive images such as those of the (resilient) Michelin Man, (comforting, filling) Pillsbury Doughboy, (adorable, dependent) World Wildlife Federation Panda, (crafty, resilient) Asterix the Gaulois (France), (rich, royal, persuasive) Loeki the Lion (Amsterdam), or the (folkloric) Golden Nightingale (Russia). Yet

Brand Icons Go Global

INDUSTRY INSIGHTS 4.2

The core of Grand Metropolitan's food business is the Pillsbury company, comprising four major American brands: Pillsbury (bakery products), Green Giant (packaged vegetables), Häagen Dazs (frozen desserts), and Burger King (fast food). All these brands have substantial volume and profitability, and recent attempts have focused on building them into global "megabrands." In the case of Pillsbury, the most enduring symbol of the brand is the doughboy, followed by the Green Giant and the Little Sprout. Pillsbury has attempted to use evidence that these are more than animated characters, and in fact are useful vehicles for establishing Pillsbury brands with new consumers worldwide. The characters' unique, intense, and clear imagery contributes to their memorability.

Source: Sigrid Bekmeier, "Determination of Brand-Equity from a Consumer-Oriented Perspective," in European Advances in Consumer Research, *vol. 2, ed. Flemming Hansen (Provo, UT: Association for Consumer Research, 1995), pp. 224–36; and Akshay R. Rao, "Views from across the Bridge: Industry Perspectives on Brand Equity Management," in* Advances in Consumer Research, *vol. 23, eds. Kim Corfman and John Lynch (Provo, UT: Association for Consumer Research, 1996), p. 12.*

consumers do decode the metaphorical, purposeful (rhetorical) meanings of these figures as suggested by the adjectives within parentheses above. Advertisers generally do not need to resort to logical explanations. Of course, powerful associations in one culture may not apply in another, which causes problems in cross-national advertising. Nevertheless, as Industry Insights 4.2 indicates, many visual brand icons are going global.

Characters and Consumption Meanings

Cultural meanings are connected to the product not only through text but also through characters associated with ads. Some ads contain explicit characters such as a real or fictional spokesperson. When the character is a real or fictional spokesperson, such as a celebrity endorser, advertising effectiveness depends on the credibility, trustworthiness, expertise, and likeability of the spokesperson, as discussed in Chapter 15. Exhibit 4.7 shows how meaning transfer works with celebrity endorsers. The celebrity endorser (media or political figure, cartoon character) develops a meaningful **persona** as a result of the roles she or he has assumed in the past and the social context, persons, and objects with which she or he has interacted in those roles. In this way the endorser draws meaning from the culturally constituted world. For example, the characters they portray in films and television form Harrison Ford's or Hong Kong star Jackie Chan's heroic personae and Julia Robert's or Indian star Hrithik Roshan's romantic personae. The ad for the Omega Constellation watch on page 139 provides an example of the role of a persona in meaning transfer. The target market is meant to attach Cindy Crawford's fashion credibility, developed through many years of association with the high fashion clothing and make-up to the watch that she is endorsing. To interpret the visual, the target market must recognize Cindy as a fashion icon herself, that her persona is synonymous with fashion. The meaning transfer process is completed when the consumer purchases and wears the watch. He or she then has the opportunity to capture and enjoy some of the meanings associated with the endorser's persona. In the endorsement process, the meanings move from the celebrity to the product through figures of speech, contiguity (closeness), similarity, and so forth.

In one study, researchers found that the meanings attributed to previously unendorsed products—bath towels and VCRs—changed dramatically when they were linked to Madonna or to model Christie Brinkley. Interestingly, the meanings picked up from the two celebrities were similar across the products, although the meanings differed significantly between the two endorsers. Managers need to be sensitive to both the desirable and the undesirable attributes of potential endorsers since either meaning may be passed on to the products.[42]

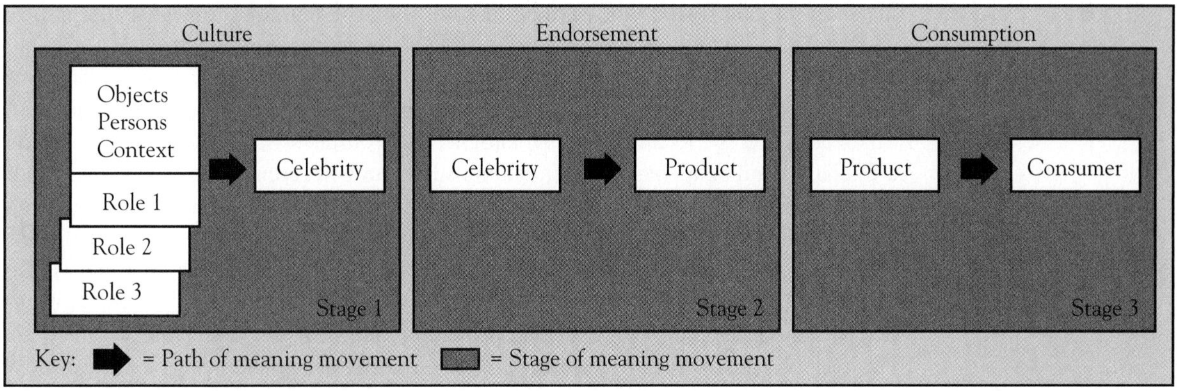

EXHIBIT 4.7

Meaning Movement and the Endorsement Process

Source: Grant McCracken, "Who Is the Celebrity Endorser? Cultural Foundations of the Endorsement Process," *Journal of Consumer Research* 16 (December 1989), pp. 310–21.

Advertising connects market segments and particular goods. Once having established these links, advertisers can use these symbolic relations as given, and so do consumers. For example, diamonds may be marketed by likening them to eternal love (a cultural category of time and emotion), creating a symbolism where the mineral (object) means something not in its own terms, as a rock, but in human terms, as a sign. Thus, a diamond comes to mean love and endurance (interpretants) for consumers. Once advertising has successfully made the connection, consumers may also begin to read

Cindy Crawford's persona is synonymous with high fashion.

Ortega gives its family brand a consistent image by using conventional associations between color and national culture.

meaning the other way; that is, they take the sign, the diamond, for what it signifies, enduring love. Symbolic associations like this are powerful marketing tools.[43] Silk Cut, a brand of cigarettes marketed in Great Britain and Europe, makes a symbolic reference to desirable qualities of creaminess and mildness it would like to associate with Silk Cut indirectly. Its ads do so by using a color (purple swirls) and typeface used on a Cadbury's milk chocolate bar. The famous (to European consumers) "glass and a half of full-cream dairy milk" (interpretant), which *another* advertisement has told them goes into Cadbury's chocolate, can be evoked by Silk Cut cigarettes symbolically.

The principle by which a subtly modified sign evokes a familiar set of meanings is also discussed in Chapter 8. This stimulus generalization, or halo effect, can be seen underlying the principle of product line packaging and in brand extensions of all types. For example, the distinctive red and yellow colors and design elements on Ortega Mexican food products are those that have already been established through previous media portrayals as those associated with Mexican cuisine and culture. Of course, this symbolic association is purely conventional; there is nothing intrinsically red or yellow about Mexican culture![44]

LINKING PRODUCT MEANINGS AND CONSUMPTION MEANINGS

Neither advertising nor other cultural production systems simply bestow meanings on objects or consumers. Consumers play an active role in linking product and consumption meanings.[45] The success of many marketing campaigns depends on actively engaged consumers. This is true of markets in the Triad nations as well as in the emerging markets of the NICs and transitional economies. In fact, as shown in Exhibit 4.5, consumers are actively involved in meaning transfer. In some senses, they create product meanings. They also take meanings from products. They even create themselves both in interpreting marketing communications and through consumption of the goods and services promoted.

Consumers provide products or their advertising images with meaning through their recognition of what they stand for, what they symbolize, at least within the space of an ad. Thus, consumers give the clarinet in the Johnny Walker ad mentioned earlier its meaning for use in the ad. By presenting the instrument and the scotch together, marketers invite consumers to transfer meaning from the culturally constituted world of meanings associated with clarinets to the product, Johnny Walker. Similarly, in a series of television ads for Grey Poupon mustard, Rolls Royce automobiles are prominently featured. Again, no explicit claim is made about the luxuriousness, quality, good taste, and timeliness of either the automobile or the mustard. Consumers draw on their already constituted fund of cultural knowledge to decode the meaning of the automobile and link it to the mustard. Thus, in the sense just indicated, advertisers are correct when they claim that they cannot create meaning; consumers create the meaning of the ad through their interpretations.[46]

Second, people take meanings from ads and products. By using particular products, with particular associated meanings and not others, consumers differentiate themselves from other people who consume different products with presumably different meanings. The woman who wears Chanel No. 5, advertised by French actress Catherine Deneuve, differs from the woman who wears Babe, advertised by American actress Margaux Hemingway. By consuming one and not the other of these products, people partake of the meanings associated with the products and the characters that serve as signs for the products. Consumers may use products to create meaningful new dis-

Using the rhetorical device termed apostrophe.

tinctions between groups. This is discussed more thoroughly in Chapter 11 on lifestyles. Third, there is a sense in which consumers allow themselves to be created by ads and products. People sometimes buy not just to become a part of the group that the product represents but because they *already* feel that they *naturally* belong to that group and therefore will buy the product on offer. In some cases a consumer does not so much choose products from an array, nor in response to an advertisement, but more powerfully, by recognizing oneself as the kind of person who will use a specific product or brand. Some successful ads and acts of consumption create their own consumers. They tell the consumer what he or she is like.

It is easy to think of ads for products that hail consumers directly. This technique of *direct hailing* is a rhetorical device termed **apostrophe.** A Kirin Light Beer can label in Japan reads, "I'm off. I'll gladly work off 12 ozs. to savor a good beer." Similarly an outdoor ad for Bang & Olufsen music systems reads, "I want, I want . . . a life less ordinary" (see advertising banner above), and the print ad below for a French

This print ad from the French discount retailer TATI reads, Tati is me! This illustrates the persuasive tactic called apostrophe.

discount store reads, "Tati, it's me." Using first- and second-person pronouns in ads suggests that the consumer is already a person desirous of savoring a good beer in the first case and of possessing the features of extraordinariness in the second. Advertisements of the Bang & Olufsen and Tati variety invite the consumers to read their individual qualities into the product, implying they had them in the first place. In other words, having been attributed with the qualities connected with a product, viewers are projected as buyers. Given that they embody the beliefs implied in the ad, they will act in accordance and buy products that symbolize those beliefs.

Direct hailing is consistent with the ideas of marketing communication held by many copywriters. Copywriters argue that they create effective advertisements when they develop an empathic emotional connection between some product meaning and the desires of an imagined consumer. That is, they seek to make ads so that consumers recognize the product is hailing them directly.[47]

MODES AND RITUALS OF MEANING TRANSFER

The final step in meaning transfer involves more than just interpretation of marketing communications; it involves temporary or permanent acquisition of goods and services. Various forms of symbolic action transfer meaning from goods to consumers. Among these forms of symbolic action we can distinguish ordinary behaviors that consumers engage in on a regular basis and behaviors that have a ritual character.

Exhibit 4.8 suggests four main categories of ordinary consumption modes and provides some examples of these behaviors. The four modes are experiencing, playing, integrating, and classifying. Experience and playing are hedonic meaning transfer activities, whereas integrating and classifying are utilitarian ones. This division is consistent with the distinction made earlier between utilitarian and hedonic meanings.

Playing and classifying are more social activities, whereas experiencing and integrating are more individual activities. The former types of meaning transfer activities help consumers to establish social identity. For instance, dressing in team colors to symbolize fandom is a form of classification through objects commonly seen among world soccer fans. Experiencing and integrating help consumers establish individual identity. Contrasting features of different brands of major appliances provides a form of utilitarian meanings—evaluation—to a consumer, for example. Or taking a solo hiking trip through Germany's Black Forest might provide a form of hedonic meanings—appreciation—to a consumer.

In addition to the ordinary modes of meaning transfer, we can also identify a number of special behaviors. Among the special behaviors consumers employ to transfer meaning from objects to themselves are possession rituals, grooming rituals, exchange rituals, and divestment rituals. The first two types are mechanisms by which people invest personal, idiosyncratic meanings in goods. The latter two, discussed in Chapters 16 and 19, respectively, involve the further movement of goods and the meanings they hold to other consumers.[48]

Possession rituals allow consumers to assume ownership of product meanings. Customizing, decorating, personalizing, cleaning, discussing, displaying, and photographing are some of the activities consumers engage in to assert possession and draw from the object the qualities that advertising, the fashion system, or retailing generally have invested in them. At the simplest level, consumers may remove tags, packaging, pins, labels, and other markers of the retail origins of goods. To assert possession of paperbound books sold in Great Britain or bedding and cushions sold in North America, consumers tear off covers and tags, respectively, which prohibit commercial resale. One

EXHIBIT 4.8

Modes of Meaning Transfer

Modes	Definitions	Examples
Experiencing		
Accounting	Typifying actions and objects, assigning them specific meanings and values, then contextualizing the account to enrich it.	Doing play-by-play of a live or televised sports event or dance recital.
Evaluating	Making comparisons to norms, history, and conventions.	Citing historical games or players to characterize recent ones; comparing pizzas in terms of crust, toppings, cheese, delivery speed, price.
Appreciating	Applying aesthetic and emotional frameworks to actions and to objects.	A graceful play in sports is much discussed; a hot dog is said to taste special at the ballpark.
Playing		
Communing	Sharing consumption experiences with others so that consumption becomes a mutual experience.	The temporary community that develops among participants in sporting events, tours, adventure recreations, religious pageants, community festivals, and so on.
Socializing	Consumers use their personal (past or present) consumption experiences to entertain one another.	Consumption-related storytelling of all kinds; acting as a market maven.
Integrating		
Assimilating	Methods by which consumers become competent participants (see Experiencing above).	Joining "the wave"; following one's preferred football team to away games; adopting the jargon of the consumption context; creating personalized, traditional holiday celebrations.
Producing	Methods by which consumers act to enhance their perception that they are significantly involved in production of the object or action.	The variety of celebrity-worship activities that enable people to feel bonded with those celebrities; contributing comments or suggestions; predicting the outcome of sports events.
Personalizing	Practices through which consumers add extrainstitutional elements to consumption to assert the individuality of their relationship to the object or action.	Developing innovative uses for products; modifying holiday celebrations significantly; customizing dress, cars, houses, bodies, and other products.
Classifying		
Through objects	Using shared meanings of consumption objects to classify oneself or others.	Using documentary markers such as souvenirs, T-shirts, bumper stickers, matched clothing, jewelry, cycles, or cars.
Through actions	Using the manner in which one experiences a consumption object or event to classify oneself or others; mentoring novice consumers.	Engaging in novice/expert behaviors; expressions of connoisseurship in sports, crafts, or the arts.

Source: Douglas B. Holt, "How Consumers Consume: A Typology of Consumption Practices," *Journal of Consumer Research* 22 (June 1995), pp. 1–16.

study found that inner-city children left the tags on their clothing to display to their peers. The tag provided evidence that the item was purchased at a prestigious retail outlet and became a potent personal statement.[49]

Customizing is a more elaborate procedure for asserting possession. Customization allows for the encoding of personal meanings into products. For example, tailoring and monogramming of new clothing are devices that allow consumers to assert unique claims to ownership. Custom building of homes enables consumers to express elaborate personal meanings. In one study, the authors found that custom-made homes in North America express the idea of the home as a process that starts with the anticipation of building and extends into the living experience. A colonial-style home symbolizes traditional values to one consumer. The construction of a solar home symbolizes a harmonious, natural lifestyle to another.[50]

Evidence of repeated interaction with possessions seems to be one way in which meaning and value are asserted. Many kinds of collections are cleaned, arranged, and displayed for public view. Postage-stamp collectors, for example, compete for prizes at international competitions on the basis of quality and creativity of the arrangements and displays they make of the stamps. These displays may include stories (called postal history) about the stamps and their use. Unique, personal arrangements may dramatically increase the value of the stamps. Note that in these collections, canceled stamps without instrumental value are generally more valuable than unused stamps.

Various institutions, including governments, engage in possession rituals to assert ownership of public property. For example, historical preservation commissions lobby to apply the label "historical" to landmarks, buildings, and even neighborhoods. This device asserts special ownership qualities and may even protect these items from resale or redevelopment.

Grooming rituals are repeated actions necessary to draw perishable meanings from goods. Human grooming behavior is a form of body language communicating specific messages about an individual's social status, maturity, aspirations, conformity, and morality. The meaning of certain items of clothing, hairstyles, makeup, and even certain "looks" are coaxed out through the performance of a sequence of special behaviors. Ritual paraphernalia such as shampoo, lotions, henna, paint, hair curlers, hair dryers, and false hair are valued for their transformational properties. Sometimes modern consumer products are invested with the same sort of energizing magical power

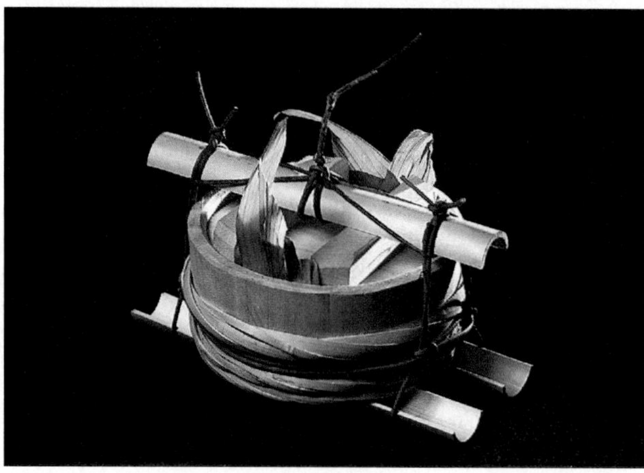

In Japan, packaging may convey more meaning than the product it contains.

that indigenous peoples may ascribe to herbal concoctions devised by local shamans. The aim of many grooming rituals is to enable the consumer to take on the powers of confidence, beauty, defense, glamour, and so forth, perceived to reside in certain brands. Events ranging from "voguing" to Carnival are examples of events related to extended grooming rituals.

Often, it is not the consumer but the good that needs to be groomed in order to maintain meaning. In North American culture, automobiles and homes are highly likely to be subject to such attention. In Japan, wrapping and packaging are important art forms, and most retail stores will wrap or package even the most conventional purchase with great care. Packaging conveys more meaning than the gift itself. An example of traditional Japanese packaging appears on page 144. The Chinese or Indian family altar is also subject to such special care. Collections are typically subject to grooming rituals. Cleaning, rearranging, sorting, and labeling these objects are symbolic behaviors that allow consumers to freshen the meanings they draw from them.[51]

MALLEABILITY AND MOVEMENT OF MEANINGS

The meanings of products and services are malleable; that is to say, there is considerable variation in the extent to which consumers share meanings. This malleability can be examined either at the product level or at the social level. For marketers, the choice depends on whether one is more interested in the development of positioning strategy or segmentation and targeting strategies, as discussed in Chapter 5. Both approaches provide insight into consumer behavior.

It may be useful to think about product meaning as a multilevel construct. Meaningful associations attached to product concept might be arranged into four levels: (1) tangible attributes, (2) cultural associations, (3) subcultural associations (those relevant to a particular group), and (4) unique, personal associations. These four categories of meaning are a continuum, ranging from commonly shared judgments about the tangible qualities of products to unique, intangible personal meanings. For example, in evaluating a sofa (or a commode in British English), most consumers could agree if it was covered in leather, a tangible attribute. At a cultural level, many consumers could also agree that leather is a sign of luxury. At a subcultural level, some consumers might regard a leather sofa as appropriate for a den or library, but not for a formal living room. Members of another subcultural group might object to leather as a by-product of treatment of animals they find objectionable. Color might play a role here: black leather might evoke a bachelor apartment; white might evoke an idle wealthy lifestyle. The possible personal meanings of a leather sofa are probably too numerous to identify. Some might see purchasing such a sofa as a status symbol; for others, it might represent a nostalgic memory of a childhood home. People are more likely to agree about the physical attributes of products than about their personal meanings.[52]

Products may be viewed as displaying varying proportions of common cultural, subcultural, and unique, personal associations. The elective quality of personal meaning in advanced consumer cultures means that consumers often define themselves through the meanings of consumer goods.

T-shirts are vehicles consumers use to assert a variety of personal meanings. Emblazoned with words and pictures, they are used to indicate occupation of a cultural category such as sports fan (Texas Longhorn), affiliate of a university or corporation, member of a family (Smith family reunion, Provo, Utah, 1995) or other group (I am a UFO); to indicate passage through a social status change (U2 Unforgettable Fire, 1985 Tour; I survived Woodstock 94); or as a trophy of some personal accomplishment (Beautiful

British Columbia) or group success (Run for Cancer). Savvy marketers use consumers' chameleon-like behavior to advantage by providing them with promotional T-shirts and other identity-bestowing giveaways.[53]

Special possessions, those regarded as *extensions of the self* (see Chapter 10)—pets, collections, memory-laden objects, and symbols of core cultural values, for example—often proclaim idiosyncratic meanings.[54]

By contrast with idiosyncratic meanings, heavily advertised, branded consumer goods carry a shared set of meanings, even if these are taken for granted by consumers. For example, T-shirts emblazoned with brand names assert the consumer's acceptance of the meanings associated with the brand. Individuals, groups, and firms might exploit differences in widely shared product meanings. Thus, Harley-Davidson motorcycles carry a general set of meanings recognized by North American consumers, other subcultural sets of meanings recognized by members of HOG (Harley Owners Groups) and outlaw motorcycle groups, and still other sets of meanings recognized by individual Harley owners contemplating a customized bike. Please note, however, that all goods are invested with varying proportions of meaning types. It makes no sense to speak of goods without cultural meaning since meaning, however idiosyncratic or general, is a cultural phenomenon.

Marketers commonly work to change meanings at each of the four levels cited above in order to align their products with the desires of target markets. This is central to the product repositioning strategies discussed in Chapter 5. Consider tangible attributes. The North American beef industry has worked hard to promote beef as a low-fat food in response to concern about the fat content of red meats. It has done so in part by re-engineering beef cattle so that they are leaner than they were 30 years ago. In this way, the beef industry has changed the tangible attributes of beef to reflect consumers' beliefs about the link between fat and health. You can explore these industry marketing efforts at the industry website.

@ www.beef.org

Marketers seek to exploit the unique, personal meanings that develop between people and products. IBM's ad campaign for its Powerbook computers was called "What's on Your Powerbook?" This campaign showed unique semicelebrity spokespersons with their Powerbooks and lists of the idiosyncratic but meaningful items stored on their computers. Photographs, creative works, personal phone numbers, and other personalized items figure prominently in these lists, suggesting that the Powerbook is a vehicle for the expression of customers' unique qualities.

Marketers also work to change the subcultural associations between brands and meanings. Again, this is often part of a product repositioning strategy. For example, lumber and hardware stores have traditionally appealed primarily to men. The Lowe's do-it-yourself lumber and hardware company is working to reposition itself to appeal to women. Similarly, Las Vegas has sought to reposition itself away from the meanings of gambling, gangsters, and prostitution that appealed to a niche market, and towards the meanings of a family-friendly, spectacular resort that appeals to a mass market.[55]

COLLECTING AND MUSEUMS

Collecting is *the selective, active, and longitudinal acquisition, possession, and disposition of an interrelated set of differentiated objects (material things, ideas, beings, or experiences) that contribute to and derive extraordinary meaning from the set itself.* Collecting provides consumers with important benefits. These include opportunities to experience hedonic and sacred meanings and to engage in possession and exchange rituals. Once items enter a collection they stop serving their utilitarian functions as, for

Some Examples of Collecting Phenomena

CONSUMER CHRONICLES 4.3

- Movie memorabilia is especially rewarding to collectors. A pair of ruby slippers worn in *The Wizard of Oz* fetched $1,650,000. Someone purchased a uniform worn by Elvis Presley in *G.I. Blues* for $12,000. A large poster of the movie *Casablanca* sells for $17,500.
- The founder of the G.I. Joe Club of America, himself an avid collector of more than 500 of the action figures, desires to build a national monument to the character. Early model versions of the toy now sell for more than $2,000.
- A teddy bear was recently sold at Sotheby's for a record $85,000. The auction house also sold 152 cookie jars owned by Andy Warhol for $247,830 and three Campbell's soup can banks for $7,150.
- Among the rapidly appreciating speculative investments some experts view as a hedge against inflation are Elvis memorabilia, presidential autographs, rare books, toy figurines, and American muscle cars (1950–1960s).
- Collecting behavior radiates to increasingly novel niches. In Japan, prepaid magnetic cards intended to render service encounters more automatic and convenient have spawned a market of more than 200,000 collectors. In France, several magazines specialize in displaying automatic telephone credit cards on which advertising appears for avid collectors. Even junk mail has become a collectible for some consumers.

Source: Russell W. Belk, Melanie Wallendorf, John F. Sherry Jr., and Morris B. Holbrook, "Collecting in a Consumer Culture," Highways and Buyways: Naturalistic Research from the Consumer Behavior Odyssey, *ed. Russell W. Belk (Provo, UT: Association for Consumer Research, 1991), pp. 185–86.*

instance, advertisements, shells on a beach, postage stamps, or dolls for ordinary play. For collectors, the meaning of even those objects that retain their original uses, such as antique furniture or recordings, is more than utilitarian. Through collecting, objects are imbued with a personal significance. Products leave the marketplace and become **singularized** through *possession and grooming rituals (accounting, evaluating, appreciating, and assimilating).* Consumer Chronicles 4.3 provides some evidence of the monetary value and importance of collecting to consumers.[56]

Items are added to collections according to some systematic pattern, although the cultural principles that provide a blueprint for the collection and meanings that consumers derive from them may be highly personal. Consumer Chronicles 4.4 concerns boys who trade superhero cards. In this case, aesthetic and textual meanings and market value are the guiding criteria for collecting. Older boys focus more on market value and **textual meanings,** that is, the character's role in comics, television shows, video games, and so forth. Younger boys focus more on aesthetic meaning, the way the cards look and feel. They prize holographic and specially coated cards. Boys value trading for itself, as an extended game (hedonic meaning) that builds social networks among the boys. Older boys also calculate both current and future market values in building their collections.[57]

Collecting is a behavior characteristic of both individuals and institutions. Individual collectors come in so many guises that it is difficult to generalize about the profile of serious collectors. If you are familiar with the British or American television series *Antiques Roadshow,* you've probably encountered all sorts of collectors. Religious institutions have long been repositories of collections of art and other relics. The Catholic

Boys and Their Trading Cards

CONSUMER CHRONICLES 4.4

Andrew Foster, then five years old, had been attending his new school, a private progressive day school in Rochester, New York, no more than a few weeks when he came home with two trading cards and a plastic sheet into which to insert them. He had received these cards from one of the oldest and most popular boys in his school, a boy whose collection of cards was perhaps the largest and most extensive. As it happened, there was a box of baseball cards in the attic, and Andrew added some of these to his sheet. The next day, Andrew returned from school with no baseball cards; but he did have an assortment of other cards, including football cards, a GI Joe card, and a Batman card. Andrew had been recruited into a social network of card traders.

Soon, Andrew would sit with two of his newcomer friends on the edge of a circle of older boys who were examining and trading their cards. The young ones would say nothing but watch and listen avidly as the older boys discussed the relative merits of the cards and negotiated trades. Later, Andrew became a participant in this sort of trading. He acquired a binder and many more plastic display pages. He developed a repertory of phrases he had heard from the older boys and learned how to talk about cards, to evaluate trades, and to articulate trading rules. While Andrew managed to enlarge his collection through trading the baseball cards, he also asked his parents to buy packs of certain super hero cards, Marvel Masterpieces Series 2 and Skybox's Marvel Universe Series 4, that were extremely popular at school.

Source: Nancy Foster and Robert J. Foster, "Learning Fetishism? Boys Consumption Work with Marvel Super Heroes Trading Cards," paper presented at the 93rd annual meeting of the American Anthropological Association, Atlanta, November 30, 1994.

www.exhibitionsonline.org/artbrief/corpart1.htm

Church holds enormous stocks of art and relics. The political and economic strength of corporations and nations is judged in part by the size and diversity of their collections.[58] The British Museum (Great Britain), the Hermitage (Russia), the Imperial Library (China), the Louvre (France), the Rijksmuseum (Netherlands), the Smithsonian Institution (United States), and the National Museum of Anthropology (Mexico) are just a few among the great collections held by nations.

What do collections mean to consumers? Among the important overlapping meanings collections appear to hold are control; magical power; evocation of other times, people, and places; legitimization for materialism; an expanded sense of self; and, of course, hedonic pleasure. Evidence for magical meanings of collections can be seen in the setting apart of collections from the ordinary, the reverent care given them, and the treasure tales that surround collecting arenas.

Some collections allow collectors to enter into fantasy worlds represented by their dolls, baseball cards, stamps, and so forth. One of the authors of this text knew a young man whose passion for the Victorian Age led not only to furnishing his home in Victoriana but to wearing Victorian clothing, using no electricity or electric appliances, driving a turn-of-the-century vehicle, and earning his living as a vintage player-piano restorer.

Collecting is big business. The modern collecting industry consists of a cultural production system that, like the advertising system discussed above, serves to transfer meaning from the culturally constituted world to collectibles as well as to distribute them among the collectors. Auction houses such as Sotheby's and Christie's are widely known. Museums and retail galleries display collections of various kinds and place the stamp of connoisseurship on them. Media vehicles for every type of collectible exist. Other institutions mass merchandise presingularized collectibles to consumers who desire special objects. Firms such as Hummel, Lladro, and Waterford encourage collecting by producing items whose principle value or point-of-difference resides in their collectibility. These firms reinforce the social and economic significance of collecting behavior by prepacking the experience for consumers and providing the comforting assurance of authenticity. They have commercialized a social activity, co-opting it and reinforcing collecting behavior.[59]

CROSS-CULTURAL PERSPECTIVES ON THE MEANINGS OF POSSESSIONS

We suggested in Chapters 2 and 3 that possessions and their meanings vary cross-culturally. There we mentioned a number of key differences between consumption priorities in different regions of the world. Any attempt to document differences in the dictionaries of consumer meaning cross-culturally is doomed. Either we'd end up cataloguing great long lists of differences and mountains of examples to illustrate them, or we'd be reduced to making such general characterizations of differences in meanings that they would provide little guidance to marketers or to students of consumer behavior.[60]

Since we have emphasized the malleability and dynamism of consumption meanings in this chapter, we can mention a number of dimensions along which consumer researchers can expect to find differences in meaning between cultural areas. One obvious dimension is the cultural meaning of consumer goods.

We can contrast the meanings of goods in different cultural contexts. Contrast the meaning of a house in the United States, where customization and self-expression are often prized, to its meaning in Great Britain, where conformity, solidity of construction, and longevity are favored. Or contrast the meanings of personal property expressed in the Anglo-American belief that "a man's home is his castle" with the Swedish view that the countryside is public space open to everyone, even parts immediately adjacent to the country homes that dot the Swedish countryside. On a darker note, many critics have pointed out that loss of meaning occurs when arts and crafts made by indigenous peoples for utilitarian, sacred, or artistic (hedonic) purposes are reused in Western interior decorating or placed behind museum glass.

Another dimension along which consumer meaning varies cross-culturally is the identity of goods that are the focus of consumption meanings. For North Americans, the home, including the lawn, and the car are extremely meaningful consumer goods. Interesting homes and cars are important sources of meaning to women and men, respectively, on the island of Trinidad as well. The home but not the car is also critically important in Sweden, Great Britain, Belize, and many other nations. We discussed some differences in how homes are valued in Ethical Dilemma 4.1. By contrast, the apartment is a focus of attention for many Japanese. The family altar concerns some Chinese. Some young Congolese focus intense interest on French designer fashions.[61]

A third dimension is the quantity of meaningful possessions in circulation. Consumers in the more economically and socially differentiated societies of the Triad nations invest meanings in many types of objects. T-shirts and bumper stickers reading "The person that dies with the most toys wins" are playful examples of the value of quantity in U.S. consumer culture. By contrast, consumers in less developed economies may attach

Sanse, Fashion, and Meaning in Urban Senegal

CONSUMER CHRONICLES 4.5

Sanse, dressing up or dressing well, is highly valued among women in the cities of Senegal and The Gambia, West Africa. The elegant style of Senegalese women—the well-starched copious folds of their colorful garments, accompanied by matching headdresses and abundant qualities of gold jewelry—draws praise when well executed from men and women alike. Achieving such a style is expensive and appears to reflect the dominance of Western consumerist values in which foreign commodities are valued symbols of cosmopolitanism. *Sanse* forges a link between having and being, displaying both wealth and social identity. But *sanse* is an indexical communicative act [that is, it is indicative of true social status]; it derives its meaning from its context of use, pointing to a larger social hierarchy within which the actor is situated and can only be understood in this context.

Sanse and the practices that surround it reflect accents of identity and difference (heteroglossia) on a number of different levels: tradition and modernity, Western and African style, religious devotion and heterodoxy, women's autonomy and dependence. Thus, urban tailors create a rapidly changing array of styles often incorporating design elements of apparent Western origin such as flounces, lace, and fitted, zippered bodices drawn from Western fashion magazines. On the important public occasions at which *sanse* is performed, the preferred costume is the *mbubb,* a voluminous unfitted garment that is less tailored and more African. In addition, two types of cloth figure among the most highly prized in the execution of *sanse.* One is the imported machine-made, polished [cotton] damask. Sometimes a less expensive, locally manufactured version that is never confused with the luxury fabric it imitates is worn. It signals social difference, reinforcing the distance between women of greater and those of lesser means. But its display also reinforces a sense of identity, through exclusion, among lower-class women. The other type of fabric used in the *mbubb* is luxurious, hand-woven strip cloth with its brightly colored designs that originated in the cloth currency produced by slaves as early as the mid-1500s. This hand-loomed cloth provides an alternative to factory made textiles and partial autonomy from the circuits of mass-produced commodities. Thus, both tradition and modernity, African and Western meanings fluctuate within the overall practice of *sanse.*

In addition to these contending meanings, *sanse* also reflects the social organization of women's independence in urban Senegal. Many women amass the cloth necessary to execute *sanse* through complex networks of gift giving and exchange. Women exchange cloth at baptisms and weddings, for example. More commonly, a prospective groom, a husband, or a suitor offers cloth to a woman on the occasion of a life-cycle ceremony. Such gifts make a public statement about what the women's suitor or husband has and who he is. In this way, *sanse* serves as a public display of someone else's generosity and is viewed as a service, a communicative act for someone else's behalf. A woman also may be expected to carry out a display of *sanse* to display her husband's wealth. In this case, he is then considered her master. However, in Senegalese culture, the possession and display of material goods through *sanse* is tied to the notion of generosity and hospitality. Related to this is the notion that wealth is an aspect of honor and respectability. Thus, wearing cloth and clothing contributed by her husband, a woman conveys a message designed to enhance the latter's reputation for honor. Paradoxically, by communicating that her male kin are men of means, a woman may also be communicating the possibility that she too is a person of means, capable of displaying generosity toward others. In this way, she may be making a statement about her independence rather than dependence. Thus, the meaning of *sanse* is always ambiguous, always moving, always slightly in dispute.

In contrast to these complex symbolic statements in fashion, true antifashions may be found in urban Senegal as well. Adepts of the Baay Fal Muslim sect use scraps of brightly colored locally manufactured wax print cloth to fashion voluminous patchwork pantaloons. Along with other behaviors, such as the rejection of imported tea or Nescafé, their patchwork costumes exemplify their rejection of Western consumerism and what some of them characterize as worldly materialism in general.

Source: Deborah Heath, "Fashion, Anti-Fashion and Heteroglossia in Urban Senegal," American Ethnologist *19 (February 1992), pp. 19–33.*

meaning to a smaller number of goods. With the globalization of markets this is changing rapidly.

In the newly industrialized countries of Asia, for example, what some herald as a new stage in consumer demand may also be seen in the emergence of young people with ever-expanding consumer wants. The emergence of individual consumers who are concerned with both quantity as well as quality in consumer goods in the NICs and transitional economies is likely to continue with the expansion of the global market system.[62]

A fourth dimension of interest cross-culturally is the stability of consumer meanings. The development of a global market economy creates a situation in which consumers' demand for meaningful goods becomes nearly insatiable, as the money economy reduces the intrinsic differences in value between them. Global growth in marketing communications may be expected to continue for the foreseeable future, especially in the NICs and the transitional economies. With its growth may come the generalization of certain characteristics of consumer culture found in the West. Cultural categories and principles become less and less fixed. Consumption meaning moves ever more quickly, becoming more differentiated, more compartmentalized, more transitory. At the same time, we may expect that ad effectiveness will continue to rely on the elicitation of shared meanings from a dictionary common to members of particular target markets. Cross-national studies of advertising themes and executions do not reveal a tendency toward simple convergence on a set of global conventions. Instead global conventions combine with recycled national and regional conventions. Thus, national or regional markets are likely to continue to differ in the symbols and meanings they find compelling. Managing meaning transfer processes will remain central to successful global marketing.[63]

Consumer Chronicles 4.5 illustrates each of these aspects of consumer meaning cross-culturally. The meaning of fashion in Senegal clearly varies from its meaning in Western and Eastern cultures. *Sanse* is also a focus for consumer meaning particular to Senegal. It also concentrates a great many personal, social, and hedonic meanings in one product category. Notice too that Senegalese consumers contest the meaning of *sanse*. Finally, the system is open to outside influences, as Western fashion elements are eagerly incorporated into the Senegalese fashion system.

SUMMARY

Consumption meanings are at the core of demand for products (goods, services, experiences, and ideals). Central to understanding consumer demand is the idea of semiosis, or the nature of meaning. Semiosis is a meaning-making process linking objects, meanings, and symbols of various kinds. Consumer meaning is a set of cultually particular and fundamentally arbitrary associations consumers connect with commercial products such as those linked to blue jeans, street fashions, or diamond rings. Meaning attaches to objects as signs, symbols, or indexes. In consumption, people extract both individual and social meanings from products and services. Five general kinds of consumption meanings may be derived from products: utilitarian, sacred, secular, hedonic, and social. Often these overlap in a single product, yet specific meanings associated with a product may vary between market segments and individuals.

The origin and movement of consumption meanings can be understood through the meaning transfer model. Meaning develops in the culturally constituted world as a natural part of human experience and our interpretations of sensory stimuli. Cultural principles and

SUMMARY

categories help us to organize novel experiences into meaningful ones. Next, in consumer culture available meanings are linked to products through the advertising and fashion systems. Marketing communications professionals and other tastemakers link products to cultural categories of time, place, emotion, and person. Advertising formats and treatments portray the world in ways designed to associate desired meaning with products. Verbal conventions such as metaphors and similes, and visual ones like familiar celebrities whose persona are well-known, are used to provide the recipients of advertising messages the clues to decode the intended links between product and meanings.

Consumers play active roles in interpreting and assimilating advertising meanings. They interpret the meanings in marketing communications; they sometimes seek to take on the meanings of products as portrayed in marketing communications. In other cases, they allow themselves to be identified as a participant in the meanings linked to a particular brand through consumption of the brands. Sometimes consumers use products to physically or mentally transform themselves. We identify a set of ordinary activities that consumers may use to assimilate meanings from goods such as personalizing and categorizing, and also discuss the possession and grooming rituals that they employ. The meanings of consumer goods are malleable and dynamic. Meanings fluctuate both within and between market segments.

Collecting is a peculiar and economically significant vehicle for the consumption of meaning. It provides consumers with opportunities to experience hedonic and sacred meanings and to engage in possession and exchange rituals. Both individual and institutional collecting take place; institutional collecting of art and antiques enables corporations and governments to appropriate sacred meanings for their secular purposes. Providing collectibles to individual consumers is big business.

Consumption meanings vary cross-culturally. Cataloguing all possible consumption meanings is impossible, given the fluid quality of demand in a global economy. The underlying meaning of products varies, as do the particular goods valued in different cultural contexts. Cultures also vary both in the terms of the quantity of possessions that are meaningful to them and the stability of the meanings valued within a particular culture. Seeking to manage the apparently universal human propensity to invest products with meaning requires that marketers pay attention to the ever-shifting play of cultural meanings.

KEY TERMS

1. Choose a number of your favorite consumer goods for which you can find print ads or commercials. Describe a semiotic triangle for each of them.
2. Choose a number of products for which you are brand loyal. Can you explain the meaning of these products for you? Explain why alternative brands just wouldn't mean the same to you.
3. Make a list of your favorite possessions. Can you list the kinds of meanings your favorite possessions have for you?
4. Clip a number of print advertisements. Can you identify the main consumption meanings contained in the ads?
5. Using this same set of ads, identify the kind of advertising format (lecture, drama, fairy tale, allegory, soap opera) and some rhetorical elements (metaphor, simile, symbol) employed.
6. Take as an example a common consumption event such as a visit to a fast-food restaurant or attendance at a sports or musical event, a birthday party, a garage sale, or any similar event. Can you identify examples of the many modes of consumer meaning transfer described in the chapter?
7. Some morning as you prepare for the day, make a list of your grooming rituals. What are they? How many? What do they mean to you? Identify any that you consider essential, that is, you wouldn't leave the house without performing it. What products are involved with these rituals?
8. Are you a collector? Try to take stock of your possessions and see. If so, try to make an objective appraisal of the meanings you derive from collecting in terms of the modes and rituals of meaning transfer described in the text.
9. Given the *sanse* system of meaning transfer, how would you market wax print cloth in Senegal?
10. The chapter discussed cases of dispute over the meaning of products between and within consumer segments. Can you think of examples of products for which you have been involved in some such dispute? (*Hint:* Perhaps you and some family members have quarreled about consumption at some point.)

REVIEW QUESTIONS

CASES

YOU MAKE THE CALL

KOLA NUT SHORTAGE IN NIGER

"Give me a kola nut!" "It'll cost you more than that!"

Get it? Probably you don't unless you are familiar with kola nuts and West African markets and celebrations. But this You Make the Call describes a very real crisis in meaning.

In Chapter 1 of Nigerian author Chinua Achebe's novel *Things Fall Apart,* Okoye says to Unoka, "He who brings kola brings life," referring to the kola nut and showing people of the Ibo culture's reverence of this native nut. The kola nut is actually the seed of a large African tree with the Latin name *Cola acuminata.* The nut is reddish gray in color, about an inch in size, and grows in long pods containing from five to twelve seeds each. The shape is irregular, with one side being flat and round, and the other side irregularly scooped or unfolded. Kola has the consistency of an unripe apple and is bitter in taste. Chewing kola is an acquired taste. According to fans throughout West Africa, kola nut makes ideas clearer, thoughts flow more easily and clearly, and fatigue and drowsiness decrease. Laborers use it to increase physical endurance, and people use it to treat a variety of illnesses.

As to the kola's spiritual nature, it's not hard to see why the Ibo and many other West African peoples hold it in such high esteem. It makes them feel good, and in this respect they use it at the beginning of important functions to heighten their senses both physically and mentally. In Chapter 3 of *Things Fall Apart,* Okonkwo presents kola nut and alligator pepper to a wealthy clansman, and typical of its use in ceremony, the kola nut is passed around for "all to see," then returned to Okonkwo to be broken and distributed among the men present. Okonkwo, affirming the group's desire for a long and happy life with children and good harvests, says a small prayer. Achebe goes into detail here to show the importance of kola in the Ibo culture and the ceremony surrounding it.

This same use of kola can be found in Niger and indeed throughout West Africa, where the collection and redistribution of kola nut accompanies all important celebrations. Family members contribute to the kola fund, and at the ceremony, the host breaks and distributes the kola to the participants. Kola is essential for weddings and baptisms, during which the nuts are distributed to all the guests. It is also common to offer kola nuts in a variety of social situations, and, with its heavy concentration of caffeine, it is virtually the only stimulant allowed by Islam.

Nigerians have been suffering a serious kola nut shortage for several weeks. This is due in part to a poor harvest in the kola-producing countries of Nigeria and Ghana, and the crisis has been exacerbated by a recent transport workers strike. In the capital Niamey's Katako Market, the price for a single kola nut has risen from a range of 15–50 CFA francs to 100–250 CFA francs (US$0.15–0.35), if one can even find it. As for the 100-kilogram sack, its price has risen from a range of 40,000–70,000 CFA to as much as 300,000 CFA (US$414), or the equivalent of three metric tons of millet, the staple food grain.

Because of its importance in social life, the current shortage is a real crisis for many Nigerians. To cope with the crisis, hosts have been offering their guests dates at various types of ceremonies, and state-controlled media have urged people not to be offended if given dates instead of kola.

QUESTIONS

1. What do you think are some of the types of meanings Nigerians attach to kola nuts?
2. Can you explain the meanings Nigerians attach to kola nuts using the meaning transfer model described in this chapter?

3. What factors will determine whether dates make an effective substitute for kola nuts?
4. If you were a Nigerian kola marketer, how might you respond to this crisis in meaning?

This case is adapted from Kakaki: News of Niger, *users.idworld.net/jmayer/kakaki.*

CASES

ENDNOTES

1. This chapter draws heavily on the work of a small number of researchers, especially Grant McCracken, *Culture and Consumption* (Bloomington: Indiana University Press, 1986).
2. Center for Chicano Studies and Coleccion Tloque Nahuaque University Library, *Dia de Los Muertos: An Illustrated Essay and Bibliography* (Santa Barbara: University of California Press, 1983); Juanita Garciagodoy, *Digging the Days of the Dead: A Reading of Mexico's Dias de Muertos* (Niwot, CO: University Press of Colorado, 1998); Maria Garza-Lubeck and Ana Maria Salinas, *Mexican Celebrations* (Austin: University of Texas, Institute of Latin American Studies, 1986); and Judith Winningham, "Beyond Halloween," *Texas Monthly,* October 1986, pp. 140–47.
3. Elizabeth C. Hirschman, "Comprehending Symbolic Consumption: Three Theoretical Issues," in *Symbolic Consumer Behavior,* ed. Elizabeth C. Hirschman and Morris Holbrook (Ann Arbor, MI: Association for Consumer Research, 1981), pp. 4–6: and Marsha L. Richins, "Valuing Things: The Public and Private Meanings of Possessions," *Journal of Consumer Research* 21 (December 1994), pp. 504–21.
4. Kent Grayson and David Shulman, "Indexicality and the Verification Function of Irreplaceable Possessions: A Semiotic Analysis," *Journal of Consumer Research* 27 (June 2000), pp. 17–30.
5. U. Beck, *Risk Society: Towards a New Modernity,* trans. M. Ritter (London: Sage Publications, 1992); Mike Featherstone, *Consumer Culture and Postmodernism* (London: Sage Publications, 1991); S. Lash and J. Urry, *Economies of Signs and Space* (London: Sage Publications, 1994); Melanie Wallendorf and Eric J. Arnould, "'My Favorite Things': A Cross-Cultural Inquiry into Object Attachment Possessiveness and Social Linkage," *Journal of Consumer Research* 14 (March 1988), pp. 531–47; and David Lewis and Darren Bridger, *The Soul of the New Consumer,* (London: Nicholas Brealey Publishing, 2000).
6. Colin Campbell, *The Romantic Ethic and the Spirit of Modern Consumerism* (Oxford: Basil Blackwell, 1987); Fred Davis, *Fashion, Culture, and Identity* (Chicago: University of Chicago Press, 1992); Ed Housewright, "Do Church Ads Work or Compromise Gospel?" *Marketing News,* March 13, 1995, p. 21; Robert H. Frank, *Luxury Fever* (New York: Free Press, 1999); and Lewis Hyde, *The Gift: Imagination and the Erotic Life of Property* (New York: Vintage Books, 1983).
7. Hirschman, "Comprehending Symbolic Consumption"; and Richins, "Valuing Things."
8. Brad Herzog, "They're Great!" *Attache,* August 1999, pp. 54–59.
9. Dawn Dobni and George M. Zinkhan, "In Search of Brand Image: A Foundation Analysis," in *Advances in Consumer Research,* vol. 17, ed. Marvin Goldberg, Gerald Gorn, and Richard Pollay (Provo, UT: Association for Consumer Research, 1990), pp. 110–19; B. G. Gardner and Sidney J. Levy, "The Product and the Brand," *Harvard Business Review,* March–April 1955, pp. 33–39; W. Noth, "The Language of Commodities Groundwork for a Semiotics of Consumer Goods," *International Journal of Research in Marketing* 4 (1988), pp. 173–86; and E. M. Timmerman, "Starting from Scratch: Rethinking Brand Images Research and Identifying Cues and Context as Influential Factors," in *Asia Pacific Advances in Consumer Research,* vol. 4, ed. Paula Tidwell (Provo, UT: Association for Consumer Research, 2001), pp. 156–61.
10. John Clammer, "Aesthetics of the Self: Shopping and Social Being in Contemporary Urban Japan," in *Lifestyle Shopping: The Subject of Consumption,* ed. Ron Shields (London: Routledge, 1992), p. 210; David Crockett and Melanie Wallendorf, "Sociological Perspectives on Imported School Dress Codes: Consumption as Attempted Suppression of Class and Group Symbolism," *Journal of Macromarketing* 18 (Fall 1998), pp. 115–32; Deborah J. MacInnis, Stewart Shapiro, and Gayathri Mani, "Enhancing Brand Awareness through Brand Symbols," in *Advances in*

Consumer Research, vol. 26, ed. Eric Arnould and Linda Scott (Provo, UT: Association for Consumer Research, 1999), pp. 601–9; D. Martin and P. Herbig, "Marketing Implications of Japan's Socio-Cultural Underpinnings," *The Journal of Brand Management* 9, no. 3 (2002), pp. 171–79; Barbara Olsen, "Brand Loyalty and Consumption Patterns: The Lineage Factor," in *Contemporary Marketing and Consumer Behavior,* ed. John F. Sherry Jr. (Thousand Oaks, CA: Sage Publications, 1995), pp. 245–81; and Deborah Orr, "Why Can't We Say No to Brands?" June 12, 2002, http://www.commondreams.org.

11. B. Wansink and S. Seed, "Making Brand Loyalty Programmes Succeed," *The Journal of Brand Management* 8, no. 3 (2001), pp. 211–22; Cynthia Huffman and Brian Wansink, "Revitalizing Mature Brands," in *Advances in Consumer Research,* vol. 24, ed. Merrie Brucks and Deborah J. MacInnis (Provo, UT: Association for Consumer Research, 1997), pp. 251–252; Michael Korchia, "A New Typology of Brand Image," in *European Advances in Consumer Research,* vol. 4, ed. Bernard Dubois, Tina M. Lowery, L. J. Shrum, and Marc Vanhuele (Provo, UT: Association for Consumer Research, 1999), pp. 147–54; and Timmerman, "Starting from Scratch."

12. Junichi Kamekura, Gideon Bosker, and Mamoru Watanabe, *Ekiben: The Art of the Japanese Box Lunch* (San Francisco: Chronicle Books, 1989); and David Glen Mick, James E. Burroughs, Patrick Hetzel, and Mary Yoko Brannen, "A Global Review of Semiotic Consumer Research: Progress Problems and Prospects," working paper (Madison: University of Wisconsin–Madison, School of Business, 1999).

13. Jennifer Edson Escalas and James M. Bettman, "Using Narratives to Discern Self-Identity Related Consumer Goals and Motivations," in *The Why of Consumption,* ed. S. Ratneshwar, David Glen Mick, and Cynthia Huffman (London and New York: Routledge, 2000), pp. 237–58; and Grayson and Shulman, "Indexicality and the Verification Function of Irreplaceable Possessions."

14. Davis, *Fashion, Culture, and Identity;* Hyde, *The Gift;* Igor Kopytoff, "The Cultural Biography of Things: Commoditization as Process," in *The Social Life of Things,* ed. Arjun Appadurai (Cambridge: Cambridge University Press, 1989), pp. 64–94; Barbara Olsen, "Exploring Women's Brand Relationships and Enduring Themes at Mid-Life," in *Advances in Consumer Research,* vol. 26, ed. Eric Arnould and Linda Scott (Provo, UT: Association for Consumer Research, 1999), pp. 615–20; and Larry Rohter, "Who Is Vainest of All? Venezuela," *New York Times,* August 13, 2000, p. A4.

15. Mark Ligas and June Cotte, "The Process of Negotiating Brand Meaning: A Symbolic Interactionist Perspective," in *Advances in Consumer Research,* vol. 26, ed. Eric Arnould and Linda Scott (Provo, UT: Association for Consumer Research, 1999), pp. 609–14.

16. Kathleen Brewer Doran, "Symbolic Consumption in China: The Color Television as a Life Statement," in *Advances in Consumer Research,* vol. 24, ed. Merrie Brucks and Deborah J. MacInnis (Provo, UT: Association for Consumer Research, 1997), pp. 128–31.

17. Pierre Bourdieu, *Distinction: A Social Critique of the Judgment of Taste* (Cambridge: Harvard University Press, 1984); Davis, *Fashion, Culture, and Identity;* Dick Hebidge, *Subculture: The Meaning of Style* (London: Methuen, 1976); Johanna L. Holland and James W. Gentry, "The Impact of Cultural Symbols on Advertising Effectiveness: A Theory of Intercultural Accommodation," in *Advances in Consumer Research,* vol. 24, ed. Merrie Brucks and Deborah L. MacInnis (Provo, UT: Association for Consumer Research, 1997), pp. 483–89; John W. Schouten and James M. McAlexander, "Subcultures of Consumption: An Ethnography of the New Bikers," *Journal of Consumer Research* 22 (June 1995), pp. 43–61; and Malene Djursaa and Simon Ulrik Kragh, "Syntax and Creolization in Cross-Cultural Readings of Rooms," in *European Advances in Consumer Research,* vol. 4, ed. Bernard Dubois, Tina M. Lowery, L. J. Shrum, and Marc Vanhuele (Provo, UT: Association for Consumer Research, 1999), pp. 293–303.

18. Elizabeth C. Hirschman, "Commonality and Idiosyncracy in Popular Culture: An Empirical Examination of the 'Layers of Meaning' Concept," in *Symbolic Consumer Behavior,* ed. Elizabeth C. Hirschman and Morris Holbrook (Ann Arbor, MI: Association for Consumer Research, 1981), pp. 29–34; David Glen Mick, "Consumer Research and Semiotics: Exploring the Morphology of Signs, Symbols, and Significance," *Journal of Consumer Research* 13 (September

1986), pp. 196–213; David Glen Mick and Laura G. Politi, "Consumers' Interpretations of Advertising Images: A Visit to the Hell of Connotation," in *Interpretive Consumer Research,* ed. Elizabeth C. Hirschman (Provo, UT: Association for Consumer Research, 1989), pp. 85–96; and Richins, "Valuing Things."

19. Nabil Razzouk and Jamal Al-Khatib, "The Nature of Television Advertising in Saudi Arabia: Content Analysis and Marketing Implications," *Journal of International Consumer Marketing* 6, no. 2 (1993), pp. 65–90; Richins, "Valuing Things"; Jagdish N. Sheth, Bruce I. Newman, and Barbara L. Gross, *Consumption Values and Market Choices: Theory and Applications* (Cincinnati: South-Western, 1991), pp. 18–19; and Wallendorf and Arnould, "My Favorite Things."

20. Russell W. Belk and Nan Zhou, "Learning to Want Things," in *Advances in Consumer Research,* vol. 14, ed. Melanie Wallendorf and Paul Anderson (Provo, UT: Association for Consumer Research, 1987), pp. 478–81; Barry J. Babin, William R. Darden, and Mitch Griffin, "Work and/or Fun: Measuring Hedonic and Utilitarian Shopping Value," *Journal of Consumer Research* 20 (March 1994), pp. 644–56; Jean-Marie Floch, "The Contribution of Structural Semiotics to the Design of a Hypermarket," *International Journal of Research in Marketing* 4 (1988), pp. 233–52; Marshall D. Rice and Zaiming Lu, "A Content Analysis of Chinese Magazine Advertisements," *Journal of Advertising* 17, no. 4 (1988), pp. 43–48; and Jean Umiker-Sebeok, "Meaning Construction in a Cultural Gallery: A Sociosemiotic Study of Consumption Experiences in a Museum," in *Advances in Consumer Research,* vol. 19, ed. John F. Sherry Jr. and Brian Sternthal (Provo, UT: Association for Consumer Research, 1992), pp. 46–55.

21. Russell W. Belk, Melanie Wallendorf, and John F. Sherry Jr., "The Sacred and Profane in Consumer Behavior: Theodicy on the Odyssey," *Journal of Consumer Research* 16 (June 1989), pp. 1–38; and Annette Weiner, *Inalienable Possessions* (Berkeley: University of California Press, 1989).

22. Raj Mehta and Russell W. Belk, "Artifacts, Identity, and Transition: Favorite Possessions of Indians and Indian Immigrants to the United States," *Journal of Consumer Research* 17 (March 1991), pp. 398–411; Wallendorf and Arnould, "My Favorite Things"; and Gregory Starrett, "The Political Economy of Religious Commodities in Cairo," *American Anthropologist* 97 (March 1995), pp. 51–68.

23. Janeen Arnold Costa and Gary J. Bamossy, "Culture and the Marketing of Culture: The Museum Retail Context," in *Marketing in a Multi-Cultural World,* ed. Janeen Arnold Costa and Gary J. Bamossy (Thousand Oaks, CA: Sage Publications, 1995), pp. 299–328; Carole Duhaime, Annamma Joy, and Christopher Ross, "Learning to 'See': A Folk Phenomenology of Contemporary Canadian Art," in *Contemporary Marketing and Consumer Behavior: An Anthropological Sourcebook,* ed. John F. Sherry Jr. (Thousand Oaks, CA: Sage Publications, 1995), pp. 399–432; David Glen Mick et al., "A Global Review of Semiotic Consumer Research," p. 35; and Ira G. Zepp Jr., *The New Religious Image of Urban America: The Shopping Mall as Ceremonial Center* (Westminster, MD: Christian Classic, Inc., 1986).

24. Elizabeth C. Hirschman, "Point of View: Sacred, Secular, and Mediating Consumption Imagery in Television Commercials," *Journal of Advertising Research* 36 (December–January 1991), pp. 38–43.

25. David A. Aaker, *Managing Brand Equity* (New York: Free Press, 1991); Eric J. Arnould and Linda L. Price, "River Magic: Extraordinary Experience and the Extended Service Encounter," *Journal of Consumer Research* 20 (June 1993), pp. 24–45; Morris B. Holbrook and Elizabeth C. Hirschman, "The Experiential Aspects of Consumption: Consumer Fantasies, Feelings, and Fun," *Journal of Consumer Research* 9 (September 1982), pp. 132–40; Morris B. Holbrook, "Nostalgia and Consumption Preferences: Some Emerging Patterns of Consumer Tastes," *Journal of Consumer Research* 20 (September 1993), pp. 245–56; Barbara Olsen, "Brand Loyalty and Consumption Patterns: The Lineage Factor," in *Contemporary Marketing and Consumer Behavior: An Anthropological Sourcebook,* ed. John F. Sherry Jr. (Thousand Oaks, CA: Sage Publications, 1995), pp. 245–81; John W. Schouten, "Selves in Transition: Symbolic Consumption in Personal Rites of Passage and Identity Reconstruction," *Journal of Consumer Research* 17 (March 1991), pp. 412–25; Richins, "Valuing Things"; and Sheth, Newman, and Gross, *Consumption Values and Market Choices,* pp. 20–21.

26. Arnould and Price, "River Magic"; Babin, Dardin, and Griffin, "Work and/or Fun"; Richard L. Celsi, Randall L. Rose, and Thomas W. Leigh, "An Exploration of High-Risk Leisure Consumption through Skydiving," *Journal of Consumer Research* 20 (June 1993), pp. 1–23; Elizabeth Chin, "Bullfighters in the China Shop: Children, Consumption, and Social Process," paper presented at the annual meetings of the American Anthropological Association, Chicago, 1991; Pauline McLaran and Lorna Stephens, "Romancing the Utopian Marketplace: Dallying with Bakhtin in the Powerscourt Townhouse Center," in *Romancing the Market,* ed. Stephen Brown, Anne Marie Doherty, and Bill Clarke (London and New York: Routledge, 1998), pp. 172–86; John F. Sherry Jr., "The Soul of the Company Store: Niketown Chicago and the Emplaced Brandscape," in *Servicescapes,* ed. John F. Sherry Jr. (Chicago: NTC, 1998), pp. 109–46; and Peter Varley and Geoff Crowther, "Performance and the Service Encounter: An Exploration of Narrative Expectations and Relationship Management in the Outdoor Leisure Market," *Market Intelligence and Planning* 16, no. 5 (1998), pp. 311–17.

27. Elizabeth C. Hirschman, "Secular Immortality and the American Ideology of Affluence," *Journal of Consumer Research* 17 (June 1990), pp. 31–42; Elizabeth C. Hirschman, "The Consciousness of Addiction: Toward a Generalized Theory of Compulsive Consumption," *Journal of Consumer Research* 19 (September 1992), pp. 155–79; Thomas C. O'Guinn and Ronald J. Faber, "Compulsive Buying: A Phenomenological Exploration," *Journal of Consumer Research* 16 (September 1989), pp. 147–57; and Rob Shields, ed., *Lifestyle Shopping: The Subject of Consumption* (New York: Routledge, 1992).

28. Albert M. Muniz Jr., "Brand Community and the Negotiation of Brand Meaning," in *Advances in Consumer Research,* vol. 24, ed. Merrie Brucks and Deborah J. MacInnis (Provo, UT: Association for Consumer Research, 1997), pp. 308–9; and Richard Elliott and Mark Ritson, "Practicing Existential Consumption: The Lived Meaning of Sexuality in Advertising," in *Advances in Consumer Research,* vol. 22, ed. Frank Kardes and Mita Sujan (Provo, UT: Association for Consumer Research, 1995), pp. 740–45.

29. Douglas B. Holt, "Why Do Brands Cause Trouble? A Dialectic Theory of Consumer Culture and Branding," *Journal of Consumer Research* 29 (June 2002), pp. 70–90.

30. Crockett and Wallendorf, "Sociological Perspectives on Imported School Dress Codes."

31. David A. Aaker and R Jacobson, "The Financial Information Content of Perceived Quality," *Journal of Marketing Research* 31 (May 1994), pp. 191–201; Thomas Andresen and Thorsten Muller, "Brand Equity: Theoretical Phenomenon or Practicable Instrument for Market Control," in *European Advances in Consumer Research,* vol. 3, eds. Basil G. Englis and Anna Olofsson (Provo, UT: Association for Consumer Research, 1998), pp. 223–26; Sigrid Bekmeier, "Determination of Brand-Equity from a Consumer-Oriented Perspective," in *European Advances in Consumer Research,* vol. 2, ed. Flemming Hansen (Provo, UT: Association for Consumer Research, 1995), pp. 224–36; Franz-Rudolf Esch, "New Insights Into Communication Effects and Brand Equity," in *European Advances in Consumer Research,* vol. 3, eds. Basil G. Englis and Anna Olofsson (Provo, UT: Association for Consumer Research 1998), p. 222; and Akshay R. Rao, "Views from across the Bridge: Industry Perspectives on Brand Equity Management," in *Advances in Consumer Research,* vol. 23, eds. Kim Corfman and John Lynch (Provo, UT: Association for Consumer Research, 1996), p. 12.

32. The following sections were inspired by and rely heavily on material presented in Grant McCracken, "Culture and Consumption: A Theoretical Account of the Structure and Movement of the Cultural Meaning of Consumer Goods," *Journal of Consumer Research* 13 (June 1986), pp. 71–84.

33. This paragraph paraphrases Herbert Blumer, "Fashion," in *International Encyclopedia of the Social Sciences* (New York: Macmillan, 1968), pp. 341–45; see also Ligas and Cotte, "The Process of Negotiating Brand Meaning."

34. Holt, "Why Do Brands Cause Trouble?" and John W. Schouten and James M. McAlexander, "Subcultures of Consumption: An Ethnography of the New Bikers," *Journal of Consumer Research* 22 (June 1995), pp. 43–61.

35. Clammer, "Aesthetics of the Self"; and Dorinne Kondo, "The Aesthetics and Politics of Japanese Identity in the Fashion Industry," in *Re-Made in Japan,* ed. Joseph J. Tobin (New Haven: Yale University Press, 1993), pp. 176–203.

36. This section of the chapter relies heavily on the work of Barbara Stern and Linda Scott. Specific references are cited in the text.
37. Clammer, "Aesthetics of the Self."
38. Anthony Lewis, "Boom Box," *New York Times Magazine,* August 11, 2000, pp. 36–41, 51, 65–67; and Barbara J. Phillips, "Advertising and the Cultural Meaning of Animals," in *Advances in Consumer Research,* vol. 23, ed. Kim P. Corfman and John G. Lynch (Provo, UT: Association for Consumer Research, 1996), pp. 354–60.
39. Edward F. McQuarrie and David Glen Mick, "On Resonance: A Critical Pluralistic Inquiry into Advertising Rhetoric," *Journal of Consumer Research* 19 (September 1992), pp. 180–97.
40. Barbara B. Stern, "How Does an Ad Mean? Language in Services Advertising," *Journal of Advertising* 17, no. 2 (1988), pp. 3–14.
41. William Leiss, Stephen Kline, and Sut Jahly, *Social Communication in Advertising: Persons, Products, and Images of Well-Being* (Toronto: Methuen, 1986).
42. C. Anthony Di Benedetto, Mariko Tamate, and Rajan Chandran, "Developing Creative Advertising Strategy for the Japanese Marketplace," *Journal of Advertising Research* 32 (January–February 1992), pp. 39–48; Grant McCracken, "Who Is the Celebrity Endorser? Cultural Foundations of the Endorsement Process," *Journal of Consumer Research* 16 (December 1989), pp. 310–21; and Mary Walker, Lynn Langmeyer, and Daniel Langmeyer, "Celebrity Endorsers: Do You Get What You Pay For?" *Journal of Consumer Marketing* 9 (Spring 1992), pp. 69–76.
43. Lance State, "The Cultural Meaning of Beer Commercials," in *Advances in Consumer Research,* vol. 18, ed. Rebecca H. Holman and Michael R. Solomon (Provo, UT: Association for Consumer Research, 1991), pp. 115–19.
44. Judith Williamson, *Decoding Advertisements: Ideology and Meaning in Advertising* (New York: Marion Boyars, 1993), pp. 7, 12; and Coleman, Lipuma, Segal & Morrill, Inc., *Package Design and Brand Identity* (Rockport, MA: Rockport Publishers, 1994).
45. Stephanie O'Donohue and Caroline Tynan, "Beyond the Semiotic Strait-Jacket: Everyday Experiences of Advertising Involvement," in *Consumer Research: Postcards from the Edge,* ed. Stephan Brown and Darach Turley (London: Routledge, 1997), pp. 220–48; and Mark Ritson and Richard Elliott, "The Social Uses of Advertising: An Ethnographic Study of Adolescent Advertising Audiences," *Journal of Consumer Research* 26 (December 1999), pp. 260–77.
46. Arthur J. Kover, "Copywriters' Implicit Theories of Communication: An Exploration," *Journal of Consumer Research* 21 (March 1994), p. 603; and Williamson, *Decoding Advertisements,* pp. 40–44.
47. Kover, "Copywriters' Implicit Theories of Communication"; and Williamson, *Decoding Advertisements.*
48. Kopytoff, "The Cultural Biography of Things."
49. Elizabeth Chin, "Fettered Desire: Consumption and Social Experience among Minority Children in New Haven, Connecticut," unpublished Ph.D. dissertation (New York: Graduate School of the City University of New York, 1996).
50. C. B. Claiborne and Julie L. Ozanne, "The Meaning of Custom-Made Homes: Home as a Metaphor for Living," in *Advances in Consumer Research,* vol. 17, ed. Marvin Goldberg, Gerald Gorn, and Richard Pollay (Provo, UT: Association for Consumer Research, 1990), pp. 367–74.
51. Clammer, "Aesthetics of the Self"; Patrick Geary, "Sacred Commodities: The Circulation of Medieval Relics," in *The Social Life of Things,* ed. Arjun Appadurai (Cambridge: Cambridge University Press, 1986), pp. 169–91; Martin J. Gannon and Associates, *Understanding Global Cultures* (Thousand Oaks, CA: Sage Publications, 1994); Joy Hendry, *Wrapping Culture: Politeness, Presentation and Power in Japan and Other Societies* (Oxford: Clarendon Press, 1995); and Hideyuki Oka, *How to Wrap Five More Eggs* (New York: Weatherhill, 1975).
52. Hirschman, "Comprehending Symbolic Consumption."
53. T. Bettina Cornwell, "T-Shirts as Wearable Diary: An Examination of Artifact Consumption and Garnering Related to Life Events," in *Advances in Consumer Research,* vol. 17, ed. Marvin E. Goldberg, Gerald Gorn, and Richard W. Pollay (Provo, UT: Association for Consumer

Research, 1990), pp. 375–79; and David Glen Mick, et al., "A Global Review of Semiotic Consumer Research."
54. Marsha L. Richins, "Special Possessions and the Expression of Material Values," *Journal of Consumer Research* 20 (December 1994), pp. 522–33.
55. "Lowe's Is Sprucing Up Its House," *Business Week,* June 3, 2002.
56. Russell W. Belk, Melanie Wallendorf, John F. Sherry Jr., and Morris B. Holbrook, "Collecting in a Consumer Culture," in *Highways and Buyways: Naturalistic Research from the Consumer Behavior Odyssey,* ed. Russell W. Belk (Provo, UT: Association for Consumer Research, 1991), pp. 185–86.
57. Nancy Foster and Robert J. Foster, "Learning Fetishism? Boys Consumption Work with Marvel Super Heroes Trading Cards," paper presented at the 93rd annual meeting of the American Anthropological Association, Atlanta, November 30, 1994.
58. S. R. Howarth, "Corporate Art: An Integral Part of the Company Image," manuscript, The Humanities Exchange/International Art Alliance, Largo, FL.
59. Belk, Wallendorf, Sherry Jr., and Holbrook, "Collecting in a Consumer Culture," pp. 178–215.
60. Di Benedetto, Tamate, and Chandran, "Developing Creative Strategy for the Japanese Marketplace"; Geert Hofstede, *Culture's Consequences: International Differences in Work-Related Values* (Thousand Oaks, CA: Sage Publications, 1984); Carolyn A. Lin, "Cultural Differences in Message Strategies: A Comparison between American and Japanese TV Commercials," *Journal of Advertising Research* 33 (July–August 1993), pp. 40–47; Barbara Mueller, "Standardization vs. Specialization: An Examination of Westernization in Japanese Advertising," *Journal of Advertising Research* 32 (January–February 1992), pp. 15–24; Richard Tansey, Michael R. Hyman, and George M. Zinkhan, "Cultural Themes in Brazilian and U.S. Auto Ads: A Cross-Cultural Comparison," *Journal of Advertising* 19, no. 2 (1990), pp. 30–39; Ludmilla Gricenko Wells, "Western Concepts, Russian Perspectives: Meanings of Advertising in the Former Soviet Union," *Journal of Advertising* 23 (March 1994), pp. 83–93; and Fred Zandpour, Cypress Chang, and Joelle Catalano, "Stories, Symbols, and Straight Talk," *Journal of Advertising Research* 32 (January–February 1992), pp. 25–38.
61. Gannon and Associates, *Understanding Global Cultures;* Igor Kopytoff, "Leisure, Boredom, Luxury Consumerism: The Lineage Mode of Consumption in a Central African Society," in *Consumption and Identity,* ed. Jonathan Friedman (Chur, Switzerland: Harwood Academic Publishers, 1994), pp. 207–32; Witold Rybczysnski, *Home* (New York: Viking Press, 1986); Valene L. Smith, ed., *Hosts and Guests,* 2nd ed. (Philadelphia: University of Pennsylvania Press, 1989); and Polly Weissner, "Reconsidering the Behavioral Basis for Style: A Case Study among the Kalahari San," *Journal of Anthropological Archaeology* 3 (1984), pp. 190–234.
62. Nancy Rosenberger, "Images of the West: House Style in Japanese Magazines," *Re-Made in Japan,* ed. Joseph J. Tobin (New Haven: Yale University Press, 1992), pp. 106–25.
63. Marieke de Mooij, *Global Marketing and Advertising: Understanding Cultural Paradoxes* (Thousand Oaks, CA: Sage Publications, 1998).

LEARNING OBJECTIVES

After completing this chapter, you should be able to:

- Explain why effective marketing strategy depends on understanding consumer behavior.
- Identify the keys to adopting a market orientation and a customer focus.
- Understand the importance of marketing imagination to business success and know some keys to being an imaginative company.
- Describe market segmentation and identify a process for segmenting markets.
- Identify useful segmentation variables and criteria for effective market segmentation.
- Describe different kinds of market segmentation strategies and when they are appropriate.
- Understand the relationship between positioning and targeting.
- Describe different product positioning strategies.

CONSUMER BEHAVIORS AND MARKETING STRATEGIES

LET'S GO SHOPPING!

If you want to go shopping from the comfort of your own home, a good place to start might be the Lands' End catalog or else the website, landsend.com. Lands' End was founded in a basement along the river in Chicago's old tannery district. The original product line consisted of equipment for racing sail boats (e.g., duffle bags, rain suits, some sweaters). A lot of people ask why the apostrophe in Lands' End is in the wrong place. Originally, this mistake came as the result of a typographical error, but, in recent times, this feature serves to set the company apart from the competition.

In the second year of operation, the company started its famous catalog operation, which, in the year 2001, distributed more than 269 million catalogs. The organization's basic premise for winning customers remains constant: "Sell only things we believe in, ship every order the day it arrives, unconditionally guarantee everything, and help customers as much as we can with advice on how to use the things we sell."

Lands' End was an early adopter of the Internet, launching its website in 1995. Initially, the site featured 100 products as well as stories, essays, and travelogues. Now, the website offers every Lands' End product. Localized versions of the website are available in the United Kingdom, Japan, Germany, France, Ireland, and Italy. At present, landsend.com is the world's largest apparel website (in terms of business volume). It is also a leader in developing new ways to enhance the online shopping experience. Examples include

- A virtual model, where customers create a 3-D model of themselves by providing critical measurements. After this virtual model is created, the customer can use it to "try on" items and outfits and see how they look.

This Lands' End display, constructed for a trade show, emphasizes the familiarity and intimacy of the company.

Source: Lands' End trade show display by Boss Display. Reprinted by permission of Boss Display.

- A chat feature that allows customers to talk, any time of day or night, to a customer service representative over the phone or via a text-based chat screen.
- Shopping with a friend, where two shoppers can browse the site together and communicate with each other. It's exactly like going on a shopping trip with someone else, except that you don't have to leave your home!

"Can I call you back? I'm shopping."

The retail industry now finds itself in a state of flux. On the one hand, online retailers (e.g., Excite.com) find it difficult to survive. On the other hand, traditional "bricks-and-mortar" retailers sense that there is a growing competition and that many customers are interested in experimenting with shopping in cyberspace. In this respect, traditional retailers can view e-tailing as just another kind of channel for delivering products, services, or information. Lands' End, as a direct merchant, reaps the benefits of two large marketplaces: catalog sales and online sales.[1]

OVERVIEW

We aim primarily to provide you with a basic understanding of consumer behavior from the consumer's perspective. We also provide many examples throughout the text of how marketing managers use consumer behavior theory and research. This chapter focuses specifically on the intersection between managerial marketing strategy and the insights provided by consumer behavior research. **Strategy** can be defined simply as *the actions managers take to attain the goals of the firm.* **Marketing strategy** concerns *the actions managers take to improve the likelihood marketplace exchanges will occur between a firm and its target markets.* To this end, the opening vignette illustrates how important it is to anticipate the needs of consumers; it also illustrates how quickly the environment for marketplace exchange is changing.

A marketplace is the physical space where economic and social transactions occur. In the twenty-first century, more and more buyer–seller transactions will occur in an *information-defined arena,* coined **marketspace.** Business-to-business (B2B) online commerce is a growing area, and it's expected to account for more than one trillion dollars in sales by 2003. By the year 2005, it is estimated that online B2B commerce will account for more than 42 percent of all B2B trade. On the business-to-consumer (B2C) side, more than 60 million (out of 107 million) U.S. households are currently online. By 2007, 44 percent of European households will have broadband access to the Internet. However, wireless access to the Internet is quite popular in Europe. By the year 2006, it is estimated that the majority of European wireless phone subscribers will own Internet-enabled phones. E-commerce is fast developing in Asian nations such as Japan (which is currently third in the world, behind the United States and Germany) and China (which is currently eighth in the world with more than 9.4 million Internet users). Australia ranks 10th in the world, with more than 6 million users.[2]

The contents of marketspace transactions, the contexts in which they occur, and the support activities that enable them are all likely to be very different from exchanges in the physical marketplace. Consider one dramatic example. FreeMarkets, Inc., is a business-to-business Internet auction company that enables suppliers of components for manufactured goods to compete for manufacturers' orders in live, open, electronic auctions. FreeMarkets helps buyers standardize every item of their orders, finds and screens potential sellers, and runs the electronic auctions. The company's clients, such as GE, Raytheon, Quaker Oats, and United Technologies, save more than 15 percent on parts, materials, and even services. During the online auctions, sellers can see exactly what the competition is bidding and how low they must go to pocket the order. FreeMarkets makes millions on its services. Carrier Aircon is the India-based operation of Carrier Corporation, which is the world's largest manufacturer of heating, air-conditioning, and refrigeration systems. When Carrier Aircon started manufacturing products in India, their

@ carrierindia.com

procurement of raw materials was conventional and rudimentary, at best. Everything was done manually, including finding suppliers and writing requests for quotations. Negotiations with suppliers could drag on for days and were often unproductive. Now, Carrier Aircon uses FreeMarkets' services, and, as a result, they have expanded their supplier outreach globally. In addition, Carrier Aircon reports that they have increased their competitiveness among suppliers and now negotiate on a level playing field. Carrier Aircon estimates that they experience an 18 percent cost saving via their interactions with FreeMarkets. "Technology is a facilitator, and we have adopted the solution provider which creates the most value for us," says Ashish Kaul, general manager, supply chain at Carrier Aircon India. In this way, business auctions have created a new business interface between buyers and companies. At the same time, the competitive dynamics of industries is altered, both for business-to-consumer and business-to-business marketers.[3]

In this chapter we first discuss marketing strategy. We also discuss two essentials for developing effective strategy from insights from consumer research: a market orientation and a customer focus. We then talk about the idea of **marketing imagination.** Companies with marketing imagination *go beyond what consumers are able to tell researchers to find new ways to create value for them.*

@ landsend.com

Lands' End, featured in the vignette, seems to have that kind of imagination. Note how Lands' End offers consumers a variety of ways to "stretch" the website so that it begins to take on some of the features of shopping in an "on-ground" store. Through My Virtual Model™ customers simulate the experience of looking into a store mirror. Through My Personal Shopper, customers create a virtual wardrobe consultant who suggests outfits that best suit the user's unique taste, style, and preferences. Through Shop with a friend™, two Internet users can simulate the experience of shopping together. In all of these instances, Lands' End has found a way to introduce a personal and human touch into the potentially sterile Internet setting.

Although every successful marketing strategy is built on important skills and resources, none is more critical than the ability to sense the market. Effectively sensing the market produces knowledge, not just information. This kind of knowledge increases a firm's market orientation and results in improved service levels and more innovative products. Listening carefully to customers and remaining market focused leads to market offerings that are different from competitors' products and to improved profit margins. FreeMarkets and Lands' End are great examples of organizations that are adept at market sensing.

In this chapter we also outline the segmentation, targeting, and positioning process and provide examples. Organizations need to understand consumer behavior in order to segment markets, choose market segments to serve, and develop and position products and services to attract current and potential customers. Developing and positioning products and services involves not just deciding on the form of the product or service but also determining what communications and promotions, distribution systems, and pricing techniques to use.

MARKETING STRATEGIES

As we discuss in Chapter 6, consumer research can be used in numerous ways to assist managers in understanding their customers. One of the most important applications of consumer research is to improve marketing strategies. In general, customer-oriented marketing strategies improve the value customers derive from products or decrease the costs of products to customers.

Defender strategy: The McIlhenny Company uses market penetration strategy to increase sales and defend its brand's position.

One useful categorization of strategies identifies four strategy types: prospector, defender, analyzer, and reactor. **Defenders** are *firms with a narrow product market, a stable customer group, and an established organization structure typically managed by older executives.* Church & Dwight, maker of Arm & Hammer baking soda (founded 1846), and the McIlhenny Company, maker of Tabasco sauce (founded 1868), might be considered defenders. Nevertheless, Church & Dwight has successfully implemented both *product and market development strategies* by creating new products containing baking soda and new uses for those products. McIlhenny has implemented a *market penetration strategy* by extending its core brand and suggesting new uses for it to stimulate increased sales.[4]

www.churchdwight.com/company/company_information.htm

www.tabasco.com/cgi-bin/historian.pl

The essence of the defender strategy is maintaining an established market position. The defender focuses on protecting its current markets by lowering costs and/or improving the performance of current products. One good example here is UPS, which competes successfully in the business-to-business delivery market by consistently beating their competitors on a price basis. UPS constantly tries to find ways to develop cost-efficient methods for delivering goods. The defender strategy may be particularly effective when markets are stable and the firm can, therefore, focus on efficiency. Key methods for competing include the introduction of

Defender strategy: Church & Dwight creates new uses for existing products through product line extensions.

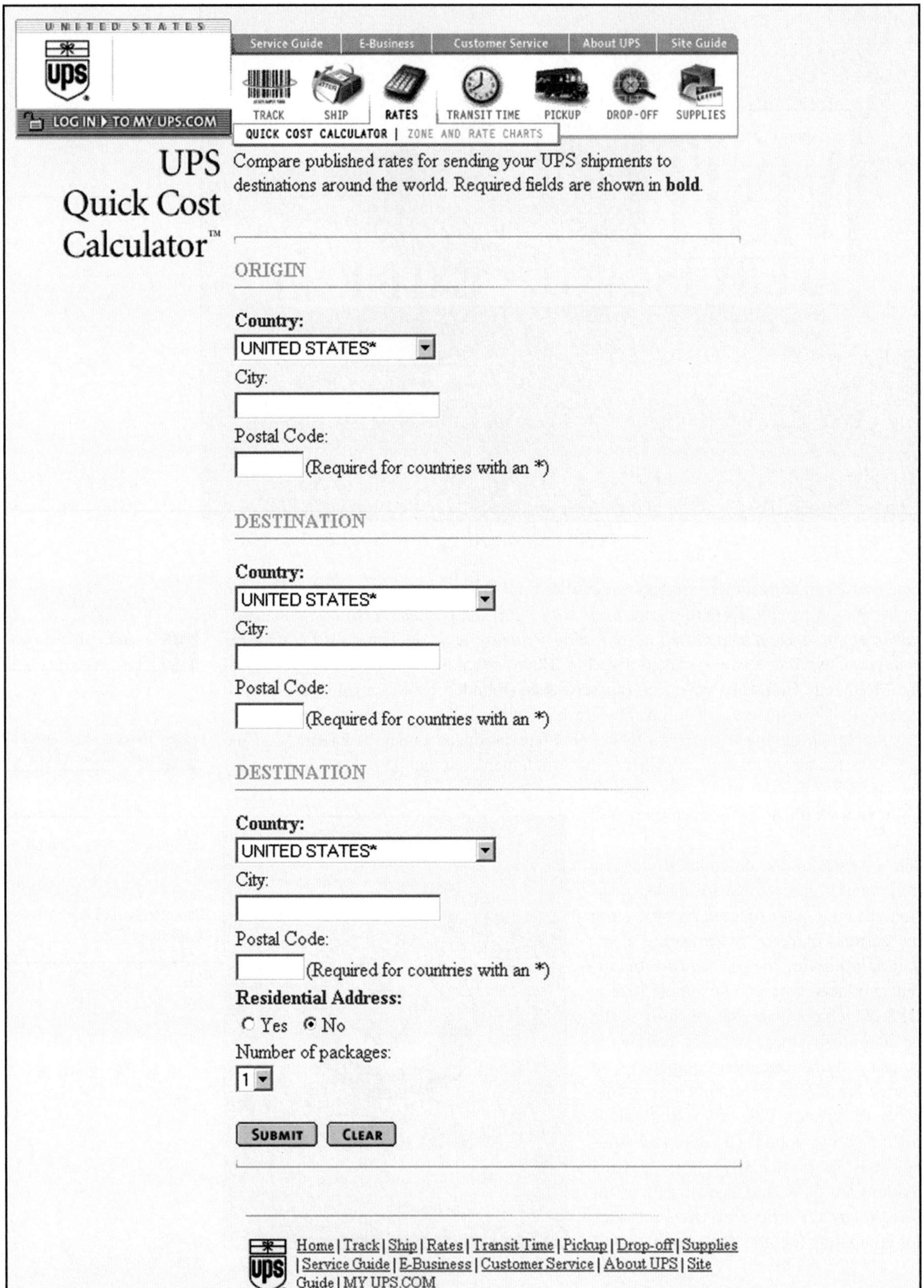

The Quick Cost Calculator™ is one way that UPS implements cost-effective methods in a B2B context.

3M's Major Innovations, 1997-2001

Year	Invention
2001	A halon-replacement alternative to hydrofluorocarbons and perfluorocarbons for extinguishing fires.
	3M™ Inflata-Pak™ Air Cushion Packaging. Plastic packaging designed for protecting items in shipping. This product conforms to shapes and is self-sealers.
2000	3M™ SandBlaster™ Sponge Products. A line of sanding products designed to sand three times faster and last three times longer than sandpaper.
	3M™ Laminating Products. Products provide lamination without the use of any heat.
1999	Scotch® Photo and Document Tape. This tape is acid-free and is resistant to yellowing.
	3M™ Light Management Technology makes strides in telecommunications, photonics, lighting, medical, automotive, packaging and horticulture.
1998	Scotch-Brite® High Performance Cloth. This microtextured cloth can be used wet or dry for dusting or other household cleaning chores, without the use of additional cleaners.
	3M™ Microflex Circuits. Circuitry that is used in ink jet printers and link integrated circuits to printed circuit boards. Also used in disk drives, hearing aids and cellular phones.
1997	3M™ Volition™ Fiber Optic Cabling System. First fiber optic network cable system for data-intensive communications network applications.
	Scotch® Pop-Up Tape Strips and Dispensers. For one-hand dispensing and access to tape strips.

planned upgrades and the implementation of strong customer service, so as to retain key customers. There is also an emphasis on protecting the market from new competitors. For instance, there is a premium on creating barriers to entry. An illustrative example of this strategy is provided in the soft-drink industry. Coca-Cola and Pepsi have created strong brand images (e.g., through advertising), and they monopolize shelf space. As a result of these twin strategies (brand image and shelf space), it is quite difficult for a new competitor to enter the soft-drink market.

Samsung didn't invent the PDA, but they market it well.

Source: Nexio by Samsung. www.samsung.com

Prospectors have a *changing product market, a focus on innovation and change, and a flexible organizational structure headed by younger managers*. A more specific example of a prospector strategy is a **differentiation strategy.** Such a strategy *emphasizes a product that is perceived as unique in the industry, provides a distinct advantage, or is otherwise set apart from competitors' brands in some way.* Entrepreneurial firms such as Lands' End and FreeMarkets tend to be prospectors.

A main goal of the prospector is to shake up the market, and this approach works best when the marketplace (and the environment) are dynamic and growing. There is a premium on effectiveness (doing things right) and innovation. In terms of marketing, there is an emphasis on developing the most up-to-date and sophisticated (or fashionable) offering. 3M Worldwide is a good example, as they continually seek to develop the newest technology or product. Employees are encouraged to follow their entrepreneurial spirit and set aside time to develop pet projects. For instance, 3M management attributes its 100 years of successful operation to "perseverence, ingenuity, and creativity." 3M employees strive to "solve problems for [consumers] and make their lives easier and better."[5] Prospector firms take risks. They are organized to be creative, innovative, and decentralized. The managers of these entrepreneurial firms actively seek new opportunities in the marketplace. Such entrepreneurial spirit is exemplified by

Samsung, an electronics firm, which is creating a stir in the marketplace with innovative products such as cell phones and personal digital assistants (see photograph).

Caterpillar is an analyzer.

Source: Reprinted courtesy of Caterpillar, Inc.

Defenders and prospectors lie on opposite ends of a continuum of competitive strategies. That is, defenders try to maintain the status quo, while prospectors are risk takers and focus on innovation. The **analyzer** strategy falls between defenders and prospectors on the continuum. Analyzers *generally operate in two types of product/market domains: one relatively stable and the other changing. In their stable areas, they operate routinely and efficiently through the use of formalized structures and processes. In their turbulent areas, top managers watch their competitors closely for new ideas and then rapidly adopt those that appear to be the most promising.* Analyzers, through careful evaluation, quickly identify innovations in the marketplace, and then try to improve upon these innovations. However, they are also conservative and attempt to maintain the core of their effective practices and markets. Korean electronics firms such as Hyundai, Samsung, and Lucky Goldstar entered the U.S. market using this approach. The essence of the analyzer strategy is to maintain stability while, at the same time, exploring innovation in the sense of creating rapid copies of successful market offerings. Such an approach works especially well in a climate of moderate change. This is an in-between strategy in the sense that there is an effort to maintain the current market share while, at the same time, attempting to pursue a moderate level of innovation. Analyzers seek to follow prospectors into new markets, but they also try to improve on their technological advances. Caterpillar Tractor provides a good example. Caterpillar strives to maintain its current business practices by producing high-quality equipment; however, it is quick to create and focus on new product lines as they develop. CarMax is another example. CarMax followed AutoNation into the quality used-car market, but they were creative in terms of providing a satisfying shopping experience for customers. They were more effective with respect to distribution and established retail outlets throughout the country. They also innovated by compensating their sales force in a unique manner (e.g., sales people are paid the same commission, no matter which car the consumer purchases). In brief, CarMax was not the innovator. They did not invent the "quality used-car" segment. But once AutoNation experienced some success, then CarMax was able to identify an opportunity. CarMax moved quickly and improved upon the original concept.

Reactors do not really have a consistent strategy. They are not particularly customer oriented, and they *adopt a "me-too" approach to marketing.* Reactors tend to respond slowly to environmental change, often because resources are quite limited. They also react to external developments without sophisticated analysis of costs or opportunities. As a result, they often find themselves in a crisis state, and decisions are oriented toward the short versus the long term. As they merely react to changes in the market and the moves of their competitors, they must maintain flexibility. Consider The Gap, a clothing retailer. They stuck too long with a tried-and-true clothing line and were eventually passed by more creative and adventuresome companies (e.g., Abercrombie and Fitch).

The American network ABC lost market share over a long period of time with poor programming. Their "late-night" programming continually loses high advertising dollars to more successful shows such as David Letterman's and Jay Leno's.[6]

Market Focused and Customer Oriented

To deepen our understanding of the connection between consumer behavior and effective marketing strategy we can review the **marketing concept.** The marketing concept is a business philosophy, an ideal, and a policy statement. The essence of the marketing concept is a *market-focused, customer-oriented, coordinated marketing effort aimed at generating customer satisfaction as the key to satisfying organizational needs.* A study based on interviews with managers at almost 50 different U.S. companies summarized what managers mean by a market orientation and what organizational factors encourage or discourage this orientation. The answers were revealing.[7] First, managers agreed that a **customer focus** is the central element of a market orientation. Organizations with a customer focus *constantly look for ways to deliver greater value to current and prospective customers through mutually beneficial exchanges.* A related concept is **market orientation,** which is defined as the *organizational generation of market intelligence pertaining to current and future consumer needs, dissemination of that intelligence across departments, and organization-wide responsiveness to that intelligence.*

Although every successful marketing strategy is built on important skills and resources, none is more critical than customer focus, or the ability to **sense the market.** Sensing the market refers to a *manager's ability to empathize with and gain insights from customers.* This is the single most important skill a manager can use to mobilize new technologies, develop product and service offerings, and design communications programs. In fact, all the elements of a company's strategic posture depend on this skill. We can think of many ventures that have been enormously successful because the founders brought this ability to their enterprises: Bill Gates (Microsoft), Mary Kay Ash (Mary Kay Cosmetics), Akio Morita (Sony), Sam Walton (Wal-Mart), Steve Case (AOL), Richard Branson (Virgin), and many others.[8]

Paying attention to the customer is certainly not a new idea, and yet many companies don't do it or don't do it well. For example, Encyclopedia Britannica's management disregarded the threat of CD-ROM technology and later bungled the company's entrée onto the Internet. The result has been a major decline in sales and profits. Ironically, Encyclopedia Britannica had CD-ROM technology in one of its other units, but the company failed to recognize its importance in the encyclopedia market. GE, which became one of FreeMarkets' biggest customers, initially rejected the idea when it was proposed in-house. By contrast with these bloopers, Toyota, which has a history of market sensitivity, is investing heavily in web technology, although it seems far from the company's core business, because it expects to build its web browser into its soon-to-be-computerized auto models.[9]

Managers sometimes confuse information about consumers with knowledge about consumers. Effectively sensing the market produces knowledge, not just information. We'll have more to say about this in the next chapter. General market data such as those provided by syndicated marketing research services show who is consuming what. But the data rarely show a company how customers relate to each other, the product, and the company. Attending to this kind of knowledge produces many payoffs. It increases a firm's market orientation, resulting in improved service levels and more innovative products. It leads to promoting products and services that are designed specially for different national markets. By listening carefully to customers and remaining market focused, a company can develop products that are fundamentally different from those of its competitors, which can result in increased profit margins. Finally, listening to the market favors differentiation over cost reduction even when the latter seems like the easier course of action. **Differentiation** means *offering customers something they value and that competitors don't have,* such as FreeMarkets' vertical auctions, or Toyota's hybrid energy car.[10] Differentiation can occur at any point in the consumption chain—from how and when the product is acquired, to when consumers decide they no longer want it and decide to dispose of it. Good Practice 5.1 identifies a series of questions managers can ask about their products and services to map the consumption chain and capture the consumer's total experience. The most important way to achieve differentiation is to analyze completely the consumer's experience with a company and its products: *What* are customers doing at each phase of the circle of consumption? *Where* are customers at each stage of the consumption chain? *When* are consumers engaged with an element of the consumption circle? *Who* else is with the customer points in the cycle of consumption? *How* are consumers' needs and desires being addressed at each stage of consumption? Yankelovich Partners' Brand Intelligence and Corporate Reputation Studies are examples of innovative research on customers' experience that answers these kinds of questions for firms.[11] Firms that have established effective differentiation have also created a sustainable competitive advantage. Consider the cartoon, where Burger King is offering a rare Fabergé egg with each purchase. However, this strategy is not attracting customers. MacDonald's mass market appeal to children is quite difficult for Burger King to overcome. In this sense, the cartoon pokes fun at the differentiation concept.

GOOD PRACTICE 5.1

Questions to Map the Consumption Chain

1. How do people become aware of their need for your product or service?
2. How do consumers find your offering?
3. How do consumers make their final selections?
4. What happens when your product or service is delivered?
5. How is your product installed?
6. How is your product or service paid for?
7. How is your product stored?
8. How is your product moved around?
9. What is the customer really using your product for?
10. What do customers need help with when they use your product?
11. Are there any patterns in returns or exchanges? What are the causes?
12. How is your product repaired or serviced?
13. What happens when your product is disposed of or no longer used?

From *The Red and Black,* syndicated by Tribune Media Services, Inc., May 12, 1997.

Prospector strategy: The Toyota hybrid energy vehicle may satisfy consumers' future needs for energy-efficient transportation.

Next, many of the managers surveyed emphasized that a customer focus goes beyond conducting customer research. It involves taking actions based on market intelligence. **Market intelligence** includes *knowledge of environmental factors that affect both current and future needs and preferences of customers.* The concern for future needs drives companies such as Xerox, 3M, Toyota, and Procter & Gamble to invest heavily in new-product development and The Coca-Cola Company to invest heavily in trends research provided by companies such as Yankelovich Partners. The idea that market intelligence includes anticipated customer needs is important because it often takes years for an organization to develop new product offerings.

Third, the managers emphasized the need for **coordinated marketing,** stressing that a market orientation is not just the responsibility of a marketing department. This means that market intelligence must be distributed across the organization. Effectively sharing intelligence is important because it provides a basis for joint action by different departments. For example, the vice president of a manufacturing firm indicated that her organization spreads customer information by telling stories about customers, their needs, their personality characteristics, and even their families. The idea is to have the secretaries, engineers, and production personnel "get to know" customers. If they do, they are more likely to incorporate knowledge about customer needs into activities at every level of the firm.

Fourth, the managers emphasized that certain kinds of environmental conditions may make a market orientation more or less important to overall business performance. One example is a change in customer base. Two U.S. consumer food products companies included in the survey on which this section is based marketed their products in a specific region in the United States without doing much market research. The population in this region had remained unchanged and the preferences of customers were known and stable. Over the last few years, however, the region has received a new influx of population, forcing both companies to initiate research and develop new products. Similarly, the rapid transition to market-driven economies in countries such as Poland and Turkey has led to a rapid growth in customers and an increase in customer sophistication. Old state-run firms that cannot deliver value to meet changing consumer demand in these markets decline as market-oriented foreign firms rush in.[12]

www.yankelovich.com

Finally, the managers stressed that the degree of competition in an industry affects the importance of a market orientation. Increased competition makes it difficult for firms to develop distinctive product positioning strategies. A sales manager for an industrial product firm explained his firm's response to competitive pressure: "Historically, we were a technically driven company. In the early years it was a successful approach. If we had a better mousetrap, customers would search us out. However, as more companies came up with more solutions, we had to become more market oriented. Find out what solution the customer is looking for, and try to solve it."

Simply engaging in market-oriented activities does not ensure the quality of those activities. For organizations to become more market oriented, they often must acknowledge gaps between their current orientation and a market orientation. For example, a manager of a service organization (a hospital) noted that the company's employees felt they were very responsive to customer needs. However, when service interactions between these employees and customers were videotaped and played back to the employees, they were horrified at the callous ways they saw themselves treating cus-

A Few Rules for Becoming Market Focused

GOOD PRACTICE 5.2

1. **Recognize that "customer" means more than the next step in the distribution chain. An important corollary: Do not think of your marketplace offering as a commodity.**
   In many cases, businesses may have consumers (end users of products and services) as well as clients (organizations that may dictate or influence the choices or end users). Organizations must pay attention to both.
2. **Count on your customers for information, not for insight.**
   Customers can describe their experiences and define their immediate needs. But only you can interpret their data and help them solve their problems. Being market focused is about your own creativity uncovering and solving your customers' problems.
3. **Don't expect brilliant insights each time you study a customer. Small operational shifts made from a market-focused perspective can also add up to significant improvements.**
   Through a succession of small moves it's possible to take critical steps toward delivering a new set of benefits to a market. It may be as simple as coming up with a more effective way to handle customer complaints or streamlining the sales organization on the basis of recent information about the distribution of customers.
4. **Involve all levels of the organization in the drive to become market focused.**
   Senior management's commitment and participation are vital for an organization to become market focused, but not sufficient for prolonged success. For maximum results, the market-focused mind-set must invade the entire organization.

Source: Francis J. Gouillart and Frederick D. Sturdivant, "Spend a Day in the Life of Your Customers," Harvard Business Review *(January–February 1994), pp. 116–27.*

tomers. The videotape identified a gap between the hospital's current orientation and a preferred market orientation. Incorporating simple rules into interactions with customers—illustrated in Good Practice 5.2—can help managers improve their market orientation.[13]

The Context of Strategy Development

The cornerstone of market orientation is a customer focus. Marketing and organizational strategies must be designed around an understanding of consumers' thoughts, feelings, and behaviors. Exhibit 5.1 summarizes the crucial relationship between marketing strategies and understanding consumers. Companies must avoid a narrow focus when trying to understand consumers. As discussed further in Chapters 2 and 3, these understandings must be formulated with due attention to the economic, social, and cultural environment of consumption. Consistent with the views of the managers discussed above, many global corporations from GM to GE to Nestlé to Mattel are organized into geographic units so that production and marketing are better coordinated and market offerings are more closely tailored to the demands of consumers in the United States, Europe, Asia, or Latin America. Global companies believe this will help them produce well-adapted products and will introduce economies of scale and scope. Mattel's Global

EXHIBIT 5.1

Marketing Strategy and Consumers

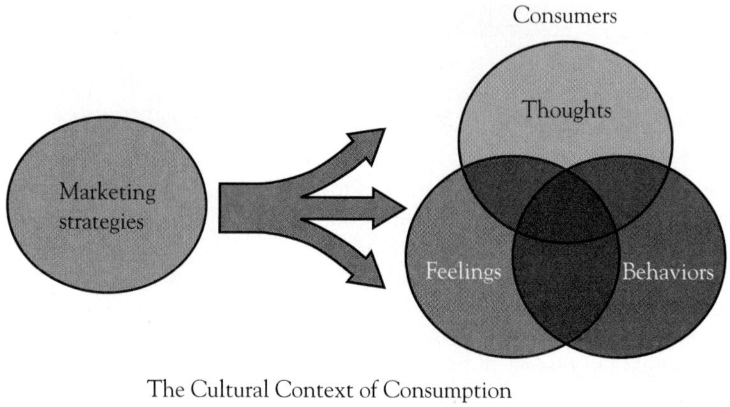

Friends line of dolls is produced to appeal to consumers in each major global city. Gaining a global focus for Mattel is very important. Although Mattel is the world's largest toy company and currently holds about 16 percent of the market share for toys sold in the United States, its share in Europe is less than 8 percent. With 800 million children in Asia, 120 million in Latin America, and 70 million in Europe, toy makers are challenging each other to make an impact in international toy sales.[14]

Global consumer marketing usually requires firms to tailor their strategies in response to variations in their environment. Typical sources of pressure to respond to local conditions include (1) differences in consumer tastes and preferences, (2) differences in infrastructure and customary marketing practices, (3) differences in distribution channels, and (4) host government rules and regulations. We discuss differences in consumer tastes and preferences throughout this book so we need not dwell on them here.

Differences in infrastructure include variation in measurement units (metric versus English measures), electrical current (110 versus 220 v), and telephone service (land versus microwave systems). Examples of differences in customary marketing practices include restrictions on advertising to children in Denmark and comparative advertising in Germany, rules about business-to-business gift giving, and the like. Such restrictions may even limit firms' abilities to commit to a marketing orientation, as researchers have found in Germany.

Differences in distribution channels include such things as channel penetration and retail concentration. Japanese distribution systems have more intermediaries than typical U.S. distribution systems, for example. By contrast, transition economies in eastern Europe or in China often lack developed marketing channels or experience a breakdown in channel penetration when centralized state-owned firms lose their monopoly on importing. Retail concentrations may also vary greatly between countries. For example, the packaged-rice industry is fragmented among a number of firms in Brazil and Italy and, until recently, was virtually nonexistent in Poland. The recent aggressive expansion of Wal-Mart and the French retailer Carrefour has dramatically increased retail concentration for clothing and housewares in many Latin and Asian nations.

Examples of host country regulations are many. A specific example concerns rules about the use of genetically modified seed materials. The United States is quite favorable, the European Community not. Similarly, pharmaceuticals are subject to an array of testing, registration, and pricing restrictions in different countries. Some countries, such as France or Canada, have moved to enforce rules requiring a certain percentage of locally produced content in their radio, television, and film media.[15]

In international consumer marketing, what foreign resources and capabilities do local firms typically want? In addition to capital, expertise in marketing strategy is one of the most universally sought capabilities. This function is almost completely absent in many organizations in transition economies and the less affluent world, yet it is a necessity if a company is to compete effectively. Unfortunately, local firms may be less interested in developing the managerial skills that make implementation of a marketing orientation possible.[16]

Consumers' Thoughts, Feelings, and Behaviors

Within a particular context, a person may have conflicting thoughts, feelings, and behaviors toward a product or service. For example, someone may express a preference for a brand but still not purchase it—the person has positive attitudes about a brand but negative purchase behavior. By digging into the conflicts between feelings, thoughts, and behavior, managers can not only better satisfy existing customers but develop differentiated products that appeal to unserved portions of the market.

Mazda's successful Miata roadster offers a great example of using the difference between customers' feelings and behaviors strategically and imaginatively. Mazda identified a large segment of consumers who had positive feelings and nostalgia for classic British sports cars (e.g., MG, Triumph, Austin Healey). However, the old British cars are associated with a stream of negative attributes—expense, breakdowns, parts problems, and so forth—that led customers to negative purchase behavior. They abandoned these brands. The Miata was an affordable answer to this conflict between thoughts, feelings, and behaviors. It retained the look and feel of a British sports car but without the associated problems. By examining both what consumers feel and what they do, marketers will have a better chance of developing a marketing mix that delivers superior value to a chosen target market segment. Indeed, Ford has subsequently revived the Jaguar brand by attending to the positive feelings but negative thoughts and behavior toward this brand.

Exhibit 5.2 illustrates a strategic analysis of consumers that involves an examination of both their purchase behaviors and their thoughts and feelings about a brand. Let's consider an

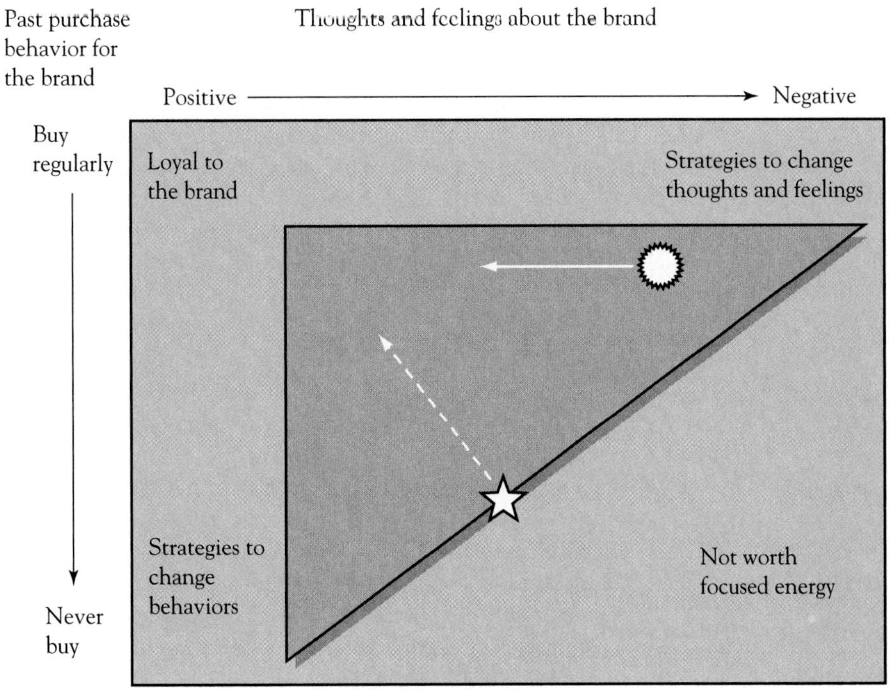

EXHIBIT 5.2

Strategic Analysis of Consumers

example of how such an analysis can help managers. Suppose you produce V8 brand vegetable juice (the name comes from the eight types of vegetable juice it contains) and you know that a segment of consumers know about V8 and have favorable feelings about the drink. But they only buy the brand occasionally or maybe never. This would mean they could be located about halfway down the triangle, as shown by the star in Exhibit 5.2.

Why they don't buy becomes the focus of attention. Perhaps, they haven't formed a V8 habit—they don't recognize a consumption situation that calls for a V8. In this case, advertising that reminds consumers of occasions to drink V8 would be a good tactic to reposition the product in their minds and change behavior. The manufacturers of V8 used to run an ad like this showing a consumer remarking, "Oh, I could have had a V8." This tactic aims to convert nonpurchasers with a favorable image of the product into **brand-loyal consumers,** *consumers who regularly purchase the brand and have an expressed preference for it.*

A marketer can also capitalize on brand loyalty that has been built up over time, so as to create innovative appeals to the target audience. Consider the ad for Fisherman's Friend, a throat lozenge being promoted in Bangkok. For this ad to have meaning, the reader has to have previous familiarity and experiences with the brand and its package. Thus, the advertiser can take advantage of this preexisting brand loyalty to produce a creative execution such that the package is folded into an origami *Tyrannosaurus rex,* which communicates the strength of the lozenge itself, as well as the strength of the brand.

Perhaps you can identify a segment of customers who buy V8 regularly, but when you explore in more depth you find their feelings about the product are mostly negative, as shown by the sunburst on Exhibit 5.2. These customers are vulnerable to competitors. Perhaps because of inertia or a lack of alternative vegetable juices they continue to buy your product, but they are ripe for the picking. Again, identifying why these consumers are unhappy and resolving their complaints can convert them into brand-loyal consumers.

Public transportation offers a case of customers who buy regularly out of necessity but often feel negatively about the product. Public transportation has typically not been market focused. In many places, people use public transportation regularly, but only because they have no other alternative; many people consider public transportation to be neither safe nor convenient. In a recent effort to make public transportation a preferred choice, managers of the Denver, Colorado, public transportation system listened to what customers didn't like about the service. They identified a segment of people commuting to an industrial park area of a nearby city where there was no convenient direct access. The transport authority added a special bus two times a day that provides direct, convenient access. This made their current customers more satisfied and more regular users of the service, and it attracted a number of new users who now found public transportation more convenient. Similarly, in the Niger Republic in West Africa the National Transportation Company (NTC) introduced an air-conditioned, on-time express bus service linking major cities in this very poor country. Although the service was costly by local standards, NTC always filled the bus, and this service helped NTC become one of the few profitable state-run companies in Niger.

"Be Warned!" Not only is the throat lozenge strong, but so is brand loyalty to the product, which allows for minimalist and whimsical ad execution.

Finally, analyzing both consumer attitudes and behaviors can help managers pinpoint consumer segments that are not worth trying to develop. Anytime a company attracts new customers it is asking them to do something different from what they would have done in the absence of the marketing programs directed at them. They have to change their attitudes and their actions. Changing attitudes is difficult, as is changing behavior—changing both is expensive and sometimes impossible.

A growing consumer segment that dislikes a product and never buys bodes poorly for the company that makes it. Creative and future-oriented strategies are needed to respond. For example, some U.S. classical music orchestras have found that their audiences are aging and may not be replaced. Because of cutbacks in funding of public school music programs, many U.S. children reach adulthood with little exposure to classical music. In the short term, orchestra marketing directors can attempt to resolve the problem of shrinking audiences by offering them benefits other than classical music—meeting singles, firework displays, family picnics, and more popular musical fare. This, however, is an uphill battle because of other competitive options. In the longer term, orchestras like to play classical music and would like to develop audiences that enjoy their music. This suggests an active outreach program to replace cutbacks in school music programs and to attract future concertgoers by building positive consumer attitudes early. The Pacific Symphony Orchestra in Orange Country, California, has a very aggressive community outreach program. For example, they offer an "adopt a musician" education program serving 17,000 students in 20 schools. But one wonders whether and which school children could be targeted effectively with this outreach program. What do you think?[17]

Marketing Imagination

The connection between understanding customers and designing effective marketing strategies requires creativity and imagination.[18] Customers can often tell marketers what's important to them, and they can identify problems they face in their lives; but they usually can't identify what they'd like the company to do about it. Marketing

An imaginative company: Benetton promotes its casual clothing along with the virtues of multiculturalism through global marketing communications.

An imaginative company: Rollerblade, Inc., continues to grow through innovation. In 1995, *Business Week* magazine selected Rollerblade's Bravoblades with automatic braking technology (ABT) as one of the best new products on the market.

intelligence attempts to find out what problems customers are trying to solve, and marketing imagination offers solutions. Great consumer examples of marketing imagination include the following. Rollerblades invented not merely a product and a sport, street hockey, but an entire youth lifestyle tailored to urban living. Rollerblade has now attracted a global following. Benetton promotes its casual clothing along with the virtues of multiculturalism to a global market segment, allowing its brand to cross many political, social, and cultural borders. There are almost 30 Benetton outlets in Syria, for example, a country known neither for its promarket policies nor its fashion-forward orientation. In Bangladesh, GrameenPhone provided a solution to the notorious isolation of rural villages through small loans to village women that enable them to buy cellular phones. The women use the phones to sell airtime to their neighbors. The women entrepreneurs profit from the difference between retail and wholesale airtime costs, approximately $50 per month, twice Bangladesh's per capita income.[19]

FreeMarkets' vertical auctions described earlier offer a business-to-business example of marketing imagination. Nalco Chemical and Betz Laboratories, two highly successful chemical companies, offer another. Originally, both of these companies thought of themselves as manufacturers and distributors of chemical products for use in water treatment. Over time, both companies concluded that everyone would benefit if they took over their customers' water-treatment processes themselves. For a monthly fee, Nalco and Betz guarantee the best available handling of all water-treatment issues. By having the imagination to connect a consumer problem with a marketing solution, both companies created new businesses that turned out to be immensely profitable. Industry Insights 5.1 provides another clever business-to-business example of the marketing imagination.[20]

Marketing imagination doesn't just involve finding solutions to consumer problems; sometimes it involves a different type of matching of consumer problems and solutions. Many companies develop new technologies and then attempt to determine what consumer problems these technologies can solve. When the goal is truly innovative products and markets, being customer-led is not enough.[21] Kodak offers an example.

Beach'n Billboard

INDUSTRY INSIGHTS 5.1

Beach'n Billboard is a company that brings the marketing imagination to life. The firm makes interchangeable impression mats that are mounted to a custom-designed cylinder and donates the apparatus to towns that own beaches. The company then pays a town a daily fee to hitch the trailer behind the town's beach-cleaning vehicles. In return, Beach'n Billboard retains the right to market the beach as a giant billboard. For as much as $2,500 a month, the firm guarantees that a client's message will be embossed onto the beach every day—as many as 5,000 impressions. In addition, each imprint is tagged with an antilittering message that helps reduce beach trash. Thus, clients get a "green" rub-off. Skippy peanut butter, Snapple, ABC television, and the 1999 Super Bowl have been clients. The technology is already under license to the Netherlands, Portugal, and Japan.

Source: Bennett Daviss, "The Subtle and Not-So-Subtle New Science of Advertising and Marketing," Ambassador, *April 2000, pp. 18–20.*

The company searched explicitly for markets that combined its traditional competence in chemicals (film) and electronic imagining (copying). What emerged was an idea for a new kind of film and camera system. The result was the Advantix system.

www.kodak.com/global/en/consumer/aps/index.shtml

A decade or two ago we weren't asking for portable computers, cellular telephones, CD players, digital video disks, automatic tellers, Palm Pilots, or the Internet. Nevertheless, each of these products has been successful and solves important customer problems. To realize opportunities, companies like FreeMarkets have the imagination to envision markets that do not exist and to stake them out ahead of the competition. Similarly, NEC is pursuing a telephone that can interpret between callers speaking in different languages, and Motorola envisions a world in which telephone numbers are attached to people rather than places. The marketing imagination requires deep insight into the needs, lifestyles, and aspirations of today's and tomorrow's customers. Companies with marketing imagination are able to lead customers where they want to go before customers know it themselves. A few important guidelines to nurturing the marketing imagination are described in Good Practice 5.3.

In this chapter we discuss tools for segmenting markets and positioning products; in Chapter 6 we discuss tools for learning about consumers. We will not be able to give you a marketing imagination, however. Standing at the top of a ski slope, it helps to have good boots, appropriate skis and poles, and good instruction. However, only dedicated practice, many mistakes, and good luck make for a successful run. Although companies such as GE, Shell, Microsoft, Nestlé, Toyota, and Procter & Gamble are among the largest and most successful in the world, each has experienced many failures. But they learned from their mistakes and tried again. This book will help you develop deeper insight into the lives of consumers, but only diligent attention to consumer behaviors around you will give you a marketing imagination.

GOOD PRACTICE 5.3

The Imaginative Company

1. **Escapes the tyranny of the served market.** The imaginative company views itself as a portfolio of core competencies rather than as a portfolio of products. It avoids overly narrow business charters.
2. **Searches for innovative product concepts.** The imaginative company (1) adds important new functions to well-known products (Yamaha's digital recording piano); (2) develops novel forms to deliver an important function (automated teller machines and electronic pocket calendars); and (3) delivers new functions through entirely new product concepts (camcorders and home fax machines).
3. **Overturns traditional price/performance assumptions.** The imaginative company challenges existing price/performance trade-offs. To do this means envisioning the possibility that the function of a $50,000 technology can be delivered with a $500 price tag (this is what happened with VCRs) and so on. Often it means distinguishing functions from the traditional product form used to deliver those functions.
4. **Gets out in front of customers.** The imaginative company goes beyond traditional modes of market research. These companies observe up close the world's most sophisticated and demanding customers. They work to anticipate consumers' future problems. These companies develop marketers with technological imagination and technologists with marketing imagination.

Source: Gary Hamel and C. K. Prahalad, "Corporate Imagination and Expeditionary Marketing," Harvard Business Review, *July–August 1991, pp. 81–92.*

From a consumer behavior standpoint, the core of marketing strategy concerns market segmentation, targeting, and product positioning. We discuss each of these in detail in the next several sections of this chapter. Throughout the book, we will give many examples of how consumer behavior theory and research enable and improve marketing strategies.

MARKET SEGMENTATION AND MASS CUSTOMIZATION

Market segmentation is based on a simple idea: in general, not everyone wants the same things. From this idea comes **market segmentation,** which is *the process of dividing a market into identifiable groups of similar consumers.* By similar, we mean groups that are alike in their responses to marketing mix tactics that an organization can effectively and profitably develop. The **marketing mix** refers to *those basic building blocks of marketing strategy—a product, its price, promotional communications, and its place of purchase and delivery.* A potential segment, for example, might consist of people who share the attribute "red hair." But this attribute only becomes relevant to marketers if, as consumers, the people with red hair exhibit purchase behavior or have consumption needs that are similar and, at the same time, differ from those of other groups, such as people with black and brown hair. As it turns out, several shampoo manufacturers, including L'Oréal, Paul Mitchell, and Aveda, market shampoos especially for red-haired consumers.

Until the 1980s, many consumer products firms were content to make a few products for large mass markets. One of the earliest examples was Henry Ford's Model T auto produced from 1909 to 1927. For much of the twentieth century, marketers spoke of marketing to the "average" consumer. However, in the **Triad regions** (*North America, Europe, and the Asian Pacific Rim*) by the 1980s, the satisfaction of basic needs and the glut of competitive goods and services led to market saturation. As a result, the process of market segmentation has now become increasingly complex as marketers identify more specialized market segments, such as consumers interested in Ford's limited-production, retro Thunderbird. National markets have fragmented into smaller, more demanding, and more market-wise consumer segments. If they are to meet these markets' needs, global companies face the additional complexity of responding to the cultural differences that exist between international markets (see Chapters 2 and 3).

www.mtfca.com

Soon market segmentation may give way to **mass customization,** which a growing number of manufacturers are adopting. *Customization means manufacturing a product or delivering a service in response to a particular customer's needs, and mass customization means doing it in a cost-effective way.*[22] Saturn, Toyota, and even jeans maker Levi Strauss and Co. are moving in this direction. Hallmark Cards and American Greetings installed electronic kiosks in stores and other public places to enable people to create their own greeting cards. However, these systems have not fully exploited the potential of mass customization—they offer no opportunities to customize graphics and don't learn and remember customer preferences.

With the growth of the Internet, mass customization is likely to be a significant force in the next few decades, as more companies try to cultivate **learning relationships** with their customers. *By learning about the customer during each exchange,* companies can more precisely tailor products and services to the particular needs of that customer. Thus, Amazon.com provides suggestions to repeat customers on the basis of their previous orders. In the short-run, market segmentation will remain the tool of choice for most consumer marketing organizations. In this section we focus primarily on market segmentation, but many of the same principles apply when mass customization is the goal.

To develop a competitive advantage for a product or service with specific market segments, the organization needs to ask what consumer variables may affect the success of a particular marketing strategy. Many of the chapters that follow identify these kinds of consumer variables. A firm achieves a competitive advantage when it is able to deliver a bundle of benefits or values that consumers perceive to be unique to the product. If this happens, the firm is in a position to benefit from repeated exchange relationships with product- or brand-loyal consumers, those who purchase the product repeatedly and feel positively about it. An approach to segmenting markets is illustrated in Exhibit 5.3. This process begins with a thorough investigation of consumer–product relationships.

Investigating Consumer–Product Relationships

From our perspective, the first step in developing a useful understanding of market segments is investigating consumer–product relationships. Throughout this chapter we have emphasized that marketing imagination, effective product differentiation, and

EXHIBIT 5.3

The Market Segmentation Process

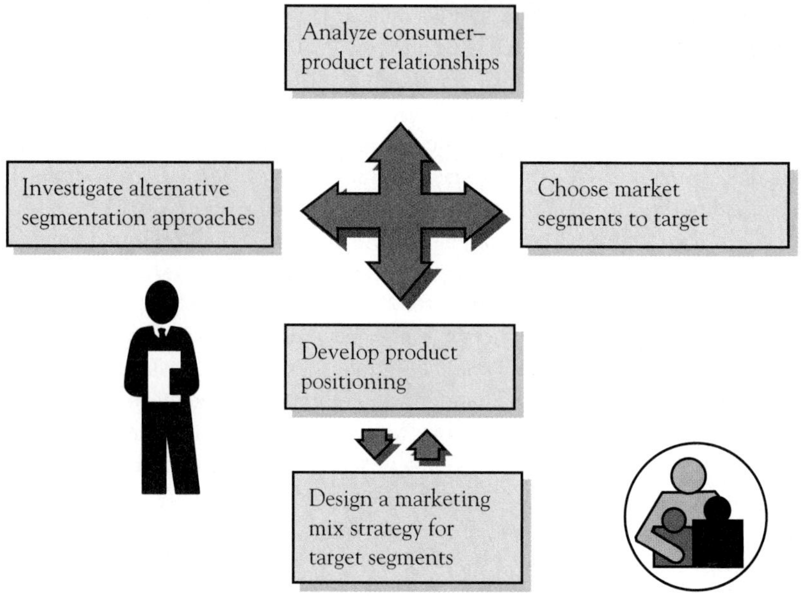

market segmentation begin with a thorough understanding about consumer–product relationships for each phase of the circle of consumption. This involves answering a number of questions. Recall that Good Practice 5.1 identifies a series of questions managers can ask to capture the consumers' total experience and identify potentially unique ways to differentiate their products. In this section we discuss three questions about how consumers relate to particular products. At the most general level, marketers need to ask, *What kind of environmental factors are involved in the purchase–consumption process for the product?* This question has many parts. What effect do macroeconomic factors have on product purchase and consumption? For example, in poorer countries with a low average income, companies may need to modify the product by selling in smaller quantities or reduce the price by developing more cost-effective production strategies. An economic downturn might inspire a firm to make its products more attractive by initiating creative credit policies for its products. Industry Insights 5.2 identifies an imaginative response to environmental factors in Germany.[23]

A second general sort of question marketers should ask is, *What does the product category mean to consumers and how involved are they in purchasing and consuming it?* This includes a wide range of questions

Innovative Auto Leasing in Germany

INDUSTRY INSIGHTS 5.2

The automobile has long been revered as an emblem of freedom and prosperity in Germany; but the price of maintaining this cherished icon keeps rising. Germans pay some of the highest fuel prices in the world (more than $5 per gallon); they are also complaining about traffic congestion, accidents, and air pollution. In response, Bremen's public transportation system introduced a new approach to automobile use—car-sharing. A smart card provides access to 10 different car models available at 37 locations, and when the car is returned, a swipe of the card locks the car and records mileage for billing information. Rates are lower than for conventional car rentals: about $7 for a six-mile shopping trip and $85 for a two-day, 120-mile excursion. There has been much interest in similar programs in other German cities and in other European countries sharing the Bremen context of high fuel prices, good public transit, and road congestion.

Source: Thomas T. Semon, "Program Steers Germany in Right Direction," Marketing News, *May 8, 2000, p. 27.*

such as, What sensory properties are associated with this product? What emotions are associated with the product? How does it relate to other consumption activities and products? How does it relate to the self and other people important to the consumer? What images and memories are associated with the product? What risks are associated with the purchase and use of the product? and so on.

A European campaign for Evian attempts to associate a variety of emotions with the branded bottled water. On the one hand, the campaign features a series of ads that communicates the message over time, as is necessary for a relationship to be established and maintained. On the other hand, individual ads communicate emotions such as fun, excitement, youthful energy, and sexuality. Besides communicating emotions, the ad also makes a link with other consumption activities and products. The ad campaign is entitled "Evian Jetiquette," so that the potentially mundane product category of water is now linked with an affluent, hip lifestyle, as represented by the models and jet interior appearing in the ad. To take another example, a program like the Bremen car-sharing system, described in Industry Insights 5.2, would be a difficult marketing challenge in the United States. Not having your own car is more inconvenient in the United States than in Europe; in addition, car use is much cheaper and the environmental movement, which supports the program in Europe, is far weaker in the United States. But most important, many U.S. citizens are emotionally involved with their cars.[24]

Frequently people use a product not because of its functional attributes but because of its meanings. Chapter 4 deals extensively with issues of product meaning. Watching soccer matches is an activity that traditionally is not very popular in the United States.[25] However, in the rest of the world, soccer (or football) is the most popular spectator

World Cup Madness in Turkey

CONSUMER CHRONICLES 5.1

All government offices shut down for the morning. Throughout the nation, people gathered together and huddled around their TVs. Chanting voices raised up and flags were waved. This same scene repeated seven times during the month of June 2002 in Turkey, which was in the midst of its worst economic downturn in history. Even though the economy had fallen over 9 percent in one year and layoffs were becoming the norm, the citizens of Turkey were able to forget those problems for one month, and they united in a common cause. Of course, the events that triggered this euphoria was the World Cup Finals, which are held every four years.

There's a whole website culture in the soccer world. In addition, the World Cup is the most watched event in the history of television. Fans come out at all hours of the day or night to watch their country's footballers compete, live, with teams of other nations. Fans dress in their country's colors—often donning full replica uniforms and painting their faces. They chant in unison to patriotic songs. They dance in the streets after thrilling victories and sometimes pillage or damage public buildings or marketplaces after heartbreaking losses.

In 2002, Turkey was making its first appearance in the World Cup Finals since 1954. But with gutsy determination and fierce play, the Turkish team raised the hopes of their countrymen and went all the way to the semifinals before ending up as the third-place team.

Such a remarkable outcome means a lot for Turkish citizens who are battling economic and political woes. The spectator sport proved to be a welcome distraction from these serious hardships. Fans showed their appreciation with a crowd of over 10,000 welcoming home their heroic footballers to the capital city of Ankara. Now the fans are looking forward to World Cup 2006, which will be staged in Germany, where over 2.6 million people of Turkish heritage already make their home. As the coach of the Turkish team noted. "We were guests here (in South Korea and Japan). But we will be the host in Germany!"

Sources: Steven L. Hellerman, Offside: Soccer and American Exceptionalism *(Princeton: Princeton University Press, 2001); and fifaworldcup.yahoo.com/en.*

sport, and, as illustrated in Consumer Chronicles 5.1, there are an elaborate lifestyle and a bundle of meanings associated with this spectator sport. Procter & Gamble's introduction of disposable diapers in Japan, described in Consumer Chronicles 5.2, provides another example of the importance of product uses and meanings to purchase behaviors. Learning from its Japanese mistakes, P&G was more careful introducing disposable diapers in Korea, China, and elsewhere. It stuck to unisex white in these markets. In these countries sexism is very strong. Buying a pink diaper package as in the United States would make visible that the family has a less prestigious daughter instead of a more prestigious son.[26]

@ fifaworldcup.yahoo.com/en

Another example concerns McDonald's in China. In the twenty-first century, McDonald's has become a favorite destination for children celebrating birthday parties. But birthday celebrations are themselves a recent innovation in China. Now many kids in China celebrate birthdays with McDonald's food and with "Auntie McDonald" playing hostess; it has become a preferred mode of consumption. Thus, the particular ways in which people consume McDonald's products are important to marketing strategy in Beijing. This example is useful since it also illustrates that marketers must often communicate not only with the end user of a product like a McDonald's Happy Meal but also with the purchaser, perhaps the child's grandparent, and possibly other decision makers, such as a child's parent or parents.[27]

It may sound strange to some readers to ask what kind of relationships consumers have with products and brands. After all we are talking about inanimate objects not people or pets. But people do develop complex relationships with some products and brands they use. Consumer Chronicles 5.3 summarizes some of the different types of relationships that people may form with products and brands.

At the extreme, some brands become the focus of **brand communities,** *groups of people who share a consciousness of a kind, share moral responsibility for other members, and perpetuate rituals and traditions associated with the brand.* Brand communities grow up around specific brands. They boost customer retention. For instance, Saturn owners are fairly loyal, even cultish. Thousands show up for the annual Saturn birthday party in Tennessee. And Saturn has been a leader in customer service and satisfaction, consistently ranked at the top of the J. D. Power and Associates sales satisfaction index. Followers of the rock group Phish and the 25,000 members of the Winnebago-Itasca (mobile homes or caravans) Travelers Group are other examples.[28]

A final question that marketers must ask about consumer–product relationships is, *What behaviors are involved in the purchase–consumption process for this product?* This includes questions such as, Where do they buy or use it? How do they buy or use it? How often and when do they buy or use it? The impact of Internet retailing on some categories of goods, especially those that can take digital form such as computer software, travel and event tickets, financial products, music, video, and books, illustrates the importance of these questions. On the other hand, websites are not much good for replicating precisely the social function of shopping, nor for browsing around, nor for producing impulse purchases, all of which come from visiting a shopping center. Nor can e-commerce offer instant purchase gratification that many consumers expect. Traditional retailers continue to compete increasingly on these attributes.[29]

Diaper Use in Japan

CONSUMER CHRONICLES 5.2

In the late 1970s, Procter & Gamble introduced Pampers diapers in Japan, the world's second-largest consumer market. At first, the efforts paid off, but at $50 a month they were expensive. More important, they were too bulky. Procter & Gamble had overlooked a critical culture difference. Japanese mothers change their babies' diapers about 14 times a day—more than twice as often as most Americans. They wanted a thin diaper that was easy to store and use. A Japanese manufacturer caught on, and its thinner disposable—the Moony—soon snared 23 percent of the market. A Procter & Gamble executive recalled, "It was clear that we were out of the ballgame."

Source: Alecia Swasy, "Don't Sell Thick Diapers in Tokyo," New York Times, *October 3, 1993, p. F9.*

Investigating Alternative Segmentation Approaches

An organization can segment a market in many ways. Although there is no best basis for segmenting a market, a firm must start somewhere. Usually segmentation of consumer markets is based on one or more of three basic criteria: consumer needs as related to (1) some geographic or demographic criteria, (2) psychographic variables, or (3) behavioral variables. The major segmentation variables for consumer markets are illustrated in Exhibit 5.4. Ultimately, the **segmentation bases** for a firm's customers are determined by continual refinement of market offerings as consumers respond to them through purchase and use.

Geographic segmentation *divides the market into different geographical units such as nations, states, regions, counties, cities, or neighborhoods.* Chapter 11 describes how lifestyle segments are often associated with geographic location. For example, the

Examples of Consumer–Brand Relationship Forms

CONSUMER CHRONICLES 5.3

Relationship Form	Definition	Case Examples
Arranged marriages	Nonvoluntary union imposed by preferences of third party; intended for long-term exclusive commitment, although at low levels of affect	Adopting an ex-husband's preferred brands of cleansers or packaged foods
Casual friends, buddies	Friendship low in emotion and intimacy, characterized by infrequent engagement and few expectations for reward	Household cleaners
Best friendships	Voluntary union based on reciprocity principle; endures because of continued provision of voluntary rewards	Performance products such as athletic equipment; personal products such as soaps and moisturizers
Kinships	Nonvoluntary union with lineage ties	Brand preferences inherited from one's parents or grandparents
Flings	Short-term, time-bounded engagements of high emotional reward but devoid of commitment and reciprocity demands	Vacation of a "lifetime"; trial-size products; products bought on deal, e.g., a coupon
Enmities	Intensely involving relationship characterized by negative feelings and desire to avoid or inflict pain on the other	Partners' brands postdivorce or separation; recommended but rejected brands
Secret affairs	Highly emotive, privately held relationship considered risky if exposed to others	Treats of all kinds; racy lingerie

Source: Susan Fournier, "Consumers and Their Brands: Developing Relationship Theory in Consumer Research," Journal of Consumer Research *24 (March 1998), pp. 343–73.*

PRIZM system clusters U.S. consumers according to their zip code, socioeconomic status, and urbanization to derive 62 different kinds of neighborhoods.[30] Think about your own neighborhood. Are there certain products and services that could be targeted effectively to your entire neighborhood? In many parts of the world, degree of urbanization is an important segmentation variable that influences what products are distributed, how they are distributed, and how they are priced and promoted—in other words, the full marketing mix. To see regional taste differences in action consider a simple food such as soup. Industry Insights 5.3 illustrates differences in preferences for chicken noodle soup in different parts of the United States.[31]

Demographic segmentation consists of *dividing the market into groups on the basis of variables such as age, sex, income, occupation, education, religion, family size, family life cycle, and ethnicity.* Demographic variables are the most popular bases for distinguishing customer groups. Even when the target market is described in nondemographic terms (say, a lifestyle), a link to demographic variables is necessary in order to identify and reach the target segment.

We can use the example of Campbell soup to illustrate the value of demographic segmentation.[32] Campbell Soup began making its first ready-to-serve soup in 1892, and today the company remains the U.S. market leader. Campbell has extended its reach worldwide, acquiring well-known brands in Great Britain, Japan, and other countries. Campbell's philosophy is to target markets locally. In the United States, Campbell has segmented on several demographic variables, including age (with products for the children's market and the aging baby boomer interested in low-fat, healthy alternatives); income (with upscale, premium brands marketed under the Pepperidge Farm name); and ethnicity (for example, selling spicy nacho-flavored cheese soup in California and Texas and using different promotional campaigns to reach Caribbean- and Mexican-Americans).

INDUSTRY INSIGHTS 5.3

Regional Preferences in Campbell's Chicken Noodle Soup Line

Detroit	Chicken Noodle with Mushrooms
Cincinnati	Red-and-white-labeled Chicken Noodle
Seattle	Home Cookin' chicken with broad egg noodles
Milwaukee	Microwave Chicken Noodle
Baltimore	Healthy Request Chicken Noodle
Salt Lake City	Family Size Chicken Noodle
Denver	Chicken-flavor Ramen Noodle

Source: Ronald D. Michman and Edward M. Mazze, The Food Industry Wars: Marketing Triumphs and Blunders *(Westport, CT: Quorum Books, 1998).*

Geographic and Demographic

Region	Age
County size	Gender
City or SMSA size	Family size
Density	Family life cycle
Climate	Income
	Occupation
	Education
	Religion
	Ethnicity

Psychographic

Social class
Lifestyle
Subculture
Personality

Behavioral

Occasions
Benefits
User status
Loyalty status
Buyer readiness stage
Attitude toward product

EXHIBIT 5.4

Major Segmentation Bases

Psychographic segmentation divides buyers into *groups on the basis of differences in consumer lifestyle.* We can think of **lifestyle** broadly as *how people live; this includes their activities, interests, and opinions.* In some cases, researchers measure lifestyles in very broad terms by asking questions such as, Do you prefer to read a book or go to a party? For example, one market research group has segmented high-tech buyers into nine attitude categories, including cyber-snobs, media junkies, and sidelined citizens, the latter a technophobic group.[33] An illustration of a "cybersnob" appeal is shown in the ad for the Macro Media Flash Player. As illustrated in the ad, the consumer who doesn't use Flash appears to be toothless, psychotic, and scary. In other situations, lifestyles are measured in very specific terms. Kellogg's has been serving the health-conscious consumer market segment since the early 1900s and now has several distinct market subsegments, as illustrated in Industry Insights 5.4. Lifestyles are certainly related to demographics such as income, occupation, gender, family life cycle, ethnicity, and so on, but they also reflect a complex composite of a person's self and experiences. We talk more about psychographic segmentation in Chapter 11.

www.macromedia.com

Increasingly, hybrid approaches that combine demographics, geographics, and psychographics are employed to segment markets more precisely. For example, using all three criteria, one recent study divided the Chinese market into four main segments: the nouveau riche (*baofahu*), yuppies (*dushi yapishi*), salary class (*gongxin jiceng*), and the working poor (*qiongiaogong*). Details about these groups can be found in Good Practice 5.4. Lifestyle orientations of these four segments hint at possible marketing opportunities. What ideas do you have?[34]

With **behavioral segmentation,** *buyers are divided into groups on the basis of differences in their knowledge, attitude, use, or response to a product.* Many marketers believe that behavioral variables offer the best starting point for identifying market segments. One powerful form of behavioral segmentation is benefit segmentation. **Benefit segmentation** divides buyers according to the *different benefits they seek from the product.* Behavioral segmentation is so important because segmentation only has value if it is related to consumer–product relationships. Perceived benefits of product consumption anchor such relationships. For instance, the Hong Kong ad for Kiwi shoe polish uses a humorous approach to depict two benefits associated with the product: cleanliness and respect.

Marketers have tried to explore what sorts of benefits are desired by different groups of consumers and which of these benefits leads to the greatest amount of consumer satisfaction (see Chapter 18). Benefits can take a variety of forms. For example, some derive benefits from the functions products perform. Others derive social benefits, for example, from anonymous disposition behaviors such as charitable giving to social service agencies. Still other consumers derive benefits from innovation, such as being the first to acquire a particular product or service. Some derive benefits from creative use of products that manufacturers did not intend, such as using carbonated water to remove wet spills from clothing or carpets. Others, as illustrated in the cartoon on page 194, are like Calvin, the six-year-old comic strip hero who won't eat any cereal that doesn't turn his milk purple. Not only do consumers derive different types of benefits from products in general, but also different consumers may derive different benefits from the same product. Suntan lotion, for example, may provide tanning, sun protection, moisturizing, or scenting benefits. Attention to benefit segmentation provides marketers with multiple positioning bases (see Good Practice 5.4) for their products.

Kellogg's Cereals for Health and Nutritional Needs

INDUSTRY INSIGHTS 5.4

Brand	Market Segment
Special K	Low cholesterol
Product 19	Dieters
Müeslix	Nutrition oriented
Just Right	Natural ingredients
All-Bran	High fiber

Another kind of behavioral segmentation concerns how much of a product people use. Several different types of segmentation associated with product use are possible. Consider that for many products over three-quarters of the purchases are made by half of the customers. Often markets can be segmented into light, medium, and heavy user groups. This makes **usage rate segmentation,** *segmenting the market by amount of the product purchased or consumed,* valuable. For example, a recent study in Hong Kong segmented the green market into light and heavy green consumers. Heavy consumers enjoyed a higher education and a higher household income than light green consumers. Heavy green consumers reported that they liked to buy environmentally friendly products and that buying such products was considered good for their health and the environment and easy. Light users perceived that environmentally friendly products were difficult to obtain, were more expensive, and did not have better quality. What strategies and marketing mix tactics would you use to reach these two groups of consumers?[35]

Another aspect of benefit segmentation relates to the occasions consumers associate with product use. Consumers reserve some purchases for particular occasions, wedding gifts, for example. They do not consider it appropriate to purchase them on other occasions. Americans like to purchase china and small appliances for weddings, whereas Nigerians purchase beds and bedding, for example. And it is hard to imagine French consumers drinking the aperitif *pastis* at any time except the cocktail hour. In the United States the poultry industry has had a difficult time expanding sales of turkey because of its strong symbolic associations with a particular occasion, Thanksgiving Day. Thus, **occasion segmentation** *divides buyers according to when they acquire or use a product.*

GOOD PRACTICE 5.4
A Hybrid Approach to Segmenting Chinese Consumers

Segment/Attribute	Nouveau Riche	Yuppies	Salary Class	Working Poor
Size of segment	100,000	60 million	3,000 million	840 million
Geographics				
Residence place	Coastal urban areas	Major urban areas	Small cities	Small towns and rural areas, especially in the west of China
Demographics				
Household income	Above $5,000	$2,000–5,000	$1,000–1,999	Less than $1,000
Age	30–65	25–45	18–60	All age groups
Education	Various	College	High school	Elementary school
Occupation	Entrepreneurs, businesspeople, government officials, celebrities	Managerial, professional, technical	Office clerks, factory workers, teachers	Manual laborers, peasants, migrant workers
Psychographics				
Orientation	Optimistic	Hopeful	Status quo	Uncertain
Innovativeness	Innovators, trend setters	Early adopters, opinion leaders	Early majority, emulators	Late majority, laggards
Risk aversion	Low	Moderate	High	Very high
Readiness for foreign goods	High	Moderate	Low	Minimum
Lifestyles				
Mobility	Active	Mobile	Confined	Immobile
Activities	Wheel and deal, dine and wine in exclusive clubs; frequent shopping binges	Busy work schedule; frequent dining out and excursions	Trapped 8 to 5; limited disposable income; occasional outings; cameras and parks	Menial labor; hand-to-mouth; mass entertainment such as sports on TV

Occasion segmentation can help firms expand product usage. Frequently, an excellent way to increase demand is to get current consumers to use the product for more occasions. Numerous companies have promoted more usage occasions as a way to expand demand. In addition to the new uses promoted for Arm & Hammer baking soda and McIlhenny's Tabasco sauce discussed earlier in the chapter, a campaign by the Florida Orange Growers provides another example: "Orange Juice isn't just for breakfast anymore."

Selling Shandy: Targeting Underage Drinkers

ETHICAL DILEMMA 5.1

Jolly Shandy is a low-alcohol beverage that was launched in 1984 by Carlsberg Malaysia. The drink is a mixture of lemonade and beer, and it is "specially formulated for young adult drinkers." It's enriched with vitamin C and appeals to those with a trendy lifestyle. In fact, shandy is a popular beverage around the world, and it is frequently targeted toward younger drinkers. In Britain, an 11-year-old girl was sent home from school for bringing a can of shandy into a classroom. Even though the level of alcohol is low enough for the shandy to be classed as a soft-drink in Britain, the Holt School in Wokingham sent the pupil home. Is it ethical for brewers to produce and sell a beverage like Jolly Shandy? In many parts of the world, this drink is targeted to younger drinkers, who may be especially vulnerable to messages that feature groups of youthful people having fun. For instance, in the UK, there is growing concern about the increasing number of young girls who regularly drink alcohol. Even if the official target market is those of legal drinking age, marketers are aware that those who fall below the legal age will still be attracted to the product. And peer pressure is a very strong influence among this cohort of teenagers. If a person starts to drink a sweet alcoholic beverage at a young age, then the odds may be increased that this same person will move on to other alcoholic beverages later in life.

As illustrated by this brief example, traditional marketing methods (e.g., segmentation and targeting) are quite powerful. Is it ethical to use these techniques to promote socially harmful products to those who are vulnerable (e.g., young teens)?

Sources: http://www.carlsberg.com.my/product/jolly.cfm.

Another type of use segmentation focuses on **buyer readiness.** We discuss this in greater detail in Chapter 15. Buyer readiness refers to the fact that *at any time people are in different stages of willingness to buy a product.* For example, some people may be unaware of the product, others aware, some knowledgeable, some interested, and some intending to buy. The marketing program for new technological innovations, for example, will be dramatically affected by the relative numbers of people at different stages of readiness to buy. Notice that the Chinese market segments profiled in Good Practices 5.4 vary in their readiness to buy foreign goods. Whichever segmentation criteria an organization chooses, four general **rules of good segmentation** can be identified. They are summarized in Good Practices 5.5. First, in selecting market segments, a firm should assess whether a segment is *measurable.* In other words, can the segment be clearly identified on the basis of measurable criteria? For example, we might like to know the number of Thai males ages 21–30, making between US$7,500 and US$15,000 annually, employed in the banking sector in Bangkok, the capital city of Thailand, to target for the sale of securities sold on the Hong Kong stock market. Good Practices 5.4 supplies measures of Chinese market segments.

GOOD PRACTICE 5.5

Effective Segmentation Criteria

1. **Measurability.** Can the size and purchasing power of the segment be clearly identified and measured?
2. **Substantiality.** Is the segment large enough or profitable enough to warrant a separate market offering?
3. **Accessibility.** Can the segment be effectively reached and served?
4. **Responsiveness.** Does the segment respond differently to one or more elements of the marketing mix?

A second important criterion is that of *substantiality.* Is the market segment large enough to warrant the expense of developing a market offering to meet its needs? In other words, does the segment exhibit adequate market potential? Revenues derived from exchanges with the segment must cover the costs of developing a differentiated market offering and provide the desired profits. Ideally a segment should be growing. For this reason, the over-55-year-old market in the Triad countries (North America, Europe, Japan) is attracting a lot of attention from marketers. Likewise, the Chinese yuppie market profiled in Good Practice 5.4 is attractive because it is growing. Because of its growth, the Hispanic market has become attractive to mainstream marketers in North America. By contrast, niche marketers (see cartoon below) may be content with merely stable market segments with whom they can develop multiple, recurrent exchange relations. Above all, marketers should avoid fickle segments. For this reason, while it might be perfectly feasible to develop a line of off-road inline skates, or specialized surfboards for parachute surfing, there may not be adequate market potential to merit the costs of developing and marketing these items.

A third criterion for effective market segmentation is *accessibility.* Accessibility refers to the ability of an organization (1) to communicate with its customers and (2) to deliver products and services to its customers reliably. The ability to communicate relates to issues such as the existence of media that reach the market segment and the firm's skill at using those media.

Many factors affect accessibility. In the Triad countries, market and media fragmentation complicate accessibility. Some Hollywood studios, for example, are trying new strategies to communicate, such as showing prerelease screenings at conventions, providing sneak previews for online film critics, and even offering first-run films to college film studies courses, all to stimulate demand. Some groups are just hard to reach—college students, for example. Residential instability and constraints on media exposure due to studying are two of the factors that make them inaccessible. Media content significantly affects accessibility. Studies indicate that communication in the appropriate language and use of same language/same ethnicity spokespersons have a significant positive effect on attitudes toward commercial messages.[36] Media type also affects accessibility. Consumer Chronicles 5.4 reminds us that cultures vary in their respon-

Source: CALVIN AND HOBBES © Watterson. Reprinted with permission of UNIVERSAL PRESS SYNDICATE.

siveness to particular media.[37] Until recently it has been difficult to communicate with the vast markets of east Asia due to the absence of television satellites. It is difficult to reach these markets because of high rates of illiteracy as well. Sound trucks remain popular advertising tools in such markets.[38]

The other component of accessibility is the ability to deliver goods and services reliably. Accessibility problems are sometimes self-inflicted. The 1999 holiday season was infamous for customer order fulfillment and distribution problems at new e-tailers such as Toys "R" Us, Wal-Mart, and Etoys, for example. A variety of intrachannel barriers may keep firms away from potential markets. For example, many small firms cannot afford the slotting allowances charged by major retailers to place their products on the retailers' shelves. Sheer distances from point of production and geographic dispersal of the market are two geographic factors that may place some markets beyond an organization's reach. Limited production capacity may constrain a firm's ability to meet market demand, as happened in the early 1990s to the manufacturers of Super Soakers water pistols. Finally, in international contexts, a variety of trade barriers erected by protectionist policies (currency controls, domestic content limits, size and labeling requirements) may make some markets inaccessible.[39]

Direct Mail in Japan

CONSUMER CHRONICLES 5.4

The avalanche of junk mail they receive on an almost daily basis has jaded U.S. consumers. As a result, many Americans don't even open this mail. By contrast, a Japanese is much more likely than an American to open the envelope and respond to the offer. A word for "junk mail" does not exist in the Japanese language. Although the number of Japanese consumers who shop by mail is currently quite small, these sales are growing at a rate of more than 20 percent per year. The Japanese are receptive to direct mail, making them accessible. However, Japanese are extremely resistant to having their names sold among list companies. This makes measurability of target segments more difficult. The sale of financial information about Japanese consumers is already restricted in Japan, and other legal restrictions on consumer listings are in the process of being formulated.

Source: Michael J. McDermott, "Fishing for Customers," Profiles, *November 1992, pp. 44–48.*

The final criterion of effective market segmentation is *responsiveness.* A particular segment is likely to react differently than others to the elements of the marketing mix. For example, the Chinese nouveau riche profiled in Good Practice 5.4 are very responsive to Western market offerings. By contrast, the Chinese working poor—a large segment of 840 million—may not be very responsive to market offers because of low incomes. Similarly, in the Triad nations it is easy to identify working wives, and they can be accessed through specialized media and are a large percentage of the adult female population. However, working women's consumption behaviors do not differ dramatically from those of nonworking women despite the problems of time constraints and overload they experience. Hence, they may not be as responsive to convenience-based appeals as some have thought. The mosquito-borne disease malaria provides a final, tragic example. Malaria kills millions of people each year in the tropics, but pharmaceutical companies have little incentive to develop a vaccine since most of the victims are poor and could not respond to a marketing campaign for it.[40]

CHOOSING MARKET SEGMENTS TO TARGET

From a consumer behavior perspective, the next task in developing marketing strategy is selecting the most appropriate group or groups for the firm to serve. In choosing whom to serve, a firm may adopt three basic strategies. The first strategy is to *ignore differences between groups within a market and offer a single marketing mix to the entire market.* We refer to this strategic choice as mass or **undifferentiated marketing.**

"Who can afford *not* to moisturize?"

Source: © 2001 The New Yorker Collection from cartoonbank.com. All rights reserved.

The cartoon of the elephant buying moisturizer suggests the logic of this approach; it applies when the product meets important needs of a large, responsive market. Classic examples include Ford's Model T automobile or the Hershey chocolate bar. Contemporary examples include the marketing of agricultural commodities such as soybeans or early versions of Internet portals such as Yahoo! and AOL. Until recently, most hospitals adopted undifferentiated marketing; each hospital tried to offer a full range of services to all the customers in a market area. Many state-owned consumer product firms in formerly socialist countries adopted such a strategy. Some firms offering new products and services find themselves adopting this approach if they do not precisely know the characteristics of their target market. Du Pont's Kevlar fiber was available for some years before it was adapted for specific uses such as in baseball bats, skis, and bulletproof vests.

Some benefits accrue to a firm using undifferentiated marketing, most notably cost economies in production and marketing. In the developed markets of the world, however, such an approach entails numerous disadvantages, including customer dissatisfaction and organizational vulnerability to competitors offering more differentiated products and services to market subsegments. Consumer dissatisfaction with the undifferentiated segmentation approach of state-owned firms in the former socialist countries was widespread.

A second strategic option available is to operate in several segments of the market and design separate marketing mixes for each segment. We refer to this as multisegment or **differentiated marketing.** A classic example is General Motors' old "price ladder." Younger, first-time buyers were directed to buy inexpensive Chevrolet models; older, repeat customers were urged to buy Oldsmobiles or Buicks; still older, wealthier repeat buyers could move up to a Cadillac. Contemporary examples include the strategies of Nike or Reebok, which seek to offer a perfect shoe for nearly every kind of active person participating in nearly every kind of activity and sport. The recent evolution of the diaper business has been in the direction of multisegment marketing, making differently sized and padded diapers available for children from newborns to age five and for boys and girls as well. Cisco Systems pursues a similar strategy in the B2B computer switching and networking market.

The multisegment option entails both benefits and costs for an organization. On the one hand, by creating special market mixes for each segment, the organization hopes to create more total sales, or in the case of nonprofits, to obtain more donations. On the other hand, multisegment marketing is likely to increase the research and development, production, and marketing costs incurred as a result of creating multiple marketing mixes. These costs make it crucial that firms carefully choose segments, using the criteria outlined above.

Igor goes shopping.

Niche Marketing at Szczecin Shipyard, Poland

INDUSTRY INSIGHTS 5.5

With the collapse of the Soviet Union, the historic Polish shipyard Szczecin was plunged into financial crisis. Headed by a new management team installed in 1991, the shipyard embarked on a turnaround in three ways. First, to raise money, new management sold or gave away all but its core ship-building assets. Second, a new product strategy was chosen to more efficiently utilize the shipyard's capacity. Virtually all of the shipyard's capacity was moved to medium-sized container ships, resulting in a drastically shortened product-cycle time. Turnaround for a single ship was reduced from three years to 11 months. Finally, management began courting Western buyers. Two German firms placed a small order and received delivery six months earlier than they could have in Germany, and also realized 20 percent to 30 percent cost savings. Because these two firms were opinion leaders among German shippers (see Chapter 17), their order was quickly followed by a large number of other orders. By 1993, Szczecin had achieved a 40 percent world market share in its category.

Source: S. Johnson, D. Kotchev, and G. Loveman, "How One Polish Shipyard Became a Market Competitor," Harvard Business Review *73, no. 6 (1995), pp. 53–72.*

The final option available to an organization is to seek a large share of one or a few submarkets. We call this approach **concentrated** or **niche marketing.** The cartoon of Igor shopping for brains (p. 197) provides a humorous illustration of a peculiar niche-marketing strategy. There are many examples of successful niche-marketing strategies across a range of products and services. Celestial Seasonings offers a wide range of brewed, noncaffeinated beverages to the tea-drinking market; Bang & Olufsson offers a line of high-end stereo products to the audiophile; Goya foods in the northeast United States for many years has enjoyed more than 80 percent share of the Hispanic packaged foods market; Aston Martin targets its handmade automobiles toward the luxury car market; Orvis markets a line of specialty products to the advanced fly fisherman. Industry Insights 5.5 provides a dramatic business-to-business example in a transitional economy.[41]

Organizations that adopt a concentrated marketing strategy can enjoy a number of benefits. Among them are greater knowledge of their market segment's needs and wants, operating economies of scale, and increased loyalty from grateful customers. Some costs accompany this strategy too. The impact of product failure on the firm may be greater since risk is spread over fewer products; likewise, a loss of customer confidence might be difficult to mend. Perhaps more serious is the vulnerability to rapid and unpredicted changes in the segment's needs and wants. For example, Szczecin, featured in Industry Insights 5.5, was hardly prepared for the collapse of its assured Soviet ship market in 1990. Some firms in the Western aerospace defense business were likewise unprepared for the end of the Cold War and the abrupt decline in government arms procurement. Club Med struggled for a while when its "singles" vacation market changed to a family market. Further, a firm with a concentrated strategy may be vulnerable to competition from larger multisegment marketing firms that suddenly recognize opportunities in the niche market. In the United States, a number of cosmetics firms that operated in ethnic marketing niches now face competition from large firms such as Revlon.

In making the decision about what strategy to adopt, an organization's management needs to examine a number of questions. First, it must assess the skills and resources available to the organization. The more limited the skills and resources, the more likely undifferentiated strategies should be adopted. If only resources are lacking but the firm has good skills, as in the Szczecin case, concentrated strategies may be attractive. Second, the firm should assess market variability as suggested in the section on segmentation. If the market is not composed of identifiable, sizable, accessible, responsive segments, an undifferentiated strategy may be appropriate. Perhaps one size really does fit all. Alternatively, if many segments are identified, a differentiated or concentrated strategy is appropriate. A third, related issue is to ask, Just how variable is the product? For example, the market for bananas, mushrooms, or potatoes is relatively undifferentiated in the United States. Consumers perceive few differences between varieties. However, a firm marketing potatoes in Peru or Denmark, where numerous varieties of potato are grown, or mushrooms in France, where dozens of mushroom varieties are recognized, might be best advised to adopt a differentiated strategy. A fourth issue concerns the stage of the product life cycle. Typically, as in the case of Internet portals such as Yahoo!, undifferentiated strategies may be used early in the product life cycle. Differentiated strategies become more common during the growth and maturity phases, and concentrated strategies may become fruitful during the maturity and decline phases. A nice example of this is the maintenance, repair, and operations supply company Richardson Electronics, whose motto is "on the trailing edge of [industrial] technology." Richardson specializes in providing outmoded electronic parts.

Niche marketer: Celestial Seasonings positions a wide variety of caffeine-free beverages to appeal to the tea-drinking market.

A final issue that a firm must evaluate in adopting a segmentation strategy is its competitors' strategies. Although we noted above that bananas are a relatively undifferentiated product in U.S. markets, Chiquita has sought to differentiate its product from other bananas on quality and image. In so doing it follows the lead of Sunkist, which successfully differentiated its brands of oranges from other nonbranded varieties. The costs of inattention to competitors' strategies can be great. In the United States, canvas shoe companies such as Keds and Converse that failed to adopt the multisegment strategies of Reebok and Nike experienced a drop in market share, and only recently have they fought back by adopting their own niche-marketing strategies.

PRODUCT POSITIONING

Product positioning means *deciding how the organization wants the company and its brands to be perceived and evaluated by target markets.* In general, product positioning requires an organization to differentiate its market offerings from those of its competitors. However, it's not enough for the firm to distinguish its market offerings; it must do so in ways that are meaningful to its target market segments. For example, if the company has identified a profitable segment of skiers who are especially annoyed with the mechanics of skiing—getting their skis to and from the airport, from their car to the ski lift, picking up their lift tickets, and so forth—it might decide to offer a differentiated ski area. The key question is, What changes in what characteristics will clearly differentiate this ski area from competitors and communicate "ease of skiing" to the target skier segment? Deer Valley, located next to Park City, about half an hour from Salt Lake City, Utah, appeals to this segment of skiers with "valet ski service" and other amenities that make skiing more hassle free. Bear Hollow, another Utah ski area just north of Park City, caters to athletes in training and "weekend warriors" who want to experience the rush of ski jumping. Recreational ski jumping is a unique option not offered at most ski resorts.[42]

Firms seeking to enter their brands in another country's market may face large expenditures to build brand awareness and a positive brand image. Often, new market entrants use a particular kind of co-branding called a **brand alliance** to position brands. A brand alliance amounts to *renting a brand name known to target consumers from another firm.* Fuji–Xerox, Northwest–KLM, and British Air–USAir are examples of international brand alliances. Montana-grown barley gets increased visibility through a brand alliance with Budweiser beer. Experiments with Japanese and U.S. consumers have shown that consumer evaluations of an unknown brand from another country become more positive when a brand alliance is used to position the product. Brand alliances also increase consumers' evaluations of the brand's parent firm.[43]

To effectively position products and services for a target segment, an organization often begins by identifying competitors. Competitors are identified as those companies that offer similar benefits to the target consumers. The organization then undertakes research to determine how consumers perceive and evaluate the competitors. This step provides the organization with information about how competitors are positioned in the market. By analyzing consumers' preferences, the company can determine a profitable, differentiated position for their product or service. For example, Lee brand jeans positioned its product as offering "best fit" for women. Competitor Levi Strauss offered "Levi's for Women," using an ad campaign featuring drawings of graceful female forms by women artists. Both firms seek to differentiate their product from traditional jeans made for men. Consumer research can then be used to monitor the organization's success in attaining or maintaining that position in the market. Levi's has sought to further differentiate itself from competitors by setting up in-store kiosks where customers order custom-fit jeans that are home delivered in 48 hours.

One technique often used to position products and services is **perceptual mapping.** A perceptual map is a *spatial picture of how consumers view products or brands within a market.* Exhibit 5.5 illustrates a perceptual map of 15 products and services that could be purchased over the Internet. A nationwide sample of Internet users in the United States and Canada was polled to produce this map. Whether or not respondents have purchased (specific products and services) online in the 15 product and service categories provides the basis for the map. It is important to note that this pattern of results is culturally biased. The same study conducted in a different culture would include a different set of offerings and may result in a different pattern for the map.

In this study, a key research question is, How do Internet purchases cluster together? For instance, is the person who buys a book online also likely to purchase an airline ticket online? The answer to such a question could help advertisers plan their cross-promotions (e.g., does the book retailer want to advertise on the travel agent's

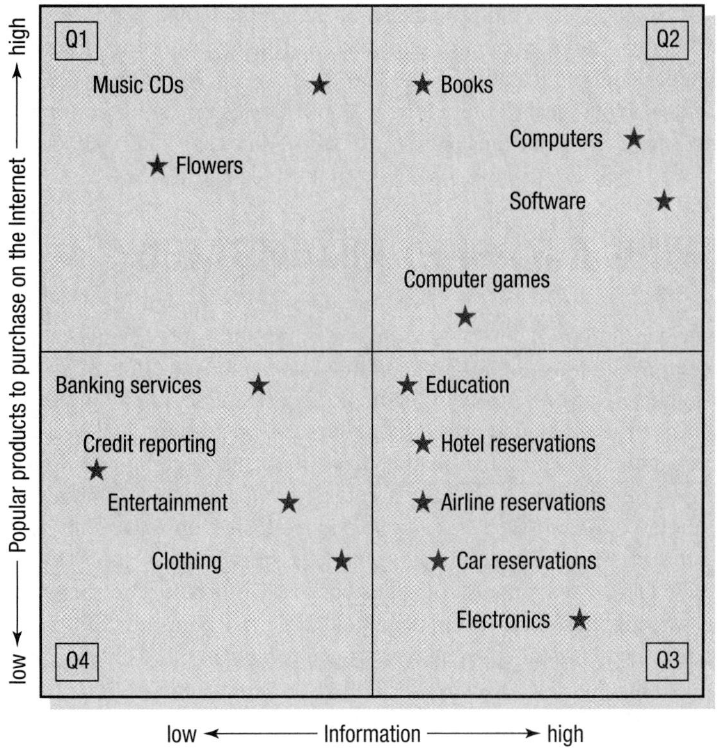

EXHIBIT 5.5

Perceptual Map for Internet Purchasing

Source: Expanded and adapted from Hyokjin Kwak, Richard Fox, and George M. Zinkhan, "What Products Can Be Successfully Promoted and Sold via the Internet?" *Journal of Advertising Research* 42, no. 1 (2002), pp. 23–38; and Hyokjin Kwak and George M. Zinkhan, "Global and Cultural Perspectives on Web-Based Chatting: An Exploratory Study," University of Georgia working paper, No. 199-03 (1999).

website?). In this study, the two most important dimensions turned out to be "information content" and "frequency of purchase on the Internet." Books and computer-related products are positioned together in the "high-information and high-frequency zone." Travel services and education appear in the "high-information and low-frequency" quadrant. Products that are perceived to have lower information content include music CDs, flowers, and entertainment. Some examples of entertainment on the Internet include online gaming and gambling sites. However, caution must be exercised in interpreting the information dimension. For instance, products and services (e.g., music CDs) on the low end of the spectrum are not necessarily purchased without careful thought and deliberation.[44]

Marketers could use the results of this perceptual map to design specific strategies for each of the four quadrants shown in Exhibit 5.5. In this sense, each quadrant represents a unique segment (Q1, Q2, Q3, and Q4). Consider Q1. Music products appear in this segment, as they are frequently purchased on the Internet and score relatively low on information content. In the 1980s, music manufacturers enhanced exposure to the product through radio and then sold it through retailers such as Tower Records.[45] However, in the twenty-first century, Internet music startups (e.g., CDNow) have revolutionized the way the industry and consumers transact business. Without going to retail shops (e.g., Circuit City), buyers can now sample music on the Internet. Through numerous product trials and free information on the web, customers accumulate a great deal of knowledge. The product category is quite mature, so frequent promotional campaigns (e.g., featuring free product trials) are an effective strategy for music products on the Web.[46]

Consider quadrant 3 (Q3). Consumers purchase products and services in this group only after seeking a large amount of information. Thus, a promising strategy is to offer aided consumer communications on the Web (e.g., extensive product illustrations and demonstrations on purchasing sites along with banner ads that guide consumers to these informative sites). Also, the installation of online, interactive service sites may help consumers who seek extensive information in these categories.[47]

DESIGNING A MARKET MIX STRATEGY

Once management knows how it wants the company's product to be perceived and evaluated by consumers, it must then design a market mix strategy to accomplish that. This includes developing tactics for communicating the position of the product to target consumers. Many elements of the marketing mix associated with the product—its distribution, promotion, and price—communicate positioning to the customer. Consider, for example, two products marketed by the same company and based on the same chemical innovation.[48] L'Oréal markets both Niosome and Plenitude face cream to fight wrinkles. Niosome face cream is sold in exclusive, upscale beauty shops. Plenitude sells for one-sixth as much in supermarkets and discount stores. L'Oréal is one of the world's largest cosmetics companies because of its ability to span both the luxury market with brands such as Lancôme and Helena Rubinstein and the mass market with Elsève and L'Oréal. L'Oréal first launches innovations as luxury products and then simplifies them and then relaunches the innovations under different brand names for the mass market. Niosome and Plenitude are distinguished by marketing mix tactics: their product formulation, packaging, advertising, media placement, distribution, and price.

Often a company will attempt to *change its image and position* in the market. This is accomplished by changing the marketing mix. Many bricks-and-mortar businesses, such as UK retailer Tesco and global retailer Wal-Mart, have developed a strong presence on the Internet. Fast-food retailer Burger King is following a more conventional repositioning strategy in an effort to regain its quality image. First it's remodeling its retail outlets. Second, it is reinforcing its movie-licensing program that gives it a boost with kids, through such items as *Men in Black II* merchandise, and it has new menu items as well. Third, it has launched an innovative website, with state-of-the art graphics, so as to appeal to younger consumers. In a different product category, retailer Ann Taylor went through a complete overhaul in the early 1990s.[49] In the 1980s the company was known for its tailored business suits and pants. Then workplaces grew less formal and women wanted more choice. Ann Taylor evolved to meet their needs. In 1992 a big-selling item became Ann Taylor jeans costing only $30. Similarly, Abercrombie and Fitch recently went from being a stuffy, conservative, high-end clothing retailer to a lower-end, fashion-forward, youth marketer by changing its product line, pricing, retail formats, and so on.

@ www.burgerking.com

It is difficult to *maintain a position in the market.* Constant monitoring and innovation are required simply to stay in the same place. Fast-food franchiser Burger King's repositioning effort comes because it lost its point of differentiation when McDonald's remodeled its kitchens to handle made-to-order food, long Burger King's single greatest advantage in the burger wars. A final example of how changing tastes and competitive conditions alter the position of products within a market is offered by the dramatic decline of the French café. Some 4,500 traditional cafés close each year, dwindling in France from 200,000 in 1960 to less than 70,000 today. Some of the reasons for this decline are described in Consumer Chronicles 5.5.[50]

Reasons for the Decline of the Traditional French Café

CONSUMER CHRONICLES 5.5

In his guide, *Le Pieton a Paris,* Leon-Paul Fargue described the quintessential French café, with its long zinc bar and little round tables under gaily colored parasols spilling out over the pavement, as "the most solid of the institutions." That was 60 years ago. Now, if the experts are to be believed, the traditional corner café, the bistro (from the Russian word for quickly), the brasserie—call it what you will—is threatened with extinction.

In 1960, when France had 46 million people, there were reputed to be over 200,000 café-brasseries (defined as places with a license to sell alcohol on the premises as well as serving simple meals). Today, in a France of 58 million, only 50,000 remain, and even they are disappearing at a rate of around 3,000 a year. In Paris alone, more than 1,500 cafés closed last year, bringing the total down to half what it was in 1980.

There are several reasons for these closings. First, Parisians have no time to go to cafés. They are always in theirs cars. Cars and TV killed the café. Second, people can't find what they're looking for in a café. Surveys show that ambience is the first thing people look for when they go to a café. Third, we used to say cafés were *salon de pauvres,* the living room of poor people who had no heat. Today, everybody has central heat and air conditioning. A sharp rise in property prices in the 1980s put many struggling cafés into the hands of property developers. Alcohol consumption has fallen from an average of 18 liters of pure alcohol per person per year in 1960 to around 11 liters today (and the government, in an effort to discourage alcoholism, has introduced tax incentives to encourage cafés to give up their alcohol licenses). Desertification of the countryside has led to the closure of the traditional village café. And, finally, it costs a lot to go for lunch at the café in town. So people prefer to go to a fast-food restaurant like McDonald's, which arrived in France 25 years ago and has replaced the café for young people. With its 353 McDonald's fast-food restaurants, France ranks sixth among the 79 countries where the fast-food chain has outlets.

Source: Mark Seal, "Paris' Café Revolution," American Way, *July 15, 1993, pp. 40–43; "Mais Ou Sont Les Cafés D'antan?"* The Economist, *June 10, 1995, http://www.economist.com/tfs/aarchive_tframeset.html.*

SUMMARY

Marketing strategy concerns the actions managers take to improve the likelihood marketplace exchanges that meet firm and customer goals will occur. In general, customer-oriented marketing strategies improve the value customers derive from products or decrease the costs of products to customers. Firms may adopt any of four general strategic positions: prospector, analyzer, defender, and reactor. More specific strategies include differentiation, market penetration, and cost leadership.

One of the most critical skills for a successful business is to empathize with and gain insights from customers. A customer focus is the central element of this market orientation. A market orientation is not solely the responsibility of a marketing department, however; it requires the concerted action of everyone in the organization. The degree of competition in an industry affects the importance of a market orientation. When there are many competitors, it is difficult to develop a distinctive product position.

The connection between understanding consumers and designing effective marketing strategies requires creativity and imagination. Marketing intelligence attempts to find out what problems consumers are trying to solve, and marketing imagination offers solutions. But beyond the traditional modes of market research, marketing imagination

SUMMARY

requires deep insight into the needs, lifestyles, and aspirations of the customers of today and tomorrow.

Market segmentation, targeting, and positioning are central elements of marketing strategies. The process of market segmentation begins with a thorough investigation of consumer–product relationships. This investigation includes examining environmental factors involved in the purchase–consumption process for the product; what the product means to consumers and how involved they are in purchasing and consuming it; and the behaviors involved in the purchase–consumption process for the product. Then, an organization can investigate alternative market segmentation approaches. Geographic or demographic criteria, psychographic variables, and behavioral variables are bases for identifying market segments. Whichever segmentation approach an organization chooses, four general criteria of good segmentation are measurability, substantiality, accessibility, and responsiveness. After investigating alternative segmentation approaches, managers must select the most appropriate group or groups for the firm to serve. They can use undifferentiated marketing, differentiated marketing, or concentrated or niche marketing as the basis for choosing the segment or segments.

Next, the firm's managers must decide on product positioning: how they would like the company and its brands to be perceived and evaluated by target markets. One general technique that's often used to position products and services is perceptual mapping. Once they know how they want the company and its products to be perceived and evaluated by consumers, managers must design a market mix strategy to achieve or maintain the position. Everything associated with the product—its distribution, promotion, and price—communicates the position of the product to the customer. By managing the market mix, companies can establish, change, or maintain desired product positions.

KEY TERMS

analyzer 171
behavioral segmentation 190
benefit segmentation 190
brand alliance 200
brand communities 187
brand-loyal consumers 178
buyer readiness 193
concentrated, or niche, marketing 198
coordinated marketing 174
customer focus 172
defender 167
demographic segmentation 189
differentiated marketing 196
differentiation 173
differentiation strategy 170
geographic segmentation 187
learning relationships 183
lifestyle 190
market intelligence 174
market orientation 172
market segmentation 182
marketing concept 172
marketing imagination 166
marketing mix 182
marketing strategy 165
marketspace 165
mass customization 183
occasion segmentation 191
perceptual mapping 200
product positioning 199
prospector 170
psychographic segmentation 190
reactor 171
rules of good segmentation 193
segmentation bases 187
sense the market 172
strategy 165
Triad regions 183
undifferentiated marketing 195
usage rate segmentation 191

1. Identify a firm in your community that you feel is highly customer oriented. Make a list of the firm's activities or behaviors that illustrate its market orientation. You might include tools the firm uses to sense the market.
2. Identify the marketing strategies adopted by some familiar consumer goods companies in terms of whether they resemble prospectors, analyzers, defenders, or reactors.
3. Suppose that the McIlhenny Company has discovered that its market can be segmented into light and heavy users of Tabasco sauce, with the smaller heavy-user group accounting for 75 percent of sales. What strategies and marketing mix tactics would you use to reach these two groups of consumers? (*Hint:* Consider market penetration and market development strategies.)
4. Use the dimensions of popular products to search on the Internet and information identified in the example perceptual map. Construct your own perceptual map using a selection of six websites that you know. If your perceptions were representative, what would be the managerial implications?
5. How could benefit segmentation be used to develop marketing strategy for the following?

    a. Health clubs
    b. Bath soaps
    c. Cosmetics
    d. Ice cream
    e. Education
    f. Bicycles

6. Using cars as a product category, investigate different segmentation approaches (e.g., geographic and demographic, psychographic, and behavioral). Provide illustrations of different brands and models that segment the market using these different bases.
7. Review a popular commercial magazine and record the content of a series of print ads. Try to identify the positioning bases of the products featured in the ads.
8. Visit a local shopping district, such as a main street or mall. Go from store to store and observe the customers. Make a detailed composite portrait of the customers at each store using as many criteria as possible. Then, name the market segment you have described.

YOU MAKE THE CALL

ROYAL CARIBBEAN CRUISES

The cruise industry represents the most exciting growth category in the entire leisure market. The cruise industry is commonly divided into three segments: luxury, premium, and volume. The volume segment has per diem rates of less than $300 and lasts seven nights or less. Target customers for the volume segment are normally first-time cruise passengers.

Carnival targets the volume market with its Carnival Fun Ship line. These customers include mostly younger, less affluent passengers and families with children. These customers typically take land resort vacations. The Carnival line is the standard by which all lower-priced cruise lines are measured. Carnival is known to deliver all that it promises: Activities and entertainment are nonstop; the food is plentiful; and the cabins are comfortable. According to Bob Dickinson, CEO of Carnival, "If you tell people you

CASES

are the Fun Ships you are going to attract people disposed to having fun." Everything about Carnival—the brand name, ship names like "Mardi Gras" and "Fantasy"—connotes fun. Many younger customers see the type of crowd Carnival attracts as a significant factor in their decision. While traditional cruise advertising has promoted ports of call, Carnival hypes the ships, where vacationers spend 80 percent of the time during a cruise. The product strategy has been centered on structuring fun ship tours into inexpensive, easy-to-book packages for the masses.

Royal Caribbean focuses on superior service to differentiate it from the other major competitors for first-time cruisers. However, consumers do not always perceive the higher quality and service to be worth Royal Caribbean's higher price, as evidenced by the lower number of first-time cruisers on the line relative to Carnival. (The actual difference in average price is quite small, $209 compared to $187 per night.) Consumers see Royal as being similar to Carnival but slightly more sophisticated and professional and less energetic. Royal appears to pursue an undifferentiated strategy targeting different markets with essentially one product. The strategy is to offer a quality product, with multiple activities and destinations at a reasonable price. Royal sees itself marketing to the lower-premium market and the upper-end of the volume market. The image one gets is that the service is likely to be very good, but the product a passenger gets in terms of atmosphere, types of people, and activities is somewhat unclear. Further, the company lacks a strong, consistent message such as Carnival's "Fun Ships" slogan.

Although both Carnival and Royal Caribbean continue to enjoy strong growth and profitability, Royal Caribbean seems to be losing ground to Carnival, especially in the volume market. Their appeal as a provider of high-quality cruise vacations seems to be losing out to Carnival's "fun" concept.

QUESTIONS

1. What should Royal Carribbean do?
2. Outline some steps Royal Caribbean can take to decide whether and how to target the volume segment of the cruise market.

This case was adapted from student reports and Eileen Ogintz, "Ignore Children's Needs and Risk Minor Mutiny," Los Angeles Times, *September 13, 1992, Travel Section; Shirley Slater and Harry Basch, "The Right Ship for You,"* Los Angeles Times, *September 8, 1991, Travel Section; Shirley Slater and Harry Basch, "Short Sailings Making a Big Impact,"* Los Angeles Times, *September 27, 1992, Travel Section; and Shirley Slater and Harry Basch, "Ship Builds Up for Caribbean Duty,"* Los Angeles Times, *November 10, 1991, Travel Section.*

ENDNOTES

1. Vignette sources include landsend.com/cd/fp/help/0,,1_26215_26859_26908___,00.html?refer=/cd/frontdoor/0,,,00+en-USS_01DBC.html&sid=6278074277113109780; digitrends.net/ebna/index_1315.html; and Margaret Kane, "Auction Gavel Strikes Excite@Home," News.Com, May 29, 2002.

2. Jupiter Communications, July 2002, www.jup.com/home.jsp.

3. Robert D. Hof, David Welch, Michael Arndt, Amy Barrett, and Stephen Baker, "E-Malls for Business," *Business Week,* March 13, 2000, pp. 32–34; Jeffrey F. Rayport and John J. Sviokla, "Managing in the Marketspace" *Harvard Business Review,* November–December 1994, pp. 141–50; Shawn Tully, "The *B2B* Tool That Really *Is* Changing the World," *Fortune,* March 20, 2000, pp. 132–45; David Welch, "Oh, What a Feeling: *B2B,*" *Business Week,* May 15, 2000,

p. 14; Richard T. Watson, Pierre Berthon, Leyland F. Pitt, and George M. Zinkhan, *Electronic Commerce: The Strategic Perspective* (Fort Worth, TX: Harcourt, 2002); and www.freemarkets.com/en/benefits/case_studies/carrier.asp.

4. R. Miles and C. Snow, *Organizational Strategy, Structure and Process* (New York: McGraw-Hill, 1978); and William G. Zikmund and Michael D'Amico, *Marketing,* 5th ed. (Minneapolis/St. Paul: West Publishing Co., 1993).

5. www.3m.com/about3m/century.

6. This section draws heavily from Ajay K. Kohli and Bernard J. Jaworski,"Market Orientation: The Construct, Research Propositions, and Managerial Implications," *Journal of Marketing* 54 (April 1990), pp. 1–18.

7. Francis J. Gouillart and Frederick D. Sturdivant, "Spend a Day in the Life of Your Customers," *Harvard Business Review,* January–February 1994, pp. 116–27.

8. David W. Cravens, Gordon Greenley, Nigel F. Piercy, and Stanley F. Slater,"Mapping the Path to Market Leadership," *Marketing Management* 7 (October 1998), pp. 29–39; and Emily Thornton, Larry Armstrong, and Kathleen Kerwin, "Toyota Unbound," *Business Week,* May 1, 2000, pp. 142–46.

9. Bryan A. Lukas and O. C. Ferrell, "The Effect of Market Orientation on Product Innovation," *Journal of the Academy of Marketing Science* 28 (Spring 2000), pp. 239–47.

10. This discussion and Good Practice 5.1 are adapted from Ian C. MacMillan and Rita Gunther McGrath, "Discovering New Points of Differentiation," *Harvard Business Review,* May–June 1997, pp. 133–45; and "Shopping around the Web: A Survey of Ecommerce," *The Economist* 26 (February 2000), p. 33.

11. Michael W. Peng, *Business Strategies in Transition Economies* (Thousand Oaks, CA: Sage Publications, 2000); and C. K. Prahalad and K. Lieberthal, "The End of Corporate Imperialism," *Harvard Business Review* 76, no. 4 (1998), pp. 68–79.

12. Gouillart and Sturdivant, "Spend a Day in the Life of Your Customers."

13. Lisa Bannon, "Mattel Plans to Double Sales Abroad," *The Wall Street Journal,* February 11, 1998, pp. A1, A8.

14. Charles W. L. Hill, *International Business,* 3rd ed. (New York: McGraw-Hill/Irwin, 2000); Christian Homburg, John P. Workman, Jr., and Harley Krohmer, "Marketing's Influence within the Firm," *Journal of Marketing* 63 (April 1999), pp. 1–18; Nathalie Laidler and John Quelch, "Gallo Rice," Case No. 9-593-018, Harvard Business School Publishing, Boston, 1993; Peng, *Business Strategies in Transition Economies;* and Prahalad and Lieberthal, "The End of Corporate Imperialism."

15. Peng, *Business Strategies in Transition Economies,* pp. 220–21.

16. A detailed list of education and community programs is offered on the Pacific Symphony Orchestra user-friendly website at www.ocartsnet.org.

17. Theodore Levitt, *The Marketing Imagination* (New York: Free Press, 1983).

18. Note that our discussion of the "marketing imagination" follows upon Wright's idea of the "sociological imagination." C. Wright Mills, *The Sociological Imagination* (New York: Oxford University Press, 1959).

19. Catherine Arnst, "Developments to Watch," *Business Week,* December 1, 1997, p. 119; "UpFront," *Business Week,* December 15, 1997, p. 8; "The Road from Damascus," *The Economist,* August 15, 1998, p. 57; Michael Hoechsmann, *Benetton Culture: Marketing Difference to the New Global Consumer* (Thousand Oaks, CA: Sage Publications, 1997); and "Cell Phones Transform Bangladesh," *Lincoln Journal Star,* February 23, 2000, p. 7A.

20. Bennett Daviss, "The Subtle and Not-So-Subtle New Science of Advertising and Marketing," *Ambassador,* April 2000, pp. 18–20; and Gouillart and Sturdivant, "Spend a Day in the Life of Your Customers," pp. 123–24.

21. This section draws from Gary Hamel and C. K. Prahalad, "Corporate Imagination and Expeditionary Marketing," *Harvard Business Review,* July–August 1991, pp. 81–92.

22. B. Joseph Pine II, Don Peppers, and Martha Rogers, "Do You Want to Keep Your Customers Forever?" *Harvard Business Review,* March–April 1995, pp. 103–14.

23. Thomas T. Semon, "Program Steers Germany in Right Direction," *Marketing News,* May 8, 2000, p. 27.
24. Ibid.
25. Steven L. Hellerman, *Offside: Soccer and American Exceptionalism* (Princeton: Princeton University Press, 2001).
26. Irene Lacher, "The Era of Fragments," *Los Angeles Times,* January 2, 1994, p. E4; and Alecia Swasy, "Don't Sell Thick Diapers in Tokyo," *New York Times,* October 3, 1993, p. F9.
27. Ynuxiang Yan, "McDonald's in Beijing: The Localization of Americana," in *Golden Arches East,* ed. James L. Watson (Stanford: Stanford University Press, 1997), pp. 77–109.
28. Rebecca G. Adams and Robert Sardiello, eds., *Deadhead Social Science* (Walnut Creek, CA: Altamira Press, 2000); Susan Fournier, "Consumers and Their Brands: Developing Relationship Theory in Consumer Research," *Journal of Consumer Research* 24 (March 1998), pp. 343–73; Albert Muniz Jr. and Thomas O'Guinn, "Brand Community," *Journal of Consumer Research* 27 (March 2001), pp. 412–32; Kendra Parker, "Customer Retention: The Next Big Thing," *American Demographics,* January 2000, pp. 38–39; and John Schouten and James McAlexander, "Brandfests," in *Servicescapes,* ed. John F. Sherry Jr. (Homewood, IL: NTC Publications, 1998), pp. 377–402.
29."Shopping around the Web," pp. 11–12; and Ellen Neuborne,"Sites Not Worth Seeing," *Business Week e.biz,* May 15, 2000, p. EB16.
30. Michael J. Weiss, *The Clustering of America* (New York: Harper and Row, 1988).
31. Ronald D. Michman and Edward M. Mazze, *The Food Industry Wars: Marketing Triumphs and Blunders* (Westport, CT: Quorum Books, 1998).
32. Michman and Mazze, *The Food Industry Wars.*
33. Priscila A. LaBarbera and Zeynep Gurhan,"The Role of Materialism, Religiosity, and Demographics in Subjective Well-Being," *Psychology and Marketing* 14 (January 1997), pp. 71–97; Forrester Research, Inc.,"Why Consumers Buy," *The Forrester Report,* December 1996; and Paul C. Judge,"Are Tech Buyers Different?" *Business Week,* January 26, 1998, pp. 64–66.
34. Geng Cui,"Segmenting China's Consumer Market: A Hybrid Approach," *Journal of International Consumer Marketing* 11, no. 1 (1999), pp. 55–76; and Dexter Roberts,"China's Wealth Gap," *Business Week,* May 15, 2000, pp. 172–80.
35. Kara Chan,"Market Segmentation of Green Consumers in Hong Kong," *Journal of International Consumer Marketing* 12, no. 2 (1999), pp. 7–24.
36. Ronald Grover,"Come See My Movie—Please!" *Business Week,* May 8, 2000, pp. 153–54.
37. Michael J. McDermott,"Fishing for Customers," *Profiles,* November 1992, pp. 44–48.
38. Rohit Deshpandé and Douglas Stayman,"A Tale of Two Cities: Distinctiveness Theory and Advertising Effectiveness," *Journal of Marketing Research* 31 (February 1994), pp. 57–64
39. "Shopping around the Web," pp. 27–29; Hill, *International Business,* pp. 296–97; and Ellen Neuborne,"E-Tail: Gleaming Storefronts with Nothing Inside," *Business Week,* May 1, 2000, pp. 94, 98.
40. Linda L. Price, Lawrence F. Feick, and Audrey Guskey-Federouch,"Couponing Behavior of the Market Maven: Profile of a Super Couponer," in *Advances in Consumer Research,* vol. 15, ed. Michael J. Houston (Provo, UT: Association for Consumer Research, 1989), pp. 354–59; and Michael A. Reilly, "Working Wives and Convenience Consumption," *Journal of Consumer Research* 8 (March 1982), pp. 407–18.
41. S. Johnson, D. Kotchev, and G. Loveman,"How One Polish Shipyard Became a Market Competitor," *Harvard Business Review* 73, no. 6 (1995), pp. 53–72.
42. Kurt Repanshek,"White Gold: Utah's Invaluable Ski Industry," *Utah Business,* January–February 1994, p. 38.
43. Kevin E. Voss and Patriya Tansuhaj, "A Consumer Perspective on Foreign Market Entry: Building Brands through Brand Alliances," *Journal of International Consumer Marketing* 11, no. 2 (1999), pp. 39–58.
44. Hyokjin Kwak and George M. Zinkhan, "Global and Cultural Perspectives on Web-Based Chatting: An Exploratory Study," University of Georgia working paper, No. 1999-03 (1999).

45. Hyokjin Kwak, Richard Fox, and George M. Zinkhan, "What Products Can Be Successfully Promoted and Sold via the Internet?" *Journal of Advertising Research* 42, no. 1 (2002), pp. 23–38.
46. Ibid.
47. Ibid.
48. "L Oréal Aiming at High and Low Markets," *Fortune,* March 22, 1993, p. 89.
49. "Ann Retaylored," *Business Week,* May 17, 1993, p. 70.
50. Aixa M. Pascual, "The Whopper Plays Catch-Up," *Business Week,* May 15, 2000, pp. 98, 100; and Mark Seal, "Paris' Cafe Revolution," *American Way,* July 15, 1993, pp. 40–43.

chapter 1
chapter 2
chapter 3
chapter 4
chapter 5
chapter 6
chapter 7
chapter 8
chapter 9
chapter 10
chapter 11
chapter 12
chapter 13
chapter 14
chapter 15
chapter 16
chapter 17
chapter 18
chapter 19

LEARNING OBJECTIVES

After completing this chapter, you should be able to:

- Describe the basics of consumer research and have an understanding of available consumer behavior research techniques.
- Explain the complexities in doing international consumer research.
- Outline the steps in the research process.
- Describe generally how to ask consumers questions.
- Identify some of the changes the Internet brings to consumer behavior research and some of the problems of evaluating secondary research.
- Appreciate the ethical issues raised by market research.

LEARNING ABOUT CONSUMERS

ADVENTURE TRAVEL

Check out gorptravel.gorp.com for adventure travel the world over, spanning Africa, Antarctica, Asia, and the Caribbean. A trip summary for Kahikatea, New Zealand, features a photo of white-water river rafting and promises eight days of adventure with upscale accommodations for the entire trip. And you can be back in your office on Monday morning. Or perhaps you'd prefer to sea kayak in Belize or take a white-water river expedition in Alaska with Adrift Adventures. To see what you are missing check out www.adrift.com. Adventure travel, including commercial white-water river rafting, is a fast-growing outdoor leisure services industry; commercial rafting trips are booked in many nations from Canada to Zimbabwe.

@ gorptravel.gorp.com

@ www.adrift.com

Our example focuses on Colorado and Utah, where many small firms operate on a half-dozen rivers and provide half-day to multiday trips to thousands of clients every year. The managers of a group of Colorado River Basin outfitters wanted to know how to increase consumer satisfaction and repeat business for their multiday river trips. They wanted to make their business more predictable.

We conducted applied consumer research with several river-outfitting companies to help answer questions of interest to managers. Depth interviews with management and river-rafting guides suggested the hypothesis that customer satisfaction is related to concerns with the quality of food and amenities provided, safety, and lore about the natural and historical setting of the trips. We then collected written descriptions of river rafting from experienced rafters. Through content analysis of these descriptions, we found that rafters rarely mentioned food, safety, or information. Instead they spoke of exhilaration, personal growth, and growing closer to family and friends through their rafting experiences.

A river-rafting adventure

Next, we undertook participant observation research with rafters. That is, we accompanied participants on a number of multiday river trips to explore the experience of rafting and the meaning of rafting to customers. In addition, we conducted posttrip focus groups, and we sent mail surveys to customers both before and after their river trips. Our research revealed that participants had difficulty expressing what was really important to their satisfaction. It included experiencing personal growth, a sense of harmony with nature, and community with family, friends, and other participants. Management was only vaguely aware of these benefits to customers because their perception of what customers wanted was primarily based on pretrip inquiries rather than posttrip memories and reminiscences.

Our research showed that river guides are critical in orchestrating customer satisfaction, but customers hardly ever mention the guides' role. We, as researchers, didn't know why. We undertook surveys, focus groups, and further participant observation to describe more adequately the guides' role in orchestrating customer satisfaction. Because of the duration, intimacy, and purpose of the trips (fun, fantasy, and adventure), effective river guides became like friends to customers over the course of the trip. When things went well, customers were satisfied with the guides; but when things went badly they tended to blame the weather or other external factors rather than guides. The role of temporary friend is one that guides find stressful, management vaguely understands, and customers take for granted. These findings helped reorient some outfitters' training and promotional efforts.

The various research projects described above provide important insights about river-rafting customers and their experiences. In turn, this feedback suggests opportunities for the River Basin rafting companies to improve their services so as to enhance customer satisfaction and loyalty. While managers see their consumers as concerned with the tangible services of a trip, the rafters seem more focused on the actual rafting experience and the intangible feelings that a trip can foster. It is, therefore, important for managers to structure both their advertising and the rafting excursions to meet consumers' desires for personal growth. It is quite likely that, initially, rafters may perceive that an "adrenalin rush" is what they are seeking. And it is certainly the case that customers will complain about the food and other amenities during the actual excursions. Nonetheless, note how the research provides an important means for stimulating managerial insight and suggesting promising directions for strategic changes—especially in the areas of stimulating repeat business. Specifically, the research exposes the types of experiences that customers seek in leisure consumption contexts, and it also highlights the behaviors of front-line personnel in communicating expectations, values, and meanings to customers.[1]

OVERVIEW

Learning about consumers is the key to implementing the marketing concept and exercising marketing imagination. The aim of this chapter is to introduce you to consumer research. Consumer research is not the only way we learn about consumers, but it is certainly one of the most important ways. **Consumer behavior research** is *the systematic and objective process of gathering, recording, and analyzing data for aid in understanding and predicting consumer thoughts, feelings, and behaviors.* With the globalization of markets, consumer research has assumed a truly international character, and this trend is likely to continue. At the simplest level, international consumer research involves studies in a single market outside the firm's domestic market. More elaborate and complex are international consumer research programs that are intended to help solve multicountry marketing problems. We will discuss examples of each type in this chapter.

The opening vignette mentions several kinds of research as well as several techniques for conducting it. We discuss these issues in more detail in this chapter. The value of consumer research can be measured by its contribution to solving practical problems or by advancing our general understanding of human behavior. The practical problems addressed by consumer behavior research range widely from those of organizations seeking to increase their customers' purchase frequency (see Chapter 9) to those of advocacy organizations seeking to enlist increased support from their constituents. It could even include research on disadvantaged consumers designed to promote changes in society or changes in the marketplace. Public policymakers also use consumer behavior research (e.g., to study how to enhance healthy or life-saving behaviors).

CONSUMER RESEARCH IN THE TWENTY-FIRST CENTURY

This chapter illustrates the important role that consumer research plays in creating a solid foundation for marketing understanding and marketing strategy. There are a variety of ways that organizations can gain insights about buyers. One method relies upon managerial insights, judgments, and experiences. However, as illustrated in the opening vignette, this approach is not always sufficient. Another way is to rely upon methods of scientific inquiry. For instance, random sampling (introduced in the 1940s) and telephone interviewing (introduced in the 1970s) revolutionized consumer research in the twentieth century. It is important to realize that there is not necessarily a single approach for conducting social science research, and there are a variety of ways of "learning" about consumers. Here, we briefly mention three scientific approaches: (a) an emphasis on prediction; (b) an emphasis on cultural understanding; and (c) an emphasis on understanding the individual world of the consumer.

Marketing managers are interested in making predictions about how their customers will behave in the future, and prediction plays a central role in traditional approaches to science (e.g., as practiced by physicists or chemists). For instance, a researcher could use quantitative analysis to make a prediction about expected sales levels for the next fiscal year. However, marketing is an applied social science, so other approaches need to be considered.[2] As described in Chapter 3, a cultural approach to knowledge emphasizes understanding in a symbolic sense. That is, understanding is like grasping a proverb or catching an allusion.[3] From another perspective, social scientists attempt to understand consumers' perceptions of reality, and the researcher strives to "feel one's way inside the experience of the actor."[4] This last approach has value to marketers because they are charged with representing the customer perspective, inside the organization.

Four broad themes affect human life in the twenty-first century: speed, the Internet, globalization, and data overload. As a result, today's consumer researchers need to be trained to take account of these trends, and they need to learn a wide variety of skills.

Speed

Many technologies and services have speeded up delivery of information. Big companies such as Ford Motor Company used to spend several years researching and developing a new product. Now they attempt to shorten the length of time between the idea for a new product and the introduction of that product to the market. In addition, they attempt to better gauge not just what consumers say they want but how consumers actually use the product. The importance of observing use was brought home when Ford unsuccessfully introduced Fiesta into Thailand in the 1970s. Thai vehicles are regularly overloaded two to three times beyond their designed capacity, and so the Fiesta had frequent breakdowns. A sturdier model was introduced, but too late, and Ford incurred heavy losses.[5] Market research companies increasingly emphasize speed, combined with international research capabilities. Marketing decision makers require information that is insightful, timely, and global in perspective.

The Internet

The Internet has the potential to transform every relationship on the planet. From a research perspective, the Internet represents a new data collection tool that organizations must harness to remain competitive. At present, the Internet represents the fastest-growing segment of the marketing research industry.[6] Sotheby's site on the Web is typical. It posted a questionnaire to encourage visitors to give personal information and their tastes and opinions. Responses can help the art auction gallery modify its website to suit the needs of potential clients. In addition, the site provides a list of all the Sotheby's galleries around the world.

/sothebys.ebay.com

The Internet can be used to enhance quantitative data collection. For instance, a consumer's responses to a questionnaire can be captured electronically, so there is no need to keypunch data and then check that data-entry process for accuracy. Data can be analyzed continuously, in real time. Thus, if there is a problem with one of the questions, that question can be changed on the spot. In the same way, the Internet offers new possibilities for qualitative data collection. Traditionally, it is difficult to get participants to show up for a group interview, all at the same place and the same time. Through use of the Internet, group interviews can be conducted online so that respondents don't have to leave the safety and comfort of their home or office.

/www.acm.org/ubiquity/views/r_watson_1.html

The Internet also provides new opportunities for one-to-one interactions with potential customers. For instance, firms ask visitors to their websites to provide personal information. In turn, this information can be used to customize a product (e.g., for that particular customer), or it can be used to customize a promotional strategy. In addition, opinion leaders (see Chapter 14) can be better located and targeted online (as opposed to offline). For instance, chat rooms or personal home pages can be used to gain insights about opinion leaders.[7] In brief, researchers can take advantage of the one-to-one customization opportunities that are offered by the Internet.

Of course, the Internet is one of the technologies that quickens the pace of globalization. A novel aspect of the Internet is its capacity to cut across vast distances in no time.[8] Under previous systems of international contact (e.g., the telephone), different parts of the world might be connected to relatively few others. With the Internet, the number of paths between different people and locations has exploded. In the middle of the twentieth century, we imagined a world that was connected with a variety of commercial and communication lines. In the twenty-first century, it is more accurate to think of the globe as connected by a web, and the number of international interactions increases exponentially. That is, there is an expanding web of political, economic, and cultural interconnections.[9]

Globalization

Global inhabitants have much more to do with one another and interact more often than they once did. More and more people live their professional, family, and intellectual lives in more than one country.[10] An expanding variety of goods and services are being exchanged across traditional boundaries. As a result, two common themes of globalization are interdependence and integration. The "world" economy emerged in the sixteenth century, but, in the twenty-first century, we now have a "global" economy.[11] Consumer researchers expand their methods and perspectives to monitor and interact with this global economy. For instance, globalization demands that consumer researchers have experience and knowledge about individual countries and international conditions. Researchers must have the ability to synthesize data from different countries and interpret the factors on which they are based. Meaningful synthesis and comparison demand not just proficiency in statistical methods and languages but insights into cultural differences. Increasingly, international researchers understand that multicountry research requires comparability of meanings and not just comparable questions.[12]

Globalization and the Internet are dramatically changing the face of consumer research. Things move at lightening speed, and this in turn brings a sense of heightened vulnerability. Issues can spread rapidly across borders. A local mistake translates into a global blunder nearly instantly.[13] Globalization and the Internet have combined to create increased interest in standardizing both technical and ethical research procedures and reporting. For example, Canada, the United States, and Mexico are working to standardize how they report basic industry and demographic data. This is partially a response to NAFTA, but it also reflects marketers' needs to formulate strategy on a global basis.

As implied above, the themes of Internet technology and globalization are intertwined. On the one hand, the Internet is an engine that accelerates globalization and provides a web of connections between users (e.g., the users and providers of consumer research). On the other hand, the Internet is a tool that consumer researchers can use to overcome spatial and temporal barriers (such as international borders). From a consumer research perspective, the Internet can be used to provide background information on a topic of interest. It can also be used as a tool by a firm that is looking for a research provider. For example, BBC Radio could use a search engine (such as Yahoo!) to locate a firm that could deliver a research study about sports fans and their listening preferences. In the same way, as a student of consumer research, you could use Internet search engines to locate key associations that promote good practices and ethical behavior in consumer research. Exhibit 6.1 gives the URLs of important marketing research associations. Consider ESOMAR. **ESOMAR** is the *World Association of Opinion and Marketing Research Professionals*. It is European in origin (founded in 1948), but it is global in nature, with more than 4,000 members in 100 countries. ESOMAR's mission

@ www.bbc.co.uk

@ www.intersearch.tnsofres.com

EXHIBIT 6.1

Marketing Research Associations Online

Domestic

AAPOR: American Association for Public Opinion Research (www.aapor.org)
AMA: American Marketing Association (www.ama.org)
ARF: The Advertising Research Foundation (www.arfsite.org)
CASRO: Council of American Survey Research Organizations (www.casro.org)
MRA: Marketing Research Association (www.mra-net.org)
QRCA: Qualitative Research Consultants Association (www.qrca.org)
RIC: Research Industry Coalition (www.researchindustry.org)

International

ESOMAR: World Association of Opinion and Marketing Research Professionals (www.esomar.nl)
MRS: The Market Research Society (UK) (www.marketresearch.org.uk)
MRSA: The Market Research Society of Australia (www.mrsa.com.au)
PMRS: The Professional Marketing Research Society (Canada) (www.pmrs-aprm.com)

Source: Marketing Research: An Applied Orientation, 3E by Naresh K. Malhotra ©. Reprinted by permission of Pearson Education, Inc., Upper Saddle River, NJ.

Guidelines on Conducting Marketing and Opinion Research Using the Internet

GOOD PRACTICE 6.1

- Respondents' cooperation is voluntary and no personal information should be sought from or about respondents without their prior knowledge and agreement.
- The researcher's identity must be disclosed to respondents.
- Respondents' rights to anonymity must be safeguarded.
- Adequate security of data must be provided.
- Researchers are encouraged to post their privacy policy statement on their online site.
- Survey reports should describe the methods used.
- Special care must be taken when interviewing children and young people.
- Researchers should not send unsolicited messages online to respondents who have indicated that they do not wish to receive such messages relating to that specific research project.

Source: Adapted from www.esomar.nl/codes_and_guidelines.html.

is to promote the use of opinion and marketing research, for improving decision making in business and society. Members come from all industry sectors and include representatives from ad agencies, media providers, universities, and government agencies. ESOMAR (and the other associations in Exhibit 6.1) are very sensitive to the issue of protecting respondents and their privacy. For instance, one new initiative that ESOMAR is undertaking is a project to develop measurement guidelines for online media (e.g., radio broadcasts over the Internet, web-based ads). Given the fast-changing and global nature of online media, ESOMAR believes that suitable standards must be developed to assess the effectiveness of these communications (e.g., in terms of informing consumers).[14]

To examine some of ESOMAR's recent press releases, check out the organization's website. Research ethics are of particular concern as international researchers adopt Internet-based methods. For instance, ESOMAR posts a set of ethical guidelines on their website. A version of these guidelines are shown in Good Practice 6.1. Visit some of the other websites shown in Exhibit 6.1 in order to get an idea of other emerging topics in international research. You will find that important and interesting topics are being posted and updated on a daily basis.

@ www.esomar.nl

Data Overload

Data overload is a reality for both consumers and professionals. Historically, managers faced the problem of insufficient information. Much has changed with the information revolution that has been driven by dramatic developments in computer and telecommunications technology, including the Internet. Now, the managers' problem has shifted because huge amounts of information are readily available to organizations, even to small ones. While some may struggle with collecting information in transitional and developing economies, most organizations are more concerned with the dissemination and effective use of information within their organizations.

Data Mining

In the sixteenth century, the philosopher Erasmus wrote that it is a good part of wisdom to learn the foolish desires of the crowd and their unreasonable notions. In the twenty-first century, due largely to the implementation of new technologies (e.g., scanners, bar codes), organizations are accumulating vast volumes of data about their customers. A **database** is a *collection of data and information describing items of interest.*[15] The world's data are estimated to be doubling every 20 months. As a result, data management has become a key function for many organizations.[16] The management of an organization's data requires skills in designing, using, and managing the memory systems of modern organizations. Data managers need to see the organization as a social system and to understand data management technology (e.g., data storage, data retrieval, and the methods of management science such as cluster analysis).[17]

In today's complex and changing marketplace, organizations need to identify reliable and consistent data sources in order to remain current. **Data mining** is an important tool that provides the opportunity to gain such knowledge. In brief, data mining is *the process of analyzing large amounts of data and scouring through databases in order to discover the meaning of data by discovering trends or uncovering hidden patterns and relationships.* These patterns and relationships might be used to formulate predictions about consumer behavior and to identify future trends allowing marketing managers to make proactive and knowledge-based decisions.

Consumer activities that might end up in a marketing database include such behaviors as (a) completing a bank transaction, (b) scanning a loyalty card from the local grocery store, (c) making a phone call, or (d) surfing the Internet. Any one of these everyday events could result in an entry in an electronic database. As a result, corporate databases contain enormous amounts of raw data. A data warehouse stores these raw data by specific categories, making the data easier to retrieve, sort, and analyze. However, merely storing data in a warehouse does not benefit an organization. Firms must find a way to efficiently convert terabytes (one trillion bytes) of raw data into valuable

Dominick's uses customer information to create a marketing database.

The check-out aisle is an important source for data about the marketplace.

insights about customers and markets. Finding meaning from these data can provide the basis for successful marketing strategies.

Data mining can be successfully applied in the twenty-first century due to the development of three technologies: powerful multiprocessor computers, enormous capacities for (automatic) data collection, and data mining algorithms. Data mining has successfully been used by science, government, and business organizations to solve issues relevant to their fields. Companies in many different industries including aerospace, health care, finance, retail, and transportation already use data mining to learn about their customers by collecting and analyzing historical data. Data mining is largely used for business purposes, but has applications across many fields. For example, police detectives use techniques from data mining to detect patterns in statements made by suspects in criminal investigations. In fact, most activities that generate enormous amounts of data can benefit from data mining.

In a business setting, data mining can assist in finding sales trends, predicting customer loyalty, and creating improved marketing campaigns. Some of the specific uses of data mining for business are fraud detection, market-basket analysis, customer churn, interactive marketing, trend analysis, market segmentation, and direct marketing. Other possible applications consist of warranty analysis, customer profiling, pharmaceutical research, claims processing, ad revenue forecasting, customer retention, setting of government policies, and targeted marketing.

Data mining offers an opportunity to change the very nature of communication with customers. A database provides a memory of customer relationships, a record of every message and response between a firm and a customer.[18] Some companies keep track of customers' preferences and customize messages to their needs (e.g., via direct mail). Catalog retailers send customers only those catalogs for which they estimate that there is a high probability of a purchase. For instance, a customer with a history of buying detective novels is sent a catalog of mystery books, instead of one featuring romance novels.[19]

Visitors to this web site "leave tracks" that might wind up in a marketing data base.

GOOD PRACTICE 6.2

Clusters of Service Purchases

Industry Insights
Patterns of Consumer Satisfaction

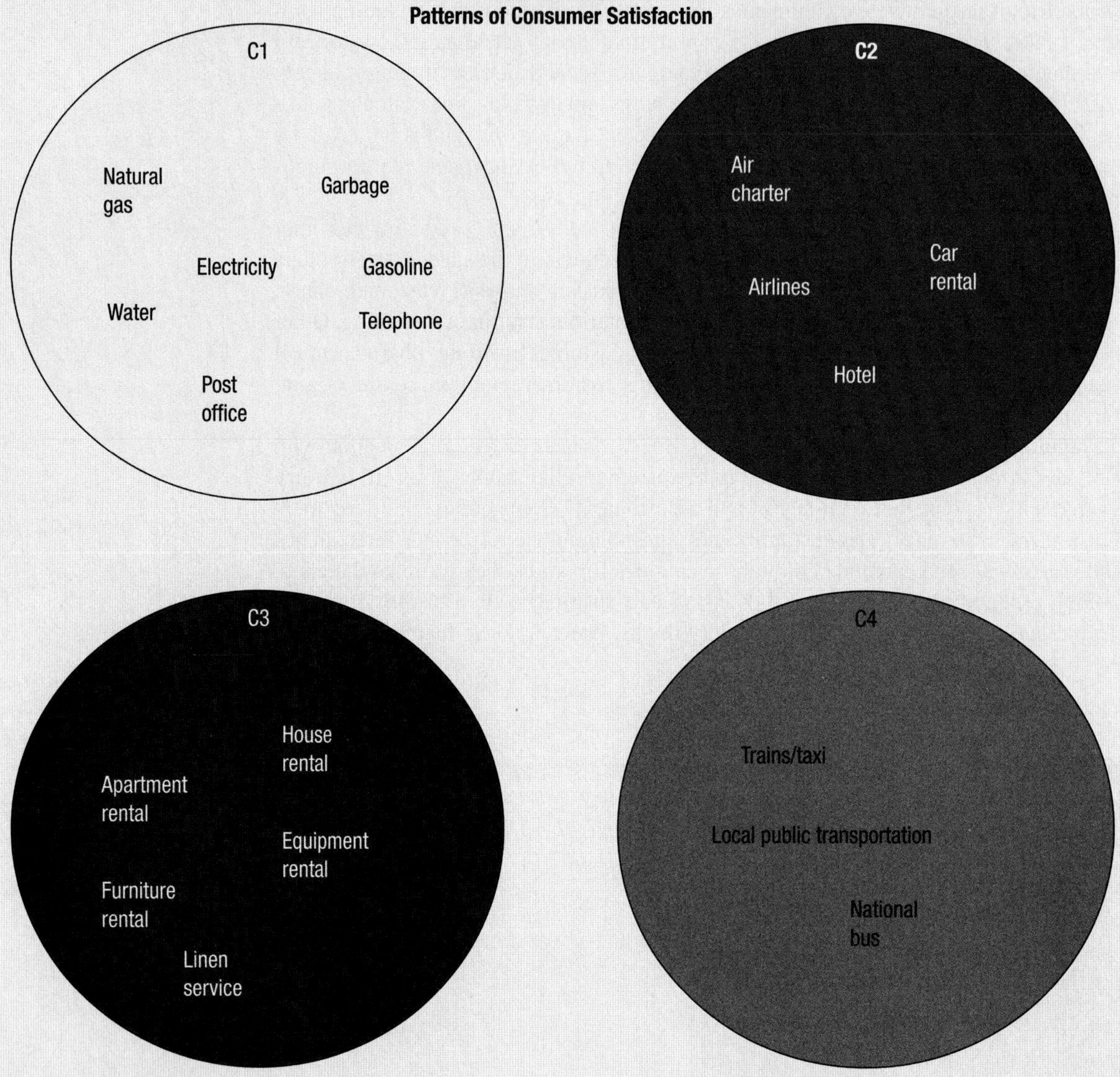

- ❖ C1 = Cluster 1 — Utilities
- ❖ C2 = Cluster 2 — Upscale Travel
- ❖ C3 = Cluster 3 — Downscale Travel
- ❖ C4 = Cluster 4 — Housing

Note: These data were collected in Canada from English-speaking and French-speaking consumers.

Source: Adapted from George M. Zinkhan and Melanie Wallendorf, "Service Set Similarities in Patterns of Consumer Satisfaction/Dissatisfaction," International Journal of Research in Marketing *2, no. 4 (1985), pp. 227–35.*

Examples of Data Mining

GOOD PRACTICE 6.3

- Insurance companies increase sales by predicting where customers are in their life cycles and using those predictions to suggest products that might be needed at those stages of life.
- Supermarket and health care information are analyzed to detect changing patterns and changing consumer lifestyles.
- Investment companies use cluster analysis (a data-mining technique) in order to predict what products are likely to be purchased together.
- Telecommunication companies analyze past behavior of customers and use this model as a means to predict future behavior.
- Lenders predict the probability of default for loan applications.
- Investment companies adopt advanced data mining to pick stocks and bonds.
- Research companies predict the audience share of television programs.
- Credit card firms, the health care industry, and the Internal Revenue Service detect fraud by searching for unusual purchasing behavior through monitoring millions of transactions.

Good Practice 6.2 illustrates an application of a data mining technique (i.e., cluster analysis) to answer the research question: "What bundles of services are Canadian consumers likely to purchase (use) together (i.e., in clusters)?" In the graph, those items that appear close together (e.g., bus and train service) are likely to be used or purchased by the same person, while those that appear far apart (e.g., car rental, natural gas) are not likely to be purchased together by the same person. Other, specific examples of current data-mining uses are shown in Good Practice 6.3.

The FBI, the United States Treasury Department, USAA Insurance, Fidelity, AC Nielsen, American Express, Capital One, and AT&T are some of the growing list of companies using data mining. Why? These firms and others are trying to obtain a competitive advantage and increase profitability. Financial analysts are sifting through financial data and information to improve investment decisions. Medical records are examined by health care organizations to understand past trends and reduce future costs. In brief, data mining is a valuable tool that allows companies to interact with and learn about their customers and anticipate their needs, accurately and efficiently.

@ /www.acnielsen.com

During the process of data mining, data integrity, storage, and cleaning become critical. Decision makers must consider the purpose and objective of a data-mining project, implementation and integration problems, the type of data-mining tools available, what form the output should take, and ease of use. In addition, they must have a specific plan for integrating data mining into everyday business operations.

Database Marketing: A Service Encounter

ETHICAL DILEMMA 6.1

Mr. Robert Beken, a computer software consultant, has a long-standing dislike of unsolicited mail or e-mail. One day, Mr. Beken purchased a software guidebook for $35 at a Computer City outlet in San Diego. When he noticed that the clerk was typing his address off a check into a computer, Mr. Beken asked if he would be placed on a mailing list. The clerk assured Mr. Beken that he wouldn't be included in such a list. As a precaution, Mr. Beken wrote the following message on the back of his check:

> Computer City agrees NOT to place Robert Beken on any mailing list or send him any advertisements or mailings. Computer City agrees that breach of this agreement by Computer City will damage Robert Beken and that these damages may be pursued in court. Further, that these damages for the first breach are $1,000. The deposit of this check for payment is agreement with these terms and conditions.

What do you think happens next? Here is the order of events. First, Computer City cashes the check. Second, Computer City sends several fliers to Robert Beken. Third, Mr. Beken sues the retailer in San Diego Municipal Court.

The Small Claims judge, Jerome Varon, agreed with Mr. Beken and ordered Computer City to pay Mr. Beken $1,000, plus $21 in court costs. In describing his ruling, Judge Varon wrote, "The attempt to protect one's privacy can hardly be viewed as unreasonable." When contacted by a reporter from *The Wall Street Journal,* the retailer declined to comment on the case or on its use of databases.

This court case offers a lesson for marketers who desire to establish a relationship with a customer via database marketing. First, many customers do not want to have a "relationship" with a corporation. Second, the term "relationship" means something quite different when the two parties carrying on the relationship are not both human beings. Third, corporations should be careful about their applications of data mining techniques and relationship marketing (see Dilbert cartoon). Fourth, organizations that want a long-term association with a customer should find ways to reward that customer for maintaining the association. For example, consider the free trips that airlines offer as an incentive to their loyal customers. And finally, notice the ethical issues that are raised by the practice of database marketing. Organizations need to balance a customer's right to privacy with their own need to gather consumer information.

Source: "Litigious Crusader Uses Checks to Ensure No Junk Is in the Mail," from The Wall Street Journal, Eastern Edition. [Staff produced copy only] by Ross Kerber. Copyright 1996 by Dow Jones & Co. Inc. Reproduced with permission of Dow Jones & Co. Inc. in the format textbook via Copyright Clearance Center.

Data Mining or Spam?

ETHICAL DILEMMA 6.2

Source: DILBERT reprinted by permission of United Feature Syndicate, Inc.

LEARNING ABOUT CONSUMERS

Successful companies try to gauge consumers in many different ways. The Coca-Cola Company uses a three-pronged approach to gather information from customers and potential customers in all the countries in which it operates. Trend research seeks to understand broad societal and cultural factors that influence customer behavior. Traditional market research seeks to track real-time purchase and consumption behaviors. Under this approach researchers predict sales and utilize sophisticated mathematical modeling techniques. Finally, research is employed to predict customer responses to changes in the marketing mix for Coca-Cola products. All of the products of this research are available to marketing managers through the company's user-friendly intranet information system.

Some manufacturing companies go to great lengths to encourage information exchange between nonmarketing employees and customers. To cite one example, a manufacturer holds an annual open house for which manufacturing, not marketing, personnel hand deliver invitations to customers. Customers interact with shop floor personnel as well as white-collar employees. The president of this company notes that this impresses on manufacturing personnel that there are people who buy the product—"real, live-bodied, walking-around people."[20]

As another illustration of the range of ways to learn about consumers, consider Japanese companies. Many Japanese companies rely heavily on personal observation as a way of learning about customers. For example, when Canon Cameras was losing ground to Minolta, Canon sent three managers to the United States to look into the problem. The head of the team, Tatehiro Tsuruta, spent six weeks in the United States entering camera stores and acting like a customer. He noted how the cameras were displayed and how the clerks served customers. He realized that some dealers were not enthusiastic about Canon and drugstores and other discount outlets were not advantageous outlets. As a result of this research, Canon opened its own sales subsidiary.[21]

@ www.unitedmedia.com/comics/dilbert

Finally, consider the strategy of a Weyerhaeuser sawmill for learning about customers. This sawmill was located far from company headquarters in the small community of Cottage Grove, Oregon. A cross section of employees, from the general manager to forklift drivers, began spending a week at a time as "employees" of their customers. For example, customer service representatives worked as sales assistants in Home Depot and other home centers. Buyers soon found that they were dealing with personnel who not only understood their problems but also frequently anticipated them because Weyerhaeuser employees were actively learning about them.[22]

International consumer research includes two different kinds of research. First, it includes **single-country consumer research**—*research carried out in a country other than that of the research-commissioning organization.* For example, if a company is considering entering a new foreign market, it might conduct extensive research to understand foreign consumers as related to that product. In this case, the company is not necessarily trying to make comparisons between foreign consumers and other consumers of that product. Second, international consumer research includes **multicountry consumer research**—*research conducted in more than one country with the intent of making comparisons.* For example, a company might be interested in contrasting health attitudes in Russia with those in the United States. International consumer research presents challenges that arise out of political, legal, economic, social, and cultural differences between nations. These national and cultural differences also contribute to problems of comparability of research results, especially in multicountry studies.

THE RESEARCH PROCESS

Consumer researchers engage in a systematic process to ensure that the resulting market intelligence is relevant, timely, efficient, accurate, and ethical. The research is considered **relevant** if it *anticipates the kinds of information that will be required by decision makers, scientists, or policy advocates.* This is information that improves the quality of exchanges between organizations and their customers or stakeholders. **Timely** research is *completed in time to influence decisions.* Research is **efficient** when it is of *the best quality for the minimum expenditure and the study is appropriate to the research context.* Research is considered **accurate,** or valid, when *the interpretation can account for both consistencies and inconsistencies in the data.* An important way to improve accuracy is to incorporate multiple methods and perspectives in the research effort as both Colgate-Palmolive and The Coca-Cola Company do, for example. Finally, careful attention to the research process can ensure that it is **ethical,** that it *promotes trust, exercises care, observes standards, and protects the rights of all the participants in the research process.*[23] We discuss research ethics in greater detail later in this chapter.

Defining the Problem and Project Scope

A general outline of the research process is shown in Exhibit 6.2. The research process begins by defining the problem and scope of the project. Very often it will require numerous conversations with decision makers, experts, and consumers before the problem can be precisely defined. In the rafting research discussed in the vignette, for example, we would have misunderstood the nature of customer satisfaction, and indeed measured the wrong things, if we had relied solely on the impressions of the river outfitters. An especially important part of problem definition is clarifying the boundaries of the study. For example, we set out to study consumer behavior as it related to white-water river rafting in the United States; we quickly learned that such rafting in the eastern part of the country differs substantially from that in the west. After some

EXHIBIT 6.2

Outline of the Research Process

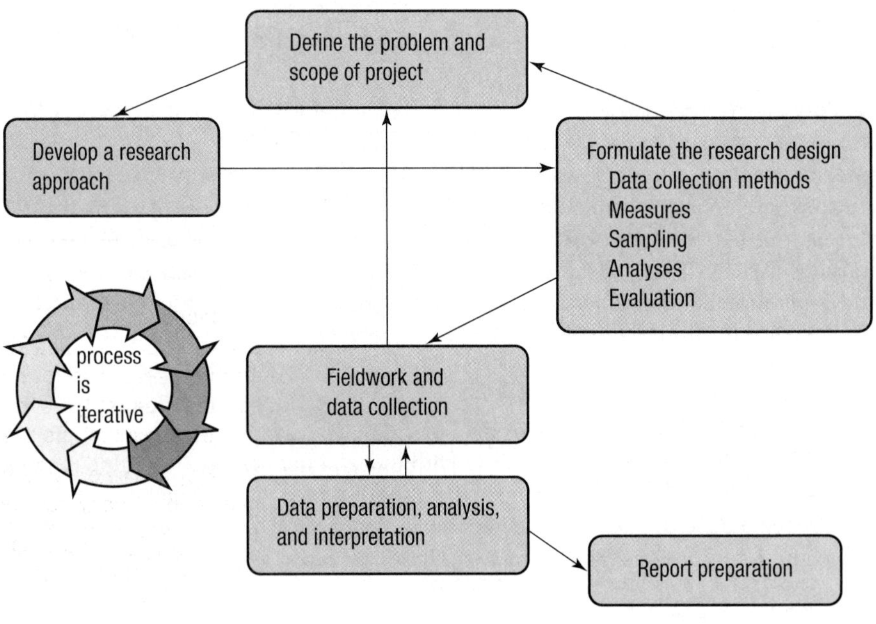

preliminary research on both one-day trips and multiday rafting trips, we learned that these two types of trips have very different characteristics and attract different segments. We ended up focusing on multiday (mostly three- to five-day trips) white-water river-rafting trips in the Colorado River Basin. Subsequently, in discussing this research in Europe, we discovered that there are important differences in the meanings of nature and wilderness between the North American and European contexts that further limit the generalizability of our results.[24]

A famous proverb summarizes the importance of this first step of the research process—"garbage in, garbage out" (GIGO). In other words, a mistake made at the first stage of the research project is fatal. No matter how skilled the researcher may be at statistical analysis or interpretation or report writing, the research project will fail if the initial steps in the research process are not completed in a thorough and competent manner.

www.webopedia.com/TERM/g/garbage_in_garbage_out.html

The Research Approach

The second step of the process shown in Exhibit 6.2 involves development of a research approach to the problem. This involves deciding on what types of research are implied by the research objective. We can outline three basic types of research: exploratory (such as the basic research described above), descriptive, and causal. The three types of research have complementary roles; that is, each can contribute something to the overall research process.

Causal research *investigates a very specific relationship between two or more variables.* To take a very simple example of causal research, a firm might like to know if coupons mailed to prospective customers result in an increase in sales subsequent to the mailing. In other words, do coupons cause increased sales? Measuring retail sales before and after the mailing provides the answer. To take a more complex example of causal research, a researcher might be interested in whether female college students exposed to highly attractive models in ads will be less satisfied with their own physical attractiveness. To answer this question, the researcher might conduct an experiment that exposes female college students to different kinds of advertising models, some of whom are very attractive, and then measures the students' satisfaction with their own attractiveness.[25]

After finding that highly attractive models in ads do make women feel less satisfied with their own appearance, the researcher might be interested in finding out more about the thoughts and feelings that lead consumers to report less satisfaction with their own appearance. In this case, as in the participant observation rafting research described in the opening vignette, the research approach is exploratory. **Exploratory research** *seeks insights into the general nature of the problem, possible decision alternatives, or identification of relevant variables.* In this case, the research is attempting to identify the thoughts and feelings associated with exposure to attractive models in ads. The researcher does not know what variables or relationships between variables will be identified. The researcher conducts a focus group in which female college students first look at ads taken from fashion magazines featuring highly attractive models. Then, the students are asked to write their thoughts and reactions to the ads on a blank piece of paper. Finally, they discuss them as a focus group. The thoughts and feelings shared in this session offer a more textured understanding of the types of comparisons that occur. For example, this research suggests women tend to focus on that part of the model's body that they are most dissatisfied with. One woman noted, "I have wide hips. I always look at the hips. I guess I'm just jealous." This type of discussion can also give a richer understanding of the intensity of feelings associated with these

Selected Focus Group Comments: Negative Self-Feelings from Viewing Ads

CONSUMER CHRONICLES 6.1

"You look at these ads and you feel inadequate, like you can't measure up."

"It's frustrating when you start to realize you should look that way—I mean—I can't."

"I used to go through these magazines every day and look at [models in the ads] and wish I looked like them. I used to go running every day, and I really thought maybe I could look like them. I remember, I even picked one model in particular and cut out ads with her in them. I was pretty obsessed. And I finally realized this wasn't realistic. But I sometimes still look and think, 'Well, maybe.'"

"Sometimes [ads with models] can make you feel a little depressed."

"They make me feel self-critical" [participant viewing models in swimsuit ads].

Source: Marsha Richins, "Social Comparison and the Idealized Images of Advertising," Journal of Consumer Research *18 (June 1991), p. 75.*

comparisons. Consumer Chronicles 6.1 illustrates selected negative self-feelings from viewing ads that came out of the focus groups. Researchers could also undertake a study to profile the characteristics of women most likely to make negative self-assessments following exposure to highly attractive models. This type of study would be **descriptive research**—*research designed to profile some aspect of the consumer environment.*

The Research Design

The third step in the research process is to formulate the research design. A **research design** is *a framework or blueprint for conducting the marketing research project.* It includes deciding on the appropriate data collection method or methods. It also reports decisions about how to translate the research problem into specific measures (specific questions, observations, and stimuli), decisions about the sampling plan, decisions about how to analyze the data, and a critical evaluation of what the payoff from the research is likely to be. Many critical decisions are made in formulating the research design. Often the research design will be revised as data collection proceeds, according to changing needs and understandings. For example, in international consumer research, the unit of analysis may shift from a country to a region as the researcher gains greater insight into consumers. Consider Belgium, which is divided in half between Wallonia in the south and Flanders in the north. Walloons use butter, but Flemish people use margarine. As preliminary investigation uncovers regional differences, additional research might be modified to better represent these regions.

Data collection methods can be divided into secondary and primary data collection approaches, and then each of these approaches can be further divided into several additional types. In this chapter we just provide an overview of some of the major approaches used to learn about consumers. Exhibit 6.3 outlines some secondary data collection approaches, including some examples, uses, and advantages and disadvantages. **Secondary data** are *data that have already been collected for purposes other than the problem at hand.* These data can be located quickly, easily, and inexpensively, and they should represent the starting point for any data collection effort. Because secondary data have been collected for purposes other than the problem at hand, they may lack accuracy, relevancy, or currency.

Secondary data are especially important in the case of international consumer research because primary international research projects can be very costly in terms of time and money. H.J. Heinz Company failed to successfully introduce Ketchup in Brazil. A more intensive look at the Brazilian food distribution system through secondary research might have helped avert this problem. Heinz concentrated on distributing through neighborhood shops, a strategy that worked well in Mexico. However, 75 percent of grocery

EXHIBIT 6.3

Secondary Data Collection Methods

Types	Examples	Uses	Pluses and Minuses
Scanner data	An "intelligent" terminal records the bar code on a product. Consumer panels are recruited to track purchase patterns and link to consumer profiles.	Scanners cover more and more product groups. Penetration is highest in the United States and Canada, but there is adequate scanner penetration in most European countries.	Large database that provides detailed information about consumer purchases; actual behavior. Often purchases can't be tied back to buyer, and in other cases buyers may not be very representative of general population. Links between retail outlets are not typically available.
Syndicated data sources	Global Scan provides detailed brand and category information on more than 1,000 products. Research International provides continuous panel data for 40 countries in the world. The ESOMAR website provides information on sources of syndicated data in various countries.	Syndicated data are collected for a set of information users with a common need. Scanner data, consumer panels, store audits, television viewer audits, and so on are examples of syndicated data.	The researcher must identify syndicated data sources for the country of interest. Subscription is expensive and data collection categories may not be relevant; quality is highly sensitive to sampling quality. Lots of information is available on a real-time basis.
Databases	National Trade Data Bank maintained by the U.S. Department of Commerce. World Atlas and World Development Report maintained by World Bank. Census of the Population from the U.S. Bureau of the Census.	There are thousands of sources of information that may be relevant to business decisions.	Many developing countries have data that are outdated or inaccurate. May be impossible to compare data collected from different countries. Very inexpensive and more accessible due to the Internet.
Internet	The PRIZM website provides extensive demographic and media use information organized by zip codes in the United States.	Information for research can be obtained at the company level, industry level, or macro level. Access to the information can be received directly by using the Internet address, but search engines and agents can also help obtain the information.	The Internet has only a limited number of search tools and does not provide extensive user support; information is not well structured; and quality of information is highly variable. The Internet is very low cost and offers information on a broad spectrum of topics.

EXHIBIT 6.4

Primary Data Collection Methods: Qualitative Techniques

Types	Examples	Uses	Pluses and Minuses
Depth interviews	A consumer tells a trained interviewer how she feels about a trip to the dentist. Consumer stories reveal the meanings they assign to "homemade" food and holiday meals.	Detailed probing of the respondent. Discussion of confidential, sensitive, or embarrassing topics. Situations where strong social norms exist and the respondent may be easily swayed by group. Detailed understanding of complicated behavior. Situations in which the product consumption experience is sensory in nature, affecting mood states and emotions.	Excellent method for understanding consumer motivation and the ***why*** of behavior. Time-consuming and costly, difficult to interpret. Should be used to identify the range of beliefs, attitudes, and behaviors on a particular topic, but not the frequency or prevalence of those beliefs. Requires interviewing and interpretation skills; opportunities for interviewer bias.
Focus groups	A group of French consumers describe their image and use of herbal teas for a Chinese tea manufacturer. Focus groups with Japanese consumers reveal perceptions, preferences, and behavior regarding laundry detergent.	Understanding consumers' perceptions, preferences, and behavior concerning a product category; generating new ideas about products or impressions of new product concepts; developing creative ideas for marketing programs or preliminary consumer reaction to marketing programs.	Great opportunities for group synergies that result in unique insights. In international settings, the researcher must understand cultural traits and adapt process accordingly. Requires interviewing and interpretation skills; opportunities for interviewer bias.
Projective techniques	Word associations are used to help American marketers better understand Japanese consumers' perceptions of foreign countries. Consumers, asked if their neighbor fears flying, are able to discuss more openly reasons for fearing flying than when asked if they themselves fear flying.	Encourages respondents to project underlying motivations, beliefs, attitudes, or feelings through use of unstructured, indirect forms of questioning. Projective techniques should be used when the required information can't be accurately obtained through direct methods.	Requires highly trained interviewers and skilled interpreters. Tends to be expensive. Analysis and interpretation are difficult and subjective. There is risk of interpretation bias. Establishing the equivalence of meaning across cultures is especially difficult in the case of projective techniques and their use in international research should be carefully considered. Can elicit responses that consumers would be unable or unwilling to give if they knew the true purpose of the study.
Ethnography	Intense observation combined with consumer interviews and consumer diaries are used to learn how U.S. consumers purchase beef. Interviews and participant observation are used to better understand an experience such as white-water river rafting. Mechanical observation (using video cameras) combined with consumer interviews is used to learn how consumers, especially children, use microwave ovens. Observation and consumer interviews are used to learn how Mexican women purchase and use laundry cleaning products.	Ethnographic research is especially useful for showing companies how consumers purchase and use products in their everyday lives. This technique was developed in anthropology, but it is becoming increasingly popular in market research. It can be used in new-product development, product promotion, and understanding competitive market structure from the consumers' perspective.	The diversity of the global marketplace and increasing demands for customization contribute to much greater interest in ethnographic studies. Such studies can offer rich insights into consumer meaning and use behavior. Ethnographic research requires very special training, and typically requires apprenticing with someone well-trained in this methodology. The research is very time-consuming and intensive, and data interpretation is difficult.

shopping in São Paulo, Brazil, is done in supermarkets and not the smaller shops.[26] Many countries offer extensive data about their populations through departments of commerce. Much of this information can be obtained online, and because of the importance of foreign trade, many national commerce departments offer links to trade data relevant to other countries.

www.fedstats.gov

Exhibit 6.4 outlines some primary data collection approaches, again including examples, uses, advantages, and disadvantages. **Primary data collection** is *research carried out for a specific purpose.* Management decisions may seem in many cases as if they rely on pure instinct. Primary data collection can help managers counterbalance these intuitions, monitor consequences, and review and refine a course of action. Of course, as compared to secondary data collection, primary data collection is difficult, expensive, and time-consuming. Exhibit 6.4 overviews some qualitative techniques: **depth interviews, focus groups, projective techniques,** and **ethnography. Qualitative techniques** *provide insights and understanding of a problem or topic* rather than trying to quantify the data and apply some form of statistical analysis. Most accomplished researchers treat qualitative and quantitative data as complementary input into understanding and predicting consumers. Qualitative research typically relies on a small sample and should not be used to infer a population distribution. Analysis and interpretation of qualitative data are particularly challenging, requiring skills of categorization, abstraction, comparison, integration, and so on.[27] Qualitative techniques are gaining in popularity as consumer researchers attempt to stay in touch with global diversity and the demand for customization.[28] Successful international consumer research is highly dependent on qualitative research.

Observation, survey research, and experiments are other very important primary data collection techniques. They are overviewed in Exhibit 6.5. **Observational techniques** *record actual behavior* (e.g., consumers eating spaghetti) *or traces of actual behavior* (e.g., an audit of spaghetti sauces, noodles, and so on in the consumer's pantry). Observation may yield either qualitative or quantitative data. For example, an observer may simply count the number of cars crossing an intersection as input on a decision about whether to locate a minimart at that location. This observation would yield quantitative data. Alternatively, an observer could record all relevant aspects of children playing with new toys, including their emotional responses, how long they played with the toys, what they did with them, and so on. For each child this could render a unique, detailed, qualitative account of his or her interaction with the toys.

"For crying out loud, gentlemen! That's us! Someone's installed the one-way mirror in backwards!"

A humorous look at observational techniques.

Survey research is probably the most popular way of collecting primary data. Surveys are usually *conducted with the help of questionnaires, and questions and responses are typically structured.* There are a number of ways surveys can be administered, including via face-to-face interviews, telephone, mail, fax, e-mail, and the Internet. The survey method has several advantages. Questionnaires are simple to administer, and coding, analysis, and statistical interpretation are relatively simple. However, wording questions properly is not easy, and respondents may be unable or unwilling to provide the desired information. It is very important for the survey instrument to be applicable in a given country and in a given situation. The researcher must be culturally sensitive. For example, respondents in many Asian countries provide responses they think will please the interviewer; Japanese people consider telephone surveys impolite; Middle Eastern respondents tend to exaggerate class, income, and position; Latin Americans are touchy about alcoholism; and Indians consider sex a taboo topic.[29]

Experiments are based on the principle of *manipulating one or more variables (termed independent variables) and observing changes in some other variable or variables (dependent variables).* So, for example, a company might test consumer preference toward two different packages, or three different promotional appeals, or a set of price and package size combinations. Experiments are especially useful for doing causal research, but they are extremely difficult to implement meaningfully in multicountry studies. All experiments must balance the need for precision with the need to make the experiment meaningful for the decision at hand.

The principle of GIGO is also appropriate for thinking about the importance of research design. If the research design is not appropriate for the research question, then the project will fail. No level of analytical sophistication can make good information out of bad (or inappropriate) data. Suppose a British radio station (BBC Radio 3) wanted to identify ways of attracting new listeners—those who currently patronize competing radio stations. If the subsequent research project resulted in 240 interviews, all conducted with current Radio 3 listeners, then there is not an appropriate match between the research purpose and the research design. The resulting data can be classified as "garbage" because they do not allow the managers to make any progress in meeting their objective (i.e., finding ways to attract new listeners). Perhaps in a similar way, Arnold's classmates in the cartoon do not see the relevance of his data.

Skepticism is a key aspect of scientific inquiry

Source: Copyright © Kevin McCormick. Reprinted with permission.

Fieldwork and Data Collection

The fourth step in the research process is fieldwork or data collection employing some or all of the techniques outlined in Exhibits 6.4 and 6.5. Many researchers agree there is no substitute for doing a portion of the fieldwork or data collection themselves. This is particularly true of data collection techniques that require enormous skill and flexibility, such as depth interviews, participant observation, and certain projective techniques. However, this is also true of other data collection techniques. Even if the primary investigators intend to contract with a service to do a large-scale telephone interview, they may do a small number of calls themselves to get a firsthand feel for the survey process, response types, and potential problems. Proper selection, training, supervision, and evaluation of the field force helps to minimize data collection errors. Research

EXHIBIT 6.5

Other Primary Data Collection Methods

Types	Examples	Uses	Pluses and Minuses
Observation	Ford Motor Company invites guests to test drive prototype models through a predetermined route. A trained observer rides along, making notes on the driver's reaction to the car. Content analysis is used to compare the information content in American and Japanese magazine advertising. A trained researcher participates with other consumers in a Harley-Davidson Brandfest to learn more about the behaviors and activities associated with these events.	Observational techniques can range from direct or even mechanical observation of particular consumption behaviors to observation of the natural "residue" of consumption behaviors (e.g., consumer's garbage). It is useful for learning what consumers do and can provide new ideas for product development, product complements, and substitutes.	Certain types of behavioral data can only be collected through observation. Observation, used alone, cannot determine underlying motives, beliefs, attitudes, and preferences. Observation can be difficult and time-consuming and in some cases may be unethical. The researcher's observations may be selective and biased.
Survey research	Interviewers are stationed at the entrance to a shopping mall in Toronto, Canada, to invite respondents to answer a questionnaire about snack-food preferences. Telephone interviews are conducted with members of a small art theater located in Lincoln, Nebraska, to profile members and learn more about their film and theater preferences. Busy German executives are first contacted by phone and then e-mailed a brief questionnaire to e-mail or fax back. The questionnaire is used to measure market potential for a U.S. software company's products.	Personal interviewing is the most flexible method of survey research and used most frequently in international consumer surveys. Telephone interviews are dependent on the quality of lines and also telephone etiquette, and these vary considerably between countries. Mail surveys depend on the availability of mailing list and literacy levels, which can also vary substantially between countries.	Conducting a survey is a complex task of gaining trust and building rapport with a respondent. The researcher needs to be familiar with important national and cultural traits of the countries where the research is being conducted and fluent in the local language. Designing good questions and good questionnaires requires considerable expertise laced with creativity. There are vast differences in the way different cultures react toward surveys. The respondent, the interviewer, and the topic can all bias the research results.
Experiments	How will a point-of-purchase promotion affect juice sales in the United States, the United Kingdom, and Japan?	Firms that sell on the Internet can create field experiments that test different prices, atmospheres, or service details.	Experiments by their very nature incorporate cultural differences. Transferring the same design across countries could result in erroneous conclusions. Experiments are probably the best way to do causal research. It is very difficult to ensure that all relevant variables have been measured or controlled. Laboratory experiments may be too contrived or artificial to provide much information about real consumer settings.

experience can make a difference in the quality of the data attained. For example, research has found that inexperienced interviewers are more likely to commit coding errors, misrecord responses, and fail to probe; have a difficult time filling respondent quotas; and have larger refusal rates and more "don't know" responses or unanswered questions.[30]

Data Analysis and Interpretation

The fifth step involves data preparation and analysis or interpretation. This step will proceed very differently depending on the type of data collected and the general purposes of the research. For example, for some research projects, the data collected might include garbage, photos, videotapes, brain waves, eye movement traces, as well as or instead of written or recorded responses to probes and questions. In general, preparing data for interpretation includes editing, coding, transcribing, and verifying data. Data analysis includes all of the techniques used to interpret and give meaning to the collected data.

Analysis includes a broad range of techniques, both statistical and nonnumerical. In Chapter 5 we introduced the concept of perceptual maps, a product positioning tool based on a statistical technique called *multidimensional scaling.* In the river-rafting research, by contrast, interpretation was based on coding interview and observational data into thematic categories related both to progression through time and typical events that occurred on a given day.

As mentioned in the introduction, interpretation is one of the biggest problems that leading organizations face today. Their problem is that they are drowning in data compiled from secondary sources, **syndicated data,** and exploratory, descriptive, and causal consumer research. Managers are often too busy to examine all the data available to them. In many cases, they lack the training that would enable them to interpret one or more of the specialized studies they receive. One response to this problem is to standardize report formats. Thus, when managers are constructing reports from diverse data sources, they cannot reanalyze data or modify reporting formats. While this simplifies their task, it also robs them of opportunities to mine the data available to them.

Report of Findings

Generally, the final step of the project is a written or oral report describing the entire research process and presenting the results and major findings. Decision makers are likely to evaluate the report in terms of whether it addresses the problem, has a complete and understandable research design, uses appropriate research procedures and executes them correctly, provides a complete and objective interpretation, and clearly identifies the boundaries of the study and the generalizability of the findings. One of the most important and difficult aspects of market research is evaluation. A marketing manager needs to know what the research *means.* In a study of the Norwegian food marketing industry, one researcher found that managers felt deeply insecure about the meaning of research conducted by well-regarded advertising and marketing research firms. Since market success or failure often hangs on the meaning of research, their anxiety is understandable. In evaluating any explanation of data, readers will look for "symptoms of truth." These symptoms of truth are summarized in Good Practice 6.4.[31] These symptoms provide guidelines for evaluating the quality of a research project. Together these guidelines suggest that researchers must "tell a good story," a story that holds together

Symptoms of Truth for Evaluating Interpretations

GOOD PRACTICE 6.4

1. The interpretation must be **exact,** so that no unnecessary ambiguity exists.
2. It must be **economical,** so that it forces us to make the minimum number of assumptions and still explains the data.
3. It must be mutually **consistent,** so that no assertion contradicts another.
4. It must be **externally consistent,** so that it conforms to what we independently know about the subject matter.
5. It must be **unified,** so that assertions are organized in a manner that subsumes the specific within the general, unifying where possible, discriminating when necessary.
6. It must be **powerful,** so that it explains as much of the data as possible without sacrificing accuracy.
7. The interpretation must be **fertile,** so that it suggests new ideas, opportunities for insight.

Source: Grant McCracken, The Long Interview *(Newbury Park, CA: Sage Publications, 1988), pp. 50–52.*

internally and externally, grabs our attention, explains the data, and provides future direction.

Summary Features of the Research Process

Several general features characterize the research process we have just outlined. First, as suggested in Exhibit 6.2, *the research process is iterative.* The initial research problem may be completely reformulated as the researcher learns more about the consumer from initial data collection efforts. For example, Avon Products, Inc., which markets cosmetics to women, began a strategic initiative with the research question how to capture an increased share of the Hispanic market. At first, this seemed like the appropriate question since secondary data from the U.S. Census Bureau treats Hispanic females as one cultural group. However, depth interviews, pilot surveys, and observations of Hispanic communities revealed many segments of Hispanic females that differ in cultural and historic background as well as in attitudes and beliefs. On the basis of this early research, Avon redefined the research problem as one of how best to segment the Hispanic female market. Similarly, if Avon or any other firm were to conduct research in Australia, it would want to be sure to distinguish between the many national varieties of Asian-Australians such as Koreans, Vietnamese, and Chinese. A study of how women express assertiveness conducted by The Coca-Cola Company revealed that it needed to look at the issue in many national contexts.

@ avon.avon.com

Second, *the use of different methods and perspectives affects the research results.* It is impossible to be completely objective. That's why it is so important to incorporate multiple approaches and perspectives in research efforts. Very often researchers will find from observation that consumers behave in ways that are very different from how they report they behave in a questionnaire. For example, Ernest Dichter, the famous expert on consumer motivation, once conducted a study on the reasons people wear

A fashion-statement for Batman.

Does this woman need glasses to protect her eyes from the sun?

sunglasses. Sunglass-wearing people who were questioned on a cloudy day in New York City frequently maintained that sunglasses protected their eyes from the sun. Clearly their behavior contradicted their verbal responses, suggesting, as we all know, that there are other reasons for wearing sunglasses. See two photographs above. The task of the researcher is to provide an interpretation that makes sense of the differences between the results of different kinds of data.[32] Similarly, by incorporating only one perspective on the research, findings may underrepresent or misrepresent other perspectives. For example, a study of consumer research showed that much of it makes inappropriate assumptions and presents misleading findings because researchers fail to take into account differences in the viewpoints and behaviors of men and women.[33] Third, *no research is perfect.* Researchers must constantly make trade-offs between the costs and benefits of conducting different types and amounts of research as well as different types of error. For example, by asking several questions to measure a concept, researchers can feel more confident that they have actually measured the concept and not omitted important aspects of it. However, asking more questions can lead to respondent fatigue, resentment, and nonresponse, which can significantly bias the findings. Of course, the more researchers ask, the more it costs to collect, analyze, and interpret the data.

ASKING QUESTIONS

One of the most important problems in data collection is how to ask research questions. Even if researchers collect data by observing behaviors, they generally want to be able to relate those behaviors to consumers' thoughts and feelings. To do this, they need to know how to ask questions. In this section we focus on a simple review of the basics for asking questions; but it's important to keep in mind that the type of questions asked in a focus group or depth interview will differ from those asked in telephone, mail, or mall-intercept surveys. Even mail and telephone formats cannot be used to ask the same type of questions. For example, mail questionnaires can generally ask people to make finer discriminations (using 7- or 10-point scales) than telephone surveys. Similarly, mall-intercept surveys or personal interviews can use visual and other sensory stimuli, whereas telephone interviews cannot.

The Importance of How Researchers Ask Questions

You may be able to recall examples of promotions that feature responses to consumer surveys of one sort or another. For example, a car company may claim that it is number one in customer satisfaction, or a cough syrup manufacturer may claim to be the brand doctors recommended most, or a pharmaceutical company may claim a specific brand of aspirin is preferred by physicians if they are going to be stranded on a desert island. All of these claims imply valid research. In fact, the results are often based on biased questions.

Similarly, polls conducted for particular political parties report voter preferences based on very specific questions that may bias the results. What happens if the companies that make these claims ask questions differently? Some years ago, fast-food company Burger King ran a series of commercials in which it claimed that consumers preferred its method of cooking hamburgers over that of McDonald's by three to one. The question used to generate these data was, Do you prefer your hamburgers flame-broiled or fried? An independent researcher asked the "same" question a different way: Do you prefer a hamburger that is grilled on a hot stainless steel grill or cooked by passing the raw meat through an open gas flame? This version of the question resulted in 53 percent preferring McDonald's grilling process. When further description was added by noting that the gas-flame hamburgers are kept in a microwave oven before serving, the preference for grilled burgers was 85 percent. In this case, three technically correct descriptions of cooking methods produced preferences ranging from 3 to 1 for Burger King to 5.5 to 1 for McDonald's.[34] This example illustrates a critical principle of consumer research: How researchers ask questions is very important.

Three Questions Researchers Should Ask about Research Questions

To build a quality questionnaire, the researcher should begin by asking three questions about each research question.[35] First, *can potential study participants understand the question?* The cartoon shown on the next page illustrates the reaction of more than one consumer to what seems like gobbledygook from the researcher. Researchers bring their own perspectives and biases to questions, and these can be very different from those of the respondents. An appealing illustration involves the pretest of a telephone survey to look at people's understanding of corporate profits. One of the first questions was, When I say profits, what comes to your mind? The first

Next question: I believe that life is a constant striving for balance, requiring frequent trade-offs between morality and necessity, within a cyclic pattern of joy and sadness, forging a trail of bittersweet memories until one slips, inevitably, into the jaws of death. Agree or disagree?

couple of interviews went fine, but in the third interview, an elderly woman responded, "Well, I know about Moses and Isaiah, but that is about all I know about prophets." This question was changed to ask about "corporate or business profits."[36] Obviously, the difficulty of ensuring that study participants understand the question is greatly increased when conducting international research. Consumer Chronicles 6.2 offers a short, humorous illustration.

Second, *can potential study participants answer the question?* Sometimes, the researcher will ask a question that study participants can understand but can't answer. For example, a researcher doing a telephone interview may call and ask, Exactly how much did your household spend on groceries last month? Participants may have an approximate idea about how much their household spent on groceries; but it's likely that the majority of respondents won't know exactly. To ensure that participants can answer the question also means making sure that response categories are mutually exclusive (nonoverlapping) and collectively exhaustive (everyone has something to mark). It's very easy to make mistakes in setting up response categories that make it impossible for study participants to answer the question accurately.

Third, *will potential study participants answer the question?* Even if you ask a simple, nonsensitive question, you might not get an answer. More than a third of all Americans contacted routinely shut the door or hang up the phone on interviewer questions. One Singaporean researcher conducting mall-intercept interviews in three Asian countries found that Chinese in the People's Republic were willing to answer his questions in part because he was a foreigner, whereas most of those in his own country refused to answer.[37] Sometimes it's possible to predict that at least a portion of potential study participants will find a particular question too personal and refuse to answer. For example, approximately 10 percent of U.S. survey respondents refuse to answer questions related to income. In Scandinavia, however, where salaries are more highly standardized, such questions are felt to be less personal. In countries with large informal economies, such as those of the transitional economies of eastern Europe, considerable resistance to such questions should be expected. Other times, the researcher needs a deep understanding of potential participants to predict what topics they will be sensitive about. Many years ago, while still in school, one of us did research for a Southwestern art magazine to profile their customers. The magazine was interested in establishing what type of advertising would appeal to its customers, with the hope of broadening its advertiser base. The mail survey was university sponsored, and care was taken to establish the legitimacy of the project and confidentiality of the respondents. However, questions about art types (not specific pieces or values) engendered a significant number of refusals. One respondent wrote that he was afraid that the chances of a break-in would increase if the type of art he owned were publicized (by his answering the questionnaire). As a poor graduate student hanging poster art on the walls, the researcher (one of us) was too distant from the experience of the potential respondent to have predicted this attitude.

Understanding the Question?

CONSUMER CHRONICLES 6.2

Four men—a Saudi, a Russian, a North Korean, and a New Yorker—are walking down the street. A marketing researcher says to them, "Excuse me, what is your opinion on the meat shortage?" The Saudi says, "What's a shortage?" The Russian says, "What's meat?" The Korean says, "What's an opinion?" The New Yorker says, "'Excuse me'? What's excuse me?"

Source: V. Kumar, International Marketing Research *(Englewood Cliffs, NJ: Prentice Hall, 2000), p. 202. Adapted from* India Herald, *May 22, 1998, p. 27.*

Specific Guidelines for Asking Questions

To help answer the preceding three primary questions about questionnaire items, the researcher can apply what are known as the **BRONS guidelines.** The acronym BRONS serves to reinforce the important criteria—brevity, relevancy, objectivity, nonambiguity, and specificity—and to suggest a warning about poorly constructed questions: Be Right Or Necessarily Suffer.

Brevity is the first important criterion. A good rule of thumb is that questions should contain 20 words or less, excluding answer categories. Perhaps you've had the experience of a telephone interviewer asking a question that's so long you can't remember the beginning of the question by the time she gets to the end. Overly long questions can lead to confusion or misleading responses or nonresponses and should be avoided.

Relevancy is a second important criterion. Every question and every word in every question has a cost associated with it for all the participants. Relevancy in words and in questions is critical. Quite often, after the research problem and scope of the study have been defined, the client will begin to remark, "Wouldn't it be interesting to know . . ." This can be very dangerous. Sometimes, of course, this can lead to reconsidering the problem and scope and enrich the project, but very often this approach simply detracts attention from the intended purposes of the research. Before including the question, the researcher needs to be fairly sure that it's not just interesting, but it's interesting given the purposes and scope of the research.

Objectivity is a third important criterion. There are three common ways in which nonobjectivity arises. First, questions may suggest an answer. For example, if a focus group moderator exploring television show preferences in Egypt said, "You watch *Hilmiyya Nights,* don't you?" or if one in Brazil asked, "You watch *Torre de Babel* don't you?" she or he would be implying a socially desirable answer to focus group participants.[38] Asking leading questions like this could lead to very misleading results.

Second, questions may have answer categories that are biased (unbalanced response categories). For example, consider the following question: About how many soft drinks do you drink per week, with response categories 0–4, 5–8, 9–12, 12–15, over 15. Answers to this question could be very misleading because people who don't drink any soft drinks would be lumped with those who drink up to four per week. In general, a soft-drink manufacturer would be interested in separating out people who don't consume soft drinks. It's easy to imagine other, more sensitive topics where results reported without a "none" category would be very misleading (e.g., questions about alcohol consumption, drug use, sexual activity).

Finally, questions may be nonobjective because they don't contain sufficient information to allow respondents to make an informed choice. For example, a question such as, Do you favor abortion? does not contain enough information. Most people in the United States would agree that abortion is an unfortunate act. Many favor abortion only under particular circumstances. And most people in the United States do not favor abortion after the first trimester. Thus, the question lacks specificity. Very often researchers exploring consumer preferences are misled because the preference questions are not specific enough to allow informed choice.

Nonambiguity is the fourth important criterion to ensure good questions. Ambiguity can arise in two ways. Ambiguity arises when unfamiliar words are employed or when words have multiple meanings. Sometimes this is very difficult for researchers to judge themselves. After all, the researcher uses the word because he or she is familiar with it. Very frequently, we acquire specialized vocabularies that are widely shared by our circle of friends and co-workers. We are so familiar with these words and acronyms and use them so frequently that we may not realize that they are not used in other social circles.

Differences in familiarity and vocabulary are particularly relevant when study participants differ culturally from the researchers. Language creates highly sensitive issues in multicultural societies like those of North and South America, South Africa, Australia, and New Zealand. Language can also create problems when marketers whose countries of origin are culturally homogeneous (e.g., those of Scandinavia) find themselves working in multicultural or foreign environments.

Ambiguity also occurs in response categories. Perhaps you have filled out a questionnaire that asks about your consumption of some food or beverage using terms like "never," "rarely," "occasionally," "frequently," "all the time." Researchers ask questions this way because they are not sure how to be more specific. Unfortunately, what is "rarely" for one person may be "frequently" for someone else. Doctors and medical personnel commonly use this type of question in reference to alcohol consumption. A consumer whose social group drinks three or more portions of alcohol each day will see his or her own behavior differently than someone whose social group drinks only on holidays or not at all. A member of the first group who happens to drink one or two glasses of wine per week may report "rarely"; but someone from the second group who drinks one or two glasses per week may report "frequently." A Saudi Arabian will view the question differently than a German. In Saudi Arabia, all alcohol is taboo; in Germany beer is considered a food.

"I'm sorry, sir, but this survey does not allow for that opinion."

Source: Copyright © Graham Wilson.

Avoiding ambiguous response categories is especially important for international consumer research. Qualitative research can help researchers understand what level and frequency of usage is normal. For example, from depth interviews with consumers and product managers in Budapest we learned that Hungarian consumers rarely wash their hair every day and commonly wash their hair about once per week, and many wash their hair less frequently. To compare Hungarian and American consumers in terms of shampoo usage requires specific response categories that include a wider range of likely responses, or response categories tailored to each country.

The fifth and final criterion is *specificity.* The researcher wants to try and balance the information requirements of the manager with the abilities of study participants to answer a question. Using an earlier illustration, the manager may want to know exactly how much the household spent on groceries last month, but the potential participant can at best give an estimate of what was spent. The goal is to provide the information needed without overtaxing the respondent. Sometimes no matter how specific the question, participants cannot answer accurately. When this is the case, it may be appropriate to use another form of data collection, such as observation, consumer diaries, or some unobtrusive measures, for example, a study of garbage to see how much alcohol is really consumed in a neighborhood.

We have outlined only the essentials of how to ask questions efficiently and effectively. The researcher would also need to evaluate the research instrument or questionnaire to ensure that it's appropriate in terms of sequencing, order, and other aspects of design.

CONDUCTING INTERNATIONAL CONSUMER RESEARCH

We have already provided numerous examples in this chapter of the difficulty of conducting international consumer research. In this section we provide a more detailed description of some of the major problems. In developing theory, models, research questions, and hypotheses it is important to remember that differences in the sociocultural environment and other environmental factors may lead to differences in the formation of perceptions, attitudes, preferences, choices, and behaviors.

Cross-national consumer research is especially difficult because the researcher is attempting to produce comparable data in two different countries. That is, there is an interest in comparing what is discovered in one culture with what is found in another

GOOD PRACTICE 6.5

Questions to Ask in Constructing Cross-Cultural Research Instruments

- Is the word or concept relevant in both cultures?
- Is the explicit meaning of the word or concept the same in both cultures?
- Are the suggested, implied, or hinted-at meanings of the word or concept the same in both cultures? Is there congruence between cultural experiences with the word or concept?
- Are both cultures equally experienced and fluent with the research techniques employed?

Source: Adapted from the material contained in Eric J. Arnould and Melanie Wallendorf, "On Identical Methods in Cross-Cultural Research or the Noncomparability of Data Obtained with Seemingly-Comparable Measures," working paper, California State University, Long Beach, 1993.

culture. Nevertheless, this type of research is extremely important to companies that market global brands such as Mercedes automobiles, Nokia cell phones, Fuji film, Schweppes tonic water, Coca-Cola, Procter & Gamble's Tide detergent, or Nescafé instant coffee. To collect comparable information, the researcher may have to use nonidentical methods because of differences between the cultures. Good Practice 6.5 summarizes some important questions to ask when constructing a survey instrument for use in cross-cultural research.

The questions in Good Practice 6.5 are based on five specific problems that arise in trying to construct questions to compare two or more different cultures. One problem is that questions used in one cultural context may simply not be relevant in another cultural context. Research comparing valued consumer objects in Niger, West Africa, with valued consumer objects in the United States is illustrative of this problem.[39] One part of the study measured people's attachments to other people. The scale used in the United States included items asking the number of club memberships the respondent has and the frequency of talking on the phone with friends. These questions would not be relevant for the Nigerian sample. While telephone use is quite widespread in the United States, one-half of the world's population has never placed a phone call. In this instance, comparable data were obtained from the Nigerian sample by including items that ask how frequently the respondent attends village association meetings and the frequency of visiting friends and participating in village gossip. Despite the fact that these items are not identical, they attempt to measure attachment to other persons through organized group activities and informal communications comparably.

A second problem is that the explicit meaning of a word, its denotation, may differ between cultures. For example, Nigerians and Nepalese understand perfectly well the notion of markets as locations where things are sold. They will easily talk about "going to market," "buying things at the market," or "attending the market." However, a question like, Has the market for cosmetics/cloth/yogurt changed in recent years? may make little sense to them. (This problem may also still apply in many transitional economies.) In this question, *market* refers to an abstract notion of the market as an accumulation of exchanges between sellers and buyers taking place in many locations and at many times.

Finding comparable words is essential in cross-cultural research, and it can be difficult. In Chapter 3 we discuss the List of Values as a way to measure consumer values. To conduct a comparative study in Germany, researchers used a standard process of translation and back translation. However, it was very difficult to translate the English concepts of "warm relationships with others" and "self-respect" into German. The results revealed that significantly fewer Germans than Americans hold these as their most important values. However, the researchers concluded that imprecise translation might be more responsible for these results than actual differences in value orientations.[40]

A third problem is that the suggested, implied, or hinted meanings of words (connotative meanings) may differ between cultures. This stems from a lack of overlap between dimensions of cultural experience. Anytime the cultural experience of an object or process varies between cultures, the issue of connotative meanings arises. For example, research might find that both Japanese and American consumers value courteous service providers in fast-food restaurants.[41] However, what does *courteous* mean in these two cultural contexts? In the United States, courtesy implies warmth and friendliness, whereas in Japan it implies formality and respect. For a company planning to open a service establishment in Japan, knowing that the customers like courteous service doesn't help very much. The company needs to know what *courteous* means and implies in that culture. Similarly, originality in product design carries different connotations with regard to innovativeness to the Dutch than it does to Americans.

Differences in the connotative meaning of words can cause confusion about how to interpret responses to questions as well. For example, in Japan, it is considered impolite to disagree. Japanese respondents are much more reluctant to disagree than their American counterparts when asked about their level of agreement with a set of statements. This might leave the researcher with the false impression that a new product will be well received, when in fact the respondent is simply trying to be agreeable. Some interesting cross-cultural research shows significant patterns of difference in reported customer satisfaction across cultures.[42]

A fourth problem is that respondents in various cultures may have different experiences with and fluency in research techniques. For example, respondents in Euro-American samples have little difficulty rating their degree of preference or agreement with statements on a seven-point scale like the following:

1	2	3	4	5	6	7
Strongly Agree						Strongly Disagree

Researchers have found that three- or four-point scales work best in Ghana and other developing countries because people there are not as used to making as fine a distinction in their opinions as those in highly developed consumer cultures are.[43]

A fifth, related, but even more profound problem is that most research techniques rely on collecting verbal information. Although this approach may work in cultures with high literacy rates, this method is much less appropriate in other cultures. The Diné people (Navajo) of northern Arizona, for example, are extremely close-mouthed, and Indonesian inhabitants of the island of Bali might not even interact with outsiders. The approach of most consumer research techniques makes very important assumptions about how people acquire, process, and retrieve information. Survey instruments are not very good at accurately retrieving data on certain kinds of sensory information such as smells and tastes, because people don't easily express this information using words. Nonetheless, survey research is still the norm in consumer research.

Of course, the problems we've talked about so far have to do with how to ask comparable questions in two different cultures. Anytime a company undertakes international research, it faces a host of other equally complex problems. Methods for collecting data and sampling techniques have to be carefully matched to the cultures. Again, we emphasize that to ensure comparability in cross-cultural research does not mean using identical methods. It means using data collection methods that have comparable levels of reliability. For example, in the United States and Canada, nearly every household has a telephone. As a consequence, telephone interviewing is the dominant mode of questionnaire administration in those countries. By contrast, in the transitional economies of central and eastern Europe, a telephone is still very much a luxury good. In India, less than 1 percent of households have telephones.[44] In one country, telephone interviews may be known to have a given level of reliability; in another country, inhome interviews, rather than telephone interviews, may have an equivalent level of reliability. Thus, telephone interviews should be used in the first country, and in-home interviews should be conducted in the second. In the same way, the penetration of Internet technology varies widely between countries. An Internet survey may provide representative data in the United States or Japan but be infeasible in India or eastern Europe.

Let's take another example. As we noted earlier, focus groups are a popular mode of data collection in the United States and are widely used in Europe and Australia. Focus groups tend to concentrate on particular activities, products, or problems; they are often used in the development of new products or services and to evaluate advertising copy and formats. Agree shampoo and conditioner, a familiar Australian brand, and Pantene shampoo and conditioner both employed focus group research in their development, for example.[45] However, sophisticated levels of cultural awareness become crucial when trying to conduct focus groups in a foreign culture. For example, in Japan, conformity is highly valued, as is deference to superiors, including anyone older. Conducting focus groups in Japan requires special attention to how group dynamics operate in that culture. In many countries in the Middle or Far East, people are hesitant to discuss their feelings in a group setting, and personal interviews should be used to ensure comparable reliability.[46] In the United States, a simple focus group may contain both males and females. Mixed-gender focus groups pose a challenge in the Middle East.

CONDUCTING RESEARCH ON THE INTERNET

As we have already discussed, the Internet is a revolutionary tool that has the potential to change the nature of human interactions. Here, we provide a detailed framework for thinking about how the Internet can influence consumer behavior research, concentrating on three major ways: it can automate, inform, and transform (see Exhibit 6.6). We view all three of these functions from an organizational perspective: how an organization, such as Ford Motor Company, can use the Internet to communicate better with its stakeholders, such as research suppliers, customers, and dealers.

Automate means that paper-and-pencil methods are replaced with electronic transactions or communications. As suggested by the exhibit, Ford could collect and analyze consumer complaints online. Such an application would be classified as "automation." Of course, it is also possible for organizations to try to solve consumer problems online, either with a cleverly designed website or through e-mail communications.

Inform means that the organization finds new ways to communicate (e.g., with customers). As shown in the exhibit, a researcher could include a pop-up window in a web-based survey to provide definitions and explanations for respondents who request such information. As a result of this information transfer, there should be less confusion, and consumers have a better chance of understanding the meaning of the words and concepts that appear on a data collection instrument.

Transform means that a new industry is created or that the organization finds a completely new way to transact business. As shown in the exhibit, virtual focus group interviews have the potential to revolutionize the research industry. A major problem with in-person focus groups is that researchers have to convince a group of respondents to show up at the same time and place. A major advantage of the virtual (online) focus group is that the limitations of geography can be overcome. Twelve people, all in different nations, could simultaneously participate in a focus group discussion, either using video cameras or e-mail. At the present time, most consumers do not have video cameras hooked up to the Web. So in the near future, this method would be more suitable for specialized audiences (e.g., managers who may be more likely to have access to such advanced technology).

Automation applications are usually the easiest changes to implement. Quite often, this type of application results in considerable cost savings, as paper-and-pencil methods are replaced by electronic data storage. Transforming applications are difficult to identify and difficult to implement successfully. Nonetheless, these transforming opportunities are what make the Internet such a potentially revolutionary force in society. If a transforming application is successful, then the entire industry changes for good.

In Exhibit 6.6, we also differentiate between three types of communication networks: Internet, intranet, and extranet. The **Internet** is *a global network of networks.* Any computer connected to the Internet can communicate with any server in the system. Thus, the Internet is well suited for communicating with a wide variety of stakeholders (e.g., customers, business partners, stockholders). Adobe, for example, uses its website to distribute software changes to customers and to provide financial and other reports to investors.[47]

An organization can establish an **intranet,** which is *an intraorganizational network that enables people within the organization to communicate and cooperate with each other.* Thus, an intranet is essentially a fenced-off, mini-Internet within an organization. A firewall is used to restrict access so that people outside the organization cannot access the intranet. Although an intranet may not directly facilitate cooperation with external stakeholders, its ultimate goal is to improve an organization's ability to serve those stakeholders by increasing the ability of employees to interact and communicate customer information with one another.[48]

Both the Internet and an intranet, as the names imply, are networks—arrays of computers that can connect to each other. In some situations, however, an organization may want to restrict connection capabilities. An **extranet** is designed to *link a buyer and supplier to facilitate greater coordination of common activities.* Thus, an extranet could link an organization with its alliance partners. It could link an organization with its suppliers or business customers. Communication is confined to the computers linking the two organizations. An extranet is specialized to support partnership coordination.

The examples shown in Exhibit 6.6 are related to the marketing research industry, which consists of research firms that collect a wide variety of consumer behavior data, along with other kinds of information. The exhibit is constructed from the point of view of a marketing research firm. For example, the entries in the exhibit show the kinds of automation changes a research firm could implement on an extranet. Thus, ACNielsen could use an extranet to send status reports to Ford Motor Company to describe the progress of a research project that has just gotten underway in California. Managers at Ford could examine an electronic database as it accumulates. Alternatively, they could look at a video of a focus group interview over the Web, or they could listen to an audio broadcast on the Web to hear customers' reactions to driving a new car model in Tokyo.

At this point, it is somewhat difficult to predict all of the changes that the Internet will bring to business and society. However, Exhibit 6.6 provides a framework for thinking about the kinds of changes that might emerge. In the end, it is consumers themselves who will decide which technologies are successful and in what forms.

EXHIBIT 6.6

Internet Technology and Consumer Behavior Research

Network	Automate
Internet—Global	Develop interactive questionnaire design; the online questionnaire adapts to respondents as they supply answers Establish Internet consumer panel Observe chat room behavior Collect data on viewing habits on websites and TV Use e-mail for purchase satisfaction surveys; customers reply via Internet to report consumption experiences Use incentives to increase response rates or identify committed customers Administer consumer questionnaire online (i.e., click-through data collection) Facilitate flow with online questionnaires (e.g., in terms of skip patterns, closure) Use chat rooms or newsgroups to reduce the number of concepts for new-product development and factor analysis Conduct follow-up verifications (e.g., to verify that a consumer has participated in a particular study) via e-mail instead of phone Recruit consumers online to participate in research studies; collect and analyze consumer complaints (e.g., customer satisfaction) online Create a website to explain the purpose of a study more fully to consumers
Intranet—Internal communications and processes	Provide repository of research information for internal access (library); for instance, online "book of scales" or tested measurements (e.g., to aid in questionnaire design); automate questionnaire design using online templates Automate the coding of open-end responses by key words Use search engine techniques to enhance qualitative analysis; create automated databases to summarize findings of previous studies
Extranet—Link between researcher and supplier (researcher) and research user (client)	Conduct interactive focus groups online (this could also be an Internet application) Use to send status reports to organizations that purchase consumer behavior research Send final results via extranet to organizations that purchase consumer behavior research Provide online access to presentations for clients Use to deliver a multimedia summary of results (e.g., using audio, video, graphics) Share automated databases with clients and other business partners; simplifies selection of a research supplier (via online databases, prior bids, and histories of project satisfaction)

Network	Inform	Transform
Internet—Global	Communicate with consumers in a more cost-effective manner, via ongoing, online panels and interactive interviewing Use the Internet to tap into libraries of marketing research; undertakes customized searches Collect information about competitors more quickly and more effectively Create pop-up windows to provide definitions and explanations for respondents who request additional information; thus, there is less confusion, and consumers understand a questionnaire better	Creates a new industry in the sense that online data collection replaces data collection by traditional means (telephone, mail, face-to-face interviews) if current problems (e.g., the sampling bias inherent in the Internet) can be overcome Provides syndicated Internet purchase data (i.e., Nielsen purchase data for e-commerce purchases, visits) Supplements or replaces in-person focus groups with virtual focus groups, thus overcoming the inherent limits of geography Lessens importance of time of day in collecting data from consumers Tests product concepts online Changes sampling methods: The use of self-selected samples increases (e.g., consumers are part of sample if they choose to participate by responding to e-mail solicitation and incentives)
Intranet—Internal communications and processes	Create a database of past research projects and best demonstrated practices Use to facilitate the flow of information between various participants in the research process (e.g., manager, questionnaire designers, coders, data analysts, report writers)	Data collection faster and less labor intensive; requires researchers who are highly technical and highly skilled Transforms the offices of research providers (e.g., the triumph of the "paperless" office); less need for central offices as the "virtual" office becomes common
Extranet—Link between researcher and supplier (researcher) and research user (client)	Communicate with business partners more effectively; work more efficiently with business partners via extranet Communicate with research clients as the project unfolds, using a digital camera	Provides real-time syndicated data sites Transmits information such as surveys, results, methods, and so forth to business partners online

ETHICS IN CONSUMER RESEARCH

Globalization and technology have also contributed to increased attention to ethical issues. When companies operate abroad, they run up against all sorts of new moral issues and ethical standards that differ among countries. Today, large organizations normally have a corporate ethics officer, although such a job description barely existed a decade ago. As many as one in five big firms has a full-time office devoted to ethics. At United Technologies, for example, the business ethics department includes an international network of 16 business-ethics officers working in 24 different languages.[49]

Collecting, analyzing, and using the results of consumer research raise a number of ethical issues. Many people are concerned that marketing is essentially a manipulative profession that collects information in order to induce consumers to buy things they neither want nor need. Others are concerned about erosion of privacy and corporate control of huge quantities of information about the private lives of individuals. As a result, many people around the world refuse to respond to requests for information from polling organizations, market research firms, corporations, and individual researchers. In response, consumer researchers should resist pressures to construct even more intrusive data collection procedures and instead strive to construct and then adhere to professional standards for research practice. Some guidelines for professional research practice are shown in Good Practice 6.6. What are some examples of unprofessional research behavior? A number of unprofessional practices can be identified. For example, participants in research have a right to confidentiality unless they specifically waive that right. This principle seems straightforward, but with the profusion of catalog retailing and telemarketing (telephone marketing) and the advent of the Internet, much data are collected from and about consumers, sometimes almost incidentally. In some countries, these data are shared a little too liberally between firms, sometimes resulting in the invasion of consumers' privacy.

In addition, researchers are generally obligated to avoid deception. However, some deception is common in many types of research. For example, in experimental research, the true purpose of the study is often hidden from subjects so that their knowledge does not influence their responses to experimental stimuli. In participant observation research, continuous interaction between researchers and informants makes it impossible to ask for research consent every time data are recorded. Participant observation always involves some deceit, since researchers are trying to develop relationships with informants in order to collect data. Thus, limited deception is a part of most consumer research. As a result, researchers should strive to adhere to the research standards adopted by most professional research organizations.

www.bayer.be

Several types of unacceptable lapses in the obligation to avoid deception can be identified. Perhaps the least of these problems concerns deceiving participants about the length of a research task. If a personal interview is going to take 30 minutes, but the researcher does not specify this, it may be considered an unethical deception by omission. Reaction to this type of time deception varies a lot from culture to culture. For example, Germans are very conscientious about time and will cut off the interview if you go over. French and Italians are more flexible with their time, and many people living in Mediterranean countries like to converse.

More serious is misidentification of the researcher or research sponsor. Sponsor concealment is acceptable if it serves legitimate purposes of interviewer security or data integrity, not if disclosing the sponsor's identity will affect peoples' willingness to participate in the study. Worse still is sales prospecting and fund-raising under the guise of surveys. In one case, a major car company conducted a large phone survey. Partic-

Guidelines for Ethical Consumer Research Practice

GOOD PRACTICE 6.6

1. Expect and prepare to encounter ethical dilemmas in consumer research.
2. Do not harm participants physically, emotionally, or psychologically.
3. Do not deceive participants.
4. Ensure that participation is willing and informed.
5. Employ proper research procedures.
6. Hold data in confidence.
7. Be guided by ethical maxims (e.g., the Golden Rule).
8. Where possible, debrief participants about the true purposes of disguised research.
9. Do not overpromise the benefits of research.
10. Do not distort research results to please clients.
11. Refuse to conduct research you consider unethical.
12. Be clear about your values, because no research is value-neutral.

ipants were told the purpose of the survey was to measure their buying intentions and attitudes about cars. However, the data were turned over to local dealers who made sales calls to likely buyers. This example illustrates an unethical deception of respondents and leads to reduced cooperation in legitimate surveys.[50]

Emerging technology creates ethical dilemmas. For instance, the creators of websites may want to remember facts about a customer's visit to that site. Thus, many websites include "cookies," a mechanism for remembering details of a single visit or storing facts between visits. A **cookie** is *a small file (not more than 4K) stored on the consumer's hard disk by a web application.* Thus, a cookie is a kind of instant, and automated, research tool that records details about consumer behavior.[51] A website such as CNN uses cookies to customize its service. That is, CNN uses a cookie to remember that a site visitor is mainly interested in news about basketball or cooking. A cookie might also be used to determine what pages a person views on a particular website so as to improve site design. Similarly, a cookie can be used so that particular advertisements can be targeted to specific consumers. For example, if you frequently visit travel sites, you might get a banner ad from Delta popping up the next time that you do a search (e.g., on Google).

@ www.google.com

Of course, some consumers do not like the fact that the creators of websites are secretly monitoring their behavior. Such an intrusion is viewed as an invasion of privacy. Both Internet Explorer and Netscape Navigator allow surfers to set options for various levels of warnings about the use of cookies. Concerned consumers can turn these features off altogether. Some marketers feel that service levels are diminished when cookies are turned off and the flow of information from consumer to website owner is disrupted. In this way, the advent of new technology creates ethical dilemmas. To what extent are firms allowed to collect information in an electronic way? Does such automated information collection provide better service, or does it invade consumer privacy?

Online Focus Group Interviews

ETHICAL DILEMMA 6.2

Group interviews are the most popular form of commercial marketing research. The Internet provides an opportunity to complete the entire research project online, including recruitment, screening (which can be conducted via e-mail), moderation of the group discussion, and debriefing. Despite these opportunities, there are also ethical challenges associated with online qualitative research. Consider the following situations.

- Ms. Tomala, working with Bayer Belgium NV, has only a few days to recruit nine online participants for an upcoming focus group interview. She is tempted to contact some members of a consumer panel that completes an online survey every month for Ms. Tomala's firm. However, Ms. Tomala is concerned that she may be creating a "professional class" of online research participants.
- In cyberspace, consumers and research participants can never be sure who has access to their information. How can interviewers protect focus group members' comments from prying computer hackers?
- In Ms. Tomala's group interview, she plans to serve as the moderator of the group interview and ask nine European males to discuss their attitudes toward different birth control products and methods. She is thinking that the participants might discuss the topic more freely if the moderator is also a male. Should she become "another self," and identify herself as a male, when she initiates the group interview?

Source: Journal of Business Ethics *33 (2001) pp. 271–86. "Ethics and the Internet: Issues Associated with Qualitative Research," Denise DeLorme, George M. Zinkhan, and Warren French, copyright ©2001. Reprinted with kind permission of Kluwer Academic Publishers.*

One key concept in ethics is the principle of "doing no harm."[52] Many of the issues discussed in the previous paragraphs fall into this category (e.g., avoiding deception, not invading privacy). Another key concept in ethics is beneficence (i.e., actively "doing good"). Consumer research can also be viewed from this perspective.[53] In other words, consumer researchers can try to extend their own values into the real world. For instance, a researcher may recognize a consumer problem such as credit card abuse or compulsive spending and then try to design a study that suggests some ways to solve this problem.[54] Alternatively, a researcher may design a study that has potential to generate social change strategies that could prove useful to legislators or consumer-rights organizations. In this way, consumer research and imagination are used to actively promote a better world.[55] Note the link between this idea and the concept of "marketing imagination," as discussed in Chapter 5.

@ /gort.ucsd.edu/newjour/j/msg03158.html

SUMMARY

Learning about consumers is the key to implementing the marketing concept and exercising marketing imagination. Consumer behavior research is concerned with systematically collecting and analyzing information in order to improve the quality of exchanges between organizations and their customers or constituents. That is, organizations create value by improving the quality of exchanges. There are five main steps in the research process, including definition of the problem and project scope, development of a research approach, formulation of the research design, fieldwork and data collection, and data interpretation and communication of results.

SUMMARY

The research process is iterative; different methods and perspectives lead to different research results, and no consumer research is perfect. Because collecting verbal and written information from consumers is so central to the research process, researchers must be particularly careful that they ask questions effectively. To build a quality questionnaire, the researcher should begin by asking three questions about each research question. First, can potential study participants understand the question? Second, can potential study participants answer the question? Third, will potential study participants answer the question? Brevity, relevancy, objectivity, nonambiguity, and specificity are also important criteria for evaluating questions.

Conducting international consumer research is even more complicated than conducting consumer research in a single, national context, so we also explore some of the problems encountered in cross-cultural consumer research. Here, we review special problems associated with conceptual equivalence, and sources of response bias.

The Internet is likely to have a dramatic impact on how consumer research is done over the next five years: by replacing paper and pencil methods with electronic transactions or communications, by enabling the organization to communicate in new ways, and by creating completely new ways to collect data. Collecting and analyzing information about consumer behavior raise a host of ethical questions. Consumer researchers should resist pressures to construct even more intrusive data collection procedures and instead strive to construct and then adhere to professional standards for research practice.

KEY TERMS

REVIEW QUESTIONS

1. Go to the grocery store and observe four different consumers as they select a cereal brand to purchase. Write a diary to describe your experience. What process do the consumers go through? Do they look at packages and labels? Can you tell what specific aspect of the package they look at? Are prices important? How do consumers gather price information? Do some seem to purchase by habit? Do others (e.g., purchase pals, children) get involved in the decision?
2. Visit a local shopping district, such as a main street or mall. Go from store to store and observe the customers. Make a detailed composite portrait of the customers at each store using as many criteria as possible. Then, name the market segment you have described.
3. Outline a research design to determine the effects of attractive advertising models on males and females. Be specific. What is your design (e.g., experiment, survey, observation)? Who are your subjects? How are they selected? What do you measure? How can you be certain that your results are valid?
4. What are the strengths and weaknesses of secondary data? What questions should you ask when examining secondary data?
5. Conduct secondary research on the Internet to describe the auto industry in Brazil. How could a company such as Volkswagen use this information to understand their competitive marketplace in Brazil? (*Hint:* You might want to begin with a search on "Brazil automotive".)
6. Write a questionnaire that you would use to carry out the research project introduced in question 3. Be certain to include the following measures: demographic data; perceived body image; media use (e.g., television programs watched, magazines read); estimated amount of time looking at ads on a typical day; overall attitude toward advertising in general. Also, include an introduction and an ending in your questionnaire. Include both open-ended and closed-end questions. Make certain that your questionnaire flows well. Pretest your questionnaire by having three friends fill it out. Ask them if they have any comments for improvement. Apply the criteria introduced in this chapter to evaluate the effectiveness and validity of your questionnaire.
7. British consumers are reluctant to talk about cockroaches in a focus group setting, but French consumers are happy to talk about them in a focus group. Describe at least five topics that people in your home country would be reluctant to discuss in a focus group.
8. Consider the focus group interview. Describe, in detail, a specific research question that could be well addressed by this method. Do the same for syndicated data.
9. What kinds of consumer behavior research do you consider unethical? Have you ever been asked to participate in a research study that you thought was unethical? If so, provide specific details.

YOU MAKE THE CALL

BIZRATE.COM

Karl Schrieber wants to buy a birthday gift for his friend, Erich, who likes to read mystery novels. Karl doesn't know much about mystery novels, so he decides to search the Internet. Starting with Crawler.de, he identifies a long list of sites that sell books. He visits three of these sites to gather information and get some ideas about gift possibilities. He spends quite a bit time on the de.yahoo.com site, and finally decides to buy *Death in Holy Orders* by the British writer P.D. James. Karl orders the book directly from the Yahoo! website.

Once the purchase transaction is completed, Karl is presented with an online survey from Bizrate.com, and he rates the site with respect to "ease of ordering," "product selection," and so forth (see Exhibit 6.7). This questionnaire is designed to solicit information about Karl's online shopping experience, and customers use the Smiley Scale™ to indicate their responses to the various questions (see Exhibit 6.8).

www.bizrate.com

BizRate continuously seeks feedback from more than 10 million real online shoppers each month, based on transactions with more than 2,000 online merchants. This information is summarized for each merchant with an easy-to-use report card on

EXHIBIT 6.7

BizRate Questions

What are the twelve quality ratings and what do they mean?

Six of the twelve quality ratings are determined at the point-of-sale or "checkout." These are collected by asking a store's customers to evaluate their purchase experiences immediately after completing the online transaction. The remaining four quality ratings are determined when the purchase is expected to be received as an "after delivery" follow-up. Explanations of each rating's attribute are found below:

Source	Rating	Explanation
at checkout	Ease of Ordering	Convenience and speed of ordering
at checkout	Product Selection	Breadth/depth of products offered
at checkout	Product Information	Information quantity, quality & relevance
at checkout	Price	Prices relative to similar stores
at checkout	Web Site Performance	Layout, links, pictures, images & speed
at checkout	Shipping & Handling	Charges & Options
after delivery	On-Time Delivery	Expected vs. actual delivery date
after delivery	Product Met Expectations	Product description/depiction vs. what you received
after delivery	Customer Support	Status updates and complaint/question handling
after delivery	Order Tracking	Ability to effectively track orders
after delivery	Would Shop Here Again	Likelihood to return to this store
after delivery	Overall Rating	Overall experience with store

Source: http://www.bizrate.com/content/merchant_ratings_faq.xpml.

EXHIBIT 6.8

BizRate Rating Scale: The Smiley Scale™

What is the BizRate.com Smiley Scale™?

The **BizRate.com Smiley Scale** is a simple and intuitive way to visualize a lot of rigorous research about a store's capabilities, so you, the consumer can, at a glance tell the good from the not-so-good when comparison shopping.

How should I use the rating?

The Smiley Scale can quickly help you find stores with the level of quality you like for the price that you want. Example: Is it worth saving $10 on a bouquet of flowers when the merchant has a Red Sad-face for "On-time delivery"? Not if it's the day before Valentines!

Source: http://www.bizrate.com/content/merchant_ratings_faq.xpml.

BizRate. BizRate also provides information to customers as they engage in information search. That is, BizRate aids consumers by reporting how online stores score in categories such as site usability, product descriptions, and shipping time. These scores are based on consumers' ratings of individual e-stores, over time. Such a service is potentially quite valuable, as less than 30 percent of Internet users trust websites that sell products and services. BizRate designers believe that their site helps consumers distinguish between sites so that they can shop with more confidence. There is even a feature that allows users to compare prices from one site to another with sales tax and shipping included so that buyers can complete a total price comparison.

It is important to understand that BizRate receives its revenue from merchants. While BizRate does not collect fees for including company/product descriptions on their site, they do receive royalties if a consumer purchases goods by clicking through to the e-commerce site. For example, if Karl had initiated his gift search on BizRate and then clicked through to Yahoo! to make the purchase, then BizRate would receive a monetary reward for this referral. Sellers are charged on a pay-for-performance basis, according to sales leads generated through BizRate. As of July 2002, BizRate achieved a level of financial success by reporting a small profit for the second quarter.

QUESTIONS

1. Evaluate the questionnaire (Exhibits 6.7 and 6.8) that BizRate uses to collect customer feedback. Apply the BRONS criteria to the questionnaire.
2. From a research perspective, what drawbacks are associated with BizRate's method for generating revenue (e.g., accepting money from the merchants that are rated by consumers and subsequently "evaluated" by BizRate)?
3. Before committing to a purchase, what are the top three questions that a consumer wants answered about an e-commerce site?

ENDNOTES

1. Eric J. Arnould and Linda L. Price, "'River Magic': Hedonic Consumption and the Extended Service Encounter," *Journal of Consumer Research* 20 (June 1993), pp. 24–45; and Linda L. Price, Eric J. Arnould, and Patrick Tierney, "Going to Extremes: Managing Service Encounters and Assessing Provider Performance," *Journal of Marketing* 59 (April 1995), pp. 83–97.
2. George M. Zinkhan and Rudy Hirschmann, "Truth in Marketing Theory and Research: An Alternative Perspective," *Journal of Marketing* 56 (April 1992), pp. 80–88.
3. Clifford Geertz, *Local Knowledge: Further Essays in Interpretive Anthropology* (New York: Basic Books, 1983).
4. Herbert Blumer, "Mead and Blumer: The Convergent Methodological Perspectives of Social Behaviorism and Symbolic Interactionism," *American Sociological Review* 45 (June 1980), pp. 409–19; Laurel Hudson and Julie Ozanne, "Alternative Ways of Seeking Knowledge in Consumer Research," *Journal of Consumer Research* 14 (March 1998), pp. 508–21.
5. For a discussion of Ford Motor Company's changing approach to new-product development, see Kirk Damon, *Innovative Market Research for Breakthrough Product Design,* Report No. 99–113 (Cambridge, MD: Marketing Science Institute 1999). For more discussion of the Ford Fiesta case, see Vern Terpstra, *International Dimensions of Marketing,* 3rd ed. (Belmont, CA: Wadsworth Publishing, 1993), p. 91.
6. Anthony Romeo, "The Changing Role of the Consumer: Implications for Selling and Marketing," speech at iGrocer Conference, San Diego, California, July 17, 2000.
7. George M. Zinkhan, Margy Conchar, Ajay Gupta, and Gary Geissler, "Motivations Underlying the Creation of Personal Web Pages: An Exploratory Study," *Advances in Consumer Research,* vol. 26, ed. E. Arnould and L. Scott (Provo, UT: Association for Consumer Research, 1999), pp. 69–74; and George M. Zinkhan, Hyokjin Kwak, Michelle Morrison, and Cara Peters, "Web-Based Chatting: Consumer Communications in Cyberspace," *Journal of Consumer Psychology* 12 (forthcoming, 2002).
8. Richard T. Watson, Pierre Berthon, Leyland F. Pitt, and George M. Zinkhan, *Electronic Commerce: The Strategic Perspective* (Fort Worth, TX: The Dryden Press, 2000).
9. Eszter Hargittai and Miguel Angel Centeno, "Introduction: Defining a Global Geography," *American Behavioral Scientist* 44 (June 2001), pp. 1545–60.
10. George M. Zinkhan, Denise DeLorme, and Richard Watson, "Information Sources and Government Research: Ethical Conflicts and Solutions," *Cambridge Review of International Affairs* (forthcoming, 2002).
11. Hargittai and Centeno, "Introduction: Defining a Global Geography."
12. V. Kumar, *International Marketing Research* (Upper Saddle River, NJ: Prentice Hall, 2000).
13. For a discussion relevant to several marketing industries, including market research, see Dana James and Kathleen V. Schmidt, "Getting Good Listing Attracts Volumes," *Marketing News,* January 3, 2000, pp. 8–9.
14. www.esomar.nl.
15. See Alvin C. Burns and Ronald F. Bush, *Marketing Research,* 3rd ed. (Upper Saddle River, NJ: Prentice Hall, 2000), for a discussion of databases. See also Raymond C. Pettit, "Data Mining: Race for Mission-Critical Info," *Marketing News,* January 3, 2000, p. 18.
16. Richard T. Watson, *Data Management: Databases and Organizations* (New York: Wiley & Sons, 2002).
17. Ibid.
18. Richard Fox, Hyokjin Kwak, and George M. Zinkhan, "What Products Can Be Successfully Promoted and Sold via the Internet," *Journal of Advertising Research* 42, no. 1 (2002), p. 36.
19. Watson, *Data Management.*
20. This example is taken from interviews summarized in Ajay K. Kohli and Bernard J. Jaworski, "Market Orientation: The Construct, Research Propositions, and Managerial Implications," *Journal of Marketing* 54 (April 1990), p. 5.
21. Johnny K. Johansson and Ikujiro Nonaka, "Market Research the Japanese Way," *Harvard Business Review,* May–June 1987, pp. 16–18.
22. This example is taken from F. Gouillart and F. Sturdivant, "Spend a Day in the Life of Your Customers," *Harvard Business Review,* January–February 1994, p. 125.

23. For a more complete description, see *The Code of Professional Ethics and Practices,* Marketing Research Association, Inc., Chicago, IL.
24. For a full description of this study, see Arnould and Price, "River Magic."
25. This example is based on the research reported in Marsha L. Richins, "Social Comparison and the Idealized Images of Advertising," *Journal of Consumer Research* 18 (June 1991), pp. 71–83. However, we've taken some license in ordering the studies reported in order to illustrate that research can iterate between the basic research types in many different ways.
26. Dagnoli Judann, "Why Heinz Went Sour in Brazil," *Advertising Age,* December 5, 1988.
27. A good description of how to analyze and interpret qualitative data is provided in Susan Spiggle, "Analysis and Interpretation of Qualitative Data in Consumer Research," *Journal of Consumer Research* 21 (December 1994), pp. 491–503.
28. For an interesting discussion of the application of ethnography in applied consumer research, see Kendra Parker, "How Do You Like Your Beef?" *American Demographics,* January 2000, pp. 35–37.
29. For these and many other examples of the need for cultural sensitivity in survey research, see Kumar, *International Marketing Research.*
30. Martin Collins and Bob Butcher, "Interviewer and Clustering Effects in an Attitude Survey," *Journal of the Market Research Society* 25 (January 1983), pp. 29–58; and R. F. Q. Johnson, "Pitfalls in Research: The Interview as an Illustrative Model," *Psychological Reports* 38 (1976), pp. 3–17.
31. M. Bunge, "The Weight of Simplicity in the Construction and Assaying of Scientific Theories," *Philosophy of Science* 28, no. 2 (1961), pp. 120–49. See also Grant McCracken, *The Long Interview* (Newbury Park, CA: Sage Publications, 1988), pp. 50–52; and Marianne Elisabeth Lien, *Marketing and Modernity* (Oxford: Berg, 1997).
32. For a discussion of how to build interpretations that consider different kinds of data collection, see Eric J. Arnould and Melanie Wallendorf, "Market-Oriented Ethnography: Interpretation Building and Marketing Strategy Formulation," *Journal of Marketing Research,* November 1994, pp. 484–504.
33. Julia M. Bristor and Eileen Fischer, "Feminist Thought: Implications for Consumer Research," *Journal of Consumer Research* 19 (March 1993), pp. 518–37.
34. *Advertising Age,* April 4, 1983, p. 18.
35. For this section on asking questions we are indebted to Robert Peterson, who taught one of us market research. This approach is also outlined in Robert A. Peterson, *Constructing Effective Questionnaires* (Thousand Oaks, CA: Sage Publications, 2000).
36. This example is provided in ibid., p. 19.
37. Randall Rothenberg, "Surveys Proliferate, but Answers Dwindle," *New York Times,* October 5, 1990, pp. A1, A5; and Ian Phau, Internet query, July 1998.
38. *Hilmiyya Nights,* a soap opera, was a major media event in modern Egypt. See Lila Abu-Lughod, "The Objects of Soap Opera: Egyptian Television and the Cultural Politics of Modernity," in *Worlds Apart,* ed. Daniel Miller (London: Routledge, 1995), pp. 190–210. According to *The Economist,* August 5, 1998, *Torre de Babel,* a soap opera, was the third most watched show in Brazil at the time.
39. Eric J. Arnould and Melanie Wallendorf, "On Identical Methods in Cross-Cultural Market Research or the Noncomparability of Data Obtained with Seemingly-Comparable Measures," working paper, California State University, Long Beach, 1993. Also see Melanie Wallendorf and Eric J. Arnould, "'My Favorite Things': A Cross-Cultural Inquiry into Object Attachment, Possessiveness and Social Linkage," *Journal of Consumer Research* 14 (March 1988), pp. 531–47.
40. S. C. Grunert and G. Scherhorn, "Consumer Values in West Germany: Underlying Dimensions and Cross-Cultural Comparison with North America," *Journal of Business Research* 20 (1990), pp. 97–107.
41. Kathy Frazier Winsted, "Dimensions of Service Encounter Satisfaction: A Cross-Cultural Analysis," unpublished doctoral dissertation, University of Colorado, Boulder, 1993.
42. Kumar, *International Marketing Research.*
43. Wallendorf and Arnould, "My Favorite Things."

44. D. Sopariwala, "India: Election Polling in the World's Largest Democracy," *European Research,* August 1987, pp. 174–77.
45. Betty Holcomb, "The Focus Groupie," *Madison Avenue* 27 (September 1985), p. 47.
46. Naresh K. Malhotra, *Marketing Research: An Applied Orientation* (Englewood Cliffs, NJ: Prentice Hall, 1993), p. 780.
47. Richard T. Watson, Pierre Berthon, Leyland F. Pitt, and George M. Zinkhan, *Electronic Commerce: The Strategic Perspective* (Fort Worth, TX: Dryden, 1999).
48. Ibid.
49. "Business Ethics: Doing Well by Doing Good," *The Economist,* April 22, 2000, pp. 65–66, 67.
50. Eric J. Arnould "Ethical Concerns in Participant Observation/Ethnography," in *Advances in Consumer Research,* vol. 25, ed. Joseph W. Alba and J. Wesley Hutchinson (Provo, UT: Association for Consumer Research, 1998), pp. 72–74; Seymour Sudman, "Survey Research and Ethics," in *Advances in Consumer Research,* vol. 25, ed. Joseph W. Alba and J. Wesley Hutchinson (Provo, UT: Association for Consumer Research, 1998), pp. 69–71; and N. Craig Smith, "Ethics in Consumer Research," in *Advances in Consumer Research,* vol. 25, ed. Joseph W. Alba and J. Wesley Hutchinson (Provo, UT: Association for Consumer Research, 1998), p. 68.
51. Watson, Berthon, Pitt, and Zinkhan, *Electronic Commerce.*
52. Denice DeLorme, George M. Zinkhan, and Warren French, "Ethics and the Internet: Issues Associated with Qualitative Research," *Journal of Business Ethics* 33, no. 4 (2001), pp. 271–86.
53. Ibid.
54. Hyokjin Kwak, George M. Zinkhan, and Joseph R. Dominick, "The Moderating Role of Gender and Compulsive Buying Tendencies in the Cultivation Effects of TV Shows and TV Advertising: A Cross-Cultural Study between the United States and South Korea," *Media Psychology* 4, no. 1 (2002), pp. 77–111.
55. Jeff B. Murray and Julie L. Ozanne, "The Critical Imagination: Emancipatory Interests in Consumer Research," *Journal of Consumer Research* 18 (September 1991), pp. 129–44.

LEARNING OBJECTIVES

After completing this chapter, you should be able to:

- Explain relationships among consumer motives, goals, involvements, and goal-striving.
- Describe how consumers' cultural and social contexts influence motives and consumption goals.
- Identify classic approaches that account for human motivation and derive managerial implications from these theoretical approaches.
- Explain the concepts of goal-striving and consumer involvement and how they influence consumer behavior.
- Describe some research methods for uncovering consumer motives.
- Describe approaches to measuring consumer involvement.

CONSUMER MOTIVES, GOALS, AND INVOLVEMENT

CARMEN'S ATTENTION TO HER APPEARANCE

Carmen is 22 years old and is just completing a degree in computer science. She lives in Cluj, Romania. She is professionally ambitious and dreams of traveling and learning about other cultures. Consistent with her dreams of world travel, Carmen is attracted to media images of women outside Romania. She sees Romanian women as "sad, hopeless, just trying to survive" and depicts American women as "relaxed, open, taking care of themselves." She believes Romania "needs more foreign influences," and "being open is absolutely necessary." Carmen's stories about herself reflect the determination and self-efficacy that she associates with media images of non-Romanian women, and she too wants to "have a different air and a different attitude toward life." A particular story that Carmen speaks of as "an important moment in her life" involves her decision to lose weight. She started to do sports even though her parents didn't encourage her. Carmen claims, "I proved to them in two years that I was a pretty good athlete and became attractive."

When we met Carmen she was not wearing makeup but had taken care with her appearance, wearing a nicely ironed, slightly worn, white blouse and short black skirt. Although Carmen claims to use some beauty products every day, she feels she can't "afford to use good quality products that I trust and know they are good." Carmen works with programmers, who mostly don't pay attention to their appearance. Nevertheless, Carmen believes that appearance is a reflection of who you are—it defines your personality. She observes, "I feel better if I look good. This brings a better feeling to the people around me. By feeling better myself, I can make others feel better." For Carmen, attractiveness is linked to internal qualities she sees as important in her own life, for example, being open and having good taste. Carmen's primary concerns are quality and taste.

Carmen believes makeup and clothes are important to looking attractive. "Fashion, cosmetics make a woman more appealing. But more than this is taste, according to age, situation, occasions, maybe how you feel." Carmen notes her mother is "concerned with beauty products" and "uses them with taste." She feels she is like her mother, who is "very different from my grandmother." Carmen emphasizes, "It is important to be attractive. For me comfort is also important. I don't dress up to meet X or Y, or because I go to a theater. I dress up because I feel good. I like to feel good; that's why I dress up." Nevertheless, Carmen observes with regard to her boyfriend, "He lets me do what I want . . . but I notice every time I am more elegant, or I look better, I can feel he is happy." Carmen would like to purchase high-quality brands of clothing and cosmetics but sees both accessibility and money as obstacles. Rather than purchase cheap things now, she is investing in her professional goals, observing that if she accomplishes these goals, then she will be able to purchase the products and brands of fashion and cosmetics products that she would like.

OVERVIEW

Why do people do the things they do? More specifically, why do they buy and consume the products, services, experiences, and brands they do? This question is at the core of consumer behavior, and this chapter provides some answers. Although human motives have been studied for a long time, there are many ways of thinking about motives. The vignette above stresses that consumers are motivated to achieve goals. This means they are willing to direct time and energy to accomplish their aims. Carmen's interview reminds us that consumers have multiple and even conflicting ambitions and encounter numerous obstacles trying to reach important goals. Striving to reach goals is not easy, and depends on effort, ability, and opportunity. One of the most important points illustrated in the opening vignette is that consumer motivations and goals evolve within a particular cultural and social context. Consumers interpret the world around them based on their personal history and current concerns.

We overview in this chapter concepts that can help us understand consumers' motivations and goals. We illustrate how macro-environmental factors and social context mold consumers' motivations and goals. Many classic theories of motivation can help us understand consumers. We briefly describe these classic approaches to motivation with attention to their implications for management and public policy. One potential limitation of these theories is that they are not always attentive to ways that consumer motives and goals vary cross-culturally. In this chapter we describe how some important consumer motives vary around the world. Throughout the chapter we recognize that consumers have multiple and conflicting goals. Marketing managers can often benefit by understanding how to help consumers resolve motivational conflicts. We illustrate some common types of motivational conflict and implications for managers. To understand consumer goals requires special research tools. We introduce some tools that can prove helpful in uncovering linkages between consumer goals and preferences and behaviors. When consumers are motivated by a goal, they feel involved with stimuli that relate to their goal. The final portion of the chapter is devoted to understanding consumer involvement. We describe different kinds of involvement and ways that marketers create or stimulate involvement. We also describe some ways to measure consumer involvement.

CONSUMER MOTIVATION AND GOALS

We define **motivation** as *an inner drive that reflects goal-directed arousal.*[1] A **drive** is *an internal stimulus.* For example, hunger, thirst, pain, and other physically experienced states are described as drives. Emotionally experienced states such as the desire for affiliation or self-esteem can also be described as drives. In the opening vignette, Carmen feels better when she looks good and feels this also makes others around her feel better. **Goals** are *ends or aspirations that direct action.* Motivation drives behaviors consistent with the goal and creates a willingness to expend time and energy to achieve the goal. For example, Carmen is motivated to look attractive. In order to achieve this goal, she gets involved with sports, loses weight, chooses her clothing carefully, and uses beauty products. She believes these actions will help make her attractive. In consumer behavior contexts, the result of an internal drive is a desire for a product, service, or experience.[2] The motivated consumer is aroused, ready, and willing to engage in an activity. Carmen is ready and willing to purchase high-quality brands of clothing and cosmetics because she believes this will contribute to her goal of being attractive. **Involvement** is *the psychological outcome of motivation.* We can further define it as *the perceived level of personal importance or interest evoked by a stimulus within a specific situation.* Pursuing goals, motivated consumers may feel interest, excitement, anxiety, passion, engagement, and flow. These are feelings of involvement with goals.

It is important to remember that consumers have multiple and even conflicting goals, and they encounter numerous obstacles in trying to achieve their goals. For instance, Carmen feels lack of money and accessibility prevent her from purchasing products that would enhance her attractiveness. Hence, she is prioritizing professional goals, believing that accomplishing these goals will make other goals more attainable. The vignette illustrates that achieving consumer goals requires effort, ability, and trade-offs among various goals. **Effort** reflects *the time and energy consumers are willing to commit to a goal.* When motivation to achieve a goal is high, consumers are likely to commit substantial effort. When motivation to achieve the goal is lower, they commit less time and energy to accomplishing the goal, although they may still engage in activities relevant to that goal. Carmen was able to lose weight, but many other consumers struggle endlessly with weight loss, continuously unhappy with their bodies. Advertising promotes that you can give yourself a body you will feel "confident" and "powerful" in. However, as most of us know, such a body is likely to entail considerable effort!

Because of competing or conflicting goals, pursuit of certain goals may be delayed so long that they change or are forgotten. Alternatively behavior consistent with these goals may show up unexpectedly when resources or opportunities enable goal attainment.[3] Consumer Chronicles 7.1 illustrates unexpected ways goal-striving can be activated.

The vignette suggests something we all know: Striving to obtain goals is complicated. **Goal-striving** is *the execution of actions needed to achieve a particular goal.* Carmen is delaying purchasing expensive clothes and cosmetics, spending her limited income

Goal Striving

CONSUMER CHRONICLES 7.1

One of our favorite stories, told to us by a colleague, is of a young professional architect who one day, while attending an out-of-town tennis tournament, walks across the street to a Porsche dealership and purchases a Porsche. He returns to the hotel intent on changing his airline reservations so that he and his wife can drive their new automobile home. Taken by surprise, his wife asks how he could walk across the street and buy a $50,000 car. To her, this looks like a crazy example of an impulse purchase. He explained, "Susan, I've been buying this car all of my life." And in fact, he had. From the time he was a young boy, eagerly poring over automobile-enthusiast magazines, he intended to own a Porsche someday. Finally, he had both the resources and the opportunity to do so. Why delay! Chris remains involved with cars and over the past several years has invested substantial time and money into restoring an old British sports car.

on education instead. However, she intends to use her degree to enable other consumption experiences. The question remains whether new goals will further delay or interrupt her intentions. A consumer may have a goal of losing weight but postpone that goal until work is less harried, or the weather is cooler, or she has fewer social commitments. Losing weight is a goal, but effort, ability, and opportunity are required to implement pursuit of that goal. Can you think of a personal goal that you are actively pursuing—striving toward? Now, can you think of a personal goal that is "on hold"—waiting for more favorable circumstances? As a full-time student in a poor country, Carmen has a modest income. She can't afford to buy high-quality cosmetics and fashion clothing. Consumer ability impacts goal-striving. **Ability** can be thought of as *the extent to which consumers have the necessary resources (including knowledge, intelligence, and money) to make the outcome happen.*[4]

Consumer Goal Hierarchies

As evident in the vignette, *goals can be thought of at many different levels,* represented with a **goal hierarchy.**[5] For example, Carmen's decision to lose weight can be thought of as a **focal goal**—*what she is striving for*—but this goal is connected to a goal of looking attractive, which is connected to other goals of feeling better and making others feel better too. We might refer to these as **superordinate goals,** or *reasons why she wants to achieve the focal goal.* Moreover, Carmen has identified playing sports and exercise as strategies for losing weight. Playing sports or exercising each day could then become **subordinate goals,** *actions that contribute to the focal goal* of losing weight. Consumers could be involved with sports for many different reasons, that is, sports could be used to fulfill many different goals. Also, for other consumers sports would not be identified as a strategy for losing weight. What constitutes focal, superordinate, or subordinate goals will vary among consumers and situations. For example, playing football with the Nebraska Cornhuskers college football team could become a focal goal. There could be many reasons why a young athlete might want to attain this goal, and he could pursue a variety of actions to contribute to this focal objective.

Marketers are often interested in the connections that consumers make between and among various goals. Managers can learn which goals to emphasize in advertising and personal selling by identifying the goals and linkages that relate best to consumer preferences or intentions. For example, other Romanian women linked attractiveness to keeping a job, finding a husband, and/or being more cosmopolitan.[6] A perfume, lipstick, or other beauty product might use different appeals depending on a woman's reasons for wanting to be attractive. Later in this chapter we will describe some research techniques for identifying linkages between goals and consumer preferences and intentions. A major insight for marketers is that although many consumers may have a similar preference, there may be substantial variability in the reasons given for their preference. Of particular note is the finding that when asked for reasons for a preference or behavior, cross-cultural differences come to the forefront.[7] For example, while Japanese, Chinese, American, and European men may all express a preference for a particular clothing brand, when probed for reasons, they may generate substantially different goal hierarchies reflecting cultural norms. These findings underscore that cultural influence is dynamic, fragmented, and specific—whether and how cultural norms are activated depends on the situation and the person.[8] We turn next to a further exploration of motives in context.

Consumer Motivation in Context

Human motivation and goal-striving develop within a cultural and social context and reflect the desire to live, hope, and enjoy life and its promises.[9] Consumers' goal hierarchies reflect and conform to the shared language and social conventions within which people unconsciously function. Although all human cultures probably share some common bases of motivation (because of their common biology), motivation researchers have been unable to identify a single set of universal motives, spot them in behavior, and explain situational variation in their expression.[10]

THE CONSUMER AS INTERPRETER In this chapter and the next three chapters, we will focus special attention on how consumers interpret their world. Research on the mind can help us understand the relationship between culture and the consumer as interpreter. One of the leading experts in the evolving debate about human consciousness is Nobel Prize–winner Gerald Edelman. Edelman's theory draws very directly from Darwin; in fact, he refers to his theory as **neural Darwinism.** He argues that *each individual brain, even before birth, uses a process that resembles natural selection to develop during its own lifetime.* This means that every person's individual mind is shaped by Darwinian rules of selection to provide a structure (networks of connections between neurons) that will enable that person to cope with the world. Genetics predisposes certain connections, for example, those related to reaching for and grasping objects (which most babies seem to do instinctively). However, the actual pattern of connections in a brain is unpredictable. Those connections that prove most helpful in the outside world become stronger; those that prove unhelpful weaken and disappear. This and other emerging theories have profound implications for the study of motivation.[11]

These theories lead us to a central conclusion: Consumers are uniquely shaped by cultural and social settings, and they are constantly adapting based on what works and what doesn't. Our brains are not like computers; they are more like the ecology of a jungle. Each of us is a product of our environment—our minds are dynamic entities defined by our relationship to the world around us, and each of us has at least a somewhat unique set of experiences that shape our particular mind. Motivations are likely to be both unique to an individual and variable across social and cultural environments more than we previously thought. Consumers' interpretation of culture messages will depend on the specific connections and strength of those connections in their minds.[12] Moreover, motivations are more likely to change as the world around us changes. Consumers will adapt their motivations and actions to fit with what works in that new environment. Industry Insights 7.1 discusses how the basic and primitive human skill of foraging is shifted to foraging on the Internet in contemporary society.

Foraging on the Internet: An Ancient Skill and a Contemporary Application

INDUSTRY INSIGHTS 7.1

Foraging theory has established a secure place in archeological analyses of economic decisions in prehistoric societies. Much of the use of these foraging models has focused on the survival behavior of hunter-gatherers or pastoralists. One can imagine applications in urbanized, industrial economies. For instance, taxi drivers act as predators seeking to optimize the benefit-to-cost ratio of encountering and "harvesting" their prey. Routinely, they must decide whether to actively search or to use a sit-and-wait, ambush tactic. Political scientists have also applied foraging theory to lobbying in state legislatures.

One of the more interesting recent applications of foraging theory is to analyze and optimize patterns of "information foraging" on the Internet. Computer scientists are applying these models to design effective information-gathering mechanisms from the World Wide Web and other large-scale databases. It turns out that a theory that was designed to understand prehistoric hunter-gatherers is now proving useful in understanding information-seeking readers on the Internet.

Source: Adapted from Bruce Winterhalder and Eric Alden Smith, "Analyzing Adaptive Strategies: Human Behavioral Ecology at Twenty-Five," Evolutionary Anthropology *9, no. 2 (2000), pp. 51–72.*

Following from our discussion of the mind, there is not a direct relationship between culture and motivation. Not everyone in a particular culture behaves the same because each has an individual set of experiences that shape how he or she interprets and responds to his or her world. Nevertheless, our discussion of the mind does suggest that motivations vary between cultures. Particular motivations would be better supported in some cultures than in others. Exhibit 7.1 illustrates that consumers' goals depend on how they interpret macro-environmental factors, local context and social networks within their own personal history, circumstances, life themes, and values.[13]

We see in the vignette that Carmen's involvement with beauty products and her appearance have been influenced by media images of women outside Romania. The cultural production system, including manufacturers, advertisers, retailers, news reporters, media producers, and fashion merchandisers, discussed in Chapter 4, has been significant in shaping women's perceptions of attractiveness, products that contribute to being attractive, and end goals attractiveness can achieve.[14] Other aspects of Carmen's cultural background and consumer context have also influenced her life themes, motives, and goals. For example, Carmen's goals reflect her desire to be different from other Romanian women. Because of the revolution and post-socialist reforms in Romania, Carmen expects to be able to travel to many cultures and to afford and acquire expensive clothes and cosmetics—things her grandmother did not expect. Romania is slowly sloughing off the remnants of the Ceauşescu era.

Local context and social networks also influence consumer motives and goals. For example, Carmen's boyfriend, mother, and friends influence her attention to appearance. They reinforce her belief that attractiveness is important and help shape her strategies for being attractive. In Chapters 13 and 14 we will discuss in more detail how families,

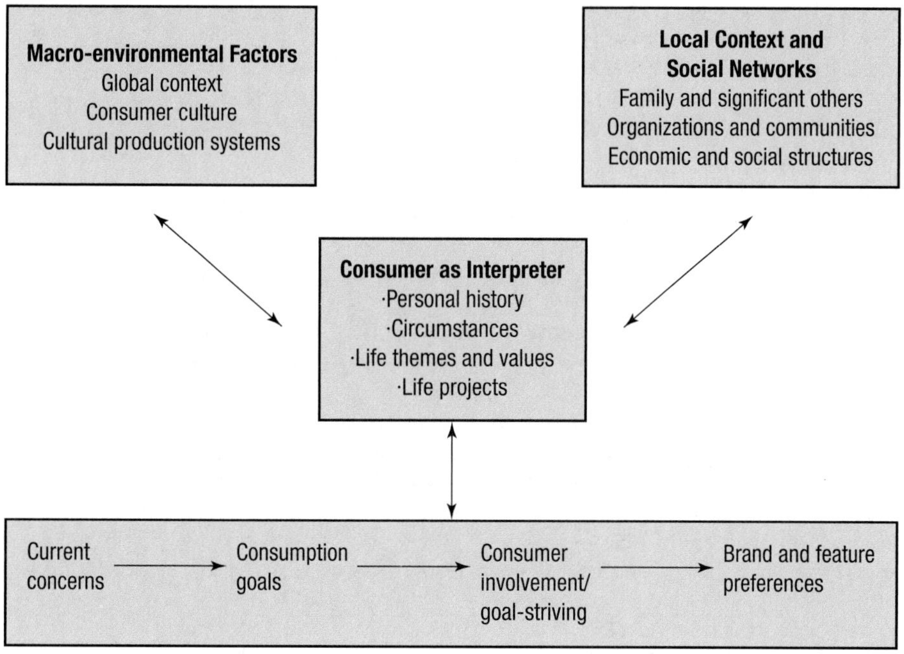

EXHIBIT 7.1

Consumer Motivation in Context

Source: Cynthia Huffman, S. Ratneshwar, and David Glen Mick, "Consumer Goal Structures and Goal-Determination Processes: An Integrative Framework," in *The Why of Consumption: Contemporary Perspectives on Consumer Motives, Goals, and Desires*, ed. S. Ratneshwar, David Glen Mick, and Cynthia Huffman (New York and London: Routledge, 2000), pp. 9–35; and Robin A. Coulter, Linda L. Price, and Lawrence F. Feick, "Origins of Product Involvement and Brand Commitment: Women and Cosmetics in Post-Socialist Central Europe," working paper, University of Connecticut, Storrs, CT (2002).

friends, and organizations influence consumers' motivations, goals, and preferences. Her age, gender, social class, and geographic location further shape Carmen's goals. For example, compared to Bucharest, the capital of Romania, Cluj offers a modest selection of high-quality fashion clothing. Romanian women in their 40s and 50s reflect different attitudes about consumer culture than Carmen. In Chapter 12 we will expand on how economic and social structures mold consumer motives and behaviors.

We can also see that Carmen's ideas about herself influence her motives and goals. She sees being open to new experiences and ideas as essential life themes, and because of her personal history she feels confident that she can attain her goals through effort and determination. Chapter 10 further describes how personality and self-concept relate to consumer motives and behaviors. Chapter 11 expands on that topic by discussing consumers' lifestyles. **Life themes** are *basic concerns that consumers address in everyday life* (e.g., being educated, being cosmopolitan, showing good taste) and **life projects** are *the construction and maintenance of key life roles and identities* (e.g., being a responsible mother, a loyal employee, a successful teacher). Of course, life goals and themes are modified and shaped by macro-environmental factors, but are also distinctly rooted in personal history and social context and networks.[15] Life themes and projects are often linked to consumption goals, goal-striving, and involvement. Can you name some life themes or projects that are important to you? Can you think of ways they influence your consumption behavior? Exhibit 7.2 profiles three different people illustrating how life themes and projects influence consumption goals, goal-striving, and involvement.

Again, it is important to remember that most people have multiple life projects that proceed simultaneously. For example, you may be striving to be a good employee, a good student, a good friend, and a good family member (to name just a few roles). Different roles are situationally evoked and emotionally activated and they are embedded in distinctive role relations.[16] Consider how you behave around your parents versus

EXHIBIT 7.2

Examples of Goal Structures for Three Consumers

Goal Level	*Ito, Now Living in Colorado, U.S. (22 years old)*	*Yvonne, California, U.S. (30 years old)*	*Aturo, El Salvador (58 years old)*
Macro-environmental factors	Economic and political prosperity, but views Japan as small, crowded, expensive, with many formal rituals	Economic and political prosperity	Severe economic and political instability leading to breakdown of public safety and job security
Local context and social networks	Father owns a business, but never talks with him about it Loves living in America but finds English difficult to learn	Friends and relatives around the world; stays in touch through e-mail Has lived in several different countries	Grew up in a poor family; first of his family to go to college, with the financial support of an older brother
Life themes and projects	Be a professional golfer Improve his English Be economically successful	Explorer Independent Family and friends are important	Education as a way out of poverty Family safety and financial security Dedicated to profession as a doctor
Current concerns	Improve his golf skills; plays golf everyday. His major reason for living in the United States: he couldn't afford to play regularly in Japan Improve education Have fun	Be physically attractive Explore different places and cultures Support herself Find a life partner Find a professional passion	Ensure his children's financial success Keep his family from growing apart from each other Share experiences with his grandchildren
Consumption intentions	Golf, cars, fast food, and education	Maybe go to college, maybe move to Europe, maybe invest in a modeling career Clothes and experiences	Products to keep his family safe and secure Travel to ensure time with grandchildren
Consumer involvements	Involved with golf, his sports car, American fast food, Japanese traditions	Travel, clothes, music, friends, movies	Involved with programs to improve public life in El Salvador
Brand and feature preferences	Buys brands that reflect status, success, American youth, and involvement with golf	Avid and talented clothes shopper Buys on sale and through connections to stretch her meager budget	Buys features and brands that promise safety, security, and family values

how you behave around an employer or your friends. Sometimes these roles complement and reinforce each other. Perhaps your studies help you do your job better and/or your job helps you understand your classes differently. But sometimes, it is difficult to juggle these many different roles, and sometimes they conflict. Can you recall an occasion when two important life projects seemed at odds with each other? Most of us can. Moreover, just being a good student involves trade-offs among subgoals that contribute to this life project; for example, should you skip your 9 A.M. class to study a little extra for your 11 A.M. exam? An Australian advertisement for a simple food item, chicken stock, recognizes that consumers have multiple goals, and feelings of self-esteem may depend on maintaining all these key life roles and identities.

Although life themes and life projects may remain relatively stable over a number of years or even a lifetime, **role transitions** may dramatically shift life projects and even life themes. In Chapter 10 we will describe how *major changes in the rights, duties, and responsibilities expected of an individual by a social group* can alter a consumer's self-concept. Here, we want to acknowledge that role transitions impact consumers' motives and goals in significant ways. For example, Carmen anticipates changes in her goal hierarchy following graduation. The Australian advertisement for Zafira depicts how parenthood can influence automobile preferences by introducing a new role and the demands that accompany that role, but eases the transition by promising a versatile car that can seat two, five, or seven. Can you think of role transitions that have shifted your personal life projects or life themes?

Consumers have multiple roles and goals.

MOTIVATIONAL DYNAMICS Social life is an important source of consumer motives and goals. Here we introduce a simple motivational model that drives many consumer behaviors. Shown in Exhibit 7.3, this model will be helpful in all of the chapters that follow. Within society two opposing motivational tendencies together drive many consumer behaviors. One we may call the motive toward integration or affiliation with other people; the other is the motive toward differentiation or distinction from other people. For example, sports fans communicate their affiliation with a team and fellow fans by sporting team colors and merchandise; at the same time, they communicate their differentiation from other teams and fan groups.

Consumers' taste preferences are expressed through recurring patterns of acquisition, consumption, disposal, and production. In consumer culture, marketers encourage people to go to the market to purchase goods and services that help them define with whom they are affiliated and from whom they are separated. These patterns of consumer preference are defined and refined through a third motivational process, a process of individual and social comparison. In other words, most of us are motivated to scan our social environment continuously for cues in the consumer behavior of others to help us define who we are and who we are not and the social groups to which we belong and the groups to which we do not.

Designed to fit changing consumer goals.

These motivational drivers may not always be conscious, but they are reflected in the large number of consumption choices we make daily, choices that reflect and maintain the division of societies into distinct classes, ages, neighborhoods, ethnicities, lifestyles, occupations, personalities, nationalities, and so on. In other words, these motives and the consumer behaviors they stimulate integrate individuals with some groups and distinguish them from others. Thus, we are able to say that Germans differ from the French in their avid consumption of beer rather than wine. And within Germany we may distinguish groups of Germans by their preferences for brands of beer produced in

EXHIBIT 7.3

Motivational Dynamics

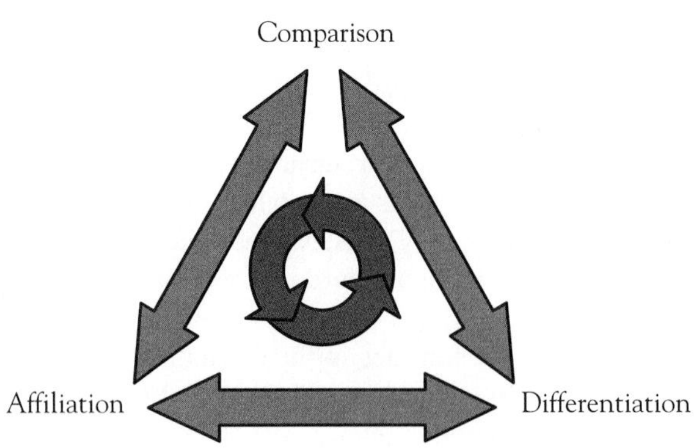

Fitting in by standing out. Colors, June/July 2002

particular regions. Examine the advertisement for Diesel. How could we interpret this ad in terms of the motivational dynamics of differentiation, integration, and social comparison? In what ways does Diesel clothing promise to help you fit in? In what ways does it promise to help you stand out? How does it help you define a comparison group?

CLASSIC THEORIES OF MOTIVATION

No discussion of consumer motivation would be complete without some reference to Sigmund Freud, Carl Jung, Abraham Maslow, and their many followers who have struggled to advance our understanding of why people behave the way they do. Their theories form the background for any discussion of motivation and it is quite likely that you have been exposed to some of their ideas before. To some extent, it may seem confusing that there are so many (sometimes conflicting) accounts and lists of human motives. One reason for this is that motives are not directly observable. They are psychological constructs. We hypothesize that they exist, but it is hard to prove. We cannot see or touch a motivation; we can only infer its existence. We will briefly overview four motivational frameworks with particular emphasis on how these concepts can be useful in understanding consumers:

- Sigmund Freud's concept of drives (e.g., as mediated by the id, ego, superego).
- Carl Jung's concept of archetypes (e.g., the self, the great mother, the hero).
- Abraham Maslow's concept of need hierarchy (e.g., physiological needs, safety needs).
- Henry Murray's list of human needs (e.g., abasement, acquisition, affiliation).

Overview of Freud's Theory

Freud believed the human psyche is broadly divided into the conscious and the unconscious.[17] The **ego** represents *the conscious mind.* It is composed of perceptions, thoughts, memories, and feelings. The ego gives the personality a sense of identity and continuity. In many respects, Freud's notion of ego is a precursor to modern theories about self-concept (see Chapter 10). The *unconscious mind* is called the **id.** It includes all the instincts and psychic energies that exist at birth. In this sense, the id (to a large extent) is biologically determined. The motivations that derive from the unconscious mind are both innate and unique to the individual. The power of the unconscious is so strong that ignoring its impulses can cause the rational processes of the ego to become distorted and result in neuroses, phobias, delusions, and other irrationalities. In this sense, Freud concentrated his attention on abnormal individuals—people who, for one reason or another, had trouble fitting into society. The **superego** is the third structure hypothesized by Freud. It represents the *traditional ideas and values of society.* These values are learned at childhood and are transmitted largely through identification with parents. The superego serves as a conscience and attempts to curb the passions that emanate from the id. The superego attempts to compel the ego to pursue goals that match the morality dictated by society and culture.[18]

Freud's simple framework provides a way to think about the interplay between biological forces (represented by the id), societal forces (the superego), and human consciousness (the ego). These three forces are the foundations for explaining human motivations and needs as they influence behavior. Whatever model we create to explain human motivation has to include a role for each of these major influences: biology, society, and facets of the self. It is important to recognize that Freud's three psychological structures do not necessarily have biological counterparts in the human brain. Nonetheless, these are interesting concepts for thinking about human motivation and how consumers balance conflicting desires. New-product managers may try to create brands that fulfill needs of the id, ego, or superego. As illustrated in Good Practice 7.1, it is sometimes difficult to uncover consumer motives.

Similarly, advertising managers can use Freud's concepts to inspire creative copy. For instance, advertisers often use sexual symbols in ads, and the effectiveness of these ads is easily explained through Freudian theory. Many observers declared that the cartoon character Joe Camel looked like a phallus. Thus, many promotional themes appeal to consumers' unconscious motivations, and Freudian theory provides an interesting framework for thinking about these unconscious urges.

Overview of Jung's Theory

Jung conceived of the unconscious as being subdivided into the personal unconscious and the collective unconscious, which together hold all the hidden contents of the mind. The personal unconscious holds previously conscious experiences that have been repressed, forgotten, suppressed, or ignored. Although stored in the unconscious, these experiences can become conscious in the form of intuitions or similar inexplicable urges. The concept of the collective unconscious is the most difficult of Jung's ideas about human motivation. Jung saw **archetypes** as *a common reservoir of images that represent the collective unconscious.* He believed the collective unconscious is a storehouse of latent memory traces, or archetypes, inherited from the human ancestral past.[19] Jung proposed archetypes predispose humans to react to the world in a selective fashion. For Jung, the collective unconscious explains why spiritual concerns are so deeply rooted in human life across cultures and why people in different cultures share certain myths and images, such as "mother" as a symbol of nurturing.[20] Jung was careful to point out that the archetypes, while shared universally, are also universally individualized.

GOOD PRACTICE 7.1

Uncovering Consumer Motives

Consumers often have difficulty articulating exactly why they like something or why they have purchased something. For this reason, marketing researchers often make use of techniques (e.g., the depth interview) that facilitate an understanding of *unconscious motives.* In a depth interview, a consumer is asked to explain in great detail the impressions that he or she has about a product or brand. Sometimes, the services of a trained psychoanalyst are employed to help elicit and decipher a consumer's hidden motives. Depth interviews were quite popular in the 1950s, and they are becoming more popular again. For example, Ernest and Julio Gallo is experimenting with depth interviews to learn more about how people perceive wines and how they buy them. John Bowen, director of the Center of Global Brand Management at Columbia University, consults with a psychoanalyst to understand how consumers react to brand names and how they interpret their experiences in the marketplace.

Jung's approach is important for marketers because it provides a way to explore myths, images, and symbols. In turn, myths and symbols are the building blocks for creating marketing phenomena, such as advertisements and promotions. For example, the advertisement for Degree Gel Antiperspirant draws on a hero myth. The graphics remind us this is a story, not reality, that nevertheless has strong archetype appeal.

The hero and rescuer archetype in advertising.

To make use of Jung's archetypes, advertisers need to isolate the positive characteristics associated with myths or symbols, as discussed in Chapter 4. According to Jung's theory, humans share deep-seated, eternal similarities. To the extent that this is the case, Jung's theory provides one way marketers' messages can be globalized. By selecting universal symbols, marketers may use similar promotional campaigns in many different cultures. Following Jung's analysis, advertising can operate on the unconscious mind and create strong impressions by appealing to universal archetypes. Promotional campaigns that appeal to the consumer's unconscious can be controversial. How do you feel about such campaigns? Check out Ethical Dilemma 7.1 describing Calvin Klein's promotional campaign.

Overview of Maslow's Theory

The most popular and well-known approach to human motivation is based on the research of psychologist

Appeals to Universal Archetypes

ETHICAL DILEMMA 7.1

The Calvin Klein jeans promotion is one of the most controversial and memorable ad campaigns in the last decade. From teen actress Brooke Shields purring "Nothing comes between me and my Calvins" to a fantasy spread featuring couples attired in the product and little else, Calvin Klein jeans promotions are heavily imbued with the sensuality and suggestiveness of the shadow. One of Jung's archetypes, the shadow is where hide all the inadvertent aspects of the personality that may be unfavorable, nefarious, or suppressed, in addition to the instinctive and creative impulses. When the ego attempts to see what is hidden in the shadow, it becomes aware of those forbidden qualities and impulses that are denied in the self but seen in other people. The erotic promotions, often featuring very young models, invite the consumer to experience the urges of the shadow by wearing Calvin Klein jeans. This campaign is controversial because it operates on the unconscious mind by appealing to universal archetypes. What do you think? What limits, if any, should be imposed on the types of appeals involved in promotional campaigns? Do the Calvin Klein ads you've seen cross that limit? Why or why not?

Abraham Maslow. **Maslow's need hierarchy** specified that *needs are arranged in a sequence from lower-level needs to higher-level needs.* He identified five needs:

1. **Physiological**—*the biological needs for food, water, and sleep.*
2. **Safety and security**—*shelter, protection, and security.*
3. **Social**—*affection, friendship, and acceptance.*
4. **Ego**—*prestige, success, accomplishment, and self-esteem.*
5. **Self-actualization**—*self-fulfillment and enriching experiences.*

Lower-level needs (starting with the physiological) are considered to dominate higher-level needs. That is, consumers must satisfy lower-level needs before they begin to pursue higher-order needs. For example, once a consumer feels satisfied in terms of biological and safety needs, then that person is capable of relating to other people (i.e., pursuing social needs). According to Maslow the highest level of need is related to self-actualization. Consumers desire to live up to their full potential. They want to maximize the use of their skills and abilities. This need for self-actualization only becomes activated if all four of the lower-level needs have already been satisfied. Maslow's hierarchy provides a useful organization for thinking about needs and motives, but it is overly simplistic. The hierarchy ignores the intensity of the needs. For example, how hungry does a person need to be before that need dominates the need for friendship, self-esteem, or self-fulfillment? The avid consumption of luxuries in poor transitional economies illustrates aspects of this oversimplification.[21] For example, Romanian families forgo needed food in order to afford refrigerators that then remain empty and Turkish families sell nutritious cow's milk in order to buy candy for their children who have seen it advertised on TV. These examples may seem extreme, but each of us can probably think of instances where it seems as if higher-level needs won out over basic needs. Even in ancient cultures, in which people often struggled to meet basic needs, we see evidence of human tendencies to make art and assemble collections. For example, cave paintings can be traced back at least 30,000 years. Some researchers argue that the desire for the beautiful is a basic need.[22] In addition, Maslow's ordering of needs may not be consistent across cultures. Research supports a somewhat different hierarchy in the East.[23] Some cultures certainly put more value on social needs and belonging and less on ego needs and self-actualization. As we discuss in Chapter 10, different cultures have varying conceptions of the self that are likely to influence whether they value self-fulfillment or collective fulfillment.

Maslow's need hierarchy provides a useful summary or inventory of human needs that can be useful for marketing managers who are interested in understanding their customers' needs. However, marketing managers should be cautious in assuming that a hierarchy of needs holds.[24] Maslow's list of needs can serve as key input for product design. For example, the core product can be designed to represent a basic physiological need, reliability and ontime product delivery or warranties can be equated with safety, and customer interaction can be related to belongingness.[25] Many ad campaigns are designed to appeal to one or more of the needs represented in Maslow's hierarchy.

Overview of Murray's Theory

Henry Murray shifted attention away from motives as internal states or drives, to thinking about motives in terms of goal-striving. His research continues to influence many students of motivation.[26] Murray set out to list an inventory of every possible need he could distinguish. A major criticism of Murray's work is that it is just a lengthy inventory of needs—difficult and impractical for marketers to use. Just his basic list of major human needs includes 22 different ones. He believed that people differ in their priority ranking of these needs. Modern interpretations of his list suggest some of these needs are never salient while others assume great importance, depending on social and cultural circumstances. Like Freud, Jung, and Maslow, Murray had a view of the self and motives that derived from Western psychology, and his theory is **culture-bound;** that is, *it doesn't necessarily apply outside the society where the theory was developed.*[27] However, because his inventory of motives is so comprehensive, it is more adaptable to different cultural traditions. We later describe how Murray's work can be used to provide a more cross-cultural perspective on motives, but first we outline a unique contribution of Murray's theory for marketers.

Murray's detailed list identifies several needs specifically associated with objects. He identified acquisition needs (to gain possessions and property), order needs (to put things in order; to achieve cleanliness, arrangement, organization, and balance), and retention needs (to retain possession of things; to hoard; to be frugal, economical, and miserly) as among the most basic human needs. Marketers often appeal to these needs for acquiring and retaining possessions. Acquisition may be a basic human need, but major religions discourage excess in acquisition and encourage restraint. Judeo-Christian, Buddhist, Taoist, Hindu, and Native American traditions all encourage restraint in materialist desires. Acquisition can be tied to four of the seven deadly sins in the Judeo-Christian tradition: greed, pride, gluttony, and envy.[28] Nevertheless, we give examples throughout this book from many different cultures about the desire to acquire, order, and retain possessions. Although the meaning and importance of possessions vary substantially among different peoples both within a given culture and between cultures, as we discussed in Chapter 4, most people seem to need to acquire and retain certain special objects.

Contrasting Independent and Interdependent Selves

CONSUMER CHRONICLES 7.2

In America, "the squeaky wheel gets the grease." In Japan, "the nail that stands out gets pounded down." American parents who are trying to induce their children to eat their suppers are fond of saying, "Think of the starving kids in Ethiopia and appreciate how lucky you are to be different from them." Japanese parents are likely to say, "Think about the farmer who worked so hard to produce this rice for you: if you don't eat it, he will feel bad for his efforts will have been in vain." A small Texas corporation seeking to elevate productivity told its employees to look in the mirror and say, "I am beautiful" 100 times before coming to work each day. Employees of a Japanese supermarket recently opened in New Jersey were instructed to begin the day by holding hands and telling each other that "he" or "she is beautiful."

Source: Hazel Markus and Shinobu Kitayama, "Culture and the Self: Implications for Cognition, Emotion, and Motivation," Psychological Review *98 (April 1991), p. 224.*

FIVE CONSUMER MOTIVES IN CULTURAL PERSPECTIVE

One important difference among how consumers interpret their world is whether they grew up in a culture that stresses independent or interdependent goals. Some cultures stress **independent goals.** Americans and many western Europeans *stress a unique, self-contained, autonomous entity mastering his or her potential.* In these cultures, parents want their children to learn independence and separateness, to sleep in their own bed at night and not go along with the crowd. No wonder Maslow, coming from this tradition, frames the highest goal as self-actualization. However, many cultures stress **interdependent goals.** Japanese, other Asians, Africans, Latin-Americans, and some southern Europeans all emphasize the importance of fitting with the family, group, and society. In this view, *goals are formulated as part of an encompassing social relation, and behavior is dependent on and organized by perceptions of the thoughts, feelings, and actions of others in the relationship.* Goals depend on social context and the social unit. Parents in these cultures teach their children to seek connectedness, social integration, and interpersonal harmony. Consumer Chronicles 7.2 illustrates how an independent versus interdependent view influences motivations.

Research has demonstrated that these differences translate very directly into what types of advertising strategies work. For example, ad messages featuring "older people" and "experts" are more persuasive to consumers from the People's Republic of China than to Australians. This appeals to the interdependent need to admire and defer to a superior. The Chinese from the PRC are less likely to lodge a complaint for a faulty product, consistent with the need to comply, behave well, and not stand out. They are less likely to purchase new products when compared with Australians. Being different and standing out are not valued; staying with tradition is.[29] In the next few pages, we outline some motives that marketers often use in promotions. These motives are sensitive to whether the culture stresses independent or interdependent goals. Two of these—power and uniqueness motives—are likely to be much higher in independent than interdependent cultures. Three of these—achievement, affiliation, and self-esteem motives—are likely to be important in both but have different meanings and actions associated with them. Advertisements often emphasize more than one of these motives.

The Achievement Motive

One of the most studied and talked about motivations is the need for achievement. The **achievement motive** is defined as *the drive to experience emotion in connection with evaluated performance.*[30] This definition allows for variety in the type of performance involved. Whereas the individually oriented achievement motive implies striving for its own sake, the socially oriented achievement motive has the goal of meeting expectations of significant others. Several studies have distinguished between these two types of achievement motivation, showing that the motive to achieve goals can be for social and collective reasons. For example, Chinese children strive to achieve the goals of others, such as family and teachers.[31] Some research compares Anglo-Irish and Chinese-Vietnamese mothers' gifts to their children. It shows that Anglo-Irish mothers, representing extreme individualism, prefer not to give gifts to reward their children's academic endeavors; they feel achievement should have an internal/intrinsic basis. Chinese-Vietnamese mothers, representing extreme collectivism, give gifts to reward their children's academic progress. These mothers also registered different gift-giving motivations. Anglo-Irish mothers give gifts to gain short-term benefits for their children, such as enhanced self-concept, and for themselves (their children's love). Chinese-Vietnamese mothers give gifts to attain long-term benefits for their children and mention no personal benefits.[32]

The Power Motive

The **power motive** is defined as *the drive to have control or influence over another person, group, or the world at large.*[33] One specific (appropriate or inappropriate) manifestation of the motive—to "make a splash" or create excitement—is particularly situation dependent.[34] Researchers have reached the general conclusion that people who have a high need for power strive to be assertive.[35] Although everyone may have some desire for agency and control, assertiveness may not be the control strategy of choice. For example, people in many Asian cultures appear to use what is termed **secondary control.** This involves *accommodating existing circumstances* and may mean limiting individualism in order to fit with present circumstances. For example, feng shui is practiced to control the environment through harmony with the environment. Feng shui is sometimes referred to in advertisements for products ranging from real estate and cars to home and personal care, playing on the idea of control through harmony with the environment.

One socially acceptable way for people to fulfill their power need is by collecting prestige possessions, or symbols of power. These possessions may include credit cards, watches, computers, cars, cellular phones, and so on.[36] If a man has an important interview coming up, he may purchase a "power" tie. Similarly, a woman may wear a power suit to such an interview. With the growth in popularity of the World Wide Web, new opportunities exist for image projection. For example, as Consumer Chronicles 7.3 illustrates, creating a personal web page can be a source of power. In this study, technologically sensitized college students wrote a brief story or commentary about the likely motives of an imaginary web page creator (i.e., a projective technique).

Nevertheless, there are many opportunities for creating unique images using existing signals (e.g., related to clothing). To promote her book, author Jane Gallop wears a skirt that is made of men's silk ties. This skirt turns the traditional dress code on its head while at the same time creating a unique image for the author.[37] Advertisers often try to position products as symbols of power or as means to achieve power and control.

The Uniqueness/Novelty Motive

In this chapter we introduced a basic model of motivational dynamics. Blending in and not standing out (e.g., integration or affiliation) are very important in cultures that stress interdependent goals. By contrast, individuals in cultures that stress independence

Power-Related Motives for Creating Personal Web Pages

CONSUMER CHRONICLES 7.3

1. **Ego-enhancement.** Some consumers are motivated to create web pages by the feeling of importance that a home page on the Web provides. They use it as an opportunity to show off, impress others, or look cool. They enjoy the awareness that many people will be looking at their home page.
2. **Social status/prestige.** Individuals who are motivated by social status feel that a home page on the Web provides prestige and establishes a place for them in society.
3. **Gain attention of others.** The creation of a web page provides an opportunity to attract attention to the page owner on two levels. First, it is a topic of conversation. It can attract attention and admiration related to the achievement of being at the cutting edge of the new technology. Second, the author gains attention through having others visit the home page.
4. **Control/mastery over the environment.** Some consumers gain a feeling of having conquered technology by creating a personal home page. They feel that understanding now will create leverage in the future, allowing them to take advantage of the benefits the Internet has to offer. Other consumers feel they impact the environment by sharing what they know with the world.

Source: Adapted from George M. Zinkhan, Margy Conchar, Ajay Gupta, and Gary Geissler, "Motivations Underlying the Creation of Personal Web Pages: An Exploratory Study," in Advances in Consumer Research, *vol. 26, ed. Eric J. Arnould and Linda M. Scott (Provo, UT: Association for Consumer Research, 1999), pp. 69–74.*

express the desire to be independent and unique (e.g., differentiation or distinction). The **uniqueness motive,** that is, *the drive to perceive oneself as different from others,* has been called the "pursuit of difference."[38] Apple Computer's famous slogan "Think Different" typifies appeals to the need for uniqueness. Many Western cultures, and Americans in particular, put a premium on standing out and being unique. Americans struggle to enhance self-perceptions of uniqueness.[39] In much of the modern world, the majority of products are mass marketed. In this climate, many people feel that it is difficult to create and project uniqueness. One way consumers can differentiate themselves is through attitudes and beliefs. Another way a person can be different is through uniqueness attributes, for example, physical qualities, information, or experiences. For example, consumers with a high need to express uniqueness are especially attracted to scarce products.[40] These consumers search for new and special products to maintain a sense of specialness relative to others.[41] Youths in many Triad cultures focus on irreverence, nonconformity, noncommitment, detachment, difference, and fragmentation in their consumer behaviors.[42] Again, computer technology can be used to create a unique image or to express individuality. Communicating in cyberspace can provide thrills, excitement, and a feeling of uniqueness. Consumers' interactions on the Web can be exciting to the senses.[43]

The Affiliation Motive

The **affiliation motive** is defined as *the drive to be with people.*[44] As noted earlier in this chapter, one of people's most basic social behaviors is the urge for contact.[45] Our ancestors evolved in small, cohesive groups. The universality of the motive to belong is revealed by the use of ostracism as a punishment in many societies. Brain research now supports a social view of the brain, believing that a kind of sociality that does not distinguish self from other is woven deeply into the primate brain. Many research studies have shown the importance of mutual imitation and shared action for both infants and mothers.

We might expect that the desire for affiliation would be higher in interdependent than independent cultures. Surprisingly, however, studies have not found this. But researchers have discovered that the meaning of affiliation and the behaviors that accompany affiliation do differ. For example, a person's concern with adjusting to occupy a proper place with respect to others is more important in interdependent cultures.

One recent trend in industrialized society is that consumers feel more and more detached as the twentieth century unfolds.[46] Large institutions and mass media have the effect of insulating and detaching consumers from their fellows. As a result, consumers sometimes experience a strong motivation to reconnect and associate with groups of kindred spirits. Many consumers are eager to find a way to overcome feelings of detachment, depersonalization, and isolation. Advertisers often try to position products and services as symbols of affiliation or as means that will enable consumers to achieve connection with people.

The Self-Esteem Motive

Another motive that has received a lot of attention is the need to maintain a positive view of the self, or self-esteem need. This is discussed in more depth in Chapter 10. Studies of Americans show that even at a very early age they *take credit for successes, explain away failures, and see themselves as better than most others* in most ways.[47] This is referred to as a **self-enhancing bias.** Studies of Japanese college students show a strong bias in the reverse direction—that is, self-effacing.

The self-esteem goal is seen as fundamental in Western cultures. Themes such as "express yourself" and "be yourself" are common appeals to self-esteem used in American advertising. However, these appeals are perceived quite negatively in Japanese culture. In Japan, expressing the inner self is not valued. What is important is to control the expression of the inner self in order to fit in with others and maintain harmony. Research has demonstrated that Japanese put much less emphasis on consistency between feelings and actions than Americans.[48] In fact, self-esteem among cultures stressing interdependent goals may heavily depend on self-control and self-restraint that enable belonging and fitting in.

MOTIVATIONAL CONFLICT

Faced with multiple goals and obstacles, consumers weigh how to allot their resources and efforts. Many consumer decisions evoke both positive and negative feelings. Mixed emotions and ambivalence are prominent with important decisions such as choosing a college, buying a house, having a baby, or moving to a new job. We talk more about consumers' mixed feelings following a purchase decision in Chapter 18. Western cultures tend to encourage resolution of these mixed feelings, emphasizing the anxiety and stress evoked by the experience of emotional and motivational conflicts. Other cultures, for example East Asian, are likely to perceive these conflicts as natural and common. There is greater acceptance of contradictions and conflicts and less of a sense that such conflicts must be resolved.[49] However, even within a particular culture, there

Resolving an approach/avoidance motivational conflict.

are many differences in how consumers deal with motivational conflict. For example, when decisions are extended and complex, when consumers have higher levels of education, and when they are more motivated, they are better able to process and accept these conflicts.[50] How motivational conflicts are resolved also depends on culture. For example, individuals with more interdependent goals focus more on avoidance goals (selecting a car that will withstand an accident), while individuals with more independent goals focus more on approach goals (selecting a car that offers an enjoyable driving experience).[51]

Here we focus on three motivational conflicts consumers may feel as they strive to fulfill their various consumption goals. Marketers are likely to benefit from recognizing these conflicts. In some cases it may be appropriate to help consumers resolve them, while in other cases marketers may benefit from confronting consumers with the inevitability and naturalness of these conflicting feelings.[52]

Approach-Avoidance Conflict

Some outcomes are viewed as both desirable and undesirable because while they satisfy some goals, they fail to satisfy others. At the simplest level, resources or efforts directed toward one goal are not available for other goals. In the opening vignette, Carmen feels good about investing in her education, but feels sad that she has no money for other things. The benefits of a product or service are always offset to some degree by the price we pay in time and money. Marketers use lots of strategies to evoke motivational approach over avoidence. For example, credit cards, 90-days-of-no-interest credit, and other tactics that separate benefits from paying help delay avoidance feelings. By identifying consumers' feelings of approach and avoidance, marketers can communicate to strengthen approach feelings and diminish avoidance feelings. The advertisement for Equal recognizes an **approach-avoidance conflict** many consumers face and encourages consumers not to say no to everything with calories, but to use Equal. This advertisement explicitly recognizes that the conflict will remain and the consumer will continue to make trade-offs.

Approach-Approach Conflict

Another common type of conflict occurs when consumers choose between two or more desirable options that fulfill different goals. Identifying consumers' **approach-approach conflicts** can be an important source of new product ideas. For example, a consumer may feel that a manual car transmission provides feelings of power and control, but for driving around town in traffic, automatic transmissions provide comfort and convenience. The Australian ad for the VR-X resolves this conflict by providing a transmission that does both.

Avoidance-Avoidance Conflict

An **avoidance-avoidance conflict** occurs when consumers must choose between two equally undesirable options. Can you think of an example? Prominent examples might include going to the dentist, getting a shot, buying new tires, buying insurance, and

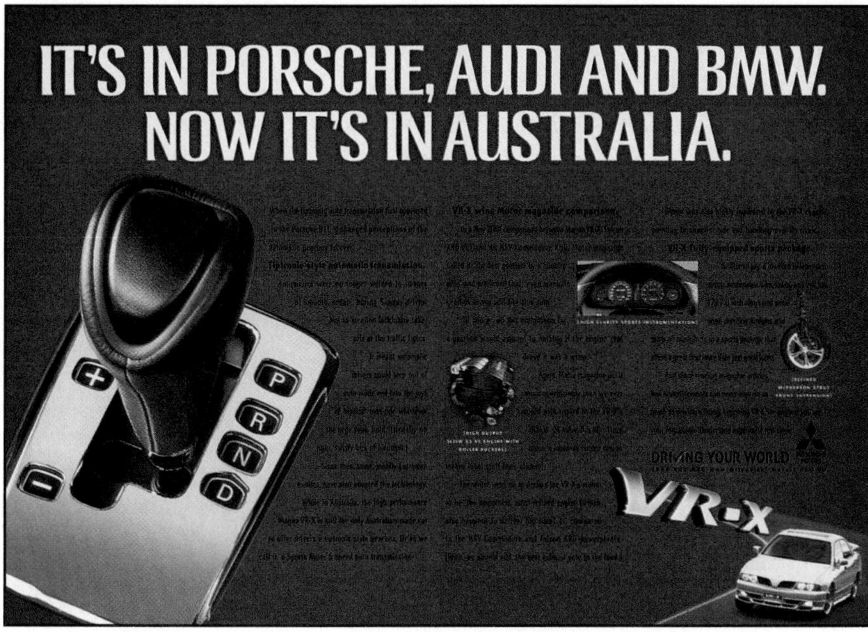

Resolving an approach/approach motivational conflict.

product repair or replacement. Some products and services are purchased in order to avoid negative outcomes. Most of us don't like spending hundreds of dollars on new tires, but we don't want the alternative of an unsafe car that breaks down. Sometimes marketers can make one of the alternatives more attractive. For example, many dentists work hard to make regular checkups a rewarding and pleasant experience. Nevertheless, marketers of products and services characterized by avoidance-avoidance conflict are most likely to promote how bad the alternative is. For example, many insurance companies implicitly focus on negative outcomes that will be offset or minimized if you have their product.

RESEARCHING MOTIVES

Motivational research can provide insights into the whys of consumer behavior and can reveal unsuspected motivations concerning product and brand usage. It can be used to develop new ideas for products and promotional campaigns and to explore consumer reactions to new products and appeals. There are many different motivational research techniques, some of which were discussed in Chapter 6. The means-ends chain and laddering provide a basic way of moving from product attributes to underlying motives; the Zaltman Metaphor Elicitation Technique (ZMET) combines consumer images and stories to help researchers understand motives. Both of these techniques can help uncover how a similar preference may be motivated by very different consumer goals. These techniques could be fruitfully employed in cross-cultural contexts to uncover the different goals and varied meanings associated with a brand.

The Means-Ends Chain and Laddering

As discussed in Chapter 5, consumers don't buy products or services; they buy benefits.[53] A chief goal of the marketing department is to understand the underlying consumer

Administering Means-Ends Chains

GOOD PRACTICE 7.2

Find two consumers who you can talk to for about 5–10 minutes each. Try to find a quiet place where you won't be interrupted.

- Begin the interview by stating:
  Assume that you were in the market for [insert product name]. What factors [or benefits] do you consider when you are deciding what brand of [product name] to buy for yourself?
- Then ask:
  What two factors [or benefits] are most important to you in making your decision?
- Then do the laddering:
  Why is [factor one] important to you? Why is [factor two] important? What does [factor one or two] give you?
- Continue this process until the consumer cannot go on, and then end the interview.
- Draw out the two means-ends chains you measured for each person. Discuss what you have learned about these consumers' product knowledge and what implications this analysis could have for developing marketing strategies. Finally, discuss problems that you had with the measurement procedures. Was this process easy or hard for the consumers? Why do you think so?

motivations for purchasing and then to communicate these motivations to the rest of the organization. The **means-ends chain** provides a way to dig beneath the surface and to discover layers of consumer meaning. The name is derived from the assumption that a brand is a consumer's means of achieving a desired end or goal.[54] The means-ends chain suggests a clear method for discovering a consumer's pattern of motivations. Instructions for administering a means-ends chain are shown in Good Practice 7.2.

At the first step, the respondent narrows down the list of important factors, or benefits, to the two that are seen as most important. At the second step of measurement, the respondent is asked to say why that particular benefit is important. This is the start of the laddering process. The interviewer keeps asking Why? until the informant responds with a value (e.g., achievement, affiliation) or until the informant becomes fatigued and can no longer answer. In this sense, the interviewer is a bit like a two-year-old, interminably asking Why? Why? Why? This succession of "why" questions is referred to as the laddering process. Presumably, the majority of consumer means-ends chains will culminate with a basic motive or value. As the consumer proceeds through the laddering process, he or she can respond with concrete product attributes (e.g., "Crest toothpaste has fluoride") or with product attributes that are more abstract (e.g., "Crest protects my teeth"). Note that the laddering technique requires an in-depth interview that is potentially time-consuming and possibly frustrating for the respondent (e.g., being continually confronted with why questions). Thus, the means-ends chain method is usually applied to small samples. It is not particularly feasible for large-scale applications.

The Zaltman Metaphor Elicitation Technique

With the Zaltman Metaphor Elicitation Technique, or **ZMET,** researchers use pictures and nonvisual images generated by consumers to elicit and probe the metaphors that represent consumers' thoughts and feelings about a topic.[55] *The use of one form of expression to describe or represent feelings about another* is called a **metaphor;** for example, earlier in this chapter we said the brain is like the ecology of a jungle. By having people select their own images, the ZMET process gives participants control of the research stimuli and a sense of involvement with the topic. Participants are able to represent their thoughts and feelings more fully and personally than when responding to stimuli created and presented by the researcher. The technique is especially effective at helping consumers uncover hidden or **tacit knowledge**—*understanding they didn't know they had.* It has been used to help many companies develop promotional campaigns or identify new product ideas. For example, the technique was useful at early stages in helping Procter & Gamble develop ideas for their Swiffer product, a new style "dust mop" that uses disposable cloths to pick up air and dirt.

Each ZMET interview is a one-on-one discussion, approximately two hours long. In preparation for the interview, participants spend considerable time thinking about the topic and locating appropriate visual images. As a result, participants arrive for their in-depth interview at an advanced stage of thinking, ready to discuss their thoughts and feelings.

The ZMET interview employs several steps to identify consumers' key thoughts and feelings. The technique is based, in part, on the fact that most human communication is nonverbal and that much of nonverbal communication is visual. Each step in the ZMET process provides a different window for identifying and understanding metaphors, thereby gaining a deep understanding of consumers' thoughts and feelings. The use of multiple steps also increases the likelihood of uncovering an important idea that might be missed by more narrowly focused techniques. At the same time, each step provides validation of ideas from other steps. ZMET capitalizes on consumers' ideas about stories and movies to get at deeper meanings. Storytelling is a technique that focuses on individuals rather than on arguments or averages. Consumers use stories to give feelings and experiences personal relevance and meaning. They develop the context and relevant relationships instead of merely positing raw data. Stories unfold in time, and a specific place, instead of being presented as timeless, and they are emotionally evocative.[56] The central steps of the ZMET interview procedure are described in Good Practice 7.3.

ZMET offers researchers a way to tap into the unconscious mind. It provides a way to understand consumer motivations that are not necessarily tied to verbal expressions. One advantage of the technique is that it can provide unique input to advertising copywriters. Much of marketing research is summarized by statistics or by a written report. ZMET provides consumer-based images that can become part of the visual portion of an ad campaign.[57] In the example offered here, the ZMET technique was used to explore consumers' impressions of advertising better.[58] Two consumers' views of advertising are represented in their summary images. These images are described in detail by the consumer so that researchers can understand what the consumer intends to represent. These images along with others helped researchers uncover basic feelings about advertising. In both these summary images we can see good and evil, pleasure and harm represented. This affirms that consumers have both positive and negative feelings about advertising and its effects. Consumers see advertising images as a source of temptation and despair. How would you interpret these collages and what would your collage look like?

Steps in the ZMET Process

GOOD PRACTICE 7.3

1. **Storytelling about pictures.** Participants describe how each picture they brought to the interview represents thoughts and feelings about a particular topic of interest. Stories are excellent sources of metaphors and important sources of insight about participants. Participants spontaneously state the theme (overall meaning) of each picture during storytelling for that picture.
2. **Laddering.** During the storytelling step, the interviewer often uses laddering. The interviewer asks the participant to describe why something is important or relevant.
3. **Missing pictures.** Participants are asked if there were important ideas they wanted to express but for which they could not find relevant images. If this happens, a record is made of the idea and kind of image that might represent those thoughts and feelings.
4. **Kelly grid and laddering.** The Kelly repertory grid seeks to identify concepts, distinctions, and concepts at a higher level. The interviewer asks the participant to examine three pictures and to indicate how any two pictures are similar, but different from the third, with regard to the topic.
5. **Metaphor probe/expand the frame.** ZMET employs several other probing techniques to encourage participants to elaborate their thoughts and feelings (meanings) more deeply and completely. For example, participants are asked to widen the frame of one or more selected pictures and describe what else might enter the picture that reinforces the original idea. Participants imagine themselves in the picture and discuss what might take place and what they are thinking and feeling. Participants invite someone or something into the picture that will help them with their problem and describe who or what it would be.
6. **Sensory (nonvisual) metaphors.** Each participant is asked about other sensory images that are related to the topic of interest. For instance, the interviewer might ask participants what is (and what is not) the color, taste, smell, touch, sound, and emotion of "a product to refresh the spirit." The interviewer probes each answer to explicate its meaning and relevance for the participant.
7. **Vignette.** Participants may be asked to create a short story or movie that expresses important ideas about the topic. If necessary, participants are prompted to describe the location, time of day, and season; who, if anyone, was present; what else was happening; and so on.
8. **Digital imaging.** Finally, at the end of the interview, each participant creates a summary digital image with the skilled assistance of a computer graphics imager. When the image is finished, the participant gives a verbal description, which serves as an interpretative tour through the summary image. Thus, the digital image provides a visual and verbal summary of the participant's thoughts and feelings about the topic of interest.

This ZMET collage represents one consumer's view of advertising. How would you interpret this collage?

This is another consumer's view of advertising represented in a ZMET collage. What would your collage look like?

CONSUMER INVOLVEMENT

Motivation evokes an experience of involvement for consumers. The final portion of this chapter discusses this important outcome of motivation. Consumer involvement is a function of the goal object, the individual, and the decision situation. Consumers' interests and involvements fluctuate over time and situations. Stimuli within a specific situation evoke a level of personal importance or interest for the consumer.[59] Involvement becomes activated when personal needs, values, or self-concept are stimulated within a given situation. Consumers can be involved with various goal objects, including product categories, brands, ads, media, decisions, and activities.[60] For example, a consumer may be involved with motorcycles, or with Harley-Davidson motorcycles, or advertisements that feature motorcycles because they remind him of his youth, or male-oriented adventure magazines that also happen to promote motorcycles, or he may simply be trying to purchase a form of transportation for his teenage son, or perhaps he loves the physical feeling of riding motorcycles. Of course, he may be simultaneously involved with motorcycles in all these different but potentially complementary ways. This is true for Delia and cosmetics. Delia is a 21-year-old Romanian woman who works as a clerk, but has in the past year become both an Avon and an Oriflame representative. She is involved with cosmetics and her involvement is clearly evidenced by the prominent way she displays her cosmetics, right under the TV, for everyone to see. She feels that TV and magazines were more important than other people in her evolving interest in cosmetics, but she also observes that "today for any job, they ask you to be attractive." Delia illustrates that involvement can be aroused by many related

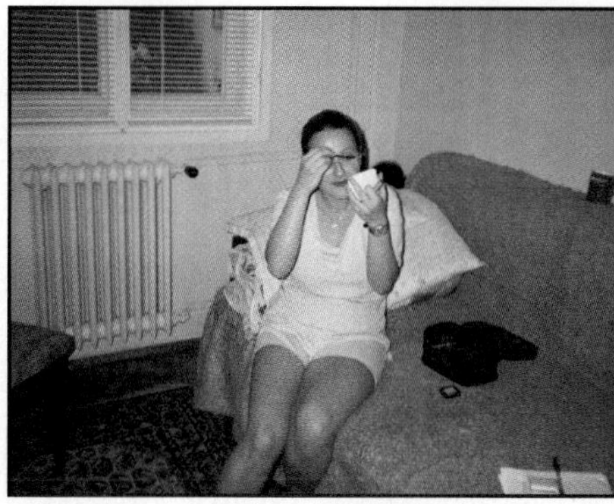

This young Romanian woman is involved with cosmetics.

goal objects including product categories, brands, media, and activities. Delia believes mascara is especially important because it "gives light to the eyes." In this photo Delia illustrates her use of mascara. It's very important for marketers to understand the object(s) of consumer involvement. Consider the advertisment for Yoplait drinkable yogurt that appeared in a male-oriented British soccer magazine. This ad may provoke involvement, exclusive of the product, brand, or decision situation. This picture is visually surprising, perhaps even disgusting, puzzling us at first as to its meaning. In Chapter 8 we draw attention to a variety of advertising and marketing techniques employed to involve consumers, capturing their attention and interest.

Creating involvement in the ad through shock.

Types and Characteristics of Consumer Involvement

Involvement can include *heightened thinking and processing information about the goal object,* referred to as **cognitive involvement.** Ads that provide a detailed enumeration of information about a product or websites that include comprehensive brand comparisons appeal to cognitive involvement. Involvement can also or instead *include heightened feelings and emotional energy,* referred to as **affective involvement.** Ads that encourage people to experience the feelings and sensations associated with a product are stimulating affective involvement. Marketing can stimulate one or the other or both types of involvement. Consider the ad for Agria that appeared in a Swedish hunting dog magazine. Even outside of this highly specialized context, the ad stimulates positive emotional involvement because of the objects included in the ad.

Two car advertisements taken from the same issue of *Motor Trend* magazine illustrate how cognitive and affective appeals can be used with different brands of the same product. Shown on page 284 are two pages of a six-page ad for Infiniti QX4. The promotion includes lots of detailed information about the specific features of the car. This ad appeals to cognitive involvement. By contrast, a two-page

Creating involvement in the ad through positive emotions.

spread for Jaguar promotes the sensation of driving the car, especially the first 5.4 seconds. This ad appeals to affective involvement.

People who purchase *Motor Trend* magazine are probably involved with cars. Some may be car enthusiasts who are intrinsically interested in cars over a long period of time. Consumers who show *interest in an offering or activity over a long period of time* are said to have **enduring involvement.** Consumer Chronicles 7.1 introduced a consumer, Chris, who has enduring involvement with cars. Some people who read this magazine are currently in the market to purchase a car and are trying to gather information to reach this goal. These consumers have *a temporary interest in the goal object* and are characterized by **situational involvement.** Many aspects of the decision situation can influence situational involvement. The more important the reason for purchase, the greater the consumer involvement. The greater the social pressure for purchase, the greater the involvement. The faster that a decision has to be made, the greater the involvement. The more irrevocable, or final, a decision is, the greater the involvement. Situational purchase or consumption involvement levels increase when financial risk and social risk are high. If consumers are required to invest a lot of money to buy a product or service, then this financial risk catches their attention. They are highly motivated to make the right choice and find this choice to be personally relevant. In the same way, if the potential social costs are high, this decision situation becomes both interesting and relevant.

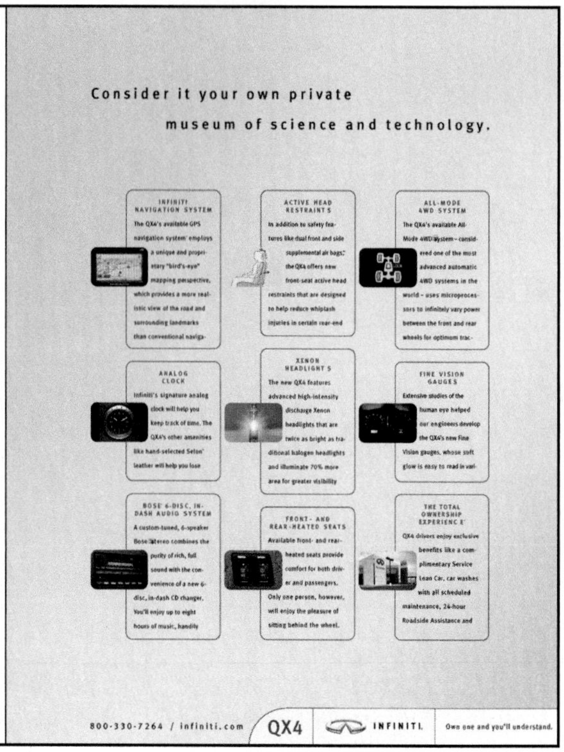

The Infiniti ad encourages cognitive involvement, while the Jaguar ad encourages affective involvement.

When involvement peaks, it is referred to as **flow.** A flow experience is when a person's *attention is completely absorbed by the activity or the goal object.* This kind of experience creates a merging of action and awareness. Achieving flow requires a clear goal, a strong sense of whether progress is being made, and skilled performance—accomplishing the goal requires effort and demands the individual's capabilities. Many people report flow as an outcome of engaging in leisure activities.[61] The copy for an L.L. Bean advertisement, shown below, reflects the centrality of flow activities in con-

Many leisure activities provide a sense of flow to participants.

sumers' lives. Any activity that fully engages an individual can be a source of a flow experience. Can you think of activities that are fully absorbing for you? How do these activities make you feel?

Marketing Implications of Different Levels of Involvement

High involvement and low involvement affect attention, information search, purchase, and consumption satisfaction differently. Thus, the marketing strategies used vary with level of involvement, and marketers use involvement to identify segments in the market. Because involvement affects decision making, attitudes, and shopping activities, we will revisit some marketing implications of involvement in Chapters 15 and 16.

HIGH-INVOLVEMENT PURCHASE AND CONSUMPTION When consumers are highly involved with a purchase, they are willing to expend greater levels of shopping effort. They are concerned with the purchase and feel that it is important to their life.[62] Consequently, they are willing to spend more time and money and visit a greater number of stores. With high involvement, attention is increased and more importance is attached to the stimulus object. Memory is also enhanced. The purchase process is more complex for highly involved consumers, and they are motivated to make a careful purchase decision.[63] They search extensively for relevant information about products or brands that are personally relevant. They consciously evaluate alternatives and make detailed comparisons before making a final selection. High-involvement consumers may have strongly held beliefs about brands and perceive great differences between brands in a product class. They often have a favorite or preferred brand and are brand loyal, but may also use brand experimentation as a way of learning about new alternatives for future purchase decisions.[64]

Consumers with high involvement place greater importance on major information sources and engage in an active search process, and they are heavy users of newspapers and advertising.[65] However, they are more likely to generate negative cognitive responses to product-related messages.[66] Highly involved consumers find shopping more interesting and enjoyable. They are more likely to value purchasing and shopping activities than consumers of low involvement.[67] Involved consumers like to get the best value for their money and are much more concerned with attributes that assure value in purchasing, such as favorable return policies.[68]

Highly involved consumers often show more satisfaction with products.[69] Since high involvement motivates consumers to spend time and effort to avoid postpurchase dissatisfaction, these consumers generally report higher satisfaction and less negative disconfirmation with the product they purchase. However, there is some question about how satisfaction levels change over time. For example, two months after purchase, highly involved automobile owners showed a decline in their satisfaction. In contrast, low-involvement consumers' satisfaction increased after the two-month period.[70] As in many areas of consumer behavior, we don't know much about how involvement levels ebb and flow over time and how the relationship between involvement and other variables, such as satisfaction, may vary over time.

LOW-INVOLVEMENT PURCHASE AND CONSUMPTION It is important to keep in mind that in many purchase situations the consumer couldn't care less; that is, there is low involvement. For paper towels, consumers may make the purchase, switch brands, and ignore commercials. Consumers are thinking about the important decisions in their lives; they don't have time to worry about what paper towels to buy.[71] The average supermarket has more than 10,000 brands on display. By way of comparison, the average U.S. college graduate has a vocabulary of 7,000 words. Given these numbers, there is great risk of information overload. The only way to survive is to take many decision shortcuts. Decision making is minimal for low-involvement products.

Low-involvement consumers are not active information seekers or active information processors. They tend to make few comparisons among brands or among product attributes.[72] Often, low-involvement consumers are indifferent among a group of brands. They don't see a lot of differences between these brands and view them as reasonable substitutes for one another. That is, they don't have special preferences for a particular brand, and brand loyalty is not very strong. The purchase decision may result from simple recognition of the product on the shelf. Since low-involvement purchasers are not paying much attention, they may get easily confused, or they may make mistakes. In many instances, however, the low-involvement purchaser may not really care too much about the mistakes. If a purchase error is made, the consumer might not even notice.

Consumption experiences may also not involve much arousal or involvement. For instance, if an employee is late for work and rushing, she may not really notice which breakfast cereal she is eating. Later in the day, if a co-worker asks what she had for breakfast, she may not be able to say with certainty. There definitely was eating and chewing involved. But attention levels may be so low that the behavior is barely noticed and quickly forgotten.

Marketers of a product that evokes low involvement may consider strategies that will increase consumers' involvement with a product or brand over a short period or for longer periods. For example, special promotions such as sweepstakes or seasonal clearance sales may temporarily raise consumers' involvement levels. The level of involvement consumers have with a certain product can be influenced over longer periods of time by creative marketing strategies, such as effective advertising or product usage campaigns. Also, marketers may link low-involvement products with high-involvement issues, such as health. For example, marketers may link low-involvement food products with a high-involvement health attribute such as cancer prevention.

On the one hand, brand managers of low-involvement products may not be thrilled with the idea that consumers don't really care about their product. On the other hand, consumers in low-involvement situations are willing to try unfamiliar brands without a full search for information and without forming a strong preference first. Complete evaluation of the brand comes after the brand has been purchased and used. Thus, marketers can appeal to low-involvement consumers through extensive distribution networks or through clever in-store displays.

INVOLVEMENT AS A SEGMENTATION VARIABLE Involvement can be a useful segmentation variable. For instance, consumers can be segmented into the following four groups based around their involvement with a product category and with particular brands:

1. **Brand loyalists**—*those who are highly involved both with the product category and with particular brands.*
2. **Information seekers**—*those who are highly involved with a product category but who do not have a preferred brand.*
3. **Routine brand buyers**—*those who are not highly involved with the product category but are involved with a particular brand in that category.*
4. **Brand switchers**—*those who are not involved with the product category or with particular brands.*

For each of the above descriptions, try to list a product category or brand for which you would fall into that segment.

MEASURING INVOLVEMENT Both means-ends chains and ZMET can also be used to understand involvement because they show how product attributes are related to important aspects of the self and basic consumer problems and goals. Because we lack a clear definition about the essential components of involvement, there is a lot of variation in the measurement of involvement. Some measures focus on cognitive involvement, others on behaviors or outcomes of involvement, and others on measuring the enduring involvement the product has for the consumer. In short, there are many different quantitative measures to assess the degree of involvement people have with products, promotions, purchases, consumption experiences, and so on.[73] Most agree that involvement should be measured on a continuum rather than as a dichotomy of high and low involvement, and many use multi-item scales.

One measure of involvement is called the Revised Personal Involvement Inventory, the **RPII,** shown in Exhibit 7.4.[74] The scales displayed in the exhibit make use of the semantic differential method. The semantic differential consists of a series of bipolar items, each measured on a seven-point scale. There are three main advantages of the RPII. First, it contains only 10 items. This makes it easy to include in a survey or experiment. Second, the RPII is divided into two overall factors—cognitive and affective—consistent with involvement theory. A third major advantage of the RPII is that it can be used to measure involvement with a wide variety of stimulus objects, including products, ads, or purchase decisions.

EXHIBIT 7.4

The Revised Personal Involvement Inventory (RPII)

Five cognitive items:

Important	___	___	___	___	___	___	___	Unimportant
Relevant	___	___	___	___	___	___	___	Irrelevant*
Means a lot to me	___	___	___	___	___	___	___	Means nothing to me
Valuable	___	___	___	___	___	___	___	Worthless
Needed	___	___	___	___	___	___	___	Not needed

Five emotional items:

Interesting	___	___	___	___	___	___	___	Uninteresting
Exciting	___	___	___	___	___	___	___	Unexciting*
Appealing	___	___	___	___	___	___	___	Unappealing*
Fascinating	___	___	___	___	___	___	___	Mundane*
Involving	___	___	___	___	___	___	___	Not involving

*Indicates item is reverse scored.

SUMMARY

This chapter stresses that consumers are uniquely shaped by cultural and social settings and are constantly adapting based on what works and what doesn't. As such, consumers' motivations and goals depend on how they interpret macro-environmental factors, local context and social networks within their own personal history, circumstances, life themes, and values. Although all human cultures probably share some common bases of motivation, there is not a single set of universal motives that apply cross-culturally. Sigmund Freud, Carl Jung, Abraham Maslow, Henry Murray, and their many followers have struggled to advance our understanding of motivation and their theories are an important background for discussion. However, these theories fail to provide a cultural perspective on motivation. For example, one important difference among how consumers interpret their world is whether they grew up in a culture that stresses independent or interdependent goals. Consumer goals such as power and uniqueness are likely to be much more important in independent than interdependent cultures. Goals such as achievement, affiliation, and self-esteem may be important in both but have different meanings and actions associated with them. Motivation is an inner drive that reflects goal-directed arousal. Goals are ends or aspirations that direct action. Motivation drives behaviors consistent with the goal and creates a willingness to expend time and energy to achieve the goal. Involvement is the psychological outcome of motivation and reflects the perceived level of personal importance or interest evoked by a stimulus within a specific situation. Consumers can be involved with various goal objects, including product categories, brands, ads, media, decisions, and activities. It's very important for marketers to understand the object(s) of consumer involvement. Involvement in a goal object can be enduring or situational and can be cognitive and/or affective. High-involvement consumers differ in many important ways from low-involvement consumers. They have different search patterns, knowledge, attitudes, decisions, consumption experiences, and consumption outcomes. Pursuing goals, motivated consumers may feel interest, excitement, anxiety, passion, engagement, and flow. We describe a measure that can be used to profile consumers' involvement in a goal object.

Consumers have multiple and even conflicting goals and encounter numerous obstacles in trying to achieve their goals. Achieving consumer goals requires effort, ability, opportunity, and trade-offs among various goals. Goal-striving is the execution of actions needed to achieve a particular goal. Goals can be thought of at many different levels represented with a goal hierarchy. Marketers are often interested in the connections consumers make between and among various goals. We describe two techniques that can be used to uncover relationships among consumer motives and goals. Although many consumers may have a similar preference, they may have very different reasons for that preference that reflect cultural, situational, and individual differences. For example, media, social networks, self-concept, life themes, and life projects all help shape our consumption motives and goals. And role transitions such as graduation, marriage, or birth of a child can dramatically alter our motives and goals. Social life is an important source of consumer motives and goals, and many consumer behaviors are motivated by our desire to be integrated or affiliated with other people and by our desire to be different or distinct from other people. We accomplish this through the process of social comparison.

KEY TERMS

ability 260
achievement motive 272
affective involvement 282
affiliation motive 274
approach-approach conflict 276
approach-avoidance conflict 276
archetypes 268
avoidance-avoidance conflict 276
brand loyalists 286
brand switchers 286

KEY TERMS

cognitive involvement 282
culture-bound 271
drive 259
effort 259
ego 267
ego needs 270
enduring involvement 283
flow 284
focal goal 260
goal hierarchy 260
goals 259
goal-striving 259
id 268
independent goals 272
information seekers 286
interdependent goals 272
involvement 259
life projects 263
life themes 263
Maslow's need hierarchy 270
means-ends chain 278
metaphor 279
motivation 259
neural Darwinism 261
physiological needs 270
power motive 273
role transitions 265
routine brand buyers 286
RPII 287
safety and security needs 270
secondary control 273
self-actualization needs 270
self-enhancing bias 275
situational involvement 283
social needs 270
subordinate goals 260
superego 268
superordinate goals 260
tacit knowledge 279
uniqueness motive 274
ZMET 279

REVIEW QUESTIONS

1. Choose a product, brand, or activity that you are involved with. Drawing on Exhibit 7.1, illustrate how macro-environmental factors, local context and social networks, personal history, life themes, and life projects have or have not influenced your level of involvement with this goal object.
2. Drawing on your own experience, outline three different consumer situations where you felt motivational conflict: approach-approach, approach-avoidance, and avoidance-avoidance. What were your feelings? Did you resolve the conflicts? If so, how?
3. Describe a consumer goal you are actively pursuing, striving toward. How do effort, ability, and opportunity influence your goal-striving behavior? Can you think of goals that you have put on hold? What were the reasons?
4. Build a collage that represents your various life themes and life projects and how they influence your consumption behavior. In a few paragraphs provide an interpretation of your collage.
5. Select an advertisement that seems to be based on an independent view of the self and appeals to the achievement need. How might this advertisement be adapted for an interdependent view of the self?
6. Select a need described in this chapter as salient in cultures with an interdependent view of the self. Design an ad that would appeal to one of these needs.
7. Survey three friends that use a particular brand of a product. Use the means-ends chain technique to find out why they use that product. Compare and contrast their chains as well as their termination points. Do they all have the same basic reason for using that particular brand?

8. Evaluate the following statement: Advertisers manipulate consumers and create wants and desires that wouldn't exist otherwise. Do you agree or disagree? Identify an example from the marketplace where this statement seems to be true. Identify another example where the statement appears to be false.
9. Find a print ad designed to appeal to each of the five needs discussed in depth in this chapter. Describe in detail how the need is represented in the ad, emphasizing both visual and verbal cues.

CASES

YOU MAKE THE CALL

"WHY HAGGLE?"

"Name your own price . . . and save!" That may be the slogan of Priceline.com. But name your own price is a misnomer. You might not realize this from news reports, but almost without exception, the analyses of these so-called name-your-price businesses have missed the most basic point: Priceline has never run a name-your-own-price business. It is a propose-your-own-price business—something altogether different.

The so-called name-your-price approach to business may well harness the power of the Internet, data mining, and other software secrets patented by Jay Walker, the founder of Priceline. But in the end, the business is not about naming prices, but haggling.

Haggling is a venerable and preferred price-making mechanism for certain goods in the Arab world, in sub-Saharan Africa, and even in Latin America. Haggling can even be found in exchange economies lacking money such as historic societies in the South Pacific. But generally haggling is most developed for high-value goods and luxuries. Over the past century or so, consumers in Western capitalist societies have agreed, via social contract, that for everyday commerce it is more efficient not to haggle over everyday goods.

Indeed for many consumers, one true breakthrough of the Web has been to reduce the haggling and bickering involved in buying a car and other big-ticket items. Do your research online and you can get a pretty good idea of the dealer's invoice price for any given automobile or home theater, for example.

Brian Elk, chief spokesman for Priceline, says that seven million customers have used the company's service and that nearly 40 percent have come back again. "In our view," Mr. Elk said, "name your price means make a reasonable offer, and we'll see what we can do for you." Generally, he said, Priceline's consumers of air tickets, hotel rooms, and car rentals are college students, retired people, or parents of large families—"People who have time they are willing to trade, if they can get deep discounts." Some think the model can be extended to items such as airline seats, theater seats, and other goods for which the seller bears a fairly low marginal cost for each additional item, particularly if the items have no value at all if they go unsold by takeoff or curtain time.

So maybe it's worth saving $300 on an airline ticket to Barcelona, Spain, next Wednesday at 0200 h via Istanbul even if a direct flight at noon was what you originally had in mind. But isn't life too short to go online and dicker over a jar of JIF peanut butter—particularly if there is no certainty that the price you "name" bears any relationship to what somebody's willing to sell it for? At a time when the Web is dangling the promise of ending car-dealer dickering in our lifetimes, would anyone think the public is eager to bring haggling to the meat case at Safeway or any other grocery store?

Not surprisingly perhaps, WebHouse is unwinding its operation after its founder, Mr. Walker, pulled the plug. He and other WebHouse executives blamed the current investment climate, not their business model, for failing to give the grocery-haggling service enough time to prove itself. A WebHouse spokesman said the company's typical customer was "a woman, shopping for her family, who would be flexible on the brands she wanted and who wanted to save money." He conceded that the system—make an offer for Ragu and wait for a response, bid on Cream of Wheat and see if it takes—demanded more time and patience than many people might tolerate. "One of the complaints we hear overwhelmingly from consumers and manufacturers was, 'Look this takes too long; it's too hard,'" the spokesman said.

QUESTIONS

1. How might Maslow's hierarchy help to position Priceline and other similar services more effectively?
2. How might Murray's theory be used to improve marketing communications for Priceline and other similar services?
3. In what ways will a knowledge of consumer involvement be relevant to the success of offerings such as Priceline and other similar services?

Source: Adapted from Tim Race, "There's Just One Thing Wrong with Name-Your-Own-Price Businesses: You're Not Naming Your Own Price," The New York Times, *October 23, 2000, p. C4.*

CASES

ENDNOTES

1. Deborah J. MacInnis, Christine Moorman, and Bernard J. Jaworski, "Enhancing and Measuring Consumers' Motivation, Opportunity, and Ability to Process Brand Information from Ads," *Journal of Marketing,* October 1991, pp. 32–53; Roy G. D'Andrade, "Schemas and Motivation," in *Human Motives and Cultural Models,* ed. Roy D'Andrade and Claudia Strauss (Cambridge: Cambridge University Press, 1992), pp. 23–44; and Douglas G. Mook, *Motivation: The Organization of Action* (New York: W. W. Norton, 1987).
2. Brian Mullen and Craig Johnson, *The Psychology of Consumer Behavior* (Hillsdale, NJ: Lawrence Erlbaum, 1990), p. 3.
3. Richard P. Bagozzi and Utpal Dholakia, "Goal Setting and Goal Striving in Consumer Behavior," *Journal of Marketing* 63 (special issue, 1999), pp. 19–32; Richard P. Bagozzi and Elizabeth A. Edwards, "Goal Setting and Goal Pursuit in the Regulation of Body Weight," *Psychology and Health* 13, no. 4 (1998), pp. 593–621; and Richard P. Bagozzi and Paul R. Warshaw, "Trying to Consume," *Journal of Consumer Research* 17, no. 2 (1990), pp. 127–40.
4. MacInnis and Jaworski, "Information Processing from Advertisements".
5. Jim Bettman, in *An Information Processing Theory of Consumer Choice* (Reading, MA: Addison-Wesley, 1979), pioneered thinking about how a desired end state is related to goals and subgoals, and how goals interface with decision processes. See, also, Bagozzi and Dholakia, "Goal Setting and Goal Striving in Consumer Behavior."
6. Robin A. Coulter, Linda L. Price, and Lawrence F. Feick, "Origins of Product Involvement and Brand Commitment: Women and Cosmetics in Post-Socialist Central Europe," working paper, University of Connecticut, Storrs, CT (2002).
7. Donnel A. Briley, Michael W. Morris, and Itamar Simonson, "Reasons as Carriers of Culture: Dynamic versus Dispositional Models of Cultural Influence on Decision Making, *Journal of Consumer Research* 27 (September 2000), pp. 157–78.
8. Paul DiMaggio, "Culture and Cognition," *Annual Review of Sociology* 23 (1997), pp. 263–87.
9. For an eloquent and elaborated discussion see Russell W. Belk, Güliz Ger, and Søren Askegaard, "The Missing Streetcar Named Desire," in *The Why of Consumption: Contemporary Perspectives on Consumer Motives, Goals, and Desires*, ed. S. Ratneshwar, David Glen Mick, and Cynthia Huffman (New York and London: Routledge, 2000), pp. 98–139.

10. Claudia Strauss, "Models and Motives," in *Human Motives and Cultural Models,* ed. Roy D'Andrade and Claudia Strauss (Cambridge: Cambridge University Press, 1992), p. 3.
11. There are many books and articles on evolving ideas of the mind. Two good articles are Steven Levy, "Dr. Edelman's Brain," *The New Yorker,* May 2, 1994, pp. 62–73; and Gerald Zaltman, "Consumer Researchers: Take a Hike!" *Journal of Consumer Research* 26 (March 2000), pp. 423–28. See, also, Leslie Brothers, *Friday's Footprint: How Society Shapes the Human Mind* (New York: Oxford University Press, 1997); Gerald M. Edelman, *Bright Air, Brilliant Fire: On the Matter of the Mind* (New York: Basic Books, 1994); and J. Allan Hobson, *Consciousness* (New York: Scientific American Library, 1999).
12. Naomi Quinn and Claudia Strauss, "Cognition and Culture," in *Cultural Models in Language and Thought,* ed. D. Holland and N. Quinn (Cambridge: Cambridge University Press, 1993), pp. 3–40; and Michelle Z. Rosaldo, "Toward an Anthropology of Self and Feeling," in *Culture Theory: Essays on Mind, Self, and Emotion,* ed. R. Shweder and R. A. LaVine (Cambridge: Cambridge University Press, 1984), pp. 137–57.
13. Cynthia Huffman, S. Ratneshwar, and David Glen Mick, "Consumer Goal Structures and Goal-Determination Processes: An Integrative Framework," in *The Why of Consumption: Contemporary Perspectives on Consumer Motives, Goals, and Desires*, ed. S. Ratneshwar, David Glen Mick, and Cynthia Huffman (New York and London: Routledge, 2000), pp. 9–35.
14. Kathy Peiss, *Hope in a Jar: The Making of the American Beauty Culture* (New York: Metropolitan Books, 1998); and Craig J. Thompson and Diana L. Haytko, "Speaking of Fashion: Consumers' Uses of Fashion Discourses and the Appropriation of Countervailing Cultural Meanings," *Journal of Consumer Research* 24 (June 1997), pp. 15–43.
15. Huffman et al., "Consumer Goal Structures," pp. 15, 18; and David Glen Mick and Claus Buhl, "A Meaning-Based Model of Advertising Experiences," *Journal of Consumer Research* 19 (December 1992), pp. 317–38.
16. DiMaggio, "Culture and Cognition."
17. Gerald Zaltman and Melanie Wallendorf, *Consumer Behavior* (New York: Wiley, 1979), p. 365.
18. Ibid.
19. Carl G. Jung, M. L. von Vranz, Joseph L. Henderson, Jolande Jacobi, and Aniela Jaffe, *Man and His Symbols* (Garden City, NY: Doubleday, 1964).
20. David G. Meyers, *Psychology* (New York: Worth Publishers, 1998).
21. Russell W. Belk, "Third World Consumer Culture," in *Marketing and Development: Toward Broader Dimensions,* ed. Erodoan Kumcu and A. Fuat Firat (Greenwich, CT: JAI Press, 1988), pp. 103–27; Güliz Ger; "The Positive and Negative Effects of Marketing on Socioeconomic Development: The Turkish Case," *Journal of Consumer Policy* 15, no. 3 (1992), pp. 229–54; and Güliz Ger and Russell W. Belk, "I'd Like to Buy the World a Coke: Consumptionscapes of the 'Less Affluent World,'" *Journal of Public Policy* 19, no. 3 (1996), pp. 271–304.
22. Güliz Ger, "Human Development and Humane Consumption: Well-Being beyond the Good Life," *Journal of Public Policy and Marketing* 16 (Spring 1997), pp. 110–25. Recent research on the brain, discussed later, also lends support to the primacy of beauty/aesthetics as a need.
23. Edwin C. Nevis, "Cultural Assumptions and Productivity: The United States and China," *Sloan Management Review* 24, no. 3 (Spring 1983), pp. 17–29.
24. For some examples of research related to this, see Lynn Kahle, David Bousch, and Pamela Homer, "Broken Rungs in Abraham's Ladder: Is Maslow's Hierarchy Hierarchical?" in *Proceedings of the Society for Consumer Psychology,* ed. David Schumann (Nashville, TN: The Society for Consumer Psychology, 1988), pp. 11–16; and Richard Yalch and Frederic Brunel, "Need Hierarchies in Consumer Judgments of Product Designs: Is It Time to Reconsider Maslow's Theory?" in *Advances in Consumer Research,* vol. 23, ed. Kim Corfman and John Lynch (Provo, UT: Association for Consumer Research, 1996), pp. 405–10.
25. Mike Herrington, "What Does the Customer Want?" *Across the Board* 30 (April 1993), p. 33.
26. Henry A. Murray, *Explorations in Personality* (New York: Oxford University Press, 1938); see also E. R. Hilgard, *Psychology in America: A Historical Survey* (New York: Harcourt Brace Jovanovich, 1987). For example, see Hazel Rose Markus and Shinobu Kitayama, "Culture and

the Self: Implications for Cognition, Emotion, and Motivation," *Psychological Review* 98 (April 1991), pp. 224–53.
27. M. M. Suarez-Orozco, "Psychological Aspects of Achievement Motivation among Recent Hispanic Immigrants," in *Anthropological Perspectives on Dropping Out,* ed. H. Trueba, G. Spindler, and L. Spindler (London: Falmer Press, 1989), pp. 99–116.
28. John L. Lastovicka, Lance A. Bettencourt, Renée Shaw Hughner, and Ronald J. Kuntze, "Lifestyle of the Tight and Frugal: Theory and Measurement," *Journal of Consumer Research* 26 (June 1999), pp. 85–98; and Russell W. Belk, "Worldly Possessions: Issues and Criticisms," in *Advances in Consumer Research,* vol. 10, ed. Richard P. Bagozzi and Alice M. Tybout (Ann Arbor, MI: Association for Consumer Research, 1983), pp. 514–19.
29. Anthony Chun-Tung Lowe and David R. Corkindale, "Differences in 'Cultural Values' and Their Effects on Responses to Marketing Stimuli: A Cross-Cultural Study Between Australians and Chinese from the People's Republic of China," *European Journal of Marketing* 32, no. 9–10 (1998), pp. 843–67.
30. David C. McClelland, *The Achievement Motive* (New York: Appleton-Century-Crofts, Inc., 1953), p. 79.
31. See Markus and Kitayama, "Culture and the Self," for a discussion and bibliography.
32. Constance Hill and Celia T. Romm, "The Role of Mothers as Gift Givers: A Comparison across Three Cultures," in *Advances in Consumer Research,* vol. 23, ed. Kim Corfman and John Lynch (Provo, UT: Association for Consumer Research, 1996), pp. 21–29.
33. D. G. Winter, *The Power Motive* (New York: Free Press, 1973).
34. J. Veroff, "Assertive Motivations: Achievement versus Power," in *Motivation and Society,* ed. D. G. Winter and A. J. Stewart (San Francisco: Jossey-Bass, 1982).
35. David C. McClelland, *Human Motivation* (New York: Cambridge University Press, 1987).
36. Winter, *The Power Motive.*
37. Courtney Leatherman, "A Prominent Feminist Theorist Recounts How She Faced Charges of Sex Harassment," *Chronicle of Higher Education,* March 7, 1997, p. A45.
38. C. R. Snyder and Howard L. Fromkin, *Uniqueness: The Human Pursuit of Difference* (New York: Plenum Press, 1980), p. 198.
39. Ibid.
40. M. Lynn, "Scarcity Effects on Value: A Quantitative Review of Commodity Theory Literature," *Psychology and Marketing* 8 (1991), pp. 43–57.
41. C. R. Snyder, "Product Scarcity by Need for Uniqueness Interaction," *Basic and Applied Social Psychology* 13, no. 1 (1992), pp. 9–24.
42. Alladi Venkatesh, "Modernity and Postmodernity: A Synthesis or Antithesis?" in *Proceedings of the 1989 AMA Winter Educators' Conference,* ed. T. Childers (Chicago: American Marketing Association, 1989), pp. 99–104.
43. A. Fuat Firat and Alladi Venkatesh, "Postmodernity: The Age of Marketing," *International Journal of Research in Marketing* 10 (1993), pp. 227–50.
44. McClelland, *Human Motivation,* p. 347.
45. An excellent discussion of the social dimension of brain activity and the social mind is provided in Leslie Brothers, *Friday's Footprint: How Society Shapes the Human Mind* (New York: Oxford University Press, 1997).
46. Firat and Venkatesh, "Postmodernity."
47. Susan Harter, "Causes, Correlates and the Functional Role of Global Self-Worth: A Life Span Perspective," in *Competence Considered,* ed. Robert J. Sternberg and John Kolligian Jr. (New Haven, CT: Yale University Press, 1987), pp. 67–97; and B. E. Whitley Jr. and Irene Frieze, "Children's Causal Attributions for Success and Failure in Achievement Settings: A Meta-Analysis," *Journal of Educational Psychology* 77 (1985), pp. 608–16.
48. L. T. Doi, *The Anatomy of Conformity: The Individual versus Society* (Tokyo: Kodansha, 1986).
49. Patti Williams and Jennifer L. Aaker, "Can Mixed Emotions Peacefully Coexist?" *Journal of Consumer Research* 28 (March 2000), pp. 636–49; and Richard P. Bagozzi, Nancy Wong, and Youjae Yi, "The Role of Culture and Gender in the Relationship between Positive and Negative Affect," *Cognition and Emotion* 6 (November 1999), pp. 641–72.

50. Lynn R. Kahle, Raymond R. Liu, Gregory M. Rose, and Kim Woo-Sung, "Dialectical Thinking in Consumer Decision Making," *Journal of Consumer Psychology* 9 (January 2000), pp. 53–58.
51. Jennifer Aaker and Patti Williams, "Empathy versus Pride: The Influence of Emotional Appeals across Cultures," *Journal of Consumer Research* 25 (December 1998), pp. 241–61; and Jennifer Aaker and Angela Y. Lee, "'I' Seek Pleasures and 'We' Avoid Pains: The Role of Self-Regulatory Goals in Information Processing and Persuasion," *Journal of Consumer Research* 28 (June 2001), pp. 33–49.
52. Linda M. Scott, "Images in Advertising: The Need for a Theory of Visual Rhetoric," *Journal of Consumer Research* 21 (September 1994), pp. 813–38.
53. Jagdish N. Sheth, Banwari Mittal, and Bruce Newman, *Customer Behavior: Consumer Behavior and Beyond* (Fort Worth, TX: Dryden Press, 1999).
54. William D. Wells and David Prensky, *Consumer Behavior* (New York: John Wiley, 1996).
55. ZMET is a patented process. Any use of the process or its constituent elements is prohibited unless under license or by other written permission of the patent holder. This includes indirect, unauthorized third-party use of any aspect of ZMET. Also included under this prohibition is inadvertent use where any party unknowingly uses or accepts use of the process or its elements. Gerald Zaltman, "Rethinking Market Research: Putting People Back In," *Journal of Marketing Research* 34 (November 1997), pp. 424–37.
56. John Allen Paulos. *Once Upon a Number: The Hidden Mathematical Logic of Stories* (New York: Basic Books, 1998); and Catherine Kohler Riessman, *Narrative Analysis* (Newbury Park, CA: Sage Publications, 1993).
57. Jerry Zaltman and Robin Higie Coulter, "Seeing the Voice of the Customer: Metaphor-Based Advertising Research," *Journal of Advertising Research* 35, no. 4 (1995), pp. 35–51.
58. Robin A. Coulter, Gerald Zaltman, and Keith S. Coulter, "Interpreting Consumer Perceptions of Advertising: An Application of the Zaltman Metaphor Elicitation Technique," *Journal of Advertising* 30 (Winter 2001), pp. 1–21.
59. J. H. Antil, "Conceptualization and Operationalization of Involvement," in *Advances in Consumer Research,* ed. T. C. Kinnear (Provo, UT: Association for Consumer Research, 1984), pp. 203–9; and Joel B. Cohen, "Involvement and You: 1,000 Great Ideas," in *Advances in Consumer Research,* ed. R. Bagozzi and A. Tybout (Ann Arbor, MI: Association for Consumer Research, 1983), pp. 325–28.
60. Marsha L. Richins, Peter H. Bloch, and Edward F. McQuarrie, "How Enduring and Situational Involvement Combine to Create Involvement Responses," *Journal of Consumer Psychology,* September 1992, pp. 143–54; J. Craig Andrews, Syed H. Akhter, Srinivas Durvasaula, and Darrel D. Muehling, "The Effect of Advertising Distinctiveness and Message Content Involvement on Cognitive and Affective Responses to Advertising," *Journal of Current Issues and Research in Advertising,* Spring 1992, pp. 45–58; and Richard L. Celsi, Randall L. Rose, and Thomas W. Leigh, "An Exploration of High-Risk Leisure Consumption through Skydiving," *Journal of Consumer Research,* June 1993, pp. 1–23.
61. Mihaly Csikszenthmihalyi, *Flow: The Psychology of Optimal Experience* (New York: Harper and Row, 1990); and Celsi, Rose, and Leigh, "An Exploration of High-Risk Leisure Consumption through Skydiving."
62. R. Ohanian and A. Tashchian, "Consumers' Shopping Effort and Evaluation of Store Image Attributes: The Roles of Purchasing Involvement and Recreational Shopping Interest," *Journal of Applied Business Research* 8, no. 4 (1992), pp. 40–49; and M. E. Salma and A. Tashchian, "Selected Socio-Economic and Demographic Characteristics Associated with Purchase Involvement," *Journal of Advertising* 18, no. 30 (1985), pp. 9–20.
63. G. Laurent and J. N. Kapferer, "Measuring Consumer Involvement Profiles," *Journal of Marketing Research* 22 (1985), pp. 41–53; Salma and Tashchian, "Selected Socio-Economic and Demographic Characteristics Associated with Purchase Involvement"; and Judy L. Zaichkowsky, "Measuring the Involvement Construct," *Journal of Consumer Research* 12 (December 1985), pp. 341–52.
64. Brian Ratchford, "The Economics of Consumer Knowledge," *Journal of Consumer Research* 27 (March 2001), pp. 397–411.

65. Ohanian and Tashchian, "Consumers' Shopping Effort and Evaluation of Store Image Attributes."
66. Peter H. Bloch, "An Exploration into the Scaling of Consumers' Involvement in a Product Class," in *Advances in Consumer Research,* ed. Kent B. Monroe (Ann Arbor, MI: Association for Consumer Research, 1981), pp. 61–65.
67. Laurent and Kapferer, "Measuring Consumer Involvement Profiles."
68. Ohanian and Tashchian, "Consumers' Shopping Effort and Evaluation of Store Image Attributes."
69. Sharon E. Beatty, Lynn R. Kahle, and Pamela Homer, "Theory and Implications," *Journal of Business Research* 16, no. 2 (1988), pp. 149–67.
70. Bloch, "An Exploration into the Scaling of Consumers' Involvement in a Product Class."
71. Judy L. Zaichkowsky, *Defending Your Brand against Imitation* (London: Quorum Books, 1995).
72. Harold H. Kassarjian, "Low Involvement: A Second Look," in *Advances in Consumer Research,* vol. 8, ed. Kent B. Monroe (Ann Arbor, MI: Association for Consumer Research, 1981), pp. 31–34; and Beatty, Kahle, and Homer, "Theory and Implications."
73. For a review of involvement measures in advertising and consumer research, see J. Craig Andrews, Srinivas Durvasula, and Syed H. Akhter, "A Framework for Conceptualizing and Measuring the Involvement Construct in Advertising Research," *Journal of Advertising* 19 (1990), pp. 27–40.
74. Judy L. Zaichkowsky, "The Personal Involvement Inventory: Reduction, Revision, and Application to Advertising," *Journal of Advertising* 23, no. 4 (1994), pp. 59–70; Zaichkowsky, "Measuring the Involvement Construct," p. 342; and Charles Osgood, George J. Suci, and Percy H. Tannenbaum, *The Measurement of Meaning* (Urbana, IL: University of Illinois Press, 1957).

LEARNING OBJECTIVES

After completing this chapter, you should be able to:

- Explain the meaning of and relationship between perceptions and sensations and discuss some basic facts about the classic five sensory receptors: vision, smell, hearing, touch, and taste.
- Describe how sensory thresholds are used by marketers, including marketing applications of Weber's law.
- Outline the process through which our sensory systems select, organize, and interpret stimuli, including preattentive processing, perceptual selection, organization and categorization, interpretation, and elaboration.
- Describe some basic tools consumers use in primitive categorization, including grouping, figure and ground, and closure, and develop marketing applications using these three tools.
- Explain how elaboration of marketing stimuli influences consumer perceptions and preferences.
- Define some basic features of perceptual preferences and consumer tastes.

THE TOTAL PACKAGE[1]

Few experiences in contemporary life offer the visual intensity of a Safeway, a Kroger's, a Piggly Wiggly, a TESCO, or a Woolworth's grocery story. No marketplace in the world, neither the bazaars of Morocco nor the Indian markets of Guatemala's Lake Atitlan offer so many different goods with such focused salesmanship as your neighborhood supermarket. You're exposed to a thousand different products a minute; no wonder it's tiring to shop. There are some major differences between the supermarket and a traditional marketplace. The cacophony of the traditional market has given way to programmed, innocuous music, punctuated by enthusiastically intoned commercials. A stroll through a traditional market offers an array of sensuous aromas; if you are conscious of smelling something in a supermarket, there is a problem. But the most notable difference is it replaces people who sell with packages that do the work.

Packages are an inescapable part of modern life. They are omnipresent and invisible, deplored and ignored. During most of your waking moments, there are one or more packages within your field of vision. Packages are so omnipresent they slip beneath conscious attention, though many packages are designed so that people will respond to them even if they're not paying attention.

The package is useful to the shopper. It is a tool for simplifying and speeding decisions. Packages promise, and usually deliver predictability. One reason you don't think about packages is that you don't need to. The candy bar, the aspirin, the baking powder, or the beer in the old familiar package may, at times, be touted as new and improved, but it will rarely be very different.

With its thousands of images and messages, the supermarket is as visually dense, if not as beautiful, as a Gothic cathedral. It is as complex and predatory as a tropical rainforest. It is more than a person can possibly take in during an ordinary half hour of shopping, and some researchers have spoken of the trancelike state that pushing a cart through this environment induces. The visual intensity that overwhelms shoppers is precisely the thing that makes design of packages so crucial. Just because you're not looking at a package doesn't mean you don't see it. And most of the time, you see far more than a container and a label. You see a personality, a familiar friend, an attitude toward life, perhaps even a set of beliefs.

The similar appearance of supermarkets throughout the world should not be interpreted as the evidence of a single global consumer culture. In fact, most companies that do business internationally redesign their packages for each market. The principal reason is that people in different places have different expectations and make different uses of packaging.

The United States and Japan, the world's two leading industrial powers, have almost opposite approaches to packaging. Packaging is recognized as an expression of culture in Japan and largely ignored in America. Japanese packaging is designed to be appreciated; American packaging is calculated to be accepted. Foods that only Japanese eat—even humble ones like refrigerated prepared fish cakes—have wrappings that resemble handmade paper or leaves. Beautiful, traditionally designed wrapping accommodate scannable bar codes. Such products look Japanese and are intended to do so. Products that are foreign, such as coffee, look foreign, even to the point of having only Roman lettering on the can.

We speak of global villages and international markets, but packages reveal some unexpected cultural boundaries. Why are Canadians willing to drink milk out of flexible plastic pouches that fit into reusable plastic holders, while residents of the United States are believed to be so resistant to the idea that they have not been given the opportunity to do so? Why do Japanese consumers prefer packages that contain two tennis balls and view the standard U.S. package of three as cheap and undesirable? Why do Germans insist on highly detailed technical specifications on packages of videotapes, while Americans don't? Why do Swedes think that blue is masculine, while the Dutch see the color as feminine? The answers to all these questions lie in unquestioned habits of perception and deep-seated imagery.

OVERVIEW

Perception is a process of giving meaning to sensory stimuli. People act and react on the basis of their **perceptions,** *the way they sense and interpret the world around them.* Consumers' perceptions are fundamental to understanding acquisition, consumption, and disposal of goods and services. The symbols used in language and writing, in marketing communication in all its forms, gain meaning by reference to perceptions. Hence, in a basic way, perceptions underlie preferences. When consumers order curry chicken for dinner or buy silk lingerie or listen to Nine Inch Nails or select Magie Noire as their evening fragrance or refuse to buy plaids even when plaids are the fashion statement for the year, they reflect their **sensory preferences**—*sights, sounds, tastes, smells, and feelings that they like over other sensations.* Of course, culture, family, friends, motivations, experience, and a myriad of other factors influence these sensory preferences. Sophisticated understanding and management of sensations and perceptions are necessary if marketing communication, packaging, design of food products, and creation of retail environments are to be effective. As we examine perceptions, we continue to consider consumers as active interpreters of the marketing environment, and their uses of this environment in production, acquisition, consumption, and disposition processes.

The study of perceptions is a basic way to understand consumers. Nonetheless, there is something elusive about perceptions, and they have many aspects. Consider the vignette that opens this chapter. It suggests that some packages may attract or repel us without our being conscious of this effect or why we experience these feelings. For example, a package that we associated with pleasant childhood memories of the breakfast table may evoke warm feelings without awareness of specific memories. Perception, in this sense, does not use the symbols or rules of language or logic. Clearly, cognitive or symbolic knowledge comes *after* these perceptions, although experiences, learning, and memories may be bound up with them. In contrast, when we speak of the perceived quality, perceived risk, or perceived value, we are clearly talking about something that refers to perception, although the actual sensations at the root of these judgments may seem far away, transformed by judgment, thought, and logic.

Underlying both meanings of perception (i.e., the immediate sense of delight in the taste of something sweet versus the judgment that the colors in a gown do or do not go together) is **sensation,** *the immediate and direct response of sensory systems to stimuli.* Sensations vary between persons, social groups, and cultures. Nevertheless, sensation is an important ingredient of consumer learning and decision making (see Chapters 9 and 15).

In this chapter we examine the cultural, social, psychological, and physiological bases of perception. You will learn first about sensation and the sensory systems. Then, we introduce the four phases of perception. Next, we discuss some inference processes of particular importance in consumer behavior. Finally, we discuss the perceptual and sensory preferences that constitute what people call matters of taste. As you read about perception, you will understand that it is closely related to topics we will take up in other chapters. For example, perception is closely related to needs, motivation, and involvement (Chapter 7); experience, learning, and knowledge (Chapter 9); and decision making and attitude formation (Chapter 15).

THE SUBJECTIVE NATURE OF PERCEPTION

Many aspects of perception remain mysterious to science. While we know considerably more about the way neurons work when exposed to light, sound, taste, smell, and touch than was known even 30 years ago, we still do not understand much about our

The Subjective Nature of Perception

CONSUMER CHRONICLES 8.1

Global marketers are constantly brought face to face with the subjective nature of perception. Procter & Gamble recently scrapped the claim "Reduces cavities by 80 percent" for a Hungarian spot for Blend-a-Med toothpaste in a test campaign via DMB&B, Budapest. It reminded viewers too much of the false statements used in five-year plans under the old communist regime, and was thus perceived as false also. And in February, P&G used an ad in Polish dailies to try to quash rumors that Vidal Sassoon's Wash N'Go shampoo-conditioner made hair go, that is, fall out.

Source: "Road to Eastern Europe Paved with Marketing Mistakes," Advertising Age, *October 26, 1992, p. 13.*

subjective awareness of perceptual phenomena. Consciousness is the experience of knowing our sensations as though they were displayed before us, but how this display works is not well understood.[2] We often do not recognize that our perception of the world is created through indirect inference. Psychologists call this bias **phenomenal absolutism** and point out that we often assume that all other observers perceive sensations as we do. If others respond differently than we do, we assume it is because of error or bad intention rather than, as is often the case, because they are acting on different perceptual inferences. An important conclusion is that perceptions are learned as part of the enculturation process; as a result, they may be manipulated and altered.[3]

The subjective nature of perception presents challenges for global marketers, as illustrated in Consumer Chronicles 8.1. Of course, culture and the social world can play an important role in influencing consumers' subjective perceptions and interpretations. As the P&G experience in Poland illustrates, the media can also play an important role in influencing perceptions.

SENSATION AND SENSORY THRESHOLDS

Sensory stimuli are inputs to the senses. People detect stimuli through **sensory receptors.** These are the organs of perception. Although we may think of them in terms of the classic five—vision, smell, hearing, touch, and taste—it turns out that the organs of perception are more numerous and specialized than this. Indeed, some researchers suggest there are as many as 32 different sensory systems! There are, for example, separate sensory pathways in the eye for color, motion, form, and depth; separate pathways in skin to detect pressure, pain, and temperature; and multiple pathways connecting the olfactory organs of the nose to the multiple limbic structures in the brain (e.g., prepiriform cortex, amygdala, hypocampus).[4] While recognizing the diversity of the perceptual apparatus, we nonetheless organize our discussion of sensation around the five traditional systems.

Sensory Systems and Marketing Effects

There is debate about whether sensations are **autonomic responses** (i.e., automatic neural responses) or **learned responses** (the product of enculturation). This issue is important for marketers because they may rely on simple physical stimuli to produce certain responses in consumers. If these responses are autonomic, they are more predictable and more universal than if they are learned.

VISION Human eyes have separate mechanisms that gather the light, pick out an important or novel image, focus it precisely, pinpoint it in space, and follow it. They work like top-flight stereoscopic binoculars. Vision can rush through fields and travel across time, country, and outer space. Seventy percent of the body's sense receptors cluster in the eyes. People often vividly remember scenes from days or even years earlier, viewing them in their mind's eye. Of course, humans can even picture completely imaginary events, if they wish.

Because vision is a dominant sense in humans, it has been studied in great detail and more is known of it than the other senses. Studies find that exposure to warm hues (red-orange-yellow) raises blood pressure, heart rate, and perspiration, whereas exposure to cool hues (green-blue) has opposite effects. Applying these findings to commercial environments, studies show that yellow booths speed up phone calls; yellow walls and fixtures move people through stores faster; orange fixtures in fast-food joints stimulate hunger; and blue and pink hues reduce patient anxiety in doctors' waiting rooms and hospitals.

Color can play an important role in the success of marketing stimuli, such as the colors used in advertising or package design. In a study of a print ad for a fictitious paint company, the researchers found that the colors used in the ad influenced consumers' feelings of excitement and relaxation.[5] Colors that stimulate excitement appear whitish, as if the color white had been mixed in to create a pastel effect. Colors that evoke relaxation are fully saturated. That is, they have a high level of pigment in them. Much of the research on the role of color in marketing is anecdotal. Generally, red is an effective color to use in restaurants because it leads people to eat more.[6] Red also makes people lose track of time, making it a good color for use in casinos.[7] One intriguing study showed that when the background color on which a potential purchase was presented to viewers in the United States was changed from red to blue, people held different and more positive beliefs about it and the benefits of ownership. However, the authors found that only a fountain pen among the objects they employed in their experiments benefited from the change in background color. Another found that when U.S. consumers devoted little effort to processing ads, they developed more positive attitudes to ads with color highlighting rather than to all black-and-white ads. Curiously, when they are distracted by competing information, black-and-white and color-highlighted ads are more persuasive than color ads. Thus, while the specific findings about color effects are complex and vary from study to study, research suggests that colors have significant effects on consumer behaviors and often operate at an unconscious level.[8]

Most of the work on vision in consumer research has examined color or more complex visual stimuli such as words and pictures. We've discussed this in Chapter 4 and discuss it further later in this chapter. One little-studied aspect of vision is size and area perceptions. Yet consumers' varying estimates of size and area of products affect their judgements about prices they are willing to pay. Wouldn't you pay more for a box of breakfast cereal you perceived to be BIG than you would for a small one? But consumers' perceptions are biased. For instance, it turns out that the more equal the sides of a rectangle like a cereal box, the more consumers underestimate the area of the rectangle. Research on perceptions of size and area can help determine if cereal boxes should be rectangular or square or pizzas round or rectangular when a firm wishes to increase consumers' perceptions of value for money.[9]

SMELL The sense of smell is less important for humans than for many other animals. Yet, odors have a persistent and enveloping quality that may be difficult to escape. Smells can be extraordinarily precise, but in many cultures it's almost impossible to describe how something smells to someone who hasn't smelled it. Smells tend to be described

Smellevision

INDUSTRY INSIGHTS 8.1

When YTV Canada Inc. launched its fall programming in 1999, the network wanted a wild and wacky way to introduce its new line-up, promote one of its sponsors, and add a new dimension to its slogan, "Keep it Weird." Toronto-based YTV sought a promotion that kids could really sink their teeth—or in this case their noses—into. Targeting the 6- to 11-year-old crowd, YTV teamed up with Kraft Canada to create an unusual scratch-and-sniff, watch-and-win contest that turned viewers' TV sets into "Smellevision." The campaign drove increases both in YTV viewership and Kraft sales while reinforcing the network's "weird" brand image.

For three consecutive weekends in September and early October, while kids watched YTV's weekend morning programming, an animated nose sniffed across the screen and took bits of Kraft food items. Viewers then scratched the box next to the matching Kraft product on their game cards and decided what the correct smell was. Actual smells included dill pickles and orange peels. Other options were swamp gas and grandma's toenails. "Kids like the gross-out factor," says Tim McCormick, YTVs co-marketing director. The 100th caller to a toll-free number to identify the smell correctly won a $500 gift certificate from Roots, a popular Gap-like clothing retailer with stores throughout Canada.

Besides being an unusual gimmick, Smellevision really drew kids to interact with the promotion, an effective technique for targeting teens and "tweens," according to Pascale Le Blanc, president of Toronto-based Youthopia Communications, a public relations and marketing firm.

Source: Paula Lyon Andruss, "'Smellevision' Wafts Fresh Air into Canadian Kids' Network," Marketing News, *April 9, 2001, p. 4. Reprinted by permission of the American Marketing Association.*

in terms of how they feel emotionally (e.g., disgusting, delightful). Try it yourself. Can you describe the smell of your favorite pastry, flower, sauce, chair, or room? Smell is the most direct of the senses. Nothing is more memorable than a smell. Exposure to odors remembered from childhood can induce mood effects like those experienced in childhood. Marketers are attuned to this and have found ways to build mood effects into products through their odors. For example, three of the best-selling perfumes in the U.S. market are scented with baby powder. The appeal of the perfumes may be more basic than the flashy promotional campaigns with which they are associated—rooted in the warm feelings associated with the fragrance of baby powder. Odor greatly affects an individual's evaluation of things and other people. For example, if consumers are handed two cans of identical furniture polish, one with a pleasant odor and one with no odor, they will swear the scented one works better. Odor also affects consumer responses in a multitude of other ways. For example, people are more alert in a room with a light, pleasant smell. Psychologists have found that the odor of spiced apple has a calming effect and that various food odors, including spiced apple, can lower blood pressure in some people by inducing a relaxation of respiratory patterns. As marketers seek to tap consumers' feelings and memories directly, aromachology and the home fragrance industry have become a growing aspect of the economy.[10]

Sometimes odors are used as a way of communicating product attribute information, such as with perfume or household cleaners. Sometimes they are directly related to the product being sold, such as the scent of fresh-baked bread in a grocery store or the aroma of ground coffee in specialty shops. However, marketers have become interested in the notion that pleasant scents that are not necessarily related to the products being sold can also affect consumer feelings, thoughts, and behaviors. For example, research has found that pleasant odors increase lingering and the amount of time spent in a store.[11] Industry Insights 8.1 provides an off-beat example of the use of smells to influence consumer behaviors.

HEARING Sound is an onrushing, cresting, and withdrawing wave of air molecules that roll to the ears, where they make the eardrum vibrate and move the three tiniest bones in the body. These three bones press fluid in the inner ear against membranes, which brush tiny hairs that trigger nearby nerve cells, which telegraph messages to the brain. As a result, people hear.

What people hear occupies a large range of intensities. People have a surprising ability to move some sounds to the almost unnoticeable rear and drag others right up front. For example, a mother wakes quickly to the sound of her colicky baby at the other end of the house, but she may sleep through the louder and more abrasive sound of a garbage truck. At a busy cocktail party, people can slice straight through all the noise when they hear their name mentioned across the room.

Sound patterns can create a mood of relaxation or stimulation. Religions and cults have long made use of music to induce trances or other mood states. The Muzak Corporation, among others, offers functional music to relax, stimulate, or liven up shoppers. Other piped-in music is designed to reduce absenteeism among workers.

Research into the impact of music upon consumers within a commercial context is still relatively sparse. Some recent research has examined the effects of music tempo on several aspects of consumer behavior. For example, a recent study employing digital technology showed that experimental subjects' perceptions of time varied with tempo. This research is of potential value because if music can be harnessed to make perceived advertising time shorter than actual advertising time, it might be used to reduce boredom and "zapping" and increase viewers' attention span. Another field study in the UK explored the effects of music tempo on actual and perceived time spent dining and the amount of money spent. Results showed that when slow music is playing, British customers spend a significantly greater amount of time dining than when fast music is playing. The slow music tempo was also found to increase amounts of money spent on food and drink at the restaurant.[12]

TOUCH Our skin stands between the world and us, and it serves many functions. It protects us and imprisons us. It gives us individual shape, cools us down, and heats us up. Most of all, it harbors the sense of touch. There are many complex sensations that constitute touch, and various parts of the body are much more sensitive than others. In language, there are many metaphors for touch. We call our emotions "feelings," and we care most deeply when something "touches" us. The importance of touch is not just represented in language and poetry; it is evident in many other ways. Touch affects the whole organism.

Numerous studies detail the vital affects of touch. For example, massaged babies gain weight as much as 50 percent faster than unmassaged babies. Touch is critical in the psychological and physical development of children. Sustained touching reduces heart rate and has a calming effect. Stroking of pets has a similar effect; in one study of longevity following heart attack, the single most important factor was the presence of pets in the patients' environment. The capacity of fabrics such as wool, silk, and fur to evoke associations directly has apparently fueled the development of synthetic fabrics with the tactile associations of the natural ones. Given a recent increase in concern with animal rights, interest is especially high in developing false fur with the feel of the original.

TASTE What people eat suggests the powerful role of culture in determining taste. Thus, the Masai drink cow's blood; some Asians eat stir-fried canine; Germans eat rancid cabbage (sauerkraut); North Americans eat decaying cucumbers (pickles); Italians eat whole deep-fried songbirds; Vietnamese eat fermented fish dosed with chili peppers; Japanese and others eat fungus (mushroom); French eat garlic-soaked snails. People eat rodents, grasshoppers, snakes, flightless birds, kangaroos, lobsters, and bats. When the explorer Dr. Livingston died in Africa, his organs were apparently eaten by two of his native followers as a way to absorb his strength and courage.

The Taste of Olive Oil

CONSUMER CHRONICLES 8.2

"Artisan-made olive oil is like silk or velvet in your mouth. It has the beautiful aroma of olives, but is more earthy. What I like is as you swallow it, there's a long finish of black pepper in the back of your throat," says Michelle Anna Jordan, author of *The Good Cook's Book of Oil and Vinegar.* In the United States, consumption of olive oil increased 50 percent from 1987 to 1992, according to the USDA. Forecasted consumption for 1993 is 278 million pounds, putting per capita consumption at about one pound per person. So how do you judge olive oil? Taste it.

Source: Kristen A. Conover, "Olive Oil Branching Out," Christian Science Monitor, *March 3, 1994.*

Taste is also an intimate sense. As Consumer Chronicles 8.2 illustrates, how people taste things may be as individual as fingerprints. Every culture uses food as a sign of approval or commemoration. Some foods are eaten symbolically or ritualistically or for their supernatural powers. Food gods have ruled the hearts and lives of many peoples. Food is a big source of physiological and emotional pleasure in most people's lives. So, how do people taste? Taste buds are exceedingly small, and adults have about 10,000, grouped by theme (salt, sour, sweet, bitter), at various sites in the mouth. Inside each one, about 50 taste cells busily relay information to a neuron, which will alert the brain. People use the tip of the tongue to taste sweet things, the back to taste bitter, and the side to taste sour. Up front and along the surface, they taste salty things. Smell is also important to taste, and it hits us faster. It takes 25,000 times more molecules of cherry pie to taste it than to smell it. In fact, a food's flavor includes its texture, smell, temperature, color, and painfulness (as in spices), among many other features. Food engineers create products to assault as many of the taste sensors as possible. There has been considerable interest in creating substances that fool taste buds, such as artificial sweeteners and fats that mimic the taste of sugar and the saturated fats that give many meat and dairy products their flavor. At any one time, there are multiple and conflicting trends related to culinary fashions. In the Triad nations there is a growing segment of health-conscious consumers who are concerned about the cholesterol and the fat contents of the foods they eat. At the same time, there is a segment of consumers who indulge and prefer foods that are high in fat, those as rich and savory as possible (see Consumer Chronicles 8.3). Marketers can position products on taste in many creative ways, as suggested in Industry Insights 8.2.

Obviously our senses do not work in isolation but together. Retailers have long understood the importance of a store's overall sensory environment in enhancing consumers' experience. However, surprisingly little research addresses the interaction of the senses on consumers' experiences in retail and other commercial settings. One recent study showed that when both music and scent shared an arousing quality, consumers rated the retail environment more positively and expressed more satisfaction with the shopping experience and spent more money than when the cues were at odds with one another. Themed retailers seem to understand this intuitively, but more research is needed in this area to provide improved managerial guidance.[13]

Sensory Thresholds

Sensation is provoked, not by some unit of sensation but by changes in sensory input. It's these differences in input that people perceive. Several differences in input, or **sensory thresholds,** are important in marketing; these include the absolute threshold and the differential threshold, or the just noticeable difference.

ABSOLUTE THRESHOLD The **absolute threshold** is *the lowest level of input to be detected by the various sensory receptors in the human body.* Some examples are given in Consumer Chronicles 8.4. The absolute threshold should not be confused with the threshold of consciousness. Perceptual scientists recognize that there are sensations to which people attend and those to which they do not attend. Some of the latter may nonetheless affect behavior, if they exceed the absolute threshold of perception.

Marketers sometimes make use of sensations that are not obvious to customers. Although customers may not notice the background music in a grocery store (i.e., it does not receive conscious attention), the music nevertheless affects buyer behavior. The Magic Kingdom and Epcot Center at Walt Disney World in Orlando, Florida, use a machine called a "smellitzer" that dissipates scents on their rides, including the odors of oranges, bubble gum, and volcanoes.[14]

Marketing stimuli must reach the absolute threshold if they are to affect consumers. Receptors adapt quickly to environments. Hence, any continuous low-level sensation quickly becomes mere background, and the sensory receptors stop responding. The absolute threshold may increase for physiological reasons, such as increasing age. Physiological factors may reduce the likelihood of some persons receiving sensory input. Thus, younger people tend to be more sensitive to smell than elderly people. Research has found that smell decreases more with age than taste sensitivity, a fact related to loss of appetite and undernourishment among the elderly.

A Sensory Preference for Fatty Foods

CONSUMER CHRONICLES 8.3

North American fast-food restaurants have gone off their diet. Their menus are increasing with grease-laden sandwiches: Wendy's International, Big Bacon Classic; McDonald's MegaMac; KFC's Popcorn Chicken; etc. The fast-food industry hasn't had much luck with skimpy dietetic products. The reason for these flops: People crave large quantities of fatty foods. Food trends experts say North Americans are tired of the stern dietary warnings issued by physicians. Rebellious consumers want their food indulgences to be rich and savory. Fast-food chains have been inspired by the popularity and higher margins of specialty sandwiches, which tend to be larger and more expensive than regular burgers.

Source: Gabriella Stern, "In a Turn About Fast-Food Fare Becomes Fattier," The Wall Street Journal, *August 8, 1993, pp. B1, B6.*

The absolute threshold also varies with demographic factors. Women seem to be more sensitive than males. For instance, women seem to exhibit superior performance in a variety of tasks involving odor information than men.[15]

Thanks in part to commercial media (the saturation of the media with marketing messages), consumers in the Triad countries live in a stimulus-rich environment. Consumers adapt to this sensory environment in part by "disattending," by applying **perceptual filters** to screen out unwanted stimuli. As an illustration of perceptual filters, consider the experience of Northwestern Mutual Life Insurance Company when it placed coupons worth $10 in an informational mailing. To redeem it, all one had to do was find the coupon in the mailer. Virtually no one redeemed the coupon. People simply tuned this input out.

Marketers frequently attempt to provoke consumers into re-attending by crossing the absolute threshold in novel ways. One technique that radio or TV advertisers may use to increase attention is to alter the volume of certain frequencies. Another technique is to remove sounds that tend to drown others out—just as low-frequency wind and road noise tend to cancel out the highs on a car radio, making the music harder to hear. To avoid this effect, advertisers may try to filter out as much masking noise as possible, which

Bertie Bott's Every Flavor Beans

INDUSTRY INSIGHTS 8.2

Every pouch of Bertie Bott's Every Flavor Beans candy is a treasure hunt of unusual flavors. Intermingled among "usual" jellybean flavors such as strawberry jam and lemon drop are unusual flavors such as sardine, black pepper, dirt, earwax, and booger. Earwax? Booger? Yes, booger . . . Yum! While your taste buds might be screaming at the idea, the Jelly Belly Candy Company has found renewed success making Bertie Bott's Every Flavored Beans under license to Warner Brothers, producer of the Harry Potter film series. The beans do indeed taste like the flavors described, but kids love them anyway. Why? They represent a clear-cut example of perceptual inference. These gross-out flavors convey authenticity and coolness and provide a tangible link to Harry Potter, Hermione Granger, and Ron Weezely, the beloved youthful heroes of the successful book and film series. In other words, the beans are perceived as true artifacts from the book. The story of the beans and the flavors comes straight off the pages of the first Harry Potter book, encouraging the kids to imagine themselves as junior wizards like Harry! The Jelly Belly Candy Company, a family candy-making company since 1869, is headquartered in Fairfield, California. A second manufacturing plant is located in North Chicago, Illinois, a location where they have produced candy since 1912.

Source: www.jellybelly.com; Melissa Fogarty and Beth Mosher, "The Second Time's a Charm: Cap Candy Conjures up a Line of Candy Based upon the Theatrical Release of Harry Potter and the Chamber of Secrets," *press release (Hoboken, NJ: Litzky Public Relations, 2002).*

could make a sound track seem quieter than it is. In addition, some frequencies are more piercing than other frequencies. Acoustic researchers have found that the human voice has the most impact in the frequency range between two and six kilohertz. Thus, by electronically manipulating a voice sound so that it always stays within that band, audio engineers can enhance its effect on a listener. Even the way a commercial is written can make a difference because the ear is more sensitive to consonants than vowel sounds.[16]

Weber's Law and the JND

Another important sensory threshold is the **just noticeable difference (JND),** or **differential threshold.** This conveys the idea of the *minimum change in sensation necessary for a person to detect it.* Note that the JND differs from absolute threshold in that the former focuses on *changes* in sensations not *minimum* sensation.

Any first-time touch or change in touch (from gentle to stinging, say) sends the brain into a flurry of activity. However, an additional dose of stimulus at the same level results in a much lower level of excitation of sensory receptors. To explain this phenomenon, a theorem known as **Weber's law** states that *the stronger the initial sensory stimulus, the greater the additional intensity needed for the second stimulus to be perceived as different.* A corollary of this theorem is that an additional level of stimulus equivalent to the JND must be added for the majority of people to perceive a difference between the resulting stimulus and the initial stimulus.

The most important implication of Weber's law for marketers is the necessity of determining the JND to optimize any changes in the marketing mix. Sometimes it will be optimal to introduce stimuli or changes in the marketing mix that are equal to the

JND. In this case, the challenge for marketers is to determine the amount of change necessary in a given component of the marketing mix, in particular marketing environments for particular market segments. Change less than the JND is wasted because it is not perceived. More than the JND is wasted because it may stimulate no additional response—no more repeat business, no further sales. For example, a household cleaner might distinguish itself with "more lemon scent." In this case, the lemon scent should be noticeably stronger than it was in the original version.

According to Weber's law, the level of a just noticeable difference will depend on the strength of the initial stimulus. Hence, the JND is in contrast to economic principles that would contend that a $5 savings is a savings, whether the savings is on $10 or $10,000. In contrast, Weber's law suggests that a $5 savings on $10 is likely to be noticeable, but on a larger amount, say $10,000, a $5 savings is likely to go unnoticed. On a related note, a study was done of U.S. consumers' response to retailers' price promotions. This study found that consumers *discount* the price discounts; that is, consumers are so used to discounts that small discounts fail to stimulate a reaction. Consumers do not change their intentions to buy unless the promotional discount is above a threshold level. Moreover, this threshold point differs for name brands and store brands. The threshold for name brands is lower than for store brands. In other words, stores can attract consumers by offering a smaller discount on name brands than they would have to offer on store brands.[17] Weber's law applies to many stimuli. If a product is generally unsalted, just a little salt will be readily discernible. However, that same amount of salt added to potato chips is likely to go unnoticed.

Sometimes a marketer's objective is to change the product *without* the consumer noticing. The key is to stay just below a noticeable difference. For example, a marketer might advertise "all the same good taste with only half the sodium." In this case, the marketer would continue to cut salt until the consumer noticed that the product didn't taste as good—that is, just below the JND for reduced salt. This may be easy to do with very salty products but much more difficult with products already low in sodium. Often, firms want to introduce changes in products and services that are not readily discernible to customers in order to save money or else reposition the brand (e.g., reductions in product size, changes in package design). Thus, they may try shrinking candy bars slightly while retaining the same size package. The strategy of downsizing the package or decreasing contents is a popular way of implementing price increases. Often consumers more readily notice a price change, especially on relatively inexpensive products, than a change in the quantity. During periods of rising coffee prices, a slight increase in the percentage of inferior coffee beans may be introduced into ground coffees.[18] Packaged-goods marketers frequently change the package design but usually

Some Approximate Detection Threshold Values

CONSUMER CHRONICLES 8.4

Sense Modality	Detection Threshold
Light	A candle flame seen at 30 miles on a dark clear night.
Sound	The tick of a watch under quiet conditions at 20 feet.
Taste	One teaspoon of sugar in two gallons of water.
Smell	One drop of perfume diffused into the entire volume of a three-room apartment.
Touch	The wing of a bee falling on your back from a distance of one centimeter.

Source: Introduction to Sensation/Perception *by Donald H. McBurney and Virginia B. Collings, ©. Reprinted by permission at Pearson Education, Inc., Upper Saddle River, NJ.*

do so in small stages. As a result, consumers often do not notice these subtle changes in package design, color, or wording.

THE PERCEPTUAL PROCESS

People think of the senses as windows on the world, but a primary function of sensory systems is to discard irrelevant or useless information. As such, the sensory systems serve as selection systems. Humans may agree on certain events only because we share a common biology and thus are similarly limited by our sensory selection systems. Perhaps the most striking trend in the psychology and physiology of perception in the past two decades is the increasing understanding of the interactive and constructive nature of ordinary awareness.

Our experience of the world involves a wide range of unconscious inferences about perceptual categories that we create from personal experience.[19] In this section we look in more detail at how sensory systems make predictions, that is to say, how they select, organize, and interpret stimuli. For the sake of discussion, we divide the process of perception into four parts:

1. Preattentive processing
2. Selection
3. Organization
4. Interpretation and elaboration

Preattentive Processing

Preattentive processing refers to *the simultaneous preconscious monitoring of all sensory channels for events that will require a shift in attention.*[20] This kind of preattentive processing is what makes it possible for us to suddenly hear our name spoken across a crowded, noisy room or wake at the cry of a baby but not a garbage truck. Considerable research suggests that preconscious processes operate in the selection of stimuli for further processing. However, some recent research has demonstrated that preattentive processing *may* also have an effect on preference formation. The possibility that consumer attitudes can be influenced without consumers being able to identify the factors responsible for that influence has many implications for marketers.[21]

EXPOSURE Our understanding of perceptual **exposure** to information derives from the theory of cognitive consistency (see Chapters 7 and 15). This theory states that information search continues as a consumer weighs the advantages and disadvantages of various purchase and consumption alternatives. Consumers will be receptive to new information that is consistent with their decisions, values, beliefs, and attitudes and will avoid information that is discrepant. Thus, consumers who engage in a particular behavior or who hold positive attitudes about a product or activity will be more receptive to information that supports those attitudes and behaviors (see Chapter 15). In addition selective exposure theory also suggests that receptivity will be biased by certain factors in decision-making and attitude formation processes such as freedom of choice in developing the decision or belief, level of commitment to cognition, and the reversibility of the decision. For example, one study showed that ecological concern was associated with greater receptivity to ecological information among

Anglo-American and Mexican-American consumers. Finally, consumers may choose to be exposed to dissonant or discrepant information when they believe that they may have the chance to revise their decision in the near future or when future similar decisions are anticipated. Acquisition behavior, particularly for consumer nondurables, is a reversible decision at the time of the next purchase, and, in most cases, future similar decisions are anticipated.

Selection

There's an extraordinary amount of competition for people's attention in the marketplace. Media environments everywhere are becoming increasingly rich, led, of course, by the commercial media based in the Triad countries. As explained by the principle of sensory thresholds, as the background becomes more saturated with sensation, peoples' filters become stronger and more immune to each individual sensory input. In effect, the perceptual system is a nonconscious, parallel information-generation device that selects and creates the small array of information that the higher-order system will process.[22] **Perceptual selection** refers to the fact that *consumers select only a small portion of the stimuli to which they are exposed for conscious processing,* or what we might term *focal attention.* To get the consumer's focal attention, an escalation of sensory impulses is required. Evidence is easy to find in a comparison of the staid, single-shot TV commercials of television's first decades with today's rapid-fire explosions of sounds and images pioneered in many cases by MTV and entertainment advertisers.

Merely escalating the intensity of stimuli is likely to be an ineffective way of cutting through perceptual filters and provoking potential customers to pay attention. Consumers will concentrate on some stimuli, be unaware of others, and avoid some commercial messages. Many poorly targeted direct-mail pieces, for example, are discarded, unopened and unread. A variety of factors will lead to increased selection, as we outline in the next several paragraphs.

MOTIVES One of the most important factors influencing selection of stimuli for further processing is consumers' motives and goals, discussed in Chapter 7. Consumers are more likely to attend to stimuli that relate to themselves or their current needs. In addition, consumers' goals serve to direct their attention to information that is relevant or important to those goals.[23] Perhaps you've noticed how once you get interested in purchasing a particular product, all of a sudden there seems to be lots of information available on that product. Or perhaps, right after purchasing a new car it seems like you suddenly see that model of car everywhere you look. Both of these common examples illustrate information selectivity. This type of need-specific attention is called **perceptual vigilance.**

The idea of perceptual vigilance has important implications for marketers. For example, producers of radio commercials are advised to include personal references in their spots. The use of a question format in advertisements appears to have the capacity to draw attention to a message and thus engage listeners. Incidentally, the philosopher Protagoras introduced the question format as a persuasive technique in the fourth century B.C.[24]

An important application of perceptual vigilance for marketers is to target consumers whose needs have changed. During transitional periods, consumers may be especially attentive to relevant information that addresses their changing needs. For example, when consumers make a long-distance move, they must establish relationships with many new services (everything from schools and insurance to laundries and barbers) and buy many new and replacement goods (tools, furnishings). Some marketers keep careful track of new home purchases, a matter of public record in the United States, and target new buyers with promotional materials. Other marketers keep track of birth, marriage, and divorce records for similar purposes, secure in the knowledge that consumers faced with these life-changing events will be more attentive to campaigns focused on meeting their needs.[25]

Many studies indicate that consumers are raising their perceptual filters to avoid exposure to commercial messages in their media viewing. Practices include channel surfing, and zipping (fast-forwarding recorded programs) and zapping (muting) commercials. These behaviors have been observed in media-rich environments such as the United States and Australia. Further, it has been shown to be increasing as consumers' attitudes toward marketing communications throughout the Triad nations become more negative. Interactive media such as the Internet will afford the consumer even greater influence over and choice of the material available for selective attention. Thus, consumers are becoming more selective over what they view, when they view it, and how much of the media content they will view.

These trends suggest that exposure to marketing messages and commercial communication in interactive media will be voluntarily sought by the consumer, such as clicking on an icon or button in order for exposure to occur. In addition, the consumer will increasingly exercise a choice of different levels of interactive messages. In other words, consumers will increasingly vary levels of exposure. From a managerial perspective these findings indicate that to achieve exposure, marketing communications must strive for relevance, timeliness, and quality of execution, while more precisely targeting consumers who are at least momentarily receptive to information. For example, one study showed that well-placed silence in a television ad evoking the silent operation of a brand of air conditioner produced not only more exposure to the ad, but heightened recall of product attributes and a favorable attitude towards the air conditioner.[26]

Size matters: Salvatore Ferragamo shoes

NATURE OF THE STIMULUS Some of the time, the perceptual stimulus attracts the consumer's attention. **Involuntary attention** can occur via the **orientation reflex,** when *surprise, threat, or violation of expectations elicits attention automatically.* A variety of mechanisms increase attention to messages. For example, **atypicality** of execution format can provoke perceptual selection. Thus, black and white commercials on color television and clear advertising pages in opaque magazine pages will elicit attention. These particular examples also illustrate that **contrast effects** elicit attention. The contrast effect is illustrated in the ad shown below for Medips Dental Clinic. More generally, perceptual surprises may increase the likelihood of selection. Increased size of advertisements or life-size images of products are surprising, as in the Salvatore Ferragamo shoes ad on page 310. Especially vivid images such as those employed in a series of Benetton ads during the late 1980s and early 1990s can also evoke the orientation reflex. Benetton drew both attention and controversy with ads depicting actors dressed as a priest and nun kissing, a young man dying of AIDS in his parents arms, and a shipping disaster. Good Practice 8.1 provides some practical guidance for cutting through the clutter and eliciting selective attention from consumers.

Organization

The third part in the perceptual process is **perceptual organization.** Consumers classify perceptions into categories (categorization) and apply prior knowledge about the categories to organize them. Basically, **categorization** involves *comparison between a perceived target and categorical knowledge.*[27] Categorization is a fundamental sense-making activity that encompasses all forms of stimulus situations. When we identify a moving object in a tree as a bird, we are categorizing. Whenever we reason about *kinds* of things, we employ categories. Whenever we intentionally perform any *kind* of action,

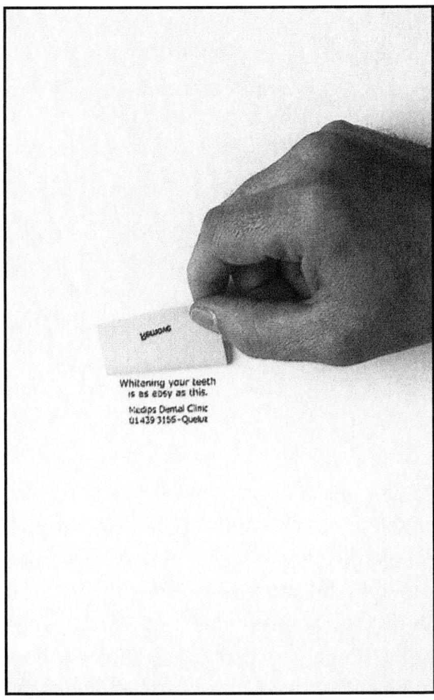

Three contrast points for the Medips Dental Clinic ad shown here. First, the ad lacks color. Second, very little text is used. Third, unlike most print ads, this one is interactive; the consumer peels back the sticky note.

Getting the Attention You Need

GOOD PRACTICE 8.1

The scarcest resource in marketing communications today is no longer land, capital, or labor, and it is certainly not information. Selective attention is what's in short supply. And human attention behaves like an economic good in the sense that we buy it and measure it. On an individual level, we are deeply aware when we don't have enough of it. Some lessons from the experts on attention management:

1. Manage attention knowing that there's only so much to go around. The stickiest websites capitalize on this by providing high returns on attention investment. For example, Yahoo! is a successful search engine because its human-based approach to classifying sites yields fewer irrelevant hits than a computer-based approach.
2. People are hardwired to fight for survival; use that to fight for survival. Web designers and managers alike can use this natural reaction to get and hold attention. For example, online grocers in Brazil noted Brazilians' response to years of hyperinflation was to buy huge amounts of groceries whenever they received a paycheck. Online grocers have exploited this survival reaction: 39 percent of total e-commerce in Brazil is grocery sales compared to about 3 percent in the United States.
3. People are infinitely distractible. One of the most popular banner ads of 1999 featured an animated monkey quickly bounding across the top of the screen. Many people found the manic monkey an irresistible target. Great news for the gambling site where you were whisked if you "punched the monkey."
4. People want to feel engaged, so help make that happen. Customized or personalized communications whether off- or online get attention, hence the effectiveness of MyYahoo!.com or Amazon.com's customized recommendations.
5. Clutter distracts from attention. So it is in advertising, so it is on websites.
6. Contrast always draws attention. Devising communications to take advantage of the latest fads and the latest technologies leads to homogeneous, hence boring media environments.
7. Attention can and should be measured. Measurement enables firms to identify what to improve to get attention. Ad agencies know which TV ads pull in which consumers, how much those consumers spend, and their return rates. On the Web stickiness is measured as a combination of the number of unique visits to a site and the total time spent by the average user across multiple visits.

Source: Thomas H. Davenport and John C. Beck, "Getting the Attention You Need," Harvard Business Review, *September–October 2000, pp. 118–26.*

say something as ordinary as drinking a soda, attending a class, or exercising, we are using categories. Whenever we talk for a reasonable length of time we employ dozens, if not hundreds, of categories. Categorization schemes allow people to give coherence to their general knowledge about other people, objects, and situations. By putting stimuli into categories, consumers are able to decide how they should behave in certain situations and also what they can expect. For example, some recent research looks at how the outside facade and the inside seating arrangement of an eating establishment lead consumers to categorize the establishment as a fast-food, family, or fancy restaurant. This classification, in turn, affects how consumers believe they should behave and should be treated by service staff. Simple aspects of restaurant appearance (e.g., the intimacy of the lighting, the flexibility of seating arrangements) lead to different categorizations of the stimuli.[28]

A key feature of categories is that they are functional and, as such, are shaped by personal goals, values, or the need to respond. Recent research emphasizes that categories are influenced by context and by goals or judgment purposes.[29] By altering context, systematic differences in category judgments occur. In fact, a different context invites people to organize their knowledge structures differently and create categories appropriate to the context. The formation of a particular goal also leads people to create categories to fit that specific goal. Such categories are referred to as **ad hoc categories.** For example, a student residing in a university town may construct a category of "places to go with friends for FAC (Friday afternoon club) on Friday afternoon." This particular category reflects the context and consumer goals of the student.[30]

Another key feature of categories is that they are socially and culturally constructed and learned.[31] For example, the Australian aboriginal language Dyirbal has a category, *balan,* that includes women, fire, and dangerous things. Native speakers of Dyirbal use the category *balan* automatically and effortlessly, but speakers of English try to comprehend it and ponder it in terms of their normal categories of thought and are rarely able to employ it.

Categorization operates at different levels of abstraction. In this section, on organizing perceptions, we are interested in some principles that affect the initial, often automatic, and unconscious categorization of stimuli. We refer to this *initial classification of an object into a category* as **primitive categorization.** To appreciate the problem of primitive categorization, we need to understand that people derive meaning from the perceptual information they receive at a given moment. They frequently derive meaning from partial perceptual data, inferring the rest from previous learning. So, for example, it is no problem to infer the weather outside is very cold, if from inside we view falling snowflakes. Marketers often make use of our human tendency to make sense of perceptual data through primitive categorization on the basis of partial information. The ad shown below relies for its effectiveness on primitive classification. We "see" the wood as an animal. Three especially common illustrations of this tendency are grouping, figure-and-ground discriminations, and the closure principle. Each of these shows how, when presented with ambiguous stimuli, people try to impose familiar categories on their perceptions.

Viewers ability and willingness to see this image as an animal illustrates the idea of categorization.

GROUPING In the first case of primitive categorization, **grouping,** people tend to *assume that options found in proximity to one another go together.* Advertisers and retailers, through grouping, try to create perceptual environment for their goods and services that creates a particular image for them. Architects, designers, and

Target stores makes use of figure-and-ground principles to attract attention to featured products.

landscapers use perceptual cues to suggest an overall landscape. Ralph Lauren has gone to considerable lengths to create an overall perception of his Polo line that conveys a classic, old money, country-club image. In the 1980s, the American wine producer Gallo sought to upgrade its down-market image among wine consumers by picturing upgraded products with gourmet foods, a linen napkin, and a napkin ring as shown on page 315, images that some consumers would associate with a more formal, upscale dining situation. One practical illustration of the grouping principle can be found in television scheduling. Networks schedule promising new shows to follow proven winners, hoping for a rub-off from the winner onto the newcomer. Of course, this technique improves the likelihood the newcomer at a minimum will arouse the viewers' attention.[32] All these examples use the principle of grouping to suggest to consumers that the objects are all members of a single category.

FIGURE AND GROUND In the second case of primitive categorization, referred to as **figure and ground,** people try to *determine what aspects of stimuli they should focus on.* People tend to place "important" stimuli in the foreground and move less important stimuli to the background. Classic figure-and-ground tricks developed by psychologists illustrate how we may perceive something as foreground, until an alternative perception is pointed out to us. Exhibit 8.1 illustrates the vase/face trick. The figure and ground will shift back and forth as we attempt to see one element, such as the faces, and then the other, the vase, as foreground. An interesting aspect of figure-and-ground problems is that people cannot perceive both objects as figure simultaneously.

Gallo wine: Upscale dining. This ad employs the principle of grouping.

There are many instances of the use of figure-and-ground principles in marketing. For example, people often say that contrast attracts attention. But what they are really saying is that a stimulus has forced something into the foreground that would otherwise have been treated as background. Thus, in a U.S. campaign, Toyota, using a sports figure as a celebrity spokesperson, brought an otherwise ordinary figure into the foreground of our attention with the line, "I'm Eric Karras, the *lowest-paid* player in baseball!" Target Stores uses figure-and-ground effects to draw attention to the merchandise displayed in its print ads, as shown in the example on page 314. Viewers have to exert cognitive effort to distinguish figure and ground.

EXHIBIT 8.1

A Classic Figure-and-Ground Problem

What Do You See?

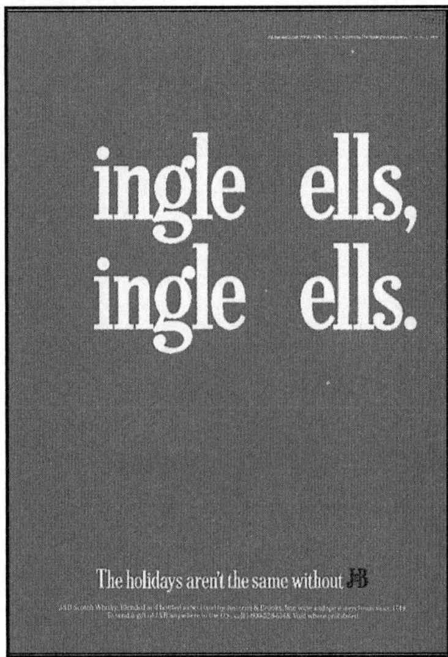

An application of the principle of closure.

The literature on the effects of background and foreground music in retail settings is mixed. Foreground music differs from background music in that it includes original artists and lyrics, unlike background music that uses primarily instrumental treatments played by anonymous musicians. A number of studies have reported that playing slow-paced background music results in increased sales in grocery settings. A study in a restaurant found that more alcohol, but not food, was consumed when slow music was played. Soft, soothing music may be an appropriate background in retail settings requiring extensive sales interaction and in those where customers make infrequent, big-ticket, high-risk purchases.[33]

CLOSURE The third principle of perceptual organization that illustrates the consumer's use of partial cues to complete an image is **closure.** In radio or television ads, it is not uncommon to repeat a jingle or slogan several times and then to leave it incomplete as the advertisement ends. Advertisers know that the listener will imagine the final bars of the tune. Through this heightened level of involvement with the ad, the listener is then more likely to remember the message itself. Print and outdoor advertising examples are also common. Justerini & Brooks' clever Christmastime ad for J & B Scotch relies on the audience's tacit knowledge of a popular seasonal song "Jingle Bells" to get them to fill in the missing letters in the ad shown above. Similar techniques are employed by Vin & Spirit to promote their Absolut brand of vodka in the United States and by Schweppes to promote their tonic water. On bus kiosks in Europe, there are two versions of the Schweppes ad shown above, one that includes the brand name and one that does not. Consumers are supposed to fill in the brand name for themselves, after having viewed the first ad.

GESTALT PSYCHOLOGY Gestalt psychologists are responsible for much of the work on perceptual organization.[34] These researchers attempt to identify the rules that govern how people perceive patterns in the world. In German, *gestalt* means "pattern" or "configuration." The gestalt perspective is the study of how individuals make sense of the stimuli to which they are exposed. Many of the rules pertain to the ways in which people decide what things go together. Some of the rules are grouping, figure and ground, and closure.

Interpretation and Elaboration

The fourth part in the perceptual process is interpretation. Obviously, organization and interpretation are intertwined. Both have to do with comprehension and sense making. Whereas the principles of perceptual organization are most often applied unconsciously, at least part of the time, interpretation is a conscious process. The interpretation of perceptual stimuli involves the application of learned associations between perceptual cues, or signs, and meanings to novel stimuli. These associations are, in turn, based on individual expectations, motivations, and experiences grounded in cultural convention. Hence, interpretation depends on consumers' knowledge structures.

At least two different sorts of knowledge structures are important to interpretation. One type, called **schemas,** includes *organized collections of beliefs and feelings that a person has about objects, ideas, people, or situations.* As illustrated earlier, many consumers have a schema for a "fancy restaurant" that includes beliefs, feelings, and likely attributes of such an eating establishment. The second type of knowledge structure, called **scripts,** includes *sequences of actions associated with objects, ideas, people, or situations.* For example, when going to a "fancy restaurant" in the United States, the consumer probably expects to be seated or told to wait, expects to give an order to a waiter, expects to have a sequence of ordering steps, expects to receive the bill at the end of the meal, and may expect to have the waiter handle the payment transfer. Even schemas and scripts for something as basic as going to a restaurant are quite complicated and typically allow for many different contingencies and context effects.[35] Whether we are aware of it or not, knowledge about cultural roles, settings, goals, and event sequences are basic to interpretation. We will talk more about knowledge structures and how they influence consumer choices and behaviors in Chapters 9 and 15.

PERCEPTUAL INFERENCES An important aspect of interpretation is **perceptual inferences.** Inferences are *interpretations that go beyond the information given.* Our understanding of how and when consumers make inferences is still limited. Yet, we do know that consumers rarely have complete information. They have to make judgments and purchase decisions about products on the basis of limited or incomplete information. Frequently, consumers use a small number of cues to make inferences. For example, Westerners associate a dark-brown color with rich flavor for both coffee and chocolate. Merely darkening the color of the product will lead people to insist the product is indeed richer in flavor. As you can see from this example, some inferences are made more or less automatically, and we are largely unconscious of the cues we use in making them. Ethical Dilemma 8.1 shows how perceptual inferences can vary across customer segments and may lead to ethical dilemmas for marketers.

ELABORATION Sometimes consumer interpretation of perceptual stimuli also includes high levels of **elaboration.** Elaboration reflects *the extent to which perceptual stimuli are integrated with prior knowledge structures.* Interpretation always involves

Marketing to Perceptually Challenged Consumers

ETHICAL DILEMMA 8.1

Some 10 to 15 percent of the population suffers from some type of activity limitation resulting from a chronic condition. From 1.5 to 2 percent suffer from visual impairments. Should marketers adapt their tactics to meet the needs of such consumers? In some countries such as the United States, legislation such as the Americans with Disabilities Act (ADA) mandates that they should, and some retailers do provide amenities to facilitate their shopping. What are some of the perceptual effects of disability? In one study, the author found that visually impaired people still sought out perceptual information about products including color. They relied on shopping companions for this information, but also on store personnel. The lesson for retailers is to provide training for personnel in how to communicate product attributes effectively to visually impaired customers. Visually impaired customers also rely heavily on tactile information to evaluate product quality and draw perceptual inferences concerning product aesthetics from touch. The lesson for marketers is the need to ensure tactile information communicates product quality effectively. This study also found visually challenged consumers were highly loyal to responsive retailers. In another study, the authors found that physically challenged customers drew negative inferences about retailers from physical cues. For example, when wheelchairs and electric carts were placed in inaccessible locations or were dirty, when store aisles and dressing rooms were too narrow to maneuver carts easily, when doors were too heavy to open from a seated position, or when signage was too far above their line of sight, physically challenged customers inferred that retailers did not really value their patronage in spite of the presence of some amenities such as electric carts. The lesson for retailers is to adapt their facilities to these challenged patrons. However, many retailers resist these adaptations citing the small size of the disabled market segment and the expense of installing automatic doors, Braille signage, electric carts, and so on. Recent court decisions in the United States have rolled back some ADA provisions. How do you think marketers should respond to the special perceptual needs of the segment of physically challenged consumers and manage the perceptual inferences they draw from physical cues in retail landscapes?

Source: Carol Kaufman-Scarborough, "Sharing the Experience of Disabled Consumers: Building Understanding Through Ethnography," Journal of Contemporary Ethnography *30 (August 2001), pp. 430–64; and Richard Vezina, Alain d'Astous, and Sophie Deschamps, "The Physically Disabled Consumer: Some Preliminary Findings and an Agenda for Future Research,"* European Advances in Consumer Research, *vol. 2, ed. Flemming Hansen (Provo, UT: Association for Consumer Research, 1995), pp. 277–81.*

some elaboration, that is, some accessing of prior knowledge structures; but this can be at low levels such as simple recognition. At high levels of elaboration, people engage in processes such as counterarguing, problem solving, daydreaming, and fantasizing. Elaboration produces freedom of memory and attitude from the specific details of the original message or its setting. It can even result in a **boomerang effect** where *the attitude change is opposite to that advocated in the persuasive message.*[36]

Of course, stimuli that encourage elaboration can also be enormously effective. Such stimuli are likely to be remembered longer, and attitudes formed are likely to be much stronger than those associated with stimuli processed at a lower level of elaboration. For example, one form of high elaboration would be **role taking.** In the context of advertising, role taking involves placing the self into the ad or product experience. Through this transformation into the person or situation depicted in the ad, the potential consequences of product use or nonuse become more vivid and concrete for the viewer. **Transformational advertising** encourages this kind of identification, because it figuratively transforms the viewer watching the ad. Such transformations are likely only when the viewer is highly motivated to process the ad and when the ad contains

By picturing yourself in the experience portrayed, transformational ads make the consequences of product use more vivid.

sufficient cues to allow for such a transformation. For example, a strictly informational ad that contains no cues about feelings or emotional consequences is unlikely to elicit role taking.[37] A transformational ad can also serve to transform the product-use experience. For instance, drinking a soft drink may be perceived as more than just quenching a thirst. Through the influence of advertising imagery, consumers may feel that sipping the soft drink is now akin to playing volleyball on the beach with a group of friends on a beautiful summer day. The Clif Bar ad shown above is a good example of a transformational ad.

PERCEPTUAL JUDGMENTS AND MARKETING STRATEGIES

Most consumer perception research deals with perceptual interpretation. This is fundamental to issues of perceived product and service quality, for example. In the global marketplace, the issue of product-country image comes to the fore. Although we are dealing with perceptual judgments, sensations at the root of these judgments seem far away, transformed by knowledge and beliefs (see Chapter 9).

Perceptual judgments begin with selective attention to perceptual stimuli in the marketing landscape. Through selective exposure and attention, consumers form basic images of brands, products, and marketing communications, for instance. They draw basic perceptual inferences about the attributes of these marketing stimuli. Through learning and experience, consumers eventually form summary perceptual judgments that link the sensory stimuli to outcomes they consider probable. These judgments may be thought of as schemas, as discussed earlier. Depending on the judgment in question, quality, or product-country image (PCI), for example, both the perceptual stimuli to which people attend and the importance of those stimuli in forming judgments vary. Because consumers use information selectively, marketers must examine such issues as perceived quality and PCI in developing an understanding of particular consumers' perceptual judgments of particular market offerings.[38]

Perceived Quality

Perceived quality has been a central preoccupation in consumer and organization marketing. **Perceived quality,** whether in reference to a product or service, has been defined as *the consumer's evaluative judgment about an entity's overall excellence or superiority in providing desired benefits.* Quality is a key determinant of national competitiveness, responsible in part for the economic ascendancy of Japan and Germany. Perceived quality can reduce costs, extend market share, increase profitability, and create a differential advantage by erecting barriers to entry and lessening price elasticity. Research suggests that customers may care more about quality than economy; hence, marketers believe that providing evidence of incremental quality is a key to competitive advantage. While something is known of the way in which some consumers evaluate quality in the West, very little research has been conducted on quality judgment cross-culturally. Even in the West, however, the study of perceived quality is incomplete. For example, research on product and service quality tends to be conducted separately.[39]

Perceived quality is a judgment derived by a comparison of performance perceptions against expectations or evaluative standards. According to one theory, consumers use an array of sensory cues as indicators of quality. Cues are used according to their **predictive value,** *the degree to which consumers associate a given cue with product quality, the confidence value of a cue, and the degree to which consumers have confidence in their ability to use and judge that cue accurately.* The value of cues varies across product categories. Consumers in developed markets find it relatively easy to interpret cues for shopping goods such as personal care items; consumers in transitional markets do not always find this so easy. Cues must be learned of course. Even in the West, consumers find it less easy to interpret cues for credence goods such as auto repair or medical care.

Consumers rely on both **extrinsic cues,** such as price, brand name, packaging, store name, country of origin, color, and prior experience, and **intrinsic cues,** such as taste, texture, and aroma, when assessing product quality. Purchasing of wine, for example, involves both extrinsic and intrinsic product features. The more extrinsic cues include the shape of the bottle, the color of the wine, and the price. The intrinsic cues include taste, smell, and grape type. People vary in their use of cues, and we can segment markets by the cues typically employed by consumers to assess quality. For example, the Australian wine market can be divided into four segments: connoisseurs, a wine-knowledgeable segment, who rely heavily on intrinsic cues in making purchase decisions; aspirational drinkers, concerned with the social aspects of wine drinking, who rely heavily on extrinsic cues such as fashionable brands and labels; beverage wine consumers whose choice is dependent on a mix of cues—brands, taste, price, and price-related promotions—but who value consistency; and new wine drinkers, who are strongly influenced by the occasion where wine may be consumed, and often use price as a determinant for purchase.[40]

In developed markets, consumers frequently use brand name as a gestalt cue. That is, the brand name represents a composite of information about product attributes. A brand's perceived quality may exert a positive influence on the perceived value of a retail firm, for example. Depending on the product category, intrinsic cues also have high predictive and confidence value for consumers. Consider, for example, shopping for fruit and vegetables. Color, texture, firmness, and aroma all help cue whether the fruits and vegetables are fresh and ripe.[41]

Belief in price–quality relationships has been found to differentiate groups of U.S. consumers and affect marketplace behavior. This means that consumers who believe in a positive price–quality correspondence rely on price as a cue to quality, often preferring high-priced products, and demonstrate higher price-acceptability levels. Younger, lower-income, and less-experienced consumers tend to use belief more strongly in this perceptual schema. Recent research in urban China has found two groups of consumers: those who believe in a price–quality relationship and are likely to pay more for products, and those who are less trusting of a price–quality relationship and are likely to pay lower prices for products. This suggests that in some transitional markets, price does not yet have the same cuing value as in Western market economies.[42]

In the West, studies comparing private labels (retailers) to national brands (manufacturers) show that consumers often use both intrinsic product attributes and extrinsic attributes to discriminate against private-label brands. In one study, extrinsic cues such as a national brand name are more predictive of consumers' quality judgments than intrinsic cues, such as ingredients. Nonetheless, many large retailers, including Lobo's, a Canadian firm, and Carrefour, a French firm, have successfully leveraged private-label brands for competitive advantage.

Perceived service quality has often been measured using the **SERVQUAL scale,** which contains *five generic dimensions of perceived quality: tangibles, reliability, responsiveness, assurance, and empathy.* The tangibles dimension refers to characteristics of the service provider and the service delivery environment, also called the *servicescape.* Perceived service quality also varies with the participative role of the service provider, including the length of contact with the service provider, spatial intimacy, and affective content of the service delivered. Little research has been conducted on combined product/service-quality perceptions, although it has long been recognized that much of what is purchased in the marketplace combines features of products and services.[43] However, one study combining automobile product quality and automobile dealership service quality suggested both were better predictors of perceived quality than either alone.[44]

Product-Country Image Effects

Research on product-country image (PCI) has mainly studied **country of origin,** or country of manufacture, as a cue used by consumers and industrial buyers to infer beliefs about product attributes. Country of origin is conveyed through packaging, promotional materials, ingredients (e.g., Kobé or Nebraska corn-fed beef), and conventional symbols such as national flags. Country-of-origin cues are like other extrinsic cues in that they can be manipulated without changing the physical product. Sometimes, however, product-country image is clouded by confusion between country of origin and country of manufacture. Nike, for example, has a positive image as a U.S. origin brand, but it suffers from negative connotations as a company that uses low-paid labor in Southeast Asian manufacturing facilities.[45]

Provided that the basic criteria for perceptual selection such as vividness, clarity, and intensity are met, consumers' use of country-of-origin cues is determined by their power to predict positive consumption outcomes. This predictive relationship is shaped by **product-country image,** which is a *schematic mental representation of a country's people, products, culture, and national symbols.* A particular PCI may contain information about place of design (e.g., Italy), origin, manufacture (e.g., Germany or Japan), raw materials (e.g., cashmere from Kasmir), and so forth. Product-country images contain general impressions of countries and idiosyncratic beliefs about a country's products formed through direct or indirect experiences. They also contain information about the competitive market context, that is to say, the value of a product made in the United States compared to a product made in Japan, in the Japanese market, for example. Thus, Starbucks has become very successful in Japan, not known as a coffee-drinking country, because Starbucks conveys an "authentic" American coffeehouse image. Finally, PCI contains meanings pertaining to the usage scripts (see section on interpretation and elaboration above) it evokes. Each of the elements of the PCI may be used in targeting and positioning the product in a particular market context.[46]

Consumers' evaluations of country of origin are based in part on a match between product and country. Consumers prefer country X as an origin for a specific product when they believe that there is a match between the perceived strengths of country X and those needed to produce a particular product. Thus, high-tech products from Japan and Germany enjoy a kind of halo effect, or positive perceptual gestalt, because of a perceived match between their national strengths and what is required to make high-tech products. McDonald's has enjoyed a positive reception in some Asian markets because of its association with the United States and the idea of "modern" consumption. Similarly, some NICs and LAW nations such as India face market resistance based on less positive country stereotypes.[47]

Product-country images contain widely shared cultural stereotypes, or simplifying categories. For example, French-sounding brand names have a positive effect on consumers' evaluations of hedonic products such as perfume and wine. For this reason, the Champagne and Cognac regions of France have zealously guarded the use of these regional names as product cues. These effects persist even when consumers actually experience products.

Symbolic aspects of PCI may influence consumer preferences and contribute to brand loyalty. For example, some authors found that in India a Western origin had a substantial positive effect on brand attitudes, even holding quality constant. This effect was most powerful for consumers with a high admiration for Western lifestyles and for publicly consumed products. Similar findings have been reported in Romania and Turkey, whereas Muslim consumers in West Africa attach symbolic value to products alleged to come from Mecca in Saudi Arabia.[48]

The term **consumer voting** captures *the normative dimension of product-country images.* In other words, by deciding to purchase or avoid a country's products, consumers "vote" for or against the policies of its government. There are numerous global examples, including Jewish consumers boycotting German products because of the Holocaust, Australians boycotting French products because of French nuclear tests in the Pacific, and African-Americans boycotting products made in South Africa during the apartheid (racial separation) regime. Some Chinese consumers' willingness to buy Japanese products is negatively affected by the rivalry between these two countries. There are also instances where consumers reward sympathetic countries through selective purchase of their products.

PCI may also trigger the norm to buy domestically. Some consumers consider it morally appropriate to buy products that are manufactured or grown domestically. Trends in Poland suggest a resurgent preference for venerable Polish brands, although a number of these have been taken over and brought up to Western quality standards by Western firms. A study in South Africa showed that groups with an African national identity were more likely to use brands with South African or ambiguous product-country images, whereas groups with a European national identity were more likely to use brands with British or American product-country images. The United States, Canada, and the UK have sponsored buy-domestic campaigns, although there is limited evidence for the effectiveness of these. Consumer ethnocentrism, discussed in Chapter 3, serves as an important motivation of the decision to purchase domestically.[49]

Not all products evoke strong product-country images, and not all consumers use product-country images in developing product preferences. For example, a study in Singapore showed that a product's country of origin has a stronger effect on purchase choice when considering luxury products than necessities.[50] A study of Israeli consumers found they were indifferent to country of origin for shoes but attended to country of origin for consumer durables. And a study comparing U.S. and Canadian consumers found low rates of country-of-origin knowledge.

In short, PCI plays a role in judgments of product and brand quality. The influence of product-country image on behavior varies, but there is no doubt that it plays a role and that its relative importance may in fact equal or exceed that of other extrinsic cues depending on situational and other factors.

MATTERS OF TASTE: AESTHETIC BRIDGES BETWEEN GOODS

The idea of taste is fundamental to the success of many industries, including architecture, interior design, packaging, and fashion. A variety of specialized institutions, including fashion, food, wine, architecture, magazines, department stores and shopping malls, fashion shows, museums, and even television, have become important sources for the dissemination of perceptual judgments that we call fashion, style, and taste. The department stores that emerged in Paris and London at the end of the nineteenth century were intended as taste-making instruments, designed to teach and market good taste. American department stores offered for public consumption both elite consumer lifestyles and democratic consumer lifestyles promoted by the decorative arts movement. Interestingly, Crate and Barrel and Renovation Hardware have revived the decorative arts look. In 1926, Wanamaker's department store in Philadelphia offered interior design consulting to its patrons. Contemporary Japanese department stores, or *depato,* not only feature elaborate displays of Western goods and classes in their appreciation, they also offer classes in kimono wearing, pottery making, calligraphy, flower arranging, the preparation of Japanese delicacies, and the tea ceremony. In Sweden, the annual IKEA catalog distributed in August is an anxiously awaited repository of taste; a corporate effort to limit distribution only to consumers above a certain income threshold was hotly debated in the national press. The catalog is now translated into 17 languages for 28 different countries. In each case, the stores display a commitment to exploring and conveying conventional symbols of shared cultural identity, or taste.[51]

www.ikea.com

In this chapter we have explained how consumers' perceptions underlie preferences. Just about every consumer decision reflects sensory preferences and perceptual judgments. Often, we refer to differences between consumers in their sensory preferences as a "matter of taste." Take a moment and imagine what you think we mean by the term **taste.** You've probably heard it used in a variety of ways, for example, in ways that simply imply a difference in taste (That's more to his taste than mine) or in ways that imply evaluation (That was in bad taste). Modern use of the term obviously extends beyond sensory preferences and perceptual judgments to include combinations of sensory stimuli (e.g., home decor) and even behaviors and activities (table manners or jokes). However, discussions of taste are closely linked to perception. We will use the term to refer to *the making of judgments based on ideas of beauty, order, and arrangement.* The Japanese ad for a Motorola cell phone shown below, provides a good example of the role of beauty, order, and arrangement in making aesthetic judgments. The image exudes the harmony and appeal to emotions characteristic of much Japanese advertising and packaging.

There are a few important general points to make about taste. First, taste is a culturally and historically specific preference for certain things. A quick look at your parents' photo album is likely to reveal clothes and looks that to you seem absolutely ridiculous. But don't laugh too hard because you may be wearing those same styles in a few months or years. Second, taste is not only about raw sensory stimuli; it's also about the interpretation of those stimuli. It's possible to like short skirts in one fashion cycle and find them distasteful in a different cycle. Third, tastes as a form of cultural capital (see Chapter 12) give us membership in some groups and exclude us from others. They are used to signal and distinguish who we are. Sometimes these tastes are very subtle, and people are hardly aware of how they cue social class or cultural heritage. For example, research both in the United States and in the Netherlands shows that people of higher social status tend to be more omnivorous in their musical tastes (that is, they are more familiar with and like more different musical genres) than those from lower-status groups.

Japanese taste—a distinctive sense of beauty, order, and arrangement is reflected in this advertisement for cell phones.

At the same time, research in the United States showed that those musical genres whose fans have the least education—gospel, country, rap, and heavy metal—are also those most likely to be rejected by the musically omnivorous. In the Netherlands, statistical analysis showed that musical tastes are structured on the basis of three basic genres (highbrow, pop, folk). The omnivores' tastes (and purchase and consumption behavior) combine elements of all these genres. In both cases research confirmed other findings suggesting omnivorous consumers tend to be of higher status than univorous consumers, those with more exclusive tastes.[52] Sometimes tastes are adopted or acquired in order to signal membership in a group (e.g., a taste for tattoos, body piercing).[53] Fourth, each culture has arbitrators of taste, such as Martha Stewart, discussed in Chapter 11, or the late Princess Diana, who function to define and change what's tasteful and what's not. This is what fashion and home-decorating consultants do.

Specialized taste-making institutions have been around a long time. Royal courts in both Europe and Asia were important taste-making centers in the past. Prevalent in Tudor England (fifteenth century) was a concern for the aesthetic value of "patina," or the perceived age of durable consumer goods. An elaborate, highly prescriptive eleventh century guide to the court fashion of imperial Japan survives. This guide focuses on the creation of subtle color effects geared to the season of the year, to occasions, and to the age and social status of the wearer. Fashion broadside sheets from England and several different types of block-print fashion publications from eighteenth-century Japan also survive. Of the latter, one type resembles global fashion magazines such as *Cosmopolitan*. The Web has become a hugely influential taste-making environment. Sites for connoisseurs and would-be connoisseurs of all things from garage bands to motor scooters and alternative lifestyle ideas abound.

@ www.garagebands.com

@ http://members.aol.com/vespavamp/main.htm#top

@ www.utnereader.com

We do not want to leave you with the impression that consumers are passive recipients of perceptual meanings. Consumers often develop their own tastes from elements provided by the taste-making institutions and perceive consumer goods in terms of them. That is, taste is a matter of individual perception and judgment. But at the same time, taste is part of the social world and helps consumers find their place in that world.

SUMMARY

In examining perception, we are moving to a consideration of those factors that more directly influence acquisition and consumption. Perception is a process of giving meaning to sensory stimuli.

Underlying perception is sensation. By sensation we mean the immediate response of the sensory systems to stimuli. Sensations vary between persons, social groups, and cultures. People detect stimuli through a variety of sensory receptor. These are the organs of perception. Sensation is provoked in large part by changes in sensory input. Two different sensory thresholds are important in marketing. One is the absolute threshold and the other is the just noticeable difference or differential threshold. A related idea, Weber's law, states that the stronger the initial sensory stimulus, the greater the additional intensity needed for the second stimulus to be perceived as different.

A primary function of sensory systems is to discard irrelevant or useless information. That is, sensory systems serve as selection systems. Perception begins with an exposure to a stimulus. Preattentive processing refers to the simultaneous preconscious monitoring of all sensory channels for events that will require a shift in attention.

SUMMARY

Perceptual selection refers to the fact that consumers select only a small portion of the stimuli to which they are exposed for conscious processing.

Perceptual organization is the third part in the perceptual process. Categorization schemes allow people to give coherence to their general knowledge about other people, objects, and situations. Three illustrations of this tendency—grouping, figure-and-ground discriminations, and the closure principle—are especially common. In all cases, when presented with ambiguous stimuli, people try to clarify their perceptions.

The fourth part in the perceptual process is interpretation. While the principles of perceptual organization are often applied unconsciously, interpretation is usually a conscious process. At least two different sorts of knowledge structures are important to interpretation: schemas and scripts.

One important aspect of interpretation is perceptual inferences. Inferences are interpretations that go beyond the information given. Perceptions of quality and country-product images are examples. Sometimes consumer interpretation of perceptual stimuli also includes high levels of elaboration. Marketing stimuli that encourage elaboration can be enormously effective.

Finally, sensory preferences, or taste, are primary influences on the decisions consumers make. The idea of taste is important to the success of design and business practice (e.g., creating effective advertisements).

KEY TERMS

absolute threshold 305
ad hoc categories 313
atypicality 311
autonomic responses 300
boomerang effect 318
categorization 311
closure 316
consumer voting 322
contrast effects 311
country of origin 321
differential threshold 306
elaboration 317
exposure 308
extrinsic cues 320
figure and ground 314
grouping 313
intrinsic cues 320
involuntary attention 311
just noticeable difference (JND) 306
learned responses 300
orientation reflex 311
perceived quality 320
perceptions 299
perceptual filters 305
perceptual inferences 317
perceptual organization 311
perceptual selection 309
perceptual vigilance 309
phenomenal absolutism 300
preattentive processing 308
predictive value 320
primitive categorization 313
product-country image 322
role taking 318
schemas 317
scripts 317
sensation 299
sensory preferences 299
sensory receptors 300
sensory thresholds 304
SERVQUAL scale 321
taste 323
transformational advertising 318
Weber's law 306

1. Discuss how cereal manufacturers can apply their knowledge of differential threshold during periods of (*a*) increasing competition, (*b*) rising ingredient prices, and (*c*) changing consumer attitudes regarding nutrition.
2. Find two or three ads that use the grouping technique to influence consumers' interpretation of the ad. Explain how grouping is being used in the advertisement.
3. Midas International Corporation wants to be known for more than mufflers. It wants to reposition itself as an auto systems expert. Although the company has been offering services such as computerized alignment and suspension work for years, consumers still view Midas as a muffler shop. How would you recommend that Midas go about changing its image?
4. Develop a description of your own schema for (*a*) a cruise, (*b*) a movie theater, and (*c*) a birthday party. Talk about the different sensory systems that are engaged in your schemas. Do your schemas involve sights, sounds, smell, tastes, and tactile sensations? Now, take just one of your descriptions and indicate the potential importance to marketing managers if your description represents a significant segment of consumers.
5. For each of the following product categories, develop a basic example of how role taking might be used in advertising to encourage high elaboration of the message:
    a. Mountain bikes
    b. Portable phones
    c. Airline travel
6. As the owner of a small bed and breakfast in the Colorado Rockies, you rely on favorable word-of-mouth messages and repeat patronage to attract guests each year. What sensory and perceptual tactics could you use to help people remember their experience with you so that they pass the word on and also come back again?
7. Zapping is a common problem for marketers. Consumers use remote controls to switch between channels during commercials or mute out commercial messages. What perceptual tactics can advertisers use to get the prime-time television audience to pay attention to their ads and brands?
8. Try to imagine cellular phones, cars, lamps, bottled water, and chocolate made in Sweden, Mexico, and Japan. For each of these three countries, write down a list of the words you might associate with each product (e.g., Swedish chocolate), including beliefs, feelings, and any moral ideas you might attach to them. Try to explain whether and why your product-country images are positive or not.

REVIEW QUESTIONS

CASES

YOU MAKE THE CALL

THE CALL OF THE WILD CAR ALARM

The familiar urban "song" goes like this: 16 siren wails as an introduction, followed by 16 more, in a different pattern. Then eight descending swoops, then two long upward swoops, then the so-called European ambulance sound, like a shrill grunt. Finally, as a coda, a truly annoying staccato of warning tones follows.

Summer in New York and other big cities is the noisiest time of the year—open windows, blaring stereos, and screaming kids home from school all contribute to the background din. The "song" is the tone sequence of many car alarms installed to inhibit car theft and vandalism, and it adds its own distinct sound to urban noise pollution problems.

"I've seen cars driving down the street with these things in full blare and nobody—not even police officers—seems to take notice," Rick Karr of National Public Radio reports. "What kind of theft deterrent is that? These car alarms are pretty much for the birds."

But Brooklyn, New York, artist Nina Katchadourian has a novel solution. With help from the Sculpture Center in the New York City borough of Queens, she's taken three cars and fitted them with a new kind of alarm. Instead of those six annoying electronic tones, her alarms ring out with bird songs that more or less follow the same sonic pattern as standard alarms.

"They're all real birds," Katchadourian says of her Natural Car Alarms. "They are all a little bit re-edited so that I could . . . get this patterning to work. And they are—like car alarms—quite loud, quite shrill."

She built the hardware for her alarms from car stereos and microprocessor chips. She got the basic bird sounds from the Macauley Library of Natural Sounds at Cornell University. Her sonic aviary includes the mating call of the three-wattled bellbird, the everyday song of the northern bobwhite, and the rare ivory-billed woodpecker—which hasn't really been seen for about 70 years, and may be extinct. You can listen to these bird alarms at the website listed below.

Katchadourian says she got the idea for Natural Car Alarms while she was on an artist's residency last year on the island of Trinidad. "One day deep in the jungle I heard a bird that I mistook for a car alarm . . . and I thought, my urban New York mindset is creeping in, even here."

Out in the country, bird sounds are perfectly natural, blending into the background—much like the sound of a car alarm in an urban environment. "But here in the city, a bobwhite is almost unheard of," Karr reports. "Its sound is especially jarring when it's blaring from the underside of a late-model Honda sedan."

Nina Katchadourian says the whole point of her Natural Car Alarms is to get people to think about what we mean when we use the word "natural." Her "flock" of natural car alarms will be alighting throughout the summer at art events across New York City. She says she didn't start out with any intention of actually selling her alarms, but she's received so many requests that she's looking into having the alarms mass-produced.

Under the hood: the electronic "guts" of the bird call alarm.

QUESTIONS

1. What perceptual effects explain why people do not pay attention to standard car alarms in urban environments?
2. What perceptual effects explain why people do pay attention to car alarms featuring bird sounds?
3. Does perceptual theory suggest it would be better to use a different sonic pattern for the bird alarms or the standard pattern as Katchadourian's alarms currently do?
4. If Katchadourian is successful at mass-marketing Natural Car Alarms, does perceptual theory suggest they will be more successful than standard alarms in alerting people to potential car thefts in progress?

Source: Rick Karr, "The Call of the Wild Car Alarm," July 11, 2002, All Things Considered, *National Public Radio, http://www.npr.org/programs/atc/features/2002/july/car_alarm/index.html.*

CASES

ENDNOTES

1. Thomas Hine, *The Total Package* (Boston: Little, Brown and Company, 1995).

2. Edmund Blair Bolles, *A Second Way of Knowing* (Englewood Cliffs, NJ: Prentice Hall, 1991).

3. Marshall H. Segall, Donald T. Campbell, and Melville J. Herskovits, *The Influence of Culture on Visual Perception* (New York: Bobbs-Merrill, 1996); and Linda M. Scott, "Images in Advertising: The Need for a Theory of Visual Rhetoric," *Journal of Consumer Research* 21 (September 1994), pp. 252–73.

4. Bolles, *A Second Way of Knowing;* Alan R. Hirsch, "Effect of Ambient Odor on Slot Machine Usage in a Las Vegas Casino," working paper, Smell and Taste Treatment and Research Foundation, Chicago, 1994; and Michael E. Long, *National Geographic* 182 (November 5, 1992), pp. 3–41.

5. Gerald J. Gorn, Amitava Chattopaduyay, Tracey Yi, and Darren W. Dahl, "Effects of Color as an Excutional Cue in Advertising: They're in the Shade," *Management Science* 43, no. 10 (1997), pp. 1387–400.

6. Ibid.

7. J. Argue, "Color Counts," *Vancouver Sun,* June 10, 1991, p. B7.

8. Joan Meyers-Levy and Laura A. Peracchio, "Understanding the Effects of Color: How the Correspondence between Available and Required Resources Affects Attitudes," *Journal of Consumer Research* 22 (September 1995), pp. 121–38; and Susan E. Middlestadt, "The Effect of Background and Ambient Color on Product Attitudes and Beliefs," *Advances in Consumer Research,* vol. 17, ed. Marvin Goldberg, Gerald Gorn, and Richard Pollay (Provo, UT: Association for Consumer Research, 1990) pp. 244–49.

9. Robert E. Krider, Priya Raghubir, and Aradhna Krishna, *Asia Pacific Advances in Consumer Research,* vol. 3, ed. Kineta Hung and Kent Menroe (Provo, UT: Association for Consumer Research, 1998), pp. 216–17.

10. Wayne Weiten, *Psychology: Themes and Variations* (Pacific Grove, CA: Brooks/Cole Publishing Company, 1998); and Deborah J. Mitchell, Barbara E. Kahn, and Susan C. Knasko, "There's Something in the Air: Effects of Congruent and Incongruent Ambient Odor on Consumer Decision Making," *Journal of Consumer Research* 22 (September 1995), pp. 229–38.

11. See Mitchell, Kahn, and Knasko, "There's Something in the Air"; and Susan C. Knasko, "Lingering Time in a Museum in the Presence of Congruent and Incongruent Odors," *Chemical Senses* 18 (October 1993), p. 581.

12. Clare Caldwell and Sally A. Hibbert, "Play That One Again: The Effect of Music Tempo on Consumer Behavior in a Restaurant," *European Advances in Consumer Research,* vol. 4, ed. Bernard Dubois, Tina M. Lowry, L. J. Shrum, and Marc Venhuele (Provo, UT: Association for

Consumer Research, 1999), pp. 58–62; James J. Kellaris and Susan Powell Mantel, "Shaping Time Perceptions with Background Music: The Effects of Congruity and Arousal on Estimates of Ad Durations," *Psychology and Marketing* 10 (January/February 1996), pp. 15–29; Steve Oakes, "Examining the Relationship between Background Music Tempo and Perceived Duration Using Different Versions of a Radio Ad," *European Advances in Consumer Research,* vol. 4, ed. Bernard Dubois, Tina M. Lowry, L. J. Shrum, and Marc Venhuele (Provo, UT: Association for Consumer Research, 1999), pp. 40–44; and Linda M. Scott, "Understanding Jingles and Needledrop: A Rhetorical Approach to Music in Advertising," *Journal of Consumer Research* 17 (September 1990), pp. 223–326.

13. Jochen Wirtz and Anna Mattila, "Congruency of Scent and Music as a Driver of In-Store Evaluations and Behavior," *Asia Pacific Advances in Consumer Research,* vol. 4, ed. Paula Tidwell (Provo, UT: Association for Consumer Research, 2001), p. 363.

14. The idea of using scents in Disney World and the Epcot Center came from Disney Imagineering, which designs and develops all of the company attractions. Disney purchases its scents from Selton International.

15. William S. Cain, "Physical and Cognitive Limitations on Olfactory Processing in Human Beings," in *Chemical Signals in Vertebrates,* ed. D. Muller-Schwarz and M. M. Mozell (New York: Plenum, 1977), pp. 287–301; William S. Cain, "Odor Identification by Males and Females: Predication vs. Performance," *Chemical Senses* 7, no. 2 (1982), pp. 129–42; B. J. Cowart, "Development of Taste Perception in Humans: Sensitivity and Preference throughout the Lifespan," *Psychological Bulletin* 90 (1981), pp. 43–73; Joseph C. Stevens, Linda M. Bartoshuk, and William S. Cain, "Chemical Senses and Aging: Taste versus Smell," *Chemical Senses* 9, no. 2 (1984), pp. 167–79; and M. Schleidt, B. Hold, and G. Attili, "A Cross-Cultural Study on Attitude toward Personal Odors," *Journal of Chemical Ecology* 7 (1981), pp. 19–31.

16. John Koten, "To Grab Viewer's Attention, TV Ads Aim for the Eardrum," *The Wall Street Journal,* January 26, 1984, Eastern Edition, p. B1.

17. Sunil Gupta and Lee G. Cooper, "The Discounting of Discounts and Promotion Strategies," *Journal of Consumer Research* 19 (December 1992), pp. 401–11.

18. John B. Hinge, "Critics Call Cuts in Package Size Deceptive Move," *The Wall Street Journal,* February 5, 1991, p. B1.

19. Robert E. Ornstein, *The Psychology of Consciousness* (New York: Pelican Books, 1972). See also Jerome Bruner, "On Perceptual Readiness," *Psychological Review* 64 (1957), pp. 123–52; and George Kelly, *The Psychology of Personal Constructs,* vols. 1 and 2 (New York: Norton, 1955).

20. Anthony G. Greenwald and Clark Leavitt, "Audience Involvement in Advertising: Four Levels," *Journal of Consumer Research* 11 (June 1984), pp. 581–92; and Chris Janiszewski, "Preconscious Processing Effects: The Independence of Attitude Formation and Conscious Thought," *Journal of Consumer Research* 15 (September 1988), pp. 199–209.

21. Janiszewski, "Preconscious Processing Effects"; Philip M. Merikle and Jim Sheesman, "Current Status of Research on Subliminal Perception," in *Advances in Consumer Research,* vol. 14, ed. Melanie Wallendorf and Paul Anderson (Provo, UT: Association for Consumer Research, 1987), pp. 298–302; and William R. Wilson, "Feeling More Than We Can Know: Exposure Effects without Learning," *Journal of Personality and Social Psychology* 37, no. 6 (1979), pp. 811–21. A related area of research also speaks to the question of whether consumers' preferences and behavior can be influenced by factors independent of cognition. This stream of research regards what has been termed the "mere-exposure" effect. Because much of this research relies on *remembered* exposure or attention, we reserve this important discussion for Chapter 15 where we explicitly discuss attitude formation.

22. Geoffrey Hall, *Perceptual and Associative Learning* (Oxford: Clarendon, 1991); Keith J. Holyoak, Koh Kyunghee, and Richard E. Nisbett, "A Theory of Conditioning: Inductive Learning within Rule-Based Default Hierarchies," *Psychological Review* 96 (April 1989), pp. 315–40; and Chris Janiszewski and Luk Warlop, "The Influence of Classical Conditioning Procedures on Subsequent Attention to the Conditioned Brand," *Journal of Consumer Research* 20 (September 1993), pp. 171–89.

23. Greenwald and Leavitt, "Audience Involvement in Advertising"; and Richard L. Celsi and

Jerry C. Olson, "The Role of Involvement in Attention and Comprehension Processes," *Journal of Consumer Research* 15 (September 1988), pp. 210–24. The topic of involvement and attention is also discussed in Chapter 7. See also Cynthia Huffman and Michael J. Houston, "Goal-Oriented Experiences and the Development of Knowledge," *Journal of Consumer Research* 20 (September 1993), pp. 190–207.

24. Rhonda Gibson, Huiuk Yi, and Dolf Zilmann, "Incidental Learning from Radio Advertisements with and without Curiosity-Arousing Questions," in *Advances in Consumer Research,* vol. 21, ed. Chris Allen and Deborah Roedder John (Provo, UT: Association for Consumer Research, 1994), pp. 282–85; Robin Coulter Higie, "A Test of Prescriptive Advice from the Rossiter-Percy Advertising Planning Grid Using Radio Commercials," in *Advances in Consumer Research,* vol. 21, ed. Chris Allen and Deborah Roedder John (Provo, UT: Association for Consumer Research, 1994), pp. 276–81; Romain Laufer and Catherine Paradeise, *Marketing Democracy* (New Brunswick, NJ: Transaction Books, 1990), p. 8; Richard E. Petty, John T. Cacioppo, and Rachel Goldman, "Personal Involvement as a Determinant of Argument-Based Persuasion," *Journal of Personality and Social Psychology* 41, no. 5 (1981), pp. 847–55; and Richard E. Petty, John T. Cacioppo, and Martin Heesacker, "Effects of Rhetorical Questions on Persuasion: A Cognitive Response Analysis," *Journal of Personality and Social Psychology* 40, no. 3 (1981), pp. 432–40.

25. James Heckman, "Say 'Buy-Buy': Baby Product Makers School Marketers in Reaching Elusive Targets," *Marketing News* 11 (October 1999), pp. 1, 19.

26. Swee Hoon Ang, Siew Meng Leon, and Wendy Yeo, "When Silence Is Golden: Effects of Silence on Consumer Ad Response," *Advances in Consumer Research,* vol. 26, ed. Eric J. Arnould and Linda M. Scott (Provo, UT: Association for Consumer Research, 1999), pp. 295–99; Mike Ewing, "From Medium to Mild: Tracking Australian Consumers' Indifference Towards Television Advertising," *Asia Pacific Advances in Consumer Research,* vol. 4, ed. Paula Tidwell (Provo, UT: Association for Consumer Research, 2001), pp. 53–59; Linda L. Golden, Judy K. Frels, Vern C. Vincent, and Gilberto de los Santos, "Ecological Information Receptivity of Hispanic and Anglo Americans," *Advances in Consumer Research,* vol. 23, ed. Kim Corfman and John Lynch (Provo, UT: Association for Consumer Research, 1996), pp. 189–95; Thomas J. Olney, Morris B. Holbrook, and Rajeev Batra, "Consumer Responses to Advertising: The Effects of Ad Content, Emotions, and Attitude toward the Ad on Viewing Time," *Journal of Consumer Research* 17 (March 1991), pp. 440–53; V. Raman, "A Qualitative Investigation of Web-Browsing Behavior," *Advances in Consumer Research,* vol. 24, ed. Merrie Brucks and Debbie MacInnis (Provo, UT: Association for Consumer Research, 1997), pp. 511–16; and Roland Rust and Richard W. Oliver, "The Death of Advertising," *Journal of Advertising* 23, no. 4 (1994), pp. 71–78.

27. Joel B. Cohen and Kunal Basu, "Alternative Models of Categorization: Toward a Contingent Processing Framework," *Journal of Consumer Research* 13 (March 1987), pp. 455–72; and Carolyn B. Mervis and Eleanor Rosch, "Categorization of Natural Objects," in *Annual Review of Psychology,* vol. 32, ed. Mark R. Rosenzweig and Lyman W. Porter (Palo Alto, CA: Annual Reviews, Inc., 1981), pp. 89–115.

28. Anat Rafaeli, "When Appearance Matters: Visible Aspects of Organizations as Precursors of Service Expectations," in *Proceedings of the Fourth International Research Seminar in Service Management,* ed. Pierre Eiglier and Eric Langeard (Aix-en-Provence, France: I.A.E., 1996), pp. 83–86.

29. Lawrence W. Barsalou, "Ad Hoc Categories," *Memory and Cognition* 11 (1983), pp. 211–27; William D. Wattenmaker, Gerald I. Dewey, Timothy D. Murphy, and Douglas Medin, "Linear Separability and Concept Learning: Context, Relational Properties, and Concept Naturalness," *Cognitive Psychology* 18 (1986), pp. 158–94; Craig J. Thompson, "The Role of Context in Consumers' Category Judgments: A Preliminary Investigation," in *Advances in Consumer Research,* vol. 16, ed. Thomas Srull (Provo, UT: Association for Consumer Research, 1989), pp. 542–47; and Emilie M. Roth and Edward J. Shoben, "The Effect of Context on the Structure of Categories," *Cognitive Psychology* 15 (1983), pp. 346–78.

30. Recent research suggests that *frames* rather than independent feature lists provide the fundamental representation of knowledge. Frames include both abstract attributes and specific values for those attributes; and also connect attributes into a pattern of relationships. For a more complete

discussion, see Lawrence W. Barsalou, "Frames, Concepts and Conceptual Fields," in *Frames, Fields, and Contrasts: New Essays in Semantic and Lexical Organization,* ed. Eva Kittay and Adrienne Lehrer (Hillsdale, NJ: Erlbaum, 1992), pp. 11–35.

31. For an entertaining discussion and many examples of how categories vary cross-culturally, see George Lakoff, *Women, Fire and Dangerous Things* (Chicago: University of Chicago Press, 1987); Roy G. D'Andrade, "Cultural Meaning Systems," in *Culture Theory: Essays on Mind, Self, and Emotion,* ed. Richard A. Shweder and Robert A. LeVine (Cambridge: Cambridge University Press, 1984), pp. 88–119; and Ajay K. Sirsi, James C. Ward, and Peter H. Reingen, "Microcultural Analysis of Variation in Sharing of Causal Reasoning about Behavior," *Journal of Consumer Research* 22 (March 1996), pp. 345–72.

32. Thomas H. Davenport and John C. Beck, "Getting the Attention You Need," *Harvard Business Review,* September–October 2000, pp. 118–26.

33. Ronald E. Milliman, "Using Background Music to Affect the Behavior of Supermarket Shoppers," *Journal of Marketing* 46 (Summer 1982), pp. 86–91; Ronald E. Milliman, "The Influence of Background Music on the Behavior of Restaurant Patrons," *Journal of Consumer Research* 13 (September 1986), pp. 286–89; Lee Rath, "Store Music Directly Affects Buying Trends: Expert Advises Tailoring It to Suit Clients," *Merchandising,* August 1984; Jeff Ware and Gerald L. Patrick, "Gelson's Supermarkets: Effects of MUZAK Music on the Purchasing Behavior of Supermarket Shoppers," *MUZAK Research Report,* 1984; and Richard F. Yalch and Eric Spangenberg, "Effects of Store Music on Shopping Behavior," *Journal of Consumer Marketing* 7 (Spring 1990), pp. 55–60.

34. Gestalt psychology was founded by Max Wertheimer (1880–1943). Other influential pioneers in this area include Kurt Koffka and Wolfgang Kohler.

35. For examples directly relevant to restaurant scripts, see Roger Schank and Robert Abelson, *Scripts, Plans, Goals and Understanding* (Hillsdale, NJ: Erlbaum, 1977).

36. Deborah J. MacInnis and Linda L. Price, "The Role of Imagery in Information Processing: Review and Extensions," *Journal of Consumer Research* 13 (March 1987), pp. 473–91; and Greenwald and Leavitt, "Audience Involvement in Advertising."

37. Deborah J. MacInnis and Bernard J. Jaworski, "Information Processing from Advertisements: Toward an Integrative Framework," *Journal of Marketing* 53 (October 1989), pp. 1–23; and Chris Puto and William D. Wells, "Informational and Transformational Advertising: The Differential Effects of Time," in *Advances in Consumer Research,* vol. 11, ed. Thomas Kinnear (Ann Arbor, MI: Association for Consumer Research, 1984), pp. 638–43.

38. Güliz Ger, "Country Image: Perceptions, Attitudes, Associations, and Their Relationships to Context," in *Proceedings of the Third International Conference on Marketing and Development,* ed. R. R. Dholaki and K. C. Bothra (New Delhi: Academy of Marketing Science, 1991), pp. 390–98; D. Maheshwaran, "Country of Origin as a Stereotype: Effects of Consumer Expertise and Attribute Strength on Product Evaluation," *Journal of Consumer Research* 21, no. 2 (1994), pp. 354–65; and David Mazursky, "Forming Impressions of Merchandise and Service Quality," in *Perceived Quality: How Consumers View Stores and Merchandise,* ed. Jacob Jacoby and Jerry C. Olson (Lexington, MA: Lexington Books, 1985), pp. 139–53.

39. Robert Jacobson and David A. Aaker, "The Strategic Role of Product Quality," *Journal of Marketing* 51 (October 1987), pp. 31–44; Leonard A. Morgan, "The Importance of Quality," in *Perceived Quality: How Consumers View Stores and Merchandise,* ed. Jacob Jacoby and Jerry C. Olson (Lexington, MA: Lexington Books, 1985), pp. 61–64; Joseph A. Limprecht and Robert H. Hayes, "The Incline of Quality," *Harvard Business Review* 60 (September–October 1982), pp. 137–45; Michael E. Porter, *Competitive Strategy* (New York: Free Press, 1980); and Michael E. Porter, "The Competitive Advantage of Nations," *Harvard Business Review* 69 (March–April 1991), pp. 73–93.

40. John Hall and Maxwell Winchester, "Empirical Analysis of Spawton's (1991) Segmentation of the Australian Wine Market," *Asia Pacific Advances in Consumer Research,* vol. 4, ed. Paula Tidwell (Provo, UT: Association for Consumer Research, 2001), pp. 319–27.

41. Dhruv Grewal, R. Krishnan, Julie Baker, and Norm Borin, "The Effect of Store Name, Brand Name and Price Discounts on Consumers' Evaluations and Purchase Intentions," *Journal of Retailing* 74, no. 3 (1998), pp. 331–52; Jacob Jacoby, Jerry Olson, and Rafael Haddock, "Price,

Brand Name and Product Composition Characteristics as Determinants of Perceived Quality," *Journal of Applied Psychology* 55 (December 1971), pp. 570–79; Jerry Olson and Jacob Jacoby, "Cue Utilization in the Quality Perception Process," *Proceedings, 3rd Annual Conference,* ed. M. Venkatesan (Urbana, IL: Association for Consumer Research, 1973), pp. 167–79; Jacob Jacoby and Jerry C. Olson, eds., *Perceived Quality: How Consumers View Stores and Merchandise* (Lexington, MA: Lexington Books, 1985); Ashkay R. Rao and Kent B. Monroe, "The Effect of Price, Brand Name, and Store Name on Buyers' Perceptions of Product, Quality: An Integrative Review," *Journal of Marketing Research* 26 (August 1989), pp. 351–57; Valarie A. Zeithaml, "Consumer Perceptions of Price, Quality, and Value: A Means-End Model and Synthesis of Evidence," *Journal of Marketing* 52 (July 1988), pp. 2–22; and Jan-Benedict E. M. Steenkamp, "Conceptual Model of the Quality Perception Process," *Journal of Business Research* 21 (December 1990), pp. 309–33.

42. Ann Veeck and Alvin C. Burns, "An Investigation of the Use of Price-Quality Schema by Urban Chinese," in *Advances in Consumer Research,* vol. 22, ed. Frank Kardes and Mita Sujan (Provo, UT: Association for Consumer Research, 1995), pp. 297–302; and Rose L. Johnson and James J. Kellaris, "An Exploratory Study of Price/Perceived-Quality Relationships among Customer Services," in *Advances in Consumer Research,* vol. 15, ed. Michael Houston (Provo, UT: Association for Consumer Research, 1988), pp. 316–22.

43. Mary Jo Bitner, "Servicescapes: The Impact of Physical Surroundings on Customers and Employees," *Journal of Marketing* 56 (April 1992), pp. 57–71; Mary Jo Bitner, "Evaluating Service Encounters: The Effects of Physical Surroundings and Employee Responses," *Journal of Marketing* 54 (April 1990), pp. 69–82; Linda L. Price, Eric J. Arnould, and Patrick Tierney, "Going to Extremes: Rethinking Service Encounter Management and Provider Performance," *Journal of Marketing* 59 (April 1995), pp. 83–97; and Valarie Zeithaml, A. Parasuraman, and Leonard L. Berry, *Delivering Quality Service: Balancing Customer Perceptions and Expectations* (New York: Free Press, 1990).

44. Joseph A. Bellizzi, Harry F. Krueckeberg, John R. Hamilton, and Warren S. Martin, "Consumer Perceptions of National, Private, and Generic Brands," *Journal of Retailing* 57 (1998), pp. 56–70; Ronald P. Brensinger, *An Empirical Investigation into Consumer Perceptions of Combined Product and Service Quality: The Automobile,* doctoral dissertation, Department of Marketing, University of South Florida, Tampa, 1993; Isabella C. M. Cunningham, Andrew P. Hardy, and Giovanna Imperia, "Generic Brands versus National Brands and Store Brands," *Journal of Advertising Research* 22 (October–November 1982), pp. 25–32; Christine T. Ennew and Martin R. Binks, "Impact of Participative Service Relationships on Quality, Satisfaction and Retention: An Exploratory Study," *Journal of Business Research* 46 (October 1999), pp. 121–32; Paul S. Richardson, Alan S. Dick, and Arun K. Jain, "Extrinsic and Intrinsic Cue Effects on Perceptions of Store Brand Quality," *Journal of Marketing* 58 (October 1994), pp. 28–36; and Steenkamp, "Conceptual Model of the Quality Perception Process."

45. Peter W. J. Verlegh and Jan-Benedict E. M. Steenkamp, "A Review and Meta-Analysis of Country-of-Origin Research," *Journal of Economic Psychology* 20, no. 5 (1999), pp. 521–46.

46. Søren Askegaard and Güliz Ger, "Product-Country Images: Toward a Contextualized Approach," in *European Advances in Consumer Research,* vol. 8, ed. B. Englis and A. Olofsson (Provo, UT: Association for Consumer Research, 1997), pp. 50–58; and N. Papadopoulos, "What Product-Country Images Are and Are Not," in *Product-Country Images: Impact and Role in International Marketing,* ed. N. Papadopoulos and L. Heslop (New York: International Business Press, 1993), pp. 3–35.

47. M. C. Han, "Country Image: Halo or Summary Construct?" *Journal of Marketing Research* 26 (May 1989), pp. 222–29; Irwin P. Levin, J. D. Jasper, John D. Mittelstadt, and Gary J. Gaeth, "Attitudes toward 'Buy America First' and Preference for American and Japanese Cars: A Different Role for Country-of-Origin Information," in *Advances in Consumer Research,* vol. 20, ed. Leigh McAlister and Michael L. Rothschild (Provo, UT: Association for Consumer Research, 1993), pp. 625–29; Aysegul Ozsomer and S. Tamer Cavusgil, "Country-of-Origin Effects on Product Evaluations: A Sequel to Bilkey and Nes Review," in *AMA Educators' Proceedings,* vol. 2, ed. Mary C. Gilly et al. (Chicago: American Marketing Association, 1991), pp. 269–77;

Nader T. Tavassoli, Lauren Goldberg Block, Bernd H. Schmitt, and Morris B. Holbrook, "Perceptions of Western Products in Transforming Socialist Countries," in *European Advances in Consumer Research,* vol. 1, ed. Gary J. Bamossy and W. Fred van Raaij (Provo, UT: Association for Consumer Research, 1993), pp. 226–31; and James L. Watson, ed., *Golden Arches East* (Stanford: Stanford University Press, 1997).

48. Eric J. Arnould, "Toward a Broadened Theory of Preference Formation and the Diffusion of Innovations: Cases from Zinder Province, Niger Republic," *Journal of Consumer Research* 16 (September 1989), pp. 239–67; Güliz Ger, Russell W. Belk, and Dana N. Lascu, "The Development of Consumer Desire in Marketing and Developing Economies: The Cases of Romania and Turkey," in *Advances in Consumer Research,* vol. 20, ed. Leigh McAlister and Michael Rothschild (Provo, UT: Association for Consumer Research, 1993), pp. 102–7; Rajeev Batra, Dana L. Alden, Jan-Benedict E. M. Steenkamp, and S. Ramachander, "Effects of Brand Local/Non-Local Origin on Consumer Attitudes in Developing Countries," *Journal of Consumer Psychology* 9, no. 2 (1999), pp. 113–18; David McQuaid, "Poland: After the Gold Rush," *Business Eastern Europe,* October 24, 1994, p. 7; and Tavassoli, Block, Schmitt, and Holbrook, "Perceptions of Western Products in Transforming Socialist Countries."

49. Steven M. Burgess and Mari Harris, "Social Identity in an Emerging Consumer Market," in *Advances in Consumer Research,* vol. 26, ed. Eric J. Arnould and Linda M. Scott (Provo, UT: Association for Consumer Research, 1999), pp. 170–75; K. G. Dickerson, "Imported versus U.S.-Produced Apparel: Consumer Views and Buying Patterns," *Home Economies Research Journal* 10 (March 1982), pp. 241–52; Susan B. Hester and Mary Yuen, "The Influence of Origin on Consumer Attitude and Buying Behavior in the United States and Canada," in *Advances in Consumer Research,* vol. 14, ed. M. Wallendorf and P. Anderson (Provo, UT: Association for Consumer Research, 1987), pp. 538–42; and M. Wall and L. A. Heslop, "Consumer Attitudes toward Canadian-Made versus Imported Products," *Journal of the Academy of Marketing Science* 14 (Summer 1986), pp. 27–36.

50. Francis Piron, Go Kiah Kiah, Pang Kah Meng, and Wong Li Peng, "Country of Origin Effect on Product Usage Conspicuousness," in *Asia Pacific Advances in Consumer Research,* vol. 4, ed. Paula Tidwell (Provo, UT: Association for Consumer Research, 2001), p. 97.

51. Stephen Bayley, *Taste: The Secret Meaning of Things* (New York: Pantheon Books, 1991), p. 125; Millie R. Creighton, "The *Depato:* Merchandising the West while Selling Japaneseness," *Re-Made in Japan: Everyday Life and Consumer Taste in a Changing Society,* ed. Joseph J. Tobin (New Haven: Yale University Press, 1992), pp. 42–57; Liza C. Dalby, *Kimono: Fashioning Culture* (New Haven: Yale University Press, 1993); Grant McCracken, "The Making of Modern Consumption," *Culture and Consumption* (Bloomington: Indiana University Press, 1988), pp. 1–30; and Rosalind H. Williams, *Dream Worlds: Mass Consumption in Late Nineteenth Century France* (Berkeley: University of California Press, 1982), p. 71.

52. Bethany Bryson, "'Anything But Heavy Metal': Symbolic Exclusion and Musical Dislikes," *American Sociological Review* 61 (October 1996), pp. 884–89; Koen van Eijck, "Social Differentiation in Musical Taste Patterns," *Social Forces* 79, no. 3 (2001), pp. 1163–85; and Richard A. Peterson and Albert Simkus, "How Musical Tastes Mark Occupational Status Groups," in *Cultivating Differences: Symbolic Boundaries and the Making of Inequality,* ed. Michèle Lamont and Marcel Fournier (Chicago: University of Chicago Press, 1992), pp. 152–86.

53. Dorothy George and George M. Zinkhan, "Why People Get Tattoos," *Skin & Ink,* July 2000, pp. 25–34.

chapter 1
chapter 2
chapter 3
chapter 4
chapter 5
chapter 6
chapter 7
chapter 8
chapter 9
chapter 10
chapter 11
chapter 12
chapter 13
chapter 14
chapter 15
chapter 16
chapter 17
chapter 18
chapter 19

LEARNING OBJECTIVES

After completing this chapter, you should be able to:

- Describe the relationships among consumer experience, learning, memory, and knowledge and the distinctions between these concepts.
- Discuss the different kinds of consumer experiences, their relationship to other kinds of consumer behavior, and marketing implications.
- Explain the role of anticipated consumption and provide examples and details.
- Describe the different ways that consumers learn and remember and understand the marketing implications.
- Distinguish between the two types of behavioral theories—classical conditioning and operant conditioning—and apply these concepts to consumer behavior settings.
- Appreciate the intricacy and diversity of human memory and relate memory concepts to marketing actions.
- Understand basic ways memory fails and how marketers can influence and enhance memory.

EXPERIENCE, LEARNING, AND KNOWLEDGE

A VISIT TO SEA WORLD SAN DIEGO

Jorja, Dave, and Maddie booked a flight and hotel for almost a week of fun in San Diego. They planned to visit the Scrips Aquarium and San Diego Zoo for sure. Both Jorja and Dave had visited these attractions before and had many pleasant memories. They wanted to share these places with Maddie. Neither of them had been to Sea World, and, in fact, viewed Sea World in the same category with other big amusement parks such as Disney World, Six Flags, and Busch Gardens. To Dave and Jorja, these parks are synonymous with long lines and crying, tired, and overstimulated young children; it was exhausting just thinking about it! However, Jorja's brother recommended including a trip to Sea World, guidance Jorja simply filed away as a remote possibility. Arriving in San Diego, Jorja encountered a friend who had just returned from taking her children to Sea World, and Beth, too, gave the park high marks. The Sea World brochure in the hotel lobby captivated Maddie, and she anticipated, imagined, and lobbied for a visit. Scrips Aquarium and the San Diego Zoo were both wonderful, as expected, with some pleasant surprises too! Expecting the worst, Jorja agreed to take Maddie to Sea World.

Have you ever visited Sea World? Visit Sea World San Diego's website. There are three Sea World locations in the United States: one in Orlando, Florida; one in San Antonio, Texas; and one in San Diego, California. Sea World San Diego opened in 1964 and has hosted over 100 million guests on the 189.5-acre park. Their mission statement is: "To entertain, amaze and educate, creating memories that last a lifetime." You might be surprised to learn Sea World rescues, rehabilitates, and releases more marine animals than any other organization and has won many awards for achievement in education, breeding, and display of marine wildlife. Nevertheless, standing in a ticket line outside the park at 9 A.M. Monday morning, it looked

@ http://www.seaworld.com/seaworld/ca

altogether similar to other amusement parks, and Jorja felt a sinking feeling in her stomach. A voice in the background warned visitors that if they wanted good seats for a show, they should arrive 45 minutes in advance, and called attention to an opportunity to buy a two-day visit for just a little more than the one-day price, plus this ticket would provide a special behind-the-scenes look at the park. At the time, Jorja couldn't imagine that she would want to come back here a second day! She had visions of waiting hours in the sun for half-hour shows. Once inside the park, Jorja and Maddie quickly learned several valuable things. First, when the show has rows of seats labeled "Soak Zone," they mean "Soak Zone," not just a little wet zone. Second, there are lots of fun things to do outside of the shows. Jorja and Maddie especially liked feeding and touching dolphins and rays and feeding sea lions. They also enjoyed all the wildlife displays—penguins, freshwater aquariums, manatees, sharks, tide pools, and more. Third, although getting to a show early provides better seats, there are plenty of seats if you just walk in at the last minute and the shows are surprising and fun. Jorja and Maddie had a wonderful day at Sea World. They took lots of pictures and purchased a Shamu T-shirt for Maddie to preserve their memories. Jorja and Maddie vowed to take Dave back the next day. The next day was great too, but on the whole Maddie felt the shows were not as good as they had been the first day. Nevertheless, Maddie looks forward to another visit to Sea World and vividly recalls her experience for friends. Her stories improve with each retelling. The next visit they'll know better. They'll buy the two-day pass, take appropriate gear or avoid the soak zone, and only see each show once!

OVERVIEW

How do consumers learn about and understand the world around them? More specifically, how do they integrate their consumption experiences with what they already know—their prior knowledge? What do they remember, and forget? And how do memories influence future beliefs and behaviors? These questions are fundamental to understanding consumers as interpreters of their worlds, and they are the subjects of this chapter.

The opening vignette illustrates there is a dynamic interplay among experience, learning, memory, and knowledge. Jorja and Dave have unpleasant memories of theme parks. Their memories are so vivid that recalling them makes them feel tired and sick to their stomachs. They put Sea World in the category of theme parks and assumed the same emotional experience would unfold. As we noted in Chapter 8, categorization is a fundamental sense-making activity and helps people understand what something is by relating it to prior knowledge. Consumers learn things in different ways. Jorja, Dave,

Is Sea World a Theme Park or a zoo?

and Maddie don't just rely on their own experiences. They learned that friends and relatives had enjoyed Sea World, and they read brochures about the park attractions. From this information, at odds with their own experiences, they decided to try it, and they anticipated the experience. As the experience unfolded replete with decisions, positive feelings, and regrets, Jorja, Dave, and Maddie learned many things and they made memories—good and bad. They changed how they think and feel about Sea World, and formed intentions to do this again. Their pictures and story telling help them remember their experience in a particular way. Experience, learning, knowledge, and memories are interactive in this vignette and in consumers' lives.

Consumer experiences, learning, and knowledge evolve within a particular cultural and social context based around consumers' motives and goals. For example, Jorja neglects to mention the price of admission to Sea World, or the fact that to feed the animals you must first buy them food. She's conveniently forgotten how many $5 bills disappeared for tiny trays of slimy, smelly fish and squid, and remembers instead the look on Maddie's face as she petted the dolphins. Jorja and Dave want Maddie to have fun, enriching experiences—their role as parents is motivating this visit, and her pleasure and enrichment are their primary goals. Many poor and disadvantaged families can't afford the steep ticket price that provides access to the tidy, idealized, and self-contained world of the American theme park. The very fact that Jorja and Dave have a category called theme parks reflects their social class and cultural heritage. The United States has approximately 450 theme parks, and theme parks are a favorite destination not just for American families, but increasingly that is how foreign visitors experience America. Moreover, the template for an American theme park has influenced shopping malls, retail spaces, restaurants, retirement communities, and theme parks around the world.[1]

We overview in this chapter concepts that can help us understand consumers' experiences, ways of learning, memories, and knowledge. We first briefly situate these concepts in consumers' lives and broadly outline relationships among them. Next we talk about consumer experience. Consumer experiences are at the heart of consumer behavior and have an important impact on what consumers learn and remember. We further classify consumer experiences by considering the phases from anticipation, purchase and other decisions, the consumption experience itself, and the remembered experience. Each of these phases is important in understanding how consumers interpret the world around them, and each of these phases is evident in the opening vignette. Consumer learning plays a fundamental role in many consumer theories and models. Learning is adaptive and determined by consumers' motives, goals, and environment. We provide a simplified model of how consumers learn, describe different types of learning, and discuss two useful behavioral learning theories. Almost all consumer decisions rely to some extent on memory. Memory and knowledge are closely related and are crucial for understanding consumer decisions, experiences, and postconsumption satisfaction. First, we overview different types of memory and how memories are retrieved. We describe several ways that memory fails us and some tactics marketers can use to enhance consumer memory. In the opening vignette, Jorja and Dave make inferences about Sea World from their prior knowledge of theme parks. Consumers' inferences are important for marketers and policy makers to understand. We conclude the chapter with a discussion of knowledge focusing on consumer inferences and use of analogies.

EXPERIENCE, LEARNING, AND KNOWLEDGE IN CONTEXT

Exhibit 9.1 illustrates that the four key concepts of experience, learning, memory, and knowledge discussed in this chapter are part of how consumers interpret and understand

EXHIBIT 9.1

Consumer Experience and Learning in Context

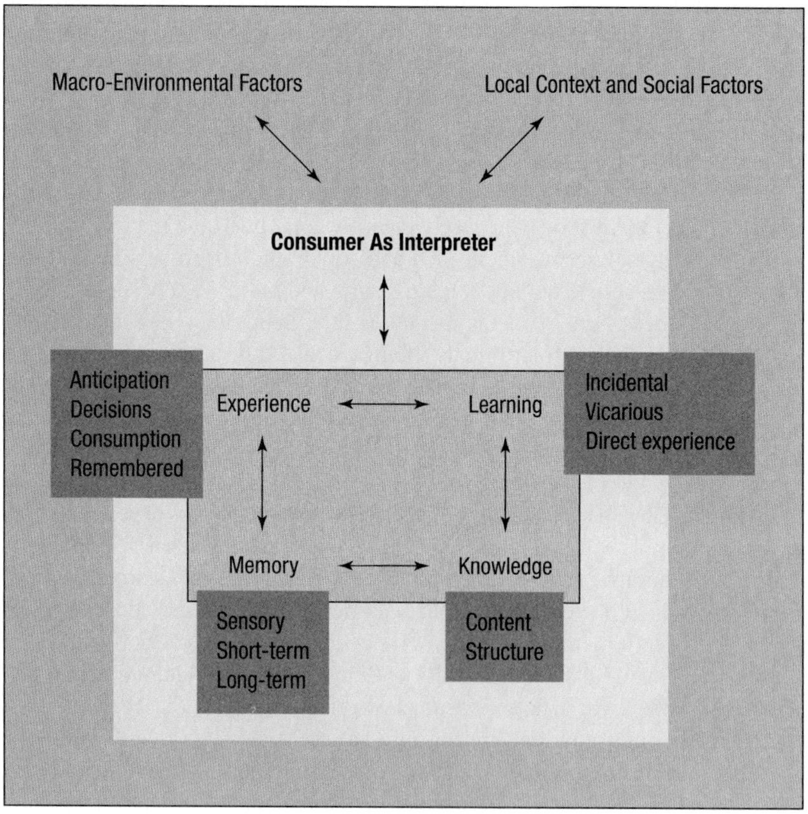

their world. As with Chapters 7 and 8 the focus of this chapter is on consumers as interpreters of their world. It is important to remember that experience, learning, memory, and knowledge happen within a particular cultural context and social setting. Even how we learn and remember is affected by culture and context. Of course, many of the things we experience and know are because of our specific context.

As we observed in Chapter 3, this is most evident when we change contexts, and experience and learn many different things. Consumer Chronicles 9.1 provides a partial list of common questions refugees ask when they first arrive in the United States. If you live in the United States, you may take many of these things for granted.

In this section we briefly overview the four major concepts in this chapter and how they are related to each other. In subsequent sections we elaborate on the key elements of experience, learning, memory, and knowledge.

Common Questions Refugees Ask after Arriving in Lincoln, Nebraska

CONSUMER CHRONICLES 9.1

- How to order food in a café.
- How to use escalators, stairs, elevators, and revolving doors.
- How to use a water fountain.
- What to put in a refrigerator.
- How to read the want ads.
- How to shop at a grocery store.
- What a washing machine is.
- How to wear socks.
- How and when to call 911.
- How to get a prescription and get it filled.
- What dry cleaning is.
- How to walk on snow and ice.

Source: Adapted from Mary Pipher, The Middle of Everywhere: The World's Refugees Come to Our Town *(New York: Harcourt, 2002), pp. 90–94.*

Experience

Everything we experience—joy or pain, interest or boredom—is represented in the mind as information. How we feel about ourselves depends on how our minds filter and interpret everyday experience. One important way that we order and filter experience is through goals.[2] **Experiences** are *physical, cognitive, and emotional interactions with an environment*. To each experience we bring a level of effort and skills that impacts our physical, cognitive, and emotional interactions. For example, watching television involves few challenges, hence little effort or skill. Our emotional response to watching television may be apathy or boredom. Driving in a car has physical activities that are affected by certain features of the automobile: is it an automatic or manual transmission; does it have power brakes, air conditioning, cruise control? Driving also has cognitive elements: watching for lights or pedestrians and perhaps daydreaming or planning daily activities. Finally, as you drive you may feel various emotions depending on the driving context—bored, fearful, in control, relaxed. Emotion and cognitions can't be separated. **Emotions** are *a combination of a mental evaluation process with responses to that process that result in a body state and additional mental processes*. Let's take a simple example. Think of a time you were very frightened. Replay the event in your mind. Do you feel some of the same emotions you felt then? Your mind and body are working together—the content of your thoughts is changing your body state, and your thoughts are again reflecting on those changes. Experiences are at the heart of consumer behavior.[3] When marketers sponsor a car, they are promoting a driving experience, and when marketers advertise a cleaning product, they are promoting a cleaning experience. Direct experience is an important way consumers learn. Compared to other ways of learning, it is more motivated, vivid, and sensory and under the control of the consumer.[4]

Learning

We define **consumer learning** as *connecting categories to behaviors that have adaptive value in terms of consumer goals.*[5] Fundamental to this definition is that learning is adaptive and determined by the value systems, desires, and needs of the learner. Also, of course, it depends on what the learner already knows. That is, new information is assessed in terms of existing beliefs and past experiences. Learning requires both forward and backward thinking. Sometimes people engage in backward reasoning to understand their actions; in other situations they look forward and anticipate likes and dislikes based on previous experiences. Thus, actions are partly a response to **preferences**—*feelings and beliefs about what a person likes and dislikes.* But actions also help consumers identify and predict new preferences.[6] For example, through product trial, Jorja and David learn that they like Sea World San Diego. Sometimes consumers have firm and stable preferences, but more often they compare new alternatives with old favorites or find that, because of their own changing circumstances, they need or require different things. People use context and other cues to help them guess what they will like and dislike. For example, Jorja uses certain cues at the entrance of Sea World as cues to what she can expect. Cues compete against each other for predictive value. Consumers decide which cues to pay attention to and which to ignore.[7]

Memory

Memory and retrieval work together. We extract *key elements from our and others' experiences and store them.* These constitute our **memories.** Information, including false information, often passes into memory without being "tagged" as to source or credibility. We then *recreate or reconstruct these experiences.* In the process of reconstructing our experiences, we add on feelings, beliefs, and even knowledge that we obtained after the experience. Inference is often required to identify the source of the information when it is recalled and such inferences may be incorrect. This process is termed **retrieval.**[8] Many times situations arise that make consumers reflect on the past, comparing and contrasting it with the present. Here again, categories, concepts, and the stories consumers build around them are important in how and what they describe about the past. In this sense, remembering is constructive. The past is filtered through recent understandings to create and rework social worlds. Telling stories helps consumers make sense of events and actions in their lives.[9] Sometimes, however, consumers feel they are "reliving" an experience when they remember. In fact, brain research confirms that when people remember a particular episode, the neurons that were active together during the episode are reactivated, recreating a representation of the event. This is why, with especially significant events, people may feel the emotions and physical sensations they experienced at that time.[10] This has many implications for marketers, which we will discuss in this chapter.

Knowledge

To "know" something means we recognize it and understand what it is like and what it means. **Knowledge** includes *the information we have in memory* (**knowledge content**) and *the way that information is stored* (**knowledge structure**). Culture and social conditions shape both the content and structure of knowledge. For example, the introduction of new media for recording, transmitting, and accumulating knowledge changes knowledge itself.[11] Categories become naturalized through social use and conventions. Minivans offer a great example. The minivan category is now a taken-for-granted one, but in the mid-1980s there was little knowledge of or agreement about what a minivan is or how it relates to station wagons, sedans, and full-size vans. Over time the minivan category stabilized and producers began to introduce models into this category, and consumers began to search within this category.[12] The cultural system affects what associations are linked to a concept, what members belong in a category, and what is prototypical for a category. Knowledge is also shaped by consumer goals. *People create unique groupings of things (people, objects, places, etc.) that serve a particular goal—goal-based categories.* For example, a mother might have a category called "things for children to do on a rainy day," and a college student might have a category called "good places to eat close to campus." Conflicting goals and ambiguous (uncertain or unknown) goals change how people group objects and make choices.[13] For instance, consumers sometimes use unusual, creative categories to help them resolve goal conflicts or clarify goals.

Knowing includes the *process of labeling or identifying an object based on what we already know*—**categorization**—and the *process of using prior knowledge to understand more about what we have categorized*—**comprehension.** For example, in the opening vignette, Jorja and David believe they know what theme parks are like and based on available information they categorize Sea World as a theme park. Their visit leads them to reconsider the category of theme parks to include ones that do not have long lines and crying children. Sea World is still a theme park, similar in many respects to other ones they have visited. Based on this new information, they may further consider the features of Sea World that contributed to their enjoyment and look for those features in other theme parks or leisure activities.

When we say we know something, we mean that we believe we have valid information that can be useful in understanding the world. However, as illustrated in the vignette, consumer knowledge is seldom complete or errorless. Marketers and public policy makers are interested in what consumers know, but also what they think they know, and the correspondence between these two. The *relationship between what consumers know and what they think they know* is termed **knowledge calibration.**[14] If there is a close correspondence, the consumer's knowledge is well calibrated; if there is a weak correspondence, the consumer's knowledge is poorly calibrated. Notice that a person may think they know more than they actually do (overconfidence), or they may think that they know less than they actually do (underconfidence). Knowledge calibration is important because it influences consumer search, assessments of risk, and weighing of alternatives. For example, if Jorja were quite certain about her assessment of theme parks, she would have refused to take Maddie to Sea World. Ethical Dilemma 9.1 outlines the importance of considering carefully what consumers know and what they think they know about a topic, and how this impacts their risk assessments.

Many factors can affect knowledge calibration. For example, some counterintuitive research suggests that Chinese may be more overconfident than Americans about at least some things. Experts too are sometimes more confident than their superior knowledge justifies, reluctant to admit uncertainty and more likely to express confidence in incorrect responses. However, some experts seem more inclined toward overconfidence than others. It will perhaps come as no surprise that financial analysts are susceptible to wishful thinking. Meteorologists appear to know their limitations (e.g., well-calibrated), whereas doctors do not (e.g., poorly calibrated).[15]

CONSUMER EXPERIENCES

Often, the best way to sell a product is by associating it with a more fundamental life experience. The advertisement for REI is an example of linking products and experiences. Marketers need to remember that consumers buy products and services hoping

What Do Women Know about Alcohol Consumption during Pregnancy?

ETHICAL DILEMMA 9.1

A continuing health objective in the United States is a public commitment to decreasing the percentage of women who consume alcoholic beverages during pregnancy. But what's the best way to accomplish this objective? You may be surprised to learn that women who continue to drink during pregnancy are older and have a higher income than those who abstain. It turns out that the problem is not that women are unaware of the link between alcohol consumption and birth defects. In fact women who continue to drink during pregnancy reduce alcohol consumption over this period. Instead, the problem in that these women may not believe that consuming small amounts of alcohol is risky, and in fact they may not even consider consumption of small amounts of alcohol to be drinking. Part of the problem might be that they engage in counterfactual thinking. That is, they may recall examples of women who consumed alcohol during pregnancy and gave birth to normal children to justify continued occasional or moderate drinking. Public education strategies that merely discuss the risks of alcohol during pregnancy may be insufficient. A more sophisticated approach is called for. Persuasive appeals need to identify the risks of low levels of alcohol consumption during pregnancy. For example, messages could indicate that low levels of alcohol consumption correlate with low-birth-weight infants that in turn can interfere with a child's development.

Source: Adapted from Louis A. Morris, John L. Swasy, and Michael B. Mazis, "Accepted Risk and Alcohol Use during Pregnancy," Journal of Consumer Research *21 (June 1994), pp. 135–43.*

that those purchases will contribute to how they, and others they care about, experience life. Examples abound of retailers and manufacturers (click and brick) that offer more than an array of goods and services for sale—they offer a shopping experience. You can adventure on the climbing wall at REI, enjoy the playground at McDonald's, be enveloped in a sensory exploration at Victoria's Secret, and enter into an interactive

Linking Products to Experience

Polus Shopping Center: Themed retailing in Hungary.

sports museum at Niketown USA. A short walk down Michigan Avenue in Chicago offers an array of themed retailing that combines experience and shopping. The Polus Center, a shopping mall in Budapest, Hungary, that opened in 1998, illustrates a Western theme.

Whether extraordinary or mundane, experience has an important impact on what consumers learn and remember. Positive experiences may lead to repeated behaviors. Negative experiences may lead to avoidance behaviors. Some peak experiences (e.g., climbing a mountain while on vacation) may come to dominate wake-time thoughts. Other experiences (e.g., TV shows watched two months ago) are quickly forgotten.

The New Experience Economy

Some industry experts argue that economic value now turns on more than a high-quality product or good service delivery; it turns on engaging consumers in a memorable way—offering them an experience or, even better, transforming them by guiding them through experiences. These experts argue that economic value increases as offerings move from commodities to transformations. In Chapter 6 we talked about how adventure tourism such as white-water river rafting is frequently viewed and valued as a **transformational experience,** that is, it *changes how consumers think and feel about themselves and the world around them.* Exhibit 9.2 illustrates this revised economic pyramid.[16] Notice that when marketers shift the economic offering from commodities toward experiences and transformations they also alter the way they view consumers. Many aspects of the offering change along with this shifting perspective. For example, when offering experiences marketers are concerned with staging the experience—making it memorable and personal. When the offering is

EXHIBIT 9.2

The Economic Pyramid

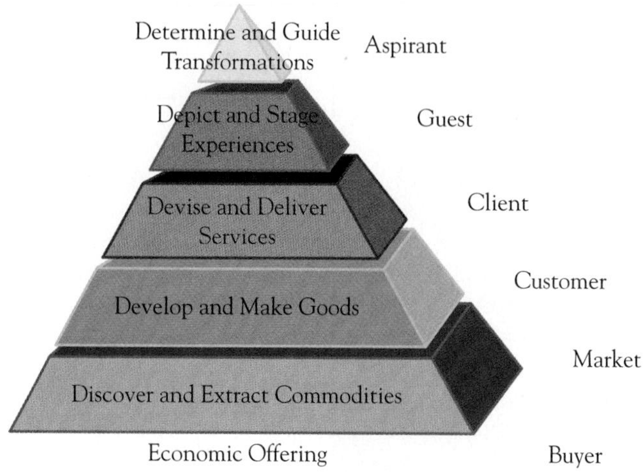

transformational, the buyer (aspirant) is the product. The marketer only succeeds if the individual is changed. Many product and service promotions are organized around promising a transformation. A classic example would be an advertisement in a fashion magazine that portrays "before" and "after" images, suggesting that the reader too can be transformed.

In many parts of the world, a great deal of effort goes into designing the best store layout, so that consumers' shopping experiences will be positive and rewarding. Likewise, designers attempt to construct websites so that consumers' search experiences will be efficient and fun. Nonetheless, consumers' shopping experiences are more than just those behaviors that can be directly observed.[17] Shopping experiences also include the mental events and emotional states surrounding purchase events.

For some product categories (e.g., a snack food), the consumption experience is over quickly. For example, a consumer may buy a candy bar on the way out of the grocery store and eat it entirely before the groceries are packed in the car. Other consumption experiences stretch out long after the time of actual purchase. For instance, when consumers purchase some entertainment services such as a concert or a sporting event, the allocation (and expenditure) of time is perhaps more important than the allocation of money. Many service experiences (e.g., taking a vacation, attending a concert) stretch out over time. Consumers invest their time in these activities, just as they invest their money. Transformational experiences typically unfold over time and must be sustained through time. Losing weight, stopping smoking, or changing personal patterns through therapy are all potentially transforming but also arduous, effortful investments.

As shown in Exhibit 9.3, experiences related to consumer behavior can be classified into four groups: (1) anticipated consumption (including search behavior), (2) the actual purchase of the good or service, (3) consumption experiences, and (4) remembered consumption (experiences that are relived over a period of days or weeks or months, perhaps retold to others). Over the next several chapters we will be discussing these aspects of experience in more detail. In this chapter we will focus primarily on anticipated consumption and how it relates to learning and knowledge and on remembered consumption as one dimension of memory.

Anticipated Consumption	Purchase Experiences	Consumption Experiences	Remembered Consumption and Nostalgia
Searching (in person, using traditional media, via the Web, talking to friends)	Choice	Sense experiences (taste, touch, feel, sight, sound)	Reliving past experiences; looking at photographs
Planning for future purchases	Payment	Satiation	Telling stories
Daydreaming	Bundling product (for transport)	Satisfaction/dissatisfaction	Comparing (old times to new)
Budgeting	Service encounter	Arousal/flow (other experiences shown in Exhibit 9.3)	Talking with friends from days gone by
Fantasizing	Atmospherics (in-store environment)	Transformation	Playing "what if"; remembered consumption
			Daydreaming
			Sorting through memorabilia and other mementos

EXHIBIT 9.3

A Classification of Consumer Experiences

Anticipated Consumption

Anticipated consumption experiences include **prepurchase search** that *occurs in response to the activation of a consumption problem or desire*. For instance, Sam is a typical college student in the southeastern United States. He has several CDs recorded by the rap artist Coolio. He is interested in attending a Coolio concert, so he checks appropriate websites for information about upcoming performances near his hometown. He talks with some of his friends about dates that best suit their schedules. He finds out the costs of attending the concert, including ticket prices and travel expenses. He sets aside money in his budget to cover these expenses; and he checks his exam schedule to make certain that there are not critical conflicts.

Anticipated consumption can also include thoughts, feelings, and sensory images that surround the upcoming event. Imagined consumption is an important element. Prior to attending the Coolio concert, Sam finds that it is difficult to concentrate on his studies. His mind wanders to the concert arena. After class, he rushes to find his friends so that they can further discuss their upcoming plans for attending the concert. He completes more web searches to find the best places to stay and eat near the concert venue. All of these activities come under the rubric of anticipated consumption.

Anticipated consumption may begin a long time before actual purchase. For example, many parents begin college funds for their children even before those children are born, and young boys in the United States start anticipating car purchases well in advance of when they are old enough to drive or rich enough to sustain car payments. Their attention to information about cars has an ongoing quality—they are building a bank of information for future use.[18] Of course, much anticipated consumption never results in a purchase. Colette, a third grader, is saving earnings and windfall profits for a pony, but her parents are hoping that her intentions waver before she has amassed sufficient capital to go pony shopping. In Chapter 10 we will discuss in more detail why purchase intentions often don't translate into purchase behavior.

Anticipated consumption is related to consumers' aspirations, which in turn are based on their environment, knowledge, and experiences. Colette believes it is reasonable to save for and acquire a horse because her friend Willie is saving for one, her father had one when he was growing up, and her uncle and grandfather have horses. The relationship between anticipated consumption and consumer knowledge is important to pay attention to. Consider as an example the transitional economies of eastern and central Europe. Many consumers in these environments are experiencing an increasing **aspiration gap,** *a disparity between the consumption level they earnestly desire and strive for and the level actually attainable.* The explosion of media and consumer goods that promote a new consumption standard create disillusionment and frustration for many consumers who view these things as unattainable. Seeing ads with nice houses, cars, and clothes, they are frustrated and disillusioned because they can't see how they will ever attain these things.[19] Marketers can influence consumers by changing their aspirations or the perceived aspiration gap. For example, attractive auto loan programs available in the late 1990s in Hungary reduced the aspiration gap—Hungarian consumers were able to buy the cars they dreamed of for years, and they did.

A Typology of Consumer Experiences

As implied in the previous section, there are many kinds of consumer experiences. In his best-selling book *Finding Flow,* Csikzentmihalyi provides a typology for understanding different types of human experiences.[20] This typology, which is particularly applicable for understanding consumer experiences, is shown in Exhibit 9.4. We briefly discussed flow in Chapter 7 but did not distinguish other types of experiences. Two key dimensions distinguish experiences: level of skill and level of challenge. For instance, when skills and challenges are low, experiences are boring. When skill levels are high and challenges are low, people have relaxing experiences.

When challenges are high and skill levels are moderate, consumers have arousing experiences. Learning is one example of such arousal. People's favorite activities are

EXHIBIT 9.4

Flow: A Combination of Challenge and Skill

Source: Mihaly Csikzentmihalyi, *Finding Flow* (New York: Perseus Books, 1997).

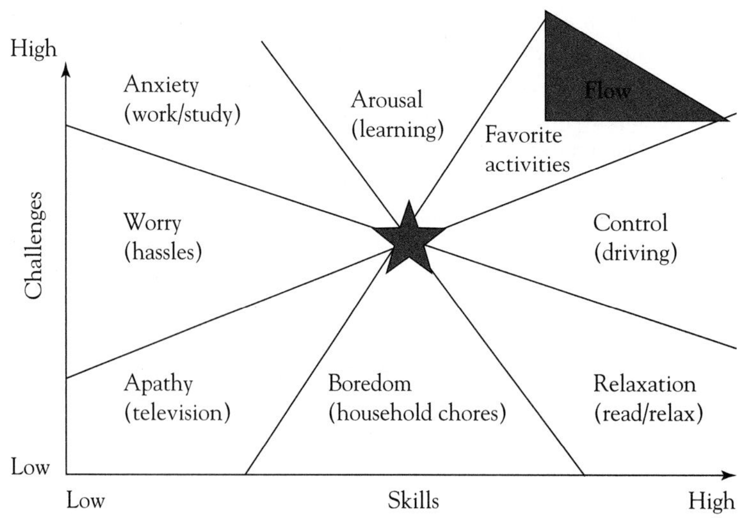

classified as flow experiences. As shown in Exhibit 9.4, flow results when both skills and challenges are at their maximum. This is what makes flow experiences favorite activities. Some examples of flow experience include a pilot flying a test aircraft, a doctor performing surgery, a professor teaching a class, the process involved in making social contacts and forging intimate relationships, playing a video game, climbing a mountain, and participating in a professional conference. Remember, a flow experience for one consumer may be boring or irritating to another consumer—it depends on their skills and challenges.

Only a small fraction of consumer experiences can be classified as flow activities. Nonetheless, flow activities are pivotal because they represent peak experiences. They may come at work or in leisure time. To a large extent flow experiences may come to dominate leisure time. A large portion of nonwork time is spent on rest or relaxation. But through anticipating future flow experiences or by looking back nostalgically at such past experiences, consumers may devote quite a bit of their active leisure time to pursuing or remembering these flow periods.

From a marketing perspective, it is difficult to underestimate the importance of the experiences that consumers have with products and services. Now that we have introduced a classification scheme (Exhibit 9.4) for thinking about and understanding the kinds of experiences that consumers have, we'll highlight one specific kind of consumer experience: learning.

CONSUMER LEARNING

What Is Learning?

Learning is a mysterious and challenging concept even for neuroscientists.[21] Imagine this. Consumers (not to mention pigeons, dogs, and monkeys) encounter a small number of events or objects and after this exposure adaptively categorize or recognize an indefinite number of novel objects (even in a variety of contexts) as being similar or identical to the small set that they first encountered. This is an amazing process and nobody understands exactly how it happens. Learning is complicated because it involves object definition and generalization in a world that is not prelabeled by any a priori scheme. Moreover, consumers can learn, retain, and act on information via unconscious and implicit learning processes that are hard to identify and poorly understood.[22] An example might be how adolescents acquire an understanding of the way advertising works. Some research illustrates that as early as sixth grade, consumers begin to discern advertiser tactics and effects. For example, they begin to connect a tactic such as using a popular TV, music, or movie star with what the advertiser hopes to accomplish—grab your attention and get you to remember the ad. However, by eighth grade consumers' ability to connect advertiser tactics with effects improves significantly. What's interesting is that general skepticism about advertising doesn't change with age, but consumers' ability to discern tactics does.[23]

Although learning plays a fundamental role in many consumer theories and models, it is seldom investigated directly. Only a few studies have looked at the basic ways in which consumers learn. That research suggests that we can think of consumers as generating guesses or hypotheses about the way the world works, in order to make adaptive choices that move them toward their goals. Sometimes these guesses may be unconscious or implicit, sometimes so much a part of consumers' cultural background that the guesses are completely taken for granted. Visiting Denmark for the first time and not speaking the language, we went grocery shopping and selected something that we guessed from the picture would be chocolate-covered ice cream bars. To our surprise, they were licorice-covered ice cream bars, a product concept our young daughter found totally disgusting. Coming from the United States, we never considered this possibility. Similar to other consumers in these types of situations, we didn't generate very many hypotheses (only one) and we clearly underestimated the likelihood of unspecified alternative hypotheses.[24] Exhibit 9.5 provides a simplified model of consumer learning based on consumer guesses and exposure to evidence.

The model provided in Exhibit 9.5 suggests that as consumers are exposed to events that seem to require explanation, they trigger a search from prior experiences and among existing beliefs to develop a hunch about what might be going on. Their exposure to evidence, encoding of evidence, and integration of evidence with prior beliefs depend on their familiarity with other things that they believe relate, their motivation to learn, and characteristics of the information environment. **Encoding** evidence is the process by which *consumers select a word or visual image to represent a perceived object.* **Integration** is how *they relate that evidence to other information and beliefs.* Both encoding and integration rely on learned cultural categories as well as individual experiences. How people encode and integrate information also depends on other factors such as gender and age.[25] For example, color is used in packaging to convey properties of the product.[26] The use of color in packaging is powerful and, unlike the use of words, it is outside government intervention. Consumers respond to colors physiologically, culturally, and associationally and they respond on all of these levels at once. In Japan, soft gray shades are used for products such as tea and seaweed that are distinctively Japanese in character. These shades coincide with Japanese consumers' appreciation for extremely subtle distinctions. Yellow is one of the most used packaging colors, but for Japanese, Americans, and Europeans it evokes "cheap." Nevertheless, consider the power of marketers to alter even what we see. Decades of McDonald's promotion of "the golden arches" have turned their otherwise yellow color into gold—and gold evokes associations of purity and changeless high quality.

A few comments are appropriate. First, consumers only generate guesses when objects or events are unexpected or novel or block goals. Much of the time consumers just apply already "good enough" learned rules to make decisions and take action.[27] Second,

EXHIBIT 9.5

A Simplified Model of Consumer Learning

Source: Adapted from Stephen J. Hoch and John Deighton, "Managing What Consumers Learn from Experience," *Journal of Marketing* 53 (April 1989), pp. 1–20. Reprinted by permission of the American Marketing Association.

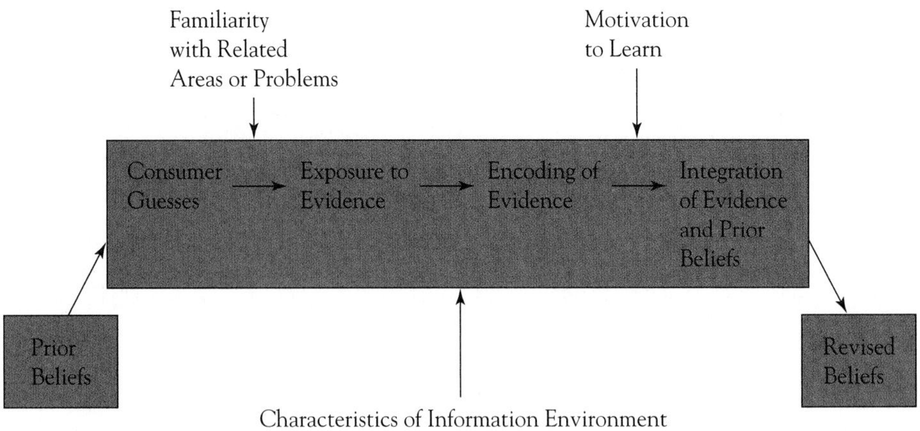

as in the example of licorice ice cream bars, previous experience can interfere with generating new guesses or recognizing new diagnostic evidence. For example, had we looked closely at the package picture, the coating on the ice cream bar would have appeared more black than brown (new diagnostic evidence). Third, when consumers scan through what they know to decide what to do in a new situation, they often make guesses by drawing on their familiarity with unexpected domains. Marketers can't always determine inferences consumers will make to formulate guesses and achieve goals. For example, in trying to decide about the safety of food that has been genetically modified, some U.S. consumers apply inappropriate rules they have learned about food safety, such as the need to cook meat thoroughly or wash vegetables properly.[28] These rules in turn derive from deeply embedded, culturally learned ideas about food and the ability to transform nature.[29] Finally, the information environment can have a dramatic impact on consumers' exposure, encoding, and integration of evidence to accomplish goals. For example, in Central and Eastern Europe, there is an explosion of interest and involvement with all kinds of consumer goods spurred by a dramatically altered retail and media landscape. Prior to 1989 in Central and Eastern Europe, consumer goods manufacturers and retailers were state-owned. They offered few product alternatives and consumers saw few choices within product categories. Over the decade of the 90s Central and Eastern Europe also generally moved from tightly controlled and minimal media to an explosion of cable alternatives. For example, The Act on Radio and Television Services, also known as the Media Law, was enacted in 1995 in Hungary to "promote the freedom and independence of television and radio broadcasting" and privatize the television and radio markets. The result was a flood of new TV channels available to Hungarian consumers. As in the United States and in Western Europe, various cable programming packages were available to consumers.[30]

Types of Learning

Consumers can learn from description.[31] This is a very efficient way to learn and includes listening to, observing, and remembering what other people tell us. Parents, teachers, books, friends, TV, billboards, magazines, sales representatives, Internet sites, package labels, and instruction manuals are just a few of the ways that people learn by description. Consumers may imitate or model a fashion look they see on MTV, carefully follow a recipe on the back of a soup can, or check out a critic's movie recommendations on the Internet. *Through repetition, people learn lots of things almost by accident.* This type of learning is referred to as **incidental learning.** In fact, advertising information may be most likely to influence consumers when they are not aware of its influence.[32] **Learning by description** includes *acquiring information from vicarious or indirect encounters.* For marketers, advertising is a primary tool for teaching consumers, and it relies on learning by description. For example, advertisers use celebrity spokespersons in their campaigns to provide consumers with opportunities for **vicarious learning.** A cartoon character can also serve this purpose, as can an appealing advertising model who is not necessarily a well-known entity but with whom the consumer can identify. Even though consumers do not have their own direct experience, they can learn by observing the experience described in advertising. In the United States, kindergarten children can recall brand names within several different categories, and even preschoolers can associate brand names with picture and color cues for several different types of products.[33]

Do Cigarette Ads Lead Youth to Smoke?

ETHICAL DILEMMA 9.2

Numerous studies have attempted to discover whether cigarette ads encourage underage smoking. There are many good reasons to think they do. For example, some research found that adolescents are three times more responsive to cigarette brand advertising than adults. However, whether cigarette advertising simply affects brand choice or impacts initial decisions to smoke has not been resolved. In 2002 a study was published that shed light on that question. Using an experimental design, the researchers conclude that first advertising primes or makes salient a positive smoker stereotype and this happens even among adolescents who hold contrary beliefs. Adolescents need not even be aware that they saw the advertising. In the second step this primed positive stereotype enhances adolescents' perceptions of peers that smoke. Thus repeated exposures to advertising and peers who smoke have a cumulative effect. One implication is that self-reported reasons for smoking may be misleading. Adolescents may understate the impact of cigarette ads and overstate the impact of peers in the decision to start smoking.

Source: This is abstracted from Cornelia Pechmann and Susan J. Knight, "An Experimental Investigation of the Joint Effects of Advertising and Peers on Adolescents' Beliefs and Intentions about Cigarette Consumption," Journal of Consumer Research *29 (June 2002), pp. 5–19.*

Consumers also learn from firsthand, **direct experience.** Learning from experience differs from indirect or vicarious learning because of its *interactive character* and because consumers tend to privilege conclusions drawn from experience. Experiences are easier to remember because they are more vivid and concrete; they are also more credible than someone else's reported experiences and are likely to be more involving and motivating. Consumers may also gain feelings of competence, or flow (as we discussed earlier), from their experiences. A paradox of experiential information is that while it is learned fast, it is also the most fragile, context-dependent, and subject to distortion.[34]

It would be a mistake to think that experience provides a perfect match between action and consequence, making it easy to learn what to do next time. Much experience is ambiguous. For example, often consumers don't know what went wrong when a product or service fails and may feel confused about how to avoid future failures. Whether they actively search for explanations and how they explain what happened depend on their cultural knowledge and experience. For example, many people in non-Western cultures are content to leave the mystery of what happened unquestioned and unresolved, often attributing the outcome to fate or magic.[35] Some research has shown that consumers rely on the consumption experience when evaluating brands *if* the experience is unambiguous, but they rely on prior opinions or advertising claims when the experience is ambiguous. For example, coffee prepared to taste bitter (an ambiguous and relative experience) tastes less bitter to individuals who have been exposed to advertising claiming the coffee has no bitterness. Moreover, exposure to advertising *after* an ambiguous experience can affect how consumers report on and evaluate that experience.[36]

Some research on learning supports a two-step model of advertising effects such that advertising plus evidence promotes more positive product beliefs, even when neither factor alone is able to do so. Recently this hypothesis has been further explored in the context of adolescents' beliefs and intentions about cigarette smoking. Ethical Dilemma 9.2 argues that this two-step model is very important in understanding how youth who hold contrary beliefs take up smoking.

In addition, it would be a mistake to think that experiences are recalled just the way they happened. For example, research has shown consumers' recollections of product or service experiences can be influenced and shaped by marketing communications following the experiences. Consumers' memories often include interpretation and details that help the experience make sense within the broader scope of their lives and in terms of the outcomes that transpired and the audience for whom the story is told. The mental procedures used in putting together a memory rely as much on constructive processes as on retrieval.[37]

Much of how people make sense of things happens after the fact, sometimes a long time after. How consumers describe their first car purchase will differ depending on when they are asked and what has happened since then. For example, an accident, a birth, a marriage, or anything that makes certain attributes more or less salient may change how consumers describe the factors they considered when they bought the car. Consumers are very vulnerable to **hindsight bias,** the "*I knew it all along" effect.* After experiencing a product or service, consumers tend to *falsely believe that they knew the outcomes in advance of their experience.*[38]

Behavioral Learning Theories

Up to this point in our discussion we have described learning as a mental process that is adaptive and directed toward advancing consumer goals. Based on the most recent understandings of how the brain works, our perspective has emphasized the mysterious and contextual quality of learning. Nevertheless, by just looking at behavior researchers have discovered a lot about learning, both in humans and in animals. Two **behavioral learning theories,** briefly discussed here, are classical conditioning and operant conditioning. Both take a behaviorist approach to learning. They treat human memory processes as a black box—processes that are not really necessary to understand. Under the behaviorist approach, consumers operate on the environment (e.g., people do things). In turn, consumers experience consequences from the environment (e.g., rewards, punishments, pairings of stimuli). These consequences determine the probabilities of future behavioral responses.

CLASSICAL CONDITIONING THEORY **Classical conditioning** is a specific procedure that creates a learning environment, but other learning processes may operate simultaneously with this procedure.[39] Classical conditioning became well known from the Russian psychologist Ivan Pavlov. Pavlov is most famous for his experiments with dogs. When he administered meat powder to dogs, they would naturally salivate. Every time that he administered the powder, he would sound a bell. Through repetition, the dogs learned to associate the sound of the bell with the coming of food. Eventually, the dogs would salivate upon hearing the sound of the bell, even when the meat powder was not present. In this way, Pavlov took a neutral object (the bell) and over time associated it with a meaningful object (the meat powder). An important part of this procedure is that the bell and the meat powder occur close together in time as opposed to far apart in time. The **temporal contiguity principle** states that *stronger associations are learned when events occur close together in time as opposed to far apart in time.* This principle has been used to explain why people spend more freely using credit cards than cash. Credit cards separate the joy of consuming from the pain of paying by at least 30 days, whereas with cash the costs and benefits occur close together.[40] The classical conditioning procedure can be applied in a media or an advertising environment. An important feature of classical conditioning is that it does not require conscious attention or involvement of the audience. Consider the popular Steven Spielberg movie *Jaws.* In this film, the man-eating shark (presumably hungry for beachgoers) is paired with a signature piece of music. This pairing takes place repeatedly throughout the film. By the movie's end, the music itself elicits fear and anxiety.

Unconditioned Stimulus	**Unconditioned Response**
Shark ------------------------->	Emotion (fear, anxiety, panic)
Paired with	
Music (neutral stimulus) ------------>	No response
Conditioned Stimulus	**Conditioned Response**
Music ------------------------->	Emotion (fear, anxiety, panic)

EXHIBIT 9.6

An Example of Classical Conditioning: Steven Spielberg's *Jaws*

This happens even though the audience wasn't really paying attention to the music.[41] This example is shown pictorially in Exhibit 9.6. Advertisers today try to accomplish the same purpose. They start with a neutral object (a new brand name) and make it a symbol of something else by repeatedly associating it with stimuli that naturally evoke positive emotions or physical responses. For example, cuddly puppies, cute kittens, and pets in general frolic in ads for many products unrelated or only tangentially related to pets. Why? Many viewers have natural positive emotional (affective) responses to these animals.

Classical learning research helped generate early understanding of stimulus generalization. **Stimulus generalization** refers to the tendency of *stimuli that are similar to evoke similar responses*. That is, consumers make a leap of sorts. They make a judgment that one stimulus is similar enough to another that it warrants a similar response. This is exactly what happened in the case of the licorice ice cream bars we described earlier. Categorizing new stimuli in order to guide action is a basic learning principle and doesn't just apply in the case of classical conditioning. Nevertheless, Pavlov's research drew attention to the power of stimuli generalization. He was able to get his dogs to salivate based on a variety of sounds that were similar to the original bell.

Marketers use stimulus generalization to devise branding and product strategies. These strategies include family branding, brand extensions, licensing, and look-alike packaging. **Family branding** is the practice of *using a company name (or umbrella name) on a set of brands*. For instance, Heinz puts its name on catsup, canned tomatoes, mustard, pickles, and many other food products. Similarly, Kellogg's is a family brand name for cereals. However, within this family brand there are recognized individual brand names, such as Rice Krispies and Apple Jacks. **Brand extension** refers to the practice of *using an existing brand name to promote a new product*. The new product may be in the same category as the original brand, or it may be in a very different category. For instance, Kellogg's could introduce a new kind of cereal (e.g., a Korean rice porridge), or it could use the Kellogg's name to promote a noncereal brand (e.g., by introducing a Kellogg's energy bar). **Licensing** means *lending an established brand name to a new venture*. For example, Kellogg's could license its name to a toy manufacturer, which could then include small facsimiles of Kellogg's cereals as part of a child's cooking set. As the name implies, **look-alike packaging** means *introducing a package that appears to be very similar to existing packages*. The hope is that consumers will make an inference that the brand with the similar package will have all of the traits of the original brand, whose package was imitated. For all four of these strategies—family branding, brand extensions, licensing, and look-alike packaging—the perceptual process of stimulus generalization is crucial. All four strategies depend on the consumer perceiving a new stimulus to be similar to an existing stimulus that evokes positive response. Because of this perception, consumers will respond favorably to the new brand (the new stimulus).

OPERANT CONDITIONING **Operant conditioning,** also called *instrumental conditioning,* occurs as *consumers shape their behaviors to respond to rewards and punishments in the marketplace*. Under operant conditioning, the frequency of occurrence of a behavior is modified by the consequences of the behavior. That is, the frequency of behavior is conditioned by the extent of reinforcement associated with that behavior.[42] Responses are made deliberately, as opposed to the involuntary responses illustrated by classical conditioning. Under operant conditioning, consumers' satisfaction with purchases serves to reinforce future behavioral responses, specifically, repeat purchases. The stream of associations that occur during consumption (e.g., imagery, daydreams, emotions) may also serve as important reward mechanisms.[43]

The American psychologist B. F. Skinner is the social scientist who did a lot of the early work to discover and support the operant conditioning model of learning. His original work used pigeons as subjects. He placed them in a "Skinner box," where, among other things, the pigeons could peck appropriate objects to receive rewards. In some experiments, pigeons learned to peck a lever multiple times to receive a reward (food). In other experiments, pigeons were rewarded for pecking other objects. Of course, the pigeons may not have been conscious of their learning. In contrast, the same kind of mental processes in humans are often available to conscious thought.

Operant conditioning involves several important concepts for our understanding of consumer behavior, including shaping, reinforcement, and punishment schedules.

Shaping Under **shaping,** *the desired behavior is learned over time, as intermediate actions are rewarded.* For example, a new retail store may offer several activities during opening week, encouraging visitors to enter the store. Next, the retail store may offer discounts, encouraging visitors to buy. The retail store may also offer a gift just for getting a store charge card, thus encouraging commitment. Strategies such as these help shape consumer responses.

Reinforcement Both **positive reinforcement** (*the presence of reward*) and **negative reinforcement** (*the absence of punishment*) strengthen or increase the probability of a target response. Marketers make use of many different rewards such as coupons, trading stamps, loyalty programs, rebates, and prizes. In some countries, however, some or all of these tactics are considered unfair marketing practice and prohibited. An example of both shaping and positive reinforcement that is common in the United States and parts of Europe (where it is legal) is the use of gifts offered in some cosmetic departments and described in Consumer Chronicles 9.2. Learning occurs faster through **continuous reinforcement,** when *a reward is given each and every time the response occurs;* but **partial reinforcement,** when *the reward is given only some of the time the response occurs,* causes learning to persist for longer after the reinforcement is discontinued.

Punishment *Punishment weakens the probability of a target response.* When consumers have a bad product or service experience, they may feel punished for their product choice; they may explain this punishment in terms of the choice rule they used, saying "that's what happens when you buy the cheapest brand." Some advertisements advise that you will be "punished" if you do not use a product or brand. In a Korean

The Free Gift

CONSUMER CHRONICLES 9.2

Marie, a U.S. college freshman, tells the following story about her mother's shopping behavior.

As my mother walks into the cosmetics section of Rich's Department Store, her eyes dart hungrily from side to side, hot in pursuit of a good deal. Any customer, entering any cosmetics department, at any time of year, is certain to observe my mother's so-called good deal. Out of the 20-odd cosmetics houses that are usually represented, at least 3 or 4 will be offering a "free-with-purchase gift." Clinique may require a $20 purchase, upon which the proud customer will receive a free mirror and two lipsticks, whose colors seem especially designed for circus folk. Lancôme will have an offer for customers who buy a fragrance. Upon purchase, they receive a free beach bag.

"Marie, look at that special offer from Estée Lauder!"

"Incredible," I think. A sample perfume, lipstick, and a comb—all free for customers who spend $20!

Inevitably, on display, will be a revolutionary new product for combating the aging process. Given half a chance, the sales clerk can easily convince my mother to scoop up $60 worth of cream, guaranteed to enhance a youthful appearance. And don't forget that "fabulous" free gift!

"What a deal!" exclaims my mother.

I, of course, remain perfectly silent. I don't want to spoil her fun.

It doesn't really matter that my mother is not a regular user of Estée Lauder. If mother gets something for free, then it was a successful shopping trip.

ad for milk, the headline promises that "your bones will be full of holes" if you don't drink milk. The image of a chair that is full of holes like a piece of Swiss cheese reinforces this claim, making an analogy between the support that a piece of furniture supplies and the support provided by the human spine. The sponsor is an agricultural association (dairy farmers).

MEMORY AND RETRIEVAL

How Memory and Retrieval Work

A crucial piece in the puzzle of how and what people learn is memory.[44] Memory begins as an internal experience: an image, a fragment of recalled conversation, a vivid scene. It travels outward and then returns to the privacy of one's own mind. People build up neural pathways for memories, and the more often a particular memory is invoked, the stronger that neural pathway becomes. Memory depends on a variety of neural activities that converge to create recollections. How and what someone remembers depends on a host of factors: the person's brain, the specific clue that triggers a particular search for memory, age, how the person took in the information in the first place, how much time has elapsed since the original experience, frequency of recall of the memory, and what the person is doing and feeling at the moment of recall. These are just some of the factors that influence the quality and precision of a particular act of recollection.

Recent years have brought great advances in what we know about memory and retrieval. For example, we know that the neural mechanisms that lead to memory are similar to those used for imagining things. Research now shows that each time people say or imagine something from their past, they are putting it together from bits and pieces that may have, until now, been stored separately. No wonder people change, add, and delete things from a remembered event. Research on cultural differences in how people organize information implies that how people think about what they are doing may influence the process of remembering.[45] In addition, cultural differences affect whether and how people recall the past. For instance, compared to people in Western cultures, Korean mothers and their children refer to the past less frequently and focus less on personal experience of a past event. One study compared **self-narratives**—*stories about the self*—of four- to six-year-old Korean, Chinese, and U.S. youngsters. The research suggested that although all the children were equivalent in their overall memory capacity, they differed in what they recalled. American children were more likely to include descriptive terms, references to internal states, and evaluations. Compared to Korean and Chinese children, they also mentioned themselves as opposed to others more often.[46] This finding is consistent with our discussion of motivation (Chapter 7) and our discussion of self (Chapter 10).

The Social Nature of Memory

The more we know about the physiological and social bases for memory, the more we are left in awe and bewilderment when trying to explain people's shifting, and vivid recollections. Memory must be understood as a kind of dynamic interplay between inner and outer settings. Memories are shaped by the complex and potent settings that involve other people. Moreover, memories are both private and public. The moment that an internal image, sound, smell, or scene is told to another person, it becomes something else, something that depends as much on motivation and social context as neural network. For example, the moment a person tells another about his or her most recent purchase decision, what may have been fleeting takes on substance, what may have been disorganized or irrational takes on sequence and reason, what may not have even been clearly marked as a memory is now embedded as something remembered, something from the past.

Like many American children, Colette likes to "recall" for anyone who will listen the story of the day she was born. She tells the story in vivid and imaginative detail from the moment mom left for the hospital to the time daddy cut the umbilical cord and laid her washed, clean, and hungry on mommy's breast, and she will go on from there. Of course, one of the unique qualities of this recollection, however vivid and autobiographical the story appears, is that her parents *created the memory*. She has internalized their shared and verbalized memories of the event in which she was clearly an important participant. By telling her this story, they signaled the drama and significance of this past moment and, like other parents, helped establish and sustain a sense of unique and ongoing intimacy.[47]

There are three interesting aspects of Colette's "recollection." First, people talk about collective or shared memories. Many times people feel *vividly familiar with events they never actually experienced.* They are able to construct an image, scene, or constellation of information that serves as a kind of **vicarious memory.** These vicarious memories are an important source of individual meaning as well as cultural life. The cartoon shown in Exhibit 9.7 illustrates vicarious memory of activities

EXHIBIT 9.7

The Doonesbury cartoon illustrates the concept of vicarious memories. Here, Zonker Harris describes a series of student high jinks, including an incident with the dean's Volvo. Finally, Doonesbury interrupts him to say, "Uh . . . Zonker? We never did any of those things." Zonker replies, "I know, but one day we'll think we did."

Source: DOONESBURY © G. B. Trudeau. Reprinted with permission of Universal Press Syndicate.

common to a time. Moreover, even when people share the common experience of an event, they do so from their own particular reference point. Consumer Chronicles 9.3 illustrates that these accounts of what happened may be at odds with a formal record of what happened. As people tell and trade stories around an event or a time in history, they communicate what is idiosyncratic and private, but they also exchange and build on shared versions of what happened.[48] Consumers' idiosyncratic reference points can provide a richer and more complex picture of an event. For example, one study asked husbands and wives to remember long lists of information. In each list, some of the information drew on the women's expertise and some drew on the men's expertise. Each couple acted as a team, with the man and woman in each spontaneously taking responsibility for the terms they would most easily remember. This type of *collaborative remembering* is referred to as **transactional memory.**[49] In trying to accomplish household consumption tasks (preparing meals, grocery shopping, getting the children to soccer practice), it is quite likely that collaborative remembering plays a significant role.

Second, with her birth story Colette reflects a society that values and uses autobiographical memories as an important source of information about the self. By telling the story, she is projecting a cultural point of view about life stories and about what is worth talking about. This viewpoint is reinforced in many conversations she has with other children and adults. For example, a small American child reporting to first grade with her arm in a cast is immediately bombarded by peers' questions about what happened, how it happened, what the doctor did, and how it felt. The story is told and retold, each retelling responding in detail to the parts the audience likes best. These questions communicate that in this social setting it is appropriate to tell a story about the self that includes an ordered sequence of events and emotions. In many other cultures such a story would be inappropriate. In focus groups with Hungarian women in the early 1990s, several reflected hesitation at talking about cosmetics, stressing the many more pressing social problems. Raised in a culture that abhorred the use of makeup, these women had been trained to believe that recalling stories about personal use of cosmetics was not appropriate for conversation.

Finally, and most important, the birth story reflects that there is no meaningful representation of the past outside of the one constructed in exchanges with others. Remembering is a culturally constructed, social activity. The influence of others on memory is startlingly powerful. In fact, there are now a number of studies suggesting people can be led by others to remember what they have not really experienced.[50] In everyday consumer life, beyond the courtroom or therapy session, remembering and reminiscing are consequential, influencing how others see us, our relationship with others, others' behaviors (including the memories they share), and the stories others share with yet others.

CONSUMER CHRONICLES 9.3

British Psychologists Try to Remember

Two British psychologists secretly recorded a discussion that took place after a meeting of the Cambridge Psychological Society. Two weeks later, the psychologists contacted all the participants and asked them to write down everything they could remember about the discussion. When these accounts were checked against the original recording, it turned out that respondents typically omitted more than 90 percent of the specific points that had been discussed. Moreover, of the points that were recalled, nearly half were substantially incorrect. Respondents recalled comments that were never made, they transformed casual remarks into lengthy orations, and they converted implicit meanings into explicit comments.

Source: Ian M. L. Hunter, Memory *(Harmondsworth, UK: Penguin, 1968).*

What Are the Types of Memory?

Scientists still don't know exactly what it means to say that a memory stays in the brain. This remains a black box in memory research. In this section we talk about three types of memories—sensory, short-term, and long-term memory—and how we use each of these. However, most of what we know about memory is inferred from what we have learned about retrieval. We do know that what is available in memory is different from what is accessible from memory.[51] As we have emphasized throughout this chapter, memories are constructed at the time of retrieval.[52] That is, memories are reconstructed, in a split second. At the time of recall, people use logical inferences to fill in missing details and use associated memories to add detail to the original memory. People put past experiences together from bits and pieces of memories stored separately to respond to individual needs in a particular context.

SENSORY MEMORY Memory researchers distinguish a particular category of short-term memory called **sensory memory.** This information is *stored for only a few seconds and is stored in its actual sensory form.* Sensory memory doesn't require the individual to pay attention to it or try to store it. For example, you might be listening to the radio while you do homework. Your roommate walks into the room and indicates she loves that group. You haven't really been paying attention, but you realize that you have been listening to Stone Temple Pilots and you say, "Yeah, I like that too!" If information is relevant, you will process it further. For example, your roommate may cause you to attend to the music and you may realize you haven't heard this piece before, but if it is not analyzed, the information is lost. Sensory memory can house information from any of the senses, but **echoic memory,** *memory of things we hear,* and **iconic memory,** *memory of things we see,* has received the most research attention.

SHORT-TERM MEMORY **Short-term memory** *encodes and interprets incoming information based on prior knowledge.* Most processing of information happens in short-term memory, making it very important for marketers to understand. When Jorja compares the entrance at Sea World with the entrances for other theme parks, she does this in short-term memory. We can hold only a limited number of things in short-term memory at any one time. Research suggests consumers can only hold an average of seven units or chunks of information, plus or minus two, in short-term memory.[53] In fact, that's why U.S. telephone numbers are seven digits long. Marketers can further facilitate consumers' memory for telephone numbers, or e-mail addresses, by providing words rather than individual numbers or digits. For example, 1-800-4-A-Yukon is a number to call to learn about GMC's Yukon XL sports utility vehicle. Short-term memory is also short-lived, only a few minutes. Unless we actively try to remember information or transfer that information to long-term memory, it will be lost.

Information in short-term memory can take different forms.[54] For example, Jorja used imagery processing to compare Sea World with other theme parks. That is, she represented the sounds, sights, and other sensations of being at the entrance to a big theme park. **Imagery processing** *represents information in sensory form.* **Discursive processing** is another way to represent information. In this case, *information is represented in words and symbols.* For example, if Jorja compared the price of Sea World with the price of DisneyLand she would be using discursive processing. Information in short-term memory also varies in terms of how much we elaborate on it, and this in turn depends on motives, goals, and context. In Chapter 8 we talked about elaboration as varying from simple recognition to counterarguing, problem-solving, daydreaming, and fantasizing. The use of imagery processing and especially elaborated imagery processing has many interesting implications for marketers.[55] For example, consumers value certain products such as books and music because of their ability to stimulate multisensory imagery. Imagery can also stimulate memories of past experiences and consumers may retain products that help them relive the event. Maddie's T-shirt from Sea World and her family's collection of pictures are partly valued for this reason. Imagery processing also can impact how consumers evaluate products because it allows them to chunk a lot of information together in a vivid image. Finally, imagery may affect how satisfied we are with a product or consumption experience. Sometimes these images may affect consumers' expectations for a product. For example, a family traveling to Utah for a rafting trip on the Green River was so disappointed to find the river was brown that they wanted to head home. Luckily they persevered and had a wonderful rafting experience. However, imagery also can enhance satisfaction by allowing consumers to elaborate the experience itself in ways that make it more enjoyable.[56]

LONG-TERM MEMORY Anything that is retained for more than a few minutes becomes long-term memory. **Long-term memory** is that part of *memory where information is* *placed for later use*. Researchers have identified two different types of long-term memories: **semantic** and episodic.[57] **Semantic memory** refers to *things people recall without any sense of when they learned them*. Semantic memory is often thought of as knowledge. **Consumer knowledge** is one type of semantic memory that *includes the structure and content of information related to aspects of purchase and consumption.*[58] Consumers have vast amounts of information about brands, market environments, consumption experiences, and so on that have been acquired over time, often without knowing when or how. For example, most consumers would be stumped with a question such as "when did you first learn about the brand Coca-Cola?" Many people, even in rather remote parts of the world, have grown up with Coca-Cola. Similarly, knowledge of many purchase and consumption activities such as ordering food at a restaurant, grocery shopping, or skiing are not attached to a particular event or experience but acquired through repetition over time.[59]

Consumers also have **episodic memory,** *memories that come tagged with information about when and where they happened*. Because episodic memory focuses on things that have happened to the individual, it is sometimes termed autobiographical memory. You may distinctly remember the first time you went on a roller-coaster ride, your first trip alone, the first time you bought a new car, a recent trip to the dentist, or a variety of other purchase and consumption events. As we have already noted, consumers in many cultures value products that help them cue and relive autobiographical memories. Possessions consumers value highly are often special to them because of their association with autobiographical memories.[60] Advertisements too often evoke positive emotions by recalling autobiographical memories, as we discussed in Chapter 8. Many of consumers' memories are a blend of semantic and episodic memory. For example, many people eat and enjoy Chinese food. They have general knowledge about going to a Chinese restaurant, ordering food, and determining what foods go together and how to eat Chinese food. Depending on a variety of circumstances, they also may recall particular salient episodes of eating Chinese food.

One type of semantic memory that marketers are especially interested in is consumer thoughts about brands. **Brand image** is the *perceptions about a brand as reflected by the associations held in consumer memory*. Consumers have a variety of different associations with brands. To take a specific example of the application of brand image, consider the French brand Kookaï, a very popular ready-to-wear clothing brand for European women. An advertisement for Kookaï is shown on the next page.

www.kookai.fr

Kookaï's target market is composed of young women between 15 and 25. The prices are quite low and the advertisements show attractive and sassy young women as illustrated on their website and in their advertising. When women between 19 and 39 were interviewed about the brand, many had a very clear image of the typical user, called a "kookaïette." Associations for Kookaï ranged between 17 and 176 and included all the types shown in Exhibit 9.8 on page 363.[61]

Exhibit 9.8 is an example of an associative network. This is one way that memory researchers represent semantic memory or prior knowledge. An **associative network** is a *set of ideas and memories that are linked to a concept*. The different links shown in Exhibit 9.8 may have different strengths. For example, the link to clothes may be very strong whereas the link to accessories may be much weaker. Strong links are firmly established in memory, whereas other links may have been encountered infrequently, or not accessed for a long time and their establishment in memory is weak. The entire associative network represents what is available in a consumer's long-term memory about Kookaï. In the section on knowledge, we will talk more about how associative networks structure the content of long-term memory.

Who's Kookaï's target market?

Retrieving Memories

Associative networks provide some insights into how information gets retrieved from memory. For example, the stronger a link between information and a product or brand, the more accessible or available the information is. **Accessibility,** then, *refers to the likelihood that an item will be retrieved from long-term memory.* Consider the outdoor poster shown on page 364 that was part of an antidiscrimination public service campaign in Southhampton, England. What associations are encouraged by this poster? Do you have strong positive autobiographical or episodic memories linked to crayons? What other kinds of associations does this poster recall for you?

Strong links are important to marketers because they enhance an item's accessibility in memory. For example, Kookaï benefits if it is closely linked to clothes shopping. However, weak links also can be important to marketers. Ethical Dilemma 9.2 discussed earlier illustrates one way that weak links can be important. In this case advertising primes a link between positive role models and cigarette smoking, although youth are unaware that has happened. Later, the link primed by advertising is reinforced by exposure to peers who smoke. **Priming** is *activation of a node in memory, often without conscious awareness.*

How Memory Fails Us

Perhaps you've had the frustrating experience of wasting valuable time looking for misplaced keys, or returned from the grocery store to discover you forgot the very item you most intended to purchase. Can you remember an occasion where you felt you had the answer "on the tip of your tongue" but simply could not retrieve it? Memory is adaptive and it serves us well in many respects, but the very qualities that boost our chances of survival and our ability to pursue and achieve goals occasionally get us into trouble.[62] In this section we outline some important ways that memory fails us.[63]

MEMORY FADES Forgetting occurs with the passage of time. One of the most documented findings about memory is that over time we forget many details even when

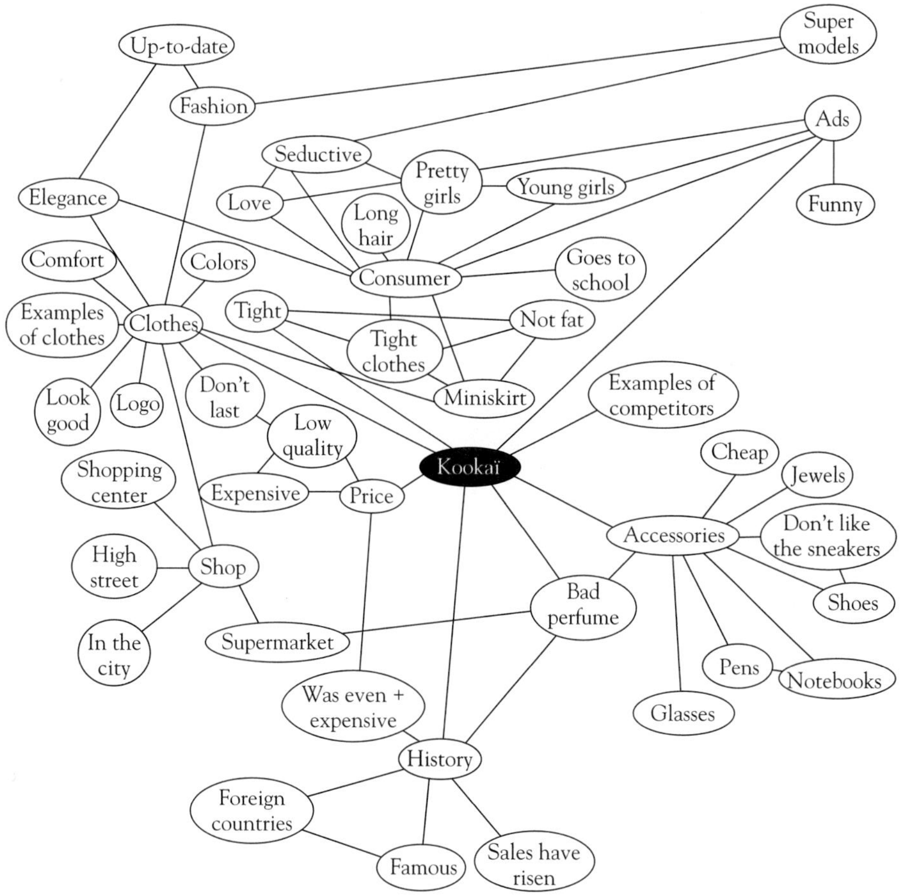

EXHIBIT 9.8

An Associative Network of Memory for Kookaï

Source: Michaël Korchia, "Brand Image and Brand Associations," working paper (Paris, France: ESSEC).

the person or event is of considerable personal significance to us. In fact, we can talk about a forgetting curve. For days memory may preserve a relatively detailed record that allows us to reproduce the past with reasonable accuracy, but with the passing of time opportunities for interference multiply, generated by similar experiences, and blur recollections. When we try to recall last year's Thanksgiving celebration, we end up inferring some of the details from our more general knowledge of how our family celebrates Thanksgiving.

Although fading memory is pervasive, it increases as people age. By the time people reach their 60s and 70s, the forgetting curve is more marked and consistent. However, there is still considerable variability among older adults. For example, better-educated older adults have fewer problems than less-educated older adults. Of course, forgetting can be offset by various factors as well. For example, Maddie's telling and retelling of her trip to Sea World is one of the best ways to counter forgetting. Also, events that are more distinctive are less vulnerable to interference from everyday experiences. Maddie finds it easier to recall her trip to Sea World than what she did a month ago in school. Finally, certain events or cues may dredge up seemingly lost information. In Chapter 8 we talked about how familiar smells can powerfully recall past events otherwise lost in memory.

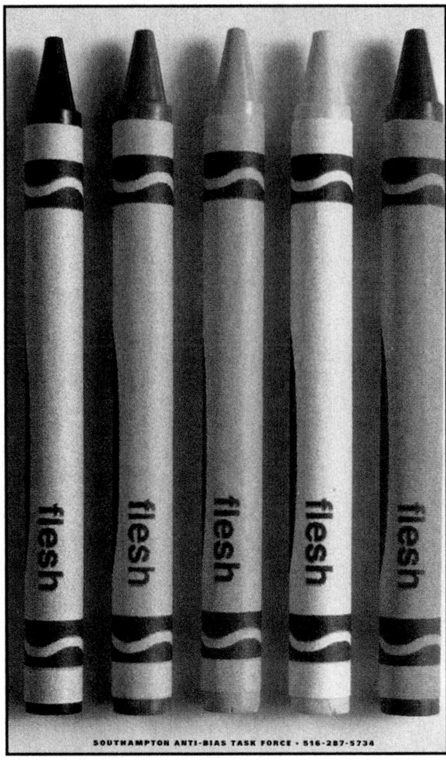

An outdoor poster campaign against discrimination stimulates associations.

ABSENTMINDEDNESS **Absentmindedness** is *lapses in attention that result in failing to remember information because it was not encoded properly or is overlooked at the time we need to retrieve it.* Consumers and marketers constantly contend with absentmindedness. For example, the "Got Milk" billboard campaign was designed to help consumers remember to stop for milk on their way home from work. It seems marketers are constantly bombarding consumers with reminders to use their products. And sometimes, when you open the refrigerator and realize you don't have that key ingredient, you wish they were more effective. A big reason for absentmindedness is the divided attention that pervades our daily lives. Insufficient attention at the time of encoding is an important problem. For example, you may quickly glance in the refrigerator and make note of three or four things to stop for on the way home, but unless you give a certain amount of attention to remembering those three or four items, there's a good chance that you'll forget one or more of them later on. Similarly, when we meet a group of new people and we later encounter one of them again, we may remember her face as familiar, but we may not have engaged in sufficient elaboration to remember anything else about her—our attention was divided among too many competing pieces of incoming information. Of course, this is a big problem for advertisers who are often competing against other incoming information that the consumer is more motivated to pay attention to. In Chapter 8 we described some ways for marketers to grab consumers' attention so that they encode messages completely, enhancing the likelihood that the consumer will be able to recall them later.

A fascinating related problem is associated with the failure of prospective memory. **Prospective memory** is *remembering to do things in the future*. For a long time researchers concerned themselves with remembrance of things past, but people are more concerned with remembering to carry out future actions. What tools do you use to remember to make a lunch appointment, or send in your credit card payment? The success of products such as Palm Pilots turns on the importance of prospective memory. When people fail to remember future intentions, they are considered unreliable. But, since many people consider following through on such intentions important, why do they forget? Again, we tend to call this absentmindedness, but in this case the culprit is often the failure of a retrieval cue. There's an old joke about tying a string around your finger to remember something, but forgetting what the string is there to remember. This is not so far-fetched. We sometimes put something in our calendar, but then forget to look at our calendar, or put a Post-it note on the refrigerator, only to forget to look at the Post-it note. One of the authors of this textbook is guilty of writing appointments in her calendar that she later can't decipher—she's supposed to meet with someone at 11:00 A.M., but who and where escapes her—at the time she made the entry it all seemed perfectly clear. A very important policy and marketing problem related to failures of prospective memory is described in Ethical Dilemma 9.3.

Don't Forget to Take Your Medicine!

ETHICAL DILEMMA 9.3

An important prospective memory task for many older adults is remembering to take their medications at the right time of the day. Surveys suggest that between one-third and one-half of older consumers do not stick with their medication schedules. Failing to remember medications is especially prevalent among consumers over 70. Lots of different factors contribute to the problem of taking medications at the right time. However, one way to help is to make sure retrieval cues work better. For example, remembering a time-based task, for example, take your medication at 8 A.M. in the morning, is more difficult than remembering an event-based task, for example, take your medication when you brush your teeth in the morning. Encouraging older adults to pair medications with daily events can improve their adherence to medication schedules. For example, a medication can be set next to the toothpaste to encourage retrieval. Can you think of other contexts where this tactic would be useful?

Source: Adapted from Daniel L. Schacter, The Seven Sins of Memory *(New York: Houghton Mifflin, 2001), pp. 55–56.*

BLOCKING **Blocking** occurs *when a name or word has been encoded and stored and a retrieval cue may be available that would normally trigger recall, but the information remains just out of reach when needed.* It can occur in numerous situations and is especially prevalent among older adults. Although it can occur for names of objects and abstract words, it occurs most frequently for proper names for people. Without fully describing how blocking occurs in memory, one fundamental problem is the word or name has only a tenuous link with the attributes of that person or object. We can easily recall our friend's face and his occupation, but his name is not logically linked to this easily retrieved information and we can't quite activate that information. Of course, in some cultures, people's names incorporate attributes of their bearers. In cultures where names reflect specific properties of individuals, blocking might be less problematic.

Of course, blocking has important implications when we talk about brand names. It helps explain why a consumer could regularly use a product, easily picture the product and how it tastes and smells in her mind, but not be able to recall the brand name. Marketers can benefit from understanding how activation works in memory to ensure that brand names incorporate attributes of their bearers, or, using the behavioral learning theories described earlier, are inextricably linked in consumers' minds. If brand names are strongly linked to visual images and actions, they will be easier for consumers to retrieve. Industry Insights 9.1 illustrates how Orangina links to vivid actions to strengthen brand image.

INDUSTRY INSIGHTS 9.1

Orangina Wants You to "Shake It"

An important quality Orangina wants to associate with its drinks is naturalness. According to Orangina, the orange pulp proves its naturalness. That means that before you drink it you should "shake it." Orangina has enlisted big names in entertainment to do just that. In 1972, the concept "Shake the bottle to wake the taste" was featured in "Barman" films produced by Jean Jacques Annaud and Pierre Etaix. In 1994–95, a series of films produced by Alain Chabat introduced the new signature "Shake it." The shaking action included new heights of humor and daring. They are now broadcast worldwide.

Source: Adapted from the Orangina website. www.orangina.fr

Blocked retrieval is another aspect of blocking that is particularly vexing. Blocked retrieval can happen for a variety of reasons and has numerous public policy implications. One important finding is that retrieving information from memory can inhibit subsequent recall of related information. Consider an eyewitness of a crime. When the eyewitness is asked about certain aspects of the crime, recalling those aspects can make parts of the event not asked about more difficult to recall. Other research suggests that we remember better what we are told to remember than what we are told to forget. Of course, a modest implication is that as consumers recall brand information, related information about competitive products or even other information about that brand may become less accessible. This also could have implications for market research. Comments in a focus group may make certain related information easier to recall for focus group participants, but might make other information that the researcher would like to access more difficult for participants to recall.

MISATTRIBUTION **Misattributions** in remembering are quite common. Sometimes we remember events that never happened. We attribute ease of processing or vivid images to familiarity—"it must be something I experienced in the past." Sometimes we recall correctly what happened, but misattribute it to the wrong time or place. And sometimes we credit a spontaneous image or thought to our own imagination, when in fact we are recalling it from something we read or heard. Misattributions have serious policy ramifications. Many people are sent to prison on the basis of eyewitness accounts that may later turn out to be misattributions—the accused person may be familiar to the eyewitness, but from a different time and place. And, of course, unintentional plagiarism may occur when we attribute something to our imagination that is actually the product of someone else's imagination. **Source misattributions** occur when *people recall a fact they learned earlier, or recognize a person or object they have seen before, but misattribute the source of their knowledge*. Psychologists explain this in terms of **memory binding**—*the linking of various components of an experience into a unitary whole*. When an action, object, or person is not properly bound to a particular time and place, memory binding fails. Thus, when there is a strong sense of general familiarity but an absence of specific recollections, misattributions are likely.

Source misattributions can work for or against marketers, and are certainly of concern to policy makers. Misattributions can lead consumers to attribute to their own experience things they have only read or heard about from others. For example, a failure of memory binding is at work when consumers remember as an experience something they saw in an advertisement. Such a misattribution is consequential because experience is considered more credible than advertising.

SUGGESTIBILITY Suggestibility is actually a specific case of misattribution. **Suggestibility** *is the tendency to incorporate misleading information from external sources* *into personal recollections*. There are many dramatic even frightening cases of suggestibility. One of the most dramatic involves false confessions to crimes. Coercive questioning by police can lead people to mistakenly believe in their own guilt. False memories from childhood are especially common because we don't expect to have clear and detailed memories of something that far back in the past. Consequently, suggestions or guided imagery can lead us to interpret fuzzy images or vague feelings of familiarity as something that actually happened. The Doonesbury cartoon in Exhibit 9.7 used to illustrate vicarious memory also illustrates how suggestibility works.

BIAS Throughout this chapter we have emphasized the constructive, narrative quality of memory. Nowhere is this more apparent than in a consideration of the types of bias our memories are vulnerable to. **Bias** refers to how *our present knowledge, beliefs, and feelings may distort and influence our encoding of new experiences or our later memories of them.* Luckily we can ameliorate many of these biases just with awareness and attention. Memory bias takes several different forms. Here we will describe just a few. Evidence suggests that we *reinterpret the past both to show how it is like how we are now*—**consistency bias**—*and to show how we have changed*—**change bias.** For example, our recollections of the history of close personal relationships is colored by the current status of that relationship. This has implications for marketers. For example, if a service provider fails to provide good service, customers may under certain circumstances reinterpret past service to be consistent with this failure. The hindsight bias that we talked about earlier is another illustration of memory bias. We also noted earlier cultural differences in how prominently the self is encoded in memories. The **self-enhancing bias,** or *tendency to remember past experiences so as to see the self positively,* is a common type of bias, at least in the West. As indicated earlier, categories are important devices for comparing incoming information to prior knowledge. However, stereotypes also can lead to biases, causing us to activate feelings and beliefs based on membership in a category that actually don't apply. We saw that kind of "guilt by association" in Jorja's initial assessment of Sea World. Of course, it has much more serious repercussions when it affects ethnic, racial, and gender relations. Marketers have to be sensitive to how membership in a category affects beliefs that consumers have about their product. Beliefs about new products may depend importantly on what categories consumers draw on to understand those products. We will talk more about this when we describe consumer inferences and analogies.

PERSISTENCE **Persistence** involves *remembering things you wish you could forget.* All of us have had the experience of memories that distract us from more important tasks—for example, a song running through our heads. However, sometimes we are haunted by memories of emotionally charged experiences that we would prefer to forget or at least control. Why does this happen? Emotional information attracts attention quickly and automatically. Then emotional information is evaluated in terms of our current goals and concerns. That elaboration, as discussed earlier in the chapter, promotes subsequent memory for the experience. In the case of painful emotional events, people often replay the event, sometimes falling into a destructive cycle of persistent remembering. The powerful impact of emotion on memory makes biological sense. Remembering what causes pain and evokes pleasure is adaptive and when functioning in a healthy way is one of our greatest strengths. We see it's adaptive power in the learning theories we discussed earlier. Nevertheless, it's wise to be wary of the risks of persistence.

Enhancing Consumer Memory

Throughout this section we have provided insights into how memory works and fails to work. People may remember certain things and not others for a variety of reasons, including the mood they're in when they recall them, the uniqueness of the memory, or because they have rehearsed them a number of times. Several characteristics of consumers influence what they recall. For example, being in a positive mood can enhance recall both by encouraging elaboration and by affecting rehearsal of information.[64] However, mood congruency is also important, so someone in a negative mood may be more likely to recall negative information. Expertise also affects what people recall. For example, providing a consumption vocabulary facilitates encoding and retrieval in addition to influencing decisions. Helping consumers label a sensory experience such as a taste, smell, sound, or visual image can help them encode it, retrieve it, and use it in future decisions.[65] Even the existence of categories makes it easier to encode new information. Compared to novices, experts have more complex categories in memory, with a greater number of higher- and lower-level categories and more detail within each category. Because of involvement and interest, experts also have rehearsed the associations among and between related categories, making the paths between them stronger.[66] Exhibit 9.9 compares the types of thoughts generated by an expert and a novice in response to memory probes about motorcycles.

Can you guess which thoughts represent those of the expert and those of the novice? The novice has never owned a motorcycle and does not read motorcycle magazines, but she does have friends who own motorcycles. The expert has owned eight motorcycles, is an avid reader of motorcycle magazines, and has five friends who own motorcycles. Looking at these two sets of thoughts about motorcycles, it is easy to see that the expert has much greater awareness and knowledge about alternative models and organizes information around product types. Experts also have information about the characteristics of different alternatives, making it easier to compare models and infer the performance of new models or performance in different usage situations.

Of course, marketers are interested in enhancing consumer memory for their own products and services and may be interested in interfering with consumer memory for competitive products and services. Good Practice 9.1 summarizes research on how marketers can influence consumer memory. Of course, this list is overly simple and does not include how these factors might interact in making a choice.[67]

Marketers are also interested in learning and measuring what consumers remember. Consumer researchers must decide carefully about what type of retrieval cues, if any, to provide to consumers. Industry Insights 9.2 illustrates the procedure for looking at what consumers recall using **aided recall.** In this example, *consumers are given cues to recall slogans and brand names.* **Free recall** exists *when consumers can recall something from memory without any cues or help.*

Marketers also can partner with technology to assist consumers in learning and remembering information. A pressing need is to provide consumers with useful tools to help them navigate through the morass of information that has become available through satellite, cable, and the World Wide Web. Ideas that a short number of years ago were just possibilities are rapidly becoming realities.[68] One alternative for information-weary consumers is a "knowbot," a type of robot. A knowbot may serve to screen out and organize the flood of information that bombards people every day. It thus has the potential to reduce information overload.

A knowbot may be designed to attach itself to a combination TV/VCR. A consumer might program the knowbot to tape his favorite program. Then, he may ask the knowbot

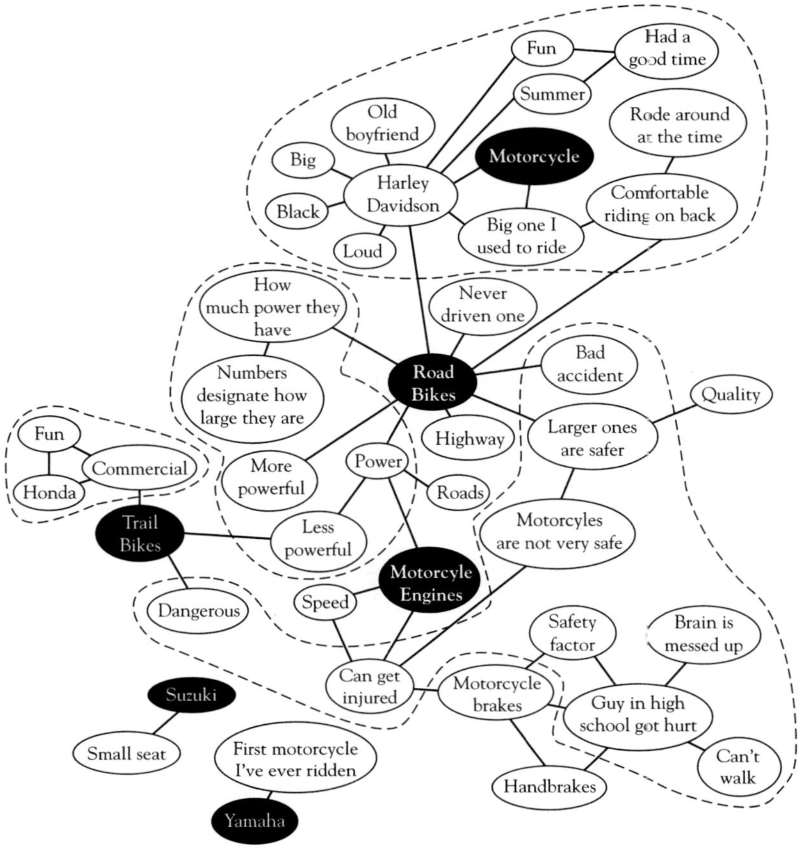

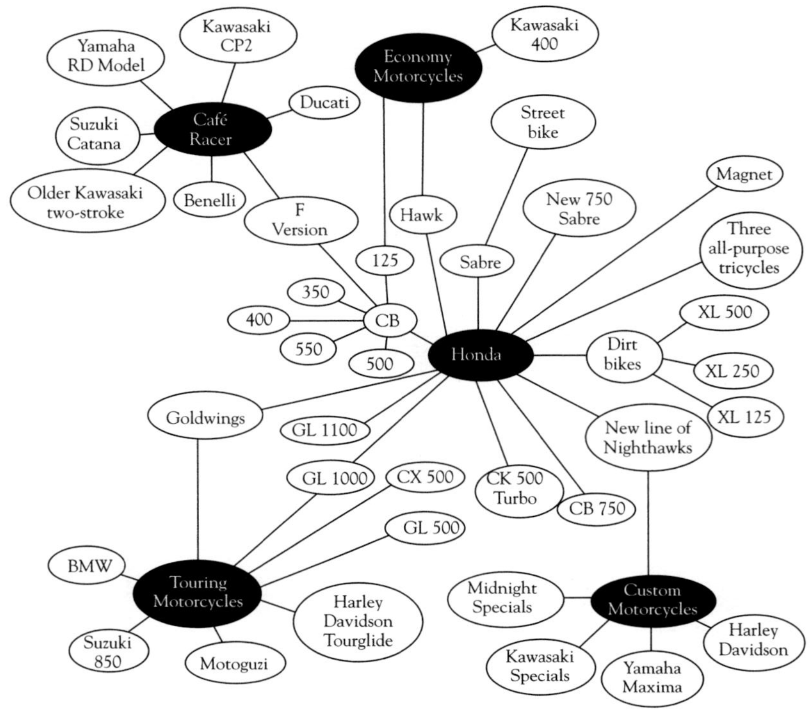

EXHIBIT 9.9

Motorcycle Associations

Can You Name the Expert?

Source: Andrew A. Mitchell and Peter A. Dacin, "The Assessment of Alternative Measures of Consumer Expertise," *Journal of Consumer Research* 23 (December 1996), pp. 219–39.

Enhancing What Consumers Remember

GOOD PRACTICE 9.1

Chunking	Helping consumers put a group of relevant information about a brand into a single chunk will make it easier to hold in short-term memory and increase the chance that it will move to long-term memory.
Rehearsal	The use of catchy jingles and slogans can encourage consumers to repeat and think about the information.
Recirculation	Consumers should be repeatedly exposed to marketing communication. This effect can be enhanced if varied executions are employed.
Elaboration	Stronger memory traces are established when consumers think about the information and consciously relate it to existing information. Advertising that encourages consumers to relate to important past experiences may be an effective way of encouraging elaboration.
Primacy	Consumers seem to remember best what they learn first. Marketers can try to control the order of consumer exposure to information. However, be advised, less knowledgeable consumers are more susceptible to this effect than more knowledgeable consumers. And a competitor advertising right after another can sometimes cause interference.
Emotion	Overall evaluations or feelings tend to be more accessible than specific brand information. Marketers can encourage consumers to generate positive feelings about their product or service.
Salience	Information that stands out as unique or important will be more accessible than other information. Marketers can work to make their product-relevant information salient to the consumer.
Prototypicality	Brands that are considered typical of a product class also tend to be more accessible. Marketers that are first to market have an advantage over later entrants because they define the product class. Category leaders may also have this type of advantage.
Congruence	When multiple associations for a product are congruent or consistent with one another, the information tends to be more accessible. Marketers can work to ensure that information about a product is consistent, thereby strengthening the associative links that connect a set of ideas to the product.
Priming	When items are commonly recalled together, activating one item may prime other items that consumers commonly link with it. If marketers understand these links, they can effectively promote their product through links to other associations. An effective example of this would be the "Got Milk" campaign that primed consumers' appetite for milk by promoting products that go with milk such as cereal, cookies, cupcakes, and so on.

to screen out all of the commercials. The next day, he may decide that he's in the market for some new athletic shoes. He asks the knowbot to tape all of the athletic shoe commercials and put them together into a block. Then, because of prior experiences, he asks the knowbot to delete all of the Keds commercials. In this way, the knowbot

Procedure

Consumers are told that a new magazine is coming out and the publisher wants to test the concept and the appeal of the articles. This cover story is called an experimental "guise."
Consumers enter a reading room and are given the magazine to read through. Most consumers read the magazine for about one hour, front to back. The magazine contains a mixture of news articles, features, and advertisements. Altogether there are approximately 20 ads in the magazine for a wide range of products and services. In this particular instance, the researchers are interested in the 5 ads for hair care products that are placed throughout the publication. The ads are for five different brands and are quite distinct from one another in terms of creativity, copy points, and layout.

Questionnaire

The following day, respondents are contacted again and asked some questions about the ads and the articles. For instance, respondents answer some of the following questions about the shampoo ads:

14. Which of the following brands do you remember seeing advertised in the magazine (check all that apply)?

    a) Pert Shampoo
    b) Prell Shampoo
    c) Givens Shampoo
    d) Crest Shampoo
    e) Head and Shoulders Shampoo

15. Which of the advertised shampoos uses the slogan, "Shower and go!" (fill in the brand name)?
    Check here if you don't know

serves as a buffer between the consumer and the commercial world. Advertisers will have to design commercials to appeal to mechanical intermediaries. It may not be enough to create a commercial message that is eye-catching and attention-getting for humans. In addition, advertisers may have to create commercials that can get past mechanical screens (such as knowbots).
Of course, such screening already takes place on the World Wide Web when consumers use search engines. Web page designers try to include key words that will be popular when consumers conduct a guided search. In addition, web designers have methods to ensure that their page will appear at the top of any search list that is generated. As knowbots become more sophisticated, advertisers in turn find clever ways to subvert the system. In the next generation, the knowbots are more sophisticated again. This is true technological warfare. Of course, one dilemma is how to design intelligent agents that can learn and respond to the needs of consumers.[69] Researchers argue that consumers need help on at least three fronts: formulating preferences, finding and organizing relevant information, and evaluating attractive alternatives and choosing among them. Good Practice 9.2 summarizes the goals of electronic agents.

Knowledge

Very often, consumers' understanding of marketing communications depends on their prior knowledge and experiences. A great example is an advertisement for Wrigley's

GOOD PRACTICE 9.2
Goals of an Electronic Agent

Goal	Features
Improve decision quality	Assist consumers in learning about the product and preferences Reduce decision complexity Be a warehouse for good information Provide an appropriate consideration set for evaluation Adapt over time in response to new information and feedback
Increase satisfaction	Be flexible and responsive to users' requests Increase the match between consumers' taste and products Be simple to operate and use Allow consumers to have good experiences Set realistic expectations
Develop trust	Satisfy and protect users' best interests Reassure users that they are getting a good value

Source: Adapted from Pat West et al., "Agents to the Rescue?" HEC Symposium on Advances in Choice Theory, *Marketing Science Institute, report no. 99-121, 1999, pp. 5–7.*

"long-lasting" Extra Sugarfree Gum. This ad appeared in *Good Housekeeping,* a family-oriented magazine. The Advertisement shows a complicated set of instructions with the tagline "Assembles in minutes." The advertisement is most effective if the audience can relate to the experience of complicated assembly instructions tagged with the promotion "Assembles in Minutes."

In this final section we look more closely at the content and structure of knowledge to better understand how consumers integrate prior knowledge to make inferences and judgments. In Chapter 8 we introduced the basic ideas of schemas and scripts, and we have given several examples of associative networks in this chapter. Associative networks are another way of representing a consumer's schema for a brand such as Kookaï (as in Exhibit 9.8) or a product category such as motorcycles (as in Exhibit 9.9). Both Chapters 4 and 8 talked about consumers' interpretations of marketing communications. Here we will focus on a few examples that emphasize how prior knowledge is integrated with new stimuli to assign meaning.

Assigning Products to Categories

When a product is new, marketers must help consumers understand it, the benefits it offers, and how it is different from other offerings in the market. Consumers will rely on marketers, and other cues about how they should categorize the product and what images, beliefs, and even personality characteristics they should assign to it. In this

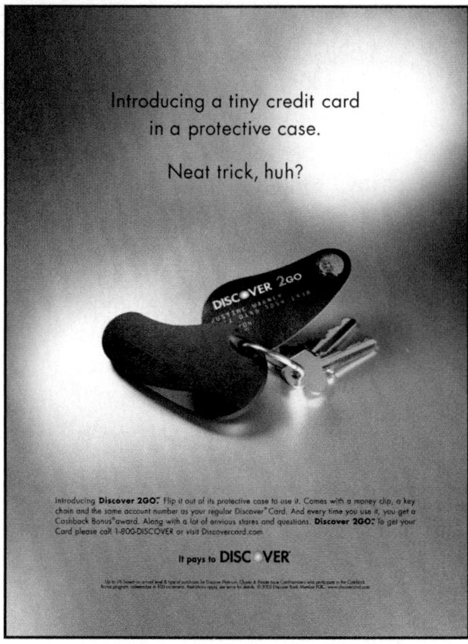

Helping consumers learn a new product concept.

sense, the marketer attempts to create and elaborate consumer schemas. Consider the advertisement shown for Discover 2Go. This advertisement introduces a new product, and even acknowledges that consumers are confused about what it is. How do you think consumers will respond to this new product? What category or categories will consumers put this product in?

When a firm introduces a brand extension *(a new product with a familiar brand name),* they are hoping that the qualities of the familiar brand will be associated with the new product. They also may be hoping that the new product will enliven and extend images of the familiar brand. Sometimes a product is logically linked to multiple categories. The comparative advantage and success of such a product will often turn on how consumers categorize and think about it. Consider the brief life of Motorola's Envoy, described in Industry Insight 9.3.

The problem of how products get thought about is especially important in the case of really new and innovative products such as Motorola's Envoy. In such cases analogies can sometimes offer consumers a useful frame of reference. We can think of **analogical learning** as *using a familiar domain to understand a novel domain.* Let's take an example. Suppose you are interested in the offline web readers used to download web pages to your computer's disk drive. You could learn more about this by relating it to something you understand better, such as a VCR. Using this knowledge, you might note that both allow you to retrieve and store media content, that both use a storage device (tape, disk), and you might surmise, on the basis of your VCR experience, that both will be difficult to program.[70] E-commerce companies rely heavily on analogical learning—just flip through any e-company or e-shopping magazine. The Bowstreet ad shown on page 375 encourages viewers to make an analogy between roads and business webs.

As with the failed Motorola Envoy, for many really new products, multiple categories are useful in understanding the product benefits and features. Unfortunately, consistent

What Category Should Your Product Compete In?

INDUSTRY INSIGHTS 9.3

Motorola launched a personal digital assistant, Envoy, in 1994. The product was withdrawn from the market in 1996. Shortly before Envoy was withdrawn, the PalmPilot 1000 was launched and became the most rapidly adopted electronic device ever. The PalmPilot 1000, however, had only a fraction of the capabilities of Envoy. Why did Envoy fail? The problem was that Envoy lacked a clear category consumers could use as a frame of reference. It could receive messages wirelessly like a pager, but it was too large and expensive to compete in this category. It could send e-mail and faxes like a laptop but lacked a keyboard and sufficient storage to be a substitute. Envoy could store calendar and contact information like an organizer but was too expensive and cumbersome to compete well in this category. By contrast the PalmPilot was clearly positioned as an improvement over existing organizers. Consumers knew how to think about it.

Source: Adapted from Kevin Lane Keller, Brian Sternthal, and Alice Tybout, "Three Questions You Need to Ask About Your Brand," Harvard Business Review, *September 2002.*

with the blocking memory problem described above, the first category that consumers activate can significantly influence their categorizations, expectations, and preferences. However, it is possible for marketers to encourage consumers to use information from multiple categories in evaluating a new product.[71]

Analogical thinking is not only useful for understanding new products but can frame more familiar products in new ways. For example, consider the upscale Australian advertisement for Hydrotherm, a heated towel rack. What analogies does this advertisement draw on? The analogies a firm employs are often intended to tell us something about the personality of the brand. **Brand personality** refers to *the set of human characteristics associated with a brand.*[72] Some research has suggested most brands can be described along five dimensions of brand personality. Industry Insights 9.4 outlines these five dimensions. Can you think of brands that are prototypical of each dimension? A category **prototype** is *a member that we perceive to be the best example of the category.* If you are American, there is a good chance you can, but people from some other cultures probably find the idea of brand personality bizarre.

Consumer Inferences

If marketers understand consumers' prior knowledge, they can manipulate elements of their offering to affect inferences consumers make about the brand. We have seen many illustrations in other chapters of how marketers use symbols, packaging, prices, and promotion to influence the meanings consumers assign to objects. Here we wish only to stress how such tactics rely on consumers' prior knowledge. Consider the South African ad for Land Rover on page 376. Perhaps you need to reflect a moment to decide exactly what this ad is hoping to communicate.

This ad encourages analogical learning.

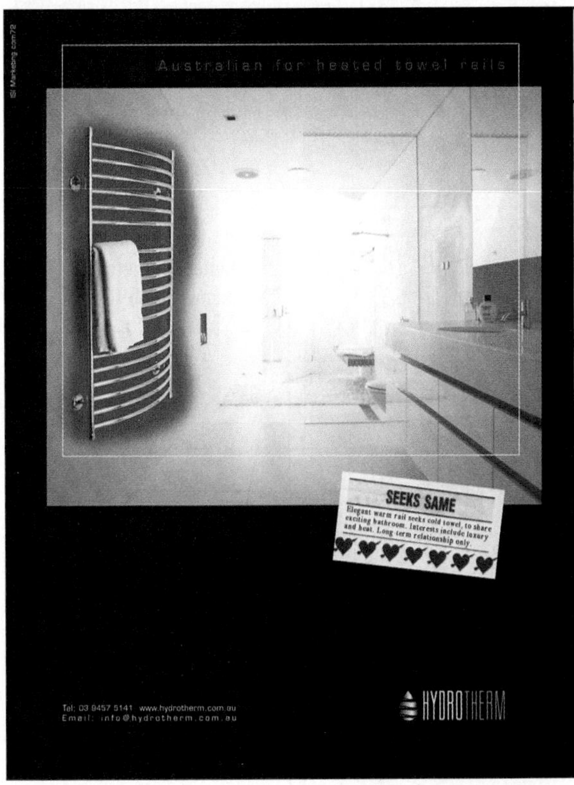

Encouraging consumer analogies.

Brand Personality Dimensions

INDUSTRY INSIGHTS 9.4

Name	Descriptors
Sincerity	Domestic, honest, genuine, cheerful
Excitement	Daring, spirited, imaginative, up-to-date
Competence	Reliable, responsible, dependable, efficient
Sophistication	Glamorous, pretentious, charming, romantic
Ruggedness	Tough, strong, outdoorsy, rugged

Source: Adapted from Jennifer L. Aaker, "Dimensions of Brand Personality," Journal of Marketing Research *34 (August 1997), pp. 347–56. Reprinted by permission of the American Marketing Association.*

To communicate the theme of original and authentic, the marketer makes several assumptions about thoughts and images consumers have about these terms. Perhaps the use of small carvings encourages the consumer to go back in time, recalling toy animals and trucks. Wooden carvings, especially of African animals, also connote authenticity. Even the colors are imbued with these feelings. Of course, the ad is also distinctive with puzzling components that encourage our further elaboration, enhancing the likelihood that the information will be stored and remembered.

Promoting theme of authenticity through consumer inferences.

This fear appeal relies on consumer inferences.

Let's consider one additional example. The advertisement for Boeri delivers a very scary message to consumers about wearing a helmet when skiing and snowboarding, but consider the way it communicates this threat. Now reflect on what other associations you have with chocolate and bunnies. The stimuli used in the advertisement create some humor and positive feelings, but make an effective analogy as well.

SUMMARY

Consumer experiences, learning, and knowledge evolve within a particular culture and social context based around consumers' motives and goals. Consumer experiences are at the heart of consumer behavior and have an important impact on what consumers learn and remember. Marketers can benefit by considering what experiences their products and services offer consumers. Consumer experiences include preconsumption, consumption, and postconsumption activities.

Consumer learning is adaptive and determined by value systems, desires, needs, and what the learner already knows. Consumers generate guesses or hypotheses about the way the world works, in order to make adaptive choices that move them toward their goals. There are lots of different ways to learn, including learning from experience and learning by description. Two important behavioral learning theories are classical conditioning and operant conditioning. These two approaches have helped researchers discover useful techniques for stimulating learning.

Almost all consumer decisions include a memory component. Each time consumers say or remember something, they put it together from bits and pieces stored separately in their brain. Memory is constructive, and it is a culturally constructed, social activity. Memories can be distinguished as sensory, short term and long term, and long-term memories can be further categorized as semantic or episodic. Associative networks represent what is available in a consumers' long-term memory about a concept. They

SUMMARY

provide some insights into how information gets retrieved from memory. Although memory is adaptive and serves us well in many respects, it also can get us into trouble. We describe seven different ways memory fails us: memory decay, absentmindedness, blocking, misattribution, suggestibility, bias, and persistence. Marketers can use several different techniques to influence and enhance memory.

Knowledge includes the information we have in memory and the way that information is stored. Culture, social conditions, and consumer goals shape the content and structure of knowledge. Knowledge includes categorization and comprehension. Consumer knowledge is seldom complete or errorless. It is important for marketers to consider both what consumers know and what they think they know. Consumers' understanding of marketing communications depends on their prior knowledge and experiences. Consumers rely on marketer and other cues to determine how they should categorize a product and what images, beliefs, and even personality characteristics they should assign to it. The category with which consumers associate a product can significantly influence consumers' inferences, expectations, and preferences. If marketers understand consumers' prior knowledge, they can manipulate elements of their offering to affect inferences consumers make about a brand.

KEY TERMS

absentmindedness 364
accessibility 362
aided recall 368
analogical learning 373
aspiration gap 348
associative network 361
behavioral learning theories 353
bias 367
blocking 365
brand extension 354
brand image 361
brand personality 374
categorization 343
change bias 367
classical conditioning 353
comprehension 343
consistency bias 367
consumer knowledge 361
consumer learning 342
continuous reinforcement 355
direct experience 352
discursive processing 360
echoic memory 360
emotion 341
encoding 350
episodic memory 361
experiences 341
family branding 354
free recall 368
hindsight bias 353
iconic memory 360
imagery processing 360
incidental learning 351
integration 350
knowledge 342
knowledge calibration 343
knowledge content 342
knowledge structure 342
learning by description 351
licensing 354
long-term memory 360
look-alike packaging 354
memory 342
memory binding 366
misattribution 366
negative reinforcement 355
operant conditioning 355
partial reinforcement 355
persistence 367
positive reinforcement 355
preferences 342
prepurchase search 347
priming 362
prospective memory 364
prototype 374
punishment 355
retrieval 342
self-enhancing bias 367
self-narratives 357
semantic memory 361

sensory memory 359
shaping 355
short-term memory 360
source misattributions 366
stimulus generalization 354
suggestibility 366
temporal contiguity principle 353
transactional memory 358
transformational experience 345
vicarious learning 351
vicarious memory 357

REVIEW QUESTIONS

1. Select a product category that you know a lot about and make a picture of your network of product associations. Now ask a less knowledgeable friend to do the same. How is his or her picture similar and different from your picture?
2. Think of your own examples of the different levels of the economic pyramid shown in Exhibit 9.2. How do you think the role of the marketer changes? How do you think the role of the buyer changes?
3. Operant conditioning is said to occur through positive reinforcement, negative reinforcement, or punishment. Name some products that promise that "good things will happen" if you buy or use them. What are some products that tell you that you will be "punished" if you don't buy them? Try to name products or behaviors for which you are told that you will be "punished" if you do buy or use them. Discuss and expand.
4. Can you think of some products that have similar packaging? Similar shapes? Similar names? Do you think that these look-alikes are effective at taking sales away from existing, popular brands? Explain and relate to principles of how learning and memory work.
5. What can marketing managers do to encourage consumer learning and knowledge development? Identify some advertisements that seem to be following your suggestions.
6. Give some examples of anticipated consumption. Is there a consumption experience that you are anticipating now? Describe the elements and details of that anticipation.
7. For each of the seven ways that memory fails us, outline one marketing opportunity and one public policy implication.
8. Draw on your own experiences to give examples of three of the seven ways that memory fails us.
9. Select three advertisements. Outline what prior knowledge the consumer needs to have in order to interpret the ad.
10. Pick one of your favorite brands and outline that brand's personality. What problems if any did you encounter? Is this a good or bad description of how you think and feel about the brand?

CASES

YOU MAKE THE CALL

AFFINITY.COM

Affinity Internet, Inc., is a web-hosting and applications services provider (ASP) that guides small and medium-sized businesses seeking to build a successful e-business.

Harnessing learning, experience, and knowledge to enhance product positioning.

The Los Angeles–based company offers a wide range of turnkey Internet solutions, including web hosting, e-commerce, dedicated servers, and advanced hosting services to business customers in more than 100 countries.
Examine the advertisement for Affinity above. This company promotes that it will help your business harness the strength of the Internet.

QUESTIONS

1. How is memory important in this advertisement?
2. Do you think analogical learning plays a role in this advertisement? Explain.
3. Can you identify cultural models or schemas that are important in the meaning of this advertisement?
4. Who is the target audience for this advertisement?
5. What are the strengths and weaknesses of Affinity's approach?
6. Affinity provides services in 100 countries. How global is this advertisement? Explain.

This case is adapted from material found on the Affinity website, www.affinity.com.

ENDNOTES

1. Stephen F. Mills, *The American Landscape* (Edinburgh: Edinburgh University Press, 1997); Chris Rojek, *Ways of Escape: Modern Transformations in Leisure and Travel* (London: Macmillan, 1993); and Pamela Shurmer-Smith and K. Hannam, *Worlds of Desire, Realms of Power: A Cultural Geography* (London: Edward Arnould, 1994).
2. Mihaly Csikszentmihalyi, *Flow = The Psychology of Optimal Experience* (New York: Harper and Row, 1990).
3. B. Joseph Pine II and James H. Gilmore, *The Experience Economy* (Boston: Harvard Business School Press, 1999).
4. Stephen J. Hoch and John Deighton, "Managing What Consumers Learn from Experience," *Journal of Marketing,* April 1989, pp. 1–20.
5. A more common definition of learning is to gain knowledge, understanding, or skill by study, instruction, or experience, but this definition tells us little about how it happens. Our definition derives from Gerold M. Edelman, *Bright Air, Brilliant Fire: On the Matter of the Mind* (New York: Basic Books, 1992).
6. Hillel J. Einhorn and Robin M. Hogarth, "Decision Making: Going Forward in Reverse," *Harvard Business Review* 65 (January–February 1987), pp. 66–70; James R. Bettman, Mary Frances Luce, and John W. Payne, "Constructive Consumer Choice Processes," *Journal of Consumer Research* 25 (December 1998), pp. 187–217; and Patricia M. West, Christina L. Brown, and Stephen J. Hoch, "Consumption Vocabulary and Preference Formation," *Journal of Consumer Research* 23 (September 1996), pp. 120–35.
7. Stijin M. J. van Osselaer and Joseph W. Alba, "Consumer Learning and Brand Equity," *Journal of Consumer Research* 27 (June 2000), pp. 1–16.
8. Paul DiMaggio, "Culture and Cognition," *Annual Review of Sociology* 23 (1997), pp. 263–87; and Daniel L. Schacter, *The Seven Sins of Memory* (New York: Houghton Mifflin Company, 2001).
9. Catherine Kohler Riessman, *Narrative Analysis* (Newbury Park, CA: Sage Publications, 1993); Leslie Brothers, *Friday's Footprint: How Society Shapes the Human Mind* (New York: Oxford University Press, 1997); and James R. Bettman, "The Decision Maker Who Came in from the Cold," in *Advances in Consumer Research,* vol. 20, ed. Leigh McAlister and Michael L. Rothschild (Provo, UT: Association for Consumer Research, 1993), pp. 7–11.
10. Brothers, *Friday's Footprint;* and Antonio R. Damasio, *Descartes' Error: Emotion, Reason and the Human Brain* (New York: Avon Books, 1994).
11. Ann Swidler and Jorge Arditi, "The New Sociology of Knowledge," *Annual Review of Sociology* 20 (1994), pp. 305–29.
12. José Antonio Rosa, Joseph F. Porac, Jelena Runser-Spanjol, and Michael S. Saxon, "Sociocognitive Dynamics in a Product Market," *Journal of Marketing* 63 (special issue 1999), pp. 64–77. See also Paul Thagard, *Conceptual Revolutions* (Princeton: Princeton University Press, 1992).
13. Lawrence W. Barsalou, "Deriving Categories to Achieve Goals," in *The Psychology of Learning and Motivation,* vol. 27, ed. Gordon H. Bower (New York: Academic Press, 1991), pp. 1–64; and S. Ratneshwar, Cornelia Pechmann, and Allan D. Shocker, "Goal Derived Categories and the Antecedents of Across-Category Consideration," *Journal of Consumer Research* 23 (December 1996), pp. 240–50.
14. Joseph W. Alba and J. Wesley Hutchinson, "Knowledge Calibration: What Consumers Know and What They Think They Know," *Journal of Consumer Research* 27 (September 2000), pp. 123–56. Some researchers also talk about subjective knowledge as what consumers think they know and objective knowledge as what they actually know.
15. See, for example, J. Frank Yates, Ju-Whei Lee, and Julie G. Bush, "General Knowledge Overconfidence: Cross-National Variations, Response Style, and 'Reality,'" *Organizational Behavior and Human Decision Processes* 57 (January 1997), pp. 1–25; and Alba and Hutchinson, "Knowledge Calibration."
16. B. Joseph Pine II and James H. Gilmore, *The Experience Economy.*
17. Morris B. Holbrook and Elizabeth C. Hirschman, "The Experiential Aspects of Consumption: Consumer Fantasies, Feeling, and Fun," *Journal of Consumer Research* 9 (September 1982), pp. 132–40.

18. Peter H. Bloch, Daniel L. Sherrell, and Nancy M. Ridgway, "Consumer Search: An Extended Framework," *Journal of Consumer Research,* June 1986, p. 120.
19. Russell W. Belk and Güliz Ger, "Problems of Marketization in Romania and Turkey," in *Research in Consumer Behavior: Consumption in Marketizing Economies*, vol. 7, ed. Clifford J. Shultz II, Russell W. Belk, and Güliz Ger (Greenwich, CT: JAI Press, 1994), pp. 123–55; Brian Lofman, "Polish Society in Transformation: The Impact of Marketization on Business, Consumption, and Education," in *Research in Consumer Behavior: Consumption in Marketizing Economies,* vol. 7, ed. Clifford J. Shultz II, Russell W. Belk, and Güliz Ger (Greenwich, CT: JAI Press, 1994), pp. 29–55; and Lawrence F. Feick, Robin A. Higie, and Linda L. Price, "Consumer Search and Decision Problems in a Transitional Economy: Hungary, 1989–1992," *Marketing Science Institute,* report no. 93–113, August 1993.
20. Mihaly Csikzentmihalyi, *Finding Flow* (New York: Perseus Books, 1997).
21. This section draws primarily from these sources: Edelman, *Bright Air, Brilliant Fire;* Stephen J. Hoch, "Hypothesis Testing and Consumer Behavior: 'If It Works, Don't Mess with It,'" in *Advances in Consumer Research,* vol. 11, ed. Thomas Kinnear (Provo, UT: Association for Consumer Research, 1984), pp. 478–81; Stephen J. Hoch and John Deighton, "Managing What Consumers Learn from Experience," *Journal of Marketing* 52 (April 1989), pp. 1–20; and J. Wesley Hutchinson and Joseph W. Alba, "Ignoring Irrelevant Information: Situational Determinants of Consumer Learning," *Journal of Consumer Research* 18 (December 1991), pp. 325–45.
22. Gilles Laurent, "Introduction—HEC Symposium on Advances in Choice Theory: Conference Summary," *Marketing Science Institute,* report no. 99–121, 1999.
23. David M. Boush, Marian Friestad, and Gregory M. Rose, "Adolescent Skepticism toward TV Advertising and Knowledge of Advertiser Tactics," *Journal of Consumer Research* 21 (June 1994), pp. 165–75.
24. Charles G. Gettys, Thomas Mehle, and Stanley Fisher, "Plausibility Assessments in Hypothesis Generation," *Organizational Behavior and Human Performance* 24 (1986), pp. 93–110.
25. For a discussion of male and female differences based on Joan Meyer-Levy's and others' work, see Malcolm Gladwell, "Listening to Khakis," *The New Yorker,* July 28, 1997, pp. 54–57.
26. Thomas Hine, *The Total Package* (Boston: Little Brown and Company, 1995), Chapter 8, pp. 204–37.
27. Barsalou, "Deriving Categories to Achieve Goals"; and C. Whan Park and Daniel C. Smith, "Product-Level Choice: A Top-Down or Bottom-Up Process?" *Journal of Consumer Research* 16 (December 1989), pp. 289–99.
28. Ahmet Ekici and Linda L. Price, "Exploratory Study of American Consumers' Knowledge and Responses to Genetically Modified Food Products," Proceedings, American Marketing Association Winter Educators' Meetings (Chicago: AMA, 2001).
29. Claude Lévi Strauss, *The Raw and the Cooked* (London: Cape, 1964).
30. Coulter, Feick, and Price, "Making Up Time in Hungary." For related descriptions from Moscow, see Caroline Humphrey, "Creating a Culture of Disillusionment: Consumption in Moscow, a Chronicle of Changing Times," in *Worlds Apart*, ed. Daniel Miller (London and New York: Routledge, 1995), pp. 43–68.
31. Hoch, "Hypothesis Testing and Consumer Behavior," and Hoch and Deighton, "Managing What Consumers Learn from Experience."
32. Elizabeth F. Loftus and Jacqueline E. Pickrell, "The Formulation of False Memories," *Psychiatric Annals* 25 (December 1995), pp. 720–25.
33. Scott Ward, Daniel Wackman, and Ellen Wartella, *How Children Learn to Buy: The Development of Consumer Information Processing Skills* (Beverly Hills: Sage, 1977); and M. Carole Macklin, "Preschoolers' Learning of Brand Names from Visual Cues," *Journal of Consumer Research* 23 (December 1996), pp. 251–61.
34. Kathryn A. Braun, "Postexperience Advertising Effects on Consumer Memory," *Journal of Consumer Research* 25 (March 1999), pp. 319–34. See also Alice A. Wright and John G. Lynch, "Communication Effects of Advertising versus Direct Experience When Both Search and Experience Attributes Are Present," *Journal of Consumer Research* 21 (March 1995), pp. 708–18;

and Gay Snodgrass, "The Memory Trainers," in *Mind and Brain Sciences in the Twenty-First Century,* ed. Robert L. Solso (Cambridge: MIT Press, 1997).
35. Lee Ross and Richard Nisbett, *The Person and the Situation: Perspectives of Social Psychology* (New York: McGraw-Hill, 1991).
36. John Deighton and Robert Schindler, "Can Advertising Influence Experience?" *Psychology and Marketing* 5 (1988), pp. 103–15; Stephen Hoch and Yi Ha, "Consumer Learning: Advertising and the Ambiguity of Product Experience," *Journal of Consumer Research* 13 (1986), pp. 221–33; Jerry Olson and Phillip Dover, "Disconfirmation of Consumer Expectations through Product Trial," *Journal of Applied Psychology* 64 (1979), pp. 179–89; and Braun, "Postexperience Advertising Effects on Consumer Memory."
37. A delightful book that summarizes much recent memory research is Susan Engel, *Context Is Everything: The Nature of Memory* (New York: W. H. Freeman and Company, 1999).
38. Rik Pieters and Rami Zwick, "Hindsight Bias in the Context of a Consumption Experience," in *European Advances in Consumer Research,* vol. 1, ed. Gary Banossy and Fred van Raaij (Provo, UT: Association for Consumer Research, 1993), pp. 307–11.
39. Chris Janiszewski and Luk Warlop, "The Influence of Classical Conditioning Procedures on Subsequent Attention to the Conditioned Brand," *Journal of Consumer Research* 20 (September 1993), pp. 171–89; and John Kim, Chris T. Allen, and Frank R. Kardes, "An Investigation of the Mediational Mechanisms Underlying Attitudinal Conditioning," *Journal of Marketing Research* 33 (August 1996), pp. 318–28.
40. R. A. Feinberg, "Credit Cards as Spending Facilitating Stimuli," *Journal of Consumer Research* 13 (1986), pp. 348–56.
41. A study that used pleasant background music to evoke higher brand evaluations is Gerald J. Gorn, "The Effects of Music in Advertising on Choice Behavior: A Classical Conditioning Approach," *Journal of Marketing* 46 (Winter 1982), pp. 94–101. See also Terence A. Shimp, Eva M. Hyatt, and David J. Snyder, "A Critical Appraisal of Demand Artifacts in Consumer Research," *Journal of Consumer Research* 18 (December 1991), pp. 273–83.
42. Harold W. Berkman, Jay D. Lindquist, and M. Joseph Sirgy, *Consumer Behavior* (Lincolnwood, IL: NTC Business Books, 1997).
43. Holbrook and Hirschman, "The Experiential Aspects of Consumption."
44. This section draws heavily from Engel, *Context Is Everything.* See also Daniel Schacter, *Searching for Memory* (New York: Basic Books, 1996).
45. M. Cole, J. Gay, J. Glick, and D. Sharp, *The Cultural Context of Learning and Thinking* (New York: Basic Books, 1971); and Michael Cole and Sylvia Scribner, "Cross-Cultural Studies of Memory and Cognition," in *Perspectives on the Development of Memory and Cognition,* ed. R. V. Kail Jr. and J. W. Hagen (Hillsdale, NJ: Lawrence Erlbaum, 1977), pp. 239–72.
46. M. Mullen and S. Yi, "The Cultural Context of Talk about the Past: Implications for the Development of Autobiographical Memory," *Cognitive Development* 10 (1995), pp. 407–19. See also Shinobu Kitayama and Hazel Rose Markus, *Emotion and Culture: Empirical Studies of Mutual Influence* (Washington, DC: American Psychological Association, 1994).
47. Susan Engel, *The Stories Children Tell* (New York: W. H. Freeman, 1995); and R. V. Kail, *The Development of Memory in Children* (New York: W. H. Freeman, 1990).
48. An excellent discussion of this intersection of the internal and external aspects of human experience can be found in Bradd Shore, *Culture in Mind: Cognition, Culture, and the Problem of Meaning* (New York: Oxford University Press, 1996).
49. Daniel Wegner, "Transactive Memory: A Contemporary Analysis of the Group Mind," in *Theories of Group Behavior,* ed. Brian Mullen and George R. Goethals (New York: Springer-Verlag, 1987), pp. 185–208.
50. Saul M. Kassin and Katherine L. Kiechel, "The Social Psychology of False Confessions: Compliance, Internalization and Confabulation," *Psychological Science* 7 (May 1996), pp. 125–28.
51. Gabriel Biehal and Dipankar Chakravarti, "Consumers' Use of Memory and External Information in Choice: Macro and Micro Perspectives," *Journal of Consumer Research,* March 1986, pp. 382–405; and John G. Lynch, Howard Marmorstein, and Michael F. Weigold, "Choices from

Sets Including Remembered Brands: Use of Recalled Attributes and Prior Overall Evaluations," *Journal of Consumer Research,* September 1988, pp. 225–33.

52. Scott Plous, *The Psychology of Judgment and Decision Making* (Philadelphia: Temple University Press, 1993); and E. F. Loftus, *Eyewitness Testimony* (Cambridge: Harvard University Press, 1979).

53. The first one to develop this idea was G. A. Miller, "The Magical Number Seven, Plus or Minus Two: Some Limits on Our Capacity for Processing Information," *Psychological Review* 63 (1956), pp. 81–97. This research has subsequently been replicated many times. See, for example, A. Newell and Herbert Simon, *Human Problem Solving* (Englewood Cliffs, NJ: Prentice Hall, 1972).

54. Deborah J. MacInnis and Linda L. Price, "The Role of Imagery in Information Processing: Review and Extensions," *Journal of Consumer Research,* March 1987, pp. 473–91.

55. Morris B. Holbrook and Elizabeth C. Hirschman, "The Experiential Aspects of Consumption: Consumer Fantasies, Feelings, and Fun," *Journal of Consumer Research,* September 1982, pp. 132–40; and MacInnis and Price, "The Role of Imagery in Information Processing."

56. Deborah J. MacInnis and Linda L. Price, "An Exploratory Study of the Effect of Imagery Processing and Consumer Experience on Expectations and Satisfaction," *Advances in Consumer Research,* vol. 17, ed. Marvin E. Goldberg, Gerald Gorn, and Richard W. Pollay (Provo, UT: Association for Consumer Research, 1990), pp. 41–47.

57. Endel Tulving, *Elements of Episodic Memory* (New York: Oxford University Press, 1983).

58. Merrie Brucks and Andrew A. Mitchell, "Knowledge Structures, Production Systems and Decision Strategies," in *Advances in Consumer Research,* vol. 8, ed. Kent B. Monroe (Ann Arbor: Association for Consumer Research, 1981), pp. 750–57; and A. Mitchell and P. F. Dacin, "The Assessment of Alternative Measures of Consumer Expertise," *Journal of Consumer Research* 23 (December 1996), pp. 219–39.

59. Alba and Hutchinson, "Knowledge Calibration."

60. Kent Grayson and David Shulman, "Indexicality and the Verification Function of Irreplaceable Possessions: A Semiotic Analysis," *Journal of Consumer Research* 27 (June 2000), pp. 17–30; and Linda L. Price, Eric J. Arnould, and Carolyn Folkman Curasi, "Older Consumers' Disposition of Special Possessions," *Journal of Consumer Research* 27 (September 2000), pp. 179–201.

61. Michaël Korchia, "A New Typology of Brand Image," in *European Advances in Consumer Research,* vol. 4. ed. Bernard Dubois, Tina M. Lowry, L. J. Shrum, and Marc Vanhuele (Provo, UT: Association for Consumer Research, 1999), pp. 147–54. For a detailed review of brand image from a consumer memory perspective, see Kevin Keller, *Strategic Brand Management* (Upper Saddle River, NJ: Prentice Hall, 1998).

62. Shelley Taylor, *Positive Illusions* (New York: Basic Books, 1989).

63. A vast amount of research addresses memory's failings. For this section we primarily draw on an excellent book by one of the world's foremost memory experts, Schacter, *The Seven Sins of Memory.*

64. Angela Y. Lee and Brian Stemthal, "The Effects of Positive Mood on Memory," *Journal of Consumer Research* 26 (September 1999), pp. 115–27.

65. Stewart Shapiro and Mark T. Spence, "Factors Affecting Encoding, Retrieval, and Alignment of Sensory Attributes in a Memory-Based Brand Choice Task," *Journal of Consumer Research* 28 (March 2002), pp. 603–17; and Patricia M. West, Christina L. Brown, and Stephen J. Hoch, "Consumption Vocabulary and Preference Formation," *Journal of Consumer Research* 23 (September 1996), pp. 120–35.

66. Gordon H. Bower, "Mood and Memory," *American Psychologist,* February 1981, pp. 129–48; and Joseph Alba and J. Wesley Hutchinson, "Dimensions of Consumer Expertise," *Journal of Consumer Research* 13 (March 1987), pp. 411–54.

67. This list draws from a number of references already listed. A more in-depth discussion of many of these factors is provided in Plous, *The Psychology of Judgment and Decision Making;* and Wayne Hoyer and Debbie MacInnis, *Consumer Behavior* (New York: Houghton Mifflin, 1997), pp. 171–85. See also Elizabeth Cowley, "Primacy Effects: When First Learned Is Best Recalled." in *European Advances in Consumer Research,* vol. 4, ed. Bernard Dubois, Tina M.

Lowry, L. J. Shrum, and Marc Vanhuele (Provo, UT: Association for Consumer Research, 1999), pp. 155–60.
68. Roland T. Rust and Richard W. Oliver, "Notes and Comments: The Death of Advertising," *Journal of Advertising* 23, no. 4 (December 1994), pp. 71–78; and Mark Pesce, "Toy Stories," *The Sciences*, September–October 2000, pp. 25–31.
69. Pat West et al., "Agents to the Rescue?" *HEC Symposium on Advances in Choice Theory,* Marketing Science Institute, report no. 99–121, 1999, pp. 5–7.
70. This example and discussion comes from Jennifer Gagen-Paxton and Deborah Roedder John, "Consumer Learning by Analogy: A Model of Internal Knowledge Transfer," *Journal of Consumer Research* 24 (December 1997), pp. 266–84.
71. C. Page Moreau, Arthur B. Markman, and Donald R. Lehmann, "'What Is It?' Categorization Flexibility and Consumers' Responses to Really New Products," *Journal of Consumer Research* 27 (March 2001), pp. 489–98.
72. Jennifer L. Aaker, "Dimensions of Brand Personality," *Journal of Marketing Research* 34 (August 1997), pp. 347–56.

chapter 1
chapter 2
chapter 3
chapter 4
chapter 5
chapter 6
chapter 7
chapter 8
chapter 9
chapter 10
chapter 11
chapter 12
chapter 13
chapter 14
chapter 15
chapter 16
chapter 17
chapter 18
chapter 19

LEARNING OBJECTIVES

After completing this chapter, you should be able to:

- Explain the relationship between personality traits and self-concept and discuss applications of personality theory to consumer behavior.
- Know the characteristics of self-concept and understand more about how you characterize yourself and how others are likely to describe you.
- Recognize the I-self, the me-self, and the looking-glass self.
- Explain how self-concept affects intrapersonal processes such as self-narrative, information processing of self-relevant information, and the regulation of affect.
- Describe how self-concept affects interpersonal processes such as lifestyle, interaction strategy, and interpersonal influence.
- Discuss the relationship between people's self-concepts and their consumption behavior, including relating self-concept to the circle of consumption.
- Recognize how the self-concept varies cross-culturally.

ISLAM, FASHION, AND IDENTITY IN TURKEY[1]

Despite the Turkish Republic's attempt to reduce religious influence in social life since the 1920s, secularization remains problematic in Turkey today. Since 1980 Islam has assumed a prominent role in politics and in the marketing and sociocultural arenas as well. Liberalization of the economy created an Islamic upper middle class. Islamic businesses have grown rapidly. These businesses began to offer alternative products for those consumers to whom their religious identity was important. As wealth accumulated among religious population segments, an Islamic upper middle class, conservative in values but avant-garde in consumption, has emerged.

Today, rich and prolific Islamic media ranging from Islamic pop music to romance novels, women's magazines, and movies compete with the secular media for audience, ratings, and advertising money.

Fashion is one of the most visible arenas in which Islamic identities are played out. The Koran and the practices recommended by the prophet Mohammed provide a definition of what dress is religiously acceptable. However, different interpretations coexist. Such diversity in the meaning of fashion enables women to justify different practices. As the meanings of religious dressing become more plural, diversity in dress becomes more prevalent and classificatory. The covering and dressing style operates not only to signify being religious but indicates the identity of the wearer in relation to subgroups of Islamists and secularists. Islamic identity appears to be more and more fragmented, as various segments of the Islamists seek to construct distinct identities. Newly evident urban, upper-middle-class, covered women do not simply differentiate themselves from the Westernized, secular Turkish women; they equally distance themselves from traditional Islamic women who wear a headscarf out of habit and from the Islamic newly rich with their gaudy and pretentious styles of dress. Urban, upper-middle-class women reject both the image of covering as a sign of cultural backwardness and as a sign of extravagance and flaunting.

At a broader level, through fashion an Islamic elite seeks to assert itself as an alternative to the secular elite that has traditionally been dominant in Turkish public life. Drawing both from Islam and local and global cultural resources, this elite crafts new consumption practices—modern, casual, and trendy clothes; natural goods; traditional cuisine; Ottoman artifacts; alternative vacations; books; educational programs on Islamic television channels—in an attempt to differentiate itself from the secularist moderns and other groups of Islamists.

OVERVIEW

Understanding perceptions of the self, the social world, and relationships between the self and others is among the most central concern in consumer behavior. Self-concept organizes the wants and goals of individuals. As the opening vignette suggests, individuals use possessions such as scarves and consumption activities such as vacationing to define who they are, to say things about themselves, and to make conjectures about how, when, and what kinds of other people buy, use, and discard products. Consumption and ideas such as self-concept, self-image, and self-presentation are closely intertwined. Topics such as motivation, perception, information processing, and interpersonal influence, which are the subjects of other chapters, rely on understanding the self.

Self-concept is a complex topic because of competing definitions and cross-cultural and historical variations in concepts of the self. In addition to marketers, philosophers, social scientists, and literary critics are interested in self-concept and identity issues. The definition of **self-concept** we will use in this chapter is *an organized configuration of perceptions of the self, which are available to awareness.* In other words, self-concepts are perceptions people have about themselves.[2] Self-concept is an active configuration that influences many *intrapersonal,* or inner, processes, including motivation (Chapter 9) and information processing (Chapter 15). Self-concept also affects a variety of *interpersonal* processes, including perception (Chapter 8), interpersonal influence (Chapter 4), and reaction to others' feedback.[3]

Perhaps the most important thing to be said about self-concept is that it is *not* distinct from society and culture. The sense of self grows out of interactions with three aspects of one's environment. First, individuals with whom people interact in various roles are crucial to forming the self. Consumers vary in the importance they place on others in determining self-definition. Second, materials and objects (including the physical environment) that support and intervene in people's social relations, affect the development of the self. Consumers also vary in the importance they place on products in determining self-definition.[4] Third, ideas, beliefs, and values—such as those associated with Turkish secular nationalism or conservative Islam mentioned in the vignette—influence the way people perceive and respond to their environment. Individuals develop a concept of self through interaction with all three elements, which are themselves related to each other.

A basic relational approach to how self-concepts develop is depicted in Exhibit 10.1.[5] This four-part framework gives us a way of thinking about the changing concepts of

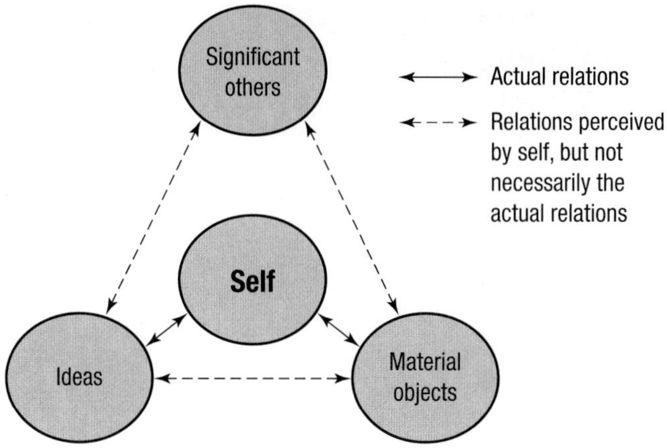

EXHIBIT 10.1

The Relational Self

self and a way to compare self-concepts between cultures. When there is a major change in any of the three elements—in significant others, the material environment, or the ideas and beliefs surrounding an individual—we can expect change to take place in the self and in consumer behavior.

Virtually any **role transition** creates changes in one or more of the three entities in the environment of the self. A role transition is *a major change in the rights, duties, and responsibilities expected of an individual by a social group.* Consequently, role transitions are likely to influence purchase and consumption behavior.[6] Of course, many other factors beyond the self influence consumption behavior.

In this chapter, we first discuss the challenge of measuring dimensions of the self and relating these dimensions to consumption behaviors. In this discussion, we introduce the idea of personality, some methods for measuring personality, and relating personality to other aspects of consumer behavior. Then, we discuss the self and its relationship to some of the factors depicted in Exhibit 10.1. We introduce some ways of understanding self and the relationship of self to consumer behavior. We also compare Western concepts of the self with concepts of self in other parts of the world.

PERSONALITY

Personality is a traditional construct for describing the self. We define **personality** as *the distinctive and enduring patterns of thoughts, emotions, and behaviors that characterize each individual's adaptation to the situations of his or her life.* An individual's consistent self-representations form the basis for what we understand as personality. For example, an individual may have an image of herself as hardworking and honest. This image or schema may be activated in a variety of situations, initiating behavior consistent with these traits.[7]

The study of personality addresses a question critical to all of us: How can we best judge other people's characters and know what to expect of them? Early Egyptian, Chinese, and Greek efforts to understand personality relied on astrology. About 2,500 years ago, early Western philosophers such as Hippocrates and Aristotle compiled lists of connections between facial characteristics and character traits. Contemporary interest in personality dates from the twentieth century founder of modern psychology, Sigmund Freud, and his popularizers in marketing, the so-called motivation researchers who were

GOOD PRACTICE 10.1
Examples of Personality Traits

Label	Definition	Consumer Behavior Application
Dogmatism	An individual's tendency to be more or less resistant to new ideas and change	Dogmatic consumers will be more resistant to new marketing practices
Interpersonal trust	An individual's expectation that the behavior, promises, or statements of others can be relied upon	Those high in individual trust may find salespeople and product endorsers more believable
Introversion/ extroversion	Introverts are shy, prefer to be alone, and are anxious socially; extroverts are outgoing, sociable, and often conventional	Introverts may be less likely to find out about new products from others because they avoid social channels
Locus of control	Degree to which individuals attribute responsibility for events to themselves or to external forces	Externally oriented persons place responsibility of product or service failure on manufacturers or service providers; internally oriented consumers may blame themselves for product or service failures
Need for cognition	Degree of pleasure individuals derive from effortful thinking	Consumers with a high need for cognition enjoy products with a heavy learning component, enjoy product search, and react positively to technical product information
Powerlessness	Low expectations for control of events	Powerlessness favors conforming behaviors
Self-esteem	An individual's overall feelings of self-worth or self-acceptance	Low self-esteem is related to a number of dark-side consumer behaviors
Self-monitoring	The degree to which individuals look to others for cues about how to behave	High self-monitors are more responsive to image-oriented ads; low self-monitors are more responsive to quality claims in ads

Source: Lawrence A. Pervin, ed., Handbook of Personality: Theory and Research *(New York: Guilford, 1990).*

prominent in marketing research after World War II. Over the years, a number of psychologists (e.g., Freud, Carl Jung, Henry Murray, and S. H. Schwartz) have created theories of personality. The long-standing desire to predict behavior on the basis of character traits endures in personality theory and its consumer behavior applications.[8]

Traits

Personality **traits** are *characteristics in which one person differs from another in a relatively permanent and consistent way;* that is, personality traits are supposed to endure over time and over situations. Tests of personality based on measuring so-called personality traits were initiated during World War I (1914–18). Today many psychologists regard personality psychology as synonymous with the study of traits, and psychologists have developed many trait inventories. Good Practice 10.1 shows some examples of personality traits that are of interest to psychologists and consumer behavior researchers.[9] As illustrated, some traits are negative (e.g., powerlessness) and some are positive (e.g., interpersonal trust). Relative stability is a key aspect of personality traits. Marketing researchers frequently measure personality with respect to specific traits, using a tool such as the Social Character Scale shown in Good Practice 10.2, which comes from a study relating the traits of introversion and extroversion to mass media preferences.[10]

Recently, a book of consumer behavior scales has been compiled that includes numerous individual differences shown to affect consumer behavior.[11] Among the scales represented in this book are social character (i.e., inner- and other-directedness), self-concepts, need for cognition, consumer ethnocentrism, and the sexual identity scale. Good Practice 10.2 shows some of the items used to measure inner- and other-directedness.[12] For instance, a respondent who prefers partying with a smaller group is likely to be inner-directed. A respondent who likes larger parties ("the more the merrier") is more likely to be other-directed (see item 1 in Good Practice 10.2). As illustrated in the measurement instrument, inner-directed consumers look to their own inner values and standards for guiding their behavior. In contrast, other-directed consumers depend on the people around them to provide direction for their actions.

Marketers' interest in traits is practical. Do personality traits predict consumer behavior? One review across numerous studies found that personality traits only explain about 10 percent of the variation in consumers' purchase, product preference, and innovation behaviors. This suggests trait-based approaches should be combined with other variables to improve predictions.[13]

The development of the Five Factor Personality Structure, consisting of five clusters of traits, has recently reinvigorated the trait literature. Research over several decades indicates that the dimensions of emotional stability (or neuroticism), extroversion (or outgoingness), openness to experience, agreeableness, and conscientiousness provide a good catalog of personality traits. Research in China, Germany, Holland, Japan, Korea, Norway, the United States, and the United Kingdom lend support for the generality of the "big five" traits. These traits have demonstrated a bit more explanatory power than other personality traits, but relating these traits to buying behavior has just begun. In a Korean study, these traits were shown to differentiate shopping styles and product preferences.[14] Overall across dozens of studies, the results of trying to relate personality traits to consumer behaviors have been mixed. These difficulties have led some researchers to other methods for learning about the self.[15] We discuss some other traits such as self-esteem and self-monitoring later in this chapter.

Some approaches for measuring personality traits allow individuals more leeway to describe themselves in their own ways on dimensions of their own choosing. For example, participants might be presented with open-ended probes such as, Tell us about yourself, Tell us what you are not, and so on. One innovative tool for studying personality is the personal project. A personal project is a set of interrelated acts extending over time that is intended to maintain or attain a state of affairs foreseen by the individual. A wide range of related, goal-driven activities might constitute a personal project. Learning to ski, graduating from a university, achieving a career goal, and building a house are examples of personal projects. The method for investigation of personal projects is not outlined in detail here, but an example of a matrix of personal projects that can be used for data collection is reproduced in Good Practice 10.3. Take a few minutes and think about your personal projects. Think about how these projects do or do not reflect your personality. Do some of your personal projects involve consumption? Many personal projects constitute core aspects of a person's life and have a great deal of consumption content.[16]

A Sample of Items from the Social Character Scale (Inner- and Other-Social Preference Scale)

GOOD PRACTICE 10.2

1. With regard to partying, I feel
   a) The more the merrier (25 or more people present).
   b) It is nicest to be in a small group of intimate friends (6 or 8 people at most).
2. If I had more time,
   a) I would spend more evenings at home doing the things I'd like to do.
   b) I would more often go out with my friends.
3. I believe that
   a) It is difficult to draw the line between work and play and therefore one should not even try it.
   b) One is better off keeping work and social activities separated.
4. I would rather join
   a) A political or social club or organization.
   b) An organization dedicated to literary, scientific, or other academic subject matter.
5. I would be more eager to accept a person as a group leader who
   a) Is outstanding in those activities which are important to the group.
   b) Is about average in the performance of the group activities but has an especially pleasing personality.
6. I like to read books about
   a) People like you and me.
   b) Great people or adventurers.
7. For physical exercise or as a sport, I would prefer
   a) Softball, basketball, volleyball, or similar team sport.
   b) Skiing, hiking, horseback riding, bicycling, or similar individual sport.
8. I believe
   a) Being able to make friends is a great accomplishment in and of itself.
   b) One should be concerned more about one's achievements rather than making friends.
9. It is more desirable
   a) To be popular and well liked by everybody.
   b) To become famous in the field of one's choice or for a particular deed.
10. With regard to clothing,
    a) I would feel conspicuous if I were not dressed the way most of my friends are dressed.
    b) I like to wear clothes which stress my individuality and which not everybody else is wearing.
11. On the subject of social living,
    a) A person should set up his own standards and then live up to them.
    b) One should be careful to live up to the prevailing standards of the culture.
12. I would consider it more embarrassing
    a) To be caught loafing on the job for which I get paid.
    b) Losing my temper when a number of people are around of whom I think a lot.

Source: Lawrence A. Pervin, ed., Handbook of Personality: Theory and Research *(New York: Guilford, 1990).*

GOOD PRACTICE 10.3

Personal Project Matrix

List of Projects	1 Importance	2 Enjoyment	3 Difficulty	4 Visibility	5 Control	6 Irritation	7 Stress	8 Time adequacy	9 Outcome	10 Self-identity	11 Others' view	12 Value congruency	13 Positive impact	14 Negative impact	15 Progress	16 Challenge	17 Absorption	18 With whom?	19 Where?
1																			
2																			
3																			
4																			
Etc.																			

Source: Brian R. Little, "Personal Projects: A Rationale and Method for Investigation," Environment and Behavior *15 (May 1983), pp. 273–309.*

Self-Esteem and Self-Efficacy

Self-evaluation, how a person feels about him- or herself, is an important aspect of personality. Self-evaluations affect the goals people set; their motives; the anxiety, stress, and depression they experience in various situations; and their selection of preferred environments.

Self-esteem is one way of talking about personal evaluation. **Self-esteem** is *the pattern of beliefs an individual has about self-worth.* Conceptions of self-esteem have a social dimension. William James, one of the founders of psychology, recognized one aspect of personality as an object of personal reflection (the Me). Modern conceptions of self-esteem also include an interpersonal dimension. Self-esteem is one's subjective self-evaluation developed from personal experiences of success or failure, interactions with others, maturation, heredity, and social learning. In short, self-esteem is linked to the reflected appraisals of others and can be seen as a prism through which an individual views the world. It is a broad trait that influences both self-perception and social behavior. Individuals with high self-esteem are less influenced by the opinions of others, more independent, and less likely to conform to group pressure than individuals with low self-esteem.

Some research shows that high self-esteem is related to spending. One series of studies found that people who feel good about themselves, particularly those who perceive themselves to be competent in domains that they feel are important, are more likely than others to spend more on a variety of products and services that make them feel good. This affects the marketing of a whole host of products, including entertainment, alcoholic beverages, and especially beauty enhancers.[17]

Low self-esteem is related to exaggerated concern with the self as viewed through others' opinions. Quite a bit of research suggests that consumer culture, with its exaggerated emphasis on the beauty of the physical self, may lead to lower self-esteem among consumers. Very low self-esteem in turn is related to compulsive and addictive behaviors, such as eating disorders, compulsive gambling, television addiction, shoplifting, and compulsive buying. In one series of focus group interviews about skin care, conducted with groups of women with similar demographic profiles, it was found that low self-esteem women avoid buying certain products because they don't feel that it is worth spending money on themselves. Therefore, low self-esteem may sometimes lead to overconsumption and sometimes to underconsumption, depending on other individual characteristics.[18]

In contrast to the large amount of social science research on compulsive gambling and eating disorders, the investigation of compulsive buying behavior is relatively new. We can define compulsive buying as the inability to restrain the impulse to buy. Most of us make impulse purchases at one time or another, but when the impulse results in repetitive and excessive buying, we term it **compulsive buying.** Reports estimate that 10 percent of the U.S. population and up to 7 percent of the Mexican population may be considered compulsive shoppers. Studies in the United States, Mexico, and Germany show that compulsive spenders have relatively lower self-esteem than other consumers, and they believe in the power of money to enhance self-esteem or to influence others.[19]

Research has found that self-esteem is an effective advertising appeal as it is one of the strongest intrapersonal needs. Further, people with low self-esteem have been found to be more susceptible to persuasion, and therefore may be more susceptible to self-esteem appeals in advertising. While marketing research recognizes self-esteem as a dimension of the self-concept, there has been little research on its direct impact beyond advertising.

Studies have focused on the social development of self-image during adolescence. Self-esteem derives from a series of self-estimates and the evaluation of self is linked to the reflected appraisals of others. People have a basic need to evaluate their opinions and abilities. Comparing oneself with others can satisfy this need. Lacking an objective basis of comparison as during the period of rapid personal change that characterizes adolescence, people use a social basis of comparison, such as their peers. Consequently, interpersonal influence should be a particularly important aspect of self-esteem judgments among early adolescents. Self-esteem should be related to other characteristics such as gender.

A study examined the effect of adolescent self-esteem and susceptibility to interpersonal influence on the relative importance placed on the utilitarian (e.g., ease of care, value) and display aspects of clothing (e.g., brand name and what others wear). The researchers found that adolescent consumers' susceptibility to interpersonal influence was positively related to sensitivity to the display aspects of clothing. This helps to explain young adolescents' tendency to conform to peers' dress codes, and the value to them of brands with clear meanings shared by their peer group. They further found that this association was stronger for girls than for boys. And they found that self-esteem was positively related to greater sensitivity to the utilitarian aspects of clothing. That is, adolescents with high self-esteem place more value on the nonnormative aspects of clothing.

A recent extension of this kind of work in France examined use of lipstick to present an older desired sense of self. The desire for social recognition with age should depend on an individual's self-esteem and elements of the self linked to physical appearance. When self-esteem is low, ego defense mechanisms could strengthen the aspiration to aging. The social character of makeup use allows individuals to improve their physical appearance and their impact on others. Makeup therefore satisfies the imperatives of defending one's image, with respect to others and to oneself, and is a means of consolidating an individual's sense of self. Makeup can also compensate for negative self-esteem.

The researchers found that adolescent girls typically perceive earthy lipstick colors as more appropriate to their age but as adult women, they use brighter colors. These colors allow them to affirm the different social roles they play as individuals, and therefore strengthen their identity. Therefore, the color of lipstick can symbolize a preferred age for a group to which the girls belong, and girls may claim an older subjective age and enhance their self-esteem by wearing a brighter shade of lipstick.[20]

Another way of talking about self-evaluation is self-efficacy. **Self-efficacy** is defined as *people's beliefs about their capabilities to exercise control over events that affect their lives.* Within the context of a set of tasks, some people will believe that they can succeed (take effective action), whereas other individuals will believe that they will fail. Some research has related self-efficacy to consumer behavior. Studies in Denmark and the United States have found that perceived consumer effectiveness (PCE) influences environmental concerns and some behaviors such as recycling. Greater PCE was related to greater concern. Several researchers have suggested that self-efficacy influences decisions involving technological innovations. One study sought to relate perceptions of self-efficacy to the use of new technologies, finding that consumers' perceptions of their ability to use a technology reduce their resistance to accepting that technology.[21]

Self-efficacy should vary cross-culturally. Euro-Americans tend to score relatively high on measures of self-efficacy and sometimes believe that buying power can be used to solve social problems. By contrast, a study conducted in Thailand found that Thais scored low on perceived efficacy to preserve the environment.[22]

Applications to Consumer Behavior Research

Consumer behavior research is filled with examples of personality trait measures or individual difference measures. Motivation research conducted in the 1950s and 1960s examined the relationship between consumers' perceptions of products and actual or ideal personality traits using self-administered questionnaires. In general, it proved difficult to predict consumer brand choices using personality traits alone. For example, knowing that a particular consumer was a risk taker did not help predict whether that person would purchase a Ford or a Chevrolet. Nonetheless, even in recent years it has become quite common to see an ad for a sports car targeted toward consumers who like to take risks.

Going beyond the realm of brand choice, personality variables are related to consumption behaviors. For instance, materialism (a personality trait discussed in Chapter 3) is related to both impulsive and compulsive buying behavior. Similarly, self-esteem, need for cognition, and locus of control are related to the likelihood that a buyer might consult a friend or expert prior to making a purchase. Self-efficacy, as noted above, is related to belief in the influence of buying power on social change. Advertisers often use such personality traits to segment markets.[23]

NEED FOR COGNITION One personality trait that has received some attention recently is **need for cognition.** Need for cognition is *a tendency to engage in and enjoy thinking.* The value of this trait has been well established in the communication and persuasion literature. Need for cognition can be reliably measured and is stable over time and situations. Individuals who are classified as high in their need for cognition, compared to those classified as low, recall more information with which they have been supplied, search for more information, are more responsive argument quality rather than argument style, possess more knowledge, and display a stronger link between thoughts and attitudes over time.

What is the relevance of the need for cognition to consumer behavior? Distinguishing customers in terms of their need for cognition holds promise for tailoring the market mix to their varying needs. Research has shown that consumers high in need for cognition process advertisements longer and remember them better. Such consumers should respond more positively to marketing communications that provide them with greater amounts of information. Some other research shows that consumers scoring high on need for cognition tend to compare brands in terms of their attributes rather than in terms of their overall attitudes toward the brands. This behavior increases the importance of well-known brands in the preferences high-need-for-cognition consumers form between competing brands. Preferences of low-need-for-cognition consumers by contrast are more affected by holistic information such as opinions of others. Finally, some research has looked at consumers' responsiveness to deals and their need for cognition. One study suggests that consumers with a high need for cognition do not respond to featured product displays, because they recognize that displays do not reliably signal price cuts. Other research argues consumers use the presence of a restriction (i.e., purchase limit, purchase precondition, or time limit) as a source of information to evaluate a deal. These restrictions serve to highlight deal value and "promote" promotions. While a large set of scanner data shows that a sales restriction (e.g., "limit X per customer") results in higher sales, an experiment suggests that restrictions only have a positive effect on low-need-for-cognition individuals.[24]

LOCUS OF CONTROL **Locus of control** is a significant personality trait in psychology. Individuals having an external locus of control tend to ascribe the influences on their lives to luck, fate, chance, other people, or strong forces they cannot overcome—the externals. People having an internal locus of control tend to attribute the influences on their lives to forces such as their own skills that are within their control—the internals. Externals attribute causality to environmental forces while internals assign such attribution to personal forces.

Does locus of control affect consumer behavior? Internal-locus-of-control and external-locus-of-control individuals differ not only as to their attentiveness to information immediately present in the environment, but also in terms of their actively seeking additional relevant information. In a U.S. survey of 1,401 new car buyers, internals were found to engage in greater information search than externals.[25] In another study, consistently greater perceived influence of children in family consumption decision making was reported by parents scoring high in external locus of control than by parents scoring low on an internal-locus-of-control parents measure. Thus, we can say that consumers with a more external locus of control are likely to seek out information external to themselves such as marketing communications or the opinions of valued others and to use it in making purchase decisions. Good Practice 10.4 provides a social marketing example of the relevance of locus of control to consumer behavior.[26]

How does locus of control affect consumer behavior across cultures? Respondents with an external locus of control may be more resistant to innovation. Some research among Singaporean Chinese supported this notion.[27] Respondents with an external locus of control may form less accurate behavioral purchase intentions. Since they believe they have less control over their behavior, they would feel less able to predict their behavior. For example, in many Muslim cultures people feel that Allah determines future

Locus of Control and Protective Health Behaviors

GOOD PRACTICE 10.4

People should be more likely to perform health protective behaviors if they believe that what happens to them is due to their own actions rather than to chance or fate. However, general attributions of control may be less important than specific ones. For example, although one may feel that one has little control over one's life (in general), one may nevertheless believe that one has control over one's health. Similarly, even though one may not believe that one has control over one's health (in general), one may believe that whether or not one is exposed to HIV is under one's control. Thus, it is generally assumed that the more specific the locus-of-control measure, the stronger its association with a particular behavior.

In a study of health protective consumer behaviors on one Caribbean island, researchers explored this hypothesis. Consistent with expectations, the more one attributes outcomes to internal rather than external factors, the more likely is one to have used a condom to protect against HIV infection. However, as expected, this relationship varied with item specificity. That is, general locus of control did not predict condom use, but health locus of control was a better predictor of condom use. The authors of this study suggested that in a population with a generally low internal locus of control, social marketing campaigns to encourage health protective behaviors against HIV infection should focus on reinforcing social norms rather than individual health protection.

Source: Martin Fishbein, Susan E. Middlestadt, and David Trafimow, "Social Norms for Condom Use: Implications for HIV Prevention Interventions of a KABP Survey with Heterosexuals in the Eastern Caribbean," in Advances in Consumer Research, vol. 20, ed. Leigh McAlister and Michael Rothschild (Provo, UT: Association for Consumer Research, 1993), pp. 292–96.

events. Trying to predict the future is considered either stupid or irreligious. Data from Jordan (Muslim sample), Thailand, and the United States (non-Muslim samples) partially support the claim that locus of control influences a consumer's ability to form accurate purchase intentions. The American students scored the highest on internal locus of control, while the Jordanians had the lowest scores on internal locus of control. An analysis of academic-related purchase behavior (a highly involving, financially and socially significant, and infrequent purchase) supports the hypothesis. A stronger internal locus of control leads to smaller discrepancies between intentions and behavior.[28]

Not so fast! Measuring locus of control across cultures is not so straightforward. One study showed that, as expected of an Asian sample, Korean students scored higher on a general external-locus-of-control measure than U.S. students. However, a scale that tried to measure internal control did not provide reliable results. The authors speculated that high levels of external control might have meant that Korean respondents found questions about internal control confusing. Further relationships between different subscales were unstable across Korean and U.S. student respondents. The authors speculated that the scales were actually measuring different things in the two cultural groups, what they did not know.[29]

Although it may be difficult to predict single instances of behavior from personality measures such as those discussed above, it is possible to predict behavior averaged over a sample of situations or occasions. For example, we cannot predict whether the novelty-seeking trait will lead an individual consumer to seek out information about a particular new product, but we might predict that a high level of novelty seeking would lead to higher levels of new-product awareness when averaged over a sample of new products.[30] Following this approach, advertisers can use personality traits to segment markets and target their market offerings.

SELF-CONCEPT

Studying personality traits is not the only way to understand the self. Another way to think about the self is to answer this question: Tell me about yourself. Take a few minutes right now and think about how you would respond. Surely you have been asked to talk about yourself many times, in very different situations by different people. A normal and important aspect of social exchanges is a sharing of information about selves. You may have noticed several things about your own responses to this question that we now discuss.

Self-Concept Is Multifaceted

You might observe that your *self-concept is multifaceted.* It includes a collection of images, activities, goals, feelings, roles, traits, and values. If you ask a small child to tell you about herself, she might respond by describing that she has a big brother who teases her all the time and a kitten that she loves very much. She might also tell you that her favorite color is pink and she's seen the movie *Spirit* three times. She answers

This Balnéo Grandform ad plays on the concept of the extended self in referring to your body ("votre corps") as your most precious possession.

The *tuku* headscarf worn by Herero women in Botswana is central to their social selves.

the question of who she is with a catalog of characteristics and relationships, including consumption behaviors. Social scientists now refer to the *multiplicity* of identity, indicating that selfhood is a collection of diverse but related self-perceptions. In fact, *the self includes a multiplicity of things that people are to themselves and to one another.* Consumer researchers want to know which aspects of the self are most relevant in marketing communications and how these aspects are linked to products and product images.

The multiple nature of the self has long been recognized in psychology.[31] Psychologists recognize the **I-self,** *the active observer, the knower, or the information processor.* The I-self attends to matters of importance to the individual and helps that person maintain self-esteem (as we discuss below). The I-self may come into play when consumers choose inconspicuous products such as the many shopping goods that do not have a well-developed image.

Psychologists also recognize the **me-self,** that is *the known, observed, and constructed self-image.* One influential formulation of the idea of the me-self concept is the **looking-glass self.** In this view, the me-self concept is formed as an individual gathers the reflected opinions of significant other people toward him or her. These others' opinions are gradually incorporated into the me-self concept. The looking-glass self may come more into play when consumers are choosing status goods, conspicuous products, or heavily advertised products with a well-developed product image that incorporates the opinions of others.

Psychologist William James, who formulated the I-self idea, thought it produced self-concept. Charles Horton Cooley, who formulated the concept of the looking-glass self, thought the opinions of others matter most in producing self-concept. Both elements mold self-concept, in Euro-American cultures at least, and from these ideas, we get two elements of the contemporary four-element model of the self, shown in Exhibit 10.1. The third element of Exhibit 10.1 is material things and goods. Things also help to

GOOD PRACTICE 10.5

Your Name Everywhere

The craze for customized products—what social scientists might see as support for Professor Belk's theory of the extended self—has moved into all sorts of product arenas. For instance, L. L. Bean customers can design their own boat and tote bags in honor of the company's 90th birthday. The heavy canvas bags, introduced in 1944 as "Bean's ice carriers," more recently became standard issue in the fashion world. Customers can choose among a dozen colors and prints, and each bag bears a label identifying the customer as its designer. C. O. Bigelow Chemists offers FlavoRx, a service that spikes unappetizing medicines with your favorite flavor from among 40 choices for $5. Now, the New York pharmacy is extending the service to pets! Boutique cosmetics maker Pookie for You will infuse its lip gloss with your favorite color and flavor. Customers can also name the flavor and write the label copy to create a one-of-a-kind tin. Minimum order, 50 tins!

Source: Ellen Tien, "Your Name Everywhere," New York Times, *Style section, February 24, 2002, p. 3. Copyright © 2002 by the New York Times Co. Reprinted with permission.*

form a person's sense of self, even though they are outside the actual self. Considerable research has established the idea that purchase, display, and use of consumer goods communicates meaning to the individual and to others. *Individual consumer behavior is often directed toward enhancing self-concept through the consumption of goods as symbols.* (Symbolic consumption is discussed in Chapter 3 and at further length in Chapter 4.) *Self-concept is enhanced through the transfer of socially accepted meanings of the product or brand to oneself.* This then enhances the value of the self. Interaction with others, as well as the products and brands, is also required since social recognition provides meaning to products and brands. In short, individual consumers use products and brands to express something about themselves, and self-concept is reinforced as positive responses from others support their consumption behaviors. This is called the **image congruence hypothesis.** Thus, since consumers evaluate brands partly in terms of how those products might enhance their self-image, marketers should build self-enhancement meanings into marketing communications.[32]

Russell Belk says that *external objects to which we are emotionally attached and that we consider a part of ourselves* comprise the **extended self.**[33] Belk found that things consumers incorporated into the extended self symbolize key elements of the self; in other words, they are highly congruent with or match a person's sense of self. U.S. women, for example, generally see their bodies as more central to their identities than U.S. men do.[34] The text of an ad for Balnéo Grandform, French maker of bathtubs, plays on this idea of the body as part of the extended self. It reads, "Balnéo Grandform . . . because your body is your most precious possession." Dwellings, automobiles, and favorite clothes are among the material possessions Belk found most closely related to the self. Subsequent research has led to a measure to determine the extent of possession incorporation into the extended self; some people's extended selves include collections, pets, mountain bikes, and tattoos.[35] Good Practice 10.5 illustrates one consumer behavior application of the extended self idea—personalized products.

Most work on the extended self has been conducted with people in the United States. However, findings from some other parts of the world show that the relation between possessions and an extended social self assumes some importance. To Maya farmers of Central America, for example, *milpa* cornfields represent a collaboration between man and the gods that is the basis for life. Even Maya who don't need corn still make a *milpa.* Keeping a *milpa* is considered very close to the Maya conception of self. Similarly, the elaborate dress and *tuku* (headscarf) worn by Herero women in Botswana shown on page 399, and the reggae music and material goods associated with Rastafarianism (a Jamaican folk religion) are important sources of personal and social (ethnic) selfhood simultaneously.[36]

The concept of extended self has numerous implications for consumer behavior. For example, people may live vicariously through things incorporated into the extended self. Pets are a good example. North Americans spend $23 billion a year on pet food and supplies and more than $2 billion on pet goodies. The worldwide market is very large indeed. As another example, the accompanying advertisement for the Jaguar XK8 invites consumers to live vicariously through this automobile. The tendency to care for something within the extended self will lead the individual to purchase accessories for the particular object and devote resources to its care and improvement. This has considerable relevance for marketers of lifestyle products such as mountain bikes, collections, and heirlooms, for example, not to mention pets, cars, and scooters.[37]

Self-Concept Depends on Situations and Motives

You might observe that your response to the invitation to tell others about yourself *depends on situations and motives.* Some research suggests that individuals focus on whatever *aspects of themselves that are most relevant in a particular social setting or situation.* Consumer researchers term this idea the **working, or activated, self-concept.**[38] Culture, gender, ethnic, and other characteristics of identity become

An appeal to consumers to live vicariously through a Jaguar sports car.

The Activated Immigrant Greenlandic Self

CONSUMER CHRONICLES 10.1

When I came from Greenland, I brought my jewelry, I can't live without them. I don't wear it here, but I have to bring them. They are various amulets and the like, made from bone or stone. . . . I take them out occasionally and look at them, but, uh-oh, I don't wear them because I think it is a bit . . . In Qaportoq [Greenland] I often wear them but here in Denmark people look at me and think: "What is it made from? Oh, it's made of bone! Poor animal!" So maybe it is mostly to spare people for that, that I don't wear it. A bear claw I have or something like that would scare them to death. "Are you into voodoo or something like that?" So you are a little afraid of what people might think. You don't want them to believe you're some kind of cannibal.

Occupation: student; gender: female; age: 25; residence: from the Disco Bay, living temporarily in Vanløse.

Source: Søren Askegaard, Dannie Kjeldgaard, and Eric J. Arnould, "Identity and Acculturation: The Case of Food Consumption by Greenlanders in Denmark," Paper presented at the First International Conference on Consumption and Representation, Plymouth, UK, September 1–3, 1999.

significant to consumers in particular circumstances, for example, when marketers invite consumers to attend to them as in the ad on page 403 that focuses on African-American pride, or when consumers find themselves in a consumption context that brings such characteristics into view. Consumer Chronicles 10.1 illustrates how the ethnic identity of Greenlandic immigrants to mainland Denmark is activated by Danes' reactions to some traditional Greenlandic possessions.[39]

Marketers and policymakers should be sensitive to how different self-concepts get activated in social situations. In some university communities, *not* drinking alcohol is a distinctive consumer behavior and thus becomes a relevant dimension of self-concept. In a sample of undergraduate students at a small U.S. college (61 percent under legal drinking age), only 20 percent were nondrinkers. Their reasons for drinking included "Because people I know drink," "So I won't feel left out," and "Because of pressure from others." In this case, reducing alcohol-related problems on campus might require changes in social relationships to change drinkers' activated self-concept.[40]

People selectively retrieve different aspects of their self-concept depending on goals and motives. Think about how your answer to "tell me about yourself" might vary as a function of who is asking the question: your teacher, your date, or a potential employer. The part of your self-concept that comes to mind—what we call the working self-concept—would be different because you are motivated to communicate different things about yourself in each situation.

Even during a single day, as situations change a consumer may desire to represent self either publicly or privately in a variety of different ways through consumption. Fashion offers a way to express different aspects of the self and helps people create and represent different identities, as illustrated in the opening vignette.[41] As another example, a successful woman executive may go into board meetings with an audacious Vivienne Westwood leggings outfit underneath her conservative attire.

Depending on the situation, consumption may activate different aspects of the self. For example, setting out crystal wine glasses for a dinner party may activate self-schemas of pride and competence, creating both memories and expectations. A study in the UK found that drink choice in pubs might activate different aspects of the self. Sometimes consumers may contrive to use products to trigger aspects of the self. For example, you may have noticed that the clothes you wear subtly change your body language. More formal attire triggers, almost unconsciously, more formal aspects of your self. Try staging a candlelight dinner on a weeknight. Does it trigger different aspects of your self-concept? Marketers position products to take advantage of the power of products to activate aspects of the self, such as in the nostalgic advertisement for Lands' End, shown on page 405.[42]

Behavioral Constraints and Possible Selves

When you think about your answer to the question, Tell me about yourself, you might observe that your own *behavior is constrained by factors other than your self-concept.* For example, you may describe yourself as fun loving and carefree but have trouble, especially during exams, remembering the last time those self qualities were reflected in your behavior. In a recent study of self-concept, one man in his late 20s said, "I am torn between two ideas of the real me. There is the day-to-day real me, how I usually function, and the rare occasion of the real me I want to be. These times are a total reversal of everyday life."[43] As a consequence of restrictions on behavior, self-concept will not always be directly revealed in behavior. Its impact may be revealed more indirectly in mood changes, in what aspects of self-concept are dominant and accessible, in the nature of self-presentation, and in the choice of social setting.

Thus, one way of thinking about self-concept is that it is composed of self-image, or **self-schemas,** each *consisting of a system of knowledge structures organized in memory and self-relevant information,* including ideas and information about others and things.[44] Some self-representations are more important and more elaborate than others. Some are positive, some negative. Consumers are aware of some self-representations, but they are unaware of others because they are either fairly automatic or repressed in daily life. For marketers, these constraints on self-expression may modify the relationships between expressions of self and consumption behaviors. By identifying barriers to self-expression, marketers can develop or position products and services to alleviate them. Frozen dinner entrees and bread- and pasta-making machines, for example, are products that allow consumers to express a nurturing "homemaker" self when other time commitments frustrate the expression of this aspect of self.

Self-representations may refer to actual I-selves and also to **possible selves**—selves we could be, would like to be, or are afraid of becoming.[45] Possible selves consist of *self-schemas created for domains of activity that give personal meaning to the past and*

This ad seeks to activate an aspect of African-American self-concept, and, perhaps, a schema representative of self-concept.

The Self Is Dynamic

CONSUMER CHRONICLES 10.2

In response to research about experiences that make one feel like "this is really me," one young woman said:

> Last summer, I took a course called "Copy and Layout" in which I learned how to design advertisements for the first time. On the first day of class, we were given an assignment which entailed coming up with a newspaper advertisement for any product we wanted as long as we sold the product in the ad. Immediately, I came up with several ideas, and within an hour after class my advertisement was finished. I found out right then that creative work in advertising was truly me—my senses seemed to come alive as I started thinking about different products and how I could advertise them.

the future. People are likely to attribute certain consumption behaviors to these possible selves, both negative and positive.[46] For example, one of the attractions of Las Vegas for consumers willing to take risks is the opportunity to take on a possible self. This is the composed, self-confident "player" like the Tom Cruise character Charlie Babbitt in the movie *Rain Man.*[47]

Because of the existence of possible selves and different working selves, consumers may have conflicted self-conceptions. Some research suggests that conflicted self-representations can cause emotional disorders, anxiety, and depression. However, other research suggests that complex self-conceptions and multiple identities can lead to better mental health. Part of the key seems to be whether or not the identities can be successfully integrated with each other.[48] Often purchases and possessions can help facilitate an integration of different aspects of the self. Islamic fashion and resorts with separate facilities for men and women serve this role for some Turkish consumers. The specialty catalog retailer The J. Peterman Company sought to build this idea into its corporate mission, noting that "people want things that make their lives the way they wish they were."[49] Marketers can develop new product positioning by identifying key problems of self-integration and designing products that help consumers do this; for example, high-quality packaged convenience foods that integrate a woman's self as nurturing mother and self as high-achieving corporate executive.

Self-Concept Is Changeable

When you think about your answer to the question, Tell me about yourself, you might recognize that your *self-concept is flexible and changeable,* not only between situations but in a more enduring way. New self-conceptions are added periodically, self-conceptions change in meaning, and the relationship among self-conceptions changes. For example, you may contrast your self-concept in secondary school with your self-concept at university. You may have added new roles (perhaps joined new clubs and organizations), new relationships (friends, classmates, co-workers), new activities, new traits (hardworking, studious), or new goals (career success). In Consumer Chronicles 10.2, one young woman describes the discovery of new self-aspects.

Consumers' self-concepts are particularly dynamic during certain role transitions, such as between secondary school and university, when changing jobs, or after a divorce. Role transitions are often accompanied by changing consumption patterns that reflect changing conceptions of the self.[50] For example, before heading for college, a young woman who has worn her hair long all through high school may decide it's time for a new look to go with the new self that she intends to be. She may associate her new haircut with being more outgoing, athletic, or a variety of other desired selves. Consumer Chronicles 10.3 illustrates a Japanese role transition and the important relation-

Nostalgic ad for Lands' End activates consumer self-expression.

ships between identity, material goods, and the influence of society that together work to transform the identity of Japanese young adults.[51]

Some very interesting research has been conducted with consumers who have undergone plastic surgery. Patients seem to seek plastic surgery during role transitions. Plastic surgery allows these consumers to take greater control of their bodies and their appearance. As a result of the surgery, their self-esteem—or degree to which they have a positive attitude toward themselves—improves substantially. Plastic surgery has many elements of a rite of passage, discussed in Chapter 3, including separation from old roles, considerable physical and mental pain, and a period of isolation (convalescence) before the new self emerges.[52]

Many products are designed to facilitate role transitions, and role transitions are often marked by changes in consumption patterns. Weddings and baby showers typically incorporate products that mark role transitions. The traditional baby shower serves the economic purpose of equipping the new mother with the clothes, toys, and furnishings she will need. Such an event also serves the social function of reinforcing the mother's dependence on a network of kin and friends. "Insider knowledge" about the usefulness of products is communicated to the new mother, as each gift is opened. Similarly, on April 1 of every year a million new employees at Japanese businesses receive business cards and corporate lapel badges and learn their corporate songs during annual entering-the-company ceremonies held throughout Japan. Consumer behaviors such as these that mark role transitions are a nearly universal feature of human cultures, and marketers may position products to take advantage of this fact. Thus, participants in Japanese

A Japanese Role Transition

CONSUMER CHRONICLES 10.3

Of the countless ceremonies held regularly in Japan, my favorite was Seijin-shiki, the coming-of-age ceremony held annually on January 15. On that date, each year all the Japanese who will turn 20 during the year are toasted and honored in official ceremonies during which they are officially recognized as adult citizens of Japan, with all the associated rights and many responsibilities. This is considered so important that January 15 is a national holiday. Every city, town, and rural hamlet in the country—3,200 jurisdictions in all—gathers its newly minted adults into the town hall or school auditorium for a combination reunion/party/lecture.

New clothes are a key part of coming of age. The Seijin-shiki is generally the first occasion in a young woman's life when she can wear a formal adult kimono. Most girls jump at the chance. After all, a halfway decent kimono, together with the necessary obi, sandals, hair ornaments, handbag, handkerchiefs, pins, and other assorted accoutrements, runs about $6,500 nowadays. The men's business suits, in contrast, were probably priced under $500, even for those who chose the seven-point *setto* (or set). These prices, well beyond the reach of most 20-year-olds, constitute one reason why so many kids show up for a formal ceremony on their day off. There's an implicit deal at work: Parents want their kids to attend Seijin-shiki, so they pay for the expensive outfits. The kids want the formal kimono or business suit, so they agree to attend.

Source: T. R. Reid, Confucius Lives Next Door *(New York: Vintage Books, 1999), pp. 161–66.*

coming-of-age ceremonies receive gifts of promotional consumer goods provided by marketers interested in cashing in on their changing consumer needs, in addition to receiving their kimonos and business suits.[53]

THE DYNAMIC SELF-CONCEPT

Exhibit 10.2 illustrates a dynamic model of self-concept that summarizes a lot of what we have described above. The currently active set of dynamic self-representations is the working self-concept, which regulates both intrapersonal and interpersonal processes.

Intrapersonal Processes

The working self-concept regulates intrapersonal processes in several important ways. First, the self-concept integrates and organizes an individual's self-relevant experiences into a self-narrative. **Self-narratives** consist of *stories that are coherent, context-sensitive accounts of experiences that provide a sense of personal continuity in time and space.* These stories often refer to events past, present, and future; they contain a judgmental or evaluative component and are woven together to appear coherent to the storyteller.[54]

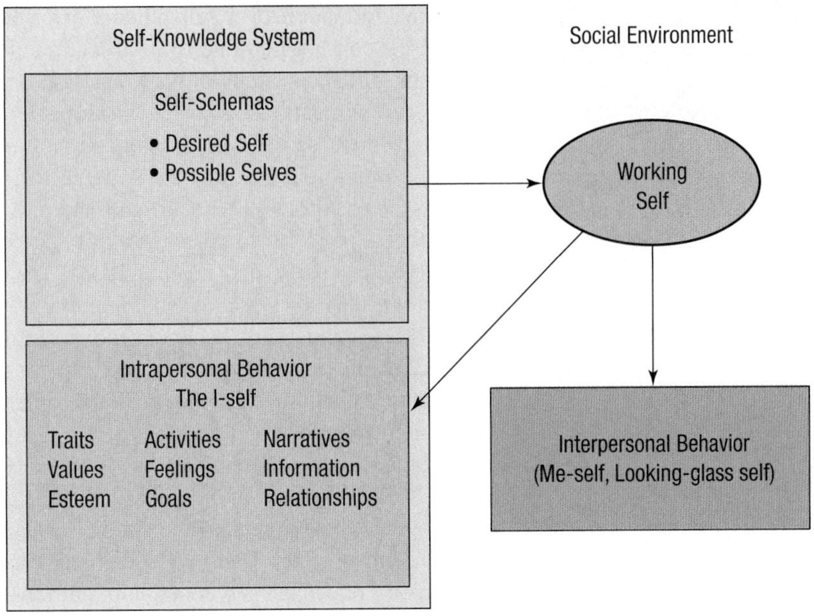

EXHIBIT 10.2

A Dynamic Model of Self-Concept

Often people use consumption to give coherence to their stories about the self. For example, cherished possessions are cherished in part because they become a repository for stories about the self. Some research has shown that consumers try to build preferred elements of self-narratives into custom-made homes.[55]

Consumers also may use consumption to create new self-narratives and change self-concept. A tattoo artist describing his clients' motivations for getting tattoos in Consumer Chronicles 10.4 provides one example of the relationship between using consumption and self-narrative to change self-concept during a role transition.[56] The contribution of commercial high-risk adventures to self-narrative and identity construction is illustrated in Consumer Chronicles 10.5. In this example, skydiving affords a young woman skydiver a way to organize a new and possibly central self-concept. As the skydiver's story indicates, consuming high-risk experiences may provide psychological resources to guide behavior in other contexts.[57]

Second, self-concept influences the processing of **self-relevant information,**[58] the *internalized self-schemas that represent a reference value or standard of comparison for new information from the environment.* In other words, people pay attention to information, including marketing communications, that reinforces self-concept. Individuals are more sensitive to information that is self-relevant. Self-relevant information is more efficiently processed; and people remember and recognize self-relevant information better. Finally, consumers are resistant to information that is incongruent with their self-representations. For example, a recent study presented individuals with a pair of letters, each pair containing a letter from their name. Asked to quickly choose which letter they preferred, individuals reliably chose the letter from their own name. When given a chance to study the letter pairs carefully, they had no awareness that a letter from their name was embedded among the pairs of letters.[59]

It is important for marketers to understand the effect of product self-relevance on self-concept and processing of information. Regular acquisition and consumption of a particular brand, say Prada fashions, or a product category, say designer clothing, may

Tattooing and a New Sense of Self

CONSUMER CHRONICLES 10.4

I do see that many people get tattooed to find out again . . . to say, "Who was I before I got into this lost position?" It's almost like a tattoo pulls you back to a certain kind of reality about who you are as an individual. Either that or it transfers you to the next step in your life, the next plateau. A woman will come in and say, "Well, I just went through a really ugly divorce. My husband had control of my ______ body and now I have it again. I want a tattoo. I want a tattoo that says that I have the courage to get this, that I have the courage to take on the rest of my life. I'm going to do what I want to do and do what I have to do to survive as a person." That's a motivation that comes through the door a lot.

Source: Clinton R. Sanders, Customizing the Body: The Art and Culture of Tattooing *(Philadelphia: Temple University Press, 1989), p. 43.*

lead to the formation of a self-schema or reference point in self-concept that one is an affluent, fashionable person. If the consumer of the Prada fashion then receives compliments about being fashionable from significant others or receives promotions from other designer-clothing retailers, and these messages match her self-schema, this will tend to reinforce and consolidate this aspect of self-concept. In this way, being fashionable in general, and being a Prada consumer in particular, may also become more central to self-concept. If fashionability becomes more central to self-concept, the consumer is then more likely to be open to other fashion-based appeals. At the same time, brands such as Prada may become self-relevant product symbols, and repeat purchase is more likely. By the same token, any kind of brand or product category that becomes a widely recognized symbol of particular kinds of people, say Tommy Hilfiger fashions and hip-hop stars or Hickey Freeman suits and business executives, leads people to adopt such product symbols as a vehicle to create their own possible selves.[60] Self-relevance is likely to be an important determinant of consumer involvement with and processing of marketing communications. Because people attend to self-relevant information, many studies suggest that personalized advertising should attract subscribers' attention. At a more subtle level, of course, advertisers employ images they hope will be congruent with consumers' self-concepts and associate those images with their product.[61]

Third, self-concept influences the *regulation of affect.* Individuals defend their self-concepts against negative emotional states and interact with others and interpret events in ways that enhance and promote their self-concept. Many studies have documented self-serving biases in how individuals interpret events. One way that people regulate negative affect is by reducing self-awareness. For example, as discussed in Chapter 8, people may not pay attention to marketing communications that conflict with preferred self-image.[62]

Some related recent research has focused on **self-gifts** (see Chapter 16). Many Euro-Americans give themselves presents, that is, they think of certain purchases or consumption activities as gifts for themselves. Often, these presents help people regulate their emotional balance. For example, a person may treat himself to an ice cream cone because he had a hard day at work; another may buy herself flowers as a way to maintain an especially good mood. As messages from and to the self, self-gifts can be elevating, protective, or soothing.[63] Self-gifts frequently carry messages about identity and self-distinctiveness, which contributes to self-esteem.

Body image is commonly defined as a mental construction, embedded in self-schema that can deviate substantially from a person's objective physical characteristics. In this view, the body is understood through a cognitive schema, and this cognitively structured image regulates understanding of the physical body. Body image research in consumption has tended to focus on the psychological problems that stem from cultural ideals of beautiful bodies such as distorted perceptions of weight, eating disorders, and lowered self-esteem.[64] But a range of cultural ideals, social relationships, and norms affects body image. For example, the desire to transform the body into a more desired form and the belief that this can and should be done is widespread among Western consumers. This belief also seems to spread globally with consumer culture. Several multi-billion dollar industries cater to this desire such as diet programs, fitness equipment and services, cosmetic surgeries, and diet- and health-oriented foods and media. Consumers' desire to resist or alter the body nature has given us may seem self-evident, but it rests on three longstanding Western beliefs. First is the idea that our body does not limit our true or essential self but merely houses it. Second is the idealization of youth and health. Third is the idea that scientific knowledge can liberate the true self from natural forces including aging. Effective commercial messages that build on this idea have helped create markets for a range of plastic surgery techniques and fueled the recent mass market success of botox as a treatment for wrinkling in the United States. Together, these ideas take on a kind of moral force; body appearance is sometimes treated as an indicator of character. Deviations from ideals can be punished. And eating disorders such as anorexia and obesity are sometimes misunderstood as character failings. Often portrayed in ads and infomercials as a decision to take control of one's life and reconstruct a more desirable appearance, these ideas about the body's relationships to the self apparently drive consumers' use of products and services offered by the cosmetic, beauty, medical, and fitness industries. While Western ideals of feminine beauty tend to impose stricter standards of youthful appearance on women than on men, men too are driving sales growth in these industries. The ad for Diesel clothing shown on page 411 appeals to Western values of youthfulness, science, and body control.[65]

CONSUMER CHRONICLES 10.5

High-Risk Leisure Consumption and Self-Narrative

A young woman, interviewed after 325 jumps, said about skydiving,

> I work for the weekend. I work to make a living and to make jump money. The DZ (drop zone) is the enjoyable part of my life.

In recollections of a river-rafting experience, one participant noted:

> [You] develop a personal enrichment especially if you encounter a situation in which you become frightened and overcome the obstacle of the situation. And finally, long after it's done, even years later, you'll find your mind escaping/returning back to the journey and reliving the thrill and when you encounter a situation in life where you're afraid or unsure the river experience often enables you to overcome it because you are inevitably more self-assured.

Source: Richard L. Celsi, Randall L. Rose, and Thomas W. Loigh, "An Exploration of High-Risk Leisure Consumption through Skydiving," Journal of Consumer Research *20 (June 1993), p. 9.*

Finally, self-concept has important effects on motivation, discussed in Chapter 7. In considering the effect of self-concept on motivation, notice that the self-concept includes many images of possible selves, feared and desired. **Desired selves** comprise a particularly important subset of people's possible selves, that is, *what they would like to be and think they really can be.* Depending on the importance and commitment to these self-definitions, desired selves can define goals and move individuals to action. As suggested by the Eileen Fisher ad shown on the next page that invites consumers to "compose our own lives," marketing communication often appeals to consumer behavior directed at closing the gap between actual and desired selves.[66]

Often, advertising appeals to a consumer's desired self-concept; thus, an ad for a Piaget gold watch might appeal to a consumer's desire to appear wealthy or chic. Exhibit 10.3 shows a decision process that advertisers might use to create effective advertising. First,

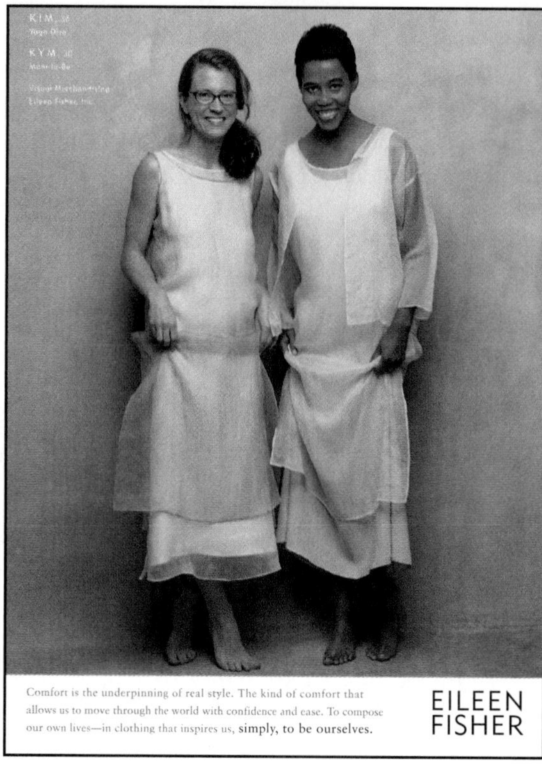

Closing the gap between desired and actual selves: This ad invites consumers to compose their own lives.

This ad appeals to the real self of older women. The text reads: "good fashion sees not only the beauty of youth."

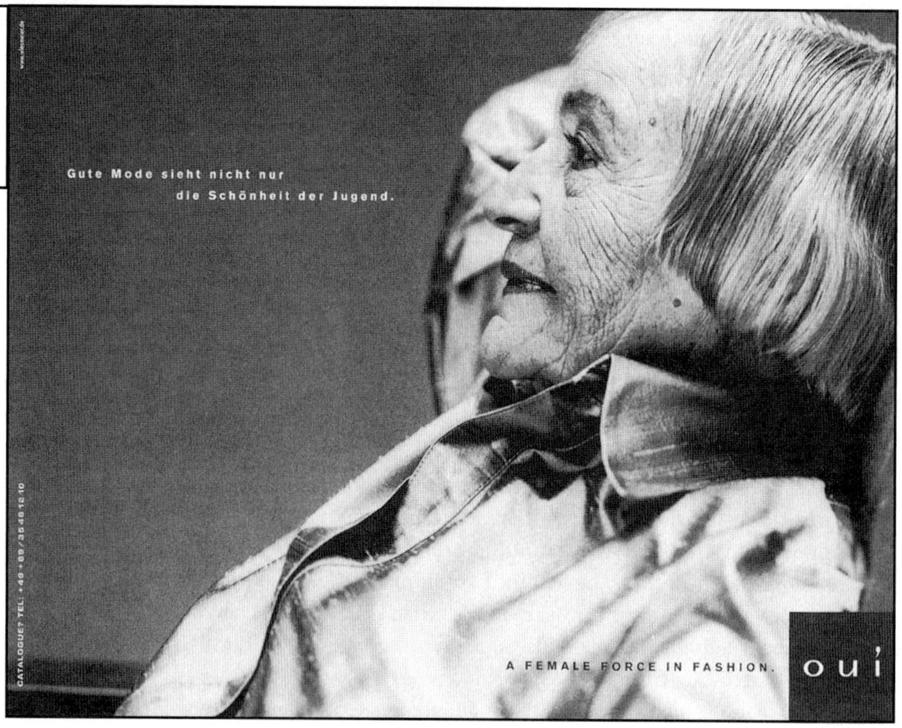

Diesel appeals to Western beliefs about the body, science, and youthfulness.

the diagram shows that ads that are congruent with a consumer's self-concept will be more effective than one that is not. Second, it shows that an appeal to actual self-concept is more effective in evoking associations in memory than is an ad that appeals to desired self-concept. If advertisers want to change consumer attitudes, just the reverse is true. Appeals should be made to the desired self-concept.[67]

A group of 24 ad agency personnel were interviewed about self-concept and its potential application to advertising strategy. The results of these interviews are shown in Industry Insights 10.1. Here, advertised products are separated into three groups: convenience (e.g., frozen food), shopping (athletic wear), and speciality (a luxury automobile). Services are separated into two groups: tangible (a retail grocery chain) and intangible (a leasing company). For each entry, the agency personnel identified (1) the target audience, (2) the main appeal of the ad, and (3) the relevance of that appeal to self-concept, or product attribute. For instance, athletic wear that is targeted to young consumers may project a main appeal of health and sex. In turn, this "health and sex" message can be viewed as an appeal to desired self-concept. As shown in the table, self-concept can have value for advertisers and their agencies as they create promotional strategies and advertising copy.[68]

EXHIBIT 10.3

Self-Concept and Advertising Effectiveness

Source: Adapted from George M. Zinkhan, Diana Haytko, and Allison Ward, "Self-Concept Theory: Applications in Advertising," *Journal of Marketing Communications* 2 (1996), pp. 1–19.

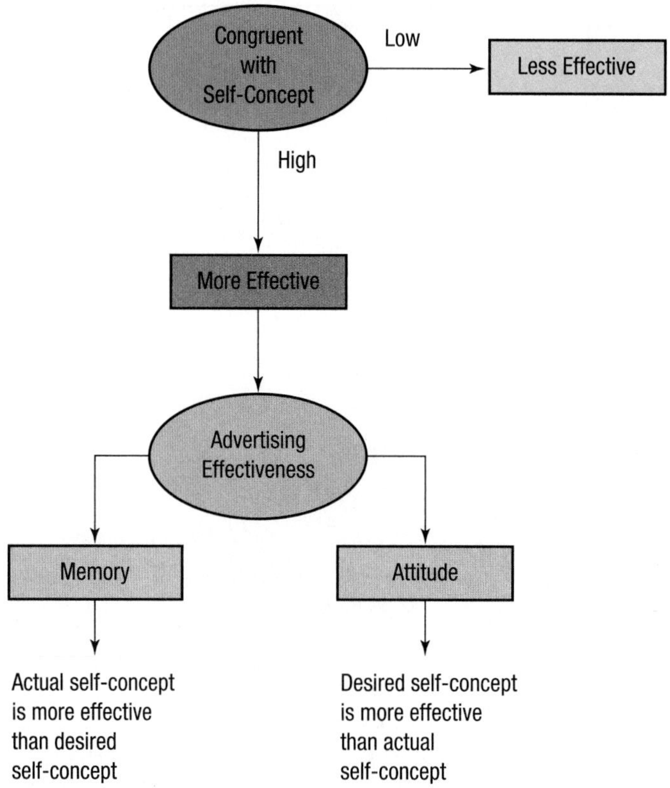

Interpersonal Processes

The working self-concept provides a guide for interpreting social experiences. People use self as a reference point for evaluating other people, selecting friends, and directing interactions with others. People tend to judge others on characteristics that are personally important, tend to choose friends and partners who reinforce beliefs about their desired selves, and use a variety of strategies and tactics to present preferred identities to others. Just as individuals use products as symbols of various aspects of the self or as vehicles to create a self, simultaneously those same products present identity externally to others. In Western societies, for example, consumers expect a home to be decorated in a fashion that meaningfully represents the character of its inhabitants. Consequently, consumers expend considerable resources on personalized home decoration. Consumer goods used to convey meaning to others vary cross-culturally. In earlier chapters we discussed how in China successive groups of consumer durables were used over time to convey their owners' conventional middle-class status to others for example.

Because of the link between self-concept and consumption, audiences infer characteristics of self by using consumption as a reference point. Consumer goods thus help create communication systems of socially shared meanings about identity. As suggested in Chapter 4, consumption expresses and defines the self through group membership and values conveyed by the shared symbolic meaning of consumer goods. Researchers have examined whether and how consumers attribute characteristics to others on the basis of their clothing choices, preferred possession, and lifestyle choices.[69]

Adopting shared consumption patterns enables people to construct and maintain a sense

Self-Concept Examples from Ad Agency Personnel

INDUSTRY INSIGHTS 10.1a

Category	Product or Service	Target Audience	Main Appeal	Relevance to Self-Concept
Products	Frozen food	Single working people	Romantic appeal	Desired self-concept
Convenience Shopping	Domestic beer	Blue-collar men	Adventure and macho appeal	Desired self-concept
	Instant rice	Working women	Quick dinner	Product attribute
Specialty	Athletic wear	Ages 16–49 years	Healthy, sexy image	Desired self-concept
	Distinct tequila	Upscale educated women	Cosmopolitan and party image	Desired self-concept
	Luxury car	Wealthy men	Display of wealth	Desired self-concept
Services				
Tangible	Retail grocery chain	Upper-income women aged 25–49 years	Ideal family image	Desired self-concept
	Major airline	Frequent business traveler	Need for praise from the boss	Desired self-concept
	Real estate company	Families	Portray believable lifestyles	Mix of actual and desired self-concept
	Department store	Wide target	Models are average	Mix of actual and desired self-concept
	Hospital	Nurse recruitment	Actual nurses enjoying hobbies	Mix of actual and desired self-concept
	Auto parts store	Men 16–49 years	Products and prices	Product attribute
	Fast-food restaurant	Wide target	Fun place to go	Product attribute
	Mass-transit system	Wide target	Actual bus riders	Actual self-concept
	Craft and home warehouse	Wide target	Actual customers having fun in store	Actual self-concept
Intangible	Staff leasing company	Small business	Relieve time pressure	Actual leading to desired self-concept
	Long-distance 800 service	Individuals	Hope for broken marriage	Actual leading to desired self-concept
	ATM card	Anti–high-status person	Product information	Product attribute

of personal and group identities simultaneously. Thus, people derive significant psychological benefits from shared consumption. In Western cultural contexts, shared consumption also often creates some conflicts because of the exaggerated value Westerners place on individual identity. Research has examined how the individual identities of members of a few well-defined market segments vary.[70]

Appeals in Magazine Advertisements: Product Attribute versus Desired Self-Concept

INDUSTRY INSIGHTS 10.1b

Category	Product or Service	Main Appeal	Relevance to Self-Concept
Products	Beef	Benefits of eating steak	Product attribute
	Carlton cigarettes	Lowest tar and nicotine	Product attribute
	Arid deodorant	Nonwhitening features	Product attribute
	Nonalcoholic beer	Tastes as good as regular beer with fewer calories	Product attribute
	Rémy Martin	Relaxed and comfortable feeling	Desired self-concept
	Mazda sports car	Owner will stand out in a crowd	Desired self-concept
	Calphalon cookware	Quality cookware	Product attribute
	Nike	Self-image of conquering any obstacle	Desired self-concept
	Piaget gold watch	Wealthy image	Desired self-concept
	First Colony coffee	Buyer has expensive and good taste	Desired self-concept
Services	Intercoiffure salons	Glamorous and beautiful look	Desired self-concept
	Ritz Carlton hotels	Relaxation and luxury	Desired self-concept
	United Airlines	First-class amenities	Product benefit and desired self-concept
	NationsBank	Many different services offered	Product attribute
	American Express	Owner is self-sufficient	Product attribute
	Communication in schools: Nonprofit	Invest in our children	Product benefit and desired self-concept

Sources: http://www3.itu.ch/virtexh/botswana/botdoll4.htm; Hazel Rose Markus and Shinobu Kitayama, "Culture and Self: Implications for Cognition, Emotion, and Motivation," Psychological Review *98 (1991), pp. 224–53; Harold H. Kassarjian, "Social Character and Differential Preference for Mass Communication,"* Journal of Marketing Research *2 (May 1965), pp. 146–53; and George M. Zinkhan, Diana Haytko, and Allison Ward, "Self-Concept Theory: Applications in Advertising,"* Journal of Marketing Communications *2 (1996), pp. 1–19.*

Some research on interpersonal self-processes has studied self-presentation, or impression management. The tendency to manage self-presentation to fit the social situation through consumption differs between people. Some people are **high self-monitors;** *they are concerned that their behavior is consistent with their conception of how people behave in a particular situation.* Other people are **low self-monitors;** *they are more concerned with being themselves in various situations* and less with whether their behavior matches how other people look and act.[71] Degree of self-monitoring varies over the life cycle, between cultures and individuals, and between situations.

How does the self-monitoring personality trait affect consumer behavior? A British study showed that high self-monitors chose alcoholic soft drinks that helped them support the image they wished to project within different consumption situations. Low self-monitors reported a more pragmatic range of influences on their drink choices.

This ad appeals to high self-monitor's desire to conform to fashion stereotypes.

Another British study showed that high self-monitors try to conform to the identity depicted in ads for the fashion brands they purchase. The ad for Rivets by Lee shown above is a good example of an ad that will appeal to high self-monitors' desire to conform to idealized images of fashion and beauty.[72]

Several studies have shown that individuals who are high versus low in self-monitoring differ in the types of messages that they find persuasive. In the product domain, low self-monitors tend to be concerned with dimensions related to product quality, such as the taste of a brand of whiskey or the cleaning performance of a shampoo. Marketing communications that focus on the inherent qualities and benefits of the product appear to be particularly effective for low self-monitors. High self-monitors, in contrast, tend to be concerned with the self-presentational significance of products, such as the popular or successful image associated with fashion or a certain brand of whiskey, shampoo, and so forth. Marketing communications that focus on the impressions created by using the product tend to be especially effective for high self-monitors.

Age, product characteristics, and culture interact with individual differences in self-monitoring to influence consumers' response to marketing communications. Teenagers tend to be higher self-monitors than adults and hence more responsive to image appeals. Japanese consumers, like others from cultures with an interdependent sense of self (discussed on the next page), tend to adapt their self-presentation, including consumption choices, to social situations. The persuasiveness of image-based versus quality-based marketing communications varies with product characteristics. Specifically, to the extent that a product can be thought of in terms of both pragmatic utility and image, high self-monitors prefer image appeals, whereas low self-monitors prefer quality appeals. However, when judging the persuasiveness of appeals for products that are primarily utilitarian or imagistic, both high and low self-monitors prefer appeals that focus on how well the product fulfills that function.[73]

Regardless of whether they are high or low self-monitors, all people present various identities to different audiences.[74] Sometimes the audiences are internalized others;

You Are Where You Live

CONSUMER CHRONICLES 10.6

- Psychologist Edward Sadalla of ASU and his colleagues selected 12 upper-middle-class homeowners, questioned them on 36 aspects of their personality, and took slides of the living room and front exterior of their homes. The homeowners themselves all believed their homes expressed their identity "fairly well" or "very well."
- The researchers showed 99 students slides of the insides or outsides and asked them to try to infer the personalities of the owners using the same 36-item questionnaire.
- Students made especially accurate judgments about personalities after only a glance at the living room. They also formed relatively accurate impressions by viewing the outside of the house.
- The inside and outside reveal different aspects of personality. For example, interior areas communicate accurate information about intellectualism, venturesomeness, and family orientation. Exterior areas communicated about privacy and artistic proclivities.

Source: Vincent Bozzi, "You Are Where You Live," Psychology Today *22 (May 1988), p. 12.*

other times the audiences are external. Advertising commonly appeals to consumers' internalized audiences. An advertisement might show a woman looking at shoes or makeup and picturing herself wearing them, deciding whether she approves of how she will look. Such an ad appeals to a tendency for a person's I-self to stand outside the self and evaluate the self-image, the me-self.

In Japan, *enka* music and musicians provide a looking-glass image that appeals to the external audience of older, blue-collar Japanese listeners. According to one critic, *enka* music encodes Confucian values of rank and hierarchy, traditional gender roles, striving and hardship, and nostalgia for old village times (*furasato*), all values close to the selves of the *enka* consumer. In listening to or singing *enka,* consumers uphold and personify these values to an audience of which they are a part. Recall that researchers have referred to this process of trying to look at self-identity through the eyes of others as the looking-glass self.[75]

People infer characteristics of the self from the sets or patterns of consumer goods others consume. But do internal and external audiences agree on what is being communicated? Often they do. Even at very young ages, U.S. children make connections between consumption objects, such as houses and cars, and characteristics of their owners. Moreover, subtle consumption patterns such as food preferences (e.g., salty or sweet), drink preferences, and location of television set communicate social class and cultural influences. By observing consumption constellations believed to express identity, strangers are able to accurately match the owner's own reported personality profile. Consumer Chronicles 10.6 describes a study reported in *Psychology Today* relating pictures of the interiors and exteriors of homes to the owners' selves.[76]

Exhibit 10.4 summarizes some of the ways that consumer behaviors are linked to self-concept. People use consumption to illustrate or symbolize aspects of their self-concept. They acquire and consume goods that contribute to their self-narrative. Consumers may also use goods to close the gap between actual and possible selves or to experiment with desired selves. Finally, consumption behaviors often make evident a change in self-concept during role transitions.

The Postmodern Self

Postmodernity is another name for the post–cold war world in which market capitalism has become the main organizing force globally. Postmodernity is characterized by three conditions that affect identity: (1) declining allegiance to unifying belief systems, such as national purpose, democratic values, scientific progress, or religious doctrines;

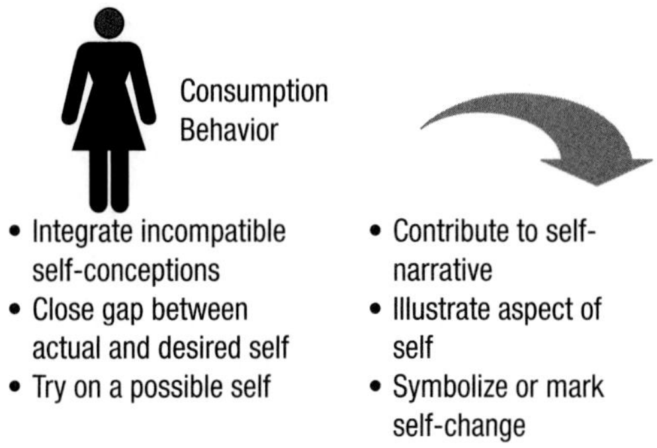

EXHIBIT 10.4

Consumer Goods and Consumption Behavior

(2) a fragmentation of the self-concept; and (3) the decentering of the subject, by which is sometimes meant a loss of purpose and coherent sense of self. As a consequence, the postmodern consumer is free to choose—with little sense of enduring commitment from a wide range of identities—to become the person she or he wants to be in any given moment or situation. Whereas modern self-identity was defined through labor and tradition, the **postmodern self** is an ongoing consumption project continuously in flux and in flight from the past and the status quo.[77]

This postmodern self is an optimistic idea because it implies that each of us can select identities at will from a catalog of cultural identities that can be worn and then discarded free from anxiety and uncertainty. Evidence in support of such a model of the self is the wild popularity of role-playing games and activities. Fervent participants in activities such as Renaissance Fairs or Mountain Man rendezvous provide U.S. examples. In Korea, online role-playing games are hugely popular and some research says that a majority of Koreans participate in creating and interacting through imaginative computer-generated avatars.[78]

Certainly consumer culture provides many opportunities to experiment with identity. However, much research suggests that consumers' self-knowledge, self-narratives, and personal projects are structured by long-standing cultural and cognitive models that mold their consumption choices. Identity does not seem to be a free-floating choice. For example, research in several Triad nations finds that a range of purchases and consumption experiences is sought that provides one of two kinds of supports for identity. Some consumers seek out products and experiences that are seen as highly authentic and help them express their true selves, but are, in fact, mass merchandised. Signature merchandise or adventure travel can serve this end. Others look for products and commercial experiences that are seen as authoritative and help them express values they believe are widely shared. Tours of national monuments and participation in community festivals and ethnic and national holidays can serve this end.[79]

Self-Concept and the Circle of Consumption

Self-concept affects consumption patterns during each phase of the circle of consumption (introduced in Chapter 1). In this section, we offer a few related examples of how self-concept influences the phases of consumption, but we encourage you to think of your own examples.[80]

PRODUCTION An important segment for marketers of high-end kitchen products are people who are into cooking (e.g., the production of gourmet meals). For these customers, the production of elegant meals is used to make a statement about who they are. Men and women have different notions of what types of meal production are consistent with their self-image. For example, men grill and make cappuccino. An example of how cooking can feature prominently in self-narratives is provided in a recent movie entitled *Household Saints*. In this movie, an old Italian mother tells a self-narrative of how in the early years she and her husband were so poor they dug clam shells out of the garbage can outside a local seafood restaurant, but she still managed "to make a very good soup" from them. The retail and catalog store Williams Sonoma, makers of high-end barbecue equipment such as Weber, and department stores in Japan such as Mitsukoshi and in the UK such as Fortnum and Mason cater to market segments that imagine gourmet cooking as part of self-concept.

www.mitsukoshi.co.jp

www.fortnumandmason.com

ACQUISITION Consider how self-image enters into decisions about how to redesign a kitchen. At a time when household size was declining, consumers in the United States spent $88 billion in 1991 alone to remodel their kitchens. Research suggests that these decisions had more to do with self-image than with food. For example, men want a high-tech look where everything is flush and sleek, so as to convey the feeling that there is a professional in charge, although that is rarely the case. By contrast, women see the kitchen as the heart of the home, the nerve center of the household. For them, the kitchen is about nurturing, and it is likely to be a more significant element of their extended self—a reflection of their care and nurturing of the family. Empty-nest couples whose children have left the home (see Chapter 13) often have powerful emotional attachments to their kitchens. It is frequently a central aspect of their self-concept. Consequently, they are good prospects for kitchen remodeling jobs.

Often, the desired self enters into kitchen remodeling decisions. For example, working women have a dream of having husbands who help them prepare meals. Consequently, their dream kitchens are being designed so two people can cook at once.

CONSUMPTION In the United States we think of kitchens as a place for consuming food, but many more important things get consumed in the kitchen. Thus, a recent advertisement for General Electric appliances reads, "You may call it a kitchen, but we know it's your living room." People use their kitchen for family socializing, entertaining, study, or work and as a place for solitude and relaxation. Family socializing in the kitchen is tied to self-concepts of warmth and nurturing. Of course, the multipurpose consumption occurring in the kitchen makes certain features more important. Quiet appliances become a priority, because families want to be able to have household conversations in the kitchen. Thus, if you go to the GE website you can find out all about the Triton dishwasher, advertised as "The Cleanest Wash You Never Heard."

www.geappliances.com/triton

DISPOSAL Concern with caring for the environment is a much more important self-aspect than it was in the past. Fifteen years ago, few families recycled or needed storage areas for recyclable materials. Now more than half of all U.S. households recycle cans, bottles, or newspapers, and recycling rates are much higher in some European countries. Self-concepts have changed to include the belief "I care about the environment," and that change is reflected in recycling behaviors. Consequently, kitchens must change to include storage areas for recycled materials. So if you go to the Real Goods website you can find out about countertop composting crocks, aluminum can crushers, and compost bins, all products designed to make recycling in the kitchen easier.

www.realgoods.com/products

SELF-CONCEPT AROUND THE WORLD

In 1938, anthropologist Marcel Mauss wrote that the self is primarily a product of social factors and remains an imprecise, delicate, and fragile category. His essay and much subsequent work show that the self varies substantially across cultures.[81] How then do different cultures define the self? What is universal and what is culturally variable in people's thinking about the self? How can these variations be explained? How do an individual's notions of the self inform that person's ability to comprehend alternative formulations? And what is the significance of cultural differences in the self for consumer behavior?

These questions are of compelling interest and importance. However, we don't know all the answers. What we do know is that the self is configured differently in different cultures. We can refer back to Exhibit 10.1 to help us understand some of the variability. For instance, role relations may be primarily oriented toward the individual (self) or toward significant others. Or cultural ideas or materials and objects may be the primary basis for defining self-other relations. As different aspects of the relational self are emphasized in different cultural contexts, the self and associated consumer wants are likely to vary.[82]

Individualism, autonomy, and self-assertion—doing your own thing—rather than accommodation of others characterize the Euro-American self. The Euro-American self strives for a high degree of self-reliance and independence. Materials and objects play an important role in self-realization and in defining relationships with others. Consequently, in successful Euro-American advertising, consumer goods are often depicted as ways of realizing personal aspirations, expressing the real self or possible selves, and creating family togetherness or other social relationships.

The traditional Chinese self, by contrast, is more oriented toward significant others rather than toward the individual. Even among the most rapidly modernizing segments of the Chinese population, *people tend to act primarily in accordance with the anticipated expectations of others and social norms rather than with internal wishes or personal attributes.* A traditional male Chinese would consider himself a son, a brother, a husband, a father, but more rarely *himself.* In contrast to Euro-Americans, for Chinese people, cultural ideas and values rather than materials and objects are also dominant in defining self-other relations. Thus, the traditional Chinese self, like the self in other Asian societies and those in the less affluent world, is a **relational self** built on enduring social relations and cultural ideas.[83] Differences in the traditional Chinese and Euro-American self have broad implications for consumer behavior. For example, the relational self enjoys a high degree of security, but at the same time relations and ideas may be so rigidly defined that there is a higher degree of resistance to innovation and change than among Western consumers. On the other hand, when change occurs, it tends to move quickly through the group.[84]

The principal, overarching concept of an Asian society imbued with Confucian teaching is that of harmony and order. This ordering principle is reflected in Chinese society and is also fundamental to the Japanese perception of self. The Japanese word for self, *jibun,* refers to one's share of the shared life space; thus, belonging, or a sense of identification with others, is central to the Japanese sense of self. *Proper role behavior and behaviors that convey identification with the needs of others and contribute* to **relationship harmony,** rather than a constant sense of self, are dominant components of the Japanese self.[85] In Japanese companies, morning rituals symbolize the collectivity and the sense of belonging. Employees do gymnastics together or sing company songs. In Japan, "belonging" is often cemented with material objects. For example, lapel pins and company shirts and baseball caps are popular ways of signaling belonging and membership. Japanese youth subcultures also like to use brands and logos to symbolize their group memberships.[86]

Japan offers an interesting example of how a change in the individual's relationship with material objects can begin to alter self-definitions. Being satisfied with one's lot in life has been an old-fashioned Japanese virtue. However, the Japanese are not as satisfied with their lives as Americans. One explanation is that learning to be content was a necessity in post–World War II Japan. However, today's economic success makes self-denial more difficult. As more Japanese travel abroad, they learn that their material possessions do not measure up to those of people in many Western countries. Perhaps this explanation accounts in part for the popularity in today's Japan of designer products, which provide a globally recognized standard of quality.[87]

We summarize some contrasts between self-concepts in the Triad nations of the West with those in Japan, China, and the NICs of east Asia in Exhibit 10.5. Particularly noteworthy is the conception of tasks for the self that may well be expressed in consumer behavior. Thus, Exhibit 10.5 suggests that hard selling is inappropriate in east Asian cultures because the seller should try to feel and think what customers are feeling and thinking without being told and should try to help customers satisfy their wishes and realize their goals rather than those of the seller. The consumer behaviors of the Japanese undergoing role transition to adulthood or employment mentioned earlier reflect the interdependent self. We say more about the contrasts between Western and Eastern concepts of the self in our discussion of motives in Chapter 7.[88]

Next, consider the self proposed by Hinduism, an important religious tradition among the 1.5 billion people of India, Sri Lanka, and Indonesia. The Hindu self-concept is part of religious doctrine dating to at least 700 B.C. (the ideas and beliefs component of the relational self). The Hindu conception of self is that there is one and only one being in existence, the absolute. This absolute (Brahman) is without form. The multitude of other beings, souls, selves, beasts, stars, and planets is a mistaken imposition on the

EXHIBIT 10.5

Key Differences between an Independent and Interdependent Self-Concept

Characteristics	Independent Western Self-Concept	Interdependent East Asian Self-Concept
Definition	Separate from social context	Connected to social context
Structure	Bounded, unique, separate, stable	Fluid, flexible, variable
Tasks, often realized through consumption	Be unique, separate from others Express self Realize internal qualities Promote own goals Be direct—say what's on your mind	Belong; connect and fit in with others Occupy one's proper place Engage in appropriate action Promote other's goals Be indirect—read others' minds
Role of others	Self-evaluation: others are important for social comparison and reflected appraisal	Self-definition: relations with others in specific contexts comprise the self

Source: Hazel Rose Markus and Shinobu Kitayama, "Culture and Self: Implications for Cognition, Emotion, and Motivation," *Psychological Review* 98 (1991), pp. 224–53.

One. The goal of individual human life is to break through this delusion of multiplicity and achieve identity with the One. Also, the apparent self (which is part of the delusion of multiplicity) is not sovereign and infinitely varied; rather, it is ill defined and weak in the Hindu conception. The person is not viewed as individual but as "dividual," or divisible—made up of varied substances, which may reproduce in others something of persons from whom they have originated. Thus, as for people in east Asian cultures, for Hindu people family and lineage are a more prominent aspect of self than they are for an American or European.

The ways in which this self-concept resonates across south Asian societies are complex and well beyond the scope of this book, but they have profound implications for how south Asians think about what is self and not self. In simple terms, whatever the body is, it is not the self. Thus, if Belk did his study of the extended self in India, we might expect that body parts would not be viewed as central aspects of self. Concepts of self and nonself in south Asian thought influence intrapersonal and interpersonal information processing as well. Indian movies produced by a successful studio system based in Mumbai, India, always depict stereotyped personages. Everyone is either good or bad. There are no shades of gray. Woody Allen's or Ingmar Bergman's films, built around individuals' murky existential struggles, would have little appeal to most south Asians.[89]

Africa provides examples of other conceptions of self. Africa is characterized by great cultural diversity, but some common characteristics can be identified. First, while practical, the African self is simultaneously spiritual. Second is the idea that persons are part of an all-encompassing, vital life force. Third, the self is not a bounded entity as in Western notions but a permeable one subject to the influence of many forces. Fourth, the African self is an interdependent self linked to the individual's kin group and often to ancestral spirits. As one result, there seems to be a **socially oriented achievement motivation** among many Africans. A socially oriented achievement motivation means *an individual's striving for success is bound up with the success of others,* as, for example, in a tendency for small-scale marketers to prefer to profit together rather than through purely individual initiative.[90]

The consumer consequences of such conceptions are many, although little research has been conducted on the relationship between the self and consumption on the African continent. For example, in some contexts, conspicuous consumption is regarded as evidence of an individual's or family's control of the vital life force. The permeability and interdependence of the self may be seen in the tendency for groups of people to dress in identical clothing, based on a variety of social bonds, on public occasions. In other contexts, people's desire to ensure ancestorhood for themselves leads to significant consumption expenditures associated with death and mortuary rites. In still other contexts, consumption may be inspired by the desire to fulfill one's role as a family member rather than personal desires.[91]

SUMMARY

Self-concept is a dynamic interpretive structure that influences both intrapersonal and interpersonal processes. Self-concept varies both cross-culturally and historically. The self develops out of interactions with significant others; materials and objects; and ideals, beliefs, and values. Whenever any of these entities changes, we can expect some change to take place in self-concept. Several observations are helpful in understanding self-concept. First, the self includes the multiplicity of things people are to one another and to themselves. A person's body, objects, places, time periods, other people, and pets may be considered central to the self and are part of what is called the extended self. The self includes many self-schemas or self-representations, both positive and negative, actual and possible, compatible and incompatible. Second, a person's working self-concept depends on situations and motives. People selectively retrieve different aspects of themselves depending on the situation and our goals. Third, because of restrictions on behavior, self-concept is not always directly revealed in people's actions. Finally, self-concept is malleable or dynamic both between social settings and over time. Self-concept is especially dynamic during role transitions.

Self-concept regulates intrapersonal processes in several important ways. Self-narratives are important in helping to integrate and organize self-relevant experiences. Also, self-relevance is important to every aspect of information processing, to the regulation of affect or mood, and as a motivator of behavior. Self-concept is also important in interpersonal processes, offering a guide for evaluating people, selecting friends, and directing interactions.

Self-concept is closely linked to many consumption behaviors. People use consumption to symbolize, change, integrate, or experiment with aspects of their selves. Studying the communication properties of consumption provides many insights about the activated, working self-concept. We suggest that consumption can accurately communicate aspects of self to others, the meaning of consumption objects changes between different times and social settings, and even young children can make connections between consumption objects and characteristics of their owners.

The self is configured differently in different cultures. By looking at how people relate to significant others, materials and objects, and ideas and values, we can form comparisons between the concepts of self in different cultures. We can ask whether role relations are oriented toward the individual or toward significant others and whether cultural ideas or materials and objects are the primary basis for defining self.

This chapter focuses on self-schemas and self-representations rather than on personality. Nevertheless, personality trait measures (e.g., risk taking, materialistic) can be used to gain insights about consumer behaviors (e.g., compulsive buying) and to segment markets. Newer approaches for measuring traits give consumers more leeway to describe themselves in their own ways on dimensions of their own choosing. Many trait measures have been developed in consumer behavior. In general, they are not very effective in predicting specific brand choices. However, they may predict behavior averaged over a sample of consumption situations or occasions.

As you read about perception, learning, information processing, lifestyle, the diffusion of innovations, and many other consumer behavior topics, your own thinking about self-concept will be valuable. The interpretive structure that constitutes self-concept is central to the way that you will process this learning experience. For example, if you can make consumer behavior self-relevant by relating it to aspects of your own life, you will find it easier to learn and remember and more fun to think about and discuss.

KEY TERMS

body image 408
compulsive buying 394
desired selves 409
extended self 400
high self-monitors 414
image congruence hypothesis 400
I-self 399
locus of control 396
looking-glass self 399
low self-monitors 414
me-self 399
need for cognition 395
personality 389
possible selves 403
postmodern self 417
relational self 419
relationship harmony 419
role transition 389
self-concept 388
self-efficacy 395
self-esteem 393
self-gifts 408
self-narratives 406
self-relevant information 407
self-schemas 403
socially oriented achievement motivation 421
traits 390
working, or activated, self-concept 401

REVIEW QUESTIONS

1. Draw a picture of your extended self. Draw your perception of the extended self of a close friend or family member. How are they different? How are they similar?
2. Lori has just graduated from a state university in the southern United States, where she shared an apartment with some friends she's known since high school. She has taken a job with a medium-sized manufacturing company in the Midwest and has rented a small, one-bedroom apartment about two miles from her new office. Would you expect Lori's self-concept to change? Explain.
3. How could the concept of desired selves be used to develop marketing strategy for
   a. Health clubs
   b. Bath soaps
   c. Sports cars
   d. Cosmetics
   e. Cruises
   f. Towels
4. Some research suggests that individuals focus on whatever aspects of themselves are most distinctive in a particular social setting or situation. How could this finding be used by an advertiser? Describe the target market and the nature of an appeal for swimming suits.
5. Think about features of your own home or your parent's home. Can you relate these features to your personality or the personalities of your parents? Explain.
6. Build your own set of examples to illustrate the relationship between self-concept and the circle of consumption. (*Hint:* In the book we used examples related to the kitchen.)
7. Add more entries to Industry Insights 10.1a. For instance, identify a specialty product other than a luxury car. Find an ad for that product, and identify the target audience for that ad. What is the main appeal in the ad? Is that appeal related to a product attribute or to a desired self-concept? In the same way, find an ad for an intangible service and repeat the assignment.
8. Think of a brand that you frequently purchase and list the characteristics and image of that brand. If that brand were a person, what kind of person would that brand be? What is the brand's personality? Now, make a list of personality traits that describe who you are. Compare the two personality lists (your personality and your favorite brand's personality). How are these lists alike? How are they different? Why do you like this brand?

YOU MAKE THE CALL

SHOULD YOU GET AN MBA?

After college, Tad Glauthier didn't have much of a career plan. He knocked around as a ski instructor, then as a TV sitcom stand-in. But when he decided at the age of 28 to get serious, he applied to one of the most respected career-building institutions in capitalism: Stanford University's Graduate School of Business (GSB). "I thought B-school would catch me up," he says.

Asked about his educational experience, he fails to mention the 4Ps, discounted cash flow analysis, the chi-square test, or any other morsels of wisdom from the MBA curriculum. Instead he cites his role as executive producer of the 2002 GSB student musical and "All About Beer," a one-week elective about organizational dynamics in the brewing industry. As for his future? Glauthier hopes to start a business he describes as "a cross between *Moulin Rouge* (the movie), Angkor Wat (the temple), and Burning Man (the anti-marketing festival)—in a supper club."

But an upcoming study by Jeffrey Pfeffer, a management professor at Glauthier's own business alma mater, Stanford, challenges the bedrock assumption of business school: that those who make the effort to get an MBA degree have more successful careers than those who don't. Pfeffer combs through 40 years' worth of data for evidence that this is true—and uncovers almost none.

So, is an MBA worth the investment? In the wake of a scolding report from the Association to Advance Collegiate Schools of Business (AACSB) about lack of relevance, and Pfeffer's study—and the on-the-ground experience of consulting firms and other employers—it's hard to maintain that learning what's taught in B-school will make you a business leader. But the question is broader than that.

For one thing, there's more to a B-school education than the curriculum. Two years of shared projects and all-nighters link graduates in a social network that would take years to reproduce in the real world. Employers these days give more weight to your experience than to your degree, but they're still more likely to favor people they know. Harvard's famously close-knit MBA network is a huge leg up. There's also the screening effect: Employers assume, with some justification, that someone who managed to get into an elite school (and pay the tuition, to boot) is ambitious, intelligent, and motivated. But are a foot in recruiters' doors and a supercharged Rolodex really worth two years of your life and a total investment that could top $100,000? It depends on how hard it would be for you to re-create them outside B-school—and how much your career path depends on such advantages. Even Pfeffer concedes that they are worth something. "The connections, the networking, the 'being anointed'—all that has value," he says. "What we are questioning is whether the education has value."

Ironically, one group that seems to have no doubts about the MBA is the one most at risk—the students. Applications are at record levels again this year, and according to a *Business 2.0* survey, those who have the degree view a rich, rewarding career as all but ensured. Indeed U.S. MBA programs are a global magnet for ambitious students from all over the globe, and U.S.-style MBA programs have cropped up in nations as diverse as France, Australia, India, and China.

Presented with the news that his MBA does not ensure him a fabulous career, Glauthier brings up that beer class again. That's because one day, Pete Slosberg—founder of Pete's Brewing—showed up as a guest lecturer and floated an idea for a startup. Glauthier and some classmates showed interest, so Slosberg invited them to write a business plan. Two weeks after spring break, Slosberg had the company funded and Glauthier had an offer to work for it: competitive salary, options vesting over four years.

Glauthier politely declined so he could get moving on the supper club project. And for him, that's proof enough that his MBA experience has prepared him for a rewarding career. "Salary is important, but the real measure of success is your ability to go after your dreams," he says. "That sounds pretty Disney, but I suspect I just turned down a job that would have made me a lot more money."

In this way, Glauthier is not unlike many MBA graduates *Business 2.0* surveyed. If they appear to be money-grubbers set for the good life, they'd say it isn't so. At the top of their list of important post-graduation values: leadership, integrity, a caring family life, and discipline. And Kristin Greene, a 30-year-old graduate of the Wharton School at the University of Pennsylvania, says business school gave her skills that she hadn't developed during her five years as a management consultant in New York and Tokyo. "It taught me the importance of teamwork," she says.

Source: Damon Darlin, "Tomorrow Belongs to Them," Business 2.0, *July 2002, pp. 46, 48, 50; and Andy Raskin, "So What's an MBA Really Worth,"* Business 2.0, *July 2002, pp. 40, 42–44.*

QUESTIONS

1. How might concepts in this chapter help us to understand a person's decision to seek an MBA?
2. How might the concept of the extended self help us explain the value of Harvard's MBA network?
3. How might the concept of consumer self-narratives help account for the enduring popularity of MBA programs?
4. Do you think MBA students on average would score higher or lower on a measure of self-monitoring than the average person? Justify your answer.
5. Do you think MBA students on average would score higher or lower on a measure of need for cognition than the average person? Justify your answer.

1. Özlem Sandikci and Güliz Ger, "In-Between Modernities and Postmodernities: Theorizing Turkish Consumptionscape," in *Advances in Consumer Research,* vol. 29, ed. Susan Broniarczyk and Kent Nakamoto (Provo, UT: Association for Consumer Research, 2002).
2. For theory and research consistent with this definition, see Valerie S. Folkes and Tina Kiesler, "Social Cognition: Consumers' Inferences about the Self and Others," in *Handbook of Consumer Behavior,* ed. Thomas S. Robertson and Harold H. Kassarjian (Englewood Cliffs, NJ: Prentice Hall, 1991), pp. 281–315; Hazel Markus, "Self-Schemata and Processing Information about the Self," *Journal of Personality and Social Psychology* 35 (February 1977), pp. 63–78; and Beth A. Walker and Jerry C. Olson, "The Activated Self and Consumer Behavior: A Cognitive Structure Perspective," working paper, Arizona State University, 1993.
3. This section draws on the work of Hazel Markus, who is arguably the most influential contemporary psychologist doing research on the self. See, for example, Hazel Markus and Elissa Wurf, "The Dynamic Self-Concept: A Social Psychological Perspective," *Annual Review of Psychology* 38 (1987), pp. 299–337. An excellent review of how cognitive processes influence ways in which consumers think about the self and the relationship of self-concept to consumer behavior is provided in Folkes and Kiesler, "Social Cognition."
4. Eugene Sivadas and Karen A. Machleit, "A Scale to Determine the Extent of Object Incorporation in the Extended Self," in *Marketing Theory and Applications,* vol. 5, ed. C. Whan Park and Daniel C. Smith (Chicago: American Marketing Association, 1994), pp. 143–49.

5. This conception of the self largely follows ideas presented in George Herbert Mead, *Mind, Self, and Society* (Chicago: University of Chicago Press, 1934); Godwin C. Chu, "The Changing Concept of Self in Contemporary China," in *Culture and Self: Asian and Western Perspectives,* ed. Anthony J. Marsella, George Devos, and Francis L.K. Hsu (New York: Tavistock Publications, 1985), pp. 252–77; and Brian Morris, *Anthropology of the Self: The Individual in Cultural Perspective* (London and Boulder, CO: Pluto Press, 1994).

6. For a general theory and some empirical support, see Alan R. Andreasen, "Life Status Changes and Changes in Consumer Preferences and Satisfaction," *Journal of Consumer Research* 11 (December 1984), pp. 784–94. Several recent treatments examine this topic in specific contexts. For example, see Melissa Martin Young, "Disposition of Possessions during Role Transitions," in *Advances in Consumer Research,* vol. 18, ed. Michael Solomon and Rebecca Holman (Provo, UT: Association for Consumer Research, 1990), pp. 33–39. Teresa Pavia, "Dispossession and Perceptions of Self in Late Stage HIV Infection," in *Advances in Consumer Research,* vol. 20, ed. Leigh McAlister and Michael L. Rothschild (Provo, UT: Association for Consumer Research, 1993), pp. 425–28, balances out perspective by showing how much more important loss of control of self-defining activities and behaviors (such as jobs) is than loss of possessions.

7. For an insightful review of the relationship between personality, the core self, and the self-schema that gets activated in a particular purchase or consumption situation, see Walker and Olson, "The Activated Self and Consumer Behavior."

8. Harold H. Kassarjian and Mary Jane Sheffet, "Personality and Consumer Behavior: An Update," in *Perspectives in Consumer Behavior,* 4th ed., ed. Harold H. Kassarjian and Thomas S. Robertson (Englewood Cliffs, NJ: Prentice Hall, 1991), pp. 281–303.

9. Curtis R. Haugtvedt, Richard E. Petty, and John T. Cacioppo, "Need for Cognition and Advertising: Understanding the Role of Personality Variables in Consumer Behavior," *Journal of Consumer Psychology* 1, no. 3 (1992), pp. 239–60; Carl G. Jung, *Man and His Symbols* (Garden City, NY: Doubleday, 1964); David Glen Mick and Claus Buhl, "A Meaning-Based Model of Advertising Experiences," *Journal of Consumer Research* 19 (December 1992), pp. 317–38; John P. Robinson, Phillip R. Shaver, and Lawrence S. Wrightsman, eds., *Measures of Personality and Social Psychological Attitudes* (San Diego: Academic Press, 1991); Leon G. Schiffman, William R. Dillon, and Festus E. Nkrumah, "The Influence of Subcultural and Personality Factors on Consumer Acculturation," *Journal of International Business Studies,* Fall 1981, pp. 137–43; Mark Snyder and Kenneth G. DeBono, "Appeals to Image and Claims about Quality: Understanding the Psychology of Advertising," *Journal of Personality and Social Psychology,* September 1985, pp. 586–97; and Bernard Weiner, "Attribution in Personality Psychology," in *Handbook of Personality: Theory and Research,* ed. Lawrence A. Pervin (New York: Guilford, 1990), pp. 465–84.

10. Harold H. Kassarjian, "Social Character and Differential Preference for Mass Communication," *Journal of Marketing Research* 2 (May 1965), pp. 146–53; and J. W. Hong and George M. Zinkhan, "Self-Concept and Advertising Effectiveness: The Influence of Congruency and Response Mode," *Psychology & Marketing* 12, no. 1 (1995), pp. 53–77.

11. William O. Bearden, Richard G. Netemeyer, and Mary F. Mobley, *Handbook of Marketing Scales: Multi-Item Measures for Marketing and Consumer Behavior Research* (London: Sage Publications, 1993).

12. David Riesman, *The Lonely Crowd* (New Haven: Yale University Press, 1950).

13. Kassarjian and Sheffet, "Personality and Consumer Behavior: An Update."

14. R. R. McCrae, P. T. Costs Jr., G. H Del Pilar, J.-P. Rolland, and W. D. Parker, "Cross-Cultural Assessment of the Five Factor Model: The Revised NEO Personality Inventory," *Journal of Cross-Cultural Psychology* 29 (1998), pp. 171–88; Woonbong Na and Roger Marshall, "Validation of the 'Big Five' Personality Traits in Korea: A Comparative Approach," *Journal of International Consumer Marketing* 12, no. 1 (1999), pp. 5–19; and Samp V. Paunonen, Moshe Zeidner, Harald A. Engvik, Paul Oosterveld, and Rodney Maliphant, "The Nonverbal Assessment of Personality in Five Cultures," *Journal of Cross-Cultural Psychology* 31 (March 2000), pp. 220–39.

15. Kassarjian and Sheffet, "Personality and Consumer Behavior: An Update."

16. The work of William J. McGuire and his colleagues is especially important in breaking free of reactive measures of self. See, for example, W. J. McGuire, "Search for the Self: Going beyond

Self-Esteem and the Reactive Self," in *Personality and the Prediction of Behavior,* ed. R. A. Zucker, J. Aronoff, and A. I. Rabin (New York: Academic Press, 1984), pp. 73–120. Work on personal projects is reviewed in Brian R. Little, "Personal Projects: A Rationale and Method for Investigation," *Environment and Behavior* 15 (May 1983), pp. 273–309. A fun novel built around an important personal project is Tracy Kidder, *House* (Boston: Houghton Mifflin, 1985).

17. This example is taken from Nancy Giges, "Buying Linked to Self-Esteem," *Advertising Age,* April 13, 1987, p. 68.

18. Susan Harter, "Vision of Self: Beyond the Me in the Mirror," in *Developmental Perspectives on Motivation,* ed. J. E. Jacobs (Proceedings of the Nebraska Symposium on Motivations, Lincoln: University of Nebraska Press, 1993), pp. 99–144.

19. For a general discussion of the relationship between self-esteem and addictive and compulsive behaviors, see D. Krueger, "On Compulsive Shopping and Spending: A Psychodynamic Inquiry," *American Journal of Psychotherapy* 42 (1988), p. 454. On compulsive buying, see Thomas O'Guinn and Ronald Faber, "Compulsive Buying: A Phenomenological Exploration," *Journal of Consumer Research* 16 (1989), pp. 147–57; Alice Hanley and Mari S. Wilhelm, "Compulsive Buying: An Exploration into Self-Esteem and Money Attitudes," *Journal of Economic Psychology* 13 (1992), pp. 5–18; James A. Roberts and Carlos Ruy Martinez, "The Emerging Consumer Culture in Mexico: An Exploratory Investigation of Compulsive Buying in Mexican Young Adults," *Journal of International Consumer Marketing* 10, no. 1–2 (1997), pp. 7–32; James A. Roberts and Cesar J. Sepulveda M., "Money Attitudes and Compulsive Buying: An Exploratory Investigation of the Emerging Consumer Culture," *Journal of International Consumer Marketing* 11, no. 4 (1999), pp. 53–74; Gerhard Scherhord, Lucia A. Reisch, and Gerard Raab, "Addictive Buying in West Germany: An Empirical Study," *Journal of Consumer Policy* 13, no. 4 (1990), pp. 355–87; and J. Trachtenberg, "Shop Until You Drop?" *Forbes,* January 11, 1988, p. 40.

20. Denis Guiot, "Subjective Age Biases among Adolescent Girls," in *Advances in Consumer Research,* vol. 27, eds. Steven J. Hoch and Robert J. Meyer (Provo, UT: Association for Consumer Research, 2000), pp. 215–23; William O. Bearden and Randall L. Rose, "Attention to Social Comparison Information: An Individual Difference Factor Affecting Consumer Conformity," *Journal of Consumer Research* 16 (March 1990), pp. 461–71; William O. Bearden, Richard G. Netemeyer, and Jesse E. Teel, "Measurement of Consumer Susceptibility to Interpersonal Influence," *Journal of Consumer Research* 15 (March 1989), pp. 473–81; Rachel Maldonado and Patriya Tansuhaj, "The Relationship between Self-Esteem and Latino Consumer Acculturation," in *Advances in Consumer Research,* vol. 25, ed. Joseph W. Alba and J. Wesley Hutchinson (Provo, UT: Association for Consumer Research, 1998), pp. 252–57; and Gregory M. Rose, David M. Boush, and Marian Friestad, "Self-Esteem, Susceptibility to Interpersonal Influence, and Fashion Attribute Preference in Early Adolescents," in *European Advances in Consumer Research,* vol. 3, ed. Basil Englis and Anna Olofsson (Provo, UT: Association for Consumer Research, 1998), pp. 197–203.

21. S. Grunert and R. Rohme, "Consumers' Environmental Concern: Are We Really Tapping True Concern That Relates to Environmentally Ethic Behavior?" presented at the *ESOMAR Conference on Marketing Research and a New World Order* (Amsterdam: ESOMAR, 1992); Pam Scholder Ellen, Joshua L. Weiner, and C. Cobb-Algren, "The Role of Perceived Consumer Effectiveness in Motivating Environmentally Conscious Behaviors," *Journal of Public Policy and Marketing* 10 (Fall 1991), pp. 102–17; and Pam Scholder Ellen, William O. Bearden, and Subhash Sharma, "Resistance to Technological Innovations: An Examination of the Role of Self Efficacy and Performance Satisfaction," *Journal of the Academy of Marketing Science* 19, no. 4 (1991), pp. 297–307.

22. Gillian Rice, Nittaya Wongtada, and Orose Leelakulthanit, "An Investigation of Self-Efficacy and Environmentally Concerned Behavior of Thai Consumers," *Journal of International Consumer Marketing* 9, no. 2 (1996), pp. 1–21.

23. George M. Zinkhan and Ali Shermohamed, "Is Other-Directedness on the Increase? An Empirical Test of Riesman's Theory of Social Character," *Journal of Consumer Research* 13, no. 1 (1986), pp. 127–30.

24. Hans Baumgartner, "An Exploratory Investigation of Holistic and Analytic Modes of Product Perception," in *Advances in Consumer Research,* vol. 20, ed. Leigh McAlister and Michael Rothschild (Provo, UT: Association for Consumer Research, 1993), pp. 673–77; J. Jeffrey Inman, Anil

C. Peter, and Priya Raghubir, "Framing the Deal: The Role of Restrictions in Accentuating Deal Value," *Journal of Consumer Research* 24 (June 1997), pp. 68–79; Donald R. Lichtenstein, Scot Burton, and Richard G. Netemeyer, "Psychological Correlates of a Proneness to Deals: A Domain-Specific Analysis," in *Advances in Consumer Research,* vol. 24, ed. Merrie Brucks and Debbie MacInnis (Provo, UT: Association for Consumer Research, 1997), pp. 274–80; Susan Powell Mantel and Frank R. Kardes, "The Role of Direction of Comparison, Attribute-Based Processing, and Attitude-Based Processing in Consumer Preference," *Journal of Consumer Research* 25 (March 1999), pp. 335–52; James W. Peltier and John A. Schibrowsky, "Need for Cognition, Advertisement Viewing Time and Memory for Advertising Stimuli," in *Advances in Consumer Research,* vol. 21, ed. Chris Allen and Deborah Roedder John (Provo, UT: Association for Consumer Research, 1994), pp. 244–50; and Michael Sherrard and Ronald Czaja, "Extending Two Need for Cognition Scales: Need for Cognition and Need for Evaluation for Use in a Health Intervention," in *European Advances in Consumer Research,* vol. 4, eds. Bernard Dubois, Tina M. Lowry, L. J. Shrum, and Marc Venhuele (Provo, UT: Association for Consumer Research, 1999), pp. 135–42.

25. Narasimhan Srinivasan and Surinder Tikoo, "Effect of Locus of Control on Information Search Behavior," in *Advances in Consumer Research,* vol. 19, ed. John Sherry and Brian Sternthal (Provo, UT: Association for Consumer Research, 1992), pp. 498–504.

26. William K. Darley and Jeen-Su Lim, "Family Decision Making in Leisure-Time Activities: An Exploratory Investigation of the Impact of Locus of Control, Child Age Influence Factor and Parental Type on Perceived Child Influence," in *Advances in Consumer Research,* vol. 13, ed. Richard Lutz (Provo, UT: Association for Consumer Research, 1986), pp. 370–74.

27. Subhash C. Mehta and Kau Ah Keng, "Correlates of Materialism: A Study of Singaporean Chinese," *Historical Perspective in Consumer Research: National and International Perspectives* (Provo, UT: Association for Consumer Research, 1985), pp. 326–30.

28. Joseph A. Cote and Patriya S. Tansuhaj, "Culture Bound Assumptions in Behavior Intention Models," in *Advances in Consumer Research,* vol. 16, ed. Thomas Srull (Provo, UT: Association for Consumer Research, 1989), pp. 105–109.

29. Gary Ko and James W. Gentry, "The Development of Time Orientation Measures for Use in Cross-Cultural Research," in *Advances in Consumer Research,* vol. 18, ed. Rebecca Holman and Michael Solomon (Provo, UT: Association for Consumer Research, 1991) pp. 135–42.

30. For a summary of individual difference measures used in studying consumer behavior, see William Bearden and Richard Netemeyer, eds., *Handbook of Marketing Scales* (Walnut Creek, CA: AltaMira Press, 1998). For excellent reviews of predicting behavior with personality, see Seymour Epstein, "The Stability of Behavior: I. On Predicting Most of the People Much of the Time," *Journal of Personality and Social Psychology* 37 (July 1979), pp. 1097–126; and Seymour Epstein, "The Stability of Behavior: II. Implications for Psychological Research," *American Psychologist* 35 (September 1980), pp. 790–806.

31. J. Michael Munson and W. Austin Spivey, "Assessing Self Concept," in *Advances in Consumer Research,* vol. 7, ed. Jerry C. Olson (Ann Arbor, MI: Association for Consumer Research, 1980), pp. 598–603.

32. Richard Elliott, "Existential Consumption and Irrational Desire," *European Journal of Marketing* 31, nos. 3–4 (1997), pp. 256–89; E. Grubb and H. Grathwohl, "Consumer Self-Concept, Symbolism and Market Behavior: A Theoretical Approach," *Journal of Marketing* 31 (October 1967), pp. 22–27; Margaret K. Hogg, Alastair J. Cox, and Kathy Keeling, "The Impact of Self-Monitoring on Image Congruence and Product/Brand Evaluation," *European Journal of Marketing* 34, nos. 5–6 (2000), pp. 641–67; Rebecca H. Holman, "Clothing as Communication: An Empirical Investigation," in *Advances in Consumer Research,* vol. 7, ed. Jerry C. Olson (Ann Arbor, MI: Association for Consumer Research, 1980), pp. 372–77; and M. Joseph Sirgy, "Self-Concept in Consumer Behavior: A Critical Review," *Journal of Consumer Research* 9 (December 1982), pp. 287–99.

33. Russell B. Belk, "Possessions and the Extended Self," *Journal of Consumer Research* 15 (September 1988), pp. 139–68; and Russell B. Belk, "My Possessions Myself," *Psychology Today,* July–August 1988, pp. 50–52.

34. A touching portrayal of how self-concept is related to body parts is provided in Marilynn J. Phillips, "Damaged Goods: Oral Narratives of the Experience of Disability in American

Culture," *Social Science Medicine* 30, no. 8 (1990), pp. 849–57. She talked with 33 people with visible physical disabilities. These conversations revealed how disability frames social interactions between disabled and nondisabled individuals and how such interactions affect the self-images of disabled persons. The narratives reveal that society perceived disabled persons to be damaged goods, and the popular media of language and images perpetuate the notion of the wrongness of their bodies. Not surprisingly, the self-concept of disabled individuals is dramatically influenced by these cultural themes.

35. Russell W. Belk, *Collecting in a Consumer Society (Collecting Cultures)* (London and New York: Routledge, 1995); Kimberly J. Dodson, "Peak Experiences and Mountain Biking: Incorporating the Bike into the Extended Self," in *Advances in Consumer Research,* vol. 23, ed. Kim Corfman and John Lynch (Provo, UT: Association for Consumer Research, 1996), pp. 317–22; Elizabeth C. Hirschman, "Consumers and Their Animal Companions," *Journal of Consumer Research* 20 (March 1994), pp. 616–32; Eugene Sivadas and Ravi Venkatesh, "An Examination of Individual and Object-Specific Influences on the Extended Self and Its Relation to Attachment and Satisfaction," in *Advances in Consumer Research,* vol. 22, ed. Frank Kardes and Mita Sujan (Provo, UT: Association for Consumer Research, 1995), pp. 406–12; and Anne M. Velliquette, Jeff B. Murray, and Elizabeth H. Creyer, "The Tattoo Renaissance: An Ethnographic Account of Symbolic Consumer Behavior," in *Advances in Consumer Research,* vol. 25, ed. Joseph W. Alba and J. Wesley Hutchinson (Provo, UT: Association for Consumer Research, 1998), pp. 461–67.

36. Peter Canby, *The Heart of the Sky: Travels among the Maya* (New York: HarperCollins, 1992), pp. 23–24; Deborah Durham, "The Predicament of Dress: Polyvalency and the Ironies of Cultural Identity," *American Ethnologist* 26 (May 1999), pp. 389–411; Barbara Olsen, "Consuming Rastafari: Ethnographic Research in Context and Meaning," in *Advances in Consumer Research,* vol. 22, ed. Frank Kardos and Mita Sujan (Provo, UT: Association for Consumer Research, 1995), pp. 481–85; and http://www3.itu.ch/virtexh/botswana/botdoll4.htm.

37. Dodson, "Peak Experiences and Mountain Biking"; and Arlene Weintraub, "For Online Pet Stores, It's Dog-Eat-Dog," *Business Week,* March 6, 2000, pp. 78, 80.

38. McGuire and his colleagues have done quite a bit of work on how individuals selectively represent the self. Their research suggests how many aspects of the situation affect the self that's represented. See, for example, William J. McGuire and Claire V. McGuire, "Content and Process in the Experience of Self," *Advances in Experimental Social Psychology* 21 (1988), pp. 97–144. A nice paper that draws the connection between the activated self and consumer behavior in various situations is Walker and Olson, "The Activated Self and Consumer Behavior."

39. Søren Askegaard, Dannie Kjeldgaard, and Eric J. Arnould, "Identity and Acculturation: The Case of Food Consumption by Greenlanders in Denmark," paper presented at the First International Conference on Consumption and Representation, Plymouth, UK, September 1–3, 1999.

40. Jean C. Darian, "Social Marketing and Consumer Behavior: Influencing the Decision to Reduce Alcohol Consumption," in *Advances in Consumer Research,* vol. 20, ed. Leigh McAlister and Michael L. Rothschild (Provo, UT: Association for Consumer Research, 1993), pp. 413–18. See also John L. Lastovicka, John P. Murray Jr., Erich A. Joachimsthaler, Gaurav Bhalla, and Jim Scheurich, "A Lifestyle Typology to Model Young Male Drinking and Driving," *Journal of Consumer Research* 14 (September 1987), pp. 257–63.

41. Craig J. Thompson and Diana L. Haytko, "Speaking of Fashion: Consumers' Use of Fashion Discourse and the Appropriation of Countervailing Cultural Meanings," *Journal of Consumer Research* 24 (June 1997), pp. 15–42; and Fred Davis, *Fashion, Culture, and Identity* (Chicago: University of Chicago Press, 1994). For a collection of readings on how the clothing we buy and wear reflects our identities, see Juliet Ash and Elizabeth Wilson, eds., *Chic Thrills: A Fashion Reader* (Berkeley: University of California Press, 1993).

42. Munson and Spivey, "Assessing Self-Concept." This discussion is adapted from Walker and Olson, "The Activated Self and Consumer Behavior," which provide a richer discussion of the role of products in triggering the working self or activated self.

43. This research was based on the authors' investigation of "really me" experiences, purchases, and possessions of graduate and undergraduate business students at two different state universities.

44. Hazel Markus, "Self-Schemata and Processing Information about the Self," *Journal of Personality and Social Psychology* 35 (February 1977), pp. 63–78; and Hazel Markus and Keith Sentis, "The Self in Social Information Processing," in *Psychological Perspectives on the Self,* ed. Jerry Suls (Hillsdale, NJ: Erlbaum, 1982), pp. 41–70.
45. Hazel Marcus and Paula Narius, "Possible Selves," *American Psychologist* 41 (September 1986), pp. 954–69, discuss the motivating power of "possible selves." They note that possible selves function as incentives for behavior and provide an evaluative and interpretive context for the current view of self.
46. Amy J. Morgan, "The Evolving Self in Consumer Behavior: Exploring Possible Selves," in *Advances in Consumer Research,* vol. 20, ed. Leigh McAlister and Michael L. Rothschild (Provo, UT: Association for Consumer Research, 1993), pp. 429–32.
47. Norman K. Denzin, "Rain Man in Las Vegas," *Symbolic Interaction* 16, no. 1 (1993), pp. 65–77.
48. For some of the research on this topic, see Edward T. Higgins, "Self-Discrepancy: A Theory Relating Self and Affect," *Psychological Review* 94 (July 1987), pp. 319–40; Patricia Linville, "Self Complexity as a Cognitive Buffer against Stress-Related Illness and Depression," *Journal of Personality and Social Psychology* 52 (April 1997), pp. 663–76, on self-concept complexity; and Paula R. Pietromonaco, Jean Manis, and Katherine Frohart-Lane, "Self-Complexity as a Cognitive Buffer Against Stress-Related Illness and Depression," *Psychology of Women Quarterly* 10, no. 4 (December 1986), pp. 373–81, on integrating identities with each other.
49. The J. Peterman Company, *Owner's Manual,* no. 14 (1991), cited in Amy J. Morgan, "The Evolving Self in Consumer Behavior: Exploring Possible Selves," in *Advances in Consumer Research,* vol. 20, ed. Leigh McAlister and Michael L. Rothschild (Provo, UT: Association for Consumer Research, 1993), p. 431.
50. Andreasen, "Life Status Changes and Changes in Consumer Preferences and Satisfaction."
51. T. R. Reid, *Confucius Lives Next Door* (New York: Vintage Books, 1999), pp. 161–66.
52. Shay Sayre, *Consumption, Markets, and Culture* 3, no. 2 (1999), pp. 99–128; and John Schouten, "Selves in Transition: Symbolic Consumption in Personal Rites of Passage and Identity Reconstruction," *Journal of Consumer Research,* March 17, 1991, pp. 412–25.
53. Eileen Fischer and Brenda Gainer, "Baby Showers: A Rite of Passage in Transition," in *Advances in Consumer Research,* vol. 20, ed. Leigh McAlister and Michael L. Rothschild (Provo, UT: Association for Consumer Research, 1993), pp. 320–24; Cele Otnes and Tina M. Lowry, "'Til Debt Do Us Part: The Selection and Meaning of Artifacts in the American Wedding," in *Advances in Consumer Research,* vol. 20, ed. Leigh McAlister and Michael L. Rothschild (Provo, UT: Association for Consumer Research, 1993), pp. 325–29; and Reid, *Confucius Lives Next Door,* pp. 153–55.
54. Jennifer Edson Escalas, "Advertising Narratives: What Are They and How Do They Work?" in *The Why of Consumption: Contemporary Perspectives on Consumer Motives, Goals, and Desires,* ed. S. Ratneshwar, David Glen Mick, and Cynthia Huffman (New York and London: Routledge, 2000); Clifford Geertz, "Making Experiences, Authoring Selves," in *The Anthropology of Experience,* ed. Victor W. Turner and Edward M. Bruner (Urbana: University of Illinois Press, 1986), pp. 373–80; Kenneth J. Gergen and Mary M. Gergen, "Narrative and the Self as Relationship," in *Advances in Experimental Social Psychology,* vol. 21, ed. Leonard Berkowitz (San Diego: Academic Press, 1988), pp. 17–56; Kristin M. Langellier, "Personal Narratives: Perspectives on Theory and Research," *Text and Performance Quarterly* 9 (October 1989), pp. 243–76; and Theodore R. Sarbin, ed., *Narrative Psychology* (New York: Praeger, 1986).
55. C. B. Claiborne and Julie L. Ozanne, "The Meaning of Custom-Made Homes: Home as a Metaphor for Living," in *Advances in Consumer Research,* vol. 17, ed. Marvin E. Goldberg, Gerald Gorn, and Richard W. Pollay (Provo, UT: Association for Consumer Research, 1990), pp. 367–74; and Linda L. Price, Eric J. Arnould, and Carolyn Curasi, "Older Consumer's Disposition of Cherished Possessions," *Journal of Consumer Research* 27 (September 2000), pp. 179–201.
56. Clinton R. Sanders, *Customizing the Body: The Art and Culture of Tattooing* (Philadelphia: Temple University Press, 1989), p. 43. See also Kathleen A. O'Donnell, "Good Girls Gone Bad: The Consumption of Fetish Fashion and the Sexual Empowerment of Women," in *Advances in*

Consumer Research, vol. 26, ed. Eric J. Arnould and Linda Scott (Provo, UT: Association for Consumer Research, 1999), pp. 184–89. Similar examples of the use of consumption to give agency and coherence to life narratives is provided in Eric J. Arnould and Linda L. Price, "Questing for Self and Community in Post Modernity," in *The Why of Consumption: Contemporary Perspectives on Consumer Motives, Goals, and Desires,* ed. S. Ratneshwar, David Glen Mick, and Cynthia Huffman (New York and London: Routledge, 2000).

57. Richard L. Celsi, Randall L. Rose, and Thomas W. Leigh, "An Exploration of High-Risk Leisure Consumption through Skydiving," *Journal of Consumer Research* 20 (June 1993), pp. 1–23; Eric J. Arnould and Linda L. Price, "River Magic: Extraordinary Experience and the Extended Service Encounter," *Journal of Consumer Research* 20 (June 1993), pp. 24–45; and Jerry Adler, Daniel Glick, Patricia King, Jeanne Gordon, and Alden Cohen, "Been There, Done That," *Newsweek,* July 19, 1993, pp. 42–49.

58. Folkes and Kiesler, "Social Cognition"; and Anthony G. Greenwald and Anthony R. Pratkanis, "The Self," in *Handbook of Social Cognition,* vol. 3, ed. Robert S. Wyer Jr. and Thomas K. Srull (Hillsdale, NJ: Erlbaum, 1984), pp. 129–78.

59. The name-letter effect is documented in Joseph R. Nuttin, *Motivation Planning and Action: A Relational Theory of Behavioral Dynamics* (Hillsdale, NJ: Lawrence Erlbaum, 1984). Markus and Wurf, "The Dynamic Self-Concept," provide a review of this literature. Herbert A. Simon, *Reason in Human Affairs* (Stanford: Stanford University Press, 1991), and Richard E. Nisbett and Lee Ross, *Human Inference: Strategies and Shortcomings of Social Judgment* (Englewood Cliffs, NJ: Prentice Hall, 1980), are also good references for these kinds of self-relevant stimuli effects.

60. Newell D. Wright, D. B. Claiborne, and M. Joseph Sirgy, "The Effects of Product Symbolism on Consumer Self-Concept," in *Advances in Consumer Research,* vol. 19, ed. John Sherry and Brian Sernthal (Provo, UT: Association for Consumer Research, 1992), pp. 311–18.

61. Anthony G. Greenwald and Clark Leavitt, "Audience Involvement in Advertising: Four Levels," *Journal of Consumer Research* 11 (June 1984), pp. 581–92; Michael L. Rothschild, "Perspectives in Involvement: Current Problems and Future Directions," in *Advances in Consumer Research,* vol. 11, ed. Tom Kinnear (Ann Arbor, MI: Association for Consumer Research, 1984), pp. 216–17.

62. For a discussion of how drugs and alcohol are used to protect self-representations see Jay G. Hull, Ronald R. Van Treuran, Susan J. Ashford, Pamela Propsom, and Bruce W. Andrus, "Self Consciousness and the Processing of Self-Relevant Information," *Journal of Personality and Social Psychology* 54 (March 1988), pp. 452 65. For a more general discussion of self-serving biases and how they affect information processing, see Anthony G. Greenwald, "The Totalitarian Ego: Fabrication and Revision of Personal History," *American Psychologist* 35 (1980), pp. 603–18.

63. David Glen Mick and Michelle DeMoss, "Self-Gifts: Phenomenological Insights from Four Contexts," *Journal of Consumer Research* 17 (December 1990), p. 325.

64. Peter H. Bloch and Marsha L. Richins, "You Look 'Marvelous': The Pursuit of Beauty and the Marketing Concept," *Psychology and Marketing* 9 (January 1992), pp. 3–15; Philip N. Myers and Frank A. and Biocca, "The Elastic Body Image: The Effect of Television Advertising and Programming on Body Image Distortion in Young Women," *Journal of Communication* 42 (Summer 1992), pp. 108–16; and Marsha L. Richins, "Social Comparison and the Idealized Images of Advertising," *Journal of Consumer Research* 18 (June 1991), pp. 71–83.

65. Craig J. Thompson and Elizabeth C. Hirschman, "Understanding the Socialized Body: A Poststructuralist Analysis of Consumers' Self-Conceptions, Body Images, and Self-Care Practices," *Journal of Consumer Research* 22 (September 1995), pp. 139–53; Elizabeth C. Hirschman, "The Consciousness of Addiction: Toward a General Theory of Compulsive Consumption," *Journal of Consumer Research* 19 (September 1992), pp. 155–79; and Melanie Wells, "Smooth Operator," *Forbes,* May 13, 2002, pp. 167–68.

66. Barry R. Schlenker, *Impression Management: The Self-Concept, Social Identity, and Interpersonal Relations* (Melbourne, FL: Krieger, 1980), introduces the concept of desired selves. Robert A. Wickund and Peter M. Gollwitzer, *Symbolic Self-Completion* (Hillsdale, NJ: Lawrence Erlbaum, 1982), stress the importance of commitment to these self-definitions in motivating behavior. For a review of literature on the relationship between self-concept and product preference, see Sirgy, "Self-Concept in Consumer Behavior."

67. George M. Zinkhan, Diana Haytko, and Allison Ward, "Self-Concept Theory: Applications in Advertising," *Journal of Marketing Communications* 2 (1996), pp. 1–19.
68. Ibid.
69. Marsha Richins, "Valuing Things: The Public and Private Meanings of Possession," *Journal of Consumer Research* 21 (December 1994), pp. 504–21. For research on the relationship between self-concept and social perception, see G. G. Sherwood, "Self-Serving Biases in Person Perception: A Reexamination of Projection as a Mechanism of Defense," *Psychological Bulletin* 90 (1981), pp. 445–59. B. R. Schlenker provides a discussion of the relationship between self-concept and relationships in Barry R. Schlenker, ed., *The Self and Social Life* (New York: McGraw-Hill, 1985).
70. Mark Ritson, Richard Elliot, and Sue Eccles, "Reframing IKEA: Commodity-Signs, Consumer Creativity, and the Social/Self Dialectic," in *Advances in Consumer Research,* vol. 23, ed. Kim Corfman and John Lynch (Provo, UT: Association for Consumer Research, 1996), pp. 127–31; and Ajay K. Sirsi, James C. Ward, and Peter H. Reingen, "Microcultural Analysis of Variation in Sharing of Causal Reasoning about Behavior," *Journal of Consumer Research* 22 (March 1996), pp. 345–72.
71. The psychology of self-monitoring is developed extensively by Mark Snyder in numerous articles and books. A fairly comprehensive treatment of the topic is provided in Mark Snyder, *Public Appearances Private Realities: The Psychology of Self-Monitoring* (New York: W. H. Freeman and Company, 1987).
72. Susan Auty and Richart Elliot, and "'Reading' Advertising and 'Writing' Identity," in *Advances in Consumer Research,* vol. 26, ed. Eric J. Arnould and Linda M. Scott (Provo, UT: Association for Consumer Research), pp. 439–44; and Margaret K. Hogg, Alastair J. Cox, and Kathy Keeling, "The Impact of Self-Monitoring on Image Congruence and Product/Brand Evaluation," *European Journal of Marketing,* 34, nos. 5–6 (2000).
73. Jacques A. Nantel and William Strahle, "The Self-Monitoring Concept: A Consumer Behavior Perspective," in *Advances in Consumer Research,* vol. 13, ed. Richard Lutz (Provo, UT: Association for Consumer Research, 1986), pp. 83–87; and Sharon Shavitt and Tina M. Lowrey, "Attitude Functions in Advertising Effectiveness: The Interactive Role of Product Type and Personality Type," in *Advances in Consumer Research,* vol. 19, ed. John Sherry and Brian Sternthal (Provo, UT: Association for Consumer Research, 1992), pp. 323–28.
74. One of the most influential books on the subject of the self is Erving Goffman's *The Presentation of Self in Everyday Life* (New York: Doubleday, 1959). For a discussion of internal and external audiences for the self, see Schlenker, *The Self and Social Life.* For a general discussion of impression management strategies, see Schlenker, *Impression Management;* and Michael R. Solomon, "The Role of Products as Social Stimuli: A Symbolic Interactionism Perspective," *Journal of Consumer Research* 10 (December 1983), pp. 319–29. See also Raj Mehta and Russell W. Belk, "Artifacts, Identity, and Transition: Favorite Possessions of Indians and Indian Immigrants to the United States," *Journal of Consumer Research* 17 (March 1991), pp. 398–411.
75. Diane Barthel talks about advertising that appeals to self-presentation by representing the voices of internal audiences in her book *Putting on Appearances: Gender and Advertising* (Philadelphia: Temple University Press, 1988). She argues that advertising constantly reinforces males as the audience for women's consumption behaviors. A classic example is the long-running advertising campaign that asserts "Gentlemen prefer Hanes" and shows a model in a short skirt getting all the attention. See also John V. Canfield, *The Looking-Glass Self* (New York: Praeger, 1990); and Christine Yano, "Inventing Selves: Images and Image-Making in a Japanese Popular Music Genre," *Journal of Popular Culture* 31, no. 2 (1997), pp. 115–29.
76. There is a lot of novel and interesting research on this topic. A good review is offered by David Mick, "Consumer Research and Semiotics: Exploring the Morphology of Signs, Symbols, and Significance," *Journal of Consumer Research* 13 (September 1986), pp. 196–213. See also Rebecca H. Holman, "Apparel as Communication," in *Symbolic Consumer Behavior,* ed. Elizabeth C. Hirschman and Morris B. Holbrook (Ann Arbor, MI: Association for Consumer Research, 1981), pp. 7–15. A fun study using Halloween costumes as the consumption context

is reported in Trudy Kehret-Ward and Richard Yalch, "To Take or Not to Take the Only One: Effects of Changing the Meaning of a Product Attribute on Choice Behavior," *Journal of Consumer Research,* March 1984, pp. 410–16. Russell Belk, Kenneth Bahn, and Robert Mayer, "Developmental Recognition of Consumption Symbolism," *Journal of Consumer Research* 9 (June 1982), p. 417, study children's consumption symbolism. Of course, we shouldn't neglect the classic work of Sidney J. Levy, "Symbols for Sale," *Harvard Business Review,* July–August 1959, pp. 117–24.

77. Thompson and Hirschman, "Understanding the Socialized Body."

78. Russell W. Belk and Janeen Arnold Costa, "The Mountain Man Myth: A Contemporary Consuming Fantasy," *Journal of Consumer Research* 25 (December 1998), pp. 241–61; and A. Fuat Firat and Alladi Venkatesh, "Liberatory Postmodernism and the Reenchantment of Consumption," *Journal of Consumer Research* 22 (December 1995), pp. 239–67.

79. Eric J. Arnould and Linda L. Price, "Authenticating Acts and Authoritative Performances: Questing for Self and Community," in *The Why of Consumption: Contemporary Perspectives on Consumer Motives, Goals, and Desires,* ed. S. Ratneshwar, David Glen Mick, and Cynthia Huffman (New York and London: Routledge, 2000), pp. 140–63.

80. These examples are adapted from Susan Kraft, "The Heart of the Home," *American Demographics,* June 1992, pp. 46–50.

81. Marcel Mauss, "A Category of the Human Mind: The Notion of Person; the Notion of Self," in *The Category of the Person: Anthropology, Philosophy, History,* ed. M. Carrithers, S. Collins, and S. Lukes (Cambridge: Cambridge University Press, 1985), pp. 1–25.

82. Michael Carrithers, Steven Collins, and Steven Lukes, eds., *The Category of the Person: Anthropology, Philosophy, History* (Cambridge: Cambridge University Press, 1985); and Brian Morris, *Anthropology of the Self: The Individual in Cultural Perspective* (London and Boulder: Pluto Press, 1994).

83. C. Kagitcibasi, "The Autonomous-Relational Self: A New Synthesis," *European Psychologist* 1 (1996), pp. 180–86; and Hazel Rose Markus and Shinobu Kitayama, "Culture and Self: Implications for Cognition, Emotion, and Motivation," *Psychological Review* 98 (1991), pp. 224–53.

84. M. H. Bond, *The Psychology of the Chinese People* (New York: Oxford University Press, 1986); and Chu, "The Changing Concept of Self in Contemporary China."

85. V. S. Y. Kwan, M. H. Bond, and T. M. Singelis, "Pancultural Explanations for Life Satisfaction: Adding Relationship Harmony to Self-Esteem," *Journal of Personality and Social Psychology* 73 (1997), pp. 1038–51.

86. E. Hamaguchi, "A Contextual Model of the Japanese: Toward a Methodological Innovation in Japan Studies," *Journal of Japanese Studies* 11 (1985), pp. 289–321; George DeVos, "Dimensions of the Self in Japanese Culture," in *Culture and Self: Asian and Western Perspectives,* ed. Anthony J. Marsella, George DeVos, and Francis L. K. Hsu (New York: Tavistock Publications, 1985), pp. 141–84. See also Yumiko Ono, "Designers Cater to Japan's Love of Logos," *The Wall Street Journal,* May 29, 1990, p. B1.

87. Robert Levine, "Why Isn't Japan Happy?" *American Demographics,* June 1992, pp. 58–60.

88. Markus and Kitayama, "Culture and Self."

89. For a more complete discussion of Hindu views of the self, see Agehananda Bharati, "The Self in Hindu Thought and Action," in *Culture and Self: Asian and Western Perspectives,* ed. Anthony J. Marsella, George DeVos, and Francis L. K. Hsu (New York: Tavistock Publications, 1985), pp. 185–230.

90. R. Agarwal and G. Misra, "A Factor Analytic Study of Achievement Goals and Means: An Indian View," *International Journal of Psychology* 21 (1986), pp. 717–31; Gracia Clark, *Onions Are My Husband* (Chicago: University of Chicago Press, 1994); Paul Clough, "The Social Relations of Grain Marketing in Northern Nigeria," *Review of African Political Economy* 34 (December 1985), pp. 16–34; and A.-B. Yu and K.-S. Yang, "The Nature of Achievement Motivation in Collectivistic Societies," in *Individualism and Collectivism: Theory, Method, and Applications,* ed. U. Kim, H. C. Triandis, C. Kagitcibasi, S.-C. Choi, and G. Yoon (Thousand Oaks, CA: Sage Publications, 1994), pp. 239–50.

91. Morris, *Anthropology of the Self,* pp. 118–47.

chapter 1
chapter 2
chapter 3
chapter 4
chapter 5
chapter 6
chapter 7
chapter 8
chapter 9
chapter 10
chapter 11
chapter 12
chapter 13
chapter 14
chapter 15
chapter 16
chapter 17
chapter 18
chapter 19

LEARNING OBJECTIVES

After completing this chapter, you should be able to:

- Identify role-related product constellations.
- Describe psychographics and lifestyle research.
- Understand the use of lifestyles data to profile lifestyle segments, identify related lifestyle interests, and locate lifestyle segments geographically.
- Recognize lifestyle typologies such as VALS, LOV, Japan VALS, and Global Scan.
- Understand how lifestyle may be used at various levels of aggregation.
- Identify the value and limitations of lifestyle research.

LIFESTYLES: CONSUMPTION SUBCULTURES

KEEPIN' IT REAL: THE HIPHOP ENGINE[1]

Hiphop culture is now more than 25 years old. The term itself derives from two underlying words: "hip" (trendy) and "hop" (jump or dance). The Hiphop lifestyle emerged in the Bronx, New York, out of broader African-American cultural roots. In July 2002, the Rock Steady Crew (one of the founding Hiphop rap groups) hosted a four-day party to celebrate their 25th anniversary. They have appeared in such films as *Beat Street,* and they've toured worldwide. Other performers participating in this four-day celebration included DJ Cash Money, Pack FM & Tone Deff, The Awesome Two, and Gangstarr. In addition to music, fashion is a prominent part of the Hiphop style. In the language of Hiphop, "street fashion" refers to the clothing trends of the inner city. Street fashion is an important way to present Hiphop identity and ideology. This audience is media-oriented, but one that perceives media messages as a kind of living experience rather than a stream of cognitive themes.

Hiphop is, in many respects, a classic youth subculture. It rejects the norms and values of the mainstream, measuring success in terms of peer approval. This culture's insider cues, language, tastes, and values are constantly evolving. Its strengths are its energy, creativity, and worldwide appeal. An estimated 97 percent of urban African-American teens follow rap music. It is the universal element in their experience. This lifestyle demands adherence to its orthodoxies as a condition of acceptance, and this adherence is rendered hazardous by the culture's macho encouragement of risk taking (e.g., violence, substance abuse, promiscuity).

Hiphop has become a global lifestyle. In Paris, a French adaptation of the American genre is becoming quite popular, with producers such as "Prince Charles" recreating the musical sound that's identified with rap. The fundamental difference in language inflection between French and English gives the French version of rap its distinctive pattern. In a similar way, Greenlandic performers rap in both the Inuit language and Danish to express their multicultural angst. Algerian rap music cross-fertilizes with sounds made by North African artists living in France's immigrant districts. Rap music is used by Palestinian youths to express their displeasure with Israeli rule.

South Africa's musical craze, Kwaito, sounds rather like American gangsta rap, and this is no coincidence. Kwaito stars admire and emulate transatlantic rappers. But their music is more than imitation. The songs are about life in the townships and about the experiences of the post-apartheid generation. Kwaito's popularity in South Africa depends a lot on the incorporation of local rhythms and bass lines, and it reflects young black South African culture in a way that no imported dance track could.

www.krs-one.com

www.zulunation.com

http://www.angelfire.com/tx3/thugappeal/

"Keepin' it real," or authenticity, is the key to reaching the Hiphop audience, but it is a moving, mutating target. "True Hipphoppas" are suspicious that corporate exploiters show no respect for "Hiphop Kulture." Corporate exploiters are sometimes identified by the spellings that they use for "Hiphop" (e.g., "hip-hop"). Such a spelling refers to a trendy dance, not the full range of Hiphop Kulture.

www.defjam.com

www.nauticajeans.com

Although the charge of going "commercial" is often the kiss of death to rap musicians, Hiphop has become a marketing phenomenon. Annual revenues from rap music exceed $1 billion. Hiphop street culture is a positioning device for all sorts of companies, including Nautica jeans and Bizo shoes and skateboards. Visit the Temple of HipHop website.

www.bizo.com

www.Rapstation.com

For marketers, the task of incorporating the "street life" in their promotions poses two challenges. First, the message has to be shareable. Second, the message must have sufficient longevity for the sharing to take place. The promotion has to be entertaining, engaging, and couched in terms that conceal its link to mainstream values. This is no easy task in a culture characterized by constant change and dynamism.

OVERVIEW

The focus of this chapter is on consumers' lifestyles—that is, how consumers live. Lifestyle includes consumers' activities, interests, likes and dislikes, attitudes, consumption patterns, and expectations. The term *lifestyle* suggests a patterned way of life into which consumers fit various products, activities, and resources.[2] We can trace the origins of the interest in lifestyle to the work of Thorstein Veblen's turn-of-the-century classic *The Theory of the Leisure Class,* in which the conspicuous consumption of the

Caterpillar clothing uses a lifestyle positioning in this global ad campaign.

nouveau riche (Chapter 12) was first identified and ridiculed. In making use of the lifestyle concept, marketers often rely on the idea that consumer lifestyles are a reflection of individuals' attempts to realize a desired or ideal self-concept, a notion discussed in Chapter 10.[3]

Marketing's conception of lifestyle emerged from four main developments: (1) the desire to develop an easily measurable, more objective variant of motivational research that was popular in the 1950s and 1960s; (2) the emergence of more sophisticated statistical techniques and the computer power to run them; (3) the desire to give traditional personality research a narrower consumer focus; and (4) the inability to describe increasingly diverse consumption patterns with then-existing tools (for example, demographic or social class analysis). The concept that resulted combines the attitudinal clustering typically associated with personality research with a wider domain of person measures.[4]

Consumers' lifestyles influence many of their production, acquisition, consumption, and disposition activities. In many cases we might think of marketers as selling pieces of a style of life, not isolated products.[5] A series of ads for Caterpillar clothing provides a good illustration of how a product is depicted as a part of a style of life. Two examples from this international ad campaign are provided here. Notice the gritty urban settings and the "ordinary" look of the models. What style of life do you think these ads are trying to convey?

Decisions that consumers make about purchase, consumption, and disposal can alter or reinforce their lifestyles. Hence, lifestyles are dynamic and constantly changing. For example, a consumer may decide to start jogging in order to get into better shape. This decision may reinforce her already health-oriented lifestyle. However, as she integrates this behavior into her life, she may find that this change also alters her lifestyle—when she gets up in the morning, her meals, her bedtime, her reading, and her other leisure or vacation activities. Jogging may even influence her social groups, her wardrobe, her hairstyle, and other seemingly unrelated aspects of the way she lives. Hence, deciding to jog doesn't just influence the purchase of a pair of shorts, a running bra, and a pair of running shoes; it also has the potential to alter many other facets of a consumer's daily life.

Lifestyles are influenced by many factors, including demographics, social class, reference groups, and family. As illustrated in the vignette about Hiphop, many aspects of the cultural environment can influence lifestyle. An individual's self-concept, as

PowerBar tailors its lifestyle message to two slightly different segments.

discussed in Chapter 10, serves as the basis for one's lifestyle. In fact, we might think of lifestyle as an outward manifestation of aspects of the self. This means that, in some ways, each person, family, and household has a unique lifestyle. It also means that individuals, families, and households may practice multiple lifestyles. For example, many households with school-age children have a different lifestyle during the summer months than during the school year.[6]

Of course, many products and marketing strategies focus on an explicit recognition of a particular lifestyle that is shared by a market segment. We show two ads for PowerBar. One appeared in *Sierra* (the magazine of the Sierra Club); the other appeared in *Runner's World.* The ads are each tailored to appeal to consumers who share a particular lifestyle, in this case backpacking and running. Such advertising is very common. In fact, lifestyle differences or lifestyle patterns constitute one of the most important bases for segmenting markets.

Lifestyle differences might be recognized and targeted by marketers at various levels of aggregation. The Hiphop lifestyle describes a form we might consider a global structure of common differences as discussed in Chapter 3. It has mutated into a variety of national and transnational forms that nonetheless always incorporate values connected with youth, authenticity, opposition to the mainstream, poetry, and rhythm into the local variations. Similarly, some authors have described a cosmopolitan lifestyle, where participants organize around concepts of self, personal goals, consumption of "exotic" foreign products, and adventuresome travel. We might define the lifestyle characteristics of a whole generation, such as generation Xers. Alternatively, we could talk about the lifestyle of a

This lifestyle ad appeals to enthusiasts of a particular leisure activity.

This tongue-in-cheek ad disclaims a particular lifestyle.

particular segment within a generation, such as the "privileged poor." This is a subset of generation Xers who cobble together a lifestyle combining some lavish consumer spending on fashion with handouts from parents and odd jobs. Or we might identify migrating seniors, a group of older consumers who retire to take up new lifestyles in retirement communities in subtropical climates.[7]

Marketers often define a lifestyle segment around a single activity such as cycling, soccer, bowling, or hiking. For example, the Football Collector ad on page 439 invites soccer enthusiasts to buy merchandise reflective of their favorite teams and heroes. Marketers may also create an ad campaign to appeal to consumers reacting against a lifestyle rather like the disclaimant reference groups discussed in Chapter 14. For example, with so many restaurants promising low-fat, healthy, and even vegetarian food, Wienerschnitzel appeals to consumers who want, at least occasionally, to rebel against that healthy lifestyle in the cheeky ad shown on page 439.

Lifestyle research can be applied to solve a variety of marketing problems, including identifying the target market, positioning a brand, locating where the target group lives, identifying how to communicate with the target group, and gaining insight into why the target group acts the way it does.[8] For instance, if a medical center wanted to offer a new line of service (for example, treating and preventing sports-related injuries), then a lifestyle segmentation might be completed to determine who would want such a service and who would be willing to pay for such a service. In addition, a lifestyle segmentation would be useful to help choose a media vehicle (for example, a specific magazine such as *Women's Soccer World*) for promoting the new hospital service.

The key for lifestyle marketers is to figure out what goes with what and, in many cases, to help define product and service assortments for particular lifestyles. This often involves figuring out what attitudes and values go with what activities and products. An example of a creative application of lifestyle marketing is the highly successful marketing behind the No Fear Apparel company. Sales for the company rose to $200 million in less than five years. Jim Hancock, the marketing director, sought to convey a particular feeling with the marketing strategy and the logo. The apparel is designed to speak to a myriad of subcultures (for example, auto racing, rock climbing) that have as a common emotional link the "No Fear" attitude. According to Jim Hancock, the No Fear attitude is about taking on the challenge and fear that's in every and any kind of task and overcoming it.[9]

www.xoutfitters.com/nofear/

www.yesterdayland.com/popopedia/shows/fashion/fa1678.php

This chapter will introduce you to some of the most important tools marketers use to figure out what goes with what. We begin with a brief discussion of product clusters, or constellations. This will help you to understand and identify different behavioral lifestyles. Then, we introduce some important tools for implementing lifestyle marketing, including psychographic segmentation schemes such as VALS, LOV, PRIZM, and Global Scan. We also discuss the use of psychographic methods to chart social and cultural trends. We conclude the chapter with a discussion of emerging criticisms of lifestyles research.

PRODUCT CONSTELLATIONS

Products are important for communicating social information. For example, what image do you have of a minivan driver versus a sports car driver? The term *lifestyle* implies a pattern of behavior that is reflected in and reflects the consumption not merely of single products but of interrelated product clusters, or **product constellations.** Product constellations are *clusters of complementary products, specific brands, or consumption activities.* Product constellations are socially meaningful sets of consumption stimuli that are used by consumers both for self-definition and for the categorization of others. Some early analyses of supermarket purchases demonstrated that purchases do fall into meaningful bundles and that groups of consumers with shared consumption patterns also shared demographics, tastes, and values such that consumption lifestyle groups could be meaningfully identified. In the mid-1980s, Levi Strauss and Company divided the U.S. men's clothing market into five product-based segments, including the utilitarian jeans wearer, who wears jeans for work and leisure, and the classic independent, a tailored, pinstripe-suit professional, who shops alone.[10]

In the late 1960s, two U.S. researchers employed product usage data concerning 80 products in an attempt to identify behavioral lifestyles. They identified 10 groups of men who used multiple products, such as the car-conscious man, who bought aftermarket products and accessories; the cosmopolitan traveler, who engaged in air travel and car rental; the cigar and pipe smoker, who purchased many smoking articles; and so forth. Industry Insights 11.1 shows the contents of product constellations elicited for some male social roles in the United States.[11]

Lifestyle profiles can be organized around a single product category. Such profiles are the bread and butter of many marketing research firms and offer valuable insights on specific appeals and vehicles to use in targeting product category users. Consumer Chronicles 11.1 profiles the *Otaku,* a youth-oriented hacker lifestyle associated with *anime* (Japanese animation) and an antisocial orientation. The Otaku even inhabit a weird novel by famed sci-fi author William Gibson called *Idoru.*[12] On a more mainstream note, Industry Insights 11.2 describes an activity-based lifestyle profile designed to get a handle on the characteristics and golf-related spending of 24 million U.S. golfers.

www.levi.com/

Some particularly strong product-to-role relationships have led researchers to speak of **brand tribes** for *people who are devoted to a particular brand,* such as clothes by No Fear in the United States or by Naf Naf or Clark's in Europe. The ad for Clark's shown on page 445 was featured in an issue of the UK pop magazine *The Face* devoted to Great Britain's garage band scene. When product-to-role relationships are especially strong, the brands become a defining symbol of a communal identity, hence the term *brand tribe.*

www.zenith.com/

Product symbolism plays a key role in lifestyle appeals in marketing. Look again at the discussion of core symbols in Chapter 3. From a managerial perspective, a marketer can rely upon symbolic, socially defined relationships to match products with consumers' desires. Consider a potentially mundane product such as toothpaste. In modern advertising, toothpaste has become separated from its original use—a paste to cleanse teeth. Instead, the product is attached with new, symbolic meanings such as sexiness, beauty, happiness, and attractiveness.[13] It is important to note that cultural and commercial symbols often acquire their meanings and associations without direct actions by marketers.[14] However, consider all of the commercial opportunities that members of the Hiphop culture have for expressing themselves. They can enter chat rooms, get a tattoo, wear clothing that conveys a message, or recommend a commercial website to their friends. In brief, members of any subculture can express themselves by purchasing symbols that marketers have preassembled and prepackaged. When viewed as a whole, these brands, symbols, and services make up a product constellation.[15]

Lifestyle profiles such as those shown in Industry Insights 11.2 have both strengths and weaknesses from a marketing perspective. Such profiles aid in identifying consumer segments. Each role can be associated with a specific constellation, or collection, of products and services. Marketers may offer new products to reinforce role identities or reinforce product and brand loyalty by emphasizing product-to-role

Examples of Product Constellations Elicited for Occupation Social Roles

INDUSTRY INSIGHTS 11.1

Professional	Salesman	Suit Salesman	Businessman
Seiko watch	Farrah slacks	Zenith TV	Tiffany jewels
Burberry raincoat	Budweiser beer	Oldsmobile 98	Steuben glass
Lacoste shirt	Buick Skylark	Whirlpool freezer	Italian leather briefcase
Atlantic magazine	Coca-Cola	Gillette shaver	Cross pen
Brooks Bros. suit	McDonald's	Old Spice cologne	Cuff links
Bass loafers	M & M's candy	Miller beer	Ralph Lauren shirt
Silk tie	Puritan golf shirts	JVC stereo	VCR
French wine	Fayva shoes		Lincoln Continental
BMW	Samsonite luggage		*The Wall Street Journal*
	Timex watch		

Attorney	Blue-Collar Worker	Public Defender	Unskilled Worker
Prince tennis racket	Schaefer beer	Levi's cords	Chevrolet
Leather briefcase	AMF bowling ball	Wallaby shoes	Goldstar TV
American Express gold card	Ford pickup truck	Calvin Klein glasses	*NY Daily News*
Cadillac Eldorado	Levi's jeans	Molson beer	Hanes T-shirts
Michelob beer	Marlboro cigarettes	L.L. Bean shirts	Levi's jeans
Vantage cigarettes	RCA TV	RCA VCR	Coca-Cola
Cigars	*Field and Stream*	Volkswagen Rabbit	Miller beer
Johnston & Murphy shoes	Black & Decker tools	*Esquire*	McDonald's
L.L. Bean catalog	McDonald's		Camel cigarettes

Source: Michael R. Solomon and Henry Assael, "The Forest or the Trees?: A Gestalt Approach to Symbolic Consumption," in Marketing and Semiotics: New Directions in the Study of Signs for Sale, *ed. Jean Umiker-Sebeok (New York: Mouton de Gruyter, 1987), p. 206.*

relationships. Product constellations can be matched with demographic profiles and media preferences to improve targeting. Advertisers can use product constellations to engineer the context of ads (e.g., to indicate what other products should appear alongside the advertised brand). Product constellations also have implications for store layouts. For example, merchandisers may place complementary items together rather than organize the store by product categories.[16]

Lifestyle profiles constructed from product constellations also have some weaknesses. For instance, the same person may enact multiple social roles, such as manager, mother, wife, daughter, runner, and Red Cross volunteer. If a product is too closely associated with one role that conflicts with other roles, it may not suit the consumer's needs. Further, lifestyle profiles are insensitive to effects of potential innovations, environmental influences, and changes in corporate strategy. For example, two products in Industry Insights 11.1 would no longer be included in their product constellations. Lacoste

The Obsession of Otaku

CONSUMER CHRONICLES 11.1

The blurring of man and machine, of reality and what comes in over the video display terminal, is spawning a generation of Japanese kids who are opting out of the conformity of Japan, Inc., in favor of logging onto computer networks. They have been dubbed the *Otaku* by the Japanese media, from the most formal way of saying *you* in Japanese, the implication being that there is always some kind of technological barrier between people. The Otaku came of age in the 1980s with "prehistoric" 186 computers and Atari Pac-Men as playmates. They were brought up on junk food and educated to memorize reams of context-less information in preparation for multiple-choice high school and college entrance exams. They unwind with ultraviolent slasher comic books or equally violent computer games. They discovered that, by interacting with computers instead of people, they could avoid Japanese society's dauntingly complex web of social obligations and loyalties. The result: a generation of Japanese youth too uptight to talk to a bank teller but who can go hell-for-leather on the deck of a personal computer or workstation. First identified by the Japanese lifestyle magazine *SPA!*, 200,000 hardcore Otaku are Japan's newest information age product. "These kids are unlike any who preceded them in Japan," *Lap Top* magazine editor Abiko Seigo says of the subculture of 16- to 25-year-olds. "Where they are coming from is a world where all the usual perspectives—like whether something is good or bad, smart or stupid—are irrelevant, because all of those things are judgments based on social relations. If you don't socialize, you don't have much sense of morality. The only thing that matters to them is data. How much do you have, and how much can you memorize?"

An alternative version of what Otaku means is as follows: Otaku is a Japanese expression for an obsessive fan or hobbyist, taken from *otaku-zoku,* which translates as "home tribe." Otaku mythology roughly corresponds to America's antisocial computer hacker, but the passion for obscure trivia (often traded as databases over computer networks) also attaches to a wide variety of pop enthusiasms from video games, Ultraman, and manga to teen-idol singers, American Hiphop, and Hong Kong action movies. Though still something of an insult in Japan, along the lines of "homebody" or "fanboy," the term has gained currency, in part via the Internet, as a badge of honor among American anime (Japanese video animation) devotees. A large number of websites, such as http://www.otakuworld.com, are devoted to each of the consumer "obsessions" mentioned above.

Source: Karl Taro Greenfeld, "The Obsession of the Otaku," Los Angeles Times Magazine, *September 12, 1993, pp. 40–43; and www.altculture.com/aentries/o/otaku.html.*

shirts lost their position in the American marketplace during a recession in the 1980s, in part because of their association with a yuppie lifestyle. The Lacoste brand is making a strong comeback in the twenty-first century. Nonetheless, the brand's positioning within the consumer segments shown in Industry Insights 11.1 has shifted over time. Camel cigarettes were repositioned with a juvenile image for a more youthful market. Marketers using such lifestyle profiles need to be especially sensitive to changing trends that may alter the product constellation in either subtle or dramatic ways. Marketers must also avoid allowing the product constellation to become a cliche (à la Lacoste shirts) so that potential customers begin to shun it.[17]

@ www.lacoste.com/lcl_pe02/

PSYCHOGRAPHICS AND LIFESTYLE

Psychographics is *an operational technique to measure lifestyles.* Psychographics is more comprehensive than demographic, behavioral, and socioeconomic measures. Using a psychographic technique involves systematically linking individual psychological

Lifestyles of American Golfers

INDUSTRY INSIGHTS 11.2

Seven golfing consumer segments were identified in a study by the Professional Golfers' Association of America:

- **Dilettante Duffers:** Male, comprise 27 percent of American golfers, average age of 41, annual household income of $64,200. They play only 16 rounds of golf per year, mostly on weekends. When they do golf, they want to look good, and they spend a larger than average share of their annual vacation time golfing.
- **Tank Tops 'n Tennis Shoes:** These male golfers make up 17 percent of U.S. golfers and are the youngest segment, average age of 35 with annual incomes of $36,700. They do much of their golfing on weekends, only golf 13 rounds a year, and spend less on golfing than any other segment.
- **Pull-Carts:** These male golfers make up 15 percent of U.S. golfers, with an average age of 52 and annual income of $32,200. Six out of 10 are retired or unemployed. They play 32 rounds of golf annually and spend $1,400 per year on the sport.
- **Public Pundits:** These zealous middle-aged male golfers are 13 percent of U.S. golfers. They play almost 52 rounds a year, but almost entirely on public golf courses despite an average income of $50,600. They do spend $2,000 per year on the sport, well above average.
- **Junior Leaguers:** These female golfers are about 15 percent of U.S. golfers, play around 24 rounds of golf a year, and spend close to the average for the sport ($1,600 annually). Their annual household income is $57,800.
- **Country Club Traditionals:** These men are only about 9 percent of U.S. golfers, but with annual household incomes of $77,300, they fork out an average of $4,400 on golf. They play an average of 60 of their 69 rounds a year on private courses.
- **Swingin' Seniors:** These women make up 6 percent of U.S. golfers. Although they report a lower than average household income, they may be enjoying retirement on tidy nest eggs. They play over half their 42 annual golf rounds on private courses, and almost half belong to a golf club.

Source: Deborah Bosanko, "Seven Ways to Swing a Club," American Demographics, *July 1995, pp. 16–18.*

factors to characteristic patterns of overt consumer behavior to determine who the market segment is. The basic idea is that cognitive processes or properties, including values, aptitudes, beliefs, and opinions, affect the likelihood of groups within the market to make a particular decision about a product, person, or ideology; to hold an attitude, or to use a communication medium such as TV or the Internet. Psychographic techniques are employed to give flesh and blood to sample demographic surveys that provide little information about the *why* of consumer behavior.

Psychographic techniques divide the total market into segments on the bases of activities, interests, values, opinions, personality characteristics, and attitudes using various statistical procedures. The term *psychographic* is often used interchangeably with **AIO measures,** or *statements to describe the activities, interests, and opinions of consumers.* AIO statements may be general activities and motivations, or they may focus on statements that are product or brand specific. Psychographic methods might be termed

This ad is strategically placed in a lifestyle magazine to appeal to a specific segment.

backward segmentation because they group people by behavioral characteristics before seeking purchase and consumption correlates.[18]

To execute a psychographic analysis, researchers poll prospective or actual members of a market segment using standardized survey instruments. Researchers can administer these forms in person, by phone, by mail, or electronically (for example, on the Web), or they might send such surveys in the form of warranty cards, sweepstakes entries, or customer profiles. These data are then analyzed in a statistical sense to tease out various consumption typologies.

Profiles may be very general, as in a study by the Newspaper Advertising Bureau that produced eight male psychographic segments, including the quiet family man (8 percent of the total) and the ethical highbrow (14 percent of the total). At the other extreme, they may be product specific, as in a segmentation of stomach-remedy users that produced four segments, including severe sufferers, active medicators, hypochondriacs, and practicalists. Good Practice 11.1, entitled "The Average American Consumer Quiz," provides a few examples of the many statements that have been used in psychographic surveys of American consumers.[19]

Most of you are probably familiar with psychographic research since many products now include lifestyles surveys with their warranty cards. Consumers are asked to mail in these cards to ensure their warranty (Good Practice 11.2). The data contained on the card are then added to computer databases to help marketers pinpoint buyer characteristics. That

GOOD PRACTICE 11.1
The Average American Consumer Quiz

How well do *you* know the average American consumer? Try guessing the answers to these AIO inventory items. If your intuition is not too good, you have demonstrated the value of careful psychographic research to marketers. Find the answers in the footnote.

Statements	Percentage of Consumers Agreeing: % Men	% Women
1. A nationally advertised brand is usually a better buy than a generic brand.	________	________
2. I went fishing at least once in the past year.	________	________
3. I am a homebody.	________	________
4. Communism is the greatest peril in the world today.	________	________
5. The government should exercise more control over what is shown on television.	________	________
6. Information from advertising helps me to make better buying decisions.	________	________
7. I like to pay cash for everything I buy.	________	________
8. The working world is no place for a woman.	________	________
9. I am interested in spices and seasonings.	________	________
10. The father should be the boss in the house.	________	________
11. You have to use disinfectants to get things really clean.	________	________

Source: Steven J. Hoch, "Who Do We Know: Predicting the Interests and Opinions of the American Consumer," Journal of Consumer Research *15 (December 1988), pp. 315–24. Answers to the quiz are (1) M = 36, W = 35; (2) M = 52, W = 34; (3) M = 75, W = 71; (4) M = 63, W = 61; (5) M = 29, W = 33; (6) M = 66, W = 74; (7) M = 72, W = 70; (8) M = 17, W = 11; (9) M = 57, W = 79; (10) M = 68, W = 50; (11) M = 48, W = 54.*

is, marketers can combine the information from the warranty card with other kinds of consumer information to create a lifestyle inventory. Such an inventory could include demographic, purchase, and psychographic information.

Many products, including household soap, stomach remedies, and automobiles, have been successfully positioned or repositioned using lifestyle segmentation. In the early 1970s, the Ford Pinto was advertised as a friendly, romantic little car not unlike today's updated VW Beetle. The Pinto was subsequently repositioned as economical, basic transportation when typical buyers' lifestyles were identified more carefully. An unsuccessful example of lifestyle repositioning was Oldsmobile's "It's Not Your Father's Oldsmobile" campaign, which alienated its traditional, conservative male buyers without attracting a new generation. Oldsmobile is the second oldest automobile brand in the world (after Daimler). Nonetheless, poor positioning and declining market share have resulted in its elimination from the world marketplace. At the retail level, the restructuring of many department stores in the Triad nations into lifestyle

@ inventors.about.com/library/inventors/bldaimler.htm

GOOD PRACTICE 11.2

VTech Warranty Card

1 1. ☐ Mr. 2. ☐ Mrs. 3. ☐ Ms. 4. ☐ Miss **244C**

First Name: Initial: Last Name:

Address: (Number and Street) Apt #:

City: State: Zip Code:

2 E-Mail Address:

3 Phone #: (Example: kaimathi@aol.com)

4 Date of Purchase: Month Day Year

5 Model Purchased: (Example: CSD-EX110)

6 Serial #:

7 Purchase Price: $ .00 (Excluding Tax)

8 Store Name:

9 Is this: (Check all that apply)
1. ☐ A first time purchase of this product type?
2. ☐ A replacement purchase of this product type?
3. ☐ An additional purchase of this product type?
4. ☐ A gift for you or someone else?

10 What three (3) factors most influenced your purchase of this Aiwa product?
1. ☐ Size
2. ☐ Special Features
3. ☐ Price/Value
4. ☐ Quality
5. ☐ Aiwa Reputation
6. ☐ Magazine/Newspaper Article
7. ☐ Previous Aiwa Experience
8. ☐ Friend/Relative Recommendation
9. ☐ Salesperson Recommendation
10. ☐ Other________________

11 What other brand(s) did you consider?
1. ☐ RCA 5. ☐ Sanyo 9. ☐ Magnavox
2. ☐ Koss 6. ☐ Fisher 10. ☐ Kenwood
3. ☐ Sony 7. ☐ JVC 11. ☐ Other
4. ☐ Panasonic 8. ☐ GPX ________

12 Which of the following products do you own or plan to purchase?

	Own	Plan to Buy
1. Head Phones	1. ☐	2. ☐
2. Portable CD Player	1. ☐	2. ☐
3. Portable Cassette Player	1. ☐	2. ☐
4. Mini Audio System	1. ☐	2. ☐
5. Multi Media Computer Speakers	1. ☐	2. ☐
6. VCR	1. ☐	2. ☐
7. Mini Disc	1. ☐	2. ☐

13 If you purchased a clock radio, what 3 features would you like most?
1. ☐ Dual Alarm 5. ☐ Cassette Player
2. ☐ Red LED Display 6. ☐ Digital Tuner
3. ☐ Green LED Display 7. ☐ Color________
4. ☐ CD Player 8. ☐ Other________

14 If you purchased a portable CD player, how much buffer memory would you want?
1. ☐ 3 seconds 3. ☐ 20 seconds
2. ☐ 10 seconds 4. ☐ 20+ seconds

15 What type of radio do you prefer to have in your headphone stereo, portable stereo or radio?
1. ☐ Digital 3. ☐ No preference
2. ☐ Analog

16 Do you own a personal computer?
1. ☐ Yes 2. ☐ No

17 Date of Your Birth: Month Day Year

18 Marital Status: 1. ☐ Married 2. ☐ Single

19 Education (Check which category applies):
1. ☐ High School 3. ☐ Completed College
2. ☐ Some College 4. ☐ Graduate School

20 Which best describes your family income?
1. ☐ Under $15,000 5. ☐ $50,000-$74,999
2. ☐ $15,000-$24,999 6. ☐ $75,000-$99,999
3. ☐ $25,000-$34,999 7. ☐ $100,000-$149,999
4. ☐ $35,000-$49,999 8. ☐ Over $150,000

21 Including yourself, what is the total number of people living in your household?

22 NOT including yourself, what are the AGES of any other people living in your household?

Age (in years)

Male:

Female:

23 In the last six (6) months have you or your spouse:
1. ☐ Purchased clothes through the mail?
2. ☐ Purchased gifts through the mail?
3. ☐ Worked in your garden?
4. ☐ Traveled on vacation?
5. ☐ Purchased a PC or PC software?
6. ☐ Purchased two or more books?
7. ☐ Purchased cassettes/CDs?
8. ☐ Donated to wildlife/environmental causes?
9. ☐ Donated to charities?

Thank you for filling out this questionnaire. Please check here [ ] if you would prefer not to participate in additional market research for Aiwa or obtain information on new and interesting opportunities from other companies.

boutiques and the success of Nike Town and Virgin megastores, which are divided into lifestyle meccas, are notable examples of the successful application of lifestyle segmentation.[20]

VALS, LOV, AND OTHER PSYCHOGRAPHIC SEGMENTATION SCHEMES

In this section we describe some widely used approaches to lifestyle marketing. Although each of these has gained rapid acceptance and widespread use, each has certain limitations. For example, marketers must be careful about the cultural assumptions they make in their use of these psychographic segmentation schemes. Sometimes these approaches can be used to identify lifestyle segments across country borders, but this requires considerable managerial judgment and expertise.[21]

Values and Lifestyles Systems (VALS 1)

A team of researchers at the Stanford Research Institute (SRI) developed several influential values-based lifestyle segmentation schemes widely used by firms in North America. **VALS 1** was based on the work of two psychologists: Abraham Maslow's hierarchy of human needs and David Reisman's concept of social character. The researchers sent questions concerning both general and specific attitude statements and demographic items to a national probability sample of Americans in a 1980 mail survey. Using the data gathered, they partitioned the market into nine groups, or VALS 1 segments, based on Maslow's hierarchical model of human needs (from most basic physiological needs to most abstract self-actualization needs) and Reisman's model of external or internal basic goal orientations. Exhibit 11.1 compares a profile of North American and European VALS 1 segments and shows the approximate percentage of U.S. residents in each group. The size of some segments is extremely small; others are extremely large.

VALS 1 enjoyed massive early success for clients as diverse as Merrill Lynch, Dr Pepper, Clairol, and Folonari wine. Some versions of Merrill Lynch's long-running advertising campaign featuring a lone bull were targeted to achievers. By the late 1980s VALS 1 had outlived its usefulness. Among the criticisms were that the classifications were too abstract and general. In addition, its origin in developmental psychology does not seem especially applicable to consumer markets. As a result, there are too many similarities and too few differences between groups. Also, given the imbalance in size between segments, the system was not useful for identifying markets.

Values and Lifestyles Systems (VALS 2)

In response to criticisms of VALS 1, the team at SRI developed the **VALS 2** scheme that classifies people into segments on the bases whether they control abundant or minimal resources and three aspects of their basic motivational self-orientations: principles, status, or action. Using the dimensions of self-orientation and resources, VALS 2 has defined eight consumer segments with differing attitudes and behavior patterns. The groups are fairly balanced, proportionately ranging from 8 percent to 16 percent of the population, so that each represents a viable consumer target. The VALS 2 framework is shown in Exhibit 11.2, along with brief descriptions for each of the eight segments. Marketers are advised to take different approaches when dealing with principle-oriented consumers versus status- or action-oriented ones. **Principle-oriented people** are *guided by intellectual matters.* The principle-oriented segments are labeled as fulfilleds and believers. **Status-oriented people** *alter their behavior to fit their surroundings to win the approval of important reference groups and individuals.* The two status-oriented segments are labeled as achievers and strivers. One difference between these two segments is the amount of resources available, indicated by the vertical axis in Exhibit 11.2. Achievers have access to more resources than strivers, as defined by the VALS 2 framework.

Action-oriented people *thrive on new social or physical activities.* Experiencers and makers are two such segments. The resource measure (the vertical axis in Exhibit 11.2) indicates the ability of a particular group to respond to an appeal to buy. VALS 2 recognizes that a wide range of constraints, from financial to psychological, can prevent a person's values from having free expression in the way they live. As shown in the exhibit, increasing resources are associated with increased ability to indulge their self-orientation through consumption.

www.sric-bi.com/VALS/

The VALS 2 survey can be found at the SRI websites. The survey itself is relatively short, and some example questions are shown in Exhibit 11.3. By studying the actual questions in the exhibit, you may get a better idea of what the various VALS 2 segments mean. If you go to the website and take the survey yourself, you will find that you will be segmented into one of the following VALS types: actualizers, fulfilleds, achievers, experiencers, believers, strivers, makers, and strugglers. Actualizers are the highest in terms of resources. Strugglers are the lowest. Also on the website, you have the option of reading about each individual segment and the activities that are popular with each.

Some problems with the survey may include the wording of the questions and the lack of a neutral response. Most questions are worded in such a way that respondents may choose an answer that is socially desirable rather than one that is strictly honest. Questions are repeated several times with hardly any word changes. Thus, the survey might seem to be rather repetitive to some respondents. Finally, respondents are forced to agree or disagree with each statement. Thus, there is no option to be neutral about any of the questions.

Other problems with the survey have been identified by Douglas Holt. According to Holt, segmenting people according to their values and lifestyle will give researchers some idea of what they consume, but how they consume will still be missing. Thus, it is important to take into account the context of consumption in order to understand the segments. Ethnographic research provides a way to understand various contexts, including in-depth interviews about how people use the products and services that they buy.[22] In contrast, psychographic research relies on a personality or values-based approach, where consumption patterns are identified for categories of goods owned and activities pursued. For instance, by administering a survey, it is discovered that achievers tend to own patio furniture at a higher than average rate.[23] Patio furniture is assumed to express the achiever lifestyle regardless of how it is understood and used by the actual consumers. Holt argues that an ethnographic approach (as an improvement on the survey method shown in Exhibit 11.3) allows for a deeper understanding of how people interact with consumption objects. He also points out that it is important to understand the full constellation of objects that people consume.

Like VALS 1, VALS 2 clarifies understanding of consumer segments for targeted marketing. As a first step, marketers might identify the light, heavy, and nonusing segments of the product category in question. For example, Industry Insights 11.3 compares pain reliever users by VALS 2 segments. The graphs show that experiencers, achievers, and strivers are most likely to use Advil, whereas achievers, strivers, experiencers, and makers are likely users of Nuprin. The graph also shows that Nuprin has a lower usage index among actualizers and experiencers than does Advil. The manufacturer might wish to target these groups. Alternatively, the marketer could investigate further to

	The Needy		Outer-Directed Goal Orientation		
Country	**Survivors**	**Sustainers**	**Belongers**	**Emulators**	**Achievers**
United States	Elderly, extremely poor, deprived, marginalized, lost. Highly price conscious, focused on basic, immediate needs. (4%)	Embittered, insecure persons. Streetwise. Near poverty; live off part-time, casual jobs. Price wise and cautious buyers. (7%)	Elderly, conservative patriots, sentimental, stable, traditional, middle class. Middle and lower mass markets; family and home-centered buying behavior. (35%)	Young, ambitious machos, dandies; upwardly mobile; demanding of themselves and others; dream of a future of self-fulfillment. Conspicuous consumers; purchase trends; imitative. (9%)	Middle-aged, prosperous leaders; sure of themselves; materialist; satisfied; defenders of the status quo. Want products showing success; luxury and gift markets; new and improved products; top of the line. (22%)
France	Few in number but similar to the American segment. Share traits with sustainers and belongers.	Retirees and elderly persons often living in the country, poorly educated, creatures of habit, unwilling or unable to change.	Elderly; attached to the family, financial security, appearances, health, and others' opinions of oneself.	Young, but older and more reserved than in the United States. Better educated, suspicious of ideologies, preoccupied with health.	Two groups: the first is more mature and similar to Americans; the second is younger and more intuitive, concerned with ecology and the environment.
Italy	Similar to North American survivors; often live in the slums around northern industrial cities.	The elderly. Poorly educated, originally from the country. Welfare recipients, fugitives.	Aging, authoritarian, fatalists, savers; reflective of their society and its problems.	Young, male, well-educated; independent of their families. Materialists, avid readers.	Between two ages: tied to their family and to religion (especially women), preoccupied with success.
Sweden	This group can be subdivided into two categories: an elderly group similar to that in the United States and a group of young school dropouts.	Typically better off than in the other countries. Anxious for their children, suspicious of public institutions, concerned about their security and their retirement.	Similar to the United States, but more critical of social institutions and business.	A bit older, more preoccupied with their status. Desire a comfortable house and a calm lifestyle.	As interested by social standing as by money. Buy things that their children can inherit. Middle-class values.
Great Britain	Similar to Sweden. The school dropouts tend to be more aggressive and often organized into marginal subcultures: soccer hooligans, skinheads, and punks.	Traditional bearers of working-class values. Focused on their families. Critical or suspicious of public institutions; women are overrepresented.	Two groups: one similar to the United States: the other more active and demanding.	Older, often female. Concerned with fashion and their social status.	Not very numerous; rich; older and fairly traditional.
Germany	More psychologically than materially disadvantaged. Fearful, alienated, envious, antibusiness. Women are overrepresented.	Negative and pessimistic, resigned and apathetic. More psychologically than materially disadvantaged; hypochondriac.	Similar to those in the United States, but richer and better educated. Preoccupied with social status and prestige.	Very young, knowledgeable, masculine; preoccupied with social status and prestige.	Similar to those in the United States, although more politically active and more concerned with the "green" movement.

EXHIBIT 11.1

Comparison of VALS 1 Segments in North America and Europe

determine which groups are the heaviest users of pain relievers. It turns out that 43 percent of actualizers are heavy users of pain relievers but seem to prefer Advil. In response to this situation, Nuprin might try to alter its approach to attract more actualizers. One possibility is to use promotional appeals that are attractive to this segment,

Inner-Directed Goal Orientation

I Am Me	Experiential	Societally Conscious	Integrated
Exhibitionistic and narcissistic; young, impulsive, creative, active. Display their taste; clique buying; source of far-out fads. (5%)	Young, educated, artistic types eager for direct experience; person centered. Outdoor adventure; makers and doers. (7%)	Societally responsible; well-educated; interested in inner growth; small is beautiful, simplicity. Conservation emphasis in consumption. (9%)	Psychological maturity; tolerant; self-actualizing; global perspective; sense of fittingness. Esthetically oriented; one-of-a kind buying. (2%)
Older, informed, contemplative; high job satisfaction; little concern with financial success.	Young, male, dissatisfied with their jobs; invest more in their leisure activities; hedonists and bon vivants.	Few in number; more occupied with societal responsibilities than those in the United States.	Similar to the U.S. group; arbiters of cultural taste.
Knowledgeable; 25–35 years old; reject traditional values; extreme political views; live for the moment; easily bored.	Few in number; similar characteristics to the I am me's.	Well-informed; very young; born after the 1960s; activists; strong cultural appetites.	Similar to the U.S. group; arbiters of cultural taste.
Older; entrepreneurial; reject alcohol and drug use. Favor an intense and highly emotional lifestyle.	Hedonists; like high risk and dangerous activities. Ready for anything.	In search of an authentic life; active members of the community. Preoccupied with the environment and society in general.	Similar to the U.S. group; arbiters of cultural taste.
Few in number; exhibitionistic but also societally conscious.	Knowledgeable, adventurous, creative; want jobs that allow them to demonstrate these qualities.	Young, well-educated, creative, family-oriented; want jobs that allow them to achieve. Critical of authority and technology.	Similar to the U.S. group; arbiters of cultural taste.
Older; invest in their work. Would like to influence society. Anxious, searching for ideals.	Few in number.	Few in number.	Similar to the U.S. group; arbiters of cultural taste.

such as variety, personal freedom, and excellence. Another possibility is to use symbols that are popular with actualizers, such as people who are happy or people who are active.

The VALS systems have been used to segment markets and to target new product introductions. For each group one may define key product constellations as well as

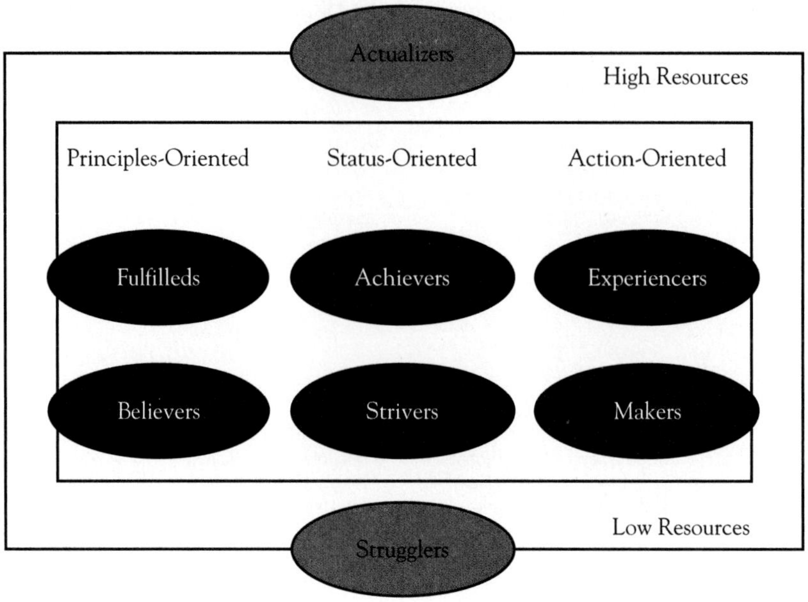

Actualizers are successful, sophisticated, active, take-charge people with high self-esteem and abundant resources. They are interested in growth and seek to develop, explore, and express themselves in a variety of ways—sometimes guided by principle, and sometimes by a desire to have an effect, to make a change.

Fulfilleds are mature, satisfied, comfortable, reflective people who value order, knowledge, and responsibility. Most are well educated and in (or recently retired from) professional occupations. They are well informed about world and national events and are alert to opportunities to broaden their knowledge. Content with their career, families, and station in life, their leisure activities tend to center around the home.

Achievers are successful career and work-oriented people who like to, and generally do, feel in control of their lives. They value consensus, predictability, and stability over risk, intimacy, and self-discovery. They are deeply committed to work and family. Work provides them with a sense of duty, material rewards, and prestige. Their social lives reflect this focus and are structured around family, church, and career.

Experiencers are young, vital, enthusiastic, impulsive, and rebellious. They seek variety and excitement, savoring the new, the offbeat, and the risky. Still in the process of formulating life values and patterns of behavior, they quickly become enthusiastic about new possibilities but are equally quick to cool. At this stage in their lives, they are politically uncommitted, uninformed, and highly ambivalent about what they believe.

Believers are conservative, conventional people with concrete beliefs based on traditional, established codes: family, church, community, and the nation. Many believers express moral codes that are deeply rooted and literally interpreted. They follow established routines, organized in large part around home, family, and social or religious organizations to which they belong.

Strivers seek motivation, self-definition, and approval from the world around them. They are striving to find a secure place in life. Unsure of themselves and low on economic social and psychological resources, strivers are concerned about the opinions and approval of others.

Makers are practical people who have constructive skills and value self-sufficiency. They live within a traditional context of family, practical work, and physical recreation and have little interest in what lies outside that context. Makers experience the world by working on it—building a house, raising children, fixing a car, or canning vegetables—and have enough skill, income, and energy to carry out their projects successfully.

Strugglers live constricted lifes. Chronically poor, ill educated, low skilled, without strong social bonds, elderly, and concerned about their health, they are often resigned and passive. Because they are limited by the need to meet the urgent needs of the present moment, they do not show a strong self-orientation. Their chief concerns are for security and safety.

Source: www.sric-bi.com/VALS/.

EXHIBIT 11.2

VALS 2 Segment Profiles

Question	Related VALS 2 Dimension
I love to make things I can use everyday.	Makers
I follow the latest trends and fashions.	Strivers
Just as the Bible says, the world literally was created in six days.	Believers
I like to learn about art, culture, and history.	Resource/skills question
I often crave excitement.	Experiencers
I would rather make something than buy it.	Makers
I dress more fashionably than most people.	Strivers
The federal government should encourage prayers in public schools.	Believers
I like trying new things.	Experiencers
I like to lead others.	Actualizers
I like doing things that are new and different.	Experiencers

Response format: mostly disagree; somewhat disagree; somewhat agree; mostly agree.
Demographic information is also collected: gender; age; level of formal education (a resource question); income (a resource question).

EXHIBIT 11.3

Example Questions from the VALS 2 Survey

appropriate communication styles, media of communication, and particular elements of the marketing mix to emphasize.

Japan VALS

SRI has recently extended the VALS system to Japan. Like VALS 2, its typologies are based on product usage and behavior as well as attitudes. The **Japan VALS** identifies leaders of change and their relationship to emerging social trends. Japan VALS identifies five important dimensions:

Exploration—an individual's active involvement and motivation to master new challenges.

Self-expression—sociable, enjoys sports, and impulsive shoppers.

Achievement—career, status, leadership, and culture.

Tradition—stability, order, community, and traditional beliefs.

Realists—follow a reactive orientation to life; relatively unconcerned with self-improvement or fashion.

The exploration and achievement dimensions are designed to predict activities related to innovation, consumption, production, and social control or mediation. Four main groups—change leaders, adapters, followers, and change resisters—divided into 10 standard segments emerge from the Japan VALS analysis. The Japan VALS analysis and characteristics of the groups are shown in Exhibit 11.4. In addition to the standard segmentation, Japan VALS defines three other levels of analysis that allow subscribers to focus on specific industry markets, niche segments for specific products and market opportunities, and international comparisons.

Understanding pressures experienced in different cultures can translate into market opportunities. For example, U.S. strivers want fun, stylish, fast, good-value cars. Japanese strivers consider their car like an extra room and will spend to add lace curtains

INDUSTRY INSIGHTS 11.3

Pain Reliever Use by VALS 2 Type

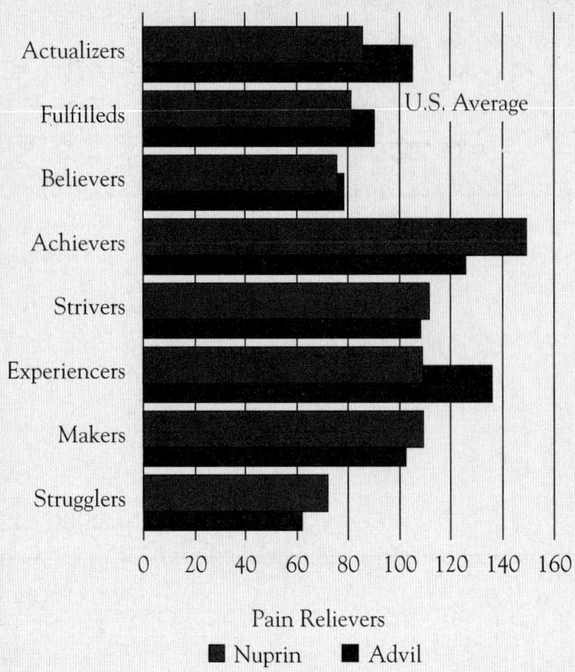

Source: SRI International.

or expensive stereos to them. A value appeal that might work well with a U.S. striver would be lost on a Japanese striver.[24]

List of Values (LOV) Approach

An alternative to the VALS scheme is the List of Values (LOV) approach developed at the University of Michigan. This approach was introduced in Chapter 3 in our discussion of cultural values. The LOV approach aims to assess adaptation to various roles through value fulfillment. People's dominant values are identified from a list of nine, including self-respect, security, warm relationships with others, sense of accomplishment, self-fulfillment, sense of belonging, being well respected, fun and enjoyment in life, and excitement. Research has found a significant number of predicted relationships between LOV dimensions and various criterion variables such as participation in certain commercially available activities such as skiing, backpacking, camping, and consumption of certain products.

Certain LOV values are associated with the values identified in VALS, such as an inner- or outward orientation, self-fulfillment, and accomplishment. Unlike VALS, there is no implicit evaluative dimension in the LOV such as the developmental contrast between marginal survivors and wealthy, healthy integrateds.

Cohort Analysis

Another useful way of anticipating lifestyle trends is to understand the power of cohorts. We provide additional discussion of age cohorts in Chapter 12. In lifestyle terms, an age cohort is the group of people born over a relatively short and contiguous time period who are deeply influenced and bound together by the events of their formative years. In twenty-first-century America, the passage to adulthood occurs roughly between the ages of 17 and 21. Events that happen when people first come of age create habits and attitudes that often last a lifetime and influence future attitudes and behaviors toward savings, sex, a good meal, musical preferences, and product preferences. Exhibit 11.5 outlines four of the six age cohorts that define the U.S. consumer market.[25]

Understanding cohort effects can improve predictions about changing lifestyles by sensitizing marketers to how generations will age differently than they have in the past. For example, consider coffee consumption. Over the past 40 years, coffee consumption has risen with age, while cola consumption has declined with age. Also, the number of 18- to 34-year-olds declined by 4 million in the 1990s, while the number of

EXHIBIT 11.4

Japan VALS Segments

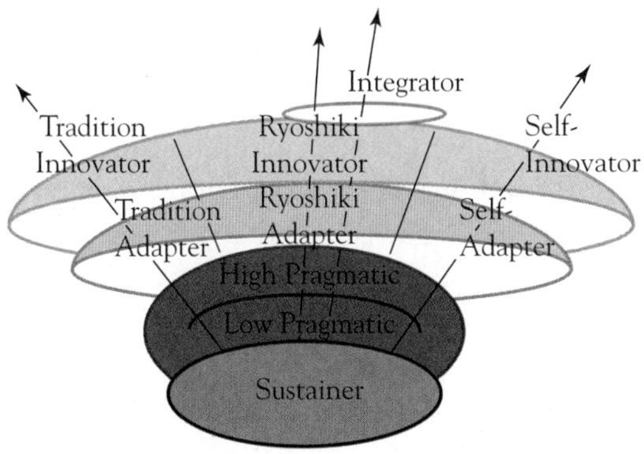

- Change leader segments show high levels of consumer activity, a clear distinct self-concept, and high interests in many areas of life.
- Adapter segments tend to follow the trends of change leaders near them, but at moderate levels of activity.
- Follower segments tend to show no distinct pattern except risk avoidance.
- Change resister segments show low consumer activity, generally reserved attitudes, and few strong interests.

Exploration

Integrators are well educated, very affluent, sociable adventurous, and stylish. Their values are modern and include Western values and some traditional ideas. They enjoy the new and risky and rank highest on a variety of consumer indicators. Integrators travel and read widely and are attracted to high-quality, prestigious products.

Sustainers are at the low end of the exploration dimension. They are resistant to change and lead lives of calm simplicity and traditional routine.

Self-expression

Self-innovators are young, active, sociable, and very interested in fashion and leisure sports. They spend more on themselves in proportion to their income and are able to do so because many live with parents or friends. Some "office ladies" would be found in this group.

Self-adapters pattern their activities and product choices after the self-innovator group but are somewhat older and less active. They have below-average incomes and are less educated. They are shy, unassertive, and sensitive to others' opinions. They enjoy sports, tend to be impulsive shoppers, and read comics (which are huge in Japan) and fashion and lifestyle magazines.

Achievement

Ryoshiki innovators are committed to career and the social status quo. They have high education but average income, and many are middle-aged specialists or teachers. Their tastes tend toward cultural pursuits, fashion, exercise, socializing with spouses, and continuing education for self-betterment.

Ryoshiki adapters have higher incomes than Ryoshiki innovators. They are less assertive, less stressed, and more down to earth, well adjusted, and active. They have a moderate, modern outlook on life. Many own European furniture, expensive artwork, and home computers, and many play golf. They read the business newspaper *Nikkei* and business magazines.

Tradition

Tradition innovators are mostly middle-aged homeowners with jobs in middle management and primary industries who are active in community affairs. They are successful but avoid risk. They are highest in use of organic foods, health magazines, home repair, carpentry, local newspapers, and large luxury cars.

Tradition adapters are high but not extreme in the traditional orientation and have adapted the traditional innovator lifestyle. They are younger and better educated than traditional innovators and are the second most affluent of all the groups. Many are managers, entrepreneurs, or farmers, or work in primary industries. They travel frequently on business, read health magazines, and enjoy doing home repair, fishing, and playing golf. They put their money into real estate and postal insurance funds.

Realists

High pragmatists are middle-aged, above average in income and education, but average in consumption. The group least likely to agree with any attitude statement, they seem withdrawn and suspicious. They are unconcerned about self-improvement, fashion, leading others, or preserving traditional customs. They appear to follow a flexible, even reactive, orientation to life with few fixed beliefs.

Low pragmatics are attitudinally negative and show a strong psychological tendency, except a slightly more positive stance, toward traditional customs. This group includes married women who take care of children at home and men who work as laborers, farmers, and fishermen. Their housing is modest, and many commute by bicycle. They are below-average consumers and prefer inexpensive goods and established brands.

Source: SRI International.

The World War II Cohort—born: 1922 to 1927; coming of age: 1940 to 1945; age in 1994: 67 to 72; current population: 11 million; share of adult population: 6 percent.
People who came of age in the early 1940s were unified by a common enemy and shared experiences. A sense of deferment was especially strong among the 16 million Americans in the military and their loved ones at home. Consequently, the World War II cohort became intensely romantic. Although it was not a boom time, unemployment was no longer a problem.
The Boomers I Cohort—born: 1946 to 1954; coming of age: 1963 to 1972; age in 1994: 40 to 48; current population: 33 million; share of adult population: 17 percent.
The two boomer cohorts are separated by the end of the Vietnam conflict. The Kennedy assassination, followed by those of Martin Luther King and Robert Kennedy, signaled an end to the status quo and galvanized the large boomer cohort. Still, the boomers I cohort continued to experience economic good times and wants a lifestyle at least as good as the one experienced as children in the 1950s.
The Boomers II Cohort—born: 1955 to 1965; coming of age: 1973 to 1983; age in 1994: 29 to 39; current population: 49 million; share of adult population: 25 percent.
After Watergate, something changed people coming of age in America. The idealistic fervor of youth disappeared. Instead, the boomers II cohort exhibited a narcissistic preoccupation with themselves, which manifested itself in everything from the self-help movement to self-deprecation in the media. Changes in the economy had a profound effect on this group. Debt as a means of maintaining a lifestyle made sense.
The Generation X Cohort—born: 1966 to 1976; coming of age: 1984 to 1994; age in 1994: 18 to 28; current population: 41 million; share of adult population: 21 percent.
Generation X has nothing to hang on to. These are children of divorce and day care, the latch-key kids of the 1980s. They are searching for anchors with their seemingly contradictory retro behavior: the resurgence of proms, coming-out parties, and fraternities. Their political conservatism is motivated by a what's-in-it-for-me? cynicism. Their alienation is reflected in the violence and brutal sex of their popular culture.

Sources: J. Walker Smith and Ann Clurman, Rocking the Ages: The Yankelovich Report on Generational Marketing *(New York: Harper Business, 1997); and Geoffrey Meredith and Charles Schewe, "The Power of Cohorts,"* American Demographics, *December 1994, pp. 22–31. See also Joseph O. Rentz and Fred D. Reynolds, "Forecasting the Effects of an Aging Population on Product Consumption: An Age-Period-Cohort Framework,"* Journal of Marketing Research *28 (1991), pp. 355–60; and Norman B. Ryder, "The Cohort as a Concept in the Study of Social Change,"* American Sociological Review *30 (December 1965), pp. 843–61.*

EXHIBIT 11.5

Cohort Cartography: Some Age Cohorts That Define the U.S. Consumer Market

older adults grew by 24 million. This might on the surface suggest that demand for coffee will increase while demand for cola declines. However, this is based on a crucial premise that historic consumption rates by a particular age group will prevail in the future. A **cohort analysis** might instead suggest that younger, cola-intensive cohorts will continue to consume soft drinks even as they age. Meanwhile, older, coffee-intensive groups will age and move out of the marketplace. Baby boomers and other lower-consuming cohorts will replace them. This trend indicates that, despite an aging population, demand for cola will not decline (e.g., the reverse effect). As other examples, consider food and music preferences. Certainly some eating habits are affected by aging. However, baby boomers aren't going to start baking lots of tuna casseroles and listening to Lawrence Welk when they turn 50. Because the enduring taste preferences of cohorts are often formed during the teenage years, they probably will still eat pizza and listen to rock 'n' roll. For example, the popularity of the Rock 'n' Roll Hall of Fame in Cleveland and Paul Allen's Experience Music Project outside of Seattle both speak to the enduring involvement of North American baby boomers with this music.[26]

www.emplive.com/

www.greatbuildings.com/buildings/Experience_Music_Project.html

REGIONAL LIFESTYLES

For a variety of reasons, consumer culture varies geographically, or by region. These reasons include climate and topography, ethnic history, and the distribution of jobs and industries. For example, in Latin America, economic resources are often concentrated in a few large cities. Mexico City alone represents 60 percent of the purchasing power of Mexico. Southern Germans with their Catholic heritage differ in outlook from people in northern and eastern Germany with their Protestant and Prussian heritage. Those from southern and northern Germany differ from eastern Germans who experienced 50 years of Soviet domination. French-speaking, Catholic Quebecois differ in outlook from Anglican and Protestant English-speaking Canadians. Inclusive civic institutions and parenting styles in east Asian countries such as Singapore and Japan moderate the rebelliousness and permissiveness associated with teenage lifestyles. The point here is that lifestyle marketing needs to take regional variations into account.[27]

Regional differences affect consumption. In northern Europe, for example, butter is a prime ingredient in traditional cooking, whereas southern Europeans favor olive oil. In northern India, the staple food and drink are wheat (bread) and tea; in the south, they are rice and coffee. In the United States, light vegetable, pasta, and fruit-laden California cuisine contrasts with the meat, potatoes, and gravy traditions of the Midwest, the Mexican-influenced cuisine of the Southwest, and the Caribbean-influenced cuisine of south Florida.

A number of segmentation systems have been developed to take **regional lifestyles** into account. Take, for example, the **nine nations of North America.** North America has been divided into "nations" according to differences in cultural value orientations and lifestyles. Exhibit 11.6 summarizes these differences for eight of these regions (excluding Quebec). Fun, enjoyment, and excitement are valued most by inhabitants of the Islands (the southern tip of Florida). A sense of belonging is most highly prized by residents of the Empty Quarter, comprising Idaho, Montana, Wyoming, Utah, Nevada, and parts of some other states. Like other values-based schemes, the nine nations model has some intuitive appeal, but it has limited power to predict the values of any given consumer. Because of intracultural variation, other factors must be taken into account in explaining individual consumer behaviors.[28]

China too has been divided into regional lifestyle segments, seven in this case. Regional markets in the south and east represent China's growth markets. They are more economically developed and contain more affluent consumers. South China represents the Min-Yue culture, with plenty of contact with the outside world and great emphasis on mercantile entrepreneurship. South Chinese speak Cantonese and Fukienese. East China, located around the Yangtze River Delta, is densely populated, urbanized, and prosperous. Shanghai, the financial and industrial capital of China, is located here. East China represents the Hai-pai culture, well known for producing products that enhance quality of life. Consumers here are highly innovative and fashion trendsetters.

China's emerging markets are to be found in the north, central, and southwest. Each has its own distinctive culture and language differences. For example, in the north China city of Beijing, the capital of the country, the Jing-pai culture is strong, which attaches great value to Confucian doctrines. Consumers here are relatively more conservative

Values	New England	The Foundry	Dixie	The Islands	Breadbasket	Mex-America	Empty Quarter	Ecotopia
Self-respect	22.5%	20.5%	22.5%	25.0%	17.9%	22.7%	35.3%	18.0%
Security	21.7	19.6	23.3	15.6	20.2	17.3	17.6	19.6
Warm relationships with others	14.2	16.7	13.8	9.4	20.5	18.0	5.9	18.5
Sense of accomplishment	14.2	11.7	10.0	9.4	12.4	11.3	8.8	12.2
Self-fulfillment	9.2	9.9	8.4	3.1	7.5	16.0	5.9	12.7
Being well respected	8.3	8.7	11.0	15.6	10.1	2.7	2.9	4.2
Sense of belonging	5.0	8.4	7.5	12.5	7.8	6.7	17.6	7.9
Fun, enjoyment, excitement	5.0	4.5	3.5	9.4	3.6	5.3	5.9	6.9

[a]The French-speaking region of Canada is excluded in this table.

EXHIBIT 11.6

Psychographic Differences between the Regional Nations of North America[a]

than in the south. Finally, China's untapped markets are to be found in the northeast and northwest. Northwest China contains a large number of ethnic minorities. A few of the many intriguing psychographic and lifestyle differences between these complex regions are summarized in Exhibit 11.7.[29]

PRIZM

PRIZM is *a lifestyle segmentation system that deals with regional lifestyles at a micro level.* It is based on the principle that people with similar lifestyles tend to live near one another. As the familiar saying predicts, birds of a feather flock together. Claritas Inc.—a market research firm in San Diego, California—originally created PRIZM nearly 30 years ago. It describes every U.S. neighborhood in terms of 62 distinct clusters, based on census data, consumer surveys, and other methods.[30] Industry Insights 11.4 shows some examples of the PRIZM clusters. In brief, the clusters are defined in terms of buying habits and media patterns. For instance, members of the Upward Bound cluster are more likely than the average household to read *Vogue* magazine and watch *The Tonight Show.* At the same time, this cluster is brand loyal and more likely to purchase a new station wagon. As the name implies, the Upward Bound cluster consists of professional workers with relatively high incomes. People in this cluster live in towns such as Simi Valley, California, and Herndon, Virginia.

PRIZM is useful for marketers because it can identify groups of consumers who perform at or above average levels for product purchases. PRIZM identifies neighborhoods where existing customers live, and it can be used to predict where prospective customers are likely to be found. The reports generated by PRIZM can be used to answer such questions as: Who are my targets? What are they like (e.g., in terms of demographics)? Where can I find them? For instance, PRIZM software can be used to create prospect lists for direct-mail campaigns, or it could be used to suggest media vehicles (e.g., magazines) for an ad campaign.

PRIZM data can be accessed via postal zip codes. Each zip code may contain many clusters. Industry Insights 11.5 shows the top five clusters for the zip code 30605, which

	South	East	North	Central	Southwest	Northeast	Northwest
Household income	$27,481	$24,659	$12,993	$13,831	$14,008	$8,683	$7,770
Psychographics							
Satisfaction with life	66.6%	67.5%	81.3%	80.2%	66.8%	81.3%	67.6%
Work hard and get rich	33.3	31.6	30.7	34.6	42.3	44.2	67.1
Favor foreign brands	36.4	27.5	22.2	24.1	19.6	28.1	35.7
Lifestyle activities							
Going to movies	33.3	41.0	40.4	37.2	41.4	2.4	10.0
Listening to music	75.0	62.5	42.4	50.0	43.6	35.6	36.6
Traveling	25.0	23.1	17.7	27.9	22.3	32.9	4.3
Media usage							
Cable TV	83.3	69.2	68.3	68.9	68.8	28.3	14.3
Magazine	25.0	30.8	40.1	44.7	36.7	32.9	9.9
Consumer durables							
Refrigerator	91.7	94.9	74.7	69.6	64.2	39.6	24.7
Color TV	100.0	97.5	90.8	85.4	79.0	87.3	44.3
PC	18.2	7.7	4.5	3.2	4.5	2.7	2.9

Source: Geng Cui and Qiming Liu, "Regional Market Segments of China: Opportunities and Barriers in a Big Emerging Market," *Journal of Consumer Marketing* 17, no. 1 (2000), pp. 55–70.

EXHIBIT 11.7

Psychographic and Lifestyle Differences in the Seven Nations of China

@ yawyl.claritas.com

is part of a college town, Athens, Georgia. Important clusters in this zip code include the Towns and Gowns, college-town singles who are likely to own a computer and have a school loan. Another key cluster in 30605 is the New Homesteaders (young, middle-class families). This group is likely to shop by direct mail, buy microwave cookware, and read *Southern Living*. Go to the Claritas website and look up your own zip code to learn more about the PRIZM system of lifestyle segmentation. Do the PRIZM clusters that appear for your zip code make sense? Why or why not? It is important to realize that a single zip code can contain more than 15 significant clusters, so the five that appear on the website may not always seem complete to you.

SHIFTING LIFESTYLES

In this chapter we have talked mostly about psychographic segmentation schemes designed to identify and profile similar groups in the current marketplace. However, another very important focus for lifestyle research is to provide general insights into emerging social trends and evolving lifestyles. Identifying lifestyle trends is one of the most difficult applications of psychographic research, and yet it is perhaps one of the most vital. Lifestyle trends are triggered by major demographic shifts, such as Japanese women entering the workforce, U.S. women having babies later in life and returning to work sooner, or U.S. baby boomers aging. But lifestyle trends are also triggered by important attitudinal shifts, such as European consumers' growing commitment to organic food or the casual dress trend in corporate America. Lifestyle trends such as

Examples of PRIZM Clusters

INDUSTRY INSIGHTS 11.4

PRIZM Cluster	Upward Bound	New Ecotopia	River City, USA
Description	Young, upscale, white-collar families	Rural, white/blue-collar, farm families	Middle-class, rural families
Demographics			
Age group	Under 18, 35–54	45+	Under 18, 45–54
Work status	Professional	White-collar, blue-collar, farming	Blue-collar, farming
Household income	$62,000	$39,000	$39,000
Percent of U.S. households	1.81%	0.89%	1.80%
Most likely to . . .	Be brand loyal Buy a new station wagon Have a 401(k) plan Watch *The Tonight Show* Read *Vogue*	Go cross-country skiing Own a dog Have a Keogh account Watch *Jeopardy!* Read *Prevention*	Go target shooting Travel by train Own a cat Watch TNN Read *Country Living*
Live in neighborhoods like . . .	Simi Valley, CA Herndon, VA Nashua, NH	Sutter Creek, CA East Chatham, NY Grafton, VT	Silver Creek, MN Springville, IA Coopers Mill, ME

Source: Adapted from yawyl.claritas.com.

these affect the welfare of numerous industries. Successful strategic planning relies on identifying these trends early and separating out trends from fads (see Chapter 17 for a discussion of trends versus fads). Let's look at just a couple of specific lifestyle trends and consider their implications for products and services.

Consider the dramatic increase in the number of Japanese working women. Although Japanese women haven't become as liberated as Western women, they are at least as busy. More than half of Japan's married women now hold full- or part-time jobs, and women account for 40.5 percent of the Japanese workforce. Although many Japanese advertisers still use images of the stereotypical housewife, others are addressing the new breed of working women in products as diverse as frozen vegetables, cigarettes, and nonsmear lipstick.[31] Nonsmear lipstick didn't even exist 10 years ago, but now it's a $45 million a month business in Japan. The popularity is attributed to the working Japanese woman who prefers brands that eliminate time-consuming reapplications. As an aside, it solves a common problem for Japanese men as well. A survey by a Japanese cosmetics manufacturer (Shiseido) found that 40 percent of all male commuters have been smeared by lipstick in Tokyo's jam-packed trains and subways. "This can cause a riot at home," a Shiseido spokesman said. In a culture that abhors a loss of face, the nonsmear lipstick helps avoid this problem.

PRIZM Clusters for a Specific Zip Code: Athens, GA 30605

INDUSTRY INSIGHTS 11.5

PRIZM Cluster	Towns and Gowns	Southside City	New Homesteaders	God's Country	Middleburg Managers
Description	College-town singles	African-American service workers	Young middle-class families	Executive exurban families	Midlevel, white-collar couples
Demographics					
Age group	18–34	Under 18, 18–34	35–54, 65+	35–64	35–44, 65+
Work status	White-collar, service	Blue-collar, service	White-collar	White-collar	Professional, white-collar
Household income	$19,700	$17,000	$40,400	$65,300	$42,000
Percent of U.S. households	1.35%	1.89%	1.69%	2.69%	1.81%
Most likely to . . .	Be college basketball fans Own a $1,000 + computer Have a school loan Watch *Friends* Read *Glamour*	Be pro wrestling fans Buy gospel music Own a Mazda Watch BET Read *GQ*	Shop by direct mail Buy microwave cookware Have a Sears credit card Watch country music TV Read *Southern Living*	Shop online each month Own a garden tiller/tractor Have tax-sheltered annuities Watch *This Old House* Read *Colonial Homes*	Jog or run Own a laptop computer Have a home equity loan Watch the QVC channel Read *PC* magazine
Live in neighborhoods like . . .	Madison, WI Bowling Green, OH Gainesville, FL	Saginaw, MI Shreveport, LA Mobile, AL	McQueeney, TX Opolis, KS West Rockport, ME	South Austin, TX Forsyth, IL Watertown, CT	East Olympia, WA Charleston, WV Panama City, FL

Source: Adapted from yawyl.claritas.com.

Another subtle lifestyle shift that has important implications for clothes makers is the trend toward dressing down in corporate America, as suggested by the photo on page 462. A recent study revealed that almost 90 percent of U.S. workers are dressing down at least some of the time. The casual Friday trend has created an important growth in corporate casual clothing. Companies such as Levi Strauss are aggressively attempting to capitalize on the trend. Levi Strauss is targeting businesses with newsletters to human resources managers about why casual dress codes should be adopted and following up with how-to kits, videos on the fine art of dressing down, and casual dress fashion shows. Its competitor, Haggar, long known for custom-fit suits and sports suits, is moving toward casual wear with a line called City Casuals.

Sometimes, a single person can personify a lifestyle. One example in the United States of such a person is Martha Stewart, a woman who has created an empire to promote

Levi Strauss (Dockers) and Banana Republic are just two examples of clothing lines capitalizing on the lifestyle trend toward casual business dress.

her ideas about a style of elegant living. She is viewed as the "ultimate homemaker," and she strives to teach the masses how to create "the good life." She provides an example of a marketer who teaches cultural capital—knowledge of specialized consumption genres—to the upwardly mobile nouveau riche, as will be discussed in Chapter 12.

The Martha Stewart lifestyle did not exist in the early 1960s, but it is a conspicuous force in the early twenty-first century. In fact, Martha Stewart, Inc., is a public corporation with the following components: magazines (*Martha Stewart Weddings, Martha Stewart Entertaining*), books (*Martha Stewart Cookbook*), cable TV (*From Martha's Kitchen*), Internet sites (chat groups, *askMartha*), catalogs (Martha by Mail), specialty products (lines of linens and garden equipment for Kmart), and others. Martha Stewart sees herself as a purveyor of information. She got her start by catering elaborate parties in the 1970s. Subsequently, she published her landmark book, *Martha Stewart Entertaining,* which has sold more than 500,000 copies. In brief, the Martha Stewart lifestyle represents investing a large amount of time in adding ornamentation to life, especially in the areas of cooking, home decor, design, gift giving, celebrations (e.g., weddings), and parties. It involves a search for casual elegance and sometimes is seen as embodying the "perfect housewife" image. As with any trend, however, there is a countertrend. For instance, detractors say her name has become synonymous with an unobtainable and slightly ridiculous standard in the domestic arts. Many of Martha Stewart's recommended household projects seem as if they require hours, if not days, to complete. Some U.S. consumers put out welcome mats that say, "Martha Stewart doesn't live here."[32]

In the twenty-first century, the strong association between Martha Stewart, the person, and her commercial empire has caused some problems. For instance, when Martha Stewart was accused of insider stock trading, the popularity of her TV shows and magazines declined a bit.

The Martha Stewart lifestyle is seen as an upscale, idealized version of the American Dream.[33] As the CEO of Martha Stewart, Inc., Ms. Stewart had the vision to recognize lifestyle trends and the determination to turn this vision into an unprecedented success. In fact, many American CEOs and their families live out some of the good-life fantasies that are described, in detail, in Martha Stewart's media and retail empire. Nonetheless, there are emerging questions about the degree to which such lavish lifestyles are sustainable. See Ethical Dilemma 11.1.

INTERNATIONAL LIFESTYLE SEGMENTS

Lifestyle segmentation schemes are popular worldwide. National and international schemes have been developed in all the major European countries and for European consumers as a whole. In France, the COFRECMA Sociostyles scheme is widely used, and in Denmark a popular scheme called Minerva identifies lifestyle segments by color.

Global Scan

Backer Spielvogel & Bates Worldwide (BSB) has created **Global Scan,** *an evolving psychographic segmentation scheme including at least 18 countries* (mostly Triad and Pacific Rim countries). Global Scan measures a wide variety of attitude and consumer values, media use, and buying patterns. Repeat surveys are conducted annually in each country to ensure the model remains reflective of the population. Both higher-order values such as self-sufficiency and self-esteem and personality characteristics are included in the survey, as are political opinions and attitudes about social issues. To improve applicability, consumers are questioned directly on their use of more than 1,000 brands and products.

BSB claims 95 percent of the combined population of all the countries surveyed can be assigned to five segments: **adapters** (18 percent), **traditionals** (16 percent), **pressureds** (13 percent), **achievers** (22 percent), and **strivers** (26 percent). A three-country comparison is shown in Industry Insights 11.6. As can be seen from the diagram, the five general groups are found in varying proportions in the countries studied. For example, there are fewer traditionals in the United States than in Japan or the UK, while the UK has proportionately more strivers and Japan has more adapters.

Global Scan allows marketers to identify cross-cultural and local differences. Canadian strivers are more open-minded and liberal than their U.S. counterparts, but they are also more materialistic, ambitious, optimistic, and risk taking. Canadian achievers, the affluent opinion leader segment, enjoy one of the highest-quality lifestyles of any country surveyed. The pressured segment, those with familial and financial worries, are found in greater proportion in Quebec than in any other Canadian province.

In the next section, we briefly present examples of lifestyle segments that exist in three countries: Turkey, New Zealand, and China. It is interesting to note how these lifestyle segments differ across the three nations and how they differ from lifestyle segments that have been identified in the United States (for example, VALS 2). These three countries are discussed because recent lifestyle research has been completed there and because they represent regions where lifestyles are likely to be quite different from those discussed in traditional schemes.[34]

TURKISH LIFESTYLES In a recent study, three lifestyle segments were identified for Turkish consumers. The first segment is labeled liberals/trendsetters. These consumers are somewhat similar to those in Western nations. They are mostly college educated and high-income earners. Important characteristics for these consumers include quality,

A Contrast in Lifestyles: On Walden Pond and the CEO

ETHICAL DILEMMA 11.1

On Walden Pond

Henry David Thoreau describes his time on Walden Pond as follows.

> I went to the woods because I wished to live deliberately, to front only the essential facts of life. I wanted to live deep and suck all the marrow of life, to live so sturdily and Spartan-like as to put to rout all that was not life. I say, let your affairs be as two or three, and not a hundred or a thousand; instead of a million count half a dozen . . . Simplify, simplify.

The CEO

Born in Russia and trained as a geophysicist, Alexander E. Benton founded an oil-and-gas exploration business in 1988. At first, Benton Oil & Gas Co. did well, developing the first Russian oil field funded with foreign investment. Like many successful chief executives, Mr. Benton enjoyed the good life. As CEO, he owned a $4 million estate on more than six acres near Santa Barbara, complete with Pacific views, pool, formal garden, and a wine cellar. In Carmel, California, he and his wife had another home, valued at about $1.7 million. Then there was a house in Ventura, which sat on an 8,712-square-foot lot. Mr. Benton had his

It takes a folk-rock poet (president) to describe the impact of business leaders' ethical lapses.

Source: By permission of Mike Luckovich & Creators Syndicate, Inc.

ETHICAL DILEMMA 11.1

pick of six cars, including a 1963 Jaguar and a 1964 Porsche, two other sports cars, and a Land Rover. He owned 15 antique watches and expensive collections of fine art.

Much of Mr. Benton's luxury acquisition spree was funded with debt, and when it came to shopping for credit he found some easy-going loan officers. They were Benton Oil's directors, and, over nearly five years, they extended him roughly $6.6 million in loans. It turned out that Mr. Benton was not a very good credit risk. The loans were secured by his company stock and options. When oil prices dropped in the late 1990s, so did Benton Oil's share price. By the summer of 1999, the balance owed on the loans exceeded the collateral's value. The directors demanded early repayment and ultimately ousted him.

Mr. Benton, 59 years old, now lives in a rented London flat and doesn't own a single car. He has earned the dubious distinction of being the first head of a public company in recent memory to file for bankruptcy over his corporate IOUs. See the cartoon, where the rock/poet (president) describes the societal fall-out associated with ethical lapses in the business world.

A contrast

When many consumers imagine a lifestyle that embodies the good life, they may be tempted to pursue some of the opulent trappings that Mr. Benton acquired. In contrast, Thoreau describes how "less can be more." It is from this perspective that Thoreau is sometimes called the father of the environmental movement in the United States.

As life becomes more complex, there are many connections between citizens and consumers. An ethical lapse, at the top, reverberates throughout the economy. There are many hidden costs associated with luxurious lifestyles. In Thoreau's *Walden,* the author describes his retreat from the encroaching civilization, and he outlines a philosophy of self-reliance that still serves as an inspiration to those interested in designing a "sustainable" lifestyle.

Sources: Joann S. Lublin and Jared Sandberg, "Uneasy Money: Deadbeat CEOs Plague Firms as Economy and Markets Roil," The Wall Street Journal, *August 1, 2002, pp. A1, A8; and Henry David Thoreau,* Walden; or, Life in the Woods *(1854).*

workmanship, prestigious brand name, and style. Price is not especially important to this group.[35]

The second and third clusters are labeled moderates/survivors and traditionalists/conservatives. A major difference between clusters two and three is that the former contains mostly males. Group three contains many females, but key purchase decisions (for example, automobiles) are made by male family members. Prestige and style are not so important. Price is very important. As a whole, the traditionalist segment does not have a favorable attitude toward imported Western products, in contrast to the relatively positive attitudes of the liberals/trendsetters.

NEW ZEALAND LIFESTYLES In a 1998 study of 3,773 New Zealanders, six major segments were identified (see Exhibit 11.8). These include active family values people, conservative quiet lifers, educated liberals, accepting mid-lifers, success-driven extroverts, pragmatic strugglers, and social strivers. Some of the segments have parallels in VALS 2. For instance, the pragmatic strugglers are somewhat like the strugglers in VALS 2, but this group also shares something in common with the VALS's makers. As the name implies, the strivers and the social strivers are similar. The VALS's achievers and the New Zealand extroverts share common characteristics.[36]

The accepting mid-lifers is one group that doesn't have a clear counterpart in the VALS 2 classification system. The mid-lifers are generally accepting of their lives and of society.

INDUSTRY INSIGHTS 11.6

Global Scan Segments in Three Countries

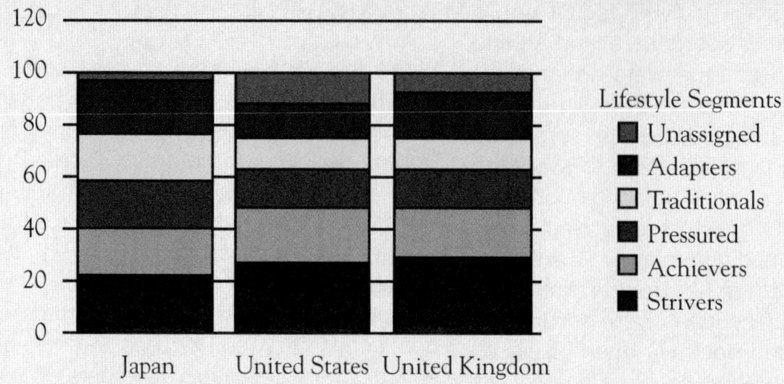

	Japan	United States	United Kingdom
Unassigned	2	12	8
Adapters	22	14	17
Traditionals	18	12	16
Pressured	19	14	12
Achievers	17	22	18
Strivers	22	26	29

Source: Rebecca Piirto, Beyond Mind Games *(Ithaca, NY: American Demographics Books, 1991).*

They lack a strong feeling regarding political and social issues. They like things as they are and are not so willing to try new things (for example, new brands or products). With regard to food products, their most important criterion is taste. They are not so concerned with sugar or cholesterol intake. Mid-lifers don't receive much enjoyment from shopping. At the same time, they are not very brand loyal. They are likely to use credit cards and purchase items such as videocassette recorders, compact disc players, and more than one television. The New Zealand study illustrates the value of combining psychological variables (for example, novelty seeking) with marketing information (for example, data about the purchase of specific brands or products).

SEGMENTS FOR CHINESE FEMALES A segmentation study for females living in greater China was completed in 1998.[37] A total of four segments was identified for females between the ages of 18 and 35: conventional women (40.7 percent of the population), contemporary women (21.9 percent), searching singles (19.4 percent), and followers (18.1 percent).

It is interesting to note that the conventional segment corresponds somewhat to the traditionalist/conservative segment identified in Turkey. Conventional women are proud of having a close-knit family, and they consider family to be the most important aspect of their life. In terms of recreation, they are indoor types and prefer reading newspapers and books or watching television.

Contemporary women share some characteristics in common with conventional women, especially with regard to the importance of family. However, this group believes that

Segment Name	Population	Description
Active family values people	15.5%	Family and community focus Traditional principles Positive outlook
Conservative quiet lifers	13.5	Homebodies Conservative views Reflective and nostalgic
Educated liberals	9.0	Socially concerned Progressive and egalitarian Enjoy variety and diversity
Accepting mid-lifers	17.1	Observe rather than partake Accepting of status quo Content
Success-driven extroverts	16.4	Self-oriented Value free enterprise Actively ambitious
Pragmatic strugglers	14.7	Family survival focus Politically conservative Determined
Social strivers	13.0	Outer directed Conformist Feel life is a struggle

Source: Sarah Todd, Rob Lawson, and Fiona Faris, "A Lifestyle Analysis of New Zealand Consumers," *Asia Pacific Journal of Management and Logistics* 10, no. 3 (1998), pp. 30–47. Reprinted by permission of John Wiley & Sons, Inc.

EXHIBIT 11.8

Lifestyle Segments in New Zealand

work is also important, and they try to combine family and work into their lifestyle. Unlike the conventional women, contemporary women are likely to voice a complaint when they are dissatisfied with a product or service. They are very concerned about their appearance and prefer imported and branded products.

Searching singles have more progressive ideas about the role of women in society. For instance, they are more career oriented, and they postpone marriage longer. Females in this group like to go shopping and are concerned with the image of the store where they shop. They are especially influenced by sales announcements and the image of the brand. Also, they are heavy users of fast food and entertainment services.

Women in the fourth and final segment, followers, are not very active in social, cultural, or other physical activities. They don't make as many shopping trips as those in some of the other groups. More than half of them are single, and they have achieved relatively low levels in both education and income. Followers lack confidence and are somewhat uncertain about the future. Consequently, they like to seek advice from salespeople about the products they buy.

In general, the Chinese segments do not share much in common with the segments identified in New Zealand. The New Zealand segments are more like those that might be found in a European or North American country. The Chinese segments are more similar to those found in Turkey. This makes sense in that China and Turkey are both developing nations, and both have a culture that sometimes clashes with consumption values as they are represented in the Triad nations.

CRITICISMS OF LIFESTYLES RESEARCH

It is important to note the major criticisms of lifestyles research. These criticisms warn of overenthusiastic use of psychographic data and point out challenges for future marketing research. First, there is a general conceptual problem. The central concepts (i.e., lifestyles, psychographics, AIO research) tend to be ill-defined. Also, it is not always clear *why* particular segments express particular consumer preferences. Predictions of emerging patterns are especially difficult. Are psychographic profiles predictive of consumer behaviors (e.g., purchase behaviors)?

Second, there is a problem associated with the secret, often ad hoc, nature of the methods used to develop lifestyle schemes. To what extent are lifestyle segments stable over time? Current lifestyle measures are not very good at capturing the fluidity of lifestyle segment membership. That is, people are likely to change lifestyle segments over time. Finally, there tends to be a fairly low correlation between lifestyle segments and particular behaviors such as brand choice that are of great interest to many companies. For instance, the consumption of many low-involvement products may not be closely related to lifestyle variables.[38]

SUMMARY

In this chapter, we describe the concept of consumer lifestyle. We then introduce the notion of role-related product constellations and the idea that consumers can perceive sets of products as belonging together to help them express personal and group identity. We next discuss psychographics and AIO as ways of implementing lifestyle research. We show how lifestyles segmentation studies have been used by firms to link segments and products, to position products, and to target media vehicles effectively. Several highly influential commercial lifestyles segmentation schemes (VALS, LOV, PRIZM, Global Scan, and cohort analysis) are explored. The chapter also shows that lifestyles may be profiled at different levels of aggregation depending on marketers' purposes. We discuss regional, national, and international lifestyles schemes such as one used in China, PRIZM, and Global Scan in some detail. Brief portraits of lifestyles in Turkey, New Zealand, and China are introduced. We conclude with a discussion of some limitations associated with lifestyle research.

KEY TERMS

achievement 453
achievers 463
action-oriented people 449
adapters 463
AIO measures 444
brand tribes 441
cohort analysis 456
exploration 453
Global Scan 463
Japan VALS 453
nine nations of North America 457
pressureds 463
principle-oriented people 448
PRIZM 458
product constellations 440
psychographics 443
realists 453
regional lifestyles 457
self-expression 453
status-oriented people 448
strivers 463
tradition 453
traditionals 463
VALS 1 448
VALS 2 448

REVIEW QUESTIONS

1. Assume you have recently been employed by Starbuck's coffee to prepare an analysis of the market for iced coffee. The marketing director is interested in doing a psychographic study and has asked you to prepare a questionnaire. Be sure to indicate the specific content of the questionnaire and some sample questions.
2. According to United Nations statistics, U.S. birth rates have risen slightly between 1975 and 2002. The arrival of a new baby causes lifestyle changes for a family. This trend is heightened by the fact that many women choose to return to work rather quickly after giving birth. Develop a list of products and services that are affected by this trend. For one product or service, develop a promotional appeal incorporating the lifestyle of a new mother, over 30 years old, who returned to a professional job eight weeks after her baby boy was born.
3. Develop a short description of your own lifestyle and the lifestyle of a close friend or relative. How are they similar? How are they different? Now consider all of the psychographic measures presented in this chapter. Which scheme fits best with your lifestyle and that of your friend? Try to label yourself and your friend using one of the breakdowns given.
4. Assume that you are in charge of targeting a new no-fat, premium-priced cookie that tastes sinful. What lifestyle segments can you identify for this type of product?
5. Assume that you are in the hosiery industry and are attempting to forecast future demand for pantyhose. What lifestyle trends can you identify that might affect the growth of pantyhose sales over the next five years? Explain your answer.
6. You are in charge of marketing, attendance, and membership for a new independent film theater that has just opened in your city. Using the VALS 2 framework, develop different appeals to reach principle-oriented, status-oriented, and action-oriented consumers.
7. Your company markets a fashionable, expensive, and high-performance line of ski clothing. You are finalizing partnering arrangements to distribute your line in Japan. Which Japanese VALS segments would you target with your ski clothing? Outline some promotional appeals that you might use.
8. Suppose you have been asked to design a social marketing campaign to encourage a drug-free lifestyle to run on Planet Hip-Hop Radio DJ-ed by KRS-One (Kris Parker), found at www.planet-hiphop.com. Describe some key elements of source and message that you would use.

CASES

YOU MAKE THE CALL

EARTH'S BEST BABY FOOD

@ www.earthsbest.com

Have you heard of Earth's Best Baby Food? Maybe not. But in the 15 years since Earth's Best Baby Food was born, it has moved into a solid number four position behind category powerhouses Gerber, Beech Nut, and Heinz—despite the fact Earth's Best's retail price is at least 50 percent higher. Earth's Best Baby Food is a tiny Colorado company with only a few dozen employees. Unable to afford big-budget ad campaigns, Earth's Best opts for folksy direct mail, co-marketing with other green marketers, and development of a user-friendly website.

This strategy is in keeping with its wholesome image as a purveyor of pure, healthy baby foods. The website provides information on organic foods and links to related websites. Earth's Best communicates that it is a little company that really cares and is out to do something right for babies and the world. According to Mike Mondello, vice president of marketing, "The idea moves beyond organic." An important part of the company's promotion is a periodic newsletter *Earth's Best Family Times.* The newsletter promotes brand loyalty with the sale of items such as Earth's Best place mats, T-shirts, and bibs as well as rebate and coupon offers. The newsletter also includes an invitation to send the company the name of a new mother who might like receiving the newsletter. The website includes a Q&A section where a physician will answer health care questions related to pregnancy and baby care. The newsletter and website serve to nurture the caring image of the company by including advice from pediatricians and answers to parents' questions.

The whole company is built around relationship marketing, but a key question is, Who buys Earth's Best Baby Food and what is their lifestyle? By answering this question, Earth's Best hopes it can be more effective in developing a relationship with their customers and growing in a way consistent with their customers' lifestyle needs. Management believes that positioning the product as a cut above other baby foods is a surefire hook with working mothers who feel a bit guilty about spending less time with their children.

QUESTIONS

1. Take a look at the website. Then, see if you can profile the Earth's Best Baby Food buyer.
2. Assume the vice president of marketing is interested in doing a psychographic study and has asked you to prepare a questionnaire. Describe the specific content you would put in and give some sample questions.
3. Describe the lifestyle segments that Earth's Best appeals to.
4. Discuss the strengths of Earth's Best's system for research and strategy.
5. Describe some alternative strategic/promotional directions for Earth's Best.

This case is adapted from public corporate communications.

ENDNOTES

1. Sources for this vignette are "From Raï to Rap," *The Economist,* June 10, 2000, p. 91; "Moreover: One Way to Get Rich in Soweto," *The Economist,* March 4, 2000, pp. 85–86; Ayse S. Caglar, "Popular Culture, Marginality and Institutional Incorporation: German-Turkish Rap and Turkish Pop in Berlin," *Cultural Dynamics* 10 (November 1998); Wayne Friedman, "Converse Hopes Master P Can Dunk Shoe Sales Trend," *Advertising Age,* Midwest region edition, June 7, 1999, p. 50; Scot Johnson and Amanda Bernard, "The New Arab Woman," *Newsweek International,* June 12, 2000, pp. 22–23; Devin Leonard, "Living without a Leader," *Fortune,* March 20, 2000, p. 218; Kembrew McLeod, "Authenticity within Hip-Hop and Other Cultures Threatened with Assimilation," *Journal of Communication* 49, no. 4 (Autumn 1999), pp. 134–50; Allison Samuels, "Rap's Ultimate Outsiders," *Newsweek,* February 28, 2000, p. 67; Scott Stossel, "Gate Crashers," *The New Republic,* August 30, 2000, pp. 16–18; Juliana Verdone, "Music to the People," *Inc.,* May 16, 2000, p. 98; www.krs-one.com; www.zulunation.com; www.templeofhiphop.org; and Craig D. Frazier, "Hip-Hop Appreciation Week Is a Big Hit," *New York Amsterdam News,* May 24–30, 2001, p. A4.

2. See David G. Moore, "Life Style in Mobile Suburbia," in *Toward Scientific Marketing,* ed. Stephen A. Greyser (Chicago: American Marketing Association, 1963), pp. 140–49; and W. Thomas Anderson Jr. and Linda L. Golden, "Lifestyle and Psychographics: A Critical Review and Recommendation," in *Advances in Consumer Research,* vol. 11, ed. Thomas C. Kinnear (Provo, UT: Association for Consumer Research, 1984), pp. 405–11.
3. Anderson and Golden, "Lifestyle and Psychographics."
4. Ibid.
5. See Eugene J. Kelley, "Discussion," in *Toward Scientific Marketing,* ed. Stephen A. Greyser (Chicago: American Marketing Association, 1963), pp. 164–71.
6. Douglas B. Holt, "How Consumers Consume: A Typology of Consumption Practices," *Journal of Consumer Research* 22 (June 1995), pp. 1–16; and William Wells, *Lifestyle and Psychographics* (Chicago: American Marketing Association, 1974).
7. Julie Caniglia, "Lifestyles of the Privileged Poor," *Utne Reader,* July–August 1993, pp. 21–22; and Craig J. Thompson and Siok Kuan Tambyah, "Trying to Be Cosmopolitan," *Journal of Consumer Research* 26 (December 1999), pp. 214–41.
8. future.sri.com/vals, May 25, 2000.
9. Jim Hancock and No Fear Apparel are profiled in "The Marketing 100," *Advertising Age,* June 26, 1995, p. S28.
10. Susan Fournier, David Antes, and Glenn Beaumier, "Nine Consumption Lifestyles," in *Advances in Consumer Research,* vol. 19, ed. John Sherry and Brian Sternthal (Provo, UT: Association for Consumer Research, 1991), pp. 329–37.
11. Michael R. Solomon and Henry Assael, "The Forest or the Trees?: A Gestalt Approach to Symbolic Consumption," in *Marketing and Semiotics: New Directions in the Study of Signs for Sale,* ed. Jean Umiker-Sebeok (New York: Mouton de Gruyter, 1987), p. 206.
12. Karl Taro Greenfeld, "The Obsession of the Otaku," *Los Angeles Times Magazine,* September 12, 1993, pp. 40–43; and www.altculture.com/aentries/o/otaku.html.
13. A. Fuat Firat, "The Consumer in Postmodernity," in *Advances in Consumer Research,* vol. 18, ed. Rebecca Holman and Michael Solomon (Provo, UT: Association for Consumer Research, 1991), pp. 70–71.
14. Dawn Dobni and George M. Zinkhan, "In Search of Brand Image: A Foundation Analysis," in *Advances in Consumer Research,* vol. 17, ed. M. Goldberg, G. Gorn, and R. W. Pollay (Provo, UT: Association for Consumer Research, 1990), pp. 110–19.
15. Susan Fournier, "Consumers and Their Brands: Developing Relationship Theory," *Journal of Consumer Research* 24 (March 1998), pp. 343–73.
16. J. N. Kapferer, "Publicité: Une révolution des méthodes de travail," *Revue Française de gestion,* September–December 1985, pp. 102–11.
17. Lewis Alpert and Ronald Gatty, "Product Positioning by Behavioral Lifestyles," *Journal of Marketing* 33 (April 1969), pp. 65–69; Brenda Gainer and Eileen Fischer, "Community and Consumer Behavior," working paper, Queen's University, Ontario, Canada, 1995; Jeff Kaye, "The Raves of Europe," *Los Angeles Times,* 1993, pp. F1, F7, E1, E3; Michael R. Solomon, "Mapping Product Constellations: A Social Categorization Approach to Consumption Symbolism," *Psychology and Marketing* 5 (Fall 1988), pp. 233–57; Michael R. Solomon and Punam Anand, "Ritual Costumes and Status Transitions: The Female Business Suit as Totemic Emblem," in *Advances in Consumer Research,* vol. 11, ed. Thomas Kinnear (Provo, UT: Association for Consumer Research, 1984), pp. 315–18; Solomon and Assael, "The Forest or the Trees?" pp. 189–218; and Pierre Valette-Florence, *Les styles de vie: Bilan critique et perspectives* (Paris: Nathan, 1994).
18. Harold H. Kassarjian and Mary Jane Sheffert, "Personality and Consumer Behavior: An Update," in *Perspectives in Consumer Behavior,* 4th ed., ed. Harold H. Kassarjian and Thomas S. Robertson (Englewood Cliffs, NJ: Prentice Hall, 1991), pp. 281–303.
19. Steven J. Hoch, "Who Do We Know: Predicting the Interests and Opinions of the American Consumer," *Journal of Consumer Research* 15 (December 1988), pp. 315–24; and William D. Wells, "Psychographics: A Critical Review," *Journal of Marketing Research* 12 (May 1975), pp. 196–213.
20. Kassarjian and Sheffert, "Personality and Consumer Behavior"; Wells, "Psychographics: A Critical Review"; "Consuming Images," video, Corporation for Public Broadcasting; and Shirley

Young, "Research Both for Strategic Planning and for Tactical Testing," *Proceedings,* 19th Annual Conference, Advertising Research Foundation, New York, 1971, pp. 13–16.
21. Arnold Mitchell, "Nine American Lifestyles: Values and Societal Change," *The Futurist* 18 (August 1984), pp. 4–13; and Wagner A. Kamakura and Jose Alfonso Masson, "Value Segmentation: A Model for the Measurement of Values and Value Systems," *Journal of Consumer Research* 18 (September 1991), pp. 208–18.
22. Douglas B. Holt, "Poststructuralist Lifestyle Analysis: Conceptualizing the Social Patterning of Consumption in Postmodernity," *Journal of Consumer Research* 23 (March 1997), pp. 326–50; and Douglas B. Holt, "Does Cultural Capital Structure American Consumption?" *Journal of Consumer Research* 25 (June 1998), pp. 1–25.
23. Arnold Mitchell, *The Nine American Lifestyles* (New York: Warner, 1983).
24. Rebecca Piirto, *Beyond Mind Games: The Marketing Power of Psychographics* (Ithaca: American Demographics Books, 1991).
25. J. Walker Smith and Ann Clurman, *Rocking the Ages: The Yankelovich Report on Generational Marketing* (New York: Harper Business, 1997); and Geoffrey Meredith and Charles Schewe, "The Power of Cohorts," *American Demographics,* December 1994, pp. 22–31; see also Joseph O. Rentz and Fred D. Reynolds, "Forecasting the Effects of an Aging Population on Product Consumption: An Age-Period-Cohort Framework," *Journal of Marketing Research* (1991), pp. 355–60; and Norman B. Ryder, "The Cohort as a Concept in the Study of Social Change," *American Sociological Review* 30 (December 1965), pp. 843–61.
26. Meredith and Schewe, "The Power of Cohorts," p. 31.
27. Ronald A. Fullerton, "Marketing and the Economic Redevelopment in East Germany: Field Observations and Theoretical Analysis," in *Marketing and Economic Restructuring in the Developing World,* ed. Luis V. Dominguez (San Jose, Costa Rica: INCAF, 1993), pp. 145–51; T. R. Reid, *Confucius Lives Next Door* (New York: Vintage Books, 1999); and Thomas Tan Tsu Wee, "An Exploration of a Global Teenage Lifestyle in Asian Societies," *Journal of Consumer Marketing* 16, no. 4 (1999), pp. 365–75.
28. Joel Garreau, *The Nine Nations of North America* (Boston: Houghton Mifflin, 1981); and Lynn R. Kahle, "The Nine Nations of North America and the Value Basis of Geographic Segmentation," *Journal of Marketing,* April 1986, pp. 37–47.
29. Geng Cui and Qiming Liu, "Regional Market Segments of China: Opportunities and Barriers in a Big Emerging Market," *Journal of Consumer Marketing* 17, no. 1 (2000), pp. 55–70.
30. yawyl.claritas.com, May 2000.
31. Jack Russell, "Working Women Give Japan Culture Shock," *Advertising Age,* January 16, 1995, p. 124; and Jack Russell, "At Last, a Product That Makes Japan's Subways Safe for Men," *Advertising Age,* January 16, 1995, p. 124.
32. Diane Brady, "Inside the Growing Empire of America's Lifestyle Queen," *Business Week,* January 17, 2000, pp. 63–72.
33. Christopher M. Byron, *Martha Inc.: The Incredible Story of Martha Stewart Living* (New York: Omnimedia, 2002).
34. Bernard Cathelat, *Styles de vie: Courants & scénarios,* vol. 2, Collection CCA (Paris: Les Editions D'Organisation, 1985); Bernard Dubois, *Comprendre le consommateur* (Paris: Duboz, 1994), pp. 195–97; and Valette-Florence, *Les styles de vie: Bilan critique et perspectives.*
35. Orsay Kucukemiroglu, "Market Segmentation by Using Consumer Lifestyle Dimensions and Ethnocentrism: An Empirical Study," *European Journal of Marketing* 33, no. 5–6 (1999), pp. 1–9.
36. Sarah Todd, Rob Lawson, and Fionna Faris, "A Lifestyle Analysis of New Zealand Consumers," *Asia Pacific Journal of Marketing and Logistics* 10, no. 3 (1998), pp. 30–47.
37. Jackie L. M. Tam and Susan H. C. Tai, "Research Note: The Psychographic Segmentation of the Female Market in Greater China," *International Marketing Review* 15, no. 1 (1998), pp. 25–41.
38. Dubois, *Comprendre le consommateur,* pp. 195–97; Wells, "Psychographics: A Critical Review"; and William D. Wells, "Discussion," in *Advances in Consumer Research,* vol. 7, ed. Jerry C. Olson (Ann Arbor, MI: Association for Consumer Research, 1980), p. 473.

LEARNING OBJECTIVES

After completing this chapter, you should be able to:

- See how the concept of cultural capital can be used to position products and services.
- Explain the impact of social class, ethnicity, age, gender, and religion on consumption choices.
- Understand the bases for ethnic segmentation and targeting.
- Appreciate the difference between acculturation and assimilation and their relevance to consumer behavior.
- Understand the idea of age cohorts and recognize the different kinds of cohorts relevant to marketing.
- Recognize some of the key differences in consumer desires between class, ethnicity, gender, and age segments.
- Understand the difference between sex and gender and its relevance for marketing.

ECONOMIC AND SOCIAL SEGMENTS

COCA-COLA CONFRONTS THE GLOBAL YOUTH MARKET[1]

Kazuki Yamane and Makoto Sato hop out of their chauffeured car at the corner of a busy Tokyo intersection. The two men, wearing suits, make their way into the teeming bustle. They brush past some sort of shrieking dance squad handing out free cosmetic samples to the crowd. Multiple massive TV screens beam loops of commercials down to the street. The pedestrian flow is a blocks-thick surge of teenagers tapping at their cell phones. This neighborhood, Shibuya, is the frenzied, wired heart of nearly all Japanese teenage culture. It is also an important consumer lab for Coca-Cola Company. Yamane and Sato have come to view the newest Coke innovation. They're sure it's another triumph of Coca-Cola marketing genius, and angling fast through the crowds now, dicing up flocks of school girls, the main attraction is drawing near. The excitement builds on Sato's face. Their steps slow. And then, at last, beside the entrance to a busy boutique, they come face to face with the future of soft drinks. The Coke execs are beaming and gesturing toward it . . . a vending machine.

There are a number of remarkable things about this vending machine—most of all the range of drinks it offers, about 30 of them. Colas, juices, waters, teas, coffees, sports drinks, and a few beverages defying any category familiar to a Euro-American consumer jostle for attention. But for Japan, it's very normal. Surprisingly, what the Coke guys want to see is not what kids buy from this machine, but *how* they buy it.

As they watch (and Yamane snaps several pictures), a uniformed schoolgirl approaches with her DoCoMo cell phone at the ready. First she presses some buttons on the phone—and waits about 10 seconds. Then she holds the phone up to the infrared scanner on the machine and waits again—for her purchase to go through. And then finally the machine tumbles out her selection: Water Salad, a vitamin-enhanced meal in a can that Coke targets to Japanese women.

The whole routine is awkward and slightly ridiculous. If she had taken a 100-yen coin from her pocket, she would have saved at least 45 seconds. Yet this is what it takes now to sell drinks to a Japanese teenager, perhaps the most demanding breed of consumer who ever lived. You offer her endless choices, in dozens of beverage categories, then top it all off with a nifty bit of novelty. Anything less will bore her and lose the sale.

OVERVIEW

The above vignette illustrates a number of points we discuss in this chapter. Most obviously, it draws attention to the value of teenagers—generation Y—in many firms' global marketing plans. Demographic factors such as age and the other economic and structural segments we discuss in this chapter are important marketing segmentation variables. Second, marketers in the Triad nations are interested in this group because of the large discretionary income they enjoy. The resources each economic and social segment controls are of bottom-line concern to marketers. Third, the vignette shows that competition for markets is increasingly focused on how people consume, rather than merely what they consume. Consumer value increasingly lies in stylistic variations in the purchase and consumption process. Fourth, it suggests that how people consume varies with a resource called symbolic capital, a kind of cultural knowledge we discuss below.

Consumers identify with, aspire to membership in, or may be identified as members of a number of economic and social segments. Their participation integrates them with and differentiates them from other consumers. The segments discussed in this chapter—class, ethnicity, caste, religion, gender, and age—are major organizational categories in societies around the world. Membership in these categories is often expressed through the purchase and use of products and services. Clusters of goods and services purchased and consumed are often connected to and help define these economic and social segments. Marketers increasingly play a role in the identification of social and economic segments, such as the ethnic category of Hispanics in the United States or non-English-speaking background (NESB) immigrants in Australia, by marketing identity-defining and enhancing products to them.[2]

Affiliation with individual segments varies in its effects on our purchase and consumption options in particular contexts. For example, religion may have a significant impact on core values, influencing whether we wear particular clothes (veils for women) or purchase products at particular times (Sabbath days, religious holidays). Other consumption choices may have little to do with religion, and more with ethnic affiliation, such as a Danish Inuit's taste for whale blubber and animal bones.[3] Situations often influence which source of identity we choose to emphasize through consumption behavior. A woman may enjoy some "downtime" curled up with a formula-driven Harlequin Romance novel or watch a clichéd "women's movie" on one of the women's television networks. These products may supply values and meanings that cut across class or ethnic segments that influence her consumption choices at other times.[4]

Membership in or affiliation with economic and social segments is dynamic. Groups and individuals may experience **social mobility,** *improvements or deterioration in social status as a result of changes in resources,* which may in turn change consumer behavior. Social mobility is more common in some countries, Hong Kong, Australia, and the

United States, for example, and less common in others, Guatemala or Mozambique, for example. The preferences and consumption behavior of market segments may be relatively consistent over time. For example, boys yearn for the freedom afforded by independent transportation in many parts of the world—whether they imagine this freedom can be provided by a car, scooter, motorcycle, or bicycle. At the same time, individuals' preferences may shift over time as they undergo social mobility or life transitions.[5]

In the Roman and Ottoman (Turkish) Empires, **sumptuary laws** attempted to *restrict certain types of consumption based on social segment characteristics*.[6] Sumptuary laws that mandate consumption behaviors are less common today, although gender-based sumptuary rules apply in some conservative nations and communities. Instead, less formal social norms and consumer skills are employed to defend consumption niches and the social boundaries they create. For example, luxury good prices are kept artificially high to restrict access to all but elite consumers. Crossing economic and social segment boundaries is not necessarily easy. In Indonesia, small groups of friends will share a single Benetton sweater to wear in public places in an effort to signal middle-class status that their incomes do not warrant. Mainstream retailers sometimes discriminate against ethnic teenagers because their fashion preferences are inappropriately used as indicators of lower social class affiliation.[7] Some universities include extracurricular courses such as formal dining and wine tasting designed to equip their graduates with consumer skills that facilitate crossing social segment boundaries.

Marketing and advertising managers find economic and socially defined segments a useful basis for targeting to the extent such segments possess characteristics that distinguish their desires, choices, media preferences, and decision-making styles from other groups. For example, ethnicity- and gender-targeted media are growing in popularity.[8] Over 110 newspapers and magazines in 30 languages are published regularly in Australia, and Telstra, Inc., scored a major marketing success with Australia's Chinese-language Yellow Pages.[9] In the United States, there are 350 Asian language newspapers and magazines.[10] A study in the United Arab Emirates showed that ethnicity—Western, Asian, Arab—affected product attributes consumers considered important in 12 product categories.[11] Every element of the marketing mix may require adjustments to match the distinctive characteristics of economic and social segments we discuss in this chapter.

ECONOMIC AND SOCIAL SEGMENTS

Social class, ethnicity, caste, and religion influence consumers' behaviors, both directly and indirectly. For example, economic status directly affects purchasing power and sets a floor on consumption possibilities. Further, economic status may indirectly affect a person's identity (Chapter 10) and lifestyle aspirations (Chapter 11), and these in turn directly influence consumption behaviors. As with culture, the influence of economic and social structures is easiest to discern in people whose class, ethnicity, gender, or caste differs from our own, but it is important to become sensitive to these differences as national and global markets become more diverse. Adding complication is that some part of a consumer's identity may relate to social class and another part to ethnicity, for example. Many American middle-class blacks struggle with this issue, perhaps embracing their ethnicity during Black History month, while on other occasions feeling their social class alienates them from their ethnic roots. Purchase and consumption decisions may be employed to express these multiple sources of identity.[12] Another complicating factor is that consumers now embrace and switch between some social segments, up, down, and across the social ladder, depending on situational contexts.

For example, a study showed that middle-class Haitian immigrants to the United States in one context distanced themselves from Creole (as the language of lower-class Haitians) and in another context embraced it as the all-Haitian language.[13]

Symbolic Capital

Social structure has loosened as consumer culture has become global. Global marketing has created an environment increasingly filled with consumer goods, services, and experiences. Technological advance has led to increased information flows, communication across segment boundaries, and wider accessibility to consumption by all but the poorest members of society. Innovative styles and designs now diffuse rapidly between elite and mass markets and between Triad and less affluent countries. With globalization and economic development, simple models of preference that link social segments with a stable set of products and brands decrease in their value to marketers. Lower-class consumers now consume many of the same goods and participate in many of the same activities as higher-class consumers. And low-income ethnic consumers may be the source of fashions that subsequently spread to upper-income consumers. In a sense, as suggested by the opening vignette, what really differentiates consumers in different economic and social segments is how, rather than what, they consume.[14]

In this regard, it is useful to segment consumption across segments on the basis of how people *compete for status,* or what some call **symbolic capital.**[15] To obtain symbolic capital, people draw on three types of resources: economic, social, and cultural capital. **Economic capital** means *financial resources, including income, investments, or inherited wealth.* Inherited wealth tends to provide more symbolic capital, hence higher social status, than income. **Social capital** includes *relationships, organizational memberships, and social networks.* Ethnic and neighborhood clubs, service organizations such as the Lion's Clubs, or a sorority would be examples of social capital resources. **Cultural capital** is more complicated. Building on our definition of culture in Chapter 2, we can say that cultural capital consists of specialized knowledge about how to get along in a given consumption context. It is a product of a person's class, ethnic, religious, and national heritage. One aspect of cultural capital is *unspoken knowledge and skills,* such as how to set a formal dining table, appreciate diverse musical styles, or consume foreign food. In some contexts, cultural capital is referred to as the possession of "good taste," the ability to appreciate the finer things (see Chapter 8). A second aspect is *access to high-status consumer goods and objects* such as fine arts or heirlooms. And a third is *degrees, diplomas, and memberships that certify certain valued qualities.*

People with a lot of symbolic capital can use it to cross social segments in which particular cultural knowledge is valued. So, for example, movie stars from national cinemas like Chow Yun Fat from Hong Kong or Hrthik Roshan from Bollywood (India) can trade their national screen chops into credibility in Hollywood.[16] And people with a lot of cultural capital in one domain can sometimes translate it into other kinds of capital, such as social capital. So Irish rock band U2's front man, Bono, has been able to translate his rock star credibility into access to political networks involving members of the World Bank and the U.S. Congress. With these high economic and social capital individuals, Bono lobbies for debt relief for less affluent nations.

Consumer researchers might find it useful to think of cultural capital as knowledge of high-status consumption activities. The ad for Smeg refrigerators may be unappealing to some consumers, but very meaningful to those with expert knowledge of design history, who recognize the 1950s retro look of the refrigerators, and who also see the Italian language slogan, "Art and Technology," as a cue to indicate fine Italian design. This ad appeared in an up-market Australian magazine.

A preference for retro Italian design reveals one kind of high cultural capital.

Knowledge of specialized consumption domains, whether it is Italian design or stock car racing, comes about in part through informal learning and socialization. Shared consumption experiences, such as attending a particular class at a particular school or working under a particularly visionary leader, can help equip a person with cultural capital. Cultural capital, in the form of codes of proper consumption behavior among the old elites of New York, the British aristocracy, or feudal Japan, for example, was very elaborate. While we might see behaviors indicative of high levels of cultural capital depicted in popular movies, an ordinary person cannot really become fluent in these codes of behavior unless socialized into them from any early age. Increasingly, consumer culture places value on cultural capital that is more widely accessible to people, as expressed, for example, in status symbols.

Globally, across economic and social segments, we see a heightened emphasis on **status-oriented consumption,** that is, *behavior involving competition for symbolic capital often associated with status symbols.* **Status symbols** are *consumer products, activities, or services that indicate a person's position in a hierarchy of classes, ethnic groups, or castes.* The domains of competition for status symbols vary across segments, from unique sports cars such as a Masserati Spyder among the wealthy to "Precious Moments" porcelain dolls and ceramic plates among working-class consumers. The "Precious Moments" ads shown on next page were targeted to lower-middle and working classes in the United States. Notice how each ad makes it easy to buy with multiple small payments. This appeals to persons with a modest income. And the ad guarantees authenticity and ensures a "limited edition." These appeals to status cross segment boundaries.[17]

Consumer status symbols vary internationally. Taking an expensive cruise may be an indicator of cultural capital among upwardly mobile Thais, while knowledge of fast-food restaurants may serve this role among lower-middle-class Brazilians living in a Rio de Janeiro *favella* (slum). The point is that even when what is consumed overlaps, lower social status groups consume differently than upper social status groups. A member of the old French bourgeoisie buys a piece of fine china to add to a family heirloom set, whereas a new economy entrepreneur buys a whole new set to demonstrate social mobility, for example. A poor African-American child making a modest jewelry purchase in a retail mall is also self-consciously claiming her right to participate as a consumer in an environment that generally devalues poor consumers. Marketers must position status symbols for different economic and social segments in different ways to accommodate differences in how people purchase and consume symbolic capital.[18]

These ads promote attainable status symbols for lower-middle- and working-class North Americans.

Class Variation in Consumer Behavior

As detailed in Chapter 5, many firms and organizations focus their efforts on fine-tuned marketing strategies targeted to different segments of consumers. Some of these consumer segments are based on social class differences. We might say **social class** refers to *a hierarchy of large groups across society, broadly recognized by members of that society, involving inequalities in such areas as power, authority, wealth, income, prestige, working conditions, lifestyles, and culture*. People of any one class tend to associate more with one another than they do with members of other classes and they tend to share endowments of cultural capital and values and to display similar consumption patterns. Most authors measure class distinctions using some combination of factors, including inherited wealth, income, occupation, residential location, and educational attainment.[19]

The way in which elements of income, education, occupation, and residential location combine to form a specific **social class hierarchy,** *whereby some individuals have higher cultural capital than others,* differs according to a society's history. Social class is deeply significant in a number of Latin American nations, where stark class differences exist. Nevertheless, the life of a middle-class Latin American household is different from middle-class life in the United States or much of Europe. The French and the British, who share a tradition of a landed aristocracy, are more aware of class differences than are Americans or Australians, who lack this tradition. The Japanese express socioeconomic differences in numerous fine gradations of consumption practices rather than in a small number of distinct social classes. In the transitional economies of Eastern Europe, new economic elites have emerged by staking out controlling interests in productive resources formerly owned by the state. Many of these people were part of the political elite under old Communist Party regimes. While the traditions differ, class differences themselves are not soft and temporary. Instead, they are tough and persistent patterns of customary social relationships that affect consumption behaviors and translate into different consumer preferences.[20]

HOW SOCIAL CLASS IS DETERMINED Social classes are measured in different ways. **Self-attribution measures** invite *people to assign themselves to a class stratum.* This method produces profiles that reflect people's preferred status and give hints about their value orientations. In an Australian study, 5 percent of respondents identified themselves as upper or upper-middle class, 52 percent middle class, 28 percent working class, and 16 percent other. The popularity of middle class self-attribution suggests that middle-class values guide consumption. Such subjective perceptions do relate to product usage and consumption preferences. However, in countries that value equality such as France, the United States, and Australia, this method of measuring class has the disadvantage that people over-identify as middle class.[21]

Another technique is the **reputational approach.** This method is *based on surveying well-informed community members to identify the social class positions of others.* Marketers have made little use of this method. Instead, marketers and other social scientists have turned increasingly to **objective measures** of class, typically *employing one or more of the following criteria: income or wealth, education, occupation, and residential location.*

One key measure of social class is income. For example, in countries as diverse as the United States and Zimbabwe, people draw socioeconomic boundaries on the basis of income differences. And differences of income are especially significant for marketers as these resources are related to purchasing power. Also, absolute income and differences in income levels indicate the size of potential markets.[22] One system of measurement produces a fourfold classification of French households, of which 15 percent may be considered upper class, 30 percent upper middle class, 40 percent lower middle class, and 15 percent lower class.[23]

Despite the importance of income as an indicator of social class and of consumption patterns, it also can be inaccurate, or misleading. Even in the United States, income level plays an unclear role in class identification. In 1994, 74 percent of the working class and 63 percent of the middle class reported household incomes between $15,000 and $74,999. But 10 percent of the upper class also reported making less than $15,000, and 4 percent of the lower class reported making over $50,000 a year.[24] Reasonable estimates of income are frequently unavailable in the developing world and inaccurate or unavailable in transitional economies.

A useful concept here is **discretionary** or **contestable income** (see Chapter 4), *the amount of income left over after necessities have been covered.* Discretionary or contestable income is an important indicator of the resources consumers may spend on consumer goods. Discretionary income increases as overall income goes up. Discretionary income tends to increase with class position, but the association is not perfect. Consumers often desire to translate improvements in discretionary income into evidence of social mobility through changes in consumer goods. Discretionary income is used for this purpose.[25] But discretionary income goes further in some places than in others. For these reasons, the World Bank distinguishes countries by **purchasing power parity** rather than income alone. The index allows marketers to compare *the relative purchasing power of goods in a particular country to what those same things cost in the United States.*[26]

In the Triad countries, people typically perceive their own class position as based on **relative income,** that is, *how one's purchasing power seems to compare to others of similar occupation or lifestyle.* In many countries, this aspect of socioeconomic status is growing in importance as a result of the globalization of the consumer economy. Income-based status is readily signaled and easily communicated through some consumption activities that are not strongly related to other aspects of social class but require money, such as the purchase of designer brands and foreign travel to expensive destinations. In some contexts, furniture, clothing, automobiles, cuisine, and housing have been found to convey relatively consistent messages about socioeconomic status. For example, automobile models sold in Britain come in more variations than anywhere else in Europe because of Britons' desire to precisely convey their socioeconomic status. And, as marketers know, by adding and subtracting gadgets and options, consumers can create a hierarchical system of great complexity. Similarly, in Sydney, Australia, citizens define themselves in terms of residential location. Evaluating social position according to residence is based on consumers' widespread knowledge of relative real estate values and implied socioeconomic status.[27]

Throughout the Triad nations, education, occupation, and social background are mutually reinforcing criteria that more precisely define social class than income. A landmark study asked Americans what class they belonged to and then went on to analyze why they classified themselves the way they did. Topping the list of reasons they belonged to a particular social class was occupation, followed by education and then lifestyle values and attitudes.[28] Occupation is a reasonably reliable indicator of social class, and occupations tend to be ranked in terms of symbolic capital. However, rankings vary cross-culturally. In many less affluent nations, government positions are relatively prestigious; engineers are highly regarded in south Asia; university professors are highly regarded in France and Israel; and judges, cabinet ministers, and medical specialists top the list of occupational rankings in Australia.[29]

Education is a determinant of occupation, and it increases social and cultural capital; hence it is a critical element of social class and social mobility. However, in many parts of the world, the quality of education is partially determined by the social status of parents.[30] Consequently, middle-class people in many countries value education highly, viewing it as a ticket to social mobility. African-Americans' social mobility can be directly attributed to dramatic gains in education in the last quarter of the twentieth century. Sweden, Denmark, and Norway show the highest levels of population literacy.[31] Consistent with this equitable distribution of education, these Nordic countries also have less pronounced social class distinctions (see Exhibit 12.2 on p. 484). New Zealand has a strong tradition of accessible education and more than 54 percent of New Zealanders are categorized as middle class. Vietnam's success at reducing poverty through growth in the past decade is in large part attributable to the equitable distribution of education across the population. Even in the poorest households, the educational attainment is similar to that of the wealthiest households. As it has in Vietnam, education has been key to growth in many of Asia's NIC countries. Other developing countries tend to have highly inequitable distributions of education assets, which makes it difficult for them to replicate Vietnam's success.[32]

THE GEOGRAPHY OF SOCIAL CLASS On a global level, most of the world's poor live in the less affluent world, where some 4.4 billion have been mostly left out of the consumption explosion of the last two decades. Although per capita gross domestic

Rank	County	Per Capita Income (U.S. Dollars) 2000	2010
1	New York, New York	69,157	99,088
2	Marin, California	54,608	85,243
3	Pitkin, Colorado	54,076	79,455
4	Fairfield, New Jersey	53,474	80,234
5	Somerset, New Jersey	51,605	81,320
6	Alexandria, Virginia	50,752	78,225
7	Westchester, New York	50,402	74,206
8	Morris, New Jersey	49,640	76,613
9	Bergen, New Jersey	48,137	72,053
10	Arlington, Virginia	47,252	71,679

Source: John Fetto, "Counties with Cash," *American Demographics*, April 2000, pp. 42–43.

EXHIBIT 12.1

U.S. Counties with the Highest Per Capita Income

product (see Chapter 2) is growing at a brisk rate in China, still less than 15 percent of households have income sufficient to buy a refrigerator. Only about 5 percent of Colombians have the purchasing power to afford a car.[33]

The richest one-fifth of the world's population live in the Triad nations, where they consume the bulk of goods and services produced in the world. On a national level, wealthy, middle-, and working-class residential areas are reasonably stable. Therefore, it is possible to target groups, site retail outlets, and deliver effective market communications to them. For example, Exhibit 12.1 identifies the 10 counties with the highest per capita incomes in the United States. In Europe and Latin America, wealthy people tend to inhabit inner cities and enjoy second homes in rural areas. Although only 3 in 10 Mexican households are middle class, 58 percent of Mexico City households are classified as middle class. Cities such as São Paulo, Brazil, and Mexico City also have significant numbers of upper-class households with the economic power to buy high-end and luxury goods. Income per capita in Buenos Aires province is roughly double that of poorer Argentina provinces. Lower-socioeconomic-profile consumers live in the near suburbs either in high-rise apartment blocks or shantytowns. In North American and Australia, by contrast, the poor are concentrated in the inner cities, and wealthier consumers inhabit the suburbs. Japanese "salarymen" also inhabit the suburbs, while remnants of the old nobility are clustered in the oldest urban neighborhoods. Demographic shifts made possible by development of the information economy have weakened residence as a predictor of class and resulted in the emergence of local pockets of affluence in America, Europe, and South Asia.[34]

CLASS-BASED SEGMENTS AND CONSUMPTION PATTERNS The globalization of a market economy and of consumer society has changed class structure and the relationship between class and consumption. Social mobility is dramatic in many NICs and the LAW nations. Upper-income groups of the "new rich" have emerged in these markets. Three decades of economic growth produced a huge Korean middle class of 36 million people. India's middle class officially numbers 32.5 million households, or about 162 million people.[35] In the 1990s, financial stability and economic growth in Latin America meant that 10 million people a year have moved into the middle consumer classes, yet recent financial instability has reversed some gains. New middle and elite classes have emerged in the transitional economies of Eastern Europe as well. Many Triad countries also have seen their class structures change to reflect more pronounced gaps between the haves and have-nots.

It can be misleading to look for neat social class divisions segmented on the basis of income, education, occupation, and residence. Nevertheless, it is valuable to develop measures of the rough size of such groups for targeting purposes, because social class affects how people consume. Three main class-based segments are upper class (including both old, established elites and the upper echelons of technical and managerial groups), middle class, and lower class (including the underclass). Exhibit 12.2 shows various models of class structure found around the world. The Japanese and Nordic (Denmark, Finland, Norway, and Sweden) models contain the three segments noted above, with smaller upper and lower classes bracketing a large middle class.

Often finer class distinctions can be made. For example, the European Union uses a sevenfold class division to categorize citizens of the 28 member nations. Group A consists of the most highly educated persons working as corporate presidents and managers or skilled professionals. Group E3 consists of semi- and unskilled workers with few educational qualifications. Exhibit 12.3 shows how dramatically the distribution of social classes may vary even between European countries, using Denmark and Portugal as examples. Denmark has a relatively large number of upper-middle-class consumers, category B, while Portugal has a large number of semi- and unskilled workers, category E3.

We can make a number of points about social class hierarchies for marketing purposes in a global context. One is that globalization reproduces a similar sort of class hierarchy around the world. This has led to **upward mobility,** *a move to a higher social*

EXHIBIT 12.2

Class Structure by World Areas

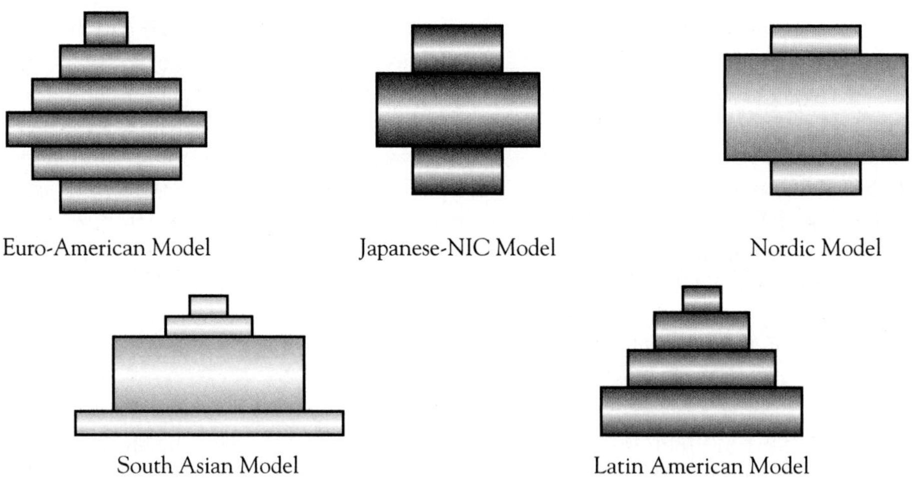

Source: Adapted from Wayne D. Hoyer and Deborah J. MacInnis, *Consumer Behavior*, 2nd ed. (Boston: Houghton Mifflin, 2001), Exhibit 13.4, p. 327.

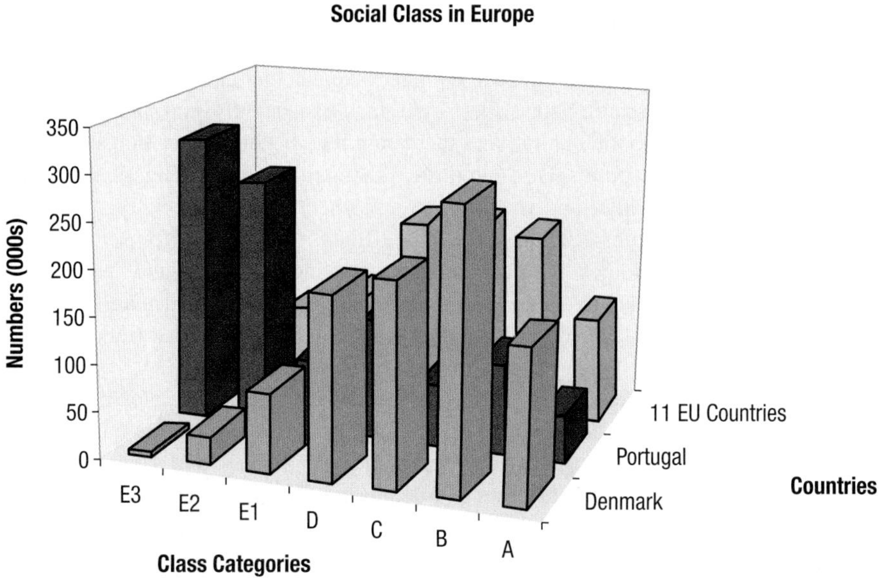

EXHIBIT 12.3

Social Class in Europe

Source: Bernard Dubois, *Comprendre Le Consommateur,* 2nd ed. (Paris: Dalloz, 1994), p. 173.

class, usually associated with educational or occupational achievement, in many transitional, NIC, and LAW countries. In turn, this has led to growth in demand for consumer durables and branded consumer goods. It also has led to **downward mobility,** *a move to a lower social class,* for millions of people in some of the Triad countries and in many transitional and LAW countries as well. Downward mobility has been associated with a loss of agricultural and low-level manufacturing and managerial jobs in the Triad countries due to the move to an information economy, the collapse of state enterprises in the transitional economies, and a failure of many enterprises to produce for competitive global markets in LAW countries.[36]

A second point of significance is that global class segments may be over- or underrepresented in different countries. Thus, upper-class segments are now overrepresented in the Triad countries while the traditional industrial working class is now overrepresented in the developing world. Companies as diverse as Louis Vuitton Moet Hennessey (LVMH), the luxury-brand conglomerate, and Wal-Mart have globalized their retail operations to reach similar class-based segments in different national markets. At this time, Wal-Mart is the largest retailer in the world and operates stores in Argentina (10), Brazil (16), Canada (166), China (8), Germany (95), Korea (5), Mexico (460), Puerto Rico (15), and the United Kingdom (236), in addition to all 50 United States. In the United States, Wal-Mart promotes a working-class image, but at home and abroad the store appeals to a wider spectrum of social class.

A third point is that members of the very lowest classes, ranging from native peoples in the developing world to ghetto gang-bangers in the Triad nations, now play an important role as sources of images and styles. Companies incorporate these images and styles in their global marketing plans, capitalizing on the **status float** that occurs when *fashion trends start in the lower class and spread upward.* Products as diverse as sneakers, tattoos, and some musical styles such as rap and world beat have benefited from status float.[37] Chapter 11 includes more discussion of these global consumption lifestyles.

Social class influences a variety of consumer behaviors. Social class is a variable for segmenting product markets that satisfy needs related to such lifestyle expressions as housing, clothing, furniture, travel, sports, cuisine, and entertainment. It is also a variable with positioning implications. For example, store patronage is related to social class. Further, people tend to avoid retailers that have a social class image very different from their own. Research shows that Americans consistently rank retail outlets in terms of perceived symbolic capital, and these rankings become more consistent with higher social class of respondents.[38] Similarly, in Australia, Kmart, Big-W, and Woolworth's target lower-middle- and working-class segments, while specialty stores such as Grace Bros. and Robins Kitchen target the affluent.[39] In Hong Kong, lower-class consumers buy their clothes in local chain stores such as Giordano and Theme. Middle-class consumers shop at Japanese department stores such as Isetan, Sogo, and Yaohan. The newly wealthy shop at boutiques such as Seibu and Le Cadre and designer boutiques such as Yohji Yamamoto and Dolce and Gabbana.[40]

Brand loyalty also is related to class. Displaying branded products helps newly middle and wealthy classes signal upward social mobility. For instance, one author found the Indonesian middle class highly committed to the display and consumption of branded products. Brand name use tends to decrease in the highest social classes, but this depends on degree of purchase and consumption experience. Purchase and consumption experience may outweigh the effects of social class on brand loyalty. For example, in Latin America brand knowledge is less developed than in the United States; buyers tend to go for what looks good at the moment rather than drawing from a standard list of favorite brands.[41]

Upper-Class Segments

Because of its wealth, marketers have targeted upper-class consumers around the world with distinctive media and product offerings. In addition, some marketers have segmented this group into subsegments such as Old Money, Nouveau Riche, and the upper-middle-class Get Set.

This ad uses architectural design elements that appeal to the old money elite.

This ad should appeal to the nouveau riche communities.

Old money corresponds to the capitalist class or *the upper-upper class* whose wealth derives from inheritance and investments. In French bourgeois circles, for example, "earned" money is deemphasized in favor of inherited wealth. Old money individuals distinguish themselves through organized philanthropy and other activities that have more to do with the way in which money is spent and less with what is purchased. This is the world of America's old WASP (White Anglo-Saxon Protestant) elite, the British and Japanese nobility, and the old French bourgeoisie, for example. First-generation computer billionaires have begun to mimic the pattern of philanthropic concern associated with the old money elite. Old money tends to value products that they view as simple, comfortable, and refined and engages in heavy consumption of unique products.

The old money bourgeois lifestyle remains strong in many European and Latin American national cultures. It is a segment that prizes quality and spending with good taste, as well as being distinctively recognized for doing so.[42] The ad for Forbes magazine shown on page 486 uses classical design elements in a playful way to suggest the stability of old money. Old money consumers are likely to buy clothing free from the supporting associations provided by brand names or licensing. In France, money is a means of maintaining a distinctive social identity rather than signaling one's progress on the consumption ladder. The old money French bourgeois rarely talk about prices and purchases; they play down commercial relationships; hence, marketing to such groups must focus on other factors such as aesthetic appreciation. True to popular perceptions, upper-class French spend disproportionately on distinctive food products.[43]

Nouveau riche means *new money*. Nouveau riche consumers are upwardly mobile. These groups *combine qualities of the middle class with those of the upper classes*. Like new economy entrepreneurs throughout the world, they tend to consider hard work to be the source of their newfound wealth; but besides working hard, they spend or play hard as well. This is the group people associate with conspicuous consumption, discussed in Chapter 3. Social mobility has enabled them to afford luxury goods.

Advertising to Old Money

INDUSTRY INSIGHTS 12.1

This image consciousness is one of the factors that upscale furniture retailer Maurice Villency counts on when marketing to this demographic. Three years ago, the New York–based company switched from a product-oriented marketing strategy to an image-and-brand-focused marketing strategy, says Eric Villency, the company's president. After all, since these consumers already have all the furniture that they need, a furniture purchase will more likely fall in the discretionary category. "When you're aiming for this upscale luxury customer, it's really about setting a tone and image for your advertising," he says. In the company's print ads, a glamour photo of a single piece of furniture has replaced the industry standard of packing as many pieces onto a page circular-style. Although Villency won't reveal specific numbers, he says that the strategy has been "very effective."

Source: "What They Spend on Easy Street," American Demographics, *Forecast, August 20, 2001.*

Conspicuous consumption refers to people's desire to provide prominent visible evidence of social mobility, the passage of individuals from one social class to another. Conspicuous consumption often involves purchase and display of status symbols, conventional indicators of wealth and power. Conspicuous consumption tends to be very conformist, because the nouveau riche want to convey meanings that are conventional indications of success.

To give some examples of nouveau riche consumption, members of southern China's new rich spend enormous amounts of money on first-growth French Bordeaux wines, restaurants, and karaoke entertainment. In Shanghai, public wearing of pajamas serves as a status symbol for the newly affluent.[44] The text of the ad for the Finnish firm Marja and Kurki on page 487 should appeal to nouveau riche consumers.

Being rich enables nouveau riche consumers to buy beauty through such services as personal trainers, prestigious health spas, and plastic surgery. The nouveaux riches tend to have expensive hobbies such as auto racing or yachting. Often, imagined European aristocratic consumption norms provide inspiration to this group. Thus, exports to Asia's nouveaux riches account for more than 50 percent of total turnover for LVMH, the French conglomerate of luxury labels. Because of their unfamiliarity with the goods and services appropriate to their new station, the nouveaux riches are a valuable target for fashion and design professionals.[45]

The emergence of newly affluent market segments in the NICs—with many people learning how to be affluent—represents a market opportunity. The growth of affluence in Asia includes China, whose standard of living has doubled in the last quarter of the twentieth century. It is also likely that the Triad nations of North America and Europe will retain their affluent segments; in those countries, a significant share of national wealth, at least 25 percent, is controlled by less than 5 percent of the population.[46]

Finally, as a result of income gains among information workers and changing attitudes toward consumption brought about by the globalization of marketing and consumer culture, *the upper middle class* is reemerging as what some U.S. marketers call the **Get Set.** Some limitations on income may cause this group to be more selective in their purchase behavior than the other two upper-class groups. However, firms such as Mercedes and Waterford Crystal find that the quality appeal of their brands can be used to encourage members of the Get Set to trade up. It is possible that the increasing ability of middle-class consumers to purchase the goods and services normally reserved for upper-class groups is reviving status competition through consumption of status symbols. Industry Insights 12.1 suggests one upscale furniture retailer believes this. Similarly, theme weddings have become popular with the Indian Get Set. U.S. and Australian Get Set members buy aggressively functional or very expensive practical things (e.g., big SUVs or Smeg gas ranges, for example; see ad on opposite page). Such goods continue to enjoy the prestige of authenticity and high quality that mass-produced, mass-marketed consumer goods do not provide.[47]

Targeting the affluent is not always easy. One reason is that the numbers are small. Second, the truly affluent may own multiple residences. And wealth may be used to purchase some degree of anonymity. Nevertheless, from social registers, real estate maps, listings of boards of directors of major companies and charitable organizations, and other census data, it is often possible to pinpoint the wealthy. Geodemographic segmentation schemes, discussed in Chapter 11, target finely graded affluent segments. Another reason is that vertical lifestyle variations have emerged over the past generation within upper-class groups, sometimes incorporating people from other classes (and ethnic groups; see Chapter 11). These lifestyle subdivisions are sometimes more important for positioning goods and messages than are the named classes in the Triad nations. For example, the Roy Morgan International geodemographic scheme in Australia identifies four high-class lifestyle groups (Champagne and Chardonnay, Asset Rich Commuters, Educated Influentials, Suburban Success Stories) representing about 7 percent of the population, and Claritas identifies three highly affluent geodemographic clusters in the United States (e.g., Blue Blood Estates, Winner's Circle, and Urban Gold Coast), representing about 4 percent of U.S. households.[48]

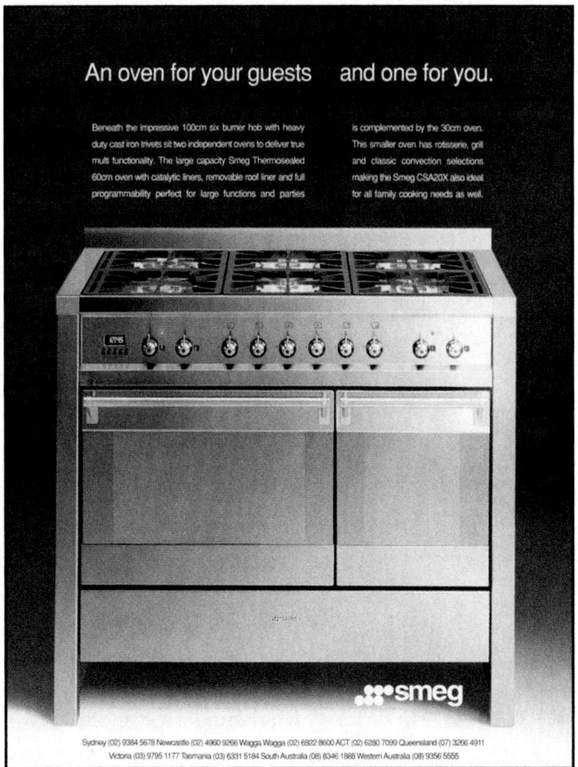

The get Set buys very expensive practical things like Smeg ranges.

Middle-Class Segments

Sizable and relatively stable middle-class segments can be found in at least half of the 190 nations of the world. Most Americans think of themselves as middle class. In 1978, 75 percent of Americans enjoyed middle-class status, although this number has since decreased somewhat. In the United States, middle-class status would generally include households with incomes between $37,000 and $70,000. Possessing a college education and marriage are defining criteria for this segment. Members of this class possess specialized managerial or professional skills. As suggested by Exhibit 12.2, middle-income segments now predominate in European societies as gross domestic product quadrupled in the last quarter of the twentieth century. Thus, the British government classifies half of its citizens as middle class. Similarly, over half of New Zealanders consider themselves middle class, and when asked, 90 percent of Japanese reply they too are middle class.[49]

The middle class in the Triad nations is increasingly multiethnic. Incomes in the average black household rose more than six times faster than in white households between 1989 and 1997, and about one million black households (of 8.4 million) now have an income of $50,000 or more. The trend of a slowly shrinking education gap in the United States is leading to changes in class position and lifestyle choices of African Americans. Indeed, minorities in the United States perceive access to education to be a key to class advancement and attaining related lifestyle and consumption prerogatives.[50]

Globally, economic booms in the early 80s and 90s led to the emergence of upwardly mobile middle-class groups; their newfound economic well-being fueled a huge demand for "modern" consumer goods to express their new middle-class identities.[51] New middle classes represent growth opportunities for international marketers. In India, for example, only 2.8 percent of the population was middle class at independence in 1947, but today it accounts for 32.5 million households—about 162 million people. In Asia, the middle class is expanding dramatically. Just prior to the Asian economic slowdown of the late 1990s, 80 percent of Koreans self-identified as middle class. Up to 20 percent of Thailand's and Malaysia's populations (11 and 3 million people, respectively) may be considered middle class, and even in China 120 million people, or 10 percent of the population, already own their own homes and TVs. The growth of Malaysia's middle class fueled a recent boom in up-market condominium apartments. Overall, the number of non-Japanese Asian households earning $18,000 annually was expected to quadruple, or reach 75 million in 2000.[52]

In many countries, middle classes adopt values familiar to many Americans, such as education, upward mobility, a future orientation, and material self-improvement. These values lead to heightened expenditures on education and culture (e.g., theater attendance and foreign vacations), household furnishings, electronics, and popular leisure activities like sports, and they increase brand loyalty. The Mexican middle class spends much of its disposable income on cars, clothing, vacations, and household goods. Newly middle-class residents of Hong Kong eat out, shop, and go to the movies a great deal.[53]

Marketing to middle-class segments in Asia, the Middle East, and Africa requires appeals that meld innovative values with great consideration of local norms and traditional values. For example, Indians are ambivalent about the values of Western consumerism as consumer individualism conflicts with core Hindu values. The Indonesian middle class is relatively passive and conformist. Part of the explanation lies with the internalization of traditional Confucian-style values.[54]

An increase in discretionary or contestable income characterizes the gains in income of these middle-class households. Thus, in the NICs, these income trends are fueling increasing demand not only for consumer durables but for higher-quality food products and luxuries such as recreation and private transportation as well. For example, some Malaysian yuppies developed an unusual taste for large motorcycles such as Harley-Davidsons to signal their upward mobility.[55] Volkswagen, GM, and other automakers were quick to establish plants in China in anticipation of the emergence of a middle class with increased discretionary income.

Working-Class and Underclass Segments

Working- and underclass segments constitute a majority of the population of the world. Half of the nations of the world have per capita incomes of less than $2,000; in two-thirds of the world, per capita income is less than $5,000. In China, 285 million people, mostly in the western half of the country, earn incomes of $150 to $750 annually. In the United States, ranking 10th in per capita income in the world ($22,000), more than 30 million Americans live in poverty and 40 million U.S. households have annual incomes of less than $25,000. In the UK, almost 20 percent of households have incomes below half the average national income. From a demographic standpoint, what best characterizes the working class is low levels of education and inadequate income. In the United States, in terms of race and household composition, the working class closely resembles the middle classes.[56]

Although the middle class is expanding in some developing nations, relatively rapid growth of per capita GDP is often accompanied by extreme income inequality. The problem of rapid growth without redistribution to a middle class afflicts most developing countries. For example, in spite of improvements in quality of life that have accompanied the transition to popular democracy in South Africa, in 1994 the poorest 20 percent of South Africans earned a GDP per capita of only $516, compared to the richest 20 percent, who earned $9,897.[57]

Studies of the working poor and working class in the United States and in developing countries show that official income figures conceal numerous sources of informal income. In addition, intense networks of exchange of goods and services among kin and neighbors effectively increase demand for many goods and services among poorer consumers. In the Triad nations, these groups also receive a disproportionate amount of public assistance.[58] Networks of reciprocal exchange also act to improve standards of living. Such networks redistribute consumer goods, as suggested in Consumer Chronicles 12.1. The fact that many working-class consumers may spread the cost of acquiring desired goods among kin and neighbors by charging user fees or pooling income suggests marketers need to develop strategies to target these supra-individual consumer groups among the lower classes.

Redistributive Consumption Networks in Lima, Peru

CONSUMER CHRONICLES 12.1

It is customary for kin, visiting from the highlands of Peru, to bring with them as gifts large sacks filled with the product of the land. These delicacies, which are difficult to obtain in the city, include potatoes, quinoa, the flat coarse highland bread, goat cheese, chickens, and guinea pigs. These foods are distributed to urban kin, who savor small symbolic remembrances of their homelands. When residents of the squatter settlements make trips to their highland villages, it is their obligation to take bags of used clothing for their side of the reciprocal exchange and on their return to bring home some bags of food for their kin who had to remain on the coast. The use of food as the basis for initiating and continuing reciprocal relationships is an example of one mechanism for getting along with others.

Source: Susan Lobo, A House of My Own: Social Organization in the Squatter Settlements of Lima, Peru *(Tucson, AZ: University of Arizona Press, 1982).*

Studies in Triad nations as well as in some developing nations have found that working-class consumers are resistant to changes in the basic characteristics of their lifestyles. Other characteristics include limited social and geographic horizons, centrality of family and clan influences on behavior, and devotion to nation and neighborhood. Loyalty to specific musical genres, and local sports teams is also common.[59] These characteristics have been little altered by broader patterns of global change, even in the technological environment. Similarly, heightened brand loyalty and value consciousness are characteristic of lower-class consumers. So-called dollar stores, bargain-basement, packaged-goods retailers, are well positioned to deliver benefits to the working class.

Working-class consumers tend to be externally oriented and emulative of the behaviors of others in their face-to-face networks. They take status goods and other markers of the good life to heart. Fatalism and magical beliefs in luck, astrology, psychic powers, and miracles are not uncommon. Typical of down-market magazines, *Australian Women's Day* magazine features a section containing features and advertisements for products and services promising magical diagnoses and psychic cures.[60]

Working-class consumers seek to participate in the consumer economy through consumption of goods and services that strengthen existing social relationships. They use consumption to claim status in a straightforward way. In working-class homes in many industrial nations, products exemplifying values such as orderliness, religiosity, abundance, and prosperity are often favored. Lower- or working-class cultures value group conformity, localism, and authority. A characteristic behavior is keeping up with the Joneses, so to speak, but not getting ahead of them. This often means preferring regional and mass-merchandise brands. The home and family are a focus for working-class consumption, with home repair being a typical activity in countries as diverse as the United States, France, and Norway.[61]

Working-class demographics and value orientations might suggest that these consumers represent unattractive markets. However, mass merchandisers and discount retailers that offer quality basics at fair prices, such as Wal-Mart and Kmart, may expect to cultivate loyalty with such groups. Recognition of the size of the working-class segment has led to what is sometimes called **two-tiered marketing.** In two-tiered marketing, *firms differentiate their retail outlets or product or service offerings into two groups, targeted at upper- or lower-class consumers, respectively*. In addition, these firms minimize offerings to middle-income segments.

Working-class groups are not uninterested in innovative products that resolve basic needs. For example, in the United States, the working class often lacks access to financial services. In response, Fleet Bank's Community Banking Group has profitably targeted lower-income segments with check cashing and other banking services, some in ATM-like vending machines. In India, a young start-up company, iNabling Technologies, has spotted a promising business opportunity in narrowing the digital divide separating the working class from the affluent. The centerpiece of the company's efforts is a small portable gadget called iStation, capable of sending or receiving text-based e-mail, the major use of the Internet, but costing only 7,000 rupees or about US$150. iNabling Technologies hopes to place their machines in public telephone booths.[62]

In distinction to the working class, a behavioral **underclass** composed of poor, chronically unemployed, and ill-educated people who are deprived of most consumer options has emerged globally. This group is increasingly socially isolated from mainstream society as the deindustrialization of First World and devaluation of unskilled labor in the transitional and LAW nations cut off the bottom rungs of the employment ladder. Members of this underclass allegedly engage in antisocial behaviors, especially crimes against property and persons. Shoplifting, burglary, and looting linked to urban disturbances and ethnic or caste-based (see below) warfare also are associated with this group. Overconsumption of alcohol, tobacco, and illegal drugs are also an affliction for them. Across urban America, some authors estimate that this group numbers between 1.5 and 2.5 million people. A similar class may be found in some of the UK's worst housing estates, among the "lost generation" of former East Germany, and in places such as Haiti and Sierra Leone. Even countries with significant consumer welfare policies are facing challenges from the problems of alienation and economic marginalization experienced by the underclass.[63]

Ethnicity

Quick, what do the United States, Canada, Indonesia, Australia, and Germany have in common? Ethnic diversity is the answer. Twenty-nine percent of Americans (70 million) and 25 percent of Australians are of non-Anglo origin. Germany is home to over two million Turks and five million other ethnic minorities. Eleven percent of the Canadian population is of non-Anglo origin; the largest group is Chinese. Indonesia is a mosaic of hundreds of ethnic groups. Many countries, including the United Kingdom, Russia, and China, have significant ethnic minority populations. In fact, 91 million Chinese belong to one of 55 different ethnic minority groups. Thus, ethnic diversity is widespread globally, and the dramatic increase in economically motivated migration in recent years results in increasing ethnic diversity, especially in richer countries.[64]

Europe's Explosive Identity Crisis

ETHICAL DILEMMA 12.1

There's an ill wind blowing across Europe. It can be felt in a string of deadly attacks on immigrant hostels in Germany. In the summer of 2001, race riots wracked northern Britain. On May 5, 2002, almost six million French voters cast their ballots for hard-right xenophobe Jean-Marie Le Pen. It can be felt in the meteoric ascent and assassination of anti-immigrant Dutch politician Pim Fortuyn on May 6, 2002. You can feel it in the increasing shrillness of current political debate in Italy, Denmark, and France. Amid the many currents feeding this rising tide of European malaise, one stands out: Europeans are in the midst of a monumental identity crisis.

From Berlin to Lisbon, people are stuck in a kind of existential halfway house. Behind them are the old nation-states of Europe, each defined by language ethnicity, and varying economic models with national champions such as Fiat, Renault, or Siemens. Ahead is the post-modern construct of the European Union. The problem is the first is fast collapsing, but the second has not yet been fully built.

Two other factors make this unstable mixture explosive. One is the growing presence of immigrant populations in a Europe that for the most part cannot accept nonwhite and non-Christian residents as full citizens. The other is a relentless economic anemia that keeps unemployment high in a context of growing consumer expectations. Dutch alderwoman Fatima Elatik, 28, thinks the growth of commercial television has put tremendous pressure on youth to acquire expensive shoes and mobile phones. "When I was a kid, I didn't give [a damn] if I had Nike's or not," she says. "Now everyone wants Prada shoes." Thus, in many European towns and cities, a vicious circle of crime, violence, and racism has taken hold. In this season of distrust, violence, and death, it's hard to believe Europe will find its way again. "When I look back, each step of building Europe has been a miracle," says Gerard Mestrallet, CEO of French-Belgian energy and water giant Suez. But forging a true European identity—untainted by nationalism and ethnic hatred—will take many miracles more.

Sources: Reprinted with permission from Stanley Reed (2002), "Murder in the Netherlands," Business Week, *May 20, 2002, pp. 32–35; and John Rossant, "Europe's Explosive Identity Crisis,"* Business Week, *May 20, 2002, p. 35, copyright ©2002 by The McGraw-Hill Companies, Inc.*

As a result of slow growth in mainstream market segments, more competition, and more diverse consumers with relatively strong purchasing power, marketing consultants from the United States to Australia and South Africa extol the virtues of **multicultural marketing,** or *special targeting of ethnic consumers*. Multicultural marketing programs differentiate the interests of one firm from another. To succeed, multicultural marketers aim to acquire customers who are more satisfied because their needs and interests overlap with those of the organizations they patronize. Greater buyer satisfaction can evolve when firms play a broader role in the cultural lives of consumers than simply producing products they desire. Recognition of target groups in advertising campaigns, sponsorships, and cause-related marketing leads to cultural partnerships that can build more profitable relationships than traditional ethnic niche marketing. Multicultural marketing is not the same as recognizing ethnic diversity in markets. It implies a general social acceptance that cultural diversity is not an impediment to economic advancement. In other words, a country may be ethnically diverse, but this diversity may not be socially acceptable to, or recognized by, majority segments. In France, for example, the census only identifies immigrants, unlike the U.S. and Australian censuses that recognize the ethnic origins of citizens. In countries where ethnic identification is not associated with claims to special treatment in the marketplace, multicultural marketing is not so likely to succeed. Ethical Dilemma 12.1 suggests that even in the Triad nations, consumer culture and ethnic diversity are not always harmoniously linked.[65]

What Is Kwanzaa?

CONSUMER CHRONICLES 12.2

Kwanzaa is based on ancient East African harvest celebrations. Kwanzaa is celebrated for seven days from December 26 to January 1, a period that represents the end of an old year. Kwanzaa shares a number of elements with East African harvest celebrations:

- Gathering of the people.
- Special reverence for the Creator and creation.
- Commemoration of the past, especially paying homage to ancestors.
- Recommitment to the highest ethical and cultural values, especially the Nguzo Saba, The Seven Principles.
- Celebration of the Good of life, especially family, community, and culture.

The estimates predict that over 18 million people, worldwide, participate in the seven-day celebration of family, community, and culture. But even in Southern California, where Kwanzaa was created about 30 years ago by Dr. Maulana Karenga—chair of the Black Studies Department at California State University–Long Beach—many people are unaware of its existence, and uninformed about its specifics. However, that's changing. Kwanzaa, a holiday founded amid the activism of 1960s America, and spread globally by word of mouth and the nurturing of spirits, is about to be embraced by capitalism and modern mass media. Hallmark has been selling Kwanzaa greeting cards since 1992. American Greetings also has added its line of Kwanzaa cards to gift shop shelves from coast to coast. An African-American-owned publishing company markets 21 styles of Kwanzaa cards and activity books for children. Bookstores offer the story of Kwanzaa in the children's section along with stories of Hanukkah and Christmas. Even the U.S. post office is in on the act with a special issue of Kwanzaa holiday stamps each year.

Sources: Dave Wielenga, "Kwanzaa Goes Mainstream," Press-Telegram, *December 19, 1993, pp. J1, J10; and Jerome Williams and Marye C. Tharp, "African Americans,"* in Marketing and Consumer Identity in Multicultural America, *ed. Marye C. Tharp (Thousand Oaks, CA: Sage Publications, 2001), pp. 165–211.*

DEFINING ETHNICITY What is ethnicity? **Ethnicity** is defined in terms of *frequent patterns of association and identification with common national or cultural origins of a subgroup found within the larger society*. In addition to a sense of common origin, four elements often define ethnicity: (1) a self-perpetuating population; (2) shared cultural values; (3) a field of communication and interaction, facilitated by a common language; and (4) members who define themselves and are identified by others as a distinguishable category. As mentioned earlier in this chapter, social class is based on economic capital, then elaborated through social and cultural capital. By contrast, ethnicity is based more on social capital (relationships, networks, and personal connections) and then elaborated through economic and cultural capital expressed in consumption.[66]

At the individual consumer level, ethnicity involves self-identity, of **felt ethnicity,** defined as *an individual's perceptions of him- or herself as a member of an ethnic group or his or her desire to express valued aspects of their sense of self through ethnic group affiliation*. Worldwide felt ethnicity has increased in the last two decades as consumer loyalty is moving from brand to company to identity groups. In the United States, as Consumer Chronicles 12.2 shows, consumers who feel drawn to their ethnic African roots mark felt ethnicity by celebrating Kwanzaa. In addition to consumption of symbolic products like those associated with Kwanzaa, felt ethnicity affects reactions to advertising. When felt ethnicity is aroused by an ethnic context such as a tel-

Ethnic festivals like Carnival offer lucrative marketing and sponsorship opportunities.

evision show or a favorable magazine article, for example, consumers may feel more positively toward ads using ethnic models as well as the products they promote.[67] When *expressions of ethnicity vary with social context,* this is termed **situational ethnicity.** In other words, while some values may be stable, the expression of ethnic values varies with the social situation. Individuals attending an ethnic festival on the basis of their felt ethnicity may consume foods and entertainment associated with their ethnic background, whereas in mixed-ethnic company their consumption choices might not reflect their ethnic background. During an African-American football weekend in Tampa, Florida, consumers actively build social capital, renewing networks and reestablishing school ties. As importantly, they consume the "black experience" through an intense round of dinners, parties, tailgating, sports events, and dressing up. A multitude of ethnic festivals are celebrated in the United States. But consumer assertions of ethnic identity occur in many countries. As shown in the photo above, West Indian Carnival is celebrated in Toronto, Canada, as well as Brooklyn, New York. Melbourne's Antipodes Festival is Australia's largest ethnic festival, promoting the culture, heritage, and tradition of Greek Australians, celebrated on Greek National Day, March 25th. Ethnic festivals offer lucrative marketing and sponsorship opportunities; by providing products or services that help consumers express ethnicity, marketers can build loyalty in ethnic communities.[68]

DYNAMICS OF ETHNICITY To understand the role of ethnicity in consumer behavior, two related concepts are needed: acculturation and assimilation. Acculturation, discussed in Chapter 3, produces changes in knowledge, beliefs, values, and behaviors when an individual member of an ethnic group comes into prolonged contact with a dominant culture. Thus, Greenlandic immigrants to Denmark noticed changes in their concepts of time, space, and nature during their years in Denmark. Acculturation produces identification with the dominant culture, including a preference for its language. It also means adopting consumption patterns of the dominant culture. Again, like acculturating ethnic groups everywhere, Greenlanders in Denmark mention changes in their consumption of food, fashions, and leisure triggered by their move to mainland Denmark.[69]

At one time, it was thought that acculturation leads inevitably to a second state, called **assimilation,** *a process of interpenetration and fusion in which persons and groups acquire memories, sentiments, and attitudes of other persons or groups and, by sharing their experience and history, are incorporated with them in a common cultural life.* The idea of a country as a melting pot reflects this process, with immigrants assimilating into the dominant culture. The gradual loss of Cajun French language and culture in Louisiana was due to assimilation brought about by the stigma attached to Cajun identity historically. Likewise, many immigrants to the United States—be they from Asia, Europe, or elsewhere—demonstrate the idea of progressive assimilation to mainstream values in their evaluation of cars, stereos, coffee, laundry detergent, and so on.[70]

A worldwide renewal of ethnic identities and the use of the metaphor of **ethnic mosaics** recognizes that assimilation is a far from certain outcome. Felt ethnic and regional ethnicities have reemerged throughout the world. Reflecting regional identity, four national languages are now recognized in Spain, for example: Catalan, Basque, Spanish, and Galician. But ethnic identities today are more voluntary than in the past; they represent a creative mix of values, beliefs, and consumption styles. Consistent with our argument in Chapter 3 that culture is now marketed, ethnic identity has become a marketed commodity. Thus, Cajun identity has been revived in part through the popularity among consumers of Cajun cuisine and zydeco music.[71]

Studies of immigrants to North America show that the outcome of the acculturation process varies. Researchers identify four reactions to the host consumer culture. Some immigrants *assimilate* to some consumption patterns associated with North American consumer cultures, yet they also *maintain* aspects of the consumption patterns they had acquired in their country of origin. Some Mexican Americans tend to buy Mexican brands and products, for instance. Informants also expressed concerns about getting caught up in U.S. consumer culture and actively *resist* its pull. So, some Mexican Americans express dislike for frozen and prepackaged foods, for example. The majority of new immigrants inhabit sites in the United States that are physically and socially segregated from members of the dominant culture. Voluntary segregation not only inhibits assimilation, it limits the ability of mainstream marketing organizations to establish trust with potential ethnic clients. Consumer Chronicles 12.3 describes a man's experience as an immigrant from Hong Kong to Canada. He continues to *operate on the margin* of both Chinese and Canadian society, referred to as *a deculturation* response to the dominant culture.[72]

Other studies have shown that some Mexican Americans, Chinese, and Koreans overacculturate, or display exaggerated conformity to perceived mainstream consumption norms. Some Mexican Americans show exaggerated consumption of Anglo food products. Some assimilated Koreans show exaggerated reliance on advertising and word-of-mouth relative to mainstream U.S. citizens. We find similarly diverse and creative consumption behaviors among ethnic consumers in other contexts. This complicates the tasks of targeting ethnic consumers and positioning products and services to appeal to them.[73]

Neither Chinese nor Canadian

CONSUMER CHRONICLES 12.3

Colin is 39 years old and arrived in Canada three years ago as an immigrant from Hong Kong. Colin has trouble coming up with an ethnic group to which he belongs, but decides it really shouldn't be Chinese, perhaps Hong Kongese. Although he is a Canadian citizen, he doesn't consider himself Canadian. He does not socialize much with non-Chinese. All his friends are Chinese and he only socializes with "gwailo" (foreign devils) in the workplace setting. He subscribes to Chinese cable television and Chinese newspapers, and grocery shops in Chinatown. However, he doesn't speak Chinese unless he is asked to; he prefers English. Many Chinese traditions are not to his liking, and he feels lucky to have escaped them by living in Canada. Colin lives on the margin of both Chinese and Canadian society.

Source: Adapted from Ed Chung, "Navigating the Primordial Soup: Charting the Lived Worlds of the Migrant Consumer," Journal of Consumer Marketing *17, no. 1 (2000). Reprinted by permission of the Universitry of Chicago Press.*

ETHNIC GROUP SEGMENTS The following section will make special reference to ethnic diversity in the United States, but the marketing implications will be similar for countries experiencing increased immigration or a renewed sense of ethnic identity among certain population segments, a trend noted in many parts of Europe and North and South America.[74]

African Americans are the largest U.S. ethnic minority, numbering nearly 36 million. They represent over $540 billion in spending power. More than 13 percent of black households may be considered affluent. Gains in education have fueled a 50 percent increase in purchasing power since 1996. Only 22 percent of blacks now live in poverty. Thirty-nine percent of blacks now live in the suburbs. Of course, African Americans are not homogeneous in their ethnic identity. For example, middle-class Haitian immigrants are lumped with African Americans in the United States, but they distance themselves from this group. African Americans frequently use consumption both as a medium for expressing participation in the mainstream and pride in ethnic roots and accomplishments depending on situational factors.[75]

Competence, empathy, respect, and self-enhancement are key value orientations or priorities that are especially meaningful appeals to African-American consumers. The ad shown on page 498 is positioned to appeal to these values. Style and trendsetting, concern with self-image and elegance, and interest in cultural heritage are also significant orientations. In response, cosmetics niche marketer African Pride combines an appeal to heritage with an appeal to style, for example. Middle-class, affluent African Americans are also cautious and conservative and respond to mainstream middle-class, value-based appeals. Many African Americans have a heightened sensitivity to interaction in the marketplace due to historic experiences of discrimination, so ethnic appeals must be handled with care. For example, a Fruity Pebbles cereal spot featuring "rapper" Barney Rubble was experienced as ridiculous and offensive. Ethical Dilemma 12.2 highlights a similar problem with niche marketing of books by African-American authors.[76]

Hispanic Americans are the next largest ethnic U.S. segment. There will be 40 million U.S. Hispanics in 2010. This is a youthful population. Hispanics contributed 47 percent of the U.S. population growth in the 1990s. Hispanics doubled their purchasing power from what it was in 1980. The Hispanic-American market is estimated to represent almost $400 billion in purchasing power.

Hispanic Americans are highly diverse in terms of national origin, lifestyle, and culture. Marketers should tailor their campaigns to capture these differences. National

This ad appeals to African-American values of self-esteem and inclusion.

origin—Mexico, Cuba, and Puerto Rico, for example—is the single most important segmentation variable among Hispanic Americans. Cuban Americans report lower levels of assimilation than most other Hispanic groups, except Puerto Ricans. Hence, Spanish language media and appeals to traditional values will be most appropriate for them. Mexican Americans report feeling most assimilated. But even highly assimilated Hispanics appreciate marketing efforts that acknowledge their characteristics and purchasing power (see "You Make the Call" at the end of this chapter).

Hispanics display some distinctive value orientations that affect product and advertising evaluation. To them, age implies acquired experience and knowledge. Hence, older spokespersons may be well regarded by target markets. Responsibility and a strong work ethic are characteristic, as is a religious orientation. Gender roles tend to be more conservative and divorce less common than among the majority population. Hispanics are family-centered; their primary loyalties are to the family. Consequently, consumption activities are generally to do with the family. Hispanics are often concerned with aesthetics and emotions and place considerable emphasis on quality of life and enjoyment. Hispanic consumers think positively about companies that advertise in Spanish, as shown in Industry Insights 12.2.[77]

Asian Americans are the fastest growing and most affluent minority market in the United States, their numbers tripling between 1980 and 2000 to 12 million, or 4 percent of the population. Four out of 10 live in California; they are youthful (mean age of 30), affluent (one-third live in households with incomes over $75,000 per year), and well educated (39 percent having attended four years of college versus 17 percent of all Americans). Asian-American purchasing power is estimated at US$254 billion per year. Asian Amer-

This ad appeals to beliefs and feelings about the extended Chinese family.

icans are diverse; as with Hispanics, there really isn't one Asian-American market. Asian Indian numbers grew especially dramatically in the last decade of the twentieth century. Chinese Americans and Filipino Americans now surpass Japanese Americans in number, and Korean and Indian Americans almost equal their numbers. Koreans and Chinese living in Chinatowns tend to be relatively unacculturated and are difficult to reach through mainstream marketing. Second- and third-generation Asians tend to be highly assimilated.[78]

Like Hispanic Americans, Asian Americans should be segmented into national groups. Family, tradition, cooperation, and a strong work ethic are among the distinctive values that affect product evaluation among Asian Americans, but each national group is tied to its particular cultural heritage and language. The advertisement for Webmiles appeals to beliefs about and feelings toward the extended Chinese family.[79]

Targeting and Positioning Issues in Multicultural Marketing

In developing targeting and positioning strategies to reach ethnic markets, marketers should consider a number of issues. First, marketers must determine empirically whether identifiable ethnic groups constitute market segments for ethnic media and ethnically targeted products and services. This will be based in part on whether their cultural values translate into distinctive preferences. For example, Asian investors tend to prefer short-term investments and frequent trades, so while the brokerage firm Charles Schwab has focused on teaching the value of diversification and long-term planning to its Asian clientele, it also has opened some of its branches on Saturdays to accommodate Asian's tendency to handle money matters on weekends.[80]

Another issue is intensity of felt ethnic identification. Consumers who strongly identify with their ethnic group will display a preference for specialized ethnic media, marketing communications that use national languages, ethnic products and services, and an

Cashing in on Black Readers

ETHICAL DILEMMA 12.2

An advertising campaign for Strivers Row, a new line of books from Random House aimed at black readers, is creating a stir among black authors and agents. The reason is that the advertisements double as plugs for Pine-Sol, a popular household cleanser. Clorox, which makes Pine-Sol, has placed the ads in a number of popular mass circulation magazines such as *Woman's Day,* spending close to a million dollars in the process. The campaign is unusual in the book business, long considered one of the few corners of the media relatively free of sponsors' pitches. After decades of complaints that the industry neglected blacks, it has touched a nerve with authors and agents. Although the industry is suddenly bringing out more books by blacks than ever, some worry that the creation of specialized imprints for blacks within several mainstream houses risks ghettoizing new black authors. Grouping books by race may limit their market potential. And the use of Strivers Row books as props to sell cleanser has aggravated these fears. Is Random House engaging in good market segmentation and co-marketing of its Strivers Row imprint, or is it a dumb move that will alienate black readers?

Source: David D. Kirkpatrick, "Cashing in on Black Readers," New York Times, *Business Day, July 16, 2001, pp. C1, C6. Copyright © 2001 by the* New York Times *Co. Reprinted with permission.*

ethnic consumer lifestyle. These preferences tend to decline with English language use and acculturation. Highly targeted media, native language advertising, and niche products and services are appropriate to less assimilated groups and can reap big rewards for marketers. Native language media tend to be much less expensive than mainstream media, exert more effective reach, and translate into higher levels of brand awareness and eventually loyalty among ethnic consumers.

Successful ethnic marketing often depends on appealing to the basic motivational drive to express integration, in this case ethnic affiliation, through benefit-and values-based segmentation. For example, since the Honda Civic has long been a favorite of young Asian Americans seeking to soup up their cars with aftermarket accessories, Honda Motor Co. chose to piggyback on Boba, a beverage developed in Taiwan that is all the rage in Asian youth circles, by developing drink sleeves featuring its products. Since family values are important to Hispanic Americans, Metropolitan Life increased sales of insurance to Hispanics by 150 percent by using a nationwide ad campaign that referred to the importance of protecting the family's future. Values-based marketing has proven successful for JCPenney and KFC. Afrocentric retailing provides a way to express situational ethnicity, discussed earlier.[81]

Successful marketing firms sometimes must adapt to subtle distinctions in the evaluative criteria employed by ethnic consumers in decision making. Many Hispanic consumers, for example, favor advertisements that indicate product purpose, benefits, or use over image-based ads. Bootchcreek Resorts in the Lake Tahoe area changed its skiing instruction techniques to accommodate Asian Americans' discomfort with frequent praising and eye contact. This has paid off in terms of increased business. Similarly, African-American media are thriving because of their distinctive value orientation. A handful of magazine titles such as *Essence, Black Enterprise,* and *Vibe* have been enjoying record advertising sales. Companies such as Cadillac have used minority ad agencies to produce ads that are sensitive to distinctive African-American values.[82]

Style is a criterion of importance to some ethnic consumers. Since style is a shared set of preferences, it is a way for ethnic groups whose social status is primarily based on social capital (networks, relationships, and connections) to transform it into symbolic capital. Ethnic groups may be recognized for a particular style or for stylishness in general. Marketers facilitate this process when, in their search for new product ideas, they mass market fashion or events like Cinco de Mayo developed by ethnic minorities. A recent example of this ongoing process of converting social into symbolic capital is shown in Consumer Chronicles 12.4, but, of course, the fashionistas have moved on to other fads by now.[83]

Understanding acculturation affects language choice in marketing communications. Advertising is more effective when it taps motivations in the language in which those drives are spontaneously expressed. The ad agency Mosaica, which specializes in marketing to Asian Americans, emphasizes the value of culturally pertinent advertising in national languages for these groups. A preference for Spanish language book titles led big U.S. book chains to double-digit sales growth in the early 1990s.[84]

Targeting ethnic minorities through special language media may sometimes cause problems. Acculturated target groups may identify with the values and goals of the dominant culture instead of the ethnic values emphasized in the ad. Or the target may perceive the ads as condescending. The ad may use the wrong dialectical variation. To avoid this problem, Goya's recent ads translate beans both as *frijoles* and *habichuelas* and show national dishes from different Latin American countries next to each other, and Campbell's soup ran an ad featuring different spokespersons speaking Cuban-, Mexican-, and Puerto-Rican-accented Spanish.[85]

"Talk to Me": Hispanic Consumers Think Positively about Companies That Advertise in Spanish

INDUSTRY INSIGHTS 12.2

- 53 percent of Hispanic consumers say they remember more about or pay more attention to products and brands that are advertised in Spanish.
- 51 percent of California Hispanics prefer listening to radio stations that broadcast specifically to Hispanics.
- 45 percent say they are much more loyal toward companies that show appreciation for their culture by advertising in Spanish.
- 46 percent feel that companies respect their heritage and really want their business when the company advertises its products in Spanish.
- 32 percent relate that Spanish-language advertising is important to them because it is the best source of information for making purchasing decisions.

Sources: John Fetto, "Targeted Media," American Demographics, *July/August 2002, p. 13, and Joan Raymond, "¿Tienen Numeros?"* American Demographics, *March 2002, p. 24.*

Caste

Caste is a social category almost unique to South Asia, primarily India, secondarily Indonesia and Bali. It cannot be compared to either ethnicity or class insofar as it *combines both hierarchical (vertical) and lateral (horizontal) systems of inequality*. The four major Indian castes from highest to lowest are (1) Brahmins (priests, scholars), (2) Kshatriyas (warriors and princes), (3) Vaisyas (merchants and artisans), and (4) Sudras (laborers and servants). These four groups are divided into over 3,000 subcastes. In addition, there are hundreds of millions of "untouchables," uncasted persons relegated to the lowest levels of society and now becoming part of the global underclass. Caste membership is associated with occupations, rights, and duties toward other castes, and castes have an explicit moral dimension. Higher-caste groups are considered morally superior to lower groups. Thus, like class in the United States, it is not terribly fashionable to discuss caste and its implications in public debate. Caste differences are very distinct and enter into many lifestyle differences; hence, marketing communications need to be sensitive to caste differences both in positioning products and presenting models and spokespersons.[86]

OTHER STRUCTURAL SEGMENTS

Age, gender, and religion are three additional systematically organized dimensions of social life that afford consumers a sense of identity, affect the distribution of symbolic capital, and consequently create opportunities for market segmentation, targeting, and

Stock Car Garb Becomes Unlikely Urban Fashion

CONSUMER CHRONICLES 12.4

Look for fashion-conscious urban youth sporting logos of companies sponsoring or supplying racing equipment for stock-car races, including Dupont, Mopar, and Champion spark plugs. Hiphop devotees are also donning authentic-looking, form-fitting, motorcycle racing jackets, retailing for more than $600 a pop.

Racing, long associated with southern good ol' boys in stock cars or European jet setters in the elite Formula One and international motorcycle circuits, is the latest object of desire for black and Hispanic city youths. Fashion firms such as Donna Karan and Tommy Hilfiger are taking note. Hiphop takes what it wants and adopts it—and what Hiphop embraces sells.

Source: Leon D. Wynter, "Business & Race," The Wall Street Journal, *June 2, 1999, p. B1.*

positioning. It is important to keep in mind that there are many interactions between each of these social segments. for example, gender roles and acceptable patterns of consumption are influenced by religion and age. And, of course, social class and caste also influence these social structures. For example, women in lower-class households tend to adopt more stereotypical gender roles than women in middle- or upper-class households. Children from upper-class households receive different allowances and spend their money differently than children from poorer households. An exhaustive discussion of age, gender, and religion segments is beyond the scope of this chapter; however, we further discuss some of these segmentation bases in Chapter 11 (on lifestyles) and Chapter 13 (on households).

Age

In using age to develop segmentation, targeting, and positioning strategies, marketers consider three aspects of age. First is the **life cycle** itself. People's wants change with physical aging over the course of the life cycle, *the movement from birth to death.* Consumers' preferences and their access to resources typically vary with age, as well. In general, young adults focus on the accumulation of functional items needed for independent living. A motor scooter or car, an MP3 player, or basic housewares are examples. Mature adults place greater value on unselfishness and emotional satisfaction than possession; they purchase a lot of financial products to protect their heirs and travel-related products, for example. Older adults are interested in products and experiences that express family and social history.

Second, age-related **life transitions**—*socially recognized changes in status*—drive demand for specialized products and services. Some examples of age-related life transitions that trigger purchase of goods and services include entering school, religious initiation, becoming a teenager, entering military service, pledging a fraternity or sorority, entering adulthood, graduating college or university, celebrating a 25th wedding anniversary, and retiring from the workforce.

Third, **age cohorts** are *groups of people who have grown up during specific time periods.* Their shared experiences and memories form the basis of shared values and cultural symbolism. These in turn translate into similarities in consumer preferences. Thus, people who were young during the turbulent 1960s differ in outlook from the youth who experienced the growing economy and horizon-expanding technological changes of the 1990s. As shown in Exhibit 12.4, U.S. marketers distinguish millennials, baby boomers, generation X, and generation Y, among other age cohorts.[87]

CHILDREN (MILLENNIALS) In the industrialized Triad nations, this age cohort affects consumer demand both directly and through their influence on their families. There are

Generation	Year Born	Age in 2000	U.S. Population (millions)	Percent of U.S. Population
GI generation	Pre-1930	71+	25.3	9.1
Depression era	1930–1939	61–70	17.8	6.5
War babies	1940–1945	55–60	15.6	5.7
Baby boomers	1946–1964	36–54	77.4	28.2
Generation X	1965–1976	24–35	44.9	16.4
Generation Y	1977–1994	6–23	70.7	25.8
Millennials	1995+	0–5	22.9	8.3

Source: Rebecca Gardyn and John Fetto, "Off the Map," *American Demographics*, June 2000, p. 72.

EXHIBIT 12.4

Vital Statistics on U.S. Generations

more than 800 million children aged 4–12 years in the Triad nations. Children's consumer demands represent considerable market opportunities for those who can meet their distinct desires and endowment of cultural capital. Triad children enjoy considerable discretionary income. American children between the ages of 6 and 14 spend approximately US$77 billion a year; their French counterparts spend US$2.7 billion. As much as a third of their income goes to candy and snacks.[88] Not surprisingly a firm like PepsiCo, through its Sabritas subsidiary, has sought a major share of the candy and bubble gum business in Mexico and is expanding into Spain and Brazil. But kids' personal spending doesn't end with snacks. As a result, many fashion retailers from the Gap to Lacoste and Sephora have extended their lines to target pre-adolescents, while others such as shoemaker Vans focus on this group. Nickelodeon, the Disney Channel, YTV, and the Cartoon Network compete for the worldwide kids' business. Sony and Sega fight for a share of the huge video game market. Denmark's Lego enjoys global recognition in construction toys. The Harry Potter craze swept the industrialized world in 2000 and will be recycled with additional film and book projects. The ad for Stevies shoes shown here is indicative of the lifestyle products increasingly now targeted at millennials.

Stevies shoes targets the increasingly market savvy preteen segment.

In Western consumer society, we now recognize the sophisticated endowment of cultural capital of consumers as young as five to seven years old, as well as children's role in influencing adult consumption. Children assume the role of consumer decision makers at a young age. Children as young as two years old rely on symbolic brand attributes when forming preferences and making choices among consumer goods. Visual cues such as television advertising and vivid packaging influence their learning and attitudes toward brands. Children as young as three recognize heavily advertised cartoon characters; this recognition produces positive attitudes toward products associated with these characters. About 50 percent of gift requests in young children's letters to Santa Claus are for specific branded items, and about 85 percent of the children mention at least one brand name in these letters.

Globally, consumer sophistication varies with the age at which kids begin their education and the amount of marketing communications to which they are exposed through the media. Thus, Danish and British kids who start school later lag French and Americans in consumer sophistication. Sometime between preschool and second grade, children begin to make inferences about people, such as occupation and age, based on things such as their cars and houses. By sixth grade, U.S. children have a keen sense of the social meaning and prestige associated with certain types of products and brand names.[89]

Children influence parental shopping and spending habits. Kids encourage over $100 billion in family spending in both the United States and France, for example (see Chapter 13). Businesses in the NICs also are waking up to kids' influence on parents' spending habits. There are about 85 million kids aged 10–19 in the region, and their economic clout is considerable. In Japan, toy sales total $3.1 billion a year and children's shoes and clothing come to about $8.8 billion. Two out of three Japanese elementary students play games on their families' computers.[90] A study reveals that urban Chinese children influence up to two-thirds of parents' purchase decisions. In part because of China's one-child policy, children have significant income from and influence on both parents and grandparents beginning as early as age four. Another study reports that urban Chinese middle-school students spent 66.3 percent of their parents' combined incomes.[91] The China case is unique in some respects, but many children globally are exerting significant influence on consumption behavior. Making retail outlets kid-friendly, as French electronics store Salon has done, can bring in shoppers and increase purchases initiated by children.[92]

The proliferation and globalization of marketing have both pluses and minuses for children. For many urban, lower-class children in the United States, watching commercial TV at home and congregating in the shopping malls are some of the only relatively safe leisure venues available to them. At the same time, limited financial resources frustrate their participation in consumer culture. In addition, poor children's consumer demands may fuel conflicts over family, class relations, and tradition, in both the Triad nations and the less affluent world. In NICs like Korea, recent rapid economic growth, industrialization, and the introduction of Western consumer culture have fueled a tremendous generation gap in values. This gap is expressed in striking differences in consumer preferences between young and old. In the less affluent world, children's power in introducing consumerism into more traditional communities cannot be underestimated. On the other hand, the growing global gap between rich and poor, and the growth in demand for commodities produced in the less developed countries, means many children enjoy few consumption options and instead spend their childhood working, as suggested in Ethical Dilemma 12.3.[93]

Another ethical controversy in consumer behavior concerns the ability of children to defend themselves against the claims advertisers direct to them. Some contend that children develop considerable abilities to counterargue against commercial messages. Others say that children, particularly young children, with less-developed problem-solving abilities have ineffective defenses against commercial claims. Most research supports the view that television advertising powerfully influences children's product preferences and choices and plays at least a moderate role in perception and usage of products such as cigarettes, alcohol, and heavily sugared, nonnutritious foods. Recent legislative and judicial decisions in the United States concerning tobacco marketing reflect the view that children's cognitive defenses against advertising are not adequate. Hence, government-financed programs to demarket tobacco products are enjoying popularity. In-school and online privacy also have begun to attract attention, particularly with regard to marketing tactics directed at children.[94]

Child Labor Fuels Commodity Trade

ETHICAL DILEMMA 12.3

According to a new United Nations report, child workers produce a high proportion of globally traded commodity crops such as cocoa, coffee, and tea. "Child labor often assumes serious proportions in commercial agriculture closely associated with global markets for coffee, cotton, rubber, sisal, tea and other commodities," the UN's International Labor Organization (ILO) said. About 246 million children worldwide are involved in unacceptable forms of child labor, the ILO said. For example, a decade after India ratified a UN convention pledging to protect children's right, the country continues to be home to the world's largest number of child laborers. It is believed there are up to 100 million of them. Both government officials and activists agree that one of the root causes of the continued prevalence of child labor is excruciating poverty. Sociologists say the lower castes of Hindu society feel this pressure the most. By contrast only 1 percent of children work in developed countries.

Sources: http://news.bbc.co.uk/hi/english/business/newsid_1970000/1970/1970563.stm; and Rayyasri Rao, "India 'Losing' Child Labor Battle," BBC News, May 6, 2002, at http://news.bbc.co.uk/hi/english/world/southasia/newsid_1970000/1970/1970708.stm.

TEENS (GENERATION Y) As illustrated in the vignette that opens this chapter, teenagers or generation Y is a popular target for marketers for many reasons. First, they are numerous. There are almost 31 million teenagers in the United States, and by 2010 there will be 35 million. One-third of China's population is younger than 20 years old. In Turkey, the young represent 67 percent of the population, and in Mexico, the young represent 71 percent of the population.[95] Second, young people in the Triad and newly industrialized nations (generation Yers) enjoy enormous discretionary purchasing power. The DoCoMo cell phone–toting Japanese consumer of Water Salad portrayed in the opening vignette is typical. Mah-jongg parlors in Tokyo have revived flagging interest in this traditional game by repositioning themselves to attract college students' discretionary spending.[96] U.S. teenagers aged 12 to 18 get an average $50 a week in cash from parents, and, not surprisingly, as household income increases, so do allowances for teens. At the same time, millions of youngsters are regularly putting money into mutual funds and the stock market. The websites Investing for Kids and Kids Bank appeal to savvy, young consumers with tips about investing and banking. A third reason teenagers comprise an attractive segment is that they are market savvy and involved with consumer culture. The preference for using one's cell phone to charge a soft drink from a vending machine described in the opening vignette is a good example of this savvy. A number of studies of teens in the UK have shown that they use advertisements and brands in creative ways to craft and comment on their lives and communities. Japanese generation Yers are innovative consumers of the latest electronic gear. One U.S. study found that 88 percent of teenage girls go to shopping malls 40 percent more often than other demographic groups. And one in nine American teenagers has a credit card. Teenagers in many of the transitional economies (e.g., Czech Republic, Poland, and Hungary) have grown up with a market economy and are much more comfortable shopping and making consumer decisions than their parents or grandparents. Many people form initial brand loyalties as teenagers, so this age group offers an ideal target market for promoting brand loyalties. Teenagers make purchase decisions for an

@ www.thinkquest.org

@ www.kidsbank.com

ever-widening variety of their own products, from books to clothes, making them attractive targets for marketing communications. Because of the way brand meanings interact with identity, teenagers appear to be extremely brand aware and often fiercely brand loyal. One study found that 50 percent of female generation Yers had already developed cosmetics brand loyalties. Consequently, global marketers from Proctor & Gamble and Kellogg's to Nestlé's and Danone produce kits targeted to secondary school kids that combine educational with brand messages. And cash-scraped schools sometimes welcome exclusive contracts with food and beverage companies that help fund school programs but that also limit kids' food and beverage choices. Do you see some ethical issues with this type of marketing?[97]

Young people are attractive because they go through rapid periods of physical, mental, social, and emotional change. This generates rapidly evolving physical, self-expression, and self-actualization needs (see Chapter 7). Teenagers and young adults often vacillate between consuming to fit in and consuming to differentiate themselves from their peers. The Japanese consumers' transitory taste for Water Salad described in the opening vignette is a good illustration. One study found that 13–17-year-old American girls tend to be conformists in their orientation to fashion trends (see Chapter 10). These characteristics make wired global teenagers attractive markets for global and regional brands of clothing, magazines, online 'zines, and comic books. Of course, at the same time, their loyalties tend to be volatile due to their rapid personal development. "Coolness" goes a long way toward determining which brands are most popular, and favored brands cycle in and out of popularity rapidly.[98]

From Singapore to Greenland, teenagers globally are increasingly wired into the Internet. This facilitates the spread of images, ideas, values, and trends among teenagers around the world, and it provides marketers with new data collection opportunities through online research. The Internet drives both increased similarity and fragmentation in generation Y consumer tastes. For example, basketball has become a global teen sport, and Nike is relentlessly promoting soccer and soccer fashions to global teens. Coca-Cola is conducting a multiyear study called the Global Teenager that it hopes will define a global teen market for its products. And many firms use the Internet to collect trend data that drives new product development.

Because generation Y consumers are so accustomed to computers, it distinguishes them as a market segment in a number of ways. First, due to zapping and surfing, generation Y consumers' preferences, fashions, and brand loyalties may be transient. Second, because the Internet makes it easy to search and compare, generation Y consumers demand customization to meet their personal preferences. More and more niche products will be required to meet their needs. Third, in a mind-set developed by clicking on a computer mouse or remote control, choices do not necessarily stick. Generation Y consumers thus like to change their minds. Fourth, since interactivity is the hallmark of the Internet, generation Y consumers prefer to try things out themselves rather than rely on promises. Giving away core products and services and charging for additional services and augmented products will probably become more common. Generation Y consumers are candidates for more relational approaches to marketing. Finally, unlike the baby boomer generation, generation Y consumers are not dazzled by technology. Good Practice 12.1 summarizes some of what marketers think they know about reaching Generation Y. You're an expert. What do you think?[99]

Common to affluent nations with large, youthful populations is the phenomenon of **youth subcultures.** First identified in the United States in the 1950s, youth subcultures are common today in Europe, Japan, and even China. In the LAW nations, universities often provide the setting for the emergence of youth subcultures. In Japan, they often

Marketing Rules to Reach Generation Y

GOOD PRACTICE 12.1

1. Don't talk down. Forget the authoritative experts who swayed the baby boomers. For example, a recent Nike ad featuring baseball pitcher Randy Johnson invites kids to form an opinion about him, rather than being told to do as Johnson does.

2. Don't try to be what you're not. Stay true to your brand DNA. Kids put a premium on straight talk. Sponsored teen spokespersons appeal to this group. They are more willing to buy from small firms run by enthusiasts. Generation Yers place greater faith in authenticity than in big brands.

3. Entertain 'em. Make it interactive, if you can. And keep the sell short. Kids like appealing ads and finding brands in unexpected places. Marketers will be forced to develop more concept-rich communications as kids will see through fluff and eye candy.

4. Show that you know what they're going through, but keep it light. Real-life dramatization is a plus.

5. Customization and interactivity are good. But don't kid yourself into thinking that new media equal cutting edge; spamming just won't work. Generation Yers are market-wise and pros at TV zapping, zipping, and channel surfing.

6. Not that they'll really let you, but get to know those savvy, plastic-wielding teens. Interactive real-time, person-to-person marketing rules. A side effect of teenagers' Internet experience has been an increasing fragmentation of the market into smaller groups that are less easy to target on national, regional, ethnic, or gender lines.

Sources: Reprinted with permission from Gerry Khermouch, "Didja C That Kewl Ad?" Business Week, *August 26, 2002, pp. 158–59, copyright ©2002 by The McGraw-Hill Companies, Inc.; and Mark Dolliver, "Creative Portfolio,"* AdWeek, *August 12, 2002, p. 27.*

take the form of parodies of familiar U.S. subcultures such as bikers, punks, and rock 'n' rollers. Youth subcultures typically *combine behaviors simultaneously expressive of values characteristic of the dominant culture and values systematically deviant from them.* Today, marketers quickly convert youth street styles into marketed commodities, even antistyles such as grunge or gangsta rap. This fuels the rapid rise and fall of youth fads and fashions as young people seek to differentiate themselves by developing consumption styles that are different from mass-market offerings.[100]

BOOMERS, DEPRESSION ERA, AND WAR BABIES Despite their virtual absence in the mass media, older consumer segments are growing and should not be neglected. The population is aging in all the Triad nations, and this is becoming a global phenomenon, as shown in Exhibits 12.5 and 12.6. By the year 2010, 18 percent of the U.S. population, or 55 million people, will be aged 60 and older. The 77-million-member baby boom generation will be the aging market of the new millennium. In other Triad nations, the aging will comprise a larger percentage of the population than in the United States, particularly so in Japan, where 30 percent will be older than 60 in the year 2010. By 2051, 24 percent of the Australian population is expected to be age 65 or over. This segment represents opportunities and challenges for marketers.

Older adults can be segmented by chronological age into young old (55 or 65 to 75), middle-aged old (75 to 85), and old-old segments (over 85). But many market

Selected Countries	Total Population over 60 Years of Age in 2010 (millions)	Percent of the Total Population
Australia	20	19.3
Canada	33	20.4
France	60	22.5
Germany	81	25.1
Italy	55	26.1
Japan	127	29.8
Sweden	9	26.0
United Kingdom	59	23.3
United States	294	18.8
High-income countries	964	21.8

Sources: Reproduced with permission from the World Bank, from *World Development Indicators*, 1998; permission conveyed through the Copyright Clearance Center. "Will You Still Feed Me?" *New York Times*, April 28, 2002, Week in Review, p. 16.

EXHIBIT 12.5

Aging of the Triad Nations' Populations

researchers have found age-based segmentation approaches less satisfactory than segmentation based on lifestyle (e.g., "healthy indulgers" and "frail recluses") or cognitive age. **Cognitive age** *represents how people see themselves and their actual levels of cognitive processing*. In youth-oriented societies like Australia or the United States, cognitive age tends to be about 10 years younger than chronological age. In any case, segmenting on chronological age alone is not very effective.[101]

To reach mature markets, marketers must abandon stereotypes concerning aging consumers. Aging consumers will be differently endowed with cultural capital than those of the past, even though this group doesn't necessarily like to think of itself as distinctive. They are better educated than in the past. The over-50 group owns three-quarters of all financial assets and accounts for half of all discretionary spending power in Triad countries. Over two-thirds of them own their own homes mortgage free. In the United States, they control four-fifths of the money invested in banks and two-thirds of all shares on the stock market. In the last two decades, consumption by over 50s in Europe increased three times as fast as that of the rest of the population. By contrast, most older people in the less affluent world, more than 250 million, live in chronic poverty and have difficulty accessing the health care products and services they need.[102]

In the Triad nations, lifestyle differences associated with distinctive values and cultural symbolism of particular age cohorts are useful in segmentation and positioning. For example, common among baby boomers is the idea that they aren't getting older no matter what the calendar says—they intend to stay young forever. To profit from this attitude, a recent film idealizes the enduring passion for surfing among a group of very senior surfers. Harley Davidson's average customer is 52 years old! Further, baby boomers tend to be sexually permissive, idealistic, self-centered, active, and somewhat hedonistic. Depression era consumers by contrast are conservative in their fiscal habits, more civic minded, and more interested in experience than in owning. One common characteristic of older consumers is the desire for connections to others, especially other

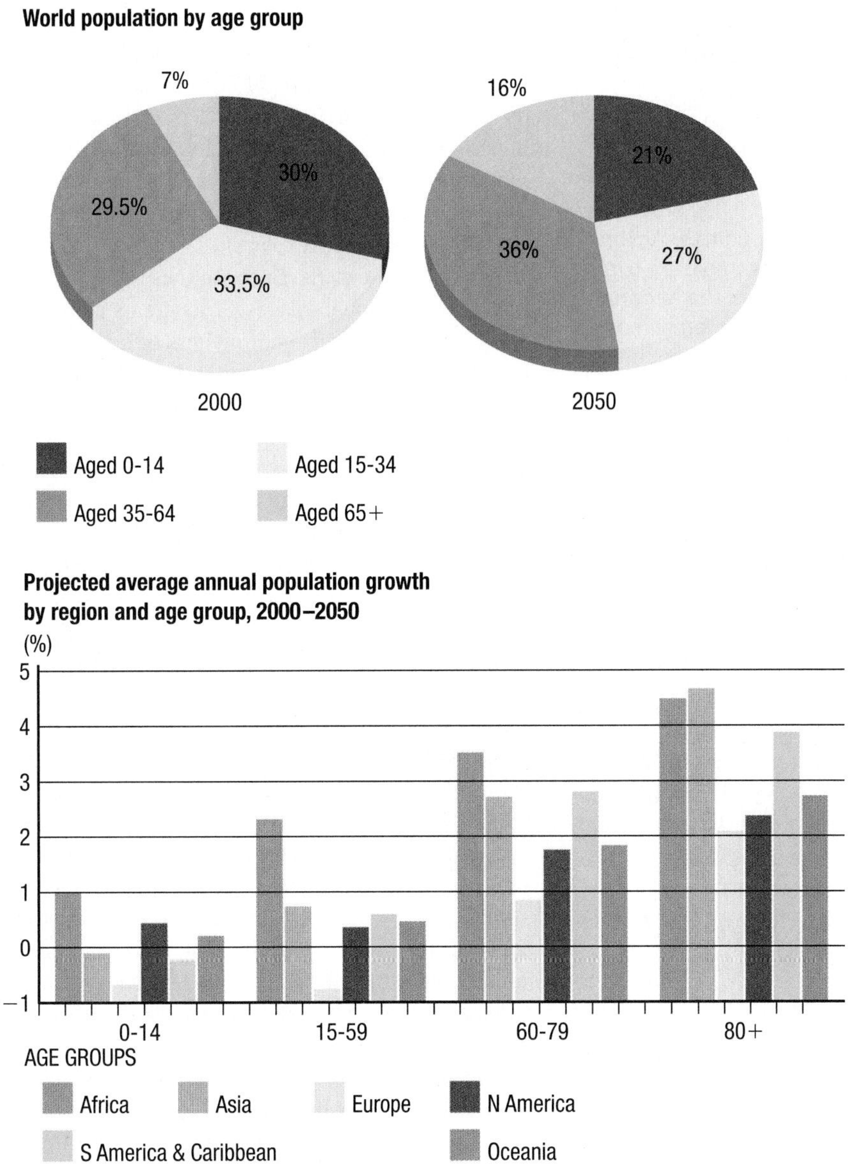

EXHIBIT 12.6

Aging of the World's Population

Source: UN Population Division.

family members. This translated into spending on grandchildren, estimated at $30 billion in the United States, and the desire for products and services that create a legacy for descendents such as genealogies, family scrapbooks, and heirlooms.[103]

Businesses enjoying the aging boom include educational, leisure, and health industries. Mature consumers in the United States account for 80 percent of all leisure travel and 30 percent of prescriptions filled, for example. The recreational vehicle industry is a beneficiary of active mature consumer lifestyles. Many seniors are taking to the road in their Winnebago RVs, as you can see at Winnebago-Itasca Traveler's Club website. Consumer Chronicles 12.5 on Elderhostel illustrates another industry that is benefiting dramatically from the aging of the Triad nations. The young-old segment is a prime

www.winnebagoind.com/html/lifestyle/wit/wit.html

Elderhostel

CONSUMER CHRONICLES 12.5

Elderhostel is a senior studies program offered at more than 1,800 educational and cultural institutions and science laboratories. Elderhostel offers over 10,000 programs a year in more than 100 countries. Anyone over 60 years of age can sample an overwhelming gamut of studies. The program has recently branched out into small-scale service programs in developing countries such as a community water project in Nicaragua. The Elderhostel movement began in 1975 when five colleges opened their campuses to 220 pioneering students. The movement now registers nearly a quarter-million participants a year. Typically classes are held in the morning and last for an hour or 90 minutes. Most courses span five or six days. The host institution often organizes free time. Many Elderhostel programs are located in world-class travel destinations and the movement has now moved into more sophisticated spaces than the college dormitories in which it started. An Elderhosteler who does not try the experience twice is virtually unheard-of.

Sources: Bern Keating, "Elderhostel: The Mature Traveler's Ticket to Intriguing Adventures," Hemispheres, *October 1992, pp. 52–54; and www.elderhostel.org.*

target for recreational and vacation activities such as those provided by Grandtravel or Familyhostel in Europe. Another example of leisure consumption indicative of the evolving lifestyles of mature consumers is participation in cyberculture. One study found that older adults spend more time online than any other age group. The American Association of Retired Persons has a very active website, as do its British and Canadian counterparts. Some of these sites have technology or computer pages. This trend is obviously good news for makers and retailers of devices that facilitate Internet access and for Internet service providers, as suggested by the photo shown on the opposite page.[104]

The growing significance of the elderly segment has generated increasing interest in the unique responses of the elderly to marketing variables. Recent research has found similarity between elderly U.S. consumers' brand sets and those of younger consumers. A study in the United Kingdom indicates a general preference among the elderly for locally operated (familiar) rather than nationally operated stores. Price discounts for senior citizens have interesting effects. Some older consumers reject such discounts because they wish to avoid thinking of themselves as being senior citizens. Others reject price discounts because they wish to avoid the negative connotations of being perceived as senior citizens by others. Finally, some elderly consumers assign positive meanings to stores that promote the use of senior citizen discounts. Mid-age old consumers patronize discount stores, perhaps because of a tendency toward frugality among war babies and Depression era seniors.[105]

@ www.arp.org.uk

@ www.aarp.org

@ www.50plus.com

The elderly are more likely to miscomprehend advertising claims. This may lead to lower levels of satisfaction with purchase choices. In addition, memory deficits may make it difficult for elderly consumers to take advantage of new information sources, such as nutritional and medical labeling, or even marketing communications designed to improve their decision making. Danone, makers of calcium-rich Talians mineral water; the Paris metro system; and DoCoMo, maker of cell phones, have responded to such information with simplified labels and signage, and larger cell phone buttons. Physical needs do change with age. Many firms from Ford Motor to Fiskars (scissors) to Oxo (cookware) have redesigned products for older consumers' physical needs, but it turns out younger people respond well to such product improvements.[106]

Age differences in processing of marketing communications have been examined. In some cases, older consumers consider fewer product characteristics and alternative brands than younger consumers because of greater experience and brand familiarity. With unfamiliar products and brands, however, older consumers may search less because they cannot hold and manipulate numerous alternatives in memory and because of diminished working memory capacity. Research on the elderly also has found that

Online computer use is growing in popularity among older consumers.

they receive information-rich ads more favorably than music-based, emotional appeals. At the same time, the use of visual information, such as symbols and pictures, and concrete language in print and television ads can improve elderly recall of ad claims. Studies have examined the effects of cognitive age in advertising. While many elderly people perceive middle-aged and older models to be more credible than younger models, companies such as Jockey find it useful to feature models about 15 years younger than their target market. L'Oreal and Estée Lauder now both employ older models keyed to age cohorts in ads targeted at the mature market. Mid-age old consumers respond best to straightforward, engaging copy and simple design; postmodern approaches nourished by MTV do not work as well, at least not yet![107]

Gender

Gender is a significant segmentation and targeting criterion in marketing. **Gender** is *the cultural definition of behavior defined as appropriate to the sexes in a given society at a given time and the cultural capital (resources, norms, values, beliefs, and customary ways of behaving) associated with a set of gender roles*. Gender is a significant segmentation and targeting variable for at least three reasons.[108]

First, every culture distinguishes at least two genders. Homosexual, bisexual, and other gender identities are recognized in some cultures, denied in others. Evident physiological differences between men and women lead to specialized product needs in nutrition, health, and personal care, for example. Marketers often use stereotypical appeals that combine biology with gender. For example, the ad for Tampax shown on page 512 associates the brand with the universal biological symbol for female and with a positive message about feminine qualities. Similarly, Kellogg's has introduced Harmony cereal fortified with calcium and folic acid, two supplements thought important to women's health.

This ad associates the brand with a positive message about qualities that many people consider to be female attributes.

GENDER IDENTITY Second, differences in psychological traits, attitudes, norms, and behavior are often associated with gender identity. Traits such as independence, assertiveness, and competitiveness are hallmarks of masculinity. The many magazines targeted to young men such as *Max, GQ,* and *Men's Health* highlight these themes. Men typically respond well to product appeals that provide feelings of control and mastery as in many pickup truck advertisements. Understanding, caring, nurturance, considerateness, and intuition are traits associated with femininity. A masculine orientation to goal seeking tends to be more impersonal and individualistic than a feminine orientation. A feminine orientation is more oriented toward social integration than is a masculine one. However, recent research suggests that gender cannot be reduced to a set of personality traits and that masculinity and femininity are just one aspect of gender identity. For example, Australian men relate positively to ads that show them in affirmative family roles.[109]

Gender-related differences in information processing and response to marketing appeals have been identified. For example, when forming judgments, a masculine orientation involves the use of a single cue or small set of highly salient cues that converge to imply a single inference or course of action. The cues that men use tend to be meaningful to the masculine self. In contrast, a feminine approach to judgment makes use of multiple cues and attempts to assimilate both highly salient and subtler cues.

Gender identity has been linked to leisure activities, gift giving, and shopping behavior.[110] As with ethnic identity, research shows that gender identity may fluctuate in different purchase and consumption situations and may vary with the degree to which a purchase and consumption situation evokes a culturally conditioned gender response. For example, buying gifts for opposite sex friends may evoke a gendered response. And research shows that sports, sports media, and sports merchandise appeal differentially to men. Industry Insights 12.3 illustrates how age and gender interact in creating appealing sports marketing.[111]

GENDER ROLES A third reason that gender is significant to marketers is because gender roles, behaviors judged both appropriate and characteristic of males and females, affect purchase and consumption. These roles are learned early and play a formative part in personality development and self-identity (see Chapters 7 and 10).[112] U.S. research on young consumers consistently finds that males report more materialistic values than females. Masculinity is associated with an instrumental orientation, that is, a concern with goals external to social relations. Femininity is associated with an expressive orientation and places a priority on dealing with others, on being actively interdependent and relational. These role orientations are sometimes described as an agentic self-based male orientation and a communal relational female orientation. Men emphasize the functional (self-oriented) benefits of clothing, and women emphasize social (other-oriented) concerns. In a Canadian study of Christmas shopping, men were found to be more object focused and women more interested in the relational meanings conveyed by the gifts chosen for purchase. Similarly, the huge international romance

Marketing Basketball to Generation Y Boys

INDUSTRY INSIGHTS 12.3

The growth of professional basketball over the past twenty-odd years from a relatively minor spectator sport to a mass-cultural phenomenon is an example of the way in which all of American culture is increasingly geared to the tastes of teen-age boys. Marketers hold that adolescent boys, with their swiftly changing appetites and their enormous buying power, are the most difficult and most critical consumers to reach. Basketball is a perfect game for teen-agers: it's fast, it's energetic, it requires little equipment, and it can be practiced in driveways and on the playground without so much as an opponent; and it has been appropriated by products that have nothing to do with sports—Coke, milk—as an excellent way to reach that desired demographic. Teen boys function, in turn, as cultural emissaries to the global population: Nikes aren't cool all over the world because Vince Carter wears them but because cool American teen-agers wear them.

Basketball itself is marketed with teen tastes in mind. The theater of a Lakers game has an adolescent-boy aesthetic: goofy and overheated. There are the whirling spotlights when the players emerge from the locker room, high-fiving; the snippets of roaring rap music and of the teen-boy anthem, "We Will Rock You" by Queen; the absurd contests held between quarters, in which competitors do things like play musical chairs on a set of huge inflatable seats. Should all this hilarity be inadequate to the task of holding a young man's interest, there is always the Laker Girls.

Source: Rebecca Mead, "A Man-Child in Lotusland," The New Yorker, *May 20, 2002, pp. 48–67.*

novel market that now extends even to Africa is driven by the communal relationship-oriented values conveyed by the books. Even generation Y girls buy in to the relational orientation. Chat-heavy websites such as Chick Click attract seven million unique visitors a month. Many gender portrayals follow gender-stereotyped roles. Some examples of gender stereotypes and reverse stereotypic normative appeals are described in Industry Insights 12.4.[113]

@ www.ChickClick.com

What constitutes stereotypically masculine or feminine roles varies across cultures and segments. For example, French men, like their American counterparts, seem to view consumption as being a feminine concern. But other stereotypes in the two cultures are different. For U.S. men, interest in sports is a masculine trait; not so for French men. Generation Y women in the United States express beliefs highly consistent with traditional feminism, but do not describe themselves as feminist. They perceive themselves to be both feminine and strong. Burton Snowboard Company got this message early and has been making women-specific boards and gear for some years. Their website shows women models looking larger than life, empowered and respected.[114]

Gender roles influence consumer behavior, but the behaviors of male and female consumers are in flux. For example, 80 percent of all households in the United States are made up of dual-career couples, and women are the chief wage earners in about a quarter of all U.S. households. As women enter the wage labor force and gain access to economic resources, a blurring of gender role differences with higher income and educational and professional attainment occurs. For some women, these changes result in role overload, sometimes called a "busy woman syndrome" or a juggling lifestyle. Such women may have to work a "double day" of eight hours in the office, then eight more cooking, cleaning, and caring for family members. Marketers are adjusting to these changing roles. For example, busy career mothers are prime targets for convenience

Communicating with Gendered Audiences

INDUSTRY INSIGHTS 12.4

Stereotypic appeals

The recent Platinum MasterCard print ad campaign targeted females with a communal message and males with an agentic theme. The communal appeal features a woman and her mother seated in a pub, with the following copy: "plane tickets to the town where she was born: $1,200 . . . train to the house where she grew up: $63 . . . pints at the pub where she met your dad: $8 . . . finally understanding where your mother was coming from: priceless." In contrast, the agentic ad targeting males depicts a narrow gravel road in the Italian countryside over which is superimposed the shadow of a man holding a bicycle. The copy reads: "18 speed bike: $1,225 . . . shipping bike to Italy: $235 . . . map of Tuscany: 9,000 lira . . . seven days without e-mail: priceless."

Reverse stereotypic appeals

When a professional working target is sought, the equation of female and communal appears to break down. Thus, in addition to using the communal format, advertisers for financial services are targeting women, especially single women, with agentic appeals. An advertisement for the Private Issue credit card, which offers an automatic 5 percent rebate on travel, depicted an attractive woman in a business suit, walking across the tarmac toward a plane. The copy included: "Mother asked why I charged Jack's ticket to my credit card. And I told her it's a Private Issue."

Existing theory clearly does not accommodate a communal male, yet these kinds of messages are appearing with greater frequency. For example, a television ad in Chevrolet's Tried, Tested, and True campaign featured a father who helped his son complete his newspaper deliveries during a downpour. Tylenol's 1999–2000 print campaign, with a man holding his sleeping daughter, tells fathers there is "nothing to add but a kiss."

Source: Maureen Hupfer, "Communicating with the Agentic Woman and the Communal Man: Are Stereotypic Advertising Appeals Still Relevant?" Academy of Marketing Science Review *[Online] 2002 (03), at http://www.amsreview.org/amsrev/theory/hupfer03-2002.html.*

products. And having recognized that 59 percent of its customers are women, quick-oil change provider Jiffy Lube is making its waiting rooms more amenable to women customers.[115]

Research suggests changes in gender roles in countries as diverse as Hungary and India. In urban China, where the one-child policy is strictly enforced, parents have strikingly similar aspirations for their female and male children and both boys and girls are receiving the same parental investments in their education and future career goals. As Consumer Chronicles 12.6 shows, even in a developing country like Thailand, gender roles are changing, presenting marketers with new opportunities. As a result of these changes, Asian businesses are targeting women travelers with specialized offerings like the Regal Airport Hotel in Hong Kong that offers Feminine Focus Rooms with special amenities.[116]

Changes in gender roles sometimes support the idea of a trend toward global standards of behavior. As suggested in Industry Insights 12.5, there is evidence that the globalization of institutions such as fashion shows and women's fashion magazines is leading to the emergence of common standards of beauty for women that provide multinational firms such as L'Oréal, Revlon, and Clarins with lucrative markets for cosmetics, fitness, and fashion. However, changes in gender roles do not necessarily mean westernization. Among conservative Islamic women in Turkey, both modest Islamic fashion and gender-segregated resorts represent growth industries, as suggested in Chapter 10.[117]

Patterns of wants and responses to market appeals vary with gender roles. Obviously, many products are designed to appeal to or even stress gender-specific roles. Even

Changing Gender Roles in Thailand

CONSUMER CHRONICLES 12.6

Life with her husband, singer Arpaporn Nakornsawan tells her audiences, was a drag. He had little time for her, and in the end she said good-bye and good riddance. "I have already left," Arpaporn's hit song of the same name begins. And she isn't in a rush to find a new man, the overnight sensation tells her fans. That never would have happened a generation ago. Thirty years earlier, girls shed tears over the wildly popular song "Wang Bua Baan (The River of Lotus Blossoms)," which told the story of a young woman who drowns herself in a river after waiting for a lover who never returns.

The contrast between the two popular songs speaks volumes about changing attitudes toward marriage among Thai women. They are, at least when it comes to men, not their mothers' daughters: Nowadays, Thai women are saying "so long" to rotten relationships instead of suffering through them. In some cases, it's not even bad relationships that women are avoiding. A growing sisterhood of women in Thailand is choosing to stay single—and loving it.

Sociologists say women's financial independence is the most important factor in the new attitude toward marriage. Greater access to education for women in recent decades has been crucial in fostering that independence. In 1993, female students at public universities outnumbered males for the first time. Over half of those graduating from public universities were women, with the proportion increasing to 57 percent in 1996. Many women feel it's difficult to find a man who suits them intellectually. This is the result of a paucity of men of the same social level in the same age group as these women. Their male counterparts tend either to have married earlier or to prefer wives who are younger.

Source: "Sole Sisters: Greater Financial Opportunities and a Flexible Culture Are Enabling a Growing Legion of Independent-Minded Thai Women to Choose the Single Life," from Far Eastern Economic Review, *September 3, 1988, p. 36 by Prangtip Daoreung. Copyright 1998 by Dow Jones & Co., Inc. Reproduced with permission of Dow Jones & Co., Inc. in the format Textbook by the Copyright Clearance Center.*

Gender boundary crossing is increasing as illustrated by this ad for cigars.

A Bra for All Seasons

INDUSTRY INSIGHTS 12.5

It may be only an exercise in band awareness but Triumph's lingerie fashion show is raising more than just a few bust lines as it shimmies its way across 30 cities in mainland China. "We're bringing lingerie out of the closet and on to the catwalk," Raymond Due, Triumph's China marketing manager told AFP on the sidelines of a show in Shenzen that was the 12th leg of the tour. Over 180,000 people are expected to have seen the "Dreams on Stage" show by the time it wraps up in Harbin, northeast China, in July. "It's eye opening for them. Most of them come out of the show surprised at what they have seen, pleasantly surprised," Mr. Due said. Five years ago a show like this would not have been possible in China. Despite a few differences such as color (blacks, whiter, and flesh tones for the West and pastels and red for the Chinese market) and compulsory padding, Chinese women are no different than Europeans when it comes to what they want from a bra. "European women might be a bit more provocative, but that's changing," according to Triumph's product manager for Asia, Harald Hindenberger. But not too quickly, according to Kavita Daswani, a Hong Kong–based fashion writer. She said that generally Chinese women are still reluctant to show off their underwear. But in more affluent areas of China, such as Shanghai and Beijing, the influence from the West is having a greater effect.

Source: "A Bra for All Seasons," The Straits Times Interactive, *May 26, 2001, at http://straitstimes.asia1.com.sg.*

research in developing and transitional economies suggests how marketers have successfully positioned products to appeal to men and women differently. Nevertheless, products may become less gender-typed as gender roles change. Team sports increasingly target women with specialized leagues and products, such as the Women's National Basketball Association. High-fashion brands such as Chanel are targeting men with cosmetics ads. Cigar smoking, a traditional male activity, has become popular among women, as shown in the ad on page 515. And the U.S. firearms industry has targeted women with campaigns that appeal to their security needs (see Chapter 10).[118]

Contemporary advertisements reflect consumers' changing conceptions of gender roles and gender boundaries.[119] Gender role stereotypes may be found along with suggestions of gender blending, bending, and boundary crossing. The photo on page 517 is typical of high-fashion images that employ stereotypical images of women, while use of a male model in the Shick ad on page 517 makes a visual joke about stereotypical depictions of female beauty.

GENDER-BASED TARGETING AND POSITIONING

Gender is highly salient in certain purchase and consumption situations. For example, in countries as diverse as Japan, the United Kingdom, and the United States, shopping is primarily viewed as women's work. In a number of Triad countries, gift giving, sending greeting cards and letters, and staging consumption celebrations that reinforce social and family ties are also primarily women's work.[120]

Research suggests that in positioning of products marketers need to be sensitive to gender-based differences in product meaning and symbolism. Products, persons, words, and even sounds convey gender-based meanings. Angularity, sharpness, and simple designs are stereotypically masculine characteristics of products. Roundness, softness, and refined design are considered more feminine product features. Brand names with numbers in them appear to have a more masculine appeal perhaps because of an association with the agentic orientation. Cross-cultural evidence indicates these associations are quite widespread. Another study found that fresh fruits and vegetables as well as prepared food have pronounced gender symbolism. Consumption of feminine foods decreases with lower social class, and women in working-class, heterosexual couples tend to consume more masculine foods. A study of celebrity endorsers also found gender-based differences in attractiveness of both male and female endorsers.[121]

In much of the developing world, gender preferences are quite separate. Such differences can be reflected in preference for a wide variety of products and services, including entertainment products. In Peru, television soap operas, or novelas, are viewed primarily by women; soccer matches by men. And gender segregation can lead to lucrative marketing opportunities. In India, the cassette market for traditional music is at least a $60 million industry and remains gender-specific in terms of performers and audiences. To take another example, Avon has done well marketing door to door to secluded Muslim women in the Middle East. The First Women's Bank of Pakistan, discussed in Industry Insights 12.6, provides another example of a gender-segregated marketing opportunity.[122]

A typical gender-stereotyped high-fashion image.

Gay Consumers

One important recent change in the role of gender in marketing efforts concerns the recognition of gays as a distinctive market segment. Several books have profiled the economic clout and distinctive value orientations of gay consumers. Further, gay households often share the greater affluence associated with heterosexual dual-income, no-children households. Marketing communications firms have emerged that specialize in the gay market. A television network is planned. And major advertisers across an array of product categories are devoting increasing resources to target the gay market. In the United States, for example, brewer Anheuser-Busch is among a dozen or so major companies that have taken the step of targeting gay and lesbian customers directly. Others include Camel cigarettes, American Express, Virgin Atlantic airline, Absolut vodka, and The Gap. Swedish furniture maker IKEA is thought to have produced the first television commercial to make use of explicitly gay spokespersons. According to some Canadian research, gay consumers can be quite loyal to firms and brands such as Levi-Strauss that are perceived to share a gay-friendly agenda.[123]

This ad uses a gender bending treatment to illustrate product benefits.

Religion

Religion is a cultural subsystem that refers to *a unified system of beliefs and practices*

Gender-Based Banking in Pakistan

INDUSTRY INSIGHTS 12.6

Pakistan's smallest bank in the public sector is a four-year-old institution run for women, by women. According to Akram Khatoon, the president, First Women's Bank (FWB) far outpaces any other public sector bank. Initially set up with reserves of 100 million rupees (US$3.34 million), FWB was meant to work as a development-oriented bank to provide credit to poor and middle-class women who often failed to get support from traditional banks. From its initial five branches, the FWB has expanded to 23 branches across the country. There are plans to set up two more this year. With that expansion, profits have soared as well. Last year, the bank earned almost 29 million rupees (US$985,000) in profits. Earnings this year are expected to jump to 50 million rupees (US$1.67 million), almost a 68 percent increase. Unlike other public sector banks, however, where clients have defaulted on a staggering 80 billion rupees (US$2.66 billion), the FWB claims that only 3 percent of its loans have gone sour. Ms. Khatoon argues that cooperation with clients and a more responsible attitude on the part of women borrowers holds the key to the bank's success. "Basically, women feel more responsible and honest in paying back their loans," she says.

Source: Farhan Bokhari, "Pakistan's Profitable First Women's Bank Carves New Niche," Christian Science Monitor, *October 25, 1993, p. 6.*

relative to a sacred ultimate reality or deity. Consumer research on the impact of religion is sparse. This is remarkable given the global resurgence of organized **religiosity,** *the degree to which beliefs in specific religious values and ideals are held, practiced, and become a badge of identity for consumers*. The spread of Christian, Islamic, and Hindu fundamentalism; the reemergence of the Russian Orthodox Church after the collapse of the Soviet Union; and religious conflict in Northern Ireland and the Balkans are just a few of the indications that religion remains a powerful influence over human behavior, including consumer behavior.[124] Religious belief is a form of cultural capital that varies within and between nations. Overall, the United States displays a high degree of religiosity. Forty-five percent of American adults claim to worship at a religious meeting place at least once a week. The only European country to exceed the United States in religiosity is Ireland, where Sunday church attendance reaches 82 percent. On the other hand 14 percent of the U.S. population identifies with no religion. Japan is a hotbed of new religions: The country boasts 200,000, most of which have emerged since the late nineteenth century. On the surface, the number is surprising, given that more than 70 percent of Japan's 125 million people do not practice any religion. To attract and keep new members, the groups combine missionary zeal with contemporary marketing strategies.[125]

In the United States alone, religion is a multibillion-dollar industry employing thousands of people in which there is intense competition between competing products. Research suggests that there is limited switching among related denominations and that religious preference interacts with social mobility and gender. Noneconomically mobile consumers prefer conservative denominations. Women are heavier consumers of religious goods and prefer conservative religious denominations, but they are also more likely to switch to liberal denominations than men. Competition is most obvious with proselytizing (the act of conversion) denominations such as the Seventh Day Adventists and the Church of Latter Day Saints. So-called Protestant mega churches and the "seeker movement" have perfected marketing techniques to lure baby boomer families back to church. The Catholic Church has launched marketing programs in many cities to attract customers to its parochial schools, using high-quality academic performance, traditional values, and discipline as positioning variables. Low-income and single-parent families are considered prime target markets.[126]

The sisters of St. Benedict have spurred something of a marketing revolution among religious orders in the United States, Ireland, and Canada by successfully pioneering aggressive, humor- and relationship-based marketing campaigns to recruit new nuns

This ad makes an appeal to core terminal values.

to its convents. The ad for the priesthood shown above makes and appeal to core values.[127]

Religious segmentation may be salient where religion becomes an important component of symbolic capital and identity. In the United States, for example, the Jewish community is notable for a high degree of congruence between social networks, values, and religion. Similarly, one author documents an interplay between religion, reputation, and repeat transactions among communities that dominate wholesale markets in India. Perhaps this is true of other historically socially isolated groups and religious minorities in other nations, such as Jains in India, Copts in Egypt, American Black Muslims, and so on. Research conducted on the American Jewish community suggests that Jewish consumers may be relatively more innovative and more prone to diffuse information about new products at least within the community. These consumers may be opinion leaders, but they also may demonstrate less brand loyalty. In terms of fund-raising, Jewish fund-raising lists respond well. The general mailing times for Jewish fund-raisers, as well as merchants of specifically Judaic things, are going to circulate around religious holidays.[128]

In addition, religion is a useful segmentation variable because it influences the cultural values discussed in Chapter 3. Value systems in turn influence preferences of all kinds. As mentioned in Chapter 10, Islamic values have fueled a fashion and leisure products industry in Turkey. Positioning on religious faith has proved profitable in some industries.[129]

An Inspirational Niche Marketer

INDUSTRY INSIGHTS 12.7

Red Rose Collection Inc. catapulted from less than $25,000 in revenues in 1986 to $13.6 million in fiscal 1994. The company has a loyal customer base of 400,000, primarily women, featuring 75 percent repeat buyers. When leafing through the catalog, a Red Rose customer enters into a warm, nurturing, and magical world. The company, which is said to be the premier purveyor of angel-related products in the United States, discovered the charm and significance angels hold in the public mind more than eight years ago, and has promoted them ever since.

Source: "Inspirational Niche Products Inspire Catalog Sales," Direct Marketing 58 *(October 1995), pp. 46–47.*

As with ethnicity, the predictive power of religion in consumer research probably varies with perceived religiosity; that is, self-identification with a religion and its values, the strength of this identification, and situational factors. The results of a study of professional marketers in the United States generally indicate that the religiousness of a marketer can partially explain his or her perception of ethical problems and behavioral intentions. A study in France showed religious orientation affected negotiation tactics. And a study comparing Australians and the United States showed that religious orientation affected ethical beliefs and that these beliefs differed cross-nationally. By contrast, in another study, there were no significant differences between the consumer behavior of the devout and casually religious Japanese, whereas the devout American Protestants had considerably different consumer behavior than the casually religious Protestants.[130] Religion-based segments and consumer behavior merit more investigation.

In the United States, the Protestant working-class segment associated with the evangelical movement represents significant marketing opportunities. This segment contains both African-American and white subsegments. Important values include literal belief in biblical texts, respect for authority, passionate expression of belief (e.g., through testimonial and gospel singing), and personal success achieved through faith in and obedience to revealed divine will.[131] Products and services targeted to Protestant evangelical segments sell well. The mega churches mentioned above earn over US$2 billion per year. The Christian publishing industry has been particularly proactive; a Women's Devotional Bible sold more than two million copies, for example, and it is increasingly seeking to brand its authors. Industry Insights 12.7 describes one catalog firm that developed a successful niche marketing strategy. Contemporary Christian music has been around for decades but was usually dismissed as woefully out of tune, especially with younger consumers weaned on MTV. That has changed as Christian labels repackage what was once viewed as the devil's music into a vehicle to spread the good word. In the United States, religious radio stations have quadrupled in the past 25 years—and the number of religious TV shows has increased fourfold in one decade—the 1980s. ARK2, a religious cable TV station, began programming in the United Kingdom in 1996. Not surprisingly, mainstream marketers have begun to invade the territory of religious niche marketers. Overall, the evangelical segment may be of broad interest for marketers in that its conservatism, traditionalism, and relatively lower tolerance of diversity may lead to greater male dominance in major purchase decisions and higher brand and store loyalty.[132] The marketing of religion is not without controversy. Some feel that this leads to a degradation of moral values and contributes to cultural chaos. Others feel that believers should not be treated like consumers, and the use of religion as a positioning strategy is a misuse of religious authority. They feel that this has undermined the fundamental purposes of religious institutions. On the other hand, others argue that the injection of religious ethics into marketing practice could help alleviate certain abuses such as heavily targeting the poor with alcohol and cigarette advertising.[133]

SUMMARY

The economic and social segments discussed in this chapter are the major organizational categories in most societies. Membership in these categories is often expressed through the purchase and use of products and services. They anchor and mold consumer preferences and consumption patterns or lifestyles, but they are dynamic. What most differs between structural segments of consumers is how they consume. Segment preferences are structured by economic, social, and cultural capital. People compete for symbolic capital through these resources. As these resources change, consumer tastes and preferences change as well.

Managers find economic and socially defined groups useful, because they possess unifying characteristics that distinguish desires, choices, and decision-making styles from other groups. Often the influence of these structures on consumption choices is indirect rather than direct. As with culture, their influence is easiest to discern when we meet people whose class, ethnicity, or caste differ from our own.

Social classes are groupings involving differences in such areas as power, authority, wealth, income, prestige, working conditions, lifestyles, and culture. People of any one class tend to associate much more with one another than they do with members of other classes. A key criterion of social class is income, but education, occupation, and social background define social class better than income measures alone. Upper classes may be segmented into distinctive subsegments. Sizable middle classes can be found in at least half of the world's nations. In many countries, middle classes adopt values that favor expenditure on education, signals of upward mobility, and material self-improvement. Working- and underclass segments constitute a majority of the population of the world. Working-class lifestyles are resistant to changes in their basic characteristics. Brand loyalty, tempered by cost consciousness, is characteristic.

Frequent patterns of association and identification with common national origins of a subgroup define ethnicity. Ethnicity is not a static demographic characteristic, but varies with individual felt ethnicity, situation, and stage of life cycle. Ethnic identities today are more voluntary than in the past and represent a creative mix of values, beliefs, and consumption styles. Marketers also must determine whether ethnicity translates into distinct consumer tastes. One issue of interest for marketers is intensity of ethnic identification, as successful ethnic marketing often depends upon appealing to the desire for ethnic affiliation. Ethnicity also affects purchases that express felt ethnicity, an individual's perceptions of him- or herself as a member of an ethnic group.

Age, gender, and religion are three additional social structures that impact consumer behavior and affect marketing strategy. Consumers' preferences vary with age, as does their access to resources. Age-related life transitions stimulate demand for specialized products and services, and age cohorts often share similar values and consumer preferences. Children's consumer demands represent considerable market opportunities. Children play an important role in influencing parental shopping and spending habits. Teens are a popular target for marketers because they make up a large part of the population and they often enjoy substantial discretionary income. Teens are market savvy and involved with consumer culture, and are undergoing many physical and emotional changes that trigger consumer demand. The population is aging in many of the most developed nations. Increasingly, elderly consumers will be more affluent, better educated, and more active. It makes sense to position goods and services to take advantage of these facts.

Gender is a significant segmentation and targeting criterion in marketing. Evident physiological differences between men and women lead to specialized product needs. Gender roles are learned early and play a formative role in personality development and self-identity. Consequently, patterns of wants and responses to market appeals vary with

SUMMARY

gender. Traditional gender-related differences in information processing and response to marketing appeals also have been identified.

Religion refers to beliefs and practices relative to the sacred. As with ethnicity, religion's influence varies with the consumer's identification with a religion and its values, the strength of identification, and situational factors. Religion may be a useful segmentation variable because religion influences value systems. Positioning on religious values has been very profitable across product categories. Religion-based segmentation and consumer behavior merit more investigation.

KEY TERMS

age cohorts 502
assimilation 496
caste 501
cognitive age 508
cultural capital 478
deculturation 496
discretionary or contestable income 481
downward mobility 485
economic capital 478
ethnic mosaic 496
ethnicity 494
felt ethnicity 494
gender 511
Get Set 488
life cycle 502
life transitions 502
multicultural marketing 493
nouveau riche 487
objective measures 481
old money 487
purchasing power parity 481
relative income 482
religion 517
religiosity 518
reputational approach 481
self-attribution measures 481
situational ethnicity 495
social capital 478
social class 480
social class hierarchy 480
social mobility 476
status float 485
status symbols 479
status-oriented consumption 479
sumptuary laws 477
symbolic capital 478
two-tiered marketing 492
underclass 492
upward mobility 484
youth subcultures 506

REVIEW QUESTIONS

1. Give an example of a form of symbolic capital consumption that provides social mobility for members of lower social classes.
2. Do social conditions in your town foster the emergence of distinctive patterns of ethnic identity and consumption behavior? Explain.
3. Identify an ethnic festival that you have attended. What products and services enabled consumers to express the defining features of ethnicity mentioned in the chapter?
4. How would you identify your own social class? Give reasons for your answer. Ask your parents about their social class and their reasons for identifying themselves in that class. How do you and your parents compare? Can you think of consumption behaviors that relate to your social class? Explain.
5. Select and compare an advertisement that you feel portrays gender stereotypes with one that breaks those stereotypes. Do you think the target audiences for these two ads would be different or similar?

6. Interview a female friend and a male friend about their perceptions of masculine roles and products and feminine roles and products. Compare and contrast their answers. Be sure to include some questions that relate to roles and products you personally see as more feminine and more masculine.
7. Rent a video movie set in a contemporary time and analyze the economic and social structures depicted in the movie. How would you describe the social class, age cohort, gender roles, religion, ethnicity, and so on illustrated in the movie? How did various consumption objects included as movie props help you decide about these economic and social structures? Explain.
8. Check out the websites for Banana Republic, The Gap, and Old Navy. If possible, check out the brick-and-mortar retail outlets as well. In what ways are the images of these brands the same and in what ways are they different? Describe the characteristics that you think might best distinguish the target markets for these brands.

YOU MAKE THE CALL

TRANSLATING "GOT MILK" FOR LATINOS

In late February 1999, Jeff Manning began to focus on a phenomenon he had never had occasion to think about before: slathering peanut butter and jelly on a tortilla. The executive director of the California Milk Processor Board, Manning was poring over a report on the Latino community, searching for a way to reverse an industry sales slump in the heavily Hispanic southern portion of the state. And there on page 12, the answer seemed to jump out at him: The ranks of Hispanic teenagers, it noted, are projected to swell to 18 percent of the U.S. teen population over the next decade.

But appealing to these youngsters, he learned, is not as simple as cutting an ad in Spanish with tried-and-true Hispanic themes. The kids often live in two worlds: one rich in traditional Latino values such as a strong commitment to family and religion; the other in which they eagerly take part is mainstream teen America. The report described how they bounce between Hiphop and rock en Español; watch *Buffy the Vampire Slayer* with their friends and Spanish telenovelas (nighttime soap operas) with their parents; blend Mexican rice with spaghetti sauce—and spread peanut butter and jelly on tortillas. When it comes to "young biculturals," the "conventional model" of straight Spanish-language advertising "is irrelevant," Roxana Lissa, a Beverly Hills public relations consultant who had prepared the report, told Manning. To Manning, who spent 25 years at major ad agencies before joining the milk board in 1993, Lissa's advice made perfect sense. Soon he was talking up the possibility of a "cutting-edge" milk ad shot in "Spanglish." He foresaw combining distinctive Latino imagery with sights and sounds that are seductive to teenagers of all backgrounds. "I want to capture both worlds," Manning declared.

Focus groups with Hispanic teenage boys and girls produced some surprising findings. A mainstream ad for Kellogg's Corn Pops was their favorite. A Spanish-language ad for Mountain Dew with the Chilean techno-rock band La Ley didn't resonate much. And they found a bilingual ad for Levi's confusing. By contrast, their response to existing Got Milk? ads was highly positive. They found them funny and compelling. They did not say a word about the English language format or the lack of a bicultural perspective. These results led Manning to a decision to take the existing Got Milk? spots and air them without any change on Spanish-language television.

Consultations with Lissa and Anita Santiago, head of a Santa Monica, California, ad agency specializing in Hispanic consumers, turned up significant discomfort with the idea on their part. Manning says in order to justify a brand-new campaign for Latino teens, "you've got to start with problems . . . Where were the big problems with Got Milk?" Santiago felt the campaign was somehow just "too Anglo." She voiced concern that its appearance on Spanish television could conflict with her agency's milk commercials targeted at Hispanic moms. Being deprived of milk—the basis for the humor throughout the Got Milk? ads—is not funny to "an older Hispanic audience," she says. Lissa raised concerns too. Unlike previous immigrant groups, she says, many Latinos embrace their language and heritage more strongly as they get older and become more established in America; advertising in English, therefore, may be a lousy way to foster long-term product loyalty. Beyond that, she worries that sticking the Got Milk? on Spanish-language television could well be perceived as an insult, especially among Latino community leaders. Mostly she and Santiago argue that, at a minimum, a lot more research into bicultural teens is needed. "You can say these teens are the same as everybody else, but they're not," Santiago says later. "They don't look the same. They don't talk the same."

But Manning would not budge. He said he'd certainly look to place more Latino actors in the regular Got Milk? campaign. And he might further explore a bicultural ad. But any urgency he felt to develop a whole new campaign was defused by the focus group results. "I don't want to look like we're backing off this group of people," he says. "But as a marketer, I can't find a rationale" for launching a bunch of new ads. He was confident that his alternate scheme would "extend the reach" of Got Milk?—without having to shell out hundreds of thousands of dollars for new creative work.

Fast forward to 2000. California milk producers began a $2 million campaign that features a ghost who cries over the loss of her children. The ghost, "La Llorona," is Spanish for weeping woman. The general legend is that there was a beautiful young Native American girl. A handsome man came riding into town and ended up marrying her. She had a child or maybe two or three, no one is really quite sure. When her husband left her, she threw her children into the river out of madness. When she realized what she had done, she ran after her children. The next day she was found dead on the river bank. They buried her, but that night they heard a shrieking cry of "AIIIEEE mis hijos," which means "Oh, my children!" in English. Legend has it that she wanders the river at night looking for her children. Parents warned their children that if they were out late at the river at night, La Llorona might mistake them for her own children and take them. La Llorona calls children who stay out at the river at night probably doing things they shouldn't be doing. Throughout the years the story has changed and newer literature associates La Llorona with the abused and neglected children of the world.

In the commercial, the shrouded ghost goes to the refrigerator for milk, finds the carton empty and leaves weeping.

Latino students of the prestigious Art Center College of Design in Pasadena, California, created the spot. It's the latest in Got Milk's nine-year campaign to promote milk in California. "Superstitions and legends such as La Llorona are prominent in the Hispanic culture," says David Delgado, one of the Art Center's students. "We wanted to take a scary childhood story and put a funny spin on it—one that would appeal to all teens." "La Llorona is a legend we were always told about as children to scare us and send us to bed," director Emmanuel Lubezki says. "My grandmother used to say 'La Llorona is coming to get you,'" said Gabriela Lemus, director of policy for the League of United Latin American Citizens in Washington. "I don't know if I'd buy milk from someone who was trying to kill me." "Are we taking a chance? Absolutely," said spokesman Jeff Manning. "I hope it's an intelligent risk." See the commercial at http://www.gotmilk.com/ads_lallorona.html.

QUESTIONS

1. Did Manning draw the correct conclusion from the focus group results? Why or why not?
2. What are some reasons the focus group results might not apply to the actual television viewing situation?
3. What additional research into bicultural teens could be done to develop campaign ideas appropriate to Hispanic teens of Mexican heritage?
4. What are some aspects of Hispanic ethnicity that Manning neglected in devising his initial campaign ideas?
5. What are the pluses and minuses of the new La Llorona campaign?

Sources: Republished by permission of Dow Jones, from The Wall Street Journal *Rick Wartzman, "When You Translate 'Got Milk?' for Latinos What Do You Get?" The Wall Street Journal, March 6, 1999, pp. A1, A8 permission conveyed through Copyright Clearance Center, Inc.;* http://www.gotmilk.com/ads *lallorona making.html; http://www.ananova.com/news/story/sm 494333.html?menu=news.quirkies; and "La Llorona: A Chicano Folktale" by Stephanie Casias, found at http://web.nmsu.edu/~tomlynch/swlit.lallorona.html.*

CASES

ENDNOTES

1. Seth Sevenson, "I'd Like to Buy the World a Shelf-Stable Children's Lactic Drink," *New York Times Magazine,* March 10, 2002, pp. 38–43.
2. Arlene Dávila, *Latinos, Inc.: The Marketing and Making of a People* (Los Angeles: University of California Press, 2001).
3. Søren Askegaard, Danny Kjelgaard, and Eric J. Arnould, "Identity and Acculturation: The Case of Food Consumption by Greenlanders in Denmark," MAPP working paper No. 67 (Aarhus, Denmark: Center for Market Surveillance, Research and Strategy for the Food Sector, 1999).
4. "Television for Women: No One's Laughing Now," *Business Week,* December 24, 2001, pp. 56–57.
5. Annie Hau-Nung Chan, "Middle Class Formation and Consumption in Hong Kong," in *Consumption in Asia,* ed. Chua Beng-Huat (London and New York: Routledge, 2000), pp. 98–134.
6. Alan Hunt, *Governance of the Consuming Passions* (New York: St. Martin's Press, 1996).
7. Elizabeth Chin, *Purchasing Power: Black Kids and American Consumer Culture* (Minneapolis: University of Minnesota Press, 2001); Solvay Gerke, "Global Lifestyles under Local Conditions: The New Indonesian Middle Class," in *Consumption in Asia,* ed. Chua Beng-Huat (London and New York: Routledge, 2000), pp. 135–58; and Miriam B. Stamps and Eric J. Arnould, "The Florida Classic: Performing African American Community," in *Advances in Consumer Research,* vol. 25, ed. Joseph W. Alba and Wes Hutchinson (Provo, UT: Association for Consumer Research, 1998), pp. 578–84.
8. "Television for Women."
9. A. W. Ata and C. Ryan, eds., *The Ethnic Press in Australia* (Melbourne: Academic Press and Footprint Publications, 1989); Leon Schiffman, David Bednall, Elizabeth Cowley, Aron O'Cass, Judith Watson, and Leslie Kanuk, *Consumer Behavior,* 2nd ed. (Australia: Prentice Hall, 2001), p. 429; and Robert Sharoff, "Diversity in the Mainstream," *Marketing News,* May 21, 2001, pp. 1, 13.
10. In the United States, two major Hispanic TV networks, Univision and Telemundo, and 230 Hispanic-targeted magazines reach this market. Marye C. Tharp, *Marketing and Consumer Identity in Multicultural America* (Thousand Oaks, CA: Sage, 2001), p. 146.

11. Julia Saurazas, "Buying Influenced by Bloodline," *Marketing News,* March 26, 2001, p. 25.
12. Tharp, *Marketing and Consumer Identity in Multicultural America.*
13. Laura Oswald, "Culture Swapping: Consumption and the Ethnogenesis of Middle-Class Haitian Immigrants," *Journal of Consumer Research* 25 (March 1999), pp. 303–18.
14. Chan, "Middle Class Formation in Hong Kong"; Doug Holt, "Does Cultural Capital Structure American Consumption?" *Journal of Consumer Research* 25 (June 1998), pp. 1–25; Geri Smith, Elisabeth Malkin, Ian Katz, and Gail DeGeorge, "Marketing in Latin America," *Business Week International Edition,* February 9, 1998, pp. 50ff; and Jennifer Veale, "Economic Crisis Robs Koreans of Money, Pride," *The Globe and Mail,* July 28, 1998, Metro, p. A11.
15. See Pierre Bourdieu, *Distinction: A Social Critique of the Judgment of Taste* (Cambridge: Harvard University Press, 1984).
16. Guy Lawson, "Escape from Planet Bollywood," *GQ,* March 2002, pp. 344–349, 359.
17. Eric J. Arnould and Linda L. Price, "Authenticating Acts and Authoritative Performances: Questing for Self and Community," *The Why of Consumption: Contemporary Perspectives on Consumer Motives, Goals, and Desires,* ed. S. Ratneshwar, David Glen Mick, and Cynthia Huffman (New York and London: Routledge, 2000), pp. 140–63.
18. Chin, *Purchasing Power;* and J. R. Whittaker Penteado, "Fast Food Franchises Fight for Brazilian Aficionados," *Brandweek,* June 7, 1993, pp. 20–24.
19. Richard P. Coleman, Lee P. Rainwater, and Kent A. McClelland, *Social Standing in America: New Dimensions of Class* (New York: Basic Books, 1978); Richard P. Coleman, "The Continuing Significance of Social Class to Marketing," *Journal of Consumer Research* 10 (December 1983), pp. 265–80; Bernard DuBois, *Comprendre Le Consommateur,* 2nd ed. (Paris: Dalloz, 1994), pp. 151–77; James E. Fisher, "Social Class and Consumer Behavior: The Relevance of Class and Status," in *Advances in Consumer Research,* vol. 14, ed. Melanie Wallendorf and Paul Anderson (Provo, UT: Association for Consumer Research, 1987), pp. 492–96; C. Kagitcibasi and J. W. Berry, "Cross-Cultural Psychology: Current Research and Trends," *Annual Review of Psychology* 40 (1989), pp. 493–531; Arthur Marwick, *Class: Image and Reality in Britain, France and the USA since 1930* (New York: Oxford University Press, 1980), p. 19; and J. L. Spates, "The Sociology of Values," *Annual Review of Sociology* 9 (1983), pp. 27–49.
20. Diana Balmori, Stuart F. Voss, and Miles Wortman, *Notable Family Networks in Latin America* (Chicago: University of Chicago Press, 1984); R. W. Connell, *Ruling Class Ruling Culture* (Cambridge: Cambridge University Press, 1977), p. 217; Ignacio Galceran and Jon Berry, "A New World of Consumers," *American Demographics,* March 1995, pp. 26–32; Anthony Giddens, *The Class Structure of the Advanced Societies* (New York: Harper & Row, 1973), p. 110; Marianne Gullestad, "The Transformation of the Norwegian Notion of Everyday Life," *American Ethnologist* 18 (August 1991), p. 483; Larissa Adler Lomnitz and Marisol Perez-Lizaur, *A Mexican Elite Family, 1820–1980: Kinship, Class, and Culture* (Princeton: Princeton University Press, 1987); Marwick, *Class: Image and Reality;* Out There News, "Who Runs Russia?" www.megastories.com/russia/power/cover.htm, May 1998; and Chip Walker, "The Global Middle Class," *American Demographics,* September 1995, pp. 40–46.
21. B. Graetz, "Social Structure and Class Consciousness: Facts, Fictions and Fantasies," *Australian and New Zealand Journal of Sociology* 2 (1986), pp. 226–47; and DuBois, *Comprendre Le Consommateur,* p. 154.
22. Russell W. Belk, *Elite Consumer Behavior in Zimbabwe* (Salt Lake City: Odyssey Film Productions, 1999); Connell, *Ruling Class Ruling Culture;* Michele Lamont, *Money, Morals, and Manners* (Chicago: University of Chicago Press, 1992), p. 70; and Scott Dawson, Bruce Stern, and Tom Gillpatrick, "An Empirical Update of Patronage Behaviors across the Social Class Hierarchy," in *Advances in Consumer Research,* vol. 17, ed. Marvin E. Goldberg, Gerald Gorn, and Richard W. Pollay (Provo, UT: Association for Consumer Research, 1990), p. 836.
23. DuBois, *Comprendre Le Consommateur,* p. 156.
24. Rebecca Piirto Heath, "The New Working Class," *American Demographics,* January 1998, pp. 51–55.
25. Jonathan H. Turner, *Sociology: Concepts and Uses* (New York: McGraw-Hill, 1994).
26. Walker, "The Global Middle Class."

27. Lamont, *Money, Morals, and Manners,* pp. 85–86; and Scott Dawson and Jill Cavell, "Status Recognition in the 1980s: Invidious Distinction Revisited," in *Advances in Consumer Research,* vol. 14, ed. Melanie Wallendorf and Paul Anderson (Provo, UT: Association for Consumer Research, 1987), p. 487.
28. Mary Jackman and Robert Jackman, *Class Awareness in the United States* (Berkeley: University of California Press, 1986).
29. Dubois, *Comprendre Le Consommateur;* and Craig McGregor, *Class in Australia* (Ringwood, Victoria: Penguin, 1997).
30. Roger Marshall, Christina Kwai-Choi Lee, and Kim Marshall, "New Zealand: Consumers in Their Market Environment—Profiles and Predictions," in *Marketing and Consumer Behavior in East and South-East Asia,* ed. Anthony Pecotich and Clifford J. Shultz II (New York: McGraw-Hill, 1998), pp. 523–48.
31. "The Uses of Literacy," *The Economist,* June 17, 2000, pp. 56–57.
32. "Vietnam in Transition: New Evidence on Growth and Poverty," *Poverty Lines,* June 1998.
33. Walker, "The Global Middle Class."
34. Marwick, *Class: Image and Reality,* pp. 347–50; Walker, "The Global Middle Class"; "It's an Unfair World," *The Economist,* May 6, 2000, p. 15; Japan Travel Bureau, *"Salaryman" in Japan,* 1997; Takie Sugiyama Lebra, *Above the Clouds: Culture of the Modern Japanese Nobility* (Berkeley: University of California Press, 1993); Sharon O'Malley, "Country Gold," *American Demographics,* July 1992, pp. 26–33; Jenny Tabkoff, "Suburb Snobs," *Sydney Morning Herald,* December 26, 1998, Spectrum, pp. 1ff; and UN Development Program, *Human Development Report* (New York: United Nations, 1998).
35. James Traub, "Keeping Up with the Shidhayes," *New York Times Magazine,* April 15, 2001, pp. 32–37.
36. Anne Kappès-Grangé, "Afrique Le Grand Perdant de la Mondialisation," *L'Expansion,* December 20, 2001, http://archives.lexpansion.com; and Katherine S. Newman, *Falling from Grace* (New York: Free Press, 1988).
37. Michael R. Solomon, "Deep-Seated Materialism: The Case of Levi's 501 Jeans," in *Advances in Consumer Research,* vol. 13, ed. Richard J. Lutz (Provo, UT: Association for Consumer Research, 1986), pp. 619–22.
38. Dawson and Cavell, "Status Recognition in the 1980s," p. 490; Elizabeth C. Hirschman, "A Descriptive Theory of Retail Market Structure," *Journal of Retailing* 54 (Winter 1978), pp. 29–48, and Arun Jain and Michael Etgar, "Measuring Store Image through Multidimensional Scaling of Free Response Data," *Journal of Retailing* 52 (Winter 1976), pp. 61–70.
39. John P. Dickson and Douglas L. MacLachan, "Social Distance and Shopping Behavior," *Journal of the Academy of Marketing Science* 18 (1990), pp. 153–61; and Brad Edmondson, "Where They Live," *American Demographics,* November 1989, p. 27.
40. Chan, "Middle Class Formation in Hong Kong."
41. Dawson, Stern, and Gillpatrick, "An Empirical Update of Patronage Behaviors," p. 833; Gerke, "Global Lifestyles under Local Conditions"; Rajesh Kanwar and Nolis Pagiavlas, "When Are Higher Social Class Consumers More and Less Brand Loyal Than Lower Social Class Consumers? The Role of Mediating Variables," in *Advances in Consumer Research,* vol. 19, ed. John F. Sherry Jr. and Brian Sternthal (Provo, UT: Association for Consumer Research, 1993), pp. 593–94; Sidney J. Levy, "Social Class and Consumer Behavior," in *On Knowing the Consumer,* ed. Joseph W. Newman (New York: John W. Wiley and Sons), pp. 146–60; and Galceran and Berry, "A New World of Consumers."
42. Jim Gullo, "Great Scott!" *Town and Country,* June 2000, pp. 166–71, 220–24; Pierre Bourdieu, *Distinction* (Cambridge: Harvard University Press, 1984); Coleman, "The Continuing Significance of Social Class to Marketing," p. 271; Bonnie H. Erickson, "What Is Good Taste For?" *Canadian Review of Sociology and Anthropology* 28, no. 2 (1991), pp. 255–78; and Lamont, *Money, Morals, and Manners,* p. 90.
43. Dubois, *Comprendre Le Consommateur,* p. 173; Lamont, *Money, Morals, and Manners,* pp. 67–68; and Beatrix Le Wita, *French Bourgeois Culture* (Cambridge: Cambridge University Press, 1994).

44. Seth Faison, "A City of Sleepwalkers? No, They Just Like PJs," *New York Times,* August 6, 1997, p. A4.
45. Nancy Y. Wong and Aaron C. Ahuvia, "Personal Taste and Family Face: Luxury Consumption in Confucian and Western Societies," *Psychology and Marketing* 15 (August 1998), pp. 423–41.
46. "Lifestyles: A Special Report," *Far Eastern Economic Review,* June 10, 1992, pp. 37–51; July 30, 1992, pp. 29–43; and August 27, 1992, pp. 27–40; see also Joseph C. H. Chai, "Consumption and Living Standards in China," *The China Quarterly* 131 (September 1992), pp. 121–49; and Marwick, *Class: Image and Reality,* p. 340.
47. "Wedding Bliss," *The Economist,* May 27, 2000, p. 64; Janeen Arnold Costa and Russell W. Belk, "Nouveaux Riches as Quintessential Americans: Case Studies of Consumption in an Extended Family," in *Advances in Nonprofit Marketing,* vol. 3, ed. Russell W. Belk (Greenwich, CT: JAI Press, 1990), pp. 83–140; Dean MacCannell and Juliet Flower MacCannell, "Social Class in Postmodernity," in *Forget Baudrillard?* ed. Chris Rojek and B. S. Turner (London and New York: Routledge, 1995), pp. 124–45; and Pia Polsa and Bai Change Hong, "China, Part II," in *Marketing and Consumer Behavior in East and South-East Asia,* ed. Anthony Pecotich and Clifford J. Schultz II (Sydney: McGraw-Hill, 1998), pp. 161–212.
48. Michael J. Weiss, *The Clustering of America* (New York: Harper and Row, 1988); Claritas, Inc., http://www.claritas.com, 1999; and materials provided by Roy Morgan International, Victoria, Australia.
49. Japan Travel Bureau, *"Salaryman" in Japan;* Peter S. H. Leeflang and W. Fred van Raaij, "The Changing Consumer in the European Union: A Meta-Analysis," *International Journal of Research in Marketing* 12 (1995), pp. 373–87; Marshall, Lee, and Marshall, "New Zealand"; and Paul Vallely, "So Which Class Do You Look Down On?" *The Independent-London,* September 26, 1998, p. 8.
50. "A Virtuous Circle," *The Economist,* July 18, 1992, p. 27; Greg J. Duncan, Timothy M. Smeeding, and Willard Rodgers, "The Incredible Shrinking Middle Class," *American Demographics,* May 1992, p. 36; Judith Waldrop, "Shades of Black," *American Demographics,* September 1990, p. 33; Matthew Grimm, "Live Large, at Home," *American Demographics,* June 2000, pp. 66–67; "Middle Class on $10,000 a Year," *American Demographics,* September 1994, pp. 15–17; and Jerome Williams and Marye C. Tharp, "African Americans," in *Marketing and Consumer Identity in Multicultural America,* ed. Marye C. Tharp (Thousand Oaks, CA: Sage, 2001), pp. 165–211.
51. Dawson and Cavell, "Status Recognition in the 1980s," p. 488.
52. Pete Engardio, Joyce Barnathan, and William Glasgall, "Asia's Wealth," *Business Week,* November 29, 1994, p. 102; Mark Clifford, "Hair-Shirt Harmony," *Far Eastern Economic Review,* May 17, 1990, pp. 40–42; Editorial, *Business Week,* October 25 1993, p. 125; and Jennifer Veale, "Economic Crisis Robs Koreans of Money, Pride. Once-Ubiquitous Middle Class Now Knows Suicides, Unemployment and Homelessness," *The Globe and Mail,* July 28, 1998, p. A11.
53. Chan, "Middle Class Formation and Consumption in Hong Kong"; and Traub, "Keeping Up with the Shidhayes."
54. Philippe Le Corré, "Raz-de-marée télévisuel sur le continent asiatique," *Le Monde Diplomatique,* January 1994, pp. 26–27; Michael Vatikiotis, "Discreet Charms," *Far Eastern Economic Review,* March 21, 1991, pp. 30–32; Clifford, "Hair-Shirt Harmony"; Eric J. Arnould, "Toward a Broadened Theory of Preference Formation and the Diffusion of Innovations: Cases from Zinder Province, Niger Republic," *Journal of Consumer Research* 16 (September 1989), pp. 239–67; Traub, "Keeping Up with the Shidhayes"; and Paul M. Lubeck, "Islamic Protest under Semi-Industrial Capitalism: Yan Tatsine Explained," *Africa* 55, no. 4 (1985), pp. 369–89.
55. Rokiah Talib, "Malaysia: Power Shifts and the Matrix of Consumption," in *Consumption in Asia,* ed. Chua Beng-Huat (London and New York: Routledge, 2000), pp. 36–60.
56. Hassan Fattah, "The Rising Tide," *American Demographics,* April 2001, pp. 48–53; Dexter Roberts, "China's Wealth Gap," *Business Week,* May 15, 2000, pp. 170–80; Jan Larson, "Reaching Downscale Markets," *American Demographics,* November 1991, p. 38; "A Virtuous Circle," *The Economist,* July 18, 1992, p. 27; and P. P. L. McGregor and V. K. Borooah, "Is Low Spend-

ing or Low Income a Better Indicator of Whether or Not a Household Is Poor? Some Results from the 1985 Family Expenditure Survey," *Journal of Social Policy* 21, no. 1 (1992), p. 54.
57. "Positive Spin-Offs from Democracy," *Africa News Service,* November 9, 1998.
58. Shirley Ardener and Sandra Burman, eds., *Money-Go-Rounds* (Oxford, UK: Berg, 1995); and Larson, "Reaching Downscale Markets," p. 39.
59. Douglas E. Allen, "Toward a Theory of Consumer Choice as a Socio-Historically Shaped Practical Experience: The Fits-Like-a-Glove (FLAG) Framework," *Journal of Consumer Research* 28 (March 2002), pp. 515–32; Fisher, "Social Class and Consumer Behavior," p. 494; Coleman, "The Continuing Significance of Social Class to Marketing," pp. 265–79; and Peter Manuel, *Cassette Culture* (Chicago: University of Chicago Press, 1993), p. 192.
60. "Your Destiny," *Australian Women's Day,* July 23, 2001, pp. 91–99.
61. Gullestad, "The Transformation of the Norwegian Notion of Everyday Life," pp. 489–90.
62. Fattah, "The Rising Tide," pp. 48–53; and Archana Sekhar, "Marketing to the Masses," *Asian Business,* July 2001, p. 19.
63. How the Other Tenth Lives," *The Economist,* September 12, 1992, pp. 63–64; William Kornblum, "Who Is the Underclass?" *Dissent,* Spring 1991, pp. 202–11; Carole Marks, "The Urban Underclass," *American Journal of Sociology* 17 (1991), pp. 445–66; William Julius Wilson, *The Truly Disadvantaged* (Chicago: University of Chicago Press, 1987); and William Julius Wilson, "Another Look at the Truly Disadvantaged," *Political Science Quarterly* 106, no. 4 (1991–92), pp. 639–56.
64. Meng Yanyan, "Analysis of a Questionnaire Survey about Minority Women in Yunnan," *Practicing Anthropology* 24 (Winter 2002), pp. 25–27.
65. Rebecca Gardyn and John Fetto, "Off the Map," *American Demographics,* June 2000, p. 72; Andrew Hornery, "Ethnic Expert Says Keep Eye on Bottom Line," *Sydney Morning Herald,* Business, Marketing, and Advertising, March 12, 1998, p. 28; Tony Koenderman, "Marketing in a Multi-cultural Society," *Financial Mail,* April 4, 1998; Marlene L. Rossman, *Multicultural Marketing: Selling to a Diverse America* (New York: American Management Association, 1994); and Tharp, *Marketing and Consumer Identity in Multicultural America.*
66. Michel Laroche, Annamma Joy, Michael Hui, and Chankom Kim, "An Examination of Ethnicity Measures: Convergent Validity and Cross-Cultural Equivalence," in *Advances in Consumer Research,* vol. 18, ed. Rebecca H. Holman and Michael R. Solomon (Provo, UT: Association for Consumer Research, 1991), p. 150; William L. Yancey, Eugene P. Ericksen, and Richard N. Juliani, "Emergent Ethnicity: A Review and Reformulation," *American Sociological Review* 41 (June 1976), pp. 391–99; and Mark H. Haller, "Recurring Themes," in *The Peoples of Philadelphia,* ed. Allen F. Davis and Mark Haller (Philadelphia: Temple University Press, 1993), pp. 277–91.
67. David B. Wooten and Tiffany Galvin, "A Preliminary Examination of the Effects of Context Induced Felt Ethnicity on Advertising Effectiveness," in *Advances in Consumer Research,* vol. 20, ed. Leigh McAlister and Michael L. Rothschild (Provo, UT: Association for Consumer Research, 1993), pp. 253–56.
68. Stamps and Arnould, "The Florida Classic"; Douglas M. Stayman and Rohit Deshpande, "Situational Ethnicity and Consumer Behavior," *Journal of Consumer Research* 16 (December 1989), pp. 361–71; May Waters, *Ethnic Options: Choosing Identities in America* (Berkeley: University of California Press, 1990); Johanna Zmud and Carlos Arce, "The Ethnicity and Consumption Relationship," in *Advances in Consumer Research,* vol. 19, ed. John F. Sherry Jr. and Brian Sternthal (Provo, UT: Association for Consumer Research, 1992), pp. 443–49; and Judith Waldrop, "The Mexican May," *American Demographics,* May 1992, p. 4.
69. Søren Askegaard, Eric J. Arnould, and Dannie Kjeldgaard, "Post-Assimilationist Ethnic Consumer Behavior: A Greenlandic Extension of Recent Theory," under review, *Journal of Consumer Research;* Søren Askegaard, Dannie Kjeldgaard, and Eric J. Arnould, "Identity and Acculturation: The Case of Food Consumption by Greenlanders in Denmark," paper presented at the 1st International Conference on Consumption and Representation, Plymouth, UK, September 1–3, 1999; and Thomas O'Guinn and Ronald Faber, "New Perspectives on Acculturation: The Relationship of General and Role-Specific Acculturation with Hispanics' Consumer

Attitudes," in *Advances in Consumer Research,* vol. 12, ed. Elizabeth C. Hirschman and Morris Holbrook (Provo, UT: Association for Consumer Research, 1985), pp. 113–17.

70. Robert Ezra Park and E. W. Burgess, *Introduction to the Science of Sociology* (Chicago: University of Chicago Press, 1924); A. Fuat Firat, "Consumer Culture or Culture Consumed," in *Marketing in a Multicultural World,* ed. Janeen Costa and Gary Bamossy (Thousand Oaks, CA: Sage, 1995), pp. 106–25; and William L. Yancy, Eugene P. Ericksen, and Richard N. Juliani, "Emergent Ethnicity: A Review and Reformulation," *American Sociological Review* 41 (June 1976), pp. 391–403.

71. Gary Boulard, "Louisiana Cajuns Celebrate Bid to Promote Their Culture," *Christian Science Monitor,* December 28, 1993, p. 7; S. P. Douglas and C. S. Craig, "Advances in International Marketing," *International Journal of Research in Marketing* 9 (1992), pp. 291–318; and L. J. Vaughan, "Cosmopolitanism, Ethnicity, and American Identity: Randolph Bourne's 'Transnational America,'" *Journal of American Studies* 25, no. 3 (1991), pp. 443–59.

72. Dominique Bouchet, "Marketing and the Redefinition of Ethnicity," in *Marketing in a Multicultural World,* ed. Janeen Costa and Gary Bamossy (Thousand Oaks, CA: Sage, 1996), pp. 68–90; Ed Chung, "Navigating the Primordial Soup: Charting the Lived Worlds of the Migrant Consumer," *Journal of Consumer Marketing* 17, no. 1 (2000), pp. 36–54; and Lisa Peñaloza, "Atravesando Fronteras/Border Crossings: A Critical Ethnographic Exploration of the Consumer Acculturation of Mexican Immigrants," *Journal of Consumer Research* 21 (June 1994), pp. 32–54.

73. Bouchet, "Marketing and the Redefinition of Ethnicity," pp. 68–104; Wei-Na Lee and Koog-Hyang Ro Um, "Ethnicity and Consumer Product Evaluation: A Cross-Cultural Comparison of Korean Immigrants and Americans," in *Advances in Consumer Research,* vol. 19, ed. John F. Sherry Jr. and Brian Sternthal (Provo, UT: Association for Consumer Research, 1992), pp. 429–36; and Melanie Wallendorf and Michal D. Reilly, "Ethnic Migration, Assimilation, and Consumption," *Journal of Consumer Research* 10 (1983), pp. 292–302.

74. Ignacio Redondo-Bellon, "The Effects of Bilingualism on the Consumer: The Case of Spain," *European Journal of Marketing* 33, no. 11–12 (1999).

75. Laura Oswald, "Culture Swapping: Consumption and the Ethnogenesis of Middle-Class Haitian Immigrants," *Journal of Consumer Research* 25 (March 1999), pp. 303–18; Joan Raymond, "The Multicultural Report," *American Demographics,* special insert, November 2001; Rifka Roesenwein, "2000 Data in a New World," *American Demographics,* January 2002, pp. 18–19; and Williams and Tharp, "African Americans," p. 190.

76. Williams and Tharp, "African Americans," pp. 165–211.

77. Dávila, *Latinos, Inc.*; Thomas O'Guinn and Timothy P. Meyer, "Segmenting the Hispanic Market: The Use of Spanish Language Radio," *Journal of Advertising Research* 22 (December 1984), pp. 9–16; Rossman, *Multicultural Marketing;* Marye C. Tharp with Ernest W. Bromley, "U.S. Latinos: The Largest Ethnic Subculture," in *Marketing and Consumer Identity in Multicultural America,* ed. Marye C. Tharpe (Thousand Oaks, CA: Sage, 2001), pp. 123–64.

78. Satomi Furuichi, Carrie La Ferle, Wei-Na Lee, and Marye C. Tharpe, "Asian Americans: In Search of the American Dream," in *Marketing and Consumer Identity in Multicultural America,* ed. Marye C. Tharpe (Thousand Oaks, CA: Sage, 2001), pp. 243–81.

79. Gardyn and Fetto, "Off the Map," p. 72; William O'Hare, "A New Look at Asian Americans," *American Demographics,* October 1990, pp. 26–31; Rossman, *Multicultural Marketing*; and "Japanese Language Ranked 11th among Foreign Languages," *Rafu Shimpo,* April 24, 1993, p. 1.

80. Hassan Fattah, "Asia Rising," *American Demographics,* July/August 2002, pp. 39–43.

81. Jonathan Burton, "Targeting Asians," *Far Eastern Economic Review,* January 21, 1993, pp. 40–41; Fattah, "Asia Rising," pp. 39–43; John P. Cortez, "KFC Stores Boast Flavor of Neighborhood," *Advertising Age,* May 31, 1993, pp. 3, 46; Eric Hollreiser, "Caddy Tweaks Ad Mix to Woo Blacks," *Brandweek,* November 21, 1994, p. 10; Maria Mallory and Stephanie Anderson Forest, "Waking Up to a Major Market," *Business Week,* March 23, 1992, pp. 70–73; and Leon D. Wynter, "Business and Race," *The Wall Street Journal,* June 2, 1999, p. B1.

82. Dan Fost, "California's Asian Market," *American Demographics,* October 1990, p. 36; Bradley Johnson, "Supermarkets Take 'Position,'" *Advertising Age,* May 10, 1993, p. S1; Lee

and Um, "Ethnicity and Consumer Product Evaluation," p. 430; and Robert E. Wilkes and Humberto Valencia, "Hispanics and Blacks in Television Commercials," *Journal of Advertising,* March 1989, pp. 19–25.

83. Eugene Roosens, "Interest Groups with a Noble Face," in *Marketing in a Multicultural World,* ed. J. A. Costa and G. J. Bamossy (Thousand Oaks, CA: Sage Publications, 1995), pp. 126–44.

84. Patricia Horn, "U.S. Book Industry Learns a New Language," *Christian Science Monitor,* March 8, 1994, p. 8; and Bickley Townsend, "Quenching Hispanic Thirst," *American Demographics,* December 1989, p. 15.

85. Dávila, *Latinos, Inc.*, pp. 120–25; Hornery, "Ethnic Expert Says Keep Eye on Bottom Line," p. 28; Carol J. Kaufman, "Coupon Use in Ethnic Markets: Implications from a Retail Perspective," *Journal of Consumer Marketing* 8 (Winter 1991), p. 44; Rossman, *Multicultural Marketing;* and Joyce Oliver, "To Reach Minorities, Try Busting Myths," *American Demographics,* April 1992, pp. 14–15.

86. "Massacres Promised," *Lincoln Journal Star,* June 20, 2000, p. 2A; and Andre Beteille, "Race, Caste and Gender," in *Society and Politics in India: Essays in a Comparative Perspective,* ed. Andre Beteille (London: Athlone Press, 1991), pp. 15–37.

87. Mihaly Csikszentmihalyi and Eugene Rochberg-Halton, *The Meaning of Things: Domestic Symbols and the Self* (Cambridge: Cambridge University Press, 1981); Vicky Goodhead, "Marketing to Mature Adults Requires a State of Being," *Marketing News,* December 9, 1991, p. 10; and Howard Schlossberg, "Expert on Aging Warns Against 'Stupid Marketing,' " *Marketing News,* September 28, 1992, pp. 2–3.

88. François Vey, "18 Millards de Francs," *L'Expansion,* no. 0652 (2001), at http://archives.lexpansion.com.

89. For an excellent review of research on children as consumers, see Deborah Roedder John, "Consumer Socialization of Children: A Retrospective Look at Twenty-Five Years of Research," *Journal of Consumer Research* 26 (December 1999), pp. 183–213; "L'Enfant Roi," *L'Expansion,* no. 635 (2000), at http://archives/lexpansion.com; Cele Otnes, Chan Kim Young, and Kyungseung Kim, "All I Want for Christmas: An Analysis of Children's Brand Requests to Santa Claus," *Journal of Popular Culture* 27 (Spring 1994), pp. 183–94; Russell W. Belk, Kenneth D. Bahn, and Robert N. Mayer, "Developmental Recognition of Consumption Symbolism," *Journal of Consumer Research* 9 (June 1982), pp. 4–17; and Robert N. Mayer and Russell Belk, "Acquisition of Consumption Stereotypes by Children," *Journal of Consumer Affairs* 16 (Winter 1982), pp. 307–21.

90. "Special Report on Asia," CNBC, June 18, 2000; and Zoher Abdoolcarim, "Consumer Kids Get Star Billing," *Asian Business* 30 (October 10, 1994), pp. 22–25.

91. James U. McNeal and Chyon-Hwa Yeh, "Development of Consumer Behavior Patterns among Chinese Children," *Journal of Consumer Marketing* 14, no. 1 (1997), pp. 45–59; James U. McNeal and Mindy F. Ji, "Chinese Children as Consumers: An Analysis of Their New Product Information Sources," *Journal of Consumer Marketing* 16, no. 4 (1999), pp. 345–64.

92. Christian Derbaix and Joel Bree, "The Impact of Children's Affective Reactions Elicited by Commercials on Attitudes toward the Advertisement and the Brand," *International Journal of Research in Marketing* 14 (July 1997), pp. 207–29; Cynthia Frazier Hite and Robert E. Hit, "Reliance on Brand by Young Children," *Journal of the Market Research Society* 37 (April 1995), pp. 185–93; M. Carole Macklin, "Preschoolers' Learning of Brand Names from Visual Cues," *Journal of Consumer Research* 23 (December 1996), pp. 251–61; Richard Mizerski, "The Relationship between Cartoon Trade Character Recognition and Attitude toward Product Category in Young Children," *Journal of Marketing* 59 (October 1995), pp. 58–70; Rodney Tasker, "Potential for Milking," *Far Eastern Economic Review,* April 3, 1997, p. 46; and Paco Underhill, "Kids in Stores," *American Demographics* 16, no. 6 (1994), pp. 22–27.

93. Elizabeth Chin, *Purchasing Power: Black Kids and American Consumer Culture* (Minneapolis: University of Minnesota Press, 2001); and Seung-Kuk Kim, "Changing Lifestyles and Consumption Patterns of the South Korean Middle Class and New Generations," in *Consumption in Asia,* ed. Chua Beng-Huat (London and New York: Routledge, 2001), pp. 61–81.

94. John, "Consumer Socialization of Children"; Merrie Brucks, Gary M. Armstrong, and Marvin E. Goldberg, "Children's Use of Cognitive Defenses against Television Advertising: A Cognitive Response Approach," *Journal of Consumer Research* 14 (March 1988), pp. 471–82; and Deborah Szynal, "New Bill Aims to Separate Kids, Cigs Online," *Marketing News,* February 4, 2002, pp. 6–7.

95. Jeff Brazil, "Play Dough," *American Demographics,* December 1999, pp. 56–61; and Anthony Pecotich and Clifford J. Shultz II, eds., *Marketing and Consumer Behavior in East and South-East Asia* (New York: McGraw-Hill, 1998).

96. Yuta Ishimori, "Mah-jongg Industry Looks to Youth," *The Nikkei Weekly,* February 26, 2001, p. 6.

97. Clotilde Warin, "Des Marketeurs Chez Jules Ferry," *L'Expansion,* September 13, 2001, no. 0652, at http://archives.lexpansion.com.

98. "Those Precocious 13-Year Olds," *Brandweek,* January 25, 1993, p. 13; Jill Brooke, "Girl Power," *ADWEEK,* Eastern ed., February 2, 1998, pp. 18–20; Robert Gray, "Keeping Up with the Kids," *Marketing,* February 24, 1997, pp. 26–29; Jane L. Levere, "A New Survey Charts the Habits of Teen-Agers around the World," *New York Times,* June 11, 1996, p. D8; Jaime Troiano, "Brazilian Teenagers Go Global—Sharing Values and Brands," *Marketing & Research Today* 25 (August 1997), pp. 149–62; "Brand Crazy," *Women's Wear Daily,* February 19, 1998, pp. S22–24; Ellen Newborne and Kathleen Kerwin, "Generation Y," *Business Week,* February 15, 1999, pp. 80–88; and Mark Ritson and Richard Elliott, "The Social Uses of Advertising: An Ethnographic Study of Adolescent Advertising Audiences," *Journal of Consumer Research* 26 (December 1999), pp. 260–77.

99. "Special Report on the Internet in Asia," CNBC, June 18, 2000; George Carey, Xiaoyan Zhao, Joan Chiaramone, and David Eden, "Is There One Global Village for Our Future Generation? Talking to 7–12 Year Olds around the World," *Marketing and Research Today* 25 (February 1997), pp. 12–16; Margaret Littman, "How Marketers Track Underage Consumers," *Marketing News,* May 8, 2000, p. 4; Don Tapscott, *Growing Up Digital: The Rise of the Net Generation* (New York: McGraw-Hill, 1998); Maureen Tkacik, "Is Soccer the New Basketball for Nike?" *The Wall Street Journal,* May 6, 2002, pp. B1, B4; Shawn Tully, "The Universal Teenager," *Fortune,* February 4, 1994, pp. 14–16; Emily De Nitto, "Brands Take a Berating at Cash Register," *Advertising Age,* August 23, 1993, pp. S4, S11; Adrienne Ward Fawcett, "When Using Slang in Advertising: BVC," *Advertising Age,* August 23, 1993, p. S6; Bruce Horowitz, "Lucrative Side of Teenage Anxieties," *Los Angeles Times,* October 4, 1992, pp. D1, D3; Jeff Jensen, "A New Read on How to Reach Boys," *Advertising Age,* August 23, 1993, pp. S10, S11; Junu Bryan Kim, "For Savvy Teens: Real Life, Real Solutions," *Advertising Age,* August 23, 1993, pp. S1, S4; Janine Lopiano-Wisdom and Jopanne De Luca, *Street Trends* (New York: Harper Perennial, 1997); Cyndee Miller, "Marketers Find Alternative Way to Appeal to Young Music Lovers," *Marketing News,* October 12, 1992, p. 18; Cyndee Miller, "The Way Xers Watch TV Has Advertisers Watching Them," *Marketing News,* December 6, 1993, p. 5; Ernie Mosteller, "In Search of Cool," *Shoot,* October 24, 1997, pp. 4–6; Fumiteru Nitta, "Shopping for Souvenirs in Hawaii," in *Re-Made in Japan,* ed. Joseph J. Tobin (New Haven: Yale University Press, 1992), pp. 204–15; Howard Schlossberg, "What Teenagers Find Hot Today Will Be Old News Tomorrow," *Marketing News,* December 6, 1993, p. 7; and Carolyn E. Setlow, "Kids Are Savvy, Affluent Consumers Who Retailers Should Court," *Discount Store News* 18, no. 36 (September 15, 1997), pp. 20–21.

100. Dick Hebidge, *Subculture: The Behavioral Basis of Style* (London: Methuen, 1979); Ikuya Sato, *Kamikaze Biker* (Chicago: University of Chicago Press, 1991); and Julie Tilsner, "From Trash Can Straight to Seventh Avenue," *Business Week,* March 22, 1993, p. 39.

101. Steve Burt and Mark Gabbott, "The Elderly Consumer and Non-Food Purchase Behaviour," *European Journal of Marketing* 29, no. 2 (1995), pp. 43–57; A. J. Greco, "Representation of the Elderly in Advertising: Crisis or Inconsequence?" *Journal of Consumer Marketing* 6, no. 1 (1989), pp. 37–44; Joan Raymond, "The Joy of Empty Nesting," *American Demographics,* May 2000, pp. 49–54; Carol M. Morgan, "The Psychographic Landscape of the 50-Plus," *Brandweek,* July 19, 1993, pp. 28–32; "Over 60 and Overlooked," *The Economist,* August 10, 2002, pp. 51–52;

and Robert E. Wilkes, "A Structural Modeling Approach to the Measurement and Meaning of Cognitive Age," *Journal of Consumer Research,* September 1992, pp. 292–301.

102. "Ageing 'Is an International Problem,'" BBC News, April 8, 2002, at http://news.bbc.co.uk/hi.english/health/newsid_1913000.1913515.stm.

103. Daniel Duane, "Silver Surfers," *New York Time Magazine,* April 15, 2001, pp. 38–39; Linda L. Price, Eric J. Arnould, and Carolyn Curasi, "Older Consumers' Disposition of Valued Possessions," *Journal of Consumer Research* 27 (September 2000), pp. 179–201; Raymond, "The Joy of Empty Nesting," pp. 49–54; and Marye C. Tharp, "Mature Americans: Fastest Growing Subculture," in *Marketing and Consumer Identity in Multicultural America,* ed. Mary C. Tharpe (Thousand Oaks, CA: Sage, 2001), pp. 91–121.

104. Bern Keating, "Elderhostel: The Mature Traveler's Ticket to Intriguing Adventures," *Hemispheres,* October 1992, pp. 52–54; Richard C. Leventhal, "The Aging Consumer: What's All the Fuss about Anyway?" *Journal of Consumer Marketing* 8 (Winter 1991), pp. 29–34; and Jim Carlton, "Web Sites, Other PC Wonders Draw Crowds of Retirees," *The Wall Street Journal,* January 29, 1998, p. B1.

105. "America's Aging Consumers," *Discount Merchandiser,* September 1993, pp. 16–28; Kelly A. Tepper, "The Role of Labeling Processes in Elderly Consumers' Responses to Age Segmentation Cues," *Journal of Consumer Research* 20 (March 1994), pp. 503–19; and Sharmistha Law, Scott A. Hawkins, and Fergus I. M. Craik, "Repetition-Induced Belief in the Elderly: Rehabilitating Age-Related Memory Deficits," *Journal of Consumer Research* 25 (September 1998), pp. 91–107.

106. Catherine A. Cole and Siva K. Balasubramanian, "Age Difference in Consumers' Search for Information: Public Policy Implications," *Journal of Consumer Research* 20 (June 1993), pp. 157–69; and "Over 60 and Overlooked," p. 52.

107. Law, Hawkins, and Craik, "Repetition-Induced Belief in the Elderly."

108. Kay M. Palan, "Gender Identity in Consumer Behavior Research: A Literature Review and Research Agenda," *Academy of Marketing Science Review* [Online] 01 (10). at http://www.vancouver.wsu.edu/amsrev/theory/palan10-01.html.

109. Peter Stickels, "The Nineties Man: Keep Me in Control and Don't Let my Family Think I'm Stupid," *Ad News,* September 24, 1993, pp. 12–14; and Kathy Evans, "Men's Interests," *Sunday Life,* May 25, 1999, pp. 8–11.

110. Palan, "Gender Identity in Consumer Behavior Research."

111. Stephen J. Gould and Claudia E. Weil, "Gift-Giving Roles and Gender Self-Concepts," *Sex Roles* 24, nos. 9/10 (1991), pp. 617–37; Stephen Gould, "Gender Identity and Gender Salience: A Dual Path, Person Situation Approach to Gender Effects in Consumer Research," in *Advances in Consumer Research,* vol. 23, ed. Kim P. Corfman and John G. Lynch (Provo, UT: Association for Consumer Research, 1996), pp. 478–83; and Adam Young, "Sport a Winner in Men's Magazine Market," *Ad News,* May 6, 1994, pp. 16–19.

112. Judy Cohen, "Gender Portrayal in Children's Advertising," in *Gender Marketing and Consumer Behavior,* vol. 5, ed. Jonathan Schroeder and Cele C. Otnes (Urbana, IL: University of Illinois Publication Service, 2000), pp. 47–68.

113. John, "Consumer Socialization of Children"; Rebecca Gardyn, "Granddaughters of Feminism," *American Demographics,* April 2001, pp. 43–47; Pamela Kiecker, Kay M. Palan, and Charles S. Areni, "Different Ways of 'Seeing': How Gender Differences in Information Processing Influence the Content Analysis of Narrative Texts," *Marketing Letters* 11, no. 1 (2000), pp. 49–65; Cele Otnes, Tina M. Lowrey, and Y. C. Kim, "Gift Selection for Easy and Difficult Recipients, a Social Roles Interpretation," *Journal of Consumer Research* 20 (1993), pp. 229–44; Janice Radway, "Interpretive Communities and Variable Literacies: The Functions of Romance Reading," in *Rethinking Popular Culture,* ed. Chandra Mukerji and Michael Schudson (Berkeley: University of California Press, 1991), pp. 465–86; Barbara Stern, "Two Pornographies: A Feminist View of Sex in Advertising," in *Advances in Consumer Research,* vol. 18, ed. Rebecca H. Holman and Michael R. Solomon (Provo, UT: Association for Consumer Research, 1991), pp. 384–91; and Eileen Fischer and Steven J. Arnold, "More Than a Labor of Love: Gender Roles and Christmas Gift Shopping," *Journal of Consumer Research* 17 (1990), pp. 333–45.

114. Gardyn "Granddaughters of Feminism"; Maureen Hupfer, "Communicating with the Agentic Woman and the Communal Man: Are Stereotypic Advertising Appeals Still Relevant?" *Academy of Marketing Science Review* [Online] 2002 (03) at http://www.amsreview.org/amsrev/theory/hupfer03-2002.html; and Allan J. Kimmel and Elisabeth Tissier-Desbordes, "Masculinity and Consumption: A Qualitative Investigation of French and American Men," in *Gender, Marketing and Consumer Behavior,* vol. 5, ed. Jonathan Schroeder and Cele C. Otnes (Urbana, IL: University of Illinois Publication Service, 2000), pp. 1–18.
115. Craig J. Thompson, "Caring Consumers: Gendered Consumption Meanings and the Juggling Lifestyle," *Journal of Consumer Research* 22 (March 1996), pp. 388–407; and "Ladies Night Out—At the Garage," *Business Week,* September 18, 2000, p. 16.
116. Ann Veeck, Laura Williams, and Naihua Jiang, "Sons and Daughters: The One-Child Policy, Education, and Gender Stratification in Urban China," pp. 78–79; Cele Otnes and Mary Ann McGrath, "Beyond the Stereotype of Male Shopping Behavior," p. 101; and Suraj Commuri, "Husbands Play 'Men': Feminist Interpretation of Women's Participation in Preserving Male Stereotypes," p. 101; all in *Gender Marketing and Consumer Behavior,* vol. 5, ed. Jonathan Schroeder and Cele C. Otnes (Urbana, IL: University of Illinois Publication Service, 2000); and "Hotels Create 'Ladies Rooms,'" *Asian Business,* July, 2001, p. 74.
117. "Amardeep Assar and George S. Bobinski Jr., "Financial Decision Making by Baby Boomer Couples," in *Advances in Consumer Research,* vol. 18, ed. Rebecca H. Holman and Michael R. Solomon (Provo, UT: Association for Consumer Research, 1991), pp. 659–60; "Automakers Learn Better Roads to Women's Market," *Marketing News,* October 12, 1992, p. 2; Elizabeth C. Hirschman, "Differences in Consumer Purchase Behavior by Credit Card Payment System," *Journal of Consumer Research* 6 (June 1979), pp. 58–66; William O. Adcock, Elizabeth C. Hirschman, and Jac L. Goldstucker, "Bank Card Users: An Updated Profile," in *Advances in Consumer Research,* vol. 4, ed. William D. Perrault Jr. (Atlanta, GA: Association for Consumer Research, 1977), pp. 236–41; and Alladi Venkatesh, "Gender Identities in the Indian Context: A Sociocultural Construction of the Female Consumer," in *Gender and Consumer Behavior,* ed. Janeen Costa (Salt Lake City: University of Utah Printing Service, 1993), pp. 119–29.
118. Carrie Goerne, "Gun Companies Target Women: Foes Call It Marketing to Fear," *Marketing News,* August 31, 1992, pp. 1, 2; Timothy Burke, *Lifebuoy Men and Lux Women* (Durham, NC: Duke University Press, 1996); Margaret Littman, "Women Fans Have Gridiron Pros Grinning," *Marketing News,* February 2, 1997, pp. 1, 14; and Lorraine A. Woellert, "For the WNBA, It's No Easy Lay-up," *Business Week,* May 1, 2000, pp. 102, 106.
119. Lisa Peñaloza, "Crossing Boundaries/Crossing Lines: A Look at the Nature of Gender Boundaries and Their Impact on Marketing Research," *International Journal of Research in Marketing* 11, no. 4 (1994), pp. 359–79.
120. Theodore Caplow, "Christmas Gifts and Kin Networks," *American Sociological Review* 48, no. 6 (1982), pp. 383–92; David Cheal, *The Gift Economy* (New York: Routledge Press, 1988); Micaela Di Leonardo, "The Female World of Cards and Holidays: Women, Families, and the Work of Kinship," *Signs: Journal of Women, Culture and Society* 12 (Spring 1987), pp. 440–53; Fischer and Arnold, "More Than a Labor of Love"; Margaret L. Rucker, L. Leckliter, S. Kivel, M. Dinkel, T. Freitas, M. Waynes, and H. Prato, "When the Thought Counts: Friendship, Love, Gift Exchanges and Gift Returns," in *Advances in Consumer Research,* vol. 18, ed. Rebecca H. Holman and Michael R. Solomon (Provo, UT: Association for Consumer Research, 1991), pp. 528–31; John F. Sherry Jr. and Mary Ann McGrath, "Unpacking the Holiday Presence: A Comparative Ethnography of Two Gift Stores," in *Interpretive Consumer Research,* ed. Elizabeth Hirschman (Provo, UT: Association for Consumer Research, 1989), pp. 148–67; Melanie Wallendorf and Eric J. Arnould, "'We Gather Together': The Consumer Rituals of Thanksgiving Day," *Journal of Consumer Research* 18 (June 1991), pp. 13–31; Eric J. Arnould, "Marketing and Social Reproduction in Zinder, Niger Republic," in *Households: Changing Form and Function,* ed. Robert Netting, Richard Wilk, and Eric Arnould (Berkeley: University of California Press, 1984), pp. 130–62; and Daniel Miller, *A Theory of Shopping* (Ithaca, NY: Cornell University Press, 1998).

121. Deborah Heisley, "Gender Symbolism and Usage Expectations in Food," p. 104; Lynn Langmeyer, "Exploring Gender Influences on Meanings in Celebrity Endorsers," pp. 158–67; and Teresa M. Pavia and Janeen A. Costa, "Gender Dimensions of the Alphabetic Characters with Implications for Branding," pp. 173–85; all in *Gender and Consumer Behavior,* ed. Janeen Costa (Salt Lake City: University of Utah Printing Service, 1991); see also Michael J. Baker and Gilbert A. Churchill, "The Impact of Physically Attractive Models on Advertising Evaluations," *Journal of Marketing Research* 14 (November 1997), pp. 538–55.
122. Susan Lobo, *A House of My Own: Social Organization in the Squatter Settlements of Lima, Peru* (Tucson, AZ: University of Arizona Press, 1982), p. 53; Peter Manuel, *Cassette Culture: Popular Music and Technology in North India* (Chicago: University of Chicago Press, 1993), pp. 66, 159–60; and Farhan Bokhari, "Pakistan's Profitable First Women's Bank Carves New Niche," *Christian Science Monitor,* October 25, 1993, p. 6.
123. Jerry Berger and Al Stamborski, "Anheuser-Busch Print Ads Begin Featuring Gay People," *St. Louis Post-Dispatch,* April 21, 1999, p. C1; Steven M. Kates, "The Protean Quality of Subcultural Consumption: An Ethnographic Account of Gay Consumers," *Journal of Consumer Research* 29 (December 2002); Steven M. Kates, *Twenty Million New Customers! Understanding Gay Men's Consumer Behavior* (Binghamton, NY: Harrington Park Press, 1998); Daniel L. Wardlow, *Gays, Lesbians, and Consumer Behavior: Theory, Practice, and Research Issues in Marketing* (New York: Haworth Press, 1996); and Lisa N. Peñaloza, "Crossing Boundaries/Drawing Lines: Gender Trouble in Consumer Research," in *Gender and Consumer Behavior,* ed. Janeen Costa (Salt Lake City, UT: University of Utah Printing Service, 1991), p. 89.
124. Richard Cimino and Don Lattin, "Choosing My Religion," *American Demographics,* April 1999, pp. 60–65; and Cyndee Miller "People Want to Believe in Something," *Marketing News,* December 5, 1994, pp. 1–3.
125. Ella Tennant, "Prophet Motive," *Far Eastern Economic Review,* March 2, 1995, pp. 34–35.
126. Cleland Kim, "Ad, Promo Strategies Make New Converts," *Advertising Age,* Midwest Region Edition, April 10, 1995, pp. 1–2; Darren E. Sherkat, "Preferences, Constraints, and Choices in Religious Markets: An Examination of Religious Switching and Apostasy," *Social Forces* 73 (March 1995), pp. 993–1026; Darren E. Sherkat, "Counterculture or Continuity? Competing Influences on Baby Boomers' Religious Orientations and Participation," *Social Forces* 76 (March 1998), pp. 1087–114; D. Paul Sullins, "Switching Close to Home: Volatility or Coherence in Protestant Affiliation Patterns?" *Social Forces* 72 (December 1993), pp. 399–419; and Dale Buss, "Peddling God," *Sales and Marketing Management* 154 (March 2002), pp. 42–48.
127. Meera Louis, "Modern Marketing Helps Sell Life as a Nun," *The Wall Street Journal,* May 11, 1999, pp. B1, B12; Malise Ruthven, *The Divine Supermarket: Shopping for God in America* (New York: William Morrow and Co., 1989); and "Public Relations Firm to Present Anti-Abortion Effort to Bishops," *New York Times,* August 14, 1990, p. A12.
128. Gopalkrishnan R. Iyer, "The Impact of Religion and Reputation in the Organization of Indian Merchant Communities," *Journal of Business & Industrial Marketing* 14, no. 2 (1999), pp. 102–17; C. Eric Lincoln, *The Black Church since Frazier* (New York: Schocken Books, 1974); Elizabeth C. Hirschman, "Effects of American Jewish Ethnicity upon Consumer Behavior," *Journal of Marketing* 45 (Summer 1985), p. 108; and Brendan Maher, "Judaica," *Target Marketing* 24 (March 2001), pp. 98–101.
129. Carole Ann King, "Pru Agent Carves out Market Niche with Religious Leaders," *National Underwriter,* Life & Health/Financial Services Edition, May 24, 1999, p. 7.
130. Mohammed Y. Rawwas, David Strutton, and Lester W. Johnson, "An Exploratory Investigation of the Ethical Values of American and Australian Consumers: Direct Marketing Implications," *Journal of Direct Marketing* 10 (Autumn 1996), pp. 52–63; Anusorn Singhapakdi, Janet K. Marta, Kumar C. Rallapalli, and C. P. Rao, "Toward an Understanding of Religiousness and Marketing Ethics: An Empirical Study," *Journal of Business Ethics* 27 (October 2000), pp. 305–20; and James Sood and Yukio Nasu, "Religiosity and Nationality: An Explanatory Study of Their Effect on Consumer Behavior in Japan and the United States," *Journal of Business Research* 34 (September 1995).

131. Nejdet Delener, "The Effects of Religious Factors on Perceived Risk in Durable Goods Purchase Decisions," *Journal of Consumer Marketing* 7 (Summer 1990), p. 27; Lawrence J. Goodrich, "Religion Is Alive and Diverse in U.S.," *Christian Science Monitor,* January 10, 1994, pp. 11–13; Hirschman, "Effects of American Jewish Ethnicity upon Consumer Behavior," p. 108; and Pamela Paul, "One Nation, Under God?" *American Demographics,* January 2002, pp. 16–18.
132. Delener, "The Effects of Religious Factors on Perceived Risk in Durable Goods Purchase Decisions," pp. 27–38; Tim W. Ferguson and Josephine Lee, "Spiritual Reality," *Forbes,* January 27, 1997, pp. 70–76; E. Franklin Frazier, *The Negro Church in America* (New York: Shocken Books, 1974 [1963]); Cyndee Miller; "Music Praises the Lord, Finds Home with Mosh Pit Crowd," *Marketing News,* March 31, 1997, pp. 1, 6; Ruthven, *The Divine Supermarket,* pp. 255–76; and Deborah Hale Shelton, "Niche Book Publishing Affects How Even the Bible Is Marketed," *Marketing News,* October 12, 1998, p. 2.
133. James G. Hutton, "Narrowing the Concept of Marketing," *Journal of Nonprofit & Public Sector Marketing* 9, no. 4 (2001), pp. 5–24; Gene R. Laczniak, "Distributive Justice, Catholic Social Teaching, and the Moral Responsibility of Marketers," *Journal of Public Policy & Marketing* 18 (Spring 1999), pp. 125–29; and John D. Mittelstaedt, "A Framework for Understanding the Relationships between Religions and Markets," *Journal of Macromarketing* 22 (June 2002), pp. 6–18.

chapter 1
chapter 2
chapter 3
chapter 4
chapter 5
chapter 6
chapter 7
chapter 8
chapter 9
chapter 10
chapter 11
chapter 12
chapter 13
chapter 14
chapter 15
chapter 16
chapter 17
chapter 18
chapter 19

LEARNING OBJECTIVES

After completing this chapter, you should be able to:

- Characterize organizations using six main dimensions: membership structure, organization, resources, motives and goals, roles, and culture.
- Understand how organizational structure and characteristics relate to consumption activities.
- Identify the basic types of organizational purchases.
- Explain how household structure and characteristics relate to consumption activities.
- Recognize the important role of the family life cycle in consumption activities.
- Distinguish decision roles and decision-making styles in households and organizations.
- Describe a variety of consuming collectives besides households and business organizations.

A NAVAJO FAMILY BUYS A PICKUP TRUCK

Ruby had been sitting in her mother's *hoogan* (the traditional octagonal Navajo house) for several hours now, helping her mother comb raw wool. They had not spoken in over an hour. Baby Ben played on the floor with a twist of wool. Without looking up, Ruby said to her mother, Agnes, "Kids wouldn't have to walk so far to the school bus stop if we had a truck." Her mother nodded her head in agreement. They went on combing the wool in silence.

Several days later Ruby was visiting her sister Edna to help dip sheep. After several hours of herding sheep through the murky water of the sheep-dip tank (to remove parasites), Ruby remarked to Edna, "Saw a used red truck over at the Begay spread." Edna said she'd seen it too. Ruby noted it sure would be good to help those kids get back and forth to the bus stop. Edna did not reply. Bertha, their grandmother, nodded.

A few weeks later at the Laundromat in Chinle, Arizona, Agnes and her sister Betty were taking clothes from the dryer. Agnes mentioned the secondhand truck for sale over at the Begay spread and how it was sometimes hard to get those kids to walk to the bus stop.

Several weeks later when Betty sold a rug to the trader at Tec Nos Pos, Arizona, she passed Agnes some money with the suggestion that she "get something for those kids." About this time, Agnes received a money order from her son Hosteen, working construction in Los Angeles. Grandmother Bertha and Edna returned from a trip to Windowrock, Arizona, with some money that Edna had received for pawning some old jewelry she had inherited from her mother. When Edna learned that Bertha and Agnes had received some money, she sold some lambs to the cooperative down in Chinle. Some days later, Agnes urged Ruby and Edna to stop by the Begay's spread. She advised them to check in on old Abigail Begay. To no one's surprise, Ruby and Edna returned to Agnes's *hoogan* with the red 1995 pickup purchased from the Begays.

OVERVIEW

The opening vignette helps us start thinking about groups and their purchase and consumption activities. A **group** simply refers to *two or more individuals who have certain implicitly or explicitly defined relationships to one another such that their behavior is interdependent.* In this chapter we will talk about two categories of groups: organizational consumers and families and households. In Chapter 14 we will talk about reference groups, a special category of groups.

Understanding groups is crucial in understanding consumer behavior because, as the vignette illustrates, many consumption activities involve groups rather than individuals. In fact, almost all consumer behavior involves groups at one or more of the stages in the circle of consumer behavior. For example, an individual acquisition decision may be followed by group consumption (e.g., individual purchase of the ingredients of a meal for a dinner party) or a group acquisition via individual consumption (Mom decides to purchase a pet for Junior). Some decisions that appear on the surface to be individual decisions often are not. For example, you may not be surprised to learn that North American students often report that their parents actively participated in their first automobile purchase.

The opening vignette illustrates things many of us already know from experience with groups. First, groups vary in terms of their **membership structure.** There are many different kinds of consuming entities, including business organizations, households, buying clubs, and even gangs. As the vignette suggests, households made up of family members are significant consumption groups cross-culturally. Second, groups vary in terms of their decision-making style or organization. Family participants in the group decision may vary. Thus, the Navajo Indian family mobilizes and pools resources from a network of people related through women. In the case of the Navajo family, the mobilization of resources to buy a truck is egalitarian and takes time and patience. The decision-making style for your household's purchase of an automobile might be quite different. Third, groups mobilize resources in order to realize their consumption choices. The Navajo family pools wages and income from selling wool, rugs, and pawned jewelry. The group's resources and mechanisms for mobilizing resources both facilitate and constrain consumption. Fourth, group consumption choices often involve a mix of motives or goals. Group consumption choices include practical and purposeful behaviors, symbolic and status concerns, and habits of which consumers are often unaware. Fifth, group members, like Ruby, Edna, and Agnes in the vignette, play different roles in the purchase process. Sixth, groups share a culture that influences their purchase and consumption behaviors. In seeking to understand, predict, and manage group purchase behaviors, these six elements need to be understood regardless of whether we are dealing with households and families or purchasing groups within business organizations. Marketers and consumer advocates should be aware of these factors and anticipate their influence on group consumption decisions, as illustrated in Industry Insights 13.1.

In the first section of this chapter we review general characteristics of organizational and domestic groups that are important for analyzing consumer behaviors. We discuss organizational consumers, beginning with a discussion of group culture and identity. Next, we describe some characteristics of organizational buyers and types of organizational purchases.

The next major section of the chapter focuses on families and households. The first part focuses on different compositions and structures for households, trends in household structure, patterns of coresidence, and the concept of family life cycle. The next part focuses on the range of domestic group activities that have implications for marketers. The final discussion of domestic groups is dedicated to distinguishing both roles and decision-making styles in the household decision processes. The chapter concludes with a brief description of consuming collectives.

Selling Pianos in Rural Montana

INDUSTRY INSIGHTS 13.1

As part of a campaign to promote a sale in a small town in Montana, the manager of a piano store was offering a $350+ hunting rifle free with the purchase of a piano. The manager, interviewed on national radio, explained. In his town the female head of household is the one who pushes for a piano for the home, but because it's a joint purchase and involves reliance on or pooling of resources with the male head of household, the female is often unable to motivate the purchase. The manager is trying to help by offering something of value for the male. The success of selling pianos lies in understanding who participates in the decision; the decision-making style and organization; the resources, motives, goals, and respective roles of the husband and wife; and something about the cultural history of the decision-making unit. Certainly, the offering of a hunting rifle with the purchase of a piano wouldn't work in many households, but it may work in many traditional households in this rural U.S. town.

GROUP STRUCTURE AND CHARACTERISTICS

One way to think about groups is in terms of their membership structure and characteristics. Important structural considerations include size, formality, voluntary or involuntary membership, primary or secondary interpersonal contact, and affect.

Group Size

Group size is a structural dimension that may vary over the phases of the circle of consumption. One family member may be the sole decision maker for routine purchases. In a large organization, a small purchasing group or even a single individual may also have decision authority for a variety of purchases, even though they constitute a significant outlay of funds. A kin group may share durable goods purchased by a single family, such as the Navajo family's truck. Married siblings and their families may purchase and share a vacation home.[1]

For marketers, another aspect of size is the **purchasing power** of the group. For example, firms are often interested in identifying large groups that make large aggregate purchases. The Center for the Persuasive Arts in San Antonio, Texas, competes for all of the marketing communications needs of corporate and government clients. Airbus Industrie and Boeing compete for national airline orders. Ford Motor uses fleet sales to corporate buyers to increase Ford Taurus's sales relative to rival Honda Accord. Maine Iron Works sells one product, naval destroyers, to one large customer, the U.S. government, although it is totally dependent on government contracts.

Group Formality

Another way in which we can classify the structure of consuming groups is in terms of formality; groups may be more or less formal or informal. **Formal groups** are *bound together by a contractual relationship.* For example, marriage, birth and baptismal certificates, wills, and titles to property provide formal bases for the existence of families and households. Employees of business organizations are often bound by contracts specifying their duties. Other documents stipulate compensation, health benefits, pensions, and other items of value they may receive from the organization.

Informal groups are not bound by such formal ties, but may be *identified by regular interaction, common lifestyle, or interests.* Market segments constitute informal groups. Informal groups can play an important role in the consumption process. For instance, a South African youth who follows Kwaito music will display a distinct style of dressing and living. In this sense, Kwaito is a sound that defines South Africa's black youth.[2] And yet, no one formally signs up to participate in the Kwaito community, and there is relatively little joint purchase behavior. We discuss further the influence of informal groups in Chapters 12 and 14.

Voluntary or Involuntary Membership

Membership in consuming groups may be **voluntary** or **involuntary.** All people are involuntary members of at least some groups. No one chose his or her culture, race, social class, or family; yet membership in involuntary groups, which might also include a church or school, may influence the person's consumption patterns and preferences. The impact of involuntary group membership on consumption patterns is extreme in the case of military personnel, prison inmates, nursing home patients, and other members of **total institutions.** Total institutions *make their members' most basic as well as discretionary consumption choices.* Such groups have often attracted the interests of marketers hoping to cater to their aggregate needs or social policy advocates eager to change their consumption regimes. A recent U.S. court case ruling in favor of inmates seeking redress from the effects of secondary cigarette smoke in jail is an example.

Exhibit 13.1 indicates that voluntary and involuntary groups can be either formal or informal. Examples in each category are provided. Corporate employees belong to formal organizations where membership is voluntary. Public school students belong to a formal organization and sometimes participate involuntarily in consumption behaviors, such as wearing school uniforms. Members of families and market segments are informal groups in which membership is involuntary. Fans are voluntary members of an informal group, unless of course they join a fan club, which is a formal group.

Primary and Secondary Groups

The structure of consumption groups may be distinguished by whether they are primary or secondary. *Groups characterized by frequent interpersonal contact* are referred to as **primary groups.** *Groups characterized by limited interpersonal contact* are called **secondary groups.** Primary consumption groups include the household and family. Primary groups play an important role in consumer socialization, discussed in depth later in the chapter; they instill core values that guide a person's consumer behaviors throughout his or her life. Secondary groups such as corporations, social clubs, and professional

EXHIBIT 13.1

Kinds of Groups

Membership	Formality: Formal	Formality: Informal
Voluntary	Corporation Religious congregation Social service organization Youth organization	Fan culture Brand tribe Brand-loyal shopper Disability group
Involuntary	Nursing home Public school Prison Doomsday cult	Family, ethnic group Culture, nation Social class Market segment

organizations, influence values and consumption behaviors but not so fundamentally as primary groups.

Affect

One additional aspect of groups that should not be neglected is the important cement provided by **affect** between group members. Affect softens the role of personal self-interest in purchase consumption decisions; group members compromise self-interest to maintain long-term relationships. *Love, attraction, commitment, and emotional support* are characteristics that motivate considerable consumer behavior in households. Affect plays a role even in relationships between industrial buyers and sellers.[3]

ORGANIZATIONAL CULTURE, IDENTITY, AND CONSUMPTION ACTIVITIES

Organizational Culture

Organizational culture refers to the meanings organizational members share about the organization—how individuals make sense of the organization. We can define group or **organizational culture** as *the pattern of shared values and beliefs that help individuals understand organizational functioning and thus provide norms for behavior in the organization.*[4] Organizations are not simply economic groups; they vary in their expressive and symbolic aspects as well. Understanding organizational culture, like the culture of other consumer groups, is useful in developing strategies to target organizational buyers.

An organization's culture often manifests itself to outsiders in terms of its reputation or image. For example, the corporate images of the largest automobile manufacturers—General Motors, Ford, DaimlerChrysler, Toyota, and Volkswagen—are distinct and diverse. The different images reflect different organizational philosophy and culture with regard to product, quality, styling, and marketing.[5]

Organizational culture often reflects more general cultural values. For example, the organizational philosophy of Amway Corporation is rooted in the American Dream. This very successful company, based on personal sales of home-cleaning products, promotes the idea that every individual can be successful through hard work and competition. How might these values affect the marketing strategy of this firm?

Any organization contains multiple cultures, such as professional, management, or technical subcultures. A study of technical professional company employees in the Silicon Valley of California illustrates that multiple cultures cut across an organization.[6] Cartoonists often poke fun at marketing subculture, for example, as shown on page 544. Looking for multiple cultures within organizations can be useful for ensuring effective targeting and positioning.

Organizational Stories, Group Rituals, and Performances

Organizations socialize new members into their culture to achieve a sense of organizational identity and commitment and to enable coordinated action. This socialization occurs through mechanisms that create and convey organizational culture. Mission statements, organizational stories, slogans, rituals, and other symbolic processes help create the organization's culture. For example, there may be an unwritten corporate ethos: "If you've got anything that is controversial, you just don't bring it up."[7]

Source: DILBERT reprinted by permission of United Feature Syndicate, Inc.

Sometimes the symbolic processes that help create the culture are subtle and difficult to uncover. Other times, as with dress codes, they are so much a part of the environment that they are inescapable. Three tools for creating and conveying culture are worth some special attention: (1) corporate mission statements, (2) organizational stories, and (3) performances and rituals.

MISSION STATEMENTS Corporate **mission statements** help *create and convey organizational culture.* Contrast the mission statements of two familiar apparel companies that offer casual and well-styled clothing, The Gap and Esprit. The business mission of The Gap is to offer well-styled clothes at affordable prices in a friendly environment. The culture at The Gap encourages responsibility to society through a companywide commitment to an in-house community program, but the focus of the culture is on consistent quality, low price, and helpful service. The business mission

Why Are There So Many Pickup Trucks in This Office Tower!

INDUSTRY INSIGHTS 13.2

The Phoenix Tower, a green-glass skyscraper with 34 floors, opened in the Greenway Plaza area of Houston, Texas, in 1984. At first, there were not so many tenants. The first large tenant was a natural gas pipeline company, Tenneco Oil and Gas, which had strong roots in the state of Texas. All of the jobs at the Tower were white-collar in nature, but almost all the Tenneco employees had been with the firm for many years. Most often, they started out their careers by riding in pickup trucks along miles and miles of remote pipelines in rural areas. There, they checked for gas leaks or other problems.

With so few tenants in the early days, there were ample parking spaces in the Tower, so the Tenneco employees parked wherever they liked. However, as the regional economy improved, more tenants moved in, and parking spots started to get scarce. In order to bring some order to the situation, managers of the Tower installed gates that would rise up when workers at the building inserted their key cards into the appropriate slot. Chaos ensued. Every morning, one employee or another from the pipeline company would smash through the gate arm, using the pickup truck as a battering ram. The Phoenix managers wrote letter after letter to the Tenneco employees. They tried every approach, but nothing worked. Every morning, the gates would be smashed to bits, and the cost of repairing the damage was substantial. The Tenneco employees had started out their careers following pipelines on the open range, and this common experience shaped their corporate culture and outlook. In this sense, the Tenneco employees share a culture with all of Texans. No one can fence them in!

www.phoenixtower.com

of Esprit is quite different. Susie Tompkins, founder of the company, was quoted as saying, "Profits are a means for Esprit to stay socially responsible; my aim is that Esprit inspires good values." When asked what the aim of Esprit was, Tompkins stated, "To have a solid business with a strong emphasis on humanistic values." The commitment reflected in Esprit's mission statement both to employees and customers is "Be informed. Be involved. Make a difference."[8] This mission statement is displayed in all employee staff rooms in the retail stores, and all employees are aware of Esprit's socially conscious philosophy. How might these differences in mission affect marketing to these two organizations?

ORGANIZATIONAL STORIES **Organizational stories** are another important way of conveying a firm's culture.[9] Stories, like the myths discussed in Chapter 3, explain and give meaning to the everyday world. An example of how stories are used in one organization is provided in Industry Insights 13.2. Stories help maintain cohesion and provide guidelines by sharing legends of the company to new employees in a powerful way. Stories often portray the organization in heroic terms to members and outsiders. Stories don't typically tell about values and feelings directly; instead, their meaning is couched in symbolic terms.[10]

Both households and companies with strong cultures are adept at recognizing and creating situational heroes. **Heroes** are those *individuals who do extraordinary things under the circumstances and who embody the culture's ethic of success.* An example of a story that features a situational hero and also embodies corporate values and beliefs is provided in Consumer Chronicles 13.1.[11]

The business press often portrays successful CEOs in heroic terms. For a U.S. company, the situational hero may be the sales manager who through an extraordinary feat of

Corporate Heroes

CONSUMER CHRONICLES 13.1

Johnson & Johnson (stock symbol, JNJ) continues to immortalize one of its past presidents to the point where his achievements have reached heroic proportions. Robert Wood Johnson took over Johnson & Johnson (J&J) during a challenging period in the late nineteenth century. Through hard work, a strong ethical standard, and a commitment to community, Mr. Johnson "righted the ship." All subsequent leaders of J&J keep a portrait of R. W. Johnson in their office and aspire to meet his high standards. Within the corporation itself, his spirit is said to exist in all endeavors. J&J employees are encouraged to view all choices with high ethical standards. Accordingly, J&J has created guidelines known as "BrightLines," whereby all employees are trained to make informed ethical decisions. R. W. Johnson was strongly committed to community service. He made provisions in his will to create a foundation to improve health care services in America. This same spirit of community continues to flourish at J&J. The Robert Wood Johnson folklore remains a key component in how J&J conducts business today.

Source: See www.jnj.com/our_company/history/history_section_1.htm.

Yankee ingenuity, timing, and finesse manages to win a big account away from the foreign competition. The story is told and retold again and again, with embellishment. The story and the hero remind members of the organization that it can triumph over strong competitors by holding onto the values of that organizational culture.

PERFORMANCES AND RITUALS Groups need a sense of identity, in addition to other kinds of resources, for their survival. Like individuals, they require tangible symbols of their status and well-being. To this end, groups typically engage in expressive consumption activities where members communicate information about their status and well-being. Thus, groups engage in performances and rituals, especially life transition rituals. **Performances** help to *express values, beliefs, status, and well-being* at different times during the year and in different ways. **Life transition rituals** *acknowledge changes in status and reassure members of the organization's continued well-being.*[12] Among U.S. business organizations, a good example of a performance that reflects organizational culture is casual dress on Fridays. Research in an insurance company showed that employees felt casual dress revealed management's trust in employees and projected a progressive image to customers, although some felt it was an imposition and others that women's preferences were not taken into account. At a more general level, the casual dress policy displays an organizational culture more tolerant of individual differences than one imposing a rigid policy.

Annual performances include corporate retreats, dinners, and parties. Among selling organizations, such as Avon or Amway, award celebrations for top sellers are not uncommon. The presentation involves a ceremony where all work comes to a halt. Although the ceremony involves some humor, it is a very serious event that makes corporate values clear to everyone and provides signs of belonging to the culture.[13] Roasts, retirement parties, Outward Bound excursions, and the like provide examples of life transition rituals undertaken by organizations. By paying attention to organizational performances and rituals, marketers can gain insight into values that may influence purchase behavior. The cartoon on page 547 takes a humorous look at corporate culture and corporate rituals.

ORGANIZATIONAL CONSUMERS

Organizational consumers constitute enormous, diverse, and complex markets. They may be categorized in a variety of ways as we discuss below.[14] Organizational consumers also share a number of characteristics. Typically, organizations rely on a small number of buyers to fill their needs. Recent moves by big organizational buyers to consolidate suppliers through online auctions are the latest example of this characteristic. Within organizations, buyers are often organized into temporary or permanent **buying**

"New Ideas for the Work Week"

centers, or buying task groups.[15] A buying center includes all those persons involved in the buying decision process. To market successfully in a B2B environment, sellers must identify and communicate with the multiple participants who enact the organizational buying process.[16] At least six important roles are included in this process:

1. The *initiator* is a person who identifies a need or who has an idea for a purchase. The initiator often plays other roles (e.g., the role of user) in the buying process. Note that there can be considerable role sharing throughout this organizational process.
2. The *gatekeeper* is a person in the organization who controls the flow of information. Many times, this person could serve in the role of administrative assistant to other actors. The gatekeeper can possess considerable power, since he or she can choose how to collect, edit, and disseminate information.
3. The *influencer* is someone in the organization who may have important technical or practical knowledge about the product category. This person can be thought of as a resident expert. Alternatively, an influencer could be someone who has lunch with key decision makers in the organization.
4. The *decider* determines whether or not to make the purchase. This person also may determine which specific models are acceptable. The decider may be the one in charge of identifying acceptable vendors and then making the final decision about which vendor to hire.
5. The *buyer* or *purchasing agent* physically acquires the product or service. That is, these actors negotiate the purchase transaction. They try to make the best deal and settle on the final terms (e.g., with respect to delivery schedules, charges, financing).
6. The *user* actually consumes the product or service. In some cases, the final user may have relatively little influence on the decision-making process and its outcome.

www.staubach.com

These buying center roles are further illustrated in the following example. Gerry Tellis (the initiator) is a salesperson for the Staubach Company, which leases and sells commercial real estate. Gerry has an idea that all the sales reps at Staubach could benefit by using a web camera with customers to provide a virtual real estate tour and, in the process, create a personal service experience for their clients.

After thinking up this idea, Gerry wants to make a formal presentation to his sales manager, Moutusi Maity (decider). However, Gerry is aware that Ms. Maity will rely upon the advice of her administrative assistant (the gatekeeper). In the past, Gerry gets the feeling that the assistant sometimes edits or screens the messages or requests that he sends to Ms. Maity.

www.earthcam.com

After listening to Gerry's formal presentation, Ms. Maity asks her administrative assistant to gather more information about web cams and their potential uses in the real estate industry. She also speaks about web cams with some of her fellow managers (influencers), in both formal and informal situations. Ms. Maity has several meetings with the head of the Tech Support Department (influencer). In the end, she decides to approve the expenditure, and she makes a formal request to the purchasing agent (buyer), who negotiates the terms of the final deal. When the new web cams arrive, Gerry and his fellow sales reps (users) have a new toy to amuse themselves and their clients! In this case, Gerry is both an initiator and a user, but his fellow sales reps fill just one role—that of users.

Organizational buyers display other characteristics. Organizational buyers are sometimes geographically concentrated in a region of a country. Good examples include Silicon Valley in northern California, home to many computer and information processing companies; Rotterdam in the Netherlands, home to many important shipping and transport companies; and Milan, Italy, home to a number of fashion and design firms. In the Internet age, there is some speculation that the era of B2B concentration may be coming to an end. The Internet opens up new possibilities for overcoming geographic distances, so organizations in the twenty-first century may cluster in "virtual space," rather than clustering so densely in geographic space.[17]

www.ism.ws

Another characteristic of organizational buyers is professionalism. Industrial goods are purchased by professional purchasing agents; in the United States many belong to the Institute for Supply Management (ISM), and there are similar organizations in other nations. Specialized organizations such as National Association of Buyers Agents in Canada, ORCAB (Organisation des Coopératives d'Achats pour les Artisans du Bâtiment), the National Association of Building Trades Buyers in France, or the international Institute of Chartered Shipbrokers also exist. Associated with professionalism is heightened formality in organizational purchasing and the use of a variety of buying instruments, such as quotations, proposals, purchase contracts, and bids.

Organizational consumers are often relatively price inelastic. But why should they be relatively insensitive to minor price changes? First, they often buy customized products that are inherently more expensive. Second, many buyers concentrate on long-term service and supply relationships with their sellers. These relationships help ensure a minimum of costly production downtime and reduce the costs of finding supplies. Third, organizational customers often require certain raw materials regardless of price fluctuations. No matter what, makers of aluminum cans require aluminum and governments require military uniforms. Fourth, organizational demand is derived from the demand for finished consumer goods. Petroleum refiners must buy oil to meet consumer demand for gasoline and heating oil.

A final characteristic of organizational buyers that is taking on increasing importance in the global marketplace is close customer–supplier relationships. In B2B marketing, buyers and sellers seek to extract advantage in the purchase process. However, many firms are finding that to compete effectively internationally, they must build interorganizational alliances. Because of the changing marketing environment, ongoing buyer–seller relationships, referred to as *relational exchanges,* have become more common.[18] Close supplier–customer cooperation is the norm in many nations and provides the industries and governments of such nations with competitive advantages. Newly industrialized countries in the Pacific Rim provide good examples of strong interorganizational alliances. Sometimes these groups are informally organized through the traditional Chinese idea of *guanxi,* loosely translated as "personal connections." And sometimes they are formally organized through interlocking firms like the Korean *chaebol* or Japanese *keiretsu.* Intraindustry alliances are also the norm in traditional businesses in Africa. Firms in a number of European Community countries also prefer intraindustry alliances to the pronounced competition more characteristic of the United States.[19]

If organizations are to develop lasting exchange relationships, they must adapt to each other's needs. Organizations adapt to each other because of power or trust.[20] The role of power in interorganizational relationships is very important. **Power** refers to *the ability of one partner in an exchange relationship to impose its preferences on the other party.* Power does not have to be used to be possessed; it is the potential that is important.[21] Power derives from having critical resources and from controlling alternative sources of those resources. Organizations respond to the demands of other organizations that control resources critical to them. We can refer to this as a **power-dependence** situation. Thus, big global retailers such as Wal-Mart and Carrefour have the power to impose requirements on their suppliers because of their financial and logistical resources.

Firms also adapt to each other to show their trust and commitment to the relationship. **Trust** refers to *one party's belief in the reliability and integrity of an exchange partner.* **Commitment** refers to *an enduring desire to maintain a valued relationship.* Commitment by industrial buyers to sellers is maintained by the costs of leaving, a perceived lack of alternatives to replace the relationship, and relational and social norms that build trust between buyers and sellers.[22] See Ethical Dilemma 13.1 for a cross-cultural view of trust and commitment in the B2B relationship.

Trust- and commitment-based adaptations are often reciprocal. Buyers and sellers adapt to each other. One organization may adapt a product to satisfy a customer. Another organization will adapt production processes to show commitment. These adaptations are also called *asset-specific investments.* They help to maintain buyer–seller relationships because it becomes costly to switch suppliers when such investments have been made. Reciprocal commitments to shared problem solving and information sharing, for example, are not based on power-dependence; instead, they are investments that strengthen relationships between organizations in expectation of positive future outcomes. Informal interorganizational relationships supplement and reinforce formal contracts.[23]

TYPES OF ORGANIZATIONAL PURCHASES

Organizational purchases can be distinguished by what is called their **buy class.**[24] We discuss three basic buy classes: new task buys, straight rebuys, and modified rebuys. **New task buys** are relatively rare, but the sale can be very large in dollar terms. The buying center for these buys tends to be large, solution of the problem is of paramount

The Binding Contract versus the Flexible Agreement

ETHICAL DILEMMA 13.1

In a B2B setting, the buyer and seller frequently engage in lengthy, complex negotiations. In Northern Europe and the United States, such a period of negotiations will be consummated as both parties sign a formal contract, and this contract is considered to be final and binding. Both parties to the contract will strive to fulfill the contract, no matter what the eventual gains and losses for their respective organizations.

In other parts of the world (e.g., South America, Asia, Southern Europe, Africa), the B2B negotiations may have a different outcome. Here, trust and commitment to the relationship are more important than the words on a contract. Both the buyer and seller expect that the final agreement might be altered in the future, depending upon the circumstances that eventually emerge. In other words, the original B2B agreement is not considered to be final and inflexible. Both parties to the agreement expect to adapt to evolving circumstances.

Of course, problems emerge when the parties to a B2B agreement come from different cultures. The Americans and the Northern Europeans are irritated when their business partners refuse to live up to the letter of the signed agreement. They expect parties to assess future risks before entering into the contract. In contrast, those from other regions can't understand why their foreign business partners insist on terms that are threatening to bankrupt their organizations!

Source: Personal communication with Dr. Warren French, I. W. Cousins Chair of Business Ethics, University of Georgia.

concern, and economic considerations are secondary. New buys are considered risky, and buyers are willing to consider many alternatives. Engineers often play a key role in these decisions.

A Japanese illustration of an industrial buying center and buying process for a new task buy is shown in Industry Insights 13.3. Note that three key individuals—the president, production chief, and foreman—as well as seven departments—financial department, sales headquarters, production department, new products development committee (NPDC), research staff, product development department, and marketing department—play roles in the process. The roles played by individuals and departments in the buying process differ. The NPDC engages in problem recognition, that is, the existence of an unmet need, and initiates the buying process. The research staff provides a general need description and, in so doing, plays an influencer role in the process. The production department coordinates the supplier's search and solicits proposals, in this case prototype machines, from potential suppliers. The NPDC includes marketing and the product development department, which influence the process through the NPDC. The production department plays a gatekeeping role by soliciting proposals from only a certain number of companies, perhaps including those from which the firm has purchased in the past. Research staff and the production chief play influential roles first in defining product specifications and then in testing the prototypes. Supplier selection and a purchase decision are made only after consultation, and perhaps negotiation, between the production chief, finance department, sales headquarters, and, of course, the president. Once a buy decision has been reached, the production department specifies the order routine for delivery with the supplier. Not shown in Industry Insights 13.3 is the final stage in the buying process, performance review, which determines whether the firm continues to buy from its chosen supplier, thus simplifying subsequent rebuying. If the firm is dissatisfied, a new buy procedure is initiated.[25]

Organizational Buying Behavior in Japan: Packaging-Machine Purchase Process

INDUSTRY INSIGHTS 13.3

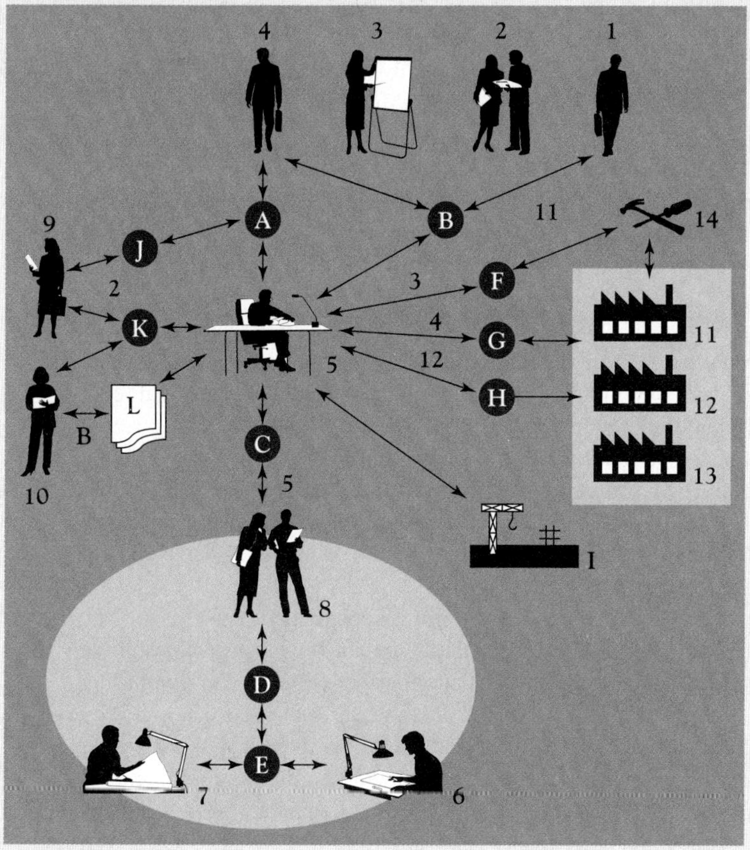

Source: Reprinted by permission of The Japan Economic Journal *23 (December 1980), p. 29, Nihon Keiza Shimbun, Inc.*

1. President
2. Finance department
3. Sales headquarters
4. Production chief
5. Production department
6. Product development department
7. Marketing department
8. New products development committee
9. Research staff
10. Foreman
11. Supplier A
12. Supplier B
13. Supplier C
14. Makers design and technical staff
    - a) Decision
    - b) Discussion of production and sales plans
    - c) Production of packing process plan
    - d) Request for consultation
    - e) Production of new product marketing plan
    - f) Discussion on design of prototype machine
    - g) Prototype machine order
    - h) Order placement
    - i) Overseas machine exhibitions
    - j) Request for testing of prototype machine
    - k) Production of basic design
    - l) Production of draft plans

The **straight rebuy** is the most common purchase situation. The purchasing agent is the primary influence, and the buying center is very small and quick to decide. To minimize purchase costs (e.g., information search, proposal solicitation and evaluation), buying organizations may seek to identify reliable sellers that deliver goods of consistent quality on time and for an agreed-upon price, thus minimizing their uncertainty. Loyalty plays a role in the process as well. Selling firms will work to convince their organizational customers of the virtue of engaging in straight rebuys for routine replacement of standardized items on a stable schedule at a stable price. Computerized, automated order systems have enabled firms to automate the straight rebuy process in many cases.[26]

The **modified rebuy** has a mix of new task and straight rebuy features. The buying center is somewhat larger and the purchasing agents somewhat less influential than for the straight rebuy. In modified rebuy situations, buyers sometimes revert to straight rebuy behavior, choosing known suppliers and thereby closing off opportunities for outside suppliers.

The extent to which organizations engage in each type of buy class depends on various factors, including environmental (e.g., the rate of technological change in an industry), organizational (e.g., the degree of hierarchy and centralization), and interpersonal (e.g., quality and character of interaction between organizations' selling and buying representatives).[27] Features of the purchase situation, including the newness of the problem to the buyer and the need for information, are the most important determinants of the buy-class decision. The size, formality, and membership of the buying center will vary depending on purchase risk, how frequently the organization encounters new tasks, and high information needs.[28]

The nature of organizational decision making varies, depending upon the specific buying situation. Thus, it is possible to identify the "type" of organizational purchase by considering the product category and by considering the nature of the purchasing organization. In the following section, we further illustrate the buy-class categories by considering three purchase decisions made by America Online, Inc. (AOL): (1) leasing office space (a new task buy), (2) ordering office equipment (a straight rebuy), and (3) purchasing a cluster of servers for Internet hosting (a modified rebuy). When understanding the type of organizational purchase, it is important to consider AOL's own needs, experiences, skills, capabilities, and business risks. At the same time, we consider the nature and expertise of the selling organizations (see B2B websites in the margins).

@ www.corp.aol.com

The decision by AOL to lease new office space in Paris, France, would be classified as a new task buy. Such a decision is not done with much frequency, and office space is not as standardized as some other product categories. Thus, it is relatively difficult to transfer knowledge and experience from one office space decision to the next. In addition, such a decision has important and long-lasting implications for the organization. Decision makers must meet the needs of the present-day organization, and they must plan strategically for the future. Since most corporate leases last more than five years and involve a major expenditure of funds, this decision is potentially risky and requires due diligence. The decision makers must make certain that the office space has all the facilities and technical equipment to house their organization. The AOL decision makers also must learn about the leasing company and its capabilities and services. Check out the websites for commercial realtors to get a sense of the services and expertise that they can provide to their corporate clients.

@ www.loopnet.com

In contrast, a decision by AOL to order office supplies would most often be classified as a straight rebuy. The organization would rely heavily upon past experiences and past vendors. From time to time, the purchasing department may solicit input from employees, users, and other key decision makers. But, in most situations, the office supplies would be ordered quickly and automatically.

www04.quillcorp.com

A B2B purchase that would fall in between these two extremes is AOL's decision to order a new cluster of servers. There is considerable risk involved in such a decision. If the new servers do not perform as advertised, then AOL's future could be placed into jeopardy. If Internet service to customers is interrupted over any considerable period of time, then a true crisis will emerge. The decision itself is relatively labor intensive. AOL decision makers will entertain formal presentations from a variety of vendors, and AOL managers must decipher how to prioritize their needs (e.g., with respect to price, technical support). Once a decision is reached, the organization must "live" with the choice for a period of time. But, at the same time, it is relatively easy for AOL to learn from past buying experiences. That is, the AOL buying center has considerable technical skills for evaluating computer hardware. They also have long-standing relationships with computer manufacturers, such as Sun Microsystems. As a result, the server purchase is classified as a modified rebuy for AOL. If the company making the purchase does not have AOL's technical sophistication and experience, then the buying task would be even more complicated and risky. Again, it is important to consider the situational and environmental influences on B2B purchases.

www.sun.com/servers/index.html

FAMILIES AND HOUSEHOLDS

Description

Domestic groups are perhaps the most widely distributed social unit. They comprise *a primary, involuntary unit of social life between the individual and the community.* Domestic groups vary in formality and the role of affect. Domestic groups are the most important unit of analysis for consumer behavior because they make most acquisition, consumption, and disposition decisions. Consumers in domestic groups decide how to choose household products and services and the amount of time to spend on different tasks and leisure activities. Because so many decisions are made in domestic groups, consumer market segmentation and targeting schemes should take domestic group structure and activities into account.

Domestic groups, families, and households differ. **Families** comprise *individuals related by blood, marriage, adoption, and emotional commitment.* However, we know from our own experience that family includes a broader range of people than the domestic group with whom we regularly reside, interact, and make consumption decisions. **Households** are another group, defined as *coresident, activity groups.* Although the terms *domestic group* and *household* are closely related, they are not necessarily the same. Some domestic groups may not share a home yet share consumption decisions. Households are often made up of family members but may also include **fictive kin,** *individuals informally adopted into a household as family members,* and nonkin. One research team found that 70 percent of African-American mothers surveyed in the United States had fictive kin as children.[29] The mother of one of the authors of this book grew up in a household comprising her mother, grandmother, sister, and a fictive kinsperson, known as M'amselle, to reflect her Belgian heritage. Does your household include any fictive kin? In the rest of the chapter, we will use the term *household* rather than *family* or *domestic group.*

Membership in Households

Membership in households varies depending on culture, class, ethnicity, and environmental influences. For example, the **nuclear family** composed of *a married couple and their children* is a common household form in many First World contexts, and it is becoming more so in many developing countries. However, the nuclear family was only briefly, if ever, the dominant form of domestic unit, even in the United States. The percentage of nuclear families in Triad nations varies substantially. About 27 percent of U.S. families, 33 percent of Kiwi families (residents of New Zealand), and 62 percent of Japanese families could be described as nuclear families.[30]

In many parts of the world, households are often composed of multiple generations of family members, and in some contexts joint households include the families of married adult brothers. These are termed the **extended family** households. The three-generation family was the norm until after WWII in much of east Asia, and the joint household persists in parts of south Asia.

In many parts of the less affluent world, poor households do best by engaging in extending strategies to increase their members. Nieces, nephews, brothers, sisters, and cousins are brought into the household around a married couple or a woman and her children. While extending is difficult and requires strict budgeting to meet expenses on food, the incremental productive labor of family members makes extended family household survival possible.

Coresidence and Dwellings

As indicated earlier, coresidence or cohabitation is one common way of defining households. In many U.S. states, lengthy coresidence is legally used to bind individuals together as family and define financial and other obligations. However, it is by no means uncommon for members of households to go on extended migrations. For example, long-distance, long-term male labor migration to obtain resources for household use is a fact of life for many poorer families in the LAW nations. Hence, coresidence alone cannot be used to define the household.[31]

Coresidence is important for marketers because it implies acquisition and maintenance of a dwelling—a home. The home is an increasingly important focus of consumer spending around the world. From a national sample of households in the Netherlands, researchers learned that households spent about 75 hours and over 2,000 guilders (US$862) a year on do-it-yourself maintenance activities. Home furnishing companies and specialized media devoted to the home may be found throughout the Triad countries and in many transitional and developing nations. As average household sizes shrink in the developed world, consumers furnish and maintain more dwellings. An example of a typical ad for home remodeling product that appeals to domestic life as lived is shown on the opposite page.

Households vary in the focus of their spending. For example, Japanese, Europeans, and middle Easterners tend to focus on interiors; North Americans often focus on exterior appearance as well. A room where guests are received may be the focus of spending in some cultures, such as among Greeks; private rooms may be the focus of spending by others. Some, like the British, neglect bathrooms; others make them splendid. Lower-middle-class North Americans prefer a homey looking dwelling. As suggested in Consumer Chronicles 13.2, expenditures on dwellings sometimes involve conspicuous consumption. And as Consumer Chronicles 13.3 suggests, for some people the home must reflect mystical associations. Household members' investments in the dwelling

The dwelling is an important focus of consumer spending.

help build loyalty to the household and also avoid conflict over alternative individual resource uses.[32]

Family Life Cycle

The **family life cycle** (FLC) is a useful conceptual tool for marketers and consumer policy advocates. The FLC is based on the idea that *domestic groups typically undergo a cyclical process of birth, growth, decay, and dissolution over time*. For marketers, an important implication is that domestic groups at each stage of the life cycle can be grouped into market segments with distinct needs, attitudes, and desires.

Exhibit 13.2 illustrates a developmental cycle for North American households. A person begins as a dependent and then moves through a sequence of household arrangements as time passes. Household types vary with the age of their members and the presence or absence of children. The frequency and sequence of stages vary across various North American subcultures. This model includes life-cycle stages that are appropriate for many upper-income domestic groups in Europe, Latin America, and Asia as well. It is probably not appropriate for many poorer urban domestic groups and certainly not for many developing nations where people make their livelihoods partly from farming. In both of these other contexts, extended, multiple-generation domestic units based on a variety of family ties are the norm.[33]

A Sri Lankan Household Builds a Carport

CONSUMER CHRONICLES 13.2

By the early 70s around 35 percent of all fishing houses in Ambakandawila [on the isolated north coast of Sri Lanka] were built of brick and tile. By the mid-70s this number had risen to over 50 percent. What was striking about these houses was their very gaudy and loud style and decoration and that their owners always compared them to other houses in Ambakandawila or other near-by villages. Thus A's house would have one more room than B's, and the reason it had one extra room would be simply to have one more room. Or C's house would have a carport not because they had a car or were likely to have a car—nor was a car likely to come to a house on top of a sand dune half a mile from the road—but because no one else in the village had a carport. One of the best examples of this sort of behavior was a house with an overhead water tank when the nearest pipe water was three miles away and the owner had no intention of installing a pump. The point about all these objects was simply to own them and for them to be displayed. The aim was to arouse jealousy in others. The prestige of these objects derived from their association with the Sinhalese middle class, yet these objects were never used in the way the middle class used them.

Source: R. L. Stirrat, "Money, Men and Women," in Money and the Morality of Exchange, *ed. Jonathan Parry and Maurice Bloch (Cambridge: Cambridge University Press, 1989), pp. 94–116. Reprinted with the permission of Cambridge University Press.*

Changing Household Segments and Demographic Trends

A number of demographic trends have emerged in the last decade in North America and other Triad nations. These trends have important implications for domestic unit structure and consumer behavior. One is a trend toward smaller households, including young people, the old, and the very old. This trend is observed in Great Britain, where 27.4 percent of households are composed of single persons, and in Japan, where 20 percent are singles. The same pattern is apparent in New Zealand, Australia, and many European countries. Larger households are still the norm in many LAW countries, although a shift toward smaller households may be discerned in the NICs like Taiwan. The result of this trend is an increased demand for basic household goods and services.[34]

Another demographic trend for First World countries is the increasing number of single-parent households. Single-parent households now account for at least 8.1 percent of all households in North America, 6.4 percent in Great Britain, and 9 percent in Australia. About 16.5 million never-married American women are now mothers, partly accounting for the growth in woman-headed households. They make up almost one-fourth of all unmarried women ages 18 to 44. Although poorer, less-educated, minority women constitute the greatest numbers of unwed mothers, the largest rates of increase are among white women, college-educated women, and professional managerial women who choose unwed motherhood. Demand for child care, other services, and convenience goods is linked to this trend toward single parenting.[35]

A third trend in First World countries is an overall aging of households. In many parts of the First World, declining birthrates, growing life expectancies, and youthful desires for independence have led to the emergence of a market segment that is likely to grow in importance throughout the 90s. Aging households may be found in both Triad and transitional countries; they comprised over 13 percent of Japanese households in 1994, for example. In the Triad these households are relatively well off; in transitional countries they tend to be poor. Indeed, in the United States, spending by older households has risen faster than for any other group. Older households need new forms of housing and are likely to spend more on various kinds of health-related products and services.[36]

Finally, later age at marriage and high rates of divorce (50 percent of first marriages) are also resulting in a diversification of household forms. A big increase in the category of "other households," including all sorts of blended and nonfamily arrangements, will challenge marketers who wish to target them. For example, recently in the United

Mystical Meanings of Home in Monterey Park, California

CONSUMER CHRONICLES 13.3

Escrow officer Catherine Chiou was working with a Chinese couple who were getting a great buy on a house they loved. But just two weeks into escrow (i.e., property is held in trust by a third party only to be turned over upon fulfillment of a condition), the couple abruptly backed out of the purchase. Chiou was not surprised. The couple's feng shui master had nixed the deal.

The ancient Chinese art of feng shui (pronounced "fung sui") takes the real estate maxim "location is everything" to a whole new plane. Feng shui links the placement of objects to fate. According to its tenets, each direction of the compass controls certain aspects of life. If you pay attention to the orientation of your house or office and the arrangement of your belongings and furnishings, you may have good feng shui. Luck, wealth, and health will follow. If you have bad feng shui, watch out. Bad luck, poor health, poverty, even death may overtake you. Literally, feng shui means wind and water. But to real estate agents and home builders it means dollars and cents. "It happens about four times a year," said Chiou, who has been with Century Escrow in Monterey Park since 1983. "People make an offer, get as far as escrow instruction, and then they have a feng shui master check it out." Chiou said she wishes people would check the feng shui before they get to escrow. But she never blames anyone who drops a deal because of unfavorable feng shui.

Source: Kirsten M. Lagatree, "The Power of Place," Los Angeles Times, *July 18, 1993, pp. K1, K6.*

States, there has been some interest in **boomerang kids,** *adult children who have returned to their parents' homes for reasons of financial insecurity or divorce.* Forty percent of young adults have experienced this boomerang.[37] A marketer could appeal to the boomerang kids using a three-step approach. First, the seller can convey the message that boomerang kids are not alone. There are many just like them. This message should be delivered in a spirit-lifting manner. Second, an attempt could be made to bring boomerang kids together. As an example, a restaurant could promote a "pink-slip" party (for people in transition between jobs), held at regular intervals and offering opportunities for networking. The third approach is to offer advice. One component of this advice might be to suggest the use of a specific product or service. For instance, online auction sites could target the boomerang kids, as a class of entrepreneurs. When faced with hard times, an increasing number of young people are looking to eBay as a source of quick cash, as they sell off items they no longer need.

U.S. households can be divided into nine main segments. Exhibit 13.3 shows the nine main household segments and how these are changing over time. These changes are consistent with changes elsewhere in the Triad nations.

How Marketers Use the Family Life Cycle

For marketers, households differentiated by the family life cycle represent promising market segments. Households' needs across FLC stages vary. Typically, households representing a small proportion of all households spend disproportionately on certain categories of goods and services. We provide a few examples in the following sections.[38]

MARRIED WITH CHILDREN In the United States, married couples with children accounted for 41.4 percent of grocery store sales in 1990, although they represented only 27 percent of the households.[39] Married couples with children 6 to 17 years old account for 49 percent of total spending on children's clothing and furnishings. Couples with school-age children, 14.3 percent of U.S. households, account for 21 percent of new-vehicle purchases. A third spending category, children's clothing, has a relatively obvious relationship to household segments. Households composed of married couples with children account for 65 percent of these expenditures. When children are present in the household, the probability of owning a personal computer increases. In 1997, 51 percent of the households with children owned computers, compared to 30 percent of households without children.[40] The ad for baby carriages illustrates an example of a need specific to this segment; the detail suggests this is a highly involving purchase for a segment of Italian households.

EMPTY NESTERS Segments whose importance will grow throughout the remainder of the century are the category of empty nesters and mature couples who tend to have

EXHIBIT 13.2

The Family Life Cycle

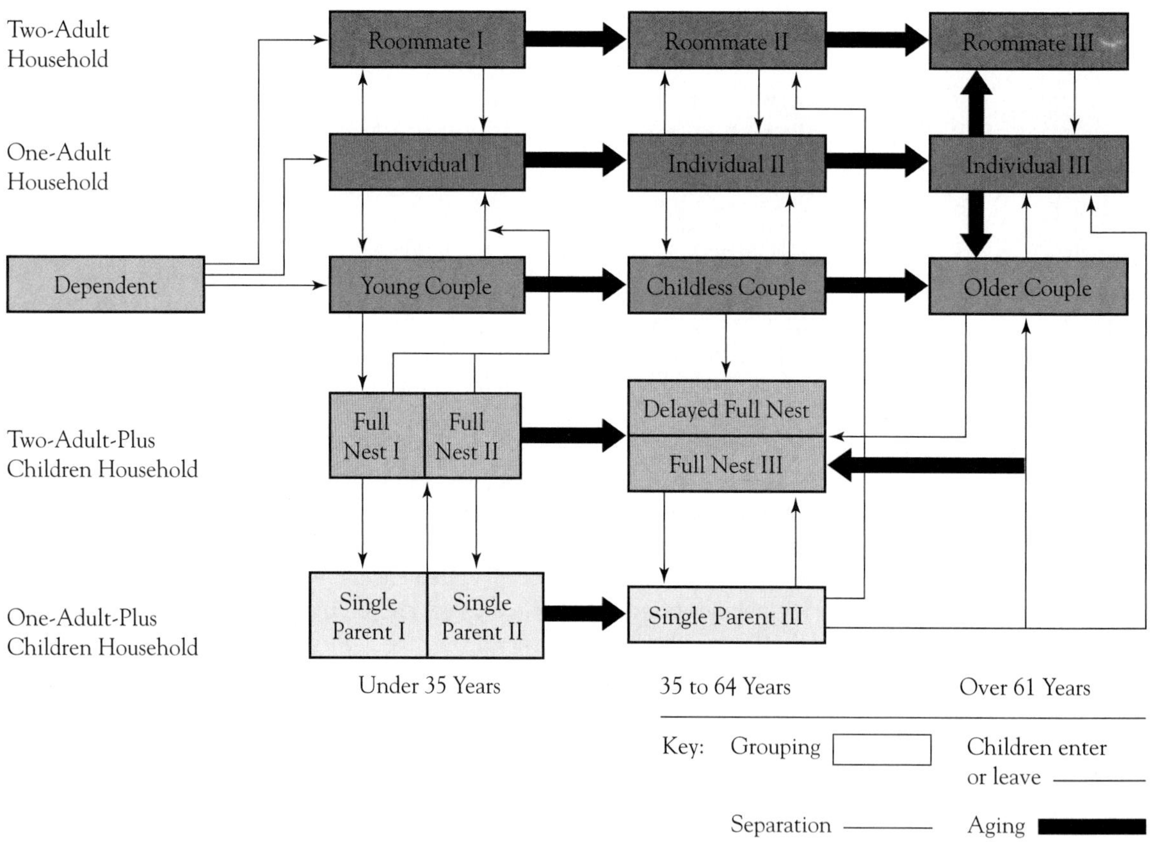

Source: Mary C. Gilly and Ben M. Ennis "Recycling the Family Life Cycle," in *Advances in Consumer Research*, vol. 9, ed. Andrew M. Mitchell (Ann Arbor, MI: Association for Consumer Research, 1982), pp. 271–76.

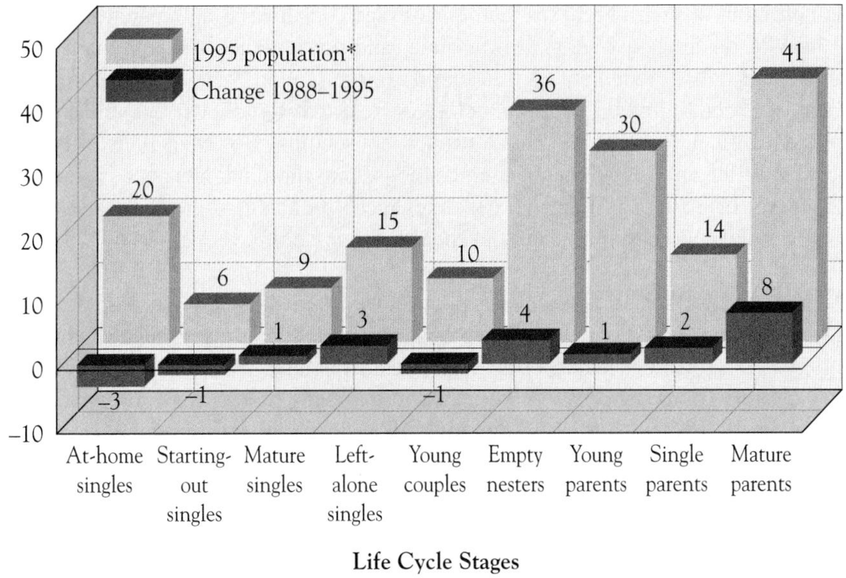

*1995 population expressed in millions.
Source: J. Walter Thompson and The U.S. Bureau of the Census.

EXHIBIT 13.3

U.S. Household Lifestyle Shifts in the Early 1990s.

a disproportionate share of disposable income. In the United States, 12.5 percent of households are composed of *empty nesters*—middle-aged adults, ages 55–64, mostly married (63.7 percent), living in households of three or less (71.2 percent), and without dependent children and the financial obligations they bring. Moreover, empty nesters had the highest net worth of all U.S. households, since many are homeowners. By comparison, 6 percent of Australian households fall into this category, and this is a growing segment in Japan. The empty-nester segment is growing fast and is attractive because of high disposable incomes. These households spend proportionately less on clothing, services, food, and transportation and more on retirement programs, life insurance, medical care, and leisure entertainment. Childless couples are a significant target market for the automobile industry. In the United States, in the early 1990s they purchased 25 percent of new vehicles.[41]

Fulfilling a need specific to an FLC segment.

SINGLE-PARENT FAMILIES Single-parent households have increased dramatically in numbers. Single-parent households face stretched budgets and severe time constraints; convenience goods appeal to them. Sole parents tend not to be brand loyal, and they are more experimental, impulsive, and style-conscious in their purchases than the average consumer. Single-parent households rely heavily on time-saving, microwaveable, and convenience food products. Single parents head only 5.8 percent of households in the United States but account for 13 percent of expenditures on children's clothes. Research has shown that children exert significant influence in single-female-headed households. However, their influence is product specific, varying with convenience foods, household maintenance products, and snack foods. Children's influence for maintenance products is somewhat elevated, perhaps given their increased role in household management.[42]

DYNAMIC HOUSEHOLDS We can expect to see more diverse household forms and consumption patterns. For example, co-housing, which first emerged in Denmark in the 1970s, is a form of cluster living where residents have their own homes but share meals, durable goods, labor, and other activities. Already there are 50 co-housing communities in the United States and hundreds more in the planning stages. How would you target a household in such a community?[43]

Implications for Marketing Management

The FLC provides marketers with clues about how to target offerings to various life-cycle segments. A key is to spot trends at early stages so that new product opportunities can be identified. The FLC also suggests "when" to market. For instance, empty nesters are likely to spend more money when they first enter the segment. At the same time, new households that enter the segment may have different needs and desires than those who have traditionally occupied the segment. Thus, it is important for organizations to implement a continuing program of consumer research in order to spot emerging trends. Another implication is that it is preferable to have a strategy that involves multiple segments of the FLC stages. That way, the company will be protected from future demand fluctuations. When a brand loses relevance to the new generation of a life-cycle stage, then the company may want to launch a new brand with a positioning that is more relevant to those just entering that life-stage segment.

@ www.cadillac.com

Consider General Motors' Cadillac brand. The Cadillac Motor Car Division of General Motors got its start in 1899 as the Detroit Automobile Company and was renamed Cadillac in 1902. In 1909, Cadillac was purchased by the young General Motors Corporation. Through the years, Cadillac was responsible for many innovations in the automotive industry, including the self-starter (1912), America's first V-8 engine (1914), safety glass as standard equipment (1929), and the world's first V-16 automobile (1930). Continuing through the twentieth century, Cadillac continued its emphasis on prestige and quality so that its brand name became the "standard of the world."[44]

@ www.lexus.com/luxury2_index.html

The average age of the typical Cadillac buyer keeps rising over time. In 1983, Cadillac controlled more than 50 percent of the U.S. luxury market, and the average age of the Cadillac buyer was approximately 62. Empty nesters were a primary target market.[45] However, by 1996, Cadillac's share of the market had declined to 15 percent, and the typical buyer was even more elderly.[46]

@ www.bmw.com

@ www.mbusa.com/brand/index.jsp

@ www.infiniti.com

From this perspective, Cadillac's target audience is dying off. As prosperous baby boomers enter the empty nest stage, they are not especially likely to consider the Cadillac brand. New entrants to the luxury car market are likely to buy a competing brand such as Lexus, BMW, Mercedes, or Infiniti. The new empty nesters associate Cadillac with the previous generation of empty nesters (their parents) who used the brand heavily. Therefore, Cadillac must shake off the perception of stodginess to entice this generation's dollars.

Note how Cadillac tries to adapt and appeal to empty nesters by introducing the Escalade, "the world's most powerful sport utility vehicle and the muscle to back it up." The division as a whole adopts a key promotional slogan: "a heritage reborn." In this way, Cadillac is able to refer to their illustrious past ("the heritage") and to their forward-looking image (e.g., "the rebirth"). Nonetheless, Cadillac's problems illustrate the difficulties associated with a corporate entity trying to remain trendy and innovative across the generations. In some respects, each succeeding generation wants a new brand to represent their image and achievements. There is no guarantee that the empty nester of 2003 will have so much in common with the empty nester of 2023. Marketers ever face the challenge of trying to hit a moving target.

And in this corner, in all black

Escalade was awarded the title of the world's most powerful SUV and it has the muscle to back up its bold, distinctive style. Take a closer look at this impressive Cadillac.

HOUSEHOLD CONSUMPTION ACTIVITIES

Households organize themselves to carry out a range of activities, many of which have implications for marketers. These activities include socialization, production, resource pooling, consumption, and disposition. We provide examples of household consumption activities throughout this book. In Chapter 19 we discuss disposition. Here we will discuss consumer socialization, production, and pooling.

Consumer Socialization

Households are a primary site for the socialization of young people. Products and services are often positioned to appeal to this household activity, as in the ad for music schools from an Australian weekly magazine, shown below.

In addition, much consumer socialization occurs within domestic groups. **Consumer socialization** refers to *imparting the values, norms, beliefs, and procedures associated with behaving as competent consumers in a given cultural setting.* Typically, we speak of parents or adults as the agents of socialization and children as the recipients of socialization.[47] Of course, it's more complicated than that. For example, young adults often may feel that they are educating their parents about new trends in the marketplace (in areas where their parents have lost touch). This pattern of socialization is especially apparent with regard to the Internet and other aspects of the information economy. Children's influence increases as they age, a finding consistent with research showing U.S. children's consumer decision-making skills are quite highly developed by adolescence. Children's influence is lessened in households with highly educated mothers with greater gender-role autonomy.

This Australian ad recognizes that household consumption behavior is directed toward children.

This ad recognizes children's influence in household consumption.

The Pokémon vitamin ad shown here pokes a little fun at the knowledgeable and influential child.[48] In developing countries and NICs, and even in Europe, which is more wedded to tradition than the newer nations of North America and the Pacific, young people are often more innovative than their parents and lead the way in the adoption of new products. For example, MTV Europe caters to a pan-European youth market with a single set of music and programs. In highland Ecuador, intergeneration conflict over the consumption of store-bought bread versus homemade barley gruel is symptomatic of a more general trend toward intergenerational conflicts associated with economic development and modernization in the less affluent world.[49]

Consumer socialization takes two forms: **direct socialization** in which *parents purposively train children in consumer knowledge;* and **indirect socialization** which *involves more passive learning through modeling of children's behaviors based on parental models.* Although parents are not the only influence on children, they do determine the degree to which their children will be exposed to other socialization sources such as television, salespeople, and peers. Consumer Chronicles 13.4 indicates that U.S. households vary in their use of direct and indirect consumer socialization efforts.[50] Research in a First World context suggests that direct consumer socialization may be characteristic of upper-class households, whereas lower-class households may focus on discussions about brand names. Middle-class households may focus on attributes of products such as price.[51] Experience in East Asian and African contexts suggests that indirect socialization is characteristic of the majority of consumers. Given these differences in socialization style, marketers may wish to direct different kinds of communication at different household segments. For example, preserving brand quality by associating it with stable brand names may be consistent with lower-class household socialization style.

Many studies have explored advertising and other types of mass media as socialization agents. Another way in which consumer socialization occurs is through **co-shopping.** Co-shopping involves *children accompanying their parents on shopping trips.* It is a good example of indirect socialization. Visiting market places, boutiques, and malls provides children with opportunities to absorb the nuances of products, prices, negotiating behaviors, market settings, times, and locations for consumption. Despite the difficulties they encounter, a majority of U.S. parents (58.4 percent) of children between the ages of 6 and 11 report that their children accompany them on major grocery shopping trips with some regularity. U.S. parents who engage in more frequent co-shopping with their children also place more value on their children's input in family consumer decision making and take a more direct role in guiding their children's consumer development.[52]

Production Activities

Most households engage in **direct** or **indirect production** activities to acquire goods for their own sustenance. In the LAW nations, direct production of goods for household survival might involve building a shelter, growing food, or, as in the Navajo

Parental Style and Consumer Socialization

CONSUMER CHRONICLES 13.4

U.S. research demonstrates that parental style helps explain whether socialization is direct or indirect and the amount of influence the household has in consumer socialization as compared to external sources of influence such as peers, teachers, and media. Five different parental styles are described that vary on warmth, restrictiveness, anxiety, and emotional involvement. The five styles are Authoritarian, Permissive, Rigid Controlling, Authoritative, and Neglecting.

Authoritarian parents believe in parental omnipotence. They show little nurturance and encouragement of interaction, expect relatively little mature behavior, enforce rules in a strict and limiting manner, and value conformity. Authoritarian parents believe their children have few rights. They have very defined expectations for their children's development, and they are very concerned with setting consumer goals and refereeing the information children receive from television and other media. They grant very limited consumption autonomy.

Authoritatives, like Permissives, are warmer than other parents. Authoritative parents encourage children to verbalize feelings more than Authoritarian and Neglecting parents. They foster responsibility less than Rigid Controlling and Neglecting parents. They favor placing early maturity demands on children more than other groups with the exception of the Rigid Controlling parents. They are the most restrictive group and strongest proponents of strict discipline. They attempt to enrich the child's environment with cultural and educational activities. They interact with children through co-shopping and asking children's opinions.

Permissive parents encourage communication but regard themselves as resources and want their children to experience the world, including the consumer world, with minimal interference. They interact with children through co-shopping and asking children's opinions. They grant greater consumption autonomy than other groups.

As you might infer, Neglecting parents do not encourage verbalization and tend to avoid communication. They don't engage in much direct socialization and don't referee or restrict information received from other media.

Source: Les Carlson and Sanford Grossbart, "Parental Style and Consumer Socialization of Children," Journal of Consumer Research *15 (June 1988), pp. 77–94.*

vignette, raising sheep for meat and wool. We return to direct production in "You Make the Call" at the end of the chapter. Many households, especially in more developed economies, engage in production activities that indirectly produce sustenance for the household. That is, the production activities are used to acquire resources that are then exchanged for needed goods.

Not all direct production activities have disappeared in First World households, and some are actually re-emerging. For example, as in the Mrs. Smith's advertisement shown on page 564, family meal preparation is an important production activity to many households. Kitchen appliances and gadgets constitute a significant share of all U.S. household spending, even though many households spend almost as much on meals taken outside the home as inside the home.[53] Restoring old cars and machinery, sewing quilts, and doing needlepoint are production activities that have inspired specialized retailing and marketing media.

Resource Pooling

It is important to understand how households pool their resources. Through this process, the household accumulates funds for use in the marketplace and for other uses (e.g., investments). Household members take on various decision roles during the pooling

Appealing to the productive function of household consumption.

process, as the domestic unit mobilizes and allocates resources. Here, we introduce several household resource allocation models, using a technique called **household resource mapping.** In essence, this technique creates a flow chart to describe the source of funds in a household and to indicate key decision makers. Specific product purchases are indicated on the map to show who is making key marketplace decisions.

All households face the problem of allocating scarce resources to competing projects. Mapping can help marketers distinguish between pooling models that households often take for granted. A combination of mapping household funds and flows could help in tailoring marketing programs to the needs and decision-making styles of particular types of households. The following descriptions of resource models will give you an idea of how much variety there is in how households manage funds. As you review these models, consider how your household pools resources.

ANGLO-AMERICAN HOUSEHOLD RESOURCE MODEL Exhibit 13.4 illustrates what we might call the Anglo-American model of household resource allocation. In this model, all cash and labor resources flow into a general fund. A portion of this fund is drawn on for necessities, determined by Engel's law (introduced in Chapter 2). The household head apportions the leftover to other uses. Investments, for example, include the purchase of a home, securities, education expenses, or even exchanges that link household resources between households. This model covers different kinds of household types, including patriarchal households, lower-income extended African-American households that may be headed by matriarchs, and entrepreneurial overseas

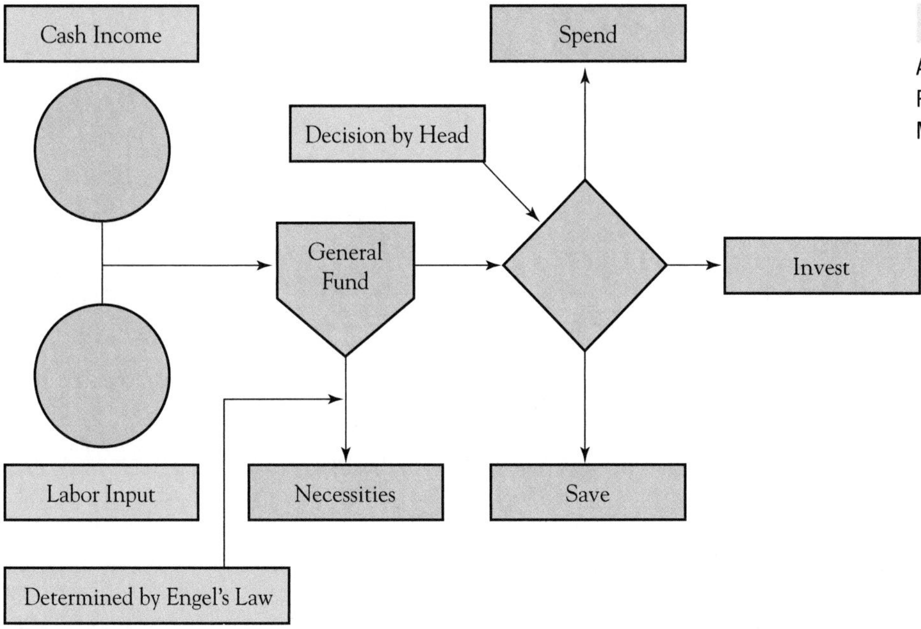

EXHIBIT 13.4

Anglo-American Household Resource Management Model

Source: Adapted from Richard R. Wilk, "Decision Making and Resource Flows within the Household: Beyond the Black Box," in *The Household Economy: Reconsidering the Domestic Mode of Production*, ed. Richard R. Wilk (Boulder, CO: Westview Press, 1989), p. 32.

Chinese households. When positioning products for market segments characterized by this model, marketers should target the household head.[54]

ASHANTI HOUSEHOLD RESOURCE MODEL We can call another common model the Ashanti resource allocation model, after the Ashanti people of Ghana. Ashanti spouses maintain a high degree of autonomy and do not necessarily share a dwelling. Husbands earn income from farming, women from trading. Each decides on some proportion of their funds that will be committed to the household's operating expenses. Wives usually contribute more to household maintenance, whereas husbands contribute to the household's capital equipment and durable goods. In addition, both husbands and wives should "invest" in their children, but wives and their lineages have much greater responsibility in this regard than do husbands. Spouses' commitments to the household vary with the emotional bonds between the two.[55] Something like this Ashanti model of pooling might apply to some dual-income, no-children (DINK) households, nonfamily households shared by roommates, or gay households. When positioning products for market segments characterized by this model, marketers should target adults in the households separately.

WORKING-CLASS ENGLISH HOUSEHOLD RESOURCE MODEL Exhibit 13.5 shows what we can call the working-class English household resource model. Here, the husband splits his income, keeping part but giving most to his wife as a housekeeping fund. A small part of his discretionary income goes to personal expenditures and some for occasional purchases of durable goods and investments. The husband's contribution and the wife's wages go to housekeeping, with an overflow returning for the wife's personal expenses. Children's earnings are turned to their mother, who allocates some

EXHIBIT 13.5

Working-Class English Household Resource Management Model

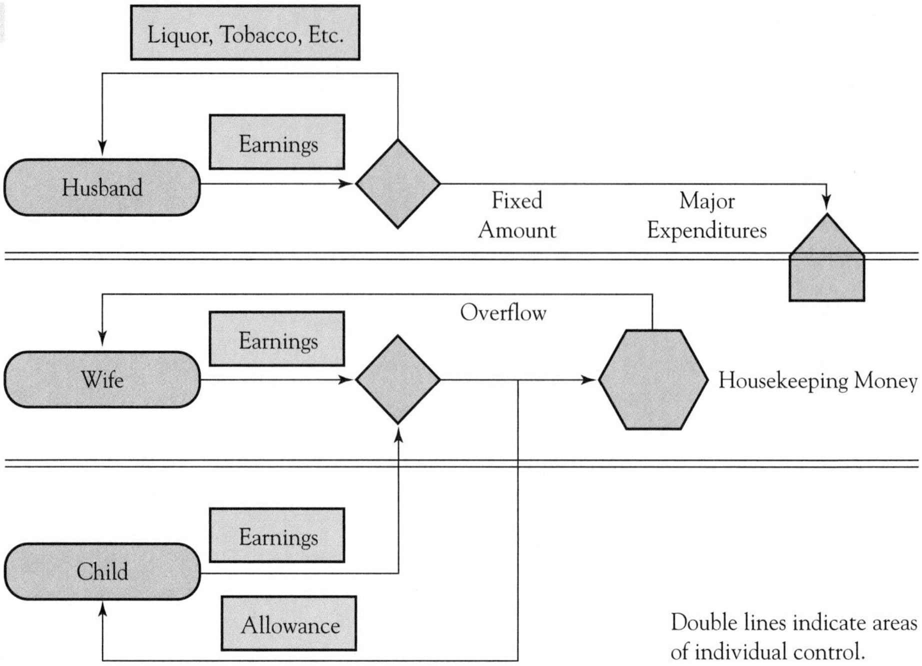

Source: Adapted from Richard R. Wilk, "Decision Making and Resource Flows within the Household: Beyond the Black Box," in *The Household Economy: Reconsidering the Domestic Mode of Production*, ed. Richard R. Wilk (Boulder, CO: Westview Press, 1989), p. 39.

back to the children as their allowance and the rest is used for housekeeping expenses. This model of resource flows and decision points suggests targeting the female household manager for many products, but there is scope for the exercise of interpersonal influence over decisions based on contributions to household resource pools. This model is not so different from the traditional Japanese household model, in which "salarymen" turn over their earnings to their wives for management.[56]

Most of the world's households probably lie somewhere between a resource model with one fund managed by the household head and one with no household fund. These models neglect the fact that resources are sometimes pooled across households, as in the Navajo family's truck purchase in the opening vignette. This is also true of the poor, of single-parent households, and of old and young family members who live in different households.[57]

HOUSEHOLD DECISION MAKING

Moral Framework for Decisions

In contrast with other organizations, household resource allocation and consumption decisions are often based on altruism and kinship—that is, they are moral rather than economic decisions.[58] Institutionalized kinship ties help to create a **moral economy** of *resource sharing, altruism, and mutual accommodation in purchase and consumption.* For example, Tommy's new bicycle is not purchased to increase the efficiency of the household but to make Tommy happy.[59]

One moral criterion for resource allocation that is particularly important in many households is fairness, or equity. Of course, what is fair is likely to be defined quite differently between different cultures. Nevertheless, individual consumption decisions are evaluated in terms of household members' feelings about the overall fairness of consumption decisions.[60]

Decision Roles and Decision-Making Styles

Each household member is influenced by background conditions, including culture, social class, and ethnicity. These conditions tend to determine individuals' attitudes concerning lifestyle norms (e.g., valued ends and acceptable means of achieving them), gender norms, and age-role norms. These norms interact with specific situational factors to determine appropriate behavior. Households negotiate purchase and consumption decisions within a given cultural and economic setting.

A greater number of household members are likely to be involved with significant household consumption decisions in more developed societies. In these societies, the number of market-based consumption choices is greater, and household income is higher. Consumer knowledge is also more widely distributed. Recognizing that households operate as consuming units, many firms target entire families with promotional materials, including Kmart, Hilton Hotels, and DaimlerChrysler, maker of minivans; even the resort town Las Vegas, Nevada, does so.[61]

In general, households act as **cooperative groups.** They are cooperative groups because the members' primary goals are compatible. In a family these shared primary goals are likely to concern affiliation, security, and trust. Studies of family decision making emphasize couples' cooperative concern for each other's preferences and for fairness. Families make compromises to maintain long-term relationships. One sort of solution is the "second-choice" solution. If household members cannot agree on a first choice, they may settle for each other's second choice. The underlying logic is that the group chooses the product alternative that perturbs individual preferences the least.[62]

In looking at household members' **decision roles** in the acquisition process, we can distinguish both roles and decision-making styles. The roles include the six roles identified for organizational buying centers (see page 547) as well as the caretaker role, the household member who services, cleans, and maintains products or services, sometimes across generations.[63]

Household decisions are well captured in the Calvin cartoons shown on page 568. In the first, Calvin is playing the role of initiator, hoping that his "goo-goo" eyes will persuade his mother, the decision maker, about his desire for a flame thrower. In the second, Calvin's mother plays initiator and gatekeeper, persuading Calvin's father of the wisdom of a joint purchase decision, a VCR. The intended VCR consumer, Calvin, is seemingly unaware of the decision making going on around him.

Household members' decision roles vary by authority structure, product category, and stage of the decision-making process. Distinguishing these roles helps marketers more effectively tailor marketing communications to the preferences and values of particular role players within the household. Thus, one study found English wives more concerned with the stylistic aspects of a new-home purchase, husbands with the financial dimensions, although shared decision making was reported. In Kenya, recruiting women to the nation's family planning staff is an effective strategy for reaching wives and daughters who are likely to be initiator, gatekeeper, buyer, and prime user of family planning aids.[64]

Consumer researchers ask what kinds of decisions are made by a group or coalition in the household, called **syncretic,** or joint, **decisions;** what kinds are made by a single household member, usually the husband or wife alone, called **autonomic decisions;**

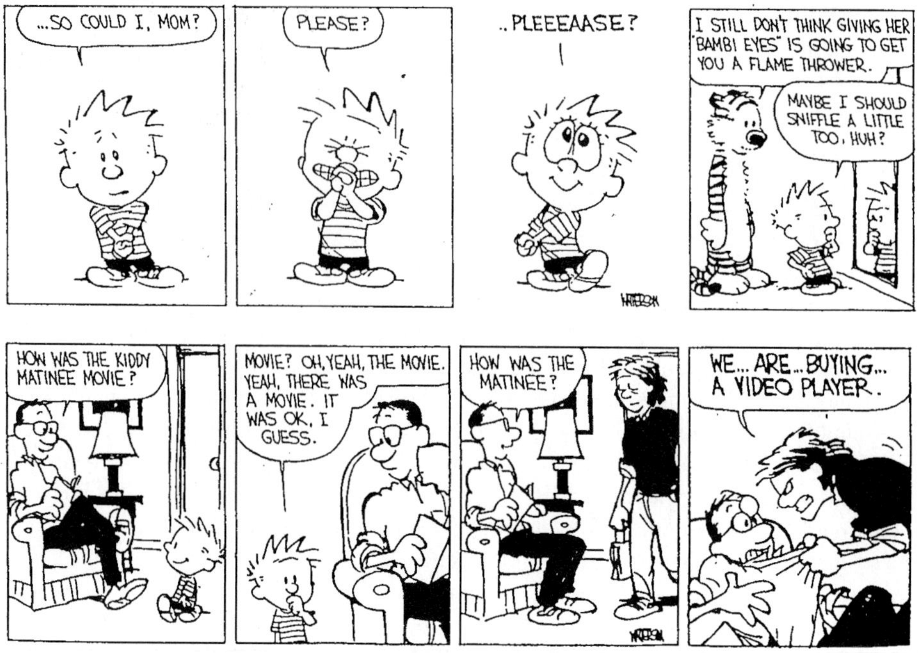

Illustrating household decision roles.

Source: CALVIN AND HOBBES © Watterson. Reprinted with permission of Universal Press Syndicate.

and what kinds are made with one spouse dominant in the process.[65] See the coalition strategy that Samir and his sister use in Consumer Chronicles 13.5.

Past research has shown that whether a decision is syncretic or autonomic depends on two types of variables. The first type consists of variables such as family life cycle, socioeconomic status, and lifestyles. The second type consists of situational factors such as perceived risk, importance of purchase, and time pressure. Members of households mention that the greater competence of one partner, preference for dividing responsibilities in household management, greater importance of the decision to one of the spouses, being too busy to decide together, and peer group norms are primarily responsible for autonomic decisions. Decisions tend to be autonomic for households with either no or grown-up children, in low or middle socioeconomic classes, and with the wife in some blue-collar occupations. Social class, education, income, family size, and the wife's employment status are all factors that influence whether a family makes syncretic or autonomic decisions. Attitudinal variables such as gender-role orientation and locus of control (whether or not members believe that events are dependent on their own behavior or not) also influence decision making. One study showed that women with modern gender-role attitudes were more likely to have their own checking accounts and individual credit card accounts, examples of autonomic behavior. Joint checking and savings accounts were related to lower incomes, whereas higher incomes were related to joint investments.

Within different product categories, role structures vary by the nature of the decision to be undertaken or the phase of the decision process. Products in the decision-making domain of men and women partners tend to be quite stable over time, but as gender roles become more flexible, decision making becomes more complex across households.[66]

Decision-making styles will vary with the quality of household interactions between parents and children. Children play influencing roles in democratic and permissive households, for example. Decision-making styles also vary with communication styles within the household: socio-oriented or concept-oriented, for example. **Socio-oriented communication** styles favor *adherence to conventional norms of authority and preservation of the domestic status quo.* Socio-oriented communication may be found in authoritarian households. **Concept-oriented communication** is *more egalitarian and favors a flow of information between all household members.* Democratic and permissive households favor concept-oriented communications. Household decision-making and communication styles also vary with culture, class, situational factors, gender-role orientation, and product category.[67]

When household members' perceptions and attitudes differ, conflict arises. The household then employs **conflict management strategies.** These strategies may include conflict-avoidance or conflict-resolution techniques that may affect decision making, purchase decisions, and satisfaction.[68] Some contentious household decisions are not made jointly; instead, individuals pursue their own decisions while attempting to minimize conflict. Although husband and wife may end up thinking they made a decision together, they actually pursued a "disjointed, unstructured, and incremental strategy," the main goal of which was to "muddle through" and keep the marriage going, whatever the actual decision reached.[69]

CONSUMER CHRONICLES 13.5

Syncretic Decision Making in Goa, India

Samir is 16 years old, and he lives with his middle-class family in a small town in Goa, India. His mother does not work outside of the home, and (as decider and purchaser) she makes most of the decisions about the household consumables. Samir could buy his own brand of toothpaste, but often he does not get around to it. So, frequently, he uses brands that he does not necessarily prefer. As the eldest son, Samir is guaranteed that his opinion will be considered in any household purchase that he wants to get involved with. However, Samir's father is the head of the household, so he has the final say in all matters. If Samir's younger sister wants to get involved, she is wise to consider a strategy of coalition building. For instance, when she wanted the family to purchase a new CD player, she first convinced Samir that such a purchase was a good idea. Then, the two of them together convinced their mother. Finally, as a group, all three approached the father. They find that this lobbying strategy is almost always successful!

To what extent do the actions of marketers and advertisers disrupt family harmony? See Ethical Dilemma 13.2.

Role Specialization

One way households cope simultaneously with individual interest and potential disagreements in purchase and consumption decisions is through **role specialization.** That is, in certain product or service domains, household members agree that they may make autonomic decisions without consulting other household members. For example, one member of the household may shop for groceries with only special requests as input from other family members. Special occasions may lead to autonomic decision making.[70]

Household members' role specialization in consumption choices is likely to be more highly developed in First World contexts where there are more consumption choices to be made in the marketplace. However, there is ample evidence of specialization of tasks between husbands and wives in most national contexts.

Role specialization may be differentially distributed over roles in the buying process. In U.S. households, children between the ages of 6 and 11 are considered experts in the categories for which they are the primary consumers. In approximately one out of

Sweets and Salty Snacks

ETHICAL DILEMMA 13.2

For many families, harmony is both a core value and a desired end state. As discussed in the text, some family members will forgo their first choice in the marketplace for the sake of the family's overall welfare and happiness. Given this state of affairs, is it ethical for marketers to appeal to children in a way that may threaten the harmony of the family?

It is well known in perceptual theory that bright, bold colors are inherently attractive to children. At the same time, children are enamored with cartoon characters, many of whom they watch on TV or see in movie theaters. Marketers utilize these bright hues and the allure of the cartoon character to promote such products as candy, presweetened breakfast cereal, and salty snacks. Some parents, on grounds of health and nutrition, strive to limit their children's intake of these very same products.

What should be the standards for marketing to children? Do you recall any disagreements in your family about the household purchase of snacks, cereals, and sweets? If so, how were these disputes resolved?

four such households, the child is credited with an expert role in purchasing snacks, ice cream, macaroni and cheese, corn and tortilla chips, soft drinks, and frozen pizza. As suggested in the Pokémon vitamin ad shown earlier, children may not often serve in the formal role of purchaser, decision maker, initiator, information seeker, or ultimate consumer. Nonetheless, they frequently exert tremendous influence on the use of household resources. In Islamic countries in West Africa, unmarried girls also have important household purchasing roles. In these contexts, it is often because of negative public attitudes toward married women appearing in public places such as the marketplace. Marketers need to tailor their targeting and promotional activities to match household role specializations.[71]

Perceived **role overload** is a situation where competing demands on the consumer's time and energy become overwhelming. Role overload may influence participation in particular purchase decisions and may lead to handing over some purchase decisions to another family member.[72] The increased role burden of professional women spills over onto teenage girls. In the United States, one-third of teen females and one in five teen males do some of the family's major food and grocery shopping.[73] Marketers must acquire a clear understanding of which household members are involved in an acquisition decision and tailor marketing communications to appeal to all concerned household members.

Gender-Role Orientation

Gender-role orientation, *the behavioral standards and cultural norms that define appropriate behavior for men and women in their society,* influences the household decision-making process. Where inegalitarian gender-role orientation prevails, we find a higher incidence of autonomic, or one-spouse-dominant, decisions, typically male dominance. This reflects a higher level of gender-role specialization in the household. Adherence to culturally prescribed gender-role orientations may increase an individual's influence over decisions considered to be within his or her domain. In the First World, it is possible to identify a trend. Women's influence in household decision making is increasing. Still, there are differences. One study found roles more highly structured by gender in a Dutch sample than in an American sample. As gender-role orientations become more egalitarian, a higher incidence of joint and one-spouse-dominant (male or female) purchase decisions occurs.[74]

Some generalizations may be drawn with respect to household decision making cross-culturally. In every cultural context, some decision situations are believed to conform to either masculine or feminine roles. In more developed consumer societies, the resources that a spouse brings to a marriage affect his or her relative decision-making power. Variations in a nation's economic and social development can also explain some patterns in household decision making. That is, LAW nations tend to exhibit greater male bias in household decision making, whereas Triad nations tend to exhibit more egalitarian household decision making. Joint decision making is more common in more developed consumer societies. Of course, this generalization does not hold in contexts with a significant number of female-headed households, such as Jamaica or Ghana. In attempting to define household purchasing decisions cross-culturally, researchers need to investigate a number of product categories, since decision-making behavior varies across categories.[75]

OTHER CONSUMING COLLECTIVES

Examples of consuming collectives other than business organizations, households, and families are endless. In the United States, a Pop Warner football league raises money by selling Fourth of July fireworks to purchase uniforms and equipment for their team. A family reunion group rents a large block of hotel rooms at a rural conference center. In Sierra Leone, West Africa, a women's saving association takes up a collection so that each woman can purchase cloth to make matching dresses for a public celebration. In Indonesia, male members of a neighborhood congregation give 10 percent of their earnings to support a popular cleric and build a modest mosque. In highland Mexico, members of the village saint's cult purchase new clothing for the images of saints in their local church and buy food and beverages to host their annual village festival.

One interesting and prevalent buying collective is the home shopping party, typically organized among women but sometimes including both genders. They originated in the United States in the 1950s by companies such as Tupperware and Avon; however, these firms have found new success in LAW markets such as Mexico, Asia, and the Middle East. At the same time, these collectives are declining in First World markets, although home lingerie parties have given the form a boost.

There are several important points to be made about buying collectives. First, all of them can probably be described in terms of the six main dimensions we mentioned at the outset of this chapter. For example, some of these groups may be formal organizations with a written charter, such as a Boy Scout or Girl Guide troop; others may be purely informal networks, such as the home shopping group or alumnae of a particular school or graduating class. Groups are likely to exhibit an internal division of labor in regard to roles in the purchasing process. Volunteers who organize a reunion of some particular affinity group may, for instance, exert special control over the choice of mementos or gifts purchased by the groups as a whole. Next, marketers may wish to target such collectives explicitly since their aggregate demand for particular goods and services may be significant. Further, home shopping clubs have been effective because of the bandwagon effects they produce. Aggregate sales are pushed higher than they might otherwise be by competition and status motives within the groups. Finally, policymakers and consumer activists might be interested in such groups for the uniqueness of their expertise and collective vulnerability to persuasive appeals.[76]

SUMMARY

In this chapter we discuss two important categories of groups: organizational consumers and households. Groups vary in terms of their membership and structure and their decision-making style and organization. They mobilize resources in order to realize consumption choices. Their consumption choices involve a mix of motives or reasons. Group members play different roles in the purchase process. Each group has a cultural history that influences purchase decisions.

Organizational consumers constitute an enormous market. Successful B2B marketing involves identification of and communication with participants in buying centers. Because of changing environmental demands, an area of increasing importance to marketers is an understanding of ongoing buyer–seller relationships. Three basic buy classes can distinguish organizational purchases: new task buys, straight rebuys, and modified rebuys.

Because so many decisions are made in domestic groups, their structure and shifts in their structure have significant implications for marketing. Four trends in household structure have emerged in the Triad nations: smaller households, increasing numbers of single-parent households, aging of households, and diversification of household forms. Coresidence or cohabitation is one common way of defining households. Coresidence is important to marketers because it requires acquisition and maintenance of a dwelling. An important tool for marketers and social policy activists is the family life cycle. Domestic groups at each stage of this cycle can be grouped into market segments with distinct needs, attitudes, and desires.

Domestic groups carry out a range of activities, including socialization, production, and resource pooling. Much, but not all, consumer socialization occurs within domestic groups. Consumer socialization takes two forms: direct and indirect socialization. Direct production of goods is most often associated with less developed economies. Greater indirect production activities characterize many First World and newly industrialized countries' households. There are big differences both between and within cultures in how households allocate resources.

Households generally act as cooperative groups. Studies on family decision making emphasize that conflict resolution is dominated by couples' cooperative concern for each other's preferences and for fairness. Changes in household structure and organization may lead to role conflicts, especially conflicts between work, family, and individual interests.

In addition to organizational consumers and households, there are various other kinds of consuming collectives. Most of them can be described in terms of the dimensions used to describe organizational and household consumer behaviors.

KEY TERMS

affect 543
autonomic decisions 567
boomerang kids 557
buy class 549
buying centers 546
commitment 549
concept-oriented communication 569
conflict management strategies 569
consumer socialization 561
cooperative groups 567
co-shopping 562
decision roles 567
direct production 562
direct socialization 562
domestic groups 553
extended family 554
families 553
family life cycle 555
fictive kin 553
formal groups 541
gender-role orientation 570
group 540
group size 541
heroes 545
household resource mapping 564
households 553
indirect production 562
indirect socialization 562
informal groups 541
life transition rituals 546
membership structure 540
mission statements 544
modified rebuy 552
moral economy 566
new task buys 549
nuclear family 554
organizational culture 543
organizational stories 545
performances 546
power 549
power-dependence 549
primary groups 542
purchasing power 541
role overload 570
role specialization 569
secondary groups 542
socio-oriented communication 569
straight rebuy 552
syncretic decisions 567
total institutions 542
trust 549
voluntary or involuntary membership 542

REVIEW QUESTIONS

1. Select an organization and characterize it in terms of membership structure, organization, resources, motives and goals, roles, and culture.
2. Using yourself as an example, characterize the groups you belong to in terms of whether they are formal or informal, membership is voluntary or involuntary, and interpersonal contact is primary or secondary. Now consider your decision role in any two of those groups. Is your decision role influenced by these factors? Explain.
3. Mission statements can help create and convey organizational culture. Below is the mission statement for The Nature Conservancy, a nonprofit U.S. corporation, formed for scientific and educational purposes.

   > The mission of The Nature Conservancy is to preserve plants, animals, and natural communities that represent the diversity of life on Earth by protecting the lands and waters they need to survive.

   What cultural values does this mission statement reflect? In what ways do you feel it might impact the culture at The Nature Conservancy? Be as specific as you can. For example, how might the mission statement influence purchase orders for raw materials to print their magazine?

4. Stories and heroes are often used to convey an organization's values and beliefs. Use an often-told story from your family or from an organization you now belong to (i.e., sorority or fraternity, student AMA chapter), and illustrate the connection between the story and the organization's culture.
5. How do the following buying situations affect the organization's buying-decision process?
   a. Purchase of a custom-designed machine to manufacture a key component part for a new toy the company is introducing later in the year.
   b. Purchase of a dedicated copier for the fifth floor office staff who have been going to the fourth floor to complete their copying.
   c. This month's purchase of particle board used in construction of inexpensive home office furniture.
6. How might the buying decision for a computer system differ between a large electronics firm and a family?
7. How would you use the family life-cycle phases depicted for North America in marketing the following?
   a. Cars
   b. Vacations
   c. Major appliances
   d. Pianos
8. Develop a resource map for your household. How could this map help marketers trying to target your household with products and services?
9. Describe in detail a recent purchase decision made by your family or household. Be sure to include decision roles, decision-making and communication styles, conflict management strategies (if any), and household satisfaction with the purchase.

YOU MAKE THE CALL

BUYING GENETICALLY MODIFIED SEED

The dusty, sleepy seed market on the North China plain in Baoding seems worlds away from any technological revolution. But here, when cotton farmers plant, they favor cutting-edge science. All but a fraction of the cotton fields in Baoding and surrounding Hebei province are sown with seed genetically implanted with a bacterium that is toxic to cotton boll worms. "The farmers really welcome these seeds," says seed-seller Meng Xinghe, standing amid sacks of corn and soybean seed in his small market stall. "Without them, they'd be wiped out." With memories of famine fresh and dwindling arable land to feed its 1.26 billion people, China has enthusiastically pursued genetically modified foods and seen little of the debate that has raged in Europe and elsewhere over their safety.

In other Asia-Pacific nations, the controversy over biotechnology has far exceeded its actual use. In India, Japan, New Zealand, Thailand, and the Philippines, consumer movements are demanding controls on the use of genetically modified crops.

Proponents contend that genetically altering crops to resist pests, drought, or other adverse conditions may be the only way to ensure food security in the developing world, particularly in densely populated Asia, home to more than half of humanity. Such crops, they argue, can drastically reduce the need for harmful pesticides, restore ravaged ecosystems, and promote public health with foods genetically enhanced with essential nutrients or vaccines. But the technique for splicing genes from one organism into another has also provoked fears of freak, unforeseen hazards to health and the environment.

In Southeast Asia, only Singapore has come out strongly in favor of biotechnology, viewing it as a promising new industry. "If it is safe for the Americans, it is safe for us," says Lee Sing Kong, a member of Singapore government's Genetic Modification Advisory Committee, brushing aside growing debate in the United States.

The source of the technology—mainly the research labs of governments and corporations in industrialized countries—raises political hackles too. Farmers in southern India torched cotton test fields operated by St. Louis–based biotech giant Monsanto (www.monsanto.com/monsanto/default.htm), complaining that the seeds were too expensive.

In the Philippines, 7 of 10 farmers are landless, renting fields from landlords or working for large corporations like Dole Foods (www.dole.com). Leftist groups (see Philippine Peasant Institute at www.ppi.org, for example) argue that genetically modified crops will give the companies that sell seeds and farm chemicals even greater power. "Big landlords and transnational corporations will call all the shots," said Wim De Ceukelaire, a consultant for the Peasant Movement of the Philippines. "In the case of small farmers, it means going deeper and deeper into debt." The Peasant Movement plans demonstrations against genetically modified foods later this year, joined by counterparts in Thailand, India, and elsewhere.

Genetic engineering has potentially explosive ramifications for ethnically divided countries such as Malaysia and Indonesia. "If people were aware that animal genes might be used in plants, maybe from cows or pigs, there would be a lot of religious objections from Hindus and Muslims," said Haji Muhammad Haji Abdul Majid, a professor of biotechnology at the University of Malaya in Kuala Lumpur, Malaysia.

Such concerns are largely absent in China. Provincial and central governments have backed research into genetic engineering. Debate over biotechnology in the state-controlled media has been muted.

QUESTIONS

1. Identify the different kinds of groups in terms of basic group characteristics (size, formality, membership, primary versus secondary, and affect) involved in the consumption of genetically modified seeds.
2. How does decision making differ between these groups?
3. Identify potential buying centers and roles for genetically modified seeds in the Chinese case.
4. Supposing you worked for a global seed company like Monsanto, how would you propose developing marketing strategy for each of these groups? In each case, what would be your product, and what would your marketing communication strategy be like?
5. Check out Watching Monsanto at www.monsanto.vigil.net. If you were Monsanto, how would you respond to this form of consumer activism?

This case is adapted from "Asians Ponder Biotech Foods Promise," Lincoln Journal Star, *July 4, 2000, p. 7A.*

1. W. E. Patton III, Christopher P. Puto, and Ronald H. King, "Which Buying Decisions Are Made by Individuals and Not by Groups?" *Industrial Marketing Management* 15 (1986), pp. 129–38.

2. www.rage.co.za/kwaito.html.

3. Linda L. Price and Eric J. Arnould, "Commercial Friendships: Service Provider Client Relationships in Context," *Journal of Marketing* 63 (October 1999), pp. 38–56.

4. Rohit Deshpande and Frederick E. Webster Jr., "Organizational Culture and Marketing: Defining the Research Agenda," *Journal of Marketing* 53 (January 1993), pp. 3–15. Our discussion of organizational culture draws heavily from this article.

5. Roy J. Lewicki, "Organizational Seduction: Building Commitment to Organizations," *Organizational Dynamics* (Autumn 1981), pp. 5–21.

6. Kathleen L. Gregory, "Native-View Paradigms: Multiple Cultures and Conflicts in Organizations," *Administrative Science Quarterly* 28 (September 1983), pp. 359–76.

7. Linda Smircich, "Concepts of Culture and Organizational Analysis," *Administrative Science Quarterly* 28 (September 1983), pp. 339–58; and David Edward Albright, *Market-Oriented Organizational Learning and Sensemaking: Shared Sensemaking Disconnects within One Marketing Research Firm's Strategic Dialogues,* unpublished dissertation, The University of Georgia, 2000.

8. For an overview of The Gap, see Alice Kahn, "Filling Every Gap," *New York Times,* August 23, 1992, section 9, p. 1. The first quote on Esprit's corporate mission comes from Laura Zinn, "Will Politically Correct Sell Sweaters?" *Business Week,* March 16, 1992, pp. 60–61. The second quote is from Elsa Klensch, "Susie Tompkins: The Spirit in Esprit," *Vogue,* August 1987, p. 376.

9. Terrence E. Deal and Allan A. Kennedy, *Corporate Cultures: The Rites and Rituals of Corporate Life* (Reading, MA: Addison-Wesley, 1982).

10. Julianne Mahler, "The Quest for Organizational Meaning: Identifying and Interpreting the Symbolism in Organizational Stories," *Administration and Society* 20 (November 1988), pp. 344–68.

11. Nancy M. Ridgway and Linda L. Price, "Creativity under Pressure: The Importance of Consumption Situations on Consumer Product Use," *American Marketing Association Proceedings,* Summer 1991, pp. 361–68.

12. Deal and Kennedy, *Corporate Cultures;* and Lewicki, "Organizational Seduction."

13. Deal and Kennedy, *Corporate Cultures;* and Mark E. Hill and Karen James, "Casual Dress Is More Than Clothing in the Workplace," *Consumption, Markets, Culture* 3, no. 3 (2000), pp. 239–82.

14. Michele D. Bunn, "Understanding Organizational Buying Behavior: The Challenges of the 1990s," *Annual Review of Marketing,* 1992, pp. 227–59.

15. F. E. Webster Jr. and Yoram Wind, *Organizational Buying Behavior* (Englewood Cliffs, NJ: Prentice Hall, 1972); and Robert Spekman and Louis W. Stern, "Environmental Uncertainty and Buying Group Structure: An Empirical Investigation," *Journal of Marketing* 43 (Spring 1977), pp. 54–64.

16. See Yoram Wind, "Preference of Relevant Others and Individual Choice Models," *Journal of Consumer Research* 3 (June 1976), pp. 50–57; Yoram Wind, "On the Interface between Organizational and Consumer Buying Behavior," in *Advances in Consumer Research,* vol. 5, ed. H. Keith Hunt (Ann Arbor: Association for Consumer Research, 1978), pp. 657–62; and Sandy D. Jap, "Online Reverse Auctions: Issues, Themes, and Prospects for the Future," *Journal of the Academy of Marketing Science* 30 (Fall 2002), pp. 502–21.

17. Richard T. Watson, Pierre Berthon, Leyland F. Pitt, and George M. Zinkhan, *Electronic Commerce: The Strategic Perspective* (Fort Worth, TX: Dryden Press, 2000).

18. F. Robert Dwyer, Paul H. Schurr, and Sejo Oh, "Developing Buyer–Seller Relationships," *Journal of Marketing* 51 (April 1987), pp. 11–27.

19. Jose Tomas Gomez Arias, "A Relationship Marketing Approach to Guanxi," *European Journal of Marketing* 32, nos. 1–2 (1998), pp. 145–56.

20. Classic references on power and trust include Peter Blau, *Exchange and Power in Social Life* (New York: John Wiley, 1964); and Richard Emerson, "Power Dependence Relations," *American*

Sociological Review 27 (February 1962), pp. 31–41. For applications of these concepts to organization relationships, see Jeffrey Pfeffer and Gerald R. Salancik, *The External Control of Organizations: A Resource Dependence Perspective* (New York: Harper and Row, 1978); and Lars Hallen, Jan Johanson, and Nazeem Seyed-Mohamed, "Interfirm Adaptation in Business Relationships," *Journal of Marketing* 55 (April 1991), pp. 29–37.

21. Kim P. Corfman and Donald Lehmann, "Models of Cooperative Group Decision-Making and Relative Influence: An Experimental Investigation of Family Purchase Decisions," *Journal of Consumer Research* 14 (June 1987), p. 2.

22. Robert M. Morgan and Shelby D. Hunt, "The Commitment-Trust Theory of Relationship Marketing," *Journal of Marketing* 58 (July 1994), pp. 20–28.

23. Christine Moorman, Gerald Zaltman, and Rohit Despandé, "Relationships between Providers and Users of Marketing Research: The Dynamics of Trust within and between Organizations," *Journal of Marketing Research* 29 (August 1992), pp. 314–29; Charles C. Nielson, "An Empirical Examination of the Role of Closeness in Industrial Buyer–Seller Relationships," *European Journal of Marketing* 32, nos. 5–6 (1998), pp. 441–63; and Sang Hyeon Kim and Ji Hea Kim, "The Relationship between Interfirm Commitment and Opportunism in Marketing Channels," in *Marketing Theory and Applications,* vol. 9, ed. Dhruv Grewal and Connie Pechman (Chicago: American Marketing Association, 1998), pp. 272–82.

24. The buy-class theory of purchasing was introduced by Patrick J. Robinson, Charles W. Faris, and Yoram Wind, *Industrial Buying and Creative Marketing* (Boston: Allyn and Bacon, 1967). A review and test of those authors' buy-class theory is provided by Erin Anderson, Wujin Chu, and Barton Weitz, "Industrial Purchasing: An Empirical Exploration of the Buyclass Framework," *Journal of Marketing* 51 (July 1987), pp. 71–86.

25. Adapted from *Japan Economic Journal* 23 (December 1980), p. 29; see also Philip Kotler, *Marketing Management,* 7th ed. (Englewood Cliffs, NJ: Prentice Hall, 1991), p. 209.

26. Ju-Young Park, Ravipreet S. Sohi, and Ray Marquardt, "The Role of Motivated Reasoning in Vendor Consideration," *Psychology and Marketing* 14 (September 1997), pp. 585–600.

27. Thomas V. Bonoma, Richard P. Bagozzi, and Gerald Zaltman, "Industrial Buying Behavior," working paper, no. 77-117, Marketing Science Institute, Cambridge, MA, 1977.

28. Robinson, Faris, and Wind, *Industrial Buying and Creative Marketing;* and Anderson, Chu, and Weitz, "Industrial Purchasing."

29. Judy Cohen and Carol Kaufman, "Consumption Choice within the Black Extended Family Network," in *Advances in Consumer Research,* vol. 19, ed. John F. Sherry Jr. and Brian Sternthal (Provo, UT: Association for Consumer Research, 1991), pp. 338–45; and Judy Cohen and Carol Kaufman, "The Cultural Variant Perspective in Black Family Research: Consumption Choice within the Extended Family Network," *Proceedings of the Households Conference,* University of California–Irvine, Irvine, CA, 1991.

30. Roger Marshall, Christina Kawi-Choi Lee, and Kim Marshall, "New Zealand," in *Marketing and Consumer Behavior in East and South-East Asia,* ed. Anthony Pecotich and Clifford J. Shultz II (Sydney: McGraw-Hill, 1998), pp. 523–48; and Tsutomu Okahashi, N. Clay Gary, and Steven Cornish-Ward, "Japan," in *Marketing and Consumer Behavior in East and South-East Asia,* ed. Anthony Pecotich and Clifford J. Shultz II (Sydney: McGraw-Hill, 1998), pp. 315–70.

31. Simon Appleton, "Women-Headed Household and Household Welfare: An Empirical Deconstruction for Uganda," *World Development* 24 (December 1996), pp. 1811–27; H. Razoun, "The Sociofamilial Impact of Labor Migration by Jordanian Family Heads," *Dirasat: Human and Social Sciences* 24 (February 1997); and Richard R. Wilk, ed., *The Household Economy: Rethinking the Domestic Mode of Production* (Boulder, CO: Westview Press, 1989).

32. Kirsten M. Lagatree, "The Power of Place," *Los Angeles Times,* July 18, 1993, pp. K1, K6; and Richard R. Wilk, "House, Home and Consumer Decision Making in Two Cultures," in *Advances in Consumer Research,* vol. 14, ed. Melanie Wallendorf and Paul Anderson (Provo, UT: Association for Consumer Research, 1986), pp. 303–7.

33. Mary C. Gilly and Ben M. Ennis, "Recycling the Family Life Cycle," in *Advances in Consumer Research,* vol. 9, ed. Andrew M. Mitchell (Ann Arbor: Association for Consumer Research, 1982), pp. 271–76; William D. Danko and Charles M. Schaninger, "An Empirical Evaluation of

the Gilly-Ennis Updated Household Life Cycle Model," *Journal of Business Research,* August 1990, pp. 39–57; and Ignacio Redondo-Bellon, Marcelo Royo-Vela, and Joaquin Aldas-Manzano, "A Family Life Cycle Model Adapted to the Spanish Environment," *European Journal of Marketing* 35, nos. 5–6 (2001), pp. 612–38.

34. Anthony Pecotich and Clifford J. Shultz II, eds., *Marketing and Consumer Behavior in East and South-East Asia* (Sydney: McGraw-Hill, 1998); and UK Department of the Environment, Transport and the Regions, *English House Condition Survey of 1996,* www.housing.detr.gov.uk/research/ehcs96/summary/2.htm.

35. UK Department of the Environment, Transport and the Regions, *English House Condition Survey of 1996;* and Roshan "Bob" D. Ahuja and Kandi M. Stinson, "Female-Headed Single Parent Families: An Exploratory Study of Children's Influence in Family Decision Making," in *Advances in Consumer Research,* vol. 20, ed. Leigh McAlister and Michael Rothschild (Provo, UT: Association for Consumer Research, 1993), pp. 469–74.

36. Thesia I. Garner, "Changing Welfare in a Changing World? Income and Expenditure Inequalities in the Czech and Slovak Republics," in *The Distribution of Welfare and Household Production,* ed. Stephen P. Jenkins, Arie Kapteyn, and Bernard van Prang (Cambridge: Cambridge University Press, 1996); Okahashi, Gary, and Cornish-Ward, "Japan"; Joan Raymond, "The Joy of Empty Nesting," *American Demographics,* May 2000, pp. 49–54; and Cheryl Russell, "The New Consumer Paradigm," *American Demographics,* April 1999, pp. 50–58.

37. Laurie Lofland and H. Razzouk, "The Changing American Household: Impact on Consumptive Behavior," *Proceedings of the Households Conference,* University of California at Irvine, Irvine, CA, 1991.

38. Alan R. Andreasen, "Life Status Changes and Changes in Consumer Preferences and Satisfaction," *Journal of Consumer Research,* December 1984, pp. 784–94; and "The Future of Households," *American Demographics,* December 1993, pp. 27–40.

39. See U.S. Bureau of Labor Statistics, *Consumer Expenditure Survey,* stats.bls.gov/csxhome.htm.

40. Alladi Venkatesh, Eric Chuan-Fong Shih, and Norman C. Stolzoff, "A Longitudinal Analysis of Computing in the Home Based on Census Data 1984–1997," paper presented at the Home Informatics Conference, Wolverhampton, UK, June 28–30, 2000.

41. Okahashi, Gary, and Cornish-Ward, "Japan"; Raymond, "The Joy of Empty Nesting"; and Simmons Market Research, *The New American Family: Significant and Diversified Lifestyles* (New York: Simmons Market Research Bureau, 1992).

42. Ahuja and Stinson, "Female-Headed Single Parent Families"; and Lynn Smith, "Mothers Go It Alone," *Long Beach Press-Telegram,* July 22, 1993, pp. E1, E2.

43. Richard Cimino and Don Lattin, "Choosing My Religion," *American Demographics,* April 1999, pp. 60–65.

44. Eric P. Andrew and Thomas C. Kinnear, "General Motors: Cadillac," in *Cases in Marketing Management,* ed. Kenneth L. Bernhardt and Thomas C. Kinnear (Homewood, IL: Richard D. Irwin, 1991); and Frank Gawronski, "Detroit's Oldest Auto Manufacturer," *Automotive News,* September 16, 1983, p. 98.

45. Andrew and Kinnear, "General Motors: Cadillac."

46. Robert L. Simison and Rebecca Bluemenstein, "Cadillac and Lincoln Try to Regain Their Cachet," *The Wall Street Journal,* July 3, 1997, pp. B1, B7.

47. See Scott Ward, "Consumer Socialization," in *Perspectives in Consumer Behavior,* ed. Harold H. Kassarjian and Thomas S. Robertson (Glenville, IL: Scott Foresman, 1980); and George P. Moschis, "The Role of Family Communication in Consumer Socialization of Children and Adolescents," *Journal of Consumer Research* 11 (March 1985), pp. 898–913.

48. Gwen Rae Bachman, Deborah Roedder John, and Askay R. Rao, "Children's Susceptibility to Peer Group Influence: An Exploratory Investigation," in *Advances in Consumer Research,* vol. 20, ed. Leigh McAlister and Michael L. Rothschild (Provo, UT: Association for Consumer Research, 1993), pp. 463–68; James U. McNeal, *Kids as Customers* (New York: Lexington Books, 1992), pp. 38–61; and Daniel Thomas Cook, "Exchange Value as Pedagogy in Children's Leisure: Moral Panics in Children's Culture at Century's End," *Leisure Sciences* 23 (2001), pp. 81–98.

49. Mary T. Weismental, "The Children Cry for Bread," in *The Social Economy of Consumption,* ed. Benjamin S. Orlove and Henry J. Rutz, Monographs in Economic Anthropology No. 6. (Lanham, MD: University Press of America, 1989), pp. 101–20; and Mary T. Weismental, "Making Breakfast and Raising Babies: The Zumbagua Household as Constituted Process," in *The Household Economy: Rethinking the Domestic Mode of Production,* ed. Richard R. Wilk (Boulder, CO: Westview Press, 1989), pp. 55–72.
50. Les Carlson and Sanford Grossbart, "Parental Style and Consumer Socialization of Children," *Journal of Consumer Research* 15 (June 1988), pp. 77–94.
51. Moschis, "The Role of Family Communication in Consumer Socialization of Children and Adolescents"; and Scott Ward and Daniel B. Wackman, *Effects of Television Advertising on Consumer Socialization* (Cambridge, MA: Marketing Science Institute, 1973).
52. Sanford Grossbart, Les Carlson, and Ann Walsh, "Consumer Socialization and Frequency of Shopping with Children," *Journal of the Academy of Marketing Science* 19 (Summer 1991), pp. 155–63.
53. U.S. Bureau of Labor Statistics, *Consumer Expenditure Survey,* 1998, Table 59, stats.bls.gov/csxhome.htm.
54. Carol Stack, *All Our Kin* (New York: Harper and Row, 1974); and Richard R. Wilk, "Decision-Making and Resource Flows within the Household: Beyond the Black Box" in *The Household Economy: Rethinking the Domestic Mode of Production,* ed. Richard R. Wilk (Boulder, CO: Westview Press, 1989), pp. 23–54.
55. Jane Guyer, "Household and Community in African Studies," *African Studies Review* 24 (1981), pp. 87–137.
56. Okahashi, Gary, and Cornish-Ward, "Japan."
57. Ritha Fellerman and Kathleen Debevec, "Kinship Exchange Networks and Family Consumption," in *Advances in Consumer Research,* vol. 20, ed. Leigh McAlister and Michael L. Rothschild (Provo, UT: Association for Consumer Research, 1993), pp. 458–62.
58. In many contemporary societies, those of both the First and Third Worlds, moral frameworks are not clear-cut and groups often have to work out entitlements. Thus, some theorists argue that the household is a mere "knot of individual interests" with self-interest governing the behavior of household members.
59. Economic organizations also consider moral issues in making decisions, but these are typically a less pervasive part of purchase decisions than in the case of families. Interesting discussions of moral elements in business decision making are available in Amitai Etzioni, *The Moral Dimension: Toward a New Economics* (New York: Free Press, 1988); and Jonghee Park, Patriya Tansuhaj, Eric R. Spangenberg, and Jim McCullough, "An Emotion-Based Perspective of Family Purchase Decisions," in *Advances in Consumer Research,* vol. 22, ed. Frank Kardes and Mita Sujan (Provo, UT: Association for Consumer Research, 1995), pp. 723–28.
60. Cohen and Kaufman, "Consumption Choice within the Black Extended Family Network"; Corfman and Lehmaan, "Models of Cooperative Group Decision-Making and Relative Influence," pp. 1–14; and Cohen and Kaufman, "The Cultural Variant Perspective in Black Family Research." For studies on African households, see Sara S. Berry, *Sons Work for Their Fathers* (Berkeley: University of California Press, 1985); Joyce Moock, "Introduction," in *Understanding Africa's Rural Households and Farming Systems,* ed. Joyce Moock (Boulder, CO: Westview, 1986), pp. 1–10; and Guyer, "Household and Community in African Studies." For studies on households in Belize, see Richard R. Wilk, "House, Home and Consumer Decision Making in Two Cultures," in *Advances in Consumer Research,* vol. 14, ed. Melanie Wallendorf and Paul Anderson (Provo, UT: Association for Consumer Research, 1986), pp. 303–7; Richard R. Wilk, "The Built Environment and Consumer Decisions," paper presented at the Annual Meeting of the Society for Economic Anthropology, Champaign, IL, 1986; Richard R. Wilk, "Houses as Consumer Goods: Social Processes and Allocation Decisions," in *The Social Economy of Consumption,* ed. Benjamin S. Orlove and Henry J. Rutz (Lanham, MD: University Press of America, 1989), pp. 297–322; and Wilk, "Decision Making and Resources Flows within the Household.
61. Kevin Goldman, "Campbell Mithun Shows Its Stuff in a Kmart Makeover Campaign," *The Wall Street Journal,* August 3, 1995, p. B3; Betsy Spethmann, "Hilton Heads toward Tie-Ins,"

Brandweek, March 8, 1993, p. 4; Betsy Spethmann, "Chrysler Rolls in the Grass Roots," *Brandweek,* March 27, 1995; and Pauline Yoshihashi, "Stars Fade as Las Vegas Bets on Families", *The Wall Street Journal,* February 5, 1993, pp. B1, B2.

62. Corfman and Lehmann, "Models of Cooperative Group Decision-Making and Relative Influence"; and Jean-Marie Choffray and Gary L. Lilien, *Market Planning for New Industrial Products* (New York: John Wiley, 1980).

63. Grant McCracken, "Lois Roget: A Curatorial Consumer," *Culture and Consumption,* 1988, pp. 44–56; and Linda L. Price, Eric J. Arnould, and Carolyn Curasi, "Older Consumer Disposition of Cherished Possession," *Journal of Consumer Research* 27 (September 2000), pp. 179–201.

64. D. J. Hempel, "Family Buying Decisions: A Cross-Cultural Perspective," *Journal of Marketing Research* 11 (August 1974), pp. 295–302; and Robert M. Press, "Kenya Manages to Slow Population Growth Rate," *Christian Science Monitor,* July 9, 1993, p. 10.

65. Robert Ferber, "Family Decision Making and Economic Behavior: A Review," in *Family Economic Behavior: Problems and Prospects,* ed. E. Sheldon (Philadelphia: Lippincott, 1973), pp. 29–64; E. Bonfield, Carol Kaufman, and S. Hernandez, "Household Decisionmaking: Units of Analysis and Decision Processes," in *Marketing to the Changing Household,* ed. M. Roberts and L. Wortzel (Cambridge, MA: Ballinger, 1984), pp. 231–63; R. J. Green Leonardi, J. Chandon, I. Cunningham, B. Verhage, and A. Straieri, "Societal Development and Family Purchasing Roles: A Cross-National Study," *Journal of Consumer Research* 9 (1984), pp. 436–42; and Jonathan Bohlmann and William J. Qualls, "Household Preference Revisions and Decision Making: The Role of Disconfirmation," *International Journal of Research in Marketing* 18 (2001), pp. 319–39.

66. David Brinberg and Nancy Schwenk, "Husband–Wife Decision Making: An Exploratory Study of the Interaction Process," in *Advances in Consumer Research,* vol. 12, ed. Elizabeth C. Hirschman and Morris B. Holbrook (Provo, UT: Association for Consumer Research, 1985), pp. 487–91; and Irene Raj Foster and Richard W. Olshavsky, "An Exploratory Study of Family Decision Making Using a New Taxonomy of Family Role Structure," in *Advances in Consumer Research,* vol. 16, ed. Thomas Srull (Provo, UT: Association for Consumer Research, 1989), pp. 665–70.

67. Carlson and Grossbart, "Parental Style and Consumer Socialization of Children."

68. W. Christian Buss and Charles M. Schaniger, "Recent Advances in Research on the Influence of Sex Roles on Family Decision Processes," in *Marketing to the Changing Household,* ed. M. Roberts and L. Wortzel (Cambridge, MA: Ballinger, 1984), pp. 69–89; and Bonfield, Kaufman, and Hernandez, "Household Decisionmaking."

69. C. Whan Park, "Joint Decisions in Home Purchasing: A Muddling-through Process," *Journal of Consumer Research* 9 (1982), p. 152.

70. Foster and Olshavsky, "An Exploratory Study of Family Decision Making."

71. Eric J. Arnould, "Marketing and Social Reproduction in Zinder, Niger Republic," in *Households: Comparative and Historical Studies of the Domestic Group,* ed. Robert M. Netting, Richard R. Wilk, and Eric J. Arnould (Berkeley: University of California Press, 1984), pp. 130–62; and Eric J. Arnould, "Toward a Broadened Theory of Preference Formation and the Diffusion of Innovations: Cases from Zinder Province, Niger Republic," *Journal of Consumer Research* 16 (September 1989), pp. 239–67.

72. Amardeep Assar and George S. Bobinski Jr. "Financial Decision Making by Baby Boomer Couples," in *Advances in Consumer Research,* vol. 18, ed. Rebecca H. Holman and Michael R. Solomon (Provo, UT: Association for Consumer Research, 1991), pp. 657–65; Ellen Foxman and Alvin C. Burns, "Role Load in the Household," in *Advances in Consumer Research,* vol. 14, ed. Melanie Wallendorf and Paul Anderson (Provo, UT: Association for Consumer Research, 1987), pp. 458–62; Judith Madill and Sheri Bailey, "Household Decision Making: The Relative Influence of Husbands and Wives in the 1990s," in *European Advances in Consumer Research,* vol. 4, ed. Bernard Dubois, L. J. Shrum, Tina Lowry, and Marc Vanhuele (Provo, UT: Association for Consumer Research, 1999), pp. 232–37; and Michael D. Reilly, "Working Wives and Convenience Consumption," *Journal of Consumer Research* 14 (September 1982), pp. 407–18.

73. Simmons Market Research, *The New American Family,* pp. 43, 48.

74. R. T. Green, B. J. Verhage, and I. C. M. Cunningham, "Household Purchasing Decisions: How Do American and Dutch Consumers Differ?" *European Journal of Marketing* 15 (1981),

pp. 68–77; William J. Qualls, "Household Decision Behavior: The Impact of Husbands' and Wives' Sex Role Orientation," *Journal of Consumer Research* 14 (September 1987), pp. 264–79; Cynthia Webster, "Determinants of Marital Power on Decision Making," in *Advances in Consumer Research,* vol. 22, ed. Frank Kardes and Mita Sujan (Provo, UT: Association for Consumer Research, 1995), pp. 717–22; Madill and Bailey, "Household Decision Making"; and Reilly, "Working Wives and Convenience Consumption."

75. P. J. O'Connor, Gary L. Sullivan, and Dana A. Pogorzelski, "Cross Cultural Family Decisions: A Literature Review," in *Advances in Consumer Research,* vol. 12, ed. Elizabeth C. Hirschman and Morris B. Holbrook (Provo, UT: Association for Consumer Research, 1985), pp. 59–64.

76. Jonathan K. Frenzen and Harry L. Davis, "Purchasing Behavior in Embedded Markets," *Journal of Consumer Research* 17 (June 1990), pp. 1–12.

LEARNING OBJECTIVES

After completing this chapter, you should be able to:

- Describe the characteristics of interpersonal influence and how interpersonal influence relates to persuasion.
- Explain the importance of interpersonal influence for consumer preferences and choices.
- Recognize how particular social contexts shape consumers' preferences and choices and how the nature of interpersonal influence varies across cultures.
- Identify different types of interpersonal influence and give examples of how they are used in marketing strategies.
- Recognize commonly used influence tactics and how and why they work and give marketing examples.
- Discuss the importance of reference groups to individuals' perspectives, attitudes, and behaviors and recognize the characteristics of reference groups that help to explain different levels of influence.
- Identify how different types of product choices and other characteristics of individuals and situations affect reliance on interpersonal influence.

PACIFIC RIVIERA: SELLING TIME-SHARE CONDOMINIUMS

In advance of an L.A. Marathon, Linda and Eric filled out cards for a "free drawing" at the entrance to the L.A. Convention Center. Some weeks later, Eric received a call announcing that he had been chosen to win a free prize. All he had to do to claim either a home computer, a Cadillac Seville, a $500 shopping spree at The Broadway department store, or a vacation package was listen to a two-hour presentation about the new Pacific Riviera Vacation Time-Sharing Package. Eric agreed, and the following Saturday he and Linda traveled to Newport Beach to see the presentation. On arrival they left their car at a valet parking stop and entered the Pacific Riviera showroom.

The walls were covered with glassed posters featuring exotic locations and a large world map that noted member vacation condos around the world. The room included mostly couples ranging in age from late 20s to late 60s. Eric filled out a short, simple form with information such as address, home ownership, and income level and then waited a few minutes before Sandy, their personal "tour guide," greeted them. Each couple was assigned their own tour guide who described that they would begin their tour of the vacation package with a short film. The small auditorium filled as show time approached. The tour guides sat with their guests. The film was introduced and the tour guides all clapped, as did almost all the guests. The film featured Robin Leach and a young woman announcer, who claimed she was neither rich nor famous, explaining the many benefits of Pacific Riviera. The film also featured endorsements from California family members who recommended the program and cute endorsements from a group of satisfied children. No money costs were mentioned in the film, only that PR condos were both elite and affordable. When the film was over, the tour guides again led the guests in applause.

After the film was over, Sandy led Eric and Linda to a table in another, adjoining, light-filled room, crowded with small tables around which dozens of tour guides and their guests sat. Balloons were tied to the backs of one guest chair at each table. Eric and Linda chatted for several minutes about themselves and their vacation history and preferences. At one point a balloon popped with a loud bang; the room filled with applause. Sandy explained that whenever a guest purchased a package, they popped a balloon.

Sandy then explained the benefits of the package, careful to write down notes on a sheet of paper, and tailored the examples she gave to Eric and Linda's vacation dreams and history. First she explained about the gold card package that was available only today and compared it to the standard package available everyday. The gold card package featured far more features at little additional cost. At one point, Eric asked how much this might cost, and Sandy demurred, explaining that she was not a licensed real estate broker, but she offered to have someone else explain the costs after her presentation. Sandy focused on how much their vacations were costing and how these costs would increase over the years. When summarizing the benefit package, she stopped and asked, "Which of these benefit features would you use most?" She then asked Linda and Eric if they would like to see a vacation alternative that would be less expensive and build equity at the same time. How could Eric and Linda say no? Meanwhile, balloons were popping around the room as a reminder that others were taking advantage of these deals.

After a short tour of the photo gallery in the front of the showroom and a mock-up of a condominium (not a real condo) complete with fireplace, kitchen, and in-bath Jacuzzi and imaginary window scenes, they returned to the table where Sandy called over her colleague Dan to go over costs with Linda and Eric. Dan spent a few minutes chatting, using as a focal point the notes he had been handed by Sandy. Dan then asked Eric how he liked the package so far. Dan again emphasized the benefits, noting that they were almost sold out of beachfront units and indicating how few there are in California and how much excess demand there is for them (30 to 1). He solicited Linda and Eric's agreement about the benefits of the package. Now was the crucial moment: Dan wrote down the price, around $13,000, available financing, and monthly payments. Eric explained he was not interested in this package, and Dan courteously said he understood and shook Eric's hand. Sandy stood up to take Linda and Eric to claim their gift, and Dan followed along.

To claim the gift Sandy took them through "The Avenue of Broken Dreams," featuring James Dean posters and many other prints and posters of that flavor. After a few minutes they were introduced to an entirely different kind of character with a heavy accent, a big mustache, a wild colored shirt, and a purple Pacific Riviera cap. He ushered them into a much smaller room again filled with people at small tables talking with agents. Surprise! The gold package only available today could be retained as an option, and Eric and Linda could get many of the accompanying vacation benefits for a mere $299. Again, Eric said no. Some conferring went on at a counter at the back of the room, and another woman came over to give Eric and Linda their prize. She explained a number-matching procedure and indicated that they had won a personal computer (by far the odds favor winning this and not a different gift). The personal computer retails for $649, but it lacks a monitor and is technologically out of date.

OVERVIEW

The opening vignette includes many basic influence principles. Some of the principles illustrated are unique to Western cultures; others are shared widely across many cultures although their power may differ. We will refer back to this vignette at several points in this chapter.

We provide a description of the tools and nature of **interpersonal influence** in this chapter. By interpersonal influence we mean *altered thinking or behavior as a result of others' accidental, expressive, or rhetorical communications.*[1] By contrast with persuasion, which is a conscious intent to change thinking or behavior, influence may be conscious but may also occur accidentally. People are often totally unintentional in their effect on others. Even when people do not intend for them to, most of their actions and words stimulate some meaning in the minds of others. Sometimes just by expressing emotional enthusiasm for a movie or a book, a person can stimulate a listener, even a stranger, to decide to see the movie or read the book.[2] In this case, the effect of an expressive communication is influence.

Rhetorical communication is typified by the story that introduces this chapter. In the story, Sandy is attempting to persuade Linda and Eric to buy a vacation condominium. As compared to accidental or expressive types of communication, **rhetorical communication** is goal-directed. It assumes that the individual is trying to *achieve a goal by stimulating a specific meaning in another person's mind.* Obviously, rhetorical communication can take an expressive form. Someone may use emotions to stimulate a specific meaning in the mind of another person. For example, many service businesses emphasize certain expressions of emotions by personnel to help persuade customers of service quality. For example, Disney World coaches prospective employees on how to look like they are having fun, and McDonald's stresses the importance of displaying enthusiasm and a sense of humor.[3] Of course, in every communication, it's important to remember that the meaning stimulated may be other than the meaning intended. For example, when McDonald's opened a fast-food outlet in Moscow, management trained staff members to conform to Western norms of good service. This included smiling at customers. However, this particular norm did not exist in the former Soviet Union, and some patrons concluded that staff members were mocking them.[4]

This chapter begins with a brief discussion of where people get their beliefs about personal and social influence. Next is an overview of the social context of personal consumption behavior and a broad-based discussion of how people rely on others in purchase and acquisition decisions. Next we discuss many important tools of influence. Interpersonal influence occurs within social systems. Understanding the role of reference groups within social systems is an important aspect of understanding interpersonal influence. Throughout the chapter we integrate a discussion of marketing strategies of persuasion.

BELIEFS ABOUT PERSONAL AND SOCIAL INFLUENCE

Over the years, a wide variety of beliefs about personal and social influence in many different spheres of life have accumulated. In forming personal beliefs about influence processes, people rely on many sources of information. For example, they may rely on cultural truisms that reflect their own cultural background. Stereotypes such as "you cannot reason with women because they are so flighty and emotional" would be one possible cultural "truism" about influence strategies (one that we sincerely hope is changing). People also rely on observation, feedback from others about their own behavior, the moral values and standards that have been instilled in them by their family and society's institutions, their specific training or education, and of course what they see and hear in the mass media. They might also look to history, religion, literature, law, and the behavioral sciences for rich and vivid ideas about the dynamics of social and personal influence.

Three behavioral sciences that have obvious and direct relevance to influence and persuasion processes are anthropology, sociology, and psychology. An anthropologist interested in influence and persuasion would investigate various cultural and cross-cultural dimensions. For example, an anthropologist might study certain attitudes and values widely shared in a given culture that affect the willingness of members of that culture to engage in certain behaviors. A sociologist interested in influence and persuasion would focus on processes existing in society, in institutions, and within groups. For example, a sociologist might study how family, friends, classmates, and work associates shape people's beliefs, attitudes, and behaviors. Finally, a psychologist interested in influence and persuasion would focus on the individual human being. For example, a psychologist might study how various influence strategies affect an individual's feelings of esteem, control, or safety.

The term *EuroKids* was coined by the pan-European advertising group Alto, which found that, increasingly, youths under 25 from Lisbon to Berlin and Stockholm to Athens have more in common with each other than with older people in their own countries.[5] They are bound not only by shared tastes in fashion, music, and food but also by lifestyle, attitudes, and values. They dance to rave music from Italy, Belgium, and Great Britain. They look for clothes from Chipie, Naf Naf, and Kookaï of France. Youth are linked globally through international style magazines and satellite television channels, primarily MTV Europe. Observe the youth shown in the photo on the opposite page. Notice how they are dressed. Although there are stylistic differences, there are also many similarities in their tastes and appearances. These youth could be from

Global youth culture.

many different parts of the world. They are part of a global youth culture that influences and is influenced by media and their own age cohort.

We have emphasized throughout this book that consumer beliefs, feelings, and actions are embedded in cultural and social contexts. Seeing pictures such as this one reminds us of the powerful impact of others on how we interpret meanings in any situation or object. What's cool and what's not is defined in these social situations. **Symbolic interaction theory** is *a sociological theory that emphasizes that consumers interact with symbols in their environment and products play symbolic roles.*[6] In Chapters 4 and 7 we talked about the social construction of meaning and the use of social comparison for affiliation and differentiation goals.

Paradoxically, one of the reasons people are not more attuned to others' influence is their tendency to assume a "not me" orientation, or an **illusion of personal invulnerability.**[7] A person may say of someone else, "he is swayed by opinions, but not me," or "she goes along with the group, but not me." Not only is this orientation illusory, but it is dangerous as well because it acts as a barrier to more effective personal control over the individual's responses to persuasion. It is through communication with others that people develop, cultivate, share, expand, and reshape their ideas and behaviors. Rarely does an individual develop an idea completely on his or her own.[8] We will give many dramatic illustrations in this chapter of the awesome power of others to alter one's thinking and behavior. In each of these cases it is not personal weaknesses that determine the degree of influence but rather the power of the situation.

Let's take one illustration. In a 1970 film, Allen Funt examined how adults conformed in a variety of unusual settings. In one instance, Funt arranged personal interviews with those who responded to a help-wanted advertisement. An interviewee is directed to a small office in which several other persons are already seated, apparently waiting. To the interviewee, the others appear to be fellow interviewees, but the movie viewers know they are really confederates of Funt. Responding to no apparent signal, the others abruptly rise from their seats and begin to take off their clothes. A close-up of the interviewee shows his apprehensive face as he surveys what is happening. After a few moments he, too, rises from his chair and begins to disrobe. During this process he does not ask any of the others why they are removing their clothing. As the scene ends, the interviewee is standing there, naked alongside the others, apparently waiting for some clue as to what happens next.[9]

Perhaps this interviewee in Funt's film later wished he had remained seated and clothed. After all, Americans are taught to admire those who are independent and not easily swayed by what others do or think. However, imitative behavior is likely to be adaptive in a variety of ways. When people are thrust into unfamiliar settings, their tendency to behave as others do may spring less from a desire to be similar to them than from a very rational belief that the others' information is better than theirs.[10] If everyone around you is yelling "fire" and heading for the door, it hardly makes sense to ask if they really know what's going on and wait to see the fire yourself.

Interpersonal influence touches on countless arenas of everyday life. It is one of the most potent factors affecting human behavior. Interpersonal influence has systematic, observable, and often surprising effects, but it is also often intangible and illusive. Several points from the above discussion are worth emphasizing: (1) interpersonal influence can be either intentional or accidental, verbal or nonverbal; (2) interpersonal influence is pervasive; (3) knowledge about influence processes derives from many sources, including people's own observations and experiences; (4) people are all personally vulnerable to influence processes; (5) people are influenced by others, at least in part, because to be influenced is adaptive—it makes people's lives more efficient, more comfortable, easier, and more successful.

THE SOCIAL CONTEXT OF PERSONAL CONSUMPTION BEHAVIOR

To emphasize the social context of personal consumption behavior is really no different than to say that the meanings of the clothing a person wears, the food she eats, the music she listens to, her furniture, her health beliefs, the totality of her consumption universe are cultural.[11] People like to think of themselves as making their own consumption choices, but in truth, such decisions are very much shaped by the individual's particular social context. From the morning voices on the clock radio (telling the listener how to smell good, have whiter teeth, or get a better job) until going to bed at night, in a single day an individual may easily have been exposed to over a hundred influence attempts.[12] Not all of these are interpersonal influence attempts, but many of them are.

Research in the United States has consistently demonstrated that interpersonal sources have a strong impact on consumer preferences and choices.[13] For example, one study indicated that up to 40 percent of a retailer's clientele were attracted by the recommendations of friends.[14] In purchases of major durables, over 90 percent of respondents reported they would be likely to use an interpersonal source in the product purchase.[15] The study suggested that a significant percent of respondents (about 20 percent) would seek out an unknown individual (a stranger or an acquaintance of an acquaintance) for information and advice. A number of studies suggest that buyers name interpersonal sources more frequently than any other source in describing their external search efforts.[16] Consumers contemplating the purchase of services or decisions involving social and financial risks show a pronounced preference for personal sources of information.[17] Studies of nondurable consumer goods opinion seeking also reveal heavy use of interpersonal sources.[18]

The power of **word-of-mouth** communication to motivate attitudes and behaviors is well known. Estimates on the power of negative word-of-mouth communication are especially compelling, suggesting that when consumers are dissatisfied almost 60 percent tell at least one friend or acquaintance.[19] In part, word-of-mouth information has so much impact because it is salient and vivid.[20] Vivid information is easier to remember and thus has greater impact. An interesting example of the vivid quality of word-of-mouth information concerned the movie *The Crying Game.* This little-fanfare, no-big-movie-star movie was described as "the most-talked-about, least-told-about movie in memory."[21] The film steadily attracted larger and larger crowds through word-of-mouth recommendations, but the word-of-mouth itself was not very informative. Many people felt that by revealing the twists in the film some of the enjoyment would be lost. Consequently, people would enthusiastically recommend the movie but refuse to reveal what it was about.

It's not just that word-of-mouth information is vivid, but also that a recommendation from someone who knows something about you is often more useful than what experts or critics have to say. For example, John Grisham, Tom Clancy, and Danielle Steel write blockbusters; but for works by lesser-known figures, word-of-mouth can turn sleepers into hits. With a sleeper sales start slowly: A friend tells a friend, and the author, actor, or some other key figure does an interview that lots of people hear, who then recommend to their friends. The book *Divine Secrets of the Ya Ya Sisterhood* and the movie *Snow Falling on Cedars* are examples of hits that followed this sleeper route.[22]

U.S. Postal Service promotes that direct mail can help your company create "buzz."

GOOD PRACTICE 14.1

Five Important Findings about Buzz

1. Not every product is a good candidate for buzz, but many are. If a product is unique in some respect and if it is highly visible, it is probably a good candidate for buzz. However, even nearly invisible products can be made visible through creating forums to exchange information about the product.
2. Buzz doesn't just happen. It happens through customers that have a disproportionate ability to shape consumer opinions, tactics that make the product seem scarce, exploitation of powerful icons, and creation of communities of users.
3. Buzz doesn't just depend on how customers feel about your product, but also whether and how they are connected to other consumers.
4. Some companies and products generate buzz, but companies can also benefit by identifying buzz early on the streets or in chat rooms.
5. Buzz is born in consumer-to-consumer communications and doesn't depend on media and advertising, although media and advertising can complement and encourage such communications.

Source: Adapted from Renée Dye, "The Buzz on Buzz," Harvard Business Review, *November–December 2000, pp. 139–46; see also Malcolm Gladwell,* The Tipping Point: How Little Things Can Make a Big Difference *(New York: Little Brown, 2000).*

A surprisingly large portion of the U.S. economy, more than two-thirds, is at least partially affected by **buzz**—*word-of-mouth promotions that can lead to explosive, self-generating consumer demand.*[23] Moreover, globalization means buzz can flourish unconstrained by geography. Consider a few of the hottest children's crazes such as Pokémon and Harry Potter that have literally swept the globe. New technologies, the

An ad for MINI Cooper encourages word-of-mouth influence.

proliferation of brands, and rising disposable incomes worldwide enable wider participation in buzz. In fact, an industry has sprung up built entirely around customer word of mouth. Check out the Epinions.com website for an example of a business designed around helping consumers make informed buying decisions through unbiased advice and personalized recommendations. Numerous websites encourage customers to share information about their websites with friends. Even the U.S. Postal Service is promoting its ability to help businesses create buzz, as shown in the advertisement on page 589. Sometimes buzz helps promote a company, but it can also hurt companies. It's important for companies to understand how buzz works and how it shapes markets. Good Practice 14.1 summarizes some findings about buzz and how it works. A great example of an attempt to activate buzz is a recent BMW campaign for the MINI Cooper. An ad that appeared in *GQ* on heavy cardstock paper with tear-out cards encourages readers to give one card with the MINI Cooper and a clever tag line to one of those people—you know, those people who play in a garage band? And so on.

www.epinions.com

The influence tactics shown in Good Practice 14.1 are discussed throughout this chapter and can help companies control and understand word-of-mouth communications. Buzz can last a long time and it can come back again and again. Hush Puppies are a

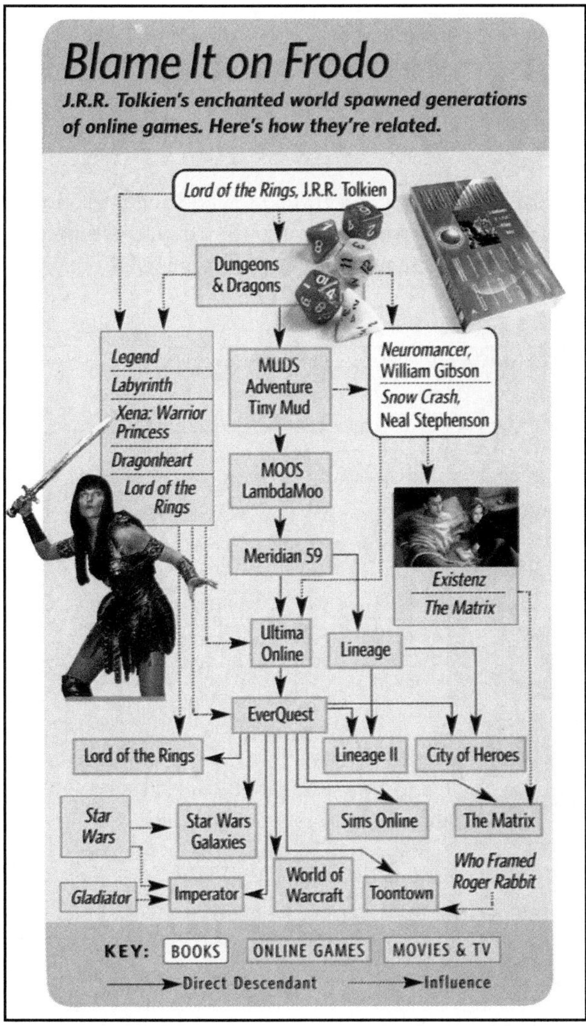

Lord of the Rings spawned generations of online games.

great example. In 1994 Wolverine, the company that makes Hush Puppies, was thinking of phasing out the shoes that made them famous; sales had fallen to a mere 30,000. However, in 1995 they sold 430,000 pairs and in 1996 they sold four times that many. Suddenly, Hush Puppies were a trend. Other products may ebb and wane, but still influence the design of numerous other products. A great example is Tolkien's classic enchanted world—*Lord of the Rings*. His books are influencing whole new generations exposed to the *Lord of the Rings* film trilogy from director Peter Jackson. However, the buzz potential of this product is easy to estimate when we examine its impact on other books, online games, movies, and TV shows, as illustrated on page 591.

Companies encourage word-of-mouth not just to create buzz, but also for other reasons. For example, companies may want to encourage responsible use of their product, as in the accompanying ad sponsored by Budweiser.

Many times interpersonal influence is invited, but interpersonal influence also operates at more subtle levels. One study of how people select consumer nondurables such as laundry detergent confirmed that many consumers simply buy the same detergent their mother used.[24] A young woman told me a story of a coat she proudly bought and wore, until she saw the same coat on an acquaintance who she disliked. She never wore the coat again. An issue of *The Nation* reported on consumption behavior in Russia in the early to mid-90s in the following fashion:

> People are mad for American culture and its artifacts. . . . School kids in Tashkent have the look down perfectly, which this year is straight out of Gap ads; a bunch of teenagers on a bus, with their colorful canvas backpacks, strategically torn jeans, hightops and oversized jackets worn loosely like shawls, puts one in mind of Ohio or Oregon as much as Uzbekistan.[25]

In his book *Beyond Culture,* Edward T. Hall offers a perplexing and subtle description of influence. He describes years of work micro-analyzing filmed interactions. He learned that when people interact, their movements become synchronized. Sometimes

Budweiser promotes parents talking to children.

Imitation is widespread.

this occurs in barely perceptible ways. In other cases, both bodies move as though the two were under the control of a master choreographer. Further studies suggest that syncing is pan-human and appears to be innate. However, the rhythms are culture specific. Each culture has its own characteristic manner of locomotion, sitting, standing, reclining, and gesturing.[26] In one study, for example, Hall found 15 differences in walking behavior between whites and Pueblo Indians of the American Southwest. Imagine how complicated service interactions between different cultures, with different culture-specific rhythms and rules for interaction, can become. Some experts attribute some of the difficulties between Korean store owners and black patrons in the Los Angeles, California, area to these differences in culture-specific rules for interaction.

The photo of Polish tourists at the Vatican illustrates that clothing can signal membership in a community, an almost unconscious bond among participants. Think about your favorite performances and events. Football games, rodeos, rock concerts, and chamber music all sport their own uniforms for belonging. As shown on the next page, fans are especially attuned to supporting their team by sporting the right colors. Nowhere is this more pronounced than at a college football game.

A useful summary point in considering the social context of personal consumption is that people tend to define their social context locally rather than globally. Face-to-face interaction tends to intensify social comparison and influence. People rarely bother to seriously compare themselves to others with whom they share little in contact, interests, culture, or geography. For example, when North Americans, Asians, or Europeans are thinking about their own social standing or well-being, they do not compare themselves to Nigerians, who have an annual per capita income of about $600, because in Europe, Asia, and North America, people do not often meet Nigerians. In fact, a powerful influence tool is to isolate an individual from the usual sources of support relied on for social rewards, feedback, and identity and to provide an alternative local social context. Religious sects often employ this local social isolation as a tool of persuasion.[27]

Moreover, even in a global, high-tech world, face-to-face interaction remains important to the free flow of news and information. Despite global events such as the World Trade Center bombing that may make travel less attractive, and new technologies such

Identification with membership groups is important to consumers.

as the Internet and videoconferencing that may make travel less necessary, people still like to get together face-to-face to do deals, woo customers, and develop new ideas. The reason? Some information requires context and trust to be meaningful, and this type of information still benefits from F2F (face-to-face) time. In fact, businesses that thrive on face-to-face communications now account for a growing share of economic activity. This would include companies that specialize in venture capital, finance, insurance, and wholesale trade, and companies whose lifeblood is creativity.[28]

Although interpersonal influence has a dramatic impact on consumption choices in the United States and many other countries, there are practical limits to personal influence. For example, a study in the early 1990s of Hungarian women's purchase of personal care and cosmetic products found little evidence of interpersonal influence despite the presence of many conditions that usually foster reliance on others. Possible reasons include a lack of interpersonal trust fostered by communism and the lack of consumers with high levels of product knowledge and experience. A replication of this study in the late 1990s revealed higher levels of interpersonal influence.[29]

TOOLS OF INFLUENCE

Three Forms of Influence

The tools of influence are numerous, but we can group the nature of influence into three categories: (1) normative (utilitarian), (2) value-expressive (identification), and (3) informational.[30] In practice it is very difficult to distinguish which form of influence is occurring; often more than one of these forms of influence comes into play in any given situation. The Chinese concept of *guanxi,* or connections, is a major component of Chinese business relationships and *connotes a form of influence that combines all three tools.*[31]

NORMATIVE INFLUENCE **Normative (utilitarian) influence** occurs when *an individual fulfills others' expectations to gain a direct reward or to avoid a sanction.*[32] In a film entitled *Consumer Behavior and Cars,* Professor Adler interviews fraternity brothers at Pepperdine University in California who indicate that a brother might be mocked or not accepted if he drove a certain type of car. To take another example of normative influence, some of the award-winning television commercials for Federal Express humorously depict the boss's sanctions visited on a hapless employee if a vital package does not arrive on time. The solution to avoid these normative sanctions, of course, is to use FedEx.

www.nshmba.org

The ad for the National Society of Hispanic MBAs shown below uses normative influence, but also an expert appeal, "Take my advice! It pays to be a member of the National Society of Hispanic MBAs." Check out their website to learn their vision, mission, and goals.

A number of marketing studies over the years have demonstrated that pressures to conform to norms affect buying decisions.[33] This is especially true when the product is conspicuous and distinct in its purchase and use, when the perceived rewards and sanctions controlled by others' are strong motivators, and when the product is viewed as relevant to obtaining rewards or avoiding sanctions. Personal care items are often promoted to help people avoid others' rejection or embarrassment.[34]

Writings on the adoption of clothing fashions assert that the diffusion of conspicuous new products like fashion goods is motivated by individuals' pursuit of social rewards through early adoption behavior.[35] The general theory states that groups in a favored social position seek out new products as a means of establishing and communicating social **differentiation.**

Others imitate these consumption patterns to affiliate themselves with the favored group and enhance their social position. As imitation threatens the integrity of the differentiating symbols, the favored group maintains their social distance by abandoning that consumption pattern and again innovating. The process of imitation and differentiation results in an ongoing cycle of change.[36] This story, in a nutshell, captures the life of 1980s "grunge" clothing, which moved from the garage bands of Seattle to

Ad for National Society of Hispanic MBAs uses normative influence.

Should You Boycott Abercrombie & Fitch Clothing?

ETHICAL DILEMMA 14.1

In April 2002 headlines across the United States featured Abercrombie & Fitch's decision to ditch a new line of T-shirts that Asian-American groups said reinforced negative stereotypes. For example, one T-shirt depicted two Asian-American males with signage that read "Wong Brothers Laundry Service—Two Wongs Can Make It White." The T-shirt caricatures are stereotypical images of Asian Americans dating back to when they were limited to manual labor jobs like laundering. University students organized protests and boycotts against Abercrombie & Fitch. Asian-American students felt the T-shirts trivialized their religion and history, but chat rooms were filled with youth of all ages and colors angry at the ethnic and racial stereotypes portrayed. The T-shirt fiasco created a chorus of angry voices demanding action and an apology. The company claims it never intended to offend anyone and that they have made fun of many other groups before. In fact, their public relations firm, Paul Wilmot Communications in New York, claimed they thought Asians would love these T-shirts. This is not the first or the last time that Abercrombie & Fitch has created a stir with their products and promotions. A&F has come under fire for promotions that endorse drinking and sex, and for producing children's-sized thong underwear that bear sexually suggestive slogans. Sometimes publicity can help a retailer more than it hurts, but pushing controversial racial or ethnic depictions is a different story. We hope Abercrombie & Fitch learned an important lesson.

Source: This case is compiled from several news articles and websites. Check out www.ecasu.org (East Coast Asian Student Union) to follow the details of this case. See also "Abercrombie & Glitch: Asian Americans Rip Retailer for Stereotypes on T-Shirts," San Francisco Chronicle, *April 18, 2002, and "T-Shirts' Ethnic Joke Flop,"* Washington Post, *April 19, 2002, p. E01.*

clothing boutiques in LA, to the Gap, and then out by the end of the decade. In the past few decades apparel designers have invested heavily in "coolhunting." **Coolhunting** involves *heading for the street, the happening streets, collecting observations and comments from the cool people, and making predictions on that basis.* Jennifer, a 17-year-old high school junior, is an early adopter of what the fringe street cultures are doing, and she's an influencer among her high school friends. She explains that it's important to her reputation to "look neat"—"you have to look good when you're walking down the street; you can't look like an idiot." Normative influence, avoiding looking like an idiot, frames her sense of style.[37]

VALUE-EXPRESSIVE INFLUENCE **Value-expressive (identification) influence** occurs when *individuals use others' norms, values, and behaviors as a guide for their own attitudes, values, and behaviors.* Implicit in value-expressive influence is the *desire for psychological association or social affiliation* with others. One desired outcome may be enhanced image in the eyes of others. However, value-expressive influence operates because of an individual's desire to be like someone he or she respects and admires, even if the attitude, value, or behavior is relatively inconspicuous or even private. The effectiveness of using celebrity endorsers to promote social causes relies in part on their value-expressive influence. Abercrombie & Fitch uses value-expressive influence and creates buzz about their products by recruiting college students from popular fraternities and sororities to work in their store. Having popular students wearing their clothes and endorsing their fashions can influence others for whom these students serve as role models. But sometimes their efforts to create and manage buzz backfire, as illustrated in Ethical Dilemma 14.1.

Identification with a valued other enhances self-esteem and self-concept. When a five-year-old boy cries inconsolably for a pair of Michael Jordan sneakers, one might conclude that he wants to be admired and respected in the eyes of his friends; but more likely he just really wants to be like Michael Jordan, and he believes that perhaps those sneakers will do the trick. Sales of gear that features the colors, logos, and numbers of sports teams and stars (a multibillion dollar industry) is a good example of value-expressive influence at work.

Value-expressive influence can be an important and positive motivator of personal change and can help individuals transcend the particular features of their local social context. A study of children from disadvantaged backgrounds who, as adults, substantially advanced their social and economic standing indicated that the presence of a significant role model was the biggest distinguishing difference between these children and their counterparts who remained in disadvantaged settings. Mentorship becomes a conduit for values and beliefs, as suggested by Consumer Chronicles 14.1.[38] Value-expressive influence can also be critical in the successful diffusion of a new product.[39] Some Third World consumers provide another vivid illustration.[40] Young inhabitants of some African countries associate themselves with the outside world and disassociate themselves from traditional village ways through the adoption of Western clothing. This behavior differentiates them from the norms within their village system and is symbolic of emotional allegiance to the perceived modernity and authority provided by this clothing. Consumer Chronicles 14.2 provides a similar example from the nation of Botswana in southern Africa.[41]

Networking among Young African Americans

CONSUMER CHRONICLES 14.1

For young African Americans contacts are invaluable. Having mentors in high places is an advantage their elders never had. An internal network at Xerox Corp. helped executive vice president A. Barry Rand break through the glass ceiling to become one of the highest-ranking black executives in the United States. As a result, he and others like him feel a strong responsibility to help open doors. "There is a tremendous sense of obligation to serve as a mentor," says Frank Savage, senior vice president of Equitable Cos.

Source: Reprinted with permission from Elizabeth Lesly and Maria Mallory, "Inside the Black Business Network," Business Week, *November 29, 1993, p. 72, copyright ©1993 by The McGraw-Hill Companies, Inc.*

Of course, for value-expressive influence to operate in a positive way, it's important that people choose role models well. An unfortunate illustration of a successful negative role model was the Joe Camel cigarette campaign. Research showed that even very young children recognize and respond positively to Joe Camel.[42] Another controversial example of value-expressive influence is the endorsement of St. Ides malt liquor by Scarface and his group Geto Boys, a hard-core rap group. Critics charged that the ads attracted the attention of rap's young audience. Research released by the Philadelphia-based firm Motivational Educational Entertainment has indicated that rap is the only medium considered credible by black, urban youth. Take a look, for example, at www.hhmoteur.ctw.cc or www.ghhr.de. Many rap stars admit that at least some kids are heavily influenced by rap music (which, as we have noted in other chapters, has a prominent role in global youth culture), constantly mouthing their favorite songs and mimicking the style and dress of their favorite performers. Some rap performers express concern that they carry a heavy burden to promote positive values because Hiphop is so influential.[43]

@ www.hhmoteur.ctw.cc

@ www.ghhr.de

INFORMATIONAL SOCIAL INFLUENCE **Informational social influence** occurs when *an individual uses the values, norms, and behaviors of others as credible and needed*

Campus Life in Botswana

CONSUMER CHRONICLES 14.2

One of the first things I noticed on campus was a distinct trend in student fashion that gave the place the feel of an American theme party: sweatshirts by California Co.; multicolored gang-style kerchiefs; imitation basketball jerseys of N.B.A. teams. In some instances the cultural costumes were in comic approximation of their models in the United States. The Yankees caps were often forest green or purple. The white X on his black cap, a student replied to my feigned ignorance, stands for "*Christ*—yes, like Xmas, you know." I'd stumbled upon a clumsy game of Telephone, played by murmuring fashion fads across the Atlantic Ocean.

Source: Nicholas Weinstock, "I Was a B.M.O.C. at Botswana U.," The Nation, *December 6, 1993, p. 693.*

evidence about reality.[44] Marketing illustrations of informational influence abound. When it is difficult to assess product or brand characteristics by observations, when acquiring the expertise required to evaluate a product choice is difficult, or when the process of purchase or consumption is frightening, consumers rely on others as guides to their own attitudes, values, and behaviors. The photo below depicts a familiar scene, two people shopping together. A *shopping companion* or **purchase pal** offers credible information and can have a significant influence on our feelings and behaviors in consumption contexts. One consumer behavior researcher provides a compelling description of the influence of a purchase pal, in the context of a tattoo service, indicating how the companion reduces purchase risk, provides social support for the decision, commiserates about the process, and acts as a social evaluator representing the opinions of others. Many other researchers have documented the frequency and extensiveness of use of a purchase pal in making consumption choices.[45] Perhaps on occasion you've been standing in the produce section of your local grocery store selecting a melon and been asked by another confused shopper how to assess the merit of the melon—do you tap it, smell it, squish it? Or perhaps your friends look to you as an expert on stereo equipment,

Illustrates purchase pal construct.

This ad uses testimonials and images of crowd approval as social proof of product merit.

photographic supplies, tools, cars, or how to get stains out of clothing. In all of these and many other cases, family, friends, and strangers may look to you for advice on how to manage their environment. They may not believe that you have any power to reward or sanction them, and they may not feel they want to be like you, but they see you as having knowledge and experience that will be useful to them.[46] One U.S. study reported that 46 percent of all respondents identified themselves as being an opinion leader or expert in some self-selected product category.[47]

Many marketing techniques rely on informational influence. Awareness of how marketers use informational influence can benefit consumers. For example, perhaps you are familiar with an advertisement for Grey Goose Vodka that ran in *GQ*. This ad claims that Grey Goose Vodka is the world's best vodka. In addition to underscoring the careful procedures of the Beverage Testing Institute and their expertise, the advertisement makes the claim more believable by providing the ranks of numerous other vodkas. A more subtle aspect of the ad's informational appeal is that it provides a vocabulary for evaluating vodkas. This in turn can have an impact on processing of future advertisements and consumer experiences.[48] Should you be skeptical? Well, that's for you to decide.

In the introductory vignette, clapping is encouraged by making sure that a salesperson sits with each customer and the salesperson claps. This offers **social proof** that clapping is the right thing to do in this situation. Social proof is used later when the balloons are popped to indicate people are buying. This lets others know that people similar to themselves recognize this offer as a good deal and have decided to make a purchase. Social proof is mimicked visually in an ad for Atomz website management software www.atomz.com

that features business customers applauding. Including a "satisfied customer" endorsement from the web management director at Sharp Electronics further extends the theme of informational influence. Check out their website and you'll see many more consumer testimonials and reports of customer satisfaction.

RELATIONSHIPS AMONG TYPES OF INFLUENCE In many, if not most, purchase and consumption circumstances, the influence of friends and acquaintances is not easily separated into normative, value-expressive, and informational forms of influence. For example, research shows a considerable amount of conformity among sorority sisters in relatively personal products such as shampoo, cosmetics, deodorants, and so forth.[49] What form of influence is operating? Well, perhaps there are social rewards and sanctions for certain brands of cosmetics and shampoo (normative influence). Anecdotal evidence from University of Colorado sorority members supports the idea that cosmetics such as Clinique, Lancôme, and Estée Lauder are more socially acceptable than Maybelline or Avon. In addition, of course, younger sisters show up on campus and hope to identify with their senior sisters who really seem to have their act together (value-expressive influence). Finally, a sorority is a wonderful environment to seek information from others about personal products. It's natural to rely on an admired and respected group for information about how to give your hair more body and what brand of lipstick really has lasting power (informational influence).

Commonly Used Influence Tactics

www.influenceatwork.com

In this section we outline some common tools for influencing others, talk about how these tools work, and give marketing examples. If you would like to learn more about this topic or if you would like to find out your Influence Quotient (NQ) with a short quiz, visit the Influence at Work website.[50]

RECIPROCITY One of the most widespread practices for human interaction is the **norm of reciprocity:** that people should *try to repay what another person or group has provided them.* This differs in important ways from an economic exchange. The most crucial distinction is that it involves *unspecified* obligations. For example, if a person gives a dinner party, she can expect her guest to reciprocate, but she can hardly bargain with them about the kind of party to which they should invite her. Many social scientists report that the reciprocity norm is pervasive within human societies and it permeates exchanges of every kind.[51] Many societies' complex rules for reciprocity perpetuate constant indebtedness between members of the culture.[52] Noted paleoarcheologist Richard Leakey and anthropologist Claude Lévi-Strauss have contended that the norm of reciprocity is the essence of what makes us human.[53]

Although the reciprocity norm exists in all human societies, it may not apply in the same way or with the same strength. A study examined employees' willingness to assist a co-worker when asked for assistance in branches of a multinational bank in four different countries: the United States, China, Spain, and Germany. In the United States, employees took a market-based approach in deciding whether to help. They felt obligated if they owed the employee a favor. In China, they felt obligated only if the employee was a member of their small group, and especially if the person was a high-status member of their group. In Spain, they helped requesters connected to their friends. If the employee had a relationship with their friends, they felt obligated to help. In Germany employees took an organizational approach to deciding to assist. They essentially asked whether the official rules and norms of the organization meant they should assist the employee. Of course, to some extent all of these different obligations to comply exist in each culture, but these results suggest that predominate norms of obligation vary from culture to culture.[54]

Relations of reciprocity can create and maintain significant social bonds. Consumer Chronicles 14.3 portrays how Mr. Dang does business in China. Interestingly, the norm of reciprocity applies not only in communications between people but between people and computers. For example, a series of experiments showed that when a computer initiates a request for information by first divulging some personal information, the subject provides more personal information than if the computer simply asks for information. This may seem strange, but it shows how important reciprocity is as a social norm for interaction.[55]

There are many studies on the impact of reciprocity on compliance. In one experiment, researchers showed that twice as many raffle tickets were sold when the request for a purchase was preceded by doing a small, unsolicited favor for the potential customer (offering someone a Coke).[56] A small bread shop based in Boulder, Colorado, illustrates an example of effective use of reciprocity. When you walk in the door, you're offered a warm slice of fresh bread with butter. There is no obligation to purchase anything, but watch the people come and go, and you will see the principle of reciprocity at work. The simple gift not only promotes the quality of the product, it also promotes the desire to reciprocate. This principle of reciprocity has been illustrated in sales techniques for centuries. There are many examples. For instance, the offering of free samples can engage the natural indebting force that requires reciprocation. Tupperware parties normally begin with a round of games that ensure everyone has received something from the company before the buying begins. Research has shown that waiters and waitresses can significantly increase the size of their tips by giving guests something as little as a single piece of candy.[57] Another illustration is the use of a small gift to accompany a request to complete a survey. The gift is often as little as 50 cents and is never intended to compensate for the respondent's efforts in completing the survey, but it is offered as a token of appreciation. The receiver is often encouraged to use the gift to brighten someone else's day. Research demonstrates that response rates are significantly increased by even this small gift.[58]

A slight variation on the reciprocity norm also plays an interesting role in many negotiation processes. This technique is commonly used in soliciting donations. The caller first asks for a rather large donation, and upon refusal, requests a much smaller amount. This technique was also used on Eric and Linda in the introductory vignette. After they declined purchasing the condominium, they were asked to make a much smaller purchase. Some writers refer to this technique as **door in the face** because it

The Rule of Reciprocity in Mr. Dang's Factory

CONSUMER CHRONICLES 14.3

Mr. Dang's approach to hiring Kaiping workers is one of paternalism. He considers his offer of employment to the children of his relatives to be a way of "looking after" them *(jiu kuo).* Both he and his wife are involved in many relations of reciprocity with local kin and friends. The depth of some of these relationships is such that Mr. Dang considers it an obligation to look after his kin through his business venture in China. In turn the employees feel obliged. Despite the unfavorable working conditions, they would not consider leaving for another factory because doing so would be a betrayal of Mr. Dang's kindness and generosity in offering them employment and taking care of them away from home. They also feel obliged to do many nonwork-related chores. It is not unusual to see one of the female workers doing the laundry for Mr. Dang.

Source: Adapted from Josephine Smart and Alan Smart, "Obligation and Control: Employment of Kin in Capitalist Labour Management in China," Critique of Anthropology *13, no. 1 (1999), pp. 7–32.*

involves *following up a large request with a much smaller request.*[59] The dramatic reduction between requests is intended to create the perception that the requester is making a concession. The approach plays on the desire to reciprocate a concession.

COMMITMENT AND CONSISTENCY The influence tools of **commitment** and **consistency** are related more generally to **attribution theory,** which suggests that people *try to explain causes to events*—people want to try to understand why things happen. **Self-perception theory,** an aspect of attribution theory, proposes that *attitudes develop as consumers look at and make judgments about their own behavior.* The influence tools of commitment and consistency relate specifically to people's desire to explain their own behavior (attribute causation) in a consistent way. It's important to note that the desire for a consistent self-image is not universally shared. For example, American businesspeople are often mystified that Indian businesspeople have very different moral codes for different parts of their lives. Many Indians live very partitioned lives, with many contradictions. They don't attempt to resolve these contradictions. Even within Western cultures the need for a consistent self-image may be much less pronounced than it used to be.[60]

Nevertheless, many societies and especially Western cultures value and support personal consistency. Inconsistency in beliefs, words, and deeds is viewed as indecisive, weak-willed, flighty, or even mentally ill. Consistency is also economical. Once a person has decided about an issue, he or she doesn't have to think about it any more; once a person has learned a particular route to work, it's easiest to just automatically go that same way each day.

Influence tactics play on the desire for consistency in a variety of ways. One popular sales technique is called **foot in the door** (FITD). FITD represents a technique where *compliance with a critical request is increased if an individual first agrees to an initial small request.* The typical explanation offered is that people who engage in a behavior may then adopt an attitude consistent with that behavior, making them more likely to engage subsequently in similar behaviors within that behavioral domain. Results studying this approach have been largely supportive, although more research is needed to identify the conditions that limit its usefulness.[61] You may have encountered this technique from an organization soliciting donations. On the first contact the organization may ask for a donation (no matter how small), hoping that you will then come to define yourself as someone who donates to that particular cause. This enhances the likelihood of continuing to get increasing donations from you. Salespeople often employ the technique of trying first to make a small sale, expecting further, much larger purchases to flow from the commitment. This technique was also employed in the opening scenario. The guests of the tour guide were encouraged to clap at the beginning and end of the film and later, at the tables, whenever a balloon went off signaling a sale. In this case clapping constituted a trivial public endorsement of the worth of the sales campaign that the tour guides hoped would prompt a larger commitment in the form of a sale.

The power of commitment as an influence tactic is substantially enhanced when the commitment is made in writing or made public.[62] The vignette at the beginning of the chapter illustrates this technique. When an individual purchased a condominium, a balloon was popped and public attention was drawn to that individual. This technique was designed to make it more difficult for the individual to back out afterward. Amway Corporation has discovered that people live up to what they have written down. They are much less likely to back out of contracts if they've made a personal commitment. The effectiveness of public commitment is used in a positive way in groups such as

This Australian promotion for Bürgen bread uses the commitment principle.

Alcoholics Anonymous. In these groups individuals publicly acknowledge their problem and their commitment to doing something about it. The visible commitment in front of family and friends enhances the likelihood of successfully breaking addiction and other consumer pathologies (e.g., compulsive shopping).

Now that you know how the consistency principle works, consider the Australian advertisement for Bürgen bread shown above. After being offered information about each of several types of Bürgen bread, the reader is asked for his or her opinion. This opinion can then be submitted to earn prizes. Notice that the opinion questions encourage the reader to endorse a particular benefit and type of Bürgen bread. This technique encourages reader commitment. Such attempts to elicit written commitment must be used carefully, because they can backfire. Good Practice 14.2 illustrates an example.

INFLUENCERS Many influence tactics revolve around characteristics of the influencer. Numerous source effects have been researched, including similarity, expertise, attractiveness, and likability. In many cases the celebrity endorser combines one or more of these qualities. All of these influencer characteristics are really ways of determining **communicator credibility,** or *overall believability of the source.* It's

GOOD PRACTICE 14.2

Reasons to Drive a BMW

A study conducted in Germany asked students to generate either 10 or 1 reason to choose a BMW. The researchers then measured students' attitudes toward both BMW and Mercedes, a competitor. What they learned has important implications for the practical limits of the consistency principle. The students who generated one reason for buying a BMW subsequently had more positive attitudes and intentions toward the brand, but those asked to generate 10 reasons found the task too hard. The difficulty of generating 10 reasons resulted in lower evaluations of BMW and more positive evaluations of Mercedes. So, if you ask consumers to generate arguments in favor of your brand, make sure it's easy; otherwise your commitment strategy may backfire.

Source: Adapted from Michaela Wänke, Gerd Bohner, and Andreas Jurkowitsch, "There Are Many Reasons to Drive a BMW: Does Imagined Ease of Argument Generation Influence Attitudes?" Journal of Consumer Research *24 (September 1997), pp. 170–78.*

important to remember that we attend to certain types of information about the source because, in general, this strategy works very well and helps people to make good and efficient choices.

Similarity An important and often effective guide to behavior is the behavior of a similar other. For example, when consumers get recommendations for movies or CDs from people with tastes similar to their own, they are likely to feel more confident that it will be entertainment they will enjoy.[63] Commercials for first-run movies often feature recommendations from "ordinary moviegoers" similar to the target audience. Under certain circumstances, consumers would prefer the advice of someone similar over someone with more expertise. In matters having to do with tastes, values, or opinions—where there is no right answer—the impact of a similar communicator is likely to be especially important.

There are other situations as well where **source similarity** may affect influence. For example, consider that you are undertaking a hike in the mountains and want to choose a route and decide what to pack. Would you prefer the advice of an expert mountain climber or someone with more experience hiking those mountains than you but with similar hiking skills? Many people might be afraid that the advice of an expert would lead them to select a route that was too difficult and carry a pack that would not serve their particular, more novice needs. An interesting variation of this theme is illustrated by Internet services that offer collaborative filtering or individualization technology.[64] Good Practice 14.3 describes collaborative filtering and how it can be used to tailor recommendations to particular user profiles. Give it a try and see what you think.

The central idea of Leon Festinger's theory of **social comparison** is that people need to compare themselves to others in order to evaluate their own abilities and opinions.[65] Of course, they don't compare themselves to just anybody; they select comparison groups on the basis of the others' similarity to them. Even though there are many pressures to use consensus to gauge reality, people's willingness to go along with a group evaluation is moderated to some extent by their judgments about the group members' similarity to them. An interesting twist on this principle is provided in some research with U.S. college students.[66] Even though previous research revealed a strong preference for a particular shade of their school color, when it was reported that students at a major rival school also preferred that shade, their preferences shifted away from that shade.

Because even small similarities can be so effective in producing a response, and because a veneer of similarity is so easy to manufacture, this tool of influence is popular in many marketing settings. For example, residents of a Los Angeles suburb who were provided with information about the recycling behavior of their neighbors immediately increased their recycling. A month later they were recycling more trash than ever. However, a request to recycle did not result in these improvements. A different study showed children a trip to the dentist's office to ease dentist office anxieties. Did it work? Yes, but only if the child depicted was the same age as the children viewing it.[67] One of the

GOOD PRACTICE 14.3

Collaborative Filtering

Collaborative filtering is simply a system that sifts through the opinions and preferences of thousands of people and systematically matches you with people who appear to have the same tastes you do and then provides you with their recommendations. A rather simple version of collaborative filtering is offered by amazon.com or by barnesandnoble.com, which recommend other books bought by people who bought books you recently purchased. However, much more sophisticated examples of collaborative filtering are available. One example is a website called MovieLens (movielens.umn.edu). After logging in to this site, you provide ratings on a series of movies and then the collaborative filtering process predicts how you will rate other popular movies, based on people like you who rate movies similarly. After you have plugged in about 15 opinions, predictions become amazingly accurate. Try it and see. Does it accurately predict your movie preferences? Will computer-generated recommendations replace the recommendations of friends? What do you think?

Source: Malcolm Gladwell, "The Science of the Sleeper," New Yorker, *October 4, 1999, pp. 48–55; and John Hagel and Marc Singer,* Net Worth *(Boston: Harvard Business School Press, 1999).*

most familiar applications is "common man" advertising. The technique employs someone prototypical of the target segment to deliver the persuasive appeal, and it may use "testimonials" from "real consumers like yourself" advocating the product. This approach can be very successful if people believe the source is similar and believe the testimonial is heartfelt. For years State Farm has been using the similarity principle in their advertising. This advertisement appeared in *Business 2.0* and is designed to appeal to small businesses.

Expertise Another way in which people may assess the credibility of another is on **expertise.** Numerous studies have demonstrated the persuasive advantage of messages delivered by an expert.[68] When consumers rely on the expertise of their stockbrokers to guide their financial portfolio, they economize on their own time and efforts.[69] People also rely on the expertise of many other professionals such as physicians and accountants. Rather than thinking through all of the arguments on a subject, consumers may seek out an expert's advice, someone who has presumably thought through those arguments. The endorsement or lack of an endorsement of a product by experts in the field can have significant consequences for the diffusion of that product. Although they are not perceived as the most influential information sources by moviegoers, film critics play a significant role in the launch of new movies. A study in France showed that moviegoers who are more knowledgeable

Source similarity is used as the basis for promoting State Farm Insurance for small businesses.

about cinema (up to a certain point) and who show evidence of high susceptibility to social influence (informational and normative) are more affected by film critics than others.[70] Use of expertise appeals is common in personal sales and in advertising.

Expertise is a common denominator in the choice of personal influencers. **Opinion leaders** are influential with consumers as sources of information and advice because of their *involvement, expertise, and experience in a product category.*[71] Opinion leaders are highly credible sources because they are perceived as neutral, they have product expertise, and they can tailor their recommendations to the specific opinion receiver. An opinion leader in one product category is likely to be an opinion receiver in a different product category.[72] **Market mavens** are distinguishable from opinion leaders because their influence stems not from product category expertise but from general knowledge or market expertise. They *possess a wide range of information about many different types of products, retail outlets, and other aspects of markets and like to share this information with others.*[73] Similar to opinion leaders, market mavens are influential because of consumers' perception that they offer an informed (expert) opinion on many market decisions. Market mavens like to share their information—they are socially motivated and want to help consumers make good choices.[74] Finally, **innovators,** or *the earliest adopters of new products,* are influential, in part because of their experience with the new product. After seeing a new trash compactor purchased by neighbors, and maybe even watching it in action, a family may decide to purchase one as well. Because of the important roles of these influencers in the diffusion of innovations, we provide a more complete description and discussion of their characteristics and how to target them in Chapter 17.

Attractiveness A number of studies have supported that physical **attractiveness** may make a source more persuasive.[75] Some particularly disturbing research suggests that attractive politicians receive more votes than unattractive candidates by a margin of more than 2 to 1, that attractive defendants are twice as likely to avoid jail as unattractive ones, and that attractive school children are viewed as better behaved and more intelligent then their less attractive classmates.[76] Why good-looking people have more influence and are regarded more favorably is something of a mystery. In some cases those who are attractive may trigger value-expressive influence—people would like to appear to others as the attractive ones appear to others; thus, the attractive people are appealing to emulate. Of course, in some cases attractiveness represents a relevant cue. A beautiful model with beautiful hair certainly seems like a more credible source of information about what shampoo to use, especially if the consumers can be convinced that the model started out with the same hard-to-manage, limp, thin hair that they are working with (e.g., combining physical attractiveness with problem similarity).[77]

Liking The effects of similarity and physical attractiveness on influence may relate to a more basic element in the influence equation: **liking.** Consumers are influenced by people they like. They may seek to obtain social rewards from those they like, wanting the liked person to like them back. This is fundamental to human processes of social bonding and social exchange.[78] When people like someone, they may also want to be perceived by others the way that individual is perceived (at least in some respects), and that too makes influence possible. Finally, people are inclined to believe the liked person is trustworthy and therefore will provide useful information in helping them manage their environment. Mounting evidence suggests that trustworthiness is a crucial factor in successful strategic alliances and other partnering arrangements.[79] Many factors in

This advertisement developed by students at Miami Ad School uses the scarcity principle to promote travel to Vietnam.

addition to similarity and physical attractiveness affect whether someone likes another. For example, some research suggests that when dissimilar people are brought together in close physical contact with each other, facing common crises that require unified action, an important bonding takes place that can create lasting and strong friendships.[80] How is this relevant to marketing? This and other research suggest that salespeople's close contact and cooperation with customers can be important ways of creating commercial friendships.[81]

Scarcity A powerful and frequently employed influence tactic is summarized by the **scarcity principle**—*something in short supply is more attractive than something that is plentiful.* Use of the tactic takes many forms. For example, in the opening vignette Linda and Eric were told that the special gold package would only be available if they signed today. Several years ago the perceived scarcity of Cabbage Patch dolls may have contributed to their popularity, and more recently the scarcity of Pokémon cards and color Gameboys made them prized. This advertisement is part of an ad campaign that encourages viewers to visit Vietnam soon, implying that it will quickly disappear, replaced by skyscrapers, multilane highways, and development projects. Students in the Miami Ad School developed this award-winning campaign. What aspects of the scarcity principle are at work in this advertisement?

One of the powers of the scarcity principle is that North Americans hate to lose opportunities, because losing opportunities or freedoms diminishes feelings of personal control.[82] They react against this by desiring the product or object about to be withheld much more than they would otherwise.[83] *Anytime the freedom to select a product or service is impeded, consumers respond by reacting against the threat.* One-day-only sales, limited editions, and last one on the shelf all appeal to this **psychological reactance** against a loss of options and control.[84] Marketers who have discontinued or changed their product line have often faced outrage and even protests by loyal consumers.[85] This happened with Coca-Cola's introduction of New Coke and with Crayola's change in their traditional crayon colors. The desire for options and control is not evenly distributed among cultures. For example, cultures with a fatalistic orientation,

Gaining Distinction in the Congo

CONSUMER CHRONICLES 14.4

An unusual example of the importance of distinction comes from the Congo and is called the *sape.* The *sape* is a ritual program for the transformation of ordinary unranked youth into great men. It begins and ends in Bacongo, with a phase in Paris. The youth moves to Paris and scrounges, living a life of incredible hardship, to obtain the cash and credit needed to accumulate a real haute couture wardrobe, called *la gamme.* Labels play a crucial role. Weston shoes, for example, are ranked among the highest. Copies are not acceptable. By returning with this haute couture wardrobe, the *sapeur* attempts to capture power via the accumulation of distinctive, authentic, effortful symbols of power.

Source: Jonathan Friedman, "The Political Economy of Elegance: An African Cult of Beauty," Consumption and Identity, *ed. Jonathan Friedman (Chur, Switzerland: Harwood Publishers, 1994), pp. 167–88.*

such as in many parts of Asia, might not react against a loss of options and control. Also, cultures in which consumers are accustomed to scarcity, such as much of central and eastern Europe and the former Soviet Union, might not experience this psychological reactance. However, even in these cultures the scarcity principle may operate, but for different reasons, as described next.

Another reason the scarcity principle works is because of a general connection, experienced over time, between demand and subsequent scarcity. Things that are in demand become scarce. In primitive societies people may observe the depletion of resources in demand, and in market-dominated societies attractive sale prices result in empty shelves. Naturally, people may infer a variant of the causality they have often experienced: Things that are scarce are in demand. Thus, scarce goods may imply popularity, also an important influencer. When a salesperson says, "They've been selling like hotcakes, I hope I have one left," the customer's interpretation is likely to be "this is a very good product since it is so popular with so many other people (consensus effect), and I may miss out if I don't buy it today." Of course, this provides an opportunity for the salesperson to take advantage of the customer. A salesperson wishing to move an especially slow item may combine a sale on the item with nearly bare shelves—just a few left, promoting the inference that this is a popular deal that won't last long. An interesting series of studies illustrates that the presence of a restriction in a promotion (i.e., purchase limit, purchase precondition, or time limit) serves to enhance value and increases sales, but not with all consumers and not all the time. Nevertheless, the public policy implications are clear. Unscrupulous marketers can use restrictions to fool some consumers into believing that a mediocre deal is a good deal.[86]

In addition, there may be a tendency to believe that things that are difficult to possess are better than those that are easy to possess. Over their lives people learn a connection between effort or investment and worth. This kicks in to explain the desire to have things that are difficult to possess. Often this feeling combines with a desire to have something that distinguishes the consumer from others—something not everyone else can have. The connection between the scarcity principle and the desire for distinction is evidenced in the limited production of many prestige goods. People in many cultures share the desire for distinction, although, as discussed in Chapter 7, it is certainly less important in some cultures than in others. An unusual example of the extreme importance of distinction is described in Consumer Chronicles 14.4.[87]

REFERENCE GROUPS

All people are influenced by both groups to which they belong and those to which they don't. As indicated in Chapter 13, almost all consumer behavior takes place within a group setting, and groups serve as one of the primary agents of socialization and learn-

Bosozoku Youth in Japan

CONSUMER CHRONICLES 14.5

On summer nights in large Japanese cities, the busiest streets reverberate to the deafening sound of hundreds of careening motorcycles and cars, astonishing onlookers and confounding police. The teenaged *bosozoku* drivers—the "violent driving tribe"—display their elegant and bizarre costumes. Kamikaze party uniforms are combined with American punk, surfer, and rock-and-roll gear, costumes imitating what they think American teens wear.

The Japanese mass media have portrayed bosozoku youths as juvenile delinquents, though in fact they are not major criminal offenders: the majority of those who participate in gang activities are from middle-class families, and gangs are rarely involved in illicit underworld activities. The photo above provides an image of these Kamikaze bikers.

Source: Ikuya Sato, Kamikaze Biker: Parody and Anomy in Affluent Japan *(Chicago: University of Chicago Press, 1991).*

ing. A **reference group,** or comparison group, is a group whose *presumed perspectives, attitudes, or behaviors are used by an individual as the basis for his or her perspectives, attitudes, or behaviors.* Consumer Chronicles 14.5 describes one important reference group for many Japanese youth, that is, *bosozoku* drivers. These youth use as referents media-made images of American youth as well as their vision of ancient symbols of power and courage such as Kamikaze warriors.[88]

Types of Reference Groups

We classify groups according to membership, attraction, and degree of contact.

MEMBERSHIP Some groups have formal membership, such that one is either a member or not. Other groups, such as cliques or informal collections of people, may have less formal rules for membership, and individuals may report confusion about whether or not they are members. For example, membership in a community may be strongly or weakly held. Many movies are built around the tension of joint membership in colliding groups that causes individuals to question their membership in one or more of the conflicting groups. Whether membership is formal or informal, strength of association with the group varies dramatically among members. For example, new initiates of a fraternity will typically feel much less secure about their membership than senior fraternity members getting ready to graduate. Similarly, a member of a group may feel

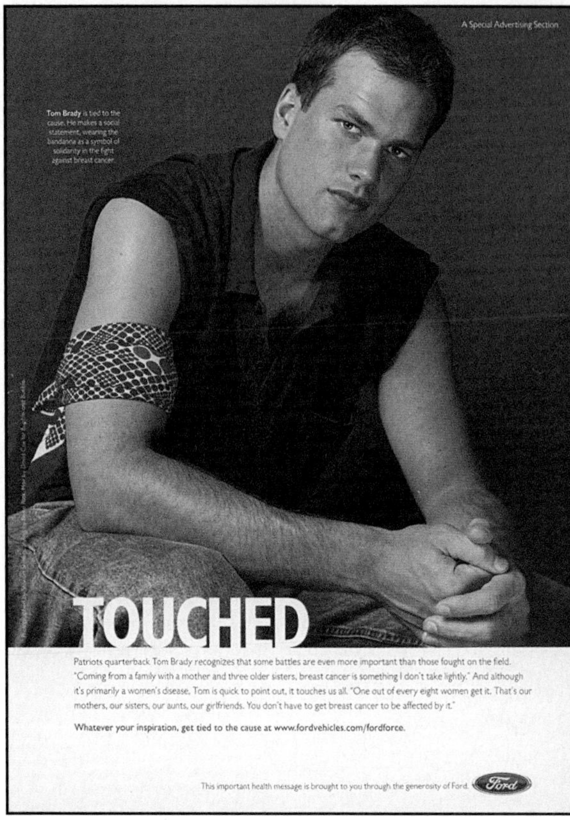

Ford teams with football celebrity to fight breast cancer.

only a very loose association with that group and hence participate only peripherally in its activities.

Group membership, and how it shapes consumer behavior, is important for marketers to understand. Many subcultures such as skydivers, Harley-Davidson club members, Jeep owners, and *Star Trek* fans draw on mass media representations of brands, products, places, and times to define their relationship to a group. As we discussed in Chapter 5, brand communities grow up around many brands and can boost customer loyalty. Companies and brands also can benefit by identifying with moral communities that consumers admire and aspire to participate in. For example, *Star Trek* fans identify with this fan community in part because of the Utopian ideals espoused in the *Star Trek* series of books, television shows, and movies.[89] The advertisement above features Patriots quarterback Tom Brady wearing a bandana as a symbol of solidarity in the fight against breast cancer. Ford encourages readers to get tied to the cause by wearing a bandana as well. This advertisement aligns Ford with the community of citizens fighting breast cancer, a worthy group to join.

ATTRACTION **Attraction** refers to *the level and direction of affect* (or emotional response) *that the group holds for an individual.* Attraction can be either positive or negative and may be associated with either membership or nonmembership groups. Exhibit 14.1 helps summarize these four major types of reference groups. For example, a high school student may confess to being "something of a nerd" (membership group) but *feel negative attraction to the group and desire to disassociate from or dis-*

EXHIBIT 14.1

Types of Reference Groups

claim membership in it. For this student, nerds are a **disclaimant reference group.** This student may attempt to avoid consumption behaviors common to the nerd group in an attempt to disassociate from it. One study that looked at how consumers think about fashion includes an interview with a young African-American woman, Gretta, who grew up in a "project-hood." She felt stigmatized by her membership in this group at the school to which she was bused. She talked about how she never had the name-brand stuff and how it made her feel bad, "seeing everyone else have something you can't have." For Gretta, people from the project-hood constitute a disclaimant group.[90]

Alternatively, a high school cheerleader may *feel positive about her membership in that group.* In this case she is likely to adhere to the group's norms and act in ways to reinforce her membership role in that group. For her, cheerleaders constitute a **contactual reference group.** Many of her consumption behaviors may be similar to those of other members of her group, as they all use similar consumption behaviors to reinforce their membership role. The use of consumption behaviors to reinforce group membership is familiar, as evidenced by the teenaged bosozoku drivers described earlier. Certain consumption objects such as Raiders caps or particular brands of sneakers have been banned in some high schools because of their strong associations with gangs. For example, a former gang member in Los Angeles reported that he can drive down the street and point out a gang member just by the way he or she dresses—the shoes, jackets, and hats are symbols, and "kids got killed over them."[91] Adidas ran an award-winning ad campaign that illustrated common runner behaviors such as nose blowing on the run and applying salves against chafing that nonrunners might find odd or even offensive. The Adidas ad tag line "Runners, Yeah, We're Different" appeals to people who feel positive about their identity as runners, and helps associate Adidas with this group.

Some important group influence can derive from a *group the individual doesn't belong to* but has either *strong positive attraction toward*—an **aspirational reference group**—or *strong negative attraction toward*—an **avoidance reference group.** Just because an individual feels a strong positive attraction to a particular group does not necessarily mean that she or he desires membership in that group, but it may mean that the group will be very influential in certain of the individual's attitudes and behaviors.

The influence of aspirational reference groups has been demonstrated in many different studies. For example, one study asked college students at a western university in the United States about their attitudes and intentions to adopt a new "cordless headphone that could be used with any current personal or home stereo system."[92] The findings suggest that aspirational group influence affects consumer attitudes and intentions in at least three distinct ways. First, the endorsement of the product by an aspirational reference group (the U.S. ski team) enhanced students' perceptions about the social desirability of new product consumption. Second, the endorsement had a direct positive effect on the perceived visibility of early adoption behavior. Finally, the endorsement had a significant influence on perceptions of sound quality. Although members of the U.S. ski team would not necessarily have any specific expertise in judging sound quality, their endorsement led consumers to infer better sound quality. One explanation for this type of aspirational group influence is provided by the **model of meaning transfer.**[93] The focus of this model is on *the transfer of culturally relevant meanings from the endorser to the product.* In the example of the cordless headphone, meanings such as "performance" and "quality" may move from the aspirational group to the new product through the endorsement process. In this case the consumer recognizes an essential similarity between the endorser (the U.S. Ski Team) and the new product (a cordless headphone). We talked about this model in Chapter 4 when we discussed consumption meanings.

What about the influence of avoidance groups? Are people influenced by nonmembership, negative-affect groups? Do consumers avoid certain clothing and behaviors out of fear that they will be mistaken for "one of them"? Certainly, in the case of gangs, the influence of avoidance groups is apparent—wearing a particular symbol could result in death. However, the influence of avoidance groups can also operate more subtly. For example, earlier we referenced a study where college students changed their color preferences to avoid sharing preferences with students from a rival school.

DEGREE OF CONTACT Degree of contact refers to *how much interpersonal contact the group members have with each other.* Groups characterized by *frequent interpersonal contact* are referred to as **primary groups.** Groups characterized by *limited interpersonal contact* are called **secondary groups.** Although, in general, we might expect primary groups to have more influence, we can think of many obvious exceptions. For example, perhaps you have a childhood friend that you don't see very often because she lives in a different part of the country. She might not influence your everyday shopping behaviors very much, but when you really need advice on something very important in your life, she may be the first person you call on. This introduces the important idea that reference groups have domains of influence. It's entirely possible to respect and be influenced by a group in one area but not in some other area.

The Degree of Reference Group Influence

A multitude of factors are likely to affect the degree of reference group influence on a particular purchase or consumption behavior. Studies have shown that some individuals are more susceptible to reference group influence than others.[94] For example, the high school girls in Shibuya and Hrajuku, Japan, will leap on any trend if the marketing is right, at least according to Sanrio's design department head. The boom-craze mentality among teens in Japan is so powerful that once 5 percent of the teen-girl market endorses a product, another 60 percent will almost certainly follow suit in less than a month.[95] A variety of studies have also shown that certain types of product and consumption choices are more likely to be influenced by reference groups than other product and consumption choices.[96] Industry Insights 14.1 illustrates some findings about influentials for the Hiphop generation. The Hiphop culture is the largest subculture of urban youth, composed of predominantly African-American teens and numbering 14 million. For members of this group, peer approval is vital, and they may well be the most difficult group to reach with mainstream messages.

Exhibit 14.2 illustrates some key dimensions that are likely to influence the degree of reference group influence. Some of these factors we have already discussed. If a behavior is not visible to others or not distinctive, then it is less vulnerable to reference group influence. The use of uniforms in schools is an attempt to take a highly visible behavior (which is vulnerable to group influence) and make it undistinguished. One aim is to reduce the feeling of children from poorer families that they don't belong. Of course, even within the rigid constraints of school uniforms students find ways to signal group and social class membership. A line of copy from a Lands' End catalog promotes "All uniform clothes are not created uniformly. See what sets Lands' End Kids Apart." Of course, one of the things that sets upscale catalog uniforms apart is their price.[97] By contrast, recycling programs in many cities attempt to make recycling a visible behavior. For example, in Boulder, Colorado, on pickup days recycled materials are prominently displayed in the front of houses in brightly colored bins. If you don't recycle, your neighbors know it.

What constitutes distinctive behavior varies from reference group to reference group. For example, college students owning skis in Pittsburgh, Pennsylvania, may be distinctive, but in Boulder, Colorado, the vast majority of college students own skis. To be distinctive in Boulder requires this year's elite brand of skis.

Reaching the Hiphop Generation

INDUSTRY INSIGHTS 14.1

- Messages perceived as being from outside the culture have little chance of getting in, and attempts to co-opt the culture will be resented and rejected.
- It is not an exaggeration to say that many of the Hiphop culture's members would rather risk death than subject themselves to peer group ostracism.
- Any authority figure telling them what to do is subject to immediate challenge. Messages perceived as persuasive are suspect. The cultural norm respects those who resist.
- When we asked who could speak to them about teen pregnancy or drugs, Hiphop members responded, "A single mother our age, someone who's going through it right now. Let her tell us what it's like. I'd listen to her."

Source: Dan Fost, "Reaching the Hiphop Generation," American Demographics *15, no. 5 (1993), pp. 15–17.*

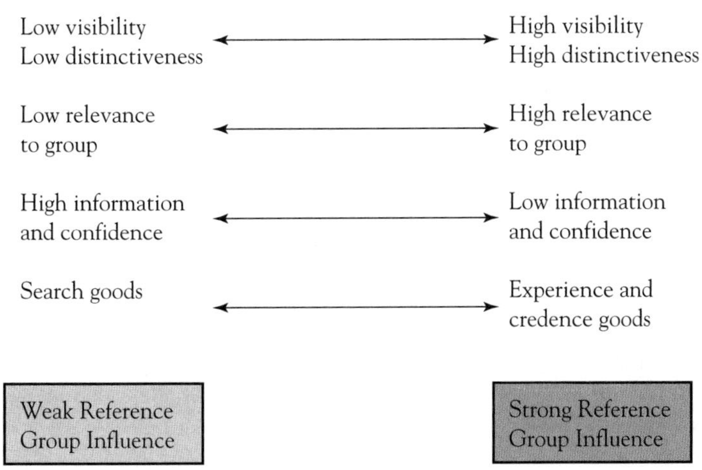

EXHIBIT 14.2

Consumption Situations and Degree of Reference Group Influence

Of course, the effect of behavior visibility and distinctiveness also depends on the relevance of the behavior to group image, standards, and norms. For example, if a neighborhood is indifferent about recycling, making recycling behavior more visible will not result in more recycling. In addition, as we discussed earlier, the opportunity to transfer meaning from the group to the object is enhanced when there is an essential similarity, that is, when the behavior seems relevant to the group image, standards, or norms. Thus, Bill Cosby is an excellent spokesperson for Jello pudding but much less effective as a spokesperson for the brokerage firm E. F. Hutton.

Finally, as we noted previously, consumers often believe that reference groups have better information than the information that they themselves have. Thus, when consumers perceive themselves to have low information as compared to a reference group and are not confident about their own attitudes or behaviors, the reference group may exert considerable influence. In unfamiliar consumption situations and complex product choices, reference groups are particularly influential. A study revealed that 25 percent of the people accompanied by a purchase pal invited that person along expressly to increase confidence in their choice.[98]

Similarly, with products and services for which consumers can't easily assess quality for themselves, reference groups may be relied on. Economist Philip Nelson talks about three types of product choices.[99] The first type is one for which *it is possible to observe the quality of the product from observation,* if the consumer has the expertise to do so. He calls products with these characteristics **search goods.** This type would include such things as fresh produce (lettuce, carrots, banana), cloth, and furniture. The second type of product choice *requires experience before it's possible to ascertain quality.* Nelson terms these products **experience goods.** For example, after seeing a movie it's easy to judge, at least for yourself, what the quality is, but it's difficult to appraise quality in advance. To decide on a movie consumers often rely on **surrogate experience,** *the reported experience of someone else,* in this case, friends or film critics. Many services are experience goods, which partially explains why interpersonal sources are so important in their selection. The third type of product choice is one for which *even after purchase and consumption it's difficult to evaluate quality.* Nelson refers to these products as **credence goods.** Checkups on people and cars are examples of credence goods. Consumers hope that if there's something wrong, the physician or car mechanic found it, but they can't really be sure. In these cases people rely on information from others about the reputation of the service provider.

RESISTING INFLUENCE

In this chapter we have talked about many different tools people and organizations use to influence consumers. In this final section we ask what techniques and strategies do we have to resist such influence when it is unwelcome? This topic is very important, but has received much less attention. Obviously, one thing that consumers try to do is screen out these influence attempts. In part they do this because they are overwhelmed with information and persuasion efforts. In fact, many businesses and products have sprung up to protect people. Consider the ads for Six Degrees and Novell shown on page 615. Both are designed to help consumers manage information boundaries, controlling information flow both in and out. Some people use their answering machines to screen out unwelcome telemarketing calls and toss direct mailings without opening them. Can you think of products that help you screen out influence attempts?

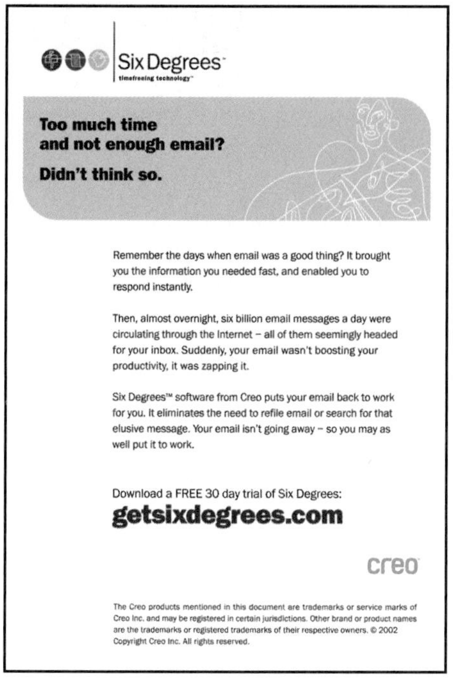

Connections can be too much of a good thing.

In addition to feeling overwhelmed with the sheer volume of influence attempts, people also know they are vulnerable. Consumers may try to protect their children from commercial TV and objectionable Internet content, avoid particular commercial encounters known to employ high-pressure persuasion tactics, avoid consumption environments that they know they can't resist, and in other ways monitor their own and others' behavior to avoid being victimized. Of course, even these avoidance strategies rely on savvy about how persuasion works! **Marketplace social intelligence** *is what consumers know about how marketing works.*[100] Some consumers know quite a lot, and *if they choose to be thoughtful* about marketplace activities, they can detect the influence strategies we have identified here and arm themselves against them. For example, after reading this chapter, you are likely to be more skeptical when someone offers you something for free.

In everyday life coping with persuasion attempts depends on: *what consumers know about how persuasion works* (**persuasion knowledge**); *what consumers know about the traits, competencies, and goals of the persuader* such as a friend, advertiser, or salesperson (**agent knowledge**); and *what consumers know about the topic of the message that may concern a product, service, social cause, or behavior* (**topic knowledge**).[101] For example, when a company such as Budweiser encourages parents to discuss responsible drinking with their children and offers a booklet to help parents, we might ask many questions. How is this message intended to make us feel about Budweiser—persuasion knowledge? What do we know about the company Budweiser and what it is hoping to accomplish—agent knowledge? What do we know about irresponsible drinking and the roles of parents and alcohol companies—topic knowledge? This may lead us to conclude that Budweiser is sincere in its attempt to encourage responsible drinking, or it may lead us to counterargue this appeal.

What's Real for Adrianna?

CONSUMER CHRONICLES 14.6

Adrianna is 40 years old, with two teenage daughters. She lives in Cluj, Romania. Adrianna views economic and political changes of the past decade in a predominantly positive light and consistent with her self-image. Although she has never traveled internationally, she is interested in the world outside Romania. "Even before the revolution we had a satellite antenna, even though it was very risky. But we wanted to see new things, America, Italy, Germany. We took chances. I like risks." Adrianna notes disbelief in media images but then indicates she likes to watch shows about "real life in America" such as "*The Young and the Restless,* and *Sunset Beach.*" Advertising and her teenage daughters have shaped Adrianna's attitudes about cosmetics brands. She experiments with Western brands of cosmetics, and believes advertising messages:

> If a product is more expensive, it is better. The advertising says this. If I had money, I would buy more expensive products, for instance an epilating cream. A Romanian epilating cream is good, but takes more time and doesn't clean completely. My daughter came with an *Oriflame* epilating cream—less time and better quality. If I had money, I would buy it.

Source: Adapted from Robin Coulter, Linda Price, and Larry Feick, "Origins of Product Involvement and Brand Commitment: Women and Cosmetics in Post-Socialist Central Europe," working paper, University of Connecticut, Storrs, 2002.

Some scholars argue that elementary and secondary education should include more information about how marketing works to provide children and youth with more effective defenses against marketplace exploitation, that is, more marketplace social intelligence. Notice we highlighted the phrase "if they choose to be thoughtful," because this is an important key. Consumers can fall victim to these techniques, even if they are knowledgeable about them, if they fail to activate their persuasion knowledge. Some research suggests that if you want to make consumers skeptical about an opponent's claims, you should provide counterarguments and make those arguments accessible (e.g., easy to recall) and linked to the opponents' message. For example, a successful antismoking ad featured a mock "Marlboro Man" commercial, but with coughing cowboys suffering from all the health symptoms associated with smoking. This ad effectively ridiculed the opponent's ads linking smoking to images of male strength and potency. One problem in developing countries and transitional economies is that they often don't have the storehouse of marketplace social intelligence to interpret the explosion of influence attempts afforded by cable TV and other global media. Consumer Chronicles 14.6 reports the beliefs of a 40-year-old Romanian woman. Growing up under communism, she is still learning how marketers persuade.

SUMMARY

In this chapter we described interpersonal influence. One of the reasons people are not more attuned to others' influence is because of an illusion of personal invulnerability. Interpersonal influence can be intentional or accidental; it is pervasive and to be influenced is often adaptive—it makes sense. Others can help people to make efficient and economical choices and can help them manage their environment.

Understanding personal influence begins by recognizing that one's attitudes and behaviors are very much shaped by the individual's particular social contexts. Interpersonal sources have a strong effect on consumer preferences and choices and influence others in both overt and more subtle ways. There are three important forms of influence, including normative (utilitarian), value-expressive (identification), and informational. In many, if not most, purchase and consumption situations, the influence of others is not easily separated into normative, value-expressive, and informational forms of influence.

There are many familiar influence tactics that consumers encounter every day. These include reciprocity, commitment and consistency, a variety of source characteristics, and the scarcity principle. The bases for some of these influence tactics are unique to one or a few cultures (e.g., psychological reactance), whereas the bases for other influence tactics are fundamental to human exchanges (e.g., reciprocity). Finally, the bases for some influence tactics are shared by many cultures but are certainly more important in some than in others (e.g., desire for distinction).

Groups are an important aspect of interpersonal influence. Consumers compare themselves to and refer to groups in forming their own perspectives, attitudes, and behaviors. Reference groups can be identified according to membership, attraction, and degree of contact. Both membership and nonmembership groups can have significant influence on an individual within a domain of purchase and consumption behavior. Characteristics of consumption situations that contribute to strong reference group influence include visibility and distinctiveness of purchase and consumption, relevance of the consumption situation to the group, low consumer information and confidence, and certain product types (experience and credence goods).

Knowledge of influence tactics can help you persuade other people, but can also help you resist persuasion attempts. Influence topics, agents, and contexts change, but the influence tactics outlined in this chapter are among the most regularly used and the most powerful. The influence processes described here also relate to many other important topics in consumer behavior. The successful diffusion of innovations relies on identifying, understanding, and managing influencers such as innovators, opinion leaders, and market mavens (Chapter 17). Persuasive advertising appeals directed at changing attitudes and behaviors also depend on many of the influence tactics we've described (Chapter 15). Source characteristics are an especially important component of many advertising campaigns, and advertisers rely heavily on endorsements by aspirational reference groups, admired celebrities, or the "common man." Discussions of group and family decision-making processes (Chapter 13), social class (Chapter 12), and lifestyle (Chapter 11) also relate to and are complemented by an understanding of interpersonal influence.

KEY TERMS

agent knowledge 615
aspirational reference group 611
attraction 610
attractiveness 606
attribution theory 602
avoidance reference group 611
buzz 590
commitment 602
communicator credibility 603
consistency 602
contactual reference group 611
coolhunting 596
credence goods 614
differentiation 595
disclaimant reference group 611
door in the face 601
experience goods 614
expertise 605
foot in the door 602
illusion of personal invulnerability 587
informational social influence 597
innovators 606
interpersonal influence 585
liking 606
market mavens 606
marketplace social intelligence 615
model of meaning transfer 612
norm of reciprocity 600
normative (utilitarian) influence 594
opinion leaders 606
persuasion knowledge 615
primary groups 612
psychological reactance 607
purchase pal 598
reference group 609
rhetorical communication 585
scarcity principle 607
search goods 614
secondary groups 612
self-perception theory 602
social comparison 604
social proof 599
source similarity 604
surrogate experience 614
symbolic interaction theory 587
topic knowledge 615
value-expressive (identification) influence 596
word-of-mouth 589

REVIEW QUESTIONS

1. Exhibit 14.1 describes four common types of reference groups. Think of examples of each of these four types of reference groups in your own life.
2. Mike is getting ready to interview for a job. He would like to influence the company to give him the job rather than someone equally qualified. Of course, he plans to be well prepared, but he'd like an extra edge. Drawing on commonly used influence tactics, give Mike advice for handling the job interview.
3. Construct a promotional appeal to illustrate
   a. Normative (utilitarian) influence.
   b. Value-expressive (identification) influence.
   c. Informational influence.
4. A sorority is planning a theme party. Major parties are important social occasions, and party themes are typically a chapterwide decision. Based on your own knowledge of social organizations, describe how interpersonal influence might operate in planning the party.
5. Think of two recent consumption situations, one for which you think reference group influence was strong and one for which you think reference group influence was weak. Describe the characteristics of these two consumption situations. Draw on Exhibit 14.2 as appropriate.
6. Assume that you have been elected to head a group on campus to reduce student abuse of alcohol. Employing the principles from this chapter, outline a campaign to influence the decision to consume less alcohol.

7. Consider the last three movies you went to see. How did you decide to go see these movies? Did other people influence your decision to see any (all) of these movies? Explain.
8. How could findings from the research on interpersonal influence be used to develop marketing strategy for the following?

a. Hospitals	d. Photographers
b. Pizza	e. Shampoo
c. Condoms	f. Cruises

9. Pick a brand, book, or movie you like, but one not many other people like or are aware of. Outline a set of strategies to create buzz around your choice.
10. Select an example of a persuasion attempt. Next, outline what you know about this persuasion appeal (persuasion knowledge), what you know about the persuader in this case (agent knowledge), and what you know about the topic. Now design a counterappeal.

REVIEW QUESTIONS

CASES

YOU MAKE THE CALL

CAN ONLINE INDIVIDUALIZATION TECHNOLOGY REPLACE INTERPERSONAL INFLUENCE?

About Direct is an online marketing company that empowers e-commerce through its individualized e-mail publications. When consumers visit one of About Direct's sites, they can customize their publications according to their tastes and interests. From consumers' preference information, About Direct matches merchants' products to a specific user's profile, determining how appropriate each item is for a particular subscriber. According to About Direct, consumers benefit because they get to hear about products and publications that are relevant to their tastes. Marketers benefit because they reach customers who most want to hear about their products. This type of mass customization was described in Chapter 5 as the leading edge in market segmentation strategy. In this chapter we also describe similar approaches such as collaborative filtering (outlined in Good Practice 14.3) designed to custom tailor recommendations to users.
By tailoring messages to each subscriber's lifestyle, budget, and tastes, About Direct is hoping to become your preferred source of information. They assume that in an age of virtually infinite choice, Internet shoppers are starved for real advice, and so far they appear to be right. BargainDog was launched in 1999 and was acquired in March 2000 by About.com network. After two years online BargainDog has over 5.5 million subscribers and was rated a top 100 shopping site by PC Data Online.

www.bargaindog.com

www.amazon.com

www.pets.com

QUESTIONS

1. In what ways is online, individualization technology like an interpersonal source, and in what ways is it different? How is online collaborative filtering like an interpersonal source, and how is it different?
2. Could a company like About Direct use an understanding of interpersonal influence to improve their service delivery? Explain.

1. See James C. McCroskey, Virginia P. Richmond, and Robert A. Stewart, *One on One: The Foundations of Interpersonal Communication* (Englewood Cliffs, NJ: Prentice Hall, 1986).
2. Mary Ann McGrath and Cele Otnes, "Unacquainted Influencers: When Strangers Interact in the Retail Setting," *Journal of Business Research* 32, no. 3 (1995), pp. 261–73.
3. David M. Johnson, "Disney World as Structure and Symbol: Re-creation of the American Experience," *Journal of Popular Culture* 15, no. 1 (1981), pp. 157–65; William B. Martin, *Quality Service: The Restaurant Manager's Bible* (Ithaca, NY: Cornell School of Hotel Administration, 1986); David Romm, "'Restauration' Theater: Giving Direction to Service," *The Cornell Hotel and Restaurant Association Quarterly* 29 (February 1989), pp. 31–39; and Maxwell Boas and Steve Chain, *Big Mac: The Unauthorized Story of McDonald's* (New York: Dutton, 1976).
4. Blake E. Ashforth and Ronald H. Humphrey, "Emotional Labor in Service Roles: The Influence of Identity," *Academy of Management Review* 18, no. 1 (1993), p. 91.
5. Jeff Kaye, "The Rave of Europe," *Los Angeles Times,* February 3, 1993, p. H1, describes the EuroKids.
6. Michael R. Solomon, "The Role of Products as Social Stimuli: A Symbolic Interactionism Perspective," *Journal of Consumer Research* 10 (December 1983), pp. 319–29.
7. See Philip G. Zimbardo, Ebbe B. Ebbesen, and Christina Maslach, *Influencing Attitudes and Changing Behavior,* 2nd ed. (Reading, MA: Addison-Wesley, 1977).
8. McCroskey et al., *One on One.*
9. This illustration comes from Allen Funt's 1970 United Artists film entitled *What Do You Say to a Naked Lady?* It is very similar in form to the classic Asch experiment. In the Asch experiment eight subjects were brought into a room and asked to determine which of a set of three unequal lines was closest to the length of a fourth line shown some distance from the other three. The subjects were to announce their judgments publicly. Seven of the subjects were working for the experimenter, and they announced incorrect matches. The order of the announcements was arranged so that the naive subject responded last. In a control situation, 37 naive subjects performed the task 18 times each without any information about others' choices. Two of the 37 subjects made a total of three mistakes. However, when another group of 50 naive subjects responded after hearing the unanimous but incorrect judgment of the other group members, 37 subjects made a total of 194 errors, all of which were in agreement with the mistake made by the group. For details on this experiment, see S. E. Asch, "Effects of Group Pressure upon the Modification and Distortion of Judgments," in *Readings in Social Psychology,* ed. E. E. MacCoby et al. (New York: Holt, Rinehart and Winston, 1958), pp. 174–83. This effect has been replicated a number of times in a variety of very different settings. For a recent example, see William O. Bearden and Randall L. Rose, "Attention to Social Comparison Information: An Individual Difference Factor Affecting Consumer Conformity," *Journal of Consumer Research* 16 (March 1990), pp. 461–72.
10. Ronald H. Frank, *Choosing the Right Pond: Human Behavior and the Quest for Status* (New York: Oxford University Press, 1985).
11. George Herbert Mead, *Mind, Self and Society* (Chicago: University of Chicago Press, 1934).
12. Richard E. Petty and John T. Caccioppo, *Attitudes and Persuasion: Classic and Contemporary Approaches* (Dubuque, IA: Wm. C. Brown, 1981).
13. Johann Arndt, "The Role of Product-Related Conversations in the Diffusion of a New Product," *Journal of Marketing Research* 4 (August 1967), pp. 291–95; and Charles W. King and John O. Summers, "Overlap of Opinion Leadership across Consumer Product Categories," *Journal of Marketing Research* 7 (February 1970), pp. 43–50.
14. A. Coskun Samli, "Interrelationships between the Market Segments and the Buyer Behavior," in *Retail Management Strategy: Selected Readings,* ed. David J. Rachman (Englewood Cliffs, NJ: Prentice Hall, 1970), pp. 79–112.
15. Linda L. Price and Lawrence F. Feick, "The Role of Interpersonal Sources in External Search: An Informational Perspective," in *Advances in Consumer Research,* vol. 11, ed. Thomas C. Kinnear (Ann Arbor, MI: Association for Consumer Research, 1984), pp. 250–53.
16. Geoffrey C. Kiel and Roger A. Layton, "Dimensions of Consumer Information Seeking Behavior," *Journal of Marketing Research* 18 (May 1981), pp. 233–39; J. W. Newman, "Consumer

External Search: Amount and Determinants," in *Consumer and Industrial Buying Behavior,* ed. A. G. Woodside, J. N. Sheth, and P. D. Bennett (New York: North-Holland, 1977); Hans B. Thorelli, "Concentration of Information Power among Consumers," *Journal of Marketing Research* 8 (November 1971), pp. 427–32; and J. G. Udell, "Prepurchase Behavior of Buyers of Small Electrical Appliances," *Journal of Marketing* 30 (1966), pp. 427–32.

17. Sharon E. Beatty and Scott M. Smith, "External Search Efforts: An Investigation across Several Product Categories," *Journal of Consumer Research* 14 (June 1987), pp. 83–95; Roger A. Formisano, Richard W. Olshavsky, and Shelley Tapp, "Choice Strategy in a Difficult Task Environment," *Journal of Consumer Research* 8 (March 1982), pp. 474–79; and Keith Murray, "A Test of Services Marketing Theory: Consumer Information Acquisition Activities," *Journal of Marketing* 55 (January 1991), pp. 10–16.

18. Lawrence F. Feick, Linda L. Price, and Robin A. Higie, "People Who Use People: Looking at Opinion Leadership from the Other Side," in *Advances in Consumer Research,* vol. 13, ed. Richard J. Lutz (Provo, UT: Association for Consumer Research, 1986), pp. 409–13.

19. Marsha L. Richins, "Negative Word-of-Mouth by Dissatisfied Consumers: A Pilot Study," *Journal of Marketing* 47 (Winter 1983), pp. 68–78.

20. Paul M. Herr, Frank R. Kardes, and John Kim, "Effects of Word-of-Mouth and Product-Attribute Information on Persuasion: An Accessibility-Diagnosticity Perspective," *Journal of Consumer Research* 17 (March 1991), pp. 454–62.

21. Steve Lowery, "Secret Raves," *Press Telegram,* January 16, 1993, p. B1.

22. Malcolm Gladwell, "The Science of the Sleeper: How the Information Age Could Blow Away the Blockbuster," *The New Yorker,* October 4, 1999, pp. 48–55.

23. Renée Dye, "The Buzz on Buzz," *Harvard Business Review,* November–December 2000, pp. 139–46; and Malcolm Gladwell, *The Tipping Point: How Little Things Can Make a Big Difference* (New York: Little, Brown, 2000).

24. Wayne D. Hoyer, "An Examination of Consumer Decision Making for a Common Repeat Purchase Product," *Journal of Consumer Research* 11 (December 1984), pp. 822–29.

25. Andrew Kopkind, "From Russia with Love and Squalor," *Nation,* January 18, 1993, pp. 44–61. See also Güliz Ger, Russell W. Belk, and Dana-Nicoleta Lascu, "The Development of Consumer Desire in Marketizing and Developing Economies: The Cases of Romania and Turkey," in *Advances in Consumer Research,* vol. 20, ed. Leigh McAlister and Michael L. Rothschild (Provo, UT: Association for Consumer Research, 1993), pp. 102–7.

26. Edward T. Hall, *Beyond Culture* (New York: Anchor, 1977); Edward T. Hall, *The Hidden Dimension* (New York: Anchor, 1990); and Edward T. Hall, *The Silent Language* (New York: Doubleday, 1959). See also John Graham, Dong Kim Chi-Yuan Lin, and Michael Robinson, "Buyer–Seller Negotiations around the Pacific Rim: Differences in Fundamental Exchange Processes," *Journal of Consumer Research* 15 (June 1988), pp. 48–54.

27. Lawrence Wright, "Orphans of Jonestown," *The New Yorker,* November 22, 1993, pp. 66–89.

28. "Press the Flesh, Not the Keyboard," *The Economist,* August 24, 2002, pp. 50–51.

29. Lawrence F. Feick, Robin A. Higie, and Linda L. Price, "Consumer Search and Decision Problems in a Transitional Economy: Hungary, 1989–1992," working paper no. 93-113, *Marketing Science Institute,* 1993; and Robin Higie Coulter, Lawrence F. Feick, and Linda L. Price, "Making up Time in the 1990s in Hungary: Are the Changes Purely Cosmetic?" working paper, University of Connecticut, 2000.

30. William O. Bearden and Michael J. Etzel, "Reference Group Influence on Product and Brand Purchase Decisions," *Journal of Consumer Research* 9 (September 1982), pp. 183–94; C. Whan Park and V. Parker Lessig, "Students and Housewives: Differences in Susceptibility to Reference Group Influence," *Journal of Consumer Research* 4 (September 1977), pp. 102–10; and Paul W. Miniard and Joel B. Cohen, "Modeling Personal and Normative Influences on Behavior," *Journal of Consumer Research* 10 (September 1983), pp. 169–80.

31. John Kao, "The Worldwide Web of Chinese Business," *Harvard Business Review* 71 (March–April 1993) pp. 24–33.

32. Normative influence can operate on a very subtle level. The Milgram experiments demonstrate the willingness of subjects, under the directive of a researcher, to deliver increasing lev-

els of electrical shocks to a victim (actually a confederate in the experiment who is acting) even after the victim begged for release with "an agonized scream." See S. Milgram, *Obedience to Authority* (New York: Harper and Row, 1974). These extremely disturbing and controversial studies illustrate the inability to defy the wishes of the boss (in this case, the lab researcher) and reveal a deep-seated sense of duty to authority within all of us.

33. Miniard and Cohen, "Modeling Personal and Normative Influences on Behavior"; and William O. Bearden, Richard G. Netemeyer, and Jesse E. Teel, "Measurement of Consumer Susceptibility to Interpersonal Influence," *Journal of Consumer Research* 15 (March 1989), pp. 473–81.

34. Pamela E. Grimm, Jagdish Agrawal, and Paul S. Richardson, "Product Conspicuousness and Buying Motives as Determinants of Reference Group Influences," in *European Advances in Consumer Research,* vol. 4, ed. Bernard Dubois, Tina M. Lowrey, L. J. Shrum, and Marc Vanhuele (Provo, UT: Association for Consumer Research, 1999), pp. 97–103.

35. Georg Simmel, "Fashion," *International Quarterly* 10 (1904), pp. 130–55; Eric J. Arnould, "Toward a Broadened Theory of Preference Formation and the Diffusion of Innovations: Cases from Zinder Province, Niger Republic," *Journal of Consumer Research* 16 (September 1989), pp. 239–67; and Grant McCracken, "Culture and Consumption: A Theoretical Account of the Structure and Movement of the Cultural Meaning of Consumer Goods," *Journal of Consumer Research* 13 (June 1986), pp. 71–84.

36. For lots of good examples related to fashion and style, see Craig J. Thompson and Diana L. Haytko, "Speaking of Fashion: Consumers' Uses of Fashion Discourses and the Appropriation of Countervailing Cultural Meanings," *Journal of Consumer Research* 24 (June 1997), pp. 15–42; and Robert J. Fisher and Linda L. Price, "An Investigation into the Social Context of Early Adoption Behavior," *Journal of Consumer Research* 19 (December 1992), pp. 477–86.

37. Malcolm Gladwell, "The Coolhunt," *The New Yorker,* March 17, 1997, pp. 78–87, describes DeeDee. She works for an advertising agency in Del Mar called Lambesis and puts out a quarterly tip sheet called the *L Report* on what the cool kids in major American cities are thinking, doing, and buying. She is a coolhunter. See also Janine Lopiano-Misdom and Joanne De Luca, *Street Trends* (New York: HarperCollins, 1998). The example about Jennifer is taken from *Street Trends,* pp. 21–22.

38. Elizabeth Lesly and Maria Mallory, "Inside the Black Business Network," *Business Week,* November 29, 1993, p. 72.

39. Fisher and Price, "An Investigation into the Social Context of Early Adoption Behavior."

40. Melanie Wallendorf and Eric J. Arnould, "'My Favorite Things': A Cross-Cultural Inquiry into Object Attachment, Possessiveness and Social Linkage," *Journal of Consumer Research* 14 (March 1988), pp. 531–47.

41. Nicholas Weinstock, "I Was a B.M.O.C. at Botswana U.," *The Nation,* December 6, 1993, p. 693.

42. Rick Pollay and Jean Kilbourne, *Pack of Lies* video. This film describes the strategic use of value-expressive influence by cigarette companies.

43. Charisse Jones, "Critics Fear Hip-Hop Is Eroding Kids' Morals and Touching Off Violent Episodes Like the Recent Rampage at Magic Mountain. Are These Entertainers Truly Poisoning Young Fans' Minds? Or Is That Just a Bum Rap? Rap's Bad Rep,"*Los Angeles Times,* May 2, 1993, Home, p. 1; and www.move.de/amm/ECON.htm.

44. Price and Feick, "The Role of Interpersonal Sources in External Search."

45. Clinton R. Sanders, "Tattoo Consumption: Risk and Regret in the Purchase of a Socially Marginal Service," in *Advances in Consumer Research,* vol. 12, ed. Elizabeth C. Hirschman and Morris B. Holbrook (Provo, UT: Association for Consumer Research, 1985), p. 20; Cathy L. Hartman and Pamela L. Kiecker, "Marketplace Influencers at the Point of Purchase: The Role of Purchase Pals in Consumer Decision Making," in *AMA Educators' Proceedings,* vol. 2, ed. Mary Gilly and Robert Dwyer (Chicago: American Marketing Association, 1991), pp. 461–69; and David F. Midgley, "Patterns of Interpersonal Information Seeking for the Purchase of a Symbolic Product," *Journal of Marketing Research* 20 (February 1983), pp. 74–83.

46. Lawrence F. Feick and Linda L. Price, "Thoughts on Search: Breaking Free of the Purchase

Paradigm," in *AMA Winter Educators' Proceedings,* vol. 2, ed. Paul Anderson and Michael Ryan (Chicago: American Marketing Association, 1984), pp. 179–83.
47. Feick, Price, and Higie, "People Who Use People."
48. Stewart Shapiro and Mark T. Spence, "Factors Affecting Encoding, Retrieval, and Alignment of Sensory Attributes in a Memory-Based Brand Choice Task," *Journal of Consumer Research* 28 (March 2002), pp. 603–17.
49. Jacqueline Johnson Brown and Peter H. Reingen, "Social Ties and Word-of-Mouth Referral Behavior," *Journal of Consumer Research* 14 (December 1987), pp. 350–62; and Peter H. Reingen, Brian L. Foster, Jacqueline Johnson Brown, and Stephen B. Seidman, "Brand Congruence in Interpersonal Relations: A Social Network Analysis," *Journal of Consumer Research* 11 (December 1984), pp. 771–83.
50. These tools and others have been described in greater depth in a variety of places. One of the best and most readable treatments of influence tactics is found in Robert Cialdini, *Influence: The New Psychology of Modern Persuasion* (New York: HarperCollins, 1983). See also Robert B. Cialdini, "Harnessing the Science of Persuasion," *Harvard Business Review,* October 2001, pp. 72–79.
51. A. W. Gouldner, "The Norm of Reciprocity: A Preliminary Statement," *American Sociological Review* 25 (1960), pp. 161–78; and Marcel Mauss, *The Gift,* trans. I. G. Cunnison (London: Cohen and West, 1954).
52. One famous institutionalized form of reciprocity called the Kula is described by Bronislaw Malinowski. The main principle underlying the regulation of actual exchange is that the Kula consists in the bestowing of a ceremonial gift, which has to be repaid by an equivalent countergift after a lapse of time. But it can never be exchanged from hand to hand, with the equivalence between the two objects being discussed, bargained about, and computed. The second important principle is that the equivalence of the countergift is left to the giver, and it cannot be enforced by any kind of coercion. If the article given as a countergift is not equivalent, the recipient will be disappointed and angry, but he has no direct means of redress, no means of coercing his partner. For more discussion, see Bronislaw Malinowski, *Argonauts of the Western Pacific* (London: Routledge and Kegan Paul, 1922); and Jerry W. Leach and Edmund Leach, eds. *The Kula: New Perspectives on Massim Exchange* (Cambridge: Cambridge University Press, 1983).
53. Claude Lévi-Strauss, *The Elementary Structures of Relationship,* trans. J. H. Bell, J. R. von Sturner, and R. Needham (Boston: Beacon, 1969); and R. Leakcy and R. Lewin, *People of the Lake* (New York: Anchor Press/Doubleday, 1978).
54. For a comprehensive outline of this and other related research, see Kelton v. L. Rhoads and Robert B. Cialdini, "The Business of Influence: Principles That Lead to Success in Commercial Settings," in *The Persuasion Handbook: Theory and Practice,* ed. M. Pfau and J. Dillard (Thousand Oaks, CA: Sage Press, 2002).
55. Youngme Moon, "Intimate Exchanges Using Computers to Elicit Self-Disclosure from Consumers," *Journal of Consumer Research* 26 (March 2000), pp. 323–39.
56. D. T. Regan, "Effects of a Favor and Liking on Compliance," *Journal of Experimental Social Psychology* 7 (1971), pp. 627–39.
57. Rhoads and Cialdini, "The Business of Influence." See also Jonathan K. Frenzen and Harry L. Davis, "Purchasing Behavior in Embedded Markets," *Journal of Consumer Research* 17 (June 1990), pp. 1–12.
58. Leslie Kanuk and Conrad Berenson, "Mail Surveys and Response Rates: A Literature Review," *Journal of Marketing Research* 12 (November 1975), pp. 440–53.
59. R. B. Cialdini et al., "Reciprocal Concessions Procedure for Inducing Compliance: The Door-in-the-Face Technique," *Journal of Personality and Social Psychology* 31 (1975), pp. 206–15; and John C. Mowen and Robert Cialdini, "On Implementing the Door-in-the-Face Compliance Strategy in a Marketing Context," *Journal of Marketing Research* 17 (May 1980), pp. 253–58.
60. Some postmodern theorists argue that increasingly consumers "don't really care whether things make sense as long as they look interesting." Consumers shift between very different and often contradictory self-images with "no such thing as an essential 'me.'" See Jack Solomon,

The Signs of Our Time: The Secret Meanings of Everyday Life (New York: Harper and Row, 1988), p. 219. For example, an individual may have many very different styles of dressing that vary between situations and moods.

61. The initial research on FITD was conducted by J. L. Freedman and S. C. Fraser in the mid-1960s. In their research, a researcher, posing as a volunteer worker, had gone door to door in a residential California neighborhood making a preposterous request of homeowners. The homeowners were asked to allow a public service billboard to be installed on their front lawns. To get an idea of how the sign would look, they were shown a photograph depicting an attractive house, the view of which was almost completely obscured by an ugly sign reading "DRIVE CAREFULLY." Although the request was understandably refused by the great majority (83 percent) of other residents in this area, a full 76 percent of this particular group agreed to the request. Why? Two weeks earlier, they had made a small commitment to driver safety. A different volunteer worker had asked them to accept and display a small three-inch square sign that read "BE A SAFE DRIVER." See J. L. Freedman and S. C. Fraser, "Compliance without Pressure: The Foot-in-the-Door Technique," *Journal of Personality and Social Psychology* 4 (1966), pp. 195–203. For a synthesis of research results on this and related compliance techniques, see Edward Fern, Kent Monroe, and Ramon Avila, "Effectiveness of Multiple Request Strategies: A Synthesis of Research Results," *Journal of Marketing Research* 23 (May 1986), pp. 144–52.

62. M. Deutsch and H. B. Gerard, "A Study of Normative and Informational Social Influences upon Individual Judgment," *Journal of Abnormal and Social Psychology* 51 (1955), pp. 629–36.

63. Robin A. Higie and Lawrence F. Feick, "The Effects of Preference Heterogeneity and Source Characteristics on Ad Processing and Judgments about Endorsers," *Journal of Advertising* 21 (June 1992), pp. 9–25; Linda L. Price, Lawrence F. Feick, and Robin A. Higie, "Preference Heterogeneity and Coorientation as Determinants of Perceived Informational Influence," *Journal of Business Research* 19 (1989), pp. 227–42; and Stewart Bither and Peter Wright, "Preferences between Product Consultants: Choices versus Preference Functions," *Journal of Consumer Research* 4 (June 1977), pp. 39–47.

64. T. G. Brock, "Communicator–Recipient Similarity and Decision Change," *Journal of Personality and Social Psychology* 1 (June 1965), pp. 650–54.

65. Leon Festinger, "A Theory of Social Comparison Processes," *Human Relations* 7 (May 1954), pp. 117–40.

66. Bearden and Rose, "Attention to Social Comparison Information." The effect of "a much despised, in-state rival institution" preference on students' reported preferences was strongest for those students high on a scale that measures attention to social comparison information (ATSCI).

67. Rhoads and Cialdini, "The Business of Influence."

68. Arch G. Woodside and J. W. Davenport, "The Effect of Salesmen Similarity and Expertise on Consumer Purchasing Behavior," *Journal of Marketing Research* 11 (May 1974), pp. 198–202. See also Dorothy Leonard-Barton, "Experts as Negative Opinion Leaders in the Diffusion of a Technological Innovation," *Journal of Consumer Research* 11 (March 1985), pp. 914–26.

69. Linda L. Price, Lawrence F. Feick, and Robin A. Higie, "Information Sensitive Consumers and Market Information," *Journal of Consumer Affairs* 21 (Winter 1987), pp. 328–41. See also Michael R. Solomon, "The Missing Link: Surrogate Consumers in the Marketing Chain," *Journal of Marketing* 50 (October 1986), pp. 208–18.

70. Leonard-Barton, "Experts as Negative Opinion Leaders"; and Alain d'Astous, "A Study of Individual Factors Explaining Movie Goers' Consultation of Film Critics," in *European Advances in Consumer Research,* vol. 4, ed. Bernard Dubois, Tina M. Lowrey, L. J. Shrum, and Marc Vanhuele (Provo, UT: Association for Consumer Research, 1999), pp. 201–8.

71. James H. Myers and Thomas S. Robertson, "Dimensions of Opinion Leadership," *Journal of Marketing Research* 9 (February 1972), pp. 41–46; Charles W. King and John O. Summers, "Overlap of Opinion Leadership across Consumer Product Categories," *Journal of Marketing Research* 7 (February 1970), pp. 43–50; and Meera P. Venkatraman, "Opinion Leaders, Adopters, and Communicative Adopters: A Role Analysis," *Psychology and Marketing* 6 (Spring 1990), pp. 51–68.

72. Feick, Price, and Higie, "People Who Use People."

73. Lawrence F. Feick and Linda L. Price, "The Market Maven: A Diffuser of Marketplace Information," *Journal of Marketing* 51 (January 1987), pp. 83–97; and Robin A. Higie, Lawrence F. Feick, and Linda L. Price, "Types and Amounts of Word-of-Mouth Communications about Retailers," *Journal of Retailing* 63 (Fall 1987), pp. 260–78.
74. Linda L. Price, Lawrence F. Feick, and Audrey Guskey-Federouch, "Everyday Market Helping Behavior," *Journal of Public Policy and Marketing* 14, no. 2 (Fall 1995), pp. 255–66. For a charming description and discussion of the market maven, see Gladwell, *The Tipping Point,* pp. 60–69.
75. Shelly Chaiken, "Communicator Physical Attractiveness and Persuasion," *Journal of Personality and Social Psychology* 37 (August 1979), pp. 1387–97.
76. Cialdini, *Influence.*
77. Lynn R. Kahle and Pamela M. Homer, "Physical Attractiveness of the Celebrity Endorser: A Social Adaptation Perspective," *Journal of Consumer Research* 11 (March 1985), pp. 954–61; and C. Whan Park and S. Mark Young, "Consumer Response to Television Commercials: The Impact of Involvement and Background Music on Brand Attitude Formation," *Journal of Marketing Research* 23 (February 1986), pp. 11–24.
78. See Peter M. Blau, *Exchange and Power in Social Life* (New Brunswick, NJ: Transaction Books, 1986).
79. For one example, see Gerald Zaltman and Christine Moorman, "The Importance of Personal Trust in the Use of Research," *Journal of Advertising Research* 28 (October–November 1988), pp. 16–24.
80. Eric J. Arnould and Linda L. Price, "River Magic: Extraordinary Experience and the Extended Service Encounter," *Journal of Consumer Research* 20 (June 1993), pp. 24–45. See also Linda L. Price, Eric J. Arnould, and Patrick Tierney, "Going to Extremes: Managing Service Encounters and Assessing Provider Performance," *Journal of Marketing* 59 (April 1995), pp. 83–97.
81. Linda L. Price and Eric J. Arnould, "Commercial Friendships: Service Provider–Client Relationships in Context," *Journal of Marketing* 63 (October 1999), pp. 38–56; and Caren Siehl, David E. Bowen, and Christine M. Pearson, "Service Encounters as Rites of Integration: An Information Processing Model," *Organization Science* 3 (November 1992), pp. 537–55.
82. J. W. Brehm, *A Theory of Psychological Reactance* (New York: Academic Press, 1966).
83. S. S. Brehm, "Psychological Reactance and the Attractiveness of Unattainable Objects: Sex Differences in Children's Responses to an Elimination of Freedom," *Sex Roles* 7 (1981), pp. 937–49.
84. Mona Clee and Robert Wicklund, "Consumer Behavior and Psychological Reactance," *Journal of Consumer Research* 6 (March 1980), pp. 389–405.
85. Suein L. Hwang, "Marketing," *The Wall Street Journal,* June 14, 1991, p. B1; and Dean Starkman, "After Hue and Cry, Crayola Will Scrap Color 'Indian Red,'" *The Wall Street Journal,* March 10, 1999, p. B7.
86. J. Jeffrey Inman, Anil C. Peter, and Priya Raghubir, "Framing the Deal: The Role of Restrictions in Accentuating Deal Value," *Journal of Consumer Research* 24 (June 1997), pp. 68–79.
87. Jonathan Friedman, "The Political Economy of Elegance: An African Cult of Beauty," *Consumption and Identity,* ed. Jonathan Friedman (Chur, Switzerland: Harwood Academic Publishers, 1994), pp. 167–88.
88. Ikuya Sato, *Kamikaze Biker: Parody and Anomy in Affluent Japan* (Chicago: University of Chicago Press, 1991), p. 1.
89. Robert V. Kozinets, "Utopian Enterprise: Articulating the Meanings of *Star Trek*'s Culture of Consumption," *Journal of Consumer Research* 28 (June 2001), pp. 67–88.
90. Thompson and Haytko, "Speaking of Fashion."
91. Rick Telander, "Senseless: In America's Cities, Kids Are Killing Kids over Sneakers and Other Sports Apparel Favored by Drug Dealers. Who's to Blame?" *Sports Illustrated,* May 14, 1990, pp. 36–49. The article contains an additional interview by Kristina Rebelo, "You See a Red Rag, Shoot," p. 46.
92. Fisher and Price, "An Investigation into the Social Context of Early Adoption Behavior."

93. Grant McCracken, "Who Is the Celebrity Endorser? Cultural Foundations of the Endorsement Process," *Journal of Consumer Research* 16 (December 1989), pp. 310–21.
94. Bearden, Netemeyer, and Teel, "Measurement of Consumer Susceptibility to Interpersonal Influence"; and Park and Lessig, "Students and Housewives."
95. "What's Up Pussy Cat?" www.tokyoclassified.com.
96. Bearden and Etzel, "Reference Group Influence on Product and Brand Purchase Decisions."
97. David Crockett and Melanie Wallendorf, "Sociological Perspectives on Imposed School Dress Codes: Consumption as Attempted Suppression of Class and Group Symbolism," *Journal of Macromarketing* 18 (Fall 1998), pp. 115–31.
98. Hartman and Kiecker, "Marketplace Influencers at the Point of Purchase."
99. Philip Nelson, "Information and Consumer Behavior," *Journal of Political Economy* 78 (March–April 1970), pp. 311–29.
100. Please see Peter Wright, "Marketplace Metacognition and Social Intelligence," *Journal of Consumer Research* 28 (March 2002), pp. 677–82, for a more extensive treatment of this important and complex topic. See also Marian Friestad and Peter Wright, "Persuasion Knowledge: Lay People's and Researchers' Beliefs about the Psychology of Persuasion," *Journal of Consumer Research* 22 (June 1994), pp. 62–74; and Robert Cialdini, "The Poison Parasite Defense: A New Way to Sap a Competitor's Persuasive Strength," APS William James Distinguished Lecture, Midwestern Psychological Association Meetings, May 2001.
101. Marian Friestad and Peter Wright, "The Persuasion Knowledge Model: How People Cope with Persuasion Attempts," *Journal of Consumer Research* 21 (June 1994), pp. 1–21.

chapter 1
chapter 2
chapter 3
chapter 4
chapter 5
chapter 6
chapter 7
chapter 8
chapter 9
chapter 10
chapter 11
chapter 12
chapter 13
chapter 14
chapter 15
chapter 16
chapter 17
chapter 18
chapter 19

LEARNING OBJECTIVES

After completing this chapter, you should be able to:

- Define attitudes and how they are acquired, strengthened, and changed.
- Distinguish cognitive, affective, and behavioral dimensions of attitudinal responses.
- Understand why consumers have attitudes.
- Apply several attitude theories to consumer behavior.
- Understand how consumer attitudes and decisions are shaped by consumer goals and involvements.
- Understand the constructive nature of consumer attitudes and decisions and how they are shaped by culture and social context.
- Distinguish the role of emotions in consumer attitudes and decisions.
- Describe several practical tools consumers use to make decisions.
- Relate consumer attitudes and decisions to other topics covered in this textbook.

CONSUMER ATTITUDES AND DECISIONS

A TASTE FOR ICE CREAM[1]

Maggie is eight years old and she loves ice cream. She is not alone. Per capita consumption of ice cream in the United States ranks second globally. New Zealand ranks number 1, with citizens consuming an average of seven gallons of ice cream each year. According to Maggie the best ice cream is made fresh at the creamery on campus, but she has other favorite brands (Ben and Jerry's and Dreyer's) and varieties of ice cream (Cookie Dough and Raspberry Chocolate Avalanche) that reflect her maturing tastes. Maggie used to only like vanilla ice cream, still the most popular flavor in America, but she is now willing to try a variety of different flavors. There are limits, however. The Ice Cream Exhibition in Tokyo, Japan, through September 2002 tests the boundaries of ice cream's versatility. Rice ice cream, common in China and Japan, is deemed tasteless by Maggie, while many other varieties offered seem too revolting to try, for example, ox tongue, crab, fried eggplant, and saury fish. And what of an ice cream made out of poisonous pit viper, which the Japanese believe increases virility? It sells for $8.50 a cup, but both Maggie and her dad Andy say, no thanks!

In the United States more ice cream is sold on Sunday than any other day of the week, and sales peak in July and August. Consistent with these cultural preferences, Maggie likes ice cream on warm summer evenings after dinner or as part of a summer afternoon excursion, and rarely favors ice cream as a winter treat. This contrasts with her young Scandinavian friends who seem willing to have ice cream almost any time and line up for it at park vendors on cold winter days after walks or ice skating. Maggie thinks of ice cream as a taste she and her father share, and they often cuddle together on a summer evening after dinner to share ice cream—sometimes right out of the carton. Of course, there are occasions and foods that seem to demand ice cream. For example, although many cakes can be served alone, birthday cakes require at least one flavor of accompanying ice cream, and the evaluation of a birthday party is diminished by its absence. Warm apple pie also seems to invite vanilla ice cream as a partner.

Although Maggie's dad loves the taste of ice cream, he also believes that it is unhealthy and frequently opts for ice cream look-alikes such as frozen yogurt. Maggie pays little attention to nutritional information about calories and fat content, so her affection for ice cream is unfettered by such information. Although Maggie initially balked at the idea of frozen yogurt, the taste convinced her that it is an acceptable, if not preferred, alternative. In addition to opting for low-fat alternatives, Andy also prefers small containers of ice cream that impose a natural limit on consumption. Ice cream may be cheaper by the gallon, but the pint size offers quantity control that Andy doesn't trust himself to exercise. Maggie likes these too, because they are cute and easy to handle. Although Maggie loves ice cream, it would be almost impossible to predict her choice between a fresh-baked chocolate chip cookie and her favorite flavor of ice cream. What is predictable is that if dad opts for ice cream and she opts for a cookie, she'll end up with some of that ice cream as well!

OVERVIEW

Consumers such as Maggie and her Dad in the vignette above formulate, strengthen, and change their attitudes about many different objects and reference these attitudes in responding to situations and deciding what actions to take. Their attitudes are impacted by many different factors, and like other consumers they are bombarded with numerous messages from various sources attempting to influence their attitudes, judgments, and decisions. Exhibit 15.1 illustrates that attitudes and decisions are nested within a cultural and social context and depend on consumers' goals, involvements, perceptions, experiences, knowledge, lifestyles, and self-concepts.

The term *attitude* is used in a variety of different ways, as shown in Consumer Chronicles 15.1. Here, we define **attitude** as *an evaluation of a concept or object, such as an issue, person, group, brand, or service that expresses a degree of favor or disfavor.*[2] As indicated by this definition, an **attitude object** is *the entity that gets evaluated,* and it can be abstract or concrete, individual or collective.

If asked, Maggie affirms she likes ice cream, but quizzed further, we learn she likes ice cream in certain situations and with certain people. She likes some brands and flavors better than others. How Maggie feels, thinks about, and uses ice cream is nested within a cultural and social context, and although her attitude toward ice cream is enduring in some respects, it is also dynamic—malleable to new information and contexts. Although Maggie has never tasted fried eggplant ice cream or even thought about

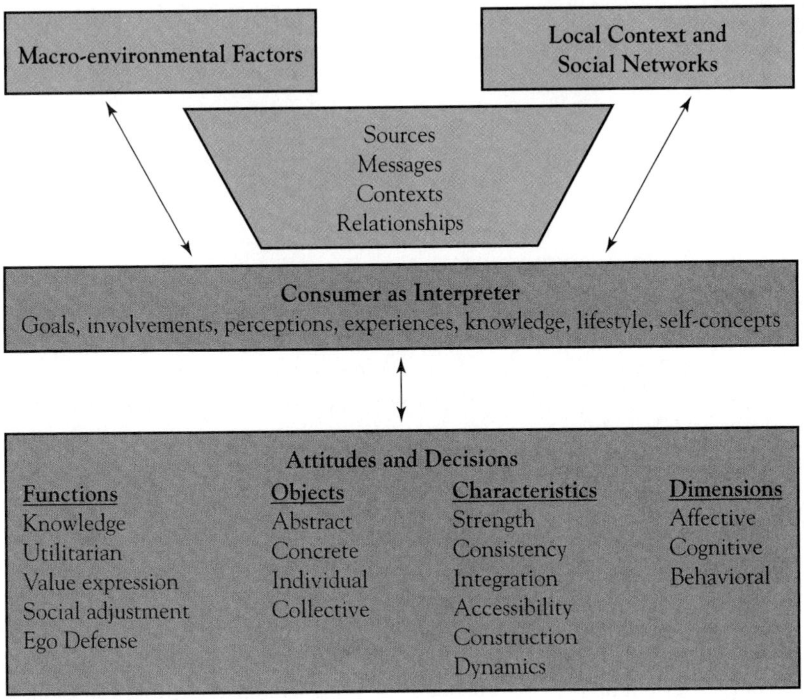

EXHIBIT 15.1

Consumer Attitudes and Decisions

it before, when presented with the idea, she accesses the set of associations this abstract concept brings to mind, and she makes a **judgment**—she *estimates the likelihood of an event,* in this case, liking eggplant ice cream. She concludes she wouldn't like it, and follows up with a decision—she won't try it. A **decision** *makes a selection between options or courses of action*. Notice the close relationship between attitudes, judgments, and decisions depicted in the introductory vignette. Although they can operate independently, they are often closely related. Maggie, like other consumers, is an **adaptive decision maker.** She *exploits and adapts to aspects of the environment in order to make decisions to achieve goals*. In Japan, rice ice cream seemed like a good way of experimenting with the exotic, but not "too exotic," supporting her self-concept, but in the United States such an option would be unlikely to catch her eye. Although frozen yogurt didn't have the descriptive appeal of ice cream, Maggie was willing to take a chance and try it, but only because ice cream wasn't an option.

This chapter will concentrate on providing an understanding of consumer attitudes and decisions and the way they vary depending on consumers and situations. We begin with a discussion of why consumers have attitudes. Next we direct attention to how attitudes are structured, describing attitude objects, characteristics, and dimensions. There are many competing and complementary theories about attitudes. Many of these turn on discussions about consumer motives and abilities, topics we discussed in Chapter 7. We focus attention on a few that are popular and have useful implications for marketing. Judgments are closely related to attitudes and crucial in whether and how consumers make decisions. We consider some common tools for making judgments and their managerial implications. Then we center discussion on consumer decisions. We begin by stressing the adaptive and constructive character of consumer decision making and the relationship between decisions and consumer action. Then we outline several

Attitude in Common Speech

CONSUMER CHRONICLES 15.1

The term *attitude* is frequently used in everyday conversations. Here are some examples:

- When Marika was young, her mother used to tell her, "Don't take that attitude with me, young lady!"
- When Marika's mother returns from a shopping trip, she tells Piet, "I didn't mean to project an attitude, but the salesclerk told me I did."
- As soon as Marika's mother leaves, Piet says, "I'm heading down to Locos for some attitude adjustment."
- Dirk's teacher tells him, "I don't like your attitude in class."
- In 1931, the psychologist L. L. Thurstone described attitude as the amount of *affect* that a person has for or against an object.

common ways that consumers make decisions, again highlighting approaches that have important implications for marketing.

WHY CONSUMERS HAVE ATTITUDES

Why do consumers have attitudes? One basic answer is that *attitudes help consumers cope with their environments.* Referred to as a **functional theory** of attitudes, this theme is evident in many attitude theories.[3] Five functions of attitudes are commonly described. Attitudes help us *organize and simplify experiences and stimuli*—**knowledge function**—and they *help us act in our own self-interest by seeking rewards and avoiding punishments*—**utilitarian function.** Attitudes provide a means for *expressing personal values and other core aspects of self-concept*—value expression. By contrast with the **value-expressive function** that allows important aspects of the self to be expressed, the **ego-defensive function** emphasizes that attitudes *provide defense against internal and external threats to self-concept.* For example, attitudes of apathy or indifference about health threats such as AIDS and breast cancer might reflect avoidance and denial—ego defense. Prejudice is also grounded in ego defense, allowing people to project their own feelings of inferiority onto other ethnic and racial groups. Attitudes also *facilitate, maintain, and disrupt social relationships*—that is, serve a **social-adjustment function.** Consumers' attitudes are embedded in broader social and cultural structures that represent their attitudes toward other people and reference groups. The social-adjustment function is very important in many contexts. For example, a consumer may believe that holding the same attitude as a liked other person will help cement the relationship.

Although an attitude can serve more than one function, typically one function will dominate. Different attitude objects may relate more to one function than another.[4] If marketers understand the dominant function a product serves, they can create brands and promotional campaigns that deliver these to consumers. The **matching hypothesis** asserts *persuasion will be maximized when message content is matched to the functional basis of the attitude.*[5] Of course, even if consumers agree that an object serves predominantly one function, that doesn't mean that they agree about the evaluation of the object on that function. For example, two consumers may agree that attitudes toward Diesel clothing reflect the self—serve a value-expressive function—but they may disagree about meaning.

The functions that attitudes serve are likely to vary in importance from culture to culture. Consistent with discussions in previous chapters, the social adjustment function is likely to be more important in more collectivist cultures such as China and Japan, and utilitarian and value-expressive functions may be more important in individualistic cultures such as the United States and Australia. A study showed that Korean advertisements tend to appeal to in-group benefits, harmony, and family integrity while

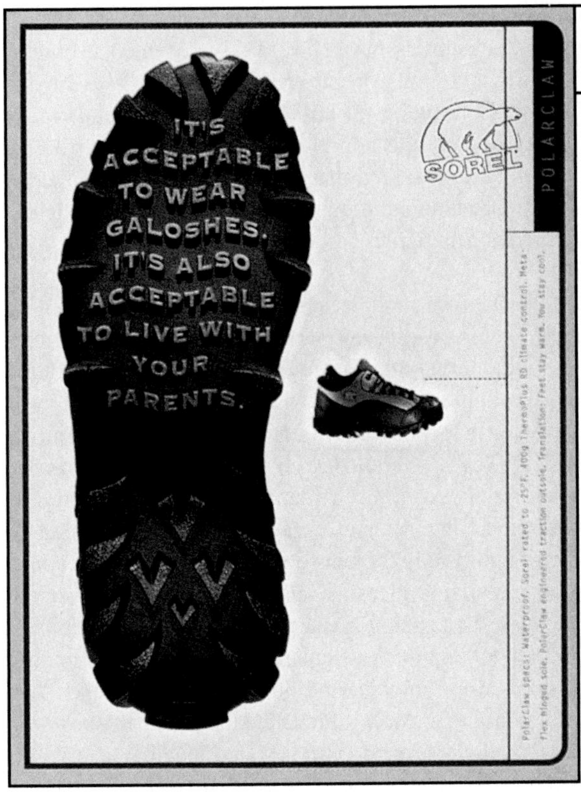

Attitudes are culturally and socially situated.

U.S. advertisements appeal to individual benefits, personal success, and independence. In Korea advertisements that stressed individual benefits were not as persuasive as those that appealed to group benefits, and in the U.S. appeals to group benefits were not as persuasive as those that stressed individual benefits.[6] The advertisement for Sorel shown above illustrates an ego-defensive appeal based on fitting in with a group, but this is not the kind of appeal you would find in a collectivist culture that values family. This advertisement implies it is "not cool" to wear galoshes or live with your parents. The advertisement also illustrates that attitudes are formed within particular cultural and social contexts.

HOW ATTITUDES ARE STRUCTURED

It's important to remember an attitude is an internal state and not directly observable. The nature and structure of attitudes is inferred from observable responses and some understanding of how the mind works. We discussed key aspects of how the mind works in Chapter 9. Drawing on these understandings we can think of attitudes as an association in memory between an attitude object and an evaluation.[7] An attitude encompasses the direct and indirect experiences that an individual has with the attitude object.

What Consumers Have Attitudes About

An attitude object can be anything that can be held in mind by the consumer. For example, attitudes toward one's self are termed self-esteem. We talked about this in Chapter 10. Attitudes toward abstract goals or end states are usually known as values.

We talked about values in several different chapters but especially Chapter 3. Marketers are especially interested in attitudes consumers have toward advertisements, brands, and stores. **Attitude toward the ad** (A_{ad}) is just *whether the consumer likes or dislikes an ad.* Determinants of A_{ad} include attitude toward the advertiser, evaluation of the ad execution itself, the mood evoked by the ad, and the degree to which the ad affects viewers' arousal levels. It is generally agreed that commercials can stimulate at least two kinds of positive emotions: pleasure and arousal. Negative emotions, such as intimidation, are also possible. **Mood-management theory** assumes *consumers strive to eliminate or at least diminish bad moods and perpetuate good ones* by selecting appropriate media. For example, when given a choice, bored subjects select exciting TV programs to watch, whereas stressed subjects opt for relaxing shows. Sometimes consumers like an advertisement so much that their positive feelings transfer from the ad to the brand. This can happen through a process of classical conditioning, as was discussed in Chapter 9. But it also can happen because consumers find the information supplied in the ad believable and accept its claims. One study shows that attitudes toward the ad affect brand evaluation not just in the United States but in countries as diverse as India, Greece, Denmark, and New Zealand.[8] Of course, what makes an ad effective will vary dramatically cross-culturally. Japanese marketing communications place special emphasis on creating affectively pleasing ads. The purpose of Japanese marketing communications is to please the consumer and to build dependency (*amae*) on the firm. This is done through indirect approaches. Japanese commercials often use serene, mood-creating nature symbols, for example, and aim to entertain rather than persuade.[9] The posters for a professional road-racer's bicycle shop in Japan shown on the opposite page are consistent with this approach. They evoke bicycle performance in a simple, powerful, and aesthetically pleasing way.

Attitude Characteristics

A consumer's attitude toward an object can be quite different at different points in time, even in the absence of new experiences with the object. That's because an expressed attitude depends on what consumers have stored in memory and how easily it can be reconstructed from memory. **Attitude availability** refers to whether consumers have *stored an evaluation of an object in memory,* and **attitude accessibility** refers to *activation potential at a particular point in time*. Attitudes vary both in their availability and accessibility.[10] These in turn can influence the strength of an attitude and how confident consumers feel about it. **Attitude strength,** or *the power to influence consumer responses,* is important to marketers because strong attitudes lead to selective information processing and are resistant to change, persistent over time, and predictive of behavior. If marketers are able to create strong, favorable brand attitudes, they protect against competitors' persuasion attempts.

Recall from Chapter 9 that memory is influenced by many contextual factors. Even an available attitude such as an evaluation of a political candidate may not be accessible standing in a polling booth registering a vote. Maggie's judgment about eggplant ice cream is a **constructed attitude,** *built up from a combination of other attitudes and guesses about combinations.* Many times consumers are asked to evaluate things they've never thought about before, attitudes that are not available. In such situations, they may formulate a judgment—that is, construct an attitude, but that attitude may not be reliable and also may be susceptible to context effects. For example, Maggie frequently responds that she likes something that her friends like even though she's never tried it. Often, after trying it, she concludes she doesn't like it after all.

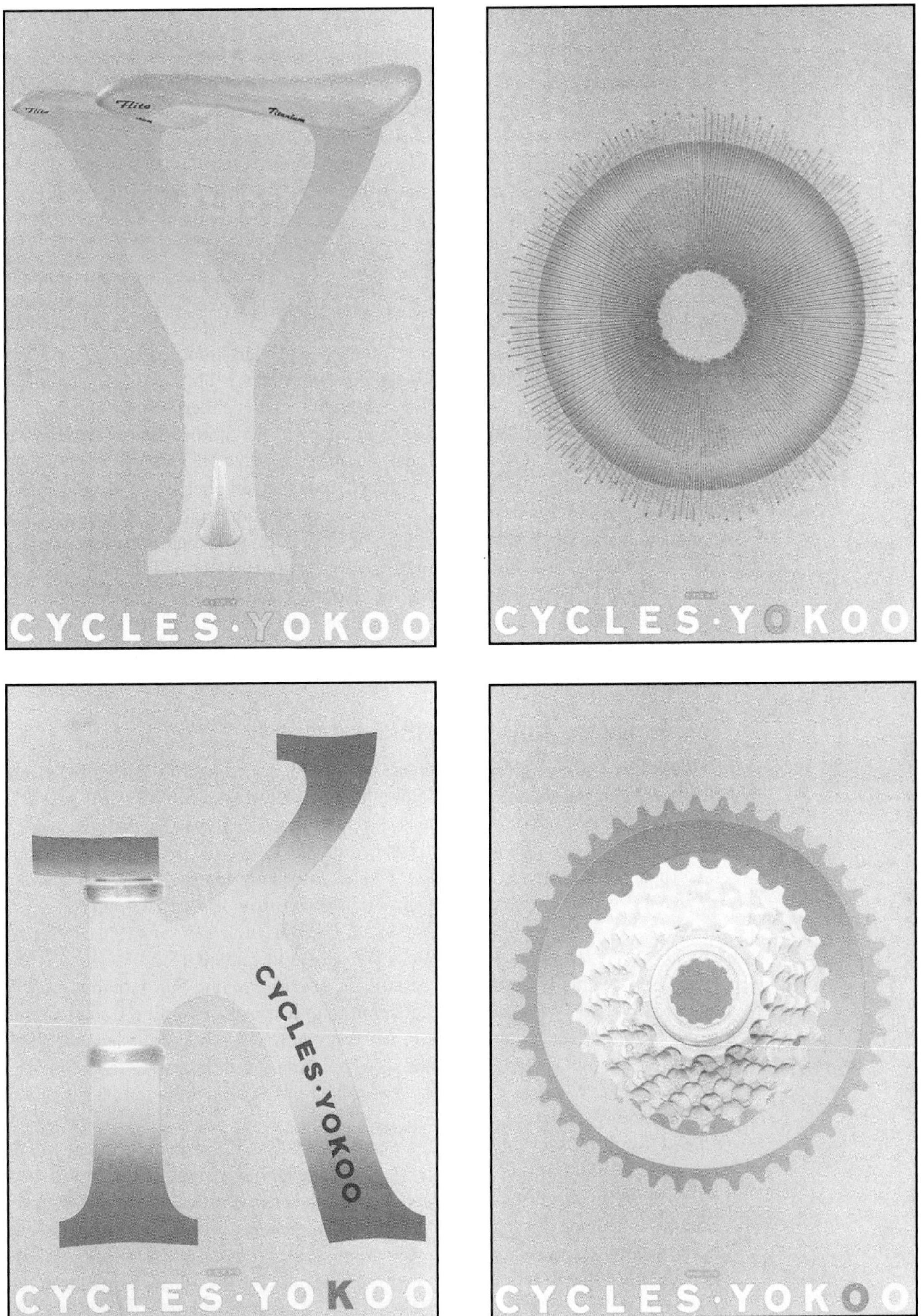

This Japanese ad evokes store quality in an aesthetically pleasing way.

Attitude Dimensions

It's convenient and useful to think of attitudes as having three dimensions: cognitive, affective, and behavioral. Maggie's attitude toward ice cream includes an **affective dimension**—*feelings, moods, emotions, and remembered sensations*—and a **behavioral dimension**—*overt actions and intentions to act toward the attitude object.* For example, she treasures the rituals of ice cream consumption (going to the creamery and cuddling with daddy) as much or more than she likes the ice cream itself. Maggie also has certain *beliefs about ice cream,* or a **cognitive dimension,** but this component figures less prominently and differently in her attitude than in Andy's, her dad's, attitude. Recall that Andy has positive feelings about ice cream, but many negative beliefs about ice cream. In this case, his overall attitude is less consistent across the dimensions than Maggie's.

It's important to remember that most objects, especially important ones, are linked to numerous feelings, thoughts, and experiences that are both positive and negative. Although we may express a summary evaluation that is either positive or negative, our feelings, thoughts, and experiences associated with an attitude object are likely to be more complicated and may conflict. The tendency toward ambivalent attitudes that express both positive and negative feelings, thoughts, and behaviors varies across consumers and cultures. For example, Asians are more comfortable with these conflicting feelings and beliefs and feel less need to resolve them in one direction or the other than Americans.[11] At the same time, once an attitude is formed, it influences subsequent thoughts, feelings, and behaviors. Attitudes can be formed through one or more of these processes and can be expressed through one or more of these dimensions. Attitude theories have typically emphasized a particular mode of forming attitudes, cognitive, affective, or behavioral, as we will discuss later.

Relationships among Attitudes

Attitudes are not isolated in consumers' minds but are linked to other attitudes. One of the most enduring theories for thinking about how attitudes are related is balance theory. In its original form, **balance theory** describes elements in the environment as appearing in groups of three. Each triad contains (1) a consumer, (2) an attitude object (such as a brand), and (3) some other person. In balance theory, *both the consumer and some other person evaluate the object as either positive or negative, and the consumer also has an evaluation of the other person. Evaluations are altered to make them consistent.*[12] An example of balance theory is shown in Exhibit 15.2.

Here, Tom originally has a negative attitude toward Evening Star mouthwash, a brand that is imported by the same organization that distributes Morning Calm. Tom originally learned about Evening Star in some promotional literature that accompanied a tube of Morning Calm. Nonetheless, Tom is quite familiar with other mouthwash brands, and he wonders why he has never heard of this brand before. Thus, his original reaction is somewhat negative.

One of Tom's best friends is Anil, a dentist who currently lives in Seattle. In a recent e-mail message, Anil told Tom that he is recommending Evening Star as an especially effective preventative of gum disease. Now, Tom is faced with a dilemma. He can either change his attitude toward Evening Star or change his attitude toward Anil. As implied in the section on attitude strength, it can be predicted that Tom's attitude toward Anil (a friend) is going to be much stronger than his attitude toward Evening Star (a mouthwash that he has seen promoted only once). Thus, Tom changes the weaker attitude. He now has a much more positive attitude toward Evening Star.

Initially, Tom has a *negative* attitude toward Evening Star Mouthwash.

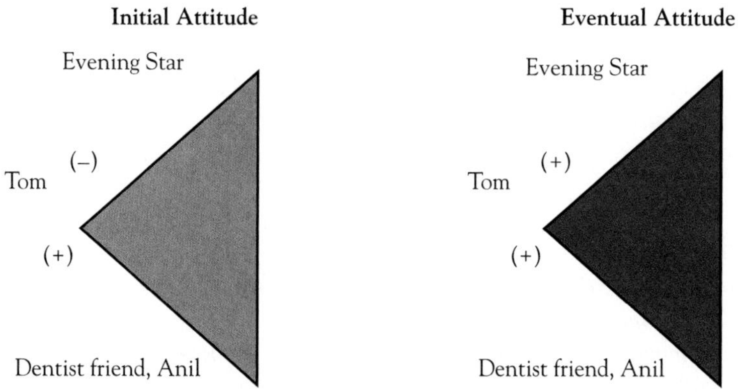

EXHIBIT 15.2

Balance Theory and Attitude Change

Consumers may believe that they ordinarily agree with people they like and disagree with people they dislike, and information is more readily learned and retained when this is the case. This is one of the reasons advertisers rely so heavily on celebrity endorsers. Celebrity endorsers are prominently featured in advertising. For instance, it is estimated that advertisers pay more than $550 million a year to famous athletes to endorse their products.[13] What do advertisers receive in return for this investment? Balance theory provides one kind of explanation. Celebrities enjoy considerable popularity among some segment of the public. Advertisers are hoping that, by using celebrities in their ads, they can convince target consumers to change their attitudes about advertised brands, in much the same way that Tom changes his attitude about Evening Star mouthwash in Exhibit 15.2.

Another useful way of thinking about how attitudes are related is based on ideologies. **Ideologies** are *clusters of attitudes and beliefs that are interdependent in the sense that they are organized around a dominant theme.*[14] This means that an attitude may be formed as an implication or deduction from a more general attitude that has already been formed. For example, attitudes toward specific environmental issues may be formed based on general values about environmentalism. This theory is consistent with the idea that attitudes are embedded in a complex network of relations between attitudes, beliefs, and values where certain core values are strongly held and are linked to many other attitudes, beliefs, and values. Of course, one implication of this theory is that marketers can benefit significantly by linking their brands to consumer's dominant themes. However, it's important for marketers to understand the cluster of attitudes and beliefs that surround that theme or the link will seem contrived. The Body Shop encourages visitors to their website www.thebodyshop.com to check out their cluster of values.

www.thebodyshop.com

DIFFERENT THEORIES ABOUT ATTITUDES

In this section of the chapter, we describe different attitude theories that emphasize different dimensions—affective, cognitive, and behavioral. These theories can help us understand how attitudes are formed, strengthened, and changed. However, the merit of these theories depends in part on consumer characteristics, such as goals, involvements, and self-concepts, and context characteristics, including characteristics of the decision task. In addition, their value also varies cross-culturally. The extent to which attitudes are formed from beliefs and/or feelings, whether beliefs are counterargued, whether dissonance is resolved, and whether objects are evaluated holistically or based on combining beliefs, all depend on culturally specific cognitive traditions about how to think.[15] We briefly describe three influential and useful attitude theories. All of these theories try to answer the question of how and why attitudes change and how attitudes are related to behavior.

Dissonance Theory

Dissonance theory proposes *that when a consumer's beliefs and behaviors don't agree, it produces discomfort and the person is motivated to alter something in order to bring them into alignment.*[16] There is a lot of evidence to support that if there is sufficient discrepancy between a belief and a behavior, consumers experience discomfort and negative feelings. The question is, what is a sufficient discrepancy? As we indicated in Chapter 14, self-consistency is often very important to people and so, if there is dissonance in any area that is important to the self-concept, this may be especially likely to create dissonance.

An important application of this is discussed in Chapter 14. If consumers can be encouraged to engage in a behavior then they may form an attitude that is consistent with that behavior. For example, the Australian ad for So Natural Soy Milk shown below is trying to encourage product trial with a contest.

Because behavior is difficult to undo, consumers often reduce dissonance by changing beliefs and attitudes to bring them in line with behavior. Of course, it depends on whether the consumer feels a need for consistency, and it also may depend on whether they feel responsible for the behavior. For example, if a high-pressure salesperson talks

This Australian advertisement encourages product trial.

a consumer into a purchase she later regrets, she may blame her behavior on the salesperson and not feel she has to revise her attitude.

The Elaboration Likelihood Model

One of the most influential theories of attitudes in recent times is the **elaboration likelihood model** (ELM). The ELM is a theory about the processes responsible for attitude change and the strength of the attitudes that result from these processes.[17] A key construct in the ELM is the elaboration likelihood continuum. We discussed elaboration likelihood in several other chapters in Part 3 of this book. The **elaboration likelihood continuum** is *defined by how motivated and able people are to assess the central merits of the attitude object (person, brand, advertisement, issue).* The more motivated and able consumers are to assess the central merits, the more likely they are to carefully scrutinize available object-relevant information. When elaboration likelihood is high, *consumers will assess information in relationship to knowledge they already possess and arrive at a reasoned attitude that is well articulated and bolstered by supporting information*—**central route to persuasion.** When elaboration likelihood is low, *information scrutiny is reduced and attitude change can result from a number of less resource-demanding processes that do not require careful evaluation of relevant information*—**peripheral route to persuasion.** Attitudes formed or changed under low elaboration are weaker than those changed the same amount by high elaboration. In short, the ELM posits *that attitude change varies to the extent that it is based on mental effort.* The perceived personal relevance or importance of the communication is one of the most important factors influencing mental effort, but other things also can influence mental effort. For example, when consumers feel they are accountable or responsible for evaluating the communication, they pay more attention. We discussed how goals and involvement influence information processing in Chapter 7.

Just because a consumer is highly motivated and able to process relevant messages doesn't mean she doesn't rely on various cues and heuristics. Rather it means she scrutinizes them for their relevance and value. For example, consider whether beautiful scenery in an advertisement for a vacation location should increase or decrease in impact as elaboration likelihood increases. If a person is not thinking about the ad very much (low elaboration likelihood), then the beautiful scenery might have a positive impact due to its association with the location. This also should happen if the beautiful scenery is included in an ad for a car. However, if the person is carefully thinking about a vacation at that location (high elaboration likelihood), then the scenery might be processed for its relevance and merit. However, beautiful scenery wouldn't be relevant for an involved consumer considering purchase of a new car. Similarly, an uninvolved consumer might rely on an expert's recommendation without scrutinizing it, while an involved consumer also might rely on an expert's recommendation but only after scrutinizing it. Marketers need to keep in mind that what may be a peripheral cue in one case may be a highly significant cue in another case. Whether and how this happens is likely to depend on consumers' existing knowledge, culture, and social context. For example, an ad targeted at Chinese consumers might feature a family celebrating a child's birthday by serving him a bowl of noodles with an egg on top. A non-Chinese viewer is unlikely to even notice this element in the overall presentation of the ad, but for a Chinese viewer this triggers tradition, nostalgia, warmth, and family. This simple cue triggers a cultural model and encourages self-referencing and communication involvement.[18]

Two examples are presented here to illustrate the ELM. The first, presented in Consumer Chronicles 15.2, shows a high-involvement situation in which the main message and

The Elaboration Likelihood Model: High-Involvement Persuasion

CONSUMER CHRONICLES 15.2

Consider a situation where Piet is surfing the Internet looking for a new piece of financial software. He is looking for "freeware," but he is also willing to pay a small fee for software that has some superior features. This choice situation is high involvement for several reasons. First, the Internet is a relatively high-involvement medium. It is interactive, so consumers have to pay attention. They have to click their mouse to move the search forward, and they have to keep responding to receive new information. Second, Piet is motivated to find just the right software package for him.

In this situation, Piet probably will not be influenced so much by peripheral cues. He may notice that a certain website has great graphics and interesting music, but these weak arguments will not convince him to download some software that does not meet his major criteria. Instead, Piet will be persuaded by strong arguments. He pays close attention to the price of the software (free versus otherwise). Also, he pays close attention to the arguments that the software companies present about their product features.

strong arguments are the main persuasive elements in the choice situation. The second example, in Consumer Chronicles 15.3, describes a low-involvement situation in which peripheral cues are more influential in guiding consumer choice.

If consumers are motivated and able to process communications, marketers want to make sure that they employ strong arguments to promote their products and brands. **Strong arguments** are *convincing presentations of the best features or central merits of an offering.* Sometimes marketers can make their message stronger or more credible by using a comparative advertisement. Comparative advertising can directly name a competitor and point out how a product or service is different, or it can make comparisons to an unnamed competitor. Direct comparative messages are especially effective for new brands or brands with low market share. The advertisement shown on page 642 is a classic example of a direct comparative message. In this case, Flonase stresses its comparative advantage over competing prescription antihistamines. However, advertisers also may use comparative advertisements to stress particular characteristics of their brand, and also encourage consumers to think differently about their product. Consider the advertisement for the Odyssey minivan shown on page 643. Honda compares their minivan to a rocking horse in order to gain attention and encourage consumers to think of the car as an investment in happy children. Don't think too hard about it though, because a rocking horse is a lot cheaper!

HOW ELM IS RELATED TO OTHER ATTITUDE THEORIES As a general model of attitude change, the ELM can account for findings related to many other attitude theories. The classical conditioning effects described in Chapter 9 can be thought of as an example of peripheral-route processing, and the kind of transfer of affect for an advertisement to a product that we discussed above would be another type of peripheral-route processing. A variety of simple inferences and judgment heuristics are also consistent with peripheral-route processing.

In addition, consider some research that has demonstrated that when objects are presented to a consumer on repeated occasions, *mere exposure is capable of making the consumer's attitude toward the object more positive*—**mere exposure effect.** Of course, familiar objects (a favorite song, stuffed animal, ring) can make us feel comfortable and give a sense of ownership, warmth, and intimacy, but this is generally intertwined with past experiences with the object and consumption meanings associated with the object—that is, high personal relevance and elaboration likelihood (see Chapter 4). What's perhaps surprising is the mere exposure effect can happen even when the consumer doesn't consciously recognize that the object is familiar—with stimuli such as foreign words, faces, and nonsense stimuli. These repeated stimuli are processed peripherally, but not consciously processed and stored. Then when they are encountered again, they are easier to perceive and process and evaluated more favorably. However, mere exposure effects are reduced if meaningful stimuli are presented or if consumers consciously think about the stimuli. Consequently, the mere exposure effect is likely to work only when elaboration likelihood is low.

The mere exposure effect has important implications for marketers. Consumers repeatedly exposed to relatively unfamiliar, low-involvement stimuli are likely to evaluate them more favorably. Perhaps Juicy Juice uses this strategy in sponsoring numerous children's shows on PBS. Their messages are short and not particularly involving, but over time the package and the message become familiar and linked to favorite shows. No wonder PBS kids and parents love Juicy Fruit 100% Juice! Can you think of other marketing applications of the mere exposure effect?

ELM is also helpful in understanding the appropriate use of various other attitude models. For example, one of the most popular frameworks for examining the relationship between attitudes and behavior is the **expectancy-value model.** This model *posits that attitudes are a function of beliefs and that attitudes (alone or with other factors) predict behavioral intentions.* We will discuss an important variant of this model in this chapter—the theory of reasoned action. The ELM recognizes that these models, in addition to neglecting the emotional dimension of attitudes, also assume high-effort, central-route processing. Thus, they are appropriately used to model attitudes and intentions only when elaboration likelihood is high and consumers are likely to rely predominantly on beliefs rather than emotions in formulating their attitudes.

CONSUMER CHRONICLES 15.3

The Elaboration Likelihood Model: Low-Involvement Persuasion

Consider a situation where Marika is tired from a long day of work, and she is watching TV. A commercial comes on for hand soap. The commercial uses a slice-of-life approach and includes appealing background music. For a variety of reasons, this is a low-involvement situation for Marika. Under most circumstances, television is a low-involvement medium. Consumers don't necessarily have to pay a lot of attention to watch it. When the commercial for a low-involvement product comes on, Marika is paying even less attention. She is not really motivated to process a complex message about the soap.

Under these low-involvement circumstances, peripheral cues will have more influence than strong arguments about the advertised brand. The background music in the ad is one type of peripheral cue that may serve as an important persuasive element. Thus, Marika may purchase this brand of soap on her next shopping trip even though she has not actively processed much information from the ad.

WHAT THE ELM DOESN'T DO The ELM has been subjected to lots of praise and criticism. In some cases it is hard to separate criticisms of the theory from criticisms of tests of the theory. Tests of the elaboration likelihood model have generally not taken symbolic, hedonic, and aesthetic motives into account. Further, they have been biased toward verbal information and linguistic performance and tended to disregard pictorial, music, and other nonlanguage aspects of marketing communications. Strong arguments could be nonverbal in nature, but these are rarely considered in tests of the theory. Thus, results to date display a Western bias and omit information that may be important in non-Western cultures. How people acquire, organize, and use information is related to the type of information they are used to processing. People in interdependent, relatively homogeneous cultures are used to processing indirect communication, symbols, and signs. People in individualistic, heterogeneous cultures, like the United States, for example, are used to words and explanations. Cultures that favor associative thinking, such as Italy, Spain, and France, for example, prefer oral, face-to-face communication that is rich in nonverbal elements, whereas cultures in which people prefer deductive thinking, such as the United States, Germany, or Austria, will tend to prefer verbal and written information.

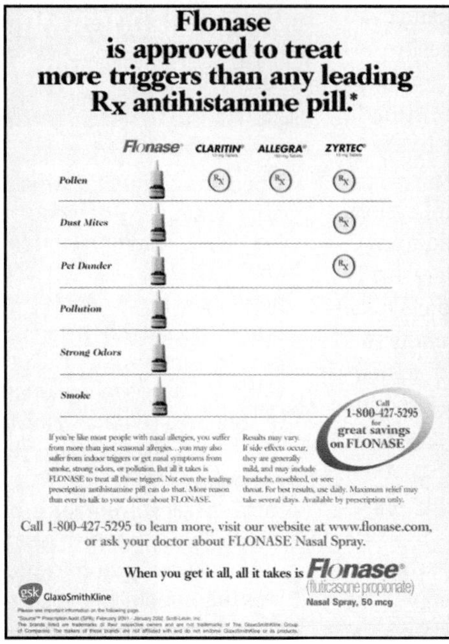

This comparative ad identifies triggers that demand Flonase antihistamine.

Differences in how people are used to processing information should affect marketing communications. For example, 90 percent of French advertising is visual, whereas 80 percent of German magazine ads are copy. In a typical Japanese ad, visuals and music are used first to develop trust and understanding, and only then is the brand, company, or product name shown. These differences suggest that the so-called central and peripheral routes to persuasion may be reversed in some way in cultures that rely more on indirection, symbols, and nonverbal information. The ELM model deals poorly with these cultural differences in information processing.

Another problem with the ELM is its emphasis on the individual as an information processor. The problem becomes clear in highly interdependent cultural contexts. If we were to ask how the individual processes persuasive information in Japan, the answer would be that there is not a persuasive process and it is not useful to look at it at the individual level. Marketing communications in this cultural context cannot persuade individuals directly. Instead, products and marketing communications must adapt to group influence, defining groups rather than the self. In their decision making, Japanese tend to depend at least in part on members of their in-group or on people who in other ways merit their trust. As a result, Japanese marketing is based more on building trust than persuasion. In sum, more different models of information processing are needed to understand persuasive processes and decision making in a global marketplace.

Theory of Reasoned Action and Planned Behavior

The theory of reasoned action is intended to predict behavior in situations where the consumer controls his behavior and is thoughtful about it.[19] That is, the aim of the theory is to explain volitional behaviors. It is not intended to explain behaviors born of habit, ritual, cravings, or impulse. It also excludes behaviors that require special skills, unique opportunities or resources, or the cooperation of others to be performed. The

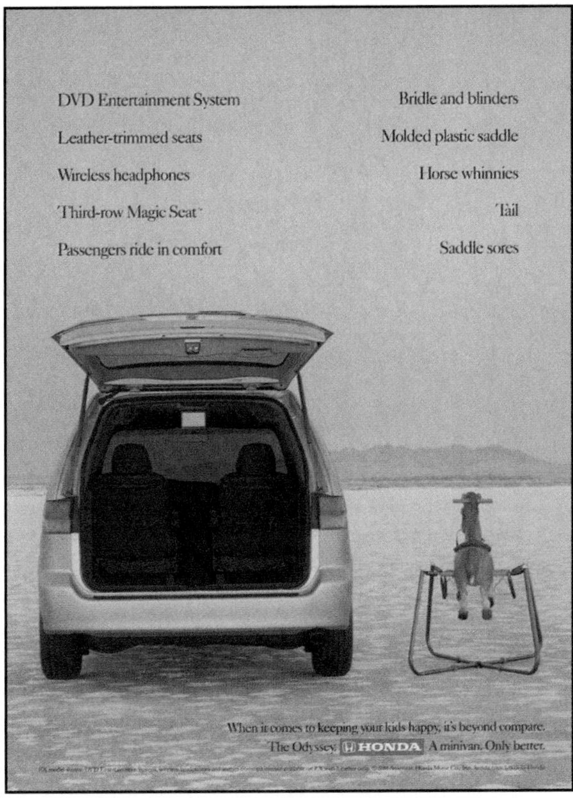

An unusual comparative ad encourages consumers to put the product in a different category.

theory of reasoned action (TORA) has been prominent in marketing, because marketers are often interested in influencing consumers' voluntary conscious choices.

COMPONENTS OF THE THEORY OF REASONED ACTION The TORA posits that *the most important determinant of consumer behavior is behavioral intentions and that depends both on a person's attitude toward performing the behavior and the influence of others' opinions about the behavior—that is, a subjective norm.* The theory of reasoned action is outlined in Exhibit 15.3. This model suggests attitudes are affected by beliefs linked to behaviors and by what others believe and how important complying with those beliefs is.

For example, Joe may believe that sports utility vehicles (SUVs) get poor gas mileage and evaluate this as a negative attribute. Further, he may believe SUVs are more likely to turn over because of high centers of gravity and evaluate this as a negative attribute. However, he also may believe that SUVs handle better in off-road conditions and evaluate this as a positive attribute. Depending on the strength of these beliefs and how positively or negatively he evaluates them, he formulates an attitude about SUVs. But in addition to his own attitude, he is concerned with other people's attitudes and beliefs. Joe lives in Colorado and loves to ski winters and hike summers. All his friends think he should purchase an SUV to travel off-road and his girlfriend teases him about his safety concerns. Because Joe's friends and girlfriend are important to him, he decides to go along with them and he forms an intention to purchase an SUV. However, whether or not Joe actually purchases an SUV still depends on what happens next. To the extent that time, changes in context, or other events intervene, the connection between

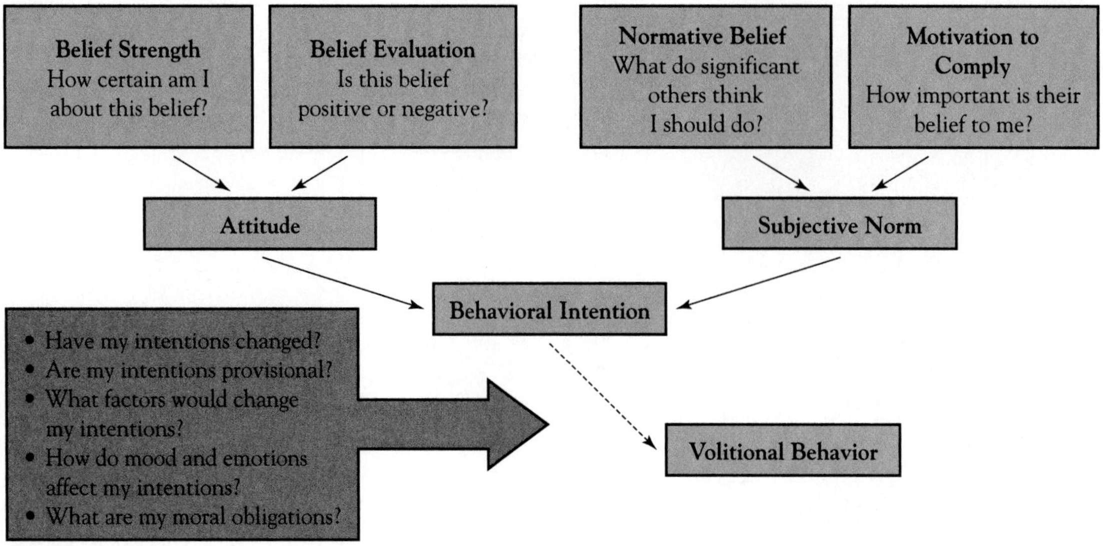

EXHIBIT 15.3

The Theory of Reasoned Action

behavioral intention and behavior may still be weak. For example, shortly after deciding to purchase an SUV, Joe breaks up with his girlfriend and also applies for a new job just outside of Chicago, Illinois. Suddenly, the purchase of an SUV for commuting on four-lane, flat, straight roads seems less appealing. Besides, in addition to what his friends think, Joe is concerned about the environment. Is it morally right to buy a gas-guzzling SUV? He's not so sure. Exhibit 15.3 illustrates that many factors may intervene between behavioral intention and behavior.

Culture too affects relationships between behavioral intentions and behavior. Cultures vary in the extent to which people make definite concrete plans. They also differ in the extent to which they believe their own actions will produce definite results. Americans believe strongly in their ability to exert control over their environments. People of Muslim and Confucian heritage do not. Cultural differences such as these can lead to wrong expectations with respect to buying intentions. For example, research suggests that if 55 percent of people who try a new product in Italy say they will definitely buy it, the product is likely to fail (because their behavior will not match their predictions); but if 5 percent of those trying the product in Japan say they will definitely buy it, the product is likely to succeed. The difference is explained by cultural difference in the strength of intentions. Consumers with a Catholic heritage and who speak Latinate languages (French, Italian, Spanish, etc.) tend to overclaim their purchase intentions. Consumers from a Protestant background may be less likely to overclaim their intentions. Consumers in Asian cultures influenced by their Confucian or Buddhist heritages follow a more middle way and avoid declarative statements like "I definitely will buy." In Asian and African cultures with an interdependent or more collective orientation or with an Islamic heritage, consumers assume that fate or other people may intervene in intentions and deflect certainty about behavior.[20]

MARKETING IMPLICATIONS OF THE THEORY OF REASONED ACTION TORA has a great deal of intuitive appeal and quite a lot of support. Of course, measurement is still a big challenge. In arriving at an attitude, how much weight should be given to Joe's belief that SUVs turn over, and how much weight should be given to Joe's belief that SUVs handle well off-road? Are there other unexpressed beliefs or feelings

Ways Marketers Can Apply the Theory of Reasoned Action

GOOD PRACTICE 15.1

1. Identify consumer attitudes and subjective norms associated with buying a brand. This theory can help marketers key in on strengths and weaknesses and how other people are influencing behavioral intentions
2. Strengthen beliefs about positive consequences associated with buying a brand. Weaken beliefs about negative consequences associated with buying a brand.
3. Change consumers' evaluations of consequences associated with buying a brand. Increase the positive evaluation of a consequence. Decrease the negative evaluation of a consequence.
4. Add a new belief. Add a positive belief that will make the attitude more positive.
5. Target normative beliefs. Emphasize normative beliefs that endorse buying a brand. Emphasize the importance of complying with others who endorse buying a brand.

that are also influencing Joe's attitude? Despite these measurement problems, the model has lots of implications for marketers attempting to influence consumers' behaviors. These strategies are summarized in Good Practice 15.1.

Each component of the TORA model can be targeted. For example, one possible strategy would be to change the strength of consumers' beliefs. The California Almonds campaign is a good example of trying to change consumers' beliefs. Many consumers believe that nuts are high in cholesterol. Their campaign emphasizes that almonds have the kind of fat that's good for you (monounsaturated), are low in saturated fat, and are cholesterol free. As another example, the advertisement shown on the next page attempts to change consumers' beliefs about Michigan, U.S.A. The hope is that biotech companies will form intentions to locate their headquarters in Michigan.

@ www.AlmondsAreIn.com

Another approach suggested by the TORA model is to make a belief more positive or less negative in order to make attitudes more positive. Although tea is central to life in China, young Chinese are turning to modern options of soft drinks and coffee. The Chinese government is bolstering tea by encouraging the belief that tea is the secret to a long life. Tea is being promoted for its healthy benefits: it can make people think fast, help in weight loss, control cholesterol, and help prevent heart attack.[21] Emphasizing a core benefit associated with a product is an important marketing strategy. Consider the Japanese billboard shown on the next page. This advertisement emphasizes a differentiating product characteristic—a nonstop action adventure channel.

In addition to increasing the positive evaluation of a belief, marketers also can add new beliefs. For example, although consumers have long believed children with growing bones need milk, the American Dairy Farmers and Milk Producers are now adding a new belief; your bones grow until about age 35. Of course, after that, milk keeps them strong. This advertisement is shown on page 647.

New Zealand is piggybacking on the success of the *Lord of the Rings* trilogy to promote tourism. They are adding the belief that New Zealand is home of Middle Earth. More than a half million dollars have been earmarked for the effort. The government has appointed a minister of Middle Earth and made maps of Middle Earth charting the

This ad attempts to change consumer beliefs.

35 locations and varied terrain featured in the trilogy. A special tour company also has been formed to promote the belief and ensure a positive evaluation.

Marketers also can target normative beliefs. Such communications would be especially important in cultures and contexts where social influence is powerful. In Singapore initiatives to increase organ donation face an uphill battle.[22] Chinese (mostly Buddhists) form roughly 77 percent of the resident population, while Malays (mostly Muslims) and Indians (mostly Hindus) make up most of the remainder. Although there are many differences, all share certain beliefs about the sanctity of the body that inhibit organ donation. In addition, they share an important regard for family and social authority. Organ-procuring organizations have learned that if a family member agrees to organ donation, his family generally accedes to his wishes. Moreover, these family members can be effective in changing beliefs of other family members. Changing attitudes is also possible, but appeals have to fit with the pattern of spiritual beliefs. For example, agencies can stress that organ donation enhances immortality, allowing donors to live

This Japanese billboard emphasizes a unique product benefit.

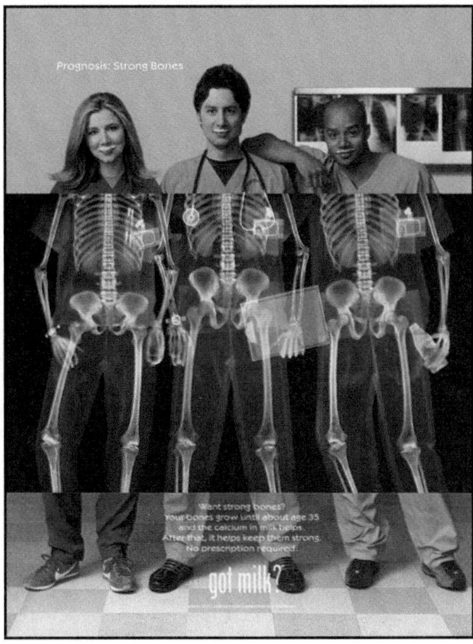

This ad provides consumers with a new belief.

on in others, and/or the selfless act of organ donation will strengthen relations in the social group.

THE THEORY OF PLANNED BEHAVIOR The **theory of planned behavior** expands the behaviors encompassed in the theory of reasoned action. This model mirrors the TORA except that it *recognizes that behavioral intentions and behavior sometimes depend on* **perceived behavioral control,** that is, *consumers' perception of how easy or difficult it is to perform the behavior.* You may recall that in Chapter 7 we talked about how achieving goals can be effortful and we used dieting as an example. Consumers may have a positive attitude that they should lose weight and subjective norms that support that belief, but still fail to lose weight. Consumers also may have difficulty controlling other aspects of consumption. For example, many consumers feel they lose control over their credit cards or can't resist purchases at the mall.[23] The Canadian ad for McDonald's shown on the next page encourages consumers to give in to their impulses.

Why do consumers yield to temptation and lose control of their own behavior? Self-control depends on standards, a monitoring process, and the capacity to alter one's behavior.[24] For example, consumers who know exactly what they want (have set standards) are less vulnerable to impulse buying and influence attempts from advertising and salespeople. Many times people have conflicting goals regarding a particular behavior, and it may be difficult to resolve the conflict between the two goals. We talked about motivational conflict in Chapter 7. Behavioral monitoring is also a key to self-control. When people keep track of their money and expenditures, impulsive purchases are less likely. Finally, *exercising self-control seems to deplete a crucial resource that is then no longer available to help a consumer exert self-control on other tasks*—we can call this **ego depletion** to indicate that the self's crucial resources have been depleted. This has numerous implications for consumers and marketers. For you as a student, it means you shouldn't go shopping, or drinking, after first forcing yourself to study several hours for an exam—you are vulnerable to losing control! For marketers it means

This ad encourages impulse buying.

that consumers in a state of ego depletion are likely to yield to temptation and buy impulsively. It turns out that making choices and decisions also seems to deplete the same resource that is used for self-control.[25] When consumers are asked to make multiple decisions, they become more impulsive and less self-controlled toward the end of the series.

CONSUMER JUDGMENTS

Judgments, like attitudes, are a crucial input into decisions, but they do not require the consumer to make a decision. As we indicated at the beginning of the chapter, judgments are just estimates regarding the likelihood of an event. Consumers don't just make judgments about the likelihood of liking something, as Maggie did with eggplant ice cream; they also make many other kinds of judgments—how likely something is to happen (for example, a plane crash or winning a lottery), or how likely a series or coincidence of events might be (for example, getting delayed going to the airport, running into long lines at check-in, a delayed plane departure, and missing the plane). When consumers are asked to make judgments, they process information differently than when they are asked to make choices; nevertheless, choices typically involve making some judgments as well. In this section we will describe some common tools consumers use for making judgments and some marketing implications.[26]

In making estimations of likelihood and goodness/badness, consumers often employ an **anchor-and-adjust process.** They first *anchor their judgment based on an initial value and then adjust it with additional information.* It's easy to see how this strategy is related to fundamental memory processes of searching through memory for something similar to the target problem and then adjusting to try to take into account the differences. For example, imagine how you might go about guessing how a friend of yours would like a movie that you recently saw. You might begin by thinking about how much you liked the movie, how similar you are to your friend in terms of movie tastes, and then guessing whether your friend would like the movie too. Now imagine that you are guessing how an average person in your community would like this movie. You might take exactly the same approach, but in this situation, you know less about how similar or different the average person is to you and how much you should adjust your guess accordingly.[27]

Consider the advertisement for Kleenex tissues shown on the next page. What is this advertisement attempting to accomplish? By encouraging consumers to imagine particular events in a typical road trip, Kleenex encourages consumers to see Kleenex use as a prominent part of the trip. In order to judge the likelihood of an event or a sequence of events, or events' goodness or badness, consumers may attempt to *imag-*

This ad encourages consumers to imagine themselves using this product.

ine or simulate events in order to make a judgment—**simulation heuristic.** Simply imagining an event or sequence of events increases the perception that it will occur. Good stories or convincing imagery can be powerful in leading consumers to believe in the possibility of an event or a sequence of events. However, the actual possibility of such an event or sequence of events may be relatively remote. Recall what you learned in statistics about conjunctive probabilities: even if two events are relatively likely (.5), the likelihood of their joint occurrence is much lower (.25). Consumers often play out consumption events in their mind, rehearsing how things will be; and they are quite likely to be disappointed, because it relies on a sequence of events unfolding exactly as planned. For example, young people and their families in many cultures work hard envisioning weddings and trying to make them happen just that way. But they hardly ever do. Of course, sometimes the things that went wrong are the very things that make the event vivid and special, and in turn these things become the source of future stories. Simulation may lead consumers to overestimate the likelihood of an event or to form an overly positive image of the event.[28] Some advertising encourages consumers to imagine use of a product, such as the ad for Pulse shown on the next page.

Judgments also can be influenced by the **availability heuristic.** The availability heuristic makes *judgments by using what comes easily to mind from memory.* For example, a person might guess at the likelihood of a delayed flight on an airline according to his or her ability to retrieve examples of such an event from memory. Unfortunately, memories are influenced by a lot more than absolute frequency of particular events. For example, events that have occurred more recently are more memorable than those that occurred long ago. Vivid and publicized events also come readily to mind. All of these memory influences, and more, can lead consumers to erroneous judgments. Marketers can capitalize on this bias by providing consumers with vivid and positive product-related experiences, or they can attempt to offset it by stressing base-rate information about actual likelihoods.

Consumers employing the **representativeness heuristic** *assign characteristics to an object based on comparing the stimulus to a category prototype or exemplar.* In many situations, consumers guess about the performance or characteristics of objects, people, and ideas based on their similarity to what consumers already know. Of course,

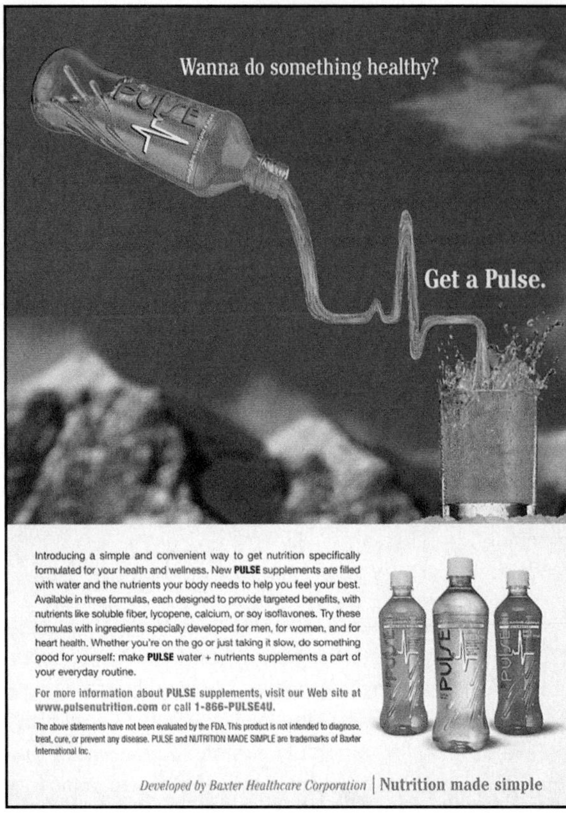

Ad encourages consumers to imagine how it will feel to use Pulse.

this is one of the reasons brand extensions can be so successful. In addition to occasionally leading consumers astray, this can be an important tool for understanding and dealing with unfamiliar things. In Chapter 9 we discussed how important it is for marketers to make sure new products and brands compare favorably to these category exemplars.

CONSUMERS AS ADAPTIVE DECISION MAKERS

As with attitudes and judgments, we often construct decisions on the spot using a variety of approaches and depending on the context and situation. Sometimes we invest time and mental effort and sometimes we don't. Consumers are **adaptive decision makers.**[29] They *exploit and adapt to aspects of the environment in order to make decisions to achieve goals.* Consumers perceive and appraise choice situations within a social and cognitive context. They attempt to determine *what aspects of the choice relate to their goals,* **goal relevance,** and what's at stake in these choices (*potential losses and gains in terms of their goals*), **goal congruence.** For example, some research suggests that how consumers make decisions and the relative weight given to thoughts versus feelings will depend on consumer goals.[30] They also decide who should decide and how the choice should be made based on the decision context. Emotions are an important aspect of this appraisal process.[31] Many of the most important decisions consumers face involve emotionally difficult trade-offs such as trade-offs between career opportunities and family needs. We discussed motivational conflict in Chapter 7.

Consumer Action without Decisions

Although it may seem reasonable to assume that consumer action is based on decisions, such is definitely not the case.[32] Much consumer action is born from habit or ritual, enactments of personal or cultural scripts. (Recall we talked about schemas and scripts in Chapters 8 and 9 and about consumer rituals in Chapters 1, 3, and 4.) For example, most of us don't decide how to drive into work in the morning, unless we have a special errand or a special context that triggers a decision. Habit, doing the same thing every time, makes life simpler and more manageable and reduces risk. Similarly, we don't decide whether to order dessert before an entrée at a restaurant; we assume a particular unfolding of events. This sequence is determined within a particular cultural and social context. If we are made aware of these behaviors and asked for reasons, it may begin to appear that we made decisions, because these scripts are often supported by underlying attitudes, judgments, or prior decisions (or we make them up), but that doesn't mean that at the time of action they are decisions. Also, if we are asked to generate reasons for our behavior, we may generate reasons consistent with how we think people should decide such issues or what we consider reasonable explanations for our behavior, rather than the reasons or nonreasons we actually had for our behavior. Although many of our nondecision actions may be characterized by low involvement or "mindlessness," we may be very involved and even very mindful of what we are doing without it seeming to entail any decisions. For example, when a consumer gathers the ingredients and then prepares a special dish, such as homemade ice cream or grandmother's special Christmas cookies brought over from the old country, there may be substantial involvement, care, and meaning without any decisions. Rather, it is a careful, even emotionally involving execution of a ritual action. In Consumer Chronicles 15.4, Peg talks about the production of homemade food as an emotionally involving ritual action.

In addition certain consumer actions are better described as the failure to make a decision, while still others are actions taken in the hope of learning enough to make a decision. For example, if a decision is especially emotional or difficult, consumers may cope by delaying making that decision.[33] In Chapter 10 we described how consumers might try an activity in order to decide whether it is consistent with their self-concept. In this case, trying the activity helps them formulate an attitude toward it.

Common Tools for Making Decisions

How do consumers make choices? How do they decide which services or brands to purchase or what retail outlets to patronize? To some extent, there may be as many choice models or strategies as there are consumers. But answering our question will depend on identifying consumers' goals, the alternatives and criteria they consider meaningful, and how they combine cognitions and feelings to make decisions.[34] Here, we attempt to identify patterns and to group consumers into overall patterns. Many times consumers combine or modify these decision models to better fit their goals, resources, and contexts. We begin with a discussion of economic models of consumer choice. We outline expected utility theory and how marketers can use utility functions to model consumer choices. Next we outline prospect theory, which is a general model for how consumers value gains and losses in decision-making tasks. We then explain cognitive models consumers use. These are generally described in terms of two dimensions: compensatory versus noncompensatory and brand versus attribute processing. Next we outline how feelings and emotions can be used in making decisions. Finally we conclude with some simple strategies consumers use to make decisions.

Peg's Homemade Cinnamon Rolls

CONSUMER CHRONICLES 15.4

For Peg, a woman in her 60s, talk of homemade food sparks idealized memories of the farm:

> What do I mean, oh, home prepared, maybe talking about fried chicken. And the good fried chicken is when years ago when we butchered our own chicken right from scratch. That was the good chicken . . . Oh ya when we butchered, we always butchered our own pigs on the farm also. Dad always butchered his own pigs. We cut it up, packaged it and everything so we could put it in the freezer.

Peg goes on to talk about how she learned to prepare recipes from her mother and grandmother, "My grandmothers on both sides were always good to teach Mom," and "Mom always passed them down to us, and I'm very fortunate that Mom's around to tell me certain things." She notes that her mother still joins her in preparing cinnamon rolls for holiday occasions.

> Uh, one thing that I picked up which, you know all the older people made was their bread and we still make bread, homemade buns. If we didn't have that at a meal, at a holiday meal it just wouldn't be a meal, may as well, they'd probably turn around and go back home. Cinnamon rolls. I, when I make the homemade rolls, I always make a pan of hot cinnamon rolls so when they (family) get there they can have a cinnamon roll before dinner. And it doesn't ruin their appetite either.

Peg feels that without the homemade rolls, the family gathering and the holiday meal couldn't happen. She feels both privileged and obligated to produce them, like her mother and her mother's mother before her.

Source: This is adapted from Eric J. Arnould and Linda L. Price, "'Bread of Our Mothers': Ruptures and Continuities in Families and Homemade Food Traditions," working paper, University of Nebraska, Lincoln.

ECONOMIC MODELS One important perspective on how consumers make choices is the **utility-maximizing view** derived from classic microeconomic theory. Marketers explore how consumers deliberately collect information, weigh alternatives, and *make decisions that lead to the largest net benefit to them in terms of the exchange resources at issue.* Consumers try to decide the utility for them of various actions.

Expected Utility Theory **Expected utility theory** typically assumes decision makers are rational and have complete information; that is, *consumers are assumed to have complete information about the probabilities and consequences attached to each alternative course of action.* They are expected to understand this information and be able to calculate the advantages and disadvantages of each alternative. Consumers compare these calculations and select the course of action that maximizes expected utility.[35] Thus, consumers make choices in a manner that maximizes a utility function, subject to the constraints of time, money income, information, and technology.

People are most likely to have well-articulated preferences when they are familiar and experienced with the choice problem, and expected utility theory may be applicable in such situations. Industrial purchasing processes may sometimes correspond to the model. But individual consumers and households rarely act in the ways that are assumed by this theory. Information about alternatives is often missing or uncertain. Perception is selective. Memory is imperfect and biased.[36] Consumers do not have unlimited time and energy to make choices. They don't want to spend all of their waking hours making

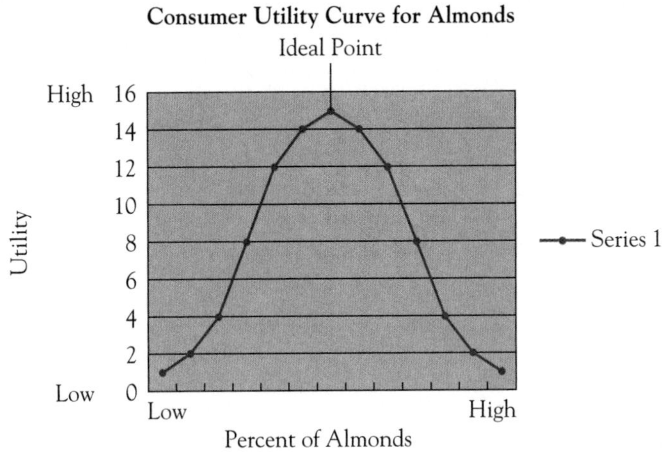

EXHIBIT 15.4

Utility Curve for Almonds in Candy Bar

consumer purchases. Thus, bounded rather than complete rationality characterizes most of us (at best!) when we make decisions. And situational factors may intrude. Thus, expected utility theory is more an idealized model than a description of how consumers actually make market choices. Nonetheless, utility theory has been adapted in marketing to provide descriptions of consumer utility for specific attribute levels. These descriptions take the form of utility functions.

Utility Functions An example of a utility function is shown in Exhibit 15.4. Here, utility refers to the amount of happiness that a consumer derives from a product or from a product attribute. The amount of utility is plotted on the *y* axis in Exhibit 15.4. The amount of an attribute present is plotted on the *x* axis. The resulting shape of most utility functions is an inverted U, which implies that consumer utility increases through the low range of an attribute but then comes to a peak at some moderate range. Exhibit 15.4 shows Melanie's utility function for the amount of almonds in a candy bar. She is generally unhappy with a small amount of nuts. For her there is also such a thing as too many almonds, which interferes with the chocolaty taste. The ideal level of almonds is shown in the exhibit.

Utility functions are useful in consumer behavior research because they can be estimated with a method called **conjoint analysis.** There are many ways of administering this method. One way is to ask consumers to rank order a series of brands, all in the same product category. As shown in Good Practice 15.2, each candy bar in the conjoint study can be represented by a profile. Good Practice 15.2 shows four different profiles with five candy bar attributes: amount of almonds, amount of chocolate, amount of sugar, number of calories, and price. To construct Exhibit 15.4, Melanie would be asked to make trade-offs between the group of four candy bars, each represented by a profile. As part of the data collection task, she would rank order the four candy bar profiles. From the rank ordering, Exhibit 15.4 can be drawn. Such a figure can be constructed for an individual consumer, for a market segment, or for an entire market.

Imagining the consumer as an individual utility maximizer is a weak strategy to adopt in marketing to members of interdependent cultures in the Asian NICs or in most developing countries. Buyers in these cultures will seek out more social information and are more likely to be interested in outcomes that produce or reinforce trust and relationships between buyers and sellers. In highly egalitarian cultural environments (e.g., Scandinavia), decisions also may emerge through a consensus-building process

GOOD PRACTICE 15.2

Conjoint Profiles: Data Collection Task for Constructing Utility Functions

Rank order the following four candy bars from 1 to 4, with 1 being your most preferred brand and 4 being your least preferred brand. All percentages are measured in terms of weight. Percentages do not add to 100 percent, because all ingredients are not included in the profiles.

Profile A:	**Rank ___**	**Profile B:**	**Rank ___**
Almonds:	15%	Almonds:	0%
Chocolate:	20%	Chocolate:	40%
Sugar:	5%	Sugar:	10%
Calories:	260	Calories:	310
Price:	80 cents	Price:	60 cents

Profile C:	**Rank ___**	**Profile D:**	**Rank ___**
Almonds:	30%	Almonds:	15%
Chocolate:	0%	Chocolate:	20%
Sugar:	5%	Sugar:	0%
Calories:	260	Calories:	210
Price:	$1.00	Price:	80 cents

in which the differing preferences of several people in a household or business buying group are worked out.[37]

Prospect Theory **Prospect theory** examines *how consumers value potential gains and losses that result from making choices.*[38] This theory is based on an individual's value function (see Exhibit 15.5). This function reflects consumers' anticipation of the pleasure or pain associated with a specific decision outcome.[39] The gains or losses are calculated with respect to some reference point. A crucial aspect of prospect theory is that the value function for gains is quite different than that for losses. As shown in Exhibit 15.5, the value function for gains appears above the horizontal axis. This gain function is concave and not so steep. In contrast, the loss function lies below the horizontal axis. It is convex and steeper than the corresponding loss function.[40] Because the value function for losses is steeper than the function for gains, losses loom larger than gains. What this means in practical terms is that *consumers resist giving up things that they already own.* This phenomenon is called the **endowment effect.** When consumers are asked to name a selling price for something they already own, they often require much more money than they would pay to own the very same item. For example, when a stranger approaches Tom on the street and offers him $45 for tickets to a Belle & Sebastian concert for which he has just paid $35, Tom rejects the offer. Due to the endowment effect, Tom values the tickets more after he owns them. To give up the tickets is viewed as a loss, and losses are felt more strongly than equivalent gains.[41]

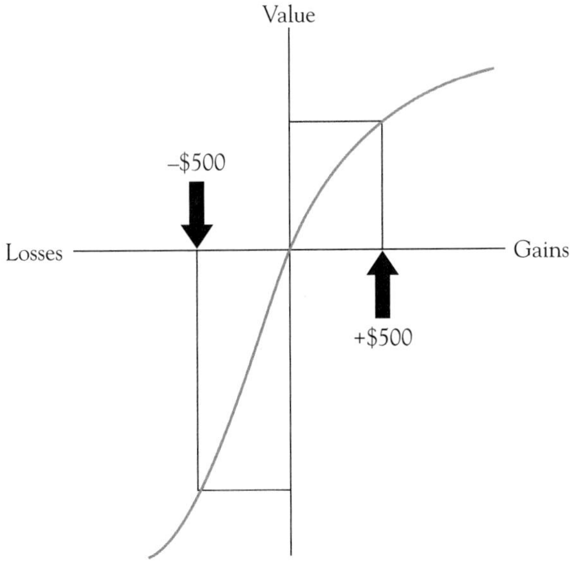

EXHIBIT 15.5

A Value Function: Gains and Losses

Source: Figure adapted from D. Kahneman and Amos Tversky, "Prospect Theory: An Analysis of Decision under Risk," *Econometrica* 47 (1979), pp. 263–91. © The Econometrica Society. Reprinted by permission.

Prospect theory predicts that preferences will depend on how a problem is framed. One of the most important contextual influences on the decision process is *the manner in which the task is defined or represented,* called **decision framing.** If the reference point is defined in a way that the outcome appears to be a gain, decision makers will be risk averse. In contrast, if the same outcome appears to be a loss, decision makers will be risk seekers. Marketers sometimes make use of consumers' differing perceptions about gains and losses. For instance, a dry cleaner has two ways of presenting a sales promotion. First, the cleaner could advertise a 25 percent price reduction. A second alternative is to offer to clean one shirt free with each order of three shirts. These two promotions offer the same gain to consumers—four shirts cleaned for the price of three. As described by prospect theory, consumers will value the free service more than the discounted service, even though the two promotions involve the same price savings.[42]

Another application of prospect theory is revealed in retail pricing. In general, it is more effective for retailers to promote cash discounts than to implement a policy of surcharges for customers who choose to use credit cards. Consumers perceive cash discounts to be gains (money retained). In contrast, surcharges are perceived as out-of-pocket losses. Even though the pricing structure may be the same, consumers will strive to avoid the surcharges, which are viewed as losses. Prospect theory also explains the retailing tactic of including "suggested retail prices" on all merchandise. Consumers use suggested retail prices to form a reference point (see Exhibit 15.5). Given this reference point, sale prices will seem like savings.[43]

There are limits associated with prospect theory. First, many positive consumer experiences do not involve receiving anything. When Tom takes his nephew, Brian, for a whitewater rafting trip, there is no monetary gain with respect to a reference point (as specified by prospect theory). In situations like this, where no monetary gains are received, it is not clear how to apply or even draw the curves shown in Exhibit 15.5. A second problem with prospect theory is that it assumes that outcomes can be scaled along a single metric, such as monetary rewards or the risk of a disease (a potential loss). For situations when consumers are forced to make trade-offs between two or more attributes, multi-attribute models (such as TORA) are more appropriate than prospect theory. When such trade-offs are made among attributes, there is not necessarily an optimal solution.[44] That is, there may be more than one type of value that a consumer derives from a positive outcome. For instance, when Tom and Brian go rafting, they derive at least three kinds of positive outcomes: (1) a close bond between two family members, (2) the aesthetic beauty of the river, and (3) skill-building in rafting. Against these positive outcomes are the costs of the trip, both monetary costs and investments of time. Prospect theory doesn't offer a coherent way to account for this kind of consumer experience, and it doesn't provide a way to explain how consumers make trade-offs when more than one attribute is involved.

Satisficing Nobel Prize–winning economist Herbert Simon proposed the idea that people **satisfice** rather than optimize when they are making decisions.[45] That is, *consumers try to make acceptable rather than optimal decisions.* For example, consumers may choose an alternative that satisfies their most important goals. Other goals might be sacrificed. As an example, consider the time that Tom rented his first apartment, after finishing university. He considered price and location to be the most important attributes. Space and safety were also key choice criteria, but he didn't consider them to be as important as the first two attributes. Tom looked at four or five apartments, but he certainly didn't make an exhaustive search of every available apartment complex. In the end he rented an apartment that passed his cutoff point on price and location. Such abbreviated search behavior is adaptive, because it saves time, an important consumer resource. However, this adaptiveness is different from the maximization described under expected utility theory. In most circumstances, expected utility theory represents an ideal model of consumer decision making, whereas satisficing theory is more descriptive of how consumers actually make choices.

COGNITIVE MODELS **Cognitive models** *describe consumers as combining items of information about attributes to reach a decision.* Cognitive models emphasize beliefs, rather than emotions or behaviors, as the key determinant of attitudes and behaviors and they assume that consumers make a decision in a thoughtful and systematic way. In consumer studies, cognitive models are typically classified as either compensatory or noncompensatory and as using either attribute (feature-based) or brand processing.

Compensatory Models A **compensatory model** assumes that a *negative evaluation on one attribute or feature can be offset by a positive evaluation on another feature.* The most familiar form of a compensatory model is the expectancy value model, one variant of which is the TORA model we described earlier. Consumers assess the importance of each product attribute and assign a subjective value to each attribute level. Then, consumers consider the alternatives, multiplying each attribute's subjective value times its importance weight and adding across these sums to obtain an overall value for each brand or product option. Product-rating schemes offered in magazines such as *Consumer Reports* in the United States and *Products* in Japan, by prestigious testing services such as Stiftung Warentest in Germany, and by some electronic agents on websites invite and assist consumers to engage in attribute-based compensatory decision making.[46] Advertisers can encourage consumers to utilize attribute-based processing models, as illustrated in the advertisement for Ford certified pre-owned vehicles. Not all attributes are treated equally. For example, consumers seem to be more resistant to trading off some quality to get a better price than accepting a higher price to get better quality. People may resist trading off attributes that encode core values such as freedom, health, or family against other less-important attributes. Some consumers also

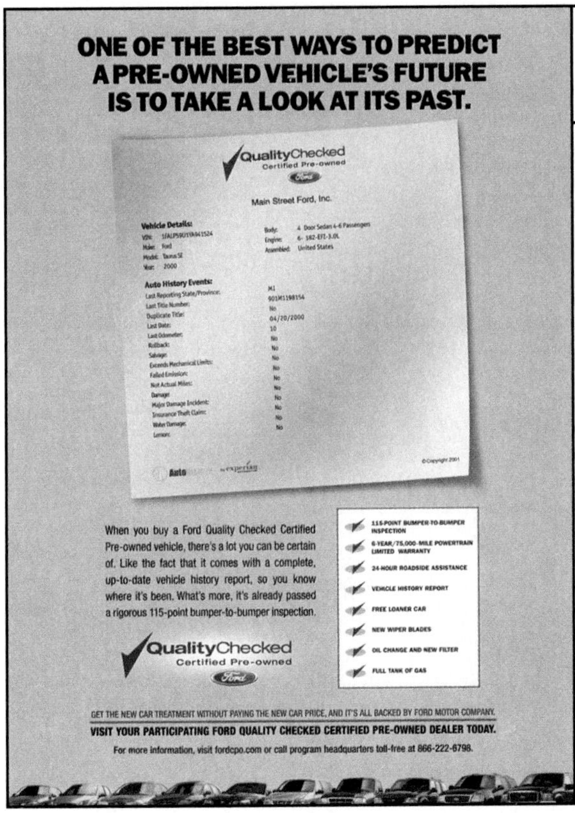

This ad uses a checklist format to encourage attribute-based decision making.

may distinguish between goals such as pleasure and resources such as time or money when they make trade-offs. Unfortunately, we do not know too much about the limits on attribute trade-offs and certainly less about this cross-culturally.[47] Compensatory models also can involve brand comparisons. For example, consumers could compare the attributes of two brands from their **evoked set**—*the set of brands a consumer would consider purchasing*—in order to form an overall evaluation. They could continue this process until one brand remains as the preferred choice.

Noncompensatory Models Consumers employ several different kinds of **noncompensatory models.** Some of these models assume processing by attribute while others assume processing by brands. The key feature of these models is that *a negative attribute rating can eliminate a brand from consideration;* that is, a positive rating on a different attribute can't compensate for that attribute. In the **lexicographic model,** for example, *consumers start with the most important attribute and compare options; if one option dominates, it is selected; if there is a tie, they compare remaining options on the second-most-important attribute, and so on.* Another example of a noncompensatory model based on attribute comparisons is the **elimination-by-aspects model.** This model *is similar to the lexicographic model but adds the notion of acceptable cutoffs.* Options remain under evaluation as long as they are over the cutoff point; options below the cutoff are eliminated.

The cartoon shown on the next page shows an example of elimination by aspects. Here, the man in the foreground decides to halt his journey where he stands. If he proceeds any further, his cell phone will be out of range. The traveler believes that the

"I can't go any farther. My cell phone will be out of range."

Source: Reprinted with permission from Dow Jones & Company from *The Wall Street Journal;* permission conveyed through the Copyright Clearance Center.

attribute—keeping within range of his cell phone—is the most important factor to consider when choosing the path and extent of his journey. When his cell phone limit is reached, he does not continue. That is, the traveler does not appear to make trade-offs between a set of attributes. The traveler is not willing to sacrifice on the cell phone attribute to receive some benefit that may accrue from some other attribute (e.g., reaching the summit that beckons in the background).

For both conjunctive and disjunctive noncompensatory models, comparisons proceed by brands rather than attributes. In the **conjunctive model,** consumers *set up minimum levels on each attribute and reject alternatives that fall below the cutoff on any attribute.* For example, if a consumer is evaluating five brands on five attributes, she would eliminate any brand that falls below the minimum on any one of the five attributes. In this case, the weight is on negative information. The **disjunctive model,** by contrast, *evaluates brands only on the most important attributes but retains options* *that are acceptable on these attributes.* Both the conjunctive and disjunctive models might be used by consumers to narrow their options. For example, a consumer may say, "I need a car that has four doors, costs less than $25,000, offers four-wheel drive, and gets at least 25 MPG." This use of a conjuctive model allows the consumer to eliminate brands that are clearly not acceptable.

AFFECTIVE MODELS Sometimes consumers make decisions in a more embodied, holistic way than suggested by the cognitive models described above. Sometimes a decision "feels right" or the decision maker has a "gut feeling" about the right choice. Sometimes a particular decision seems to "fit like a glove," or a purchase is triggered by an embodied evaluation of an object—"this is really me." In fact, emotions may sometimes summarize and capture important aspects of attitudes and behaviors that are hard to put in words but central to making a fulfilling choice.[48] Emotions may reflect deeply rooted cultural models about what's appropriate or moral, or may embody feelings we have for other people.[49] Choices of places to attend school, spouses, whether to have children, what house to buy, and what profession to pursue are often ultimately described in these ephemeral and emotional ways. Although consumers may use price, square footage, and number of rooms to narrow down a decision on a house, they then may select the home that "feels right." Although Western philosophy has emphasized cognitive models of choice, affective models may dominate in other parts of the world and in particular choice domains. We are still at the preliminary stages of understanding how emotions and cognitions are linked and how best to understand **embodied decision making**—*decisions based on a holistic perception and comprehension of a gestalt scenario.*

SIMPLE STRATEGIES FOR MAKING DECISIONS Marketers have identified numerous ways in which consumers try to simplify choices. Probably all of us use some or even most of these strategies some of the time. We use these shortcut heuristics because they save time and energy. They are often part of a satisficing strategy—an attempt to make acceptable if not optimal decisions. Here we outline just a few of the many ways consumers attempt to simplify choices. **Brand loyalty** can be a useful simplifying strategy. Often consumers just *repeatedly buy the same brand because of a strong preference.* In this case, the consumer does not have a high level of involvement in the decision but may still have a high level of involvement with the product. Sometimes **brand familiarity** is used as a basis for purchase. This can represent a mere exposure effect, but can also just be a cue to consumers that the product is acceptable. Inexperienced buyers are especially inclined to purchase a familiar brand. Visual cues such as packaging and colors also may be important simple ways of making purchase decisions. Under certain circumstances, **country of origin** also can be an important basis for making decisions. For example, consumers may look for products consistent with their image of that country—leather from Italy, electronics from Japan, entertainment from the United States. Many of these cues and their importance in choices were discussed in Chapter 8. **Price-related strategies** also can help simplify choices. For example, consumers can buy the cheapest or buy the brand on sale, or use a coupon. **Avoiding regret** also may be the basis for making decisions. Sometimes consumers may attempt to select the option they are least likely to regret.

SUMMARY

Consumers' attitudes, judgments, and decisions are nested within a cultural and social context and depend on consumers' goals, involvements, perceptions, experiences, knowledge, lifestyles, and self-concepts. Consumers formulate, strengthen, and change their attitudes about many different objects and reference those attitudes in responding to situations and deciding what actions to take. Attitudes help consumers cope with their environments and serve several basic functions. The functions that attitudes serve vary in importance from culture to culture.

Consumers have attitudes about many different people, objects, and ideas. Attitudes vary in their strength, availability, and accessibility. It's useful to think of attitudes as having cognitive, affective, and behavioral dimensions. Balance theory and ideologies are two theories for thinking about relationships among attitudes. It's important for marketers to understand the cluster of attitudes and beliefs that are linked to their offerings. There are many different theories about attitudes. In this chapter we described dissonance theory, the elaboration likelihood model, the theory of reasoned action, and the theory of planned behavior. While each of these theories has important limitations, each offers valuable perspectives on how attitudes are formed, changed, and connected to choice. Judgments, like attitudes, are a crucial input into decisions. Consumers make many different types of judgments. We outlined several common tools consumers use to make judgments and described marketing implications.

Consumers are adaptive decision makers. They exploit and adapt to aspects of the environment in order to achieve goals. Emotions are an important part of this appraisal process. It's important to remember that much consumer action is not based on decisions and that decisions or intentions don't always result in action. Consumers use many different strategies for making decisions—some simple, some complex, some based primarily on cognitions, others based more on feelings and emotions. We described expected utility theory and utility functions as useful but idealized visions of how consumers make choices. We also described consumers' valuing of gains and losses with respect to a reference point in our discussion of prospect theory. Most consumers, rather than making optimal choices, try to satisfice—make acceptable choices. In the remaining chapters in this section, we will further detail how consumers form intentions and take action.

KEY TERMS

KEY TERMS

embodied decision making 659
endowment effect 654
evoked set 657
expectancy-value model 641
expected utility theory 652
functional theory 632
goal congruence 650
goal relevance 650
ideologies theory of attitude structure 637
judgment 631
knowledge function 632
lexicographic model 657
matching hypothesis 632
mere exposure effect 640
mood-management theory 634
noncompensatory models 657
perceived behavioral control 647
peripheral route to persuasion 639
price-related strategies 659
prospect theory 654
representativeness heuristic 649
satisfice 656
simulation heuristic 649
social-adjustment function 632
strong arguments 640
theory of planned behavior 647
theory of reasoned action 643
utilitarian function 632
utility-maximizing view 652
value-expressive function 632

REVIEW QUESTIONS

1. Describe a choice that you have made in each of the following categories:
   a. A career choice
   b. A low-involvement consumer choice
   c. A high-involvement consumer choice
   d. A choice relating to your friends
   e. An academic choice

   How are these choices alike? How are they different? For each choice, describe a model or theory that explains this choice.
2. Look at some ads in a magazine that you usually read. Try to identify ads that make utilitarian appeals, value-expressive appeals, ego-defensive appeals, knowledge appeals, and social-adjustment appeals. Also, try to identify ads that have a primary goal to influence
   a. Consumer cognitions
   b. Consumer emotions
   c. Consumer actions
3. Name some celebrity endorsers who are very popular with the public. Why are they popular? Name some celebrity endorsers who have fallen into disfavor with the public. How do you suppose this has affected the sales of the product they endorsed? Did any of the companies stop using these endorsers? Do you believe celebrity endorsement works? If so, under which circumstances?
4. Describe different kinds of consumer heuristics (i.e., shortcuts). Under what examples are these heuristics used to make consumer decisions? Give examples from your own life. Describe a decision situation where you used some shortcuts. Why did you take these shortcuts? Was your resulting decision optimal or satisfying? Why or why not?
5. In plain words describe the theory of reasoned action and the theory of planned behavior. Contrast these two models. What are the limitations of these models?
6. Think of an important decision that you have made. How did you make that decision? What role did emotions, fit, or gut feelings play in this decision?

7. Compare and contrast compensatory and noncompensatory decision rules and highlight the differences between them.
8. Find a website that helps consumers evaluate one brand at a time. Now find a website that helps consumers compare brands, one attribute at a time. Evaluate how these different websites might influence consumer decision making.

YOU MAKE THE CALL

NEBRASKA CORN-FED BEEF

The Nebraska Cattlemen's Association (NCA) is exploring several international markets for entry under its Nebraska corn-fed beef (NCFB) campaign. The cattle are fed on a ration of corn and corn-products for at least 90 days prior to slaughter, which produces a juicier, better-flavored meat. The association hopes to market its end cuts (e.g., roasts), for which it feels it has a price advantage. To produce NCFB-certified meat, certain breeds of cattle with a reputation for producing tough meat are excluded from the program. The cattle are tracked from the cow and calf operations, through the feedlots, and on to the processing facilities to guarantee quality. The NCA believes that the breeding and feeding characteristics of the meat, as well as its USDA "Choice" certification, may attract Polish, Japanese, and Korean consumers. NCFB is attractively packaged and comes with advertising circulars promoting the cowboy image of rural Nebraska. American beef has a positive image in many markets. Japanese grocers sometimes display videos of U.S. cattle ranches at their beef counters. Other products with a Western and American image, such as Levi's jeans and Marlboro cigarettes, have done well in international markets, as have some food products like McDonald's.

Currently, Koreans often import grass-fed Australian beef, and Poles eat the meat of dairy cattle that have passed their milk-producing prime. Neither type of meat can compete in quality with Nebraska corn-fed beef. The NCA proposes a product trial program to demonstrate the improved flavor of corn-fed beef. Funds will be provided to train Polish chefs and meat cutters in the best ways to process NCFB beef, for example. And the association expects that attitudes about Nebraska will work in favor of the product. Images of the American West and the American cowboy figure in its marketing communications.

The beef does contain hormones and is the product of artificial insemination. It is also true that NCFB does not guarantee that the corn is free from genetically modified organisms (GMOs). The association believes that consumer education, government lobbying efforts, and consumer trial may change consumer attitudes about hormones and GMOs that are relatively negative in Europe and Asia.

QUESTIONS

1. What positive associations do consumers have with Nebraska corn-fed beef that should be reinforced? How should they be reinforced?
2. How should the NCFB program attempt to modify consumer beliefs about competing products?
3. How might balance theory be used to develop marketing communications for NCFB?

4. How might ELM models be employed in the NCFB program's marketing communications to affect behavioral intentions?

For more information about NCFB, visit their website at necornfedbeef.com.

1. This vignette was inspired by a class discussion surrounding the Wacky World of Japanese Ice Cream referenced in the Mainichi daily news through September 2002 (http://mdn.mainichi.co.jp) and also discussed in Phred Dvorak, "Something Fishy Is Going on in Japan in the Ice-Cream Biz," *The Wall Street Journal,* September 4, 2002, p. A1. For fun facts about ice cream consumption, just check this topic on the World Wide Web. Information on ice cream consumption can be found in *Latest Scoop,* 2000 edition, International Dairy Foods Association.
2. Alice Eagly and Shelly Chaiken, "Attitude Structure and Function," in *Handbook of Social Psychology,* 4th ed., vol. 1, ed. D. Gilbert, Susan Fiske, and G. Lindzey (New York: McGraw-Hill, 1998).
3. Eagly and Chaiken, "Attitude Structure and Function"; and Gregory R. Maio and James M. Olson, "Relationships between Values, Attitudes, and Behavioral Intentions: The Moderating Role of Attitude Function," *Journal of Experimental Social Psychology* 31 (1995), pp. 266–85.
4. Sharon Shavitt, "The Role of Attitude Objects in Attitude Functions," *Journal of Experimental Social Psychology* 26, no. 2, (1990), pp. 124–48.
5. For a review, see Sharon Shavitt and Michelle R. Nelson, "The Role of Attitude Functions in Persuasion and Social Judgment," in *The Persuasion Handbook: Developments in Theory and Practice,* ed. James Price Dillard and Michael Pfau (Thousand Oaks, CA: Sage Publications, 2002).
6. S. Han and Sharon Shavitt, "Persuasion and Culture: Advertising Appeals in Individualistic and Collectivistic Societies," *Journal of Experimental Social Psychology* 30 (1994), pp. 326–50.
7. Russell Fazio, David Sanbonmatsu, Martha Powell, and Frank Kardes, "On the Automatic Activation of Attitudes," *Journal of Personality and Social Psychology* 50, no. 2 (1986), pp. 229–38.
8. Durvasula Srinivas, J. Craig Andrews, Steven Lysonski, and Richard G. Netemeyer, "Assessing the Cross-National Applicability of Consumer Behavior Models: A Model of Attitude toward Advertising in General," *Journal of Consumer Research,* March 1993, pp. 626–36; and Steven P. Brown and Douglas M. Stayman, "Antecedents and Consequences of Attitude toward the Ad: A Metaanalysis," *Journal of Consumer Research,* June 1993, pp. 34–51.
9. Marieke de Mooij, *Global Marketing and Advertising: Understanding Cultural Paradoxes* (Thousand Oaks, CA: Sage Publications, 1998), pp. 166–72.
10. Fazio, Sanbonmatsu, Powell, and Kardes, "On the Automatic Activation of Attitudes"; and Eagly and Chaiken, "Attitude Structure and Function."
11. Kaiping Peng and Richard E. Nisbett, "Culture Dialectics, and Reasoning about Contradiction," *American Psychologist* 54 (September 1999), pp. 741–54.
12. Fritz Heider, *The Psychology of Interpersonal Relations* (New York: Wiley, 1958).
13. Sam Walker, "Home-Run Heroes Bring in Few Endorsements," *The Wall Street Journal,* October 21, 1998, pp. B1, B4.
14. P. C. Stern, T. Dietz, L. Kalof, and G. A. Guagnano, "Values, Beliefs, and Proenvironmental Action: Attitude Formation toward Emergent Attitude Objects," *Journal of Applied Social Psychology* 25 (1995), pp. 1611–36; and Eagly and Chaiken, "Attitude Structure and Function."
15. Eviatar Zerubavel, *Social Mindscapes: An Invitation to Cognitive Sociology* (Cambridge, MA: Harvard University Press, 1997); S. Heine, and D. Lehman, "Culture, Dissonance and Self-Affirmation," *Personality and Social Psychology Bulletin* 23, no. 4 (1997), pp. 389–400; and M. Posner and M. Rothbart, "Cognitive Science's Contributions to Culture and Emotion," in *Emotion and Culture,* ed. S. Kitayama and H. Markus (Washington, DC: American Psychological Association, 1994).

16. Leon Festinger, *A Theory of Cognitive Dissonance* (Evanston, IL: Row, Peterson, 1957); Eddie Harmon-Jones, "A Cognitive Dissonance Theory Perspective on Persuasion," in *The Persuasion Handbook: Developments in Theory and Practice,* ed. James Price Dillard and Michael Pfau (Thousand Oaks, CA: Sage Publications, 2002); Richard E. Petty and Duane T. Wegener, "Attitude Change: Multiple Roles for Persuasion Variables," in *Handbook of Social Psychology* (4th ed., vol. 1), ed. D. Gilbert, Susan Fiske, and G. Lindzey (New York: McGraw-Hill, 1998), pp. 323–90.
17. This section draws heavily from Petty and Wegener, "Attitude Change: Multiple Roles for Persuasion Variables"; Richard E. Petty, John T. Cacioppo, and David Schumann, "Central and Peripheral Routes to Advertising Effectiveness: The Moderating Role of Involvement," *Journal of Consumer Research* 10 (1984), pp. 135–47; and Steve Booth-Butterfield and Jennifer Welbourne, "The Elaboration Likelihood Model: Its Impact on Persuasion Theory and Research," in *The Persuasion Handbook: Developments in Theory and Practice,* ed. James Price Dillard and Michael Pfau (Thousand Oaks, CA: Sage Publications, 2002), pp. 155–73.
18. Anne M. Brumbaugh, "Source and Nonsource Cues in Advertising and Their Effects on the Activation of Cultural and Subcultural Knowledge on the Route to Persuasion," *Journal of Consumer Research* 29 (September 2002), pp. 258–69. The Chinese advertisement is featured in a video by Russell Belk entitled *Chinese Consumers' Responses to Advertising,* Odyssey Films, 2001.
19. This section relies on Jerold L. Hale, Brian J. Householder, and Katheryn L. Green, "The Theory of Reasoned Action," in *The Persuasion Handbook: Developments in Theory and Practice,* ed. James Price Dillard and Michael Pfau (Thousand Oaks, CA: Sage Publications, 2002), pp. 259–86. See also Martin Fishbein, "A Theory of Reasoned Action: Some Applications and Implications," in *Nebraska Symposium on Motivation,* vol. 27, ed. H. Howe and M. Page (Lincoln, NE: University of Nebraska Press, 1980), pp. 65–116.
20. de Mooij, *Global Marketing and Advertising,* pp. 130–32, 172.
21. Lynne O'Donnell, "All the Tea in China," *The Weekend Australian Magazine,* July 6–7, 2002, pp. 11–15.
22. May O. lwin, Jerome D. Williams, and Luh Luh Lan, "Social Marketing Initiatives: National Kidney Foundation's Organ Donation Programs in Singapore," *Journal of Public Policy and Marketing* 21 (Spring 2002), pp. 66–77.
23. Thomas O'Guinn and Ronald J. Faber, "Compulsive Buying: A Phenomenological Exploration," *Journal of Consumer Research* 16 (September 1989), pp. 147–57; and Dennis W. Rook, "The Buying Impulse," *Journal of Consumer Research* 14 (September 1987), pp. 189–99.
24. Roy F. Baumeister, "Yielding to Temptation: Self-Control Failure, Impulsive Purchasing, and Consumer Behavior," *Journal of Consumer Research* 28 (March 2002), pp. 670–76.
25. John M. Twenge, Roy F. Baumeister, Dianne M. Tice, and Brandon Schmeichel, "Decision Fatigue: Making Multiple Personal Decisions Depletes the Self's Resources," unpublished manuscript, Department of Psychology, Case Western Reserve University, Cleveland, OH 44106.
26. Numerous references are available on each of these topics. A couple favorites include Daniel Kahneman, Paul Slovic, and Amos Tversky, *Judgment under Uncertainty: Heuristics and Biases* (Cambridge: Cambridge University Press, 1982); and John W. Payne, James R. Bettman, and Eric J. Johnson, "The Adaptive Decision-Maker," in *Judgment and Decision Making Theory and Applications: A Tribute to Hillel Einhorn,* ed. Robin M. Hogarth (Chicago: University of Chicago Press, 1997).
27. A couple of terrific studies that illustrate these types of anchor-and-adjust effects are Stephen J. Hoch, " Who Do We Know: Predicting the Interests and Opinions of the American Consumer," *Journal of Consumer Research* 15 (December 1988), pp. 315–24; and Harry L. Davis, Stephen J. Hoch, and E. K. Easton Ragsdale, "An Anchoring and Adjustment Model of Spousal Predictions," *Journal of Consumer Research* 13 (June 1986), pp. 25–37.
28. Deborah J. MacInnis and Linda L. Price, "The Role of Imagery in Information Processing: Review and Extensions," *Journal of Consumer Research,* March 1987, pp. 473–91.
29. John Payne, James Bettman, and Eric Johnson, *The Adaptive Decision Maker* (New York: Cambridge University Press, 1993); and James Bettman, Mary Frances Luce, and John W. Payne, "Constructive Consumer Choice Processes," *Journal of Consumer Research* 25 (December 1998), pp. 187–217.

30. Rashmi Adaval, "Sometimes It Just Feels Right: The Differential Weighting of Affect-Consistent and Affect-Inconsistent Product Information," *Journal of Consumer Research* 28 (June 2001), pp. 1–17.
31. Mary Frances Luce, James R. Bettman, and John W. Payne, "Emotional Decisions: Trade-off Difficulty and Coping in Consumer Choice," *Monographs of the Journal of Consumer Research,* no. 1 (2001).
32. See Ellen J. Langer, *The Power of Mindful Learning* (Reading, MA: Addison-Wesley, 1997); and Joseph W. Alba, "Presidential Address: Dimensions of Consumer Expertise . . . or Lack Thereof," in *Advances in Consumer Research,* vol. 27, ed. Stephen J. Hoch and Robert J. Meyer (Provo, UT: Association for Consumer Research, 2000), pp. 1–9.
33. Mary Francis Luce, "Choosing to Avoid: Coping with Negatively Emotion Laden Consumer Decisions," *Journal of Consumer Research* 24 (March 1998), pp. 409–33.
34. James R. Bettman, Mary Frances Luce, and John W. Payne, "Constructive Consumer Choice Processes," *Journal of Consumer Research* 25 (December 1998), pp. 187–217.
35. Scott Plous, *The Psychology of Judgment and Decision Making* (Philadelphia: Temple University Press, 1993).
36. Ibid.
37. de Mooij, *Global Marketing and Advertising,* pp. 130–33.
38. D. Kahneman and Amos Tversky, "Prospect Theory: An Analysis of Decision under Risk," *Econometrica* 47 (1979), pp. 263–91.
39. Michal Ann Strahilevitz and George M. Zinkhan, "The Utility Consumers Derive from Giving: A Model of Donation Behavior," working paper 7, University of Georgia, Athens, 1998.
40. Plous, *The Psychology of Judgment and Decision Making.*
41. Ibid.
42. Ibid.
43. Robert Thaler, "Mental Accounting and Consumer Choice," *Marketing Science* 4 (1985), pp. 199–214; and Plous, *The Psychology of Judgment and Decision Making.*
44. Plous, *The Psychology of Judgment and Decision Making.*
45. Simon, "Rational Choice and the Structure of the Environment," *Psychological Review* 63 (1956), pp. 129–38; and Plous, *The Psychology of Judgment and Decision Making.*
46. Bettman, Luce, and Payne, "Constructive Consumer Choice Processes"; John Clammer, "Aesthetics of the Self: Shopping and Social Being in Contemporary Urban Japan," in *Lifestyle Shopping: The Subject of Consumption,* ed. Ron Shields (London: Routledge, 1995), pp. 195–215; and de Mooij, *Global Marketing and Advertising,* p. 274.
47. Jonathan Baron and Mark D. Spranca, "Protected Values," *Organizational Behavior and Human Decision Processes* 70 (April 1997), pp. 1–16; Ravi Dhar and Itamar Simonson, "Consumption Context Effects on Choice: Matching versus Balancing," working paper, School of Management, Yale University, New Haven, CT (1997); Stephen M. Nowlis and Itamar Simonson, "Attribute-Task Compatibility as a Determinant of Consumer Preference Reversals," *Journal of Marketing Research* 34 (May 1997), pp. 205–18; and Philip E. Tetlock, "The Impact of Accountability in Judgment and Choice: Toward a Social Contingency Mode," in *Advances in Experimental Social Psychology,* vol. 25, ed. Mark P. Zanna (San Diego, CA: Academic Press, 1992), pp. 331–76.
48. Seymour Epstein, " Integration of the Cognitive and the Psychodynamic Unconscious," *American Psychologist,* August 1994, pp. 709–24; George Lakoff and Mark Johnson, *Philosophy in the Flesh: The Embodied Mind and Its Challenge to Western Thought* (New York: Basic Books, 1999); Douglas E. Allen, "Toward a Theory of Consumer Choices as Sociohistorically Shaped Practical Experience: The Fits-Like-a-Glove (FLAG) Framework," *Journal of Consumer Research* 28 (March 2002), pp. 515–32; and Susan Schultz Kleine, Robert E. Kleine III, and Chris T. Allen, "How Is a Possession 'Me' or 'Not Me'? Characterizing Types and an Antecedent of Material Possession Attachment," *Journal of Consumer Research* 22 (December 1995), pp. 327–43.
49. Robert H. Frank, *Passions within Reason: The Strategic Role of the Emotions* (New York: W.W. Norton and Company, 1988).

chapter 1
chapter 2
chapter 3
chapter 4
chapter 5
chapter 6
chapter 7
chapter 8
chapter 9
chapter 10
chapter 11
chapter 12
chapter 13
chapter 14
chapter 15
chapter 16
chapter 17
chapter 18
chapter 19

LEARNING OBJECTIVES

After completing this chapter, you should be able to:

- Describe consumer acquisition strategies, behaviors, and major models of exchange.
- Be familiar with some basic approaches to consumer purchase decision making.
- Recognize some links between purchase timing, frequency, and marketing tactics.
- Explain the relationships between brand switching and marketing tactics.
- Discuss the nature of barter behavior and its implications in marketing.
- Identify the uses of countertrade in interorganizational purchase behavior.
- Recognize the importance of gift exchange in consumer behavior.
- Describe the differences between interpersonal and self-gifts.

BARTERING IN RUSSIA[1]

Wrapped tightly against chilling winds, Valentina Novikova, a pensioner, stands expectantly at a lonely crossroads outside the old glass- and crystal-making town of Gus-Khrustalny, her champagne flutes tucked neatly into cardboard boxes, stacked on makeshift birch tables.

"Don't have money for champagne," she says sheepishly, displaying the glasses to passersby under gray skies, hoping to earn a few dollars a week to feed her grandchildren. In felt boots and a padded coat, she often walks miles to the crossroads with a tote bag of crystal. "I don't have much," she sighs.

The above description provides a poignant tableau from a little understood yet pervasive phenomenon in Russia's disorderly transition to free markets. The glass and crystal sold on the roadside here are the lifeblood of the local economy. Workers are paid in glass, receive their social benefits in glass, and must sell the glass to stay alive. The glass has become a kind of substitute money. The workers and their glass factory are part of a vast transactional web of barter, trading, and debt—all using surrogates for the ruble.

In Volgograd, workers at the Armina factory decided to go on strike, according to the newspaper *Izvestia.* The reason: Their monthly wage of approximately $50 is paid in brassieres. "All our relatives and friends have got them already, and we do not know what to do with the rest," a worker laments. "See for yourself. We are paid in bras at 18,000 rubles each. That makes seven to nine bras a month. That is too many for one woman."

Movie theaters in the Siberian city of Altai started charging two eggs for admission because people had no cash to spare. However, the theaters ran into a problem in the winter when hens lay fewer eggs and audiences began to dwindle. As a remedy, the movie houses are now taking empty bottles as payment, returning them to the bottlers for cash. This flood of surrogate money has touched virtually every sector, every factory, and every worker in Russia. Thus, a trend that began a few years ago at a time of runaway inflation has persisted and become even more widespread as inflation has cooled. Nonetheless, the Russian economy still suffers from a variety of problems such as corruption, money laundering, and the effects of the recent Asian currency crisis, so industry continues to languish.

OVERVIEW

Chapter 15 focused on how consumers make decisions about consumption objects and activities, and key relationships between attitudes, judgments, decisions, and behaviors. An important aspect of consumer decision making is how, when, and where consumers acquire products and services. This topic is at the heart of consumer behavior and the focus of this chapter. As summarized in Exhibit 16.1, consumers' acquisition strategies must be understood in the context of macro-environmental factors and their local context and social networks. For example, the explosion of barter trade described in the opening vignette is a response to political and social events in Russia. Of course, as we have emphasized throughout this book, consumers interpret their environment from the perspective of their unique life experiences, perceptions, self-concepts, knowledge, and goals. Exhibit 16.1 suggests that there are many different types of **acquisition** and many locations for acquiring goods and services. In this case, we represent

EXHIBIT 16.1

Acquiring Things and Services

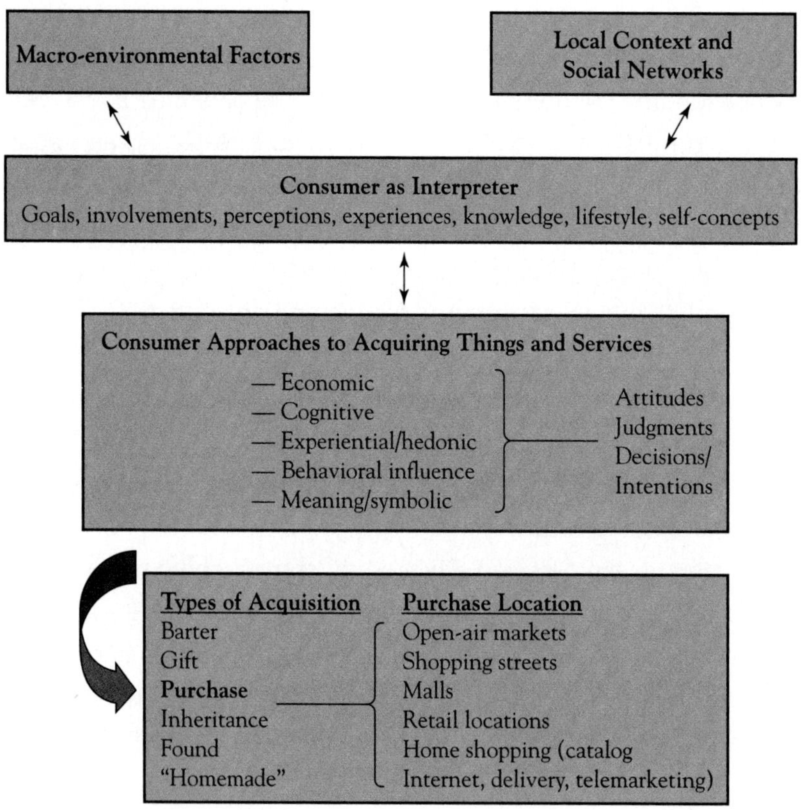

just some of the many places consumers can purchase goods and services. Think of all the many other places you might find an object, make an acquisition, or receive a gift! The vignette that introduces this chapter talks about one way that consumers acquire goods—through **barter,** *the direct exchange of goods or services between two or more trading partners.* Barter has accelerated as a mode of exchange in Russia and other parts of the world because of unstable currencies, but barter is an important type of global exchange.[2] Asia alone has a bartering business worth $90 billion a year. In 2001 there were an estimated $9 billion worth of **barter transactions** in North America, $100 million in Europe, and $350 million in Australia and New Zealand. Estimates suggest that 10 to 20 percent of all world trade involves some form of barter, and **countertrade,** used to describe *transactions where all or partial payment is made in kind* (goods and services) *rather than in cash,* currently represents about 40 percent of the world economy. Numerous bartering websites have been launched in the past several years, with many others under construction. For example, at Who's Bartering.com? you can barter over 1,000 products and services in 178 countries and 2,100 locations.

www.whosbartering.com

Of course, many consumers prefer to acquire goods and services by purchasing them, and to do this they go shopping. Shopping is a significant activity that reaches around the globe. People engage in shopping for a variety of reasons, not just to acquire goods and services, but also to learn about consumption options or to vicariously participate in consumption. In Romania, for example, window shopping gives consumers a different view of the world. We will talk more about shopping styles and goals in this chapter. From shopping on Les Champs Élysées in Paris to shopping on the Huai Hai Road in Shanghai, consumers use their currency to pursue their consumption goals and desires. In the United States there is even a magazine that proudly claims to be "a magazine about shopping." The photo on page 270 shows an open-air bazaar in Cluj, Romania. Open-air markets such as this one are commonplace around the world.

Although most U.S. consumers still purchase their fresh food through major grocery chains, farmers' markets have increased by 79 percent since 1994 when the U.S.D.A. first began keeping track, and the number of farmers who sell at them has nearly tripled.[3] Catalogs and websites enable consumers to shop from their home 24 hours a day everyday. For example, eBay, an Internet-based market for buying and selling, does $30 million a day in business with more than 35 million users.[4] The success of eBay and other top online exchanges is that they deliver value. EBay pioneered online auctions for consumer goods and its feedback system attempts to establish reputations for each buyer and seller facilitating trade in nonstandard items. For some other leading

Window shopping in Romania.

Romanian bazaar offers an affordable shopping alternative.

www.paypal.com

www.lendingtree.com

www.freemarkets.com

www.e-mart.com.sg

www.fedex.com

exchanges with shrewd marketing positions that deliver customer value, check out PayPal, LendingTree, and FreeMarkets.

Whether and under what conditions consumers will shop online remains a provocative question. In the United States, attempts to get consumers to shop for groceries online have met with resistance. However, in Singapore it's a different story. Check out e-mart to see how Singapore Food Industries has made a successful business from allowing consumers to purchase groceries online for home delivery. In this cash-rich and time-poor environment, e-mart is responsive to consumer goals. What cultural, economic, and social factors talked about in other chapters of this book might help account for this difference?

Because of the reduced overhead often associated with servicing requests online, many service providers such as travel agencies and airlines are encouraging customers to go online. This advertisement for FedEx appears in business magazines but simulates their website, encouraging potential customers to "point, click, and ship" at their website.

Beyond barter and purchase, gifts are also a significant way of acquiring goods and services. **Gift-giving behaviors** may involve money, but the tangible goods or services obtained are deemphasized in favor of the meanings or feelings evoked by the goods and services. Gift giving is at the heart of an enormous amount of consumer behavior, and the retail industry often lives or dies by its sales of gifts during Christmas and other important international holidays. In the United States, for example, consumers spend

Singapore Food Industries e-initiatives.

Numerous companies encourage online shopping.

$4 billion per day or $2.8 million per minute during the Christmas season. In Denmark, a nation of five million people, consumers spent six million crowns (about $1.07 billion) in the 1996 Christmas season.[5] Note that other kinds of acquisition behaviors exist. For example, one may find objects by accident or may have stolen them. Found objects have played an interesting role in some modern art movements, such as Dada and pop art, but are not central to the study of consumer behavior. Thefts, including what retailers refer to as "inventory shrinkage," or shoplifting, is an important "dark-side" consumer behavior, but we will not deal with it extensively here. Inheritance, another form of acquisition, is discussed further in Chapter 19. Finally, consumers may produce homemade possessions for themselves or for subsequent giving. While not discussed in this chapter, it is worth noting that handicrafts received as gifts are frequently highly valued by consumers.[6]

Acquisition can happen through exchanges that are completely impersonal (such as many Internet purchases) or they can happen through exchanges between people with intimate and enduring relationships (as is the case with many gifts). Marketers have tended to focus predominantly on impersonal marketplace transactions. But as anyone who has haggled in a Turkish bazaar, lingered in a hair-styling shop, participated in a Tupperware or Mary Kay cosmetics party, bought at auction, or even hung around in a small town café knows, much of the behavior associated with purchasing is far from impersonal. It often includes considerable amounts of emotion and interpersonal give and take. Purchase behaviors as diverse as haggling in a Turkish bazaar or buying Tupperware at a home-party sale are *embedded* in interpersonal relationships. Interpersonal ties may cause customers to buy when they have reasons for avoiding or postponing such a purchase. It may cause sellers to extend favors to good customers or cause buyers to exhibit loyalty to a particular retail outlet or service provider. Thus, purchase behaviors often include more than just impersonal acquisitions of need-fulfilling goods and services.[7] For example, **embedded purchases** are an integral part of the surrounding social world.

Discretionary purchase behavior, purchases devoted to satisfying desires rather than needs, is a relatively recent phenomenon even in the Triad countries, although it has a history in ancient China. So-called **lifestyle shopping,** *shopping as a form of leisure devoted to cultivating a consumer self-image,* is a phenomenon that emerged only in the late nineteenth century with the growth of the department store in Europe. Consumers in the transitional economies of the former Soviet bloc and emergent economies such as Turkey and India are often still learning to purchase and consume branded goods. They are still learning to understand price competition, promotions, and other marketing tools that many Euro-American marketers take for granted. Steeped in socialist values and habits, eastern Europeans often respond in surprising ways to these tactics. Shopping is still an occasional activity in developing parts of the world, especially where discretionary spending is quite limited. In these regions, acquisition behaviors are characterized by the values and habits of older, gift-based economies. In such economies, the value of possessions is realized primarily through acts of generosity, literally giving things away. Hence, the marketplace behavior in these societies often works in ways that Westerners might find peculiar.[8] Though not discussed extensively, we make some references to such economies in this chapter.

ACQUISITION MODELS

Consumer researchers and marketers examine acquisition behavior from five perspectives: (1) economic utility maximizing, (2) cognitive decision making, (3) experiential or hedonic, (4) behavioral influence, and (5) meaning transfer. As described in Chapter 15 and summarized in Exhibit 16.1, consumers reflect different approaches to forming attitudes, making judgments and decisions, and acquiring goods and services. The utility-maximizing view is derived from classic microeconomic theory. Marketers explore how consumers deliberately collect information, weigh alternatives, and make acquisition decisions that lead to the largest net benefit to them in terms of the exchange resources at issue. From the cognitive models or decision-making perspective, consumers engage in problem-solving tasks, in which they move through a series of stages.

The experiential or hedonic perspective holds that, in some cases, consumers acquire things to create feelings and experiences rather than to solve problems. This is consistent with the affective models for choice described in Chapter 15. The behavioral influence approach argues that consumers often act in response to situational, environmental pressures, such as perceptual cues in retail environments (see Chapter 8). The newest view, the meaning-transfer view, argues that acquisition and consumption behaviors are often motivated by the desire to obtain meanings that are valuable within consumers' life stories (see Chapter 4). Each approach has merit. None alone is adequate to account for the full range of acquisition behaviors.

The five perspectives are complementary because they focus on different aspects of the acquisition process. More than one type of behavior may occur simultaneously, as illustrated in The Gap interview presented in Consumer Chronicles 16.1. In this description the consumer is influenced by (1) utility-maximizing factors ("I always bought on sale. The better the sale the more I bought"; "On top of buying their clothes I also buy stock in the company"); (2) decision-making factors ("Everything in The Gap *matches* each other from belts, to socks, to slacks, and shirts"); (3) hedonic factors ("It was almost a sickness of some sort"; "I just love it. I feel like I am their friend and they are mine"); and (4) meaning-transfer factors ("They have stood the test of time and hiking in Colorado").

Similarly, automobile buyers may be influenced by utility-maximizing factors ("The dealer is offering low interest rates"); that is, they may collect comparative interest-

Shopping at The Gap

CONSUMER CHRONICLES 16.1

Excerpts from an interview with a 57-year-old female U.S. homemaker.

Consumer: I would definitely have to say The Gap is where my loyalty in clothing can be found. . . . The first time I bought an item at The Gap was around four years ago. I bought a pair of jeans on sale. . . . I have always been a shopper for clothes. It was almost a sickness of some sort. Some of my most shopped stores have been T. J. Maxx and Marshall's. I never bought things in small lots; everything I purchased was almost in what seemed to be bulk. And none of it was full-priced. I always bought on sale. The better the sale the more I bought. I also like to buy everything that matches. I do not mean by color but by label. If I bought a pair of slacks that were made by Ralph Lauren, I had to have a shirt from Ralph Lauren. When I bought the jeans at The Gap four years ago, I also had to buy a matching shirt. Nowadays, I have lost the appetite to buy in bulk (and my closet has gotten smaller). And I have stopped shopping at T. J. Maxx and Marshall's. I buy everything at The Gap. I still like to find a bargain, but now I will buy some things at regular price. Everything in The Gap matches each other, from belts, to socks, to slacks, and shirts. I have also made friends with the management team here in Brandon. They let me know when they are going to mark items down and when the new shipments will be in. I just love it. I feel like I am their friend and they are mine. On top of buying their clothes I also buy stock in the company. So, I actually own a piece of where I spend all my money. . . . The Gap makes quality clothing in my eyes. I still own that pair of jeans I first bought from them. They have stood the test of time and hiking in Colorado. The Gap has just all-around good clothing. I have never had problems with any of their clothes. And if something did go wrong I know that they will take the clothes back and give me a full return. Having a good return policy is important.

Interviewer: How would you feel if this product/company was no longer around?

Consumer: Devastated. I love their clothes and everything in my closet matches and is made by The Gap. On top of that I own a piece of the company so I would be losing money.

Interviewer: Do you feel like you have a relationship between you and the product/company?

Consumer: I have a buying relationship for their clothes and I have a friendship relationship with their workers. I feel special when I walk into The Gap and all the girls working say hello to me by my name. And these young girls don't treat me like an old lady.

Interviewer: If you could use one word to describe their product, what would it be?

Consumer: Unique.

rate information to see how to minimize the financial burden incurred through the purchase. Consumers may also evaluate automobile purchase alternatives through a consideration of attributes and benefits (e.g., seating, horsepower) in order to develop their choices. Such behavior may be understood through the decision-making perspective

("The car I buy must have room for six passengers"). In addition, they may imagine the feelings associated with riding in a convertible or impressing their friends with a sporty, luxury, or specialty vehicle ("Imagine driving along the beach with the top down"). Such behaviors can be understood through an experiential or hedonic perspective. Finally, they may think of themselves as the type whose lifestyle is realized through possession of a certain type of vehicle or whose self-image is completed by the possession of such a vehicle ("I'm a sports car kind of person"). Behaviors of this kind can be understood best through a meaning-transfer perspective.[9]

SOCIAL EXCHANGE

The sociologist George Homans proposed a model of exchange that is shown in Exhibit 16.2. One key idea presented in **Homans's model of exchange** is that buyers and sellers exchange resources (i.e., money, goods, services, social status, information, love) in varying proportions to meet their needs and in conformity with generally understood standards of fairness and propriety, subject to constraints of time, knowledge, and experience. For example, the consumer in Consumer Chronicles 16.1 states, "I buy everything at The Gap," in part because "The Gap makes quality clothing in my eyes." She also states, "the management team . . . lets me know when they are going to mark items down and when the new shipments will be in." Here, her focus is on outcomes. But Homans's exchange model also includes the idea that consumers derive value both from the things acquired and from the processes of acquisition, such as shopping, bartering, or gift giving. Thus, our consumer also states, "I have a friendship relationship with their workers." Here, her focus is on the process of exchange, from which she derives value. We discuss the outcome and process dimensions of exchange further in Chapter 18.

Exhibit 16.2 helps us to understand acquisition behavior. Successful marketers blend resources in novel ways to create distinctive market positionings and strive to ensure that both parties of an exchange derive benefit from it. In a simple purchase of a packaged good, the consumer derives the benefits of the good while the marketer derives the benefits of the money exchanged for it. But if a consumer shops for a diamond necklace at the exclusive Fred's or Bulgari jewelers, she also would expect to receive status and other benefits in exchange for her money. All acquisition behaviors can be

EXHIBIT 16.2

Homans's Model of Exchange: Resource Flows and Outcomes

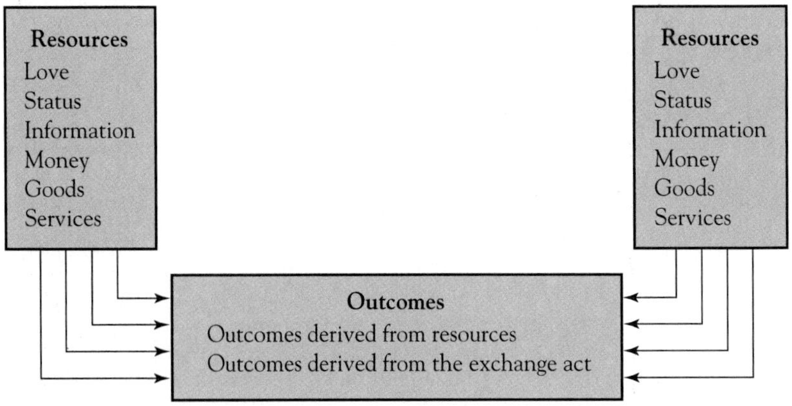

Source: George C. Homans, "Social Behavior and Exchange," *American Journal of Sociology* 63 (May 1958), pp. 597–606.

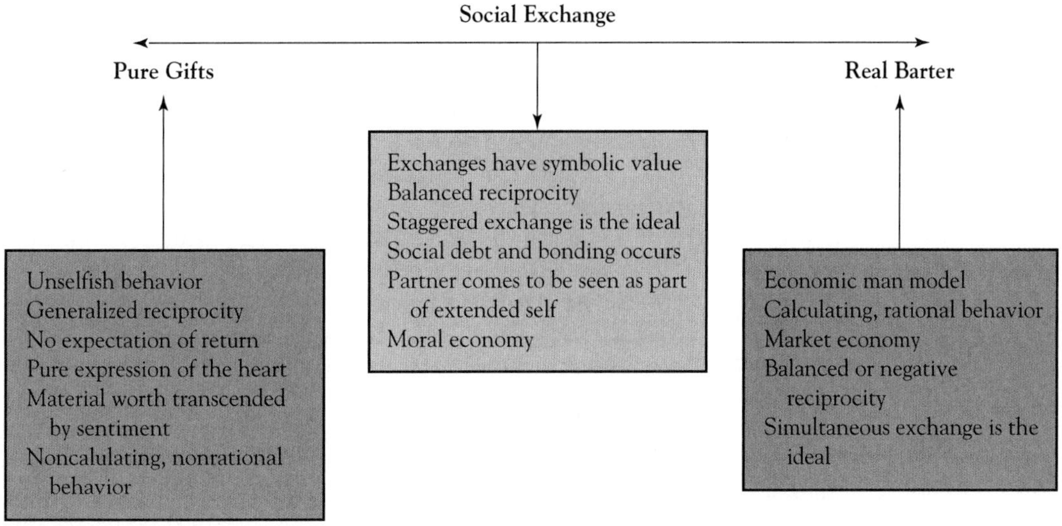

Source: Jonathan K. Frenzen and Harry L. Davis, "Purchasing Behavior in Embedded Markets," *Journal of Consumer Research* 17 (June 1990), pp. 1–12; Alvin W. Gouldner, "The Norm of Reciprocity: A Preliminary Statement," *American Sociological Review* 25 (April 1960), pp. 161–78; George C. Homans, "Social Behavior as Exchange," *American Journal of Sociology* 63 (May 1958), pp. 597–606; and John C. Mowen, "Beyond Consumer Decision Making," *Journal of Consumer Marketing* 5 (Winter 1988), pp. 15–25.

EXHIBIT 16.3

A Continuum of Acquisition Mechanisms and Motives

represented on an exchange continuum between real barter and pure gifts (see Exhibit 16.3). Social exchange also appears on this continuum, as a midpoint between real barter and pure gifts.

Real barter conforms to the economic man acquisition model, in which exchange partners are calculating and highly rational in their exchange behaviors. At this end of the continuum, transactions are a one-time phenomenon. Partners place no value on future exchanges, so they try to maximize current value of exchange resources. In such transactions the overriding norm is caveat emptor, let the buyer beware. Real barter is associated with the ideal markets of microeconomic theory. Commodities markets, used-car sales, utilitarian shopping, and flea market haggling all provide examples of such utilitarian acquisitions.

Purchases may also fall more toward the **social exchange** part of the continuum shown in Exhibit 16.3. In social exchange, utility-maximizing motives are present, but other factors moderate these motives. For instance, cultural norms of fairness may come into play. Exchange partners also may consider the long-term value of ongoing exchanges and hence be willing to sacrifice current utility for the sake of the long-term relationship. Sometimes, an emotional, personal relationship develops with the exchange partner; mutual favors are exchanged; and social debt is incurred.

Markets such as those created by in-home purchase parties can be explained as a form of social exchange in which social outcomes are equal to, or larger than, material ones. For example, many home shopping parties (where Tupperware or cosmetics might be sold) exhibit traits associated with social exchange rather than pure barter. The relationship marketing strategy in a business-to-business setting recognizes that embedding acquisition in social ties can increase customer loyalty and enhance organizational performance. Relationship marketing recognizes that firms should manage their customer interactions with a long-term view, as repeat purchase behavior is a key to creating a sustainable competitive advantage.[10]

At the other extreme from pure barter are **pure gifts.** Here, acquisition processes are embedded in relationships of **generalized reciprocity.** In such cases, exchange partners who assume things will work out in mutually beneficial ways worry little about short-term costs and benefits. Some behaviors resemble the giftlike characteristics of the Japanese *keiretsu,* the immense interlocking holding companies that dominate much of Japanese business. In these companies, member firms occasionally forgo profit or forgive the debt of another member firm that is suffering from a downturn in the business cycle. Such behavior is also characteristic of channel partners in some developing countries, such as wholesalers and retailers who may prefer to accumulate together rather than seek to maximize individual gain in their volatile marketing environments. Generalized reciprocity may also characterize gift-giving behaviors, such as those between loved ones, and may provide a motive for participants in local, self-organized barter economies and garage sales.[11]

Good marketing managers recognize that buying and selling involves multiple motives (see Chapter 7) and exchange orientations. No single orientation will drive every participant in a market transaction. Good salespeople also take a multiorientation approach knowing that customers are driven by different exchange motives. As shown simply in Exhibit 16.2, buyers are motivated both by extrinsic rewards, such as product or service performance, and intrinsic rewards, such as their enjoyment of the purchase or deal-making process.[12]

PURCHASES

Purchase Decisions

TYPES OF PURCHASE DECISIONS Consumers make many kinds of purchase decisions. We can distinguish a number of them, each of which has different managerial implications. First, a consumer may make a basic **purchase decision** in response to need recognition (see Chapter 7), as when communication needs trigger the decision to purchase a telephone. Second, the consumer may opt to make a particular **product category decision,** such as buying a cellular phone rather than a conventional phone or a shortwave radio. A cellular phone purchase decision is likely if conventional phone services are poorly developed, as in many transitional or developing countries.

Swap meets, garage, boot, and rummage sales are popular alternative marketing channels.

Of course, this decision is also affected by lifestyle (see Chapter 11) and many other factors.

Third, the consumer may make a **brand purchase decision** as when consideration of alternatives leads to the choice of a Nokia, Ericsson, Philips, or Motorola cell phone. Much marketing communication in the Triad countries, especially manufacturers' advertising campaigns, aims to influence this kind of decision. For instance, a Nokia campaign associates its digital communications products with the movie *The Saint.* Fourth, the consumer may make a **channel purchase decision,** that is, deciding whether to purchase from a retail outlet, directly from a manufacturer, through a catalog, in a duty-free airport shop, or perhaps online. In addition to television or radio advertising, newspaper circulars and direct mail often are employed to influence this type of decision. Of course, consumers are not limited to these formal channels. Our opening vignette provides an example of a direct channel between a producer and a consumer. Farmers' markets are similar. North American consumers also will be familiar with the weekend garage sale where buyers circulate between sellers; whereas UK consumers prefer the weekend car boot sale, where sellers collect in a given spot.

Fifth, a **payment decision** is made to determine the payment method and terms of payment. Both retailers and credit card companies seek to influence these types of decisions. Both institutions benefit from the interest charge on credit purchases, but the former must choose between the benefits of immediate cash flow and the potential costs of unpaid debts. Sixth, there is a distinction between an **initial purchase decision** and a **repeat purchase decision.** This is especially important in organizational buying decisions (see Chapter 13). Many utility companies and consumer marketers have become interested in trying to automate repeat purchase decisions through such devices as automatic payroll deduction plans. As suggested, marketers may seek to influence one or more of the phases of the purchase decision process just outlined.

Purchase decisions need not be made in the order indicated above. For example, a payment decision may precede and even determine a brand decision or channel purchase decision. An international business traveler may seek out a restaurant that accepts American Express cards, because she lacks local currency.

Exhibit 16.4 portrays a simple model of the brand (or product category) purchase decision model widely used in consumer behavior research. This is a variant of an expectancy value model. We discussed this type of model at length in Chapter 15. It is based on the decision-making perspective of consumer purchase behavior. Of course, many purchase decisions may not match this model very well, especially those motivated by affective or meaning-transfer desires. A good example is the impulse purchase, which we will discuss in the following section and also discussed in Chapter 15.

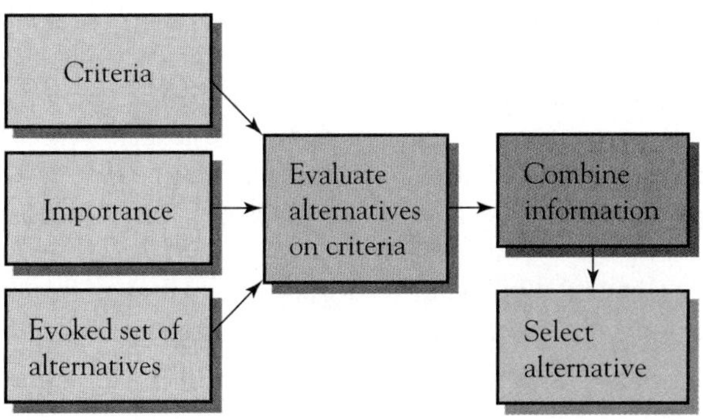

EXHIBIT 16.4

Alternative Evaluation and Selection Process

CONSUMER CHRONICLES 16.2

An Impulse Purchase Decision

I was excited to get a chance to mountain bike in this mecca for mountain bike riding (Moab, Utah). The first day the winds howled all day . . . I felt so alive to be out there by myself, me and my bike against nature. After my ride, we stopped at the visitors center so I could change. There I saw this poster of these arches that I had just experienced on my ride. I felt that this picture would always capture my adventure. I walked right up to the cashier and bought it . . . I immediately felt like this picture was my personal adventure. The price didn't matter. I just bought it. It is a picture of an adventure that I alone experienced.

The model presented in Exhibit 16.4 suggests that, in anticipation of making a purchase, consumers develop lists of criteria that are of significance to them because of the perceived benefits (e.g., needs, feelings, meanings) they provide. The consumers then rate these criteria in terms of importance. When making a product category decision, buyers might rate communication effectiveness highly, thus evaluating conventional versus cellular phones differently. In deciding where to shop, buyers might rate discount stores differently than specialty stores, depending on whether price or selection and service were more important criteria. Consumers also develop a set of alternative products, brands, or stores that they think will provide these benefits from memory, through external information search, or some combination of the two. They then combine all three types of information to reach a decision.

Marketers seek to understand the criteria that consumers use to select and rank stores or products or brands. Such knowledge can be used to position market offerings effectively by highlighting these criteria and rankings in promotional messages or other communications targeted to consumers.

Impulse Purchases

A good example of a common purchase decision *not* explained well by the decision-making model of acquisition is the impulse purchase. Although early work on the topic tried to divide products into impulse and nonimpulse goods, it is now clear that almost anything can be subject to an impulse purchase. Although impulse purchases are typically unplanned, not all unplanned purchases are impulse purchases. **Impulse purchases** *occur when consumers experience a sudden, often powerful, and persistent emotional urge to buy immediately.* Impulse purchases also entail a sudden mental match between the meaning of a product and a consumer's self-concept. Consumer Chronicles 16.2 provides a good example of the experience of an impulse purchase.[13]

Impulse purchases do not conform to economic man or decision-making man perspectives in consumer behavior. Instead, the impulse to buy is a hedonically (pleasure-seeking) complex one. High emotional activation, low cognitive control, and largely reactive behavior characterize impulse buying. In one study, more than 75 percent of impulse buyers reported that they felt better after making such a purchase. Those with positive feelings believed that they got something they needed or accomplished a necessary task. In contrast, 16 percent reported that they felt no different and only 8 percent reported that they feel worse after such a purchase. Those with negative reactions reported feelings of guilt or ambivalence.[14]

Impulse purchases have the potential to disrupt the consumer's ordinary behavioral stream. Because of the urge toward immediate action, impulse buying is prone to occur with diminished regard for the consequences of making the purchase. It may stimulate emotional conflict. Respondents often describe how the impulse arouses both pleasure and guilt. Many consumers report negative consequences from impulse buying, such as financial problems, disappointment with the product, or the disapproval of significant others. Sound familiar? Most consumers engage in impulse purchases at some time or another.[15]

Some impulse buying is related to various aspects of general acquisitiveness and materialism associated with the overall development of consumer culture. Thus, some impulse purchases are driven by the desire to fulfill imagined future needs.[16] An increase in recreational shopping is probably linked to impulse purchases too, since the positive mood generated in recreation may decrease self-control. It may also be that various marketing factors support impulsive purchase behavior, such as the availability of consumer credit, credit cards, ATM machines, television and online shopping, and long retail hours. Anonymous shopping or consumption contexts such as telemarketing or online shopping may encourage impulse buying because the threat of social sanctions that dampen the buying impulse is diminished. Finally, impulse purchase behavior varies with individual personality traits such as variety seeking and risk aversion. Variety seekers may be more prone to impulse purchases, whereas risk-averse persons may be less prone.

On the surface, impulse purchases seem harmless enough. However, in some cases, impulse purchase behavior is transformed into compulsive purchase behavior. This is a dark side of consumer behavior—a clinical condition similar to eating disorders and compulsive gambling that may require medical treatment. Good Practice 16.1 shows questions researchers have used to screen for consumers' tendencies toward compulsive purchase behaviors. Care to take the test?[17]

Managing and Controlling Purchases

One goal of marketing is to predict and manage consumers' purchasing behavior. A great deal of the work in this area has been spurred by the growth of purchase behavior databases. Begun by the hotel and airline industries, database marketing has been adopted by many retailers and financial services companies. To implement the technique, marketers combine sophisticated marketing mix tools with equally sophisticated statistical methods to manage purchase frequency and timing, repeat purchase behavior and market share, and other indicators of marketing success.[18]

Work focused on managing purchase timing and quantity traditionally adopts an economic or decision-making perspective on consumer purchase behavior, more rarely a behavioral influence perspective. In this section we discuss findings that adopt these more traditional perspectives on consumer behavior.

TIMING AND FREQUENCY Marketers are very interested in the timing of consumer purchases. **Purchase timing** refers to sequences of repetitive purchase events that occur over time. Consumers dispose of many goods (see Chapter 19) and therefore must replace them at regular intervals. Since a current purchase is worth more to a firm than a future purchase, marketers stimulate consumers to purchase frequently, and they attempt to shorten the interval between purchase occasions. Some tactics used to stimulate purchases include coupons, price cuts, point-of-purchase displays, and feature advertisements. Retail atmosphere and design can also influence purchase timing.

The notion of **purchase frequency,** especially repeat purchase behavior, is closely related to timing. A knowledge of purchase frequency helps marketers time promotional mailings, encourage greater purchase frequency, or estimate sales for particular product or service categories. Generally, it is more profitable for a firm to stimulate repeat

GOOD PRACTICE 16.1
Questions Associated with Compulsive Buying

Instructions for Q1: Indicate whether you agree or disagree with the following statements.

	Strongly agree	Somewhat agree	Neither agree nor disagree	Somewhat disagree	Strongly disagree
Q1. If I have any money left at the end of a pay period, I just have to spend it.	1	2	3	4	5

Instructions for Q2 through Q7: Indicate how often you have done each of the following.

	Very Often	Often	Sometimes	Rarely	Never
Q2. Felt others would be horrified if they knew of my spending habits.	1	2	3	4	5
Q3. Bought things even though I couldn't afford them.	___	___	___	___	___
Q4. Wrote a check when I knew I didn't have enough money in the bank to cover it.	___	___	___	___	___
Q5. Bought myself something in order to make myself feel better.	___	___	___	___	___
Q6. Felt anxious or nervous on days I didn't go shopping.	___	___	___	___	___
Q7. Made only the minimum payments on my credit cards.	___	___	___	___	___

Scoring equation $= -9.69 + (Q1 \times .33) + (Q2 \times .34) + (Q3 \times .50) + (Q4 \times .47) + (Q5 \times .33) + (Q6 \times .38) + (Q7 \times .31)$

If score is ≤ -1.34, you are classified as a compulsive buyer.

Source: Ronald J. Faber and Thomas C. O'Guinn, "A Clinical Screener for Compulsive Buying," Journal of Consumer Research *19 (December 1992), pp. 459–69.*

purchases among loyal customers than to attract new ones. Through databases that identify frequent shoppers, firms can target customers for promotional mailings that they hope, based on past purchase behavior, will stimulate increased purchase frequency.[19]

Predicting Timing and Frequency Marketers are interested in predicting and influencing purchase timing and frequency. Predicting timing and frequency makes it possible to plan production and delivery and estimate revenues and profits. By effectively managing timing and frequency, marketers can improve their knowledge of how modifications of the marketing mix will affect buying behavior.

We could assume that purchase timing is totally random. At the other extreme, we could assume *purchase behavior to be totally regular like clockwork.* We call this **deterministic timing.** Researchers have found that for consumer goods such as crackers, coffee, yogurt, toothpaste, and the like, purchase timing and frequency are neither purely random nor totally deterministic but somewhere in between. To simplify, the chance of a repeat purchase occurring varies over time. Most researchers agree that there is a kind of dead period after a given purchase. Then the probability of a purchase reoccurring increases for a while. After a certain interval, the probability of the purchase reoccurring begins to decrease. In other words, for a segment of consumers, marketers can predict the likelihood a purchase will occur, but they can never be certain when a particular household or individual will make a purchase. This means that purchase timing and frequency can be predicted using the laws of probability. The mathematical details of the models used are not important here. Probabilistic models of purchase timing do a reasonably good job of predicting timing in stable markets over short periods, and increasingly researchers are able to incorporate more marketing variables into their predictive models. As suggested by Industry Insights 16.1, models show there is significant regularity in purchase timing for some consumer goods in stable markets.[20]

In addition to product purchases, probabilistic models have also been extended to describe frequency of household trips to grocery stores over time. These models furnish good descriptions of the frequency of store trip behavior. Models that provide a standard against which repeat purchase behavior can be compared are quite useful in stable markets. They can be used to compare the purchase frequency behaviors of different consumer segments or repeat purchase patterns among products, brands, or stores. Knowledge of purchase frequency enables marketers to time promotions effectively. Probabilistic models are less useful for predicting the purchase frequency of innovative products or in dynamic, rapidly changing markets where purchase patterns are unstable. Hence, applying them to transitional or developing country markets may not be possible.[21]

INDUSTRY INSIGHTS 16.1

Modeling Purchase Timing

To understand the use of probabilistic models, consider an analysis of instant and ground coffee consumption data collected from scanner panel data. Researchers found common interpurchase times of 7, 14, and 21 days. The study found that price cuts increased purchase rates of instant coffee (by over 15 percent), that each additional ounce of coffee purchased increased the time to next purchase (by 24 percent), and that a household with two adults has a higher purchase rate than a household with one adult (12 percent higher). Among marketing mix variables, the researchers found that newspaper ads affected ground coffee purchase timing the most, while price cuts affected instant coffee purchase timing the most. They also discovered interpurchase periods in the timing of saltine crackers purchases in one U.S. market area of 7, 14, 21, and 28 days. In spite of these intriguing results, the researchers showed the difficulty of estimating interpurchase times using simple statistical predictive models, because unobserved factors have a big impact on purchase timing. This study concluded that more complex statistical procedures are required to get reasonable estimates of purchase timing.

Source: Rita D. Wheat and Donald G. Morrison, "Regularity, Recency and Rates," European Journal of Operational Research *76 (July 1992), pp. 283–89.*

Managing Purchase Timing and Frequency Promotions are often designed to increase purchase frequency and are a powerful tool for managing purchase timing. The three top promotion-using industries in the United States are all markets crowded with many similar brands: food products, toiletries and cosmetics, and beer, ale, and soft drinks. In the late 1980s, U.S. manufacturers spent over $20 billion on trade incentives and distributed over 215 billion manufacturer coupons per year. Similarly, mass merchandisers like Marks and Spencer produce reams of coupons in the UK. In the UK, "instant win" promotions have blossomed across a wide range of products.[22] Behind the promotions are fulfillment houses that process coupon redemptions and consumer mailings (e.g., sweepstakes entries, rebates), mail out checks or merchandise, and judge sweepstakes or contests. The global market research firm ACNielsen is the largest coupon redemption firm in the United States, handling coupon offers from over 180,000 U.S. retailers.[23]

Direct marketers use computerized databases to identify customers who are most likely to provide repeat business. Cooperating clients are asked to answer questionnaires and surveys in return for a coupon or premium. Results are entered into a database, and the information is used to determine the best promotional tactics for communicating with these buyers in the future. By observing the purchase patterns from their customer lists, early direct marketers developed a theory of purchase frequency known as the **RFM rule** (recency, frequency, monetary value). That is, *the likelihood of a response to a particular promotional mailing was influenced by the recency of the last purchase, the frequency of purchases over the past year, and the monetary value of a given customer's purchase history.* Segmenting markets in terms of deal proneness on the basis of criteria such as these three variables—recency, frequency, and value—helps marketers to predict the impact of promotional programs on purchase timing.[24]

Promotions are used to influence timing, especially in product categories where there is little reason for consumers to choose between competitive brands. Examples of such product categories in the United States include ground coffee, instant coffee, toothpaste, laundry detergent, aluminum foil, and bathroom and facial tissue. Purchase timing is also found to accelerate with advertised price cuts.[25]

Limitations on Trying to Control Timing and Frequency The goal of managing purchase timing and frequency is likely to remain elusive in spite of improvements in predictive models. One reason is that consumers are not passive but active agents. Marketing tactics designed to influence purchase timing and frequency can and do backfire. For example, marketing tactics may backfire in catalog sales. Common industry wisdom dictates that the more catalogs an organization sends to consumers, the more likely they are to purchase from a cataloger. In other words, purchase frequency is directly related to regular receipt of catalogs. However, consumers reach a catalog saturation point and tune out offers that exceed this threshold. Catalog purchase frequency increases at low levels as more catalogs are received within a year—until the mailbox hits tilt at some saturation point. After that point, consumers become less likely to purchase if they receive more catalogs.[26]

Promotions and other incentives designed to increase frequency can prove to be counterproductive in the long run. This occurs when consumers buy because of the promotion, not because of the product itself. In some Triad countries there is concern that consumers buy many packaged goods only when they are on some special deal or sale. Brand loyalty is thus sacrificed for purchase frequency. Consumers switch brands in favor of promoted brands. This behavior is not seen in some European countries where such deals are heavily restricted or illegal. Similarly, in Japan, discount selling remains in its infancy.[27]

PURCHASE QUANTITY AND BRAND SWITCHING Many marketing efforts are designed to create and maintain brand loyalty (see Chapter 18). Thus, marketers are concerned with **brand switching.** Brand switching is *the tendency for consumers to purchase competitors' brands within a product class.* Many factors stimulate brand-switching behavior. Environmental causes include stock-outs, price changes, deals, and advertising. Consumer-related factors include curiosity, boredom, and the need to balance among different needs and attributes possessed by competing brands and products. Consumers may also engage in switching when motivated by the desire for identification with an admired valued reference group (see Chapter 14).

Through switching, consumers sometimes seek to achieve a desired combination of attributes or benefits that do not exist in any one brand. That is, consumers may have a sense of an ideal product. If they find it in one brand, they may then stick with it, exhibiting brand loyalty. If not, they may combine switches between different brands in order to approach their ideal.

In a study of the French automobile market, it was found that brand switching patterns are nonrandom and structured. That is, managers can study these patterns and discover underlying patterns that can help them understand and predict market behavior. For instance, in the study of the French market, it was found that Citröen was not successfully implementing a targeted marketing plan. As a result, former Citröen owners were switching to other brands when it came time to make a new car purchase.[28]

Managing and Controlling Brand Switching Determination of the brand-switching cycle length can help managers develop a product line and create competitive strategies. For example, a company may wish to develop a full cycle of brands, that is, the limited set of brands among which consumers choose over time. Or a firm could specialize in one brand, which is one part of a purchase cycle that is complemented by the company's other brands. This one brand may be a large part of the cycle of a few or many consumers or a small component of the majority of the consumers. It may be that firms should not waste efforts trying to take over a full cycle with any one brand, but introduce brands that will substitute for others in a cycle.[29]

Deals and promotions affect switching behavior; that is, price differences between brands can influence brand-switching behavior. For example, retailers and manufacturers have an interest in determining the cross-price elasticities (or price sensitivity) and switching behavior associated with the complete set of ground and instant coffee brands. Such a determination enables managers to evaluate the impact of a price change, by their company or by a competitor, on the sales of all brands in a product class. Managers can also develop indicators of the clout or vulnerability of individual brands. **Clout** can be *measured by evaluating the effect of a price cut on one brand on sales of the other brands.* **Vulnerability** is *measured by summing the effects of price cuts of the other brands on sales of the brand of interest.* A study of the ground decaffeinated coffee category, for example, found that the Brim brand loses a larger percentage of its volume when two competing brands discount their prices than it gains when its price is discounted. Conversely, price increases on the other brands add substantially to Brim's sales. The net result is that demand for Brim is more sensitive to competitors' pricing actions than is either Maxwell House or Sanka, two other brands with larger market shares.[30]

Advertising affects switching behavior, as does consumers' need for novelty. Often, consumers' desires for the perceived benefits of competing brands fluctuate while perceptions of the brands remain stable, which leads to brand switching. One of the marketing implications of this idea is that advertising for an established brand, particularly a well-differentiated one, will be much more effective if it exploits the brand's positioning. Specifically, advertising should exploit the important elements of positioning that differentiate the brand from competing brands in a cluster in order to stimulate desire for the particular pattern of benefits it provides relative to other, similar brands. This kind of advertising can stimulate switching to the differentiated brand.[31]

Shopping Styles and Goals

Of course, shopping is one way that consumers gather information to make decisions. Lots of research has looked at shopping as one kind of external search. **External search** is *the process of collecting information from outside sources,* including magazines, websites, advertisements, retailers, and so on. Most research supports that the degree of search activity is limited even for purchases that are typically considered important such as the purchase of a major appliance or a car. Consumers tend to visit very few stores (most go to only one) and consult only a few sources (usually no more than two). However, as more consumers shop on the Internet, search activity may go up simply because it is easier to do.

For some consumers, shopping is like a contest or game. They like to do well at the game, and they like to succeed. Of course, there are different ways of measuring success. One measure might be "getting a good deal." So a consumer may shop for hours and make many comparisons so as to make just the right purchase. This purchase may be evaluated in terms of the amount of money saved. In other instances time may be the objective function. That is, consumers may be delighted to discover that they have saved time through a purchase or that they have completed a transaction in record time. In this sense, the deals that marketers offer can be viewed as a key motivator of behavior. Marketers offer deals to consumers for many reasons. Examples of deals include everything from coupons to rebates to free samples. From one perspective, a deal (such as a special coupon) serves to draw attention to the brand. Such a deal may stimulate or trigger purchase behavior. At the same time, a deal (such as a two-for-one offer) may appeal to a consumer's desire to be an efficient shopper. A deal may appeal to a shopper's urge to win the shopping competition (i.e., to get a good bargain). Consumers' responses to deals also can be viewed as a personality variable. **Deal-prone consumers** are *consumers who are more likely to be influenced by price.*[32] For instance, we may say that some consumers are particularly deal prone. These consumers seek out deals for a wide variety of reasons, including saving money, having fun, or being efficient shoppers. Of course, as with other motives we have discussed, the specific type of deal can influence whether deal proneness is activated.

Consumers often haggle over prices. Price haggling involves give and take by buyer and seller in order to establish a price acceptable to both. The prevalence of price haggling varies considerably between cultures. As we note in this chapter, many economies operate on a barter system and rely heavily on haggling to set prices. When consumers price haggle, we might assume that they are motivated to obtain a better dollar value for their purchases—that is, economic motives. However, noneconomic benefits are very important as well. One U.S.-based study used an analysis of depth interviews to illustrate that consumers can fulfill three primary motives, including achievement, affiliation, and dominance, by haggling over price.[33] For example, some of these depth interviews described consumers flaunting the superior deals they got on their cars. Other interviews talked about seizing control of negotiations. Finally, some price hagglers use their skill for friends' benefit. They work to negotiate effective deals that cement bonds of friendship. Deal proneness and price haggling behaviors are shaped by the shopping culture or environment the consumer experiences. Consumers in transitional economies may be particularly motivated by sales because of the previous lack of goods and lack of price differentiation among goods. Slavenka Drakulić devotes a whole chapter in her book *Café Europa* to explaining why she is particularly susceptible to sales because she grew up in eastern Europe in a nonmarket economy. Consumer Chronicles 16.3 describes some of her thinking.

Often we interpret shopping as a pleasure or a self-gift, something we talk about later in this chapter. People report that when they are feeling low or want to reward themselves, they go shopping. Bumper stickers that support this view of shopping are commonplace in the United States—for example, "When life gets tough, the tough go shopping." A perspective that may be the source of rich insights for marketers interprets shopping as self-sacrifice.[34] The findings are based on an ethnography of lower- and lower-middle-class women in the United Kingdom, although an ethnographic study of lower- and lower-middle-class Chicago women reports similar findings.

Daniel Miller, an anthropologist, argues that women shop out of devotional love for their families. Their shopping is an investment in their families and relationships with family members. Purchases are rationalized not in terms of what was spent but in terms of savings and thrift. The savings and thrift generated through shopping then constitute funds that can be given to dependents and descendants. In this perspective, provisioning of the family through shopping is an important way of constituting and preserving the family. Interestingly, many shopping centers in the United Kingdom emphasize an ideology of family shopping that is consistent with this theory. Many advertisements appearing in women's magazines around the world encourage women to buy their family something to show they care. The idea that women can use purchases to show their family they love them is common in many U.S. magazines. If shopping is viewed as provisioning the family rather than a pleasurable, self-indulgent activity, then marketers would use different appeals to encourage the purchase of their products.

The Trouble with Sales

CONSUMER CHRONICLES 16.3

It is a compulsive act for me, I have to look to avoid the feeling that perhaps I'm missing a good opportunity. Of course, I end up buying 10 T-shirts (they will always come in handy), three pairs of espadrilles (I need them), and a dozen pairs of panties I can't resist, just because they are cheap. All at the cost, as I explain to myself as soon as I am back at home, of "no money at all." What is more important is that buying so much for so little gives me a sense of satisfaction.

This is an art, I think, proud of myself for a moment. But no, it is not, and deep down I know it. Buying junk is not an art, it is only a sad necessity. Or, in my case, a bad habit that you can't get rid of, like smoking. For Christ's sake, times have changed, everything has changed, says my husband. You make some money now. You don't live in communist Yugoslavia any longer. You can buy what you want. I try to explain to him that I can't, but I am afraid he does not quite understand me. After all, he is a Western European.

Source: "The Trade with Sales", from Café Europa: Life after Communism by Slavenka Drakulić. Used by permission of WW. Norton & Company, Inc.

COUNTERTRADE AND BARTER

We now discuss a different approach to acquisition. *Countertrade* is an inclusive term used to describe transactions where all or partial payment is made in kind (goods and services) rather than in cash. The basic countertrade where goods are traded for other goods is an age-old feature of foreign trade. Countertrade moves us away from Homans's model of pure barter and toward the social exchange part of his continuum. Countertrade is a popular means of acquisition. It is a good way for firms to open new markets and establish long-term relationships with new customers, while reducing costs. Countertrade is also a good way of disposing of unwanted products and services. Policymakers have recently encouraged a number of African countries to expand countertrade. Shortages of hard currency (convertible, stable money) plus the massive foreign debt that burdens many of these countries make countertrade an attractive alternative to purchase. In Russia, some companies use countertrade to hide income and thus evade the country's confusing tax policies. It is also a way to get around protectionist policies that limit foreign imports in some countries. The countries where countertrade is popular are also those most likely to experience rapid economic growth in the coming decades.[35]

Firms engage in four types of countertrade. We have already introduced one type—barter. A simple example of corporate barter involves Sharp Electronics. Sharp arranged for 50 staterooms for 100 passengers on a major Mediterranean cruise line for its dealers, in exchange for surplus inventory traded to the cruise line. In the 1970s, the Swedish pop group Abba undertook a successful tour of Poland. They received payment for their musical services in potatoes! Subsequently, Abba organized deals for Russian heavy machinery and Czechoslovakian glass among other goods in exchange for its live concerts in these countries.

Barter can get complicated. In the early 1990s, SGD International, an American-based bartering company, supplied latex rubber to a Czech firm in exchange for 10,000 yards of finished carpeting. SGD then traded the carpeting to a hotel for room credits. The rooms were then traded to a Japanese company for electronic equipment, which was then bartered away for convention space. The cycle of exchanges ended when SGD traded the convention space for advertising space. Corporate barter is attractive because firms can usually recover their cost of goods and ultimately make a profit. It also allows them to do business in regions of the world where traditional economic transactions are somewhat difficult to secure.

Consumers also engage in barter trade. In every developed economy some people trade goods and services informally through garage sales, swap meets, or car boot sales to earn extra income, to get around the market economy, for fun, or to avoid paying income taxes.[36] A most interesting example of a consumer barter system is provided by the rapid growth of the LETS systems discussed in Consumer Chronicles 16.4. Barter systems like LETS represent a small-scale challenge to traditional business practices.[37]

Compensation deals are *barter transactions that involve payment both in goods and in cash.* The former Soviet Union made frequent requests to Western suppliers for deals of this type. In one deal, General Motors sold $12 million worth of locomotives and diesel engines to Yugoslavia and took cash and $4 million in Yugoslavian cutting tools as payment.

Counterpurchase is the most common type of countertrade. In counterpurchase, *the seller agrees to sell a product at a set price to a buyer and receives payment in cash; however, the deal is contingent on a second agreement in which the original seller buys goods from the original buyer for the total monetary amount involved in the first sale or for an agreed-on percentage of that amount.* There is often a delay between completion of the first and second transactions so that the buyer of the goods in the second transaction has the time to find markets for them.

One example of a counterpurchase comes from Russia. The Sverdlosk region around Ekaterinburg in Russia exports certain products to the UK. Proceeds from these sales are deposited in an account at the Moscow Narodny Bank in London. In exchange, the UK Health Care Consortium provides health care products and services to an integrated health care program in the region.

Another interesting case comes from two developing countries in West Africa. Merchants in Ghana sometimes send salt north to Niger for sale. A Nigerian onion merchant travels with the Ghanaian truck until it reaches the capital of Niger, Niamey. There, the Ghanaian trucker hands over the money obtained for the sale of the salt to the Nigerian merchant in the form of a loan, with a one-month payback period. With the loan, the Nigerian merchant buys onions produced in Niger, loads them onto the Ghanaian truck, and returns to Ghana, where he sells the onions and repays the loan.

LETS: A Consumer-Driven Barter System

CONSUMER CHRONICLES 16.4

LETS stands for local employment and trading system. LETS systems represent a rebellious trend in consumer acquisition strategies motivated by four principles: (1) consume less; (2) consume local products; (3) avoid mass-merchandised, mass-manufactured goods; and (4) avoid cash and use alternative acquisition mechanisms.

The first LETS system was initiated in 1983 on Vancouver Island, Canada, by a business student who observed that many local people had skills and products to offer but lacked money to permit them to trade with one another. The objectives of LETS include both stimulating trade and building community relationships. LETS organizations are local. In the UK, the average membership of the 400 or so local LETS organizations is about 250. The way it works is that a computerized system allows people to get in touch with each other and negotiate a trade at a price in the LETS currency. LETS members exchange everything from home decorating to baby sitting, time at vacation cottages to acupuncture. No money is exchanged, but individuals' accounts are credited and debited to the amount they agree on for the goods and services exchanged. Sometimes, they haggle over equivalents; other times rates of exchange are fixed. No interest is ever charged, and members are committed to the idea that accounts will balance in the long run, in conformity with the idea of generalized reciprocity. The face-to-face nature of these systems makes it easier to establish the necessary level of trust. By regularly publishing the balance position of members' accounts, members are discouraged from freeloading or running up big debts.

LETS systems can be found in North America, Europe, and Australia. Ithaca, New York, has a thriving LETS system that has even begun to develop a health insurance savings program. In Australia, it is now possible in some areas to pay local taxes in the special LETS currencies.

Source: Gabriel Yiannis and Tim Lang, The Unmanageable Consumer *(London: Sage, 1995), www.btwebworld.communities/lets. See also www.globalideabank.org/BOV/BV-98.HTML*

In this way, the Ghanaian merchant secures a loan, and the Nigerian merchant risks less capital on the trade. In addition, the Ghanaian trucker is assured of a return load, a very important asset in this region where uncertain market conditions make commerce quite risky.[38]

Product buyback agreement is the final type of countertrade. This type of agreement usually *involves an initial sale of plant, equipment, or technology.* In one kind of buyback agreement, the seller of the plant or equipment accepts as partial payment a portion of the output of the new facility. In the other, the seller receives full price initially but agrees to buy back a certain portion of the output. In an example of the first type, Polish factories producing Fiat cars and International Harvester tractors discharged their obligations by sending back part of their production to the original licensors. Levi Strauss once had this same kind of agreement with Hungary. There, Levi Strauss took part of the Hungarian output of jeans for subsequent sale in Western Europe. In such a deal, the licensor gets new market access; the buyer gets new technology and know how, in addition to the plant and equipment.

Countertrade arrangements enjoy both advantages and disadvantages. Obviously, they involve a higher level of trust and relationship management than a simple cash-for-goods purchase. Hence, countertrade gives rise to specialized firms and corporate departments (Ford Motor Company has one, for example) that act as go-betweens and guarantors of a partner's trustworthiness. Industry Insights 16.2 summarizes some of the objectives buyers and sellers have in such transactions.

Objectives in International Countertrades

INDUSTRY INSIGHTS 16.2

Sellers' Objectives

Gain access to marketing networks and expertise
Dispose of surplus, obsolete, or perishable products
Signal a high-quality product
Generate customer goodwill
Establish long-term relationships with new trading partners
Gain entry into new or difficult markets
Capitalize on strong bargaining power
Increase sales volume, market share, and profits
Help countertrade partner conceal a price cut

Buyers' Objectives

Generate goodwill
Acquire badly needed products and technology
Secure low-cost sources of production or raw materials
Establish long-term relationships with new trading partners
Conserve hard currencies
Help conceal a price cut
Reduce heavy debt burdens
Bypass trade restrictions
Free blocked funds
Circumvent an overvalued currency

Critics of business-to-business countertrade point out that it increases administrative costs, undercuts prices of competitive goods since goods are often sold at a discount, can lead to charges of dumping in the country receiving the goods, and can be used to conceal bribes or evade taxes. These criticisms have merit, but there is no doubt that countertrade is an effective means of clearing imperfect markets in a dynamic global economy.[39]

GIFT GIVING AND RECEIVING

Gift giving and receiving is the final acquisition strategy we will discuss in this chapter. As distinct from other acquisition strategies, **gifts** are *ritualized offerings that frequently represent connections to other people.* Gift exchanges have the potential to affect social relations in a way that purchases often do not. By "ritualized," we are referring to occasions when items or resources are given according to convention and occasions where the giving/receiving partners conform to cultural norms. In an increasing number of countries, if an unmarried woman accepts the ritual gift of a diamond ring, she is symbolically stating her commitment to marry the giver, for example. Similarly, in some traditional herding societies, gifts of livestock pass from the groom's family to the bride's family to solemnize the wedding commitment. In Japan, noted for the formality of its gift-giving procedures, bottles of scotch whiskey graded by the relative status of the exchange partners are often exchanged between business suppliers and customers at the New Year.[40]

The economic significance of gifts attracts marketers' attention. Consider that at least 10 percent of retail purchases in North America are given as gifts. North Americans buy eight million greeting cards a day at more than one dollar per card. The commercial value of the Christmas cards exchanged in the UK in 1991 reached 250 million

Humorous appeal promotes online shopping for wedding gifts.

pounds (about $400 million). Over 1.3 million Japanese tourists visit Hawaii (their most popular destination) each year, spending on average about $100 per day on obligatory souvenir gifts, called *omiyage.* Recognizing the social importance of gift giving, online retailers have jumped into the gift business.[41] For example, the humorous appeal for the WeddingChannel.com website shown here encourages consumers to buy wedding gifts online.

www.WeddingChannel.com

The importance that consumers attach to gift giving provides many opportunities for marketers. Although gifts often convey meanings that are difficult to put into words, many find the language of gift giving hard to master. Mistakes, disappointment, and gift-giving failures are not uncommon. These difficulties provide gift stores, online gift sites, executive gift-buying services, greeting card companies, and luxury good marketers with opportunities to facilitate consumer gift-giving exchanges.

Marketers may try to position objects to reinforce their suitability as gifts. The cut-flower market in the United States provides an example of a product category where promotional campaigns are used to strengthen the positioning of the product as a gift. Global marketers of luxury goods may try to interest new segments in luxury gifts, as you can see at the FTD website. Another good example is the success the DeBeers cartel has enjoyed in marketing diamonds in Japan and other countries where they were not given traditionally. Finally, marketers may try to provide gifts to match occasions or even create occasions for gift giving, such as Secretaries' Day in the United States, Mother's and Father's Day in China, or Christmas in non-Christian countries.

www.ftd.com

Although gift giving is universal, the language and rituals associated with gift giving are culturally specific. Guide books on doing international business sometimes feature useful discussions of the dos and don'ts associated with gift giving. In business-to-business contexts, marketers often must distinguish gifts from bribes and learn a new etiquette for appropriate gift giving to avoid embarrassment. Hence, analysis of gift giving as a mode of acquisition and consumption requires culture-specific analysis of consumer behaviors.[42]

Gift Exchange in Cross-Cultural Perspective

Gift exchange predates marketing; it is as old as human culture. The **norm of reciprocity** (also discussed in Chapter 14) describes the fact that *receiving a gift often creates a strong sense of obligation to make a return gift.* Such reciprocity may take the form of a tangible object, but it also can involve such intangible resources as deference (status) and gratitude. As the Homans model (Exhibit 16.2) suggests, such exchanges tend to strengthen social bonds. Because of the norm of reciprocity, gift giving encourages return giving, which in turn stimulates further giving. When such acts are multiplied across individuals and groups, societal stability is enhanced. Thus, the norm of reciprocity is a kind of glue that holds traditional societies together, prior to the development of written law, the marketplace, and specialized policing institutions.[43]

In premarket societies, gift exchanges organized numerous economic, social, and religious activities. Consider the **potlatch** of Native Americans in the coastal northwest. Gifts of blankets, seal oil, cedar chests, and native copper plates are given away at great feasts. Chiefs of one segment of the tribe host these feasts for other segments of the tribe in order to compete for titles and prestige. The photo on the opposite page shows a native copper valuable of the type given away at a potlatch feast.[44]

Types of Gift Exchange

Modern gift giving is different from that practiced in traditional societies. To examine modern practices we'll focus on gift relations between persons and groups, specifically, interpersonal gifts and self-gifts.

INTERPERSONAL GIFTS Exchanges of **interpersonal gifts** are provoked by specific conditions. These conditions can be either structural or emergent. Among the **structural occasions,** gift giving marks territorial passages, such as housewarmings, reunions, bon voyage parties, visiting, and farewell parties. Second, gift-giving occasions establish social placement, such as weddings, showers, baptisms, and christenings. Structural gift-giving occasions include those associated with rites of passage, such as debutante balls for society girls, initiation into a motorcycle gang, French wedding showers, bar or bat mitzvah, graduations, and retirements. Third, there are those structural occasions associated with rites of progression, such as anniversaries, birthdays, and all the **calendric holidays,** for example, Christmas, Mother's Day, Halloween, and New Year. In part due to marketing activities, many countries have imported these gift-giving holidays.[45]

There are also **emergent occasions** for interpersonal gift giving. These include occasions designed to initiate a relationship, for example, an exchange of business cards between newly introduced business acquaintances. Gifts are also used to repair relationships, such as a "peace offering" in a domestic dispute. Finally, gifts may be given to deepen or intensify a relationship, as when a young man gives a school jacket to a young woman to symbolize that they are going steady. Similarly, an organization gives an employee a bonus to reward exceptional selling, service, or performance. The significance for marketers lies in identifying products that help consumers mark both structural and emergent occasions and, in some cases, identifying and inventing occasions for gift giving such as Secretaries' Day.[46]

Exhibit 16.5 presents a two-by-two table of interpersonal gift giving. The table contrasts altruistic with self-serving gift giving and voluntary with obligatory gift giving and provides some examples. These contrasts exist cross-culturally.

Ceremonial copper ingot given in Native American potlatch ceremony.

Gift giving differs from other modes of acquisition discussed here and in later chapters. This is because gift giving, especially voluntary, altruistic giving, resists explanation in terms of the economic man model of acquisition. In terms of Homans's social exchange paradigm introduced in Exhibit 16.2, pure gifts are *noncalculating and nonrational. They are altruistic and voluntary, may express unselfish love, and are given with no expectation of return.* We sometimes refer to this form of giving as *generalized reciprocity.* Donating time at a soup kitchen, cooking a casserole for a bereaved neighbor, making a sacrifice in order to present a lover with a special gift, or even sending a greeting card to a distant relative provides additional examples of pure gifts. Notice the material worth of the gift is often less important than the sentiment it conveys. Voluntary, altruistic gifts are associated with devotion for a beloved person or even an institution, such as a university or historic building. Voluntary giving is also associated with the behavior of market mavens and opinion leaders, who are driven to share market knowledge with others (see Chapter 14).

People are often willing to make low-value charitable donations, such as a bag of old clothes or can of food, voluntarily. Such gifts are relatively easy to elicit, but contribution-driven organizations often have difficulties eliciting donations above a certain threshold. To elicit higher-value donations, contribution-driven organizations

	Altruistic	Self-Serving
Voluntary	Charitable giving Giving a stranger change for a parking meter Surprising a friend with her favorite chocolates	Inviting the boss for dinner A Christmas gift for a service provider Competitive giving
Obligatory	Family members deciding how much to spend on Christmas gifts Bequests	Wedding gifts *Omiyage* Contributing to a charitable office pool

EXHIBIT 16.5

Interpersonal Gift Giving

employ tactics to increase consumer involvement. Some may use the tactic of personal sponsorship for a poor child or a threatened ecosystem. Fund-raisers often employ the tactic of providing opportunities for personalizing contributions in this context to stimulate greater giving, such as the commemorative lists of donors seen in museums or the naming of university buildings or classrooms. The Heifer Project International (HPI) catalog page pictured on the opposite page offers donors the opportunity to send a letter to the person to whom they donate money to buy livestock. HPI also offers testimonials about the dramatic impact of livestock on the quality of life of recipients.

Unlike altruistic giving, self-serving gift giving is *undertaken with some instrumental purpose; it is a means to an end.* Of course, altruistic giving may make givers feel better about themselves, but this does not make it less altruistic. Similarly, instrumental giving to enhance personal relationships is not necessarily antisocial. Thus, dating often involves a sequence of gift exchanges intended initially to establish sincerity or express thanks, later to express confidence in or commitment to a partner or to express apology for a disagreement. Gift giving may help partners evaluate compatibility by communicating taste and lifestyle preferences or symbolize preferred images of a romantic partner. A gift to a romantic partner of housewares conveys something different than jewelry, for example.

Self-serving or instrumental giving often expresses power dynamics. This was one aspect of the traditional Native American potlatch mentioned above. In the potlatch great chiefs demonstrated their wealth and power to others. Similarly, in modern Japan the norm is that more powerful business partners should receive more valuable presents than less powerful ones. In many countries men express power over women by paying for dating expenses, giving valuable gifts, or underestimating the value of gifts women give to them. A guide to doing business in Korea warns that Korean hosts may shower visiting business partners with gifts and gestures of hospitality. The book points out that the Koreans' calculated generosity might inhibit the foreign business partner from making objective business decisions. A sense of obligation to reciprocate leads to being less critical and more cooperative in negotiations. You may recognize that this as an apt illustration of the power of the gift to command a countergift.[47]

Self-serving gifts are also employed to communicate identity. A number of studies show that gifts chosen in North America usually represent something about the giver's self-

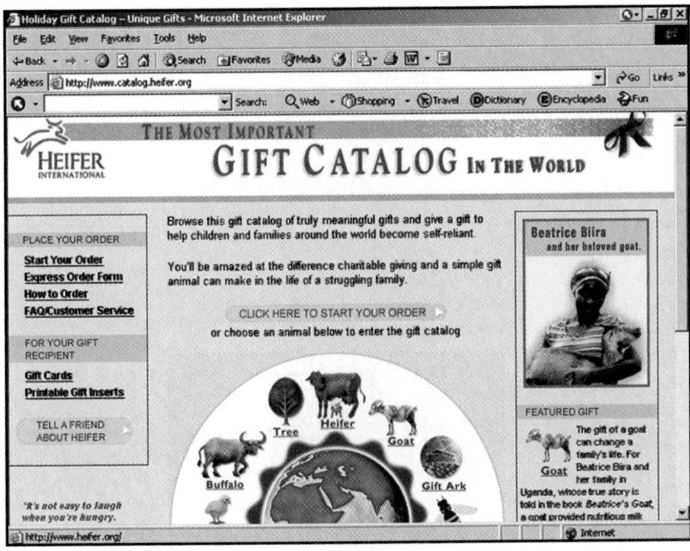

The Heifer Project increases customer involvement by personalizing charitable relationships.

concept. Unique gifts help givers express their feelings about the uniqueness of the recipient as well. Gifts to children may have a socializing function, indicating desired role identities, as when boys are given toy soldiers or girls are given tea sets or baby dolls. Elderly persons often give heirloom gifts that express aspects of self-identity they wish to pass on to their descendants.[48]

Voluntary giving is motivated by personal, idiosyncratic reasons, but *social norms or pressures drive obligatory giving.* As in the potlatch, obligatory gifts are situated more toward the social exchange part of the Homans model. Children's birthday parties share much in common with the potlatch. Both reciprocity and competition are evident. Parents feel obligated to host birthday parties and to buy gifts for other children's parties that their children attend. Parents also may compete to give the best party, with the best party favors, and to give the best gifts to their children's friends. Some structural gift-giving occasions such as an exchange of Christmas cards or wedding gifts have an obligatory dimension to them. People also may feel obliged to reciprocate a gift in order to avoid the feelings of dependence the initial gift creates. Contemporary North American consumers both accept and are sometimes troubled by the obligatory dimensions of structural gift giving. Few such problematic connotations seem to be associated with obligatory giving in countries with well-formulated gift-giving rules such as Japan.[49]

Obligatory gift giving is associated with many structural gift-giving occasions and lends itself to stereotypical giving. This is the type of gift giving to which marketers may most easily respond. For example, Christmas cards, birthday party kits, and retail wedding lists provide consumers with simplified gift giving that communicates standardized meanings and emotions. In general, marketing communications can be employed to create or reinforce associations between conventional items and conventional gift-giving occasions. In cases such as the purchase of an engagement ring, buyers often seek help from retail personnel and specialized gift consultants, thus providing marketers with opportunities to influence gift purchase decisions.[50]

Of course, gift giving doesn't fit neatly into the boxes illustrated in Exhibit 16.5, but instead gifts often combine voluntary and obligatory elements and both altruistic and self-serving motives. Another way of conceptualizing the gift-giving continuum is to

Reciprocity and competition at children's birthday parties

look at how gifts are distributed across important relationships. A study based in Hong Kong illustrates that consumers draw on a gift continuum that calibrates relationships from the most affective to the least. A simplified version of this gift continuum is shown in Exhibit 16.6. Notice family purchasing and family giving do not fall on this continuum even though family is used as a model for other social relationships. The family is a sacred sphere in this culture and falls outside the realm of reciprocity. In Hong Kong, reciprocity, sentiment, and face guide gift relations. Notice it is important in this culture to give gifts often to close friends to show you care.

Thinking about relationships as implying particular kinds of gifts also has implications for social marketing. By creating a friendship or personal relationship with consumers, social marketers can encourage consumers to adhere to social norms and provide gifts. The advertisement for friends of animals shown on the opposite page encourages you to be a friend for life.

SELF-GIFTS Self-gift behavior is not documented in premarket societies and does not seem to be recognized in China, but it is common in Western consumer societies. In **self-gifts,** *consumers give to themselves.* Self-gifts are differentiated from other personal acquisitions by their situational and motivational contexts. One study detailed two types of self-gift experiences: reward and therapeutic self-gifts. Self-gifting often occurs in a context of personal accomplishment, distress, or holiday occasion. The findings suggest that self-gifts are a form of personal, symbolic self-communication. In terms of outcomes, self-gifting can positively enhance self-concept, consistency, or esteem (see Chapter 7). Self-gifts can be products, services, or experiences, such as the Hawaiian holidays popular among single Japanese women.[51]

Who (Chinese Term)	Romantic Other (Sui láih math)	Close Friends (Yihhei)	Just Friends (Renquing)	Hi/Bye Friends (Guanxi)
When (examples)	• Birthday • Special occasion • Spontaneous • Formal/ceremonial	• Birthday • Special occasion • Spontaneous • Formal/ceremonial	• Birthday • Maintenance • Souvenir	• Birthday
Type of gift	Expressive	Expressive	Expressive/ instrumental	Instrumental
Why	Win hearts	Care	Care/build network	Build network
Face	Social/moral (obligation)	Moral (obligation)	Mostly social	Social
Risks	Guilt/shame	Guilt/shame	Loss of face	Loss of face

Source: Adapted from Annamma Joy, "Gift Giving in Hong Kong and the Continuum of Social Ties," *Journal of Consumer Research* 28 (September 2001), pp. 239–56.

EXHIBIT 16.6

The Gift Continuum in Hong Kong

Friendship infers gift giving in this promotion.

Self-gifts include ritualistic dimensions. For instance, self-gifts can involve sacrifices, such as abstaining from personal acquisitions in preparation for self-gifting. Because people consider self-gifts to be special, they may gift themselves infrequently to maintain the special qualities associated with a self-gift. Certain products are conventionally used as self-gifts. Clothing and travel are more frequently used as reward gifts than as therapy gifts, while fast food, grocery food, and personal care services are more often used as therapy gifts than reward gifts.[52]

Self-gift behavior correlates with socioeconomic traits such as age, financial condition, and gender. Older Americans self-gift less than younger ones do, for example. Wealthier consumers self-gift more than poorer ones. Similar to their use of interpersonal gifting behaviors for relationship building and maintenance, women self-gift therapeutically or to be nice to themselves. It appears men self-gift to create goal-related incentives for themselves.[53]

Self-gift purchasing may be linked to both cultural and personal values. A study showed that materialists are more likely to give self-gifts than nonmaterialists. This is especially true for occasions relating to mood management. Self-gift behavior may be particularly linked to cultural beliefs that purchasing and consumption are appropriate to the pursuit of individual happiness. In cultural contexts where purchase and consumption is not viewed in this way, self-gifting may be less common.[54]

Factors in the retail setting that affect self-gift behavior include the novelty or preselection of the brand, the brand's price, and the salesperson's empathy for the buyer's personal situation. Some managerial implications of these results are that retail advertising and point-of-purchase displays should employ themes to emphasize the increasing professional and personal independence of women. Marketing communications like these may heighten the self-gift purchase behavior of some market segments.[55]

The Power of Gifts and Marketing Implications

Marketers will be most interested in gifts that take tangible form, although understanding the intangible resources they convey (investments of love, status, and time) is critical to the successful gift marketing. Tangible gifts include items consumers have made themselves or those held in their possession for a long time, such as heirlooms, and gifts purchased with the intention to give them to others. While research indicates that handcrafted gifts often convey strong emotional and relational cues to recipients, purchased gifts are obviously of special concern to marketers. However, as shown in the Heirloom Pocket Watch ad, marketers sometimes position purchased gifts as future heirlooms because of the value of heirlooms to consumers.

Some categories of goods are only given as gifts, such as greeting cards. Other categories of goods may be treasured by particular market segments as especially appropriate to give as gifts. Flowers, perfume, expensive liquors, or diamonds often serve this function in the West. Status brands are preferred by new elite consumers in the NIC countries and many Japanese tourists who shop for *omiyage* while abroad. Tourism provides endless opportunities to create souvenirs for giving. For example, devout persons may treasure items associated with holy places such as Jerusalem, Mecca, or Lourdes in France, while Disney World seeks to provide souvenirs for every taste and pocketbook. Hence all sorts of objects may convey important meanings.[56]

Is money an appropriate interpersonal gift? There is an enormous cultural variation in the symbolism of money that influences its suitability. Not surprisingly, therefore, money is sometimes appropriate and sometimes inappropriate as a gift, depending on cultural and situational context. For example, in many gift exchanges in Japan, exact

Positioning a gift as a potential heirloom can increase its worth.

monetary repayment is the norm. Money is often given on Hanukkah and Chinese New Year. Wedding guests may pin money to a bride's wedding dress in some Mediterranean cultural contexts. Sino-Vietnamese mothers associate money with savings and future utility and so like to give it to their children as gifts. One poll conducted in the United States found that for nearly every age, education, and income group, money is the most popular gift. In North America, cash gifts are often presented in situations where the level of knowledge of the specific wants and needs of the recipient are not well known. Cash gifts can lessen the uncertainty felt by givers, but they can also increase anxieties associated with potential violations of social norms.

Some studies have revealed the existence of constraints on the use of money as a gift. For example, an investigation conducted in the UK used an extended-diary method to study aspects of the Christmas gifts given and received by 92 undergraduate students. The researchers found that cash money often lacks the attributes necessary for conveying information about intimacy and can possess attributes that may transmit inappropriate messages about the relative status of giver and receiver. Hence, in market economies, the need for tangible gifts other than money persists. Marketers can provide alternative forms of giving money as gifts, such as American Express Gift Cheques, investment accounts, cash contributions to charities, and gift certificates that provide more symbolically suitable means of giving money than cash.[57]

Gift shopping affects product category purchase selections. Sales may be affected when a product is classed as appropriate for gift giving or as product classification changes. Because sales of U.S. housewares figure in the tens of billions of dollars, U.S. manufacturers were concerned by a slump in the purchase of housewares as gifts. This slump has been attributed in part to the trend toward later marriages. As age of marriage increases in other Triad countries, do you think a similar slump will occur? Recently, some retailers have found a way to reposition novelty housewares as suitable gifts. Restoration Hardware provides an example. Consumer Chronicles 16.5 indicates that by positioning its goods on nostalgia and promising tantalizing symbols of self-completion (see Chapter 7), Restoration Hardware tempts baby boom consumers to self-gift.[58]

Restoration Hardware Encourages Self-Gifts

CONSUMER CHRONICLES 16.5

Up until this minute, I didn't even know that it was possible to have good taste in dustpans. But I am standing in front of one of the world's finest dustpans—admiring its capacious, open-mouth design, its sturdy metal construction, the elegant horsehair of the accompanying brush—and I can't tell you how much I yearn for it. If I owned this dustpan, I would be the sort of person I want to be. I'd take time to appreciate the beauty of everyday objects. I'd inhabit a world of simple craftsmanship, not of mass-produced clutter. I'd be one of those rare souls who have so much cultivation to spare that they can be thoughtful even about their cleaning equipment.

I've come across this admirable dustpan in a store called Restoration Hardware. And on my way to the sales desk I look around and find there's so much else I want. I want the ribbed steel flashlights I remember from summer camp . . . I want the old-fashioned kazoo, the mission-style magazine rack, the Moon Pies that I didn't even know were still made . . . the glass-and-steel Pyrex beakers just like the ones my doctor used to keep the tongue depressors in.

Source: David Brooks, "Annals of Consumption: Acquired Taste," The New Yorker, *January 25, 1999, pp. 36–41.*

www.restorationhardware.com

As Consumer Chronicles 16.5 illustrates, marketing communications can create or sustain the associations between goods and their suitability as gifts. For example, marketers may encourage gift givers to reduce the risks of their purchase decisions by buying status brands as gifts that may impress receivers and increase the symbolic meaning of the presents.

The behavior associated with the search for gifts tends to differ from shopping for personal use. For instance, consumers respond differently to pricing tactics when shopping for gifts than for personal use. As the success of Restoration Hardware indicates, high-status retailers can effectively merchandise highly profitable, high-status brands that are purchased as gifts.[59]

Perhaps the most dramatic influence of gift giving on retailing concerns specialty gift stores. This type of store is found throughout the Triad countries and is also common in tourist destinations that serve Triad consumers. Ethnographies of specialty gift retailers lead to several managerial propositions. First, shoppers experience the store itself as a gift. By creating delightfully fantastic environments, gift stores can impart an added significance to the merchandise that consumers in turn imbue with meanings. Second, because gift giving is the work of women in North American culture, gift stores play an important role in the giving that helps them to maintain a gift economy. Using gifts purchased at gift stores, women consumers construct intimate relationships and "networks of love" between family members and close friends. Third, personnel, browsers, and purchasers alike appreciate the objects in the store. Meanings imputed to and through these objects by all of these stakeholders create and reinforce particular values associated with the items selected as gifts. Hence, encouraging interaction in gift stores is valuable to management. Fourth, purchasers recount that gift choice often is imprecise or indescribable. Shoppers know the gift is concealed somewhere within the store and assume it will reveal itself to them eventually. Search behavior for gifts appears to be motivated by hedonic processes, involving longing, imagination, romance, and desire. This finding suggests designing stores to facilitate a kind of treasure hunt and training service personnel to aid consumers in the hunt. Fifth, successful owners are highly involved with their businesses. Merchandise selection often reflects owners' identity and values. Hence, target markets and merchandise should be allowed to evolve with the owners' interests over time.[60]

GIFTS SHAPE AND INFLUENCE BEHAVIOR Gift giving can shape and influence consumer behavior. Often marketers use gifts in an effort to command a countergift. Experimental research provides support for use of this tactic. For example, in some brand-choice experiments executed on personal computers, researchers found giving a small gift led consumers to reciprocate with greater belief in product claims and increased their willingness to try unusual or less familiar products.[61]

Gift giving can be used to improve customers' evaluations of services. Providing extras or unexpected touches can lead to an increase in customer satisfaction. Recall that the exchange model from Exhibit 16.2 stresses that both exchange outcomes and exchange processes affect consumers' evaluations and that the model proposes that every transaction involves the exchange of multiple types of resources. Analysis of service breakdowns shows that consumers' perceptions of interactional fairness (a process) influence their evaluation of breakdowns (an outcome; see Chapter 17).

Gifts are often used in direct-mail campaigns. Here they can be used as a foot-in-the-door tactic (see Chapter 14) to induce a purchase or charitable contribution or to encourage participation in marketing research. In devising direct-mail campaigns, many marketers include free gift offers to get better responses from customers. Do you or any of your family members receive gifts of calendars, cards, or return address labels from charitable organizations you support? These gifts are offered as tokens of the organizations' gratitude for your generosity. Of course, requests for more contributions usually accompany these gifts.

Tangible gifts are just one element of a successful direct-marketing campaign. Such campaigns may also stress the intangible benefits of the offer. There is value in providing a money-back guarantee, which customers may interpret as a kind of (intangible) gift that lends credibility to the offer and confidence to the buyer. Encouraging the consumer to interact with the company may also increase sales, by offering the (intangible) gift of information. One study showed that a coupon offer coupled with a requirement that the customer complete a questionnaire generated significantly more sales than the coupon alone. From a social exchange perspective, customers may view the questionnaire as a request for the gift of information in exchange for the coupon that they have received as a prior gift.[62]

The propriety of using gifts as a marketing tactic varies globally. Given its universality, exchanges of token gifts among business partners are a widespread practice. The website Management by Flowers is a good example of a business gift service, for example. Among cosmopolitan business segments, giving premiums is a widespread and effective practice to reward customer loyalty. Business gifts travel well, and business customers everywhere insist on similar (high) standards of quality. However, one must always be sensitive to the boundaries between relatively altruistic gifts and relatively self-serving bribes. With this in mind, many countries restrict the use of premiums, coupons, rebates, and other "gifts" to consumers. Germany is quite strict in this regard. Nonetheless, in most developing countries, the practice of occasionally gifting regular customers with extras is widespread.[63]

SUMMARY

This chapter explores a number of behaviors related to the acquisition of goods and services. Acquisition is a general consumer behavior concept. Marketers tend to focus their attention on the important, but relatively impersonal marketplace exchanges that we call purchase behavior. Purchase is the outcome of an array of other consumer behaviors and is often only an incidental part of these behaviors. Acquisition may involve goods and services, but it may not involve money. This is the case in barter transactions or countertrade. In gift-giving behavior goods or services may be obtained, but often the physical products are deemphasized relative to the relational significance or feelings gifts evoke.

SUMMARY

Homans's exchange model provides a framework for understanding diverse consumer acquisition behaviors. Homans showed that both outcomes and processes are important to people in exchange, and identified some of the resources people bring to exchange. A continuum of exchange transactions may also be identified with utilitarian pure barter at one extreme, pure gifts characterized by generalized reciprocity at the other, and social exchanges in the middle.

Five complementary models of purchase behavior employed in consumer research include (1) utility-maximizing, (2) decision-making, (3) behavioral-influence, (4) hedonic, and (5) meaning-transfer perspectives. Often purchase behavior is best explained by a combination of perspectives. Impulse purchases are another kind of emotionally driven purchase behavior that conforms poorly to the standard decision-making models. Compulsive purchase behavior is an extreme form of impulse behavior that occurs when normal behavioral inhibitors are somehow suppressed.

Purchase behavior management is one goal of marketing. Two main issues of concern are purchase frequency and timing, and brand-switching behavior. Purchase timing refers to sequences of repetitive purchase events that occur over time. Purchase frequency refers to patterns of repeat purchases over time. Brand switching refers to consumers' tendency to alternate purchases between different brands. Mathematical tools of purchase behavior prediction make use of large scanner panel databases that provide use models in stable markets for basic products. Marketers tend to assume consumers adopt the utilitarian norms of pure barter in their purchase behavior. Marketers face a number of limitations in managing purchase behavior including consumers' evolving marketing savvy and the disruptive role of innovations.

Four main types of countertrade can be identified: barter, compensation deals, counterpurchase, and product buybacks. Each is significant for business-to-business acquisition behaviors and helps to overcome market inefficiencies in some contexts. Consumer-to-consumer barter emerges in some economies when formal markets fail. Formal, consumer-initiated barter systems can be found in a number of countries around the world in which the exchange of resources other than money is central to the acquisition process. These systems fall toward the social exchange part of the exchange continuum.

Gift giving is close to the pure gift on Homans's exchange continuum. Gift giving motivates a very large volume of purchase behavior in all societies. In consumer culture, gift giving animates a moral economy of sentiment that parallels the formal economy. The cultural roots of gift giving may be found in premarket economies. Two major types of gifts are interpersonal gifts and self-gifts. Both structural and emergent occasions may provoke interpersonal gift giving. Interpersonal gifts may be voluntary or opportunistic. Managers may identify gift-giving occasions, influence gift-giving purchases, and design retail environments to encourage gift purchases.

KEY TERMS

acquisition 668
barter 669
barter transactions 669
brand purchase decision 677
brand switching 682
calendric holidays 690
channel purchase decision 677
clout 683
compensation deals 686
counterpurchase 686
countertrade 669
deal-prone consumers 684
deterministic timing 681
embedded purchases 671
emergent occasions 690
external search 684

generalized reciprocity 676
gift-giving behaviors 670
gifts 688
Homans's model of exchange 674
impulse purchases 678
initial purchase decision 677
interpersonal gifts 690
lifestyle shopping 672
norm of reciprocity 690
payment decision 677
potlatch 690
product buyback agreement 687
product category decision 676
purchase decision 676
purchase frequency 679
purchase timing 679
pure gifts 676
real barter 675
repeat purchase decision 677
RFM rule 682
self-gifts 694
social exchange 675
structural occasions 690
vulnerability 683

KEY TERMS

REVIEW QUESTIONS

1. Ask a friend to keep a log of some purchases for a particular nondurable consumer product category over a few weeks. Keep a log yourself of the same product category. After a few weeks, compare your purchase histories. Discuss purchase timing and frequency with your friend, and look for evidence of brand loyalty and brand switching. What are the implications of your behavior for marketing managers?
2. Does acquisition and self-gifting lead to happiness? Check out the World Data Base of Happiness at www.eur.nl/fsw/research/happiness/index.htm, maintained by Erasmus University in the Netherlands. Look at some of the national happiness scores. Compare scores between Triad, transitional, NIC, and developing nations. What do these scores suggest about the relationship between consumer culture and happiness?
3. Identify a consumer barter network in your community. Are you part of such a network? How does it work? What exchange model describes participants' motivations and acquisition strategies?
4. Describe some features that impulse purchases and self-gifts have in common. How does acquisition behavior involving gifts differ from other acquisition behaviors?
5. Not all feelings involved with gift giving are positive. What are some ways in which gift giving can evoke negative feelings?
6. What are some motivations for the purchase of self-gifts? What sorts of occasions may motivate self-gifting? Describe a recent occasion when you gifted yourself.
7. Discuss a recent gift-giving purchase with a friend. Find out how the item was chosen and what occasion stimulated the purchase. Did your friend take into account the recipient's personality? Does the gift reflect your friend's self-image? What message was your friend trying to convey? Was the gift successful? Why or why not?
8. Visit a gift store. Analyze the image created by the store in terms of the five managerial propositions discussed in the text.

CASES

YOU MAKE THE CALL

HOW TO SELL MORE TO THOSE WHO THINK IT'S COOL TO BE FRUGAL

www.patagonia.com

www.norse-log-homes.com

When the ultimate status symbols become acquiring scarce intangibles such as a happy marriage, well-adjusted children, a balanced life, and interesting vacations, marketers may need to reassess their strategies. The Yankelovitch Monitor finds that today's yardsticks of success include satisfaction with self, getting control of your life, and having a great family. The challenge for marketers then becomes, How do organizations sell more goods to segments whose shopping strategy is less is more? One approach for responding to this challenge is to reposition products so as to align them with these shifts in values. For example, Patagonia, Inc., a sportswear manufacturer, has reduced the number of items in its catalogs, offers to repair used goods, highlights its fleecewear made from recycled soda bottles, and promotes its garments as rugged enough to be passed along to the next generation. Industries affected by this change in values include clothing (e.g., the trend toward casual clothes), home builders (the price of log cabin logs has tripled; check out Norse log homes at website), fragrances, hotels and other vacation-related businesses (stress-relieving vacations are in), and high-tech gear such as computers (fewer gadgets, please). Check out a few websites, and consider what you know about acquisition strategies, purchase timing and frequency, gift giving, and retail design and image.

QUESTIONS

1. Making use of this knowledge, give specific advice to corporate clients in one of the industries affected by the belief that less is more.
2. How should they modify their marketing strategies?
3. How can this business take advantage of the evolving values of the frugal consumer?

Adapted from "How to Sell More to Those Who Think It's Cool to Be Frugal," by Ellen Graham, The Wall Street Journal, *September 30, 1996, pp. B1, B2; and "Kids, Cabins, and Free Time Say Status in Understated 90s," by Kathleen Hughes,* The Wall Street Journal, *September 30, 1996, pp. B1, B2. Copyright 1996 by Dow Jones & Co., Inc. Reproduced with permission of Dow Jones & Co., Inc. in the format Textbook via Copyright Clearance Center.*

ENDNOTES

1. David Hoffman, "Barter Now Replacing the Ruble," *International Herald Tribune,* February 1–2, 1997, pp. 1, 7.

2. For regularly updated information about barter, visit the International Reciprocal Trade Association at www.irta.com.

3. Timothy Egan, "Growers and Shoppers Crowd Farmers' Markets," *New York Times,* September 29, 2002, p. 18.

4. "What eBay Isn't Telling You," *Business 2.0,* August 2002, pp. 55–61.

5. Lars Andersen, "Julegaver for 6 milliarder," *Jyllandsposten,* December 9, 1996; and Pat Bean, "Shopping Madness Is Here!" *Ogden Standard/Examiner,* www.standard.net:80/snweb/special report/CHRISTMAS/Stories2.html.

6. Melanie Wallendorf and Eric J. Arnould, "My Favorite Things: A Cross-Cultural Inquiry into Object Attachment, Possessiveness, and Social Linkage," *Journal of Consumer Research* 14 (March 1988), pp. 531–47.

7. Linda Price and Eric J. Arnould, "Commercial Friendships: Service Provider–Client Relationships in Social Context," *Journal of Marketing* 63 (October 1999), pp. 38–56; Clifford Geertz, "The Bazaar Economy: Information and Search in Peasant Marketing," *Supplement to the American Economic Review* 68 (May 1978), pp. 28–32; and Jonathan K. Frenzen and Harry L. Davis, "Purchasing Behavior in Embedded Markets," *Journal of Consumer Research* 17 (June 1990), pp. 1–12.
8. John Brewer and Roy Porter, eds., *Consumption and the World of Goods* (London: Routledge, 1994); James Carrier, *Gifts and Commodities: Exchange and Western Capitalism since 1700* (London: Routledge, 1995); Colin Campbell, *The Romantic Ethic and the Spirit of Modern Consumerism* (Oxford: Blackwell, 1987); Güliz Ger, "The Positive and Negative Effects of Marketing on Socio-economic Development," *Journal of Consumer Policy* 15, no. 3 (1992), pp. 229–52; Rosalind H. Williams, *Dream Worlds: Mass Consumption in Nineteenth Century France* (Berkeley: University of California Press, 1982); and Terrence H. Witkowski, "Painting the Domestication of Consumption in 19th-Century America," in *Advances in Consumer Research,* vol. 26, ed. Eric Arnould and Linda Scott (Provo, UT: Association for Consumer Research, 1999), pp. 644–51.
9. Craig J. Thompson, Barbara B. Stern, and Eric J. Arnould, "Narrative Analysis of a Marketing Relationship: The Consumer's Perspective," *Psychology and Marketing* 15 (May 1997), pp. 195–214; and John C. Mowen, "Beyond Consumer Decision Making," *Journal of Consumer Marketing* 5 (Winter 1998), pp. 15–25.
10. Susan Fournier, Susan Dobscha, and David Glen Mick, "Preventing the Premature Death of Relationship Marketing," *Harvard Business Review,* January–February 1998, pp. 42–51; Jonathan K. Frenzen and Harry L. Davis, "Purchasing Behavior in Embedded Markets," *Journal of Consumer Research* 17 (June 1990), pp. 1–12; and Charles W. Smith, "Auctions: From Walras to the Real World," in *Explorations in Economic Sociology,* ed. Richard Swedberg (New York: Russell Sage Foundation, 1993), pp. 176–92.
11. Russell W. Belk and Gregory S. Coon, "Gift Giving as Agapic Love: An Alternative to the Exchange Paradigm Based on Dating Experiences," *Journal of Consumer Research* 20 (December 1993), pp. 393–417; Stewart Clough, "The Social Relations of Grain Marketing in Northern Nigeria," *Review of African Political Economy* 34 (1985), pp. 16–34; and Stewart Macaulay, "Non-Contractual Relations in Business: A Preliminary Study," in *The Sociology of Economic Life,* ed. Mark Granovetter and Richard Swedberg (Boulder, CO: Westview Press, 1992), pp. 265–85.
12. Paul F. Anderson and Terry M. Chambers, "A Reward/Measurement Model of Organizational Buying Behavior," *Journal of Marketing* 49 (Spring 1985), pp. 7–23; and Richard L. Wessler, "Premiums: The Psychology of Motivation," *Marketing Communications* 9 (May 5, 1984), pp. 29–32.
13. James E. Burroughs, "Product Symbolism, Self Meaning and Holistic Matching: The Role of Information Processing in Impulsive Buying," in *Advances in Consumer Research,* vol. 23, ed. Kim Corfman and John Lynch (Provo, UT: Association for Consumer Research, 1996), pp. 463–69.
14. Meryl Paula Gardner and Dennis W. Rook, "Effects of Impulse Purchases on Consumers' Affective States," in *Advances in Consumer Research,* vol. 15, ed. Michael Houston (Provo, UT: Association for Consumer Research, 1988), pp. 127–30.
15. Dennis W. Rook, "The Buying Impulse," *Journal of Consumer Research* 12 (December 1987), pp. 251–64; Dennis W. Rook and Robert J. Fisher, "Normative Influences on Impulsive Buying Behavior," *Journal of Consumer Research* 22 (December 1995), pp. 305–26; Peter Weinberg and Wolfgang Gottwald, "Impulsive Consumer Buying as a Result of Emotions," *Journal of Business Research* 10 (March 1, 1982), pp. 43–57; and Stephen J. Hoch and George F. Lowenstein, "Time-Inconsistent Preference and Consumer Self-Control," *Journal of Consumer Behavior* 17 (March 1991), pp. 492–507.
16. Geoff Bayley and Clive Nancarrow, "Impulse Buying: A Qualitative Exploration of the Phenomenon," *Qualitative Market Research* 1, no. 2 (1998).
17. Thomas C. O'Guinn and Ronald J. Faber, "Compulsive Buying: A Phenomenological Exploration," *Journal of Consumer Research* 16 (September 1989), pp. 147–57.

18. Kevin Lane Keller, "Conceptualizing, Measuring, and Managing Customer-Based Brand Equity," *Journal of Marketing* 57 (January 1993), pp. 1–22.

19. "The Future of Bank Card Authorization: Providing Incentives with Frequency Programs," *Chain Store Age Executive* 69, no. 10 (October 1993), pp. 86–87; and Simon Knox and Leslie de Chernatony, "A Buyer Behaviour Approach to Merchandising and Product Policy," *International Journal of Retail & Distribution Management* 18, no. 6 (November–December 1990), pp. 21–30.

20. Sunil Gupta, "Stochastic Models of Interpurchase Time with Time-Dependent Co-Variates," *Journal of Marketing Research* 28 (February 1991), pp. 1–15; Dipak C. Jain and Naufel J. Vilcassim, "Investigating Household Purchase Timing Decisions: A Conditional Hazard Function Approach," *Marketing Science* 10, no. 1 (Winter 1991), pp. 1–23; and Fred S. Zuyfryden, "The WNBD: A Stochastic Model Approach for Relating Explanatory Variables to Consumer Purchase Dynamics," *International Journal of Research in Marketing* 8 (September 1991), pp. 251–58.

21. Gil A. Frisbie, "Ehrenberg's Negative Binomial Model Applied to Grocery Store Trips," *Journal of Marketing Research* 17, no. 3 (August 1980), pp. 385–90.

22. Robin Cobb, "Marketing Services—Sales Promotion and Premiums: Lucky Dip Promo Ploys Soar," *Marketing,* July 8, 1993, pp. 22, 24.

23. Bob Gatty, "Incentives Move Products—and People," *Nation's Business* 69, no. 9 (September 1981), pp. 66–68, 70.

24. Paul Berger and Thomas Magliozzi, "The Effect of Sample Size and Proportion of Buyers in the Sample on the Performance of List Segmentation Equations Generated by Regression Analysis," *Journal of Direct Marketing* 6, no. 1 (Winter 1992), pp. 13–22; and Eileen Norris, "Direct Marketing: Databased Marketing Sets Enticing Bait," *Advertising Age* 59, no. 3 (January 18, 1988), pp. S10–S12, S15.

25. L. G. Schneider and I. S. Currim, "Consumer Purchase Behaviors Associated with Active and Passive Deal-Proneness," *International Journal of Research in Marketing* 8 (September 1991), pp. 205–22.

26. Melissa Dowling, "Mailbox Overload," *Catalog Age* 11, no. 12 (December 1994), pp. 1, 37; and Vicki G. Morwitz, Eric Johnson, and David Schmittlein, "Does Measuring Intent Change Behavior?" *Journal of Consumer Research* 20, no. 1 (June 1993), pp. 46–61.

27. "Facts Survey: Consumer Incentives," *Incentive* 165, no. 5 (May 1991), pp. 50–55.

28. Dawn Iacobucci and Geraldine Henderson, "Log Linear Models for Consumer Brand Switching Behavior: What a Manager Can Learn from Studying Standardized Residuals," in *Advances in Consumer Research,* vol. 24, ed. Merrie Brucks and Debbie MacInnis (Provo, UT: Association for Consumer Research, 1997), pp. 375–80.

29. Moshe Givon and Eitan Muller, "Cyclical Patterns in Brand Switching Behavior: An Issue of Pattern Recognition," *European Journal of Operational Research* 76, no. 2 (July 28, 1994), pp. 290–97.

30. Randolph E. Bucklin and V. Srinivasan, "Determining Interbrand Substitutability through Survey Measurement of Consumer Preference Structures," *Journal of Marketing Research* 28, no. 1 (February 1991), pp. 58–71.

31. S. Kent Stephan and Barry L. Tannenholz, "The Real Reason for Brand-Switching," *Advertising Age* 65, no. 25 (June 13, 1994), p. 31.

32. Donald R. Lichtenstein, Richard G. Netemeyer, and Scot Burton, "Assessing the Domain Specificity of Deal Proneness: A Field Study," *Journal of Consumer Research* 22 (December 1995), pp. 314–26.

33. Michael Jones, Philip Trocchia, and David Mothersbaugh, "Noneconomic Motivations for Price Haggling: An Exploratory Study," in *Advances in Consumer Research,* vol. 24, ed. Merrie Brucks and Debbie MacInnis (Provo, UT: Association for Consumer Research, 1997), pp. 388–91.

34. Daniel Miller, *A Theory of Shopping* (Ithaca, NY: Cornell University Press, 1998). This book is reviewed in Eric J. Arnould, *American Ethnologist* 26 (November 1999), pp. 999–1000. See also Marjorie L. DeVault, *Feeding the Family: The Social Organization of Caring as Gendered Work* (Chicago: University of Chicago Press, 1991).

35. "The Cashless Society," *The Economist,* March 15, 1997, www.economist.com/issue/15-03-97/fn6634.html; Beatrice B. Lund, "Corporate Barters as a Marketing Strategy," *Marketing News* 31, no. 5 (March 3, 1997), p. 8; and Dorothy A. Paun and Aviv Sholam, "Marketing Motives in International Countertrade: An Empirical Examination," *Journal of International Marketing* 4, no. 3 (1996), pp. 29–48.
36. Russell W. Belk, John F. Sherry Jr., and Melanie Wallendorf, "A Naturalistic Inquiry into Buyer and Seller Behavior at a Swap Meet," *Journal of Consumer Research* 14 (March 1988), pp. 449–70; Gretchen M. Herrmann, "His and Hers: Gender and Garage Sales," *Journal of Popular Culture* 29 (Summer 1995), pp. 127–45; Gretchen Hermann and Stephen M. Soiffer, "For Fun and Profit: An Analysis of the American Garage Sale," *Urban Life* 12, no. 4 (1984), pp. 397–421; Myriam Hivon, " 'Payer en liquide,' l'utilisation de la vodka dans les échanges en Russie rurale," *Ethnologie Française,* October 1998, pp. 515–24; and John F. Sherry Jr., "A Sociocultural Analysis of a Midwestern American Flea Market," *Journal of Consumer Research* 17 (June 1990), pp. 13–30.
37. Gabriel Yiannis and Tim Lang, *The Unmanageable Consumer* (London: Sage Publications, 1995); www.btwebworld.communities/lets; and www.newciv.org/worldtrans/GIB/BOV-.
38. Eric J. Arnould, "West African Marketing Channels: Environmental Duress, Relationship Management, and Implications for Western Marketing," in *Contemporary Marketing and Consumer Behavior: An Anthropological Sourcebook,* ed. John F. Sherry Jr. (Thousand Oaks, CA: Sage Publications, 1995), p. 168.
39. Gerald Albaum, Jesper Strandskov, Edwin Duerr, and Laurence Down, *International Marketing and Export Management,* 2nd ed. (Reading, MA: Addison-Wesley, 1994); ALM Consulting, Frere Cholmeley Bischoff, and KPMG Peat Marwick, *Doing Business in Russia* (Lincolnwood, IL: NTC Publishing, 1993); Arnould, "West African Marketing Channels"; Philip R. Cateora, *International Marketing,* 8th ed. (Homewood, IL: Irwin, 1993); Stanley Paliwoda, *International Marketing,* 2nd ed. (Oxford: Butterworth-Heinemann, 1993); and Roger C. Riddell, ed., *Manufacturing Africa* (Portsmouth, NH: Honeymoon Educational Books, 1990).
40. David Cheal, "Showing Them You Love Them: Gift Giving and the Dialectic of Intimacy," *Sociological Review* 35, no. 1 (1987), pp. 150–69; and Cele Otnes and Richard F. Beltramini, eds., *Gift Giving: A Research Anthology* (Bowling Green, OH: Bowling Green State University Press, 1996).
41. Fumeritu Nitta, "Shopping for Souvenirs in Hawaii," in *Re-Made in Japan,* ed. Joseph J. Tobin (New Haven: Yale University Press, 1992), pp. 204–15; and Mary Searle-Chatterjee, "Christmas Cards and the Construction of Social Relations in Britain Today," in *Unwrapping Christmas,* ed. Daniel Miller (Oxford: Clarendon Press, 1993), pp. 176–92.
42. Belk and Coon, "Gift Giving as Agapic Love"; Russell W. Belk, "Special Session Summary: The Meaning of Gifts and Greetings," in *Advances in Consumer Research,* vol. 23, ed. Kim P. Corfman and John G. Lynch Jr. (Provo, UT: Association for Consumer Research, 1996), p. 13; Kimberly J. Dodson and Russell W. Belk, "The Birthday Card Minefield," in *Advances in Consumer Research,* vol. 23, ed. Kim P. Corfman and John G. Lynch Jr. (Provo, UT: Association for Consumer Research, 1996), pp. 14–20; Joy Hendry, *Wrapping Culture* (Oxford: Oxford University Press, 1995); Nitta, "Shopping for Souvenirs in Hawaii"; and Deborah Scammon, Roy T. Shaw, and Gary Bamossy, "Is a Gift Always a Gift? An Investigation of Flower Purchasing," in *Advances in Consumer Research,* vol. 9, ed. A. Mitchell (Ann Arbor, MI: Association for Consumer Research, 1982), pp. 531–36.
43. Alvin Gouldner, "The Norm of Reciprocity: A Preliminary Statement," *American Sociological Review* 25 (1960), pp. 161–78; and Claude Levi-Strauss, "The Principle of Reciprocity," in *Sociological Theory: A Book of Readings,* ed. Lewis A. Coser and Bernard Rosenberg (New York: Macmillan, 1964).
44. Macel Mauss, *The Gift: The Form and Reason for Exchange in Archaic Societies,* trans. W. D. Halls (New York: W. W. Norton, 1990/1924); and Marshall Sahlins, *Stone-Age Economics* (Chicago: Aldine, 1972).
45. Dodson and Belk, "The Birthday Card Minefield"; Denise Girard, "Le shower: Enterrer sa vie de jeune fille," *Ethnologie Française,* October 1998, pp. 472–79; and Regine Sirota, "Les

copains d'abord: Les anniversaires de l'enfance, donner et recevoir," *Ethnologie Française,* October 1998, pp. 457–71.
46. David Cheal, *The Gift Economy* (London: Routledge, 1988); I. Chukwuere, "A Coffin for the 'Loved One': The Structure of Fante Death Rituals," *Current Anthropology* 22, no. 1 (1981), pp. 61–68; Miller, *Unwrapping Christmas;* Constance Classen, "Sugar Cane, Coca-Cola and Hypermarkets: Consumption and Surrealism in the Argentine Northwest," in *Cross-Cultural Consumption,* ed. David Howes (London: Routledge, 1996), pp. 39–54; John F. Sherry Jr., "Gift Giving in Anthropological Perspective," *Journal of Consumer Research* 10 (September 1983), pp. 157–68; Sherri Athay, "Giving and Getting," *American Demographics* 15, no. 12 (December 1993), pp. 46–52; Carole B. Burgoyne and David A. Routh, "Constraints on the Use of Money as a Gift at Christmas: The Role of Status and Intimacy," *Journal of Economic Psychology* 12 (March 1991), pp. 47–69; Constance Hill and Celia T. Romm, "The Role of Mothers as Gift Givers: A Comparison across Three Cultures," in *Advances in Consumer Research,* vol. 23, ed. Kim P. Corfman and John P. Lynch (Provo, UT: Association for Consumer Research, 1996), pp. 21–27; Daniel R. Horne, Shay Sayre, and David A. Horne, "Gifts: What Do You Buy the Person Who Has Nothing," in *Advances in Consumer Research,* vol. 23, ed. Kim P. Corfman and John P. Lynch (Provo, UT: Association for Consumer Research, 1996), pp. 30–34; Jonathan Parry and Maurice Bloch, "Introduction: Money and the Morality of Exchange," *Money and the Morality of Exchange* (Cambridge: Cambridge University Press, 1989), pp. 1–33; and Margaret Rucker, Anthony Freitas, and Jamie Dolstra, "A Toast for the Host: The Male Perspective on Gifts That Say Thank You," in *Advances in Consumer Research,* vol. 21, ed. Chris T. Allen and Deborah Roedder John (Provo, UT: Association for Consumer Research, 1994), pp. 165–68.
47. Russell W. Belk and Gregory S. Coon, "Can't Buy Me Love: Dating, Money, and Gifts," in *Advances in Consumer Research,* vol. 18, ed. Rebecca H. Holman and Michael Solomon (Provo, UT: Association for Consumer Research, 1991), pp. 521–27; and Margaret Rucker et al., "When the Thought Counts: Friendship, Love, Gift Exchanges and Gift Returns," in *Advances in Consumer Research,* vol. 18, ed. Rebecca H. Holman and Michael Solomon (Provo, UT: Association for Consumer Research, 1991), pp. 529–31.
48. Carolyn Folkman Curasi, Linda L. Price, and Eric J. Arnould, "You Can't Take It with You: An Examination of the Disposition Decision of Older Consumers," working paper, University of South Florida, 1996; and Mary Finley Wolfinbarger, "Motivations and Symbolism in Gift-Giving Behavior," in *Advances in Consumer Research,* vol. 17, ed. Marvin E. Goldberg, Gerald Gorn, and Richard W. Pollay (Provo, UT: Association for Consumer Research, 1990), pp. 699–706.
49. Boye De Mente, *Korean Etiquette and Ethics in Business* (Lincolnwood, IL: NTC Publishing, 1988); Cele Otnes, Julie A. Ruth, and Constance C. Milbourne, "The Pleasure and Pain of Being Close: Men's Mixed Feelings about Participation in Valentine's Day Gift Exchange," in *Advances in Consumer Research,* vol. 21, ed. Chris T. Allen and Deborah Roedder John (Provo, UT: Association for Consumer Research, 1994), pp. 159–64; and John F. Sherry Jr., Mary Ann McGrath, and Sidney J. Levy, "The Dark Side of the Gift," *Journal of Business Research* 28 (1983), pp. 225–44.
50. Cathy Goodwin, Kelly L. Smith, and Susan Spiggle, "Gift Giving: Consumer Motivation and the Gift Purchase Process," in *Advances in Consumer Research,* vol. 17, ed. Marvin E. Goldberg, Gerald Gorn, and Richard W. Pollay (Provo, UT: Association for Consumer Research, 1990), pp. 690–98; Martine Ségalen, "Où est déposé la liste? Une enquête sur les cadeaux de mariage," *Ethnologie Française,* October 1998, pp. 480–93; Belk and Coon, "Gift Giving as Agapic Love"; Sherry, McGrath, and Levy, "The Dark Side of the Gift"; and Sharon E. Beatty, Lynn R. Kahle, and Pamela Homer, "Personal Values and Gift-Giving Behaviors: A Study across Cultures," *Journal of Business Research* 22 (March 1991), pp. 149–57.
51. Annamma Joy, "When a Gift Is Not a Gift," working paper, Concordia University, Montreal, 2000; David Glen Mick and Michelle DeMoss, "Self-Gifts: Phenomenological Insights from Four Contexts," *Journal of Consumer Research* 17 (December 1990), pp. 322–32; David Glen Mick and Michelle DeMoss, "To Me from Me: A Descriptive Phenomenology of Self-Gifts," in

Advances in Consumer Research, vol. 17, ed. Marvin E. Goldberg, Gerald Gorn, and Richard W. Pollay (Provo, UT: Association for Consumer Research, 1990), pp. 677–82; and Nitta, "Shopping for Souvenirs in Hawaii."
52. David Glen Mick, Michelle DeMoss, and Ronald J. Faber, "A Projective Study of Motivations and Meanings of Self-Gifts: Implications for Retail Management," *Journal of Retailing* 68 (Summer 1992), pp. 122–44.
53. David Glen Mick and Michelle DeMoss, "Further Findings on Self-Gifts: Products, Qualities, and Socioeconomic Correlates," in *Advances in Consumer Research,* vol. 20, ed. Leigh McAlister and Michael L. Rothschild (Provo, UT: Association for Consumer Research, 1994), pp. 140–46.
54. Kim K. R. McKeage, Marsha L. Richins, and Kathleen Debevec, "Self-Gifts and the Manifestation of Material Values," in *Advances in Consumer Research,* vol. 20, ed. Leigh McAlister and Michael L. Rothschild (Provo, UT: Association for Consumer Research, 1993), pp. 359–64.
55. Mick, DeMoss, and Faber, "A Projective Study of Motivations and Meanings of Self-Gifts."
56. Sherry, "Gift Giving in Anthropological Perspective"; and Terence H. Witkowski and Yoshito Yamamoto, "Omiyage Gift Purchasing by Japanese Travelers in the U.S.," in *Advances in Consumer Research,* vol. 18, ed. Rebecca H. Holman and Michael Solomon (Provo, UT: Association for Consumer Research, 1991), pp. 123–28.
57. Athay, "Giving and Getting"; Burgoyne and Routh, "Constraints on the Use of Money as a Gift at Christmas"; Hill and Romm, "The Role of Mothers as Gift Givers"; Horne, Sayre, and Horne, "Gifts: What Do You Buy the Person Who Has Nothing?"; Parry and Bloch, "Introduction: Money and the Morality of Exchange"; and Rucker, Freitas, and Dolstra, "A Toast for the Host."
58. "Study Tracks Housewares Buying, Information Sources," *Marketing News* 17 (October 14, 1983), p. 16; and David Brooks, "Annals of Consumption: Acquired Taste," *The New Yorker* (January 25, 1999), pp. 36–41.
59. Iris D. Rosendahl, "The Search for Profits: Selling General Merchandise," *Drug Topics* 126 (March 15, 1982), pp. 52–61; Bruce E. Mattson, "Situational Influences on Store Choice," *Journal of Retailing* 58 (Fall 1982), pp. 46–58; Richard Thaler, "Mental Accounting and Consumer Choice," *Marketing Science* 4 (Summer 1985), pp. 199–214; and David M. Andrus, Edward Silver, and Dallas E. Johnson, "Status Brand Management and Gift Purchase: A Discriminant Analysis," *Journal of Consumer Marketing* 3 (Winter 1986), pp. 5–13.
60. John F. Sherry Jr. and Mary Ann McGrath, "Unpacking the Holiday Presence: A Comparative Ethnography of Two Gift Stores," in *Interpretive Consumer Research,* ed. Elizabeth C. Hirschman (Provo, UT: Association for Consumer Research, 1989), pp. 148–67; and Melanie Wallendorf, Joan Linsday-Mulliken, and Ron Pimentel, "Gorilla Marketing: Customer Animation and Regional Embeddedness in a Toy Store Servicescape," in *Servicescapes,* ed. John F. Sherry Jr. (Lincolnwood, IL: NTC Business Books, 1998), pp. 151–98.
61. Barbara E. Kahn and Alice M. Isen, "The Influence of Positive Affect on Variety Seeking among Safe, Enjoyable Products," *Journal of Consumer Research* 20 (September 1993), pp. 257–70.
62. Luther Brock, "The 10 Most Fatal Mistakes in Selling by Mail," *Marketing Times* 30 (November–December 1983), pp. 41–44; and Arthur L. Porter, "Strengthening Coupon Offers by Requiring More from the Customer," *Journal of Consumer Marketing* 10, no. 2 (1993), pp. 13–18.
63. "Barbarians at the Check-Out," *The Economist,* October 26, 1996, p. 84; and Margaret Bennett, "Premiums and Incentives: Bearing Gifts," *Marketing,* April 6, 1989, p. 47.

chapter 1
chapter 2
chapter 3
chapter 4
chapter 5
chapter 6
chapter 7
chapter 8
chapter 9
chapter 10
chapter 11
chapter 12
chapter 13
chapter 14
chapter 15
chapter 16
chapter 17
chapter 18
chapter 19

LEARNING OBJECTIVES

After completing this chapter, you should be able to:

- Distinguish characteristics of innovations that influence their rate of diffusion and help determine their market success.
- Distinguish diffusion and adoption processes.
- Describe reasons for resistance to change and for discontinuance.
- Describe strategies for changing attitudes and behavior.
- Understand how innovation and adoption processes are influenced by environmental, cultural, and social system factors.
- Identify and distinguish opinion leaders, market mavens, and innovative consumers important in the diffusion of innovations.
- Describe differences among consumers based on their time of adoption of innovations.
- Describe a common adoption decision.

THE FLOWER FOURSOME FROM TAIWAN: F4[1]

If you ask people in China to tell you their favorite "boy group," a 40-year-old woman may give the same answer as her 14-year-old daughter—"F4." This Taiwan boy group made their debut in April 2002, with the launch of a new soap opera, *Meteor Garden*. By the summer, they were one of the most popular and successful entertainment groups in Asia.

The four members of the group—Jerry Yan, Vic Zhou, Ken Zhu, and Vanness Wu—attract millions of fans with chiseled good looks, hot bodies, fantastic hair, and a "romantic love spirit," which is communicated via their TV show. On the show, the four first-time actors are all members of "a wealthy and enigmatic gang, called F4." In mainland China, even though the government discourages the program, many viewers find that they are thirsty for the "True Love" story that is portrayed in *Meteor Garden*. In this sense, the band strikes a strong emotional cord, especially among younger women. Their popularity is strong in China, Hong Kong, Taiwan, Singapore, and Malaysia.

@ devoted.to/f4

F4's debut CD, "Meteor Rain," sold more than one million copies in Asia. In China, the TV show was banned after a few episodes because the government believed that it misled young viewers. However, the ban seemed to accelerate the popularity of the group. Bootleg copies of the show sell all over the country, and the ban served to stimulate curiosity and interest.

Angie Chai created F4 to replace the Little Tigers, a boy band that disbanded 10 years ago. Since Taiwan has been without such a group for an extended period, boy bands from other cultures (e.g., Japan, Europe) gained popularity. Ms. Chai selected the four boys for the group and dubbed them F4 (short for the "Flower Four"). At present, each of the individual members is planning to issue a solo music project, and a movie project is also in the works. Young people in China imitate the clothing and hairstyle of F4. People on the street imitate the accents and slang expressions popularized by the TV show. Here's what one fan (from mainland China) has to say about F4 in a website she created:

> The first time I got to see them was in their music videos . . . I just loved their songs so much, you cannot believe that I liked Tjai Tjai [Vic] at first sight! He is just a cute babe as you can see in the pic above! Jerry is a gorgeous guy as well, he is my second fave! ☺ . . . The first time I watched "Meteor Garden," I screamed and laughed a lot as I couldn't believe how cool, how cute, how gorgeous and how funny they were! I just loved it sooooo much! As a fan, I have bought their album of course, can you believe that I listen to it every day and night?! It sounds really great, don't you know? . . . I think that's enough for now, I'd better stop, otherwise F4 will stay on my mind all night!! . . . If anyone of you is an F4 fan, just drop me a line! If you are from Taiwan, plz don't forget to drop me a line . . . hehehe . . . because I wanna meet them someday in Taiwan, so let's keep in touch!! [http://pages.ivillage.com/vickazy/]

@ pages.ivillage.com/vickazy

This fan resides in Hong Kong, but such sentiments are typical, all throughout Asia.

A number of companies have hired F4 to endorse their products. For instance, the Legend brand (e.g., laptops, cameras, personal digital assistants) has sold very well among women aged 14 to 40 since hiring F4 as celebrity endorsers. Siemens AG also finds that F4 is a good vehicle for promoting their cell phones to college students.

@ cabletv.starhub.com/eng/feature/0.1164.100-0.00.html

How long will F4's popularity last? Will they go the way of the Little Tigers, or will they persevere to the point of defining an era? How much appeal will they have, outside of areas where Chinese is a dominant language?

OVERVIEW

As described by the economist Joseph Schumpeter, product choices (really choices between technologies) drive capitalist economies and shape them into engines of **creative destruction.** That is, capitalism encourages the creation of new markets, new technologies, and new forms of industrial organization. These innovations have the potential to increase the standard of living of the populace and are quickly adopted (within a capitalistic economic system). At the same time, however, these innovations drive out old forms of doing business. For example, the creation of the transistor makes the vacuum tube obsolete; and vacuum tube manufacturers go out of business. In time, computer chips replace the transistor. Old industries, old technologies are destroyed. New industries rise up in their place, but there is upheaval and disruption and displacement. Some companies go out of business. Workers find themselves to be ill-suited for jobs in emerging industries, and they may be laid off. Consumers become dizzy with the wide array of new products and services that are introduced. Products may get more and more sophisticated over time, but consumers have less time to enjoy life, due partly to the large amount of time and energy it takes to be a consumer in the early twenty-first century.[2]

To some extent, Schumpeter's account of the triumph of technology may sound overly deterministic. In fact, it is not the technologies themselves that determine the future; rather, consumers and the individual choices they make determine how technologies are used in society. Some technologies fall by the wayside, neglected and discarded. Other technologies prosper and are adopted around the world. Nonetheless, almost all technologies evolve and adapt to the ways in which consumers use them. For instance, the radio was originally designed as a means for ships to communicate with one another and to communicate with those on land. The early pioneers of radio never imagined that they were perfecting an entertainment medium that would transform the world.

Whatever the merits of Schumpeter's arguments, this chapter focuses on innovation and change, which are at the heart of marketing. Marketers face the challenge of persuading people to change their attitudes and behaviors. Marketers ask consumers to be innovative—to buy in new places, for example. New places might include grocery stores in the developing world. Marketers ask consumers to buy in new ways. New ways might include using smart bankcards or computerized banking in the Triad countries. Marketers ask consumers to buy new products. It turns out that most new products consist of "me too" products or reformulations of brands that already exist. In the area of consumer goods, the majority of product introductions come in the industries of food, beverages, and beauty aids.[3] Sometimes, marketers even ask consumers to learn a new way of life. For example, consumers in the transitional economies of the former Soviet bloc are asked to understand and decode marketing practices, consumer culture, and a new language of promotion.[4]

For every marketer asking the consumer to believe or do something innovative, another marketer is asking that same consumer to resist change—to be loyal to the existing product or solution. Hence, it's important to understand innovation and change and, at the same time, to understand the opposite forces: conservatism and resistance to change. The individual and social dynamics associated with change and resistance to change act together. Basic tensions between pressures for change and pressures for resistance are present at every level of society, from individual to nation state.

It is the marketer's job to understand consumer tensions and to find ways to help consumers solve their problems. Marketers win awards and create customer value by working with other parts of the organization to create successful marketplace entries. Organizations find that new products are more likely to be successful when members of the marketing department are involved in the innovation process.[5] At the start of the twentieth century, most corporations did not view marketing as being an important part of the research and development process. Now, that attitude is changed, and most innovations are developed using new product teams that include a representative from the marketing department. In fact, there is evidence that the innovation process is most successful when a marketing employee is leading a new product team.[6] One explanation for this result is that new products are successful when organizations hear the voice of the market and implement the marketing concept (see Chapter 5). In addition to receiving praise, marketers' attempts to persuade people to change also form the basis for much criticism. For example, China resists the diffusion of TV satellite dishes and Singapore resists broadcasts of Star satellite TV. Both fear Western programming will erode traditional Asian values (by changing viewers' attitudes and behaviors). As illustrated in the opening vignette, the Chinese government tries to discourage the popularity of the boy band F4. To date, however, this official disapproval seems to have the opposite effect, as the group's popularity has skyrocketed in a very short period of time. Marketer-driven innovations lie at the heart of many public policy debates.

In this chapter, we introduce some of the theories and tools in marketing and the social sciences for understanding the topic of change. First, we present a perspective on diffusion, introducing some key concepts, such as innovation, diffusion, and adoption. In addition, we discuss the concepts of conservatism and discontinuance. The latter issues are important for understanding new-product/service failure. Then, we discuss the various contexts in which innovation, diffusion, and discontinuance take place. Our discussion of social system characteristics leads naturally to a discussion of individual adopter types. We discuss consumer adoption behavior and how adoptions lead to successful innovations from an organizational and societal perspective. In a market economy it is consumers who, in the end, determine how new inventions will be used and which technologies are successful.

INNOVATION

There is a vast literature on the topic of innovation, diffusion, and adoption. **Innovation** refers to *new things and ideas and new ways of behaving and interacting with things.* Innovations are defined by individuals and by social groups. What one individual or one social group perceives as novel may be old-fashioned for other individuals and groups. Innovations include ideas and business practices such as total quality management or the online reverse auction.[7] Products can be innovative, such as plastic buckets in rural Ethiopia or personal digital assistants in developed nations. In Turkish banking practice, a service such as consumer credit is innovative. Innovation also may refer to behaviors, as when designers develop resource-conserving packaging or when individual consumers adopt any product that is new for them.[8] Thus, an innovation involves new ways of thinking about the world and new behaviors (e.g., buying and using a new product).

Innovation is one component of the diffusion process. Innovations come from many sources. Users are one important source of information in both business and consumer markets. Government organizations also may become involved, as when regulators mandate the use of pollution control technologies in an industry. A key challenge for business organizations is to manage the production and diffusion of innovations.

As marketers strive for competitive advantage in the global marketplace, they seek sales and market share through the introduction of new goods and services. In fact, the rate of new consumer packaged goods introductions accelerated from approximately 6,300 in 1990 to more than 9,100 in 1997. Fewer than 100 new products may top $1 million in sales in their first year of commercialization. Eighty to 90 percent of new entrants will eventually fail in the marketplace. This flood of innovations is potentially wasteful and expensive for organizations. At the same time, it is confusing and disruptive for consumers. Hence, finding better ways to manage innovation is a critical issue for almost all organizations.[9]

Types of Innovations

Three types of innovations are discussed here: continuous, dynamically continuous, and discontinuous. These represent a continuum, with the first being relatively minor innovations and the last radically new innovations.

To improve the management of innovations, it makes sense to distinguish between types in terms of the behavioral consequences for users. At one end of the continuum lie **continuous innovations.** Continuous innovations are those that *require minor changes in user behaviors.* In other words, they have a minimally disruptive effect, while still representing a change in past behavior. One industrial example is Mazda's Miller-cycle internal combustion engine, which differs from the conventional Otto-cycle engine in producing more torque by shortening the compression stroke. In the Triad countries, consumer examples include Gillette's Mach3 razor, TopsyTail ponytail inverters, Kraft fat-free mayonnaise, Diesel wide-leg jeans, and Sony cordless headphones.[10] Technological innovations can revive an older technology and stimulate continuous innovation. Consider broadcast radio and how it adapts and thrives in the twenty-first century via web casting. For instance, Radio Locator offers a search engine with links to more than 10,000 radio stations and broadcasts around the world.

www.radio-locator.com/cgi-bin/home

Fads, fashions, and trends are examples of continuous innovations. They may be distinguished partly in terms of time of diffusion. **Fashions** refer to *particular combinations of desirable attributes.* For example, brightly colored and patterned Kente cloth (pictured on page 715), woven in thin strips in Ghana, has become a popular fashion among African Americans as a statement of ethnic pride. Ministers wear it on their vestments; high school and college graduates add it to their graduation gowns.

www.kente.net

Fads are *short-lived fashions, often adopted by relatively few people, often members of a common subculture.* Fads diffuse most rapidly and disappear most quickly. See Consumer Chronicles 17.1 for a listing of fads and fashions that were once popular in the United States. Try to think of some twenty-first century fads and fashions to add to the list. Note the distinction between fad and fashion. For instance, platform shoes are classified as a fashion item (in Consumer Chronicles 17.1). Platform shoes have been in and out of style for many years and in many places. From this perspective, platform shoes are grouped with the fashion items. However, a particular manifestation of such a style could be classified as a fad, as in the case of the Candies brand that was popular in the late 1970s among American teenagers and young adults. Candies have reemerged in the twenty-first century because of consumer nostalgia for styles of the 1970s. At the time of this writing, body branding joined body piercing as a fad among the avant-garde in the United States and Europe. The popularity of F4, as described in the opening vignette, would currently be classified as a fad. Notice that there are many aspects to this fad—clothing, speech, music, hair style, TV show, behavior patterns, romantic themes. If F4 (and its accompanying images) remains popular for a very long period of time, then they may become a signature symbol to represent an entire era. At the present, the probability of this outcome seems rather low. Most likely, F4 will remain a fad, but a fad with many features.

www.angelfire.com/fl/JackCraig/FADS.html

Trends, or styles, *last longest and may define an era.* Thus, the Victorian era emanating from Great Britain in the mid-nineteenth century was associated with certain trends in architecture, dress, and interior design. Industry Insights 17.1 defines style, and Exhibit 17.1 highlights the distinction between trends and fads.[11]

Distinguishing between fads and trends at an early stage can make a business success. The first company to identify and act on a trend gains a powerful competitive advantage. The Japanese firm Sanrio, which has made a fortune licensing Hello Kitty, claims to have capitalized on "cute."[12] See the accompanying photo of the Hello Kitty vacuum cleaner on page 716, for example. Starbucks coffee capitalized on a trend in consumer desire for higher-quality coffee by franchising a standardized service idea. By correctly identifying fads, such as licensed characters (e.g., using Pokémon characters as a company spokesperson), aggressive marketers can maximize short-term sales. But they must be careful not to invest too much in a trend or fad. As the fad loses momentum, demand can collapse quickly, as with *Star Wars Episode I* action figures.[13]

When managers are considering the introduction of continuous innovations, a major challenge is demonstrating to end users that the innovation provides a differential

Fads and Fashions: Where Are They Now?

CONSUMER CHRONICLES 17.1

It's interesting to see how fads and fashions change over the years. Sometimes, they try to make a comeback. Everyone remembers a favorite toy or fashion item that they grew up with. What would you add to this partial listing of American fads and fashions?

(a) Baby on board stickers	(b) Jeans with high heels	(b) Shag carpeting
(b) Bell bottom pants	(a) Lava lamps	(b) Slogan buttons
(b) Bobby socks	(a) Leather bracelets	(a) Sock hop
(a) Body branding	(b) Long sideburns	(b) Station wagons
(a) Campbell soup waste cans	(b) Mini, midi, & maxi dresses	(a) Tiki necklaces
(a) Cigarette holders	(a) Mood rings	(a) Velvet paintings
(a) Dance marathons	(b) Muscle cars	(a) Wearing caps backwards
(a) Dashboard hula girls	(b) Patent leather shoes	(b) Western TV shows
(b) Double-knit clothing	(a) Peace symbols	(b) White belts
(a) Earth shoes	(a) Penny loafers with pennies	(b) White shoes
(a) Fabio	(b) Plaid pants	(b) White-wall tires
(b) Fake fur	(a) Pet rocks	(b) Wing-tipped shoes
(a) Flagpole sitting	(b) Platform shoes	(a) Women's bat-winged glasses
(a) Fruit striped gum	(a) Playboy clubs	(a) Zodiac merchandise
(b) Granny glasses	(a) Poodle dresses	(a) Zoot suits
(b) Halter tops	(b) Saddle shoes	
(a) Happy face stickers		
(b) Hot pants		

Notes: (a) = fad; (b) = fashion.
Notice that fads may start out by appealing to a relatively small group of people (e.g., a subculture). However, they may gain sudden popularity and reach a wider audience for a short period of time, after which they may revert to their former state or else disappear altogether. Fashions have more staying power than fads.

Source: www.angelfire.com/fl/JackCraig/FADS.html.

advantage over existing products or solutions. Most new products fail because they do not offer a differential advantage. In a 1994 U.S. survey, 7 out of 10 new-product managers doubted their company's success rate would improve, citing products that don't deliver on their promise (35 percent) and lack of compelling or motivating positioning (33 percent) as reasons for the failure. High failure rates have driven many firms to develop innovative new-product design programs incorporating new research techniques.[14]

At the midpoint in the continuum of innovation types, we identify **dynamically continuous innovations.** Dynamically continuous innovations require either *major change*

Styles as an Example of Continuous Innovation

INDUSTRY INSIGHTS 17.1

Platform shoes and designer jeans are an example of style innovations popular in the 1970s that reemerged in the 1990s. Style begins as a risk. Then it spreads as others seeking new ways to express themselves become aware of the style, and it ends as a cliché. Style emerges in the interplay between the deliberate inventions of designers, manufacturers, and merchandisers and the spontaneous actions of innovative consumers. Style in popular culture has replaced art as a source of aesthetic pleasure. Style depends on a process of collective selection, whereby participants in a social network agree on the value of products. Bohemian ghettos (e.g., Hamburg, Germany; the Parisian Left Bank; New York's SoHo and TriBeCa; Los Angeles' Melrose district) are a frequent source of innovations. Collective selection is a future-oriented activity that allows people to adapt to and mold the rapid pace of change in a market-driven society. Styles travel widely through popular communications vehicles such as the Bombay, Hong Kong, and Californian film industries, or via MTV and other music television networks.

Styles have an internal logic of their own, although styles are often rooted in deeper societal trends. There often is interdependence of meaning across popular cultural product categories. Styles affect the design of all sorts of products. Examples include the populux (or the "space age") streamlined designs of the 1950s when the Triad nations were infatuated with the idea of scientific progress; art deco of the 1930s, which melded a romantic sensibility to an interest in machine forms and surfaces and emerging technologies; and style of the Edwardian era, based on the mythic gentility of the British royal family of the Windsors that existed between World Wars I and II.

Sources: Joshua Levine, "A Lifestyle in a Label," Forbes, *November 1996, p. 155.*

in an area of behavior that is relatively unimportant to the individual or a minor change in an area of behavior that is very important to the user. Pesticide-resistant, hybrid corn seed for use in particular microclimates is an example of a dynamically continuous innovation typical of commercial agriculture in the Triad countries. Consumer examples include such things as Internet-ready cell phones, arthroscopic laser surgery, Viagra impotency medicine, and morning-after birth control pills. Digital Satellite System television that allows individual households to receive hundreds of digitally enhanced audio and visual channels is another example. A surprising example—the Ethiopian bucket—is profiled in Consumer Chronicles 17.2. Another dramatic example is provided by the rapid adoption of snowmobiles by reindeer herders in the arctic.[15]

The Ghanaian Kente cloth is in fashion among African Americans.

At the other end of our innovation continuum are **discontinuous innovations.** Discontinuous innovations entail *major changes in behavior in an area of importance to the individual or group.* Free-market capitalism is a discontinuous innovation in the transitional economies. Green revolution rice in developing nations in Asia with its complement of new fertilizers, insecticides, and farming techniques is another example. Cyber auctions, MP3

1. The more it fits with basic lifestyle changes, the more likely the new development will become a trend.
2. The more diverse and immediate the benefits, the more likely the new development will be a trend.
3. The more adaptable the new development is, the greater chance it has of becoming a trend.
4. If the new development is an expression of a basic theme rather than just an example of it, the more chance it has of becoming a trend.
5. New developments supported by developments in other areas are more likely to represent trends.
6. If support for a change comes from an unexpected source and key market segments, the greater chance it has of becoming a trend.

Source: Martin G. Letscher, "How to Tell Fads from Trends," *American Demographics*, December 1994, pp. 38–45.

EXHIBIT 17.1

Distinguishing Trends from Fads

music technology, and wearable computers are recent examples in the Triad nations.[16] Throughout the world, the advent of inexpensive techniques of birth control has had a major effect on behavior. In the early 1950s, the frozen TV dinner revolutionized American mealtimes and may have led to more atomized family life. Even common consumer nondurables may be thought of as discontinuous innovations if their introduction creates dramatic changes in individual and social behavior. In Sri Lanka, for example, the introduction of Western cosmetics has fueled a crisis in the role of women and altered gender dynamics.[17]

Discussion of the microwave oven provides a good example of the dramatic impact discontinuous innovations can have on behavior. Microwaves became available to consumers in the 1960s, but by 1980 only 15 percent of North American households had microwaves. During the decade of the 1980s, the reentry of women into the workforce and the emergence of professional women created new time pressures. As a result, by 1989, 80 percent of North American households had microwave ovens. A *Wall Street Journal* survey found that microwaves were the respondents' favorite household product. But the widespread use of the microwave has wrought tremendous cultural changes. First, it has transformed North Americans' sense of time. The amount of time many cooks are willing to devote to meal preparation has declined from about an hour in the 1970s to a little more than 10 minutes today. Second, it has transformed the division of la-

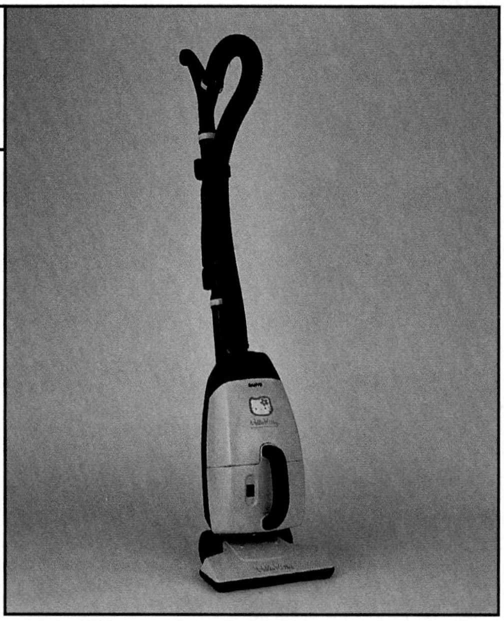

Hello Kitty merchandise represents a fad, but who knows?

bor within the household. The conventional association between mothers, nurturance, and food preparation is undermined as introduction of such products as microwavable Kid's Kitchen, Kid Cuisine, and My Own Meals turns children into food preparers. Some observers complain that Americans are no longer chefs; instead, they are a nation of "heaters," who find it difficult to prepare anything without the use of their beloved microwave oven.

These dramatic changes in behavior were facilitated by a subtle shift in North American values in the 1980s as both individualism and hedonism became more pronounced. Instant meals seem certain to remain popular as leisure time continues to shrink for many North Americans.[18]

> **CONSUMER CHRONICLES 17.2**
>
> **The Plastic Bucket**
>
> The plastic bucket has revolutionized the lives of Africans. You cannot survive in the tropics without water; shortages are always acute. Water has to be carried long distances. Before the invention of the plastic bucket, water was carried in heavy vats made of clay or stone. The wheel was not a familiar aspect of African culture; everything was carried on the head, including heavy vats of water. In the division of household labor, it was the woman's task to fetch water. The appearance of the plastic bucket was a miracle. To start with, it is relatively cheap. And it comes in different sizes; even a small child can carry a few liters! Now, it is the child's job to fetch water. What a relief for the overworked African woman!
>
> *Source: Ryszard Kapuscinski, "Plastic Buckets and Ballpoint Pens," from the Emeror (1984), Picador.*

Innovation Characteristics That Influence Adoption

When introducing new products, an organization is asking customers to change their behavior in some way. Implicitly, the organization is asking customers to take a risk by doing something new. As a result, success is more likely when marketers can optimize the benefits associated with the new behavior while also minimizing the risks or disadvantages. Indeed, many studies find that product characteristics are better predictors of adoption than personal characteristics of the adopters.

From the standpoint of a marketer, successful new-product introduction plays an important role in profitability. Being the *first firm to market a product successfully in an emerging market* often leads to what is called **pioneering advantage.** For example, Jeep defined in many consumers' minds what is now termed the sport-utility vehicle category. Curiously, British Leyland's Land Rover lost out on this opportunity. The fact that Jeep helped define the ideal point for this category meant that later entrants were inevitably compared with the pioneer and often suffered in such comparisons.[19] Can you think of examples of other products that set the standard in their categories as does Jeep for SUVs?

Extremely favorable evaluations may be formed toward the pioneer that leads. Pioneering advantage, in turn, leads to market leadership as measured by market share and return on investment. Successful new-product development is an important element in achieving long-term competitive success. For these reasons, identification of product characteristics that influence diffusion and adoption decisions has been a focus of research not only in marketing but across the applied social sciences.[20]

Probably the most important factor to the success of an innovation is its perceived **relative advantage,** that is, the extent to which it is viewed as *providing clear benefits for the target market that are superior to those offered by competitive market offerings.* Many market failures and slow adoption rates can be traced to the absence of a relative advantage. Pen- or stylus-based computing was supposed to be the new paradigm in the late 1980s. Just one problem: The handwriting recognition software never worked, and it still does not. Hence, consumers detected no relative advantage over keyboards and voice recognition software.[21]

The nature of the relative advantage varies. In the mid-1980s, Chrysler Corporation captured a significant share of the U.S. auto market by introducing a minivan that met the transportation needs of an emerging market segment of suburban professional families. In the industrial sector, containerized freight was first used commercially in 1956. In 1968, 13 percent of North Atlantic sea freight was containerized. This figure had increased to 90 percent by 1990. The benefits to shippers in the form of ease of tracking, reuse, security, simplification of sea–land shipment, and reduced costs explain the speed with which this innovation has transformed the shipping industry.[22]

The examples given above illustrate functional benefits of innovative products. Symbolism is another important source of relative advantage that works to speed the diffusion process. For example, many newly professional, young French couples have adopted home freezers in spite of the high retail density in urban France. Why? Freezers symbolize the link between young couples and their farm-dwelling parents. The parents provide the young couples with homemade farm foods. In turn, young couples introduce their parents to frozen foods bought in the city. To take another example, shoe and clothing styles often spread quickly between inner-city teens and suburban wannabes.[23]

Relative advantage must always be assessed for the target market and within the context of the consumers' current situation. Cell phones have diffused rapidly in central Asian countries where landlines are absent. Electric cars have been slow to catch on because of perceived disadvantages in terms of appearance, range, speed, handling, and cost, despite numerous advantages from an environmental perspective.[24]

The **compatibility** of an innovation refers to the extent to which the innovation is *consistent with present needs, motives, values, beliefs, and behaviors.* Another perspective might be that the more an innovation option tangibly resembles the traditional solution to a problem, the more likely it is to be adopted, regardless of its actual ability to perform the requisite task.[25]

Numerous examples of compatibility can be cited. Debit cards are a widely diffused payment option in the United States thanks to a well-wired communications infrastructure. Smart bankcards are more popular in Europe where electronic integration is less well developed. Wrinkle-reduction creams, sunscreens, and anti-aging formula vitamins are highly compatible with the baby boomer (those born between 1946 and 1964) segment's youthful self-image. In the African nation of The Gambia, sesame recently achieved dramatic success as a crop because it could be fit into the agricultural cycle after other major crops and because it provided a needed source of vegetable oil for the diet.[26]

Incompatibility, like relative advantage, may be based on either functional or symbolic properties, or both. For example, the diffusion of many quality improvement practices in business, including those designed to improve customer satisfaction, often involve cross-functional teamwork. Cross-functional teamwork is often incompatible with the top-down structure of traditional business organizations.[27] In consumer goods, electric cars have been slow to achieve popularity in part because of the incompatibility between electric fueling and gas fueling options and in part because their short range conflicts with the symbolic freedom the auto provides.

Trialability, or customers' ability to *try out an innovation without incurring risk to valued resources* (financial, esteem, status, time, information), is another factor critical to successful diffusion of innovations. All sorts of strategies may be used to improve the chances of product trial. The Japanese government facilitates trial of electric cars by offering sales tax exemptions and tax credits (see Ethical Dilemma 17.1). Celebrities may be hired to try out new consumer nondurables and report their findings to their

Innovative Technologies and Sustainable Economic Development

ETHICAL DILEMMA 17.1

Organizations evaluate innovations to determine if they will help them meet their objectives (e.g., in terms of market share, sales, shareholder value). Consumers evaluate innovations to determine if adoption will meet their needs or offer a better solution to an existing problem. However, innovations and new technologies also can be evaluated from a societal perspective. Will adoption of this innovation improve the quality of life for an entire society or community?

Consider the related areas of "sustainable economic development" and environmentalism. Nations want to achieve a level of growth and prosperity that is sustainable over a long period of time. To cite one example, the U.S. Congress establishes standards, in terms of fuel efficiency, that all new cars must meet. According to Bill Magavern, Senior Legislative Representative with Sierra Club California, "Raising auto fuel economy standards is an essential element to a balanced energy plan that offers quicker, cleaner, cheaper and safer energy solutions. Making cars go further on a gallon of gasoline is a simple solution to halting rising gas prices and global warming pollution."

In order to achieve such objectives, some governments are offering incentives to corporations to encourage them to build a new generation of automobiles. For instance, the state of California mandates that at least 4 percent of all cars produced for sale in that state be zero emission vehicles (e.g., electric cars).

@ www.prius.toyota.com

In Japan, Toyota launched the Prius, a hybrid-electric car that sells for approximately US$16,000. The Prius costs approximately $40,000 to manufacture, but government subsidies make up the difference. As indicated by Bill Magavern's quote, society has an interest in encouraging fuel-efficient innovations in the automobile industry. Since the Prius is a hybrid car, it is powered by both a gasoline engine and an electric motor. The primary target market is car buyers who are concerned about the environment and who are willing to experiment with a new technology. One of Prius's competitors is the Reva, which is manufactured in Bangalore, India. The Reva is a fully electric car and, as a result, has no engine, clutch, gears, carburetor, radiator, or exhaust system. The Reva has less power and less acceleration than the Prius, but it will travel 80 kilometers on a single electric charge. It contains eight six-volt tubular lead acid batteries that are expected to last up to five years. At present, the Reva is available in India, Nepal, Malta, Hong Kong, Switzerland, and China. Toyota makes unique versions of the Prius for sale in three distinct markets: Japan, North America, and Europe.

@ www.revaindia.com

As is apparent in the preceding paragraphs, some governments are convinced that they must intervene in the marketplace to encourage the development and adoption of innovations. After receiving sufficient economic incentives, a number of corporations accept government direction and introduce products that match their government's vision. But a key question remains. Will consumers adopt these innovations? A recent survey by J. D. Powers and Associates indicates that 75 percent of Americans don't know what a hybrid-electric is, much less how one operates. Hence, the future of the electric car is uncertain in the world marketplace.

@ www.jdpa.com

To what extent should governments subsidize the development of new technologies? How should the government select innovations to encourage? Under what circumstances do market forces fail to produce sufficient innovations (e.g., in the environmental area)? Would you purchase and drive an electric car? Why or why not?

Sources: ens.lycos.com/ens/jan2001/2001L-01-30-06.html; Sierra Club, "Higher Miles per Gallon Standards Would Save Californians More than 1 Billion Dollars Annually," San Diego Earth Times, *July 2001, pp. A13–A14; www.revaindia.com; and Eric Arnould, Linda Price, and George M. Zinkhan,* Consumers *(New York, McGraw-Hill/Irwin, 2002), pp. 569–70.*

fans. Firms may engage in sampling like E & J Gallo's online wine tastings or low-cost trials as Toyota has done in the United States with the Prius.[28]

Many products fail because of difficulties associated with trial, especially products that affect the customer's body or sense of self. Thus, radial keratotomy, a Russian surgical procedure used to correct near-sightedness, has been relatively slow to catch on in the United States, at least in part because of the perceived inability to reverse the procedure in case of error.

Observability plays an important role in the diffusion of innovations. For fashion goods and other sorts of goods consumed publicly, social visibility speeds innovation. Conversely, the nonobservability of privately consumed goods may impede diffusion. In the latter case, the evaluations of relevant opinion leaders or reference groups are less accessible to consumers.

Complexity is a factor that may impede the diffusion of innovations and hinder adoption. By **complexity,** we refer to *the difficulty of understanding product benefits and the relationship between attributes or features and those benefits.* Consider a new product marketed by Toyota—the Prius hybrid-electric car (see Ethical Dilemma 17.1). Ignorance about what a hybrid-engine vehicle is may impede the diffusion of Prius and its competitors. Almost by definition, discontinuous innovations (e.g., electric cars) are complex because they ask a consumer to undertake a new way of life.

One problem for marketers is that, as innovations become more complex, people may use shortcuts to evaluate them. That is, they may evaluate complex innovations on the basis of a small set of familiar characteristics that may or may not be appropriate for judging the innovation.[29]

There are also important societal and ethical issues associated with innovations. As described by Schumpeter, the capitalist system generates a never-ending stream of innovations. But when is that stream of innovations not enough? To what extent should the government intervene in the marketplace? What is the proper role of consumers in the innovation process? For example, will consumers make individual choices that are sometimes not in the best interest of society as a whole? See Ethical Dilemma 17.1 for an example related to environmentalism and the electric car.

KEY CONCEPTS IN THE STUDY OF CONSUMER CHANGE

Diffusion and Adoption

DIFFUSION The **diffusion process** refers to *the spread of an innovation from its creative source across space and time.* The process may take a variety of forms. An S-shaped, or sigmoid, curve has been observed in a number of marketing studies of consumer durables. In such cases a few buyers are initially convinced of the merits of adoption. Then, more decide to buy. For example, 35,000 microwave ovens were sold in one Spanish town in 1987. Later, larger, more reticent groups of buyers adopt. Thus in 1995, 650,000 microwaves were sold in the same town. Later still, a smaller laggard group adopts the innovation. The snowball effect as the product diffuses gives the adoption curve its familiar S-shaped pattern. However, diffusion may also follow an exponential adoption pattern. That is, it proceeds at a constant rate. The rate may be slow in a diverse social system. The rate may be rapid if buyers face low costs of adoption, are confident of their abilities to evaluate its benefits, or are relatively uninvolved with the innovation. Sales of Viagra, the impotence medication that sold 37,000 units in the first two weeks on the market, provides an example of a rapid exponential diffusion pattern. Fads assume an inverted V shape, exponential adoption, followed by dramatic decline in adoption and sales.[30] Diffusion curve patterns are shown in Exhibit 17.2.

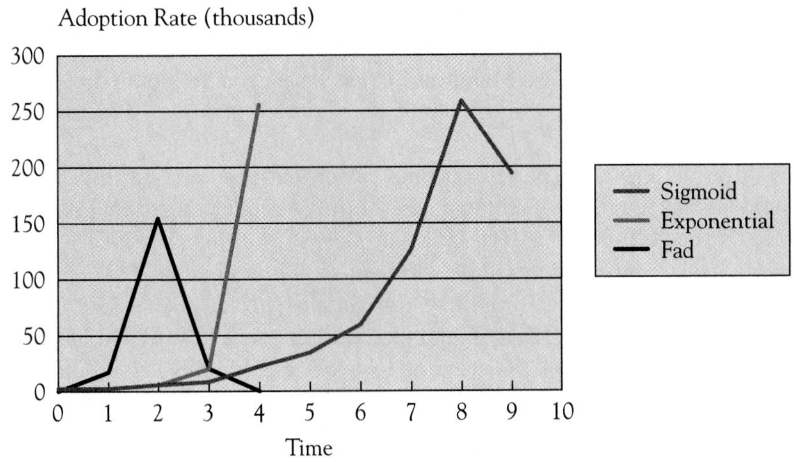

EXHIBIT 17.2

Diffusion Curves

PRODUCT LIFE CYCLE Products, just like people, undergo a life cycle. They are born. They grow and mature. They grow old and eventually die. A generic product life cycle (PLC) takes the shape of an S-curve, because it mimics the adoption pattern discussed in the previous section. A life cycle can be constructed for a product category—such as organic food products, a category that has grown by 900 percent in the United States since the 1980s. Or it can be constructed for a specific brand: the life cycle of the Plymouth brand, for example, a brand that DaimlerChrysler is now deleting from its product line. The PLC varies by product category and across world market regions, as suggested by Consumer Chronicles 17.2. There the product (the plastic bucket) was in the growth stage; in the Triad countries it is a mature product. The speed of the PLC also varies by category and world area. The Internet seems to speed up PLCs.[31]

The first phase is labeled as introduction. At this stage, consumers have relatively little knowledge about the new product, so promotional expenses are high and consumers rely on promotion for information. Profits are expected to be negative in the initial years of introduction. During the growth phase of the product life cycle, sales start to increase dramatically. Many new customers come into the market. Interpersonal influence plays a more important role in the adoption process in this phase. Attracted by this growth in sales and profits, new competitors also enter the market, and prices fall. At the maturity phase, sales begin to flatten out, and industry profits also decline. At this stage, brand loyalty is likely to be high, so it is difficult to get customers to switch to new brands. In the decline phase, industry sales begin to decline as customers lose interest in the product category, as in the U.S. chewing gum market.[32] It may be that new products are developed to satisfy the needs that were previously served by the declining industry. For instance, the microchip has replaced the integrated circuit, which previously replaced the vacuum tube. Still there are audiophiles who are loyal to audio products made from old vacuum tubes. The product life cycle is mentioned again later in the chapter, when we discuss the five adopter categories. See Exhibit 17.6.

SPACE Diffusion takes place across geographic space. For example, a dance style may diffuse from the streets to a modern dance studio, from urban areas to rural ones, or from urban areas in one country to urban areas in another country. Product innovations that present a low financial challenge may undergo more rapid diffusion.[33] The diffusion rate is faster for countries where the products are introduced later than for the countries where the product is first introduced. Hence, technologies that took a long time to diffuse in the country of origin will, in certain cases, diffuse more quickly when introduced into other countries. Microwave ovens have diffused rapidly in Spain since 1990, for example.

TIME Diffusion also takes place over time. Diffusion time varies with product category, product characteristics, and the nature of the communications environment. For example, the **neighborhood effect** says that *people who are close to the source of information concerning an innovation will tend to adopt more quickly than potential adopters situated at a distance from the information source.*

In one Spanish market, researchers found that refrigerators and washing machines diffused slowly. Laggards (see the discussion of adopter categories below) did not consider their adoption decision until 24 years had passed from the introduction of the refrigerator and 31 years from the introduction of the washing machine. It took 11 years for the dishwasher to reach early adopters! A later study found that glass-ceramic kitchen range tops also have diffused slowly in the Spanish market. The authors point out that this adoption is related to the time when people replace their kitchen, and, since this is a major purchase, the diffusion cycle will inevitably be long. Similarly, the first experimental U.S. television broadcast took place in 1933, but by 1950 only a million U.S. households owned expensive TV sets. Today, 98 percent of U.S. homes contain at least one TV set. The television market in the United States is now saturated, but television is now diffusing in rural China and Africa.

Conservatism, Resistance, and Discontinuance

Western marketers often *assume that people are predisposed to consume new or novel products, services, and experiences.* We call this a **pro-innovation bias.** Prior to the consumer revolution in the West in the mid-eighteenth century, material desires for the majority of people often focused on a relatively limited set of conventionally agreed-on goods. Of course, exceptions to the rule can be found among elite groups throughout antiquity and even prehistory, but a materialist orientation is relatively recent for most people. Further, in transitional economies, a history of political constraint has not produced the autonomous, innovation-prone consumer decision makers assumed by Western marketers. Traditional attitudes and resistance persist among older and lower-class consumers.[34]

Consumer conservatism and resistance are widespread in the world. By **innovation resistance,** we mean *a preference for existing, familiar products and behaviors over novel ones.* That is, resistance to change refers to any conduct that serves to maintain the status quo in the face of pressure to alter it. Bureaucratic organizations, including corporatives, are often allergic to changes in the status quo.

Some authors explain innovation resistance in terms of an intrinsic desire for **psychological equilibrium.** The notion of psychological equilibrium reflects *the human desire for balance, order, and consistency between beliefs and behaviors.* New ideas have the potential to disrupt existing patterns. Because changes imposed on behavior can disrupt psychological equilibrium and require psychological and behavioral adjustments, many consumers resist innovations.[35]

Some authors discuss innovation resistance in terms of **social equilibrium,** *the symmetry within social groups about the meaning of things and the meaning of one group to another.*[36] Where society is stable, innovation may be viewed as undesirable because it has the potential to disrupt the social equilibrium. Consumer Chronicles 17.3 profiles the Italian "Slow Cities" movement that represents an effort to maintain social equilibrium in the face of global marketing. Farming populations have frequently been labeled as resistant to innovations, although their conservatism is often a response to perceived risk in the social environment. Of course, periods of social upheaval are likely to be accompanied by a breakdown of innovation resistance and an influx of new ideas, products, and services. As discussed below, perceived characteristics of innovations also affect consumer resistance.[37]

Discontinuance is another aspect of the diffusion process that is important to marketers. By discontinuance we mean that *the consumer stops purchasing or using the product.* Marketing researchers have generally not focused on this aspect of the diffusion process. Discontinuance is the other side of innovation. Changing consumer need or competition may lead to discontinuance. When VCR technologies were first introduced, several competitive technologies were offered. Although many feel it was technically superior, most users discontinued use of Betamax technology. The VHS format was perceived to have superior **product complementarity.** In other words, VHS was perceived to have a fuller array of market offerings (e.g., more video titles) than the competition. As a result, consumers discontinued use of one product (technology) in order to adopt another, with negative consequences for the sales and market share of the abandoned product or brand.

Discontinuance occurs for other reasons besides changing needs and competition. For example, the state of Vermont offered its residents a really new electricity plan. Under this plan, residents were charged different rates depending on what time of day they consumed electricity. Rates were higher during peak consumption periods and lower during off-peak periods. Adoption of this discontinuous innovation required consumers to make significant behavioral changes in order to take advantage of the differential rate structure. Households that elected to adopt the new rates without being fully aware of the required behavioral changes quickly became disillusioned with the new rate plan and dropped it. Due to inertia, consumers do not like to make a lot of unnecessary changes in their lives. Thus, when consumers believe that a proposed behavioral change is too costly, then they are likely to discontinue the product that is causing this disruption in their lives.[38]

One interesting reason for discontinuance is that consumers perceive that the product or service has become too popular with other consumers or the adoption of the product by other consumers changes the benefits offered by the product. For example, people who regularly travel to Hawaii for vacations may decide it's become too commercialized and crowded and select more out-of-the-way vacation spots.

Consumer Resistance and the Slow Cities Movement

CONSUMER CHRONICLES 17.3

Nearly three-dozen Italian cities and towns have banded together to form a new league of "Slow Cities," joining a burgeoning international movement to promote homestyle food, local crafts, and all-around good living. The new Slow Cities league is a project of Italy's chief municipal alliance and of Slow Food, an international movement formed in 1989 with the aim of safeguarding culinary traditions.

Born of a backlash against fast-food, the Slow Food movement boasts roughly 40,000 members in 35 countries, a slick magazine published in five languages, and a popular biennial food show.

With 33 member towns, the Slow Cities network aims to expand internationally while remaining exclusive, network president Paolo Saturnini says. To be eligible for membership, cities and towns must introduce measures on everything from banning car alarms to the promotion of organic agriculture, including the creation of centers where visitors can sample local traditional food in a setting in harmony with nature. Towns making the slow-food grade will benefit from a joint marketing strategy to attract tourists and investors, Saturnini says. They also will be able to proudly display the Slow Cities logo—a snail crawling past two buildings, one ancient and the other modern.

Source: Peter Thayer, "Italy Says 'Yes' to Slow Value," Marketing News, August 14, 2000, p. 19. Reprinted by permission of the American Marketing Association.

THE CONTEXT OF INNOVATION, DIFFUSION, AND DISCONTINUANCE

In this section we describe the environmental, cultural, and social contexts for innovation and diffusion. In addition, we discuss how social groups influence innovation and adoption decisions.

The Environmental Context for Innovation

The environment for change is often neglected in marketing studies of innovation, but it is crucial. Environmental factors that affect innovation include the ecology, economic conditions, and market structures. Ecology, including aspects such as terrain, climate and population density, has broad effects on innovation processes. The homily "necessity is the mother of invention" is not without foundation. The diffusion of many innovations is based, at least in part, on changing environmental conditions that provide incentives for adaptive responses. For example, in arid parts of the world, farmers have often been quick to adopt drought- or pest-resistant crop varieties when these advantages are not outweighed by disadvantages such as increased labor requirements.[39] Good Practice 17.1 provides an example of an exciting innovation in water-harvesting technology designed to cope with arid environments.

Economic conditions and market structures also have broad influence on innovation processes. Diffusion of innovations is embedded within a particular market context. The developed world, the developing world, and transitional nations have radically different economic conditions and market structures that, in turn, drive different rates and types of innovative processes. True to Schumpeter's ideas, businesses in Triad economies invest heavily in innovation; this investment creates a rapid rate of introduction of new products.[40] A factor that drives receptivity to innovation on the national level is purchasing power. Greater receptivity to innovation is related to higher purchasing power. The rate of new-product introduction is also influenced by factors such as **demand density,** *the distribution and number of consumers who desire and can afford a product.*[41] Demand density is similar to the concept of "substantial segments" that we discuss in Chapter 5. A marketing manager evaluates a potential target market in order to determine if it is substantial enough to warrant a unique marketing effort (e.g., in terms of price, promotion, product, or distribution). In the same way, when the potential demand for a product is large (or dense), we can forecast that these favorable circumstances will stimulate rapid diffusion rates. When demand density is high and when market segments are substantial, then we have indications that marketing efforts will fall on fertile ground and be rewarded with success.

The overall rate of introduction of new products in a marketplace is an important environmental condition. In a quickly changing environment, consumers are generally aware of the need for change, the pace of technology, and the costs of choosing the wrong technology.[42] In such environments, many consumers are active participants in the change process.[43] In contrast, in volatile and uncertain market environments, consumers' reliance on informal exchange relationships for vital consumer goods may make them resistant to formal market system innovations.[44] Marketplace variables also influence the rate of introduction of new products. Such things as channel structure and efficiency affect the rate of new-product introduction because they affect the availability both of information and products. The rate of new-product introduction is also influenced by industry competitiveness and productivity.[45]

Fog Harvest Makes Desert Bloom

GOOD PRACTICE 17.1

The villagers of Chungungo in northern Chile are a relatively happy bunch nowadays thanks to a Canadian-Chilean project, which could soon be providing water to thousands of desert communities around the world. In certain coastal regions, where the terrain is arid and mountainous and air rolling in from the sea very cold, a dense fog collects over the hills, forming a gloomy mass of water, which is frustratingly inaccessible to the parched communities beneath it. After years of research, scientists hit on a solution as simple as it is effective. Fine mesh nets, arranged like billboards across the mountain tops, trap the water drop by drop. As billions of droplets accumulate, they trickle down into a tube. The collected water flows down the mountain to a tank above Chungungo, where it is filtered and stored. The mesh is cheap and easily maintained. Maintenance is straightforward, and the only energy required is gravity. That is good news for isolated communities in at least 22 countries around the world. Scientists have pinpointed 47 areas on six continents that have the right climatic conditions to implement this new system of fog-water collection.

Source: Miranda France, "Fog Harvet Makes Desert Bloom," Tampa Tribune, *January 15, 1995, p. A20.*

The Cultural and Social Contexts for Innovation

The diffusion of an innovation is embedded within a particular culture and social system, although it may pass between cultures and societies.[46] Focusing on macro-level cultural factors can help us understand and predict the diffusion of innovations. The cultural environment and communication system are important to the diffusion process because they determine the unique social values of a particular country and they are pervasive to all marketing activities.[47] How marketing efforts interact with a culture determine the degree of success or failure of those efforts.

SOCIAL SYSTEM VALUES AND TRADITIONS In Chapter 2 we emphasized that marketers must understand basic values in order to be effective in influencing specific behaviors within a culture. To understand the diffusion of new products, we need to consider the values related to innovation and the extent to which those values are shared across members of a culture. Important cultural values include varying degrees of pressures to engage in innovative behavior and values associated with newness, innovative behaviors, and change. Cultural attitudes toward variety, newness, and time provide norms that affect individual innovative behaviors.

Historical studies suggest that some cultures have been more open to innovation than others. For example, Europe, during and following the period of the Enlightenment, was relatively open to new ideas, as compared with China after the eleventh century or Islam after the Arabs were expelled from Spain. These differences help to account for the economic success of Western capitalism's creative destruction relative to other competing systems in the nineteenth and twentieth centuries.[48]

Although comparative consumer research on relative innovativeness is scarce, some have detected national differences in innovativeness, others not. One study found that

Muria Purchase Conformity

CONSUMER CHRONICLES 17.4

The Muria make purchases in order to express conformity, not originality or individuality. A concern with belonging marks all phases of Muria life. Muria consumption is bound up with the expression of collective identity and the need to assert commitment to the village and its institutions. For example, one year the girls of Manjapur all obtained new saris with identical borders for the Play of the Gods ritual. Innovative consumption items are sought because all villagers are attempting to live up to a particular collective image. Needless to say, innovations are hard to introduce into Muria life, and although modern and Western goods are easily accessible to the Muria by local bus, such goods are not attractive to them. The Muria are dedicated followers, and none of them wants to defy the restraints of collective style. The motives of the young men who are now starting to cut their hair and dress more like the local Hindus is not to "look smarter than before" but to look less conspicuous in a world that is perceived as increasingly Hindu dominated.

Source: Alfred Gell, "Newcomers to the World of Goods: Consumption Among the Muria Gonds," in The Social Life of Things: Commodities in Cultural Perspective, *ed. Arjun Appadurai (Cambridge: Cambridge University Press, 1986), pp. 110–38. Reprinted with the permission of Cambridge University Press.*

Irish women have less need to engage in innovative behaviors and that they achieve their optimum level of consumption variety at a lower level than their U.S. counterparts. Of course, behaviors considered innovative for Irish women, such as wine drinking and movie theater patronage, have no such connotations for American women.[49]

In general, the diffusion rate and maximum penetration level of an innovation depend on the *innovation's compatibility with social system values.* For instance, the top-down authority structures that exist in many business organizations are often incompatible with team-based innovations in quality management or information-sharing technologies.

One value that affects the diffusion of innovations within a culture is whether the traditions of a society are more interdependent-communitarian or more individualistic. The more interdependent-communitarian the traditions of a society, the greater is the importance of group goals and the more likely individual goals are subordinated to the larger interests of the group. In such societies, values of integration or fitting in take precedence over values of standing out or distinction. So powerful is the collective boom-craze mentality in Japan, that once 5 percent of the teen-girl market endorses a product, another 60 percent will almost certainly follow suit in less than a month. And if a product can reach the *kawaii* (cute) spot, it can reach almost 100 percent market saturation within a week. In this cultural context, interdependence can fuel adoption of fad products. Thus, individualism may promote individual innovativeness, whereas a more interdependent orientation can speed adoption rates.[50]

Interdependence, or valuing integration over differentiation, often favors conservatism over change. For an example, look at the exaggerated conservatism of consumption in Muria located in the north-central part of Madhya Pradesh, India, described in Consumer Chronicles 17.4. The social life of the Muria is conducted as a series of large-scale eating and drinking occasions, and this establishes the standards by which Muria evaluate the world of consumer goods. Objects are desirable only if they have meaning within the context of public feasting; otherwise, they have no consumer value. Innovations that threaten core values are subject to resistance. Promoting the use of many birth control options (male and female condoms, miscarriage-inducing drugs) is difficult for symbolic reasons related to core values. Birth control represents cultural values that make advertisers wary and some consumers resistant to their use. Another example of how core values may evoke resistance to particular innovations is provided by resistance to consumption of white bread among some Ecuadoran Indians, for whom consumption of home-prepared, barley-based gruels is fundamental to values of hearth, home, women's labor, and ethnic identity. Symbolic obstacles to diffusion have no simple technical or marketing solution.[51]

SOCIAL HIERARCHIES Social hierarchies within and between social systems affect diffusion; however, the effect is complex and varied. This is partly because the nature of social hierarchies and mobility of people between levels of a social hierarchy vary so much from culture to culture. Social class and other social hierarchies were discussed extensively in Chapter 12. We will have more to say about the diffusion of innovations within and between social groups in the next section. In this section, we want you to notice how hierarchical relations broadly influence these flows in the social system.

Early researchers proposed a **trickle-down theory of innovation.**[52] According to this theory, *status rivalry between social groups acts as a kind of engine or motive force for innovation.* Low-status social groups follow the principle of **imitation** and seek to establish new status claims by adopting the products, services, and ideas of higher-status groups. High-status social groups follow the principle of **differentiation** and embrace new products to distinguish themselves from the low-status social groups. Imitation and differentiation account for the direction, tempo, and dynamics of innovation. The **two-step flow model** is a description of communication that is closely related to the trickle-down theory.

According to the two-step flow model of communication, *new ideas flow from the mass media to influential consumers who, in turn, pass these ideas on to others who are more passive in information seeking.* The two steps imply that there is one group of influentials who are attuned to the media and quick to adopt new ideas presented there. Then, there is a second, larger group who are more passive in their media use. This second group relies on the first to learn about new developments.

Trickle-down theory is an important theory for understanding innovation, but it makes several rigid assumptions about the hierarchical nature of social relations and social interactions. Nevertheless, in some social systems, these assumptions hold up reasonably well. Trickle-down theory has been revised to include trickle-across and trickle-up models of diffusion. These models recognize that media exposure allows simultaneous adoption of new styles at all levels of society. Often, as with American Hiphop culture that arose in the ghetto or European Afro-pop that arose in poor African nations, selective innovations of low-status groups are borrowed or imitated by high-status groups. More important, the definition of high-status and low-status groups may vary from situation to situation.[53]

Looking at the diffusion of innovation within and between social systems, we can see many illustrations of social hierarchies and their effects. For example, in countries with developed market systems, fashions tend to flow outward from larger, more complex market centers such as Paris or São Paulo to smaller, simpler market centers such as Nancy, France, or Curitiba, Brazil. Similarly, the sequence of countries adopting an innovation is dominated by a hierarchical pattern. For example, digital communication technology has diffused from the First World to the Third World over a period of several decades.[54] An example of the diffusion of commercial pop culture from Taiwan to other parts of Asia is provided in the opening vignette.

CULTURAL PRODUCTION SYSTEM A **cultural production system** (CPS) is *a set of individuals and organizations responsible for creating and marketing culturally significant products.*[55] A CPS helps determine the types of products that emerge as fashion trends. It draws on a limited pool of symbols, myths, images, and rituals to create products that are anchored in cultural context. A good example is the CPS for popular music that turns out "new" hits that regularly recycle old themes, melodies, and rhythms. Country music in the United States is a highly developed example. Consider Travis

www.travis-tritt.com

Tritt, who signed his first recording contract in 1989 with Warner Brothers' Nashville Division. As the years passed, his career expanded to include television acting and awards from the Country Music Association. His 2002 release from Columbia Records is entitled "It's a Great Day to Be Alive." Travis Tritt's songs recycle classic country music themes, repackaged for a twenty-first century audience that is global in nature. Again, F4 illustrates some of the many faces of a CPS, as this boy band influences TV viewing, music sales, clothing fads, speech patterns, and hairstyles. To some extent, the images offered by Travis Tritt and F4 are "manufactured" by marketers and other communication experts.

The CPS consists of three subsystems: creative, managerial, and communications. The **creative subsystem** attempts to anticipate tastes of the buying public and generate new symbols or products that express cultural values. Examples include Milanese (Italy) fashion houses or the Bombay, Hong Kong, and Hollywood entertainment industries. The **managerial subsystem** selects and makes tangible new product ideas, producing new symbols, going so far as to create new categories of personal identity such as Euroconsumers, buppies (black urban professionals), *bon chic bon genre* French yuppies, or *GQ* (magazine) warriors. The managerial subsystem serves the needs of an economic system, which depends on growth, obsolescence, and realization of profit for its existence.

Finally, the **communication subsystem** spreads the word about what's new, upcoming, and popular to various groups of adopters. The communication subsystem includes ad agencies, fashion and style magazines, fan clubs, international consumer television networks such as MTV and CNN, national ones such as the Home Shopping Channel, and international radio stations such as France Inter or Africa No. 1 in Gabon. Mobile sound trucks exemplify the system in rural Latin America. The communication subsystem also includes lots of tastemakers and gatekeepers such as trend researchers, agents, disk jockeys, retail buyers, magazine editors, interior designers, real estate agents, and the like. Their job is to make the new seem familiar and desirable to target markets, and, of course, their services are for hire by manufacturers. Effective elements of the communication subsystem earn enormous fees.[56]

Social Group Influence on Innovation and Adoption

In Chapter 1 we introduced the idea that, within societies, there are two opposing motivational tendencies. We might call them the motive toward imitation, or integration and affiliation with the familiar, and the motive toward differentiation, or distinction from others. These twin motives can be thought of as social motives that underlie an individual consumer's innovation resistance and innovativeness. Consumers look both within and outside their social groups and make comparisons and judgments about taste. Comparative judgments, in turn, lead to recurring innovative (or conservative) purchase and use decisions. The consumer behaviors triggered by such comparisons also reconfirm the existence of groups in society and the individuals affiliated with them as distinct, although not necessarily as superior or inferior.

Innovation and conservatism in consumer behaviors serve to integrate individuals with some groups and distinguish them from others. They also provide the basis for drawing distinctions within groups. Marketers are often faced with the challenge of identifying those groups and individuals to whom others turn when making social comparisons or seeking integration. Successful adoption by these opinion leaders speeds the diffusion process.

The key to understanding innovation in consumer behavior cross-culturally lies in understanding these fundamental processes of differentiation, comparison, and integration as reflected in the goods that people value. In systems undergoing qualitative economic change, such as the NICs and developing nations, consumers' motives are complex, and the search for material symbols of these processes include novel and even bizarre goods. The supertall platform shoes worn by the Japanese *amazonesu* or the taste for designer fashion among poor Congolese migrants to France are such examples.[57]

BETWEEN- AND WITHIN-GROUP COMMUNICATION Exhibit 17.3 outlines a model of innovation and adoption processes. The model suggests that innovations spread through communications between groups about the meanings of goods and services. In many marketing situations, inducements to innovate flow between different kinds of groups, between channel members in business-to-business contexts, or from firms to consumers. The fact that the groups are different (heterophilous) may impede diffusion. This is why marketers strive to stimulate observational learning from valued role models, employ an adaptive sales force, and stimulate word-of-mouth through reference groups. These techniques shift the focus of communications from between groups to within similar (homophilous) groups.

When groups agree on the value and meanings of goods and services, consumption serves to define and defend boundaries between groups and identify members within groups. Groups are differentiated from one another, and individuals achieve group integration by consuming agreed-on goods and services. For example, consumption of snow skis might serve to distinguish skiing from nonskiing groups, athletic from nonathletic groups, richer from poorer groups, or residents from nonresidents of alpine environments. Some innovations will be consistent with the overall pattern of prior beliefs and values and will, through processes of assimilation and modification, be absorbed into the common repertoire of goods that contribute to the status quo. Thus, skiing equipment has evolved to include novice and expert gear of various kinds, distinctions that subtly encode intergroup differences.

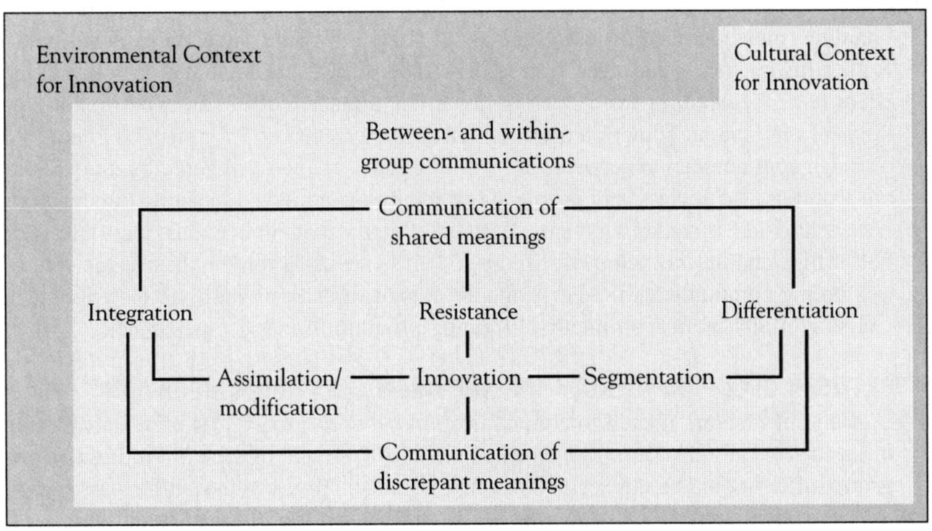

EXHIBIT 17.3

Innovation and Adoption Model

Discrepant consumption meanings fuel the snowboarding lifestyle.

In competitive, market-driven societies, discrepancies often arise about the meaning and value of products, services, and business practices. Discrepancies about consumption meanings create pressures for innovation. Some innovations are dramatically new and trigger new behavior patterns for at least some segments of the population. In some cases, innovations may lead to the creation of new population segments, causing changes in the relationships among and between groups in society. To continue the skiing example, an innovative skiing device that requires dramatic changes in skill, the snowboard, developed in the late twentieth century. Snowboards facilitated the emergence of a new youthful market segment, snowboarders. In the early days of snowboarding, snowboarders just used their ski clothing. However, snowboarders wished to further distinguish themselves from skiers. This desire, in combination with varied needs (e.g., the need for extra padding in particular places), led to an explosion of new kinds of clothing and other paraphernalia designed specifically for snowboarders.
Through communication between and within groups, changes triggered by innovations are absorbed into society, and people agree about the nature and meaning of new products, behaviors, or market segments. Without effective communications, innovations do not diffuse and are not adopted. Studies of effective diffusion emphasize the role of reinforcing communications. For example, a campaign to promote an electric car in Germany might include an intensive training program for service personnel.

BETWEEN-GROUP INFLUENCES ON INNOVATIVE, INDIVIDUAL BEHAVIOR Exhibit 17.4 outlines factors related to communication between groups and high-status group influence on individual innovative behavior.[58] As illustrated in the exhibit, **high-status group influence** has an impact on innovative behavior. To constitute a high-status group for innovation, a group must be viewed as attractive and as having ties to the innovation or consumption object, including special knowledge or expertise. The more that

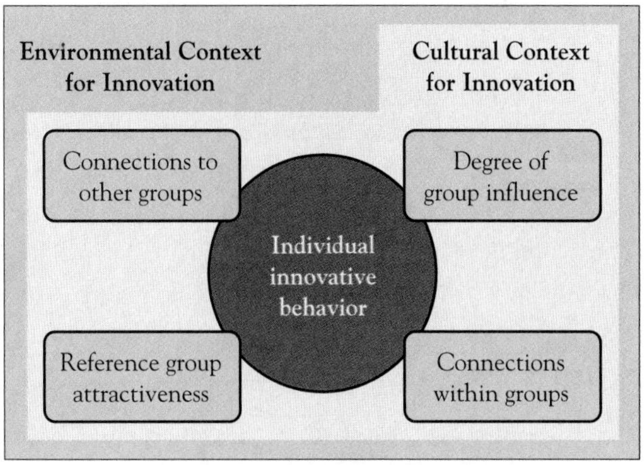

EXHIBIT 17.4

Group Influence on Innovative Behaviors

the high-status group is viewed as attractive and having an essential similarity to the consumption object, the more influential it is likely to be in purchase and possession of that product class. Japanese *amazonesu* mentioned above are a high-status reference group for Taiwanese fashion wannabes, for example.[59]

Consistent with trickle-down theory, the endorsement of a consumption object by a high-status reference group encourages innovative behavior by increasing expectations of social approval. This explains why top management endorsement consistently helps encourage the adoption of innovations within organizations.[60] Similarly, research on the diffusion of a new ethical drug among doctors in Ireland found that a trained and well-informed sales force strongly influenced doctors' adoption decisions. Research on quality improvement software in Norway and intranet technologies in South African companies confirms the influence of outside experts in encouraging adoption behavior. In another study, endorsement of a new cordless headphone system for a portable stereo system by U.S. ski team members had a positive influence on intentions to adopt the innovation among college students, living (and skiing) in the western United States. The endorsement by U.S. ski team members was related to the beliefs both that their peers would approve (adoption would have a positive effect on social approval) and that the system itself would have better sound quality (an influence on product evaluation).[61]

Another factor outlined in Exhibit 17.4 that positively influences individual innovative behavior is connections to high-status reference groups. Traditionally, this was thought of as face-to-face connections. In the case of cross-cultural diffusions, we must consider connections that occur through travel, work, and social occasions. For example, family ties between Indians living in Great Britain and India are an important channel for the diffusion of Western style and fashion into India, and travel to the West and interaction with Westerners are associated with higher levels of innovative behavior for Hungarians. Connections may be indirect as well. In many First World countries, various media offer a direct channel for learning about new products via celebrity endorsement.[62]

As suggested in Exhibit 17.4, explorations of innovative behavior must also consider the spread of novel goods and meanings *within* a social system, that is, the social communication networks for receiving information about an innovation. Exhibit 17.5 illustrates possible social communication networks for receiving information about an innovation. It depicts a **multistep media flow model** of communications. The figure reintroduces three important types of consumers discussed in Chapter 14 who pass

EXHIBIT 17.5

Multistep Media Flow Model of Communications

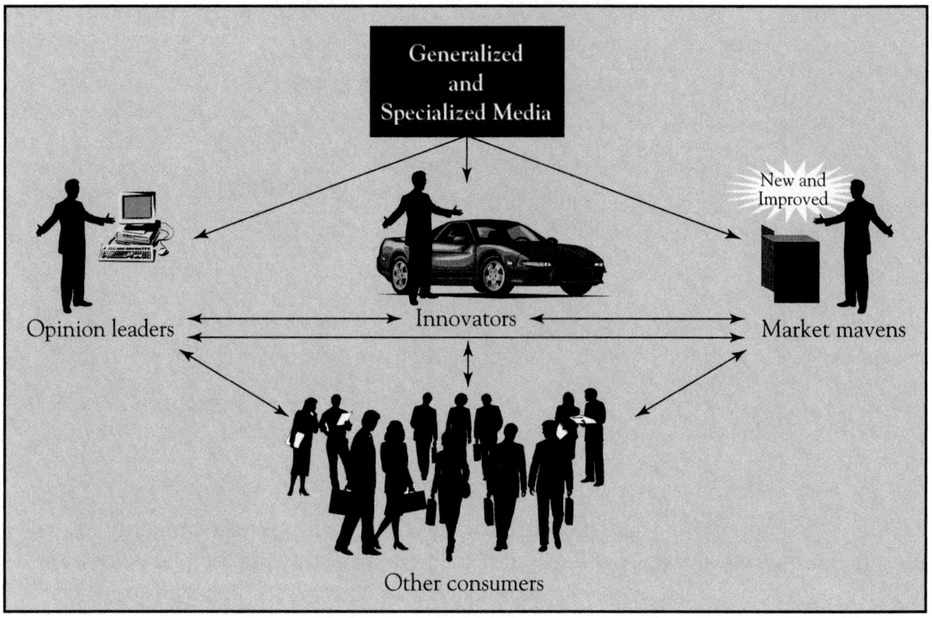

along information about innovations to other consumers in their social networks: opinion leaders, innovators, and market mavens.

Opinion leaders are individuals who act as information brokers, intervening between mass media sources and the opinions and choices of the population. Industry Insights 17.2 identifies one group of opinion leaders.[63]

Early adopters desire to look like pioneers in having purchased the new product, and they value the expertise that comes from the actual experience. Early adopters like to talk about the product and confirm their assessment.[64] Market mavens are characterized by general marketplace expertise and influence. Consumers rely on market mavens for information, and mavens provide market information across a range of topics. For instance, an online maven for fine dining can be found at The Food Maven website.[65]

@ www.thefoodmaven.com

Innovativeness turns on independence of judgment. Not surprisingly, opinion leaders, early adopters, and market mavens are all better connected to general and specialized media that provide them with more information than other consumers. Reliance on interpersonal information is also characteristic of opinion leaders and market mavens.[66]

To take advantage of interpersonal influence networks, marketers need to locate the influential consumers for their particular product or service and find a way of getting them talking about it. Toyota and Reva have done this through Internet campaigns for their electric car brands (see Ethical Dilemma 17.1). Industry Insights 17.3 illustrates how the Coca-Cola Company targets youthful opinion leaders so as to stimulate positive word-of-mouth.

Where consumers are able to identify opinion leaders, a link has been found between adoption of innovations and the views of opinion leaders about the innovation. For example, in a study of the adoption by dentists of nonprecious metal alloys in the construction of crowns and bridges, it was found that adopters of the nonprecious alloys cited experts whose evaluations of the innovation were favorable. Nonadopters and active rejecters cited experts whose evaluations of the innovations were not favorable. Furthermore, friends of experts were likely to imitate the adoption behavior of the experts, whether positive or negative. In a different context, a study of the adoption of new Western clothing styles among the Luo people of western Kenya in the early twentieth century emphasizes the role of chiefs whose influence was based on traditional authority and the role of Christian converts whose influence was based on new sources of knowledge and authority.[67]

Considering how individuals are connected within a social system is important to understanding change. In the Triad nations, we tend to take for granted that we will easily be able to find a friend or acquaintance who knows about stereo equipment. In many parts of the world, the assumption that someone knows an opinion leader in a particular product category (much less actually seeks him or her out for advice) may be misguided. In transitional economies, for example, available products and services have changed so quickly that few consumers have the expertise to help other consumers with their purchase decisions.[68]

> ## Identifying Influentials
>
> **INDUSTRY INSIGHTS 17.2**
>
> The firm Roper Starch Worldwide identifies a U.S. group termed *influentials.* These are trendsetting opinion leaders whose activism and expertise make them the natural source for word-of-mouth referrals. An estimated 10 percent of American adults aged 18 and older qualify as influentials. Many products and services that are integral parts of Americans' lives today got their initial boost from influentials, including VCRs, sport utility vehicles and light trucks, new varieties of take-out food, new kinds of restaurants, vacation spots, and health maintenance organizations. Influentials are probably giving each other advice much of the time, but the circle isn't entirely enclosed. In all, influentials account for 70 million restaurant recommendations a year, 62 million movie recommendations, 45 million TV referrals, and 44 million vacation referrals.
>
> *Source: Chip Walker, "Maximizing the Market with Influentials," American Demographics, July 1995, pp. 42–43.*

THE EFFECT OF OTHER USERS ON THE VALUE OF ADOPTION Frequently, other users influence the value of adoption to prospective users. A good example of what economists term a **positive externality** is provided by Internet price-search services. Their value is related to the number of other adopters. Their use diffuses rapidly across the hundreds of millions of Internet consumers because the cost of using and producing a search agent is largely a fixed cost: developing and updating the software and learning to use it. The greater the members of such services, the lower will be the cost of membership. The greater the consumer's use of such a service, the lower will be the cost of each search to the consumer and the greater will be the incentive to use the service. Feedback processes are everywhere, benefiting innovative and wired consumers.[69]

@ www.mysimon.com

@ www.botspot.com

There is a more subtle way in which the number of other adopters affects the value of the innovation. The number of other adopters can influence the *perception* of the quality associated with the innovation. For a dramatic example, consider the case of the transitional economies in central and eastern Europe. In this region, consumers were accustomed to a scarcity economy. Even now, as the flow of goods improves in many major cities, consumers still use lines as a cue to quality. If people are waiting in line for it, it must be good. This aspect of line psychology is illustrated in Consumer Chronicles 17.5. This bandwagon effect is found in other parts of the world too. Lines outside nightclubs and restaurants attract people who see the line as a signal of something special.

ADOPTION

So far, we have focused almost exclusively on the dynamics of diffusion. Certainly, the diffusion of innovations is a social process, so it is appropriate to focus on cultural and group variables that influence the relative time of adoption over geographic space.

Targeting Youthful Opinion Leaders

INDUSTRY INSIGHTS 17.3

The Coca-Cola Company introduced a new soft drink, Surge, that was targeted at young teenagers. One set of TV commercials showed urban youths, full of energy, drinking Surge and performing dangerous stunts (e.g., on skateboards). Surge has a relatively large amount of caffeine, so the slogan of the brand is "Feel the rush." In 1997, the soft-drink manufacturer also attempted to stimulate a positive word-of-mouth campaign by sending free copies of a CD to leaders in the teen community. The CD contained two parts: (1) a series of songs by groups popular with the target audience (e.g., Fatboy Slim, Third Eye Blind) and (2) "an arsenal of audio samples for crafting superb mix tapes." Coca-Cola managers used a variety of methods to identify teen leaders to include on their mailing list for this CD. The mailing packet also included coupons for both Surge and Tower Records. This joint promotional effort was very effective in stimulating sales for the new soft drink by targeting opinion leaders.

Source: http://www.lubbockonline.com/news/121796/cocacola.htm
http://www.teenagewildlife.com/music/Hunters/1998/coca_cola_surge/Title.html

However, the diffusion of innovations is also an individual process, and some individuals decide to adopt innovations before others do. In this section we turn our attention to the adoption process, that is, the decision by an individual to adopt an innovation.

The **adoption process** focuses on the *stages individual consumers or organizational buying units pass through in making a decision to accept or reject an innovation.* Marketers are very interested in the adoption process because knowing the profile of adopters, the numbers of adopters, and the timing of their adoption is critical to the success or failure of an innovation. This is equally true whether an organization is concerned with the adoption of innovations such as cellular phones, high-yielding seeds, or improved tillage practices; health and disease prevention behaviors; or management philosophies such as relationship marketing.

The decision to adopt or reject an innovation takes place over time. Adoption is not just an either-or decision; rather, due to the effects of the five adoption factors mentioned earlier, it involves varying degrees of acceptance or rejection. An innovation may be purchased but not really integrated into an individual's or household's life. When personal computers were first introduced, many people purchased them but then just let them sit and collect dust because they weren't sure what to do with them. This pattern persists with computer and home Internet use.[70] Similarly, many African farms are littered with unused farm equipment obtained through ill-conceived agricultural development schemes. In health care, social marketers are often very concerned about partial adoption. Consumers' erratic use of antiviral drugs is common, and it generates the awful side effect of encouraging the evolution of drug-resistant viruses.

Adopter Categories

In general, those promoting innovations want to identify customers who are most likely to change their behavior or try the new products first. Such knowledge is helpful in targeting marketing communications to reach these people. Therefore, research has sought to classify consumers into adoption classes. Several different approaches have been used. For example, the **time-of-adoption technique** defines adopter categories in terms of *purchases that occur some number of weeks, months, or years after product launch.* The **cross-sectional technique** determines how many of *a prespecified list of new products a particular individual or firm has purchased.*[71]

LEAD USERS **Lead users** play an important role in the development and spread of technological innovations. Lead users are users whose *current needs become general in a market in the future.*[72] Lead users often develop or support the development of innovations because of an industry-based need; that is, they simply can't do what they

Shopping in Russia in the Late 1980s

CONSUMER CHRONICLES 17.5

When I was about 13 years old, my family took a summer trip to Leningrad, the former capital of Russia. It is the most beautiful city I have ever visited, with summer residences of Russian emperors, fountains, and museums. All of it was fascinating. But what amazed me the most was not cathedrals or monuments. What captured my attention was the grocery stores.

Different kinds of cheeses, sausages, fish, everything already cut and packaged in small packages: 150 grams, 200 grams, 300 grams each. And customers were not grabbing 20 or 30 of those little packages but just 1 or 2. There was no sight of women carrying huge bags of groceries. Why would a person kill herself by trying to drag 10 kilograms of stuff home and then store it in her refrigerator for weeks if she could come back tomorrow and buy everything fresh? There were at least three grocery stores within walking distance from any person's home in most Russian cities, so getting to the store was not the problem. Why? I, as a teenager living in Krasnoyarsk, a big industrial city thousands of miles away from the capital in the late 1980s, thought the answer was obvious.

At that time, I was used to standing in lines. It was a big part of people's lives in all 15 republics of the Soviet Union, with an exception of only two cities, Moscow and Leningrad. Residents of these cities stood in line only to buy clothing. People would learn about what was going on in the world, hear rumors about private lives of celebrities, make friends, fall in love—all while standing in lines.

If it takes someone three hours to get sausage, would that person be satisfied with just 300 grams of it, especially if there might not be any sausage in the store for a week? Only if that person is crazy. Most people weren't, so they bought enough sausage to last for about two weeks. Five or ten kilos. There always was a limit to how much one person could buy. The limit varied by store and by how much supply the store had that particular day. Sometimes, my parents would phone me and tell me to come to the store so that we could buy more. Sometimes, on the days when a rare product (e.g., coffee or bananas) was available, my parents would call all the neighbors and friends so they, too, could stand in line to buy. Other times, we would just join a long line without even knowing for certain what was for sale. For us, a long line was a signal of something special.

In today's Russia, shopping is easy. When people in my hometown go grocery shopping, they only buy 200 grams of sausage at a time, because they will simply return the next day and get fresh meat. Now, when there are at least 20 grocery stores within easy walking area, shopping is convenient. However, if a shopper wants to buy 10 kilograms, it would cost more than a monthly salary. Now that it is possible to buy coffee and bananas in every store, is life better than it was 10 years ago? I don't know. To be honest, I don't even like coffee and bananas any more. I don't know any rumors about movie stars, and I'm not as politically informed as I was 10 years ago.

Source: "Consumer Stories: Vignettes with a Message," University of Georgia, Center for Marketing Studies, Working Paper Series (2001–1), George M. Zinkhan (editor), pages 14–15.

need to without an innovation. Lead users exist because important new technologies, products, and tastes do not affect all members simultaneously. One exploration of the rate of diffusion of important industrial goods into major firms in the bituminous coal, iron and steel, brewing, and railroad industries found that, in 75 percent of the cases, it took over 20 years for complete diffusion of these innovations to major firms. Hence, some lead users could be found far in advance of the general market.[73]

In consumer markets, some research has identified a similar group, a small segment of consumers who exhibit a great desire for unique consumer products (DUCP). This research also has produced a scale to measure DUCP, as shown in Good Practice 17.2. Care to take this test?

Desire for Unique Consumer Products (DUCP) Scale

GOOD PRACTICE 17.2

1. I am very attracted to rare objects.
2. I tend to be a fashion leader rather than a fashion follower.
3. I am more likely to buy a product if it is scarce.
4. I would prefer to have things custom-made than to have them ready-made.
5. I enjoy having things that others do not.
6. I rarely pass up an opportunity to order custom features on the products I buy.
7. I like to try new products and service before others do.
8. I enjoy shopping at stores that carry merchandise that is different and unusual.

Source: Michael Lynn and Judy Harris, "The Desire for Unique Consumer Products: A New Individual Difference Scale," Psychology and Marketing *14, June 1997, pp. 601–6.*

Exhibit 17.6 shows how the five main adopter categories map into the product life cycle. For instance, those who buy immediately after the innovation is introduced into the market are the lead users. They purchase at the early part of the introductory phase of the life cycle. Often, these lead users may have a difficult time actually finding the new product for sale, since distribution outlets are extremely limited. As such, lead users may rely on their superior marketplace and technical knowledge to ferret out sellers who carry the new product.

EXHIBIT 17.6

Relationship of the Diffusion Process to the Product Life Cycle

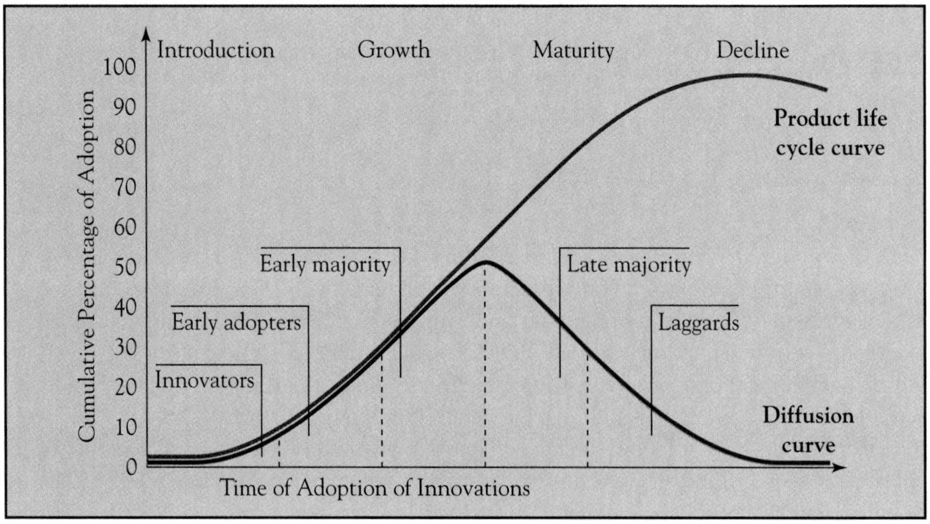

It's not easy to predict who will be innovative.

Source: DILBERT reprinted by permission of United Feature Syndicate, Inc.

INNOVATORS According to the scheme introduced in Exhibit 17.6, innovators represent less than 3 percent of adopters for a given innovation. The kids who started wearing old Hush Puppy Dukes and Columbias they bought in N.Y. thrift shops in the early 90s and fueled a subsequent sales increase of 950 percent by the peak of the fashion in 1996 are a good example.[74]

Although researchers have identified a segment with a general desire for unique consumer products, research generally shows that no generic innovators across product or service offerings can be identified. As the Dilbert cartoon above shows, it is not always easy to identify who will be innovative for particular products or which products will be the focus of innovation. For example, when first introduced, personal digital assistants proved incredibly popular with Japanese girls, who were not the original target market.[75]

Across national markets, innovative consumers share a number of characteristics. They are often venturesome, less risk averse, and younger; have higher incomes; and are better educated than later adopters. Active information seeking also characterizes their behavior. They are often more involved with media relevant to product categories that interest them and heavier users of products within a product class. Thus, researchers have found that a portion of the readers of personal computer and popular science magazines are highly involved with a range of computer and new high-tech tools and products, respectively. Innovators often have radial interpersonal networks. In other words, they are linked personally to many other people.[76]

As shown in Exhibit 17.6, the innovators purchase in the first half of the product introduction phase. These innovators play a key role in the success of the innovation by spreading the word to other consumers who might be interested in the product's benefits. When enough new users become adopters, sales start to take off, and the life cycle enters the growth phase of the life cycle.

EARLY ADOPTERS Referring again to Exhibit 17.6, early adopters typically constitute between 10 and 20 percent of adopters. They have been characterized as opinion leaders within local reference groups. This makes them important to identify since they influence others within their network.[77] They are sometimes highly involved with trends within particular product categories. When the early adopters begin to purchase, it is a sign that the innovation has entered the growth phase. Relative to the opinion-leading Japanese *yamanba* and *amazonesu* female youth tribes, the Taiwanese *hazitsu* are an example of early adopters. The *hazitsu* ape everything Japanese from the latest hairstyle to the cut of their trousers.[78]

Research on adoption of agricultural innovations among farmers has shown how complex the early adoption profile can be. In one Mexican farming community, wealthy farmers secure in their social status and the wealthiest of poor farmers, anxious to improve their standard of living, were both found to be more likely to engage in innovative behaviors than the poorest farmers and those in the middle of the social hierarchy.[79]

EARLY MAJORITY The early majority are often characterized as deliberative decision makers. They adopt innovations sooner than most of their social group but rely more heavily on interpersonal information sources than impersonal media in making their decisions. They often have interlocking personal networks that can be mobilized to facilitate the spread of innovations. For example, the diffusion of IUD birth control devices in the Philippines was accomplished by reaching interlocking circles of middle-income housewives.[80] As shown in Exhibit 17.6, early majority consumers begin to make purchases in the later portion of the growth stage.

LATE MAJORITY The late majority represents another third of the adopting population. They may be thought of as skeptical consumers, doubtful of the benefits of adoption. Lower prices that reduce risks stimulate late majority purchases, as when the cost of PCs fell below $1,000 and nudged up the U.S. penetration rate of PCs from 40 to 60 percent.[81]

Late majority consumers may be inclined to adopt in response to social pressures rather than as a result of the perceived benefits of adoption; that is, they are vulnerable to **bandwagon effects.** They adopt because "everyone is doing it," and the failure to adopt might provoke a loss of status or self-esteem. Both individual consumers (see Dilbert

Dilbert endorses the bandwagon effect.

Source: DILBERT reprinted by permission of United Feature Syndicate, Inc.

cartoon on page 738) and organizations are vulnerable to bandwagon effects. For example, most airlines have adopted frequent flier programs that reward repeat customers with reduced fares and free tickets in part because it has become expected practice. Offering such programs gives airlines legitimacy.

The bandwagon effect refers to the fact that exposure to novel information can lead to rapid shifts in mass consumption behavior, including adoption of innovations when people follow the behavior of others irrespective of what they believe or value themselves. Bandwagon effects seem to involve adoption when beliefs are not strongly held about alternatives. Bandwagon effects in politics, surgery, business, fashion, and sales of initial public stock offerings have been described. Bandwagon effects can be triggered by chance, but crucial adoptions by opinion or fashion leaders can speed adoption rates.[82]

Late majority consumers often exhibit characteristics opposite those of early adopters. Microsoft's software introduction Bob targeted the skeptical computer nonuser with what the firm hoped would be a user-friendly product.[83] Bob failed, but organizations are always looking for ways to overcome the natural skepticism of consumers, both about products and about promotional efforts.

LAGGARDS The final adopter segment is **laggards,** typically accounting for less than 20 percent of the adopting population. Laggards tend to be traditionalists, locally oriented in terms of networks and social horizons, and relatively dogmatic in beliefs and values. They also tend to be less educated. More older households and older consumers fall into the laggard category. Amazingly, 40 to 60 percent of customers at savings banks in New York City might be considered laggards. They still use passbook savings accounts that earn uncompetitive interest. Older consumers who recall the Depression of the 1930s, young technophobes, and recent immigrants belong to this group.[84]

Laggards may not begin to purchase until the product enters the decline phase (Exhibit 17.6). In this period, organizations may begin to minimize their promotional efforts and expenses. Competition may be reduced, as some firms choose to exit as sales and profitability levels decline. However, the firms that do remain in the decline phase may still prove to be profitable, as long as they continue to satisfy customer demand. In some instances, a declining product may be restimulated. Indeed, a good example of this phenomenon is designer jeans, revived by the trend toward casual business dress. Fashion items often display this cyclical product life cycle pattern, rather than the S-curve.

It is also worth distinguishing nonadopter segments. In addition to simple rejecters of a particular innovation, one may also encounter evangelical rejectionists, like those in the Slow Cities movement, who actively and publicly oppose some marketer-driven innovations, fast-food in this case. We've mentioned Adbusters and adherents of the voluntary simplicity movement in other chapters. These examples represent rejecter movements. In Japan, some oppose the importation of foreign rice. In the United States and Europe, many oppose proposals to irradiate vegetables or to alter food plants genetically.[85]

The Adoption Process

Marketers and others interested in changing consumer behavior have devoted considerable efforts to understanding the adoption process. The nature and scope of interventions in the process should be tailored to the stages adopters go through before adoption. Various models of adoption have been proposed, but the classical model of stages describes an extended high-involvement, decision-making process (see Chapters 7 and 15).

AWARENESS Awareness or knowledge of an innovation comes about through exposure to the innovation. Consumer inertia or lack of search may be a barrier to awareness. In media-rich environments in the Triad countries, the mass media generally promote awareness. In the transitional economies of eastern Europe, foreign travel or contact with people who had traveled abroad was an important source of awareness of new products prior to the collapse of communist governments. In many developing countries, periodic markets or traveling peddlers have long provided rural people with a glimpse of novel products. In a recent case involving palm cooking oil in Java, Indonesia, a mobile sales force proved crucial to creating awareness among vendors, who were the buyers. Among immigrant Mexican communities in the United States, "convenience stores on wheels," vendors selling out of trucks, provide newcomers with access to novel products.[86]

INTEREST Interest followed by evaluation and persuasion is a situation that creates awareness of relative need. Once a need or want is stimulated, information search begins. Acquisition of a mentor, access to an opinion leader, or exposure to a market maven can affect the potential adopter's perceptions of available alternatives. Online search engines have revolutionized the search process for wired consumers.[87]

At this point, innovation characteristics, such as **perceived risk,** affect the adoption process. Perceived risk may relate to product performance or to the social, personal, or financial costs of poor product performance. Lack of knowledge and inability to appreciate the relevance of an innovation's benefits cause consumers to limit information search. Marketers should take pains to address potential sources of perceived risk. Adaptive salespeople and consumer-rating services are important players in this process.

TRIAL In product trial, the adopter is moved to action. Sources of innovative goods and services are evaluated and a product is chosen. Trial often involves firsthand experience, but consumers also may "try" an innovation through the experiences of trusted acquaintances or **consumer surrogates,** *specialized expert agents retained by customers to guide, direct, or transact marketplace activities.*[88]

Trial may mean trying out the product category or just a new brand. Finding ways to try and evaluate certain new products is problematic for consumers. Often innovative products possess new and complex features (e.g., hybrid-energy vehicles, DVD disks, online books, or MP3 minidisks) that do not necessarily communicate obvious benefits over existing products. Adaptive selling, guarantees, warrantees, price promotions, and employment of surrogate consumers facilitate trial and reduce perceived risks of trial.

Ethical Dilemma 17.2 describes an example of surrogate consumers, in the context of promoting a new mobile phone that can double as a digital camera.

ADOPTION Adoption or rejection of the innovation follows trial. Although adoption is often treated as an either/or alternative, it is usually more complicated. To understand adoption, it is important to look at the ways an innovation is integrated into a consumer's lifestyle. In the case of many technologically oriented products such as home computers, the decision to purchase a technology is not as important to adoption as decisions that govern the use of the technology after adoption.[89] Does the home computer just sit in the study and collect dust, is it primarily relegated to kid's games, or is it an essential part of the household's everyday life? You may be able to think of many examples where use after purchase is important in describing adoption behavior. Perhaps you have friends who purchased exercise equipment that now sits in the garage unused or who joined a health club but now can't find time to go. In these and many other cases, consumers purchase new products or services but don't integrate them into their lifestyles. In this sense, they have not really adopted the products.

To understand adoption it is also important to consider overall adoption rates and consumption situations. For instance, studies of hospitals and retail clothing stores have found relationships between organizational adoption of innovations and overall adoption rates in competitive, urban environments. A consumer study in Taiwan showed that intentions to adopt canned Wulong tea varied, depending on the consumption situation. Specifically, the beverage was considered inappropriate for nighttime consumption because of background beliefs about the health effects of tea. A study in West Africa showed that adoption of a Western innovation, cigarette smoking, was associated with wage work in foreign, urban contexts but not with farm labor in domestic, rural contexts.[90]

A final point to emphasize is that marketing tactics can influence the adoption process. For example, a penetration strategy uses low prices, extensive distribution, and extensive communications to speed innovation. The signals conveyed by these elements of the marketing mix can induce broad consumer trial without extensive search and evaluation. By contrast, a skimming strategy makes use of high prices and selective distribution and communications to induce adoption within a narrow market, thereby limiting the scope of adoption.

ETHICAL DILEMMA 17.2

Guerilla Marketing Campaign

Sony Ericsson is a joint venture of Telefon AB L.M. Ericsson of Sweden and Sony Corp. of Japan. One of their new products is the T68i, a mobile phone that can double as a digital camera. To promote the product's launch, the firm employs a guerrilla marketing campaign. In one version, dubbed "Fake Tourist," 60 trained actors and actresses haunt tourist attractions such as the Empire State Building in New York and the Space Needle in Seattle. Working in teams of two or three and behaving as if they were actual tourists, the actors and actresses ask unsuspecting passersby to take their photographs, using the T68i. The result is an instant product demonstration. Sony Ericsson, which plans to spend $5 million on the 60-day marketing campaign, says that their campaign is all in fun and merely an effort to get people talking.

Some consumer activists disagree. "It's deceptive," says Gary Ruskin, executive director of Commercial Alert, when told about the campaign. "People will be fooled into thinking this is honest buzz."

Is such a guerrilla campaign ethical? Should the actors identify themselves as working for Sony Ericsson? Will consumers be disappointed or angry if they discover the ruse? Will the campaign be successful, in terms of generating positive word of mouth? Why or why not?

Source: "That Guy Showing Off His Hot New Phone May Be a Shill," from The Wall Street Journal, *July 31, 2002, p. B1 Eastern Edition by Suzanne Vranica. Copyright 2002 by Dow Jones & Co., Inc. Reproduced with permission of Dow Jones & Co., Inc., in the format Textbook via Copyright Clearance Center.*

SUMMARY

In this chapter we introduce several key concepts for the study of consumer change, including innovation, diffusion, and adoption. Innovation is a broad term that refers to new things, new ways of behaving and interacting with things, and new ideas, behaviors, or structures. Finding ways to improve the management of innovations is critical for organizations of all kinds. Innovations can be distinguished in terms of the behavioral consequences of the innovation for the users. Continuous innovations require only minor changes in user behaviors; discontinuous innovations require major changes. Several important characteristics of the innovation influence the adoption rate. The perceived relative advantage over existing options is the most important factor to the success of an innovation. Other important characteristics include compatibility, trialability, observability, and complexity.

Diffusion is the spread of an innovation from its creative source across space and time. Adoption refers to the stages an individual adopter goes through in making a decision to accept or reject an innovation. People in developed consumer societies may have a pro-innovation bias, but consumer conservatism and resistance are widespread. The desire for both psychological and social equilibrium contributes to innovation resistance.

Innovation and adoption processes are influenced by environmental, cultural, and social system factors. The development and diffusion of many innovations is based, at least in part, in changing environmental conditions that mandate adaptive responses. Economic conditions and market structures also have broad influence on innovation processes. The business sector of contemporary market economies invests heavily in innovation, and this investment creates a fast rate of new product introductions.

Cultural attitudes toward newness, innovative behaviors, and change provide norms that influence individual innovative behaviors. Cultural attitudes toward integration or fitting in (versus distinction or standing out) also influence rates of adoption within a social system. In general, the diffusion rate and penetration level of an innovation will depend on the innovation's compatibility with social system values. Innovations that threaten core values are subject to resistance. Cultural production systems—consisting of creative, managerial, and communication subsystems—are responsible for creating and marketing culturally significant products. Originating in the Triad countries, these cultural production systems increasingly influence the global marketplace.

Social groups have a critical impact on the diffusion of innovations. Innovations spread through communications between groups about the meanings of goods and services. Discrepancies about consumption meanings create pressures for innovation. The twin motives of integration and differentiation are key to understanding innovation and conservatism. Consumers look both within and outside their social groups and make comparisons and judgments. Looking at the diffusion of innovations within and between social systems, we can see many illustrations of the effects of social groups. One important early theory is the trickle-down theory of diffusion. The idea that innovations flow from high-status to low-status groups is still an important theory for understanding innovation.

Influential consumers often aid the spread of innovations within a social system. We review three important types of influential consumers: opinion leaders, innovators, and market mavens. The diffusion of innovations depends heavily on the flow of information, not just from media sources but between consumers as well.

In general, marketers are interested in identifying consumers who are most likely to change their behavior or try new products and services first. This has led researchers to classify consumers by their time of adoption. Adopter categories include lead users, innovators, early adopters, early majority, late majority, and laggards. The classical adoption process typical of a high-involvement decision includes awareness, interest, trial, and adoption stages. However, a number of situational factors affect this general adoption process.

KEY TERMS

adoption process 734
bandwagon effects 738
communication subsystem 728
compatibility 718
complexity 720
consumer surrogates 740
continuous innovations 712
creative destruction 710
creative subsystem 728
cross-sectional technique 734
cultural production system 727
demand density 724
differentiation 727
diffusion process 720
discontinuance 723
discontinuous innovations 715
dynamically continuous innovations 714
fads 713
fashions 713
high-status group influence 730
imitation 727
innovation 712
innovation resistance 722
laggards 739
lead users 734
managerial subsystem 728
multistep media flow model 731
neighborhood effect 722
observability 720
perceived risk 740
pioneering advantage 717
positive externality 733
product complementarity 723
pro-innovation bias 722
psychological equilibrium 722
relative advantage 717
social equilibrium 722
time-of-adoption technique 734
trends 713
trialability 718
trickle-down theory of innovation 727
two-step flow model 727

REVIEW QUESTIONS

1. Prepaid phone cards have been around for over a decade internationally, but the United States has been slow to adopt the new cards. How would you classify this innovation? What characteristics of the product are likely to influence the adoption and diffusion of this product?
2. Gridcore subpanels are lightweight, nontoxic, recycled alternatives to building materials such as particle board. They were invented and patented by the U.S. Department of Agriculture at the Forest Products Laboratory in Madison, Wisconsin. The engineered, molded fiber panels are produced from a variety of recycled materials. They come in several degrees of thickness without extensive use of toxic binders or resins. The manufacturing process uses no toxic chemicals, produces no toxic by-products, emits virtually no air pollution, and recycles 94 percent of the water used to make the boards. The ultimate goal of Gridcore Systems (exclusive licensee for manufacture and sale) is to create Gridcore panels that can be used for residential building systems. Develop a strategy for the diffusion of Gridcore panels.
3. Below is a list of six products that have recently been introduced into the U.S. market. Classify each innovation, and describe the diffusion pattern that you expect each product to have. Justify your answers.
   a. Oki color printer (www.okidata.com/mkt/html/nf/Home.html).
   b. BMW Z4 roadster (www.bmwusa.com).
   c. Celestial Seasonings Soothers, herbal throat drops (www.allergy-cold.com/conaffairs/celestialseasonings.shtml).
   d. Rayovac renewal rechargeable batteries (reusable 25 times or more) (www.rayovac.com).

e. A personal digital assistant that you wear as a wristwatch (www.informationweek.com/story/IWK20011109S0001).
f. The "second generation" Cadillac Escalade EST (www.cadillac.com/cadillacjsp/models/ext/index.html).

4. In 2002, the movie *Star Wars II—Attack of the Clones* was a big success. Discuss the cultural values that contributed to the success of this film.
5. A portable color computer, with a powerful processor, weighing in at around 7 lbs. now comes with a CD-ROM and built-in videocam. Describe how the company can develop promotional, pricing, and distribution strategies targeted to the innovators for this product. Be sure to describe who you think the innovators for this product will be.
6. The growth rate of wireless communications technologies has been phenomenal. Cellular telephone service needed only nine years to attract 10 million customers. To build a customer base of that same size, the fax machine required 22 years, cable TV service took 25 years, and the traditional landline telephone needed 38 years. Describe the product factors that have contributed to the growth of cellular telephone service. How do other users affect the spread of this product?
7. Describe a new fashion popular in your area. What factors have contributed to its successful diffusion?
8. Do you know someone who is an opinion leader for you in some category of products or services? If yes, describe the characteristics of this person that help make him or her an opinion leader. Are you an opinion leader for others in some category of products or services? Explain.
9. Explain differences between innovators, opinion leaders, and market mavens. Use examples from your own experience to help.
10. Describe the diffusion process for the World Wide Web. What factors are driving this rapid diffusion process? What kinds of businesses and consumers use the Web? Who doesn't use the Web? Why? Describe those who might be resistors of the technology.

YOU MAKE THE CALL

ONLINE PUBLISHING

@ slashdot.org/features/00/11/30/1238204.shtml

Stephen King has published more than 40 books, and he is the world's leading horror writer. He is also a pioneer in the field of e-publishing. So far, he has participated in three online experiments. In partnership with Simon & Schuster, he released *Riding the Bullet*. That novella was only available online and eventually sold 500,000 copies, even though many copies were given away free on such sites as Amazon.com.

In 2000, Mr. King bypassed his publisher altogether and sold his serial novel, *The Plant,* directly over the Internet. Readers could download each chapter for free, but, following an "honor system" payment model, readers were expected to send in one dollar if they liked the chapter. Amazon.com assisted Mr. King by collecting funds for downloads. Mr. King insisted that he would not keep posting chapters unless at least 75 percent of readers made payments. One hundred and fifty thousand readers downloaded the first chapter in July 2000, and more than 75 percent of those first-installment readers paid the one-dollar fee. Some readers paid extra, to make up for those who didn't pay. Amazon liked the system so much that they subsequently introduced their own "Amazon Payment System," where Amazon.com lends the use of its one-click payment technology to other websites in return for transaction fees. Subsequent chapters of *The Plant* did not attract so many readers or payers, and the project is currently suspended.

www.time.com/time/dreamcatcher

Mr. King's third online project was published on Time.com's website in March 2001 and offered, for free, three installments from this then-forthcoming novel, *Dreamcatcher*. The website proved to be an effective way to promote the new book.

It's not clear whether or not Mr. King's three online books scared his e-readers, but they instantly traumatized the publishing industry. We are entering an era where technologically empowered writers can bypass Stone Age marketing notions and sell their stories to readers without the benefit of traditional middlemen. Nonetheless, these online experiments were not a total success. *The Plant* is currently suspended, and later chapters did not attract the excitement and attention that was generated by the e-book's initial launch. To date, the Internet is a powerful but underutilized tool for selling books, not replacing them.

QUESTIONS

1. Identify the innovations described in the above story.
2. Classify each innovation in terms of the three categories of innovation described in the text. Justify your answers.
3. Identify barriers to adoption for each innovation, from the five identified in the chapter.
4. What marketing steps could be taken to initiate a bandwagon effect for online publishing and payment?

Sources: abcnews.go.com/sections/tech/DailyNews/king001129.html; writenews.com/2001/022601_king_dreamcatcher.htm; www.time.com/time/dreamcatcher/; slashdot.org/features/00/11/30/1238204.shtml; and news.com.com/2100-1023-243523.html?legacy=cnet.

CASES

ENDNOTES

1. Personal communications from Ms. Annie Hou, University of Georgia; pages.ivillage.com/vickazy; and www.scvmaxtv.com.sg/maxtv/eng/feature/0,1164,100,00.html.
2. George M. Zinkhan and R. T. Watson, "Advertising Trends: Innovation and the Process of Creative Destruction," *Journal of Business Research* 37, no. 3 (1996), pp. 163–71.
3. Marketing Intelligence Service Ltd., *Product Alert Weekly* (Naples, New York); and U.S. Census Bureau, *Statistical Abstract of the United States: 1999* (Washington, DC: U.S. Government Printing Office, 1999).
4. Sanford Grossbart, Lynn Samsel, and Madhavan Parthasarathy, "Diffusion, Discontinuance, and Development in Transition Economies," paper presented at the 22nd Annual Meeting of the Society for Macromarketing, Bergen, Norway, Norwegian School of Economic and Business Administration, 1997.
5. William E. Souder, *Managing New Product Innovations* (New York: Lexington Books, 1986).
6. Souder, *Managing New Product Innovations;* and Vincent P. Barabba and Jerry Zaltman, *Hearing the Voice of the Market: Competitive Advantage through Creative Use of Marketing Information* (Cambridge, MA: Harvard University Press, 1990).
7. Sandy Jap, "Online Reverse Auctions: Issues, Themes, and Prospects for the Future," *Journal of the Academy of Marketing Science* 30, no. 4 (2002), pp. 502–21.

8. Amanda Hesser, "Man Behind the Butter Pat Now Let's You Hold the Mayo, One-Handed," *New York Times,* July 30, 2000, sect. 3, p. 5; and David Midgley, "A Meta-Analysis of the Diffusion of Innovations Literature," in *Advances in Consumer Research,* vol. 14, ed. Melanie Wallendorf and Paul Anderson (Provo, UT: Association for Consumer Research, 1987), pp. 204–7.
9. Stuart Elliot, "How New Brands Become Too Much of a New Thing," *New York Times,* June 2, 1992; "New Products: Still Rising . . . Finding a Winner . . . Hassles," *The Wall Street Journal,* November 3, 1983, p. C1; Roger McMath, personal communication; Marketing Intelligence Service Ltd., *Product Alert Weekly;* and U.S. Census Bureau, *Statistical Abstract of the United States: 1999.*
10. "Mazda Develops World's First Miller-Cycle Engine for Practical Use," *Japan* 21 (July 1993), pp. 12–13; Joshua Levine, "Putting a Little Tingle in Your Kisses," *Forbes,* August 26, 1996, p. 76; and Marc Maremont, "How Gillette Brought Its Mach3 to Market," *The Wall Street Journal,* April 15, 1998, p. B1.
11. "Brand New Fad Makes Its Mark," *Tampa Tribune,* December 11, 1994, p. 18; Roland Barthes, *The Fashion System* (New York: Hill and Wang, 1983); Howard S. Becker, "Art as Collective Action," *American Sociological Review* 39 (December 1973), pp. 767–76; Fred Davis, *Fashion, Culture, and Identity* (Chicago: University of Chicago Press, 1992); Dick Hebidge, *Subculture: The Meaning of Style* (London: Methuen, 1979); Thomas Hine, *Populuxe* (New York: Alfred A. Knopf, 1987); Alfred L. Kroeber and J. Richardson, *Three Centuries of Women's Dress Fashions* (Berkeley: University of California Press, 1940); Kendall Morgan, "Dracula Dress Fever," *The Sunday Camera,* November 15, 1992, pp. 1B, 9B; Michele Santos, "Kente Cloth Not a Fad, 'It's an Awakening,' Store Owner Says," *Press-Telegram,* March 13, 1994, p. J10; and Michael R. Solomon, *Consumer Behavior,* 2nd ed. (Boston: Allyn and Bacon, 1994).
12. Sam Johnson, "What's Up Pussy Cat?" *Tokyo Classified,* 202.217.215.47/tokyofeaturestories archive/272/tokyofeaturestoriesinc.htm.
13. Martin G. Letscher, "How to Tell Fads from Trends," *American Demographics,* December 1994, pp. 38–45.
14. "It's New, but Is It Improved?" *American Demographics,* November–December 1994, p. 20; and Robert McMath and Thom Forbes, *What Were They Thinking?* (New York: Times Books, 1998).
15. William M. Bulkeley, "Portable Phones Are Prompting Change in Business and Lifestyles," *The Wall Street Journal,* January 13, 1988, pp. 2, 27; "New Products: Still Rising"; Brad Knickerbocker, "Old Ranch Traditions Blend with New Values," *Christian Science Monitor,* October 25, 1993, pp. 9–11; Brad Knickerbocker, "Forest Managers Learn How to Grow 'Green Lumber,'" *Christian Science Monitor,* November 29, 1993, pp. 11–13; and Ryszard Kapuscinski, "Plastic Buckets and Ballpoint Pens," *Granta* 48 (1994).
16. Steven V. Brull, "Net Nightmare for the Music Biz," *Business Week,* March 2, 1998, pp. 89–90; Paul C. Judge, "Care to Slip into Something More Digital?" *Business Week,* October 20, 1997, p. 42; Julie Pitta, "Competitive Shopping," *Forbes,* February 9, 1998, p. 92; N. Rain Noe, "Let's Do Talk," *Tokyo Classified,* 202.217.215.47/tokyofeaturestoriesarchive/266/tokyofeaturestoriesinc.htm.
17. Leslie Barker, "TV Dinners: 1953 Mealtime Revolution," *Press-Telegram,* May 20, 1993, pp. F1, F6; Laurent Belsie, "Powerful Internet Should Skyrocket as Firms Go On-Line," *Christian Science Monitor,* March 16, 1994, p. 8; Kirsten A. Conover, "Rock Musicians Tackle CD-ROM with an Eye on the Future," *Christian Science Monitor,* March 14, 1994, p. 15; and Lois Therrien, "The Rage to Page Has Motorola's Mouth Watering," *Business Week,* August 30, 1993, pp. 72–73.
18. Leslie Barker, "Trend Guru Focuses on TV Dinners," *Press-Telegram,* May 20, 1993, p. F6; Alix M. Freedman, "The Microwave Cooks up a New Way of Life," *The Wall Street Journal,* September 19, 1989, pp. B1, B2; and Richard T. Watson, Leyland F. Pitt, Pierre Berthon, and George M. Zinkhan, "U-Commerce: Expanding the Universe of Marketing," *Journal of the Academy of Marketing Science* 30 (Fall 2002), pp. 329–43.
19. This example of pioneering advantage is taken from Gregory S. Carpenter and Kent Nakamoto, "Reflections on 'Consumer Preference Formation and Pioneering Advantage,'" *Jour-*

nal of Marketing Research, November 1994, pp. 570–73. See also Gregory S. Carpenter and Kent Nakamoto, "Consumer Preference Formation and Pioneering Advantage," *Journal of Marketing Research* 26 (August 1989), pp. 285–98.

20. Robert D. Buzzell and Bradle T. Gale, *The PIMS Principles* (New York: Free Press, 1987); Peter N. Golder and Gerald J. Tellis, "Pioneer Advantage: Marketing Logic or Marketing Legend," *Journal of Marketing Research* 30 (May 1993), pp. 158–70; and Lyman Ostlund, "Perceived Innovation Attributes as Predictors of Innovativeness," *Journal of Consumer Research* 1 (1974), p. 23.

21. Lee Patterson, "Tanking It Five Ways: Cutting Edge Businesses Still Go Bust the Old Fashioned Way," *Forbes,* June 2, 1997, pp. 75–76.

22. *American Shipper,* July 1986, p. 9; Nicholas A. Glaskowsky Jr., Donald R. Hudson, and Robert M. Ivie, *Business Logistics,* 3rd ed. (New York: Dryden Press, 1992); and James C. Johnson and Donald F. Wood, *Contemporary Logistics,* 5th ed. (New York: Macmillan, 1993), p. 117.

23. Malcolm Gladwell, "Annals of Style: The Cool Hunt," *New Yorker,* March 17, 1997, pp. 78–87; and Anne Guillou and Pascal Guibert, "Le froid domestiqué: L'usage du congélateur," *Terrain* 12 (April 1989), pp. 7–14.

24. Reese Erlich, "Electric Car Maker Plays Down Difficulties," *Christian Science Monitor,* March 11, 1994, p. 10; and Will Nixon, "Unplugging Electric Cars," *Utne Reader,* January–February 1995, pp. 24–26.

25. Elizabeth C. Hirschman, "Adoption of an Incredibly Complex Innovation: Propositions from a Humanistic Vantage Point," in *Advances in Consumer Research,* vol. 14, ed. Melanie Wallendorf and Paul Anderson (Provo, UT: Association for Consumer Research, 1987), pp. 57–60.

26. Asif Shaikh, Eric Arnould, Kjell Christophersen, Roy Hagen, Joseph Tabor, and Peter Warshall, *Opportunities for Sustained Development* (Washington, DC. USAID/OTR/Bureau for Africa, 1988); and Gerrit Antonides, H. Bas Amesz, and Ivo C. Hulscher, "Adoption of Payment Systems in Ten Countries—A Case Study of Diffusion of Innovations," *European Journal of Marketing* 33, nos. 11–12 (1999), pp. 1123–35.

27. Thomas J. Hoban, "Food Industry Innovation: Efficient Consumer Response," *Agribusiness* 14, no. 3 (1998), pp. 235–45.

28. Nanette Byrnes, Dean Foust, Anderson Forest, William C. Symonds, and Joseph Weber, "Brands in a Bind," *Business Week,* August 28, 2000, pp. 234–38.

29. Carpenter and Nakamoto, "Consumer Preference Formation and Pioneering Advantage."

30. Antonides, Amesz, and Hulscher, "Adoption of Payment Systems in Ten Countries"; and Bruce Handy, "The Viagra Craze," *Time,* May 4, 1998, p. 57.

31. Jeffrey Ball, "So Far, the PT Cruiser Isn't Igniting Enthusiasm for Other Chrysler Cars," *The Wall Street Journal,* July 20, 2000, interactive.wsj.com/archive; Elizabeth Weise, "Families Learn to Live on 'Internet Time,'" *USA Today,* Tech Report, 1999, www.usatoday.com/life/dcovwed.htm; and S. C. Gwynne, "Thriving on Health Food," *Time,* February 23, 1998, p. 53.

32. Janet Ginsburg, "Not the Flavor of the Month," *Business Week,* March 20, 2000, p. 128.

33. Eva Martinez and Yolando Polo, "Adopter Categories in the Acceptance Process for Consumer Durables," *Journal of Product and Brand Management* 5, no. 3 (1996), pp. 34–47; and Eva Martinez, Yolando Polo, and Carlos Flavián, "The Acceptance and Diffusion of New Consumer Durables: Differences between First and Last Adopters," *Journal of Consumer Marketing* 15, no. 4 (1998), pp. 323–42.

34. Jan Adam, "Transformation to a Market Economy in the Former Czechoslovakia," *Europe-Asia Studies* 45, no. 4 (1993), pp. 627–45; Stanislaw Gajewski, "Consumer Behavior in Economics of Shortage," *Journal of Business Research* 24 (1992), pp. 5–10; Brian Lofman, "Consumers in Rapid Transition: The Polish Experience," in *Advances in Consumer Research,* vol. 20, ed. Leigh McAlister and Michael Rothschild (Provo, UT: Association for Consumer Research, 1993), pp. 18–21; and Richard Rose and Christian Haerpfer, *Europe-Asia Studies* 46, no. 1 (1994), pp. 3–28.

35. Margaret Littman, "A Dose of Reality," *Marketing News,* January 5, 1998, p. 2; and S. Ram, "A Model of Innovation Resistance," in *Advances in Consumer Research,* vol. 14, ed. Melanie

Wallendorf and Paul Anderson (Provo, UT: Association for Consumer Research, 1987), pp. 208–12.

36. Eric J. Arnould, "Toward a Broadened Theory of Preference Formation and the Diffusion of Innovations: Cases from Zinder Province, Niger Republic," *Journal of Consumer Research* 16 (September 1989), pp. 239–67.

37. Arnould, "Toward a Broadened Theory of Preference Formation and the Diffusion of Innovations"; Ram, "A Model of Innovation Resistance"; and James T. Thompson, Alfred S. Waldstein, and Karen Wiese, *Institutional Constraints on the Transfer of Agricultural and Complementary Resource-Conservation Technologies Appropriate for Semi-Arid Africa,* contract no. PDC-0000-I-00-4104-00 (Burlington, VT: Association in Rural Development/U.S. Agency for International Development, 1987).

38. J. H. Antil, "New Product or Service Adoption: When Does It Happen?" *Journal of Consumer Marketing* 5 (Spring 1988), pp. 5–16.

39. Ester Boserup, *The Conditions of Agricultural Growth* (Chicago: Aldine Press, 1965); and Miranda France, "Fog Harvest Makes the Desert Bloom," *Tampa Tribune,* January 15, 1995, p. A20. See also Robert McC. Netting et al., *The Conditions of Agricultural Intensification in the West African Savannah* (Washington, DC: USAID-PPC, 1978); and Patricia J. Vondal, "Agricultural Extension and Innovation Diffusion: A Case Example from Indonesia," paper presented at the Annual Meetings of the American Anthropological Association, Chicago, 1987.

40. Giovanni Dosi, "Sources, Procedures, and Microeconomic Effects of Innovation," *Journal of Economic Literature* 26 (September 1988), pp. 1120–71.

41. Michael Lynn and Betsy D. Gelb, "Identifying Innovative National Markets for Technical Consumer Goods," *International Marketing Review* 13, no. 6 (1996), pp. 43–57.

42. See Chris Kern, "Pulling the Reins on Computer Technology," *American Way* 18 (March 5, 1985), pp. 199, 125.

43. Consumers are often depicted as resistant or passive recipients of innovations. See, for example, Everett M. Rogers, *Diffusion of Innovations,* 3rd ed. (New York: Free Press, 1983).

44. Richard Rose, "Contradictions between Micro- and Macro-Economic Goals in Post-Communist Societies," *Europe-Asia Studies* 45, no. 3 (1993), pp. 419–44.

45. There are aspects of markets and environments that permit innovations and protect them to varying degrees against imitation. One such aspect is incentives to develop the technology. For most industries, the major mechanisms for receiving returns on innovations are lead times and learning curve advantages combined with complementary marketing efforts. For a review of the literature on business innovation, see Dosi, "Sources, Procedures, and Microeconomic Effects of Innovation."

46. For a discussion of social system variables that affect diffusion, see Hubert Gatignon and Thomas S. Robertson, "A Propositional Inventory for New Diffusion Research," *Journal of Consumer Research* 11 (March 1985), pp. 849–67; and Arnould, "Toward a Broadened Theory of Preference Formation and the Diffusion of Innovations."

47. For an interesting treatment, see George Fields, *From Bonsai to Levi's* (New York: Macmillan, 1983).

48. Peter Dickson, "Understanding the Trade Winds: The Global Evolution of Production, Consumption, and the Internet," *Journal of Consumer Research* 27 (June 2000), pp. 115–22.

49. Noel M. Murray and Lalita A. Manrai, "Exploratory Consumption Behavior: A Cross-Cultural Perspective," *Journal of International Consumer Marketing* 5, no. 1 (1993), pp. 101–20.

50. John Clammer, "Aesthetics of Self: Shopping and Social Being in Contemporary Urban Japan," *Lifestyle Shopping: The Subject of Consumption* (London and New York: Routledge, 1992), pp. 195–215; Alfred Gell, "Newcomers to the World of Goods: Consumption among the Muria Gonds," in *The Social Life of Things: Commodities in Cultural Perspective,* ed. Arjun Appadurai (Cambridge: Cambridge University Press, 1986), pp. 110–38; and Johnson, "What's Up Pussy Cat?" Under the communist regimes of eastern Europe, uniformity was an ideology; to be yourself, to cultivate individualism, to perceive yourself as an individual in a mass society are dangerous, it was said. For a very readable treatment of integration and differentiation in the

former communist countries, see Slavenka Drakulic, *How We Survived Communism and Even Laughed* (New York: Harper Perennial, 1993).
51. Arnould, "Toward a Broadened Theory of Preference Formation and the Diffusion of Innovations"; Lisa Penaloza, "Atravasando Fronteras/Border Crossings: A Critical Ethnographic Exploration of the Consumer Acculturation of Mexican Immigrants," *Journal of Consumer Research* 21 (June 1994), pp. 32–54; and Mary J. Weismantel, "The Children Cry for Bread: Hegemony and the Transformation of Consumption," in *The Social Economy of Consumption,* ed. Henry J. Rutz and Benjamin S. Orlove (Lanham, MD: University Press of America, 1989), pp. 85–100.
52. George Simmel, "Fashion," *International Quarterly* 10 (1904), pp. 130–55. For an excellent discussion, see Grant McCracken, *Culture and Consumption* (Bloomington: Indiana University Press, 1988).
53. Paul F. Lazarsfeld, Bernard R. Berelson, and Hazel Gaudet, *The People's Choice* (New York: Columbia University Press, 1948), p. 151; and Bob White, "Soukous or Sell-Out: Congolese Popular Dance Music as Cultural Commodity," in *Commodities and Globalization,* ed. Angelique Haugerud, M. Priscilla Stone, and Peter D. Little (Lanham, MD: Rowman and Littlefield, 2000), pp. 33–58.
54. Hirokazu Takada and Dipak Jain, "Cross-National Analysis of Diffusion of Consumer Durable Goods in Pacific Rim Countries," *Journal of Marketing* 55 (April 1991), pp. 48–54.
55. Solomon, *Consumer Behavior.*
56. Stuart Ewen and Elizabeth Ewen, *Channels of Desire: Mass Images and the Shaping of American Consciousness,* 2nd ed. (Minneapolis: University of Minneapolis Press, 1992); Richard A. Peterson, *The Production of Culture* (Beverly Hills: Sage Publications, 1976); and Cecilia Tichi, *High Lonesome: The American Culture of Country Music* (Chapel Hill: University of North Carolina Press, 1994).
57. Arnould, "Toward a Broadened Theory of Preference Formation and the Diffusion of Innovations"; and Gatignon and Robertson, "A Propositional Inventory for New Diffusion Research."
58. Linda L. Price, Lawrence F. Feick, and Robin Higie Coulter, "Adoption and Diffusion of Western Products in the 'New' Hungary," working paper, University of Nebraska, Lincoln, 1994.
59. McCracken, *Culture and Consumption;* and Grant McCracken, "Who Is the Celebrity Endorser? Cultural Foundations of the Endorsement Process," *Journal of Consumer Research* 16 (December 1989), pp. 310–21.
60. Susan H. Higgins and Patrick T. Hogan, "Internal Diffusion of High-Technology Industrial Innovations: An Empirical Study," *Journal of Business and Industrial Marketing* 14, no. 1 (1999), pp. 61–75; and Karen N. Kennedy, *Implementing a Customer Orientation: Viewing the Process from Multiple Perspectives,* doctoral dissertation, University of South Florida, Tampa, 1997.
61. Jam Damsgaard and Rens Scheepers, "Power, Influence and Intranet Implementation: A Safari of South African Organizations," *Information Technology & People* 12, no. 4 (1999), pp. 333–58; Robert J. Fisher and Linda L. Price, "An Investigation into the Social Context of Early Adoption Behavior," *Journal of Consumer Research* 19 (December 1992), pp. 477–86; Karlheinz Kautz and Even Åby Larsen, "Diffusion Theory and Practice: Disseminating Quality Management and Software Process Improvement Innovations," *Information Technology & People* 13, no. 1 (2000), pp. 11–26; and J. F. Ryan and J. A. Murray, "The Diffusion of a Pharmaceutical Innovation in Ireland," *European Journal of Marketing* 11, no. 1 (1980), pp. 3–12.
62. Rogers, *Diffusion of Innovations.* See also Price, Feick, and Coulter, "Adoption and Diffusion of Western Products in the 'New' Hungary"; and Naseem Khan, "From Burqah to Bloggs—Changing Clothes for Changing Times," in *Chic Thrills: A Fashion Reader,* ed. Juliet Ash and Elizabeth Wilson (Berkeley: University of California Press, 1992), pp. 61–74.
63. Lawrence F. Feick and Linda L. Price, "The Market Maven: A Diffuser of Marketplace Information," *Journal of Marketing* 51 (January 1987), pp. 83–97; David Midgley, "A Simple Mathematical Theory of Innovative Behavior," *Journal of Consumer Research* 3 (June 1976), pp. 31–41; and Marsha Richins and Teri Root-Shaffer, "The Role of Involvement and Opinion Leadership in Consumer Word-of-Mouth: An Implicit Model Made Explicit," in *Advances in*

Consumer Research, vol. 15, ed. Michael J. Houston (Provo, UT: Association for Consumer Research, 1988), pp. 32–36.

64. Feick and Price, "The Market Maven"; Steven A. Baumgarten, "The Innovative Communicator in the Diffusion Process," *Journal of Marketing Research* 12 (February 1975), pp. 12–18; and Thomas S. Robertson, *Innovative Behavior and Communication* (New York: Holt, Rinehart and Winston, 1971).

65. Feick and Price, "The Market Maven"; Linda Price, Audrey Guskey, and Lawrence Feick, "Everyday Market Helping Behavior," *Journal of Public Policy and Marketing* 14 (Fall 1995), pp. 255–66; and Mark E. Slama and Terrell G. Williams, "Generalization of the Market Maven's Information Provision Tendency across Product Categories," in *Advances in Consumer Research,* vol. 17, ed. Thomas K. Srull (Provo, UT: Association for Consumer Research, 1990), pp. 48–52.

66. David F. Midgley and Grahame R. Dowling, "A Longitudinal Study of Product Form Innovation: The Interaction between Predispositions and Social Messages," *Journal of Consumer Research* 19 (March 1993), pp. 611–25. See also Linda L. Price, Lawrence F. Feick, and Daniel C. Smith, "A Reexamination of Communication Channel Usage by Adopter Categories," in *Advances in Consumer Research,* vol. 13, ed. Richard J. Lutz (Provo, UT: Association for Consumer Research, 1986), pp. 409–13; and Lawrence F. Feick, Linda L. Price, and Robin A. Higie, "People Who Use People: Looking at Opinion Leadership from the Other Side," in *Advances in Consumer Research,* vol. 13, ed. Richard J. Lutz (Provo, UT: Association for Consumer Research, 1986), pp. 301–5. See also Chip Walker, "Word of Mouth," *American Demographics,* July 1995, pp. 38–44.

67. Dorothy Leonard-Barton, "Experts as Negative Opinion Leaders in the Diffusion of a Technological Innovation," *Journal of Consumer Research* 11 (March 1985), pp. 914–26; and Margaret Jean Hays, "Western Clothing and African Identity: Changing Consumption Patterns among the Luo," paper presented at the seminar on Transformations in African Material Culture, African Studies Center, Boston University, 1989.

68. Price, Feick, and Coulter, "Adoption and Diffusion of Western Products in the 'New' Hungary."

69. Peter Dickson, "Understanding the Trade Winds: The Global Evolution of Production, Consumption, and the Internet," *Journal of Consumer Research* 27 (June 2000), p. 120.

70. Norman C. Stolzoff, Eric Chuan-Fong Shih, and Alladi Venkatesh, "The Home of the Future: An Ethnographic Study of New Information Technologies in the Home," in *Advances in Consumer Research,* vol. 28, ed. Mary Gilly and Joan Meyers-Levy (Provo, UT: Association for Consumer Research, 2001), pp. 88–97; and Alladi Venkatesh, Lena Fagerström-Herluf, Josefine Höglund, and Minna Räsänen, "Project Noah Sweden: National Outlook for Automation in the Home," working paper, Center for Research on Information Technology and Organization, University of California, Irvine, 2000.

71. F. D. Midgley and R. G. Dowling, "Innovativeness: The Concept and Its Measurement," *Journal of Consumer Research* 4, no. 4 (1978), pp. 229–42; and Rogers, *Diffusion of Innovations.*

72. Eric Von Hippel, "Lead Users: A Source of Novel Product Concepts," *Management Science* 32 (July 1986), pp. 791–805.

73. Ibid., p. 796; and Edwin Mansfield, *Industrial Research and Technological Innovation: An Econometric Analysis* (New York: W. W. Norton, 1968), pp. 134–235.

74. Gladwell, "Annals of Style."

75. Michael Lynn and Judy Harris, "The Desire for Unique Consumer Products: A New Individual Differences Scale," *Psychology and Marketing* 14, no. 6 (1997), pp. 601–16; and Andrew Plack, "Japanese Girls Enthralled with Organizers," *N.Y. Times News Service,* December 22, 1994, pp. 1–3, America Online.

76. Martinez and Polo, "Adopter Categories in the Acceptance Process for Consumer Durables"; and Martinez, Polo, and Flavián, "The Acceptance and Diffusion of New Consumer Durables."

77. Rogers, *Diffusion of Innovations.*

78. "Advances of the Amazonesu," *The Economist,* July 22, 2000, pp. 61–62.

79. Frank Cancian, "Stratification and Risk-Taking: A Theory Tested on Agricultural Innovation," *American Sociological Review* 32 (1967), pp. 912–27.

80. W. T. Liu and R. W. Duff, "The Strength in Weak Ties," *Public Opinion Quarterly* 36 (Fall 1972), pp. 361–66.
81. Peter Burrows, Gary McWilliams, and Robert D. Hof, "Cheap PCs," *Business Week,* March 23, 1998, pp. 28–32.
82. Eric Abrahamson and Lori Ronsenkopf, "Institutional and Competitive Bandwagons: Using Mathematical Modeling as a Tool to Explore Innovation Diffusion," *Academy of Management Review* 18, no. 3 (1993), pp. 487–517; Sushil Bikhchandani, David Hirshleifer, and Ivo Welch, "A Theory of Fads, Fashion, Custom and Cultural Change as Informational Cascades," *Journal of Political Economy* 100, no. 5 (1992), pp. 992–1026; and David Scott Clark, "Venerable Beetle Survives and Succeeds in Mexico," *Christian Science Monitor,* March 2, 1994, p. 11.
83. J. Pfeffer and G. R. Salancik, *The External Control of Organizations* (New York: Harper & Row, 1978).
84. Lisa W. Foderaro, "Fat-Lane Banking Not for Everyone," *New York Times,* May 17, 1998, p. A25; and Wendy A. Rogers, Elizabeth E. Cabrera, Neff Walker, and Gilbert D. Kristen, "A Survey of Automatic Teller Machine Usage across the Adult Life Span," *Human Factors* 38, no. 1 (1996), pp. 156–66.
85. See the archive of negative coverage of GMOs at the Greenpeace website, http://www.greenpeace.org.
86. Arjun Chaudhuri, "The Diffusion of an Innovation in Indonesia," *Journal of Product and Brand Management* 3, no. 3 (1994), pp. 19–26; Price, Feick, and Coulter, "Adoption and Diffusion of Western Products in the 'New' Hungary"; and Penaloza, "Atravesando Fronteras/Border Crossings."
87. Michael D. Smith, "The Impact of Shopbots on Electronic Markets," *Journal of the Academy of Marketing Science* 30, no. 4 (2002), pp. 442–50; and A. Parasuraman and George M. Zinkhan, "Marketing to and Serving Customers through the Internet: An Overview and Research Agenda," *Journal of the Academy of Marketing Science* 30, no. 4 (2002), pp. 282–91.
88. Michael R. Solomon, "The Missing Link: Surrogate Consumers in the Marketing Chains," *Journal of Marketing* 50 (October 1987), pp. 208–18; and Praveen Aggarawal, "Surrogate Buyers and the New Product Adoption Process: A Conceptualization and Managerial Framework," *Journal of Consumer Marketing* 14, no. 5 (1997), pp. 391–400.
89. Alladi Venkatesh and Nicholas Vitalari, "A Post-Adoption Analysis of Computing in the Home," *Journal of Economic Psychology* 8 (June 1987), pp. 161–80; Nicholas Vitalari and Alladi Venkatesh, "In-Home Computing and Information Services: A Twenty Year Analysis of the Technology and Its Impacts," *Telecommunications Policy* 11, no. 1 (1987), pp. 65–81; and Nancy M. Ridgway and Linda L. Price, "Exploration in Product Usage: A Model of Use Innovativeness," *Psychology and Marketing* 11 (1994), pp. 69–84.
90. Arnould, "Toward a Broadened Theory of Preference Formation and the Diffusion of Innovations"; Albert Wenben Lai, "Consumption Situation and Product Knowledge in the Adoption of a New Product," *European Journal of Marketing* 25 (1991), pp. 55–67; Alan D. Meyer and James B. Goes, "Organizational Assimilation of Innovations," *Academy of Management Journal* 31, no. 4 (1988), pp. 897–923; and Soyeon Shim and Antigone Kotsiopulos, "Technology Innovativeness and Adopter Categories of Apparel/Gift Retailers: From the Diffusion of Innovations Perspective," *Clothing and Textiles Research Journal* 12 (Winter 1994), pp. 46–57.

LEARNING OBJECTIVES

After completing this chapter, you should be able to:

- Describe consumer satisfaction.
- Identify basic factors that influence satisfaction.
- Discuss the relationship between needs and satisfaction.
- Explain how quality and satisfaction are related.
- Describe the expectancy disconfirmation model and its limitations.
- Identify different emotions associated with satisfaction.
- Give examples of different types of satisfaction.
- Identify the consequences of satisfaction and dissatisfaction.

CONSUMER SATISFACTION

BATH & BODY WORKS[1]

There are several factors that contribute to the way I feel about the company. First of all the products are not tested on animals. I feel that animal testing is inconsiderate because there are other ways you can test products without harming or even killing the animal . . . Another important factor is customer service. This is important to me, and I feel they are a customer-oriented business because they are always friendly, not pushy, when it comes to selling their products, greet me with a pleasant smile, and assist me in finding what I am looking for. In addition, the products from Bath & Body Works give me a clean, wholesome feeling when I use them on a regular basis. They make me feel refreshed with a great smell. Most of all, the lotions and talc powder make my skin feel baby soft. I use the loofah sponge and body gel to exfoliate my skin, which also contributes to a soft, healthy look! . . . I am loyal to this company also because the prices are reasonable and each and every product is worth the price. There are always continuous sales here at Bath & Body Works. Whenever I visit Bath & Body Works and purchase accessories or toiletries, I always receive compensation such as samples of lotions and other toiletries.

@ www.bath-and-body-works.com

I have been purchasing Bath & Body Works products for about two years . . . that's a long time being loyal to a company. Just like a friendship. If you know a person for a considerable amount of time, then trust is a significant factor. I would trust my friends in many ways, such as telling them secrets, depending on them for help, and caring for them just as I would depend on Bath & Body Work products and being loyal to them as well.

Now consider this same issue of customer satisfaction from the corporate point of view. The Limited, Inc., owns Bath & Body Works. Here is a statement of their corporate values:

> The Limited, Inc. is committed to building a family of the world's best fashion and personal care brands. Why should we have this goal? To create sustained growth and shareholder value, to the benefit of our shareholders, associates, and customers . . .

> Our customers are increasingly demanding diverse and affordable merchandise of the highest quality and integrity. We are meeting their demands by developing . . . strategic partnerships with key vendors who commit . . . to our values. As our businesses continue to grow both domestically and internationally, we must take special care that the principles we hold most dear are not compromised . . .
>
> By redefining how people think about personal care, Bath & Body Works has built a brand with incredible staying power, a mix of natural but luxurious body and hair care products, grounded in world-class fragrance development.

www.limitedbrands.com/about/bbw.asp

www.limitedbrands.com/whoweare

Note that Bath & Body Works is very interested in the value of their brand, and, to create that value, they are committed to the use of natural and luxurious ingredients. In addition, Bath & Body Works recognizes that their customers demand diverse and affordable merchandise. They are determined to deliver the "highest quality," with integrity. The parent corporation, The Limited, believes that they can achieve organizational goals (e.g., shareholder value) by producing quality products and satisfying customers.

OVERVIEW[2]

Individual postpurchase consumer behavior is of growing concern to marketers as they shift their focus from inducing consumers to purchase to developing profitable, long-term relationships with them. As suggested by the opening vignette, long-term relationships are more likely if marketers concern themselves with how best to satisfy consumers in both the short and long run. This chapter describes that part of the wheel of consumption focused closely on the factors that lead to satisfaction and the outcomes of satisfaction for consumers and marketers.

All of your life people have probably been asking you questions such as, Are you satisfied? and How satisfied are you? Understanding your satisfaction is important to your parents and family, your employer, your educational institution, and the businesses that sell you products and services. For-profit and nonprofit organizations and even governments endeavor to deliver satisfactory outcomes to customers and other constituencies. As evidence of this concern, the American Consumer Satisfaction Index compiled at the University of Michigan comprehensively tracks customer satisfaction by industry sector and by U.S. governmental department. You can visit their website.

www.bus.umich.edu/research/nqrc

Aristotle once said that it is the nature of desire not to be satisfied. Thus, despite the best managerial efforts to guarantee satisfaction, it's sometimes impossible to do so. It's probably easy for you to recall at least one situation in which a presumably customer-oriented company disappointed you. At other times, your desires seem to be fulfilled in the marketplace—perhaps even to overflowing. At such times, you may experience the kind of pleasurable response reflected in the opening vignette.

The opening vignette suggests that consumption experiences evoke a range of emotions from pleasure to reassurance. Emotional extremes (including delight and distress) might accompany satisfaction with consumption experiences such as skydiving or body piercing. By contrast, when asked about their satisfaction with a favorite brand of toothpaste, consumers may say they are satisfied and brand loyal, but most often their response doesn't include much emotion. Often, consumer satisfaction reflects a neutral emotional state and perhaps little cognition as well.[3] Even with a high-involvement product such as an automobile, a segment of owners report moderately high levels of satisfaction *devoid* of strong feelings. Their experience of automobiles is a more cognitive evaluation.

The vignette suggests that satisfaction in consumer contexts responds to beliefs and thoughts (cognitive appraisals) about the outcomes of purchasing, such as the consumer's beliefs about animal testing and value for money spent. Satisfaction is also connected to the emotions that accompany purchase outcomes and related events. We will stress the hybrid emotion-cognition nature of satisfaction and the interplay between emotional and cognitive assessments.

In this chapter, we develop a definition of satisfaction. Then, we discuss factors that contribute to consumer satisfaction and discuss different types of satisfaction. Finally, we describe some consequences of satisfaction and dissatisfaction for consumers and marketers.

DEFINING SATISFACTION

What Is Satisfaction?

The definition of consumer satisfaction that we will use in this chapter incorporates the emotion-cognition characteristic of this judgment. **Satisfaction** is *a judgment of a pleasurable level of consumption-related fulfillment,* including levels of **underfulfillment** or **overfulfillment.**[4] A few comments are important in explaining this definition. First, consumers can make satisfaction judgments with respect to any aspect of the product and service experience. For example, in the context of a computer purchase, consumers could measure satisfaction associated with the purchase phase or any portion of the consumption phase (the life of the computer). In addition, they could measure satisfaction on any or all of the features of the computer (e.g., speed, software, and service) or stages and aspects of the purchase decision (salesperson, negotiations, delivery, paperwork). Because consumers make judgments about their satisfaction based on a variety of product and service aspects and events, each becomes a potential point of differentiation for a market offering. See Ethical Dilemma 18.1.

It is a mistake to assume that all these customer judgments sum to an overall level. Satisfaction is more complex than that. Consumer Chronicles 18.1 describes one consumer's river-rafting experience. This story reflects an array of positive and negative emotions, and it suggests that satisfaction emerges across the service or product experience.[5] Even when uncomfortable things happen, events may evolve in such a way as to make an experience satisfying (or fulfilling) overall. Consumer research in service environments suggests that if bad service is followed by effective service recovery, customers may be more satisfied overall than if they had not experienced bad service in the first place. In other words, apologies and gifts improve customer satisfaction. However, effective service recovery can't offset repeated service failures.[6]

A second thing to observe about this definition of satisfaction is that it focuses on fulfillment. Fulfillment comes in different varieties. For example, consumers may feel fulfilled or satisfied with the removal of a negative state (e.g., repair of a computer hardware problem). Or consumers may feel overfulfillment and satisfaction with a service experience that provides unexpected pleasure, such as expressed in the skydiving story in Consumer Chronicles 18.2. Finally, consumers can experience satisfaction when a product or service experience gives greater pleasure than anticipated.

Customer Satisfaction and Managerial Compensation

ETHICAL DILEMMA 18.1

In some organizations (e.g., public utilities, personal computing), a manager's compensation package may be partially tied to customer satisfaction ratings. In other words, the happier the customers are, the more the managers will be paid. Of course, satisfaction ratings are measured via a survey, and the survey is designed to assess a variety of factors that may be related to a customer's perception of service quality or product performance.

Consider a firm that makes and sells personal computers. Management is pleased to note that customer satisfaction ratings are consistently at 92 percent. However, customer repurchase rates hover around 65 percent over that same time period. When the satisfaction ratings are examined more closely, it is discovered that the relevant satisfaction dimensions have been selected by the product designers (e.g., the engineers). They have selected dimensions that would be appreciated by other engineers, but these same dimensions are not necessarily the main drivers of overall satisfaction for typical consumers. Thus, the product receives high marks on the items that the firm tests, but the research is not necessarily designed to test all of the factors that drive customer satisfaction. The result is a biased marketing research instrument that does not truly represent customers' impressions of product performance.

Suppose that you were a manager for this computer manufacturer and that your compensation package is tied to customer satisfaction levels. You are pleased that satisfaction ratings are so high (92 percent), as this result leads to high bonus payments for you and your colleagues. However, you have evidence (e.g., the 65 percent repurchase rates) that the satisfaction instrument may not be asking the right questions. What would you do?

Source: Personal communication from Dr. Warren French, I.W. Cousins Ethics Professor, University of Georgia.

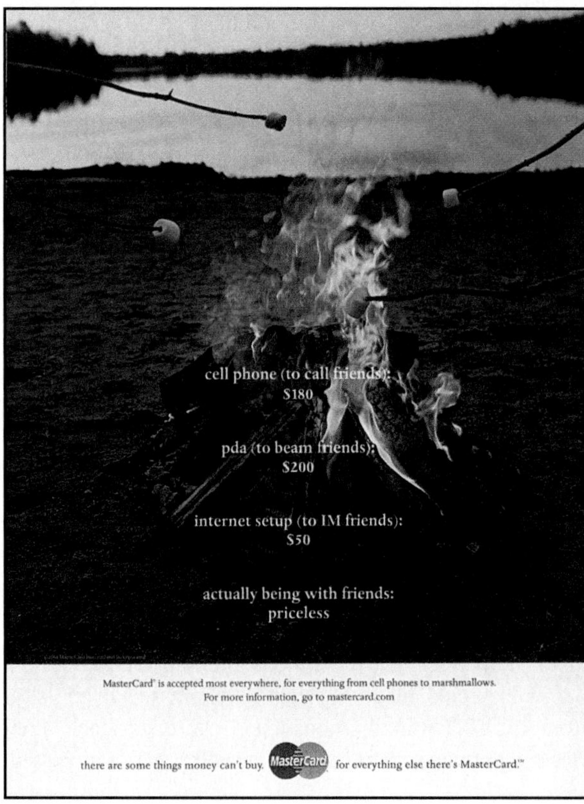

Satisfaction is social and cultural.

For example, a young child dreading a doctor visit may express satisfaction after the visit because "it wasn't so bad." Fulfillment also implies standards that form a basis for comparison. In this chapter we will discuss how consumers formulate standards and expectations.

A third thing to observe about this definition is that satisfaction is an **internal state.** This means *accounts of satisfaction must highlight the meanings that operate in the customers' field of awareness.*[7] This is important to emphasize. We can't say to managers that performance on a particular set of dimensions leads directly to customer satisfaction or make statements like "product quality leads to satisfaction" without examining customer experience. Judgments of satisfaction vary. Two customers who receive the same level of product performance may experience quite different levels of satisfaction. Because satisfaction is so variable (across customers), managers tailor market offerings to particular consumer segments.

Although satisfaction is an internal state, it is also social.[8] Marketers need to be savvy about how individual judgments express a broader system of cultural values, meanings, beliefs, emotions, group relationships, and conflicts. The satisfaction of household or buying group members often contributes to an individual consumer's satisfaction. An example of a social perspective on satisfaction is offered by some research on U.S. professional working mothers. These women grapple with an array of role conflicts, gender ideals, cultural values, and interpersonal demands. These conflicting influences color their consumption experiences and evaluations. For example, interviews reveal a disparity between ideals they envision and their actual everyday lives. One reflection of this is the ideal of an immaculate household.[9] In Consumer Chronicles 18.3, a working mother discusses her dissatisfaction with a maid service, illustrating how social expectations frame satisfaction.

Cross-culturally marketers should remember that the ideal of customer satisfaction is not a universal. Consumers in transitional and developing countries may not have learned to concern themselves so much with individual satisfaction as those in developed consumer cultures. Consumer satisfaction may still be considered a shameful luxury for some. Further, people in different cultural contexts may look to nonmarket-based situations—family interaction or religious devotion, for example—as sources of satisfaction in their lives. Consumer satisfaction is learned as part of socialization in consumer culture.[10] For instance, a MasterCard ad campaign stresses that "there are some things money can't buy." Satisfaction is both social and cultural.

CONSUMER CHRONICLES 18.1

Satisfaction with the River-Rafting Experience Is Complex

For me, river rafting is a horrible thing. I am scared to death of water . . . I have to admit—it was the most exciting thing I've done in a long time. I never felt safe, but I did start to feel like I wasn't in complete danger. For the first 15 to 20 minutes it was pure terror . . . By the end of the day—I'd been thrown all over the raft. I was soaking wet. I was very drained because I'd been tense all day long, but I felt very invigorated . . . It is challenging, exciting, thrilling, exhausting, and I'd recommend it highly.

Source: Eric J. Arnould and Linda L. Price, "River Magic: Extraordinary Experience and the Extended Service Encounter," Journal of Consumer Research *20 (June 1993), p. 40.*

What Is Dissatisfaction?

We simply define **dissatisfaction** as *an unpleasant level of consumption-related fulfillment.* Although this definition makes sense, keep in mind that factors that contribute to higher levels of satisfaction may sometimes differ from those that contribute to higher

The Magic of Skydiving

CONSUMER CHRONICLES 18.2

I would have to say the time all of us went skydiving in January was a magical experience because there is truly no other activity in the world that is more exciting, dangerous, energetic, and still just such a mental and physical rush like there is with skydiving. All of you guys made me do it. Seriously, I heard what kind of experience it was and I just had to try it. There are just some things in this world you have to do before your time is up, and I think skydiving is definitely one of them. I had a feeling it would be amazing, but I didn't really expect that feeling to be with me for as long as it has. Every time I think back to that day I just think of how exciting it really was, and it really gives me an appreciation of what life really means to me. I believe it has also changed the way I look at my life. I try not to take things for granted as much as I once did. It was just a time that I'll never forget, and in my book that is magical.

levels of dissatisfaction. Let's take a simple example. Consumers at a concert are not likely to report being more satisfied because they did not have to wait in line for tickets, but they are quite likely to report being more *dissatisfied* if they had to wait in line. Although a particular product attribute may affect both satisfaction and dissatisfaction, there are differences in what drives them.

MANAGERIAL CONCERN WITH SATISFACTION[11]

Review some key concepts on marketing strategy (from Chapter 5) to realize the key role that customer satisfaction plays in the marketing process. The marketing concept declares that the customer is king. This business philosophy advises managers to *satisfy* customer needs and wants. In a similar way, relationship marketing advises managers to cultivate a long-term relationship with customers and to reap the benefits of customer loyalty. What keeps customers coming back? Customer satisfaction is a key concept.

Exhibit 18.1 proposes a model that links together key variables such as quality, satisfaction, loyalty, and organizational performance. As illustrated in the exhibit, quality has direct effects on both customer satisfaction and organizational performance (e.g., profitability). Quality reduces failures and operating costs and lowers the cost of recovery. When a buyer experiences product failure, the selling organization incurs costs such as lost business from that potentially disgruntled customer.[12] One way to reduce failure rates is by implementing a guarantee program. With the guarantee program, the seller shifts emphasis. Instead of spending money to mop up failures, the seller now spends to prevent failures. In addition, quality leads to improved consumer reputations, channel member receptivity, and lower costs associated with attracting new customers.[13] Satisfaction has direct effects on organizational performance through its influence on retention. Satisfied customers are easier to reach with communications, more likely to increase purchase volumes, and more tolerant of price increases. By maintaining superlative levels of customer satisfaction, organizations can find new ways to compete. In essence, they have the potential to change the rules of the game for an entire industry. Consider Federal Express and how they redefined customer service in their industry. In a similar vein, consider how a pest control company that specialized in the B2B market redefined service quality in that industry (see Good Practice 18.1). As a reward for elevating customer satisfaction, that company was able to charge 10 times more than any other competitor.

Look again at the mission statement from Bath & Body Works' parent corporation in the opening vignette. The Limited strives to create shareholder value, as an ultimate objective (see Exhibit 18.1). They believe that quality products and a focus on customer satisfaction provide a promising way to reach this objective.

The pursuit of customer satisfaction is supposed to result in a customer base that is loyal to the seller. This relationship is strengthened over time. Some firms consistently enjoy a high degree of loyalty from their customers. See Industry Insights 18.1 for a listing of the top 20 brand loyalty leaders. See Industry Insights 18.2 for a listing of the most powerful Internet brands. Companies such as these can capitalize on their standing in the marketplace to accomplish other objectives (e.g., to create shareholder value). Companies can do several things to reward loyal customers. For instance, a French grocery chain lets loyal customers opt in to e-mailings of special recipes and price promotions. Loyal customers also get exclusive, early access to week-long wine festivals. Such measures result in increased purchase volumes and enhanced profitability for the chain.[14]

Now, consider the opposite sequence of events. Customers who reduce their account share or switch their account spending to a competitor exhibit disloyalty. The consequent negative effects show up in several ways. The immediate impact is loss of cash flow and market share. At the same time, competitors become stronger. As customers communicate their negative experiences to others, the seller's customer equity erodes. Thus, holding on to present customers makes sense because it may cost as much as five times as much to attract a new customer as it does to keep an existing one.[15]

In situations where key customers are about to defect, additional effort is required to understand the reasons for their imminent departure. For companies that have realized the tremendous profits available in retaining customers, it is important to institutionalize this process into the company's daily processes. The rewards of customer retention are enormous, tangible, and central to success. For instance, Ford Motor Company has estimated that the value of a 1 percent increase in owner loyalty is worth $100 million in profit. In addition, loyal customers require less attention and allow firms to weather competitor attacks and tactical maneuvers.[16]

CONSUMER CHRONICLES 18.3

Jean's Maid Service

I tried a maid service and . . . I am not fastidious by any means, but I just felt like they weren't cleaning like I would clean. I don't think I am overly critical either, but I just felt like that for that amount of money you should get one heck of a shine on things . . . I just didn't think I was getting my money's worth. And I had all these misconceptions. I thought if I had a maid service, they would come in for one day and it would stay clean for five days. I was so fussy with the kids . . . but I kept telling myself for 40 bucks I should be able to retain this for a long time.

Source: Craig J. Thompson, "Caring Consumers: Gendered Consumption Meanings and the Juggling Lifestyle," Journal of Consumer Research *22 (March 1996), p. 399.*

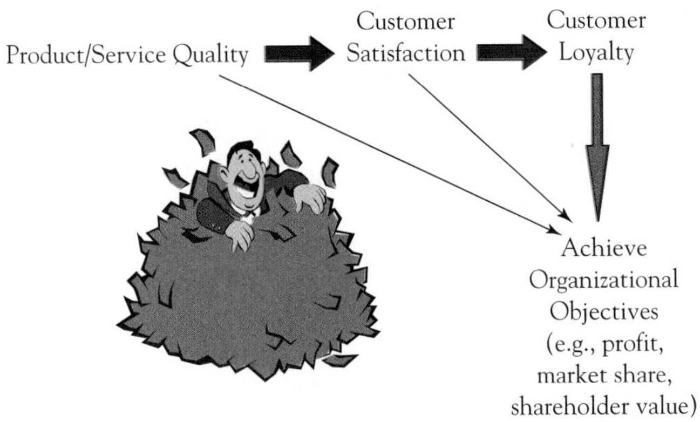

EXHIBIT 18.1

Customer Satisfaction and Organizational Performance

Source: Adapted from Richard L. Oliver, *Satisfaction: A Behavioral Perspective on the Consumer* (New York: McGraw-Hill, 1997), p. 403.

GOOD PRACTICE 18.1

"Bugs" Burger Bug Killers

"Bugs" Burger Bug Killers (BBBK) was a Miami-based pest-extermination company. Most of its competitors claim that they will reduce pests to "acceptable levels." In contrast, BBBK would promise to eliminate pests entirely. For instance, here is an excerpt from a typical guarantee offered to a hotel or restaurant client:

> You don't owe one penny until all pests on your premises have been eradicated . . . If you are ever dissatisfied with BBBK's service, you will receive a refund for up to 12 months of the company's services—plus fees for another exterminator of your choice for the next year . . . If a guest spots a pest on your premises, BBBK will pay for the guests' meal or room, send a letter of apology, and pay for a future meal or stay . . . If your facility is closed down due to the presence of roaches or rodents, BBBK will pay any fines, as well as all lost profits, plus $5,000.

In essence, BBBK is guaranteeing 100 percent level of customer satisfaction. BBBK is redefining the meaning of service for their key customers (e.g., hotels, restaurants, hospitals). Of course, BBBK is targeting a segment of price-insensitive customers who are willing to pay for superior service. In fact, BBBK commanded a price that was 10 times higher than the industry norm because it focused on those customers for whom the cost of failure was extreme. "Bugs" Burger's guarantee of "zero pests" had much more perceived value for those customers than it did for other potential accounts.

In the early 1990s, BBBK was acquired by S. C. Johnson Wax Company, and its operation base was expanded.

Sources: Robert J. Dolan, "How Do You Know When the Price Is Right?" Harvard Business Review, *September–October 1995; and Christopher W. L. Hart, "The Power of Unconditional Service Guarantees," in* Keeping Customers, *ed. John J. Sviokla and Benson P. Shapiro (Cambridge: Harvard Business School Press, 1993), pp. 151–66.*

WHAT CAUSES SATISFACTION?

We want to emphasize several basic points in our discussion of the causes of satisfaction. We can formulate these points as a series of questions that managers must answer in order to understand satisfaction processes. We certainly won't review all that has been written on customer satisfaction, but we will try to help you understand some factors that contribute to it.

How Are Performance and Satisfaction Related?

Many managers believe that product performance or service quality paves the road to satisfaction. Mission statements, company slogans, and promotional materials often claim quality as an ideal and assert a close relationship between quality and satisfaction.[17] Using a vision of quality to guide management is evident in the mission statements of two Malcolm Baldrige Quality Award winners summarized in Good Practice 18.2, for example.

As a result of the belief in the performance–satisfaction link, global management consultant firms from Mexico to Malaysia derive significant revenues from conducting quality and satisfaction studies for their corporate clients. Postpurchase research accounts for one-third of revenues of the largest U.S. market research firms, and strong

The Top 20 Brand Loyalty Leaders

INDUSTRY INSIGHTS 18.1

For its annual customer loyalty index, market research firm Brand Keys surveys 16,000 consumers twice a year on their attitudes toward 158 brands in 28 categories. (Brand Keys chooses categories at its clients' request, but a brand's rank has nothing to do with whether it is a client.) For each category, consumers are asked to describe the brand attributes most important to them and then to evaluate how the brands measure up. The firm analyzes the resulting data and assigns each brand an index score. The index baseline is 100, with anything below 93 considered a low rating and anything above 107 exceptional. This year saw significant shake-ups in nine categories, largely as a result of the economic recession and fallout in the travel industry after Sept. 11. Here are the 2002 winners in some of the most widely followed categories. For a complete list of the results, visit www.business2.com/brandkeys.

Top 20 Brand Loyalty Leaders

Rank		Index Score
1	Avis	115
2	Sprint long distance	113
3	Budweiser	111
4	Samsung mobile phones	111
5	Ritz-Carlton	110
6	Google	108
7	Canon copiers	105
8	Mobil	105
9	Amazon.com	103
10	New Balance	102
11	Diet Pepsi	101
12	Wal-Mart	101
13	Charles Schwab	100
14	Coors Light	100
15	Discover Card	99
16	Verizon Wireless	99
17	Citibank	98
18	Airborne Express	97
19	*The Today Show*	97
20	Major League Baseball	95

Source: "Taking the Measure of Customer Loyalty," Business 2.0, *July 2002, p. 85.*

annual growth is reported. Corporate clients in transitional economies and NICs worry that they must attend more to the performance–satisfaction relationship. Firms compete to win the J. D. Power awards for "initial quality," such as those won by the Maruti Zen and the Honda City automobiles in India in 1998, for example.[18]

Despite the fact that service or product quality is a frequent organizational goal, a single managerially useful meaning of quality and performance eludes us.[19] Good Practice 18.3 summarizes a few of the ways to think about quality. In that exhibit, note how item number one emphasizes the subjective nature of a consumer's quality ratings. Notice how item number five emphasizes the important fact that consumer expectations about product quality vary from person to person.

Manufacturers and consumers don't necessarily agree about product and service quality. For example, a *Fortune* survey of chief executive officers of the largest U.S. companies revealed that 60 percent of these officers believed that quality is better today, while only 13 percent believed quality was declining. A large-scale consumer survey conducted during that same period revealed that 49 percent of the respondents believed quality was declining and 59 percent believed it would continue to decline. In a General Electric study, appliance managers listed different components than did consumers as critical in quality perceptions.[20] These findings emphasize three points. There is no

INDUSTRY INSIGHTS 18.2

The Most Powerful Internet Brands

Brand Keys tracks four categories of brands that do substantial business online. According to its research, online loyalty hinges on three factors: ease of use, meaningful content, and secure transactions.

Books and music
1 Amazon.com
2 Buy.com
3 Borders[1]
4 Barnes & Noble, CDNow (tie)

Brokerage
1 Charles Schwab
2 Datek[2]
3 CSFB Direct[3]
4 TD Waterhouse
5 Merrill Lynch
6 Fidelity
7 National Discount Brokers[2]
8 Ameritrade, E-Trade (tie)

Search engine
1 Google
2 Yahoo
3 HotBot, Lycos, AltaVista, Excite (tie)
7 MSN
8 Netscape
9 AOL, Ask Jeeves (tie)

Travel
1 Expedia
2 Travelocity
3 Fodors
4 Priceline.com

[1]Online sales now handled by Amazon.com.
[2]Purchased by Ameritrade in 2001–2002.
[3]Purchased by Harris Bank in November 2001; renamed Harris Direct.

Source: "Most Powerful Internet Brands," Business 2.0, *July 2002, p. 86.*

such thing as objective quality (judgments are always based on someone's perceptions), and managers interested in customer satisfaction need to find out how customers perceive quality. Nevertheless, looking across many descriptions of quality, we can conclude that **perceived quality** involves preferences, is based on comparative standards, differs among customers and situations, and resides in product use. Moreover, quality has both cognitive (thinking) and affective (emotional) aspects.[21]

Perceived quality *is* an important predictor of customer satisfaction.[22] Several studies support the causal chain that suggests quality ⇒ satisfaction ⇒ purchase intention.[23] Although not absolute, this relationship has been documented across industries and cultural contexts. For example, research conducted over time and across industries in Sweden revealed a significant relationship between quality (product performance) and customer satisfaction.[24]

The problem is for each organization to decide how consumers perceive quality and what features or characteristics they use in judging quality. Many lists of features have been developed. Eight general dimensions of quality have been proposed, including features, performance, reliability, conformance, durability, serviceability, aesthetics, and perceived quality.[25] Some argue for a product-category-specific approach to assessing quality. For example, research on 33 food categories revealed five quality dimensions: rich/full flavor, natural taste, fresh taste, good aroma, and appetizing looks.[26] The SERVQUAL scale was devised to measure service quality. The scale, discussed in Chapter 8, was first published in 1988 and has undergone numerous revisions. It contains 21 perception items that are distributed through five service-quality dimensions:

Quality as a Mission: Two Malcolm Baldrige Recipients

GOOD PRACTICE 18.2

Cadillac

The mission of the Cadillac Motor Car Company is to engineer, produce, and market the world's finest automobiles known for uncompromised levels of distinctiveness, comfort, convenience, and refined performance. Through its people, who are its strength, Cadillac will continuously improve the quality of its products and services to meet or exceed customer expectations and succeed as a profitable business.

Motorola

It is the objective of Motorola, Inc., to produce and provide products and services of the highest quality. In its activities, Motorola will pursue goals aimed at the achievement of quality excellence. These results will be derived from the dedicated efforts of each employee in conjunction with supportive participation from management at all levels of the corporation.

reliability, empathy, tangibles, responsiveness, and assurance. It also contains expectation items.[27]

For a variety of reasons, customer satisfaction is a difficult concept to understand and measure. First, it is a highly subjective concept. It is a relative concept, with much variation between individuals. Thus, an experience that is satisfying to one consumer may be perceived to be completely inadequate and dissatisfying to another. One factor that causes this variation is differences in expectations. For instance, a person who goes on her first river-rafting trip (see Consumer Chronicles 18.1) may expect something quite different than her friend, who is going on his fifth trip.

Second, there is tremendous variation across industries. For instance, the managers of a bank, an airline, an HMO, or a dry-cleaning establishment may find that they need to measure very different things when they assess satisfaction in their unique industry. A UK specialty foods retailer learned that order processing (reliability) and food product quality (tangibles) were key drivers of satisfaction. Standard Life, an insurance company, discovered that its employees startled customers by answering the telephone more quickly than the customers anticipated. In other words, the employees were too responsive! Again, firms need to tailor their service delivery to what customers expect. This outcome for Standard Life provides a humorous example to illustrate the exacting level of behavioral knowledge that's necessary to appreciate service satisfaction and all of its consequences. Companies need to understand individual customers and their expectations. Taking that knowledge into account, they strive to deliver those service elements that are relevant in their specific industry.[28]

Third, the meaning of "service quality" varies across cultures. Consider a simple example. A study of service quality in Hong Kong hotels found that Asian travelers' satisfaction was determined primarily by value. In contrast, Western travelers were more interested in room quality.[29]

The relationship between satisfaction and purchase intention is complex. For some shopping and convenience goods, satisfaction and repurchase intentions may be closely related. However, if consumers do not distinguish between brands, satisfaction may not

Some Different Ways of Thinking about Perceived Quality

GOOD PRACTICE 18.3

1. Consumer's judgment about a product's overall excellence or superiority.
2. Totality of features and characteristics of a product or service that bear on its ability to satisfy stated and implied needs.
3. Perceived ability of a product to provide satisfaction relative to the available alternatives.
4. All attributes of a product that yield consumer satisfaction.
5. Involves the subjective response of people to objects and is therefore a highly relativistic phenomenon that differs between judges.

Source: Definitions 1 through 5 listed in the exhibit are from the following sources: (1) Valerie A. Zeithaml, "Consumer Perceptions of Price, Quality, and Value: A Means-End Model and Synthesis of Evidence," Journal of Marketing *52 (July 1988), pp. 2–22; (2) definition of the International Organization for Standardization quoted in Evert Gummesson, "Quality Dimensions: What to Measure in Service Organizations," in* Advances in Services Marketing and Management: Research and Practice, *vol. 1, ed. Teresa A. Swartz, David E. Bowen, and Stephen W. Brown (Greenwich, CT: JAI Press, 1992), pp. 177–205; (3) Kent B. Monroe and R. Krishnan, "The Effect of Price on Subjective Product Evaluations," in* Perceived Quality, *ed. Jacob Jacoby and Jerry C. Olson (Lexington, MA: Lexington Books, 1985), pp. 209–32; (4) Alfred R. Oxenfeldt, "Consumer Knowledge: Its Measurement and Extent,"* Review of Economics and Statistics *32 (1950), pp. 300–16; and (5) Morris B. Holbrook and Kim P. Corfman, "Quality and Value in the Consumption Experience: Phaedrus Rides Again," in* Perceived Quality, *ed. Jacob Jacoby and Jerry C. Olson (Lexington, MA: Lexington Books) 1985, pp. 31–57.*

predict repurchase intention all that well. Sometimes consumers have especially satisfying consumption experiences, but they have no intention of repurchasing. This may happen for a variety of reasons, including a belief that the experience can never be repeated, a desire to retain the sacred status of the experience, or a belief that other "once in a lifetime experiences" await them. Can you think of a wonderful consumption experience that you don't intend to repeat?

Finally, dissatisfying events during a consumption episode can sometimes lead consumers to repurchase or engage in other positive postconsumption behaviors. Look again at Consumer Chronicles 18.1, where the river rafter recommended her experience highly to others, even though she suffered along the way. In other words, a consumer may report high levels of satisfaction, even for a service experience where bad things happened.

How Are Employee and Customer Satisfaction Related?

Corporate slogans and mission statements sometimes link customer satisfaction to employee satisfaction.[30] Mounting evidence suggests there is a relationship. Some research in the banking industry, for example, has demonstrated that initiatives to improve employee satisfaction also affect customer satisfaction.[31] While the effect *may* be most pronounced in service industries where satisfaction with contact employees is vital to overall customer satisfaction, there are numerous examples of how nonservice industry employees contribute to performance and customer satisfaction.[32] Again, look over The Limited's mission statement, which appears at the end of the opening vignette. Here, The Limited expresses their commitment to employees (i.e., "associates"), and they implicitly believe that satisfied employees will lead to satisfied customers.

Although it seems simple and obvious to say employee satisfaction is linked to customer satisfaction, translating knowledge of that link into managerial action is not so easy. An interesting study employed the critical incident technique to look at service encounters from both the customers' and the employees' perspectives. The **critical incident technique** is *a systematic procedure for recording events and behaviors observed to lead to success or failure on specific tasks.* Respondents are asked about specific events and their accounts of these events are content analyzed.[33] The authors found that, in the case of routine service transactions, employees and customers mostly had shared notions of the sources of customer satisfaction and dissatisfaction. Nevertheless, an examination of employee reports of episodes of customer dissatisfaction made apparent several implications for management.

One implication is that the customer is NOT always right and doesn't always behave in acceptable ways. To have happy employees who make happy customers, managers need to acknowledge this fact. Employees need appropriate coping and problem-solving skills to handle difficult customers, situations, and their own personal feelings.

A second implication is that contact employees generally want to provide good service and are proud of their ability to do this. Employees express frustration when they believe that they cannot recover from a service failure or adjust the system to accommodate a customer need. Poorly designed systems or procedures, cumbersome bureaucracy, too many rules, and the lack of authority to do anything are often to blame.

How Are Choice and Satisfaction Related?

In most situations, consumers use product features to form satisfaction judgments. In other cases, the features that drive product choice may differ from those factors that drive satisfaction.[34] Exhibit 18.2 diagrams the distinction between choice criteria and drivers of satisfaction.

Research on adventure tourism activities like river rafting illustrates differences between choice criterion and **satisfaction drivers.** Consumers choose rafting companies based on such things as amenities offered, rivers accessed, length of trip, and safety claims. But variation in performance on these dimensions has relatively little to do with customer satisfaction. Satisfaction is driven by feelings of harmony with nature, connection to a community of adventurers, and personal growth experiences, such as learning to pilot a kayak. Similarly, some interesting research on Islamic banks in the Mideast

EXHIBIT 18.2

Drivers of Choice and Satisfaction

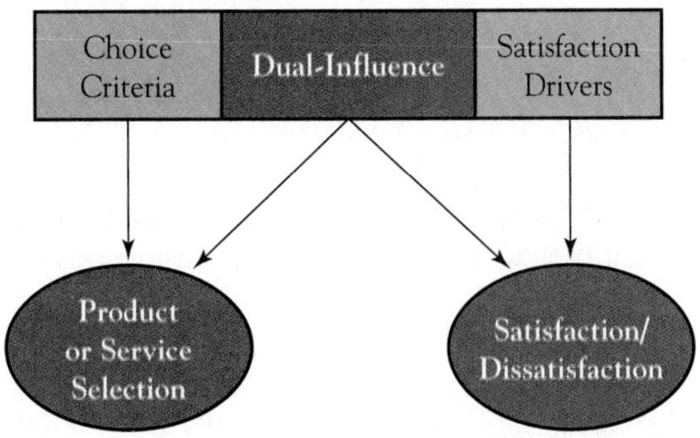

Source: Adapted from Richard L. Oliver, *Satisfaction: A Behavioral Perspective on the Consumer* (New York: McGraw-Hill, 1997), p. 42.

Purchase outcomes are unpredictable.

suggests that adherence to Islamic banking principles (e.g., interest is not charged on loans) drives choice, but product performance drives customer satisfaction.[35]

There are many reasons why choice criteria may differ from satisfaction drivers. One is that consumers have trouble foreseeing the possible problems and benefits of consumption. For complex, extended, or infrequently purchased services like an expensive tourist adventure, the discrepancy between choice and satisfaction drivers may be pronounced.[36] The same is true for complex, infrequently purchased, high-tech products that can be used to attain a variety of goals.[37]

Another reason for differences between choice and satisfaction drivers might be that aspects of the consumption situation that directly affect satisfaction are unpredictable and hence can't be used as choice criteria. For example, if you could predict in advance which airline and flight would experience turbulence, wouldn't that be a choice criterion? Unfortunately, turbulence is unpredictable and more a function of airspace than airline. In many situations, consumers find that postpurchase consumption experiences (with complex goods) differ from what they had expected or predicted.[38] The humorous ad for Northface illustrates the principle that purchase outcomes are not always easy to predict.

Consider the loyal consumer's description of her relationship with Bath & Body Works in the opening vignette. She wants to buy products that are not tested on animals. Such a desire would be classified as a choice criterion. However, using the product provides no new information about this attribute, so it doesn't really influence satisfaction ratings. In contrast, using personal care products provides more information about attributes such as aroma, and this attribute is likely to influence postconsumption satisfaction. As a third possibility, some attributes influence both choice and satisfaction. For example, customer service at the Bath & Body Works could influence a consumer's choice to visit the store and also could influence the overall satisfaction rating of the shopping experience.

Also in the vignette, notice how the loyal consumer's feelings about Bath & Body Works are built up over a long period of time. In the same way, customer satisfaction ratings are often based on a whole range of experiences that gain meaning and intensity over time. Such experiences also form the basis of consumer trust.

Consumers' satisfaction judgments often focus on purchase outcomes, whereas firms emphasize differences between brand attributes in their marketing communications.[39] If a company can distinguish itself from competitors in terms of consumer outcomes, then it may be able to closely align choice criteria and satisfaction drivers. For example, a consumer might choose Federal Express on the belief that this choice will result in rapid, reliable package delivery. One important satisfaction driver is likely to be whether rapid, safe package delivery occurs. The close alignment between choice criteria and satisfaction drivers is evident in FedEx advertising that emphasizes job-related outcomes from this versus other choices. Marketing communications that emphasize the outcomes of product use or nonuse can be viewed as attempts to align choice and satisfaction drivers. The ad for MCI advanced audio conference calling shown on page 768 is one illustration. Another is the United Airlines ad that positions the electronic ticket option as a solution to the problem of lost tickets.

How Do Consumers Judge Satisfaction?

Earlier we observed that satisfaction implies goals or standards that form a basis for comparison. How then do these standards develop, and what standards form the basis for satisfaction judgments?[40] Expectations provide one standard for later judgments of satisfaction.[41] We can define **expectations** simply as *anticipation or predictions of future events.* In fact, expectations are such a useful concept for thinking about satisfaction that we have mentioned them several times, earlier in the chapter. Expectations include predictions of future product performance and also related hopes, apprehensions, uncertainties, and probabilities. For example, the consumer in the opening vignette says that service personnel are "always friendly," there are "always continuous sales," and she always receives "compensation such as samples." These represent expectations. Consumers' basic expectation is that the products or services

Attempting to align choice and satisfaction drivers.

they purchase will fulfill their wants.

It is appropriate to outline some of the most common models for understanding the relationship between standards and satisfaction. Most research has employed some variant of the expectancy–disconfirmation model of satisfaction. However, as suggested in our discussion, there is increasing recognition that other kinds of comparative standards, such as fairness, might also affect judgments of satisfaction. We begin with a discussion of the expectancy–disconfirmation model of satisfaction and then provide a brief summary of some other comparative standards that might be used in judging satisfaction.

Expectancy–Disconfirmation Model of Satisfaction

The **expectancy–disconfirmation model of satisfaction (EDM)** states that *disconfirmation of preconsumption expectations is the key influence on consumer satisfaction.*[42] Exhibit 18.3 illustrates the expectancy–disconfirmation framework that we can use to

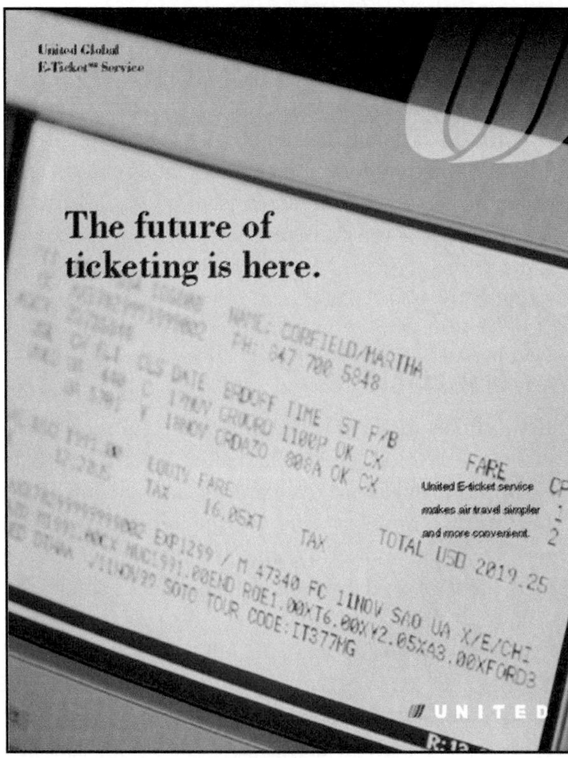

Increasing the salience of a solution to a cause of dissatisfaction: lost tickets.

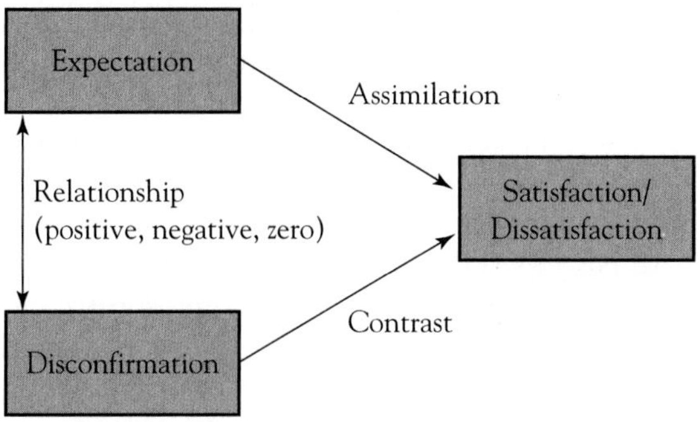

EXHIBIT 18.3

A Simplified Expectancy–Disconfirmation Framework

Source: Richard L. Oliver, *Satisfaction: A Behavioral Perspective on the Consumer* (New York: McGraw-Hill, 1997), p. 110.

understand both how these concepts are related and what this means for management strategy. This model suggests that expectations and disconfirmation operate together to jointly determine satisfaction levels. When *performances exceed expectations,* **positive disconfirmation** occurs and the likelihood of consumer satisfaction increases. When *expectations are not met,* **negative disconfirmation** occurs and the likelihood of consumer dissatisfaction increases. As was shown, for example, in a massive survey of dining in Hong Kong, positive disconfirmation leads to satisfaction and future purchase intentions. Similarly, in a large-scale study of Korean automobile purchases, negative disconfirmation negatively affected not only satisfaction but also future purchase intentions.[43] Results such as these linking disconfirmation and satisfaction have been shown for many products and services.

Now consider what happens when performance expectations are neutrally confirmed. Not much! Meeting performance expectations is probably not the key to satisfaction. Even delivering as expected when expectations are moderate or high may evoke an emotionally neutral response. Hence, the competitor that positions itself to exceed customer's expectations will likely outperform the firm that merely meets customer expectations. Look again at Good Practice 18.1, where the pest-control firm, through its guarantee, creates a service standard (and customer expectation level) that the competition finds very difficult to match.

What is most important in predicting satisfaction in the EDM is the subjective disconfirmation felt by the consumer, which may differ from disconfirmation as measured by the firm. For example, perceived waiting time for fast food is a better predictor of satisfaction than the actual clock time customers wait.[44]

To explain more fully the EDM, we need to describe assimilation effects and contrast effects. These terms and related concepts have already been described in Chapter 9. Assimilation effects imply that individuals are reluctant to acknowledge discrepancies from a previously held position. Hence, individuals will explain away (rationalize) apparent discrepancies. In the context of satisfaction, this implies that repeat consumers may minimize or rationalize away discrepancies from expectations, often with a subjective report that the product is exactly as expected or even better than expected. As modeled in Exhibit 18.3, expectations function to increase satisfaction through assimilation effects. Contrast effects have been described as the tendency to exaggerate differences, making them larger than reality. In a satisfaction context, new or infrequent consumers may exaggerate more extreme differences between expectations and outcomes.[45]

Keep in mind that disconfirmation may be of two sorts—negative (worse than expected) or positive (better than expected). In both cases, there may be a tendency to exaggerate (contrast effects) discrepancies. As modeled in Exhibit 18.3, disconfirmation functions to exaggerate differences, thereby increasing dissatisfaction (negative disconfirmation) or delight (positive disconfirmation).

Finally, we need to mention the relationship between expectations and disconfirmation. One possible relationship is a negative one, known as a ceiling-floor effect. In this case, very high expectations (ceiling) are more likely to result in negative disconfirmation, and very low expectations (floor) in positive disconfirmation. People reflect a belief in this relationship when they say, "I don't want to get my hopes too high because then I'm sure to be disappointed," or even "I'm keeping my expectations low, so I won't be disappointed." Because of these effects, firms may sometimes benefit from downplaying consumer expectations.

www.natwestfraud.com

www.consumerreports.org

Many internal and external factors influence the expectations that consumers bring to their satisfaction judgments. Some important sources of expectations include memories of past experiences, word-of-mouth communications such as consumer-maintained websites (e.g., see the natwestfraud.com site, which reports claims against the unethical practices of the Royal Bank of Scotland), explicit and implicit promises made by the organization through promotions and other media vehicles, product cues, and third-party information (e.g., from *Consumer Reports*).

Our cultural milieu is also an important source of expectations. For instance, Americans' satisfaction with technological products is linked to cultural myths about technology, human perfection, intelligence, and skill. If managers are interested in exploring the source of consumers' anger, frustration, or dissatisfaction, then they should investigate potential violations of cultural expectations.

Sometimes, cultural expectations become apparent only when you travel outside of your typical cultural setting (recall similar discussions in Chapters 1 and 3). Think about your own expectations about waiting in line for service. Now, consider the way that Danish consumers form into lines. In Denmark many services feature queuing based on taking a number when you enter the establishment. This queuing system reflects Danish cultural values of equality and freedom. Queuing eliminates the possibility that consumers will choose the wrong line and end up having to wait longer than someone else, and it allows them the freedom to move about without fear of losing their place in line.[46]

Expectations may vary in abstractness, complexity, and accessibility. For example, before their river-rafting trips, customers often articulate abstract hopes such as "I want this trip to be something completely different than I've ever experienced" or "I'm hoping this trip will change my life." Imagine the difficulty of trying to fulfill these expectations directly. When expectations are abstract or ill-formed, thinking of satisfaction as a direct result of fulfilled expectations may not be useful. In such circumstances, satisfaction derives from the benefits that were within the range of customer expectations.[47] Several examples of product attributes that contributed to customer satisfaction but were not part of expectations are provided in Consumer Chronicles 18.4.

As just described, trying to understand and identify consumers' expectations can be challenging. Sources of expectations differ, and, sometimes, consumers are only aware of their expectations when they are violated. Adding to the complexity, consumers often use multiple levels of expectations or standards. For example, a consumer taking a vacation cruise may express a goal of rest and relaxation, an expectation for good food and sunshine, and a desire for romance. It's likely the vacation will be judged satisfying even without the romance, but imagine how other goals and expectations won't matter if the consumer's hopes of a wonderful romance are realized!

In some cases the comparison object is not known at the time of purchase but is formulated during or following the consumption experience and then used in determining level of satisfaction. Consider especially trial of novel products or services. Free food samples offered in grocery stores offer a familiar example. Sometimes, consumers will try a product in a supermarket with few **active expectations** of what it will be like. That is, they haven't thought, felt, or sensed what will happen when they taste the product. That is not to say they don't have **passive expectations.** For example, consumers passively assume that they will not be poisoned and the product won't taste too bad (or stores wouldn't offer it up in a promotion). From a variety of cues, for example, the response of other consumers, color, apparent texture, and visible packaging, consumers may passively organize some ideas about what to expect. However, it may be that this jumble of thoughts and perceptual judgments gets organized into a comparison object only after the first taste: "Oh this tastes a little like a ______, only it is [sweeter, saltier, crunchier, and so on]." At this point a comparison object has been identified.

Exciting Postpurchase Product Attributes

CONSUMER CHRONICLES 18.4

When searching for a new car, one respondent found the "hill hold" feature on a Subaru to be "wonderful" and "really neat," though she had never sought out this element. Another respondent did not know his television had a sleep timer until he brought his purchase home. The sleep timer was "icing on the cake." One woman was "thrilled" when her Keds sneakers held up far beyond her expectations. One man was delighted to find the "ridiculous" heated seats in his used BMW extended the season for convertible driving and helped to sooth his chronic back troubles.

Source: Steven N. Silverman and Rajiv Grover, "Forming Perceptions of Overall Quality in Consumer Products: A Process of Quality Element Integration," Marketing Science Institute working paper, report no. 95–103, April 1995.

Marketers often attempt to identify comparison objects for consumers in a way to make their offering seem desirable or superior. An interesting example of a product that doesn't measure up to what, at first glance, appears to be its competition suggests the importance of considering comparison objects. The product is the Velo-Glide bicycle. Like a previous year's Harley limited-edition bicycle that sold out in four months, the Velo-Glide is built by GT Bicycles under license to Harley-Davidson. It too is a limited edition, with only 3,000 made, and can be purchased for a mere $1,700. At 40-plus pounds, it's a big clunker that no one would really want to ride, but it offers a Harley paint job, a fake gas tank, and the signature fenders and chrome of a Harley Softail motorcycle.[48] In this case other bicycles are not relevant comparison objects, but other Harley collectibles might be.

@ www.funbox.nl/bike_harley.html

Consumers' expectations change over time. With some service encounters, and probably with many product experiences as well, consumers update their expectations throughout the consumption process.[49] Although this seems intuitively obvious, there is actually little understanding of how this process works. In particular, it's unclear how these updated expectations are related to observed performance up to that point and how updated expectations influence satisfaction.

Consider a simple illustration. Suppose you are hoping to take your date to a nice restaurant, and on the basis of a recommendation from a friend you believe that Ambiance Unlimited is just the right place. Now suppose you walk in with your date, are seated, and given a menu. A glance at the menu and the surroundings leads you to feel disappointed. For example, the restaurant doesn't seem as fancy and exotic as you expected. At this point, you may revise your expectations downward. Although the menu doesn't seem very exotic, it turns out that many of the simple items are prepared

Ben's Telephone Answering Machine

CONSUMER CHRONICLES 18.5

Ben had definite preconsumption, predictive expectations for specific features, benefits, and uses of his telephone answering machine. However, because Ben was offered a full-time position shortly after acquiring his answering machine, the calls he expected from his supervisor did not materialize. The disconfirmation of this previously significant expectation did not appear to affect his satisfaction. Ben also came to realize that he had only four friends with whom he socialized and that he saw them regularly in class. Thus, his expectation of receiving social-planning calls was also disconfirmed, and this too appeared inconsequential to his satisfaction. In fact, by the end of six months, Ben was hardly using the device to record important calls as originally intended. Instead, he was screening calls when studying, eating, or avoiding requests to work on his day off—a usage and benefit that did not figure in his predictive expectations at purchase time. In fact, because of situational changes and new realizations in his personal and social-life world, Ben derived a complete and apparently satisfying reverse of predicted product benefits—obstructing rather than facilitating communication.

with style and fanfare at your table. The presentation of the food is exquisite. Included are some nice surprises such as a little appetizer and a chocolate dessert. Depending on a host of other things, including the interaction between you and your date, you may leave the restaurant quite satisfied or even delighted. The question remains, is your comparison standard now that first expectation of a fancy, exotic restaurant, or is it your revised expectation?[50]

The preceding discussion helps to emphasize an important point: *Satisfaction is a process extending across the entire consumption experience.* Studying consumer–product interactions following purchase is fundamental to understanding satisfaction. It is also important to consider consumer reactions over the full life of the product. For instance, L.L. Bean, in an ad campaign, specifically encourages its customers to evaluate product performance over an extended time period. In Consumer Chronicles 18.5, Ben finds that his initial expectations about a telephone answering machine need to be revised as he gains experience with the product. Also, as his personal and professional life evolve, his expectations about the product change. In summary, consumers are constantly learning, and their goals are evolving. Thus, the evaluation criteria that consumers use at the end of a product's life may be quite different from the expectations that they started out with, years ago when they made the purchase decision.[51]

Other Comparative Standards for Judging Satisfaction

In this section we consider two other possible satisfaction standards: desires and fairness.

DESIRES Individuals' goals and desires might serve as a standard against which to judge satisfaction. In a **desires model of satisfaction,** satisfaction is a function of the consumer's *assessment of the degree to which a product meets or exceeds his or her desires, the outcome being called desires congruency.* **Desires** are *the levels of products' attributes and benefits that a consumer believes will lead to, or are connected with, higher-level values,* such as the terminal values discussed in Chapter 3. Some research, discussed there, showed how a simple answering machine enabled one woman to fulfill her maternal desire to be available to her children and how a video camera enabled an older man to craft a legacy of stories for his children.[52]

Some advertisements emphasize a connection between product use and deeply held consumer desires, but delivering on these desires is hard. For example, ads for New Balance running shoes seem to promise fulfillment of the desire for a balanced life (a deeply held and oft-frustrated desire of many consumers). Yet, all these promises rely on significant effort from the consumer and may often result in dissatisfaction, sometimes attributed to the self rather than product failure. As we all know, obtaining a balanced life requires more than running shoes.

Some Ways of Asking about Consumer Desires

GOOD PRACTICE 18.4

1. Build a collage expressing the concept of desire.
2. Imagine swimming in a sea of things (objects, experiences, people) that bring you the greatest pleasure.
3. Write a fairy tale in which someone experiences great suffering, but in the end finds great happiness.
4. List states that you regard as the opposite of desire.
5. List things that you regard as the opposite of desire, and describe your feelings about those things.
6. Describe desire and the opposite of desire as taste, smell, color, shape, texture, sound, and emotion.
7. Sketch artworks that represent desire and not desire.
8. Use examples to describe differences between wants and desires. How would someone differ in their feelings and behaviors if they desire versus want something?
9. Name an object, experience, or person (X) that you desire, and list as many words or phrases as you can that might be used in the sentence "I ______ X."
10. Describe the feelings people might have about a desired thing before they get it, at the moment they get it, and after they get it.

Source: Adapted from Russell W. Belk, Güliz Ger, and Søren Askegaard, "Consumer Desire in Three Cultures: Results from Projective Research," in Advances in Consumer Research, *vol. 24, ed. Merrie Brucks and Deborah J. MacInnis (Provo, UT: Association for Consumer Research, 1997), pp. 24–25.*

Most satisfaction research has assumed that judgments are a rational and cognitive process of connecting product features to benefits. But consumption desires often spring from less rational and more affective processes, many below the threshold of consciousness.

An interesting, ongoing, multicultural research project attempts to look at the nature of consumer desire using a range of projective research techniques to tap the irrational bases of satisfaction.[53] Such research could help us refine and extend the desires model of satisfaction. Good Practice 18.4 illustrates some of the different methods these researchers have used to understand what consumers desire. One of their techniques invites consumers to make collages to illustrate their desires. Another asks informants to imagine that they are swimming in a sea of things.

FAIRNESS Perceptions of fairness affect consumers' satisfaction. The consumer in the opening vignette reports that fair prices contribute to her retail loyalty, for example.[54] When consumers feel they've been exposed to unfair or deceptive pricing practices, they may seek reparation by switching brands or firms.[55] Consumers may also seek to punish marketers for unfair treatment. When consumers perceived one bank's fees for automatic teller machine services to be unfair, they reported an intention to switch even when they gained nothing from switching, reflecting a desire to punish the firm.[56] The **fairness** concept is built into **Homans's rule of justice,** which proclaims that *parties' rewards in exchanges with others should be proportional to their investments* (or losses). (See Chapter 16 for discussion of Homans's theory of exchange.) In judging fairness, consumers compare their outcomes to their investments (or losses), but they also compare their outcomes to the perceived outcomes of other individuals or groups. Thus, senior-citizen or student price discounts do not usually provoke concerns about fairness, because consumers recognize differences in relative investments between consumer groups. However, when the comparison reveals relative inequality in the distribution of gains and losses, an inequitable, or unfair, exchange exists. Perceived inequity results in feelings of distress. Because of their socialist heritage, Eastern European consumers often feel guilty if they get a better deal than someone else. More individualistic Western consumers experience anger if someone else gets a better deal than they do. Consumers seem more inclined to act against firms in the latter situation.[57]

Exhibit 18.4 illustrates the relationship between three dimensions of fairness and satisfaction/dissatisfaction. The marketing research on fairness focuses primarily on **distributional fairness,** or *how rewards or outcomes are partitioned among the participants in an exchange.*[58] For example, preferential seating on airlines for frequent fliers appears to be considered a fair distribution of outcomes by passengers. By contrast, some Windows customers were upset that customers of WordPerfect who switched to Microsoft Word paid the same price for a software upgrade as the Word users did. They felt that their loyalty was unfairly rewarded.[59]

Research both inside and outside marketing settings suggests that two other forms of fairness are also important to satisfaction judgments. **Procedural fairness** refers to *the manner in which the outcomes are delivered.* When customers both participate in and influence the outcomes of service delivery, satisfaction increases.[60]

Interactional fairness refers to *how the consumer is treated by the marketer.* Is the customer accorded respect, politeness, and dignity? Level of satisfaction and likelihood of complaint behavior depend on whether consumers perceive the outcome following a service failure to be fair, but they also depend on interactional justice. This term refers to the degree to which the service provider provides an explanation, shows empathy and respect, and takes steps to correct service failures promptly. Similarly, a transatlantic study of customer call centers found that problem resolution on the first call was the most significant determinant of satisfaction.[61]

Consumer Attributions and the Satisfaction Process

When products or services fail, consumers may attempt to understand the reason why. The degree of disappointment and anger felt are influenced by how consumers explain the failure. We have talked about consumer attributions in other chapters. Attribution

EXHIBIT 18.4

The Relationship between Fairness and Satisfaction

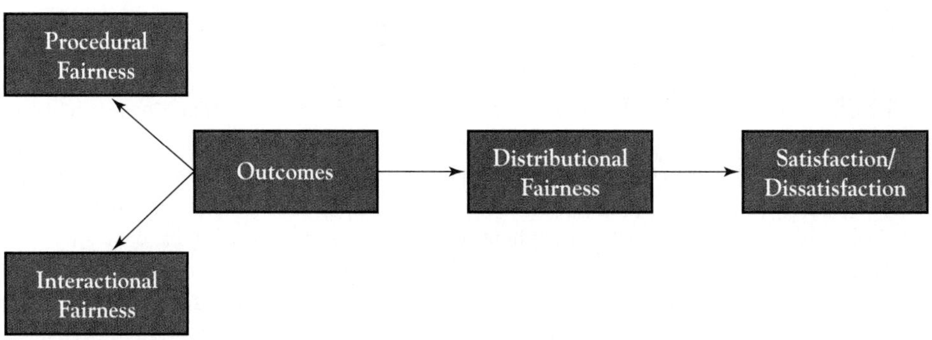

Source: Reproduced from Richard L. Oliver, *Satisfaction: A Behavioral Perspective on the Consumer* (New York: McGraw-Hill, 1997), p. 208.

theory was developed in social psychology to understand how individuals find explanations for outcomes or behaviors. In this chapter, we focus on the effects of consumer attributions on the emotions and judgments made by a consumer following the purchase and consumption experience.

A story illustrates how such attributions work in influencing consumers' feelings and judgments. Professor Arnould, one of the co-authors of this text, had spent three weeks in the war-ravaged central African nation of Chad. He'd worked for some weeks under uncomfortable conditions with refugees out in the bush. There, a local military commander had accidentally shot himself to death at his own birthday party. Disgruntled townsfolk approached Arnould with allegations of fraud against his employer, an international relief organization. In addition, he'd spent part of a night in the capital city, N'Djamena, under his bed avoiding stray bullets from a victory celebration. Following all this, he was anxious to catch one of the two weekly flights out of Chad. After he had waited patiently in the capital for one of the flights, sitting at the airport for three hours anticipating its arrival (a guy sitting next to him at the bar vomited on his shoes), the plane failed to land. The airline plausibly blamed a sandstorm. The local manager helped Arnould transfer his reservations to the other weekly scheduled flight on a different airline. Two days later, this plane also failed to land. The explanation offered: an African head of state had commandeered the plane. The second airline, popularly referred to as Air Tragique to reflect its service profile, offered no compensation. But the manager of the first company finally arranged to get the increasingly agitated passengers booked on a special charter flight that left the next day for a third country. There, after waiting in a "luxury hotel" all day, the passengers finally boarded a regularly scheduled flight for Paris. How upset was Professor Arnould, and at whom?

There are a variety of reasons to suspect that he was fairly dissatisfied with some aspects of his service experience, especially with Air Tragique. First of all, the consumption outcome in this case was very important to him. He'd done his job; he was tired and homesick. Second, there was nothing much that he could do; that is, he was not to blame for what happened. He did his part. He arrived in plenty of time for the flights, waited patiently, and followed directions. Third, he felt that Air Tragique management could have done things differently, especially since the other airline manager acted so

Waiting . . .

EXHIBIT 18.5

Consumer Attributions and Feelings of Anger with the Firm

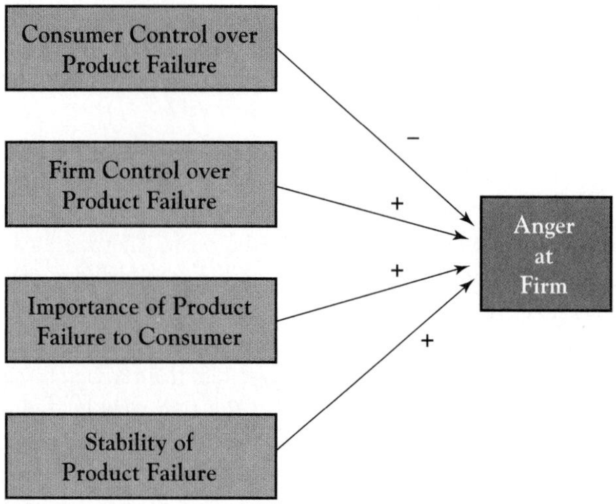

Source: Adapted from Valerie S. Folkes, Susan Koletsky, and John L. Graham, "A Field Study of Causal Inferences and Consumer Reaction: The View from the Airport," *Journal of Consumer Research* 13 (March 1987), pp. 534–39; and Valerie S. Folkes, "Consumer Reactions to Product Failure: An Attributional Approach," *Journal of Consumer Research* 10 (March 1984), pp. 398–409.

proactively. Actions that are detrimental to a person and perceived by that individual as subject to the discretion of others generate anger. If the second delay had been caused by bad weather, like the first, it would have been frustrating and stressful but understandable and less likely to generate anger toward the firm. Fourth, Air Tragique's behavior did not seem unusual; rather, it reflected the airline's service quality more generally. By contrast, the other firm went to extraordinary lengths to get the passengers out of Chad.[62] The story illustrates both successful and unsuccessful managerial tactics for influencing consumer attributions. The relationships we have outlined between attributions and anger (dissatisfaction) toward the firm are summarized in Exhibit 18.5.

In this section we have described some of the factors that influence satisfaction. We have summarized what we currently know about the relationship between performance and satisfaction, how employee satisfaction influences customer satisfaction, differences between choice criteria and satisfaction criteria, and several different kinds of comparisons that consumers use in judging satisfaction. We have also briefly outlined how consumer explanations for failure are related to satisfaction. In the next section, we examine the relationship between emotions and satisfaction.

EMOTIONS, AMBIVALENCE, AND SATISFACTION

Attention has recently shifted to the emotional content of satisfaction and especially the way in which satisfaction and emotions vary together.[63] In some cases, emotions vary quite a bit over time. Consider white-water river rafting. Satisfaction with the experience sometimes has a low-arousal emotional quality (relaxing on calm water following rapids), other times a high-arousal quality (during and immediately following rapids), and other times a cognitive appraisal quality (learning a lot about oneself and others from the experience).[64] This same mixture of emotions and cognition applies to other kinds of purchase processes, especially experiential (a museum tour, a roller coaster ride) and leisure-oriented (watching a movie, attending a ball game) consumption episodes. Five emotional response modes—contentment, pleasure, delight, relief, and ambivalence—might all be described as satisfaction.[65]

Satisfaction as Contentment

One common meaning of satisfaction is contentment. The **contentment response** is characterized by *low levels of emotional arousal and may entail disinterest.* Contentment is a passive response. This is the type of satisfaction response consumers often give when asked how satisfied they are with products that they don't think about very much. What the "satisfied" consumer means is that the product performance is within expectations, and so disconfirmation is neutral. This satisfaction response could also be associated with high-involvement products that have stable performance over time. For example, a consumer might express contentment over a family car that has functioned reliably over many years. While satisfaction may no longer have the emotional edge it had when the car was new, the consumer is still satisfied.

Sometimes, experiences with related products can lead consumers to change their post-purchase evaluations. In fact, the satisfaction rating can even switch valences, from positive to negative or vice versa. For example, Consumer Chronicles 18.4 refers to experiences with a Subaru, a BMW, Keds sneakers, and a TV sleep timer that evoked pleasure for some consumers. In each case, experience with the superior product helps reframe previous product experiences, perhaps even to the point of arousing discontent.

Satisfaction as Pleasure

Many times, purchases and product use make consumers happy. For example, when consumers choose a favorite piece of clothing, have a pleasing sensory experience at a restaurant, play a new CD they just purchased, or sit behind the wheel of their new automobile, they may have a **pleasure response.** An ad for Häagen-Dazs, shown on the next page, encourages consumers to dive into pure pleasure. In this case, *the consumer confirms expectations and has moderate to high arousal and most likely high to moderate involvement as well.* The consumer is more actively involved in processing product performance, in contrast with the contentment response mode.

Firms that consistently deliver high-quality service are likely to evoke a pleasure response. The catalog merchandiser Lands' End prides itself on being this kind of company. Lands' End has an Internet team, serving people who use the Lands' End Live feature on the company's website. With a click of a mouse, Lands' End Live allows customers to start a live chat with a Lands' End representative or get a rep to call them at home, immediately. In many cases, sales are closed by human interaction that soothes last-minute anxieties and doubts at the point of purchase. Perhaps, you can think of other products that evoke, for you, a pleasure response.[66]

@ www.landsend.com

Satisfaction as Delight

Occasionally, product or service performance evokes a combination of joy and surprise that has been termed delight. The **delight response** involves *either a positive disconfirmation of expectations or, alternatively, a positive event or outcome that the consumer did not have any expectations about.*[67] A few years ago, two of your authors stayed in a small hotel in Sweden. Right after checking in, our daughter had an accident on the bed that required changing the sheets (unpleasant even to request). An hour later when

Evoking satisfaction as pleasure.

we returned to the room, not only were the sheets freshly changed but also our daughter's stuffed animals had been gently and lovingly arranged in her little toddler bed. As consumers, we were delighted. For many complex products and services, consumers may have few expectations. As described earlier, even articulated needs are often quite abstract. In such cases, delight may come from discovering pleasurable surprises (e.g., a useful feature after purchase).

Satisfaction as Relief

Sometimes, the removal of a negative state leads to consumer satisfaction. Such a situation evokes a **relief response.** Whereas consumers actively seek out feelings of contentment, pleasure, and delight, most do not look for aversive stimuli that can then be eliminated.

A feeling of relief may come about as a response to unfulfilled negative expectations ("I didn't have to wait as long as I expected," "It didn't hurt as much as I expected"). Relief can also result from the elimination of a negative state, as with medication, a successful legal defense, or a warning instead of a ticket for speeding. The ad for Tropicana grapefruit juice, shown on the next page, taps into satisfaction as relief, the promise of quenching your thirst.

Depending on the situation, satisfaction as relief can involve high levels of arousal and involvement. For example, a patient waiting to hear the results of a test for a serious

Evoking satisfaction as relief.

illness would likely experience very high levels of emotional arousal (probably lots of fear and anxiety). These factors will strongly influence perceptions of waiting time, for example. When the marketer believes satisfaction as relief is a response to performance, timing service or product delivery and helping the customer manage expectations become crucial.[68]

Satisfaction as Ambivalence

Consumers in complex societies often deal with conflicting demands, social roles, and cultural values. Even self-concepts (as described in Chapter 10) involve conflicting aspects or even different selves. Hence, the **ambivalence response** is common in various purchase and consumption experiences. We can define consumer ambivalence as *the simultaneous or sequential experience of multiple emotional states associated with acquisition or consumption processes.* This may involve high levels of involvement and affective response. Many of our most memorable consumption and life experiences may be best described as evoking mixed emotions. For example, a bride describes the joy she got from purchasing her wedding dress. However, as the description of her purchasing process in Consumer Chronicles 18.6 shows, she also reveals anger, disappointment, and regret. Thus, satisfaction may sometimes result from achieving balance between conflicting emotions associated with product use. When the marketer believes ambivalence is a response to performance, helping the customer interpret expectations and outcomes becomes crucial.[69]

Purchasing a Wedding Dress

CONSUMER CHRONICLES 18.6

Probably the biggest joy that I got was my dress . . . I was . . . up in Chicago . . . [It was] the second dress I tried on . . . and the people there were just very, very rude, so I didn't get the dress up there . . . So the girl ordered it for me here . . . So when we got the dress, it was like the generic version [of] the original dress I tried on. What had happened was . . . it was during [the Persian Gulf] war . . . [and] people were pushing their weddings up so far, and so fast. So, instead of the actual hand-sewn dresses, they were mass-producing them . . . So, I sat in the showroom, and just cried and cried because, I mean, I didn't need the dress right away, you know. And they ended up giving my money back, and I went up and bought the sample in Chicago. It was a frustrating time, but it all worked out.

Source: Cele Otnes, Tina M. Lowrey, and L. J. Shrum, "Toward an Understanding of Consumer Ambivalence," Journal of Consumer Research *24 (June 1997), p. 80.*

THE CONSEQUENCES OF SATISFACTION AND DISSATISFACTION

In response to their consumption experiences, consumers may opt to exercise one or more of four behavioral responses: exit, voice, continued patronage, or "twist" (e.g., resistance).[70] Many different kinds of feelings and beliefs are expressed for each of these behaviors.

Exit

When a consumer has a dissatisfying purchase of consumption experience, perhaps the most common response is simply *not to purchase or use that product or service again.* That is, the consumer will **exit** as a customer of the organization. At a minimum, the dissatisfied consumer may attempt to avoid that product or service, selecting other alternatives whenever they are accessible and feasible. Of course, not all decisions to exit are based on dissatisfaction, and not all dissatisfied consumers exit. Barclays Bank in the UK found that many dissatisfied customers simply reduced their account activity to low levels, exerting a passive form of exit.[71]

We have already discussed switching behavior in Chapter 16, so we will not review the broad literature on that subject here. Sometimes consumers exit because another alternative seems superior, because they are seeking variety, or because circumstances or needs have changed. Nevertheless, the average firm is estimated to lose 20 percent of its customers in a given year, mostly due to dissatisfaction.[72] Waiting until dissatisfaction expresses itself as a decision to exit can have a disastrous effect on market share and profits. Recognizing this problem, Barclays Bank developed a tracking system to detect declining account use and to intervene in an effort to restore satisfaction.

Some consumers will exit or switch, rather than complain, when markets are heterogeneous (offer lots of different alternatives) and consumers are knowledgeable about alternatives.[73] That is, when consumers perceive that they have choices and don't have to patronize a particular organization, they will switch when they are dissatisfied. Such an exit strategy would often be employed with low-involvement or inexpensive products. Rather than make a big fuss over a little thing, the consumer simply resolves to do something different the next time. Of course, this invisible response to dissatisfaction can gradually erode market share unless the firm makes an effort to uncover the discontent behind this action.

Voice

Voice is very important for marketers. **Voice** can take several different forms, including *compliments an organization may receive when it delivers an especially satisfying* *outcome, complaints to the company about performance failure, negative and positive word-of-mouth with other consumers or consuming organizations, or third-party complaints or compliments.* Consumers' complaints and compliments to firms provide valuable feedback, and these communications influence other consumers. The Planned Parenthood advertisement shown on page 782 encourages the use of consumer voice to communicate to legislators.[74]

Loyal customers are most likely to engage in positive word-of-mouth. One study showed not only that loyal customers provided more recommendations than others but that the number of recommendations increased with the duration of their relationship with the firms studied, a bank and a dental office.

Consumers' interpersonal communications, both positive and negative, strongly influence others' purchases.[75] Unfortunately, customers are more apt to engage in word-of-mouth than to provide feedback.[76] The complaints website provides a clearinghouse, featuring complaints about dozens of U.S. firms. Chapter 14 provides a more complete treatment of how word-of-mouth communications influence purchase and consumption decisions.

www.complaints.com

Management can use complaints as an important tool.[77] Dissatisfied consumers who do not complain are more likely to discontinue purchase (e.g., exit).[78] By encouraging consumers to complain and seeking to resolve their problems, management can actually create more satisfied consumers who are more likely to talk favorably about the organization with other consumers. The very act of complaining can enhance ultimate satisfaction, not only through initiating redress but also through the cathartic effects it provides a consumer—"getting it off my chest." In contrast, consumers' negative word-of-mouth communications tend to reinforce or increase their levels of dissatisfaction with the firm.[79] At the same time, firms are very interested to minimize the incidence of "third-party" behavior. That is, the firm is better off if the complaint can be resolved before the unhappy customer complains to third parties (e.g., friends, watch-dog organizations). Thus, firms want to know about customer problems as quickly as possible, and they want complaints communicated directly to them. For instance, retailers such as Wal-Mart offer virtual space to identify and resolve consumer problems.

www.walmart.com/cservice/ca_helphome.gsp

Management should make sure legitimate complaints are handled efficiently and effectively. For example, a study from Singapore found that the more quickly complaints were responded to, the higher the satisfaction.[80] Theoretically, management can expect market share gains and decreased costs of attracting customers if the company maximizes attempts to encourage and resolve complaints (subject to cost constraints).[81]

Voice can accompany either exit or continued patronage behavior. For example, a person dissatisfied with a particular cleaning service may continue to use that service but complain in an effort to improve performance. Alternatively, a dissatisfied consumer may stop using that service and also engage in negative word-of-mouth communications.[82]

Voice varies with culture, market infrastructure (e.g., presence of a complaint channel), the economics of complaining, and consumer psychology. In a study of complaining behavior in a banking setting, researchers found that consumers from the inegalitarian and individualistic cultures (United States and Switzerland) were more likely to complain than those from the more egalitarian, less individualistic culture (Singapore). Consumers in individualistic and inegalitarian cultures are more likely to engage in negative word-of-mouth than positive word-of-mouth, whereas those in more egalitarian, less individualistic cultures may provide more positive feedback to firms. Complaining behavior in the United States varies by ethnic group or subculture. Mexican-American consumers are more likely to complain about problems such as delay or nondelivery than other consumers. Puerto Rican cultural norms and values lead consumers in that

Encouraging the exercise of consumer voice.

ethnic group to complain less than other U.S. consumers.[83] Age, income, education, attitudes, interests, and personalities have all been used as predictors of complaining behavior. Complainers tend to be younger, have higher incomes, and be less brand loyal than noncomplainers.[84]

Noncomplaining rates vary by culture.[85] For example, cultures with a more fatalistic worldview (belief in fate) complain less. Those with totalitarian political regimes complain less. Likewise, those with an interdependent orientation may be less likely to complain than those that emphasize individual agency.

Consumers in countries that have not developed market infrastructures to facilitate voice or where the consuming publics are relatively uninformed about their rights as consumers may be less likely to complain. In many developing or transitional economies, consumers lack opportunity and knowledge about how to complain. In Malaysia, one of retailer Carrefour's innovations was to offer suggestion cards to facilitate feedback that are read daily by the management team.[86] Even in developed economies in Europe, people often view complaints as bad; hence, organizational mechanisms for soliciting and responding to complaints are not as well developed as in the United States. The Internet provides increased scope for voice worldwide.[87]

There are a number of economic reasons that help explain why a consumer would or would not complain. As the price declines, so does complaining. In this case, it's not worth the cost of complaining. When a product is important for a consumer, then the likelihood of complaining is higher than when the product is not so important. The perceived costs and efforts of complaining will depress complaining behavior. Consumers will also attempt to assess the likely outcomes of complaining; a firm's reputation for addressing complaints may increase complaining behavior. But if firms institute policies that are too generous, unjustified consumer complaints may be triggered.[88] The problem of **fraudulent complaining** is a legitimate concern for management, as some consumers will try to improve their outcomes through this method.

Attributions or causal inferences for service failure influence both positive and negative word-of-mouth. Not surprisingly, consumers are more likely to complain and compliment when they hold the seller responsible and perceive the cause of the failure or success to be stable and under the seller's control.[89]

Perceived psychological costs may hinder dissatisfied but passive consumers from complaining. For example, complaining may be viewed as confrontational, and the consumer may fear being intimidated or berated by the organization. In addition, the consumer may fear being labeled a complainer or, even worse, a chronic complainer. By contrast, activist consumers perceive low psychological cost from complaining, engage heavily in complaining, and are likely to complain to a third party.[90]

The Value of Loyal Customers

INDUSTRY INSIGHTS 18.3

Some examples of the direct monetary value of loyal customers include

1. $360,000 in lifetime revenues to Federal Express.
2. $4,000 in lifetime revenues to a Baltimore Pizza Hut franchise.
3. $50,000 in 10-year revenues to a Connecticut grocery store owner.
4. $332,000 in lifetime revenues to a Texas Cadillac dealer.

Source: Dwayne D. Gremler and Stephen W. Brown, "The Loyalty Ripple Effect: Appreciating the Full Value of Customer," International Journal of Service Industry Management *10, no. 3 (1999), pp. 271–93.*

Continued Patronage

In this section, we consider the relationship between customer satisfaction and continued patronage, or loyalty. Satisfaction is a relatively temporary postpurchase state that reflects how the product or service has fulfilled its purpose. We emphasized in Chapters 6 and 16 that loyalty goes beyond satisfaction.[91] **Customer loyalty** is *a deeply held commitment to rebuy or repatronize a preferred product or service consistently in the future, despite situational influences and marketing efforts having the potential to cause switching behavior.*[92] Thus, loyalty includes both readiness to act (repeat purchase) and resistance to alternatives. For firms, loyalty leads to an increase in profits, more predictable sales and profit streams, and positive word-of-mouth. As discussed earlier in the chapter, high overall satisfaction protects firms from a reduction in loyalty after poor performance in a particular transaction.[93] Some calculations of the direct monetary benefits of loyalty are shown in Industry Insights 18.3.[94]

As indicated earlier in this chapter, customer satisfaction leads to loyalty and continued patronage.[95] Specifically, if a consumer is loyal and switching costs are high, decreases in satisfaction will not cause switching until some threshold of dissatisfaction is reached. Thus, people continue to fly on airlines they do not like because they need to go where the airline goes. However, defection rates among satisfied customers as high as 90 percent are reported. Product quality or switching costs alone are weak determinants of continued patronage.[96]

Companies should be quite interested in generating and maintaining consumer loyalty, but it's not easy. Although clusters of consumers claim that they find a good brand and stick with it, this doesn't seem to translate into consistent repurchase rates.[97] While 85 to 95 percent of automobile customers report they are satisfied, only 30 to 40 percent return to their previous make. A typical large study in Denmark that included 684 brands of consumer products found that only 13 percent of consumers claimed to use a specific brand 90 to 100 percent of the time. Consumers search for variety and respond to switching incentives provided by competitors.[98]

As suggested by our opening vignette and examples given here, enduring loyalty is a long-term consequence only of some types of customer satisfaction (e.g., pleasure and delight). Under such circumstances, loyal consumers are resistant to competitive switching efforts. If product consumption is closely associated with community membership or identity, loyalty may be stronger. Loyalty to Wrangler jeans, Justin boots, Resistol hats, and Skoal smokeless tobacco among some North American cowboys, for example, or the loyalty to particular European football teams reflects these identity and community-based types of loyalty.

Relational strength may lead consumers to ignore competitive alternatives. Consumers may remain loyal even when it is difficult to do so. Consider the case of hairstylists and consumers. Some consumers will travel long distances at considerable inconvenience to continue patronage because of their loyal feelings for the stylist. Sports and music fans also engage in this kind of behavior.[99]

With low switching costs in competitive markets, the relationship between satisfaction and continued patronage is more fluid. When people are only moderately satisfied with an automobile, they may switch since there are so many brands of cars available. Satisfaction is not enough to ensure continued patronage.

Twist[100]

Consumers may express themselves through actions other than switching, voice, or loyalty. We use the term **twist** to refer to these behaviors. Twist refers to *positive and negative ways in which consumers restructure meanings, roles, and objects in the marketplace.* The consumer reacts to consumer satisfaction/dissatisfaction with novel behaviors unanticipated by the offering organization. In one example of positive twist, loyal customers pitched in to help when the Tattered Cover Bookstore in Denver, Colorado, moved to a new location. Consumers, in effect, became partners with the firm, striving to help the organization achieve its goals.[101] In general, it seems likely that loyal consumers might be more likely to feel a sense of ownership that translates into positive, voluntary, and often novel behaviors toward the organization. Such behaviors are common for many not-for-profit organizations such as churches or public radio stations that rely on volunteers to answer phones during annual fund drives. For other types of organizations, positive twist may be more common than most people realize. Positive twist includes little things such as picking up someone else's litter in the parking lot or rehanging a piece of clothing that some other customer knocked off the rack. To date, we know very little about positive voluntary customer behaviors or how they relate to feelings of satisfaction or loyalty. Can you think of examples of positive twist you engage in?

Alternatively, consumers may reflect their dissatisfaction with a company by engaging in negative twist: unwanted behaviors or acts of resistance against the company. Sometimes these behaviors take organized form such as picketing an establishment. Resistance may also take more subtle, unorganized forms. Among the behaviors that disgruntled consumers might consider are the following: shoplifting, covert rebundling of sales merchandise (substituting a more expensive item for a less expensive item in a bundle), switching packaging to get lower prices on more expensive products, returning merchandise under false pretenses, fraudulent coupon use, and misusing memberships (e.g., allowing nonmembers to use memberships). Lately, resistance has reached the Internet, with hackers breaking into corporate websites to inject their own commentary. An example is provided in Consumer Chronicles 18.7.[102]

Alternatively, disgruntled consumers can start their own websites to publicize their grievances with specific organizations. For instance, Takako Itano, a 27-year-old systems engineer in Tokyo, was irritated when she was mistakenly charged for an Internet access fee by her phone company. She was even more irritated when her attempts to straighten out the mistake did not go smoothly. Eventually, she started writing about this problem in her diary. What's notable is that Ms. Itano keeps her diary on her website. In the two years since she started her site, complete with a bulletin board, the site has registered 32,000 hits. After updating the story of her dealings with the phone company, Ms. Itano received a flood of opinions and sympathetic messages on the bulletin board from Japanese consumers nationwide who had suffered similar experiences with the same company. In this sense, the Internet ushers in an age of real "consumer power," where the problems of one consumer can be magnified and publicized via the Internet.[103]

Nike Jam

CONSUMER CHRONICLES 18.7

Where better to place a call for global justice than on Nike's own website? Recently, an unknown hijacker redirected potential shoe shoppers to www.s11.org, the Australian website organizing the protest at Melbourne's World Economic Forum in September 1999. The jam lasted for 19 hours, and hits jumped from a low of 57 to a high of 66,000 an hour at the peak of the hijacking!

Until recently, discussions of twist have been limited and focused primarily on collective (organized) actions directed at changes in marketing mix structure and composition.[104] However, as we have suggested, there are many forms of twist. We can describe these kinds of consumers along four dimensions. First, consumers can resist as individuals or collectives. Second, consumers can have goals that vary from reformist to radical. Third, tactics of resistance can vary from actions directed at altering the marketing mix (fighting for product safety features or against ads on television) to actions directed at altering the meaning of products (using products in unintended ways).

Adbusters twists advertising conventions.

Adbusters twists advertising conventions to encourage consumer resistance.

Fourth, consumers can either appropriate marketing institutions and agents as their tools of resistance or try to use nonmarketing institutions and agents, such as the courts, as instruments of change. Most instances of consumer resistance can be described using these four dimensions.[105]

www.adbusters.org

One well-known example of organized consumer resistance is *Adbusters. Adbusters* is a quarterly magazine with the twin goals of raising consciousness of commercial excess and elevating the media awareness and skills of those in the anticonsumerist movement. *Adbusters* is a collective project with the radical goal of reducing consumerism. It uses the tools of marketing communications and employs advertising professionals to alter product meanings. Examples of *Adbusters* advertisement parodies are shown above and on page 785. Individual and organized resistance against marketing organizations and marketing practices may be on the increase among generation Xers, a group that tends to be less materialistic and more cynical about marketing than previous generations.[106]

SUMMARY

Satisfaction is a judgment of a pleasurable level of consumption-related fulfillment, including levels of under- or overfulfillment. It involves emotional and cognitive appraisals. Satisfaction judgments can be made with respect to all aspects of product and service experience. Satisfaction often reflects both positive and negative emotions. Satisfaction judgments are nested within the customer's life experience, and different customers are likely to make different satisfaction judgments about the same level of product or service performance. Individual judgments of satisfaction express a broader system of cultural values, meanings, beliefs, emotions, group relationships, and conflicts. When we look at the consumption experience over time, we realize that satisfaction with products and services shifts as current concerns and consumers' life projects shift.

Customer satisfaction plays a key role in marketing strategy (see Chapter 5) through ideas such as "marketing concept" and "relationship marketing." We introduce a general model, where satisfaction and customer loyalty are key variables that can lead to organizational success (e.g., in terms of profits or market share).

Fulfillment, or the feeling of being satisfied, implies goals or standards that form a basis for comparison. Perceived quality is one important standards-based predictor of satisfaction. Expectations are another. Most satisfaction research has employed the expectancy–disconfirmation model as a way of understanding the relationship between standards and satisfaction.

The EDM model has limitations. Attributes, features, and dimensions that contribute to heightened levels of satisfaction may sometimes differ from attributes that contribute to heightened levels of dissatisfaction. Sometimes the consumer can't foresee the problems or benefits of a product prior to purchase. In other cases, important influences on satisfaction are unpredictable. When expectations are abstract or ill formed, modeling satisfaction as a function of expectations may not be very useful.

One competing model identifies consumers' desires as a comparative standard for satisfaction. In a desires model, consumers believe that product attributes will deliver higher-level values. Fairness can also be an important comparative mechanism for judging consumer satisfaction. Three dimensions of fairness that could influence satisfaction are procedural, interactional, and distributional.

When a product or service fails, the consumer often attempts to understand why. The degree of disappointment and anger felt are influenced by the attributions consumers make to explain why the product or service failed.

Satisfaction can simultaneously include a variety of positive and negative emotions. Five different response modes that might all be described as satisfaction are contentment, pleasure, delight, relief, and ambivalence.

In response to satisfying or dissatisfying consumption experiences, consumers may exercise one or more of four behavioral options. They may exit the exchange relationship. Alternatively, consumers may respond by speaking up; this is voice. The consumer may also continue to patronize the firm. We define this loyalty as a deeply held commitment to rebuy a preferred product consistently in the future. Consumers may also express their satisfaction or dissatisfaction through twist, the term we use to incorporate both positive and negative behaviors undertaken toward the firm.

KEY TERMS

REVIEW QUESTIONS

1. Consider a recent purchase decision. Compare the criteria you used in making your choice with the factors that influenced your satisfaction. How were these criteria the same? How were they different?
2. Using the critical incident technique described in this chapter, interview three consumers about their most recent satisfying and dissatisfying service interactions. What factors do consumers name as causing them to feel satisfied or dissatisfied?
3. Consider your own purchase experiences. Try to think of examples where you used (a) desires and (b) fairness as your comparative standard in judging satisfaction.
4. Find examples of advertisements that seem to promise
   a. Contentment
   b. Pleasure
   c. Delight
   d. Relief
5. Choose a recent high-involvement or complex purchase decision. Describe the emotions you felt as you made this decision. Did you have mixed emotions? Explain.
6. During a business luncheon you sit at the table with a manager of a small electronics firm. He emphasizes that the key to customer loyalty is meeting customer expectations. Do you agree or disagree? What would you say? Explain your answer.
7. Interview three consumers about how they responded to a recent dissatisfying purchase experience. Categorize their responses in terms of exit, voice, continued patronage, and twist. See if you can use some of the models and discussion in this chapter to understand their responses.
8. What techniques could a company use to encourage their customers to complain?
9. Conduct an in-depth interview with a marketing professional. Ask him or her to describe
   a. How important customer satisfaction is to his or her business.
   b. How he or she works to generate customer satisfaction.
   c. What kinds of experiences he or she has had with dissatisfied consumers.

   Summarize your findings.

CASES

YOU MAKE THE CALL

TRANSFORMATION IN THE LAUNDRY INDUSTRY

Americans wash a whopping 200 billion pounds of laundry every year. In many parts of the world, laundry is still done as it has been for at least 4,000 years. People haul their baskets to the nearest river, pound the clothes clean on the rocks, and spread them in the sun to bleach and dry. In the United States, the chore of doing laundry has undergone a major transformation. Washing machines are one of the few commodities that cost less today than a generation ago. Doing laundry may be a lot easier than it used to be, but it is still a chore, and people are looking for ways to make it less of a chore.

The United States has about 35,000 coin-operated laundries. Most are located in urban areas with large renter populations. Singles, especially those younger than 35, are much more likely to log hours at a Laundromat. The coin-laundry business is changing, however. One change is the growth of the wash/dry/fold service. People can bring in their dirty laundry and pick it up later all clean and folded. This service is moving into suburban areas and places with middle-class and upper-middle-class consumers.

Another segment of the laundry industry is beginning to offer hip, multiservice Laundromats. At Brain Wash in San Francisco, customers can grab a bite or listen to live music and poetry readings while juggling loads. Stan Klein's Rock and Fold in Chicago treats customers to neon lights, movies on five screens, and gospel music. These Laundromats might be viewed as an attempt to change how consumers feel about doing laundry.

QUESTIONS

1. What type of satisfaction, if any, do you believe consumers associate with completing their laundry?
2. How are multiservice Laundromats trying to influence satisfaction?
3. What factors should Brain Wash consider in assessing satisfaction with its new multiservice Laundromat?

This case is adapted from material found at www.brainwash.com.

1. Based on an interview with a single, female social worker in her 30s living in the southeastern United States. See www.limitedbrands.com/about/bbw.asp; www.limitedbrands.com/whoweare/vend_intro.asp; and www.limitedbrands.com/whoweare.
2. For us, Richard L. Oliver is "Dr. Satisfaction." Our understanding of the topic and its complexity has been resolutely influenced by his work. In this chapter we draw very heavily from his book *Satisfaction: A Behavioral Perspective on the Consumer* (New York: McGraw-Hill, 1997).
3. Robert A. Westbrook and Richard L. Oliver, "The Dimensionality of Consumption Emotion Patterns and Consumer Satisfaction," *Journal of Consumer Research* 18 (June 1991), pp. 84–91; and Linda L. Price, Eric J. Arnould, and Sheila L. Deibler, "Service Provider Influence on Consumers' Emotional Response to Service Encounters," *International Journal of Service Industry Management* 6, no. 3 (1995), pp. 34–63.
4. Adapted from Oliver, *Satisfaction,* p. 13.
5. David T. Botterill, "Dissatisfaction with a Construction of Satisfaction," *Annals of Tourism Research* 14, no. 1 (1987), pp. 139–40; and John Deighton, "The Consumption of Performance," *Journal of Consumer Research* 19 (December 1992), pp. 362–72.
6. Chip Bell, "Turning Disappointment into Customer Delight," *Editor and Publisher,* August 6, 1994, pp. 38, 48; and James G. Marham III and Richard G. Netemeyer, "A Longitudinal Study of Complaining Customers' Evaluations of Multiple Service Failures and Recovery Efforts," *Journal of Marketing* 66 (October 2002), pp. 57–71.
7. Craig J. Thompson, William B. Locander, and Howard R. Pollio, "Putting Consumer Experience Back into Consumer Research: The Philosophy and Method of Existential Phenomenology," *Journal of Consumer Research* 16 (September 1989), pp. 133–47.

8. John E. Swan and Michael R. Bowers, "Services Quality and Satisfaction," *Journal of Services Marketing* 12, no. 1 (1998), pp. 59–72; and John F. Sherry, "Postmodern Alternatives: The Interpretive Turn in Consumer Research," in *Handbook of Consumer Behavior,* ed. Thomas S. Robertson and Harold H. Kassarjian (Englewood Cliffs, NJ: Prentice Hall, 1991), pp. 548–91.
9. Craig J. Thompson, "Caring Consumers: Gendered Consumption Meanings and the Juggling Lifestyle," *Journal of Consumer Research* 22 (March 1996), pp. 388–407; and Susan Fournier and David Glen Mick, "Rediscovering Satisfaction," *Journal of Marketing* 63 (October 1999), pp. 5–23.
10. Slavenka Drakulić, *Café Europa: Life after Communism* (New York: Penguin Books, 1996).
11. This section is summarized from Oliver, *Satisfaction,* pp. 403–5.
12. Christopher W. L. Hart, "The Power of Unconditional Service Guarantees," in *Keeping Customers,* ed. John J. Sviokla and Benson P. Shapiro (Cambridge: Harvard Business School Press, 1993), pp. 151–66.
13. Ibid.
14. Werner Reinartz and V. Kumar, "The Mismanagement of Customer Loyalty," *Harvard Business Review,* July 2002, pp. 86–94.
15. Madhav Srinivasan, "Keeping Your Customers," *Business and Economic Review* 43, no. 1 (1996), pp. 1–8.
16. Ibid.
17. Agnes T. Crane, "Satisfaction Guaranteed," *Business Mexico,* January 1, 1999, p. 56; Helena Ferna, "Need to Ensure That Customers Are Fully Satisfied," *Business Times,* February 8, 1999, p. 3; Richard M. Hodgetts, "Quality Lessons from America's Baldrige Winners, Malcolm Baldrige Quality Award," *Business Horizons* 37 (July 1994), pp. 74–78; and Mick James and Mary Huntington, "Customer Satisfaction: Measuring Client Satisfaction Is Anything but Straightforward," *Management Consultancy,* September 11, 1998.
18. "India: Zen Best Small Car, Says J. D. Power Asia Pacific," *Business Line,* March 24, 1999; and Richard L. Oliver, "Whence Consumer Loyalty?" *Journal of Marketing* 63, Special Issue (1999), pp. 33–44.
19. For an interesting treatment of this subject, see Steven N. Silverman and Rajiv Grover, "Forming Perceptions of Overall Quality in Consumer Products: A Process of Quality Element Integration," Marketing Science Institute working paper, report no. 95-103, April 1995; and Jan-Benedict E. M. Steenkamp, "Conceptual Model of the Quality Perception Process," *Journal of Business Research* 21 (December 1990), pp. 309–33. See also C. A. Reeves and D. A. Bednar, "Defining Quality: Alternatives and Implications," *Academy of Management Review* 19, no. 3 (1994), pp. 419–46.
20. Leonard A. Morgan, "The Importance of Quality," in *Perceived Quality,* ed. Jacob Jacoby and Jerry C. Olson (Lexington, MA: Lexington Books, 1985), pp. 209–32. See also David A. Garvin, "What Does 'Product Quality' Really Mean?" *Sloan Management Review,* Fall 1984, pp. 25–43.
21. Steenkamp, "Conceptual Model of the Quality Perception Process"; and William R. Darden and Barry J. Babin, "Exploring the Concept of Affective Quality: Expanding the Concept of Retail Personality," *Journal of Business Research* 29 (February 1994), pp. 101–9.
22. David K. Tse and Peter C. Wilton, "Models of Consumer Satisfaction Formation: An Extension," *Journal of Marketing Research* 25 (May 1988), pp. 204–12; Claes Fornell, "A National Customer Satisfaction Barometer: The Swedish Experience," *Journal of Marketing* 56 (January 1992), pp. 6–21; and Joseph J. Cronin and Steven A. Taylor, "Measuring Service Quality: A Reexamination and Extension," *Journal of Marketing* 56 (July 1992), pp. 55–67.
23. The most comprehensive of these is the structural equation modeling study performed by Cronin and Taylor, "Measuring Service Quality," which suggested that of alternative possible causal relationships between quality and satisfaction, only the quality $\Rightarrow$ satisfaction path was significant.
24. Fornell, "A National Customer Satisfaction Barometer."
25. David Garvin, "Competing on the Eight Dimensions of Quality," *Harvard Business Review,* November–December 1987, pp. 101–9.

26. P. Bonner and R. Nelson, "Product Attributes and Perceived Quality: Foods," in *Perceived Quality,* ed. J. Jacoby and J. Olson (Lexington, MA: Lexington Books, 1985), pp. 64–79.
27. A. Parasuraman, Valarie A. Zeithaml, and Leonard L. Berry, "SERVQUAL: A Multiple-Item Scale for Measuring Consumer Perceptions of Service Quality," *Journal of Retailing* 64, no. 1 (Spring 1988), pp. 12–40.
28. *The Economist,* UK Edition, May 26, 1997, p. 43; Kathryn Frazer Winsted, "Service Behaviors That Lead to Satisfied Customers," *European Journal of Marketing* 34, nos. 3–4 (2000), pp. 399–417; Li-Wei Mai and Mitchell R. Ness, "Canonical Correlation Analysis of Customer Satisfaction and Future Purchase of Mail-Order Specialty Foods," *British Food Journal* 1010, no. 11 (1999), pp. 857–70; Stewart Robinson, "Measuring Service Quality: Current Thinking and Future Requirements," *Marketing Intelligence and Planning* 17, no. 1 (1999), pp. 21–32; and Syed Saad Andaleeb, "Determinants of Customer Satisfaction with Hospitals: A Managerial Model," *International Journal of Health Care Quality Assurance* 111, no. 6 (1998), pp. 181–87.
29. D. Chadee and J. Mattsson, "Customer Satisfaction in Tourist Service Encounters," *Journal of Travel and Tourism Marketing* 4 (Fall 1995), pp. 97–108; Tat Y. Choi and Raymond Chu, "Levels of Satisfaction among Asian and Western Travelers," *International Journal of Quality and Reliability Management* 17, no. 2 (2000), pp. 116–32; and D. Scott and D. Shieff, "Service Quality Components and Group Criteria in Local Government," *International Journal of Service Industry Management* 4, no. 2 (1993), pp. 18–25.
30. Lance A. Bettencourt and Stephen W. Brown, "Contact Employees; Relationships among Workplace Fairness, Job Satisfaction and Prosocial Service Behaviors," *Journal of Retailing* 73 (Spring 1997), pp. 39–61; and James L. Heskett, Thomas O. Jones, Gary Loveman, Earl W. Sasser Jr., and Leonard A. Schlesinger, "Putting the Service Profit Chain to Work," *Harvard Business Review* 72 (March–April 1994), pp. 164–75.
31. Benjamin Schneider, J. J. Parkington, and V. M. Buxton, "Employee and Customer Perceptions of Service in Banks," *Administrative Science Quarterly,* June 1980, pp. 252–67; and Benjamin Schneider and David E. Bowen, "Employee and Customer Perceptions of Service in Banks: Replication and Extension," *Journal of Applied Psychology* 70 (1985), pp. 423–33.
32. Colby H. Chandler, "Quality: Beyond Customer Satisfaction—to Customer Delight," *Quality Progress,* October 1988, pp. 20–23.
33. Mary Jo Bitner, Bernard H. Booms, and Mary Stanfield Tetreault, "The Service Encounter: Diagnosing Favorable and Unfavorable Incidents," *Journal of Marketing* 54 (January 1990), pp. 71–84; and Mary Jo Bitner, Bernard H. Booms, and Lois A. Mohr, "Critical Service Encounters: The Employee's Viewpoint," *Journal of Marketing* 58 (October 1994), pp. 95–106.
34. Sarah Fisher Gardial, D. Scott Clemons, Robert B. Woodruff, David W. Schumann, and Mary Jane Burns, "Comparing Consumers' Recall of Prepurchase and Postpurchase Product Evaluation Experiences," *Journal of Consumer Research* 20 (March 1994), pp. 548–60; Eric J. Arnould and Linda L. Price, "River Magic: Extraordinary Experience and the Extended Service Encounter," *Journal of Consumer Research* 20 (June 1993); and Lucy L. Henke, "A Longitudinal Analysis of the Ad Agency–Client Relationship: Predictors of an Agency Switch," *Journal of Advertising Research* 35 (March–April 1995), pp. 24–30.
35. Arnould and Price, "River Magic"; Saad A. Metawa and Mohammed Almossawi, "Banking Behavior of Islamic Bank Customers: Perspectives and Implications," *International Journal of Bank Marketing* 16, no. 7 (1998), pp. 288–313; and Kamal Naser, Ahmad Jamal, and Khalid Al-Katib, "Islamic Banking: A Study of Customer Satisfaction and Preferences in Jordan," *International Journal of Bank Marketing* 17, no. 3 (1999), pp. 135–51.
36. See, for example, Michael D. Johnson, George Nader, and Claes Fornell, "Expectations, Perceived Performance, and Customer Satisfaction for a Complex Service: The Case of Bank Loans," *Journal of Economic Psychology* 17 (1996), pp. 163–82.
37. Fournier and Mick, "Rediscovering Satisfaction."
38. For a related example (dealing with road travel), see Christy Fisher, "The Not-So-Great American Road Trip," *American Demographics,* May 1997, pp. 42–49.
39. Gardial et al., "Comparing Consumers' Recall of Prepurchase and Postpurchase Product Evaluation Experiences."

40. Richard L. Oliver, "Cognitive, Affective and Attribute Bases of the Satisfaction Response," *Journal of Consumer Research* 20 (December 1993), pp. 418–30.
41. Oliver, *Satisfaction,* pp. 66–97.
42. This section draws heavily from Oliver, *Satisfaction,* pp. 98–131. See also Eugene W. Anderson and Claes Fornell, "A Customer Satisfaction Research Prospectus," in *Service Quality: New Directions in Theory and Practice,* ed. Roland T. Rust and Richard L. Oliver (Thousand Oaks, CA: Sage, 1994), pp. 241–68.
43. Jakia Kivela, Robet Inbakaran, and John Reece, "Consumer Research in the Restaurant Environment. Part 3: Analysis, Findings, and Conclusions," *International Journal of Contemporary Hospitality Management* 12, no. 1 (2000), pp. 13–30; and Sung-Joon Yoon and Joo-Ho Kim, "An Empirical Validation of a Loyalty Model Based on Expectation Disconfirmation," *Journal of Consumer Marketing* 17, no. 2 (2000), pp. 120–36.
44. Mark M. Davis and Janelle Heineke, "How Disconfirmation, Perception and Actual Waiting Times Impact Customer Satisfaction," *International Journal of Service Industry Management* 9, no. 1 (1998), pp. 64–73.
45. Jochen Wirtz and John E. G. Bateson, "Introducing Uncertain Performance Expectations in Satisfaction Models for Services," *International Journal of Service Industry Management* 10, no. 1 (1999), pp. 82–99.
46. For important early work on consumer mythology, see Sidney J. Levy, "Interpreting Consumer Mythology: A Structural Approach to Consumer Behavior," *Journal of Marketing* 45 (Summer 1981), pp. 49–61.
47. Richard L. Oliver, "Processing of the Satisfaction Response in Consumption: A Suggested Framework and Research Propositions," *Journal of Consumer Satisfaction, Dissatisfaction, and Complaining Behavior* 2 (1989), pp. 1–16; Westbrook and Oliver, "The Dimensionality of Consumption Emotion Patterns and Consumer Satisfaction"; and Abbie Griffin and John R. Hauser, "The Voice of the Customer," *Marketing Science* 12, no. 1 (Winter 1993), pp. 1–27.
48. For a product peek, see Roy Furchgott, "Rebel without an Engine," *Business Week,* September 15, 1997, p. 8.
49. A. Parasuraman, Leonard L. Berry, and Valarie A. Zeithaml, "Understanding Customer Expectations of Service," *Sloan Management Review* 32 (Spring 1991), pp. 39–48; and David J. Ortinau and Robert P. Bush, "The Propensity of College Students to Modify Course Expectations and Its Impact on Course Performance Information," *Journal of Marketing Education* 9 (Spring 1987), pp. 42–52.
50. Rami Zwick, Rik Pieters, and Hans Baumgartner, "On the Practical Significance of Hindsight Bias: The Case of the Expectancy–Disconfirmation Model of Consumer Satisfaction," *Organizational Behavior and Human Decision Processes* 64 (October 1995), pp. 103–17.
51. David Glen Mick and Susan Fournier, "Technological Consumer Products in Everyday Life: Ownership, Meaning and Satisfaction," Marketing Science Institute, report no. 95-104, May 1995; and Fournier and Mick, "Rediscovering Satisfaction."
52. Fournier and Mick, "Rediscovering Satisfaction"; Richard W. Olshavsky and Richard A. Spreng, "A 'Desires as Standard' Model of Consumer Satisfaction," *Journal of Consumer Satisfaction/Dissatisfaction and Complaining Behavior* 2 (1989), pp. 49–54; and Richard A. Spreng and Richard W. Olshavsky, "A Desires Congruency Model of Consumer Satisfaction," *Journal of the Academy of Marketing Science* 21, no. 3 (1993), pp. 169–77. See also Gardial et al., "Comparing Consumers' Recall of Prepurchase and Postpurchase Product Evaluation Experiences." On the related idea of ideals as standards, see David K. Tse and Peter C. Wilton, "Models of Consumer Satisfaction Formulation: An Extension," *Journal of Marketing Research* 24 (August 1988), pp. 204–12.
53. Russell W. Belk, Güliz Ger, and Søren Askegaard, "Metaphors of Consumer Desire," in *Advances in Consumer Research,* vol. 23, ed. Kim P. Corfman and John G. Lynch (Provo, UT: Association for Consumer Research, 1996), pp. 368–73; and Russell W. Belk, Güliz Ger, and Søren Askegaard, "Consumer Desire in Three Cultures: Results from Projective Research," in *Advances in Consumer Research,* vol. 24, ed. Merrie Brucks and Deborah J. MacInnis (Provo, UT: Association for Consumer Research, 1997), pp. 24–28.

54. Two influential papers on this general topic are D. Kahneman, Jack L. Knetsch, and Richard Thaler, "Fairness as a Constraint on Profit Seeking: Entitlements in the Market," *American Economic Review* 76 (September 1986), pp. 728–41; and D. Kahneman, J. L. Knetsch, and R. H. Thaler, "Fairness and the Assumptions of Economics," *Journal of Business* 59, no. 4 (1986), pp. 285–300.
55. Susan M. Keaveney, "Customer Switching Behavior in Service Industries: An Exploratory Study," *Journal of Marketing* 59 (April 1995), pp. 71–82.
56. Thomas Madden, Peter Dickson, and Joel Urbany, "The Perceived Fairness of Automatic Teller Machine Charges: A Field Test of the Dual Entitlement Principle," working paper, The Ohio State University, Columbus, 1994. See also Peter R. Dickson and Rosemary Kalapurakal, "The Use and Perceived Fairness of Price-Setting Rules in the Bulk Electricity Market," *Journal of Economic Psychology* 15, no. 3 (1994), pp. 427–48.
57. Drakulić, *Café Europa.*
58. Oliver, *Satisfaction;* and Cathy Goodwin and Ivan Ross, "Consumer Responses to Service Failures: Influence of Procedural and Interactional Fairness Perceptions," *Journal of Business Research* 25 (1992), pp. 149–63.
59. Marielza Martins and Kent B. Monroe, "Perceived Price Fairness: A New Look at an Old Construct," in *Advances in Consumer Research,* vol. 21, ed. Chris Allen and Deborah Roedder John (Provo, UT: Association for Consumer Research, 1994), pp. 75–78.
60. Dwayne D. Gremler and Stephen W. Brown, "The Loyalty Ripple Effect: Appreciating the Full Value of Customers," *International Journal of Service Industry Management* 10, no. 3 (1999), pp. 271–93.
61. Tor Wallin Andreassen, "Antecedents to Satisfaction with Service Recovery," *European Journal of Marketing* 34, nos. 1–2 (2000), pp. 156–75; Srinivas Durvasula, Steven Lysonski, and Subhas C. Mehta, "Business-to-Business Marketing Service Recovery and Customer Satisfaction Issues with Ocean Shipping Lines," *European Journal of Marketing* 34, nos. 3–4 (2000), pp. 433–52; Richard A. Feinberg, Ik-Suk Kim, Leigh Hokama, Ko de Ruyter, and Cherie Keen, "Operational Determinants of Caller Satisfaction," *International Journal of Service Industry Management* 11, no. 2 (2000), pp. 131–41; and Mary Ann Hocutt, Goutam Chakraborty, and John C. Mowen, "The Impact of Perceived Justice on Customer Satisfaction and Intention to Complain in a Service Recovery," in *Advances in Consumer Research,* vol. 24, ed. Merrie Brucks and Deborah J. MacInnis (Provo, UT: Association for Consumer Research, 1997), pp. 457–63.
62. For a related example, see Mary Jo Bitner, "Evaluating Service Encounters: The Effects of Physical Surrounding and Employee Responses," *Journal of Marketing,* April 1990, pp. 69–82.
63. See especially Robert A. Westbrook, "Product/Consumption-Based Affective Responses and Post-purchase Processes," *Journal of Marketing Research,* August 1987, pp. 258–70; Westbrook and Oliver, "The Dimensionality of Consumption Emotion Patterns and Consumer Satisfaction"; and Haim Mano and Richard L. Oliver, "Assessing the Dimensionality and Structure of Consumption Experience: Evaluation, Feeling, and Satisfaction," *Journal of Consumer Research* 20 (December 1993), pp. 451–66.
64. See, for example, Eric J. Arnould, Linda L. Price, and Patrick Tierney, "High Water, Low Water: The Emotional Moments of River Rafting," working paper, University of South Florida, Tampa, 1997.
65. Four of these response modes are described in Oliver, *Satisfaction,* especially pages 339–42. The fifth of these, consumer ambivalence, is based on Cele Otnes, Tina M. Lowrey, and L. J. Shrum, "Toward an Understanding of Consumer Ambivalence," *Journal of Consumer Research* 24 (June 1997), pp. 80–93; and Fournier and Mick, "Rediscovering Satisfaction."
66. Malcolm Gladwell, "Annals of Retail: Clicks and Mortar," *The New Yorker,* December 6, 1999, pp. 106–15.
67. Examples of service experiences that could be termed delightful appear in Bitner, Booms, and Tetreault, "The Service Encounter." See also Linda L. Price, Eric J. Arnould, and Sheila L. Deibler, "Consumers' Emotional Responses to Service Encounters: The Influence of the Service Provider," *International Journal of Service Industry Management* 6, no. 3 (1998), pp. 34–63.
68. Valarie A. Zeithaml and Mary J. Bitner, *Services Marketing* (New York: McGraw-Hill, 1996).

69. Otnes, Lowrey, and Shrum, "Toward an Understanding of Consumer Ambivalence"; and Fournier and Mick, "Rediscovering Satisfaction."

70. Albert O. Hirschman, *Exit, Voice and Loyalty: Responses to Decline in Firms, Organizations, and States* (Cambridge, MA: Harvard University Press, 1970). See also Albert O. Hirschman, "Exit, Voice, and Loyalty: Further Reflections and a Survey of Recent Contributions," *Social Science Information* 13 (February 1974), pp. 7–26. For a delightful and insightful follow-up that introduces the idea of "twist," see Veronique Aubert-Gamet, "Twisting Servicescapes: Diversion of the Physical Environment in a Re-Appropriation Process," *International Journal of Service Industry Management* 8, no. 1 (1997), pp. 26–41.

71. Kate Waterhouse and Ann Morgan, "Using Research to Help Keep Good Customers," *Marketing and Research Today,* August 1994, pp. 181–94.

72. Paul R. Timm, "Use the Profit Power of Customer Service," *Executive Excellence* 7 (June 1990), pp. 19–20.

73. Alan R. Andreasen, "Consumer Responses to Dissatisfaction in Loose Monopolies," *Journal of Consumer Research* 12 (September 1985), pp. 135–41.

74. Claes Fornell and Robert A. Westbrook, "The Vicious Circle of Consumer Complaints," *Journal of Marketing* 48 (1984), pp. 68–78.

75. Dwayne D. Gremler and Stephen W. Brown, "The Loyalty Ripple Effect: Appreciating the Full Value of Customers," *International Journal of Service Industry Management* 10, no. 3 (1999), pp. 271–93; and Linda L. Price and Lawrence F. Feick, "The Role of Interpersonal Sources in External Search: An Informational Perspective," in *Advances in Consumer Research,* vol. 11, ed. Thomas C. Kinnear (Ann Arbor, MI: Association for Consumer Research, 1984), pp. 250–53.

76. William O. Bearden and Richard L. Oliver, "The Role of Public and Private Complaining in Satisfaction with Problem Resolution," *Journal of Consumer Affairs* 19 (Winter 1985), pp. 222–40; Mary Gilly and Betsy Gelb, "Post-purchase Consumer Processes and Complaining Consumer Behavior," *Journal of Consumer Research,* December 1982, pp. 323–28; Prashanth U. Nyer, "An Investigation into Whether Complaining Can Cause Increased Consumer Satisfaction," *Journal of Consumer Marketing* 17, no. 1 (2000), pp. 9–19; Roland T. Rust, Bala Subramanian, and Mark Wells, "Making Complaints a Management Tool," *Marketing Management* 1, no. 3 (1992), pp. 41–45; Magnus Söderland, "Customer Satisfaction and Its Consequences on Customer Behaviour Revisited," *International Journal of Service Industry Management* 9, no. 2 (1998), pp. 169–88; and Denise T. Smart and Charles L. Martin, "Manufacturer Responsiveness to Consumer Correspondence: An Empirical Investigation of Consumer Perceptions," *Journal of Consumer Affairs,* Summer 1992, pp. 104–28.

77. Mary C. Gilly and Richard W. Hansen, "Consumer Complaint Handling as a Strategic Marketing Tool," *Journal of Consumer Marketing* 2 (Fall 1985), pp. 5–16; Mary C. Gilly, "Post-complaint Processes: From Organizational Response to Repurchase Behavior," *Journal of Consumer Affairs* 21 (Winter 1987), pp. 293–313; and Alan J. Resnick and Robert R. Harmon, "Consumer Complaints and Managerial Response: A Holistic Approach," *Journal of Marketing,* Winter 1983, pp. 86–97.

78. Claes Fornell and Nicholas M. Didow, "Economic Constraints on Consumer Complaining Behavior," in *Advances in Consumer Research,* vol. 7, ed. Jerry Olson (Ann Arbor, MI: Association for Consumer Research, 1980), pp. 318–23.

79. Bearden and Oliver, "The Role of Public and Private Complaining in Satisfaction with Problem Resolution."

80. Chow-Hou Wee and Celine Chong, "Determinants of Consumer Satisfaction/Dissatisfaction towards Dispute Settlements in Singapore," *European Journal of Marketing* 25, no. 10 (1991), pp. 6–16.

81. Claes Fornell and Birger Wernerfelt, "Defensive Marketing Strategy by Customer Complaint Management," *Journal of Marketing Research* 24 (November 1987), pp. 337–46; and Claes Fornell and Birger Wernerfelt, "A Model for Customer Complaint Management," *Marketing Science* 7 (Summer 1988), pp. 287–98.

82. William O. Bearden and Jesse E. Teel, "An Investigation of Personal Influences on Consumer Complaining," *Journal of Retailing* 56 (Fall 1980), pp. 3–20; William O. Bearden and

Jesse E. Teel, "Selected Determinants of Consumer Satisfaction and Complaint Reports," *Journal of Marketing Research* 20 (February 1983), pp. 21–28; and Rex H. Warland, Robert O. Herrmann, and Jane Willits, "Dissatisfied Consumers: Who Gets Upset and Who Takes Action," *Journal of Consumer Affairs* 9 (Winter 1975), pp. 148–63.

83. T. Bettina Cornwell, Alan David Bligh, and Emin Babakus, "Complaint Behaviors of Mexican-American Consumers to a Third Party Agency," *Journal of Consumer Affairs,* Summer 1991, pp. 1–18; Sigfredo A. Hernandez, William Strahle, Hector Garcia, and Robert C. Sorenson, "A Cross-Cultural Study of Consumer Complaining Behavior: VCR Owners in the U.S. and Puerto Rico," *Journal of Consumer Policy,* June 1991, pp. 35–62; and Ben Shaw-Ching Liu, Olivier Furrer, and D. Sudharshan, "Whether to Praise or to Complain Depends on Cultures: An Empirical Study in a Service Context," paper presented at the ninth annual Frontiers in Services Conference, Vanderbilt University, Nashville, 2000.

84. William O. Bearden and Barry J. Mason, "An Investigation of Influences of Consumer Complaint Reports," in *Advances in Consumer Research,* ed. Thomas C. Kinnear (Ann Arbor, MI: Association for Consumer Research, 1984), pp. 490–95; J. B. Liefeld, F. H. Edgecombe, and Linda Wolfe, "Demographic Characteristics of Canadian Complainers," *Journal of Consumer Affairs* 9 (Summer 1975), pp. 73–80; Michelle Ann Morganosky and Hilda Mayer Buckley, "Complaint Behavior: Analysis by Demographics, Lifestyle and Consumer Values," in *Advances in Consumer Research,* ed. Melanie Wallendorf and Paul Anderson (Ann Arbor, MI: Association for Consumer Research, 1987), pp. 223–26; and Judy Zaichkowsky and John Liefeld, "Personality Profiles of Consumer Complaint Letter Writers," in *Consumer Satisfaction, Dissatisfaction and Complaint Behavior,* ed. Ralph L. Day (Bloomington: Indiana University, 1977), pp. 124–29.

85. Ralph L. Day, Laus Grabicke, Thomas Schaetzle, and Fritz Staubach, "The Hidden Agenda of Consumer Complaining," *Journal of Retailing* 57 (Fall 1981), pp. 86–106; Hernandez, Strahle, Garcia, and Sorensen, "A Cross-Cultural Study of Consumer Complaining Behavior"; and Angelina Villarreal-Camacho, "Consumer Complaining Behavior: A Cross-Cultural Comparison," in *American Marketing Association Educators' Proceedings,* ed. Patrick E. Murphy et al. (Chicago: American Marketing Association, 1983), pp. 68–73.

86. Güliz Ger, "Problems of Marketization in Romania and Turkey," in *Consumption in Marketizing Economies,* ed. Clifford Shultz, Russell Belk, and Güliz Ger (Greenwich, CT: JAI Press, 1996), pp. 127–56; Charlotte Klopp and John Sterrlickhi, "Customer Satisfaction Just Catching on in Europe," *Marketing News,* May 28, 1990, p. 5; Trina Thomas Raj, "Customer Satisfaction Is Carrefour's Top Priority," *New Straits Times* (Singapore), February 17, 1999, pp. 2, 18; and Harry S. Watkins and Raymond Liu, "Collectivism, Individualism and In-Group Membership: Implications for Consumer Complaining Behaviors in Multicultural Contexts," *Journal of International Consumer Marketing* 8, nos. 3–4 (1996), pp. 69–96.

87. Marsha L. Richins and Bronislaw J. Verhage, "Cross-Cultural Differences in Consumer Attitudes and Their Implications for Complaint Management," *International Journal of Research in Marketing* 2 (1985), pp. 197–206.

88. Fornell and Westbrook, "The Vicious Circle of Consumer Complaints." See also Rom Zemke and Kristin Anderson, "Customers from Hell," *Training* 27 (February 1990), pp. 25–33; and "Study Says It Pays to Settle All Complaints," *DM News,* September 1, 1984, p. 21.

89. Mary T. Curren and Valerie S. Folkes, "Attributional Influences on Consumers' Desires to Communicate about Products," *Psychology and Marketing* 4 (1987), pp. 31–45; and Marsha L. Richins, "Negative Word-of-Mouth by Dissatisfied Consumers: A Pilot Study," *Journal of Marketing* 47 (Winter 1983), pp. 68–78.

90. Jagdip Singh, "A Typology of Consumer Dissatisfaction Response Styles," *Journal of Retailing* 66 (Spring 1990), pp. 57–99; Cathy Goodwin and Susan Spiggle, "Consumer Complaining: Attributions and Identities," in *Advances in Consumer Research,* vol. 16, ed. Thomas K. Srull (Ann Arbor, MI: Association for Consumer Research, 1989), pp. 17–22; and Jack Dart and Kim Freeman, "Dissatisfaction Response Styles among Clients of Professional Accounting Firms," *Journal of Business Research* 29 (1994), pp. 75–81.

91. Jacob Jacoby and Robert W. Chestnut, *Brand Loyalty: Measurement and Management* (New York: Wiley, 1978); and Alan S. Dick and Kunal Basu, "Customer Loyalty: Toward an Integrated

Conceptual Framework," *Journal of the Academy of Marketing Science* 22 (Winter 1994), pp. 99–113.
92. Oliver, *Satisfaction,* p. 392.
93. Michael A. Jones and Jaebeom Suh, "Transaction-Specific Satisfaction and Overall Satisfaction: An Empirical Analysis," *Journal of Services Marketing* 14, no. 2 (2000).
94. Gremler and Brown, "The Loyalty Ripple Effect"; and Oliver, "Whence Consumer Loyalty?"
95. Gerard J. Tellis, "Advertising Exposure, Loyalty, and Brand Purchase: A Two-Stage Model of Choice," *Journal of Marketing Research* 25 (May 1988), pp. 134–44. This study used a 20-week interval to define the loyalty exhibited toward any one brand, which although it is still only a repeat-purchase measure increases confidence that something beyond spurious or happenstance loyalty is being measured.
96. Terence A. Oliva, Richard L. Oliver, and Ian C. Macmillan, "A Catastrophe Model for Developing Service Satisfaction Strategies," *Journal of Marketing* 56 (July 1992), pp. 83–95.
97. George B. Sproles and Elizabeth L. Kendall, "A Methodology for Profiling Consumers' Decision Making Styles," *Journal of Consumer Affairs* 20 (Winter 1986), pp. 267–79.
98. Oliver, "Whence Consumer Loyalty?"; Hugo Tranberg and Flemming Hansen, "Patterns of Brand Loyalty: Their Determinants and Their Role for Leading Brands," *European Journal of Marketing* 20, nos. 3–4 (1986), pp. 81–109.
99. Robin A. Higie, Linda L. Price, and Julie Fitzmaurice, "Leaving It All Behind: Service Loyalties in Transition," in *Advances in Consumer Research,* vol. 20, ed. Leigh McAlister and Michael L. Rothschild (Provo, UT: Association for Consumer Research, 1993), pp. 656–61; and Linda L. Price and Eric J. Arnould, "Commercial Friendships: Service Provider–Client Relationships in Context," *Journal of Marketing* 68 (October 1999), pp. 38–57.
100. The term *twist* is borrowed from Veronique Aubert-Gamet and Bernard Cove, "Exit, Voice, Loyalty and Twist: Consumer Research in Search of the Subject," Workshop on Interpretive Consumer Research, Oxford, April 10–12, 1997. Although we use the term more broadly here, our use is quite consistent with their idea of a creative consumer engaged in discreet restructuring of meanings, roles, and objects in the marketplace. See also Aubert-Gamet, "Twisting Servicescapes"; and Michel de Certeau, *The Practice of Everyday Life* (Berkeley: University of California Press, 1984).
101. Leonard L. Berry, *On Great Service: A Framework for Action* (New York: Free Press, 1995).
102. Steven Skinner, "Individuals' Commission of Customer Fraud Acts: Theory Development and Managerial Insights," manuscript under review, *Journal of Marketing,* 1999.
103. Minoru Naito, "Activist Consumers Get Taste of Power," *Nikkei Weekly,* February 26, 2001, pp. 1, 3; and Leyland F. Pitt, Pierre R. Berthon, Richard T. Watson, and George M. Zinkhan, "The Internet and the Birth of Real Consumer Power," *Business Horizons* 45 (July–August 2002), pp. 7–14.
104. Monroe Friedman, "Consumer Boycotts: A Conceptual Framework and Research Agenda," *Journal of Social Issues* 47, no. 1 (1991), pp. 149–68; and Robert O. Herrmann, "The Tactics of Consumer Resistance: Group Action and Marketplace Exit," in *Advances in Consumer Research,* vol. 20, ed. Michael Rothschild and Leigh McAlister (Provo, UT: Association for Consumer Research, 1993), pp. 130–34.
105. Lisa Peñaloza and Linda L. Price, "Consumer Resistance: A Conceptual Overview," in *Advances in Consumer Research,* vol. 20, ed. Leigh McAlister and Michael L. Rothschild (Provo, UT: Association for Consumer Research, 1993), pp. 123–28; and Richard Pollay and Banwari Mittal, "Here's the Beef: Factors, Determinants, and Segments in Consumer Criticism of Advertising," *Journal of Marketing* 57 (July 1993), pp. 99–115.
106. Peter Barrow, "Marketing to Generation X," *Canadian Manager,* March 1994, pp. 23–24; Judith Langer, "Twentysomethings: They're Angry, Frustrated, and They Like Their Parents," *Brandweek,* February 22, 1993, pp. 18–19; Karen Ritchie, *Marketing to Generation X* (Lexington, MA: Lexington Books, 1995); and Laurie Freeman, "Advertising's Mirror Is Cracked: Generation X Sees Ad World's Projected Image, and Isn't Buying It," *Advertising Age* 66 (February 6, 1995), p. 27.

SUBJECT INDEX

COMPANY/BRAND INDEX

INDEXES

NAME INDEX

chapter 1
chapter 2
chapter 3
chapter 4
chapter 5
chapter 6
chapter 7
chapter 8
chapter 9
chapter 10
chapter 11
chapter 12
chapter 13
chapter 14
chapter 15
chapter 16
chapter 17
chapter 18
chapter 19

LEARNING OBJECTIVES

After completing this chapter, you should be able to:

- Understand that disposition is a growth industry that provides many marketing opportunities.
- Recognize that product disposition is an increasingly important area for public policy.
- Discuss some of the practical implications that disposition has for managers.
- Explain the differences between voluntary and involuntary disposition.
- Describe the social, individual, and situational factors that affect disposition choices.
- Realize how understanding disposition provides key insights into consumption behavior.

THE RAILS-TO-TRAILS CONSERVANCY[1]

The purpose of the Rails-to-Trails Conservancy (RTC) is to enrich America's communities and countryside by creating a nationwide network of public trails from former rail lines and connecting corridors. It began in the mid-1960s, quietly, gradually, hesitatingly. There wasn't much fanfare. It was primarily a Midwestern phenomenon, barely noticed in places like New York, Los Angeles, or Washington, D.C. People didn't say, "Is that the latest fad?" They said, "That's a really smart idea!"

The idea was to convert abandoned or unused rail corridors into public trails. Unlike the complex railroad system that was crumbling physically and financially, the concept was simple. It didn't require or even claim an inventor. Once the tracks came out, people just naturally started walking along the old grades, socializing, exploring, discovering old railroad relics, and marveling at old industrial facilities such as bridges, tunnels, abandoned mills, sidings, switches, and whatever else they could find. In the snows of winter the unconventional outdoor enthusiast skied or snowshoed on the corridor, but these were days before even running and all-terrain bicycles were common, so the predominant activity was walking. Of course, none of the corridors were paved or even graded—they were simply abandoned stretches of land.

"Rails-to-Trails" is what people started calling it, and the name was catchy and descriptive enough to give the concept a tiny niche in the fledgling environmental movement that was gathering momentum, bracing for huge battles shaping over clean air and water. However, it was destined to move into the mainstream of the conservation and environmental movements. After all, it had all the ingredients: recycling, land conservation, wildlife habitat preservation, and nonautomobile transportation—not to mention historical preservation, physical fitness, recreation access for wheelchair users, and numerous other benefits.

R-T-C is a good example of movement from disposition to use around the wheel of consumption and of a non-profit marketing opportunity benefiting from grass roots demand.

Today, more than 35 years later, rail-trails have begun to make a significant mark, with 11,703 miles of rail-trails and around 100 million users per year. But in 1965 few Americans understood the importance of the idea. Rails-to-Trails was still a highly localized movement—"we've got an abandoned railroad track, so let's use it." Only gradually did there emerge a realization that America desperately needs a national trails system and that abandoned rail corridors are the perfect backbone for that network.

The growing popularity of outdoor recreation activities, such as cycling, inline skating, walking, and running, combined with the loss of community open space, has increased the need for quality recreational facilities such as rail-trails.

Rail-trails provide places for cyclists, hikers, walkers, runners, inline skaters, cross-country skiers, and physically challenged individuals to exercise and experience the many natural and cultural wonders of the nation's urban, suburban, and rural environments. Rail-trails not only serve as independent community amenities, they also enhance existing recreational resources by linking neighborhoods and schools to parks, waterfronts, recreational centers, and other facilities. There is no doubt about the strong link between exercise and good health. By providing a place for so many types of recreational use, rail-trails can greatly help to improve public health.

Trails don't just happen. Time, money, and support from local communities and partners across all levels of government put trails on the ground. All RTC programs and activities support local efforts to transform the dream of a trail into a tangible community asset. Since its beginning in 1986, RTC has achieved notable success in promoting and protecting favorable legislation and providing assistance and leadership to the trails and greenways community.

RTC promotes policy at the national and state levels to create the conditions that make trail building possible. RTC catalyzes action at the local level by providing information, technical assistance, and training for local trail builders. RTC provides leadership and public education to the trails and greenways movement.

RTC is a 501(c)(3) nonprofit organization with more than 100,000 members and supporters. Founded in 1986, Rails-to-Trails Conservancy is located in Washington, D.C., and has offices in California, Florida, Massachusetts, Michigan, Ohio, and Pennsylvania.

OVERVIEW

In this chapter we explore the marketing implications of what consumers or organizations do with the problem of waste. This question provides a basis for developing the main ideas in this chapter. Waste includes both by-products of production and consumption processes and finished products that have outlived their value. **Disposition** encompasses *all the behaviors that consuming units undertake to divest themselves of undesired goods and services,* including reducing consumption, recycling products in multiple ways, and separating themselves from unwanted goods. Disposition is an inevitable part of the wheel of consumption, and there are a variety of markets and professions devoted to managing disposition, including auction houses, demolition specialists, flea markets, and recycling services.

First, we discuss the question of why we should be interested in the question of consumer disposition. The answer, as you will see, is that consumers, corporations, and governments are interested in it. In this section we also summarize the historical background to disposition.

Next we describe the disposition process. In this section we discuss both voluntary and involuntary disposition. We also profile various disposition behaviors. Our aim here is to emphasize both the nature of the consumer behaviors involved with disposition and the marketing opportunities they represent.

Third, we discuss some of the factors that affect disposition choices. We discuss product, competitive, life-cycle, and situational factors. We provide individual and organizational examples.

In a fourth section, we discuss what is known about the segmentation variables relevant to green consumption choices. And, finally, we bring things full circle by discussing how disposition issues enter into product acquisition choices.

Why Be Interested in Disposition?

Why should you be interested in the general question of consumer disposition? There are several reasons. Foremost, disposition is a growth industry providing many marketing opportunities in business and customer markets. Many companies have moved from a concern with pollution control to waste prevention, primarily because it is profitable. For example, Aeroquip Corporation, a US$25 million producer of hoses, fittings, and couplings, generated a $250 million business by developing products that reduce emissions. Similarly, Stonyfield Farms, a New Hampshire yogurt producer, focused its initial environmental attentions on reducing and recycling waste. Next, the company redesigned the yogurt-making process and installed heat-recovery systems to capture waste heat from process water, saving the company thousands of dollars each year. As Good Practice 19.1 suggests, some companies combine profitability, pollution prevention, and social responsibility.

As some companies have moved closer to zero emissions, **product stewardship** has become a strategic opportunity. Product stewardship *focuses on minimizing all environmental impacts of a product over its biography* (see Chapter 1). Hewlett-Packard established a product stewardship initiative in the early 1990s. Industry Insights 19.1 provides an example in another industry.

www.cfsd.org.uk

Design for environment (DFE) is *a product stewardship tool for creating products that are easier to recover, reuse, or recycle.* Go to the British Center for Sustainable Design website for more information. By reducing materials and energy consumption, DFE can be highly profitable. A decision that Xerox Corporation made in 1991 to put the environment first has been paying dividends for the company and the environment. In 1999, reuse and recycling of Xerox equipment and supplies kept 163 million pounds of materials out of landfills—equivalent to the amount of trash that 100,000 people in the United States would typically throw away in one year. And the company's Energy Star^{TM} products enabled savings of 387 million kilowatt-hours, enough energy to light more than 300,000 U.S. homes for a year. Xerox also has saved hundreds of millions of dollars by designing parts that can be recycled and products that can be remanufactured to as-new condition. In addition, reduce, reuse, and recycling initiatives in its factories saved $47 million in 1999 alone.[2]

www.rite.or.jp/English/E-home-frame.html

www.mazda.com

Going beyond stewardship, some companies are looking to develop clean technologies. Volvo, the Swedish subsidiary of Ford, decided to use water-based paints as an alternative to prepainting its products with chemical solvents. These solvents emitted volatile organic compounds (VOCs) into the environment. The new process eliminated the need for expensive air-pollution-control equipment. Volvo can market its products as cleaner and greener than those of its competitors. Japan's Research Institute for Innovative Technology for the Earth consortia of 40 Japanese corporations is focusing on the development and commercialization of clean technologies. Mazda's 2001 Environmental Report reports progress toward the commercial development of a number of clean vehicle technologies including fuel cell and hydrogen engines (see the report at the company website). The BP Amoco ad shown on page 806 states the company is committed to solving the paradox of a world that wants mobility and a cleaner environment. Good Practice 19.2 illustrates another example of the benefits of developing clean technologies.

Second, product disposition is an important area for policy activity. In the Triad nations, both the European Community and the U.S. environmental watchdog agencies monitor and pinpoint sources of waste and pollution and are encouraging sustainable consumption activities. In addition, industrial and consumer product emissions, during both

Aracruz Cellulose: A Strategy for the LAW

GOOD PRACTICE 19.1

"Poverty is one of the word's leading polluters," notes Erling Lorentzen, founder and chairman of Aracruz Cellulose. The $2 billion Brazilian company is the world's largest producer of eucalyptus pulp. "You can't expect people who don't eat a proper meal to be concerned about the environment."

From the start Aracruz has been built around a vision of sustainable development. Lorentzen understood that building a viable forest-products business in Brazil's impoverished and deforested state of Espirito Santo would require the simultaneous improvement in the natural economy and the local economy.

First, to restore the natural economy, the company took advantage of a tax incentive for tree planting in the late 1960s and began buying and reforesting cutover land. By 1992, the company had planted 130,000 hectares (338,000 acres) with managed eucalyptus. The rest was restored as conservation land. Aracruz simultaneously addressed fundamental environmental problems and created a first-rate source of fiber for its pulping operations.

Second, Aracruz has tackled the problem of poverty head on. Every year, the company gives away millions of eucalyptus seedlings to local farmers. It is a preemptive strategy aimed at reducing the farmers' need to deplete the natural forests for fuel or lumber (or poach on Aracruz plantations). Aracruz also committed to long-term capability building. In the beginning, Aracruz was able to hire desperate local people for very low wages. But instead of exploiting abundant cheap labor, the company spent $125 million to create hospitals, schools, housing, and an employee-training center. Until recently Aracruz spent more on social investments than on wages. Since that time, the standard of living has improved dramatically, as has productivity. The company no longer invests so heavily in social infrastructure.

Source: Marguerite Rigoglioso, "Stewards of the Seventh Generation," Harvard Business School Bulletin, *April 1996, p. 55.*

manufacture and use, are subject to government regulation in the developed world. Germany has passed stringent green-marketing laws that regulate the management and recycling of packaging waste, called "take-back requirements." Of course, these policies are not without controversy, as suggested by Ethical Dilemma 19.1.[3]

Enormous public policy problems surface over such questions as, What qualifies as organic food? Who bears responsibility for radioactive wastes? and What should be done about hazardous wastes? For example, six European nations in the Rhine River basin ban boats from dumping any waste into the Rhine and require them to pay a tax on fuel in return for free access to waste-disposal stations established along the river. Of course, environmental policies are frequently contentious. An ongoing dispute rages over the Black Triangle region on the common borders between Poland, Germany, and the Czech Republic that is seriously polluted by power-plant emissions. Similar disputes have flared between some Native American tribes and their off-reservation neighbors. Some tribes want to establish solid-waste dumps as a way to bring in desperately needed revenues. They often face strong opposition from their neighbors.[4]

A third reason to be interested in disposition is that it has practical implications for managers. Many opportunities for resolving customers' needs can be found at the intersection of the disposition, acquisition, and consumption phases of the wheel of

Interface, Inc., Profiting from Sustainability

INDUSTRY INSIGHTS 19.1

Interface is transforming itself from a company that sells and fits carpets into one that provides floor-covering services. Under its Evergreen Lease, Interface no longer sells carpets, but rather leases a floor-covering service for a monthly fee, accepting responsibility for keeping the carpet fresh and clean. Monthly inspections detect and replace worn carpet tiles. Since at most 20 percent of an area typically shows 80 percent of the wear, replacing only the worn parts reduces the consumption of carpeting by about 80 percent. It also minimizes the disruption that customers' experience—worn tiles are seldom found under furniture. Finally, for the corporate customer, leasing carpet can provide a tax advantage, by turning a capital expenditure into a tax-deductible expense. The result: the customer gets cheaper and better services that cost the supplier far less to produce. Indeed the energy saved from not producing a whole new carpet is in itself enough to produce all the carpeting the new business model requires. Taken together, the fivefold savings in carpeting material that Interface achieves through the Evergreen Lease and the sevenfold materials savings achieved through the use of its fully remanufacturable Solenium floor-covering material deliver a stunning 35-fold reduction in the flow of materials needed to sustain superior floor-covering service. This helps reduce the billions of pounds of nonbiodegradable carpets removed from offices each year and sent to landfills. Find out more about Interface, Inc.'s, sustainability program at its website.

Source: Amory B. Lovins, L. Hunter Lovins, and Paul Hawken, "A Road Map for Natural Capitalism," Harvard Business Review, *May–June 1999, p. 145–158.*

www.interface

consumption. Interest in environmentally responsible and sustainable consumption is growing among both individual and institutional consumers. This interest is fueled both by changes in values and by recognition of the cost-savings and value-enhancing characteristics of sustainable consumption and product stewardship. The ad for First Kick Scooters shown below illustrates consumers' interest in products refurbished for continued use. Some people enjoy the prestige benefits of using "classic" products. Attractive secondary markets for previously owned or leased goods have developed.

The text of this ad reinforces the value of restoration and productive consumption.

GOOD PRACTICE 19.2

Indianapolis-based Dow AgroSciences has developed a system for eliminating termite colonies—known by the trade name Sentricon—that does not require the usual widespread application of chemical deterrents. The Sentricon system is one technology among five that were honored with a green chemistry award at a ceremony on June 26 at the National Academy of Sciences in Washington, D.C. Dow AgroSciences received the award in the designing safer chemicals category. The Presidential Green Chemistry Challenge Awards were established in 1995 to recognize and promote fundamental green chemistry technologies that promote pollution prevention and that have broad application in industry. Green chemistry represents the pillars that hold up our sustainable future, said Daryle H. Busch, president of the American Chemical Society.

Source: Celia M. Henry, "Color Me Green," Chemical & Engineering News *28, no. 78 (July 10, 2000), pp. 49–55.*

Builders' associations advise their members that consumers are interested in green homes, primarily because of their enhanced market value, for instance. Green and recycled products are hot in many significant global markets, as suggested by Good Practice 19.3.[5]

A fourth and final reason to be interested in disposition is that it provides insight into consumption behaviors. For example, while it might be unpleasant to analyze the contents of people's garbage, such an analysis can furnish valuable information about product preferences, repeat purchase behavior, and brand loyalty. Garbage can tell us about products purchased and discarded but not consumed, and about actual, as opposed to claimed, recycling behaviors.[6]

Historical and Cross-Cultural Perspectives on Disposition

Disposition issues have been around since human beings began settling in villages, towns, and cities. From prehistoric times to as late as the periods of classical civilization in both the new and old worlds, garbage was often left where it lay in human dwellings with layers of new flooring occasionally laid over the waste. Or it was simply dumped out of doors and windows to settle where it might. Many parts of the Middle East from Syria, through Iraq, Israel, and Iran are dotted with rounded hills that are, in fact, the remains of ancient towns built up in successive levels over their garbage. In ancient Greece and Rome, garbage was thrown into the streets as well as into the rivers flowing through the towns. The Maya of ancient Central America used household refuse as fill in the construction of major civil and religious buildings like their picturesque temples.

Historically and cross-culturally, there are many examples of disposition-related behaviors. The archaeological record is crowded with artifacts that display the results of reuse and recycling behavior. In ancient times, pottery was the equivalent of modern containers made of glass or plastic. It was extensively recycled. Broken pottery, in the form of shards, was frequently ground and used as temper in the manufacture of new batches of pottery. Around the world, masonry structures are often found to

ETHICAL DILEMMA 19.1

Balancing Environmental Concern and Short-Run Profits

Whenever a firm wants to introduce a new product in Germany, it is necessary for that firm to get official permission from the government. Specifically, the firm has to prove that the new product will provide for an efficient use of resources. The new product has to be more than just a "me too" entrant into the marketplace. By policy, the country does not want to waste scarce resources through the thoughtless proliferation of new products. On the one hand, existing firms enjoy some level of protection from new competition. On the other hand, the society is able to operate in an environmentally friendly manner and conserve its natural and human resources.

harbor stone that had once been used for another purpose, such as the grinding of meal. Much of medieval Rome, to cite one famous instance, was constructed of marble and stone scavenged from buildings erected during the times of the Roman Empire. In this way, the Roman Coliseum served for centuries as a quarry. Disposition has been a particular problem in the world's cities. In the late Middle Ages in Europe, the failure to deal with urban solid-waste disposal led to the Black Plague that killed a quarter of the population. In the cities of the industrial age, livestock, especially swine, often roamed the streets feeding on garbage that accumulated there. Spas and summer resorts got their start in part because the wealthy wanted to escape the urban stench and fear of disease provoked by inadequate garbage recovery. Although Ben Franklin was the first U.S. sage to call for solid-waste disposal ordinances, it wasn't until the nineteenth century that organized waste disposal became routine in the United States.

Scavenging and recycling regimes in many Third World countries differ little, save for the matter of scale, from those employed in the past. As many do

BP Amoco repositions itself as champion of deconsumption.

Recycling Wood Products

GOOD PRACTICE 19.3

Big City Forest (BCF) was established as a for-profit corporation to advance the objectives of its parent company, the not-for-profit South Bronx 2000 Local Development Corporation. As a function of its manufacturing operations, BCF provides wood waste disposal service to metro-area companies discarding shipping pallets and other wood packaging. BCF reclaims wood shipping containers and pallets, remills the lumber, and produces pallets, furniture, flooring, fixtures, signs, plaques, dimensional lumber, and architectural millwork. The company has a proprietary remanufacturing system, a proprietary workforce-training program, and a proprietary database for identifying sources of discarded wood that are well-suited for high-value products. The company's products compare favorably in price and quality to products made with virgin wood.

BCF's wood recycling services save metro-area firms as much as 80 percent of the average disposal costs, saving local companies $1.9 million on wood waste disposal costs (this savings has, in turn, helped the companies create and retain jobs). In addition, BCF has created 100 jobs and training opportunities; diverted more than 8,400 tons of wood from landfills, incinerators, and vacant lots; reclaimed more than 5.6 million board-feet of lumber, enough to frame 335 average-sized American houses; conserved the equivalent of 1,100 acres of timberland, an area greater than the size of Central Park; saved enough trees to bank almost 12,000 tons of carbon dioxide; and conserved almost a billion BTUs of process energy, equivalent to 11,000 barrels of oil.

Sources: "Reclaiming Wood for Maximum Value," Biocycle, *January 1995, p. 38.*

in Ho Chi Minh City, Cairo, or Manila, some 17,000 garbage-pickers, or *pepenadores,* in Mexico City make their living from the city's refuse. They systematically pick through the garbage delivered to the capital's sprawling dumps, looking to reclaim cans, bottles, cardboard, scrap metal, broken appliances, paper, plastic sheeting, and meat bones (these last destined for the manufacturer of bouillon cubes and glue). The pepenadores are tightly organized by a network of *caciques,* or headmen, who are politically powerful.

This type of economy was a reality for large numbers of people in the United States as recently as the turn of the twentieth century. Boston's elegant Back Bay neighborhood, once a tidal marsh, owes its existence not only to ample loads of gravel and other kinds of fill but also to the copious amounts of garbage that Bostonians dumped into the site. An etching done by Winslow Homer in 1859 shows scavengers—"chiffoniers," he delicately called them, "pickers up of unconsidered trifles"—combing furiously among the Back Bay garbage dumps. The trade in rags was particularly important, with a class of material known as "thirds and blues"—rags that were thirdhand and blue or lighter in color—being a staple of papermaking and of reprocessed, "shoddy" clothes.[7]

A core consumption value early in American history, frugality was increasingly undermined by the norms of consumer culture. Frugality became a necessary virtue once again during the Great Depression, and then received official endorsement during World War II. Then the U.S. government's Office of War Information launched poster campaigns that advocated thriftiness, gasoline conservation, recycling, home production, obeying of price controls, and purchase of war bonds to support the war effort.

DuPont finds it pays to recycle by creating a backward marketing channel to recover used carpet.

There were some impressive achievements. Americans recycled 508 million pounds of waste fats, 23 million tons of paper, and 800 million pounds of tin. Post-war America quickly lost interest in frugality. But frugal consumption also became part of the lifestyle of "beat" poets and artists in the 1950s, and some "hippies" in the 1960s counterculture actively endorsed frugality. During the early 1970s, frugality became a conservation strategy for the rapidly emerging environmental movement and was made quite salient to all Americans by the Arab oil embargo of 1973–74. In recent years, state governments—California and in New England—often have taken the lead in promoting conservation and waste reduction. Despite advocacy groups' persistent encouragement of frugal values and behavior, thrift has been mostly noticeable in its absence from popular American consumer culture. From an environmental and public policy perspective, the successful dissemination of the principles of consumer frugality in World War II is a topic deserving of added research.[8]

THE DISPOSITION PROCESS

Disposition is not so much an event as a process. This is an important distinction. For groups and individuals alike, physical and emotional disposition processes often take place in stages; consumers often desire to place unwanted items in storage for a time to reduce their emotional connections.

Disposition consists of two interrelated components. First, there is a physical or spatial detachment from a possession object. Second, there is detachment from the meanings and emotions associated with objects. People may have nostalgic longings for lost,

destroyed, stolen, or abandoned possessions, indicating their lack of detachment from the emotions and meanings associated with the absent thing. Think for a minute about the stockpiles of possessions kept in attics, cellars, relatives' closets, and public storage facilities. Notice that there are many possessions that you don't want around all the time but can't quite part from because of emotional and meaningful associations. Auctions, garage sales, and flea markets provide consumers with mechanisms to transfer items to others through face-to-face exchanges. In such exchanges stories and information can be exchanged that ensure unwanted objects move to deserving hands.[9] A recent New York auction of Jackie Kennedy Onassis's belongings shows how physical detachment of the things from Ms. Kennedy is not at all the same as the detachment of the meanings. Many people bought items at the auction in order to obtain meanings associated with the American "Camelot" presidency of the early 1960s.[10]

A Model of Disposition

At the household or firm level, we can diagram the physical disposition process. See Exhibit 19.1 for a schematic drawing of the **model of disposition.** The physical disposition cycle starts when raw materials enter the manufacture process and then are distributed to households (or firms) X and Y that acquire, use, and dispose of them. After usage, some used-up products or their residuals are returned to the environment directly in the form of litter or waste. Alternatively, they may be returned indirectly after collection as garbage and landfill or treatment (e.g., adding rubber-tire cinder to road bedding). As suggested in the exhibit, households can also dispose of products in ways that result in reuse of various kinds.

SIMPLE REUSE **Simple reuse** occurs when a product is reused by the consumer for its original purpose or for a different purpose. Empty jars are used for storage. Newspapers line litter pans and shelves or else are used to light fires. Leftovers are fed to

EXHIBIT 19.1

Model of Disposition

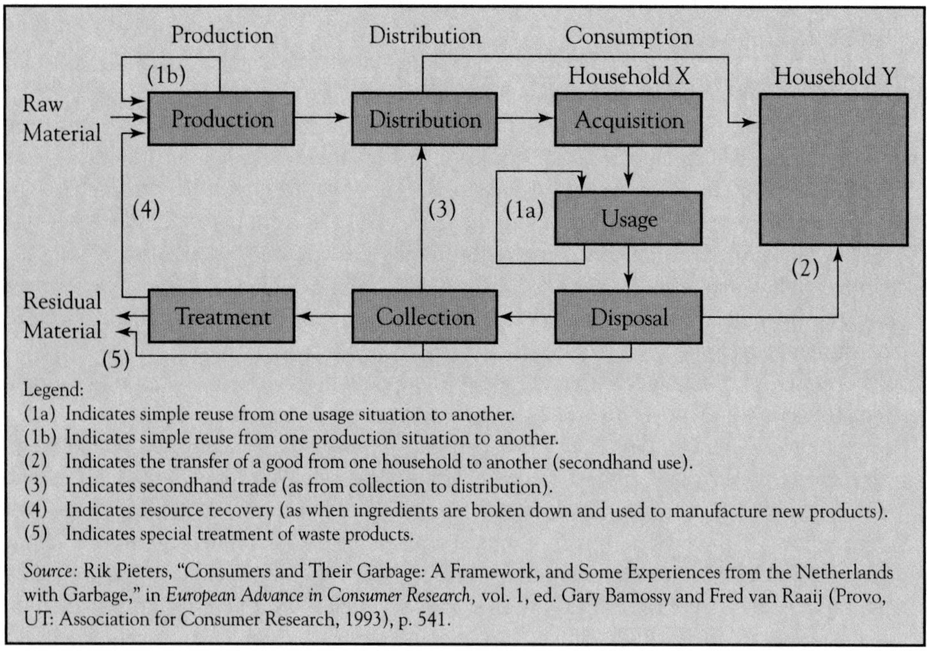

Legend:
(1a) Indicates simple reuse from one usage situation to another.
(1b) Indicates simple reuse from one production situation to another.
(2) Indicates the transfer of a good from one household to another (secondhand use).
(3) Indicates secondhand trade (as from collection to distribution).
(4) Indicates resource recovery (as when ingredients are broken down and used to manufacture new products).
(5) Indicates special treatment of waste products.

Source: Rik Pieters, "Consumers and Their Garbage: A Framework, and Some Experiences from the Netherlands with Garbage," in *European Advance in Consumer Research,* vol. 1, ed. Gary Bamossy and Fred van Raaij (Provo, UT: Association for Consumer Research, 1993), p. 541.

pets. Antique furniture may be recovered or refinished. Simple reuse is shown in the exhibit as arrows from usage to usage (1a) and production to production (1b).

SECONDHAND REUSE **Secondhand reuse** of products takes place when a product is given away—as a gift or through inheritance to friends, family, or even strangers—or sold to another household or traded for another product. This kind of transaction is called **lateral recycling.** Most people are probably familiar with boot sales and swap meets, supermarket bulletin boards, Internet auction sites, and newspaper classified sections. In Senegal, colored comics pages from newspapers are sold and used to line luggage made of hammered tin cans. Rails-to-Trails, described in the vignette, might be thought of as a kind of secondhand reuse. Interhousehold networks for hand-me-down baby clothing provide an interesting example of secondhand reuse. Inheritance networks generally provide another example of secondhand reuse. In industrial markets, some firms enter into agreements with producers to have them remanufacture the firms' used machine tools for resale back to the firm. These networks are shown in Exhibit 19.1 as an arrow (2) from household X to household (firm) Y.

SECONDHAND TRADE **Secondhand trade** takes place when the ownership for the used products is first transferred to an intermediary before distribution to new users. Such trade is depicted in the exhibit as an arrow from collection to distribution (3).[11] Many charitable organizations conduct drives to collect household goods for redistribution to the needy. Notice in this disposition process that no sale links the charitable organization to the donor. A firm called Hannah Anderson, which manufactures children's clothing, offers to buy the clothing back for redistribution to needy children. In 16 years, the firm donated 16 million garments. A U.S. organization called Second Harvest collects leftover food from restaurants for redistribution to over 200 food banks. Used auto parts firms are another example of secondhand trade. Auction houses, including the fashionable Christy's and Sotheby's, also fall into the category of firms that cater to the secondhand market. For some segments, the look of second-hand goods conveys added value. The ad for Levi's worn-in 501 jeans shown on page 811 is an example. Perhaps this look suggests the object conceals a secret biography or conveys the idea that its owner lives a glamorous or adventurous life. Such goods may also represent a possible or desired self (see Chapter 10).

@ www.hannahanderson.com

@ www.secondharvest.org

In each of these first three disposition chains, products usually retain their original form and function. Thus, deposit return bottles may be refilled with similar liquid contents for resale after cleaning. The 1930s and 1940s were the heyday of the returnable soft-drink bottle in the United States. Both retailers and consumers began to reject this system because of the inconvenience of returning bottles, and the practice declined in the United States, except in a few states (e.g., New York, Michigan) where it is required by law. In some European countries, costly deposit fees on reusable containers boost consumer recycling.

As mentioned in Chapter 1, please notice that some products may acquire additional meanings or value by virtue of their **product biography,** *the history of their movement in and out of markets and from one consumer to another.* Women often receive jewelry, china, silver plate, linens, or other consumer goods from their female ancestors. The sentimental value acquired often singularizes the objects, rendering them irreplaceable in their owners' minds. Similarly, art objects and archaeological specimens acquire a pedigree made up of previous collectors and museums. This property is called the objects' provenience. In the case of classical Chinese art, the red stamps visible on many scrolls represent the "chops" of previous owners and indicate provenience.[12]

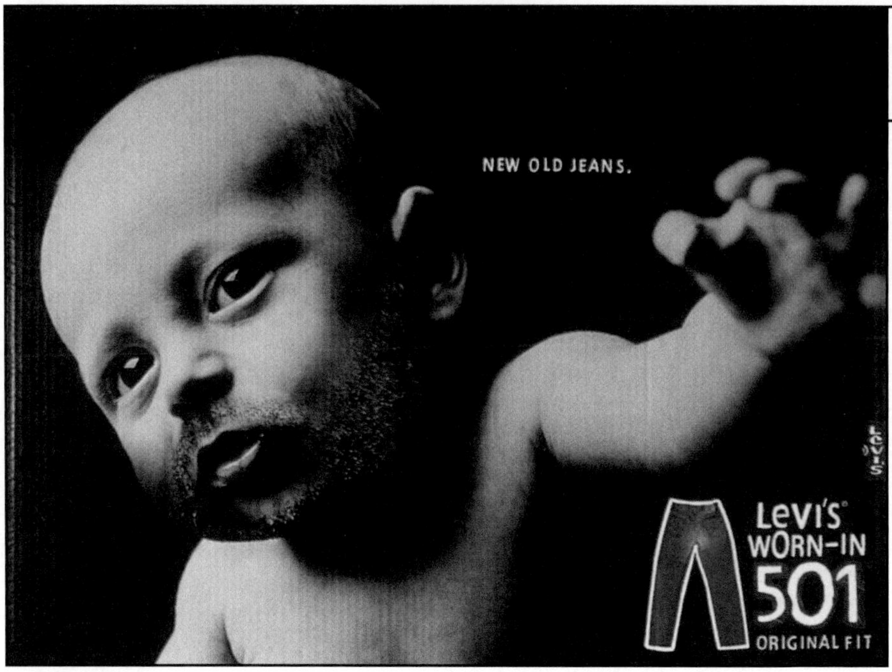

This ad promotes the appearance of reuse as a desirable product attribute.

RESOURCE RECOVERY In a fourth disposition chain, **resource recovery** (4), the product ingredients are broken down and used to manufacture new products. Resource recovery, what many think of as **recycling,** takes place when the product or its parts are used as a secondary resource in the production of new products. Glass bottles or aluminum cans may be melted down and remanufactured. Newspapers may be ground, cleaned, and added to new papermaking processes. Gypsum board can be ground up for use in agriculture. Plastic bottles may be melted down and spun into fiber for clothing. In many cities, nonhazardous waste such as yard clippings and sweepings are composted and reused in gardens, farms, or yards. Another example is provided in Good Practice 19.3. Xerox's success in turning resource recovery into a profit center has been mentioned above. In the recycling business, governments have become involved in creating markets. For instance, some U.S. state governments work to link woody materials generators, processors, and end users together to create new markets for construction materials, animal bedding, and landscaping materials. The UK set a target of 40 percent waste content in newsprint for the year 2000, for example, and helped set up a new plant to recycle newsprint and established a vigorous public relations campaign to encourage recycling.[13]

In resource recovery and retail return schemes alike, governments or marketers often face the problem of creating and managing what we call a **backward channel of distribution.** Such channels move goods in the opposite direction from traditional channels that move them from producers to consumers. Smooth backward channels are required if disposition is to lead to new production. An elaborate backward channel that recycles urban solid waste exists in Ho Chi Minh City, Vietnam, for example. It employs hundreds of people. The DuPont ad shown on page 808 highlights the successful backward channel the company created through a reclamation program. But the creation of backward channels is not necessarily a simple matter, as would-be recyclers often discover. Successful recyclers and retailers depend on the development of

Composting: special treatment to recover resources.

backward channels of distribution. These may fail to develop when markets do not form or regulations are not imposed. When this happens, resource recovery stalls. New York City recently suspended household recycling services because markets for municipal wastes failed to clear.[14]

SPECIAL TREATMENT Special treatment of waste products is depicted in Exhibit 19.1 as an arrow from treatment to residual materials (5). Metrogro™, a by-product of wastewater treatment used as a soil quality improvement aid on many farms, requires some special treatment before application to farm fields. Special treatment of hazardous waste is often required, for example, by incinerating it under controlled conditions. Household composting is a simple example of a home treatment process that has become a significant activity in both the developed and developing worlds. Entrepreneurs in Pakistan, India, and China have jumped into the resource recovery business. However, as Ethical Dilemma 19.2 indicates, when special treatment is not employed, serious problems may ensue.

In the disposition process, supply and demand are reversed. Consumers produce various kinds of waste products, and producers consume these secondary resources. One might say that the top half of Exhibit 19.1 illustrates the demand for secondary resources, while the bottom half represents the supply side.[15]

Voluntary and Involuntary Disposition

There is a distinction between voluntary and involuntary disposition behaviors. We describe both and give examples of voluntary and involuntary disposition behaviors in Exhibits 19.2 and 19.3.

Recycling High-Tech Trash Poisons Asian Villages

ETHICAL DILEMMA 19.2

In 2002, the United States will export as many as 10.2 million discarded computers to Asia, including about 9 million to China. Environmentalists estimate that the Guandong region of China, about 150 miles northeast of Hong Kong, has some 2,500 computer waste businesses, mostly family run. The industry may employ as many as 120,000 people, many of them migrants from elsewhere in China. People in the village of Guiyu, for example, have made a living out of waste collection for generations, one official said. "They used to deal in pig bones and duck feathers. But now it's integrated circuits." Workers rip through the waste looking for every reusable part. Some components are melted to extract precious metals such as gold and platinum. What's left is burned or dumped. Toxic chemicals such as mercury, lead, and dioxins have been released into the air and water. Fish have disappeared from the local river, and drinking water must now be trucked in because the wells are poisoned. Many children have been struck down with leukemia. A local teacher commented, "The villagers here are growing richer," he said, "but their wealth is built atop the health of other victims." Recycling provides a source of wealth for people in less affluent nations, and saves natural resources, but is it worth it?

Sources: Martin Fackler, "High-Tech Trash Poisons Chinese Villages," Lincoln Journal-Star, *March 1, 2002, p. 7A; and as found on www.svtc.org.*

Exhibit 19.2 presents a typology of voluntary disposition behaviors. The entries in the exhibit imply that people make considered decisions about disposition much in the way the theories of consumer decision making discussed in Chapters 15 and 16 describe acquisition behaviors. Thus, when the value derived from a good begins to lag behind the costs of having it around, consumers dispose of it in one way or another.[16] Of course, the disposition process does not always have to be so rational and considered. Feelings and emotions play a strong role in disposal. Just as there are impulse purchases, there are also impulse disposals.

In contrast to the deliberative forms of disposition discussed in the North American context where it is a means to achieve other ends, voluntary disposition is part of taken-for-granted terminal value systems in some cultures. From the Buddhist perspective, for example, a value system that influences people throughout south Asia and in the Far East, it is said that the extent of one's problems are equal to the size of one's possessions. In Buddhist psychology, the need to possess is posited to be a major cause of psychopathology and suffering. The Buddhist middle path allows for the enjoyment of possessions without attachment to them, without a need for possession. This form of voluntary disposition, then, is not rational in the narrow economic sense, but it does influence consumers' attitudes and beliefs, probably lowering generalized materialism and acquisitiveness and promoting the giving away of possessions.[17]

Most likely you can think of involuntary acquisition behaviors, such as inappropriate birthday or wedding gifts you have received. Similarly, you can imagine involuntary disposition behaviors. Losing a wedding ring down the drain, getting burgled, being compelled by poverty or illness to sell favored possessions, or giving up household goods in a divorce are all examples. Of course, death is the ultimate source of involuntary disposition since "you can't take it with you." Exhibit 19.3 presents a typology of involuntary disposition behaviors, a few of which we discuss next.

Methods	Personal Focus	Interpersonal Focus	Societal Focus
Sell—Convert objects to money	As a current example, consumers may go to the eBay website (www.ebay.com) to sell goods that they no longer want or need	Businesses of all sorts: sell personal collections and constructions; sell one's body, blood, body parts, art, crafts, or ideas; auctions; garage and yard sales; flea markets	Sell resources, waste, radio spectrum, used capital goods and weapons
Trade—Exchanging resources in kind	Trading off work, sleep, leisure, or quality time; a skin graft	Countertrades; cooperative labor exchanges, including day care; stock swaps; trading in consumer durables; exchanging ideas; trading sports players	Countertrades
Give away—Transferring objects and sometimes meanings	Possible feelings of altruism; affiliation motive	Donate body organs; charitable donations; pass baby clothes to siblings and friends; living inheritances; giving advice to others	Redistribution of land, labor, commodities, services, time from less to more needy persons
Recycle—Convert it to something else	Making a quilt from scraps, picture frames from old barn board; composting	Recycling animal waste, newspapers, aluminum, yard trimmings, tires, waste pulp and paper	Recycling buildings, neighborhoods, waste water, mining or industrial facilities, ruins
Throw away—Discard in a societally approved manner	Use of trash cans, garbage disposals, sewage systems, land fills;diet; give up an unhealthy lifestyle	Neighborhood, park, or beach cleanup; divorce, separate from, or disown, a person; diet plans	Dump garbage in space or the oceans; stockpile nuclear and chemical waste
Abandon—Discard in a societally unacceptable manner	Strew property about in public places	Abandon family members and pets; eschew accepted codes of conduct; violate a trust	Abandon social groups (poor, homeless, mentally ill, minorities); abandon political allies; abandon environmental responsibilities
Use up—Physical consumption	Eat; use nonrenewable energy sources; wear out tools or clothing	Use employees' time; use family, friends', or neighbors' resources	Use nonrenewable resources: fossil fuels, ecosystems; use citizens in war
Destroy—Intentionally damage	Suicide; burn down one's house; shred old pictures or love letters	Arson; euthanasia: infanticide; murder; terrorist bombing; redline a neighborhood	Conduct war, genocide, revolution; executions and regicides

Source: Melissa Martin Young and Melanie Wallendorf, "Ashes to Ashes, Dust to Dust: Conceptualizing Consumer Disposition of Possessions," *Proceedings*, Educators' Conference, American Marketing Association, 1989, pp. 32–37.

EXHIBIT 19.2

A Taxonomy of Voluntary Disposition Behaviors

Methods	Personal Focus	Interpersonal Focus	Societal Focus
Use up	Accidentally or unintentionally use up possessions, food, time	Loss of time at mandatory meetings; friend or family member uses up gas, tennis balls, aspirin	Ozone layer; ocean fish; fresh air and water
Legal transfer		Patent or copyright revoked or ended; lose property or children in divorce; house or car repossessed; treasured possessions dispersed after death	Eminent domain; war crimes retribution; boundary redemarcation
Illegal transfer		Burglary, theft, extortion, bribery; patent or copyright infringement; gray markets	Artwork or historical artifacts stolen; lose land or population in war; black markets
Loss	Misplace objects; forget information; lose track of time; abandon in a geographic move	Death of a loved one; losing track of people; loss of other's possessions and resources, time	Historical buildings, archives, records, heroes, values, history neglected
Destruction	Own death; breakage	Be vandalized, burgled, murdered; reputation ruined by gossip or media; gamble away an inheritance	Overpopulation or pollution destroys natural resources, or biodiversity; war or disease wipes out a population; chemical waste depresses sperm counts

Source: Melissa Martin Young and Melanie Wallendorf, "Ashes to Ashes, Dust to Dust: Conceptualizing Consumer Disposition of Possessions," *Proceedings*, Educators' Conference, American Marketing Association, 1989, pp. 32–37.

EXHIBIT 19.3

A Taxonomy of Involuntary Disposition Behaviors

Involuntary loss of possessions is relatively common. Divorce touches almost half of all marriages in the United States and is frequent in most European and African countries as well. Loss of property is commonplace for both parties to a divorce, but women suffer the most loss of property.[18]

A study of 16 countries found that over 4 percent of the citizenry became victims of one form of theft, burglary, or attempted burglary. Reactions to the loss of property accompanying burglary are relatively strong. The most intense and long-lasting reactions to burglary are found among women, the elderly, singles, and the poor. Interestingly, children's reactions to theft become increasingly harsh with age, as possession becomes progressively more a part of self-concept and perceived self-efficacy. Two characteristics of the experience may account for the special severity of adult emotional responses to burglary. The whole of the personal possessions of the victims has been

attacked. Thus, consistent with the notion of the extended self, discussed in Chapter 10, meanings of intense personal importance congealed in one's possessions are attacked and compromised in a burglary. Burglary and other forms of theft attack the boundaries of the self and the family. Feelings of alienation from the home, intrusion, loss of perceived personal control, and contamination are common. Not surprisingly, almost three-quarters of consumers in Western countries are insured against some financial consequences of residential burglary. Victims appreciate services that provide informational and emotional support, but such services are not always available. Perhaps you can identify additional marketing opportunities here.[19]

PROFILES OF DISPOSITION BEHAVIORS

In this section we provide more detail about the behaviors mentioned in the model of disposition shown in Exhibit 19.1. Specifically, we discuss discarding, selling, donating, gift giving, storing, and recovering.

Discard It

When people think about disposition, probably the first possibility that comes to mind is simply throwing something away. The United States has been accused of being a **waste-making society,** *one in which people's first thought is to discard rather than reuse or recycle unwanted possessions.* Indeed, Americans throw away a lot of trash, almost two kilograms a day. In the United States, consumers discard about 12 billion tons of material each year, of which about 209 million metric tons is the solid waste that comes from households, institutions, small businesses, towns, and municipalities. The average per capita amount of waste produced by Americans has not changed much in the past 100 years, 1.5 to 1.9 pounds per day. Americans generate over 20.5 metric tons of CO_2 per capita per year, Canadians 19.8 tons, and Germans 10.3 tons.[20]
The Japanese discard only approximately 1.1 kilograms per day, but Japan too is a throw-away culture, in part because of a high value placed on newness and a distaste for used items. In Tokyo, weekly collections of large throwaways attract tons of discarded consumer products, many in mint condition. Students and the poor enjoy attractive scavenging and reuse options.[21]
The more diversity and novelty there is in consumption patterns, the more people throw away as waste. Richer countries discard waste more than poorer ones. Marketers who thrive on providing consumers with novel and diverse product offerings contribute to the discard phenomenon.

Sell It

Flea markets; swap meets; garage, barn, and jumble sales (UK); antique dealerships; and acres of secondhand car lots are as characteristic of contemporary consumer society as the shopping mall. Together, they represent a major type of household disposition behavior, **selling.** At **swap meets,** consumers get together in informal markets to buy or trade their used goods. Such selling is a key way people get rid of unwanted possessions. For example, a study in Tucson, Arizona, found that 34 percent of household appliances that had recently been replaced had been sold to stores or strangers. Selling is often occasioned by changes in family life-cycle stage, geographic movements, and role transitions, such as divorces. Flea markets, garage sales, and yard sales

are a primary vehicle for secondhand reuse or lateral recycling from household to household, as discussed above. In lateral recycling, the use and form of used merchandise remains constant while the user changes. Under traditional recycling, form, use, and users all change.

Garage sales probably began in California in the early 1960s and spread across the continent from there. Between six and nine million North American garage sales now generate between one and two billion dollars in sales every year. Most participants are of middle- and working-class backgrounds, in their twenties and thirties.[22]

eBay.com

Internet auction sites, such as eBay, can be viewed as **electronic flea markets** that facilitate lateral recycling. Consumers come to these sites to sell goods that are no longer of use to them. The procedure is a bit different from a traditional flea market in that rival bids are posted over a period of time. Individuals, not corporations, use eBay to buy and sell items in more than 300 categories, including automobiles, collectibles, antiques, sports memorabilia, computers, toys, dolls, figures, coins, stamps, books, magazines, music, pottery, glass, photography, electronics, jewelry, and gemstones. Every day, four million new auctions are offered in 20 countries. Just like a traditional marketplace, electronic marketplaces strive to serve community needs such as social interaction and meeting with other users who share similar interests.

Disposition, just like acquisition, provides a means of expressing important values. One U.S. study identified four themes or motives for garage sales. The first is reclaiming control of one's work, which recognizes that garage sales create a sense of empowerment that middle- and working-class consumers may not have in daily life. The second is creating a sense of social justice, as reflected in the common tendency to lower prices for the deserving. A third theme or motive is beating the system, which refers to buyers' satisfaction with their reduced dependence on traditional retail outlets and their ability to acquire goods inexpensively. Fourth is feeling part of a nurturing community, which reflects the communal aspects of lateral recycling as goods pass from consumers who no longer need them to those who do.[23]

Both garage sales and the items sold in them reflect norms and values associated with gender. Gender-typed items tend to attract shoppers of the appropriate gender, and sellers may even direct men and women to the expected grouping of objects. The quintessential men's sale involves a jumble of items, focused on tools, recreation gear, and some computer equipment, for example. Prices are usually negotiated, and some men delight in drumming up enthusiasm among shoppers through a display of expertise about the items on offer.[24]

Disposition involves both physical and emotional separation from possessions. Selling household goods is one way consumers separate personal meanings from goods, or separate that part of themselves associated with objects that have been part of their lives. Sales of household goods can be a way of getting rid of the past, of an unattractive prior self, a divorced spouse, or a deceased family member. Since sales are direct, face-to-face transactions, sellers are able to maintain some control over who receives their former possessions. Because the transformation of possessions into commodities for sale may be a meaningful emotional event, sellers of household goods often engage in divestment rituals, such as cleaning, sorting, folding, arranging, and tagging them. These rituals serve to empty goods of meaning before they are passed on to others.[25]

Donate It

Giving things away is a third form of disposition. Attitudes toward the **donation** of goods and services to others vary widely around the world. Charity is enshrined in both

A Market for, Well, Almost Everything

CONSUMER CHRONICLES 19.1

The big blue-and-white trucks roll up and disgorge their cargo: A tobacco-colored vinyl lounger, a rickety croquet set, pink hair rollers, a copy of *Atlas Shrugged,* a 45-rpm Shaun Cassidy record. It's a typical day at Goodwill central out on San Fernando Road, a few miles north of downtown. Mauricio Hernandez patrols the loading dock. It's his job to see that the day's bounty—the discards of an average of 200 households—are sorted, priced, and sent on their way to some of the 26 Goodwill thrift stores throughout the county. "The show starts here," he says, as the trucks' treasures are dumped into big metal bins and wheeled to sorting tables. Clothing (8,000–10,000 items today) goes onto one conveyor belt, "hard goods"—lamps, hair dryers, pots and pans—onto another. On the fourth floor of the cavernous building, in the denim wing, recycled Guess jeans are tagged $10. Nearby, a man is "hanging" clothing and a trio of workers sift through a huge pile of shoes, seeking mates. One floor below, sofa beds are stripped and re-upholstered. Goodwill of Southern California depends on the kindness of strangers. Sale of donated items raises $12 million ot its $15-million annual budget.

Source: Beverly Beyette, "Around Town," Los Angeles Times, *July 22, 1993, pp. E1, E2.*

Catholic and Islamic religious doctrine, and charitable giving is common in many Protestant denominations as well. Millions of people donate blood to the member organizations of the International Red Cross. As such, donations are the lifeblood of thousands of charitable organizations around the world, including Second Harvest discussed above. Consumer Chronicles 19.1 provides a glimpse of how one charity that relies on donations operates. In many countries, people are encouraged to donate their body parts and to designate their eyes or other organs for reuse. Even human reproductive matter, sperm and eggs, may be donated to help redress the problem of human infertility. North Americans donate about 2.5 billion pounds of clothes to charities each year. Eighty percent of this is passed on to used-clothing firms that make cash donations back to the charities. In 2001, almost $62 million of used clothing was eventually exported from the United States to Africa, where it is retailed inexpensively, but at relatively high rates of profit to channel members. Consumer Chronicles 19.2 suggests that the charitable intent is sometimes lost in translation.[26]

The donation decision process is unique among disposition decisions. Unlike the typical marketing exchange, the donation process is often a reaction to a serious or even desperate human condition. Thus, this process may tap into feelings of joy, improved self-esteem (altruism), guilt, or denial. Donation also differs from gift giving discussed in Chapter 16 in that reciprocity and relationship maintenance are secondary considerations. Donation involves giving something tangible with little provision of any return. Moreover, rewards received are usually intangible or delayed.[27]

Gift It

Gift giving has been discussed in Chapter 16 as a form of consumer acquisition. Of course, gift giving can also be a mode of disposition. One form of gift disposition, **inheritance,** provides numerous business opportunities and is an important household consumer behavior. Family inheritance decisions involve gifts from older generations of family members to younger ones and from the departed to the living. Important distinctions are made in some societies between the way immovable property (land and buildings), movable property (other tangible property, including consumer goods), and even intangible assets (such as specialized knowledge of various kinds) are inherited. In the urban West, social norms promote relatively egalitarian inheritance decisions, especially in the United States.[28]

Between 1995 and 2000, nearly $1 trillion was passed on to baby boomers in the form of bequests. This event represents "the largest intergenerational transfer of wealth in American history."[29] As in previous generations, aging confronts consumers with

decisions about how to distribute their wealth. If populations in the Triad countries become top heavy with older citizens as expected, inheritance issues will come increasingly to the forefront, providing new entrepreneurial opportunities for visionary consumer marketers.

Cultural differences between Japan and the United States are significant with regard to inheritance. Over 75 percent of Japanese state they are unconcerned with amassing wealth to pass on to their children as compared to 57 percent of Americans. Further, 29 percent of Japanese, but only 3 percent of Americans, said they would give more or all to the child or children who took care of them in old age. Finally, 84 percent of Americans but only 44 percent of Japanese said they would divide the inheritance equally among their offspring, showing differences in cultural norms between the two countries.[30]

In south Asia and Africa, dowry and bride wealth constitute two contrasting forms of what we might call **preinheritance,** *living bequests of household resources.* In dowry, the wife's family provides important stocks of consumer goods and money to the husband's family. The custom of bride wealth works in the reverse way. The size and composition of these forms of preinheritance are often hotly debated because size and composition contribute to social status. In addition, the size and composition of dowry and bride wealth strongly affect the standard of living of the newlywed household. Both forms of preinheritance have become important systems for the diffusion of innovative consumer goods into south Asian and African societies, as they are often part of the dowry and bride wealth. Thus, these customary transfers become the vehicle for new forms of conspicuous consumption of consumer goods. Since women often contribute to and benefit from these transfers, the size and composition of dowry and bride wealth may influence the comfort and control wives exert in their new homes as well.[31]

The Meaning of Used Clothing

CONSUMER CHRONICLES 19.2

Used clothing carries different meanings in every African market. In warlord-ridden, destitute Somalia, used clothing is called contemptuously *huudhaydh*—"Who died?" In the past, some Kenyans believed used clothing was removed from the dead; they washed it carefully to avoid skin diseases. In Togo, it is called "dead white man's clothing." In Niger, it is called "small clothes" in contrast to the more prestigious traditional robes. In Sierra Leone it is called "junks" and highly prized. In Zambia, they call it *salaula,* which means "to rummage through a pile." In Rwanda, used clothing is known by the word for "choose." Some worry that the flood of charitable donations may drown traditional African fashion, but this seems far from certain since local tailors often customize used clothing to suit local tastes.

Source: Karen Tranberg Hansen, Salaula: The World of Secondhand Clothing and Zambia *(Chicago: University of Chicago Press, 2000); and George Packer, "How Susie Bayer's T-Shirt Ended Up on Yusuf Mama's Back,"* New York Times Magazine, *March 31, 2002, pp. 54–59. Copyright ©2002 by* The New York Times Co. *Reprinted with permission.*

Store It

Storage is a basic consumer necessity. Of course, some of this function is performed by retail stores and other channel members. Nonetheless, consumers make provisions for the storage of food, valuables, and sacred objects. Even Australian Aborigines, people with limited material wealth, maintained sacred sites to store elaborately carved and painted boards called *alcheringa* that served as permanent records of important myths and stories.

In the contemporary urban West, some trace of traditional storage behaviors can be seen in the frequent use of food cellars. Consistent with these traditions, many French people place modern electric freezers in their cellars. A study conducted in Tucson, Arizona, found that in 30 percent of cases in which a household appliance had recently been replaced, the old one was kept around the house somewhere. Both individual and

institutional consumers store objects in corporate, historical, and other museum collections.[32]

In most places around the world, the home has become people's most important storehouse of consumer goods.[33] Homes are used to store goods that act as objects of temporal stability in people's lives. **Time-marked goods** (e.g., trophies, souvenirs, awards, religious artifacts, wedding gifts, photos) *remind people who they once were, invite comparison with who they are now, and highlight how they have changed.* In addition, many of the items people keep around them may be thought of as stimuli for an evolving network of associated memories. Not only do such memories provide an anchor to the sense of self, they may also provide people with cues for internal search behaviors when considering future consumption choices.[34]

In homes in the West, an attic or a cellar may become a repository for special possessions. Upper-class households may contain collections that provide symbols of family distinction. That is, the things people store in attics and cellars may convey social affiliation meanings. At the same time, the things hidden away in attics and basements may also play a role in self-definition. The existence of these objects—heirloom linens, school yearbooks, yellowing photos, old dolls—are physical markers of the special beings who inhabit the house. In addition, people say they also store things because they never know when they may need them again. Hence, these stored items allow people to anticipate future needs. Finally, attics and cellars may symbolize the consumption of time. Attics and cellars allow people to remember themselves and the events and persons associated with stored objects when they periodically sort through these spaces.[35]

In contemporary consumer society, storing material possessions has assumed dramatic proportions and spawned numerous marketing activities devoted to providing companies and individuals with storage options. For example, there are firms that specialize in storage of legal documents and closet remodeling. There's a retail company called Hold Everything that specializes in storage containers and facilities. Shopping suggestions are a staple of travel guides, and souvenirs are preserved as mementos of the tourist experience. In Salt Lake City, Utah, a firm called Summum has even revived the ancient Egyptian practice of preserving bodies for posterity through mummification. For a minimum of $32,000, Summum will turn you into a museum-quality corpse! And this is just one of the many new options on offer from the trillion-dollar global funeral business.[36]

Recover It

Recycling has always been around. In the last 30 years it has become enshrined in consumer behavior and business practices as a result of a series of resource crises that hit the First World, beginning with the oil price shock in 1973. Threats of a global shortage of landfill space began in the mid-1980s. Aggressive environmental education in schools, science museums—even specialized "garbage museums"—and some media reports have also increased consumer concern and recycling behaviors. Exhibit 19.4 reports recycling and composting rates for municipal waste in several European countries. The exhibit shows that Germany composts or recycles almost 45 percent while France only composts about 8 percent. The higher rates are enforced by government regulations that impose taxes on municipal household waste that is not composted or recycled. Under pressure from European Union rules and because the country is running out of landfill space, Britain is considering adopting such legislation to reduce the simple discard rate.[37]

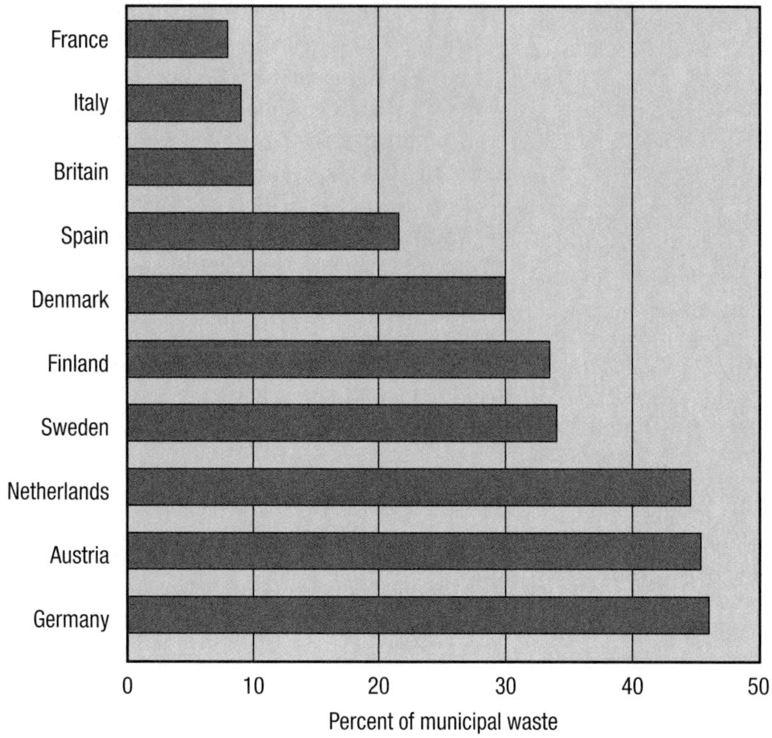

EXHIBIT 19.4

European Recycling and Composting Rates, 2001

The United States, Canada, and Mexico compost less than 4 percent of their municipal waste. Composted waste is a useful input into household gardening. Marketing easy-to-use household composting technologies is a growing business derived from the demand for household waste treatment supplies. An ad from *Biocycle* magazine for the Earth Machine, shown on page 812, illustrates this trend.[38]

Consumer Chronicles 19.3 illustrates how some entrepreneurs have taken recycling and special treatment in a surprising, weird, and presumably profitable direction and mobilized an unusual channel of distribution in the process.

Consumer activists have turned the spotlight on consumer product companies whose packaging is difficult to recycle. In the European Community and North America, recycling is written into regulatory law. One EC proposal mandates that early this century 90 percent of all packaging waste by weight must be recovered. The innovative Netherlands National Environmental Policy Plan II calls for integrated life-cycle management that will make producers responsible for whatever remains of their products after the users are through with them. The idea is that producers are more likely to design products and packaging that can be reused or recycled if they are responsible for disposal costs. As a result, some international firms, including Body Shop International PLC, Nestlé, Texas Instruments, VeryFine Products, Inc., Volvo, and BMW, have moved aggressively to recycle or to encourage employees to recycle. Of course, numerous entrepreneurs have emerged to meet the demand for recycled goods, as shown in Good Practice 19.3 and Industry Insights 19.2.[39]

Interest in **close-loop manufacturing,** where *simplified recycling is built into products from the design phase on,* is developing in Scandinavia, Germany, and to a lesser extent Japan. In Germany, for example, the so-called dual system allows for the collection of

Stones from Bones

CONSUMER CHRONICLES 19.3

If you're looking for a way to shine on in the afterlife, then Life Gem might have a solution for you. Life Gem, a company located in a suburb of Chicago, has found a way to manufacture diamonds from released carbon during cremation. This process ensures that loved ones—including pets—can now be added to the collection of family heirlooms. Several funeral homes throughout the U.S. have started to offer Life Gem's service. According to Life Gem's chief operating officer, Rusty VandenBiesen, the process was perfected in a diamond-manufacturing laboratory in Germany using the cremated remains of animals and a cadaver. The American-owned laboratory believes that one human body could yield up to 50 stones of varying sizes. Prices vary by the size of the stone—the company charges $4,000 for a .25-carat gem—and refunds are unlikely, so individuals need to be sure when investing in this costly process. Life Gem has plans to expand its service in Japan, where the cremation rate is high, as well as in veterinarians' offices across the U.S.

Source: "Stones from Bones," The Economist, *August 24, 2002, p. 49.*

all recyclable packaging materials for sorting and recycling. This effort is supported by a financing system, the Green Point, run by a former Nestlé CEO. In Europe, government regulations will tax people on their cars until they can show that they have been disposed of cleanly at an accredited disassembly plant. BMW, VW, and the PSA group, which markets Peugeot and Citroën, are actively involved in the effort. The VW Golf is designed to be recycled, and BMW has a disassembly plant in Wackersdorf, Bavaria. Detroit automakers are also involved in closed-loop recycling, experimenting with recyclable plastic body parts, brake pads, and taillights.[40] Similar efforts spurred by government regulation are under way in Japan.

SITUATIONAL AND INDIVIDUAL FACTORS AFFECTING DISPOSAL CHOICES

What factors influence the disposition choices of consumers, firms, and organizations? Here, we suggest a number of factors and group them into categories.[41]

Factors Intrinsic to the Product

Materials, purchase price, and replacement cost influence disposition decisions. For example, the materials from which products are made influence recycling significantly. Aluminum is the easiest to recycle thanks to high prices for aluminum and aluminum ore. Paper recycling is increasing, as is recycling of plastics. Organic materials such as yard sweepings and tree trimmings are recyclable through composting, fueling a global municipal composting industry as represented in the Lubo Starscreen™ ad shown on page 823. By contrast, rubber, especially vulcanized rubber used in tires, is one of the more difficult products to recycle, and markets for recycled rubber have been slow to develop. Both consumers and organizations consider purchase price and replacement costs in making disposition decisions. Interface, Inc., discussed in Industry Insights 19.1, provides a good example of how replacement costs have influenced the development of more sustainable floor-covering systems. Higher costs result in delays in disposition, and when disposition occurs, selling is a common strategy. Higher-priced goods thus tend to enter secondary markets.

Competitive Pressures

In businesses, competitive pressures play an important role in disposition. For example, new capacity for recycling fibers in the United States in 1994 created a supply shortage that drove prices for corrugated containers to $140 per short ton.[42] Competition for supply will call forth new sources of recyclable materials.

Competitive pressures also influence firms to undertake deconsumption measures or engage in special handling of waste. R. Ford has promised to boost the efficiency of its SUVs by 25 percent in the next five years, and General Motors and DaimlerChrysler have pledged to do what Ford does. As shown in the ad for Saturn on page 824, companies can then employ credible green appeals in product differentiation and market positioning strategies. Similarly, Shell Oil claims that they have reduced their net greenhouse gas emissions at a rate that puts the company ahead of the schedule in the Kyoto (Japan) agreement on the environment.[43]

Sometimes, competitive pressures are formalized as self-imposed industry norms for materials handling and life-cycle management. The new **ISO 14000** standards for environmental management are an example. The International Organization for Standardization set out to develop ISO 14000 standards that organizations can use to improve their environmental performance over time. ISO 14000 consists of five families of standards, including environmental management system (EMS), environmental auditing, environmental performance evaluation (EPE), environmental labeling,

The Re-Source

INDUSTRY INSIGHTS 19.2

Looking for a T-shirt made entirely from a plastic soda bottle? You can buy them by the caseload, thanks to environmental distributors like Mary Jarret. Jarret's Amazing Recycled Products in Denver gives retailers one-stop access to 250 unique environmental products of all shapes and sizes. A briefcase made of recycled factory wastes (from wetsuits) is a hot item; so are pens made from recycled cardboard. And Jarret sells "lumber" made from recycled milk containers for building park benches and picnic tables. "I don't have to sell the idea of using recycled products anymore," says the 45-year-old entrepreneur, who started her company seven years ago. "I'm getting 40 to 50 calls a day."

Source: Entrepreneur, *September 1993, p. 14.*

Global demand for municipal recycling fuels a growth industry.

www.shell.com/biodiversity

Saturn employs a green appeal for product differentiation.

and life-cycle assessment (LCA). EMSs allow companies to define environmental goals and then monitor progress toward reaching them. Environmental audits evaluate EMS programs. EPEs identify and quantify the effects that companies have on their environments. The measurements are made against baseline levels. LCAs provide a means of determining what effects manufacturing processes have on the environment now and in the future. LCAs also assess environmental effects over the life of a product from raw materials, through manufacturing, to disposition. Finally, environmental labeling standards will make it easier for consumers to identify and evaluate attributes of ECO-labeled products. Implementation of ISO 14000 standards should allow firms to achieve savings through waste reduction and enhanced productivity. At the same time, these standards provide assurance to consumers that a company is committed to being environmentally friendly.[44]

Competitive pressures also affect consumer disposition behaviors. Dr. Seuss, the children's author, wrote a wonderful story about two groups of creatures called Sneetches. One group had stars on their bellies; the other did not. When a clever marketer toting a pair of star-applying and star-removing machines happened along, the foolish Sneetches spent their savings alternately acquiring and disposing of their stars to stay "in with the in crowd." Thus, competitive pressures to keep up with the Sneetches may encourage consumers to dispose of faddish products merely because they are no longer in vogue.[45] Similarly, curbside recycling makes it easy to see who is and who is not recycling household waste.

Situational Factors Extrinsic to the Product

Situational factors play a role at both the individual and organizational levels. Finances, storage space, fashion change, use context, method of acquisition, legal considerations (e.g., the desire to avoid taxes and fines), and even downstream externalities may influence disposition behaviors. Fees and taxes drive numerous recycling efforts in Europe. The ad for ITT shown below suggests that pressure from the Italian fishing industry (an externality) led Sicilian industrial polluters to install a water purification system.

At the organizational level, attitudes and pressures applied by various interest groups and publics, such as a community's attitudes toward recycling or waste incineration, come into play. The Rainforest Action Network and Greenpeace have successfully lobbied large retailers such as IKEA, Home Depot, Lowe's, and others to stop selling old-growth-forest timber products, for example. Regulations applied by various governmental bodies also influence organizational practices. In 1999, for example, Shell companies paid US$2.83 million in fines and settlements for 306 violations of governmental environmental rules.[46] A final factor is the development of markets for recycled materials. This factor is probably more important than regulations on packaging or mandates for recycling.

In the area of green marketing, research shows that consumers' stated commitment to environmentally responsible consumption is only loosely tied to environmentally responsible consumption behaviors. All sorts of product (e.g., price) and situation-related factor (e.g., inconvenience) negatively affect green consumption behaviors.[47] Sometimes, consumers may not see the link between their consumption behavior and its effect on the environment. Other times, a factor such as price may influence a purchase decision more than environmental considerations.

Extrinsic factors like political pressure lead to changes in disposition.

Life-Status Changes

A life-status change occurs when consumers experience a shift in their social roles. At the same time, the norms and expectations that define interactions with others may shift. Cross-culturally, the four most common life-status changes are birth, puberty, marriage, and death. Often they are marked by rites of passage. Other life-status changes are triggered by changes in work or financial status, family life cycle, migration, losses of relationships, physical changes, and inner, psychological changes. Such changes often require the deletion, as well as the addition, of symbolic material goods.

One study conducted in the southwestern United States found that reuse behaviors are closely related to household developmental cycles. New households composed of young persons without children had the highest percentage of used items. When couples begin having children, both rented and used items in their household inventory decline. Used items plummet to near zero as households reach the stage of older couples with older children. The percentage of used items in the household inventory begins to rise again among empty nesters. Wealth and residential stability tend to depress the amount of used goods households possess.[48]

Just as we distinguished between voluntary and involuntary disposition, we should distinguish disposition related to voluntary and involuntary life-status changes. The implications for disposition vary between these two cases. With respect to voluntary changes, such as voluntary migration, first professional job, or marriage, people may willingly discard props that they associate with previous life stages. For example, young Japanese motorcycle gang members quickly give up their treasured bikes and characteristic costumes for the material trappings of adulthood after marriage or professional employment. In this way disposition comes to symbolize rejected identity.

With involuntary changes, such as those involving job loss, forced migration, retirement, death of a loved one, or divorce, the reaction to (forced) disposition may be quite different. Migrating Mormon refugees in nineteenth century North America experienced substantial anguish as a result of possessions left behind in their journey across the Great Plains to Utah. They sometimes clung to treasured possessions even at the risk of life and limb in the hazardous crossing.[49]

Deterioration in financial status is one kind of involuntary change. This situation may result in decreased consumption of leisure activities or disposal of unnecessary leisure products. In such cases consumers sometimes increase certain acquisition behaviors, perhaps to maintain face or protect self-image. Such behavior is a good example of **psychological reactance,** *a response to a threat to behavioral freedom.* At the same time, involuntary life-status changes may involve cathartic, even joyful disposition of possessions symbolic of previous roles, as when divorced people get rid of their former spouses' possessions.[50]

Elderly people, facing retirement and death, encounter special disposition problems. Decisions related to the disposition of possessions often are fraught with tension. The decision process is complicated by the fact that family members may avoid any discussion related to the disposition of the older persons' possessions.

Older consumers' possessions represent who they are and the life they have led. Possessions represent emotional connections to individuals who mean the most to them. An older person's possessions may take on value based on the length of time the person has owned them and the circumstances surrounding acquisition of that belonging. In addition, possessions help owners reminisce about significant time periods and events in their lives. The disposition of objects, possessions, and experiences that are infused with personal meanings through inheritance is often painful.[51] Deciding what will

become of those possessions, to leave a legacy that validates one's life and affirms relationships with important survivors, becomes an important responsibility for older consumers.

Disposition of older consumers' cherished possessions presents an array of mostly untapped marketing opportunities. Products and services could be devised to record and store special possession meanings and stories. Counseling and consulting services could help families confront and process the disposition needs of older consumers and help charities and other beneficiaries respond to older consumers' desires to leave a legacy. Finally, channels could be devised to more easily facilitate lateral recycling of older consumers' special possessions.[52]

Serious life-threatening illness and death may be viewed as a complex array of dispossession events. Life-threatening illness and or impending death may stimulate a chain of voluntary, and ultimately involuntary, dispossession behaviors. For the ill, dispossession may be experienced as a loss of control or a diminution of the self. Alternatively, illness may so change the sense of self that dispossession of some possessions linked to the previous sense of self may be relatively easy. Knowledge of the impending end of life sometimes stimulates a belief that material possessions are less important than other aspects of life, such as relationships with others. In turn, the relationships may be strengthened by dispossession. After death, possessions can become important symbols by which individuals wish to be remembered.[53]

DISPOSITION: SEGMENTATION AND PSYCHOGRAPHIC FACTORS

Traditionally, marketers strive to create marketing plans so as to achieve, simultaneously, two objectives. First, following the marketing concept, they attempt to satisfy customer needs. Second, they attempt to achieve organizational goals (e.g., in terms of shareholder wealth, market share, sales levels). In his pioneering book *Sustainable Marketing,* Donald Fuller argues that a third criterion needs to be added to this set. Specifically, **sustainable marketing** means that *marketing plans should be constructed so that they are compatible with ecosystems.* With an emphasis on sustainable marketing, organizations can find ways to reduce costs and serve the long-term well-being of society. Good Practice 19.1 provides one example. In this section, we review a group of segmentation strategies and issues that are congruent with Fuller's notion of sustainable marketing.[54]

Segmentation

Markets can be segmented on the basis of consumers' green orientation. Specifically, **green segments** are *consumers whose acquisition behavior is affected by proenvironmental attitudes and behaviors.* A green orientation is a variable one.[55] That is, a particular consumer may be green with respect to purchasing products with organic or recycled content but, at the same time, resist acts related to **deconsumption.** Examples of a number of green segmentation profiles of U.S. consumers are summarized in Exhibit 19.5.

These segmentation profiles assume that there is a relationship between the propensity to reuse, recycle, and consider the environmental impacts of waste disposal and a green psychographic profile (see Chapter 11 for a discussion of psychographics). At the other

Company	Segment	Characteristics
Roper/S. C. Johnson	True-blue greens (11%)	Actual behavior is consistent with strong concerns about the environment.
	Greenback greens (11%)	Commitment to the environment mainly manifested by willingness to pay substantially higher prices for green products.
	Sprouts (26%)	Show middling levels of concern about the environment and equally middling levels of behavioral response.
	Grousers (24%)	Consistently rationalize their lack of proenvironmental behavior by offering all kinds of excuses and criticizing the poor performance of others.
	Basic browns (28%)	Do not believe individuals can make a difference in solving environmental problems, and do not want to make a difference.
Green MarketAlert	Visionary greens (5–15%)	Have embraced the paradigm shift. Green is a way of life for this group, not a shopping style. Passionately committed to environmental change.
	Maybe-greens (55–80%)	Express high degree of environmental concern but act on those concerns only irregularly.
	Hard-core browns (15–30%)	Indifferent or implacably antienvironmentalist. Tend to have lower incomes and educational levels.
Simmons Market Research Bureau	Premium green (22%)	Sophisticates, totally committed, in word and deed, to protecting planet Earth. Willing to spend more, do more, vote more.
	Red, white, and green (20%)	Traditionalists, equally committed to the environment, but think more in terms of their own turf and their beloved outdoors.
	No-costs ecologists (28%)	Sound like dedicated ecologists, but less likely to commit actions and money, unless it's the government's.
	Convenient greens (11%)	Environmental attitudes strong, but actions are motivated by convenience in lifestyle.
	Unconcerneds (19%)	The name says it all.

Source: The Bridge Group, *Green MarketAlert* (Bethlehem, CT: The Bridge Group, 1991).

EXHIBIT 19.5

Green Consumer Segments

end of the continuum, it is probable that "brown" consumers, through disinterest, lower incomes, less education and environmental knowledge, or diminished sense of self-efficacy, are likely to be concerned less about the environmental consequences of manufacturing, packaging, and solid-waste disposal.

Green consumers can be found in most developed countries. A study in 1995 showed that at least 50 percent of Canadians search for products in recyclable packaging (60 percent), and a "green" (58 percent), natural, or organic (50 percent) label. The Envi-

ronmental Choice logo now covers 65 product categories in Canada. In 1992, 15 percent of the population identified itself as eco-consumers, and more than 50 percent said that environmental concerns influenced their purchase behavior. Only 13 percent of the consumers surveyed said they were not concerned about the environment.[56]

A 2001 study in the Wallonia region of the Netherlands found that 73 percent of consumers said they felt fighting pollution was an urgent problem; only 5 percent said protection of the environment was not a serious priority. Consumers between 46 and 60 years of age were more environmentally aware than people younger than 25. Seventy-eight percent of respondents claimed to have made a concrete effort to protect the environment; only 4 percent said they were disinterested in doing so. Of this 78 percent, 97 percent sorted their trash, 81 percent economized on their energy use; and 78 percent economized on their water use. About 60 percent look for green packaging. Thirty-eight percent, up 5 percent from 2000, use their cars less than before. It is worth noting that most activities were curative rather than preventative in nature.[57]

Exhibit 19.6 summarizes four types of segments for environmentally responsible corporate buying (ERB). Socially responsible purchasing includes such judgments as considering what the product is made of (e.g., office paper from recycled postconsumer waste versus virgin materials), from where it comes (e.g., wood from sustainably managed forests versus unmanaged forests), or from whom it comes (e.g., companies whose other products are unobjectionable versus companies that also make objectionable products). Politically savvy policy entrepreneurs play a key role in initiating environmen-

EXHIBIT 19.6

Overview of Organizational Segments for Environmentally Responsible Buying (ERB)

Primary Motivation/ Firm Characteristics	Type I—Founder's Ideals	Type II—Corporate Symbolism	Type III—Opportune	Type IV—Restraint
Organization type	Consumer products	Industrial products/services; business/consumer services	Consumer services; consumer/business services	Industrial products; consumer services
Policy entrepreneur	Founder or middle management	Often external relations manager	Not present	Middle manager, often in operations
Basis of demand	Founder's principles	Perceived long-term advantage	Bottom-line benefits	Consumer derived; public relations
Common focal purchase type	Product essentials	Consumption supplies	Support essentials	Product essentials
Extrinsic rewards for ERB	Yes	Yes	No	No
Attempt comprehensive approach to ERB	Yes	Yes	No	Sometimes
Meaning of environmental responsibility	What, where, who	What	What	What, frequently where, and who

tally responsible buying in the organization buying center. Successful initiation of comprehensive ERB programs involves the emergence of champions in the organization like the leader of Aracruz described in Good Practice 19.1. If organizations are to pursue ERB objectives, it is important that extrinsic rewards (i.e., monetary and career advancing) for purchasing agents be created to foster such actions.[58]

Demographic and Psychographic Factors

At the individual level, the decision maker's psychological characteristics play a role in determining disposition decisions. As with other consumption decisions, differences in motivation, knowledge, affect, experience, and involvement play a role in explaining disposition behaviors.

Green consumers tend to be younger and more highly educated and, to some extent, have higher incomes than other consumers. Gender, political affiliation, and social class are not strongly related to green consumer behaviors. Green consumers are conscious of the implicit costs of consumption and try to minimize them. Such awareness is at the root of the movement toward voluntary simplicity or to the idea of eating farther down the food chain (e.g., minimizing the processing of food products). Green consumers are motivated by a concern for social well-being. They tend to exhibit a relatively strong sense of personal efficacy; that is, they think that their daily behaviors can have a positive environmental impact.[59]

Recent research on green consumers in the United States confirms that several psychographic indicators distinguish them. These include perceived consumer effectiveness (belief that what we do as individuals makes a difference), altruism (a concern for others' welfare), and secondarily left-leaning political views. These characteristics suggest that green consumers participate in a lifestyle segment that has emerged since the 1970s labeled the Cultural Creatives. Research on Cultural Creatives finds that the most "green" group numbers about 24 million Americans, or 13 percent of the adult population.[60]

Personal values such as altruism and the **biospheric orientation,** or earth-first orientation, of committed ecologists relate to *positive beliefs and attitudes toward recycling and waste reduction behaviors.* But the link is relatively weak. One study conducted in Germany suggests a reason. The authors argue that different proenvironmental disposition behaviors such as reuse, waste reduction, garbage sorting, or recycling might be linked to different values and motives. Hence, to stimulate different proenvironmental disposition behaviors, marketers may have to appeal to different values.[61]

Voluntary simplicity, or deconsumption, may be a way to relieve stress on the environment. Consumers embracing this philosophy opt for a lifestyle that requires fewer material resources to support them. Such consumers can be regarded as a psychographic market segment with specific needs to be addressed. For example, such a segment can be labeled as true-blue greens (see Exhibit 19.5). This segment engages in the following behaviors: willing to pay more for green products, cuts down on car use, uses biodegradable soaps, writes to politicians about environmental issues, and seeks alternatives to automobile transport. Proponents of voluntary simplicity also participate in co-housing arrangements. You can find dozens of websites devoted to voluntary simplicity online. Thus, a portion of the population has decided that happiness in life does not necessarily come from owning more things. Rather, it comes from seeking simple, practical, sustainable solutions to life's problems.[62] Advertisers can attract this segment with appeals such as "slow your life down and smell the roses" or "enjoy people more

and material goods less." A spokesperson for Patagonia, Inc., a well-known seller of environmental sportswear, adds a twist: "The idea is to buy less, but buy our stuff." Patagonia appeals successfully to the true-blue greens by simplifying its product lines and by placing a heavy emphasis on the longevity and ruggedness of its products.[63]

DISPOSITION AS A PRODUCT CHOICE CRITERION

Disposition considerations can drive product choice. At the same time, the marketing of green products can benefit from a thorough understanding of disposition attitudes and behaviors.

Disposition and Product Choice

Consumers make product choices to satisfy their desires. A clean, habitable ecosystem is a legitimate need without which consumers literally cannot survive. But in many choice situations, this need is not particularly associated with the exchange process. Rather, the environmental benefits remain an underlying or latent factor. For this reason, ecological needs are unlikely to serve as the primary trigger for many consumer decisions. One challenge for marketing managers is to find ways to make ecological needs and concerns more salient.[64]

In the 1970s, researchers found that consumers became more willing to purchase phosphate-free detergents when they learned of the negative effects of phosphate pollution on water quality. In 1991 the University of Illinois found that, assuming price parity, 64.3 percent of respondents would choose paper towels labeled recycled paper over paper towels without the label. For a plastic shampoo bottle marketed as recycled, the figure was virtually identical—63.1 percent. Similar percentages of consumers reported they would choose a glass peanut butter jar labeled recyclable over one without the label and opt for a plastic shampoo bottle marked recyclable.

A study conducted in Denmark focused on the purchase of organically produced foods, which have fewer environmental costs. A wide variety of food products with labels identifying them as organic can be found in any Danish grocery store. Over half of the consumers surveyed agreed that organic foods are better than conventional foods, and 84 percent distrusted food-processing technologies. Thus, in Denmark, there is a potentially large segment of consumers whose purchase decisions might be influenced by disposition criteria. In general, Danish consumers have positive attitudes toward environmental problems, and they accept recycling as a fact of life. Nonetheless, few Danish consumers have specific understandings about the connection between specific environmental problems and the consumer behaviors they could undertake to alleviate them.[65]

As discussed above, there are segments of green consumers who recognize that the production, marketing, and disposition of products lead to social and environmental costs (e.g., pollution). They evaluate these costs negatively and try to minimize them through purchase decisions.[66] In surveys conducted over the past 25 years, a broad majority of consumers in the Triad countries say their purchase decisions are influenced by companies' environmental reputation. In the abstract, approximately two-thirds of consumers express willingness to pay more for products that are environmentally friendly. For many consumers, however, environmental concerns often remain in the background when they make decisions in the marketplace. This is

apparantly the case in Thailand too. Thai consumers of cosmetics marketed by green firms The Body Shop and Oriental Princess are impressed by product performance and ingredient quality but do not fully comprehend the firms' environmental initiatives.[67] Government-mandated schemes to introduce disposition criteria into consumer behaviors may result in negative feelings against the activity the regulation is meant to encourage. This is an example of psychological reactance. Examples of regulations might include bans on ozone-depleting chemicals in air-conditioning units, deposit fees on liquid containers, or programs requiring home garbage separation for recycling. Reactance is common where monetary effects are felt or the regulations are perceived to be unequal. Reactance may be higher in cultures with strong traditions of individual freedom, such as the United States,[68] and lower in nations with a stronger collectivist orientation (e.g., some Scandinavian nations). Denmark's bottle deposit program is successful, for example, although Danes complain about it, whereas deposit bottles have not been very successful in the United States.

Some people fear being labeled a "sucker" if they participate in green programs while others do not. Achieving environmental goals (e.g., reducing solid waste) depends on the participation of many consumers. But individual consumers cannot be sure that most others will cooperate. For example, people may believe that disposal fees applied to waste lubricants replaced by commercial garages will lead to illicit dumping and noncompliance by some, thereby aggravating existing disposition problems. Belief that others may not comply reduces compliance levels overall. This is an example of the classic **prisoner's dilemma** problem in psychology: *Everyone benefits if all comply; but if one person doesn't comply, his or her immediate benefits may outweigh the general good.* Hence, mistrust of others may reduce the likelihood of green behaviors. Marketing communications must address issues such as reactance and concerns about prisoner's dilemma if firms hope to increase the responsiveness of green marketing campaigns.

Finally, a related but separate problem has to do with the extent to which individual consumers apply private, personal cost–benefit calculations to their consumption decisions without regard for broader impacts. When many consumers are inclined to base their consumption decisions primarily on private cost–benefit calculations, as those in developed countries, it seems likely that private economic incentives (e.g., price breaks on environmentally friendly products) are necessary to encourage cooperation.[69]

Recycled and Green Products

Recycled and green products represent product categories in the introduction and growth phase of the product life cycle discussed in Chapter 17. For example, in 1989 Lever Brothers launched a $20 million campaign to reduce adverse environmental effects of its products. Canada's largest grocer, Loblaw's, also introduced a line of **green products** in 1989. U.S. sales of green products were estimated to total $8.8 billion in 1995. Elsewhere we have mentioned the skyrocketing sales of the organic foods in an industry with otherwise flat sales. Faced with a history of price disincentives for green consumption, green marketers have been working hard to dispel the idea that recycled and organic products cost more than conventional commercial goods.[70]

@ www.pg.com/docInfo/enviro/qualinit.htm

In Japan, a green purchasing law that went into effect in 2001 spurred development of clothing made from environmentally friendly fabrics. The fabrics help retain or release body heat depending on the season. Mizuno and a competing consortium of firms hope to market company uniforms made of these fabrics. The idea is that firms adopting the uniforms will then be able to reduce expenditures on air conditioning and heating, thereby lowering their greenhouse gas emissions.[71]

SUMMARY

Disposition is closely linked to other aspects of consumer behavior. By learning more about disposition trends and patterns, we can increase our knowledge about consumer behavior in general.

We present an overview of the disposition process by outlining a model of disposition. Objects may take different paths after acquisition, following various forms of reuse and recycling. The examples show how reuse is a frequent alternative to the acquisition of new goods. Consumers often sidestep the market in their disposition behaviors. From a marketing perspective, managing disposition can be viewed as a backward-channel-of-distribution problem.

There are several types of voluntary and involuntary disposition behaviors that consumers experience. These include discard behavior, donations, inheritance, giving, storage, and recycling. A variety of the situational and individual factors affect disposal choices. Factors intrinsic to the product affect disposition, as does the influence of competitive pressures both on firms and individual consumers. Self-imposed industry norms, such as the ISO 14000 principles, may well encourage organizations to pursue some green business strategies over the next decade. In addition, situational factors and consumers' life cycles affect disposition. Disposition should be thought of as a recurring social and psychological process.

Green consumers are those who take disposition issues into account either in their acquisition behaviors (e.g., buying recycled goods) or in their disposition behaviors (e.g., engaging in composting or waste reduction). In general, there are relatively weak relationships between consumers' demographic profiles, values, attitudes, knowledge, beliefs, and disposition behaviors. A variety of psychological and social psychological factors affect people's propensity to engage in particular disposition behaviors. For example, the desire for voluntary simplicity is an individual factor. Changing fashions is an example from the social world.

Product disposition may enter into consumers' product choice criteria, and there are a variety of marketing considerations related to recyclable or recycled objects. Some firms and some consumers are beginning to include disposition attributes of products when making acquisition decisions. For example, some firms are making an effort to close the loop between disposition and production by making things from recycled materials; that is, by pursuing a strategy of sustainable marketing, organizations can find ways to compete effectively in the marketplace and simultaneously pursue the goal of sustaining ecosystems.

KEY TERMS

backward channel of distribution 811
biospheric orientation 830
close-loop manufacturing 821
deconsumption 827
design for environment 802
disposition 801
donation 817
electronic flea markets 817
green products 832
green segments 827
inheritance 818
ISO 14000 823
lateral recycling 810
model of disposition 809
preinheritance 819
prisoner's dilemma 832
product biography 810
product stewardship 802
psychological reactance 826
recycling 811
resource recovery 811
secondhand reuse 810
secondhand trade 810
selling 816
simple reuse 809
storage 819
sustainable marketing 827
swap meets 816
time-marked goods 820
waste-making society 816

REVIEW QUESTIONS

1. Identify situations for different product categories in which items are no longer fit for consumer reuse and instead are discarded or recycled.
2. Think about the various paths (e.g., 1a, 1b, 2, 3) shown in Exhibit 19.1. For each path, give a specific example for firms or households. Be certain to provide examples that are different from those presented in the text.
3. Consider your household furnishings. How much of it and what types of things were obtained new? Describe the items that were obtained used. What was scavenged?
4. Identify personal possessions that you have disposed of voluntarily and involuntarily. What methods were used in the disposition process?
5. Take a look at Exhibit 19.5. What sort of green consumer segment do you fall into? Try to identify individual and situational reasons for your green and brown consumption behaviors.
6. Marketers are a long way from exploring the full range of opportunities available in the realm of disposition. Identify some untapped marketing opportunities connected with consumers' disposition behaviors.
7. Think about disposition processes at your place of business, or a place of business with which you are familiar. Identify different categories of products that are disposed of in different ways. For example, paper clips are probably reused; surplus restaurant food may be donated to charity; waste paper may be recycled. Identify some links in a backward channel of distribution that, if put in place, would change the firm's disposition behavior.
8. Do you attend swap meets, garage sales, flea markets, or other mechanisms for lateral recycling? Why or why not? What do you like or dislike about them? What do you think motivates participants apart from the obvious reasons of getting a deal or getting rid of things?
9. Speculate as to why some individuals have attachments to possessions so strong that they can throw nothing away (pack rats), whereas others regularly purge their homes of items with assumed sentimental value.

CASES

YOU MAKE THE CALL

CAN BLACK GOLD FLOW GREEN?

From its base in London, BP Amoco, the world's third-largest oil company and arguably the most powerful player in Alaskan oil, has broken ranks with most of the petroleum industry and worked to build a reputation as an environmental pioneer, while continuing to promote oil development.

Bucking industry wisdom, BP agreed with the idea that carbon-dioxide emissions contribute to global warming and pledged to cut its own emissions by 10 percent by 2010. The company is among the world's largest makers of solar panels and uses solar power at many of its own facilities. For example, 78,000 state-of-the-art photovoltaic cells supplied by BP Solar are to be used in the construction of the new TXU-Europe building in Ipswich, UK. The 200-kW project represents the largest solar installation in the UK. BP is gradually shifting the emphasis of its exploration and production from crude oil to cleaner-burning natural gas. For example, BP Trinidad and Tobago (BPTT) recently announced the discovery of one trillion cubic feet of gas in its Iron Horse field,

off the east coast of Trinidad. This is the company's second major natural gas discovery for 2002 and its fourth in three years, raising BPTT's estimated gas reserves to 17 trillion cubic feet.

A green oil company may seem an oxymoron, but some regulators, scientists, environmentalists, and investors say they cautiously believe that the company might be trying to transform itself and an industry that some equate with pollution. For the last few years, environmentalists and indigenous groups have met with BP executives and board members to try to persuade them to promise not to drill in the Arctic National Wildlife Refuge. Those who have placed some faith in BP see the Arctic Refuge, home to scarce, unique wildlife, as the crucial test of the company's environmental resolve.

BP executives repeat a companywide mantra of "no damage" to the environment, and its units have to meet certain environmental goals. "We have learned a lot in 30 years," said F. X. O'Keefe, the head of BP's Alaska Exploration unit. "Our record shows we can go into different areas with little to no impact." But the company's stock price ultimately depends on how much oil it draws out of the ground and at what cost. To ensure a steady flow of oil as supplies from Alaska's North Slope decline, BP has proceeded with projects and campaigns that pose significant risks to Alaska's ecology, said many state and federal regulators, wildlife biologists, environmentalists, and representatives of native peoples. "They're trying to present a new BP, but it's business as usual," said Francis A. Grant-Suttie, who, as director of private-sector initiatives at the World Wildlife Fund, meets regularly with BP executives. "On the P.R. level, they have been successful at differentiating themselves from others, but by virtue of what they're doing on the coastal plain, you can see it's sheer rhetoric."

Shareholders take the new corporate message seriously. At the 2001 annual meeting, 13 percent of shareholders voted for a resolution demanding that BP terminate its Northstar off-shore platform in Prudhoe Bay and stay out of the Arctic Wildlife Refuge, a proportion so high that it stunned company management and even those who introduced the measure. "Maybe it is painful for BP to have this degree of scrutiny, but being held accountable will help BP improve its environmental performance over the long run," said Simon Billenness, senior analyst at Trillium Asset Management of Boston, one of the sponsors of the resolution.

Greg Gilbert worries that underground riches will inevitably draw oil companies into the Arctic Refuge's coastal plain. A member of the 7,500-member Gwich'in Indian nation that lives scattered through the boreal forests of northwest Canada and north-central Alaska, Mr. Gilbert hunts caribou to feed his family of seven. "Caribou are sensitive," Mr. Gilbert said. "The oil companies want to drill in the refuge, but the elders say the caribou will disappear. They will change their route."

BP contends that oil development would not harm caribou, pointing to the thriving herd in the North Slope. A range of independent wildlife biologists dispute BP's argument. Moreover, the coastal plain in the refuge is far smaller than the North Slope but has 10 times the caribou population, which would make it very hard for the animals to avoid oil infrastructure. BP says it can develop oil fields on the coastal plain with what it calls "minimal" environmental impact. The acreage that its newest wells occupy, their "footprint," is much smaller than that of older wells, and pipelines are built higher to let caribou pass underneath. Often, there are no roads nearby, and workers are airlifted in.

Doubts about the company's environmental mission run deep. In London, wags say the company is Beyond Belief. In Alaska, it is said that workers on the North Slope, many of whom have weathered the harsh tundra and the industry's bad image for more than 20 years, grumble that BP looks weak for going green. BP has made sure that its interests are protected. In 2000, it contributed $50,000 to Arctic Power, a prodevelopment

CASES

lobbying group. A BP executive also serves on the board of the group. BP donates to politicians who vote regularly to open the refuge to oil development.

BP has excelled in one environmental area: In 1995, a whistleblower from BP's North Slope Endicott field reported that the contractor for which he was working, Doyon Drilling, had been illegally disposing of hazardous wastes. In 1999, the U.S. Justice Department filed criminal and civil lawsuits against BP. The company, which pleaded guilty to one violation of federal environmental laws, was fined $500,000 in the criminal proceeding and paid $6.5 million to settle the civil suit. The company also volunteered to put into place a stringent nationwide environmental management program at its exploration, drilling, and production units to improve oversight and reduce the chance of accidents and spills at a cost of about $15 million. While praising the extra step taken by BP, a federal prosecutor recognized the challenge that the company faces. "I think folks at their highest levels are committed to environmental issues," said Deborah Smith, deputy chief of the environmental crimes section at the Justice Department. "But does that reach down to their oil rig operator and change the thinking of an oil rig worker who is from an industry that hasn't always been concerned about the environment?"

Neela Banerjee, "Can Black Gold Ever Flow Green?" New York Times, *November 12, 2000, Section 3, pp. 1, 12–13.* *and www.bpamoco.com.*

QUESTIONS

1. Referring to Chapter 5, what kind of marketing strategy is BP Amoco following?
2. Again referring to Chapter 5, what, if any, evidence do you see of the marketing imagination at work in BP Amoco's corporate policies?
3. What trend in dealing with the problems of waste does BP Amoco appear to be following?
4. Does what BP Amoco is doing represent a successful strategy for differentiating itself from its competition?
5. Is the commitment of BP Amoco's corporate champions adequate to ensure success of its new corporate public relations policy?
6. What, if any, segment of consumers will be drawn to BP Amoco because of its corporate strategy?

ENDNOTES

1. www.railstrails.org.
2. Stuart L. Hart, "Strategies for a Sustainable World," *Harvard Business Review,* January–February 1997, pp. 66–76; Deanna J. Richards, "Environmentally Conscious Manufacturing," *World Class Design to Manufacture* 1, no. 3 (1994), pp. 15–22; and Xerox Investor Relations, "Going 'Green' Pays Off for Xerox, Helps Preserve the Environment: Annual Report Showcases Progress of Conservation Efforts," September 14, 2000 (Rochester, NY: Xerox Corporation), found at www.xerox.com.
3. Amory B. Lovins, L. Hunter Lovins, and Paul Hawken, "A Road Map for Natural Capitalism," *Harvard Business Review,* May–June 1999, pp. 145–58; Michael E. Porter and Claas van der Linde, "Green and Competitive," *Harvard Business Review,* September–October 1995, pp. 120–34; and Barbara Quinn, "Bottom Line: Minimizing Waste Is Good Business," *Pollution Engineering* 33 (July 2001), pp. 26–27.

4. "6 Nations Agree to Cut Pollution in Rhine Basin," *International Herald Tribune,* September 10, 1996, p. 5; Joanna Lamparska, "Curse of the Black Triangle," *Warsaw Voice,* June 4, 1995, pp. G2, G4; Dan McGovern, *The Campo Indian Landfill War* (Norman, OK: University of Oklahoma Press, 1995); and Marlise Simons, "EU's Environmental Agency Is Discovering It's Pretty Messy out There," *International Herald Tribune,* September 10, 1996, p. 5.
5. John Crowley, "Seeing Green," *Professional Builder* 65 (December 14, 2000), pp. 137–40; Minette E. Drumwright, "Socially Responsible Organizational Buying: Environmental Concern as a Noneconomic Buying Criteria," *Journal of Marketing* 58 (July 1994), pp. 1–19; and Linda R. Stanley and Karen M. Lasonde, "The Relationship between Environmental Issue Involvement and Environmentally-Conscious Behavior," in *Advances in Consumer Research,* vol. 23, ed. Kim P. Corfman and John G. Lynch (Provo, UT: Association for Consumer Research, 1996), pp. 183–88.
6. William Rathje and Cullen Murphy, *Rubbish: The Archaeology of Garbage* (New York: Harper College, 1992).
7. Ibid., pp. 191–94.
8. Terrence H. Witkowski, "World War II Poster Campaigns and the Frugality Ethos in American Consumer Culture," *Journal of Advertising,* special issue on Advertising and Consumer Culture, forthcoming.
9. Catherine A. Roster, "Letting Go: The Process and Meaning of Dispossession in the Lives of Consumers," in *Advances in Consumer Research,* vol. 28, ed. Joan Meyers-Levy and Mary Gilly (Provo, UT: Association for Consumer Research, 2001), pp. 425–30.
10. Calvin Trillin, "One More Lot," *The Nation* 262 (May 20, 1996), p. 6.
11. Simone Field, Hazel Barrett, Angela Brown, and Roy May, "The Second-Hand Clothes Trade in the Gambia," *Geography* 81, no. 4 (1996), pp. 371–74.
12. Igor Kopytoff, "The Cultural Biography of Things: Commoditization as Process," in *The Social Life of Things,* ed. Arjun Appadurai (Cambridge: Cambridge University Press, 1986), pp. 64–94; and Grant McCracken, " 'Ever Dearer in Our Thoughts': Patina and the Representation of Status before and after the Eighteenth Century," and "Lois Roget: Curatorial Consumer in a Modern World," in *Culture and Consumption* (Bloomington: Indiana University Press, 1988), pp. 31–43, 44–56.
13. "Environment," *The Futurist,* May–June 1997, p. 7; David A. Munn and James Carr, "Cropland Utilization of Ground Drywall," *Biocycle* 37 (July 1996), p. 57; and David Riggle and Gaye Wiekierak, "The Big and Small of Woody Materials Recycling," *Biocycle* 37 (July 1996), pp. 53–56.
14. Chad W. Autry, Patricia M. Daugherty, and R. Glenn Richey, "The Challenge of Reverse Logistics in Catalog Retailing," *International Journal of Physical Distribution & Logistics Management* 31, no.1 (2001), pp. 26–37.
15. Text of this section is adapted from Rik Pieters, "Consumers and Their Garbage; A Framework, and Some Experiences from the Netherlands with Garbage," in *European Advances in Consumer Research,* vol. 1, ed. Gary Bamossy and Fred Van Raaij (Provo, UT: Association for Consumer Research, 1993), pp. 541–46.
16. Jacob Jacoby, Carol K. Berning, and Thomas F. Dietvorst, "What about Disposition?" *Journal of Marketing,* April 1977, pp. 22–28.
17. Eric J. Arnould, "Toward a Broadened Theory of Preference Formation and the Diffusion of Innovations: Cases from Zinder Province, Niger Republic," *Journal of Consumer Research* 16 (September 1989), pp. 239–67; and Stuart A. Ross, "Freedom from Possession: A Tibetan Buddhist View," *Journal of Social Behavior and Psychology* 6, no. 6 (1991), pp. 415–26.
18. Scott Dawson and Gary Bamossy, "If 'We Are What We Have,' What Are We When We Don't Have?: An Exploratory Study of Materialism among Expatriate Americans," *Journal of Social Behavior and Personality* 6, no. 6 (1991), pp. 363–84.
19. Adrian Furnham and Steven Jones, "Children's Views Regarding Possessions and Their Theft," *Journal of Moral Education* 16 (January 1987), pp. 18–25; and Joop Vand den Bogaard and Oene Wiegman, "Property Crime Victimization: The Effectiveness of Police Services for

Victims of Residential Burglary," *Journal of Social Behavior and Personality* 6, no. 6 (1991), pp. 329–62.
20. Paul Hawken, "Resource Waste," *Mother Jones,* March–April 1997, pp. 44–46; and United Nations, *Human Development Report 1998* (New York: United Nations Development Program, 1998).
21. John Clammer, "Aesthetics of the Self: Shopping and Social Being in Contemporary Urban Japan," in *Lifestyle Shopping: The Subject of Consumption,* ed. Ron Shields (London and New York: Routledge, 1992), pp. 195–215.
22. Elizabeth Razzi, "A Profitable Way to Ditch Your Junque," *Kiplinger's Personal Finance Magazine* 50, no. 6 (1996), pp. 100–2.
23. Stephen M. Soiffer and Gretchen M. Hermann, "Visions of Power: Ideology and Practice in the American Garage Sale," *Sociological Review* 35, no. 1 (1987), pp. 48–83.
24. Gretchen M. Hermann, "His and Hers: Gender and Garage Sales," *Journal of Popular Culture* 29, no. 1 (Summer 1995), pp. 127–45.
25. Grant McCracken, "Culture and Consumption: A Theoretical Account of the Structure and Movement of the Cultural Meaning of Consumer Goods," *Journal of Consumer Research* 13 (June 1986), pp. 71–84; and Linda L. Price, Eric J. Arnould, and Carolyn Curasi, "Older Consumers' Disposition of Valued Possessions," *Journal of Consumer Research* 27 (September 2000), pp. 179–201.
26. Karen Tranberg Hansen, *Salaula: The World of Secondhand Clothing and Zambia,* (Chicago, University of Chicago Press, 2000); and George Packer, "How Susie Bayer's T-Shirt Ended Up on Yusuf Mama's Back," *New York Times Magazine,* March 31, 2002, pp. 54–59.
27. John J. Burnett and Van R. Wood, "A Proposed Model of the Donation Decision Process," in *Research in Consumer Behavior,* ed. Elizabeth Hirschman and Jagdish Sheth (Greenwich, CT: JAI Press, 1988), pp. 1–47; and Mitch Griffin, Barry J. Babin, Jill S. Attaway, and William R. Darden, "Hey You, Can Ya Spare Some Change? The Case of Empathy and Personal Distress as Reactions to Charitable Appeals," in *Advances in Consumer Research,* vol. 20, ed. Leigh McAlister and Michael L. Rothschild (Provo, UT: Association for Consumer Research, 1993), pp. 508–14.
28. Debra S. Judge and Sarah Blaffer Hardy, "Allocation of Accumulated Resources among Close Kin: Inheritance in Sacramento, California, 1890–1984," *Ethnology and Sociobiology* 13 (1992), pp. 495–522.
29. "Baby-Boomers Slated to Inherit Nearly $10.4 Trillion," *Trusts & Estates,* September 1994, pp. 6–10; and "Baby Boomers Slated for Inheritance Windfall," *Journal of Accountancy,* July 1994, pp. 17–21.
30. Margaret Popper, "Not So Fixated on Bequests," *Business Week,* December 24, 2001, p. 26.
31. Arnould, "Toward a Broadened Theory of Preference Formation and the Diffusion of Innovations"; Robert M. Netting, Richard R. Wilk, and Eric J. Arnould, eds., *Households: Comparative and Historical Studies of the Domestic Group* (Berkeley: University of California Press, 1983); and Tamar Rapoport, Edna Lomski-Feder, and Mohammed Masaha, "Female Subordination in the Arab-Israeli Community: The Adolescent Perspective of 'Social Veil,' " *Sex Roles* 20, nos. 5–6 (1989), pp. 255–69.
32. T. G. H. Strethlow, *Aranda Traditions* (Melbourne: Melbourne University Press, 1977); and A. Guillou and P. Guibert, "Le froid domestiqué: l'usage du congélateur," *Terrain* 12 (1989), pp. 7–14.
33. Peter Menzel, *Material World: A Global Family Portrait* (San Francisco: Sierra Club Books, 1994).
34. Russell W. Belk, "The Role of Possessions in Constructing and Maintaining a Sense of Past," in *Advances in Consumer Research,* vol. 17, ed. Marvin E. Goldberg, Gerald Gorn, and Richard W. Pollay (Provo, UT: Association for Consumer Research, 1990), pp. 669–76; and Kent Grayson and David Shulman, "Indexicality and the Verification Function of Irreplaceable Possessions: A Semiotic Analysis," *Journal of Consumer Research* 27 (June 2000), pp. 17–30.
35. N. Haumont and H. Raymond, "Habitat et pratique de l'espace: étude des relations entre l'Intérieur et l'extérieur du logement," working paper, Institut de Sociologie Urbain, Paris, 1975;

Perla Korosec-Serfaty, "The Home from Attic to Cellar," *Journal of Environmental Psychology* 4 (1984), pp. 303–21; and Kay M. Tooley, "The Remembrance of Things Past: On the Collection and Recollection of Ingredients Useful in the Treatment of Disorders Resulting from Unhappiness, Rootlessness, and the Fear of Things to Come," *American Journal of Orthopsychiatry* 48 (1978), pp. 174–82.
36. "The Death Business: Staying Alive," *Economist,* August 5, 2000, p. 61; Roy Rivenburg, "Return of the Mummy," *Los Angeles Times,* January 27, 1993, pp. E1, E27; and Thomas Lynch, "Socko Finish," *New York Times Magazine,* July 12, 1998, pp. 34–36.
37. "Waste Disposal: More Rubbish," *The Economist,* August 24, 2002, pp. 45–46.
38. OECD, *OECD Environmental Data* (Paris: Organization for Economic Cooperation and Development, 1995).
39. Laurent Belsie, "EPA Incentives Put PCS on a Diet," *Christian Science Monitor,* December 30, 1993, p. 2; Jonathan Gaw, "Dump Profit Gets Trashed," *Los Angeles Times,* July 22, 1993, pp. D1, D4; Mary Beth Jannakos, "Wastemaker Awards Go to Food Products with Lots of Wrapping," *Daily Camera,* October 21, 1992, p. 22: Zofia Jozwiak, "Dump Space Running Out," *The Warsaw Voice,* May 28, 1995, p. 8; Peter Nye, "Clean Drinking Water Becomes a National Problem," *Public Citizen* 13, no. 4 (July–August 1993), pp. 10–13; Elizabeth Ross, "Garbage Museum Aims to Change Wasteful Ways," *Christian Science Monitor,* September 21, 1993, p. 12; David Shenk, "Buy a Hat, Save the Earth," *Hemispheres,* May 1993, pp. 25–27; FTC, *The Application of Section 5 of the Federal Trade Commission Act to Environmental Advertising and Marketing Practices* (Washington, DC: Federal Trade Commission, 1992); "The Netherlands' Radical, Practical Green Plan," *Whole Earth Review,* Fall 1995, pp. 94–99; Catherine Vial, "Why EC Environmental Policy Will Affect American Business," *Business America,* March 8, 1993, pp. 24–27; and *The Wall Street Journal,* April 27, 1993, p. A1.
40. Jeff Bailey, "Two Major Garbage Rivals Find Their Profits Trashed," *The Wall Street Journal,* March 1993, p. B1; Paul A. Eisenstein, "Your Used New Car Is Here," *World Traveler,* October 1995, pp. 20–22; "Seeing Green," *Entrepreneur,* April 1993, p. 214; Naomi Freundlich, "The White House versus the Greenhouse," *Business Week,* August 19, 1996, p. 75; Paul Hawken, "A Declaration of Sustainability," *Utne Reader,* September–October 1993, pp. 54–60; Kenneth Howe, "Wanna Make Cash? Get Rid of 28 Million Tires Annually," *Press Telegram,* January 3, 1993, p. B6; Helmet Maucher, "Industry and the Environment: The Views of an Industrialist," *Columbia Journal of World Business,* Summer 1993, pp. 6–10; John McPhee, "Duty of Care," *New Yorker,* June 28, 1993, pp. 72–80; Ken Ohlson, "Seeing Green: Eco Entrepreneurs Clean Up," *Entrepreneur,* February 1993, pp. 114–18; David Taylor, "Auto Motives," *Profiles* 6 (January 1994), pp. 51–57; and Eiichiro Shimoda, "Recycling Bill puts Automakers in Catch-22," *Nikkei Weekly,* March 12, 2001, p. 4.
41. Jacoby, Berning, and Dietvorst, "What About Disposition?"
42. Raymond Communications, *News: How Do Countries Stack Up on Recycling Rates?* (Riverdale, MD: Raymond Communications, 1995).
43. Paul Raeburn, "Don't Write off Energy Conservation, Mr. Cheney," *Business Week,* May 14, 2001, p. 46; and Shell International Petroleum Company, *How Do We Stand? People, Planets and Profits: The Shell Report 2000* (London: Shell International Petroleum Company, 2000).
44. Mary Litsikas, "U.S. Perspective Varies on ISO 14000," *Quality* 36 (December 1997), pp. 28–33; and William R. Smith and Raymond J. Patchak, "So Long! Command and Control . . . Hello! ISO 14000," manuscript, Environmental Management Systems, New York City, 1996.
45. Richard R. Wilk, "Learning Not to Want Things," working paper, presented at the annual meetings of the Association for Consumer Research, Tuscon, AZ, October 1996, pp. 10–13.
46. "Curbing Pollution an Urgent Task," *Beijing Review* 39, no. 32 (1996), p. 4; Joseph Weber, "3M's Big Cleanup," *Business Week,* June 5, 2000, pp. 96–98; and Shell International Petroleum Company, *How Do We Stand?*
47. Suzanne C. Gruenert, "Everybody Seems Concerned about the Environment, but Is This Concern Reflected in (Danish) Consumers' Food Choices?" working paper, First European Association for Consumer Research Conference, Amsterdam, 1991.

48. Michael B. Schiffer, Theodore E. Downing, and Michael McCarthy, "Waste Not, Want Not: An Ethnoarchaeological Study of Refuse in Tucson, Arizona," in *Modern Material Culture: The Archaeology of Us,* ed. Michael Gould and Michael B. Schiffer (New York: Academic Press, 1981), pp. 67–86.
49. Russell W. Belk, "Moving Possessions: An Analysis Based on Personal Documents from the 1847–1869 Mormon Migration," *Journal of Consumer Research* 19 (December 1992), pp. 339–61.
50. Robin A. Higie, Linda L. Price, and Julie Fitzmaurice, "Leaving It All Behind: Service Loyalties in Transition," in *Advances in Consumer Research,* vol. 20, ed. Leigh McAlister and Michael L. Rothschild (Provo, UT: Association for Consumer Research, 1993), pp. 656–61; James H. McAlexander, "Divorce, the Disposition of the Relationship, and Everything," in *Advances in Consumer Research,* vol. 18, ed. Michael Solomon and Rebecca Holman (Provo, UT: Association for Consumer Research, 1991), pp. 43–48; Scott D. Roberts, "Consumption Responses in Involuntary Job Loss," in *Advances in Consumer Research,* vol. 18, ed. Michael Solomon and Rebecca Holman (Provo, UT: Association for Consumer Research, 1991), pp. 40–42; and Melissa Martin Young, "Disposition of Possessions during Role Transitions," in *Advances in Consumer Research,* vol. 18, ed. Michael Solomon and Rebecca Holman (Provo, UT: Association for Consumer Research, 1991), pp. 33–39.
51. Higie, Price, and Fitzmaurice, "Leaving It All Behind."
52. Russell W. Bell, John F. Sherry Jr., and Melanie Wallendorf, "A Naturalistic Inquiry into Buyer and Seller Behavior at a Swap Meet," *Journal of Consumer Research* 14 (March 1988), pp. 449–70; Mihaly Csikszentmihalyi and Eugene Rochberg-Halton, *The Meaning of Things: Domestic Symbols and the Self* (New York: Cambridge University Press, 1981); and John W. Schouten, "Selves in Transition: Favorite Possessions of Indians and Indian Immigrants to the United States," *Journal of Consumer Research* 17, no. 4 (1991), pp. 412–25.
53. Mara Adelman, "Rituals of Adversity and Remembering: The Role of Possessions for Persons and Community Living with AIDS," in *Advances in Consumer Research,* vol. 19, ed. Brian Sternthal and John F. Sherry Jr. (Provo, UT: Association for Consumer Research, 1992), pp. 401–3; and Teresa Pavia, "Dispossession and Perceptions of Self in Late Stage HIV Infection," in *Advances in Consumer Research,* vol. 20, ed. Leigh McAlister and Michael L. Rothschild (Provo, UT: Association for Consumer Research, 1993), pp. 425–28.
54. Donald A. Fuller, *Sustainable Marketing* (Thousand Oaks, CA: Sage Publications, 1999), p. 4.
55. Roper Organization, *Environmental Behavior: North America, Canada, Mexico, United States* (New York City: Roper Organization, 1992); Prem Shamdasani, Gloria Ong Chon-Lin, and Daleen Richard, "Exploring Green Consumers in an Oriental Culture: Role of Personal and Marketing Mix Factors," in *Advances in Consumer Research,* vol. 20, ed. Leigh McAlister and Michael Rothschild (Provo, UT: Association for Consumer Research, 1993), pp. 488–93.
56. Environment Canada, "Notre mode de vie," *L'état de l'environnement au Canada 1996;* found at http://www.ec.gc.ca/soer-ree/Francais/SOER/1996report/Doc/1-5-3-7-6-1.cfm.
57. Luk Joossens et Antoinette Brouyaux, "Enquête sur l'éco-consommation en Wallonie en 2001," *Du Côté des Consommateurs,* no. 116, July 30, 2002 (Bruxelles: CRIOC, Centre de Recherche et d'Information des Organisations de Consommateurs), found at www.oivo-crioc.org.
58. Minette E. Drumright, "Socially Responsible Organizational Buying: Environmental Concern as a Noneconomic Buying Criterion," *Journal of Marketing* 58 (July 1994), pp. 1–19.
59. Dorothy Leonard-Barton, "Voluntary Simplicity Lifestyles and Energy Conservation," *Journal of Consumer Research* 8 (December 1981), pp. 243–52; Pam Scholder Ellen, Joshua Lyle Wiener, and Cathy Cobb-Walgren, "The Role of Perceived Consumer Effectiveness in Motivating Environmentally Conscious Behavior," *Journal of Public Policy and Marketing* 10 (Fall 1991), pp. 101–17; and Kent Van Liere and Riley E. Dunlap, "The Social Bases of Environmental Concern: A Review of Hypotheses, Explanations, and Empirical Evidence," *Public Opinion Quarterly* 44, no. 2 (1980), pp. 181–97.
60. Paul H. Ray, "The Emerging Culture," *American Demographics,* February 1997, pp. 28–34, 56; and Robert D. Straughan and James A. Roberts, "Environmental Segmentation Alternatives:

A Look at Green Consumer Behavior in the New Millennium," *Journal of Consumer Marketing* 16, no. 6 (1999), pp. 558–75.

61. Ingo Balderjahn, "Personality Variables and Environmental Attitudes as Predictors of Ecologically Responsible Consumption Patterns," *Journal of Business Research* 17 (1988), pp. 51–56; John A. McCarty and L. J. Shrum, "A Structural Equation Analysis of the Relationships of Personal Values, Attitudes and Beliefs about Recycling and the Recycling of Solid Waste Products," in *Advances in Consumer Research,* vol. 20, ed. Leigh McAlister and Michael Rothschild (Provo, UT: Association for Consumer Research, 1993), pp. 641–46; and Paul C. Stern and Thomas Dietz, "The Value Basis of Environmental Concern," *Journal of Social Issues* 50, no. 3 (1994), pp. 65–84.

62. Henry David Thoreau, *Walden* (New York: Random House, 1937).

63. Fuller, *Sustainable Marketing,* pp. 338–41; and George M. Zinkhan and Les Carlson, "Green Advertising and the Reluctant Consumer," *Journal of Advertising* 24, no. 2 (1995), pp. 1–6.

64. Fuller, *Sustainable Marketing,* p. 322.

65. Suzanne C. Grunert, "Green Consumerism in Denmark: Some Evidence from the KO Foods Project," *Der Markt* 126, no. 3 (1993), pp. 140–51.

66. Ibid.

67. Lalit M. Johri and Kanokthip Sahasakmontri "Green Marketing of Cosmetics and Toiletries in Thailand," *Journal of Consumer Marketing* 15, no. 3 (1998), pp. 265–81.

68. Robert N. Bellah, Richard Madsen, William M. Sullivan, Ann Swidler, and Steven M. Tipton, *Habits of the Heart* (Berkeley: University of California Press, 1985).

69. Suzanne C. Grunert and John Thogersen, "Waste Handling Systems as Perceived by Citizens of Two Danish Municipalities," in *The Natural Environment: Interdisciplinary Views,* Proceedings of the First Interdisciplinary Conference on the Environment, ed. K. L. Hickey and D. Kantarelis (Worcester, MA: Assumption College, 1994), pp. 87–100.

70. Drumwright, "Socially Responsible Organizational Buying"; "Shattering a Myth: Organic Packaged Food *Can* Be the Cheapest Buy," *The Green Guide,* April 4, 1995; Michel Laroche, Roy Toffoli, and Chankom Kim, "The Influence of Culture on Pro-Environmental Knowledge, Attitudes, and Behavior: A Canadian Perspective," in *Advances in Consumer Research,* vol. 23, ed. Kim P. Corfman and John G. Lynch (Provo, UT: Association for Consumer Research, 1996), pp. 196–202; Secretary James M. Seif, "Testimony before the Pennsylvania Senate Environmental Resources and Energy Committee," Pennsylvania Department of Environmental Protection, Philadelphia, 1996; and Smart Business Supersite, "The Selling O' the Green," 1996, www.smartbiz.com.

71. Naoki Hori, "Eco-Friendly Laws Turn Fabrics Green," *Nikkei Weekly,* March 12, 2001, p. 16.

Chapter 1

CO1-1 Taxi/Getty Images, 2
CO1-2 ©DigiStock, 2
CO1-3 Walter Bibikow/Getty Images, 2
CO1-4 Kenneth Ehlers/ImageState, 2
P1-1 Courtesy Toyota Motor Sales, U.S.A., Inc., 8
P1-2 Courtesy Turkish Government Tourism Office, 10
P1-3 Courtesy of The Pleasant Company, 12
P1-4 Courtesy of The Pleasant Company, 12
P1-5 Courtesy of Phillipe Patek, 13
P1-6 Courtesy A.E.R.T, Inc., 14
P1-7 Peter Menzel/The Material World, 18
P1-8 Louis Psihoyos/The Material World, 19
P1-9 Courtesy Hard Rock Café, 20
P1-10 ©Reuters, 22
P1-11 ©Nipponia, No. 19, Heibonsha Ltd. 2001; photo by Sakai Nobuhiko, 25

Chapter 2

CO2-1 Taxi/Getty Images, 30
CO2-2 ©DigiStock, 30
CO2-3 Walter Bibikow/Getty Images, 30
CO2-4 Kenneth Ehlers/ImageState, 30
P2-1 Amr Nabil/AP Wide World, 33
P2-2 National Geographic Society, 35
P2-3 Courtesy of Eric Arnould, 43
P2-4 Courtesy of Eric Arnould, 44
P2-5 Courtesy Eric Arnould, 46
P2-6 Courtesy of Go Rving, 47
P2-7 Courtesy of Four Seasons, 48
P2-8 Courtesy of Eric Arnould, 53
P2-9 Courtesy of Eric Arnould, 54
P2-10 Courtesy of Eric Arnould, 57
P2-11 Courtesy of Eric Arnould, 59
P2-12 ©Stone Images, 60

Chapter 3

CO3-1 Taxi/Getty Images, 70
CO3-2 ©DigiStock, 70
CO3-3 Walter Bibikow/Getty Images, 70
CO3-4 Kenneth Ehlers/ImageState, 70
P3-1 Kevin Morris/Corbis, 72
P3-2 Mike Powell/GettyImages, 74
P3-3 ©Flat Earth Picture-Gallery, 76
P3-4 ©Chuck Savage/Corbis, 77
P3-5 Mark Dadswell/GettyImages, 78
P3-6 ©Paul Barton/Corbis, 80
P3-7 ©Steven Hirsch/Corbis Sygma, 98
P3-8 Everett Collection Inc., 98
P3-9 No Credit, 98
P3-10 Bill Aron/PhotoEdit, 98
P3-11 Philadelphi Museum of Art/Corbis, 99
P3-12 Jon Burbank/Image Works, 99
P3-13 Hulton Getty Picture Library/Big Picture, 99
P3-14 JIF is a trademark of Procter & Gamble. All trademarks and copyrights are used under permission, 101
P3-15 Courtesy Ferrero USA, Inc., 101

Chapter 4

CO4-1 Taxi/Getty Images, 116
CO4-2 ©DigiStock, 116
CO4-3 Walter Bibikow/Getty Images, 116
CO4-4 Kenneth Ehlers/ImageState, 116
P4-1 ©Schieffelin & Sommerset Co., 124
P4-2 ©Superstock, 125
P4-3 ©Superstock, 125
P4-4 Courtesy Phillips-Ramsey/ San Diego, 128
P4-6 Courtesy Euro RSCG Partnership/ Hong Kong, 136
P4-7 Courtesy Omega SA, 139
P4-8 Nestle U.S.A., 139
P4-9 Courtesy of Eric Arnould, 141
P4-9a Courtesy Colors Magazine, 141
P4-10 ©Sepp Seitz/Woodfin Camp, 144
P4-11 No Credit, 153

Chapter 5

CO5-1 PhotoEdit, 162
CO5-2 ©PhotoEdit, 162
CO5-3 Courtesy Rick Armstrong, 162
CO5-4 ImageState, 162
P5-1 ©Eastcott-Momatiuk/Woodfin Camp Association, 167
P5-2 Ed Carlin/Archive Photos, 167
P5-3 Courtesy Toyota Motor Sales U.S.A., Inc., 174
P5-4 Courtesy Wisit Lumsiricharoenehoke, Somporn Laokittiehok, Saranya Maleipan, Studio De Nagara, Paiboon Suwansangroj, 178
P5-5 Courtesy United Colors of Benetton, 179
P5-6 Courtesy of Rollerblade, Inc., 180
P5-7 Courtesy Messner Vetere Berger McNamee Schmetterer/Euro RSG New York, 184
P5-8a Riptide, 190
P5-8b Riptide, 190
P5-8c No credit, 193
P5-9 Courtesy Euro RSCG Partnership/Hong Kong, 193
P5-10 Courtesy The Hain Celestial Group, Inc., 199

Chapter 6

CO6-1 PhotoEdit, 210
CO6-2 ©PhotoEdit, 210
CO6-3 Courtesy Rick Armstrong, 210
CO6-4 ImageState, 210
P6-1a Courtesy of George Zinkhan, 212
P6-2 ©M. Hruby, 218
P6-3 ©Thomas Sandberg, 218
P6-4 Mystery Guild ® catalog cover image courtesy of BOOKSPAN, ©2002, 'Mystery Guild ®' is a registered trademark of BOOKSPAN, 219
P6-5a Courtesy TBWA/Anthem, New Delhi, 234

P6-5b Courtesy TBWA/Anthem, New Delhi, 234

Chapter 7

CO7-1 ©Arlene Collins/Image Works, 256
CO7-2 ©John Nordell/Image Works, 256
CO7-3 Mark Richards/PhotoEdit, 256
CO7-4 Zefa/Gulliver/Masterfile, 256
P7-2 Courtesy Unilever, 265
P7-3 Courtesy Holden Ltd., 266
P7-4 Courtesy Diesel SpA, 267
P7-5 Courtesy Unilever, 269
P7-6 Equal ® is a registered trademark of the Merisant Company, 276
P7-7 No credit, 277
P7-8 Journal of Advertising/University of Minnesota, 281
P7-9 Journal of Advertising/University of Minnesota, 281
P7-10a Courtesy of Linda Price, 282
P7-10b Courtesy of Linda Price, 282
P7-11 Courtesy General Mills, 282
P7-12 Courtesy Agria Djurforsakring, 283
P7-13a Courtesy Jaguar Cars, 284
P7-13b Copyright, Nissan (2000). Infiniti and the Infiniti logo are registered trademarks of Nissan North America, Inc., 284
P7-14 Courtesy of Outward Bound, 284

Chapter 8

CO8-1 ©Arlene Collins/Image Works, 296
CO8-2 ©John Nordell/Image Works, 296
CO8-3 Mark Richards/PhotoEdit, 296
CO8-4 Zefa/Gulliver/Masterfile, 296
P8-1 Courtesy Salvatore Ferragamo, 310
P8-2 Courtesy Edson FCB Publicidade, Lda./ Lisbon, 311
P8-3 Courtesy E&J Gallo Wines, 315
P8-4 Courtesy Target Stores, 314
P8-5 Courtesy Schieffelin & Somerset, 316
P8-6 Courtesy Clif Bar, Inc., 319
P8-7 Courtesy Motorola; Agency: McCann-Erikson/Tokyo, 324
P8-8 Ric Karr/National Public Radio News, 328
P8-10 Courtesy F Nazca Saatchi & Saatchi/ Sao Paulo, 313

Chapter 9

CO9-1 ©Arlene Collins/Image Works, 336
CO9-2 ©John Nordell/Image Works, 336
CO9-3 Mark Richards/PhotoEdit, 336
CO9-4 Zefa/Gulliver/Masterfile, 336
P9-1 PhotoEdit, 339
P9-2 ©2002–2004, Recreational Equipment, Inc. Used by permission, 344
P9-3 Courtesy of Eric Arnould, 345
P9-4 Courtesy CLM/BBDO/Paris, 362
P9-5 Courtesy Bret Wills, 364
P9-7 Courtesy Discover Bank, 373
P9-8 ©2000 Bowstreet Inc. and the Bowstreet logo are trademarks of Bowstreet, Inc. Photography by Steve Bronstein, 375
P9-9 Advertisement appears Courtesy of Faye Iliopoulos/Hydrotherm Australia Pty Ltd®, 375
P9-10 Courtesy Land Rover South Africa; Agency: Young & Rubicam/Johannesburg, 376
P9-11 Courtesy Boeri Sport USA, 377
P9-12 Courtesy Affinity, 380

Chapter 10

CO10-1 ©Arlene Collins/Image Works, 386
CO10-2 ©John Nordell/Image Works, 386
CO10-3 Mark Richards/PhotoEdit, 386
CO10-4 Zefa/Gulliver/Masterfile, 386
P10-1 Courtesy of Balneo Grandform, 398
P10-2 Kerstin Geier/Corbis, 399
P10-3 ©2000 Jaguar Cars, 401
P10-4 Courtesy Lands' End, Inc., 405
P10-5 ©Microsoft Corporation, 403
P10-6 Courtesy Eileen Fischer; Photographer: Timothy Greenfield-Sanders, 410
P10-7 RG Wiesmeier/Munich, 410
P10-8 Courtesy Diesel SpA; Agency: KesselsKramer/The Netherlands, 411
P10-9 Courtesy Fallon-McElligott, 415

Chapter 11

CO11-1 William Thomas Cain/Getty Images, 434
CO11-2 Jeffrey Aaronson/Network Aspen, 434
CO11-3 ©Ron Kimball, 434
CO11-4 Tami Dawson/Photo Resourced Hawaii, 434
P11-2a Courtesy Caterpillar, 437
P11-2b Courtesy Caterpillar, 437
P11-3 Courtesy Powerbar, 438
P11-4 Courtesy of IPC, Country and Leisure Magazines, 439
P11-5 Courtesy of The Galardi Group, 439
P11-6 Courtesy No Fear; Art Director: Erik Casillas, 440
P11-7 Courtesy of Clark's Originals, 445

Chapter 12

CO12-1 William Thomas Cain/Getty Images, 474
CO12-2 Jeffrey Aaronson/Network Aspen, 474
CO12-3 ©Ron Kimball, 474
CO12-4 Tami Dawson/Photo Resourced Hawaii, 474
P12-1 Courtesy Smeg SpA, 479
P12-2 Courtesy of Lenox Collections, 480
P12-3 Courtesy of Paradise Galleries, 480
P12-4 Courtesy Newcomm Bates/ Sao Paulo, 486
P12-5 Courtesy Pattemaa Huttunen Santala/TBWA – Finland, 487

P12-6 Courtesy Smeg SpA, 489
P12-7 Masterfile, 495
P12-8 Provided courtesy of Chevrolet Motor Division, General Motors Corporation, 498
P12-9 Courtesy WebMiles.com, 499
P12-10 ©Steve Madden, Ltd., 503
P12-11 ©Corbis, 511
P12-12 ©Procter & Gamble, 512
P12-13 Courtesy Don Diegos, 513
P12-14 ©Reuters New Media/Corbis, 517
P12-15 Courtesy J. Walter Thompson/Rio de Janeiro, 517
P12-16 Courtesy DDB Needham/Chicago, 519

Chapter 13
CO13-1 William Thomas Cain/Getty Images, 538
CO13-2 Jeffrey Aaronson/Network Aspen, 538
CO13-3 ©Ron Kimball, 538
CO13-4 Tami Dawson/Photo Resourced Hawaii, 538
P13-2 Courtesy of Lapeyre Inc., 555
P13-3 Courtesy of CAM Baby Carriages/Italy, 559
P13-4 Courtesy of Yamaha Music Schools, 561
P13-5 ©Nintendo, 562
P13-6 ©Mrs. Smith's Bakeries, Inc., 564

Chapter 14
CO14-1 William Thomas Cain/Getty Images, 582
CO14-2 Jeffrey Aaronson/Network Aspen, 582
CO14-3 ©Ron Kımball, 582
CO14-4 Tami Dawson/Photo Resourced Hawaii, 582
P14-1 Jeffrey Aaronson/Network Aspen, 587
P14-2 Trademarks and copyrights used herein are properties of the United States Postal Service and are used under license to McGraw-Hill Publishing. All Rights Reserved, 589
P14-3 Courtesy MINI USA, 590
P14-4 Todd Tankersley; Kobal Collection; PhotoFest, 591
P14-5 Courtesy of Anheuser-Busch Companies, Inc., 592
P14-6 Massimo Sambucetti/AP Wide World, 593
P14-7 Icon Sports Media, Inc., 594
P14-8 The National Society of Hispanic MBA's; National Marketing Chair: Daisy Ortiz; Editor of People En Espanol AOL Time Warner: Angelo Figueroa, 595
P14-9 Osman Orsal/AP Wide World, 598
P14-11 Courtesy Atomz Corporation, 599
P14-12 Courtesy Bürger Bread, 603
P14-13 Copyright, State Farm Mutual Automobile Insurance Company, 1996. Used by permission, 605
P14-14 Courtesy Miami Ad School; Art Director: Monica Escobar; Copywriter: Gaston Gorazi, 607
P14-15 University of Chicago Press, 609
P14-16 Courtesy Ford Motor Company, 610
P14-18 Courtesy of Creo Inc. Advertisement; designed by Brain Communications, 615
P14-19 Courtesy Novell, 615

Chapter 15
CO15-1 Masterfile, 628
CO15-2 Adam Tanner/ImageWorks, 628
CO15-3 J.C. Leacock/ImageState, 628
CO15-4 Kin Cheung/Reuters 2002, 628
P15-1 Courtesy Columbia Sportswear, 633
P15-2a Cycles Yokoo Co. Ltd.; Agency: N.G. Inc., 635
P15-2b Cycles Yokoo Co. Ltd.; Agency: N.G. Inc., 635
P15-2c Cycles Yokoo Co. Ltd.; Agency: N.G. Inc., 635
P15-2d Cycles Yokoo Co. Ltd.; Agency: N.G. Inc., 635
P15-3 Courtesy So Natural Foods Australia Ltd., 638
P15-4 Courtesy of Flonaze, 642
P15-5 Courtesy American Honda Motor Company, 643
P15-6 Courtesy Michigan Economic Development Corporation, 646
P15-7 AXN Channel 725, 646
P15-8 Courtesy National Fluid Milk Processor Promotion Board; Agency: Bozell Worldwide, Inc., 647
P15-9 Courtesy McDonald's Corporation/Canada, 648
P15-10 Courtesy Kimberly-Clark, 649
P15-11 Courtesy Baxter Healthcare Corp., 650
P15-12 Courtesy Ford Motor Company, 657

Chapter 16
CO16-1 Masterfile, 666
CO16-2 Adam Tanner/ImageWorks, 666
CO16-3 J.C. Leacock/ImageState, 666
CO16-4 Kin Cheung/Reuters 2002, 666
P16-1 ©Linda Price, 669
P16-2 ©Linda Price, 670
P16-3 Singapore Industries Limited, 670
P16-4 Courtesy FedEx Corporation, 671
P16-5 Russell W. Belk, 676
P16-6 Courtesy WeddingChannel.com, 689
P16-7 ©President & Fellows, Harvard University Museum, 691
P16-8 Heifer.org website, 693
P16-9 Chip Simons/taxi/Getty Images, 694
P16-10 Courtesy Friends of Animals, 695
P16-11 Watch catalog page, 697

Chapter 17

CO17-1 Masterfile, 708
CO17-2 Adam Tanner/ImageWorks, 708
CO17-3 J.C. Leacock/ImageState, 708
CO17-4 Kin Cheung/Reuters 2002, 708
P17-2 Young Wolff/PhotoEdit, 715
P17-3 Courtesy of Sanyo Fisher Company, 716
P17-4 ©Superstock, 730

Chapter 18

CO18-1 Masterfile, 752
CO18-2 Adam Tanner/ImageWorks, 752
CO18-3 J.C. Leacock/ImageState, 752
CO18-4 Kin Cheung/Reuters 2002, 752
P18-1 Courtesy MasterCard, 756
P18-2a School of Visual Arts/New York; Art Director: Frank Anselmo, 766
P18-2b School of Visual Arts/New York; Art Director: Frank Anselmo, 766
P18-3 Courtesy MCI Group, 768
P18-4 ©United Airlines, 768
P18-6 AP Wide World Photo, 775
P18-7 Nestle Ice Cream Company, 778
P18-8 Courtesy Tropicana Products, Inc., 779
P18-9 ©PLANNED PARENTHOOD Federation of America, 782
P18-10 ©Adbusters Media Foundation, 785
P18-11 ©Adbusters Media Foundation, 786

Chapter 19

CO19-1 Masterfile, 798
CO19-2 Adam Tanner/ImageWorks, 798
CO19-3 J.C. Leacock/ImageState, 798
CO19-4 Kin Cheung/Reuters 2002, 798
P19-1 Rails to Trails website, 800
P19-2 Courtesy First Kick, 804
P19-3 ©BP Amoco, 806
P19-4 ©Dupont, 808
P19-5 Courtesy TBWA Hunt Lascaris/Cape Town, 811
P19-6 Courtesy THE EARTH MACHINE, 812
P19-7 Courtesy LUBO USA, 823
P19-8 Courtesy Saturn Corporation, 824
P19-9 ©ITT Industries, 825